Faculty and Faculty Issues in Colleges and Universities

Second Edition

Edited by

Dorothy E. Finnegan

David Webster

Zelda F. Gamson

ASHE READER SERIES

Barbara Townsend, Series Editor

SIMON & SCHUSTER
CUSTOM PUBLISHING

Cover photos: Brian Smith
Bentley College, Waltham, MA

ISBN 0–536–59295–0
BA 95053

SIMON & SCHUSTER CUSTOM PUBLISHING
160 Gould Street/Needham Heights, MA 02194
Simon & Schuster Education Group

Acknowledgments

Grateful acknowledgment is made to the following sources for permission to reprint material copyrighted or controlled by them:

"A Comparison of Carnegie and NCES Data on Postsecondary Faculty: Ambiguities and Disjuntures," by David W. Leslie and Elaine C. Fygetakis, reprinted by permission from *Research in Higher Education*, Vol. 33, No. 4, pp. 447–465. Copyright © 1992 by Department of Educational Leadership.

"From Tutor to Specialized Scholar: Academic Professionalization in Eighteenth and Nineteenth Century America," by Martin Finkelstein, reprinted from *History of Higher Education Annual*, Vol. 3, pp. 99–121. Pennsylvania State University, 403 S. Allen St., #115, University Park, PA 16801–5202.

"'Women's Work' in Science," by Margaret W. Rossiter, reprinted from *Women Scientists in America: Struggles and Strategies to 1940*, 1982, pp. 51–72. Copyright © 1982 by The Johns Hopkins University Press. Reprinted by permission of The Johns Hopkins University Press.

"Through the Back Door:Academic Racism and the Negro Scholar in Historical Perspective," by Michael R. Winston, reprinted by permission of *Daedalus, Journal of the Academy of Arts and Sciences* from the issue entitled ," The Future of Black Colleges," Summer 1971, Volume 100, Number 3, pp. 678–719. Copyright © 1971 by *Daedalus*.

"Segmentation in the Academic Labor Market: Hiring Cohorts in Comprehensive Universities," by Dorothy E. Finnegan, *Journal of Higher Education*, Vol. 64, No. 6 (Nov./Dec. 1993, pp. 621–656) is reprinted by permission. Copyright © 1993 by the Ohio State University Press. All rights reserved.

"The Appointment Process: On Achievement and Ascription," by Lionel S. Lewis, reprinted from *Scaling the Ivory Tower: Merit and Its Limits in Academic Careers*, pp. 109–146. Copyright © 1975 by The Johns Hopkins University Press. Reprinted by permission of The Johns Hopkins University Press.

"Methods Used in Seeking Jobs," (chart) by David G. Brown, reprinted from *The Mobile Professors*, p. 119. Copyright © 1967 by American Council on Education. Reprinted by permission.

"Median Salary Differentials (in dollars)" (chart) by Michael A. La Sorte, reprinted from "Academic Women's Salaries: Equal Pay for Equal Work?" by Michael A. La Sorte, *Journal of Higher Education*, Vol. 42, April 1971, p. 269 is reprinted by permission. Copyright © 1971 by The Ohio State University Press. All rights reserved.

"Differences Between Actual Salaries of Male and Female Faculty Members and Predicted Average Salaries, 1969" (chart) by Carnegie Commission on Higher Education, reprinted from *Opportunities for Women in Higher Education*, McGraw-Hill, Inc., 1969, p. 116.

A Note to the Reader

This second edition of the *ASHE Reader on Faculty and Faculty Issues in Colleges and Universities* is expected to be printed for approximately three academic years, beginning in the Spring of 1996. It is the policy of the *ASHE Reader* series to update the collection of readings included in each *Reader* every two or three years.

A new edition of this *Reader* is anticipated. We would appreciate your comments on the current *Reader* and suggestions for improvement. Specifically, we would like to know which articles, documents and/or book chapters you found particularly helpful, thought-provoking, or informative. We would like to know how you came to use this *Reader* as well, so that future editions can be targeted to your specific needs. Lastly, we ask your help in identifying professional and academic literature which should be included in future editions of this *ASHE Reader*.

Please send your suggestions, comments, and recommendations regarding this *ASHE Reader* to the editor:

> Dorothy E. Finnegan
> School of Education
> The College of William & Mary
> Williamsburg, VA 23187

Suggestions regarding other topics which could be addressed through the *ASHE Reader* series should be sent to:

> Barbara Townsend, Editor
> ASHE Reader
> Department of Educational Leadership
> Memphis State University
> Patterson Hall 113,
> Memphis, TN 38152

The ASHE Reader Series

The ASHE Reader Series is a collection of readers on topics of current interest in higher education. Each reader represents a compendium of exemplary published works chosen by scholars who teach and conduct research in these areas. The books are designed to be used as supplementary text material in courses of higher education or as reference works.

NEW TEACHING AND LEARNING IN THE COLLEGE CLASSROOM
Edited by Kenneth A. Feldman and Michael B. Paulsen

A comprehensive review of classic and recent research in the area, TEACHING AND LEARNING IN THE COLLEGE CLASSROOM addresses issues from diverse theoretical and philosophical perspectives. Each section includes quantitative and qualitative research, a separate introductory essay, research reports, literature reviews, theoretical essays, and practitioner-oriented articles. It emphasizes teacher-student and student-student interaction. It considers multicultural and gender issues and contains practical teaching strategies based on research.

Paperbound 704 pages ISBN 0-536-58535-0

NEW ASSESSMENT AND PROGRAM EVALUATION
Edited by Joan S. Stark and Alice Thomas

This reader effectively provides the broad perspective necessary for the study of assessment by consolidating articles from a wide range of sources, some not easily obtained. By addressing such topics as the historical and philosophical context and ethical issues, this volume will help readers develop the necessary assessment skills, attitudes and knowledge to conduct and supervise studies and program reviews or to be informed clients inside or outside the academic environment.

Paperbound 832 pages ISBN 0-536-58586-5

COMMUNITY COLLEGES
Edited by James L. Ratcliff

This updated edition includes new information on the diversity of the student population and features a special focus on community college scholarship and faculty renewal. It will give you and your students a review of the current community college systems in American history, philosophy, and purpose: organization, administration, and finance; programs and services; students; professional staff; and the social role.

Paperbound 503 pages ISBN 0-536-58571-7

QUALITATIVE RESEARCH IN HIGHER EDUCATION:
Experiencing Alternative Perspectives and Approaches
Edited by Clifton E. Conrad, Anna Neuman, Jennifer Grant Haworth, and Patricia Scott

Designed to help students and teachers prepare for, enter into, participate in, reflect on, and give voice to the experience of doing qualitative research. Organized around six topics: Explicating Frames of Reference, Approaching Inquiry, Doing Fieldwork, Interacting with Self and Other, Creating a Text, Reading a Text.

Paperbound 600 pages ISBN 0-536-58417-0

WOMEN IN HIGHER EDUCATION: A Feminist Perspective
Edited by Judith Glazer, Estela Bensimon, and Barbara Townsend

Essays representing the best of feminist scholarship in the field of higher education on four main themes: Theoretical and Research Perspectives, Context Historical, Social, and Professional, Institutional, Women in Academe: As Student, Faculty, Administrators, and Trustees, and The Transformation of Knowledge: Curriculum Change and Feminist Pedagogy.

Paperbound 600 pages ISBN 0-536-58351-0

FOUNDATIONS OF AMERICAN HIGHER EDUCATION
Edited by James L. Bess

A comprehensive introduction to the basics of American higher education—45 articles by some of today's most respected leaders in the field, in six parts: The Scope of Higher Education in American Society, The Participants, The Conduct of Education and Research, The Management of the College or University, Innovation, Change, and the Future, The Study and Practice of Higher Education Administration.

Paperbound 772 pages ISBN 0-536-58013-8

THE HISTORY OF HIGHER EDUCATION
Edited by Lester E. Goodchild and Harold S. Wechsler

Included are an introductory essay on American higher education historiography; introductory overviews of each of the five chronological periods of higher education; in-depth scholarly analyses from journal articles, book chapters, and essays; and the use of primary readings to capture the flavor and meaning of important issues for each period.

Paperbound 675 pages ISBN 0-536-57566-5

ORGANIZATION AND GOVERNANCE IN HIGHER EDUCATION,
Fourth Edition
Edited by Marvin W. Peterson, with Associate Editors Ellen E. Chaffee and Theodore H. White

The selections not only reflect the changing views of colleges and universities as organizations, but also highlight the areas of literature applied to higher education that need to be addressed. The text is divided into three parts: Organization Theory and Models, Governance and Management Processes, and Leadership Perspectives.

Paperbound 475 pages ISBN 0-536-57981-4

FINANCE IN HIGHER EDUCATION

Edited by Dave Breneman, Larry L. Leslie and Richard E. Anderson

> Practical and theoretical, the selections look at the financial management of colleges and universities, higher education economies, and federal and state policies, and represent a number of divergent perspectives and opinions.

> Paperbound 450 pages ISBN 0-536-58352-8

UPCOMING TITLES IN THE SERIES:

MINORITIES IN HIGHER EDUCATION: A HISTORY

Edited by Caroline Turner, Mildred Garcia, Laura Rendon, and Amaury Nora
ISBN 0-536-59003-6

COLLEGE STUDENTS

Edited by Frances Stage, Guadelupe Anaya, John Bean, Don Hossler, and George D. Kuh

To Order:

To order copies of these titles for your class, please contact your campus bookstore and provide them with the quantity and ISBN. You can receive a complimentary desk copy with an order of 10 or more copies.

To order copies for yourself, simply call Simon & Schuster Custom Publishing at 800-428-4466 (or 617-455-7000 in Massachusetts and Canada) from 8:30 to 5:00 EST.

Contents

PART V   THE PROFESSIONAL LIFE OF FACULTY

SCHOLARSHIP ISSUES AND DEFINITIONS

PROFESSIONAL CULTURE AND AFFILIATIONS

PART VI LOOKING TOWARD THE FUTURE

Acknowledgment

The association for the Study of Higher Education wishes to express its appreciation to the following publishers, organizations, and journals for their permission to reprint copyrighted material: Agathon Press, Johns Hopkins University Press, Jossey-Bass Publishers, Open University Press, Princeton University Press, SUNY Press, University of Massachusetts Press; American Council on Education, Carnegie Commission on Higher Education, Carnegie Foundation for the Advancement of Teaching, Cooperative Institutional Research Program (UCLA), College and University Personnel Association, Office of Educational Research, and National Center for Educational Statistics; *Daedalus, History of Higher Education Annual, Isis, Journal of Higher Education, Lingua Franca, Research in Higher Education, Review of Higher Education, Social Forces, Teaching Sociology.*

The authors are especially grateful for the constructive criticism and suggestions for the content of this Reader provided by the Advisory Board and ASHE members. Those members include: Ann Austin, Roger Baldwin, Roger Boice, Dolores Burke, John Creswell, Jay Chronister, Martin Finkelstein, Judith Gappa, Carol Patitu, and Jack Schuster. ASHE members whose comments assisted our thinking include Alan Bayer and John Smart. Barbara Townsend, as Series editor, provided the much needed nudge to keep the project on track. Likewise, Kathy Kourian, our Series editor at Simon & Schuster, proved to be patient and supportive, while pressing for completion. At The College of William & Mary, Kimberly Olsen provided meticulous assistance with the construction of the volume's bibliography as well as making suggestions from the graduate student's perspective. In addition to Kim, Cindy Burns, Alan Edwards, and Douglas Adams assisted with exacting care the final proof-reading of the volume.

Introduction

Although a few researchers gathered data on faculty educational background and employment issues within and across a limited number of institutions early in the twentieth century (see Haggerty 1937), not until Logan Wilson (1942) published *The Academic Man* did scholars turn their attention in a significant way to the complexities of academic life. Following World War II, higher education scholars and planners concentrated on the quantity and quality of the academic labor pool in reaction to the initial enrollment surge after the passage of the GI Bills and in anticipation of the second and larger rush to campus when the Baby Boomers came of age (McGrath 1959; Berelson 1960; NEA 1963). Extensive enrollments translated to expanded campuses and a massive hiring of new faculty through especially the second half of the 1960s. As the structure of higher education grew more complex due to its size, public approbation, and expanded resource base, scholars began to define more elaborate questions about postsecondary issues, including inquiries into faculty life and interests.

The research on faculty since the 1960s has reflected systematically the macro and instant concerns of the professoriate. As streams of knowledge and interest have been initiated, successive cohorts of researchers have refined the ways by which we have perceived faculty behavior, beliefs, attitudes, and professional interactions. During the 1960s, when the academic labor market favored the individual, Caplow and McGee (1958) documented the mechanisms of recruitment into and retention within the professoriate, warning that the research imperative was impinging upon the quality of teaching within the largest universities. But, faculty positions abounded and research interest in the pathways and variables leading to successful professorial careers accrued (Crane 1965, 1970; Smelser and Content 1980). Merton's concept of cumulative advantage (1968) provided researchers with the framework by which to translate the realities of elite career competition for faculty aspirants (Hargens and Hagstrom 1966; Niland 1972; Reskin 1977, 1979; Pelz and Andrews 1976). Using Kerr's (1954) concept of a balkanized academic labor market, that is, that the variations among the institutional types translated into different types of professional positions and institutional requirements for the faculty, Brown (1965) demonstrated that faculty employment mobility was dependent upon institutional type. As many four-year colleges and universities contracted their hiring of faculty when traditional student enrollments dwindled in number and simultaneously shifted from disciplinary majors to vocational preparations, the academic labor market (and the accompanying research) changed. A buyers' market provided opportunities for many institutions to advance their status and student market niche by way of hiring and touting faculty with more prestigious degrees and post-doctoral publications (Muffo and Robinson 1981; Finnegan 1993). When faculty hiring contracted, stabilizing the composition of and limiting entrance into the professoriate, other faculty employment issues, such as governance (Mortimer and McConnell 1978) and unionization (Sumberg 1970; Duryea and Fisk 1972), and productivity (Fulton and Trow 1974; Allison and Stewart 1974; Bayer and Dutton 1977; Tuma and Grimes 1981) and eventually professional development (Clark and Lewis 1985), added depth to the continued research into competitive entry and retention mechanisms (Smelser and Content 1980).

Although Bernard (1960) paralleled Wilson's germinal study with a sociological analysis of women faculty in 1960, followed at the end of the decade with Astin's study of women doctorates (1969), not until the mid-1970s did scholars wrestling with feminist and minority issues find a voice. The discourse was slow to gain a hearing within the mainstream periodicals however. Nevertheless, a few scholars tentatively detailed the low status and proportional under-representation of women (Roby, 1972; Stroeber and Questar, 1977) and African Americans (Rafky, 1972; Mommsen, 1974; Thompson, 1978) within the professoriate. Thus, researchers began to challenge the generic representation within the literature on American faculty that innocently emerged from Logan Wilson's first sociological analysis of life in the academic grove. One by one, presumptions of equity across gender and ethnic lines have been displaced regarding the graduate school socialization process (Holstrom and Holstrom, 1974; Feldman 1974; Hite, 1985; Turner and Thompson, 1993; Holland, 1993), recruitment and employment conditions (Johnson and Stafford, 1974, 1979; Banks, 1984; Exum, Menges, Watkins, and Berlund, 1984; Johnsrud and Des Jarlais 1994), productivity comparisons (Reskin, 1977; Cole and Zuckerman, 1984), and career value sets (Jensen 1982).

For the past twenty years, scholars have tackled employment issues that encompass extrinsic work place elements (Bess 1973, 1982; Austin and Gamson 1983), including institutional incentive and reward systems (Fairweather 1993; Moore and Amey 1993), the intersection of professional norms with organizational requirement (London 1980; Clark 1987), and the faculty's satisfaction with their employment terms (Cares and Blackburn 1978; Plesack-Craig and Bean 1989; Bell 1992; Finnegan 1992; Tack and Patitu 1992). Analysis extends to intrinsic issues related to teaching, professional socialization and renewal. The scholarship on faculty has matured through the recognition that faculty and institutions of higher learning are not merely vanilla in nature. Gender, ethnicity, age, institutional type, and professional aspirations and activities are utilized increasingly as primary variables in the quest to understand the phenomena of faculty life and careers.

One neglected variable, however, has been social class. Perhaps in part as a measure of the acceptance of Jencks and Reisman's (1968) argument that meritocracy began to replace privilege in academe, family and class affiliations of faculty have escaped significant analysis since Ladd and Lipset (1979), using data from the 1969 National Survey of Post-Secondary Faculty, ascertained that faculty in research universities were more likely to emerge from the upper class and conversely, that faculty from the middle and lower classes filled the ranks of "less prestigious" colleges. Within the past decades, two collections (Ryan and Sackrey, 1984; Tokarczyk and Fay, 1993) of autobiographical essays by individual faculty members exploring their class and family affiliations have signaled the element's potential significance in understanding the affective side of faculty.

Finally, even with a rich collection of studies based on interviewing projects by individual or teams of sociologists (McGee 1971; Jencks and Riesman 1968; Riesman, Gusfield, and Gamson 1971), empirical data analysis has dominated this field of study. The application and acceptance of multiple methodological approaches to research questions have initiated new dialogue on faculty and related issues. Studying the life of one faculty member (Weiland 1993) or a small class of individuals (Berger 1990) can be as fertile as analyzing self-reported data from large-scale surveys. Both extremes answer very different questions.

These introductory comments serve as an historical rationale for the current edition of the *ASHE Reader on Faculty*. This edition of the *Reader* is comprised of articles and monograph chapters that have been selected to exhibit a range of subjects, philosophical perspectives, and methods. Over the past twenty years, scholars who conduct research on faculty have dilated Logan Wilson's telescoped sociological discussion of the challenges *men* faced and enjoyed as academics. The composite literature now provides a complex kaleidoscope of considerations, viewing faculty life and activities from multiple vantage points. Any one compilation of articles can never satisfy veteran scholars in this specialty, but this reader is not compiled for the experts who research faculty issues. Rather, the *Reader* has been developed with the student in mind: the student who may or may not have experience with faculty roles, obligations, and career issues; the student who questions the relation of the development of higher education as an institution to the development of the professional life of faculty; the student who wants to observe how scholars approach research questions from diverse and emerging perspectives and with heterogeneous methodologies.

Part I provides some basic data on the faculty so that students may appreciate the size and complexity of the .5M men and women who are employed as faculty in American universities and colleges. The size of the professoriate, both historical and contemporary data, demonstrate growth and permit students to perceive the various points in time when the profession expanded. Current data registering the disparate nature of the faculty by gender, rank, ethnicity, age, salary, and institutional type support further the imperative of approaching research questions from myriad perspectives. This first section is capped with an article by Leslie and Fygetakis, who introduce and interpret the purposes and content of two of the national data bases that are collected through surveys conducted at regular intervals. The Carnegie Foundation for the Advancement of Teaching and National Center for Education Statistics data provide a wealth of self-reported information on faculty; these data sets are often employed by scholars who wish to test hypotheses or to discover national trends.

Part II explores some of the primary historical issues and trends that have fostered the development of the current state of the professoriate. Higher education students learn early in their programs that American faculty began at Harvard with one president, who taught moral philosophy, and with two Fellows (Morrison 1936:18), who shepherded their charges through disputations of a contained body of knowledge. How did the profession develop from there? What have been some of the issues and concerns that have affected the profession's development since that time? Martin Finkelstein provides an overview of the growth and demographic background of American faculty through two centuries, employing an operational definition of the development of a profession. As it developed, the academic profession, however, was not as hospitable to some as it was to others. Infrequently told is the historical plight and scholarly contributions of African American faculty, who primarily taught in Historically Black Colleges. Michael Winston illustrates the effect of social barriers that precluded or limited access to professional opportunities for African American scholars prior to the Civil Rights Act of 1964.

The third section presents a variety of authors' perspectives and research on the processes involved in entering the academy. Perhaps the one phenomenon within the second half of this century that challenged and influenced the size and stratification of American higher education was the enormous growth in collegiate enrollments during the second half of the 1960s. The demand for education exceeded the supply of faculty and institutions across the country scrambled to hire faculty, while thousands of students with the promise of future professional employment flooded graduate schools. By the mid-1970s, the academic labor market dynamics shifted to favor employing colleges and universities and new government regulations forced recruitment practices to become more systematized. Dolores Burke, revisiting in the mid-1980s the questions and concerns first explored in the now classic study of faculty recruitment and retention by Caplow and McGee (1965), documents the changes from the informal networked system of the 1950–60s to current practice within research universities. She notes that the academic labor market dynamics has become more complex in recent years; rather than the market being open or closed, faculty position availability is more field-specific, reflecting changes in the curriculum taught at research universities. Dorothy Finnegan, using qualitative methods, provides an historical perspective on the labor market as she traces the career lines of faculty who are employed at two comprehensive universities. The cohorts of faculty, having been hired during very different time frames by institutions that responded to the shifts in the size of the labor pool from the late 1960s through the late 1980s, differ in dramatic ways in personal background, and professional values and activities.

Unstudied counseling on entrance into an academe career advises students to earn an advanced degree in a field and then seek employment in a college or a university. Research over the past twenty years has demonstrated that not only do an aggregate of variables influence the acquisition of an academic position, but that such qualifications within the variables as the prestige of mentors and doctoral institution affect, or even more accurately determine job attainment. Recent conceptual and methodological approaches employed by various scholars have also demonstrated that distinct conclusions and lessons may be extrapolated depending upon the unit of analysis chosen. The remaining three pieces of this section (by Lionel Lewis, by Shirley Clark and Mary Corcoran, and by Roslyn Mickelson and Melvin Oliver) represent diverse iterations of

Merton's *Matthew Effect*, the concept of cumulative advantage, and its antithesis, cumulative disadvantage. In these three selections, the evolution of the discourse on the individual's access to the range of positions within the professoriate becomes apparent as the authors argue the criteria and consequences of closed and open systems of recruitment of new faculty.

Part IV and V reflect the dichotomy of overlapping professional roles first delineated by Donald Light (1974). Faculty members are institutional actors by virtue of their employment within an institution of higher learning. All faculty belong to their disciplinary profession, although their involvement within the discipline may entail being a consumer, a contributor, or a leader of scholarship. Not all scholars, however, are faculty members, that is, employed within a university or college in an instructional role. Moreover, not all persons who teach in higher education share the same benefits that most tenured and tenure-track faculty enjoy.

Part IV, *The Institutional Life of Faculty*, is divided into three sections, Individual issues, Instructional issues, and Institutional issues, to exhibit the various perspectives that researchers can and have brought to the study of faculty in their interactions within their employment in postsecondary institutions. The authors capture the life choices and activities of faculty as they enter and pursue their professional careers. Jack Hite leads off with a fictional letter of sage albeit tongue-in-cheek advice to a young friend who has just entered the ranks of a university faculty. Through his satire, Hite instructs and counsels the young friend in the informal aspects of the everyday and long term elements of faculty life that are often neglected or simplified in other research. However, all faculty lives and careers are not the same nor has the path into the professoriate been strewn with the same hurdles and sponsorship.

When contrasted, Tony Becher and Jim Palmer demonstrate the differences between faculty who are employed in research universities as opposed to community colleges. These authors permit readers to compare and contrast the professional role options open to faculty that occur within different types of institutions. The other articles explore a variety of variables that affect or define faculty and their careers within their institutions. Anne Reynolds combines and analyzes professional age and gender to explore academic maturation processes and stages. Maria De la Luz Reyes and John Halcon direct attention to institutionalized impediments for Chicano Americans, while Suzanne Sowinska relates in an autobiographical essay the effect that her working class background has had on her academic and personal life. Finally, Richard Hamilton and Lowell Hargens investigate the changes in self-reported political orientations of faculty through a decade and a half that was marked by dramatic social and political changes.

The second sub-section addresses the instructional role of the faculty. Once again, the roles played by faculty are being explored in more and more complexity. As the state governments and the public have begun to demand more accountability and to challenge academe's definitions of productivity, research has extended into instructional issues and practice. John Braxton, Alan Bayer, and Martin Finkelstein, using quantitative methods and basic sociological principles, explore normative behaviors of faculty within their teaching role. Laura Goodwin and Ellen Stevens argue that gender influences the definitions that faculty attach to this significant aspect of faculty life. As the faculty displays more and more gray hair due to the confluence of the massive hiring of the 1960s, the closed nature of the academic labor market during the late 1970s, and the lifting of the mandatory retirement age beginning on January 1, 1994 by the federal government, postsecondary institutional administrators coupled with the faculty themselves, have been searching for methods of enabling senior faculty to stay current and interested in their careers and the changes in collegiate education. Mark LaCelle-Peterson and Martin Finkelstein offer administrators and faculty insights into the methods by which a campus culture can facilitate continued productivity.

If the employment of faculty were a simple one-to-one contract, the institutional relationship might be characterized as a *quid pro quo* interaction defining the duties and responsibilities of the faculty member to the institution and in return the institution's obligations to the faculty. However, colleges and universities are complex organizations that require flexibility to respond to the changing environment, financial exigencies, and market trends. Faculty members, on the other hand, are professionally bound to each other not only at the institutional level as colleagues, but through their disciplinary affiliations and to the national aggregation of the professoriate. As such, certain institutionalized employment policies, practices, and phenomena have developed that intimately affect both the faculty and the institution. The final sub-section of *The Institutional Life of Faculty* probes a range of issues that confront administrators and faculty as they attempt to deal with each other in a changing economic climate.

Marvin Peterson and Theodore White extend the organizational concept that faculty and administrative staff function differently as professionals while serving the same institution (Mintzberg 1979; Etzioni 1964). They frame the potential for conflict and resolution. Administrators are not merely the line officers of an institution, but often include those faculty who have assumed administrative duties at the departmental level. For some time, the effect of the environment on the productivity of faculty has been known, yet many institutions have allowed junior faculty to flounder during their first crucial years. Daniel Wheeler suggests that the chair of a department can impact positively the career and institutional longevity of a newly-hired faculty member.

Two articles follow that direct attention to issues that arise as a result of the difficult fiscal decisions which administrators face today. Although the use of part-time and full-time non-tenure-track faculty positions match the economic and short-term needs of an institution, an extensive reliance on these types of employment alternatives is of concern for various reasons. Part-time faculty can bring state-of-the-art expertise to an academic program, but continuity within academic programs may be threatened. Furthermore, hiring adjunct faculty can produce short-term flexibility and coverage of essential courses, but individuals can also be exploited by an institution if the positions are used solely to reduce budget problems. Judith Gappa and David Leslie provide a portrait of the current academics who are attached to institutions on an adjunct basis, who run the gamut of professional specialists to highway flyers or gypsy faculty. Jay Chronister, Roger Baldwin, and Theresa Bailey, on the other hand, point to a growing trend in academe of contracting full-time faculty, but who are hired outside of the normal safeguards of tenure.

As the faculty relationship with their institutions continues to evolve the issues involved in systemic rewards for defined roles are becoming more distinct, although the answers to current problems may not be as clear. Although the judicial system has deferred to academics in situations that require professional opinion, recent challenges to tenure decisions have questioned the nature and equity of the criteria and procedures used within the oftentimes closed proceedings. Kent Weeks discusses the issues of confidentiality and disclosure within the professional mechanism of peer review. Rewards for faculty productivity extend beyond tenure and include salary and various types of incentives to encourage certain types of behaviors. As James Fairweather notes, rewards reflect the values of an institution and more specifically, an institutional type. They also reflect the values of the larger academic culture. Faculty who are employed in research universities and produce scholarship reap the largest salary rewards, while faculty who are employed in teaching institutions earn less. The third leg of the employment stool is service. Although recent redefinitions of service are emerging, on-campus organizational citizenship remains an important part of contemporary faculty involvement. Barbara Lee discusses governance issues that involve faculty leadership within academic senates.

Section V delves into some of the issues associated with the advancement of knowledge. Ronald Barnett opens the section with a philosophical piece that challenges academics to pursue the relationship between teaching and research. The succeeding four selections explore the variety of definitions of productivity that are associated with the various institutional sectors. Mary Frank Fox's critical review of productivity and rewards literature details the normative expectations and dividends for faculty who drive the invisible colleges of the disciplines, most often those employed in research and doctoral universities. On the other hand, the liberal arts colleges, those that are selective and those whose missions address access, employ faculty who do and can contribute to the knowledge base. The articles by Stanley Michalak and Robert Friedrich and by Kenneth Ruscio contrast the different orientations to scholarship between faculty employed in the two different types of liberal arts colleges. Finally, Robert Blackburn and his colleagues, Jeffrey Bieber, Janet Lawrence, and Lois Trautvetter provide a quantitative analysis of the faculty productivity. Their findings tend to blow holes in many standard assumptions about the relationships among research, scholarship, and service.

Faculty do not merely interact professionally on their campuses, but also are tied to two larger entities: the academic profession and their disciplinary or field affiliation. As such, issues and concerns of faculty cross institutional lines and in turn, institutions are affected by the larger professional affiliations. The issues in this section range from conditions of academic freedom to effects of academic constraints. Sheila Slaughter begins the sub-section with an insightful discussion of the contemporary state of academic freedom. Dorothy Finnegan and Zelda Gamson demonstrate how comprehensive universities by hiring faculty from prominent graduate programs have promoted the culture of research, but are constrained by a lack of resources to support the new perspective. Burton Clark reminds us that professional associations are the foundation out of which scholars are effectively supported and knowledge is ultimately generated. Finally, Robert Merton and Patricia Gumport explore distinct social dynamics of consent and constraint in the construction and acceptance of knowledge.

The final section of *The ASHE Reader* addresses the future of the professoriate—at least a few of the issues that face faculty and institutions. Inviting young scholars to join the ranks ensures a continuation of the profession. Deborah Kirk and William Todd-Mancillas instruct graduate faculty especially about the pivotal points in graduate programs that are crucial periods that sustain or inhibit academic career interest among collegiate hopefuls. Roger Baldwin offers instructive suggestions to administrators about maintaining professional competence throughout faculty careers, while Eugene Rice challenges the status quo definition of productivity by proposing that the definition of scholarship be broadened to be more inclusive. From Rice's germinal work, Ernest Boyer's more recent definitions (1992) emerged a few years ago. The final selection returns to the beginning with a discussion of demographic trends. This time, however, Ira Robinson and Lee Everett are concerned with the future of the professoriate, not the contemporary state of the profession. As the current faculty age, replacement, renewal, and restructuring are becoming crucial elements in planning and distributing resources. With an understanding of the potential future of the academic work force, as Allan Cartter once said, the best projections should make poor predictions.

References

Allison, Paul D., and John A. Stewart. *Productivity Differences Among Scientists: Evidence for Accumulative Advantage.* **American Sociological Review** 39 (1974): 596–606.

Astin, Helen S. **The Woman Doctorate in America.** New York: Russell Sage, 1969.

Austin, Ann E., and Zelda F. Gamson. **Academic Workplace: New Demands, Heightened Tensions.** ASHE-ERIC Higher Education Research Report No. 10. Washington, D.C.: Association of Higher Education, 1983.

Banks, W. M. *Afro-American Scholars in the University: Roles and Conflicts.* **Behavioral Scientist** 27 (1984): 325–338.

Bayer, Alan E., and Jeffrey E. Dutton. *Career Age and Research-Professional Activities of Academic Scientists.* **Journal of Higher Education** 68 (1977): 259–82.

Bell, Stephen. *Research Activities and Work Satisfaction of Community College Faculty in Ontario.* **The Review of Higher Education** 15 (1992): 307–326.

Berelson, Bernard. **Graduate Education in the United States.** New York: McGraw-Hill, 1960.

Berger, Bennett M. **Authors of Their Own Lives: Intellectual Autobiographies by Twenty American Sociologists.** Berkeley: University of California Press, 1990.

Bernard, Jessie. **Academic Women.** University Park, PA: The Pennsylvania State University Press, 1964.

Bess, James L. *Patterns of Satisfaction of Organizational Prerequisites and Personal Needs in University Academic Departments.* **Sociology of Education** 46 (1973): 99–114.

_____. **University Organization: A Matrix Analysis of the Academic Professions.** New York: Human Sciences Press, 1982.

Brown, David G. **The Mobile Professor.** Washington, D.C.: The American Council on Education, 1967.

Caplow, Theodore, and Reece J. McGee. **The Academic Marketplace.** New York: Basic Books, 1958.

Cares, Robert C., and Robert T. Blackburn. *Faculty Self-Actualization. Factors Affecting Career Success.* **Research in Higher Education** 9 (1978):123–36.

Cole, Jonathan R. and Harriet Zuckerman. *The Productivity Puzzle: Persistence and Change in Patterns of Publication of Men and Women Scientists.* In **Advances in Motivation and Achievement,** edited by M. W. Steinkamps and M. L. Maehr. Greenwich, CT: Jai Press, 1984.

Clark, Shirley M, and Darrell R. Lewis (eds). **Faculty Vitality and Institutional Productivity: Critical Perspectives for Higher Education.** New York: Teachers College Press, 1985.

Clark, Burton. **The Academic Life: Small Worlds, Different Worlds.** Princeton: Carnegie Foundation for the Advancement of Teaching, 1987.

Crane, Diane. *Scientists at Major and Minor Universities: A Study of Productivity and Recognition.* **American Sociological Review** 30 (1965): 699–714.

_____. *The Academic Marketplace Revisited: A Study of Faculty Mobility Using the Cartter Ratings.* **American Journal of Sociology** 7 (1970): 953–956.

Duryea, E. D., and Robert S. Fisk. "Impact of Unionism on Governance," in *The Expanded Campus: Current Issues in Higher Education 1972*, Dyckman W. Vermilye, editor. American Association for Higher Education. San Francisco: Jossey-Bass, 1972.

Etzioni, Amitai. The *Active Society: A Theory of Societal and Political Processes.* New York: The Free Press, 1968.

Exum, W. H., Robert J. Menges, B. Watkins, and P. Berglund. *Making it at the Top: Women and Minority Faculty in the Academic Labor Market.* **American Behavioral Scientist** 27 (1984): 301–324.

Feldman, Saul D. **Escape from the Doll's House: Women in Graduate and Professional School Education.** New York: McGraw-Hill, 1974.

Finnegan, Dorothy E. **Academic Career Lines: A Case Study of Faculty in Two Comprehensive Universities.** Ph.D. diss., The Pennsylvania State University, University Park, 1992.

_____. *Segmentation in the Academic Labor Market: Hiring Cohorts in Comprehensive Universities.* **Journal of Higher Education** 64 (1993): 621–656.

Fulton, Oliver, and Martin Trow. *Research Activity in American Higher Education.* **Sociology of Education** 47 (1974): 29–73.

Haggerty, Melvin E. **The Evaluation of Higher Institutions, Volume 2: The Faculty.** Chicago: University of Chicago Press, 1937.

Hargens, Lowell, and Warren Hagstrom. *Sponsored and Contest Mobility of American Academic Scientists.* **Sociology of Education** 39 (1966): 24–38.

Hite, L. M. *Female Doctoral Students: Their Perceptions and Concerns.* **Journal of College Student Personnel** 26 (1985): 18–22.

Holland, Jearold W. *Relationships Between African American Doctoral Students and Their Major Advisors.* Paper presented at American Educational Research Association, Atlanta, 1993.

Holstrom, Engininel, and Robert Holmstrom. *The Plight of the Woman Doctoral Student.* **American Educational Research Journal** 11 (1974): 1–17.

Jencks, Christopher, and David Reisman. **The Academic Revolution.** Garden City, NY: Doubleday, 1968.

Jensen, Katherine. *Women's Work and Academic Culture.* **Higher Education** 11 (1982): 67–83.

Johnson, George E., and Frank E. Stafford. *The Earnings and Promotion of Women Faculty.* **American Economic Review** 64 (1974): 888–903.

_____. *Pecuniary Rewards to Men and Women Faculty.* In **Academic Rewards in Higher Education**, Darrell R. Lewis and William E. Becker, Jr., (eds). Cambridge: Ballinger Publishing Company, 1979.

Johnstrud, Linda K., and Christine D. Des Jarlais. *Barriers to Tenure for Women and Minorities.* **The Review of Higher Education** (1994): 335–354.

Kerr, Clark. The *Balkanization of Labor Markets.* In **Labor Mobility and Economic Opportunity**, edited by E. Wright Bakke, et al. Cambridge: MIT press, 1954.

Ladd, Everett, and Seymour Lipsett. **Survey of the American Professoriate: Selected Tabulations.** Storrs: Social Science Data Center, 1978.

Light, Donald Jr. *Thinking about Faculty,* **Daedalus,** *103* (#4, Fall) 1974:258–264.

London, Howard. **The Culture of a Community College.** New York: Praeger, 1978.

McGee, Reece. **Academic Janus: The Private College and Its Faculty.** San Francisco: Jossey-Bass, 1971.

McGrath, Earl J. **The Graduate School and the Decline of Liberal Education,** New York: Teachers College, University of Columbia University Press, 1959.

Merton, Robert K. *The Matthew Effect in Science.* **Science** 159 (1968): 55–63.

Mintzberg, Henry. **The Structuring of Organizations.** Englewood-Cliffs, NJ: Prentice-Hall, 1979.

Mommsen, Kent G. *Black Ph.D.s in the Academic Marketplace: Supply, Demand, and Price.* **The Journal of Higher Education** 45 (1974): 253–267.

Moore, Kathryn N., and Marilyn J. Amey. **Making Sense of the Dollars: The Costs and Uses of Faculty Compensation.** ASHE-ERIC Higher Education Report No. 5. Washington, D.C.: The George Washington University, School of Education and Human Development, 1993.

Morrison, Samuel Eliot. **Three Centuries of Harvard, 1636–1936.** Cambridge: Harvard University Press, 1936.

Mortimer, Kenneth, and T. R. McConnell. **Sharing Authority Effectively.** San Francisco: Jossey-Bass, 1978.

Muffo, John A. and John R. Robinson. *Early Science Career Patterns of Recent Graduates from Leading Research Universities.* **The Review of Higher Education** 5 (1981): 1–13.

National Education Association. **Teacher Supply and Demand in Colleges, Universities, and Junior Colleges.** Washington, D.C.: National Education Association, 1963.

Niland, John R. *Allocation of Ph.D. Manpower in the Academic Labor Market.* **Industrial Relations** 2 (1972):141–156.

Pelz, Donald C., and Frank M. Andrews (eds). **Scientists in Organizations: Productive Climates for Research and Development.** Ann Arbor: Institute for Social Research, 1976.

Plesack-Craig, Faye D., and John P. Bean. *Education Faculty Job Satisfaction in a Major Research University.* A paper presented at the 14th Annual Meeting of the Association for the Study of Higher Education, Atlanta, 1989.

Rafky, David M. *The Black Scholar in the Academic Marketplace.* **Teachers College Record** 74 (1972): 225–260.

Reisman, David, Joseph Gusfield, and Zelda Gamson. **Academic Values and Mass Education: The Early Years of Oakland and Monteith.** Garden City, NY: Doubleday, 1971.

Reskin, Barbara F. *Scientific Productivity and the Reward Structure of Science.* **American Sociological Review** 42 (1977): 491–504.

_____. *Academic Sponsorship and Scientists' Careers,* **Sociology of Education,** 52 (1979): 129–146.

Roby, Pamela. *Structural and Internalized Barriers to Women in Higher Education.* In **Toward a Sociology of Women,** C. Safilios-Rothschild (ed). Lexington, MA: Xerox College Publishing, 1972.

Ryan, Jake, and Charles Sackrey. **Strangers in Paradise: Academics from the Working Class.** Boston: South End Press, 1984.

Smelser, Neil, and Robin Content. **The Changing Academic Labor Market.** University of California Press, 1980.

Stoeber, Myra H., and Aline O. Questar. *The Earnings and Promotion of Women Faculty: Comment.* **American Economic Review** 67 (1977): 207–213.

Sumberg, Alfred D. "Collective Bargaining," in *The Troubled Campus: Current Issues in Higher Education 1970,* G. Kerry Smith, editor. American Association for Higher Education. San Francisco: Jossey-Bass, 1970.

Tack, Martha W., and Carol Patitu. **Faculty Job Satisfaction: Women and Minorities in Peril.** ASHE/ERIC Higher Education Reports #4. Washington, D.C.: ASHE/ERIC, George Washington University Press, 1992.

Thompson, D. *Black College Faculty and Students: The Nature of Their Interaction.* In C. Willie and R. Edmonds (eds). **Black Colleges in America: Challenge, Development, and Survival.** New York: Teachers College Press, 1978.

Tokarczyk, Michelle M., and Elizabeth A. Fay. **Working-Class Women in the Academy: Laborers in the Knowledge Factory.** Amherst: The University of Massachusetts Press, 1993.

Tuma, Nancy Brandon, and Andrew J. Grimes. *A Comparison of Models of Role Orientations of Professionals in a Research-Oriented University.* **Administrative Science Quarterly** 26 (1981): 187–206.

Turner, Caroline S. V., and J. R. Thompson. *Socializing Women Doctoral Students: Minority and Majority Experiences.* **The Review of Higher Education** 16 (1993): 355–370.

Weiland, Steven. *Writing the Academic Life: Faculty Careers in Narrative Perspective.* **The Review of Higher Education** 17 (1994): 395–422.

Wilson, Logan. **The Academic Man: A Study in the Sociology of a Profession.** New York: Oxford University Press, 1942.

PART I
DATA TABLES

HISTORICAL SUMMARY OF FACULTY IN INSTITUTIONS OF HIGHER EDUCATION: 1869–1992

YEAR	1869–1870	1899–1900	1929–1930	1959–1960	1989–1990	1991–1992
TOTAL INSTITUTIONS[1]	563	977	1,409	2,008	3,535	3,601
TOTAL FACULTY[2]	5,553	23,868	82,386	380,554	[3]824,220	826,252
MEN	4,887	19,151	60,017	296,773	577,298	525,599
WOMEN	666	4,717	22,369	83,781	246,992	300,653

SOURCE: excerpted from *Digest of Education Statistics*, 1994, p. 175.

---

[1] Prior to 1979–1980, excludes branch campuses.

[2] Total number of different individuals (not reduced to full-time equivalent). Beginning in 1959–1960, data are for the first term of the academic year. Data for 1989–1990 and 1991–1992 include only instructional faculty with the rank of instructor or above.

[3] Because of revised survey procedures, data may not be directly comparable with figures prior to 1989–1990.

NUMBER OF FACULTY AND DISTRIBUTION OF ETHNICITY AND GENDER BY CARNEGIE TYPE

INSTITUTION TYPE	# FULL TIME FACULTY	AMERICAN INDIAN		ASIAN		BLACK		HISPANIC		WHITE	
		% MEN	% WOMEN	% MEN	% WOMEN	% MEN	% WOMEN	% MEN	% WOMEN	% MEN	% WOMEN
RESEARCH	10,843	0.2	0.1	6.2	1.9	2.2	1.6	1.3	0.6	64.0	22.4
DOCTORAL¹	79,830	0.4	0.2	5.0	1.4	2.3	1.6	2.0	0.8	64.3	22.6
COMPREHENSIVE	132,898	0.2	0.2	3.3	1.0	3.2	2.8	1.4	0.7	58.0	29.4
LIBERAL ARTS	37,560	0.3	0.1	1.9	0.9	3.7	1.8	0.9	0.5	54.2	35.8
PUBLIC 2-YEAR	109,551	0.7	0.3	1.9	1.4	2.5	3.6	2.5	1.6	47.8	37.7

ORIGINAL SOURCE: U.S. DEPARTMENT OF EDUCATION, "FACULTY AND INSTRUCTIONAL STAFF: WHO ARE THEY AND WHAT DO THEY DO?"

TABLE EXCERPTED FROM: *The Chronicle of Higher Education Almanac*, September 1, 1995, p. 22.

¹ Includes medical schools

DISTRIBUTION OF AGE AND RANK OF FACULTY BY CARNEGIE TYPE

	RESEARCH	DOCTORAL	COMPRE-HENSIVE	LIBERAL ARTS	2-YEAR
AGE:					
29–younger	0.9%	1.6%	1.9%	2.2%	5.7%
30–34	9.3%	7.4%	7.1%	8.5%	6.2%
35–39	19.0%	16.4%	14.4%	14.4%	8.4%
40–44	16.4%	12.7%	17.1%	19.8%	27.2%
45–49	16.8%	18.0%	19.6%	19.9%	12.4%
50–54	13.6%	17.2%	16.1%	9.9%	19.0%
55–59	10.4%	12.0%	11.7%	13.6%	13.2%
60 or older	13.8%	15.0%	12.3%	11.7%	8.1%
RANK:					
Professor	42.3%	35.5%	34.0%	29.4%	14.1%
Associate Professor	26.7%	32.7%	28.0%	23.0%	7.1%
Assistant Professor	25.2%	27.1%	28.1%	31.2%	16.4%
Instructor	2.9%	4.4%	7.4%	9.3%	29.2%
Lecturer	2.6%	1.4%	1.7%	0.5%	0.6%

ORIGINAL SOURCE: U.S. Department of Education, National Center for Education Statistics, National Survey of Postsecondary Faculty (NSOPF), 1988.
Table excerpted from: *Digest of Education Statistics,* 1994, p. 231.

AVERAGE SALARIES OF FULL-TIME FACULTY MEMBERS, 1994–95

Doctoral Institutions	Salary	ALL 1-year Increase	PUBLIC Salary	1-year Increase	PRIVATE, INDEPENDENT Salary	1-year Increase
Professor	$71,290	3.9%	$67,560	4.0%	$84,790	3.6%
Associate professor	50,420	3.6	49,090	3.9	56,310	3.4
Assistant professor	42,500	3.3	41,320	3.4	47,390	3.1
Instructor	30,500	5.1	29,300	4.0	36,100	6.5
Lecturer	34,540	—	34,070	—	37,240	—
All	56,000	3.7	53,570	3.9	66,270	3.5
Comprehensive Institutions						
Professor	$57,850	3.0%	$57,090	2.9%	$60,830	3.0%
Associate professor	46,410	3.2	46,020	3.4	47,540	2.5
Assistant professor	38,530	3.2	38,360	3.3	39,080	2.7
Instructor	29,760	2.9	29,460	2.9	31,170	2.3
Lecturer	29,710	—	29,140	—	32,010	—
All	46,710	3.1	46,350	3.1	48,280	2.7
Baccalaureate Institutions						
Professor	$51,790	3.6%	$51,470	4.4%	$58,040	3.4%
Associate professor	41,270	3.3	42,600	3.9	44,130	3.4
Assistant professor	34,520	3.3	35,720	4.1	36,430	3.3
Instructor	27,830	3.0	28,430	3.8	28,730	2.6
Lecturer	32,370	—	30,320	—	38,910	—
All	41,120	3.4	41,420	4.1	45,330	3.3
2-year Institutions with Academic Ranks						
Professor	$51,070	3.9%	$51,490	3.8%	$41,440	6.6%
Associate professor	41,870	3.9	42,220	3.9	36,280	6.2
Assistant professor	35,640	3.8	35,960	3.7	30,460	5.6
Instructor	30,190	3.9	30,430	3.8	27,180	8.3
Lecturer	27,360	—	27,450	—	19,260	—
All	40,850	3.9	41,230	3.8	33,800	6.5

ORIGINAL SOURCE: American Association of University Professors.

Table taken from: *The Chronicle of Higher Education Almanac,* September 1, 1995, p. 22.

A Comparison of Carnegie and NCES Data on Postsecondary Faculty:
Ambiguities and Disjunctures

DAVID W. LESLIE AND ELAINE C. FYGETAKIS

This paper compares the results of NCES and Carnegie surveys of postsecondary faculty to identify points of agreement and disagreement between them, and to contrast the respective survey results to other recent research on faculty. The two surveys utilized differently constructed samples, experienced different response rates, and employed different weighting schemes for purposes of analyzing and interpreting the results. Certain important inconsistencies in the results of the two surveys were observed and the paper provides a critical analysis of methodological and interpretive issues raised in a comparison of the surveys' results.

The Carnegie Foundation for the advancement of teaching (CFAT) and the National Center of Education Statistics (NCES) conducted very nearly simultaneous national surveys of post secondary faculty in 1988-89 and 1987-88 respectively.[1] The results and technical reports for these surveys are now available publicly and have been important sources for policy-related studies and projections concerning the academic work force. This paper reviews and compares the methodologies of the two surveys and compares selected results that yield ambiguous or inconsistent conclusions about the current condition of the full-time academic work force.

The analyses in this paper are based on data drawn from the National Survey of Postsecondary Faculty, 1988 (NSOPF-88) table generation system available from NCES and from the *1989 National Survey of Faculty: Technical Report and Detailed Tabulations* available from CFAT. Concern over confidentiality precluded NCES from making original data files available for analysis, and the table generation system does not allow more than selected cross-tabulations to be performed. No inferential procedures are possible. These data sources were used because the more familiar publications of data from the two surveys offered incomplete results and did not permit full comparisons on all items of interest.[2] Small differences appear between the data sources used in this paper and the data presented in the published reports of both NCES and CFAT.

The discrepancies between the two NCES sources appear to be on the order of rounding errors, and do not appear to be serious. Occasionally, however, the table generator produces results that are not consistent with those in the published NCES data. Since there are now three versions of the table generator in circulation, it is quite possible that errors in loading the data or in the instructions to users have created significant mistakes. The analyses conducted for this paper were drawn from the first version of the table generator. (The second version appeared to have disk or system errors, and NCES so informed users in March 1991.)

Large-scale national surveys of faculty are undertaken only infrequently, yet they are the main source of data for work on faculty labor markets (e.g., Breneman and Youn, 1988), work patterns and attitudes (e.g., Bowen and Schuster, 1986), retirement plans (e.g., Bowen and Sosa, 1989), and related policy-oriented studies (Boyer, 1990). Twelve surveys conducted over the past two decades, including the two whose results are compared in this paper, are reviewed by Cresswell, Chronister, and Brown (1991). The authors identify problems in the definition and measurement of standard data elements as well as in the need to coordinate survey research among the agencies with common interests in faculty and their work (pp. 52–53). One result, we will contend, of the lack of standardization may be an important degree of measurement error in the major surveys themselves. Sources of error in these data may go undetected for a period of years between surveys, and the data may influence planning at many levels unless attention is focused on ambiguous or unclear results.

Apparent errors of measurement can be detected in comparisons of the recent CFAT and NCES survey results. Even for relatively simple variables like age and salary, differences can be observed. Such errors point to suspect instrumentation, although they leave open the question of sampling and weighting, as well. One reader of this paper pointed out that precision in the estimation of parametric values is less critical to studies employing regression methodology. While this may be true, data from the surveys are used in media stories and may become the basis for assumptions made by policymakers and the public. It therefore seems appropriate to raise questions about the level of confidence placed in parametric estimates.

Whatever errors may be due to flawed instrumentation are magnified greatly by sampling error at the level of individual cells. Very little can be learned about some subpopulations, and therefore about sources of diversity in work patterns and attitudes.

Because further surveys are planned—NCES has publicly announced its intention to repeat the survey of postsecondary faculty in 1993—it is important to assess the results of the two recent efforts and to locate potential sources of measurement error. The work on which this paper is based began with an effort to match items from the two surveys and to compare results on a selected set of key variables. By no means have all possible comparisons been conducted, nor have more than a small number of cross-tabulations been created using the NCES table generation system. An extensive amount of further work is both possible and needed.

Comparative Methodologies

Consultants

Both Carnegie and NCES relied on external consultants to design and conduct their respective surveys. Carnegie contracted with The Wirthlin Group of Princeton, NY; NCES contracted with SRI International of Palo Alto, CA.

Sampling

The NCES survey was the first of postsecondary faculty conducted by the National Center of Education Statistics in a quarter century (since 1963). It was conducted in three parts: samples of chief academic officers, department chairs, and faculty each responded to survey questionnaires. Items covered a wide range of issues affecting the current state of the faculty work force and its working conditions at institutions of postsecondary education.

Sampling for the NCES survey was conducted in two stages, with institutional samples drawn first from the framework provided by the Integrated Postsecondary Education Data System (IPEDS) file. Twelve strata were created, roughly paralleling the Carnegie classification but not technically consistent with it. No explanation is offered by NCES for the decision to use the IPEDS classification rather than the more commonly used Carnegie classification. IPEDS includes more specialized institutional types, with one consequence being a somewhat broader universe of institutions in the NCES population. The NCES sample drew from a population of 3,159 institutions; the CFAT sample drew from 2,747 institutions.

NCES ranked institutions within strata in order of faculty size, and several substrata were created to reflect varying sizes. Random sampling of institutions was performed within size substrata. Proportionally, large institutions were overrepresented in the final sample. Of 480 sampled institutions, 449 or 94 percent actually submitted lists of faculty.

Sampling faculty from institutional lists appears to have been done in stages and was not fully described in NCES reports. Certain program areas appear to have been underrepresented in the initial sampling and a supplemental sample was used. Postclassification of respondents into program areas was conducted for most fields. Education, English and literature, foreign languages, history, and philosophy faculty were drawn on the basis of their program affiliation. Once it was determined that certain fields were underrepresented in a large category defined as "all other program areas" (other than the fields mentioned above), a second round of sampling was conducted. The rationale for selecting such a narrow band of fields for the first round of sampling is not available in NCES technical reports.

In addition, part-time faculty were sampled at a lower rate than full-time faculty. It is not clear how part-time faculty were identified, but it is the experience of others conducting research on faculty that part-time temporary faculty, especially in community colleges, are difficult to identify and locate. As far as can be determined from NCES technical reports, obtained faculty samples were not compared to other data (e.g., IPEDS) to determine if individual fields were proportionately represented.

Surveys were mailed out and returned between April and October of 1988. Some concern was noted in NCES technical reports about the loss of transient faculty who may have moved between academic years. But the overall response rate was 76 percent. The total number of respondents from the initial sample (excluding those identified as ineligible) of 11,071 was 8,382. Results in the NCES statistical reports exclude responses from just over 970 temporary faculty, which reduces the effective sample size to 7,408. Of that number, 1,140 (15 percent) were part-time faculty whose responses were analyzed separately. Weighting of responses was based on five factors related to institutional size and representations of a faculty member's field in the sample.

The CFAT survey selected 306 institutions, sampling 34 from each Carnegie classification stratum. Sampling probability for each institution was based on the size of its faculty compared to the other schools within that classification. The CFAT technical report does not specify how many institutions from each stratum agreed to participate. If all 34 in each stratum agreed, 100 percent of all Research Universities II but only 2.5 percent of all two-year colleges would have been included.

A faculty sample of 9,996 was selected for inclusion in the study, according to the CFAT technical report (p. 57). The basis on which faculty were sampled is not made clear. By interpolation, it can be inferred that about 33 faculty per institution were asked to participate. Who selected them and on what basis is not reported. (The form letter to faculty soliciting replies to the survey indicates that individuals were randomly selected.) Surveys were mailed out and returned during the February - April 1989 period, meaning the first CFAT surveys were mailed about four months after the last NCES survey return was accepted. Return rates varied by stratum. As many as 62 percent (Liberal Arts I) and as few as 41 percent (Liberal Arts II) returned the survey. The overall response rate was 54.5 percent of 5,450 individual faculty. Weighting of responses was based on the proportion of faculty in each Carnegie classification stratum in the population.

Instrumentation

The two surveys emphasize substantially different kinds of variables. The NCES survey largely consists of measures of demographic and professional activity variables. CFAT concentrates more heavily on attitudinal variables.

Minimal information is provided about instrument construction or technical performance of items. No reliability or validity information is provided in reports published by NCES or CFAT. The CFAT technical appendix (prepared by The Wirthlin Group) indicates only that the survey instrument was pretested on seven faculty and several scholars and was revised as a result. NCES used advisory panels to review drafts of its survey instrument, but its published reports do not discuss instrumentation or the role(s) of panels in item validation.

Where common subjects are addressed by items on both instruments, there are important differences in both scaling and directionality of response options. In some cases, there are substantial differences in the results, far more than would be ordinarily attributable to sampling error.

Perhaps the most striking example of measurement error arises from a comparison of items asking faculty about retaining or abolishing the system of tenure. Depending on which results one reads (see Table 1), either 79 percent (NCES) or 57 percent (CFAT) support keeping tenure. The NCES result is based on the total of all responses, including temporary and part-time faculty who are not currently eligible for tenure, an estimated 57 percent of which were from tenured faculty. The CFAT result is from a respondent pool that is somewhat more tenured—66 percent. The composition of the two samples would lead one to predict a more conservative, pro-tenure response from the CFAT sample. Yet the opposite result was observed.

The two items are scaled in opposite directions. The CFAT item asks whether respondents believe that "abolition of the tenure system would . . . improve the quality of American higher education." The NCES item, on the other hand, asks respondents whether they agree or disagree that the tenure system should be preserved. A respondent to the CFAT survey would disagree to register approval of the tenure system, while a NCES respondent would agree to register the same directional response.

The items also provide for a different number of response options. The CFAT survey provides a neutral option, chosen by 13.3 percent of the respondents. NCES respondents were not given the same option, and were forced to agree or disagree. However, even if all 13 percent of the CFAT respondents choosing the neutral option were added to the total of those disagreeing that abolition of tenure would be desirable, the total still does not approach a statistical equality with the proportion of those agreeing that tenure should be preserved in response to the item on the NCES survey (75% vs. 79%).

Although a detailed item analysis was not performed for this paper, it is clear that wording, scaling, and directionality of some important items may be substantially correlated with the response patterns. There is at least enough variability between the two surveys on comparable items to suggest substantial measurement imprecision.

Results

Characteristics of Respondents

The NCES results are based on responses form 6,628 full-time faculty. CFAT results are based on responses from 5,450 full-time faculty. Table 2 compares the number of respondents from each of several large categories of institutions. IPEDS and Carnegie classifications differ in the number and definition of strata into which the universe of institutions is divided. However, certain broad categories of institution can be commonly defined. These broad categories are used in Table 2.

Table 1. Comparison of Attitudes Toward Tenure

(A negative answer to the CFAT item implies that the respondent does not want to see tenure abolished. A positive answer to the NCES item implies that the respondent wants tenure preserved.)

	NCES	Carnegie
Strongly preserve	42.7%	29.5%
Preserve w/reserve. or somewhat	36.0%	27.4%
Neutral*		13.2%
Abolish w/ reserve. or somewhat	14.9%	19.7%
Strongly abolish	6.4%	10.2%

* No neutral option provided on NCES survey.

Table 2. Proportion of Respondents from each Type of Institution

Type of Institution	NCES	Carnegie
Research Institution	27%	23%
Doctoral-granting university	15%	24%
Comprehensive college	30%	22%
Liberal arts	8%	21%
Two-year	21%	9%

Although the two surveys obviously sampled from the strata in differing proportions, this artifact is of less significance than the apparently different weighting schemes applied to the responses. Neither technical report provides illustrations or details about weighting, but it is apparent from Table 3 that they used different approaches. CFAT weighted according to the number of institutions in each stratum of the Carnegie classification; NCES weighted according to the number of faculty in the IPEDS strata. This difference alone would generate potentially important variance in the reported survey results.

Table 3. Weights Applied to Strata

Type of Institution	NCES	Carnegie
Research Institution	28.5%	23.3%
Doctoral-granting university	16.0%	9.9%
Comprehensive college	27.0%	24.8%
Liberal arts	8.2%	6.5%
Two-year	19.3%	35.2%

Gender

The two surveys estimate the full-time faculty population to be 73 percent male (NCES) and 69.6 male (CFAT), a statistically significant different ($z = 2.97$, $p < .01$). (Power is inflated by the large n in the two samples, so even small differences will be statistically significant. Nevertheless, the policy implications of these data are important enough to call attention to the statistical differences.) Substantial differences were observed in the two surveys' estimates of the gender composition of the part-time faculty population. CFAT received responses from male part-time faculty at a rate that was 30.9 percent of all part-time faculty responses. NCES, on the other hand, estimated that the population of part-time faculty was 56 percent male. Since the data considered in this study are those reported for full-time faculty only, this difference is not important. It does, however, reflect the difficulty of gathering reliable data on the substantial portion (38 percent in recent IPEDS estimates) of faculty with part-time appointments.

Race/Ethnicity

Both surveys show an overwhelmingly white professoriate: CFAT respondents were 92.5 percent white, and NCES respondents were 89.5 percent white. Applying a z-test for the difference in proportions, the two surveys differed ($p < .01$) in their estimates of the proportion of faculty who classify themselves as white and those who classify themselves as Asian (CFAT reported 2.4%, NCES reported 4.36%). Differences between the survey in estimated proportions of faculty with other racial/ethnic backgrounds were not statistically significant.

Age

The two surveys show very important differences in their respective estimates of faculty age distribution. As increasing concern develops about the retirement plans of the current cohort, establishing the age distribution of those currently working is one critical element in making projections. Bowen and Sosa (1989), in one of the most widely cited efforts to project faculty exit from the profession, based their estimate on the National Research Council's Survey of Doctoral Recipients. They estimated that in 1987, 38.9 percent of faculty in four-year institutions were over the age of 49. The CFAT survey estimated the proportion of faculty over 49 in these strata to be 44.1 percent, and NCES estimated (with interpolation of inconsistent age classifications) that 41.7 percent were over the age of 49.

Comparative age distributions for two-year institutions show that 50.1 percent of the faculty are over age 49 in one estimate (CFAT), but that 42.5 percent are over the same age in the other estimate (interpolated NCES data).

Combining age categories at all institutions into large ranges, the NCES estimates lead to the conclusion that faculty are considerably younger than would be estimated using CFAT results alone. NCES estimates that 24.7 percent are over the age of 55, while CFAT estimates that 30.0 percent are over that age. On the other hand, NCES estimates that 41.3 percent are under the age of 45, while CFAT estimates that only 34.3 percent are under that age.

Rank

Parallel biases appear in the estimated distribution of faculty in the principal ranks. CFAT estimates that 16.7 percent hold the rank of assistant professor; NCES estimates that 22.8 percent do (z = 5.17, p < .001). Conversely, CFAT estimates that 37.3 percent hold the rank of professor, while NCES estimates that 33.0 percent do (z = 4.13, $p < .001$).

Work Load

Data on work load from the two studies are not strictly comparable. Among other things, the NCES survey asked for the distribution of effort for the fall semester, while CFAT asked respondents to use their spring work load as the point of reference. At least some variance must be expected in typical patterns of assignment between the two semesters (none of which may account for variance due to assignments on a quarter system). CFAT's survey requested estimated hours spent on teaching, research, and service; NCES requested estimated percentage of total time spent on each activity. A separate item requested information on the number of hours worked at the institution. Combining percentage of time spent with number of hours worked permits at least a crude estimate of hours spent on activity.

In neither survey did the array of categories correspond with any standard array of work-load assignments or activity reports as commonly used in institutions of higher education. For example, NCES asked for an estimate of the percentage of total working hours spent seeking outside funding, taking courses, and providing [professional] services to clients. The CFAT asked for separate estimates of hours per week spent on scheduled office hours, academic advising, and preparation for teaching.

The most anomalous result has to do with reported research activity. Just short of 8 percent (7.8 percent) of CFAT respondents reported spending no time on research. But 26 percent of the respondents to the NCES survey reported spending zero percent of their time on research. Either or both of these estimates must contain substantial error. The survey items themselves may be one source of error. The NCES survey provided respondents with 12 categories of work (plus "other") and asked them to estimate a percentage of time spent on each—with instructions to force the sum of their estimates to equal 100 percent. The CFAT survey was more open-ended, allowing responses to 10 categories of work and letting the respondents estimate the number of hours spent on each. No forced closure with respect to a total percentage or number of hours was required.

Unfortunately, available data on teaching appear not to be readily comparable. NCES requested an estimate of the percentage of time on one conglomerated category of activity that included teaching, advising, and supervising students (76.5% reported spending from 1% to 50% on this category). Carnegie respondents reported separately for classroom instruction in graduate and undergraduate courses (89% reported spending between 1 and 20 actual hours on undergraduate teaching).

These numbers highlight the difficulty in establishing any common basis for measuring how much teaching faculty do from the data in these surveys. Although both studies show that faculty modally spend between one quarter and one half of their time, or 11 to 23 clock hours, teaching (41.8% per NCES), or teach undergraduates for between 11 and 20 clock hours (39.2% for CFAT), these modal estimates mask great differences among the strata. For example, only 7.3 percent of faculty (CFAT) at research universities reported spending 11-20 hours on undergraduate teaching. Yet over 36 percent of faculty (NCES) at the other sample of research universities report spending between one quarter and one half of their time teaching. The discrepancy does not seem accountable to the additional load of graduate instruction, since over 83 percent of respondents to the CFAT survey report 5 or fewer hours a week on graduate instruction. Approximately 40 percent of two-year college faculty responding to the NCES survey report spending between 26 percent and 50 percent (11-20 clock hours based on a reported 40-hour work week) of their time teaching, while 63 percent of the CFAT respondents from two-year colleges report spending between 11 and 20 clock hours a week teaching.

By inspection, the amount of variability among strata of institutions in the NCES results is smaller than it is in the CFAT results. One might assume, then, that the larger number of response options on the NCES survey, coupled with the restriction of total effort reported to 100 percent, led respondents to a less accurate, more random response pattern. In any event, these surveys do not permit confident estimates of faculty work as measured in standard categories of assignable activity.

Work Product

Both surveys provide data on publications. But the results are far from consistent, although the response categories are generally more comparable than those for work load. Both surveys requested the number of published articles in a career; NCES specified that both refereed and nonrefereed articles should be reported, while CFAT asked only for the total of published articles. Although one would expect the NCES estimate to be more conservative, the reverse appears to be true. The NCES data show a mean number of 12.9 refereed articles published and a mean number of 3.6 nonrefereed articles published, a total of 16.5 articles of all kinds. CFAT results show, however, that only 26.2 percent of all faculty report eleven or more articles published over the career. Since the upper boundary is theoretically infinite, it is possible that the two surveys would estimate the same mean. (This assumes that a small number of faculty publish very large numbers of articles over a career.) Unfortunately, CFAT's report does not provide such an estimate. It should be added that the two surveys appear much closer in the their estimates of other categories of product. Slightly more than one book (of any kind) and between one and two chapters in edited volumes are estimates that both data sets would support. Enormous variation in the predicted directions does occur: University faculty do far more publishing than do faculty at two-year institutions.

A superficially minor discrepancy appears when data on publishing activity within the past two years are considered. The NCES survey provided an extensive listing of publication possibilities, including software, patents, and presentations at conferences, among others. It also provided for responses that included works accepted for publication. Omitting categories of responses that seemed inconsistent with what would be reported on the CFAT survey (an arbitrary choice, to be sure), 43.6 percent indicated that they had no publications. CFAT, on the other hand, asked the question more restrictively: "How many of your professional writings have been published or accepted in the past two years?" A minimally different proportion of CFAT respondents (46.6%) reported that they had no publications.

One would expect the NCES survey with its more liberal provision for nonrefereed and other publications to yield a substantially different estimate of activity than the more conservatively worded CFAT item. Yet, the two surveys present only slightly different pictures of current faculty publication activity. Although it may be a case of looking for error where none exists, this anomalous similarity in result belies the clear differences in wording of the two items, and it runs counter to intuitive expectations about the resulting data pattern.

It should be noted that the data on current (last two years) publication activity presents an internally contradictory picture. NCES, which seems to project a far more active publishing career for faculty than does CFAT, estimates a lower current activity level. But CFAT, whose estimate of career publication records is the lower of the two, projects a much higher current activity level.

Salary

Reported average base salaries for the two surveys are both within a very few dollars of $40,000. There is a slight tendency for the NCES results to estimate larger numbers at both low and high ends of the salary distribution. For example, CFAT reports that 19 percent earn between $20,000 and $30,000 a year. NCES reports 25.1 percent earning salaries in this interval. On the other hand, NCES estimates that 5.1 percent of faculty earn $75,000 or more. CFAT reports that only 3 percent earn $70,000 or more. (Intervals are those used in reports of the two respective organizations.)

The greater number reporting comparatively low salaries in the NCES data is consistent with other observed biases in the same survey. Faculty responding to NCES tended to be younger and of more junior rank than those responding to CFAT. It is not clear why NCES also reports more faculty earning higher salaries. Inclusion of freestanding medical institutions in the sample may be part of the explanation, but NCES data also appear to show greater numbers of faculty in the extremely high salary category at research, doctoral, and comprehensive colleges.

Although the two surveys provide statistically equal estimates of central tendency on the variable of salary, they appear to differ with regard to their estimates of variability.

Attitudes

Both surveys covered a broad array of attitudinal variables. Items were phrased and scaled in differing ways—in some cases within the surveys themselves. Nevertheless, some general comparisons are possible. The reader is cautioned that conservative statistical comparison of attitudinal data from the two surveys has not been attempted. Sample size is so large that the inflated power of parametric tests makes the Type II error risk unacceptably large. Further, items covering similar variables are often scaled and/or coded in inconsistent ways. The goal of this analysis is, in any event, not inferential, but diagnostic. We are attempting to identify potential errors of measurement or sampling, and are not attempting to estimate parameters.

Job Satisfaction

NCES asked directly how satisfied faculty are with their current job. Over 85 percent responded that they were either very or somewhat satisfied. CFAT did not ask the same questions, but asked, "If I had it to do over again, I would not become a college teacher." Almost 77 percent disagreed strongly or with reservations. In general, both surveys seem to indicate a high level of general job satisfaction.

The actual strength of that satisfaction, however, is open to question. For example, the two surveys differ very substantially in the proportion of faculty who answered these questions at the extremes. Although 53 percent of the CFAT respondents strongly disagreed with the survey item, only 36 percent of the NCES respondents indicated that they were very satisfied.

Both surveys show higher levels of satisfaction among two-year college faculty than among faculty from other sectors. The NCES survey also shows persistently greater proportions of faculty from private institutions expressing the highest levels of satisfaction.

In addition, more specific items regarding sources of satisfaction help draw a more complete profile and highlight differences between the two surveys.

Salary and Benefits

Both surveys asked about satisfaction with salary. Table 4 compares the reported levels of that satisfaction.

Obviously, these results are open to many interpretations. One could report, for example, that more than half (58 percent) of those responding to the NCES survey expressed satisfaction with their own salary. On the other hand, the CFAT results would lead to an equally accurate conclusion that more than half (53 percent) reported that their own salaries were fair or poor.

Table 4. Satisfaction with Salary

NCES: "Satisfaction with my salary"		CFAT: "How would you rate your own salary?"	
Very satisfied:	18.7%	Excellent:	8.7%
Somewhat satisfied:	39.7%	Good:	37.7%
Somewhat dissatisfied:	24.1%	Fair:	31.2%
Very dissatisfied:	17.2%	Poor:	22.2%

Job Content/Reward Structure

Persistent questions have been raised about faculty interest in teaching as opposed to doing research. The two surveys address this issue alone and in the context of the preferred reward structure. However, it is difficult to compare the results directly. Both asked if teaching effectiveness should be the primary criterion for promotion. Although both surveys phrased the question in almost exactly the same way, they provided a different array of response options: CFAT offered two agree and two disagree categories apiece, with a neutral option. NCES did not provide a neutral option, but offered two agree and two disagree categories. Table 5 shows the results.

Support for teaching as a criterion for promotion is apparently stronger among NCES respondents than among CFAT respondents—taken at face value. But NCES respondents might not actually differ; they did not have a neutral response option. The results cannot be compared directly.

Other items address the preferred amount of teaching and research (NCES), as well as the primary focus of faculty interest (CFAT). Almost half of the CFAT respondents (45.1 percent) reported that their primary interests lie in teaching. Another 26.5 percent also reported research interests, but still prefer teaching as their principal focus. The aggregate data mask enormous divergence among strata of institutions. Over 64 percent of research university faculty report that research is their preferred emphasis, but 93 percent of two-year college faculty report that teaching is theirs.

Table 5. Teaching Effectiveness Should Be the Primary Criterion for Promotion

	NCES	CFAT
Strongly agree	30.7%	33.3%
Somewhat agree/agree w/reserv.	41.2%	30.8%
Neutral		7.2%
Somewhat disagree/disagree w/reserv.	20.2%	17.0%
Strongly disagree	8.0%	11.8%

The NCES survey asked faculty whether they would prefer to do more or less teaching and research than they presently do. Just over 60 percent indicated that they would prefer to do less teaching—superficially at variance with the CFAT results indicating that teaching is the preference of over 71 percent. Further inspection again suggests wide variance among strata. Those reporting the most substantial press to reduce their current teaching activity are faculty from research universities and faculty from community colleges. (Roughly 67% of both groups want to do less teaching.) Because the roles of faculty in these two strata are so different, it seems important to take great care in framing items that allow for a full and fair assessment of the constraints, incentives, and preferences that impinge on what faculty may realistically elect to do.

Quality of Students

Both surveys asked about the quality of undergraduate students, but the phrasing of the items is sufficiently different to leave doubt about whether they are measuring the same thing. Two-thirds (67%) of the NCES respondents reported being somewhat satisfied or very satisfied with the quality of undergraduate students at their institutions. A substantial majority of CFAT respondents (62.3%), on the other hand, agreed (strongly or with reservations) that "too many students ill-suited to academic life are now enrolling in colleges and universities."

Similar ambiguity is reflected in assessment of the quality of graduate students. Over 78 percent of those who responded to this item on the NCES survey reported satisfaction (somewhat or very satisfied) with the graduate students they have taught. The CFAT survey asked whether respondents thought the quality of graduate students had declined, and the result (omitting the scattering of responses from faculty at two-year institutions) was an even split: 32 percent agreed that a decline had occurred and 32 percent disagreed (35% were neutral). The answer to this question obviously depends on which survey results on chooses to accept.

Attitudes Toward Administration

Without reporting in detail, it is possible to generalize that faculty participate more extensively in departmental governance than in institutional governance. Similarly, results of both surveys show far greater satisfaction with departmental governance than with overall institutional administration. Over 75 percent of the CFAT respondents rated departmental administration as democratic or very democratic, and just short of 70 percent of the NCES respondents reported satisfaction (somewhat or very) with departmental leadership.

Both surveys asked about satisfaction with institutional administration, albeit with slightly different wording. CFAT asked how respondents would rate the administration and NCES asked about satisfaction with the quality of chief administrative officers. CFAT respondents apparently were less satisfied: 37 percent rated the administration good or excellent. Just over 57 percent of the NCES respondents reported being somewhat or very satisfied with campus chief administrative officers. This substantial variance in response pattern my reflect the personalization of the NCES item: When the referent is a specific person, they may be unwilling to respond negatively, but when—as in the CFAT item—the referent is as abstract as the administration, there is less hesitancy to be critical.

Opportunity for Advancement

Both surveys address faculty respondents' feelings about opportunity for career advancement. Thirty percent of NCES respondents report dissatisfaction (somewhat or very) with opportunities for advancement. But only 20.1 percent of CFAT respondents "feel trapped in a profession with limited opportunities for advancement" (strongly agree or agree with reservations). Wording and the array of response options may well account for this variation.

Projected Rates of Retirement

Among the most important numbers to policy makers is the rate of projected retirement from academe. Two major studies (Bowen and Schuster, 1986; Bowen and Sosa, 1989) have reported that faculty are likely to retire in substantial numbers in the foreseeable future. The two surveys each attempted to establish departure and retirement rates.

Although many of the most substantial concerns over retirement have focused on "uncapping" of the mandatory retirement age, faculty do not seem inclined to stay on in large numbers after age 70. Just over 20 percent of the NCES respondents and 17.5 percent of the CFAT respondents indicate plans to retire after 70. The two surveys are in more substantial disagreement over how many faculty will retire early. Over 14 percent of the CFAT respondents indicated retirement plans before age 60, while only 8.7 percent of NCES respondents did so. In addition, the NCES survey allowed respondents to indicate that they have no idea when they will retire. Ten percent chose this option. Sixty-eight percent of CFAT respondents indicated plans to retire between ages 60 and 69; 61 percent of the NCES respondents did so. Close to 15 percent indicated plans to retire (somewhat or very likely) within three years in the NCES survey.

The surveys provide some data on plans to depart from academic positions for reasons other than retirement. Almost one quarter (24.2%) of the NCES respondents had given departure serious consideration within the past two years. Those reporting that they were very or somewhat likely to depart for another full-time position within the next three years comprised 46 percent of the NCES sample. The CFAT survey reported that almost a third (32.3%) agreed (strongly or with reservations) that they were considering leaving the profession (for any reason) within five years.

Beyond this, neither survey provides a basis on which to pin down specific departure or retirement rates. If one simply takes these projected retirement and departure rates at face value, one might assume that 5 percent would retire in any given year and that anywhere from 6 percent to 15 percent would voluntarily leave the profession in any given year. This projection suggests a complete turnover in 5 to 10 years (11% a year for 9 years = 99%). That rate is more than twice as fast as the rate painstakingly established by Bowen and Sosa, who project that as many as 16 percent of current faculty (1987) would still be teaching in 2012. It is also well beyond the recent or current actual experience—and seems to contradict other data on job satisfaction, which gives little reason to expect large-scale departures from academic work. It is unlikely that much confidence can be placed in any particular forecast of departure rates based on these data.

Gender as a Control

Gender differences are not large on most items in either survey. Nor was it the central purpose of this paper to investigate gender differences in attitude. Nevertheless, gender was used as a control variable to assess whether equal differences between genders were observed on those items where there was otherwise substantial variance associated with gender. Although further exploration of control variables would be desirable, this study produced little to suggest major concern.

The two surveys differed in the level of satisfaction with salary. NCES recorded 58 percent as somewhat or very satisfied. CFAT recorded 46 percent as rating their salaries as good or excellent. Men and women did not differ more than a point or two from these overall averages. A similar observation was made on the variable relating to consulting income. Although the two surveys estimated substantially different proportions who earned no consulting income, both showed that 10 percent more women than men earned no consulting income.

The genders did respond differently to items regarding opportunity for advancement. Sixty-two percent of the women responded that they were satisfied with opportunity for advancement on the NCES survey, but 71 percent of the women responding to the CFAT item indicted that they were not seeking other work because of limited opportunity for advancement. This was the only item on which a major difference in the response patterns of either gender was found. The items are not strictly comparable, however, because the CFAT item includes the conditional phrase requiring the respondent to indicate that other work is being sought.

Gender as a control does not turn up enough error to be of concern in a general sense. The two surveys differ in their own estimates of parameters, but the differences are virtually all constant without regard to the gender of the respondent. (Few major gender differences appeared, however, so this may not be an adequate control, nor should these conclusions preclude further study.)

Conclusions

The simultaneous surveys of very large samples of faculty conducted by NCES and by CFAT have produced a wealth of data on academic work, job satisfaction, attitudes, and rates of retirement and departure. These two data bases, as well as the HERI survey data, provide investigators with their first comprehensive look at postsecondary faculty in over half a decade. The fact that both surveys were conducted at such close points in time provides an unusual opportunity to work with a far broader array of information than either survey would provide alone.

Although there are some differences in the results, it is important to look at who the faculty are and what they think and do from more than one perspective. In one sense, having two data sources with which to work should give investigators more confidence in estimating parameters. It should also help policymakers understand better that we know more about some things than about others. For example, these two surveys help illustrate the complexity of measuring faculty activity, and the difficulty of obtaining good data from self-reports. But they also reinforce certain factual conclusions where their results are mutually confirming (one useful example being agreement on the overwhelmingly white male characteristics of the professoriate). Comparing their results, however, leads to the conclusion that there are many ambiguities and disjunctures to be resolved.

It is likely that both organizations will conduct new surveys in the foreseeable future, and it will be important to build on what has been started. NCES, for example, has planned for another iteration of the National Survey of Postsecondary Faculty in 1992 or 1993. The ability of the research community to conduct longitudinal studies and to observe change in variables of universal importance will be enhanced. But this is also an opportune time to reconsider certain aspects of the design and conduct of future surveys.

Sampling is a major concern. The discrepancy in age distribution of the respondents to the two surveys considered in this paper indicates that either or both contain sampling biases. The return rates were substantially different: 55 percent for CFAT and 76 percent for NCES. Obviously, the likelihood of bias is greater in the CFAT results.

Weighting of the results proceeded from differing bases for the two surveys, but neither reports on the consequences of its choice. It is sufficiently discrepant to produce major differences in overall results, and some reconciliation between the two schemes is needed.

Instrumentation is a third major concern. The two instruments are lengthy and are designed in different formats. Individual items do not always use standard terminology (particularly in estimating faculty work patterns), nor are response options always comparable between items on the two surveys. Substantial issues related to scaling and directionality were noted, including an example in which attitudes toward retaining the tenure system appear to have been recorded in ways that correlate with item phrasing and scaling instead of in directions that would be predicted on the basis of the sample composition.

It is not at all clear that item analyses and instrument validation were handled with the attention to detail that might be expected. (For example, the CFAT instrument was pretested on seven faculty and was revised on the basis of that pretest. Published reports do not discuss the NCES instrument construction procedure, although advisory groups did meet with NCES staff to critique instrument drafts.)

Variables selected for inclusion in the survey often appear arbitrary and without benefit of a cost assessment. With such an extensive and costly instrument, and with such a high premium on attaining both valid responses and a high return rate, one might assume very tight control over the number and precision of individual items. To pick one item from each survey for the sake of illustration, it is difficult to intuit either a theoretical or policy rationale for asking how satisfied faculty are with interdepartmental cooperation at their institutions (NCES). It is equally difficult to understand what substantive question(s) might prompt a survey item asking for agreement/ disagreement with the statement that, "New developments in my discipline are not interesting to me" (CFAT). (That 9% of the respondents agreed may be worth noting, however.)

These items seem to be easy targets for criticism, but loading an already extensive survey with items for which no clear gain in knowledge can be anticipated can only result in (1) a lower rate of return/completion, and (2) a less serious/valid response pattern.

There is an inevitable institutional inertia to large-scale survey design and administration. Both CFAT and NCES may develop a vested interest in replicating past surveys to maximize the continuity and comparability of data gathered over time. This paper suggests that neither survey has achieved a level of perfection that precludes change. Users of both data bases might well explore ways in which a pooled effort could produce improved data at less cost without the inefficiencies inherent in two simultaneous large surveys. This is certainly the major policy implication of a comparison of results from the two efforts.

Notes

1. A third independent national survey of faculty was undertaken in 1989-90 by the Higher Education Research Institute at UCLA. The results of that survey are not included in this analysis, but it should be noted that the sample of over 35,000 full-time faculty was far larger than that of either the NCES or CFAT surveys.

2. Readers are referred to *Faculty in Higher Education Institutions, 1988,* Washington: National Center for Education Statistics, 1990. Also, see E. L. Boyer, *The Conditions of the Professoriate: Attitudes and Trends, 1989,* Princeton: The Carnegie Foundation for the Advancement of Teaching, 1989.

References

Bowen, H., and Schuster, J. (1986). *American Professors: A National Resource Imperiled.* New York: Oxford University Press.

Bowen, W., and Sosa, J. (1989). *Prospects for Faculty in the Arts and Sciences: A study of Factors Affecting Demand and Supply, 1987 to 2012.* Princeton: Princeton University Press

Boyer, E. L. (1989). *The Conditions of the Professoriate: Attitudes and Trends, 1989.* Princeton: The Carnegie Foundation for the Advancement of Teaching.

Breneman, D., and Youn, T. (eds.) (1988). *Academic Labor Markets and Careers.* New York: Falmer Press.

Carnegie Foundation for the Advancement of Teaching. (1989). *1989 National Survey of Faculty: Technical Report and Detailed Tabulations.* Princeton: Carnegie Foundation for the Advancement of Teaching.

Cresswell, J. W., Chronister, J. L., and Brown, M. L. (1991). The characteristics and utility of national faculty surveys. In C. S. Lenth (ed.), *Using National Data Bases.* New Directions for Institutional Research, no. 69. San Francisco: Jossey-Bass, pp. 41-59.

National Center for Education Statistics. (1990). *Faculty in Higher Education Institutions, 1988.* Washington, DC: U.S. Department of Education.

PART II
History
of the
Profession

From Tutor to Specialized Scholar: Academic Professionalization in Eighteenth and Nineteenth Century America

Martin Finkelstein

During the past decade and one-half, historians have taken the first steps toward development of an evolutionary "academetrics" of the American professoriate. In the 1960s, two quantitatively oriented studies of college teachers during the seventeenth and eighteenth centuries were published. In 1966, Wilson Smith examined the transformation of the tutorship at pre-revolutionary Harvard.[1] Two years later, William Carrell analyzed the career patterns of 124 professors at nineteen colleges in the second half of the eighteenth century.[2] Together, these analyses suggested that by the turn of the nineteenth century the academic role was emerging as an increasingly viable and distinctive career alternative to the practice of the traditional professions.

The years since have seen the publication of three quantitatively oriented case studies of the evolution of academic faculties during the nineteenth century at three quite different institutions: McCaughey on Harvard, Tobias on Dartmouth, and Creutz on the University of Michigan.[3] While these studies vary considerably in their temporal parameters and the breadth of their analyses[4] and while they hardly focus on what may be considered representative cases,[5] their results collectively require some qualification of earlier interpretations that had located the emergence of the modern, professional collegiate-based scholar in the last quarter of the nineteenth century and wedded his emergence to that of the American graduate university. Specifically, they suggested that (1) the professionalization of the academic role (i.e., the development of a specialized, secular scholarly vocation within the institutional context of the American college) was a gradual process that was already well underway in the ante-bellum period and (2) that professionalization proceeded quite unevenly across institutions, beginning quite early at Harvard and much later at Dartmouth, although the fundamental process in each case seemed to be of a single piece.

Emergence of an Institutional Career, 1750–1800

During the seventeenth and the first half of the eighteenth century, the disciplinary career strand was, of course, virtually non-existent, and even the institutional strand proved secondary to the external one. American colleges operated on a model not unlike the British universities after the Elizabethan Statutes of the late sixteenth century.[10] Assuming that any bright graduate was ready to teach all subjects leading to the degree, instructional staffs were composed entirely of *tutors*, young men (often no more than twenty) who had just received their baccalaureate degree and who were preparing for careers in the ministry. The responsibilities of tutors were both pedagogical and pastoral or custodial in nature. Ideally, a single tutor was assigned the sheparding of a single class through all four years of their baccalaureate program, both inside and outside the classroom. "Tutors were with their pupils almost every hour of the day (in classroom recitations, study halls, and at meals) and slept in the same chamber with some of them at night. They were responsible not only for the intellectual, but for the moral and spiritual development of their charges."[11] In the less than ideal practice, the tutorship functioned as a "revolving door." At Harvard, prior to 1685, very seldom did a tutor see a class through all four years. Only a half dozen of the forty-one tutors during this period remained at Harvard more than three years. While the next half century saw a progressive lengthening of the tutors' tenure at Harvard, and indeed the ultimate establishment of "permanent" tutorships in the latter half of the eighteenth century,[12] the "revolving door" condition persisted through this period at Yale, Brown, Dartmouth, and Bowdoin.

It was not until the last half of the eighteenth century that the institutional career began to take shape, as a small core of "permanent" faculty, the professors, began to supplement the cadre of short-term tutors. Carrell found that in 1750 there were only ten professors in all of American higher education, the bulk of whom were either at Harvard or William and Mary. By 1795, the professorial ranks had swelled tenfold to 105 while the number of colleges had only slightly more than doubled. All in all, some 200 individuals had served as professors in nineteen American colleges during this period.[13]

How did these professorships develop? At Harvard, they came into being slowly as a result of philanthropic bequests. During the 1720s, two Hollis professorships were endowed: one in divinity, occupied by Edward Wigglesworth for forty-four years; the other in mathematics and natural philosophy, occupied initially by Isaac Greenwood for eleven years, and then by John Winthrop for forty-one years. By 1750, President Holyoke was supported by three permanent faculty members, the two Hollis professors and Henry Flynt, a permanent tutor.[14] During the rest of the eighteenth century, four additional professorships were endowed of which three were actually filled before 1800.[15] By 1800, permanent professors had achieved near parity in numbers with tutors on the Harvard faculty.

At Yale, too, the first professorship was established by a philantrophic bequest. In 1746, the Livingston Professorship of Divinity was established, and nine years later its first occupant joined President Clap and the tutors in supervising instruction. Although Yale had established only one additional professorship by 1800, it achieved near parity between permanent and transient staff two years later with the promotion of Jerimiah Day and Benjamin Silliman from their tutorships.[16]

The pattern that developed after more than a century at Harvard and a half century at Yale was adapted quickly by several of the colleges founded during the second half of the eighteenth century. At Brown, for example, within five years of its founding a core permanent faculty was emerging with Howell's promotion from tutor to professor to join forces with President Manning. By 1800, its five tutors were supplemented by three permanent professors.[17] At Princeton, by 1767, two decades after its founding, three permanent professors had joined forces with the three tutors.[18] At Dartmouth, during the administration of John Wheelock from 1779 to 1817, several professors were appointed to supplement the single professor who together with two or three tutors constituted the faculty during the preceding administration of Eleazar Wheelock.[19]

What were the characteristics of this early core permanent faculty? How did they resemble or differ from their more transient colleagues, the tutors? With regard to similarities, both professors and tutors were drawn disproportionately from the higher socioeconomic strata of colonial and postrevolutionary society; fully one quarter came from "professional" families (with fathers engaged in the ministry, law, medicine) at a time when 1–2 percent of the labor force was "professional" and 80–90 percent were engaged in agricultural pursuits.[20] Moreover, both professors and tutors undertook very similar activities as part of their college responsibilities. Both supervised recitations and dormitories and assumed overall responsibility for student discipline and moral, as well as intellectual, development. There the similarity appears to have ended. In the first place, professors did not take charge of a class for its four years at the institution; they were appointed in a particular subject area (e.g., natural philosophy, divinity, ancient language) and were, for the most part, engaged in the supervision of instruction within that area. In the second place, professors were, on average, at least five to ten years older than the tutors. The vast majority, unlike the tutors, had some post-baccalaureate professional training in theology, law, or medicine. Among the eight professors at Brown during the eighteenth century, for example, seven had such training, as did all ten of the professors at Harvard.[21]

The most fundamental respect, however, in which professors differed from tutors was in their "permanence." Carrell's analysis of biographical sketches of 124 professors during the second half of the eighteenth century illuminates the peculiar meaning of a "permanent" faculty appointment during this period. First, a professorship implied an "institutional" career, often at his *alma mater*. Nearly 40 percent of Carrell's sample professors did this, ranging from just over one-third at the college of Philadelphia (later the University of Pennsylvania) to 83 percent at Harvard. Fully 88 percent taught at only one institution during their academic career, while barely 2.5 percent taught at three or more institutions. Second, a permanent professorship remained an "unexclusive" career. In analyzing the lifetime occupational commitment of his sample, Carrell found that less than 15 percent appeared to identify themselves exclusively as "professional teachers," less than 20 percent appeared to identify themselves primarily as a professional teacher (with a secondary occupation in the ministry, medicine, or law), while over half appeared to identify themselves primarily as practitioners of none of the traditional professions and only secondarily as professional college teachers.[22]

If college teaching was hardly the exclusive career, or even the first choice career, of a majority of eighteenth century professors, Carrell's analysis suggests that it became a long term commitment for many once the move was made. In an analysis of indicators of occupational commitment of his sample professors during their teaching tenure. Carrell found strikingly different results. Nearly 45 percent identified themselves exclusively as college teachers, while about one-quarter identified themselves, respectively, as primarily or secondarily college teachers. Among the latter two categories, clergy were disproportionately represented in the the second. This suggests that clergy were more likely than the other learned professions to develop a primary commitment to the professorial role once it was assumed.[23]

That the assumption of a professorship increasingly brought with it a heightened commitment to college teaching is further supported by at least three additional pieces of evidence. First, the average length of professors' tenures increased substantially between 1750–1800. At Yale, the average tenure of professors increased from 21.5 years to 36.8 years while at Brown it increased from 30.7 years to 36.0 years.[24] Second, Carrell reports a negative zero order correlation between age at first appointment and tenure in the professorial role of -.35 suggesting shorter tenures were, at least in part, attributable to late career entry.[25] Finally, Carrell's analysis reveals that only a relatively small proportion of professors during the period pursued subsequent non-academic careers. Just over half of the population died in office. Less than 25 percent engaged in another occupation after leaving the professorship; and among this group several either retired because of "bad health" or "were retired" by their institutions. [26] It would appear safe to conclude, then, that the professorial role, once undertaken, was pursued with a considerable degree of permanency, particularly when we consider the frequency of dual occupations (e.g., medicine and agriculture, law and agriculture, religion and education) characteristic of the late eighteenth century.

One final issue concerning the relationship of the tutor to the professor remains: the relative integration or separation of the two roles in terms of the individual career track. To what extent did the tutorship function as the first step toward a professorship? And to what extent was a professorship the reward of skillful "tutoring"? The evidence suggests that at least two contrasting patterns had developed by the close of the eighteenth century. The Harvard pattern was one of separate career tracks. Not a single Harvard tutor went on to a Harvard professorship during the eighteenth century. Indeed "tutoring" became something of a permanent career option in itself.[27] The pattern at Yale and Brown, and it would appear at most other institutions, was one of a separate, transient career track, tempered by the intermittent use of the tutorship as a very "selective" feeder for the professorship. Thus, at Brown, only four of eighteen eighteenth-century tutors (22.2 percent) went on to professorial appointments and three of the eight professors appointed during that period had served as Brown tutors.[28] At Yale, tutors were less than half as likely as their Brown counterparts to achieve professorial appointments, but all six Yale professors during the period had indeed served as Yale tutors.[29]

Ascent of the Institutional Career, 1800–1820

The first quarter of the nineteenth century has been credited by historian Frederick Rudolph as the beginnings of the "college movement," the large scale founding of small colleges throughout the west stimulated by the "community building" imperative of the period as well as by increasing competition among religious denominations.[30] It may also be credited as the beginning of the "professor movement." Between 1800 and 1820, the ratio of permanent professors to tutors dramatically reversed itself at many of the "leading" institutions. By 1820, permanent professors outnumbered tutors at both Harvard and Yale by a ratio of 10 to 6 where two decades earlier there have been parity at Harvard and a 3 to 1 majority of tutors at Yale. At Brown, the professors outnumbered tutors by a ration of 3 to 1 where only decades earlier the tutors had been in the majority by a 5 to 3 ratio.[31]

The momentum of the professor movement can be seen graphically in developments at Harvard during President Kirkland's administration from 1810 to 1828. During the entire eighteenth century, six professorships had been established at Harvard. They were created when funding to support them was obtained from private donors. If the initial gift was insufficient to support an incumbent, it was allowed to accumulate over one or more decades before the professorship was filled; e.g., the Hersey and Boylston professorships. Several professorships were allowed to go unfilled for as many as ten or twenty years. In the decade preceding the Kirkland presidency, a subscription was launched by Harvard for the creation of a single professorship. During the eighteen years of Kirkland's presidency, the number of Harvard professorships fully doubled. Seven professors were appointed while the funds destined for their support were not yet available. Indeed, in his zeal to make appointments, Kirkland frequently resorted to drawing on tuition revenues to pay the newly hired incumbents.[32]

How can this ascendance of the permanent faculty in a brief two decades be explained? While it is impossible to postulate an explicit cause and effect relationship, three developments during the period appear to have set the necessary, if not sufficient, conditions for that ascendance. The first of these was growth. The Yale faculty doubled in size between 1800 and 1820, while that of Harvard and Brown increased by 50 percent.[33] Beyond size, there was an increase in the number of institutions attendant upon the "college funding movement." Allied with growth was the progressive acceptance of the professorship as a long term, if not an exclusive, career line, reflected in progressively longer average tenures throughout the eighteenth century and the indicators of increasing career commitment reported by Carrell.[34] Yet, a third factor which may help to account for that increased ascendance of the institutional career were changes underway during the first quarter of the eighteenth century in the ministerial sector. Calhoun, in a case study of the New Hampshire clergy during the late eighteenth and early nineteenth century, reported a radical shift in clerical career patterns about this time, attributable to increasing secularization and urbanization. The average terms of service in local parishes, which throughout most of the eighteenth century had been measured in lifetimes, began to resemble the average tenures of modern college and university presidents. This job insecurity and difficulties in obtaining even so insecure positions, together with the low salaries of clergy in rural and small-town churches, led many ministers to seek to enhance their careers by building organizations such as benevolent societies and colleges and by becoming professors.[35] And the correlation of these developments in the clerical career with the ascent of the professorship is supported by Carrell's finding that clergymen became significantly more likely than their fellow professionals in law and medicine to identify themselves primarily as college teachers by the end of the eighteenth century (v. *supra*).[36]

Academic Professionalization Circa 1820

By the end of the first quarter of the nineteenth century, the "professor movement" had produced a relatively large cohort of career college teachers. While still a thoroughly homogeneous group of upper middle class, New England-born Protestants,[37] the confluence of a number of social and intellectual forces during the course of the nineteenth century wrought some fundamental changes in the group career. The progressive secularization of American society was penetrating the classical college, subjugating the demands of piety to a "religion" of progress and material-ism.[38] At the same time, the rise of science and the growth of scientific knowledge was breaking apart the classical curriculum and giving rise to the development of academic disciplines (the distinction of professional versus amateur) and of research and graduate education. By mid-century, increasingly large numbers of Americans were studying abroad in Germany and were importing their version of the German university and the German idea of research back to the United States.[39] Once graduate specialization took hold in earnest in the last quarter of the nineteenth century, it was but a short step to the establishment of the major learned societies and their sponsorship of specialized, disciplinary journals: The American Chemical Society in 1876, The Modern Language Association in 1883, The American Historical Association in 1884, The American Psychological Association in 1892, etc.[40]

These developments provided American higher education with the capability of producing graduate trained specialists and career opportunities for the specialists so produced. They shaped and reflected a fundamental restructuring, i.e., professionalization, of the academic role. Although touted by some as a veritable "academic revolution," an examination of the evolving disciplinary, institutional, and external career of faculty at the sample institutions suggests that the restructuring process actually proceeded by gradual steps over more than a half-century as successive cohorts of professors were replaced by products of the latest graduate training.

Before turning to the evolution of these three career strands during the nineteenth century, it serves to review the status of each as manifested in college faculties in 1820.

By 1820, a disciplinary career was discernible only in the cases of a few isolated individuals at selected campuses rather than among entire faculties. While a majority of individuals continued to come to the professorship with post-baccalaureate training in the traditional profession of divinity, medicine and law (mostly divinity), with the exception of Harvard few boasted post-baccalaureate training in their academic/teaching specialty.[41] For the most part without special-ized training, the majority of faculties, 50 percent at Brown and Harvard and 100 percent at Bowdoin, continued to be drawn to their initial academic appointments from non-academic jobs, primarily in school teaching and the ministry and secondarily in law and medicine.[42] Moreover, for most faculty any semblance of a disciplinary career ended with their institutional career. At Brown and Bowdoin, the modal pattern was for faculty to move into non-academic careers following their tenure as college teachers (50 percent of the full professors at Brown and 60 percent of those at Bowdoin, virtually all the junior faculty at both institutions). It should be noted, however, that those full professors who "strayed from the fold" averaged nearly two decades in their teaching positions (21.2 years at Brown and 18.5 years at Bowdoin) suggesting that even among "dropouts," college teaching still constituted a significant segment of their careers.[43]

At other institutions, most notably Harvard and Yale, patterns of career commitment ap-peared to be differentiated along senior/junior faculty lines. While no junior faculty at either institution persisted in an academic career beyond their tutorship or instructorship, the majority of permanent professors did (83 percent at Yale and 70 percent at Harvard).

Whatever their career commitments, institutionally speaking, college faculties in 1820 evi-denced fairly low disciplinary commitment as measured by their associational involvements and scholarly publications. Only a single faculty member at Brown, Bowdoin, Harvard, and Yale was involved to any significant extent in the activities of the learned societies of the day (Caswell at Brown, Cleaveland at Bowdoin, Peck at Harvard, and Silliman at Yale who had the year before founded the *American Journal of Science*).[44] And it was only those same single faculty members who were at all involved in publication in their specialized field (excluding the medical faculty). Many professors at these institutions were indeed publishing, but their work consisted chiefly of collections of sermons and public addresses/orations made at commencements and other public occasions.

While many professors in 1820 were actively pursuing external careers, virtually none did so in their academic specialization. Beyond the service of a few men such as Silliman and Cleaveland on the public lecture circuit, the vast majority of professors devoted their extra-institutional service to clerical and civic activities. Fully three-quarters of the professors at Dartmouth, two-thirds of those at Bowdoin, and half of those at Brown were engaged in itinerant preaching and work with missionary societies. Somewhat lower proportions participated actively in community life, principally by holding political office, assuming leadership roles in local civic associations unrelated to education or intellectual culture (e.g., tree planting societies) or, in fewer cases, taking membership in state historical societies.[45]

By 1820, the now familiar formalized institutional career track, i.e., the progression through the junior ranks to a full professorship, had not appeared. Indeed, in many respects, the two-track system largely operative at the turn of the nineteenth century remained intact with junior faculty holding temporary, dead-end appointments and senior faculty with long-term appointments. At Harvard, fully 80 percent of the senior faculty were initially appointed to their professorships from outside the institution, and 62 percent of these claimed no previous academic experience.[46] While Harvard was alone in this period in having established the "instructorship" as distinguished from the tutorship and the professorship,[47] instructors rarely moved to Harvard professorships and tutors did not advance to instructorships.[48]

While Yale and Brown continued to reflect some departure from the Harvard pattern by promotion of tutors to professorships, the extent of that departure appeared to be decreasing. Two-thirds of Brown and Yale arts and science professors served as tutors at their employing institutions, a significant decrement from the 100 percent who had so served on the faculties of 1800. Moreover, none of the six tutors on the Yale faculty in 1820 advanced to a Yale professorship, in contrast to two of six in 1800; and only two of the thirty-two tutors on the Yale faculty during the 1820s were so advanced.[49] Even more dramatically, at Brown, none of the ten tutors appointed during the decade of the 1820s advanced to a professorship.[50] It seems fair to conclude, then, at least on the basis of the increasing convergence of practices at Harvard, Yale, Brown, that by 1820 the dual track academic career, defined along junior-senior faculty lines, was on the ascent rather than the descent.

In sum, it may be said that there were at least two "typical" faculty members by the end of the first quarter of the nineteenth century. The first "typical" faculty member was quite young and took on a temporary assignment as either a tutor or instructor before embarking on a non-academic career, usually in the ministry. He typically came to his employing institution from the ranks of its immediate past graduates and probably undertook training in some traditional profession (usually the ministry) either during or just after his short term appointment. The second "typical" faculty member was the professor who had some post-baccalaureate training in one of the traditional professions (albeit not in his teaching specialty) and had come to the professorship at his *alma mater* perhaps from a tutorship at the same employing institution, or, more likely, from a non-academic occupation (often a pastorate). During the course of his appointment, he was engaged in itinerant preaching and a variety of community activities that were probably non-educational and non-intellectual in nature, except perhaps for membership in the state historical society. Depending on his particular employing institution, he may have moved to a non-academic occupation after a tenure of nearly two decades; or he may have continued his teaching activities for the rest of his life, most probably at his original employing institution. Together, these two types approached their role as a teaching/custodial function, oftentimes as an extension of an earlier or concurrent ministerial role.

Academic Professionalization, 1820–1880

Well before the Civil War, the disciplinary career of the American professoriate as reflected in the incidence of specialized training, publication activity, associational involvements and career commitment was undergoing significant change. The preceding discussion has already established that Harvard was at the vanguard in the area of specialized training; by 1821, 40 percent of its faculty had received such training. While isolated instances of specialty-trained faculty could be discerned during the 1830s and 1840s at Brown, Bowdoin, and Yale, these institutions did not begin replicating the Harvard pattern to any significant degree until the 1850s and 1860s. At Brown, for example, as early at 1841, John Lincoln was sent to study in Europe prior to assuming his assistant professorship. However, it was not until the mid-1850s that nearly one-quarter of the Brown faculty were to take leaves for European study (two of them returning with European doctorates).[51] At Bowdoin, as early as 1835 John Goodwin was appointed professor of modern languages and dispatched to Europe for two years to prepare for his position. Goodwin, however, remained largely alone during his thirteen-year tenure, pending several other appointments in the early 1860s.[52] At Yale, as early as 1843 Thomas Thatcher took leave to engage in European study, but it was not until 1863 that Yale appointed its first Ph.D. to the faculty.[53]

At institutions such as Dartmouth and Williams, developments began later but proceeded more rapidly. At Dartmouth, as late as the mid-1850s, nearly all of the faculty in the academic department had received training in the traditional professions but none in a specialized academic discipline. With a half dozen appointments in the late 1860s and early 1870s, however, Dartmouth had virtually reversed that condition in a single decade.[54] At Williams, the first professionally trained faculty member was not appointed until 1858 (Thomas Clark who had just received his doctorate in chemistry from the University of Gottingen) and a second did not assume professorial duties until the close of the Civil War. By 1869, however, fully five of the thirteen members of the Williams faculty could boast graduate training in their teaching specialty.[55]

As the proportion of faculty with discipline-related credentials increased, so did the proportion of those embarking on an academic career immediately following their training. At Harvard, by 1869 the proportion of faculty with no previous non-academic career had doubled since 1845 (44 percent versus 22 percent).[56] Even more dramatically, at Bowdoin, during the 1870s, nearly two-thirds of the faculty embarked on their academic careers immediately after their graduate training, compared to barely 20 percent during the preceding decade.[57]

If the pattern of increased specialized training together with assumption of an academic career immediately following that training did not take hold until the 1850s and the 1860s, other aspects of the disciplinary career (i.e., scholarly publication and participation in learned societies) were developing earlier. At Bowdoin, the largest jump in the faculty's *Professional Index* during the nineteenth century occurred during the second quarter of the century.[58] By 1845, 70 percent of the faculty were publishing in their field (although nearly half of these were primarily publishing their lectures as textbooks) and nearly 30 percent were involved in the activities of scientific associations. At Harvard, the faculty's *Professional Index* took its largest jump in the early 1840s during the Quincy presidency, nearly doubling in less than two decades.[59] The most significant jump in the Brown faculty's *Professional Index* occurred between 1845 and the end of the Civil War. By 1845, half the Brown faculty was publishing in their field of specialization (even if in the more popular media); and by the Civil War, one-half were affiliated with major disciplinary and scientific associations.[60]

By the 1850s, one unmistakable sign of the ascendance of the disciplinary career was evident. Institutional commitments built on inbreeding were breaking down in the face of disciplinary commitments which opened up opportunities at other institutions. At Bowdoin, three faculty left for positions at other institutions where only one had done so in the previous half century.[61] At Brown, while only one professor left during the decade preceding the Civil War, several junior faculty pursued career interests by moves to other institutions.[62] And during the 1850s and 1860s, the University of Michigan, and to a lesser extent the University of Wisconsin, were both serving as "revolving doors," especially for senior faculty. At Michigan, for example, among forty-three professors appointed between 1845–1868, twenty-three left, typically after relatively short tenures. While several were clearly victims of internecine strife, at least ten left for a better academic position.[63] Thus, by the eve of the Civil War, interinstitutional mobility was progressively becoming associated with academic careers.

These evolving disciplinary commitments were also extending in the 1850s to faculty extra-institutional service. Indeed, the bare outline of an external career based more on disciplinary expertise, experience as educator, and role as proponent of culture rather than proponent of religion was becoming discernible. At Brown, for example, the immediate pre-Civil War period saw the first instance of a faculty member using their expertise in the service of state government in the appointment of a professor chemistry to the head the Rhode Island Board of Weights and Measures. By the end of the Civil War, the proportion of the Brown faculty involved in itinerant preaching and other clerical activities dropped from over a third at mid-century to one-eighth. While nearly three quarters of the faculty remained involved in civic and community affairs, the nature of that involvement had changed. Only a single faculty member was directly involved in elective politics while the majority were involved in distinctively cultural, academic, and educa-tion-related activities such as membership on boards of education, holding office in national honor societies, art and historical societies, and state and federal government commissions.[64] At Bowdoin, by the eve of the Civil War, we find a majority of faculty (57 percent) engaged in extra institutional roles as specialists, educators, and men of letters. Parker Cleveland offered public lectures on minerology and Alpheus Packard on education; President Woods and Professor Packard were engaged in commissioned writing for the Maine Historical Society; and Thomas Upham was writing pamphlets for the American Peace Association.[65]

Other institutions lagged a decade or more behind in this evolution of the external career. At Dartmouth, as late as 1851 three quarters of the faculty continued to participate actively in the community as preachers, licentiates, or ordained ministers and as civic boosters. By the late 1870s, however, the proportion of faculty engaged in clerical activities had dropped precipitously to 15 percent, while more than half were engaged significantly in their fields of specialization.[66] At Wisconsin, by the early 1870s, professors at the University were being called upon to head the state geological survey.[67]

The disciplinary and discipline-based external career taking shape in the immediate pre-Civil War period also gave rise to two significant, interrelated changes in the institutional career pattern during the 1860s and 1870s. New roles as instructor and assistant professor were estab-lished and forged into a career sequence that at once gave shape to the academic career and regulated the movement through the junior ranks to a professorship. Concomitantly, the junior faculty ranks were expanded and professionalized. Together, these developments served to integrate into a single structure the dual career track system of junior and senior faculty that had characterized the early part of the nineteenth century.

The instructorship and the assistant professorship actually made their appearance quite early at some institutions. As early as 1821, one-third of the Harvard faculty were serving in instructor-ships.[68] The first instructors were appointed at Yale in 1824 and during the 1830s in arts and sciences, at Michigan in 1843, and at Brown in 1844. The first assistant professors were appointed at Brown in 1835, at Yale in 1842, and at Michigan in 1857.[69] Despite the early precedents, these new roles did not take hold for several decades even at these trend-setting institutions (with the exception of Harvard) and for an even longer period at the more insulated institutions such as Dartmouth, Bowdoin, and Williams. Thus, at Yale, only four instructors were appointed during the two decades following the first appointment; and only four additional assistant professors were appointed during the three decades following the first appointment.[70] Similarly, at Brown and Michigan, the instructorship languished until the 1860s and the 1870s, respectively; while the assistant professorship languished until the 1890s and the 1880s, respectively.[71] At Dartmouth, Bowdoin, and Williams, it was not until the 1860s that these roles first appeared and several decades later until they were firmly entrenched.[72]

These new roles represented a significant departure form the "tutorship" for their incumbents were appointed within a specific department of instruction and were likely to be the products of specialized training. Moreover, their appearance significantly transformed the tutorship, leading to its demise at some institutions (at Brown in the 1840s and at Williams in the early 1860s) and to its transformation into a junior instructorship at others. At Yale in the 1830s, for example, tutors began to be assigned to departments of instruction.[73] But, for at least several decades, they were no equivalent to their modern counterpart in at least one fundamental respect; they did not serve in a majority of cases as feeders to the full professorship. At both Harvard and Yale, it was not until the 1860s that a substantial proportion of junior faculty were advanced to a professorship (25 percent at Harvard and just over a third at Yale) and not until the decade of the 1870s that a bare majority of the junior faculty were advanced.[74] Similar patterns prevailed at Brown and, even more dramatically, at Michigan. Between 1845–1868, only one of eight junior faculty at Michigan had risen to a full professorship; a single decade later 80 percent were promoted.[75]

During the decade immediately following the Civil War, the junior faculty role, then, had changed from a temporary, dead-end appointment to the first step in the academic career ladder. At the very same time, the ranks of the junior faculty were undergoing their most rapid expansion and their largest increase in professionalization. By 1880, junior faculty outnumbered their senior colleagues at Harvard by a ratio of 8 to 5, compared to a ratio of 3 to 2 a decade earlier, had attained full parity with senior faculty at Michigan, compared with a 2 to 8 ratio a decade earlier, and were on their way to parity at Brown, constituting 40 percent of the faculty in contrast to less than a third a decade earlier. [76] They were increasingly entering their academic careers directly from graduate training in their specialty and moving from junior appointments at other institutions. At least at Harvard and Brown, they held as highly developed a professional orientation, measured by McCaughey's *Professional Index*, as their senior colleagues.

The modern academic career had come of age.

Discussion and Implications

The foregoing analysis suggests a four stage model in the evolution of the academic role by the late nineteenth century at the sample institutions: (1) the emergence of an institutional career within the matrix of the traditional professions in the latter half of the eighteenth century; (2) the rapid expansion and consolidation of that institutional career in the first quarter of the nineteenth century, at least for the permanent senior faculty; (3) the gradual professionalization of academic faculties along specialized, disciplinary lines beginning in the second and accelerating in the third quarter of the nineteenth century; (4) the formalization of the institutional career progression through the ranks, beginning in the third and accelerating in the last quarter of the nineteenth century.

This model and the data upon which it is built suggest a number of generalizations about the historical development of the American academic professions. First, they suggest that to the extent that the epithets "revolution" may be applied to the history of academic people, the first such revolution probably ought to be located at the turn of the nineteenth century. It was then that American college faculties were transformed from "revolving doors" to "permanent" bodies of careerists; and it was then that we find the first explosive growth in the size of permanent academic faculties. Second, they suggest a series of generalizations about professionalization in the nineteenth century. The process of professionalization of college faculties as self-conscious, disciplinary specialists was well underway for several decades preceding the Civil War and the emergence of the American university in the last quarter of the nineteenth century. The transformation was a gradual one; and in at least two respects it proceeded quite unevenly. Internally, different dimensions of "professionalization" proceeded according to somewhat different timetables, i.e., participation in learned societies and in specialized scholarly publication, and, to a lesser extent, the ascendance of disciplinary over institutional commitments (as reflected in inter-institutional mobility) temporally preceded the large scale shift to specialized disciplinary training and the direct movement from graduate training to full-time academic work. Interinstitutionally, these developments began and gathered momentum at different times at different institutions—quite early, for example, at Harvard and Bowdoin, considerably later at Williams and Dartmouth. Finally, the data clearly suggest that professionalization temporally preceded by at least several decades the formalization of the modern institutional career track.

That the academic faculties examined here were engaging in specialized, scholarly publication and in the activities of scientific associations on a significant scale *before* they were seeking and receiving specialized training on a similar scale and moving from such training directly to full-time academic posts suggests the situation of a rapidly transforming profession awaiting an institutional structure within which to express its new ideals and orientations. Similarly, that professionalization preceded by several decades the formalization of the institutional career track again suggests a newly arrived group awaiting an institutional structure within which to operate.

And indeed, the evidence gleaned from McCaughey's in-depth analysis of nineteenth century Harvard, [77] as well as the accounts of faculty uprisings against the ideals and organization of the "old time" college at Williams in 1868–1872 and at Dartmouth in 1881,[78] would appear to support the proposition that the growing pressures from rapidly professionalizing academic faculties were indeed a major impetus to the transformation of American higher education in the last quarter of the nineteenth century.

Having hazarded the above generalizations, it must be emphasized that both the model presented here and the inferences drawn must, of course, remain tentative. They are based on the experiences of a half dozen of the leading, eastern institutions, with the exception of Michigan. To what extent are these experiences duplicated by the younger, western institutions? How did more reform minded institutions such as Union compare with more classical institutions such as Yale and Williams? Questions such as these suggest that sound historical conclusions about academic professionalization must await comparable data on a more representative sample of institutional types and the internal comparisons that such representativeness will allow.

Quite beyond the issue of generalizability is that of explanation. How are we to account for the emergence of the institutional career during the first quarter of the nineteenth century? How much of it may be attributable to changes in the ministerial career in New England? How are we to account for the uneven development of professionalization both across institutions and across various dimensions of professionalization? While broad explanations can certainly be located in the major social and intellectual transformations occurring in nineteenth century America, the question remains as to how these broad changes were experienced at different types of institutions and reflected in the diverse conditions of academic employment. And answers to this latter question, too, must await the generation of comparable data sets on faculties at a greater diversity of institutional types.[79]

Notes

1. Wilson Smith, "The Teacher in Puritan Culture," *Harvard Educational Review* 36 (1966): 394–411.

2. William Carrell, "American College Professors: 1750–1800," *History of Education Quarterly*, 8 (1968): 289–305.

3. Robert McCaughey, "The Transformation of American Academic Life: Harvard University 1821–1892," *Perspectives in American History*, 8 (1974): 239–334; Marilyn Tobias, "Old Dartmouth on Trial: The Transformation of the Academic Community in Nineteenth century America" (Ph.D. dissertation, New York University, 1977), published by the New York University Press, 1982; and Allan Creutz, "From College Teacher to University Scholars: The Evolution and Professionalization of Academics at the University of Michigan, 1841–1900" (Ph.D. dissertation, University of Michigan, 1981).

4. They range from McCaughey's more limited focus on the timing of changes in various contemporary indicators of academic professionalization (e.g., the incidence of specialized training and publication for disciplinary audiences) between 1820–1892 to Tobias' and Creutz's broader focus on the impetus and timing of changes in faculty self concepts, ideologies and career patterns during the latter half of the nineteenth century as these both reflected and shaped the intellectual and social milieu of nineteenth century America.

5. Harvard surely had to be located at the "pinnacle" of the system. Michigan was subject to unusual internecine strife among faculty and between faculty and the Board of Regents in the early years and grew more explosively than most institutions in the last three decades of the nineteenth century. Dartmouth lingered under the paternalistic leadership of President Bartlett until 1893.

6. Both Smith, *Harvard Educational Review*, and Carrel, *History of Educational Quarterly*, limit their analysis to data for the pre-1800 period. McCaughey, *Perspectives in American History*, collected data beginning in 1821, while Tobias and Creutz collected data on faculty in the second half of the nineteenth century.

7. In the cases of Brown, Bowdoin, and Yale, historical catalogues were employed to collect data comparable to McCaughey, *Perspectives in American History*, and Tobias on faculty at five points in time: 1800, 1820, 1845, 1869, 1880. See *Historical Catalogue of Brown University*, 1764–1904 (Providence, Rhode Island: Brown University, 1905), Alpheus Packard, ed., *History of Bowdoin College* (Boston: James Ripley Osgood and Company, 1882), and *Historical Register of Yale University*, 1701–1937 (New Haven, Connecticut: Yale

University Press, 1939). The variables for which data were collected included: geographic origin, source of baccalaureate degree, the timing and nature of post-baccalaureate training, the nature of previous non-academic employment, age and years of teaching experience at time of initial appointment and at appointment to professorships, academic rank, years at focal institution, nature and timing of any subsequent occupation, nature and extent of publication activity, nature and extent of involvement with extra-institutional organization (e.g., historical and literary societies, later disciplinary organizations and local and state government), and scores on two indices developed by McCaughey, *Perspectives in American History* (The *Outsider Index* assessing the relationship of the focal individual to the institution previous to initial appointment and a *Professional Index* assessing the extent of professionalization as reflected in post-baccalaureate training, career pattern, publication/research activity, and associational involvements). A similar analysis was also undertaken for the University of Michigan faculty in 1845, 1869, and 1880, based on *The General Catalogue of the University of Michigan, 1837–1911* (Ann Arbor, Michigan: University of Michigan, 1912).

In addition to these more systematic efforts, a variety of secondary sources, ranging from standard histories of higher education to institutional histories to memoirs, were mined for data on developments related to faculty. These included: Laurence R. Veysey, *The Emergence of The American University* (Chicago: University of Chicago Press, 1965): Merle Curti; *The University of Wisconsin: 1848–1925* (Madison, Wisconsin: University of Wisconsin Press, 1949); Samuel Eliot, *A Sketch of the History of Harvard College* (Boston: Little and Brown, 1848); Samuel E. Morison, *Harvard College in the Seventeenth Century* (Cambridge, Massachusetts: Harvard University Press, 1936); Frederick Rudolph, *Mark Hopkins and the Log* (New Haven: Yale University Press, 1956); Thomas J. Wertenbaker, *Princeton 1746–1896* (Princeton, New Jersey: Princeton University Press, 1946); and Timothy Dwight, *Memories of Yale Life and Men 1845–1899* (New York: Dodd, Mead and Company, 1903).

Given the convenient, non-representative character of the institutional sample and the consequent limitations imposed on valid historical generalizations, no attempt was made to present the actual data in tabular form. Rather, it was decided to view the data as preliminary and suggestive and introduce is as necessary into the narrative.

8. In-depth institutional developments are, of course, covered in McCaughey, *Perspectives in American History*, Tobias, "Old Dartmouth on Trial," and Creutz, "From College Teacher to University Scholar." For interpretations of the cultural/social matrix of academic professionalization, the reader should consult Tobias and Creutz as well as Burton J. Bledstein, *The Culture of Professionalism* (New York: W. Norton and Company, 1976) and Dale Wolfe, *The Home of Science* (New York: McGraw-Hill, 1972).

9. Donald Light, *et. al.*, "The Impact of the Academic Revolution on Faculty Careers," *ERIC-AAHE Research Reports*, 10 (1972).

10. W. H. Cowley, *Professors, Presidents, and Trustees*, ed., Donald T. Williams (San Francisco: Jossey-Bass, 1980), pp. 18–19. Also personal communications from Allan O. Pfnister.

11. Morison, pp. 51–53.

12. Smith, *Harvard Educational Review*, shows that during the period 1685–1701 the tenure of Harvard tutors averaged 6.4 years and increased to 9.0 years during the first half of the eighteenth century.

13. Carrell, *History of Education Quarterly*, pp. 289–290.

14. At Harvard, an institutional career was provided by the appointment of "permanent" tutors as well as professors. The tutorship became institutionalized there in a way it was not at Harvard's sister institutions, largely, it would appear, as a result of the precedent set by the fifty-five year tutorship of Henry Flynt during the fist half of the eighteenth century (Smith, *Harvard Educational Review* 36, pp. 400–401).

15. When endowment funds were insufficient for the full maintenance of a professorship, the funds were allowed to accumulate for as much as one or two decades before filling the position. See Eliot, p. 107.

16. *Historical Register of Yale University*, pp. 55–56, 229 (Day), 244 (Dwight), 386 (Meigs), 477 (Silliman).

17. *Historical Catalogue of Brown University*, p. 36.

18. Wertenbaker, p. 50.

19. Cowley, p. 80.

20. Carrell, *History of Education Quarterly*, pp. 294–295.

21. *Historical Catalogue of Brown University*, pp. 37, 74 (Maxey), 77 (Messer), 518 (Howell), 528 (Fobes). Also Eliot, pp. 41–44, 61, 72, 96.

22. Carrell, *History of Education Quarterly*, pp. 296–298.

23. *Ibid.*

24. *Historical Register of Yale University*, p. 63, 202 (Clap), 223 (Daggett), 229 (Day), 244 (Dwight), 386 (Meigs), 477 (Silliman). Also *Historical Catalogue of Brown University*, p. 36.

25. Carrell, *History of Education Quarterly*, pp. 298–300.

26. *Ibid.*

27. Smith, *Harvard Educational Review*, pp. 402–405.

28. *Historical Catalogue of Brown University*, pp. 36–37.

29. *Historical Register of Yale University*, pp. 54–56.

30. Frederick Rudolph, *The American College and University* (New York: Vintage Books, 1962), pp. 51–55.

31. McCaughey, *Perspectives in American History*, pp. 316–317; *The Historical Register of Yale University*, pp. 57, 63, 229 (Day), 260–261 (Fisher, Fitch), 281 (Goodrich), 328 (Ives), 342 (Kingsley), 345 (Knight), 403 (Munson), 477 (Silliman), 484 (Smith); *The Historical Catalogue of Brown University*, pp. 36–37. Even at institutions such as Bowdoin, where the ratio of professors to tutors remained the same, appointment during the 1820s gave the permanent professors ascendance (Packard, pp. 125–136).

32. Eliot, p. 107.

33. *Ibid.*; *Historical Register of Yale University*, pp. 56–57, 244 (Dwight), 386 (Meigs), 229 (Day), 260–261 (Fisher, Fitch), 281 (Goodrich), 328 (Ives), 342 (Kingsley), 345 (Knight), 403 (Munson), 477 (Silliman), 484 (Smith).

34. Carrell, *History of Education Quarterly*, pp. 296–300.

35. Daniel Calhoun, *Professional Lives in America* (Cambridge, Mass.: Harvard University Press, 1965), p. 166, cited by Tobias, "Old Dartmouth on Trial," pp. 33–34.

36. Carrell, *History of Education Quarterly*, p. 297.

37. Among faculty at the "leading" institutions, over three-fourths had been sired by old New England families. Ecclesiastical and business family backgrounds continued to predominate, although the proportion of farm families had begun to increase. And Protestantism continued as the professorial religion, although some of the "lower" Protestant denominations, e.g., Baptists and Methodists, were now rivaling the Presbyterians, the Congregationalists, and Unitarians for hegemony, (v. Veysey, pp. 300–310).

38. Calhoun, pp. 166–168; John Brubacher and Willis Rudy, *Higher Education in Transition* (New York: Harper and Row, 1968), pp. 115–118; Richard Hofstadter and Walter P. Metzger, *The Development of Academic Freedom in the United States* (New York: Columbia University Press, 1955), pp. 320–363.

39. Hofstadter and Metzger, pp. 374–378; Veysey, pp. 121–133, 158–179; Wolfe, pp. 5–14, 33–63, 85–91; and Alexandra Oleson and John Voss, eds., *The Organization of Knowledge in Modern American*, 1860–1920 (Baltimore: Johns Hopkins University Press, 1979), pp. 3–18, 285–312.

40. Bernard Berelson, *Graduate Education in the United States* (New York: McGraw Hill, 1960), pp. 14–15.

41. While four out of ten Harvard professors had studied in Europe, at least three of these had done so on Harvard stipends provided after their initial appointment as a means of preparation for their professorship. See McCaughey, *Perspectives in American History*, pp. 250.

42. *Ibid.*; *Historical Catalogue of Brown University*, p. 69 (Drowne), 77 (Messer), 83 (Burges), 85 (Park), 117 (Adams), 212 (Peck), 122 (Brooks), 126 (Mann), 518 (Howell), 541 (Ingalls); Packard, pp. 125–136.

43. *Ibid.* These mobility patterns represent no significant change from those in 1800.

44. All of these were "professional" scientists. See McCaughey, *Perspectives in American History*, p. 254; Packard, pp. 126–129; *Historical Catalogue of Brown University*, pp. 133–134; *Historical Register of Yale University*, p. 477.

45. Packard, pp. 125–136; Tobias, pp. 29–32, 254; *Historical Catalogue of Brown University*, pp. 69 (Drowne), 77 (Messer), 83 (Burges), 85 (Park), 117 (Adams), 121 (Peck), 122 (Brooks), 126 (Mann), 518 (Howell), 541 (Ingalls).

46. McCaughey, *Perspective in American History*, pp. 250 and 330–332. While we use the term "outsiders" here and subsequently to describe these appointments, it should be noted that virtually all of these outsiders at Harvard and elsewhere were in a fundamental sense "insiders" as well: i.e., they were returning after an hiatus to their baccalaureate *alma mater*.

47. Yale did not appoint an instructor until 1824 and that in law. None were appointed in arts and sciences until the 1830s. At Brown, the first instructor was appointed in 1844.

48. While it is true that two of Harvard's ten professors in 1820 had served as Harvard instructors, this was clearly a notable exception rather than the rule. Indeed, none of the five instructors in 1820 went on to Harvard professorships. See McCaughey, *Perspective in American History*, pp. 250, 317.

49. *Historical Register of Yale University*, pp. 57–48.

50. *Historical Catalogue of Brown University*, p. 38.

51. *Ibid.*, p. 170 (Lincoln), 156 (Chace), 167 (Hewett), 183 (Boise), 192 (Harkness), 223 (Diman).

52. Packard, p. 431 (Goodwin), 743 (Young), 135 (Rockwood).

53. *Historical Register of Yale University*, p. 5–7 (Thacher), 418 (Packard).

54. Tobias, pp. 28, 53–54, 249.

55. Rudolph, *Mark Hopkins and the Log*, p. 128.

56. McCaughey, *Perspective in American History*, p. 330.

57. Packard, pp. 125–136.

58. The *Professional Index* was developed by McCaughey, *Perspective in American History*, pp. 125–136, in his study of the nineteenth century Harvard faculty. It taps primarily two dimension of faculty professionalization: specialized disciplinary training and publication in a specialty.

59. McCaughey, *Perspectives in American History*, pp. 262–263, 326.

60. Included in this latter group were a founder and future president of the American Philological Association; a future vice president of the American Chemical Society; a founder and future vice president of the American Association for the Advancement of Sciences as well as a founder of the National Academy of Sciences. *Historical Catalogue of Brown University*, pp. 133 (Caswell), 156 (Chace), 159 (Gammell), 170 (Lincoln), 183 (Boise), 192 (Harkness), 223 (Diman), 270 (Appleton).

61. Packard, pp. 431 (Goodwin), 124 (Hitchcock), 287 (Stowe).

62. *Historical Catalogue of Brown University*, pp. 183 (Boise), 195 (Day), 207 (Jillson).

63. See Creutz, pp. 55–64, for details on faculty-Board of Regents conflicts. For mobility data, see *The General Catalogue of the University of Michigan*, pp. 6–9.

64. *Historical Catalogue of Brown University*, pp. 133 (Caswell), 156 (Chace), 159 (Gammell), 170 (Lincoln), 183 (Boise), 192 (Harkness), 223 (Diman), 270 (Appleton).

65. Packard, pp. 120–124, 126–129, 131–133, 188–190.

66. Tobias, p. 254.

67. Curti, p. 53.

68. McCaughey, *Perspectives in American History*, p. 317.

69. *Historical Catalogue of Brown University*, pp. 54–55, 56–57: *The Historical Register of Yale University*, pp. 312 (Hitchcock), 507 (Thacher): *The General Catalogue of the University of Michigan*, pp. 19, 22.

70. *The Historical Register of Yale University*, pp. 148 (Bakewell), 514 (Townsend), 518 (Turner), 532 (Waterman), 290 (Hadley), 244 (Dwight), 418 (Packard), 446 (Richards).

71. *Historical Catalogue of Brown University*, pp. 54–55, 56–61; *The General Catalogue of the University of Michigan*, pp. 19–20, 22–24.

72. Tobias, pp. 42–43, 246; Packard, pp. 743 (Young), 839; Rudolph, *Mark Hopkins and the Log*, pp. 52–53.

73. *The Historical Register of Yale University*, pp. 19, 54.

74. *Ibid.*, pp. 60–61; McCaughey, *Perspectives in American History*, pp. 316–321.

75. *The General Catalogue of the University of Michigan*, pp. 6–9.

76. *Ibid.*, pp. 6–12, 18–19, 22–23; McCaughey, *Perspectives in American History*, pp. 319–321; *The General Catalogue of Brown University*, pp. 53–53, 54, 57.

77. McCaughey, *Perspectives in American History*, pp. 239–332.

78. For Williams, see Rudolph, *Mark Hopkins and the Log*, pp. 221–233. For Dartmouth, see Tobias, pp. 2–3, 61–72.

79. I am grateful to an anonymous reviewer for raising some of these questions.

"Women's Work" in Science

Margaret W. Rossiter

If by 1910 women had succeeded in being allowed to earn degrees from almost all German and American universities granting them to men, they were far less successful in these years in gaining equal treatment in the world of employment. The resistance to women's holding the same jobs as men was much stronger than it was to women's earning the same degrees as men, largely because most jobs were traditionally labelled or "sex typed." Thus, when women sought those jobs to which their hard-won degrees seemed to entitle them, they found themselves the victims of powerful social forces and traditions that channelled men and women into separate and decidedly unequal forms of employment. Systematically refused "mens' jobs" but in need of some kind of scientific employment, most women scientists of the 1880s and 1890s abandoned the aggressive tactic of "infiltration" that they were using so successfully at the graduate schools and instead advocated (publicly at least) the more moderate goal of creating separate, specifically "feminine," jobs for women in science.

Although it has often been asserted that the practice of science was open equally to both sexes (or, to use sociological terms, "universalistic" or "sex blind"), in fact a separate labor market for women emerged in the sciences in the 1880s and 1890s, when they began to seek scientific employment in significant numbers, and it was firmly established in several fields by 1910. Although the practice of such "sex segregation": was usually justified with the essentially conservative rhetoric that women had "special skills" or "unique talents" for certain fields or kinds of work, the phenomenon basically seems to have been an economic one whose origin and perpetration were the result of three forces: (1) the rise of a new supply of women seeking employment in science, including the first female college graduates; (2) strong resistance to this female work force's entering traditional kinds of scientific employment (such as university teaching or government employment); and (3) the changing structure of scientific work in the 1880s and after which provided new roles and fields for these entrants. Thus the way in which these first women were incorporated into the world of scientific employment between 1880 and 1910 give some clues as to how scientific work was expanding and research strategies changing in these years.

When the movement to give women a higher education had begun to take hold in the United States in the 1870s and 1880s, little thought had been given to the careers such graduates might take up. Because of the prevailing notion of "separate spheres" for the two sexes, it was assumed that most women were seeking personal fulfillment and were planning to become better wives and mothers. Advocates of their study of science saw it as offering a rigorous and satisfying intellectual experience to women who led essentially "aimless lives." Even such accomplished scientists as entomologist Mary Murtfeldt of St. Louis, astronomer Maria Mitchell of Vassar College, ornithologist Graceanna Lewis of Philadelphia, and physicist Edward C. Pickering of the Massachusetts Institute of Technology expected that the women would participate in science only as amateurs. There were still so few women scientists in the United States in the 1870s that there was barely a hint of sexual stereotyping or "women's work"—all fields were presumed to be open to women, who were assumed to be equally adept at all of them. Accordingly, the Reverend Phebe (*sic*) Hanaford opened her chapter on the women scientists of the 1870s with the words "Science knows no sex."[1]

As the numbers of college women increased, however, in the 1880s, expectations began to rise on all sides that their training lead somewhere. If it had been wasteful in the 1870s for women to sit idly home,[2] it was much more intolerable for college graduates to lack useful and respectable work. Accordingly the advocates of higher education for women began in the 1880s to talk hesitantly of improved job prospects as well as personal fulfillment for college graduates.[3] In her 1882 article "Scientific Study and Work for Women," Mary Whitney, Mitchell's student and successor in astronomy at Vassar, went beyond the standard view that science would hope to develop a woman's mind and "introduce a more definite purpose into her life" to proclaim that it also laid the basis for "useful, and I hope, in the future, remunerative labor" for her. Unfortunately this was not yet a real possibility for most women, since, as Whitney put it, "we cannot say the present offers many examples." Some women had been successful as physicians and others as professors, but Whitney also thought there would soon be opportunities for women in those other areas for which they were particularly well suited and in which some women (no names were given) had already been active, fields such as practical chemistry, architecture, dentistry, and agriculture. To her credit Whitney resisted the temptation to minimize the problems this pioneer generation would face. She warned them that they would have difficulty in finding any kind of employment, since even at the women's colleges "the chances are largely in favor of the man." But after urging young women to prepare themselves for such careers, Whitney showed her own ambivalence by concluding that in any case scientific training would make them excellent mothers, which after all was "the highest profession the world has to offer."[4]

Fortunately for the women seeking to enter science in the 1880s and after, at least three forces were shaping scientific work at that time which would provide new roles and opportunities for them: (1) the rise of "big science" or large budgets, which could support staffs of assistants at a few research centers; (2) a new concern for the nation's growing social problems which created the need for several new hybrid or "service" professions (or semiprofessions) designed to solve them; and (3) the need for a new faculty and other personnel at the coeducation land-grant agricultural colleges. Since some of these new jobs offered women a chance to use their special "feminine" skills in ways that did not threaten men directly (and even enhanced their dominant role), the 1880s and 1890s saw much explicit channelling of the newly available women into certain "appropriate" callings.

Advocates of such "women's work" had no trouble developing a rationale for separate kinds of jobs for women. They had merely to urge women to capitalize on the relatively warm welcome that they were already receiving in the marketplace for two kinds of jobs: those that were so low paying or low ranking that competent men would not take them (and which often required great docility or painstaking attention to detail) and those that involved social service, such as working in the home or with women or children (and which were often poorly paid as well.) The literature on "women's work" glorified these positions, considered them very suitable for women in science, and advocated more of them.[5] This message was quickly communicated to an eager audience by a new social mechanism, the middle-class magazines, whose contributors seized upon any work found suitable for such women and with evident relief advised others to enter it as well. Like the more explicit "vocational guidance" of the twentieth century, these magazines needed only a hint of a success story to unleash a torrent of articles (many written by women) extolling the new opportunities awaiting women in the newest area of "women's work."

Events were occurring so rapidly in the early 1880s that even as Mary Whitney was writing her transitional and ambivalent article in 1882, the first kinds of "women's work" in science were appearing. Although a few women (including Maria Mitchell herself) had previously worked at home as "computers" for others' astronomical projects, "women's work" in astronomy was just entering a new phase. The change apparently grew out of a fortunate but not unusual set of circumstances at the Harvard College Observatory in 1881. In that year, as the story goes, Edward Pickering, the advocate of advanced study for women cited earlier and the newly elected director of the observatory (the first astrophysicist to attain the position), became so exasperated with his male assistant's inefficiency that he declared even his maid could do a better job of copying and computing. He promptly put Williamina P. Fleming, age twenty-four, Scottish immigrant, public school graduate, divorcee, and mother, to the test, and she did so well that he kept her on for the next thirty years. She not only became one of the best-known astronomers of her generation, but she also showed such good executive ability and "energy, perseverance and loyalty," as one obituary put it, that Pickering put her in charge of hiring a staff of other women assistants whom he paid the modest sum of twenty-five to thirty-five cents per hour to sort photographs of stellar spectra. Between 1885 and 1900 she hired twenty such assistants, including the college graduates Antonia C. Maury, Vassar 1887; Henrietta P. Leavitt, Radcliffe 1892; and Annie Jump Cannon, Wellesley 1884 (who had been at home in Delaware for a decade). Several of them made such prodigious contributions not only to the observatory's main project in those years, the Henry Draper Star Catalog of stellar spectra, but to other areas of astrophysics, that they became highly regarded in their own right.[6]

Within a few years the fame of this novel employment practice began to spread, and women astronomers became the subject of several favorable magazine articles.[7] In addition, Fleming openly propagandized for the Harvard arrangement in an address on "A Field for Women's Work in Astronomy" at the World Columbian Exposition ("World's Fair") in Chicago in 1893. Like other contemporary accounts, hers praised Pickering's progressive attitude in hiring the women and talked of their many contributions, but also moved beyond this into some sex stereotyping of the skills involved. Thus Fleming was on safe ground when she urged other observatory directors to hire female assistants since such women "if granted similar opportunities would undoubtedly devote themselves to the work with the same untiring zeal." But she was on more precarious ground when she tried to describe what this case illustrated about the comparative skills and abilities of the two sexes, and in fact it is not clear what she did mean by her rather confused conclusion: "While we cannot maintain that in everything woman is man's equal, yet in many things her patience, perseverance and method made her his superior. Therefore, let us hope that in astronomy, which now affords a large field for women's work and skills, she may, as has been the case in several other sciences, at least prove herself his equal!"[8] Apparently she agreed with the prevailing idea that women were generally inferior to men, but she felt that by overachieving in the bottom ranks (or far outstripping what persons at their level were expected to do), they might prove themselves "equal" to men who had far greater opportunities.

This pattern of segregation/sex typing proved popular and spread to most other major observatories in the United States in the 1890s and after. Of the 20 women astronomers listed in the third edition of the *American Men of Science* (1921), 8 worked as assistants at major observatories (and Fleming, who died in 1911, had been listed earlier), one sign that this work attracted a sizeable proportion of the women astronomers in the country. (Seven others taught at women's colleges, as had three retirees.) Yet this count only skims the surface of the phenomenon, for Pamela Mack has collected a list of 164 women, mostly high school graduates, who worked at various observatories for a year or more between 1875 and 1920. (Of the few college graduates in her list, those trained at Vassar by Mitchell, Whitney, and later Caroline Furness were in particular demand and were sought after by many observatory directors.) Almost every large observatory hired these women; Mack found 24 at the Dudley Observatory in Albany, New York; 12 at Yerkes Observatory in Wisconsin; 12 at Mount Wilson in southern California; 6 at the U.S. Naval Observatory in Washington, D.C.; and smaller numbers at most of the other observatories, such as Columbia, Allegheny, Lick, and Yale, where talented doctorate Margaretta Palmer was especially notable.[9]

Such a wide acceptance of female assistants in astronomy in these years would seem to have been the result of something more pervasive than Pickering's personality and his practice at Harvard. More likely it grew out of certain competitive forces within the field of astronomy itself in the 1880s and after. Although still a small field, astronomy was apparently growing rapidly in the 1880s and 1890s, when several new observatories were built, and the whole new field of astrophysics was just appearing. This rapid expansion created two problems for the older observatories: maintaining a large staff of good assistants, which would be difficult because the more experienced (male) assistants might be offered better positions elsewhere at any moment, and keeping up in observational astronomy, which would be almost impossible because the newer observatories often had larger telescopes and were located in areas with better viewing conditions. Thus, as Pamela Mack has explained it, most of the newer observatories used their advantages to concentrate on the traditional observational astronomy, and they offered men from the older institutions exciting new opportunities in this field. Although these new observatories also hired some women, they restricted them to the tedious and laborious "computer" work women had long done for male astronomers. For the women the better opportunities in this period of change were not in observational astronomy at all but in the newer specialties, where they got some of the work (but not the actual jobs) that the more mobile young men had left behind. They fared much better at Harvard, for example, than they did in the West, because in order to compete with his new rivals, Pickering moved away from observational astronomy and into another specialty, the new field of photographic astrophysics. His adoption of this more advanced technology of cameras and spectroscopes had great implications for women in science, since it required a different labor force: Pickering needed fewer observers ("men's work") and many more assistants ("women's work") to classify as cheaply as possible the thousands of photographic plates his equipment was generating.[10] The term *proletariatinization* has been applied to this phenomenon of downgrading the job and then allowing it to be feminized.[11]

If Pickering (and some other observatory directors) were progressive in greatly expanding women's employment in astronomy in the 1880s and 1890s, they were not so far ahead of their time as to promote them to "men's work" or pay them men's wages, even for admittedly important or outstanding work. Most female assistants remained at the same level for decades, and thus had no alternative but to make a whole career out of a job that should have been just a stepping stone to more challenging and prestigious roles. In a sense science benefited from this practice, since these women could complete many long-term projects. One example is the massive Henry Draper Star Catalog, compiled by women when Pickering became too involved in administration and fund raising to do much astronomy himself. Knowing their "place" and having few if any options, women graciously (and for the most part gladly)[12] accepted what was offered to them and stayed as long as they were wanted. Thus the new "women's work" in astronomy trapped many into low-level jobs; Fleming, for example, appears to have had strong executive abilities, and might, had she been given the chance, have made a good director of one of the many new observatories opening up in these decades. Nevertheless, the only female directors of American observatories to date have been those at the women's colleges and at the small Maria Mitchell Observatory on Nantucket Island, a feminist memorial and outpost in the Atlantic Ocean.[13]

The most advancement these women could hope for was to a position like Mrs. Fleming's in directing the work of other women. Even she, however, seldom got a raise, a circumstance that had begun to bother her greatly by 1900—after almost twenty years of devoted services. For two months of that year she kept a private diary about her job as part of a university-wide historical project to collect and preserve for posterity descriptions of the work of the Harvard "officers," among whom she was the only female. In her account, recently uncovered in the Harvard University Archives, she describes her daily activities for the month of March and part of April. Most of the diary simply recounts her duties directing the work of eleven women and assisting the director at the observatory, but at times she records some of her own reactions to her job. There one learns that personally she would rather have spent her days making her own astronomical discoveries, but the director, whom she greatly respected, thought is was better for the observatory for her to spend most of her time preparing others' work for publication, a task she found "very trying" at times and "generally extremely difficult," especially when the would-be authors were the less articulate members of the staff. But it was her low salary that caused her greatest private complaints. On 12 March 1900 Fleming erupted with a lengthy and forthright analysis of the injustice of her salary of just $1,500 per year:

> During the morning's work on correspondence &c. I had some conversation with the Director regarding women's salaries. He seems to think that no work is too much or too hard for me, no matter what the responsibility or how long the hours. But let me raise the question of salary and I am immediately told that I receive an excellent salary as

women's salaries stand. If he would only take some step to find out how much he is mistaken in regard to this he would learn a few facts that would open his eyes and set him thinking. Sometimes I feel tempted to give up and let him try some one else, or some of the men to do my work, in order to have him find out what he is getting for $1500 a year from me, compared with $2500 from some of the other assistants. Does he ever think that I have a home to keep and a family to take care of as well as the men? But I suppose a woman has no claim to such comforts. And this is considered an enlightened age! I cannot make my salary meet my present expenses with Edward in the Institute [MIT] and still another year there ahead of him. The Director expects me to work from 9 A.M. until 6 P.M., although my time called for is 7 hours a day, and I feel almost on the verge of breaking down. There is a great pressure of work certainly, but why throw so much of it on me, and pay me in such small proportion to the others, who come and go, and take things easy?

The [rest of the] day was occupied with the usual work. . . .[14]

A month later, upon reviewing her previous entries, Fleming sought to clarify her mixed feelings of personal respect for Pickering but continuing impatience with her low salary:

I find that on March 12 I have written at considerable length regarding my salary. I do not intend this to reflect on the Director's judgment, but feel that it is due to his lack of knowledge regarding the salaries received by women in responsible positions elsewhere. I am told that my services are very valuable to the Observatory, but when I compare the compensation with that received by women elsewhere, I feel that my work cannot be of much account.[15]

A similar bureaucratization resulting in sex-segregated employment was also underway in the expanding world of natural history museums in the late nineteenth century. Although there are instances of women assistants on museum staffs as early as the late 1860s, more were added in the next few decades to help museums cope with the explosive growth in collections brought back from the increasing number of expeditions to far-off places. The whole scale of natural history was changing. A naturalist, for example, who might formerly have devoted his career to the classification of the flora or fauna of a given region would now be overwhelmed by the vast quantities of specimens that were piling up. Entire museums were necessary to house them, and staffs of bright (but poorly paid) assistants would be needed to catalog and classify them and to publish taxonomic descriptions. Although women were accepted in this new kind of work, and by 1873 twelve were listed as working at Harvard's Museum of Comparative Zoology, they received far less publicity than did the women astronomers.[16]

By the 1880s some of these museum assistants were being supported partially at least by the U.S. Fish Commission, which underwrote much zoological research in these years. Two of these were selfless spinsters from scientific families who rejoiced in even this modest opportunity to become productive marine biologists. In 1879 Addison Emery Verrill, a zoologist at Yale's Peabody Museum of Natural History, hired Katharine Jeannette Bush as an assistant. Although not a college graduate, Bush later enrolled in Yale's Sheffield Scientific Schools as a "special student," and in 1901 she became the first woman to earn a Yale doctorate in zoology. But there is no sign that the degree made much difference in her job situation. Although she worked at the Peabody Museum until 1913, she may have been paid for only twelve of these thirty-four years, and then by the federal government: by the Fish Commission in the 1880s, when she reported on the various mollusks dredged by the commission's vessels, and by the U.S. National Museum in the 1890s, when she reported on some of its collections. In time she published at least nineteen articles on marine invertebrates and was the best known woman in Yale's zoological circle at the turn of the century. Also there were two of her sisters: one, a librarian at the Peabody Museum, worked as an assistant to paleontologist O. C. Marsh, and the other was married to Wesley Coe, professor of zoology.[17]

Similarly, Mary Jane Rathbun started her long scientific career in the summer of 1881, when as a high school graduate she accompanied her older brother Richard to Woods Hole, where he was an employee of the Fish Commission, and volunteered to assist his boss, Spencer Baird. She returned each summer thereafter with her brother, and in 1884 became a paid clerk. Then in 1886 Baird transferred her to a job as a copyist at the U.S. National Museum in Washington, D.C., and she began to work on the classification of crabs. Although her job titles always remained subordinate (scientific assistant, second assistant curator, and finally assistant curator), she took over much of the general supervision of the museum's invertebrate zoology division, which her brother headed in the 1890s. Unlike Katharine Bush, Rathbun had a government salary that rose steadily from $960 per year in 1894 to $1,680 per year in 1910. In 1914, however, she returned her pay to the museum so it could be reallocated to a younger curator with a large family. She then worked unpaid for almost thirty years. By the time she died in 1943, she was one of the world's experts on crabs, having published 158 articles on them.[18]

Likewise, in the anthropological museums of this period, women began in the 1880s to hold marginal positions, from which they often made sizeable contributions to science. Women anthropologists in these years were often loosely affiliated, almost "free-lance," field workers who were only rarely paid a salary but who were allowed to publish in the museum's proceedings and to have some official museum identification, which aided them in the field. Among the most notable of these women were Alice C. Fletcher, Erminnie A. P. Smith, and Zelia Nuttall, who were affiliated with the Peabody Museum of Archeology and Ethnology at Harvard, the University Museum of the University of Pennsylvania, and the museum at the University of California at Berkeley. A few other, wealthier, women also took up the matronly role of financial patron and power-behind-the-director at late-nineteenth-century anthropology museums. Two of these powerful women were Sara Yorke Stevenson at the University Museum of the University of Pennsylvania in the 1890s and her protégé, Phoebe Apperson Heart, who stared her own museum at the University of California in 1901.[19]

Although most of the women employed by botanical gardens in the 1880s and 1890s tended to be illustrators retained on a piece-work basis, San Francisco physician Mary Brandegee became curator of botany at the California Academy of Sciences in 1883 and retained her position for eleven years, despite many controversies with others over the proper nomenclature for the region's diverse flora. She was succeeded in 1894 by Alice Eastwood, her assistant, who gained instant fame in 1906, when, after the city's earthquake, she had the courage and presence of mind to run back into the academy's building and save the "type specimens" before the oncoming fire could destroy them. Despite this heroism, Eastwood's position was long in jeopardy because of various factions among the academy's officers.[20]

All these women and their various positions are considered here together, since they typify and show, with rare exceptions, the limited range of women's opportunities in the scientific research institutions of the 1880s: they were chiefly in the marginal, subordinate positions that can be termed a hierarchical kind of "women's work." It should be noted therefore that most of the discussion of these jobs has been largely in economic terms.[21] Women were willing to do the often tedious and difficult tasks required for far lower salaries than would satisfy competent men. The women had so few other opportunities that they grabbed these low-ranking jobs and often did superbly well with little support. In addition, they were often relatives of the men in charge.

One should also pay some attention to the arguments that were not being used to restrict women's place in these scientific institutions in the 1880s and 1890s. Although many persons seem to have thought that women "naturally" made good assistants, apparently no one went a step further to use the second standard argument for sex stereotyping of occupations, claiming that the subject matter (here, the stars or the crustacea) was somehow inherently "feminine" or that the science's tools or facilities (observatories or museums) were really "homes" that women could tend better (or more "naturally") than men, a commonly held perception about libraries and public schools at the time. Thus sex stereotyping in astronomy and zoology remained "hierarchical" and did not take on the additional rhetorical and psychological trappings that "territorial" kinds of women's work—child psychology,[22] librarianship,[23] social work, or "home economics"— did at the time. Women in these fields also received low pay, but, in addition, generations of person believed (and advised others) that women "belonged" in them because there was something uniquely feminine about their subject matter.

The development of scientific employment within the federal government in the 1880s and 1890s provides another vantage point on the sex typing and sex segregation that did and did not quite occur in several other fields. These cases also help to clarify the relatively are circumstances necessary for the emergence and spread of "women's work" within a science. First, the field had to have a shortage of available men, since there was a general reluctance to appoint women scientists to any job for which men were in good supply. Yet in practice the situation was more complex than this, since the actual supply of suitable workers depended on the job description, which was often in flux in these years. Thus many scientific jobs could be upgraded (masculinized) or downgraded (feminized) over time or as the budget required, manipulating the kind of workers desired. Second (and this is closely related to the first), the employer had to want to hire women, for the appointment process required him (officially under federal Civil Service rules, unofficially elsewhere) to specify beforehand which sex he wished to appoint. Generally only those employers with strong feelings or economic incentives would request a woman. Otherwise inertia and prevailing stereotypes meant that most appointments would go to men. Third, women had to be alerted that this was work for which they would be hired. This receptivity was usually communicated by participants (like Mrs. Fleming) or enthusiastic journalists who described the job's duties almost exclusively in terms of prevailing sexual stereotypes. (Anthropology, for example, could be described as a field in which women could make unique contributions because they could study women and children better than men could.) This publicity was a kind of "market signal" to both potential workers and future employers as to what type of person would be hired.[24] The result of these processes was that what was accepted as "men's" and what was "women's work" was oftentimes not particularly logical or even consistent, but rather the result of a series of employer preferences and economic incentives. In general, however, the women got the less powerful, less prestigious, and lower-paying jobs. The rest were reserved for the men.

The prime example of sex segregation in the federal government occurred in the field of botany, or, more precisely, in the new specialty of plant pathology, in the 1880s. One sign that the signal had by this time already been passed to the public that botany was a "feminine" science was an article reprinted in *Science* in 1887 entitled "Is Botany a Suitable Study for Young Men?" Although none of its our arguments (mental discipline, outdoor exercise, practicality, and lifelong happiness) seems to be very sex linked today, popularizers had already propagandized botany's[25] suitability for young ladies so effectively that some persons though this protest necessary. Perhaps this feminine image was one reason why several divisions of the U.S. Department of Agriculture that were growing rapidly and would soon become its Bureau of Plant Industry started in 1887 to make it a regular practice to hire women as "scientific assistants." Erwin Frank Smith, the USDA's plant pathologist-in-charge, made it a point to hire a women (Effie Southworth, later Spalding), and notified the Civil Service ahead of time, as its rules required. Smith was quite proud of this practice and continued it until his retirement in the 1920s. Over the years he hired more than twenty women assistants, including such talented ones as Nellie Brown, Clara Hasse, Charlotte Elliott, Agnes Quirk, Della Watkins, and Mary Bryan, who earned modest fame for their outstanding work on such agricultural problems as crown galls, citrus canker disease, and corn and chestnut blight.[26]

This employment practice was unusual, and the motives behind it are not at all clear. There may have been economic incentives, or Smith and others at the BPI may have been taking advantage of certain highly discriminatory restrictions at the time on women's taking Civil Service examinations. Though sources on this point differ, women were presumably prohibited from taking the examinations before 1919. Until then women, even those with master's degrees in botany, could take only the exam for "scientific assistant," a lower category. Under these conditions, a shrewd laboratory director might have been able to hire highly qualified personnel at bargain rates. For their part the women might have been very glad to work at projects suited to their skills (and several praised Smith for this) rather than at the more tedious ones to which the Civil Service rules limited them. Then, too, any training given such women botanists would be a good investment, since they would not be promoted to an administrative position or leave for a better position in a state university or an experiment station, all of which were also expanding rapidly in these same years. In addition to these economic motives for preferring women assistants, there may also have been a psychological one—Smith and the other male bosses at the USDA may have (like Pickering at the Harvard Observatory) liked the "harem effect" of being surrounded by a bevy of competent female subordinates who would not be as threatening as an equal number of bright young men. Thus employing women might have been an effective way to limit the turnover and competition in a period of great opportunity and rapid growth, when maintaining a good staff might otherwise have been very difficult. In any case (and there is a 650-page biography of Smith which gives no clues as to why he preferred women assistants), the Bureau of Plant Industry was the only agency of the federal government to become so highly feminized before World War I.[27]

Yet if there were demonstrable economic and psychological advantages to hiring women subordinates in government agencies, one would expect that the practice would have become as widespread as the employment of women astronomical assistants apparently did. Since the economic potential for sex stereotyping was there, perhaps in all fields, it becomes interesting to observe where it did and did not take place in other federal agencies before 1910. Several other agencies appointed one or more women to their staffs, usually on a temporary basis before 1900, but this was apparently not enough to set a precedent, label the field, and so reserve its jobs for other women. Although no other agency became as feminized as the Bureau of Plant Industry, there were two other places (besides the Naval Observatory) where one suspects it might have happened: the Patent Office in the 1850s and the Bureau of American Ethnology in the 1880s. The appointment of three women clerk-copyists, apparently the first in the federal government and including Clara Barton, later the founder of the American Red Cross, in the Patent Office in the early 1850s might have led to a series of women patent examiners doing such detailed, painstaking, and indoor ("feminine"?) work as the job required (perhaps only on inventions submitted by women), but in 1855 a new secretary of the interior rejected even this possibility and put a stop to the "impropriety" of mixing the sexes in a government office by assigning the women elsewhere.[28]

At the Bureau of American Ethnology, Director John Wesley Powell financed the expeditions of at least two women anthropologists, Erminnie Smith and Matilda Stevenson, in the 1880s. Since there were also a great many other women anthropologists around Washington at the time (including Alice Fletcher and patron Phoebe Apperson Hearst), one suspects that female field-work was on the verge of becoming a regular feature of the bureau's projects, perhaps even justifying a separate women's division within it. But instead the opposite happened: there were so many women anthropologists in Washington, D.C., in the 1880s that a backlash developed. Not only did the BAE not start a women's branch, but the all-male Anthropological Society of Washington sternly refused to admit women members in 1885, and by 1901 Franz Boas was writing Phoebe Hearst that the way to upgrade the field was by training "a small number of young men."[29]

Meanwhile at least three other kinds of "women's work" were developing at coeducational colleges and universities in the 1890s.[30] They chiefly demonstrate the second kind of occupational sex segregation: besides the hierarchical form, such as in astronomy, where women were employed as assistants to higher-ranking persons, there was a territorial kind, where women did all the work in a specific, highly sex-typed, field or location. These jobs could be faculty position in a "womanly" subject or staff jobs concerned with the women students' "special problems."

Although one can list a series of historical "firsts" to document the trickle of women onto the faculties of coeducational schools from the 1850s on, the opposition to even these "exceptions" was usually intense. Maria Mitchell had been aware as early as the 1870s that the coeducational schools were not hiring many women and had mentioned it in an address to the Association for the Advancement of Women (AAW) in 1875. She recounted the tale of a relatively liberal president of a coeducational college who said that he would hire a woman scientist if she was as good as Mary Somerville, the renowned British mathematician. Mitchell pointed out that he was creating a double standard and requiring more of the women than he was of the men, for, as she put it, "If he applied the same standard to his choice of gentlemen professors, his chairs must be vacant today."[31]

By the 1890s the topic was no longer humorous, and other women were calling attention to the small proportion and systematic exclusion of women from the faculties of coeducational schools. In what was probably the first of that genre later known as "reports on the status of women," Octavia Bates reported to the AAW in 1891 that though women were now attending coeducational colleges and universities in large numbers, few of the faculty at these institutions were women.[32] The idea was surfacing that the proportion of women on the faculty should bear some correlation to their representation in the student body. In a way this "share-of-the-market" argument did lead to the reserving of a certain percentage of faculty jobs for women, but in a way that was very typical of the separate and subordinate world of "women's work" in the 1890s. Those women who were allowed on the faculty found themselves restricted to the segregated fields of "home economics" and "hygiene" and to the subfaculty position of "dean of women." That they were lucky to get even this much at the coeducational schools is clear from the experience at Cornell University in these years.

The opposition to having women on the faculty at Cornell University was so intense in the 1890s and after as to politicize greatly the few appointments of women that were made. Women's status and rank were deliberately lowered, thus setting precedents and limits for future appointments at that school. Cornell had opened in 1867, and after much hesitation had admitted its first women students in 1872, but had not allowed any women on the faculty until the late 1890s. Even then two women appointees were allowed only in the bottom ranks. When Liberty Hyde Bailey, Cornell's beloved and energetic professor of horticulture and later dean of its college of agriculture, urged the appointment of entomologist Anna Botsford Comstock as "assistant professor" of nature study, the trustees insisted that she be only a "lecturer." Nor would they allow Agnes Claypole to rank higher than a mere "assistant," despite her doctorate in zoology. It was thus to be expected that the appointment of the first women full professors at Cornell in 1911 would call forth a pitched battle. Faculty arguments against their promotion included those that the university would lose status by appointing women to professorships, that the women did not have families to support and did not need the money (a common fallacy), that these women were not as well trained as most men (agricultural faculties generally lacked doctorates), and that there was no need to bring the women into competition with the men. The debate was finally settled in favor of the women, but only because they were in the new department of home economics or, as the historian of Cornell has put it, "After a long and acrimonious argument, the faculty voted (18 October 1911) that 'while not favoring in general the appointment of women to professorships, it would interpose no objection to their appointment in the Department of Home Economics.'"[33] To the Cornell faculty, home economics was a field of such low status (because of its feminization or territorial segregation) that full professorships there were tolerable. But such high rank was not acceptable elsewhere, in the more masculine parts of the faculty. There were no women full professors in Cornell's College of Arts and Sciences until 1960, and not even an assistant professor there until 1947.[34] At Cornell hierarchical segregation was more rigid than the territorial kind.

The increasing numbers and percentage of women students at coeducational institutions in the 1890s played a major role in staking out an area of "women's work" for the women faculty, but in a way that now seems to have hurt them as much as it helped. When there had been only a few female students they had been tolerated without any special problem, but as their numbers grew their presence had become so visible as to disturb the men and create much pressure for segregation, both in the curriculum, with special women's subjects (the humanities plus home economics), and in student housing, with special women's dormitories. Soon this duplication would require new personnel, whose status was unclear, to take care of the women's "special problems." And who was better suited to worry about these matters than the young woman on the faculty, who would never be promoted anyway? She knew the school, was of high moral character, and had always taken special interest in the women students. Though single, she might even have the appropriate "maternal instincts" for the job. In a flash a woman chemist could become a home economist, a physiologist and instructor in "hygiene," or an assistant professor of dean of women—almost whether she wanted to or not.

Probably the largest area of scientific "women's work" in academia was the field of "home economics." Several factors contributed to its rise in the 1890s and its rapid institutionalization as an academic field for women after 1910. The subject seems, in brief (though no history of it has been written), to have been the product of two long-range trends which merged in the 1890s and after: one of nutrition research, which was creating a large supply of new information, and another of popularization, which fed a strong and increasing demand for practical advice. The feminization of the field, which had become pronounced by 1900, was the result of the men's aversion (and inability?) to advise women on domestic matters and their willingness to let the women do it instead. Had the men chosen to take over the field and make it into a profession like medicine or religion or even law, where men commonly advise female patients or clients, it is hard to see how the women could have stopped them. Apparently the field was already too "feminine" by the 1890s, since few men seemed to have tried to enter it.

The field of nutrition research grew out of the nineteenth-century sciences of analytical chemistry and biochemistry that received great impetus from the works of the great German chemist Justus Liebig, which were published in the 1840s and after. He and his many German and American followers greatly stimulated the scientific study of foods and human metabolism, which by the 1880s were being studied by workers at the young American experiment stations, especially by W.O. Atwater at Connecticut. Other scientists, such as Graham Lusk, Russell Chittenden, Lafayette B. Mendel, and Francis Benedict, were also studying these subjects, which grew up independently of medical research, at various universities and private institutes. There were no women in this classic research tradition until 1910, when Mary Swartz Rose earned her doctorate at Yale and started her own research program at Teachers College, Columbia University.[35]

There were many women, however, in the second long-term root of "home economics," the tradition of "advice literature" for the family and home, of which a classic in the 1840s and several decades thereafter had been the *Treastise on Domestic Economy for the Use of Young Ladies at Home and at School* (1841) by nonscientist Catherine Beecher. This sort of literature sought to popularize and circulate among persons who would later be called "consumers" the latest scientific advice on how best to run their lives, their homes, and their families. Here chemistry, bacteriology, and psychology would all in due course make their contributions to a primitive form of what would be later partially institutionalized and subsidized by the federal government in the Department of Agriculture's "extension service." One particularly receptive audience or market for this literature was the female one of wives and mothers whose needs and willingness to listen created a demand for a series of lay (female) advisors.[36]

Perhaps it was inevitable that the researchers or experts would be dissatisfied with much of the advice that these popularizers circulated and would want to have some hand in upgrading it. But in addition to this, two other nonscientific factors began to bring the researchers and the popularizers closer together in the 1890s and to create the need for new well-trained hybrids or "home economists" who could better fit the women's needs. These new forces were the rise of the agricultural college and the massive immigration to eastern cities which seemed to many reformers of the time to require numerous social services (including libraries, schools, settlement houses, hospitals, and social welfare agencies) to train, "Americanize," and generally homogenize and upgrade these unwashed hordes into respectable middle-class citizens. For many reasons, women, especially the new college graduates, seemed best able to take on this overwhelming social task. They were presumed to have the female's traditional interest in the home (which, because of their earlier church and charity work, could now be extended to include the neighborhood and even the whole city), to be more venturesome than their stay-at-home sisters who had not gone to college, and to be available and willing to work at low pay on these herculean social problems. Thus, like the schoolteachers, social workers, librarians, and settlement house workers, the women home economists could act as missionaries trying to save society and its victims through better nutrition and home life. There were enough diseases and other public health problems, especially among city children (who accounted for one-half of all deaths in the 1890s), to create a real demand (in the eyes of the middle-class reformers, if not among the immigrants themselves) for new and better methods of hygiene and diet. It would be easier for such self-appointed ministers to the unfortunate, however, if they had some authority or expertise other than that they thought they knew best. A scientific background and thus some claim to the role of "expert" might give these women the authority to tell others how to live. In time, of course, they, like the other women in similar subprofessional roles, would need to be upgraded with master's degrees (in education, librarianship, or social work), but in the 1890s women college graduates who "meant well" felt equal to the task.[37]

Besides this large but unorganized (and perhaps manufactured) urban demand for home economics, there was also a very strong rural interest in it, one that in the long run created more jobs for women at the university level. As a result of the Morrill Land-Grant Act of 1862 many colleges had been created in rural areas of the country to teach the "agricultural and mechanic arts" to local youths of both sexes. Since agriculture was still at that time as much an art as a science, the content of the new colleges' curriculum was somewhat problematic. On the one hand there was much antielitist sentiment for such colleges to offer "practical" instruction; on the other hand their offerings had to be more rigorous or worthwhile than the information their students could pick up at home on the farm. Some fields, like "economic entomology" or "soil chemistry," straddled this problem successfully and were both "practical" and "scientific" at the same time.

But what were the young women at such schools to study? Most chose to enroll for courses on "cookery," "sewing," and the "household arts." What sort of faculty was best for this? It apparently had to be female—the association with "women's work" was too strong for any man to teach such subjects in the late nineteenth century, though one can imagine that the agricultural colleges could have imported male (French) chefs for the purpose if they had wished. There is no evidence that men ever contested the issue. Then, too, what methods were suitable for teaching such domestic arts? Could one lecture on "cookery" or assign readings on sewing, or were demonstrations enough? The fact that the students often had little or no scientific background (and might, like the immigrants, balk at having to learn science just to cook) limited the depth of the material that could be presented. One could easily go too far, however, in pleasing the students and their parents and end up scorned by the rest of the college faculty (as well as the university administration) for not having a German doctorate and for teaching a subject that lacked intellectual rigor. Thus there was pressure on the early faculties of "domestic science" or "home economics" at the land-grant colleges to upgrade their curriculum, to make it seem "scientific" and demanding, and to hire women with doctorates to teach the subject as rigorously as the traffic would bear. These teachers should also do research in some aspect of the field and work to upgrade it into an almost (but not quite) regular academic science. Treading the narrow path between these two cultures and meeting the pressures for both prestige and practicality would be a continuing and dominant theme in the field's history.[38]

The founder of "home economics," and one whose leadership and character touched her contemporaries deeply, was Ellen Swallow Richards, Vassar 1870 and MIT 1873. Between 1880 and 1910 she almost single-handedly created the field—she propagandized for it, ran demonstration projects, raised money, performed many chemical analyses, wrote several handbooks, trained and inspired her coworkers, and organized its main activities and professional associations. In a sense she had been preparing for this role all her life. As a student at MIT she had learned how to make a place for herself (and other women) by capitalizing on woman's traditional role, or, as she put it in 1871, "Perhaps the fact that I am not a Radical or a believer in the all powerful ballot for women to right her wrongs and that I do not scorn womanly duties, but claim it as a privilege to clean up and sort of supervise the room and sew things, etc., is winning me stronger allies than anything else."[39] After marrying Robert Richards, an engineering professor at MIT (who proposed appropriately enough, in the chemistry laboratory), she volunteered her services (and about $1,000 annually) to the "Woman's Laboratory" there, which she induced philanthropic Bostonians to support from 1876 until 1883. Her curriculum there was not initially sex typed—her students were mostly schoolteachers whose normal school training had lacked laboratory work and who now wished to perform chemical experiments and learn mineralogy, one of her own specialties. In 1880, however, Richards stared stressing chemistry's value to the homemaker asserting in an address to the AAW that "laboratory work, rightly carried out, makes women better housekeepers, better cooks, better wives, and mothers more fitted to care for the versatile American youth."[40] This change in emphasis was probably the result of both the increasing interest in what would later be called "pure food and drug" issues and her own precarious position at MIT.

After MIT began to admit women directly in 1878 and the need for her separate "Woman's Laboratory" lessened (it was closed in 1883), Richards lacked a position. But when, a year later, MIT set up a new laboratory to study sanitation, apparently the first of its kind in the nation, she was appointed an instructor in sanitary chemistry, a position she held until her death in 1911. There she helped MIT professors associated with the laboratory analyze the state's water sample and also developed her interests in the composition of food and other groceries, safe drinking water, and low-cost diets for the poor. She prepared many popular works, and in 1889 she also helped several college women in Boston start their "New England Kitchen," where they prepared nutritious soups for the city's poor. It was this experience that convinced Richards that the field of nutrition education (as it is now called) offered great opportunities to women college graduates who should, she felt, be using their trained minds and special talents to understand and help solve the social problems around them. In 1890 she presented a paper entitled "The Relation of College Women to Progress in Domestic Science" to the Association of Collegiate Alumnae, of which she had been a founder (and, as Marion Talbot later put it, "like an elder sister" to the other early members). In the speech Richards stressed how challenging efficient housework could be and how much it could be improved by the application of scientific principles. She thought the new subject of "domestic science" should be taught at all the women's colleges. It would not only help college women lead more efficient home lives, but would also bring them into touch with pressing local social problems. When few liberal arts colleges seemed to follow this lead, she taught "domestic science" herself to the more vocationally oriented women students at Simmons College in Boston.[41]

By 1893 Ellen Richards was (like everyone else) at the World's Columbian Exposition in Chicago, the greatest showpiece of women's achievements since the Centennial Exposition in Philadelphia in 1876. She ran a "Rumford Kitchen" that offered nutritious and scientifically cooked lunches to visitors for thirty-two cents. Six years later Richards and Melvil Dewey, director of the New York State Library, author of the "Dewey Decimal System" of book classification, and advocate of "women's work" in librarianship, called the first of the ten Lake Placid Conferences on Home Economics. These annual meetings brought together the diverse elements within the movement—the urban cooking-school leaders, the public school supervisors, and the increasingly strong contingent of faculty members from the agricultural and teachers colleges—to discuss the field and its problems, especially its terminology and objectives, and to formulate model curricula. In 1908, at its tenth conference, the group formed the American Home Economics Association and elected Ellen Richards its first president.[42]

Yet even before her death in 1911, the movement was already moving beyond Richard's vision of it and on to a deliberately more academic phase, as it saw its future tied less to urban cooking schools and demonstration kitchens and more to the growing agricultural colleges of the Midwest and West. By 1911 many of these colleges had already formed programs and even departments of home economics, and others were eager to do so. Some of the great leaders in the field in the next few decades were getting their start around 1910: Isabel Bevier at the University of Illinois, Mary Swartz Rose at Teachers College, Columbia University, Agnes Fay Morgan at the University of California, Abby Marlatt at the University of Wisconsin, and Flora Rose and Martha Van Rensselaer at Cornell University. Yet the very success of this kind of "women's work" on major campuses helped to harden the sexual segregation for future generations still further. Rather than being accepted for other scientific employment once the pioneers had shown women could handle scientific employment, the women found themselves *more* restricted to "women's work" than ever. Since women were finding such good opportunities in this field, many persons (including the first vocational guidance counselors, a new specialty around 1910) urged ambitious young women interested in science to head for home economics. It was the only field where a woman scientist could hope to be a full professor, department chairman, or even a dean in the 1920s and 1930s.[43]

Another new and highly feminized field, which looked for a while as if it might attract women physiologists the way home economics absorbed women chemists, was that of "hygiene" or "hygiene and physical education." Started by a number of male physicians in the late nineteenth century, this field sought to understand the scientific bases of both personal and public health, especially in relation to physical exercise. About the same time, several of the early women's colleges and coeducational universities employed women doctors to teach hygiene as well as to be the college physician, since administrators were anxious to minimize the physical ailments that were suspected at the time to accompany mental exertion in females. Some women doctors apparently found this position a congenial one, as did for example the sisters Dr. Clelia Mosher, appointed at Stanford University in 1893, and Dr. Eliza Mosher, hired by the University of Michigan in 1896. Another, Dr. Lillian Welsh of Goucher College (appointed in 1894), not only taught hygiene for thirty years but also gradually developed the only full department of physiology and hygiene at a woman's college into a strong premedical program that was famed for the number of its graduates who went on to the nearby The Johns Hopkins Medical School. By the 1920s, however, and perhaps even earlier, for reasons that were then and still are unclear, the subject of "hygiene" did not flourish like "home economics" but floundered and was rarely taught in American colleges and universities. Possibly it had been downgraded; it was quickly replaced by the more popular subject of physical education, which by then had its own kinds of specialists trained in the normal schools and accredited by its own professional societies, though they often taught "health" as well in the public schools. Thus though "hygiene" might have followed the path of home economics, and many universities hired women with doctorates in physiology to do research and train high school teachers of "physical education," the field developed quite differently.[44]

A third kind of academic hybrid of "women's work" which arose at the coeducational colleges in the 1890s was that of the "dean of women." As the number of women students increased, and especially as they were required to live in dormitories on campus, the need arose for some sort of supervision. Although the duties of the office were not at first clear, most administrators considered almost all faculty women capable of the job. Accordingly the earliest office-holders included several highly trained scientists and physicians, such as Marion Talbot, assistant professor of sanitary science at the new University of Chicago, who was appointed dean of women in 1892; Eliza Mosher, M.D., became a dean of women as well as professor of hygiene at the University of Michigan in 1896; psychologist Margaret Washburn was appointed warden of Sage College (the women's dormitory) at Cornell in 1900; Mary Bidwell Breed, assistant professor of chemistry at Indiana University, was appointed its dean of women in 1901; Lucy Sprague (later Mitchell), who was later active in the child study movement, replaced a woman physician as dean of women at the University of California in 1906; and Fanny Cook Gates, formerly professor of physics at Goucher and Grinnell colleges, became the dean of women at the University of Illinois in 1916. Despite these early appointments, it soon became clear that not all women were suited to such a position of moral authority over the students, for personality and temperament were of paramount importance. Thus the research-oriented Margaret Washburn, who disliked her job at Cornell intensely, was only too glad to give it up after two years, and Fanny Gates left Illinois after two years when gossip hinted that she may have been addicted to drugs. (The president of the University of Illinois vowed never to make the mistake of hiring a Ph.D. in science for that job again.)[45] President William Faunce of Brown University had, however, sensed this nicety as early as 1900, when he described the position in these terms:

> It is a position of peculiar responsibility and opportunity; not because of the large number of students, as yet—we have about one hundred and fifty—but because things are in plastic shape, and the whole future of women's education in this region can be molded by the one who occupies this position.
>
> We want a woman who can teach, in order to emphasize the intellectual life of the College; but we want, quite as much, one who can create and maintain the right social atmosphere and keep before the young women womanly ideals.
>
> I feel that we ought to have a woman in whose nature the religious element is not lacking, and who could sympathize as well as instruct.[46]

Another problem facing these early needs of women was the declining status of their position. Although the first such deans tended to have full faculty status and taught a few classes in their specialty, the position was in constant danger of being downgraded to a staff or administrative appointment. This had apparently happened by 1911, when a report on the duties and status of deans of women at fifty-five colleges and universities across the nation revealed that, though the deans were usually required to have doctorates, they were only barely tolerated on the institutions' often nearly all-male faculties.[47]

Yet attitudes were beginning to change somewhat by 1910. The revival of the women's rights movement (which led eventually to the ratification of the suffrage amendment in 1920) emboldened some women scientists, including the archetype of "women's work," Marion Talbot, professor of household science and dean of women at the University of Chicago. She and others were beginning to realize around 1910 that sex-typed employment had not proven the opening wedge to broader opportunities that it might have. It had brought them jobs in science and academia, but it was now clear that many of these were marginal or subordinate positions, easily downgraded and rarely accorded recognition (such as a star in the *American Men of Science*).[48] Even the jobs in home economics, which were some of the best positions for women outside the women's colleges, were both separate and unequal (deliberately so, as in the Cornell faculty's vote), and thus had not brought women that much closer to the final and now for the first time, visible goal of full equality. "Womens' work" no longer seemed as progressive a step as it had in the 1880s and 1890s.

Unfortunately, however, such segregation suited so many other needs and constituencies so well that later generations would find it difficult to move beyond "women's work" and into the mainstream of scientific employment. What had formerly been a fairly nonhierarchical collection of independent investigators had become, in some fields at least, highly bureaucratized "big science" with all the gradations in the status and role that this implied: henceforth, some persons would have to be "hired hands" on projects directed by others. Government science was also expanding rapidly, as were several applied or service-oriented fields that academics scorned and tried to keep at a distance. It was a tense time of jockeying for position and status, as some jobs and roles were downgraded, others created, and still others expanded and promoted. The presence of women created new opportunities for the more liberal "empire-builders" of the time, but it worried other, more vulnerable, men, whose scientific standing it seemed to threaten. Thus a segregated, low-status, almost invisible kind of "women's work" offered a harmonious method of incorporating the newcomers into the scientific labor force: women were introduced in ways that divided the ever-expanding labor, but withheld most of the ever more precious recognition. Later women unable to change this pattern of segregated employment, would devote much energy and ingenuity to creating new forms of awards and recognition that would help to compensate for their structural invisibility in the scientific work force.

Through the Back Door: Academic Racism and the Negro Scholar in Historical Perspective

MICHAEL R. WINSTON

The Anomalous Social and Intellectual Position of the Negro Scholar

In 1939 when Rayford W. Logan was president of the Howard University chapter of the American Association of University Professors, he wrote to the national office of the AAUP to inquire about the accommodations for Howard professors at the Association's annual meeting held that year in New Orleans. Ralph Himstead, executive secretary of the AAUP, replied that the Negro members of Howard's chapter would be permitted to attend the meeting, but of course they could not be guests at the hotel and would have to enter through the back door. The incident would scarcely be worth recalling today except that it indicates the anomalous social and intellectual position of the Negro scholar in American life. Like Negro intellectuals in general, the small groups of scholars have been regarded by hostile whites as either freaks or a menace, discomfiting because their very existence challenged the prevailing racial stereotypes and the system of racial accommodation in which whites were presumed superior, blacks inferior.

Until relatively recent years, a virtually impermeable racial barrier excluded Negroes from the universities and their superior facilities for teaching and research. In addition, the Negro scholar has found himself isolated in Negro colleges and universities which were themselves marginal financially and intellectually, existing precariously on what Edward Shils has called in a slightly different connection an "intellectual periphery."[1] John Hope Franklin has written of the dilemma of isolated Negro scholars and their humiliation at the hands of racist archivists and librarians. "The world of the Negro scholar," he said, "is indescribably lonely, and he must, somehow, pursue truth down that lonely path while, at the same time, making certain that his conclusions are sanctioned by universal standards developed and maintained by those who frequently do not even recognize him. Imagine the plight of the Negro historian trying to do research in archives in the South operated by people who cannot conceive that a Negro has the capacity to use the materials there."[2] Separated by social conventions from their white peers, Negro intellectuals and scholars have been alienated also by cultural tradition from the majority of Negroes, who, in addition to sharing most of the anti-intellectual biases of most white Americans, have the traditional hostility of other basically peasant peoples to intellectuals of their own group.[3] Negro intellectuals and scholars have therefore been necessarily dependent on white philanthropy or state legislatures, with all of the limitations and difficulties such support implied in a society based on white supremacy. This essay will discuss briefly what I view as the principal forces controlling the fate of Negro scholars in America: racism, the development of Negro colleges, and the nascent mobilization of Negroes for "intellectual self-defense." Within this framework it is possible to make an assessment of what kinds of research contributions Negro scholars have made or not made to the broader world of American scholarship.

Politics and Pedagogy: The Institutional Setting of Negro Scholars

American Negroes have developed two major institutions, the Negro church and the Negro school. Of the two, only the school was a point of contact between Negroes and whites because of the problems of financial support on the one hand, and on the other the broad range of relationships inherent in any educational enterprise, no matter how caste-ridden. Because Negro colleges existed as institutions within a society dominated by whites, they were necessarily a reflection of the power relations between the two racial groups. As a consequence of this, the internal development of Negro schools has been related directly to the shifting political and social relations between whites and Negroes in the society. It has also meant that the Negro school, especially the college, has occupied a strategic intermediary position in race relations and has been therefore more of a focus of political pressures and social tension than is commonly expected to be true of educational institutions. To Negroes, denied political participation by statute, business opportunities by lack of resources and custom, and broad areas of social expression by segregation, colleges have been regarded as vehicles for expressing a variety of interests, many bearing only a slender and tangential relationship to education as a process of intellectual development. It is not surprising, therefore, that to Negroes as well as whites, Negro colleges have very often been conceived of in ways which ultimately distort the primary purposes of education. The demands of political expediency often eclipsed the educational needs of the students or the intellectual interests of the faculty. This is fundamental to an understanding of the history of the higher education of Negroes, and especially to an understanding of the peculiar conditions in which Negro scholars have had to work. A brief survey of the history of Negro higher education makes clear the range of obstacles to the development of a strong tradition of scholarship in Negro institutions. Since whites have had the dominant role in determining both the character and degree of support to Negro schools, it is useful to review shifting white attitudes to Negro education as well.

The White Dilemma: The Black Trojan Horse

The attitudes of whites toward the education of Negroes in the United States have been conditioned by three powerful and very often conflicting motives; guilt, fear, and sentimental philanthropy. Despite the passage of more than a century, the Freedmen's Aid Society's sentiments of 1868 are still relevant: "the Freedmen, though of African origin, have for the most part been born on our soil [and] reared under out institutions. . . . Their injuries appeal to our sense of justice, we must not forget that we are implicated in slavery. Our fathers covenanted to protect it. . . . By their unpaid toil [the Freedmen] and their fathers contributed largely to the wealth of our country. By their aid during the rebellion they contributed to the preservation of the Union."[4] Fear has also been the companion of guilt. The Freedmen's Aid Society report for 1872 notes, for example, that "Patriotism, philanthropy and religion with united voice, urge us to consider this subject [Negro education] and make provisions that this calamity which threatens us may be averted. Four millions of ignorant citizens in a national crisis may wreck the Republic. . . . This people . . . if neglected and left in ignorance will fall an easy prey to wicked and designing men, and become a terrible scourge to the nation."[5] J. L. M. Curry of the Peabody Fund made the point crystal clear when he addressed the general assembly of Alabama in 1889. "If you do not life them up," he said, "they will drag you down to industrial bankruptcy, social degradation and political corruption."[6] But the fear was complex and, in many instances, inarticulate. On the one hand an ignorant black rabble was a menacing Trojan horse, but on the other a truly educated class of Negroes would upset not only the cherished doctrine of the innate intellectual superiority of whites, but, more important, make impossible any prolonged maintenance of political and economic white supremacy. That has been the chief dilemma in the history of white involvement in Negro education. It explains why so-called "industrial education" appealed to white southerners and northerners alike. While the available evidence will not warrant the flat conclusion that a "conspiracy" existed among powerful whites to establish industrial education as the only type of education available to Negroes, it is clear that most of the philanthropic support for Negro education for fifty years went to the trade schools after the John F. Slater Fund adopted a policy in 1882 that it would "favor" schools with industrial programs.[7] The Peabody Fund, whose trustees had lobbied against the Civil Rights Bill in 1873, was also a powerful force for mobilizing northern support for industrial rather than collegiate education.[8] Opposition to higher education was strenuously advocated by the Peabody Fund's general agent, J. L. M. Curry, who maintained that the education provided for Negroes at Atlanta, Fisk, Howard, and other American Missionary Association—Freedmen's Bureau schools was a tragic mistake based on a fanciful view of the Negro's mental capacities. He said that the educational program of these schools "was unsettling, demoralizing, [and] pandered to a wild frenzy for schooling as a quick method of reversing social and political conditions. . . . The curriculum was for a people in the highest degree of civilization; the aptitudes and capabilities and needs of the Negro were wholly disregarded. Especial stress was laid on classics and liberal culture, to bring the race *per saltum* to the same plane with their former masters, and realize the theory of social and political equality."[9]

Caroline and Olivia Stokes, Collis P. Huntington, William H. Baldwin, Andrew Carnegie, John Wanamaker, Robert C. Ogden, George Eastman, John D. Rockefeller, Paul and Felix Warburg, and Julia Rosenwald were the most prominent supporters of industrial education and the accommodationist philosophy of Booker T. Washington.[10] In 1907 the Southern Education Association announced its policy that "in secondary education emphasis should be placed upon agriculture and industrial occupation."[11] Liberal southerners argued that in addition to practical considerations there were biological grounds for rejecting college education and favoring some "special education" for a race whose immutable destiny it was to occupy a servile status in "advanced civilizations: like the United States. "The Negro race," Charles H. McCord wrote, "is not only a child race: it is a spoilt race. It has had too much coddling on the one hand, and on the other hand it has been spanked without discretion."[12] As a southern liberal, he counseled patience to those whites exasperated by the rising tide of Negro protest. Racial peace could be achieved if they would only understand that Negroes could not be held responsible for their unfortunate inferiority, and that with the "right kind" of education the protest would cease. McCord "scientifically" demonstrated that Negro social behavior was characterized by "inordinate vanity, superstition and nonmoral religion, love of orgy and carousal, improvidence and lack of foresight, cunning and deceit, weakness of will and lack of inhibitive power, incapacity for sustained labor, lack of cleanliness and true self-respect, animal sexuality, moral insensitivity and a callousness to the suffering of others."[13] The point of the recital was that it made clear how unsuited Negroes were for higher education. McCord was, however, more candid than most white Americans about his reasons for deriding higher and favoring "industrial" education for Negroes. Characteristically, McCord argued that the colleges founded by New England whites for Negroes were "victims" of the "old Jesuitic curriculum and a discredited psychology. Their professors still worship the fetich of 'classical culture' and 'mental discipline.'" Having condemned the colleges, he praised industrial education. "It is one of the most hopeful signs of the time as regards the Negro that he is here and there in greater numbers accepting the teaching of General Armstrong and Doctor Washington.[14] And schools like Tuskegee Institute and Hampton Institute, together with the State Normal and Industrial Schools for Negroes, are forcing a recognition of the new doctrine in the old line colleges,"[15] Industrial education would draw the fangs of "the Negro menace" by reducing the worst illiteracy, social deviance, and naked anger produced by the white supremacist social system; but industrial education would not give Negroes enough education to challenge seriously their legal and political domination by whites.[16]

The grip of the industrial education lobby was strengthened by popular southern writers like Joel Chandler Harris, a purported "friend" of Negroes. Harris, as Sterling Brown has pointed out, made Uncle Remus the mouthpiece of the new white supremacist orthodoxy, which is revealed in his evaluation of Negro education:

> Hit's de ruinashun er dis country. . . . Put a spellin' book in a nigger's han's en right den en dar you loozes a plowhand. . . . What's a nigger gwineter l'arn outen books? I kin take a bar'l stave an' fling mo' sense inter a nigger in one minnit dan all de schoolhouses betwixt dis en de state er Midgigin. . . . Wid one bar'l stave I kin fa'rly lif' de vail er ignunce.[17]

Small wonder, then, that the few institutions like Atlanta, Fisk, and Howard which tried valiantly to provide a genuine collegiate education to Negroes languished in poverty and neglect while the propaganda centers for industrial education, Hampton and Tuskegee, prospered and received the lion's share of philanthropic support until the 1930's when it became clear to virtually all observers that industrial education had been a cynical political strategy, not a sound educational policy.[18]

It is not surprising that perceptive Negro intellectuals like Dean Kelly Miller of Howard University thought of the industrial education movement as a vicious scheme to destroy the higher aspirations of the race and the means of their realization. Negroes were being denied adequate opportunities for higher education, Miller said, "by the flaming sword of prejudice, kept keen and bright by avarice and cupidity."[19] The debate between advocates of industrial education and advocates of college education for Negroes is meaningless when viewed strictly in educational terms. The real conflict was about the status of Negroes in American life. One group, believing that Negroes should have no higher status than laborers, argued for industrial education and social subordination, while the other, believing that Negroes had the same intellectual aptitudes as whites, argued for higher education and social equality. Governor William C. Oats of Alabama made clear to a graduating class of Tuskegee in 1894 the views of "friendly white southerners" when he was invited to deliver the commencement address. Responding to John C. Dance's praise of higher education earlier in the program, Oats said: "I want to give you niggers a few word of plain talk and advice. . . . You might as well understand that this is a white man's country, so far as the South is concerned, and we are going to make you keep your place. Understand that."[20] Some years later, in an address to Negro students at Biddle University (now Johnson C. Smith University) in May 1909, President William Howard Taft concluded that "your race is adapted to be a race of farmers, first, last and for all times."[21] Although industrial education is a dead and now almost completely forgotten issue, it was what Buell Gallagher has called a great "detour" in the education of Negroes. The significance of this was that the colleges were forced to operate at a mere survival level, and in such circumstances faculty development, especially and sustained research program, was out of the question until relatively recent years.

Racist Scholarship and the Emergence of Negro Scholars

The growth of American universities and the spread of graduate work based on German models (beginning at John Hopkins in 1876) coincided with the defeat of Reconstruction and the triumph of social Darwinism as taught by Herbert Spencer, William Graham Sumner, and Lester Ward. Viewed in that context, it is scarcely surprising that the first two generations of Negro scholars worked in an atmosphere dominated by anti-Negro thought. From 1870, when Edward Bouchet, the first Negro to receive a doctorate at an American university, was awarded a Ph.D. in physics at Yale, to the late 1920's, when the number of Negro Ph.D.'s began to increase at a steady rate, American scholarship not only reflected the racial attitudes of the larger society, but actively propagated anti-Negro views which strengthened the "iron ring" of public policy and private prejudice designed to trap Negroes in a position of social and economic inferiority.[22] It is impossible to understand the development of scholarship by American Negroes if this background is ignored. Since these facts are usually overlooked in discussion of the type of research done by Negroes, it will be useful to review them here.

Among the leaders in the academic world who succeeded in imposing an anti-Negro bias in scholarship were the historians William A. Dunning and John W. Burgess, whose books on the Civil War and Reconstruction influenced a generation of American historians and the shapers of national policy toward the Negro. Largely through their efforts it became the dominant view that slavery was a benign institution and Reconstruction a tragic error based on the mistaken idea that Negroes should or could be citizens and enjoy the legal protections of the Constitution. At the time that Dunning was at the height of his influence as a historian he described life in the South during Radical Reconstruction as "a social and political system in which all the forces that made for civilization were dominated by a mass of barbarous freedmen."[23] Thus the oppressive racial policies of the South appeared to be vindicated by the best northern scholarship (Burgess and Dunning were at Columbia University); if it was folly to extend the franchise and education to Negroes, then it was wisdom to enforce white supremacy and segregation, and acceptable to use Ku Klux Klan terrorism and lynching to "keep the Negro in his place."

While the nation's leading historians were busy showing how "disastrous" it had been during Reconstruction for Negroes to be allowed minimal legal freedoms, a formidable body of purportedly "objective scholarship" was being produced in the emerging disciplines of sociology and psychology (at that time strongly under the influence of social Darwinism) to show that Negroes were innately incapable of rising above the status imposed by white terrorism.[24] This work was especially powerful in its influence because it was "scientific" and enjoyed the support of the leading universities of the United States. Among the distinguished social science professors was G. Stanley Hall, who held the first Ph.D. in psychology in the United States, and made an academic reputation as the founder of the psychology laboratory at Johns Hopkins (1883) and the *American Journal of Psychology* (1887). Hall used his academic authority in support of anti-Negro propaganda while he was president of Clark University (1899–1919). In 1905, his article "A Few Results of Recent Scientific Study of the Negro in America" noted that a "new scientific study of the Negro has arisen, and is fast developing established results which are slowly placing the problems of the future of this race upon a more solid and intelligent basis, and which seem destined sooner or later to condition philanthropy and legislation, make sentiment more intelligent, and take the problem out of the hands of politicians, sentimentalists, or theorists, and place it where it belongs,—with economists, anthropologists, and sociologists." What were these research findings which were to "condition philanthropy and legislation"? First, that the "color of the skin and the crookedness of the hair are only the outward signs of many far deeper difference, including cranial and thoracic capacity, proportions of body, nervous system, glands and secretions, vita sexualis, food, temperament, disposition, character, longevity, instincts, customs, emotional traits, and diseases." Speaking as the leading authority on psychology of his day, Hall associated the alleged peculiar emotional intensity of Negroes with unbridled sexuality, leading him to discuss the question of rape, lynching, and social control. "During slavery regular hard work, temperance, awe of his white masters, were potent restraints. . . . Now idleness, drink and a new sense of equality have destroyed these restraints of imperious lust, which in some cases is reinforced by the thought of generations of abuse of his own women by white men upon whom he would turn the tables. At any rate, the number, boldness, and barbarity of rapists, and the frequency of the murder of their victims have increased till whites in many parts of the South have told me that no woman of their race is safe anywhere alone day or night. . . . As a preventative of crime, lynching has something to be said for it, but more to be said against it! This wild justice is brutalizing upon those who inflict it."[25]

The brutality and viciousness and ineducability attributed to Negroes by the psychologists were explained by appeals to anatomy and physiology since these disciplines were even more "scientific." It was argued that Negroes were intellectually inferior to whites and incapable of higher education because of a genetically determined arresting of development of the brain after puberty. The most influential academic statement of this view was by Robert Bennett Bean, a professor of anatomy at the University of Virginia Medical School. The "Negro brain" developed normally as far as perception, memory, and motor responses were concerned, but logical critical thinking or the comprehension of abstract ideas were beyond its grasp because of its arrested physiological development.[26]

The degree to which this point of view prevailed is illustrated by Albert Bushnell Hart, distinguished Harvard historian and influential figure in American scholarship. Hart wrote, for example, that "the theory that the Negro mind ceases to develop after adolescence perhaps has something in it."[27] What makes Hart's statement particularly interesting is that he served for twenty-three years on the board of trustees of Howard University,[28] and had thereby a powerful voice in shaping the opportunities for Negro students and scholars. He was one of the Howard trustees in 1926 who opposed the appointment of a Negro president for the first time in its history.

An example of the sociological research sponsored by white universities was Howard W. Odum's *Social and Mental Traits of the Negro: A Study in Race Traits, Tendencies and Prospects*, published in 1910 as volume 37 of the Studies in History, Economics and Public Law, edited by the faculty of political science of Columbia University. Odum, president of the American Sociological Society in 1930, and editor of *Social Forces*, 1922–1954, was one of the most influential southern liberals in academic life, serving as Kenan Professor and head of the Sociology Department at the University of North Carolina, and director of the Institute for Research in Social Science. In recognition of his work Harvard conferred upon him an LL.D. in 1939.[29] In his *Social and Mental Traits of the American Negro*, Odum wrote a summary of his investigations, relating the proper education of the race to its genetic tendencies, which is worth quoting at length because it represents the opinion of probably the majority of American social scientists well into the 1930's and 1940's "Inherited tendency," he said,

> and environment of the race conditions constitute a powerful influence in the education of the Negro child. . . . Back of the child, and affecting him both directly and indirectly, are the characteristics of the race. The Negro has little home conscience or love of home, no local attachment of the better sort. . . . He has no pride of ancestry, and he is not influenced by the lives of great men. The Negro has few ideals and perhaps no lasting adherence to an aspiration toward real worth. He has little conception of the meaning of virtue, truth, honor, manhood, integrity. He is shiftless, untidy, and, indolent. . . . The Negro is improvident and extravagant, lazy rather than industrious, faithful in the performance of certain duties, without vindictiveness, he yet has a reasonable amount of physical endurance. But he lacks initiative; he is often dishonest and untruthful. He is over-religious and superstitious. The Negro suspects his own race and the white race as well; his mind does not conceive of faith in humanity—he does not comprehend it. . . . One of the crying weaknesses of the Negro school is the lack of moral strength on the part of the women teachers. It is but natural that children accustomed to gross immoralities at home and sometimes seeing indications of the same tendency on the part of the teachers, should be greatly affected by it at school. Thus with mental stupidity and moral insensibility back of them the children are affected already in practice and thought, in deeds and in speech.[30]

Perhaps even more revealing of the dominant patterns of thought is Odum's view of the work of the Negro colleges:

> The young educated negroes are not a force for good in the community but for evil. The Negro quickly outgrows the influence and control of his instructor; especially has this been noted in cases where the [northern] whites have taught them. . . . They imitate the whites and believe themselves thereby similar to them.[31]

Finally, his view of the problem of crime is enlightening:

> Nurtured with some hatred toward the whites, taught no morals, with fanatical religion, itself leading to erratic actions, with little regard for common decency, and bred in filth and adultery, the Negro is considered peculiarly liable to crime. The reformed Negro criminal is rarely seen, and it is well known that the Negro offender is not cured by the ordinary punishments.[32]

The Emergence of Negro Scholars

The success of white supremacist propaganda during "the nadir," 1877–1901 and after, was so great that the early efforts of Negroes to contribute to the advancement of knowledge have been largely forgotten. As early as 1787 Negroes in Philadelphia began organizing societies embracing literary and other learned interests, and as many as forty-six groups were active before the Civil War. In cities like New York, separate Negro organizations were also formed because of the racial policy of white learned societies. In 1834, for example, the New York Zoological Institute announced that "the proprietors wish it to be understood that the people of color are not permitted to enter except when in attendance upon children and families."[33]

The earliest efforts are more important for illustrating the interest of Negroes in learning and the means by which they cultivated a separate social life than for any residue of solid achievement in the advancement of knowledge. By far the most important organization not related to a university was the American Negro Academy, established in Washington, D.C., in 1897 by the Reverend Alexander Crummell.[34] Crummell was regarded by this contemporaries as "among the most scholarly black men of the age,"[35] based no doubt on his education at Queens College, Cambridge (A.B. 1853), his association in England with Bishop William Wilberforce, James A. Froude, and Thomas Babington Macaulay, his essays and addresses published while a missionary in Africa, and the character of his ministry as rector of St. Luke's Episcopal Church in Washington.[36]

The Academy had five stated purposes:

(1) The promotion of literature, science, and art,
(2) The culture of a form of intellectual taste,
(3) The fostering of higher education,
(4) The publication of scholarly work,
(5) The defense of the Negro against vicious assaults.

The Academy published occasional papers in defense of Negroes and held regular meetings with Washington until the mid-1920's. A typical product was the first paper, Kelly Miller's critique of Frederick L. Hoffman's *Race Traits and Tendencies of the American Negro*, a book published under the auspices of the American Economic Association in 1896 that maintained that genetic inferiority of Negroes was responsible for Negro social disorganization and concluded that the Negro population would be overwhelmed by disease and death, eventually disappearing altogether as an element in the American population. The Academy published too many significant papers to discuss them here, but a mere listing of a few titles will illustrate the direction of its program:

The Conservation of Races, W. E. B. Du Bois
Civilization the Primal Need of the Race, Alexander Crummell
A Comparative Study of the Negro Problem, Charles C. Cook
The Educated Negro and His Mission, William S. Scarborough
The Ballotless Victim of One-Party Government, Archibald H. Grimke

At the same time that the American Negro Academy was active, there emerged the first generation of Negro Ph.D.'s, some of whom made major contributions to American scholarship. For rather obvious reasons, the number was small. Between 1876 and 1914 only fourteen Negroes earned the Ph.D. Of this small group, two, W. E. B. Du Bois and Carter G. Woodson, stand out as the most productive researchers and organizers of efforts to counter anti-Negro scholarship.

W. E. B. Du Bois was in many respects the most outstanding pioneer Negro scholar in the United States, but a historian like George Washington Williams (*History of the Negro Race in America*, 2 volumes, 1882), although not as thoroughly or broadly trained, would also deserve the title "pioneer." After graduation from Fisk University (A.B. 1888), Du Bois studied at Harvard (A.B. 1890, A.M. 1891, Ph.D. 1895) under Albert Bushnell Hart, Justin Winsor, William James, Josiah Royce, George Santayana, and F. W. Taussig and at the University of Berlin (1892–1894) under Gustav Schmoller, Adolph Wagner, and Heinrich von Treitschke. He achieved a solid reputation in both history and the infant discipline of sociology. In 1896 his doctoral dissertation, *The Suppression of the African Slave Trade to the United States of American, 1638–1870*, was published as volume one of the Harvard Historical Studies. The most important work of Du Bois' early years as far as scholarship is concerned, however, was his study of Negroes in Philadelphia, which he worked on from August 1, 1896, to January 1, 1898. He had become convinced that social reform would result from social science research. "The Negro problem," he said, "was in my mind a matter of systematic investigation and intelligent understanding. the world was thinking wrong about race, because it did not know. The ultimate evil was stupidity. The cure for it was knowledge based on scientific investigation."[37]

Du Bois' Philadelphia research was published as *The Philadelphia Negro: A Social Study* by the University of Pennsylvania in 1899. It was the first systematic sociological study of a racial group in an American city, and, in the opinion of later sociologists, a model of the kind of social research method that many years later became standard in American universities.[38] Beyond its intrinsic value as a classic work of social research, *The Philadelphia Negro* represented a dedication to the concept of disinterested scholarship that was rare in those years, particularly when the subject involved race or class.

While engaged in his Philadelphia research, Du Bois presented an ambitious plan of systematic study of the Negro throughout the United States to the forty-second meeting of the American Academy of Political and Social Sciences in Philadelphia, November 19, 1897. At the heart of his plan was cooperative research. "We hear much of higher Negro education," he said,

> and yet all candid people know there does not exist today in the center of Negro population a single first-class fully equipped institution, devoted to the higher education of Negroes, not more than three Negro institutions in all the South deserve the name of "college" at all, and yet what is a Negro college but a vast college settlement for the study of a particular set of peculiarly baffling problems? What more effective or suitable agency could be found in which to focus the scientific efforts of the great universities of the North and East, than an institution situated in the very heart of these social problems, and made the center of careful historical and statistical research? Without doubt the first effective step toward the solving of the Negro question will be the endowment of the Negro college which is not merely a teaching body, but a center of sociological research, in close connection and co-operation with Harvard, Columbia, Johns Hopkins, and the University of Pennsylvania.[39]

Some may now smile knowingly at the almost pathetic hopefulness of the young Du Bois that white scholars would cooperate with such an enterprise. Despite the resounding silence in response to his proposal, Du Bois began what he later called his "real life's work," at Atlanta University where he was professor of history and sociology from 1896 to 1910. There he attempted to carry out his plan without the benefit or assistance of "the great Northern and Eastern universities." Each year he convened a conference to discuss cooperative research studies of particular problems related to Negroes. The studies were organized in ten-year cycles, so that there would be systematic follow-up of changes in the social and economic status of rural as well as urban Negroes. Du Bois edited the Atlanta University Studies alone from 1897 to 1910, when he was assisted by Augustus Granville Dill. A partial listing of the publications suggests the scope and significance of this path-breaking undertaking the social sciences:

(1) Social and Physical Condition of Negroes in cities,
(2) The Negro in Business,
(3) The College-Bred Negro,
(4) A Select Bibliography of the American Negro,
(5) The Negro Common School,
(6) The Negro Artisan,
(7) The Negro Church,
(8) The Negro American Family,
(9) The Health and Physique of the Negro American,
(10) Some Notes on Negro Crime, Particularly in Georgia.

Two things should be especially noted. First, even after the Atlanta University Studies received well-deserved praise from some segments of the American academic community, neither financial assistance adequate to the task, nor cooperation were forthcoming from the foundations or the large universities. Second, despite the low level of support, the Atlanta studies under Du Bois' direction were careful research efforts, the first of their kind in any American university and obviously superior to the work supported at that time by white universities. Apart from the annual *Yearbook* of the *Journal of Negro Education*, beginning in 1932, nothing comparable has been attempted since, an indictment of the black as well as white institutions. Prolonged residence in the South during the reign of terror that accompanied the movement to disfranchise and segregate Negroes destroyed much of Du Bois' faith in the efficacy of social research as a mean of achieving social reform. In his own words:

> At Wilberforce I was [my people's] captious critic. In Philadelphia I was their cold and scientific investigator, with microscope and probe. It took but a few years of Atlanta to bring me to hot and indignant defense. I saw the race-hatred of the whites as I had never dreamed of it before—naked and unashamed! The faint discrimination of my hopes and intangible dislikes paled into nothing before this great, red monster of cruel oppression. I held back with more difficulty each day my mounting indignation against injustice and misrepresentation.[40]

In 1910 Du Bois, with some reluctance, abandoned his professorial career at Atlanta to become director of publicity of the NAACP and editor of its journal, *The Crisis: A Record of the Darker Races*, which he made into the most influential publication among Negroes, and the clearest, most uncompromising condemnation of American racism and Western imperialism for the twenty-two years of his editorship. "My career as a scientist," he said later, "was to be swallowed up in my role as master of propaganda."[41]

Although Du Bois returned to Atlanta University as professor of sociology, 1933-1944, after his break with the NAACP, the turbulent years of bitter political and social struggle prevented a return to the conventions of his earlier "scientific" approach to scholarship.[42] The historical works written during this period, *Black Reconstruction* (1935) and *Black Folk: Then and Now* (1939), for example, were marked by advocacy and an understandable impulse to "set the record straight." Keenly aware of the problem of tendentious writing, Du Bois appended a chapter to his *Black Reconstruction* called "The Propaganda of History," which is not only a brilliant apologia, but also an invaluable source for understanding the preoccupation with race of the generation of Negro scholars that followed in his footsteps. Demonstrating that white scholarship, "when it regarded black men, became deaf, dumb and blind," Du Bois concluded that "in propaganda against the Negro since emancipation in this land, we face one of the most stupendous efforts the world ever saw to discredit human beings, an effort involving universities, history, science, social life and religion."[43]

Du Bois' popularization of the idea of the Talented Tenth and the encouragement he gave in the pages of *The Crisis* to younger Negroes achieving intellectual distinction may have had a greater impact on American scholarship than his own careful research efforts of the period 1896–1910. His early books were probably not read widely by contemporary white scholars, or at least I have found little evidence of it in their writing, but his inspiration of younger Negroes to undertake careers of scholarship despite awesome handicaps bore fruit in the lean years between the two world wars.

A near contemporary of Du Bois, Carter G. Woodson (1875–1950) should be mentioned also as a major force in stimulating research among Negroes, particularly historical studies. Educated at Berea College (before the state of Kentucky made it illegal in 1906 for even a private college to have a biracial student body),[44] the University of Chicago, and Harvard (Ph.D. 1912), Woodson's career was a tortuous and at times eccentric amalgam of scholarship and advocacy. At Howard University for only one year, 1919, as dean of the School of Liberal Arts and head of the graduate faculty, he withdrew from university teaching entirely after a dispute with the white president, J. Stanley Durkee, and spent the remaining thirty years in a lonely crusade to rescue the record of the Negro's past from oblivion. His own writings are rather sharply divided into scholarly efforts and energetic popularizations of Negro history for school children and general readers. Examples of the former are his superb *Education of the Negro Prior to 1861* (1915), *A Century of Negro Migration* (1918), *The History of the Negro Church* (1921), and *Free Negro Heads of Families in the United States*, which he edited in 1925. Quite different in method and quality were the popular *The Negro in Our History* (1922) and *Negro Makers of History* (1928).

As Woodson grew older and more militantly defiant, his popularizations increasingly fell heir to many of the pitfalls of that genre of writing. As far as scholarship is concerned, perhaps his development of the Association for the Study of Negro Life and History, founded in Chicago in 1915, and of the *Journal of Negro History*, founded in 1916, was more significant than his individual contributions as a historian. Woodson announced in the first issue of the *Journal of Negro History* the path it would take:

> Excepting what can be learned from current controversial literature, which either portrays the Negro as a persecuted saint or brands him as a leper of society, the people of this age are getting no information to show that the Negro has thought, and felt, and done.... The aim of the Association [for the Study of Negro Life and History] is to raise the funds to employ several investigators to collect all historical and sociological material bearing on the Negro, before it is lost to the world.... Our purpose then is not to drift into the discussion of the Negro problem. We shall aim to publish facts, believing that facts properly et forth will speak for themselves.

Almost single-handedly, Woodson made the *Journal of Negro History* into one of the respected American historical journals, a remarkable achievement by any standard. Unfortunately, within a few years of his death it began a steady and tragic decline.

Between 1920 and 1945, there emerged a more broadly differentiated group of Negro scholars, though the total number was still of course small.[45] Some sense of the numbers involved is suggested by the fact that between 1930 and 1943 a total of 317 Negroes had earned the Ph.D. By 1946, universities awarding the largest number were Chicago (40), Columbia (35), University of Pennsylvania (28), Harvard (25), Cornell (25), Ohio State (22), and Michigan (20). By 1943, 40 per cent of the Ph.D.'s held by Negroes were in the social sciences, and of those 53 percent were in the fields of history and sociology.[46] The increase was generally related to the increasing social differentiation of the Negro population, particularly the steady growth of an urban middle class able to sustain the investments of time and money required by graduate study. There was also the rapidly changing status of the Negro colleges. After the First World War there was increased pressure to upgrade the colleges and make their faculties conform more closely to what were becoming regional and national standards. This created a demand for Ph.D.'s that had scarcely existed before, when college presidents considered the degree a luxury rather than a necessity. Until the 1930's Negro colleges in the South were unaccredited, but few persons today recall that the reason had little relation to their quality as institutions. Prior to 1930 the Southern Association of Colleges and Secondary Schools had refused to consider accreditation of Negro colleges because approval of a school automatically carried with it membership in the association. Membership entitled the institution to representation at association meetings, and the majority of the members objected to attendance by Negroes. After repeated protests to the SACSS by Negro colleges because their graduates encountered difficulties in admission to graduate and professional schools in the North and West (they were, of course, excluded by law at that time from all southern graduate schools), the SACSS "solved" the problem by agreeing to review Negro colleges for rating purposes with the proviso that acceptable ratings would not entail admission to the Southern Association.[47] Only one school received an "A" rating in 1930, and as a result a strong impetus was created for the other institutions to improve their libraries, add Ph.D.'s to their faculties, and so on. This development, in conjunction with legal challenges to the gross disparities in what were supposedly separate but equal educational resources, accounted for the intense and sustained effort to upgrade the Negro colleges. After the United States Supreme Court handed down its landmark decision *Missouri ex rel. Gaines v. Canada* (305 U.S. 337) in 1938, the working conditions of Negro scholars were improved somewhat as the Negro schools were encouraged (for political rather than educational reasons) to add graduate programs, and were pressured to approximate more closely the external conditions of white schools. Although none of these added pressures resulted in equality of educational resources for either students or faculty, they did, on the whole, force some slight improvement in the position of Negro scholars. As a consequence, for a few institutions in particular, the period 1930–1945 was extraordinarily productive.

Atlanta, Fisk, and Howard (the latter not directly affected by policy changes of the SACSS, but by the decision of the federal government in 1928 to legalize its congressional appropriations and

support a "twenty-year development plan") in these new circumstances attracted the overwhelming majority of the "second generation" of Negro scholars actively engaged in research. More than
80 per cent of all Negro Ph.D.'s in 1936, for example, were employed by Atlanta, Fisk, and
Howard, and the latter had by far the largest concentration of Negro Ph.D.'s anywhere in the
United States (and the world).[48]

A change of policy on the Negro colleges by the philanthropic foundations also contributed to
what appears in retrospect to be a "golden age" of scholarship for some of these institutions.[49] In
the late 1920's two of the powerful foundations that had played a crucial role in determining the
fate of Negro colleges, the Julius Rosenwald Fund and the General Education board of the
Rockefeller Foundation, developed a plan to create, in Edwin Embree's words, "at four centers,
strategically placed throughout the South, institutions of the highest standards which are thus
able to offer careers to distinguished Negro scholars and to prepare the potential leaders of the
race." The centers were in Georgia (the Atlanta University system, Louisiana (Dillard University
and Flint Goodrich Hospital in New Orleans), Tennessee (Fisk University and Meharry Medical
College in Nashville), and the District of Columbia (Howard University's four undergraduate
colleges and the four professional schools).[50] Since white schools still excluded Negro scholars
(only three Negro Ph.D.'s were employed by white universities in 1936), the increased number of
Negro Ph.D.'s, combined with the substantial change in the fortunes of the three leading Negro
institutions, produced the first real opportunity for some Negro scholars to work in even a
second-class university environment.[51] At first it appeared that Atlanta University, under the
leadership of President John Hope, would become the principal center of Negro scholarship in the
humanities and social sciences because of the presence of W. E. B. Du Bois and the group of
scholars recruited to Atlanta like Mercer Cook (romance languages), Rayford W. Logan (history),
Frank M. Snowden (classics), William H. Dean (economics), and Ira Reid (sociology). But the
death of President Hope in 1936, the lack of an adequate system of tenure, retirement benefits, and
faculty independence, combined with the stifling and vicious atmosphere of Georgia racism,
made Atlanta less attractive than Howard, where President Mordecai Johnson had succeeded in
substantially augmenting financial resources to support a more diversified and intellectually
distinguished faculty than ever before in its history.[52] An indication of the degree to which
Howard became the leading center of research and writing by Negro scholars in the 1930's is the
composition of the graduate council of the graduate School in 1934, which included, for example,
Ralph J. Bunche (political science), Charles Eaton Burch (English), E. Franklin Frazier (sociology),
Abram L. Harris (economics), Ernest E. Just (zoology), Alain L. Locke (philosophy), Charles H.
Thompson (education), and Charles H. Wesley (history).

It is of course impossible to review adequately the research and publication of the Howard
group, but a few examples will illustrate the main lines of development. One general observation
that should be made first is that although race was the major preoccupation of these scholars, with
a few exceptions like Burch, who was a specialist on the work of Daniel Defoe, no "school" of
Negro scholarship developed. Indeed, on the whole they were methodologically conservative
and generally reflected the dominant trends of American scholarship. The only point of sharp
difference with their white counterparts was on the question of race. They reacted to the enormous body of scholarly literature designed to show that Negroes "had no history," had less
intelligence than whites, were uneducable, and so forth.

An important catalytic element in this period was the *Journal of Negro Education*, founded by
Charles H. Thompson in 1932. In its first issue, the editor said that the *Journal* was intended to
"stimulate the collection, and facilitate the dissemination of facts about the education of Negroes,"
to "present discussions involving critical appraisals of the proposals and practices relating to the
education of Negroes," and, finally, "to stimulate and sponsor investigations of problems incident
to the education of Negroes."[53] In reference to the research objective, Thompson said that "it
should be pointed out here that leadership in the investigation of the problems incident to the
education of Negroes should be assumed to a greater extent by Negro educators. This has not
been true to a greater extent, heretofore, because the average Negro student who has taken the
pains to get research training, and, in many cases, a research degree, finds his research tendencies
so dulled by the routing of 'school keeping' and by the fact that there is no ready and sympathetic

outlet for the publications of the results of his investigations that it takes a considerable amount of stimulation to overcome the inertia and discouragement produced by this combination of circumstances."[54]

During the thirty years of his editorship Thompson not only provided a "ready and sympathetic outlet" for publications of research, but made the *Journal of Negro Education* into the most potent continuing critique of the public policy of segregation. An early emphasis was on highlighting the inequities in support of white and Negro education, which worsened in the first third of the twentieth century, and did not being to improve until the legal challenges of the 1930's. Thompson pointed out that in those states maintaining separate school systems, in 1900 the disparity in per capita educational expenditures for the two racial groups was 60 per cent in favor of the whites; by 1930 the disparity had increased to 253 per cent.[55] His editorials were shrewd assessments of the changing tides of public policy and the internal developments of Negro institutions. He was critical of the low standards of most Negro schools, writing in 1946, for example, that one-half of the faculty in Negro colleges were deficient in graduate training in their fields, and commenting on the "intellectual decay" that was prevalent in the Negro college.[56] On the other hand he was critical of the often whimsical management practices of the Negro college presidents, and urged adoption of national standards of rank and tenure for faculties, something rare in most Negro institutions until relatively recent years.[57] But the most significant contribution was the publication of the annual *Yearbook* of the *Journal*, which included comprehensive studies of a wide range of problems related to Negro life (volume 8 on *The Position of the Negro in the American Social Order* is a particularly distinguished example). For many years the *Journal* was the best single source of information about the status of segregated schools and shifts in the legal strategies adopted to destroy segregation, and it was common for the *Journal* to publish articles like "The Present Status of the Negro Separate School as Defined by Court Decisions" or "Types of Potentially Favorable Court Cases Relative to the Separate School" Thompson also published a steady stream of research by Howard H. Long, Martin D. Jenkins, and others on the question of intelligence of Negroes and on intelligence testing which exposed the distortions of white psychologists and educators.[58] Because of the lack of adequate opportunity to publish articles in most of the best known journals, Negro scholars often published articles in the *Journal of Negro Education* not strictly related to "Negro education," like "Negro Character as Seen by White Authors," by Sterling Brown, the great Howard University literary critic, poet, and teacher. In addition a number of the *Yearbooks* were devoted to subjects broader than the *Journal's* name would suggest, such as the 1946 study of "The Problem of Education in Dependent Territories," with articles by Ralph E. Turner on imperialism, the system of international trusteeship by Rayford W. Logan, and "Colonies and Moral Responsibility" by W. E. B. Du Bois. Thompson also recognized the significance of "policy research," virtually all of which was done by whites before the *Journal of Negro Education* began its work in this area. In January 1936, for example, the *Journal* published an important series of articles on the New Deal and the race question, social planning, economic development, socialism, and communism by W. E. B. Du Bois, Norman Thomas, A. Philip Randolph, Ralph J. Bunche, and others. What one could call the "policy research nucleus" at Howard—Thompson, Bunche, Harris, Frazier, and Logan—was very active in criticizing public policy as well as the strategies adopted by various Negro groups.[59]

The best example of the mobilization of policy research at this time was The Howard Law School, where Professors Charles H. Houston, William H. Hastie, James M. Nabrit, Jr., Leon A. Ransom, George E. C. Hayes, and their students like Thurgood Marshall, Robert L. Carter, and Spottswood Robinson, III, pursued an unremitting attack on the legal foundations of segregation.[60] The Howard Law School's legal research on civil rights probably had an greater impact on American life than the research activities of any other Negro scholars.

Parallel to their work was the research and writing of a growing cadre in the social sciences. In history, the number of works by Negro scholars providing a corrective to the dominant view began to increase steadily. A few examples are *Negro Labor in the United States, 1850–1925* (1927) and *The Collapse of the Confederacy* (1938) by Charles H. Wesley (at Howard, 1913–1942); *The Diplomatic Relations of the United States with Haiti, 1776–1891* (1941), *The African Mandates in World Politics* (1948) and *The Negro in American Life and Thought: The Nadir, 1877–1901* (1954) by Rayford

W. Logan (at Virginia Union, 1925–1930; Atlanta, 1933–1935; and Howard since 1938); *The Negro in the Civil War* (1953), *The Negro in the American Revolution* (1961), and *Lincoln and the Negro* (1962) by Benjamin Quarles (at Dillard University, 1939–1953; Morgan State College since 1953); *The Free Negro in North Carolina* (1943), *From Slavery to Freedom: A History of American Negroes* (1947), and *The Militant South, 1800–1861* (1956) by John Hope Franklin (at Fisk, 1936–1937; St. Augustine's College, 1939–1943; North Carolina College for Negroes, 1943–1947; Howard University 1947–1956; Brooklyn College, 1956–1964; and the University of Chicago since 1964). Wesley, Logan, Quarles, and Franklin have been the best known of the Negro historians, but of course there are a number of others who made contributions to American scholarship but cannot be discussed here.

In sociology the most distinguished Negro scholar was E. Franklin Frazier, research professor in the Department of Social Science at Fisk University, 1931–1934, and professor of sociology at Howard, 1934–1962. His books and articles were a major contribution to the "scientific" study of race relations, particularly the social process by which Negro social institutions developed and interacted with the larger American society. The crude rationalizations of the subordinate status of Negroes in American life which dominated American sociology in Frazier's early years were virtually unremembered by the time death put an end to his work in 1962. Among his notable books were *The Negro Family in Chicago* (1932), *The Negro Family in the United States* (1939), *The Negro in the United States* (1949), *Bourgeoisie Noire* (1955), and *Race and Culture Contacts in the Modern World* (1957). Of his Negro contemporaries, Frazier probably received the most recognition from his white colleagues as reflected in his election as president of the American Sociological Society in 1948, and chief of the division of Applied Social Sciences, UNESCO, Paris, 1951–1953.

The work in applied social science by George Edmund Haynes and Charles S. Johnson and his associates at Fisk was also extremely important in ridding American scholarship of some of its racist excesses. Johnson was director of social science at Fisk from 1928 to 1948 when he became the university's first Negro president. His research at Fisk was more collaborative than Frazier's at Howard, and for many years his Race Relations Institutes were interracial oases in a sahara of southern bigotry and propaganda on race. Among Johnson's many books were *The Negro in American Civilization* (1930), *The Shadow of the Plantations* (1934), *The Collapse of Cotton Tenancy* (1935), and *Patterns of Negro Segregation* (1943).[61]

There were other Negro sociologists writing important articles and books, but few of them were able to secure positions which provided resources for research. And evidence mounted in the 1930's and 1940's that white philanthropy was reluctant to encourage research by Negroes, particularly in the social sciences. It appeared that virtually all of the well-prepared Negro social scientists had views considered too radical on the race question. Money was committed to Negro institutions in the hope of maintaining social peace; therefore vague programs to improve "race relations" were funded while serious research by competent Negroes literally starved for funds. In a revealing commentary on the situation, Ralph Bunche, at the time one of the forceful Young Turks in the social science division at Howard, wrote:

> Negro scholars even more completely than white, are subject to the munificence of the controlling wealthy groups in the population. Negro institutions of higher learning, particularly, are the inevitable puppets of white philanthropy. Obviously, therefore, whatever reorganization and reorientation of "Negro Education" is to be contemplated, must meet the full approval of these controlling interests. It is hardly to be expected that under such conditions "Negro Education" could ever direct itself to really effect solutions for the problems of the masses of working-class Negroes. The interests of those who contribute so much to the support of Negro education, demand that the masses of Negroes remain what they now are—a handy and docile labor supply from which additional profits can be wrung, some minute share of which will in turn find its way to the support of "Negro Education". . . . Schools like Hampton and Tuskegee train Negroes in craftsmanship but make no effort to give them any industrial or social orientation. . . . In fact, most Negro schools tread very lightly in the purely academic fields of the social sciences. They cannot afford to take the risk of losing their financial support.[62]

In the 1930's Negro scholars in the social sciences were still looked upon as "dangerous," especially if they were competent. The peculiar ambivalence, if not hostility, of foundations at that time is illustrated by the politics surrounding the organization and execution of the Carnegie Foundation's comprehensive survey of the "Negro problem" under the direction of Gunnar Myrdal. A similarly painful story was the death of the *Encyclopedia of the Negro*, which was to be edited by W. E. B. Du Bois and Guy B. Johnson, one of the most ambitious projects involving a substantial number of Negro scholars, though white scholars like Howard Odum, Robert E. Park, and Guy B. Johnson were involved, presumably to give "balance" to the encyclopedia. The project, conceived by Du Bois as early as 1909, was formally incorporated in 1932 by James H. Dillard, W. E. B. Du Bois, Charles S. Johnson, Mordecai W. Johnson, Waldo G. Leland, and Anson Phelps Stokes. After years of work a *Preparatory Volume of the Encyclopedia of the Negro* appeared in 1946 with contributions by Du Bois, Guy Johnson, L. D. Reddick, and Rayford W. Logan. Some controversy exists about the precise reason for the refusal of the foundations to support this project which included many of the most distinguished scholars on the subject, but one white anthropologist has claimed that his word alone was sufficient to "kill the encyclopedia," some indication of how scholarship reflected race relations in general.[63]

Despite these handicaps the research productivity of the Negro historians, sociologists, and economists in the 1930's is surprising, especially when the small number of Negro Ph.D.'s at that time is considered. In 1936, for example, there were only nine in history, fifteen in sociology, and five in economics.[64] As a group it is fair to say that Negro scholars made a substantial contribution to the rational study of race, and were pioneers in interracial cooperation among scholars in meetings at Atlanta, Fisk, and Howard, and in journals like the *Journal of Negro History*, the *Journal of Negro Education*, and *Phylon: The Atlanta University Review of Race and culture*. The studies of Ellis O. Knox also reveal that for the fifteen-year period 1932–1947, about 85 per cent of the 2,535 M.A. theses and 359 Ph.D. dissertations on Negro subjects accepted by American universities were done by Negroes,[65] some indication of how neglected the field was in those years, since Negro graduate students and professors were greatly underrepresented in higher education in general.

Nevertheless, on the whole the isolation imposed by segregation was a powerful deterrent to sustained research and writing by Negro scholars and the hardship on scientists was even greater than for those in the humanities or social sciences because of the high cost of laboratories. Margaret Walker's memorable lines "the struggle staggers us/for bread, for pride, for simple dignity," are not an inappropriate characterization of the situation of Negro scholars no matter how distinguished in the era of hard-edged segregation.

It is easy to forget now just how segregation operated as a powerful deterrent to sustained research or writing.[66] In the South, Negro scholars were almost universally barred from libraries, form white university laboratories, and from meetings of local chapters of learned societies. Farther north, in Washington, D.C., for example, even the meetings and dinners of a national organization like Phi Beta Kappa were closed to Negro members, most of whom were Howard University faculty who had been inducted at New England colleges and universities.[67] In the *Twenty-fifth Anniversary Report* (June 1933) of the Harvard class of 1908, Alain Locke (Ph.D. 1918, Harvard) wrote the following poignant lines to his classmates after outlining his career since his years as a Rhodes Scholars at Oxford (1907–1910) and graduate student at the University of Berlin (1910–1911): "One thing to be regretted has been the comparative isolation that separates Negro life and institutions from even academic and cultural interests at large; but I have done what I could in an interpretative way to bridge some of these barriers."[68]

A much better illustration however was the career of Ernest Everett Just (Ph.D. 1916, University of Chicago), the most distinguished (and probably most frustrated) Negro scientist in America. After a brilliant undergraduate career at Dartmouth College (A.B., Phi Beta Kappa, 1907) he began in 1909 his graduate training at the Marine Biological Laboratory at Woods Hole, Massachusetts, where he was to conduct research every summer until 1930, with the exception of two years. At the Marine Biological Laboratory Just was to become in Frank Lillie's words "more widely acquainted with the embryological resources of the marine fauna than probably any other person."[69] Just's fifty papers on fertilization and cellular physiology brought him international recognition, but that was not sufficient to escape the trap of color in the United States. As Lillie, his mentor at the University of Chicago, put it, "Just's scientific career was a constant struggle for opportunity for research, the breath of his life. He was condemned by race to remain attached to a Negro institution unfitted by means and tradition to give full opportunity to ambitions such as his."[70]

One of the things that made Howard unfit was its dictatorial president for thirty-four years (1926–1960), Mordecai W. Johnson, who, typically, succeeded in minimizing Just's opportunities for research at Howard. When Just secured research funds through the National Research Council, Julius Rosenwald, the General Education Board, and the Carnegie Corporation, there ensued power struggles in which the president sought to control the expenditure of the funds.[71] In his later years Just worked for short periods at the Kaiser Wilhelm Institut für Biologie in Berlin, at the University of Paris, and the Naples Zoological Station. The most comprehensive statement of Just's pioneering research methods and findings are in his two books, *Basic Methods for Experiments in Eggs of Marine Animals* (1939) and *The Biology of the Cell Surface* (1939). "An element of tragedy," Lillie said,

> ran through all Just's scientific career due to the limitations imposed by being a Negro in America, to which he could make no lasting psychological adjustment in spite of earnest efforts on his part. The numerous grants for research did not compensate for failure to receive an appointment in one of the large universities or research institutes. He felt this as a social stigma, and hence unjust to a scientist of his recognized standing. . . . That a man of his ability, scientific devotion, and of such strong personal loyalties as he gave and received, should have been warped in the land of his birth must remain a matter for regret.[72]

One consequence of his experience was that Just discouraged students from pursuing a career in science, pointing to his own bitter disappointment as illustrative of how race determined opportunity and access to well-equipped laboratories.[78] E. P. Lyons, dean of the University of Minnesota Medical School, summarized the conflict between racism and merit in American academic life when he discussed Just's self-exile to Europe after his rebuffs from the Rockefeller Institute. "The greatest problem in American biology," he said,

> is Professor Just. He properly belongs to an institution like Rockefeller, and he was the most logical candidate to take the place of Jacques Loeb when he died, but the Rockefeller Foundation, spending millions of dollars to combat disease internationally, couldn't summon enough courage to solve an inter-racial problem. By its example it could have set a precedent to follow that science knows no race nor creed. What is actually did was only catering to old prejudices in spite of its presumed internationalism.[74]

The case of Professor Just is noteworthy for several reasons. First, it illustrates that at least until 1940, no amount of distinction in research was sufficient for a Negro scholar to be offered the superior research advantages of white institutions, and they were as a result condemned to work in institutions on the whole unsympathetic to their work. Perhaps equally important, Just's career showed the extent to which prevailing white attitudes about stereotypes of Negroes determined the American reputation of Negro scientists. Just believed in freedom of inquiry and racial equality, and his very existence was a challenge to racist contentions about the scientific ability of Negroes. Just's manner and mien did not conform to the prevailing white idea of what a Negro scientist should be like. On the other hand, George Washington Carver, who never published a research paper in any of the standard journals, had what was considered a proper demeanor, that of a kindly, pious old man who "knew his place" around white folks. As a humble agronomist he seemed to put whites at ease, and his mystical, anti-scientific approach to his work—"Talking to the flowers" he called it—was quaint and acceptable. As a result, Carver is the best-known Negro scientist, just as Booker T. Washington was the best known Negro "educator," while Just or President John Hope are much less known. The examples could be considerably multiplied. The entomologist Charles H. Turner won an international reputation based on a steady output of research articles published in leading journals but was ignored in the United States and forced by American racial circumstances to teach biology at Sumner High School in St. Louis.[75] In physics, Fisk University's Elmer S. Imes's work on infrared spectra of the hydrogen halides, or Herman

Branson's (Howard) research on radioactive isotopes and negative ions in the mass spectra of the methylamines[76] are only the best known examples of the distinguished research done by Negro scientists. In chemistry the most productive research done by Negroes was concentrated overwhelmingly for many years at Howard University under the leadership of Percy L. Julian (physostigmine and cortisone), R. Percy Barnes (alpha and beta diketones), and others.[77] It is important to note the relationship between resources and research in this connection.

As part of President Franklin D. Roosevelt's political program with respect to Negroes, the federal government's financial commitment to Howard University, especially its building program, increased tremendously under the leadership of Harold Ickes, secretary of the Department of the Interior which was responsible at that time for administering Howard's federal appropriation. Howard was a vital symbol of "Negro progress" under the New Deal, and one which cost Roosevelt very little politically in the South since it did not alter federal policy on segregation. Roosevelt himself dedicated Howard's new chemistry building on October 26, 1936.[78] Whatever the motives involved, this was the first time that a Negro institution had received more than a million dollars for a science facility, and for many years Howard's science facilities were the best available to Negro scientists in universities. At other Negro institutions, science received a low priority in development plans, and only in the last twenty years has there been a change in policy. It is interesting to note that American industry dropped its bars to Negro scientists long before white universities. As early as 1940 there were three hundred Negro research chemists in industry.

The best known Negro industrial scientists have been James Parsons, director of research at the Duriron Company of Dayton, Ohio; Lloyd A. Hall, chief chemist of the Griffith Laboratories of Chicago; W. Lincoln Hawkins of Bell Telephone Laboratories; and William G. Haynes of the Union Pacific Railroad.[79] Charles R. Drew, the distinguished surgeon and serologist, remarked that Negroes who were employed in industrial research were especially fortunate because they did not "have to spend long years during [their] most creative period teaching in second rate institutions, which for the most part, have been totally ill-equipped for the carrying-on of productive research."[80]

In fairness to Negro colleges in the South, however, it should be pointed out that until relatively recent years, even in the white southern state universities, which had an overwhelming advantage over the Negro institutions in terms of financial support (though less than northern or western universities), achievements in scientific research were low. As one observer commented in the early 1940's about white southern institutions:

> The sort of scientific training which our students must have cannot be provided by second-rate institutions, and it has been repeatedly shown that we have relatively few institutions in the South which could, by any stretch of the imagination be regarded as approaching the status of first-rate universities. It is doubtful, however, whether there is a single institution in the South that is giving adequate attention and support to the sciences. . . . Few people actually realize how expensive graduate work in the sciences must inevitably be.[81]

In some respects, at least, the lack of support for research in Negro colleges has been a part of a regional pattern,[82] but that should not obscure the pernicious role of racism. The Hatch Act of 1887 established programs of scientific investigation and experimentations in land grant colleges and universities to make them research centers, but for half a century not one state supporting a Negro land grant college established an experiment station for the use of Negroes.[83] Only in the last decade, for example, have Negro land grant institutions received any funds from their states for research, despite the fact that the Second Morrill Act of 1890 required that where racially separate institutions were maintained "the funds received in such State or Territory be equitably divided."[84] The disparities in support, from state as well as federal sources, are shocking. The National Science Foundation has reported that in 1968 the white land grant colleges in states where there are dual institutions received $200 million from various federal agencies, roughly eleven times the amount (about $18 million) awarded to Negro land grant colleges. For example, Clemson of South Carolina received $5.8 million from the federal government while its Negro counterpart, South Carolina State, received $490,000. The *Civil Rights Digest* (Spring 1970) exposes the continuation of the long history of discrimination in this area with telling comparisons:

> The University of Georgia, with 10 times the enrollment of Fort Valley, received nearly 24 times as much Federal aid. The University of Florida with less than five times the enrollment of Florida A & M, received 24 times as much Federal aid. Virginia Polytechnic Institute, with only 1 1/2 times the enrollment of Virginia State, received five times as much Federal aid. North Carolina State, with less than 3 1/2 times the enrollment of North Carolina A & T received nearly nine times as much Federal aid.[85]
>
> Similarly the states themselves appropriate nine times as much money to support the white Land Grant institutions than their black counterparts. Georgia appropriated 20 times as much state aid, Texas more than eight times, for white schools. In no case was there an equitable distribution of funds based on enrollment.[86]

It is not surprising, in view of these gross inequities, that the state-supported Negro institution are forced to commit nearly all of their resources to teaching, and very little to research. The privately supported Negro colleges in the South are even more hard pressed for funds as the costs of instruction have risen faster than their sources of support. Earl J. McGrath reported that in 1959–1960, for example, Negro institutions spent $15 per student for organized research, while the average of all higher institutions of education in the United States was $310 per student, or twenty times as much. Put another way, in 1959–1960, Negro colleges and universities accounted for 1.91 per cent of the total expenditures in higher education, but only thirteen hundredths of 1.0 per cent of the billion dollars spent that year for research.[87] Some of the responsibility for the failure of Negro schools to become at least modest centers for research rests on their administrations.

Charles H. Thompson observed that too many administrators of Negro colleges "mistake omnipotence for omniscience," and "assume that because final authority rests with them, ultimate wisdom does also," and, finally, "confuse educational dictatorship with educational leadership."[88] E. Franklin Frazier said flatly that the failure of Negro scholars to more productively study major problems in the social sciences was partly the fault of what he called the "ignorant administration of Negro schools which have refused the intelligent proposals of Negro scholars" "As long as 25 years ago," he continued,

> I pointed out that urbanization had changed the entire relationship of Negroes to American society and that comprehensive and fundamental research should be done on Negroes in cities. But those Negroes who have controlled the destiny of Negro intellectuals ignored this and even today no Negro college or university is concerned with this fundamental problem.[89]

Similarly the shortsightedness of these institutions in not supporting, at least at Howard and several other institutions, a university press is startling. In the period of Howard's greatest research productivity, white university presses or private publishers had to be relied upon for publication opportunities. (The deceptively named "Negro Universities Press" is unrelated to Negro institutions and is a subsidiary of Greenwood Press.)

New Trends and Prospects for the Future

It has been clear that broad social and political changes in American society have had a greater impact on the fortunes of Negro colleges and their faculties than any purely internal efforts. Thus, changes in the general group status of Negroes created by urbanization, the gradual acquisition of political leverage, and the altered position of the United States as a world power, have had a profound impact on Negro scholars and their opportunities. After the Second World War, the gathering momentum of the movement to desegregate higher education gradually destroyed the basis for the upsurge of quality that marked the previous twenty years. While it is true that in 1946 Robert Maynard Hutchins reported strong opposition to the appointment of Negroes to the faculty of the University of Chicago, regarded as a "liberal" university, there was nevertheless a slow erosion of racial barriers in higher education.[90]

Since some of the first Negroes to break these barriers were naturally among the top Negro scholars (like Allison Davis who left Dillard for Chicago, Abram L. Harris who left Howard for Chicago, and John Hope Franklin who left Howard for Brooklyn) and the supply was small, token desegregation was sufficient to slowly erode the small but productive clusters of research scholars in Negro schools. Segregation had produced the situation where superior men were consigned to schools inferior in facilities and encouragement of research, not matter how commendable their commitment to provide a sound education to Negro undergraduates. By the late 1950's and 1960's token desegregation had been accelerated by the impact of "black revolution," especially the black studies explosion, and there has been heated discussion about a "black brain drain." There are numerous indications that the leading institutions of the "segregation era" have become enfeebled. The once high quality of journals like the *Journal of Negro History*, the *Journal of Negro Education*, and *Phylon* has declined precipitously in recent years and no Negro institution now publishes a really first-class scholarly journal. A number of distinguished scholars remained n Negro institutions during this period, but in virtually every case their retirement left their departments bereft of recognized scholars and many younger men were being recruited to white institutions.

There has been a countermovement away from tokenism, easily misunderstood and much maligned by older Negro scholars sensitive to its exaggeration and rhetorical excesss. High levels of racial tension in society have usually produced an acute awareness of the difficulty of existing in a "double environment," the white world and the separate black social world. The conflict between racial and national loyalties has been a persistent theme. As long ago as 1897 Du Bois asked:

> What, after all, am I? Am I an American or am I a Negro? Can I be both? Or is it my duty to cease to be a Negro as soon as possible and be an American? If I strive as a Negro am I not perpetuating the very cleft that threatens and separates black and white America? . . . It is such incessant self-questioning and the hesitation that arises from it, that is making the present period a time of vacillation and contradiction for the American Negro; combined race responsibility is shirked, race enterprises languish, and the best blood, the best talent, the best energy of the Negro people cannot be marshalled to do the bidding of the race. They stand back to make room for every rascal and demagogue who chooses to cloak his selfish deviltry under the veil of race pride. . . . Have we in America a distinct mission as a race . . . or is self-obliteration the highest end to which Negro blood dare aspire?[91]

The emergence of "black consciousness" on Negro campuses in the last five years is easily the most dramatic change in their institutional life and in the way some faculty and students regard themselves. As much a commitment to a way of life and a cluster of values as a point of view, black consciousness is the most widespread attempt to achieve an intellectual and cultural position designed to overcome the vicious heritage of racism in America. Because of the powerful psychological dimension to the movement and its rejection *en bloc* of whites, it has been a source of alarm to the leadership of Negro colleges, who realize all to clearly how dependent they are on white institutions for support. Unlike their predecessors, who despite the costs involved sought to achieve academic acceptance on white terms, many of the younger black academics reject white definitions of their situation. There is a growing disposition to challenge not only the methods of scholarship, but also its values and objectives as defined by white scholars. Many conservatives who shout cries of alarm at the dangers of this movement often forget the scandal of how American scholarship has rarely lived up to its ideals of objectivity or neutrality in matters relating to race. Unfortunately it is too late in the day and the record too blemished to feign horror at the idea that scholarship is impossible in an atmosphere overwhelmed by political and social struggle. There are increasing numbers of young black professors who see their main goal as contributing to the liberation of their people rather than acceptance by white scholars in the disciplines.

Wide differences of opinion exist, dividing principally on two questions: whether racial justice is possible in the United States, and whether it is possible to reject so-called "white standards" of scholarship without destroying all standards. There are also real differences about what the colleges should be, some arguing for them to become social and ideological centers for "liberation" in a political sense, while others insist that a college's real contribution to liberation must remain on the level of research and writing. One of the chief spokesmen for black consciousness, Nathan Hare, has written that "The black scholar can no longer afford to ape the allegedly 'value-free' approach of white scholarship. He must reject absolutely the notion that it is 'not professional' ever to become emotional, that it is somehow improper to be 'bitter' as a black man, that emotion and reason are mutually exclusive. . . . The black scholar must develop new and appropriate norms and values, new institutional structures, and in order to be effective in this regard, he must also develop and be guided by a new ideology."[92]

So far, no Negro college has agreed to support the new "black scholarship" for a variety of obvious as well as subtle reasons. Quite apart from the racial issue, many doubt that anything remotely resembling scholarship as understood in the United States can be produced by researchers whose work is dominated by an ideology. The work of white scholars on race reviewed earlier in their essay was of course also dominated by an ideology, white supremacy, and no one can doubt it who has really taken the pains to read G. Stanley Hall or Howard Odum. But for all that, and it is quite a lot indeed, no institution outside of the South, with the possible exception of Princeton under Woodrow Wilson, ever made a clear commitment to white supremacy as an ideology guiding institutional development. Nevertheless, it is likely that a growing number of black social scientists, tired of the ambiguities, evasions, and hypocrisies inherently a part of the present situation, will find the position of Abd-al Hakimu Ibn Alkalimat (Gerald McWorter) persuasive. He has written that:

> Many black social scientists seemingly have not really known the extent to which science is inevitably an handservant to ideology, a tool for people to shape if not create, reality . . . we need a revolutionary ideology that reflects the utility of a black social analysis, the inevitable correctness of African prophecy of black gods creating a new man and the immortality of communal love as the basis for a commitment to kill and die for the liberation of all black people. In other words we need to get this shit on, and for that we need a revolutionary script for the terrible black drama of cosmic forces that we're about to rain down on these pitiful ofays.[93]

It is likely that there will be more adherents to a kind of cultural nationalism in black institutions rather than to any serious effort to launch revolution in theory or fact from colleges. Like all deeply felt movements, such a nationalism has great potential for destroying any possibility of genuinely critical (that is, also self-critical) intellectual centers in black institutions. The shrill stridency of many of the propagandists of blackness seems to confirm Ralph Ellison's prophetic dismay with Americans (white and black) who have an appetite for "that intellectual abandon, that lack of restraint, which seizes those who regard blackness as an absolute and who see in it a release from the complications of the real world."[94]

It remains to be seen whether black consciousness will be another of the tragic detours taken by Negro educators. Just as the earlier movements of moral uplift, character building, and industrial education were permeated by assumptions that Negroes were not ready for serious intellectual work, there is a subtle and of course unarticulated racist assumption in some of the black consciousness position that critical reason is for whites and visceral rage is for blacks. It is not surprising that some whites, including powerful foundations, support a position which confirms the hoary view of the Negro as a surly savage incapable of genuine thought, research, or scholarship. Many whites are apparently titillated by the spectacle of black college teachers posturing as hysterical prophets of doom, just as white New Yorkers once delighted in the antiwhite plays of LeRoi Joines (Ameer Baraka). Black studies programs, growing originally out of a legitimate need to correct the distortions and omissions of WASP curricula, have become in many instances special colonies within white universities for the containment of angry blacks—the Trojan horse again. The foundations have so far been prepared to subsidize these programs, often on the flimsiest grounds, and still persist in viewing black universities as service schools which ought not to try to develop sound standards of intellectual achievement and scholarship. Whether serious scholarship by Negroes will survive this decade will depend, in the end, on the extent to which racism can be disentangled from our conceptions of the human purposes of education and scholarship.

References

1. See Edward Shils's discussion of psychological aspects of Asian and African scholars similar to those affecting Negro scholars in America in his article "Color, the Universal Intellectual Community, and the Afro-Asian Intellectual," *Daedalus* (Spring 1967), pp. 279–295. An example of the "peripheral" character of Negroes in American academic life is the still frequently heard complaint that even after years of rigorous and productive scholarship Negro scholars remain the "invisible men" of their profession. Except for one or two notable exceptions, they rarely, if ever, are invited to present papers to the national meetings of their professional organizations, despite the "high regard" some of their work is supposed to enjoy. It is not unusual for their work to be omitted from consideration entirely, behavior Americans usually believe a monopoly of Soviet historians. In John Higham, Leonard Krieger, and Felix Gilbert, *History* (Englewood Cliffs, N. J.: Prentice-Hall, 1965), W. E. B. Du Bois, Carter G. Woodwon, Rayford W. Logan, and Benjamin Quarles are not mentioned once, and although there is discussion of the *Catholic Historical Review* (begun in 1916) and the "incipient professionalization of Catholic historiography under the auspices of the Catholic University of America" (p. 34), there is total silence about Woodson's founding of the Association for the Study of Negro Life and History in 1915, the establishment of the *Journal of Negro History* in 1916, and the "incipient professionalization" of historical writing about Negroes in the United states. "To be wholly overlooked," John Adams once said, "and to know it, are intolerable. If Crusoe on his island had the library of Alexandria, and a certainty that he should never again see the face of man, would he ever open a volume?" John Adams, *Works*, VI (Boston, 1851), 239–240.

2. John Hope Franklin, "The Dilemma of the American Negro Scholar," in Herbert Hill, ed., *Soon One Morning* (New York: Alfred A. Knopf, 1963), pp. 62.76.

3. Although Negroes are now overwhelmingly urban dwellers, it is clear that the peasant heritage is still very powerful. Hardly a unique phenomenon, the anguished isolation of intellectuals in peasant cultures has been the subject of wide study. See, for example, Richard Pipes, ed., *The Russian Intelligentsia* (New York: Columbia University Press, 1961) and Edward Shils, "The Culture of the Indian Intellectual," *Sewanee Review*, 67 (1959), 239–261, 401–421.

4. *Annual Report of the Freedmen's Aid Society of the M. E. Church* (1868), p. 14.

5. An illustration of the impact of the defeat of reconstruction on the higher education of Negroes was the spectacle of William H. Councill, president of the State Normal School at Huntsville, Alabama, and Booker T. Washington's rival, insisting on trying to have none but ex-Confederate officers on his board of trustees, whose views on the education of the Negro are not difficult to imagine. Councill said, for example, that "when the old, gray-haired veterans who followed General Lees' tattered banners to Appomattox shall have passed away, the Negro's best friends shall have gone, for the Negro got more out of slavery than they did." Quoted in Horace Mann Bond, "the Influence of Personalities of the Public Education of Negroes in Alabama, I," *Journal of Negro Education*, 6 (January, 1937), 24–26.

6. Cited in Bond, "The Influence of Personalities on the Public Education of Negroes in Alabama, I," p. 24.

7. D. O. W. Holmes, *Evolution of the Negro College* (New York: Columbia University Press, 1934), p. 13.

8. Horace Mann Bond, *The Education of the Negro in the American Social Order* (New York: Prentice-Hall, 1934), p. 149.

9. Bond, "The Influence of Personalities on the Public Education of Negroes in Alabama, I," p. 23.

10. See Emmett J. Scott, "Twenty Years After: An Appraisal of Booker T. Washington," *Journal of Negro Education*, 5 (October 1936), 543–554.

11. See Lionel B. Fraser, "The Dilemma of Our Colleges and Universities," *Opportunity: Journal of Negro Life*, 15 (May 1937), 167–171.

12. Charles H. McCord, *The American Negro as a Dependent, Defective and Delinquent* (Nashville: Benson Printing Company, 1914), p.124.

13. *Ibid.*, pp. 42–44.

14. G. Stanley Hall, a warm supporter of Washington's supine acceptance of disfranchisement in return for vocational education, said, "For myself, I doubt if any educational institution in the world's history ever showed in those who attend from year to year greater progress along so many lines—dress, manners,

intelligence, morals, health than is seen in the pupils of Tuskegee." Hall did demure from Washington's opposition to higher education, however, "The only modification," he said, "of Mr. Washington's programme that seems needed is that which professor Du Bois pleads for, namely, opportunity for all the higher cultural elements of education to every Negro who can take it an make use of it." *Proceedings of the Massachusetts Historical Society*, 2d ser., 19 (Boston, 1905), 105–106.

15. McCord, *The American Negro*, pp. 66–68.

16. For a fuller discussion of industrial education see Henry Allen Bullock, *A History of Negro Education in the South from 1619 to the Present* (Cambridge, Mass.: Harvard University Press, 1967), pp. 167–193.

17. Sterling A. Brown, *The Negro in American Fiction* (Washington, D. C.: The Associates in Negro Folk Education, 1937), p. 54.

18. See Kelly Miller, "Negro Education and the Depression," *Journal of Negro Education*, 2 (January 1933), 1–4.

19. See Kelly Miller, "Howard: The National Negro University," in Alain Locke, ed., *The New Negro: An Interpretation* (New York: Albert and Charles Boni, 1925), p. 314.

20. Quoted in Horace Mann Bond, "The Influence of Personalities on the Public Education of Negroes in Alabama, II," *Journal of Negro Education*, 6 (April 1937), 174.

21. Rayford W. Logan, *The Negro in the United States*, vol. I, *A History to 1945—From Slavery to Second-Class Citizenship* (New York: Van Nostrand Reinhold Co., 1970), p. 66.

22. The first American Negro to earn a Ph.D. was Patrick Francis Healy, S.J., who received the degree from the University of Louvain in 1865. He joined the faculty of Georgetown University in 1867, and was president of the university from 1873 to 1882. Healy's career, however, was atypical in virtually every respect, and no other American Negro Catholic has since had a similar career. See Albert S. Foley, S.J., *God's Men of Color* (New York: Farrar, Strauss, & Co., 1955), pp. 23–31.

23. William A. Dunning, *Reconstruction: Political and Economic* (New York: Harper and Brothers, 1906), p. 212.

24. See Richard Hofstadter, *Social Darwinism in American Thought* (Boston: Beacon Press, 1955), chaps 3, 5, and 9.

25. G. Stanley Hall, "A Few Results of Recent Scientific Study of the Negro in American," *Proceedings of the Massachusetts Historical Society*, 2d ser., 19 (1905), 95–107. It is especially interesting to note that when Hall returned to the United States from Germany in 1872 he applied for a position on the faculty at Howard, saying that he had "strong preference" for the university. It is not known why he was not hired, but this change in point of view about Negroes may be an index of how powerful a change in public opinion had been wrought by the "New South" propagandists and their northern allies. See the facsimile of Hall's letter of March 16, 1872, in Walter Dyson, *Howard University: The capstone of Negro Education, A History, 1867–1940* (Washington, D. C.: Howard University, 1941). On page 104 of the *Proceedings* Hall writes: "For myself, an abolitionist both by conviction and descent, I wish to confess my error of opinion in those days." It seems from his comments, page 105, that Booker Washington influenced his change of mind.

26. See, for example, Robert Bennett Bean, "Some Racial Peculiarities of the Negro Brain," *American Journal of Anatomy*, 5 (September 1906), 353–432; Marion J. Mayo, The Mental Capacity of the American Negro (New York: Science Press, 1913); and George Oscar Ferguson, *The Psychology of the Negro: An Experimental Study* (New York: Science Press, 1916).

27. Albert Bushnell Hart, *The Southern South* (New York: Appleton and Company, 1912), p. 104.

28. See Rayford W. Logan, *Howard University: The First Hundred Years, 1867–1967* (New York: New York University Press, 1969), pp. 242–243, 309, 634. Even more perplexing is the fact that Hart made his 1912 statement after serving as adviser to W. E. B. Du Bois during his graduate work at Harvard. Hart highly praised Du Bois' work, and according to Du Bois, who was always sensitive to any racial slight, he was "one of Hart's favorite pupils." See Francis L. Broderick, "The Academic Training of W. E. B. Du Bois," *Journal of Negro Education*, 27 (Winter 1958), 10–16, and W. E. B. Du Bois, *Dusk of Dawn: An Essay Toward an Autobiography of a Race Concept* (New York: Harcourt, Brace & World, Inc., 1940), p. 38.

29. Howard W. Odum, *American Sociology: The Story of Sociology in the United States Through 1950* (New York: Longmans, Green, 1951), pp. 154–155.

30. *Ibid.*, pp. 38–41

31. *Ibid.*, p. 41.

32. *Ibid.*, p. 188.

33. Dorothy B. Porter, "The Organized Educational Activities of Negro Literary Societies, 1828–1846," *Journal of Negro Education*, 5 (October 1936), 565.

34. A recent history of the American Negro Academy is an unpublished 1966 M.A. thesis by Mignon Miller, "The American Negro Academy: An Intellectual Movement During the Era of Negro Disfranchisement, 1897–1924," in the Negro Collection of the Howard University Library.

35. See William Simmons, *Men of Mark, Eminent, Progressive and Rising* (Cleveland: Rewell & Co., 1887), pp. 530–535.

36. See W. E. B. Du Bois, "Of Alexander Crummell," in his *Souls of Black Folk* (Chicago: A. C. McClurg & Co., 1903), pp. 215–227.

37. Du Bois, *Dusk of Dawn*, p. 58.

38. For a contemporary scholar's appraisal of *The Philadelphia Negro*, see E. Digby Baltzell's analytical introduction to the 1968 Schocken Books reprint. E. Franklin Frazier, whose own work *The Negro Family in Chicago* is very highly regarded, said of *The Philadelphia Negro* that "Nothing better has ever been done in the United States on a Negro community." See E. Franklin Frazier, "The Role of the Social Scientist in the Negro College," in Robert E. Martin, ed., *The Civil War in Perspective: Papers Contributed to the Twenty-Fourth Annual Conference of the Division of the Social Sciences*, Howard University, 1961, pp. 9–18.

39. Du Bois, *Dusk of Dawn*, p. 62.

40. Du Bois, *Darkwater: Voices from Within the Veil* (New York: Harcourt, Brace and Howe, 1920), p. 21.

I wish to thank the following persons for consenting to be interviewed on various aspect of Negro education: Charles H. Thompson, Rayford W. Logan, Charles H. Wesley, Elsie M. Lewis, M. Wharton Young, Louis A. Hansborough, Carroll L. Miller, James M. Nabrit, Jr.

I am especially indebted to Herman R. Branson for important data on Negro scientists, and to Dorothy B. Porter for many sources on scholarship by American Negroes, and to Rayford W. Logan for information about Atlanta University and the *Encyclopedia of the Negro*. None are of course responsible in any way for any errors or interpretations in the essay.

PART III

THE ACADEMIC
LABOR MARKET:
RECRUITMENT AND RECRUITS

An Overview of the 1987 ASHE Distinguished Dissertation

Change in the Academic Marketplace: Faculty Mobility in the 1980s

DOLORES L. BURKE

Methodology

First, the replication itself provides some constraints. As general guidance, I used a paper published by Professor Caplow* that classified qualitative replications in two types: (1) a challenge, to confirm or weaken results of a study, or (2) a longitudinal study after a lapse of time to determine what changes have affected the system or subject during that period of time. These two categories are not necessarily mutually exclusive.

The research findings are based upon data obtained from 306 faculty members, primarily through personal interviews (266), but also in telephone interviews (6) and mail responses (34), with department chairs and other faculty members in the arts and sciences form December 1985 to April 1986. These individuals were at six of the universities Caplow and McGee visited in 1958; all are members of the Association of American Universities. The research used the original interview schedule, slightly modified with Professor McGee's assistance. Data analysis likewise followed the original design, with the exception that computer spreadsheets were used instead of manual coding sheets; the analysis consisted of a quantitative framework (numbers of appointments, etc.) and content analysis. (For further details, see the dissertation or forthcoming book.)

Data Comparisons

The data were organized a a natural progression, starting with process (search, selection, and separation) and moving to environment in a chapter on market and policy.

The Search

Caplow and McGee noted that the most striking feature of academic hiring procedures was the time and effort that most departments devoted to appointments. They remarked that the average

---

* Theodore Caplow, "La Repépétition des enguêtes: Une méthode de récherche sociologique," *L'Année Sociologique* 32 (1982): 9–22.

salary of an assistant professor was approximately that of a bakery truck driver—and his occupancy of the job likely to be less permanent—but that it took a large part of the time of several highly skilled people for a long period of time to hire him. That has not changed. The recruiting process is still an extremely time-consuming task; one chair characterized it as "gut-wrenching and tiring.**"

Changes have occurred in the structure of the search; for example, the Caplow-McGee assumption that a faculty departure or retirement almost automatically triggers a faculty replacement at the same rank in the same department has given way to a pattern of considerable negotiation between chairs and deans before a position is authorized. But the *position definition* generally remains within the province of the academic department.

Another change is that today's search is public knowledge through advertising in various forms. About half of the new assistant professors in the sample had learned about the position through an advertisement; the others had heard about the job before seeing it advertised. But the once-prevalent method of placement by a mentor in the "right place" seems to have vanished, and one chair expressed relief at no longer being "at the mercy of a senior man here who has a friend somewhere with a graduate student he wants to place".

At the senior level, advertising had little effect. The important consideration was, in the words of on one respondent, "Who could we get to come?"

Throughout the search process, generally a change from the 1950s, all departmental faculty members were encouraged to read the files, express opinions to members of the search committee, and argue for the inclusion or exclusion of candidates. As one experienced chair commented: "I've been chairman here for a long time, before that chairman at another university. If there is a lesson to be learned, it is that you can never please everybody all the time, but if there is one place you have to be democratic, it's in selecting new faculty".

Selection

A major change in the selection process is the importance of the campus interview for junior candidates. Fewer than half of the assistant professors in Caplow and McGee's sample were interviewed prior to being hired. Now there is general agreement that the interview is the top rung of the recruiting ladder—the place where the candidate can perform brilliantly or self-destruct. In the current study, the routine for the campus visit was fairly standard and matched the 1950s visit in the instances where it occurred. The selection decision continues to be based primarily on the research interests and capabilities of the candidate.

As in Caplow and McGee's study, the hiring departments were quite successful in hiring the people who were their first choice. New assistant professors (a group Caplow and McGee did not interview) were satisfied as well: Only six (out of seventy-four) admitted that the job was not their first choice, and more than two-thirds of the group had rejected other offers. New assistant professors were primarily attracted to the department because their personal research interests were compatible with those of the department. They were also sensitive to treatment by the department; and astute chairs, knowing that the top layer of candidates was not deep, tried, in the words of one, "to sell the place." It was a successful technique. One assistant professor said that she was impressed by "the red carpet treatment, very fine".

For the senior candidate, there was no change from the 1950s. The campus visit might not take place at all, or it might occur in a modified form—e.g., participation in a seminar series, an invitation to consult. The department is particularly interested in a good fit, as in this case: "Ostensibly her work is good and she is younger than the other candidate and therefore thought to have more potential. But really we just liked her personally a lot better."

Separation

Termination showed a rather surprising lack of change in some respects. As would be expected, there was a larger proportion of retirements and a smaller proportion of deaths in comparison to the 1958 sample. But dismissals and resignations were proportionally about the same as in the earlier study: 25 percent dismissals for Caplow and McGee; 26 percent in the current study; 47 percent resignations in 1958, in the current study, 49 percent.

Further, my expectation that a central all-discipline promotion and tenure committee would play a greater role in tenure denials was not realized. An impressive 70 percent of the tenure denials were made at the departmental level, 67 percent for Caplow and McGee. Lower-ranked departments turned people over at a higher rate; there were only eight tenure denials in top-ten departments (about 20 percent of total denials), and none in top-five department.

Colleagues of resigning assistant professors frequently cited intellectual isolation and intellectual incompatibility with senior colleagues as mobility motivators. A typical report would be, "they didn't offer him much more in the way of money, but he thought he would be more appreciated there." Senior people also left because of intellectual isolation or incompatibility, in their case with peers, and sometimes because of a lack of research support or a pronounced hostility in the department. Salary was rarely a motivator, consistent with the earlier study.

Important to the future of higher education in the more competitive market place of the 1990s may be the apparently increasing proportion of faculty members who leave higher education altogether—about a third of the assistant and associate professors in the current sample, as compared to a quarter of those in Caplow and McGee's sample. An example of the change in mindset that may be occurring is reflected in this quote from an assistant professor: "We undergo brainwashing in graduate school. We are attracted to academia by the lure of formulating and solving problems. But there are also problems to solve in the private sector. I may leave higher education.

Market and Policy

The market and policy category showed a great deal of change—change that is continuing. The study reflects the same market conditions noted by others recently—an opening up of the academic job market. One chair of classics said: "The market has improved and I think it will continue. I foresee days when we'll be right back where we were in the '60s and I'll be pulling people off the street." More than half the chairs in the sample across disciplines expressed similar sentiments. Effects like those of Sputnik n the 1950s were seen—one chair of physics talked about the "Toyota revolution" and several chairs of languages remarked on the positive effects of international trade. There was such mention of nonacademic competition for Ph.D.'s as in this comment from a chair of anthropology: "Ten to fifteen years ago all of our Ph.D.'s would get jobs in academia. Now only 10 to 20 percent get academic jobs. They work as research organizers, with computers in business and industry, in contract archaeology." So, a once-shrinking market has created new opportunities that will continue to compete for graduates.

Another change is more subtle—the reinforcement of the research culture in the university. Caplow and McGee recognized the increasing emphasis on research in the 1950s; this study shows that it is a shared emphasis, between employer and employee. There is no confusion about the basis for evaluation of an assistant professor nor any initial disagreement. The junior faculty member chooses a job and is chosen on the basis of research interests.

Related to the research emphasis is the tension between disciplinary and institutional attachment (or locals and cosmopolitans). This study identified a career cycle effect, with a strong discipline-oriented approach in assistant professors and with institutional and disciplinary orientation achieving more balance above that rank.

There are more participants in the current market, but the change in number does not necessarily connote a decline in quality. Of the chairs in the current sample, 35 percent said that today's candidates were better than those of some years ago, and the other 65 percent mostly said they were no worse—different, perhaps: "It's hard to put 'better' into perspective," commented one, "because there are a lot more things to be trained in and as chemists they know more because there is more to be known. The science has progressed. As to whether they are better, I don't really think so."

Another difference in today's participants, though, creates the spouse employment issue, now much more pronounced than the one or two occasions noted in Caplow and McGee's interview data. "The spouse problems are terrible these days", complained on chair. "It's a factor in two-thirds of our offers." In this sample, spouse employment was a factor in almost 20 percent of the appointments and resignations. For example, in appointments, 18 percent of the women and 19 percent of the men were affected by spouse employment problems.

The new problems of the academic market place have resulted in various management strategies, apparently not present at the time of the earlier study. One manifestation is a new flexibility in the central fund used for special hires—a spouse budget line and "targets of opportunity" or "superstars." Strategic planning has produced greater control over positions, but departments, too, engage in active planning: "Every two years we go off for a weekend retreat and talk about our long-term future," reported one, "not specifically about people but about research, academics." Indeed, management—a word once anathema to academics—is an important consideration for many chairs, as in this comment: "My job as a manager is to enable people to do their work."

An outgrowth of strategic management may be the aspiration to higher rankings currently found in many departments but absent from the earlier study. Chairs were highly sensitive to rankings, and there were numerous references to "moving up," "aiming for the top ten," etc. A frequent downside to these ambitions was disgruntled senior people: "I have an iron in the fire and I hope it burns," said one. "I will leave here if I can. There is a generally feeling of being unappreciated."

Conclusion

The findings led to identifying sources of change and nonchange in the academic marketplace. The source of change is the relationship between the organization and the social environment. Factors such as greater competition between universities and the composition of the labor market have also caused change. The source of nonchange, or inertia, is the academic department itself, where the personnel process resides, with its own extra-institutional relationship with the academic discipline. The organizational problem that emerged from the dissertation focused on the tension between department and institution, raising the question of how to integrate the departmental culture—the culture of the clan—into the broader organizational culture that seems necessary in the competitive environment.

Within the study, there was little variance on such items as type of institutions (public or private) and disciplinary division (humanities, natural science, or social sciences). Variance occurred principally at the departmental level, indicating the control of the department over the faculty personnel process. Therefore, an important element of the departmental culture is that process. Caplow and McGee pointed out that "the process by which a department replaces it members and maintains its immortality is as nearly central to an understanding of academic institutions as anything can be." The academic organization can be strengthened through further examination, understanding, and improvement of that process.

Note

**This and later quotes are drawn from interview data.

Dolores L. Burke is a special assistant to the president at Duke University. This dissertation, done under the direction of David Dill, University of North Carolina at Chapel Hill, is soon to be published by Greenwood Press, Westport, Connecticut.

This study replicates one reported by Theodore Caplow and Reece McGee in 1958 (The Academic Marketplace, Basic Books). The current study uses Caplow and McGee's original research framework and materials and, like the earlier study, examines the faculty personnel system in research universities.

Segmentation in the Academic Labor Market

Hiring Cohorts in Comprehensive Universities

DOROTHY E. FINNEGAN

The constituent determinants of faculty careers have been the subject of much scholarship since Logan Wilson [44] introduced the concept of self-study to the profession fifty years ago. Structural analyses have traced career pathways from entry into the profession through retirement, so much so that novices who aspire to replicate the successful careers of their research-oriented mentors have an almost complete map to guide them. For graduate students who aspire to top-tiered positions, securing entry into the professorial system means relying on sources of prestige external to themselves; the prestige of their institutions, graduate departments, and mentors plays a combined ascriptive role in securing the first academic position [12, 22, 25, 37, 38]. Following entry, responsibility for success reverts to the individual within the context of his or her academic environment [33]. Productivity, in the form of publications and especially citations, takes over as the primary mechanism to insure the appropriate rewards and, when feasible, mobility [1, 22, 36, 39].

Faculty have been alerted also to the modifying effects of fluctuations in the academic labor market on institutional recruitment and retention [12, 13, 32, 38, 43] and on institutional incentive and reward systems [33]. As the supply of faculty increased in the seventies, institutions demanded a higher price in their exchange with faculty of resources for prestige [39, 45] and boosted recruitment and retention standards. Clearly, the paths by which faculty realize success in research careers have been demonstrated to be normative.

To obtain career counseling from these various lines of research, however, research-oriented faculty or faculty "wannabes" must synthesize for themselves the varied empirical results of "the individual determinants of career outcome" [5, p. 37]. But careers are dynamic; they result from compounded individual choices and accomplishments. They also do not evolve in a vacuum. More than a compilation of singular incidents, actions, or interaction with institutions, faculty careers result from the ongoing simultaneous impact of external societal factors, such as the academic labor market, and internal organizational factors.

Moreover, the number of positions available in research-oriented universities are limited. Does the limited number of positions automatically mean that most faculty settle for positions other than their preference? What of the careers of faculty who play out their professional lives in other types of institutions? If faculty careers are a composite of continuous interactions with the labor market and with the institutions that employ them, then the essence of the missions must be taken into account. The *quid pro quo* faculty university prestige compact that Sorensen [39] suggests drives academic careers in research universities is virtually inoperative in organizations that proclaim themselves as teaching institutions. Rather than relying on the mutually beneficial exchange of resources (to faculty) for prestige (to the university), teaching institutions orient their missions to and acquire prestige from student-related factors, such as enrollment, student retention and postgraduation success. Do the career aspirations of faculty who spend their lives in colleges and universities that are primarily teaching institutions match the mission and objectives of these organizations or have they been frustrated as a result of placing lower on a meritocratic line of candidates? Existing knowledge about the professional life of faculty in non-research university contexts is scanty [16, 24, 35, 46] and provides few answers to these questions.

The purpose of this article is to broaden the study of faculty careers by exploring the career patterns of faculty who are currently employed in two comprehensive universities. I will argue three points. First, the labor market is segmented by institutional type as suggested by Brown [11] and Clark [15], in that the majority of faculty in the study have chosen deliberately to work in this sector. Second, by applying the conceptual framework of career lines [40, 41] to the professoriate, I will demonstrate that careers are not merely determined by singular incidents or a composite of incidents, but rather evolve as individuals interact with the external forces of the labor market, with continuous organizational choices made by their employing institutions, and with other faculty hired before and after them. And finally, I will establish that in this case study the normative career patterns for faculty in two comprehensive universities differ from those of faculty in research universities because their employment histories are intimately tied to different aspirations, fluctuations in the labor market, and changing institutional natures.

The Field and the Field Methods

This research, a qualitative case study, contextualizes the study of faculty careers by considering both time and space. First, in terms of space, I conducted my study at two New England universities categorized by the Carnegie Classification [14] as Comprehensive I Universities. Perhaps the most fluid in mission [9], this sector is the least often researched and therefore less understood as a group. Historically, the majority of the colleges were instituted to serve a single population or to deliver a single type of curriculum. The sector consists of former normal schools *cum* teachers colleges *cum* state colleges and universities, historically black private denominational and public land-grant colleges, technical institutes, women's colleges, and metropolitan and regional independent and denominational colleges [17]. Throughout this century, these institutions increasingly have broadened their original single-purpose missions by adopting multi-purpose objectives and an extended curriculum [21].

Comprehensives have undergone profound changes through this century, but more specifically in the past three decades. From 1960 to 1980, more institutional change occurred in the colleges and universities that offer the master's degree as their highest academic award than in any other institutional type [8]. Dunham exclaimed that "in a nutshell, the most salient characteristics of state colleges and regional universities are rapid change of function and astounding growth" [16, p. 1]. Growth and change in function were not only the experience of public institutions, but have been features of the private colleges and universities in the sector also. These two characteristics were rather complex. Characterizing institutional change between 1960 and 1980, Birnbaum found that institutions with comprehensive programs "began with the greatest number and proportion of institutions, experienced the greatest number and proportion of newly founded institutions, [and] had the greatest number of existing instititions change their programs into that category" [8, p. 113]. Today, the common characteristic across the sector is the provision of utilitarian education on the baccalaureate and master's levels.

In terms of time, within any institution, the current faculty were not hired at one time, but rather were hired over a stretch of thirty years or more. During those years, fluctuations in the academic labor market and student enrollments have affected the organization of the institutions as well as the opportunities available to faculty. Therefore, I sorted the continuous recruitment into three hiring periods that correspond with major transformations in higher education over the past quarter century. The faculty were selected to represent three hiring periods: Cohort I, the *Academic Boomers*, hired prior to 1972 during the expansion period; Cohort II, the *Brahmins*, hired between 1972 and 1982 during the academic recession; and Cohort III, the *Proteans*, hired since 1982 when the replacement period seems to have begun.

Cohort I, which nationally represents 37 percent of that nation's current comprehensive university and college faculty [29],[1] comprises 36 percent of the faculty interviewed for this study. The Academic Boomers are so named because they were hired during the surge in enrollments due to the Baby Boomers. Only 27 percent of the national comprehensive university faculty belong to Cohort II [29]. In this study, Cohort II is also the smallest group, representing 27 percent of those interviewed. Many of Cohort II were hired for their eminent credentials with the organizational intention of raising institutional prestige; hence, the name Brahmins. Cohort III, which consists of 37 percent of the case study sample, comprises 36 percent of all comprehensive university faculty nationally [29]. The dominant characteristic of the junior cohort is their versatility, and therefore they have been dubbed Proteans.

Members of three departments—English, mathematics, and management—in both universities were selected to represent faculty hiring during the three time periods. Forty full-time, tenured, or tenure-track faculty employed across the six departments participated in semidirected interviews. Both genders and a variety of ethnic, racial, and foreign national identities are represented in each cohort, given the composition of the departments. Individual interviews averaged two hours and, organized to correspond to my application [18] of Spenner, Otto, and Call's properties of career lines [40], covered family values and educational background, prior professional experience, professional and institutional affiliations and experiences (that is, recruitment and retention experiences and faculty governance), and satisfaction with professional and institutional life. In addition, department chairs, deans of the respective colleges, and the academic vice presidents were interviewed, and institutional documents were analyzed to add an institutional perspective to the three hiring times.

Typical of many private comprehensive universities, *Merger University*[2] was established in the mid-fifties as a result of a fusion of three independent postsecondary institutions. The largest of the three institutions, founded as a YMCA evening school for urban working-class men in the 1870s had offered a multipurpose curriculum combining liberal arts and professional programs as early as the 1920s. *Regional Stage University* was established first as a normal school in 1890 and subsequently was raised to the baccalaureate level as a teachers college. In the early sixties, the mission was broadened to include liberal arts. A decade later, professional curricula were added. Both New England universities today are multipurpose comprehensives, awarding baccalaureate and master's degrees. The two universities emphasize slightly different curricula. In addition o the typical liberal arts, business, and education majors, Merger offers several technology-based and fine arts programs. Regional State continues its historical mission of education, but has added programs in health-related areas and social services. Today Merger enrolls 8,000 students, 70 percent of whom are undergraduates. One-third of the students are part-time. Seventy percent of Regional state's 13,000 students are undergraduates, and slightly more than half are full-time.

This article presents each of the three cohorts within their hiring-time periods. In each time period, I analyze the interplay among the individual cohort characteristics, the institutional mission and organizational priorities, and the general characteristics of the academic labor market during the faculty's initial recruitment. As each time period unfolds, the careers of residing faculty are affected by the new priorities, the fluctuations of the labor market, and the characteristics of the new cohort. In the conclusion, I discuss the implications of my findings *vis-a-vis* a leading labor market theory to argue that the academic labor market appears to be segmented.

First Period: The Expansion, Pre-1972

Responding to an increase in postsecondary enrollment of almost six million students between 1960 and 1972, full-time faculty positions increased by 226,000 [2, p. 114]. More than half of those faculty positions were initiated after 1964, with annual increases of 18,000 to 33,000. Needless to say, employment opportunities in the professoriate abounded for persons with graduate degrees. Typical of comprehensive public institutions, Regional State's 1966–70 enrollments jumped by almost 5,000 students with a 60 percent increase in the FTEs. Among the Regional English and mathematics faculties, 61 percent (30/49) of the current faculty were hired during the period between 1962 and 1971.

The expansion, albeit welcomed, created a variety of headaches. Regional's physical plant could not adequately handle the record number of students, so the college operated on three-day shifts with faculty stacked in offices, sharing desks. The need for faculty was so great and the available supply of faculty so small that at first the demand for doctoral credentials was ludicrous. When possible, the institution tried to hire faculty with Ph.D.'s, but faculty with master's degrees were also engaged to ensure that the throngs of students were instructed.

Equally typical of private comprehensive universities, the enrollment expansion at Merger was not as dramatic. At Merger, however, the later sixties' expansion significantly improved FTEs as the historical pattern of part-time students was converted into full-time enrollment. The head count increased by only 1,500 students, but the conversion meant a 38 percent FTE increase. As the revenue stabilized with more full-time students, the institution was able to employ more full-time faculty, foregoing its reliance on part-timers, and simultaneously to build an entirely new campus. So the university was not forced to compete for quite as many faculty as Regional State during the labor market crunch of the mid-sixties. Among the English and mathematics faculty at Merger, 44 percent (13/29) were hired between 1962 and 1971, with the greater bulk hired at the end of the sixties.

Through the sixties, the number of graduate students pursuing doctoral degrees nationally increased on an annual basis so that the pool of potential faculty expanded year-by-year. Between 1955 and 1959, 1,699 English and 1,265 mathematics Ph.D.'s were awarded. During the five year period between 1965 and 1969, English and mathematics graduate departments produced 4,330 and 4,563 doctorates respectively [30, pp. 232, 269]. The number of doctorates earned in the liberal arts did not peak until the early seventies when graduate faculty and students began to realize slowly that the number of available academic positions was decreasing. As the academic labor pool widened, the course-way began to narrow. The employment choice shifted from an individual choosing one position from a variety of offers to the institution seeking one candidate out of a pile of applicants. By default, the universities were able to make demands for credentials by the early seventies that would have been unreasonable in the mid-sixties.

On an institutional level, the role requirements for faculty at both universities were relatively simple. Teaching was prized; service, in the form of intracollegiate committee participation, was assumed. On a departmental level, the liberal arts faculty were hired to teach the variety that comprised the average disciplinary set of courses. They were recruited to teach their specialties within the disciplines, but the curriculum offered to students was neither developed nor diversified. In general, the curricula at both institutions were marked by breadth, not depth. In fact, an expectation at recruitment was the expansion of the departmental curriculum. In both English and mathematics departments, the courses of study were organized to follow the traditional canons or components of undergraduate education and were thus expanded.

Few professional programs existed at Regional State. Those in place were related to the historical teaching mission of the college, such as library science. The business program was only an inchoate hope of the president and a few economics faculty.[3] At Merger, with its history of business courses for part-time local residents, the faculty required were those who had an applied orientation and background themselves in addition to their doctoral preparation. They brought stability and progressive, applied dimensions to the curriculum that had not been possible previously.

The Academic Boomers

Interestingly, both institutions originally were *access institutions*; that is they provided opportunities to students who might otherwise not have been able to attend postsecondary education. They apparently served this same function for the members of Cohort I.[4] The teaching mission of the institutions coupled with the fluid nature of the labor market during this period opened a window of opportunity to faculty who might otherwise never have entered the professoriate. With one exception, the entire hiring cohort were first-generation college students. One-third of the cohort were the children of immigrants. Unlike many of their colleagues employed in more selective colleges [23], they came from working- and middle-class families with no personal or professional experience in higher education. Only one man's parents were associated with education—they were high-school teachers. The faculty's pre-employment aspirations to the profession of teaching were formed either in college or in graduate school, mainly as a result of encouragement from their faculty and/or a discovered passion for learning and teaching. College teaching had not been a vocation within the realm of their ken or kin. Many of the cohort never even considered college teaching but were recruited from the high-school level through the sheer need for adjunct faculty.

The marked characteristic of this cohort was their deliberate choice of employment in this sector. The faculty in the sample, with one exception,[5] chose deliberately to apply to and/or accept positions in a teaching institution. Half of the faculty were *college-teaching hopefuls*. These faculty were attracted to the profession either by role models or from their experiences as teaching assistants in their graduate programs. Because the labor market was so open during the sixties, all of the *hopefuls* easily secured full-time faculty positions when they went on the market. Those who had finished their degrees found assistant professorships, while the ABDs were hired as instructors at institutions located near their doctoral programs. Convention dictated that these instructors would move on after three or four years when their degrees were finished. As a result of the fluidity of the labor market, the older faculty in this group had the luxury of teaching at several colleges prior to settling at their current university. Several resigned from their previous appointments at either liberal arts or regional teachers colleges when their ethics clashed with those of the administration.

The Merger management faculty fall into this first sub-category of *college-teaching hopefuls*, yet their original aspirations and work experience followed an entirely different pattern. These faculty spent more than a decade in managerial positions before returning to graduate school for their doctorates. They entered their doctoral programs assuming that they would teach on the collegiate level. Therefore, they not only had a considerable amount of industry experience prior to their first (and only) academic position, but they also maintained an applied professional orientation, which was manifested in the classroom as well as in their professional accomplishments. Their professional writing took the form of trade manuals for managers.

The other half of the cohort aspired to teach in secondary schools, not to the postsecondary level. A few were convinced during their doctoral programs of their ability to make a greater impact on education if they sought college teaching positions. One Boomer explained that he planned to write curriculum materials when he returned to high-school teaching from his doctoral training, but was persuaded by his mentor that he would have more support to accomplish that end on the collegiate level. These transformed *college-teaching hopefuls* were additionally attracted to the opportunities promised by the institutions. Teaching was rewarded, curriculum development was an imperative, and service to the institutions was considered a natural part of their citizenship. Those who stopped their formal education with the master's degree left teaching positions in high schools only after being offered instructorships after a year's stint as adjunct.

Recruitment

The Boomers' recruitment to their current institutions was influenced by structural forces as well as by personal preferences. The latter was characterized by personal and career values and included bounded employment searches, networking in the sector, and domestic issues. The former represented the intersection of the labor market with the needs of the two institutions and included multiple job offers and institutional hiring patterns.

First, as the labor market tightened through the late sixties to early seventies, the qualifications demanded for employment increased. Regional sought a great number of faculty throughout the entire second half of the sixties. The closer the hire to the mid-point of the decade, when the largest class of freshmen entered college, the more the market was open to faculty with only a master's preparation. Nineteen sixty-seven appears to have been the credential watershed for the former teachers college. In that year, only ABDs were hired and within two years, only doctorates. By 1971, the last Boomer, a Ph.D. with full-time teaching experience and publications, was hired.

At Merger on the other hand, the majority of the hiring began late in the sixties. Due to the swollen labor pool, faculty with doctorates were easily recruited, and the majority of faculty began the appointment with some teaching experience behind them. The fact that Merger was a university, was dedicated to teaching, and was still in the process of constructing its curriculum and its new campus attracted many of these faculty.

Second, the Boomers had recruitment opportunities yet to be equaled again. The fluid nature of the labor market furnished numerous options so that their quest for teaching positions was fairly effortless. The degree of mobility and of choice, though, was directly related to a combination of the person's highest degree, discipline, specialty, and recruitment year. Several senior Boomers had tenured appointments at other colleges prior to arriving at Merger, for example. They had the luxury of resigning without fear of being locked out of academe. Other Boomers, finishing their degrees late in the decade, had multiple offers when they sought permanent positions. But yearly, the number of options decreased. One Merger mathematician explained that two doctoral classes above him received bids from all *seven* colleges or universities to which they applied. The class directly in front of him received offers from only five of the seven. In 1968, he *only* received three offers. The Ph.D. Boomers all reported having between two and seven offers when they went on the job market.

On the personal side, the striking characteristic in the recruitment stories is that the faculty with doctorates, save one, limited their searches to teaching institutions. Teaching was (and remains) their dominant professional value. Some Boomers consciously eliminated themselves from the top-tiered sectors, whereas other deliberately sought and accepted positions based on the existing institutional cultures that supported teaching as the dominant faculty role. A Regional Boomer hired in 1968 explained: "I ended up here through a conscious decision not to have the pressure. I was a pretty good researcher during the dissertation, but I came to Regional specifically for the teaching. When I came, the Board of Trustees wanted teaching." With few exceptions, they limited their applications to liberal arts colleges with regional reputations and to comprehensive colleges, both private and public. Essentially, the Boomers were attracted to their current positions specifically because of the missions of the institutions. At Regional, many of the mathematicians were drawn to the prominent secondary education teaching emphasis of the college and their department. The English faculty at both universities were lured with the opportunity to teach in and elaborate courses for a traditional genre/period English major.

A second, but related trait that characterized the Merger Boomer's recruitment was the use of professional acquaintances to secure a match. Both the faculty within the department (to recruit) as well as the recruits (to hunt) solicited information from former colleagues. In several cases, Boomers were recruited as a direct result of recommendations from friends already employed by the university. The recruitment efforts of the university, especially when the labor market was still fairly tight, were facilitated through informal networks arising from the faculty's graduate programs and professional contacts. Rather than the vertical lineage that characterizes the research university mentor-student recruitment pattern [12, 22, 33, 34], many of the Boomers were recruited through a lateral colleague-to-colleague or former graduate student-to-graduate student linkage.

When hired, the Boomer's professional interests ranged from an active involvement in research and publication to the complete avoidance of publication. Those who wanted to pursue scholarship were attracted to their institutions *because* productivity was not required. A Regional State Boomer who has written several textbooks was offered a tenure-track position in his doctoral research university department but, "it was a *publish or perish* [position] and that would have been suicide. I was naive and would have been eaten up." The range of attitudes toward scholarly activity is reflected in the faculty's institutional and professional affiliations throughout their careers. In some cases, these attitudes as well as the activities of faculty were modified as the institutions changed and as other faculty were hired.

Finally, as a result of the availability of positions, the Boomers were able to choose their positions on the basis of domestic or geographic criteria that included family ties and the proximity of major metropolitan areas and of major research university libraries. Several Boomers, native to the state or to New England, were able to stay, or in some cases return to the region after graduate school as a result of the open labor market.

Retention

The Boomers were hired to teach. Many of the later hires were also recruited to develop the curriculum, both on the undergraduate and the graduate (master's) levels. Their teaching loads were uniformly twelve hours with three, sometimes four preparations. Meyer, Scott, and Deal have found that "the lowest levels of organizational policy are [delineated for] the type of curricular materials to be used and instructional methods or techniques teachers use." Schools (K-12) have, they continued, "few policies in the areas of greatest significance for their central goals and purpose" [26, p. 59]. While both universities declared themselves as teaching institutions, policies existed to outline the basic role requirements for the faculty, but criteria and standards for evaluation were minimal. "Good teaching" was cited by every Boomer as the primary requirement for retention during their pretenure years. Yet, reputation, perhaps hallway gossip, student praise or complaints, and other informal mechanisms served as the institutional means of faculty performance appraisals. Both institutions began to regularize faculty evaluation by the mid-seventies. At Regional, state-mandated collective bargaining drove the first specifications of policies and procedures for evaluation, albeit the criteria remained somewhat loosely defined. After having been hired by a reportedly authoritarian president who retired in the early seventies, many Boomers felt that unionization prevented further arbitrary personnel decisions. At Merger, the specifications of criteria for faculty evaluations resulted from a faculty-generated task force arising out of the senate.

The second most important role that faculty played was in service to the institution. At both universities, the Boomers generally played significant organizational roles both in temporary administrative roles, when the universities were caught short-handed, or in department, college, or university-wide governance positions. Although not selected to participate in this study on this basis, most Boomers reported having served as senate representatives or leaders at various times through their careers. At Regional, "bargaining agent" was an additional role that carried great prestige, influence, and power for a few Boomers.

At neither university was scholarship an important criterion for retention or promotion during the first time period. At Merger, publications were acclaimed but not stressed. At Regional, scholarship was originally a covert activity, a thing disdained by many and hidden from colleagues and supervisors by others. As the number of doctorates increased, production of creative professional work became legitimate by sheer force of number. As late as the early seventies, one Boomer, who had already been published in a European Royal Society journal before recruitment, was told that his continued theoretical writing was not an activity that was respected at Regional; the assumption was that this type of activity diverted his attention from the classroom. Publishing took the form of textbooks, non-scholarly writing, and non-refereed articles and presentation at both institutions, with only the occasional exception toward the more scholarly side. Faculty clearly did not have the monetary or affective support, the research facilities, or the released time from a demanding teaching and service schedule to generate much scholarly work. Nor were they particularly rewarded for these activities.

The Regional Boomers were all tenured within three years—an institutional policy that stayed in force until the union was established. By the mid-seventies, hiring in the liberal arts programs had ceased. Had there been a need for qualified faculty, the supply was so great that a short tenure-track was no longer a necessity to entice faculty to stay. By that time, however, all of the Boomers had been tenured and generally had been promoted to associate professor. All, that is, except the master's-prepared faculty. By 1970, with the probationary period set at three years, the faculty with master's degrees were tenured to positions for which, had they been in competition, they would no longer have been qualified. Many of them had to wait for several years before a higher rank was granted. The probationary period at Merger abided by the norm of the time for smaller institutions, that is, five years of probation, tenure awarded for the sixth year. Because so many Merger Boomers arrived with some teaching credit, all were tenured and promoted to associate professor by the mid-seventies.

As the Boomers were being tenured, the climate in higher education was changing and was changing dramatically. By the early seventies, the pool of potential faculty had overflowed its natural boundaries, while simultaneously students clamored for vocational curricula. In response to the early projections for the next decade's decline in the size of the traditional-aged population, many institutions looked for ways to increase their admission market-share. In light of these external forces, the nature of the institutions changed, and with it, the nature of Cohort II.

Second Period: Repositioning, 1972–1982

National postsecondary enrollments continued to grow through the seventies, but at an inconsistent and slower rate. The enrollments that had been just under six million in 1965 topped eleven million ten years later. It took ten years before the 1965 record for the single largest entering class was broken; most of the other yearly gains during this time-frame were much smaller [27, p. 90; 28, p. 126]. In terms of growth, the seventies belonged to the community colleges, with the comprehensives tagging along behind. By 1976 the community colleges registered more than one-third of the students, the highest proportion in all of the sectors. During the same years, liberal arts colleges lost 23 percent of their enrollments, while comprehensives increased their student rolls by 26 percent [14, pp. 3–4].

A burst of new professional and vocational programs was established in both the community colleges and in the state colleges. No longer were the latter instititions dual-purpose as they had developed in the sixties, adding liberal arts to their previously singular mission of teacher preparation. The comprehensive public college finally had emerged. Across the nation, fewer students were graduated from liberal arts programs as increasingly more and more students elected applied programs. English baccalaureates halved from 1971 (65,000) to 1981 (33,200); mathematics baccalaureates decreased by an even greater proportion (25,000 to 11,000) [30, p. 244].

The national complement of faculty increased by 212,000 during the seventies. Superficially, the labor market appears to have been fairly open. But the proportion of new doctorates who reported having been hired by colleges and universities declined [29, p. 92]. Two conditions explain the situation. First, 100,000 of the new positions were hires in the community colleges [30, p. 219]. During the decade, doctorates among community college faculty only increased by 2 percent [3, p. 188; 6, p. 26]. Therefore, at least one-third of the new faculty hired during this period held master's degrees and were employed in community colleges. The opportunities for Ph.D.'s obviously were reduced. Second, while the number of doctorates produced annually began to decline after 1973, the numbers had grown so much during the late sixties that it took most of the decade for the Ph.D. five-year outputs to dip below the comparable time periods in the previous decade. In other words, far too many Ph.D.'s were still being graduated throughout the decade.

The seventies proved to be a dynamic recruitment period for faculty in the right fields of study and seeking the right type of institution. For others, especially in the liberal arts, the period was a disaster. Both the community colleges and, especially for the purpose of this case study, the comprehensives continued to hire faculty through Period II, but primarily in professional or applied programs.

On the institutional level, both universities responded during this second time period to external forces in a manner that altered the role of faculty significantly. At Regional, two major occurrences affected the faculty. As noted above, the collective bargaining imposed by the state in the mid-seventies resulted in a waged battle among the Regional faculty to determine the bargaining agent. Some faculty on the losing side were severely damaged by the process. The winners went on to lead the faculty at the negotiation table. By this time, a state college consolidated system had been implemented and a board of trustees approached the negotiations with the assumption that faculty should demonstrate evidence of scholarship—a significant departure from the existing role definition. The faculty were able to stem the tide to separate scholarship from service within the criteria defined for tenure and promotion and to negotiate for a program of released time from classroom obligations. The new program, a radical departure from the previous contempt for scholarship, served as an incentive system for involvement in scholarship.

The second external force was the shift of student interest toward vocational programs. The president of the college enabled some existing faculty with applied tendencies to secede from their liberal arts departments to develop vocational/professional programs. Throughout the seventies, the major emphasis in curricular design and, therefore, in faculty hiring occurred in applied programmatic areas. Very few faculty were hired in liberal arts and education, the former mainstays of the institution.

At Merger, a new president was appointed by the board of trustees with the charge of implementing a strategic long-rang plan. The protégé of a controversial national educator, the new president took advantage of the over-supply of faculty in the labor market to "upgrade" the existing faculty. From 1978 to 1982, the university substantially raised the criteria for both recruitment and retention. The consequential effects were enormous and long-term for both the existing faculty and the newly recruited faculty.

The Brahmins

The Brahmin cohort within the two universities reflects the national group composite; that is, in comparison with the Boomers, the proportionate size of the cohort is smaller, the number of women is higher, and more professional specializations are represented.[6] The seventies academic labor market proved to be *field-sensitive* [42]. Faculty in professional fields had little difficulty obtaining positions; liberal arts faculty had to possess impeccable credentials to stand out in the crowd. At Regional State, only two faculty were hired to the mathematics departments from 1972 until the mid-eighties, and both positions were retrenched within two years. In the English department, literally no new liberal arts faculty were hired after 1972 until the mid-eighties. The only addition was a journalist who shortly defected to a newly established professional department. During the same time though, a plethora of professional programs were established throughout the state college; the management department arising out of economics, was started in the late seventies in an effort to serve the needs of the region's population. At Merger, already a comprehensive university, hiring continued across the board. In the liberal arts, however, new faculty were employed to replace retirements. In the business school, a few new positions resulting from a modest expansion of the programs and a number of replacement positions due to a "blood bath" over the future direction of the school created a need for a new faculty throughout this period.

The Cohort II sample faculty range in age from 40 to 56 with a mean of 46.6, just short of the national average for all comprehensive university faculty. As might be imagined, these faculty are Baby Boomers, who earned their baccalaureate degrees in the mid-to-late sixties. One third of the sample are women and all but one are American-born Caucasians. All were hired between 1978 and 1982. The few faculty hired after 1972 and before 1978 were not retained by either institution albeit for different reasons. Thus, the cohort spans the three departments at Merger but only includes faculty from management at Regional State. All are tenured and all but one have been promoted to associate professor.

The families of the cohort members reflect the upward mobility of the post-World War II era. All but one were raised in middle-class, native-born families; the parents of the exception were immigrants from a northern European country. At least one parent in the majority of the faculty's families was college-educated, more often the father. In general, the women's fathers have attained more education and have a higher social-class standing than the fathers of the men. College for the children was assumed, and most of the faculty's siblings pursued postsecondary education.

In contrast to the Boomers, all but two of the Brahmins earned their bachelor's degrees at selective private universities or liberal arts colleges; the exceptions were graduated from public/ doctoral universities. Some were accepted on early admissions; many had full scholarships. None went to college with the intention of a professorial career, but they were guided by their faculty advisors. The undergraduate faculty "pushed the better students and assisted them in getting into graduate school," explained one Brahmin.

All but one of the Cohort II members are research-oriented. In contrast to the Boomers' joy of finding teaching, most of the Brahmins expounded during their interviews about their discovery of research interests in graduate school. The exception is a management faculty member at Regional, who was the first member recruited to the newly established program in the late seventies and has a definitely applied perspective. The sample is very small across the cohort and especially in certain departments. As a result, implications can be discussed rather than definite patterns demonstrated.

Recruitment

Two recruitment characteristics arise from the faculty's stories: some, although highly qualified with graduate experience in research, shied away from the perceived scholarly pressure of a research university and deliberately sought employment in the comprehensive sector; most, however aspired to and prepared for research positions, but were mixed in a pool of qualified applicants who sought positions in research universities. Neither faired well in the high-supply and limited-positions labor market. These traits cross-cut the departments at Merger. One Brahmin explained, "Originally, I thought I was a hot-shot academic. My fantasy was teaching the kind of student that provided grist for the academic mill, to be able to share my work, present research, and I wouldn't be teaching four courses a term." But those type of positions were few and the competition was great. "While in graduate school," she continued, "I thought that I'd teach in a great liberal arts college, small, like the one I went to, possibly a women's college. It was my image of teaching. Then, for may years, any job would do."

The cohort could not have hit the academic labor market at a worse time. Without significant accomplishments, the Ph.D. alone bound the Brahmins into a pot of applicants identical to every other newly minted doctorate. Similar to many of their contemporaries, the cohort members initially took less-than-satisfactory or insecure positions as temporaries in order to practice their profession. Unlike many contemporaries though, these faculty pursued their scholarship during the interim, so that their credentials eventually did stand out from the crowd. The Merger administration deliberately sought faculty across-the-board with prestigious credentials during this period. Faculty hired to the liberal arts departments brought moderately superior credentials than their colleagues in management. One Brahmin, slightly above the norm perhaps, arrived at Merger after having earned his D.Phil. at Oxford, supported by a Fulbright, having started his second monograph, and having taught for four years at a historic, mid-Atlantic research university as a junior faculty member in an unofficially nontenure track position. The university, in his words, was "a Kleenex school—use 'em [junior faculty] and throw 'em away." Other faculty brought resumes with numerous refereed articles and funded textbook-writing experience in addition to years of teaching as adjuncts or as temporary replacements.

The management faculty at Regional present a slightly different picture. Rather than containing one group of faculty with homogeneous professional background, two subgroups are present. Because of the establishment of the business school, the department's development (and faculty credentials) was compressed into one short four-year period. Cohort II is comprised both of faculty hired in the late seventies who resemble the applied, industry-experienced-turned-academic of Cohort I at Merger *and* faculty hired in the early eighties with industry experience with a research-based orientation. These extremes were recruited over a four-year period and today are mixed together in one department. The philosophical arguments are extremely disruptive.

Retention

Within a few short years, both institutions were radically changed as a result of the recruitment of the new faculty. For Merger, the type of faculty recruited was intentionally modified in order to alter the professional orientation of the existing faculty. At Regional, the curricular offerings were consciously diversified and faculty were recruited to new and expanded areas. Once the second cohort was hired, the careers of the Boomers and the Brahmins became entangled. The Boomers characterize themselves as teachers. Scholarship for many of them has been an extension of their teaching; often textbooks, articles, and papers seeped out their class preparations. In contrast, most of the Brahmins embraced scholarship as a primary value, either in graduate school or during their "waiting period" prior to their current position. The interactions between the two cohorts have been largely dependent upon the ethos of their departments and are much too complicated to pursue here. Suffice it to say, the more the departments accommodated and supported the interests of both groups of faculty the more positive the interactions. Those faculty who feel that their primary professional goal (either teaching for some Boomers or scholarship for some Brahmins) has not been sufficiently rewarded are alienated or disaffected.

In the late seventies, both universities began to modify their incentive and reward systems in an effort to support scholarship. The formal and informal reward systems were grounded almost exclusively in effective teaching and service to the institution with a secondary concern for the loosely defined activity known as scholarship. Almost overnight at the end of the seventies, the Merger administration raised the criteria for promotion and tenure. By the time the Brahmins began to approach their tenure decision during the early eighties, the requirements were solidly divided between teaching and scholarship. One Brahmin, who has recently returned, originally was hired in 1978. He left the university before he would have been denied tenure:

> I was doing no research. When I came, one guy [named], had just gotten tenure with no publication. He was a great thinker, but had no publications. The next year, another [program] faculty was denied tenure. They looked at his dissertation, but he had not published. The next year, another was denied tenure and he had a book, an article. And a piece in a special edition of [a prestigious business journal], but that case was some-what political. You could see the ante was being raised.

For many of the Brahmins, the additional requirements for tenure posed few problems. But few have felt supported to conduct the type of professional lives for which they prepared and for which they thought they were being hired. Many continue to teach twelve hours a week. They are expected to be concerned with the retention of students, with service to the university, and with a continuous research agenda. Exhaustion came from the need to

> disassociate teaching from research. Teaching is over here and research is over there. It is not good distinguishing between teaching graduates and undergraduates. There is enormous guilt when I do. And it is hard for me to do, given my background. What I should do for [the undergraduates] is summarize plots.

On the other hand, many of the Boomers, hired and tenured into an organization with a strong, embedded value of teaching, advising, and institutional citizenship, did not possess the desire, the preparation, or the stamina to change. For some of these tenured faculty, promotion became a situation of *publish or languish*, a slightly different commonplace. Several Boomers have been held in rank—at Merger, generally as associates—due to their inability to meet the new requirements. To one dedicated teaching Boomer, hired in the late sixties after struggling to complete his dissertation, it has been made very clear that he will remain an associate professor for the rest of his career. "I accept that. I am dedicated to this place and I think that I deserve [promotion] as much as some others, but I'd rather be doing that I am doing [teaching]. I wouldn't like myself—it's not worth it."

The requirements for promotion and tenure did not change at Regional during the second time period, but the introduction of the incentive system of released time signaled the advent of change. Faculty who could develop scholarship-based proposals were supported and relieved for a term of three of their twelve-hour teaching load. Other faculty, primarily but not limited to those who had master's degrees, were locked out of competing for this "perk." The more new faculty who had more training and experience in research were recruited, the less competitive the existing faculty became. A certain cumulative disadvantage began. A Regional Ph.D. Boomer explained:

> The push for publications and research is coming from the university, not the faculty. In a place like this, a no mans' island—it is stuck between a teacher's college and a research university. Just because the name is changed. . . . They have supplied funds, but I can't

get into it. To get money, "What's your project? What library will you work in?" Forcing research onto the faculty who don't want to do it. Fabricating projects to get the semester off. It becomes more difficult as the language of the contract evolves. The soft criteria is good teaching. The hard criteria is how many publications with a quality hierarchy and numerical scales. Lunatics!

Similarly, a number of senior faculty are languishing in rank with no hope of promotion at Regional. Unlike Merger, no merit system exists. Promotion is the only way to increase one's base salary beyond the cost-of-living increases. Therefore, not only are many of the senior faculty stuck in rank, but they remain at the top of their salary scale, unable to move into a new strata. As these changes were beginning to take hold at the two universities, a third cohort with entirely different backgrounds and values were beginning to be added to the mix.

Third Period: Reevaluating Missions, 1982–1990

Nationally, the third time period has been characteristically a patchwork of new developments and concerns: increased faculty disciplinary specialization; recently acknowledged racial, age, gender, and sexual diversity among various constituencies; program accountability; and dwindling fiscal resources. These collective factors provide the backdrop for the operation of the labor market, the institutional articulation of mission, the recruitment of new faculty, and the retention of existing faculty.

Probably the most dramatic changes in enrollment through the late seventies and the eighties were concerned with the composition of national postsecondary enrollments rather than their size, as had been the case for the previous fifteen-plus years. Gradually the gender participation ration shifted so that by 1988 the number of women matriculants surpassed men [31, p. 19]. Attendance patterns also shifted from 73 percent of the undergraduates who were full-time matriculants in 1969 to only 59 percent. Finally, the number of students enrolled as freshmen declined through the eighties [28, p. 129; 30, pp. 176, 181].

The comprehensive sector, however, showed the strongest enrollment increase among four-year, non-specialized colleges in the eighties, augmenting their rolls by 4.2 percent overall and by almost 10 percent in the private comprehensive colleges and universities.[7] Research and doctoral institutions grew only by 2–3 percent, whereas liberal arts colleges were forced to replace their shrinking full-time enrollments (-2.3 percent) with part-time students (18 percent) [28, p. 126].

On the graduate level, the number of doctorates in the liberal arts awarded annually continued to decline. Twelve hundred mathematics doctorates were awarded in 1970, but only 752 were earned in 1988. Likewise, English doctorates halved, declining from 2,170 in 1973 to 1,180 in 1988. Business and management surpassed mathematics in the mid—seventies and approached the English awards by 1988 with 1,100 doctorates [30, p. 246].

Between 1980 and 1987, another 107,070 faculty were added to the professoriate. More than two-thirds of the new members were full-time. For the second time, half of the entire complement was employed in two-year colleges. By 1987 comprehensive colleges and universities employed 26 percent (128,000) of all full-time faculty in the United States [30, p. 220–21]. Many of the 53,500 new four-year college and university faculty positions created since 1980 were in comprehensive universities and colleges as a result of the enrollment growth in that sector. The career stories of these new faculty help to establish the existence of a segmented labor market when faculty choice and institutional mission, rather than organizational aspirations, coincided in recruitment and retention of faculty.

The Proteans

Fifteen faculty comprise the third cohort sample (37 percent) and reflect the national composite of faculty hired to the comprehensives since 1982.[8] Seven are female. Of the thirteen American citizens, eleven are native-born to the white majority, one is a native-born African American,[9] and one is a naturalized citizen from the Middle East. Two foreign nationals came to this country originally to study for their doctorates and have stayed. One is Asian and one is a Western European. Eight of the cohort are married. Of the single faculty, five are male and two are female. Five of the spouses are academics. The three associate professors have been awarded tenure; one of the assistant professors was denied tenure last year as a result of a lack of publications.

More than half of the thirty parents of the faculty pursued formal postsecondary education. Mothers were slightly more likely to purse a college education, but less likely to finish. Eight of the fathers received bachelor's degrees, four went on for graduate work, and one earned a Ph.D. The majority of families are middle-class, although three of the women came from either socially or educationally above-average families. Several of the women were raised in multigeneration academic families. The Proteans grew up with the implicit assumption that they not only would attend college, but that college would have a lasting and broadening effect on them. Only one faculty member indicated that his father assumed that college attendance was directly related to an occupation.

The Proteans, save two, received their baccalaureate degrees after 1971, with the majority having spent their entire undergraduate career in the seventies. Interestingly, therefore, most of this cohort were taught primarily by Academic Boomers in their respective colleges or universities. The faculty's education was decidedly more dispersed among the various institutional sectors than that of the other two cohorts. Two did not go straight to college after high school but experimented with alternative life-styles instead—not unusual in the late sixties and early seventies. Among the cohort members, there appears to be no pattern that links the type of control between undergraduate institutions and present employment; that is, those working in the public university are just as likely to have attended private colleges. The spread of colleges demonstrates that entry ports into the profession are no longer limited to university or elite educational patterns as they were for the Brahmins. Represented are selective and less-selective liberal arts colleges (including one Ivy League and three Catholic colleges), and research doctoral, and comprehensive universities.

Almost half of the cohort believe that they receive less career advice than they would have liked. One Protean voiced the frustration of many:

> When I was a senior, I was very active in the department, as a student rep to the faculty and in the literary club. I like classes, especially literature. I like talking about it and asked the faculty, "How can I continue?" They told me graduate school. I didn't understand what that meant. . . . I had done the research [about different graduate programs] but didn't know what to look for. My teachers' recommendations were haphazard really. Nobody said to *go to the name* [go to a prestigious department]. I hate that, so I am glad they didn't. I just wanted to continue. [Name of doctoral university] was the *alma mater* of one of my three favorite teachers.

However, many of the faculty independently researched possible types of doctoral programs available in their chosen fields. Some selected their programs specifically for the specialized nature of the faculty, for example, in mathematics, applied programs rather than theoretical. Others relied on the professional networks of their undergraduate or master's degree faculties to narrow the choice. All of the Proteans supported themselves in graduate school by teaching or research assistantships or adjunct positions and through these positions learned that teaching was a primary value to them. In many ways, the Proteans resemble their more senior colleagues than the cohort directly above them. Their recruitment patterns explain the relationship.

Recruitment

By the time the third cohort began their graduate studies, the labor market for liberal arts faculty was not promising. Nor was it any better once they approached completion. None of the faculty reported having been discouraged from entering the field by their graduate faculty, however. Like the Brahmins, most of the liberal arts faculty "hit a brick wall" when they began to search for positions. Unlike the Brahmins though, they amassed teaching and administrative experience rather than augmenting their credentials through publications. The search for an appointment took two forms. Graduates in one group waited until they had finished their degrees before going on the market. When they could not find openings, their graduate faculties continued to support their career choices by hiring them to temporary positions in the department. During this time of abeyance, they were encouraged—although few took the advice—to publish. One typical Protean explained her odyssey:

> In 1982, I began looking for tenure-track jobs. There were expectations that everybody did it. I never got a job. So I stayed [her doctoral program] as a lecturer in composition and continued to apply. There were no positions. I was one of 500 applications—a glut on the market. The faculty encouraged the best students to publish and others to go to law school. They tried to help with letters, phone calls, and recommendation for my dossier. I spent two years in the lectureship. I figured that at least the pay was better, and I was not a student anymore.

She then accepted a two-year temporary position in an American university in Europe and a three-semester temporary but full-time teaching/staff position at a doctoral university. The second pattern was for these "would-be faculty" to take full-time temporary positions as instructors while ABD, teaching freshmen service courses in mathematics or composition. Two characteristics bind these subgroups together. The Proteans were willing to go almost anywhere for these temporary positions in order to stay in their chosen fields. And while in these positions, they assumed administrative responsibilities, thereby gaining a more diversified experience. For both subgroups, temporary teaching positions allowed these individuals to stay in the profession until the demand for faculty opened ever so slightly. By this time, their resumes displayed some teaching and administrative experience, enabling them to flow to the top of the pool.

From an institutional perspective, the recruitment requirements also seemed to approach a more rational basis. At Merger especially, the departments began to seek candidates who espoused the extant values in the mission and objectives of the university rather than their organizational aspirations, as had been the case for the Brahmins. One chair, himself a Brahmin, explained that he asked a primary question of all preliminary applicants during the "meat-market" interviews at national meetings. "Would you describe yourself as a teacher, a teacher/scholar, or a researcher?" If the answer was anything other than the second, applicants were immediately eliminated.

The Proteans were attractive to the two universities as a result of their field specialties in addition to the their varied backgrounds. Possibly the most significant change in this period on the departmental level had been the diversification of the curriculum through the introduction of subspecialties. In both universities, journalism had seceded from English departments, for example, in the early eighties. By the mid-eighties, both English faculties had begun to develop programs in and to hire faculty with quasi-applied specialties, such as rhetoric and composition, cinematic studies, and creative writing, in an effort to recapture student enrollments. Many of the new faculty brought with them the new theoretical perspectives of feminism, deconstructionism, and critical theory [see 7]. In management, new specializations reflected the maturation of the field and the expansion of student interests and industry needs. Whereas one Boomer remembers teaching for three departments in his early days, Proteans were hired to specialize in organizational behavior, production management, and management information sciences—all in one department.

Most Cohort III members looked for an institution that valued teaching but also supported scholarship. Similar to most of her cohort members, a woman and her fiancé, also an academic, deliberately applied only to teaching institutions.

> I was looking for a place that would allow me to have a good life. I have the capability to be in a high-powered research institution, but the last six years have been unbelievably intense and I don't want to live like that. . . . [Fiancé's name] and I talked about this issue for two years. What kind of place do we want to be at? We decided that we wanted a balanced life. We didn't want the research university, not the straight teaching institution, unless we could be virtually involved, for example, at a Jesuit college.

The oldest of the cohort, in addition to his ABD adjunct teaching experience, was an industry analyst prior to his academic conversion. He deliberately sought a position in a comprehensive university:

> When I was leaving [Research I university doctoral program], I eliminated myself from the top tier. The publish or perish . . . you have to be a researcher, not a teacher. You are known by publications. Making a name for yourself like an actor. That was not my reason for coming into this profession. When I went to [a flagship university's extension center], there was a research emphasis to some extent, but they couldn't have hired a young graduate with no experience to stand in front of MBA students. They needed someone who was credible, and I was the right kind of person for them.

Each cohort member values a combination of all three role responsibilities—teaching, research, and service. And each expressed a desire to pursue all three areas. They were recruited for their combined talents and are already assuming responsibilities that few junior faculty would be offered normally.

Retention

While Merger has begun to reevaluate the emphasis it placed on scholarship in the early eighties, Regional State only recently has divided the combined standard of service or scholarship and now, by contract, requires faculty evaluations to assess separately teaching, service, and scholarship in promotion and tenure decision. The emphasis on scholarship at both universities surprised many of the Proteans. Some early candidates feel that they were misled during their interviews. "I got the impression at the start that teaching is the primary responsibility—that they weren't big on publications, that other activities could take place," explained one Protean. Another voiced a similar misinterpretations, "I did get the wrong impression in my interview though. I got the impression that teaching is more important than publications." Now, especially at Regional, some faculty find themselves "caught in the bind" felt by senior colleagues.

> The values are teaching as the most important thing and then publishing and service next. I took them at their word and worked on my teaching. It give me personal satisfaction. And, in fact, this was the case. I was allowed to come up for promotion within five years and was actually promoted in four years. . . . [But,] the contract has changed; research has moved up. It used to be combined with service, now it is a step above. It is going to be harder to get to full [professor] as a result of what I didn't do in publishing. So I am a little more anxious about getting something in writing.

Most of the Proteans are active scholars, though. They differ from the Brahmins in that much of their work is not limited to theory. Many are attracted to pedagogical or applied research or to creative endeavors. They are also pushing the definition of service at their institutions in new directions as a result of their experience and interest. Some of the women are intensely involved in developing women's studies curricula and extracurricular programs. Others are heavily concerned with the professional development of their students and are formalizing mentoring programs. Finally, some are exploring funding for regional scholarly programs to be sponsored and accommodated at their universities.

At Regional, the trustees have recently pushed the system toward more emphasis on research because the colleges assumed the title of university in the early eighties. Merger, on the other hand, has recently inaugurated a new president who appears to be returning the university to its comprehensive mission and redefining the concept of "service" to the advantage of both the university and the faculty. In addition to assuming that service is an intramural activity, he as invited a variety of faculty from across the university to participate in university-sponsored consulting activities on an international was well as regional level. Faculty are called on to share their professional expertise in a variety of applied projects and are encouraged to vie for research grants. Unlike in previous years, the university provides them with seed money fro the start-up phase. They also are supported to retool when necessary so that they may participate in local projects.

One Brahmin, experiencing the first phase of what could have been a severe burn-out was encouraged to learn the mechanics of computer graphics. Like so many of his colleagues in both universities, he adopted what I would call a *cosmo-local* pattern of productivity. Although time and resources are a premium, many faculty collaborate professionally with colleagues in their own departments or in other departments in the university. In this case, the Brahmin contacted an art specialist to assist him in learning computer art composition and in turn, is teaching her about computers. The pair are cooperating on a project to assist local primary and secondary teachers to integrate computers into their schools' curriculum.

All of this is not without critics from within the faculty ranks. Since some of the Boomers are left out of the incentive and reward systems, alienation and envy are natural consequences. Many of the senior faculty who are frozen in rank are suspicious of the junior faculty's motives and feel hurt by the system's persistence in providing a cumulative advantage to the research-experienced. At Regional, the emphasis has advanced toward scholarship, and those who have not participated throughout their careers in this type of endeavor are clearly left behind—seemingly with little concern from within certain departments or from an organizational level. Many of these faculty have several years before retirement and envision spending those years with little recognition for the activity for which they were hired and only the personal satisfaction that comes from their teaching. The values may be changing at Merger, reemphasizing service, but in no way are the incentive and reward systems equitably accessible or supportive across the three cohorts.

Discussion

First, this brief case study has explored the difference in the career lines of the three cohorts; each group possesses some distinctive and significant preemployment and employment traits. The family and educational background of the Boomers corresponds to Lipset and Ladd's conclusion from the 1969 Carnegie and their own 1975 faculty surveys that "[a]cademics from working-class and farm background turn up most heavily in the lower-status colleges" [23, p. 323]. For many of the Boomers, children of immigrant and working-class families, their graduate education enabled them to become first-generation professionals. Teaching institutions provided access routes into academe. But the second cohort, the Brahmins, broke the pattern that Lipset and Ladd identified.

As the academic labor market tightened in the mid-seventies the choice and flexibility previously available to prospective faculty in the mid-sixties reverted to the institutions. Had the academic labor market remained open, many of the Brahmins would [and probably should] have been hired by more selective, research-oriented institutions. Their employment at a comprehensive university matches the institution's aspirations, not theirs. Simultaneously, though, the participation rates for postsecondary education grew and achievement replaced the apparent former ascriptive advantage of class background. Although many of the Brahmins were raised in business and professional families, other families encouraged upward mobility through education in their children, which was characteristic of the post-world War II period. The academic achievements of the liberal arts Cohort II members—primarily in the form of postdoctoral productivity combined with the lack of research-oriented appointments—took precedence in this sector over the effect that ascribed class status had in determining academic placement.

By the time the Proteans were hired, entirely new patterns began to develop. The generic relationship between class background and institutional sectors has superficially all but disappeared within the cohort as an aggregate. The Proteans' families include as many working-class as professional parents. However, the family class standing of the Protean women on the whole, is higher than that of their male counterparts. Most, in fact, come from academic families. In the 1969 and 1975 studies, Lipset and Ladd found "the more prestigious, research-oriented institutions have drawn their professors disproportionately from the higher social strata. Faculty offspring do best of all. They are most likely to be found in the top schools, suggesting that family culture pays a major role in transmitting the ability to do well academically" [23, p. 323]. So, in the late sixties to early seventies, class background provided a cumulative advantage for faculty (when men significantly outnumbered women in the professoriate), as Lipset and Ladd suggested, promoting the value of academic achievement. Social class may still be an operative mechanism for some women entering and experiencing success in academe, but the interplay between the intrinsic values for the process of education held by the faculty member and the academic ethos of the institution appears to be of overriding importance in the recruitment and selection of both the men and women in this cohort.

The intrinsic values espoused by the Regional Protean faculty of both genders are centered as much on student development and culture change as on research—parallel to the mission of their university. Many of the junior faculty at Regional view their role as one of consciousness-raising. They see teaching as a "subversive" or an empowering activity, that is, a means by which to encourage social mobility among their first-generation college-going students. The Proteans at Merger, on the other hand, were clearly attracted to the more aspiring ethos and newly acquired reputation of their university and to the combined role of teaching and research enacted by the administration and the Brahmins. They are teaching students from middle-class families—some actually mentioned "spoiled children." In their interviews, the Merger faculty were more likely to value their disciplinary paradigms than the potential for empowerment. These patterns suggest that both the institutions and the faculty have reverted once again to seeking corresponding values (as was true for the Boomers) in the recruitment and selection process.

Certainly, the three cohorts' recruitment experiences differed greatly and were highly dependent upon the state of the academic labor market when they finished their highest graduate degrees. Through the three periods, the capacity to define adequate proficiency for employment switched from the candidates to the institutions and largely depended upon the relationship between enrollment demands and faculty supply. Simplisticly, the degree to which the faculty have had choice in type and location of their employing institution decreased with a larger supply of candidates and a smaller demand for their services. But in addition, the definitions of supply and demand have changed through the three periods.

During the mid-sixties, when the need for liberal arts faculty was the greatest at the public colleges across the nation and the pool of available doctorates was the smallest, faculty candidates in this sample had the greatest degree of leverage in securing their choice in employment. They could negotiate positions and security with minimal credentials or better rank and salaries with higher degrees. As the supply of liberal arts faculty increased, the pedigrees required for recruitment and retention escalated. When Regional extended its curriculum into applied areas in the seventies, the faculty-based leverage pattern was repeated at least for professional field academics. As the supply of doctorally prepared applicants in these areas has expanded, the power to regulate credentials has passed back to the institution.

During the seventies, the number of doctorates in public institutions on the national level decreased slightly, while the number and diversity of fields represented among comprehensive university faculty increased. For example, in the public comprehensives, health science (probably primarily nursing) faculty comprise 2.8 percent of Cohort I; whereas, by 1972–82, faculty in that area made up 9.2 percent of the national comprehensive sample. Less than half of the current faculty in health science have doctorates in comparison to 66 percent across the entire current faculty in public comprehensives [18, pp. 59–65].[10] During this time frame, the liberal arts departments in this study were either prohibited from hiring faculty or were limited to adding instructors in applied subfields such as journalism. Demand, then, was redefined in favor of applied or professional fields, and because the supply of faculty with doctorates at first was small in many fields, recruitment standards were lowered.

Currently, the national complement of private comprehensive university and college faculty is comprised of 71 percent doctorates, 24 percent master's, and almost 5 percent bachelors degrees. In comparison to the publics, the proportion of doctorates at these institutions increased by almost 5 percent between the first two periods. The highest percentages of doctorates of the current private university faculty nationally are in the liberal arts, while as much as 30–50 percent of the faculty in the professional fields, such as health sciences, fine arts, and business, have master's degrees [18, pp. 59–65]. During the two earlier periods, Merger, already a multipurpose university, hired faculty across more fields than Regional. The same pattern appears to have occurred on a national basis [18]. As such, one inference is that as the supply of faculty in the liberal arts increased nationally, the recruitment requirements also escalated for faculty hired to those departments. And, in fact, the case study shows that the Brahmins at Merger had credentials at recruitment unmatched by the other two cohorts when productivity is factored in.

Finally, the role expectations and their subsequent rewards for faculty through the three time periods have changed. Some faculty have managed to stay current with the changes, whereas others have not. The topic of satisfaction with their careers over time is an issue explored elsewhere [see 18]. This case study concurs with Queval [35] that institutional definitions of productivity have been transformed, and with them the criteria of the incentive and reward systems of the two universities. Again, each of the three cohorts is experiencing different reactions to the institutional expectations placed on them.

Some Boomers have continued to pursue a modest agenda of scholarship, although many have maintained their pedagogical orientation to publishing. Some, who chose to remain focused on their teaching and kept an arm's length from publishing, have become less qualified and/or less competitive as the years and new faculty are added. At Regional, for example, released time from coursework provides support for faculty to pursue scholarship. However, those who have not been publishing report that their proposals are not competitive with those of other faculty who have track records in publishing. These detached faculty, then, end up teaching the normal twelve hours each semester when the schedules of competitive colleagues reportedly are alleviated on a regular basis. At Merger, the merit system supports faculty accomplishment in any of the three areas—teaching, research, and service—but promotion is directly tied to professional productivity. At both institutions, without the terminal doctorate for some and/or a record of publications for others, promotion and the attending salary increment are out of reach. Ultimately, while the values of the senior faculty matched those of the institution at recruitment, for some, the disparity continues to increase.

For the Merger liberal arts Brahmins, hired for their established publication records, the increased demands are not the problem; they would rather spend more time at their research. They take issue, rather, with the institution's inability to uphold its part of the "bargain" struck at recruitment. Many continue to teach twelve hours a semester; some no longer have access to graduate students as a result of cut-backs. Several feel "stuck" in their situations, not able to maintain a rate of scholarly production that would allow them to be competitive for the type of institution to which they originally aspired. They also feel undervalued because the scholarly orientation for which they were hired is expected but not fully supported by the organization, and neither understood nor appreciated by the students.

The Proteans are an interesting mix of faculty. On the whole, they value all three expected responsibilities of the faculty role, but each member of the cohort appears to emphasize one over the others. As noted previously, their values appear to correspond more closely to the mission or nature of their respective institutions than had been true in the previous cohort. As a result, they have already been very successful in translating their past experience into support for their professional and institutional agendas, much to the dismay of some of the isolated senior faculty.

Burke [12], in replicating the Caplow and McGee study [13], has found extensive differentiation in the recent academic labor market for disciplinary specialties in research universities; some subfields within a discipline can be less promising for employment than others or than the field in general. Indeed, this field-specific labor market pattern is evident in the Protean recruitment cycle also. But the argument here is that the academic labor market complexity goes beyond field supply and demand. The case study demonstrates that the labor market is as focused within and for the comprehensive sector as it is within the research sector.

Because we have not understood the aspirations of individual faculty and institutional mechanisms of recruitment that operate within this sector (or those of sectors other than the research university), the assumption that the same formal and informal rules govern these processes across the professoriate limits our perspective and constructs the specifications of the models we use to analyze faculty careers and the academic labor market. One model, for instance, used in the analysis of the labor market called "institutional screening," or "queuing theory" "advocates that jobs are differentiated according to their quality and attractiveness, regardless of the current labor market situation" [45]. The implicit assumption in the concept of "queuing" is that academic employment is a singular hierarchical competition that pushes "quality and attractive" candidates to the head of the line to be "snapped up" by "quality and attractive" institutions, schools and departments, leaving the rest of the competitors to be filtered into less attractive positions. In other words, less meritorious candidates are matched with less meritorious institutions.

This case study does not support queuing theory by demonstrating that faculty hired during two different periods specifically chose to seek employment within a particular type of institution. Not only did they *not* find the research university setting "attractive," but deliberately avoided applying to the "quality" institutions as a result of their professional values and interests. Readers may ask if some would have been competitive for positions in the "attractive and quality" institutions. I would argue that this is an inappropriate question. The majority of these faculty deliberately chose, *did not settle for*, these positions. In a few cases, some faculty decided their initial career path based on what they wanted to avoid (*publish or perish*), rather than predicated on what they wanted [10]. In other words, the decision to seek employment in this sector appears to have resulted from the faculty member evaluating and subsequently eliminating what she or he perceived to be inappropriate role demands at more research-oriented institutions. Nonetheless, the majority of faculty in Cohorts I and III chose the mission and the role responsibilities advocated within the comprehensive sector. Hence the hierarchy of career sorting that exists in some minds does not exist in others.

Queues may exist and may regulate the acquisition of academic positions. However, I would argue that the queues operate within sectors rather than across institutional type, albeit modified by the condition of the labor market. In periods of equilibrium—that is, when an adequate supply of faculty is present and/or institutions utilize rational recruitment processes based on their missions—candidates are selected from an apposite queue. For comprehensives, the queue appears to consist of faculty who are not in competition with those in line for research positions. Although the acquisition of the initial academic position in research-oriented institutions has been consistently demonstrated to be governed by ascribed status mechanisms, the same mentoring and prestige instruments seem not to apply for those faculty who were able to have some control over their careers when the labor market was favorable. Disequilibrium occurs when supply exceeds demand and when institutions recruit for aspirations rather than the reality of its resources.

Those faculty who were caught in the low-demand/high-supply labor market were exploited by the university and the system. They aspired to and were trained for an entirely different career than what was available at the time. All are grateful for having managed to secure positions during a time when many new doctorates were squeezed out of the system into taxi cabs [4, 19], but they lament the incongruity between their values and those of the universities and students they serve.

As we move into a new recruiting phase, replacing the faculty hired in the sixties, institutions should recruit and faculty should search judiciously. Institutions should evaluate their aspirations and resources, and articulate their mission and values for their new recruits. Faculty aspirants should heed the advice of a Protean who waited until March to earnestly begin his search for a teaching position. After having competed for positions in comprehensives for a number of years, he has divined the appropriate timing for the application process. His analysis is that candidates from elite graduate programs not only apply to prestigious positions but blanket a variety of institutions for the sake of safety. His experience has demonstrated that these candidates are not serious contenders—either from the applicants' perspective or the university's. The university cannot support the research-support demands of these candidates, nor are these applicants drawn to this sector. These "elite candidates" undoubtedly are being advised by mentors who well remember the severe lack of choice in the seventies. So they seek a safety net with little expectation on either side of the negotiation. Once these candidates have been hired by the elite or prestigious programs and thus removed from the comprehensive sector pool, this Protean knows that his application will be seriously reviewed. The unfortunate side of this vignette is that some faculty searches at the university would obviously waste their time and money on candidates whose aspirations are not suited to the mission of the institution.

Given the findings of this case study, comprehensive universities and colleges, if they conduct their faculty searches appropriately, should not have difficulty recruiting faculty even if there is a shortage in the years to come. Some faculty, not merely the cast-offs of prestigious institutions, want to make a commitment to a mission of access and teaching. A typical Protean was adamant about her values:

> Teaching gives me a very definite high. I get results. I learn from the students. In their innocence, there are blinding insights. I learn more from them than by myself. There is serendipity in the classroom. Often I come to new insights from teaching. . . . My sense of the profession is that teaching is a political, subversive process and it is where I can do the most damage. I am not good at marching, making posters. Students here are educationally deprived. They respond to attention and are not snobs. They know that they are in an institution with the other institution down the road [an Ivy League university]. In any other town, Regional would be considered a good school. The faculty are generally good scholars.

Notes

1. The descriptive statistics from the National Survey of Postsecondary Faculty, 1988 (NSOPF-88) [29] are data that I generated from the survey data base for my dissertation [16].

2. Both universities have been assigned pseudonyms to respect the rights of the faculty who were interviewed and the confidential nature of the interviews.

3. Therefore, no management Boomers exist at Regional State.

4. Nationally, the mean age of the Academic Boomers is 54 years, seven years older than the mean for the entire composite of comprehensive faculty [29]. Within the case study sample, the faculty range in age from 48 to 65 with a mean of 58 years. Men comprise 84 percent of the group; the public comprehensives currently employ slightly more women in this cohort than men due to the substantial emphasis in education fields at the time [29]. The sample reflects the same gender distribution.

5. One faculty member wanted a research university position to pursue scholarship. Hired at the very end of the period as the labor market was closing down for liberal arts faculty, he was locked into this sector, having taught in several other comprehensive colleges while completing his degree.

6. Nationally, the comprehensive university faculty who belong to Cohort II differ from the first cohort in two distinctive ways. The faculty hired between 1972 and 1982 is the smallest of the cohorts, representing only 27 percent of the faculty. Their professional disciplinary or field distribution leans toward professional specializations rather than liberal arts. Demographically, the national mean age of the cohort is 46 years, but as of the fall 1987, 45 percent of those hired during this period were under 44 years old. Men still predominate in the cohort, but to a lesser degree. They represent 69 percent of the faculty. The private comprehensive universities and colleges gained more in gender diversity through this period but had been further behind in the previous cohort. Women comprised 12.5 per cent of Cohort I in the private institutions as opposed to 17 percent in the publics. In Cohort II, women in private universities and colleges make up 33 percent as opposed to 30 percent in the publics [29].

7. Full-time students increased by 8 percent and part-time by 12 percent.

8. Nationally, Cohort III is older than expected. Their mean age is 40.9 years, with 30 percent of the cohort over the age of 45. The cohort comprises 36 percent of the comprehensive sector faculty. Equally, 30 percent have been awarded a senior rank (either associate or full professor), and half that number had gained tenure by fall 1987 when the NSOPF was administered. The cohort does not then merely consist of young, fresh-out-of-graduate school doctorates. In addition to an age distribution, the gender mix of this newest group shows that more women are being hired than previously. They comprise 40 percent of the Proteans nationally [29].

9. Diversity extends beyond gender. Fourteen percent of the cohort are members of minority groups. The reader is cautioned though. Forty (42 percent) of the historically black colleges and universities are classified as comprehensives and make up 7 percent of the total universe of comprehensives. While the proportion of HBCUs in the sector is small, the number of minority members at those institutions is quite high. As of the late seventies, about 71 percent of the black faculty employed in public institutions were concentrated in predominantly black colleges [20]. The aggregated racial percentages therefore, are possibly skewed [see 17].

10. The NSOPF-88 [29] sample for comprehensive faculty consists of 1860 full-time faculty—1362 doctoral, 434 master's, and sixty-four bachelors degrees. To stratify the data by cohort, highest degree, and field would produce cells too small to be useful.

References

1. Allison, P. D., and J. A. Stewart, "Productivity Difference among Scientists: Evidence for Accumulative Advantage." *American Sociological Review*, 39 (1974), 596–606.

2. American Council on Education. *Fact Book on Higher Education, 1981–82*, New York: Macmillan, 1981.

3. _____. *Fact Book on Higher Education, 1986–76*. New York: Macmillan, 1987.

4. Barol, B. "The Threat to College Teaching." *Academe*, 70 (1984), 10–17.

5. Baron, J. N. "Organizational Perspectives on Stratification." *Annual Review of Sociology*, 10 (1984), 37–69.

6. Bayer, A. E. "Teaching Faculty in Academe: 1972–73." *American Council on Education Research Reports*, 8 (1973).

7. Becher, T. *Academic Tribes and Territories: Intellectual Enquiry and the Culture of Disciplines*. The Society for Research into Higher Education. Milton Keynes, England: Open University Press, 1989.

8. Birnbaum, R. *Maintaining Diversity in Higher Education*. San Francisco: Jossey-Bass, 1983.

9. _____. "State Colleges: An Unsettled Quality." In *Yearbook of American Universities and Colleges, Academic Year, 1986–87*, edited by G. T. Kurian. New York: Garland, Publishing, 1988.

10. Boice, R. University of New York at Stony Brook. Personal Communication, 1992.

11. Brown, D. G. *The Mobile Professor*. Washington, D.C.: American Council on Education, 1967.

12. Burke, D. L. *The New Academic Marketplace*. Westport, Conn.: Greenwood Press, 1988.

13. Caplow, T., and R. McGee. *The Academic Marketplace*. New York: Basic Books, 1958.

14. Carnegie Foundation for the Advancement of Teaching. *A Classification of American Colleges and Universities*. 3rd ed. Princeton: Carnegie Foundation for the Advancement of Teaching, 1987.

15. Clark, B. R. *The Academic Life: Small Worlds, Different Worlds*. Princeton: Carnegie Foundation for the Advancement of Teaching, 1987.

16. Dunham, E. A. *Colleges of the Forgotten Americans: A Profile of State Colleges and Regional Universities*. The Carnegie Commission on Higher Education. New York: McGraw-Hill, 1969.

17. Finnegan, D. E. "Opportunity Knocked: The Origins of Contemporary Comprehensive Colleges and Universities." Working Paper no. 6 University of Massachusetts at Boston: The New England Resource Center for Higher Education, 1991.

18. _____. "Academic Career Lines: A Case Study of Faculty in Two Comprehensive Universities," Ph.D. diss., University Park, Pa.: The Pennsylvania State University, 1992.

19. Flynn, E. A., J. F. Flynn, N. Grimm, and T. Lockhart, "The Part-Time Problem: Four Voices." *Academe*, 72 (1986), 12–18.

20. Galambros, E. C. *Racial Composition of Faculties in Public Colleges and Universities of the South.* Atlanta, Ga.: Southern Regional Education Board, 1979.

21. Harcleroad, F., and A. W. Ostar. *Colleges and Universities for Change: America's Comprehensive Public State Colleges and Universities.* Washington, D.C.: American Association of State Colleges and Universities Press, 1987.

22. Hargens, L. L., and W. Hagstrom. "Sponsored and Contest Mobility of American Academic Scientists." *Sociology of Education*, 39 (1966), 24–38.

23. Lipset, S. M., and E. C. Ladd. "The Changing Social Origins of American Academics." In *Qualitative and Quantitative Social Research*, edited by R. K. Merton, et al. New York: The Free Press, 1979.

24. McGee, R. *The Academic Janus.* San Francisco: Jossey-Bass, 1971.

25. McGinnis, R., and J. S. Long. "Entry into Academia: Effects of Stratification, Geography and Ecology. In *Academic Labor Markets and Careers*, edited by D. W. Breneman and T. I. K. Youn, pp. 52–73. New York: Falmer Press, 1988.

26. Meyer, J. W., W. R. Scott, and T. E. Deal. "Institutional Technical Sources of Organizational Structures: Explaining the Structure of Educational Organizations." In *Organizational Environments: Ritual and Rationality*, edited by J. W. Meyers and W. R. Scott. Beverly Hills: Sage Publications, 1983.

27. National Center for Education Statistics. *Digest of Education Statistics, 1981.* Washington, D.C.: U.S. Department of Education, 1981.

28. _____. *Digest of Education Statistics, 1987.* Washington, D.C.: U.S. Department of Education, 1987.

29. _____. 1988 National Survey of Postsecondary Faculty (NSOPF-88). Washington, D.C.: United States Department of Education, March 1988.

30. _____. *Digest of Education Statistics, 1990.* Washington, D.C.: U.S. Department of Education, 1991.

31. _____. *Digest of Education Statistics, 1991.* Early Estimates. Washington, D.C.: U.S. Department of Education, 1991.

32. Perloff, R. "Enhancing Psychology by Assessing its Manpower." *American Psychologist.* (May 1972), 355–61.

33. Perrucci, R., K. O'Flaherty, and H. Marshall. "Market Conditions, Productivity, and Promotion among University Faculty." *Research in Higher Education*, 19 (1983), 431–49.

34. Pfeffer, J. "Organizational Demography." In *Research in Organizational Behavior: An Annual Series of Analytical Essays and critical reviews*, vol 5, edited by L. L. Cummings and B. M. Staw, pp. 299–357. Greenwood, Conn.: Jai Press, 1983.

35. Queval, F. A. "The Evolution Toward Research Orientation and Capability in Comprehensive Universities: The California State System." Ph.D. diss., University of California, Los Angeles, 1990.

36. Reskin, B. "Scientific Productivity and the Reward Structure of Science." *American Sociological Review*, 42 (1977), 491–504.

37. _____. "Academic Sponsorship and Scientists' Careers." *Sociology of Education*, 52 (1979), 129–46.

38. Smelser, N. J., and R. Content. *The Changing Academic Market: General Trends and a Berkeley Case Study.* Berkeley: University of California Press, 1980.

39. Sorensen, A. B. "Academic Careers and Academic Labor Markets." Paper presented at the Ringberg Symposium, Max-Planck-Gesellschaft, Schloss Ringberg, Tegernsee, FRG, 1989.

40. Spenner, K. I., L. B. Otto, and V. R. A. Call. *Career Lines and Careers.* Lexington, Mass.: Lexington Books, 1982.

41. Spilerman, S. "Careers, Labor Market Structure, and Socioeconomic Achievement." *American Journal of Sociology,* 83 (1977), 551–93.

42. Tuckman, H. P., and K. L. Pickerill. "Part-Time Faculty and Part-Time Academic Careers." In *Academic Labor Markets and Careers,* edited by D. W. Breneman and T. I. K. Young, pp. 98–113. New York: Falmer Press, 1988.

43. Willie, R., and J. E. Stecklein. "A Three-Decade Comparison of College Faculty Characteristics, Satisfactions, Activities, and Attitudes," *Research in Higher Education,* 16 (1982), 81–93.

44. Wilson, L. *The Academic Man: A Study in the Sociology of a Profession.* New York: Oxford University Press, 1942.

45. Youn, T. I. K. "The Sociology of Academic Careers and Academic Labor Markets." Working Paper no. 3. University of Massachusetts at Boston: The New England Resource Center for Higher Education, 1990.

46. Zey-Farrell, M., and P. J. Baker. "Faculty Work in a Regional Public University: An Empirical Assessment of Goal Consensus and Congruency of Actions and Intentions." *Research in Higher Eudcation,* 20 (1984), 399–426.

This article was presented at the 1992 Annual meeting of the American Educational Research Association. The author thanks Zelda Gamson and Gary Rhoades for their encouragement and David Webster and Steven Katsinas for their helpful comments and criticisms.

Dorothy E. Finnegan is assistant professor of education at The College of William and Mary.

The Appointment Process:
On Achievement and Ascription

LIONEL S. LEWIS

An elementary distinction made by students of society, social stratification, institutions, and organizations is one between achievement and ascription, between a status acquired through effort, ability, knowledge, and skill and one acquired because of other statuses already held. There is a general assumption that placement in the academic world is determined more by achievement than by ascription.

Common sense tells us that in order to attain recognition as a scholar or scientist one has to have done something that others would be able to recognize; that is, one would have to have achieved something. To hear most people in major institutions tell it, the relationship between achievement and a desirable university appointment is pretty close. Indeed, the coupling of advancement and merit is a recurrent theme in many descriptions of the American university. Caplow and McGee reflect this consensus in their contention that "unlike other employers, who may legitimately base the preferment of their employees on seniority or the hazards of office politics, the university is committed to the ideal of advancement by merit. In a community of scholars, scholarly performance is the only legitimate claim to recognition."[1] However, accomplishing something in one's discipline does not necessarily lead to a desirable university appointment. Although the two are related, there is clearly a less than perfect relationship; this flaw has bred some differences of opinion about, and has stimulated limited inquiry into, their degree of correspondence.

If scholarly performance is to be equitably rewarded, it must first be identified. However, it defies precise definition, for there is disagreement regarding the elements it embraces and the meaning of each of these. As a consequence, what some hold to be ascriptive criteria are inevitably introduced in the evaluation of academic careers. In addition, as Parsons suggests, competitive strains and the insecurity which flows from them in a structure marked by the primacy of the universalistic-achievement pattern could weaken individual motivation.[2] An enduring concern with producing some tangible accomplishment could well lessen the drive of many. As a result there must be shelters where any set of individuals can expect to be welcome, where possessing one or another characteristic (youth, age, white skin, black skin, and so on) is enough to guarantee success or avert failure; with enough havens, almost everyone could expect a reduction of pressure at one time or another.

One consequence of this condition that in the end increases the effects of ascriptive criteria and moderates achievement is that in the academic world, as perhaps everywhere else, there is very little of what Ralph Turner has called contest mobility ("a system in which elite status is the prize in an open contest'), whereby "all the players compete on an equal footing." Victory "is taken by the aspirants' own efforts." The situation more closely approximates sponsored mobility ("a controlled selection process"), whereby "elite recruits are chosen by the established elite or their agents, and elite status is *given* on the basis of some criterion of supposed merit." As a consequence, "individuals do not win or seize elite status; mobility is rather a process of sponsored induction into the elite."[3]

One pivotal difference between these two ideal-type processes outlined by Turner is that in a system in which contest mobility is stressed, placement in an elite position is gained only after one proves himself in that province for which he is to be given a superior position—final selection to elite status is delayed as long as practicable in order to minimize premature judgments and to insure "a fair race." Where sponsored mobility holds, assessment is based on "aptitudes" or "inherent capacities" rather than on performance, and selection to an elite status occurs in enough time to enable incumbents to control effectively the training of aspirants.[4]

In this chapter, considerable evidence is presented to substantiate the thesis that ascription and sponsored mobility are at least as potent in affecting the careers of university professors as are achievement and contest mobility. Focusing first on the dissimilarity between the two examples of mobility highlighted just above, that is, whether movement is anticipatory or delayed, the findings and reflections of almost two dozen other researchers in higher education are reviewed. Particular attention is given to the matters of how departments fill vacancies and of what qualities increase or lessen the chances of individuals for obtaining these positions. Because their experiences most patently belie the contention that what you do is more important that who you are, the focus in the last half of the chapter is on academic women.

Open Recruitment: Some Exceptions

Looking initially at the degree of inbreeding among faculty, an examination by. A. B. Hollingshead of all appointments at Indiana University between 1885–1937 revealed that 43 percent were alumni, and 20 percent had family members on the staff. His striking conclusion that "these three factors (alumni, friendship, family) account for at least four-fifths of all appointments, and that only a small minority may be attributed to professional competition"[5] would certainly no longer characterize many, if any, American universities since higher education became a mass commodity and the number of faculty began mushrooming after 1945. Nonetheless, as will become evident, institutions, especially the more prestigious, are still in the habit, more often than most believe, of hiring their own graduates. Although this practice mitigates the uncertainty that waits on those who must recruit new colleagues, by significantly reducing the pool of potential candidates and enhancing the opportunities of some who may not be qualified, its overall effect is to make the academic enterprise somewhat anemic. For example, on the basis of his painstaking analysis of the relationship between academic structure and scholarship, Peter Blau, who himself is employed at the institution where he earned his doctorate, concludes that inbreeding has "adverse effects on faculty quality" in all academic settings.[6] Regardless of what the true amount of inbreeding is in various types of institutions, Hollingshead's figures are still important because they were the first to substantiate the fact that considerations other than purely professional once play more than only a minor role in recruitment.

Looking at the whole of the academic profession at the time Hollingshead was reporting his limited findings, Logan Wilson observed that "between eligible individuals [candidates] of apparently equal ability and training, preferment is always shown for 'connections.'"[7]

In the first careful examination of mobility within the wider academic marketplace, Caplow and McGee delineated "the two kinds of recruitment in general use—'open,' or competitive, hiring and 'closed,' or preferential, hiring."[8] Amplifying on this dichotomy, they added: "In theory, academic recruitment is mostly open. In practice, it is mostly closed."[9]

The recruitment ritual Caplow and McGee anatomized turned out to be insanely elaborate and complex, but after one cuts through the shell of pretense, it is evident that most of it is noncompetitive. First,

> the initial choice of a graduate school sets an indelible mark on the student's career. In many disciplines, men trained in minor universities have virtually no chance of achieving eminence. . . . [T]he handicap of initial identification with a department of low

prestige is hardly ever completely overcome. Every discipline can show examples of brilliant men with the wrong credentials whose work somehow fails to obtain normal recognition.[10]

Second, Caplow and McGee's data indicate that departments with high prestige consider fewer candidates for each vacancy and replacement and are more likely to hire those with whom they have had "prior contact" or with whom they are familiar than are departments with lower prestige.[11] For example, to recruit at Harvard an ad hoc committee is named to select the new incumbent. It proceeds by surveying the entire discipline to determine the best possible candidate—that is, it seeks the best man in the country. As a remarkable coincidence, however, in a four-year study, "the best possible candidate" for 79 percent of the appointments to associate professors and 88 percent to full professors were found to be located already at Harvard.[12]

As would be expected, Caplow and McGee's respondents generally insisted that "prior contact" made no difference in the ultimate selection of candidates, but such protestations were not entirely convincing.

> He had had some [contact] with me. His father and I had both been on the faculty at another university together, so I had known him when he was small. But this had absolutely no influence on the appointment. His father is dead now and wasn't in this discipline anyway.[13]

It is true that an individual's job history is a function of his disciplinary prestige, but Caplow and McGee are conscious that this, itself,

> is a feature of a social system, not a scientific measurement. It is correlated with professional achievement but not identical with it. A man may, for example, publish what would be, in other circumstances, a brilliant contribution to his field, but if he is too old, or too young, or located in the minor league, it will not be recognized as brilliant and will not bring him the professional advancement which he could claim if he were of the proper age and located at the proper university.[14]

In light of this, Caplow and McGee contend that there is little point in trying to determine how good someone really is; what matters is what others think of him, since this, in effect, is how good he is.[15] This evaluation is often a function of a man' specialty. When a label (a Lewinian or Boasian or Freudian) is pinned on someone, it not only denotes his point of view but implies a set of personal relationships and rights and obligations. All of this "serves the function for its adherents of automatically identifying alignments of friends, enemies, and possible allies in any academic situations."[16] Not the least of these, it should be added, would be assistance in finding the best possible position—anywhere between the Bay Bridge and the Back Bay. In outlining their tentative recommendations, Caplow and McGee sum all of this up with this melancholy aside: "Nothing at all is lost by open advertisement, except the opportunity to practice nepotism and the coyness which has become part of the employer's approach to the academic marketplace."[17]

Inferences similar to those of Caplow and McGee are reported in two separate research monographs on the academic labor market by David G. Brown. To some extent, what Brown unearthed indicates that sponsored mobility is even more widely diffused than is indicated by the interviews conducted by Caplow and McGee. One point that Brown underscores is that once someone has a position, it is unlikely that he will be dismissed unless he is grossly unfit (or, as we will see in the next chapter, too much of a bother to have around).

> Only in instances when the incompetence is excessive or where the damage that could be wrought by a slightly less than competent person is great is firing worth the trouble.
> The amount of forced movement among teachers is relatively small and concentrated at the lower ranks in the better schools.[18]

Or as Jessie Bernard puts it: "It has, in fact, been found to be practically impossible to remove academic personnel on the grounds of incompetence because there is always someone—student or colleague—who will swear that so-and-so is a wonderful teacher."[19] This reluctance to fire people means, as Logan Wilson noted many years previously,[20] that almost all hiring in universities is at the lower ranks; openings at the level of associate or full professor are filled by promoting individuals already on the faculty.

Although "the publication habits of movers differ little from their more stable colleagues,"[21] it must be noted that for those who change positions, publishers—"persons who have published more than ten articles"—"have between a 25 percent and 30 percent greater chance of increasing in each of the factors (rank, quality [of school], salary) than nonpublishers"[22]—"persons who have published nothing."

Table 5.1 shows the various sources utilized in Brown's diverse sample of mobile professors in searching for and finding a new position. In brief, it would appear that although formal liaisons for seeking a new appointment are more effective than informal ones, they are used significantly less often; only half as many faculty actually placed themselves through these sources. The blind letter is the only method that compares favorably with the assistance of former professors, graduate department contacts, and simply doing nothing as a means of successfully locating a position. These figures for Brown's over 7,200 respondents also suggest that the numerous opportunities located but not obtained through formal channels are less attractive and therefore do not culminate in a final match between candidate and position.

The use of friends, acquaintances, friends of friends and acquaintances, and acquaintances of friends and acquaintances is clearly the best way to get a job. One's future is greatly influenced by one's past. From this interviews with 103 social scientists who had recently been on the labor market, Brown concluded:

> Friends were the most frequent source of promising leads. By letter, by phone, and in person, friends and acquaintances were the ones who had made nearly 50 per cent of our respondents aware of the jobs they now hold and this figure does not include the respondents' graduate school professors, many of whom are more friends than teachers.[23]

Table 5.1. Methods Used in Seeking Jobs

Source	Percent of candidates using source in search	Percent of Mean number of jobs found per candidate using source	Percent of candidates who found current job through source
Informal			
Graduate professor	40	1.41	12
Graduate department office	32	1.72	6
Undergraduate professor	16	.82	3
Graduate school classmate	17	0.61	3
Faculty colleague	20	1.07	7
Other professional friend	25	1.01	7
Publisher's representative	2	0.86	—
Recruited	23	1.82	26
		Total	65
Formal			
Blind letters	46	2.14	19
College placement office	36	2.75	6
Church-related placement service	5	1.30	1
Professional association	14	1.96	2
Advertisement—candidate available	3	2.56	—
Advertisementposition available	9	1.73	2
Convention placement service	14	2.42	2
Public employment service	3	1.65	—
Commercial teacher's agency	7	3.05	3
		Total	35

SOURCE: David G. Brown, *The Mobile Professors* (Washington, D.C.:American Council on Education, 1967), p. 119.

Here is a sample of what some of the individuals he talked to reported:[24]

> The person who was leaving here wrote to me. We had worked together in 1951–52.

> The former department chairman had taught me when I was an undergraduate at another school.

> The dean's wife was a patient of my father who is a physician. One summer the dean visited my parents at their summer home. The job was mentioned.

> I first learned about the job while attending a meeting sponsored by the AFL-CIO, from the current dean who is a personal friend.

> While teaching botany at _____ I got to know the younger generation in the economics department through Newcomers' Club. At an August picnic I learned that economics needed another professor for September. Since my appointment in botany had not been renewed, I needed a job and got the one in economics.

> While I was teaching undergraduates at Duke on a one-year appointment, a Duke graduate student told me of the opening at _____.

> [I learned about my job] at a Russian Institute through a friend how had taught at _____ in the past and had kept up his contacts.

> A fellow graduate student of mine at Harvard had been given a letter from _____ telling of a vacancy. Since he wasn't interested, he referred the letter to me.

> A mutual friend of the department chairman and me, who was working at the Federal Reserve Bank, brought us together.

> [I found out about the job] through a friend who had a friend there.

Not only are formal channels not very helpful, but it is widely believed that only the ingenuous or desperate depend on them. On the departmental level, reverting to any type of clearinghouse for recruiting "is to admit defeat publicly,"[25] which, in turn, results in a loss of face. "To use the bureaus is to sacrifice prestige."[26]

> All of the previous studies with which this author is familiar tend to confirm that the smaller, less prestigious departments are the ones that turn to formal candidate-locating facilities in time of need.
> Further confirmation is offered by the present study. When the fifty Southeastern department chairmen were asked "How did you go about locating names of persons who might be qualified to fill your vacant position?" eleven of them indicated that they had used some type of formal service such as a university placement office, a commercial teachers' agency, or the want ads in professional journals. . . . [A]lmost all of these chairmen were from small departments located in the less prestigious schools. None of the chairmen from the larger departments (eleven or more full-time staff members) had found it necessary to use formal methods to locate personnel whereas nearly half of the chairmen from the smaller departments (ten or fewer full-time staff members) had felt such a need.[27]

It would appear that entree into any but the most marginal departments is indeed restricted for those who would hope to find a position solely on the basis of their teaching ability or research accomplishments.

> If . . . a candidate's availability has been advertised by formal means, many schools will investigate no farther. Reasoning that formal means of advertising are used only by the relatively poor candidates, the candidate will be cut immediately. Similarly, it is reasoned that the most prominent referrers suggest the most qualified candidates and cuts are made accordingly.[28]

If more support is necessary to uphold the theme that the wider academic labor market is a good deal less than fully open, there is added evidence from Brown's national survey that the most prestigious institutions fill their vacancies with graduates from the most prestigious institutions. Students from elite schools had a 16 percent chance of finding employment at another elite school, while there was only a 2 percent chance of this happening for those whose graduate training was in a school outside the top decile.[29]

Yet, the picture Brown paints is not all dark; he is convinced that individuals can publish themselves out of the academic hinterlands, though he acknowledges that it is easier to start at the top and resist downward mobility.[30] Invoking the Horatio Alger idol (or icon) he affirms: "Apparently there is no barrier to interquality movement except a lack of ability or desire."[31] On the other hand, he does recognize that promotions from within and nepotistic hiring practices create an academic labor market which is a "curious hodgepodge" of informal channels of communication where many positions and candidates "never reach the open market." All of this makes the academic scene not unlike the black market, where contacts, connections, and friendships become crucial factors for getting what one wants.[32]

Studies limited to comparing a narrower range of disciplines or to profiling a single one basically corroborate the findings of Caplow and McGee and of Brown. Howard Marshall, in his investigation of 970 departments of chemistry, economics, and English, found that between one-fourth and one-third followed no other policy but that of promotion from within, and of the 574 departments responding, only 14 indicated that they always looked outside to fill a senior position.[33] He also reported that of a sample of 420 economists, 25 percent (105) secured their last position through a friend, while only 18 found theirs through an advertisement in the *American Economic Review*, a private employment bureau, or a university placement bureau.[34]

A Prestige Degree as an Accessory: More Evidence

In their survey of political scientists, Albert Somit and Joseph Tanenhaus classified the attributes contributing to outside job offers for those with the Ph.D. After amount of publication, those factors contributing to outside job offers are school at which doctorate was taken, ability to get research support, and "having the right connections." Quality of publication was fifth, and teaching ability was tenth or last.[35] But when it came to actually getting an appointment in a ranking graduate department, the possessors of a prestige doctorate had a nearly 10:1 advantage over someone holding a lesser degree.[36] Somit and Tanenhaus charge that "these figures, however elementary, leave little doubt that the leading departments pursue a discriminatory policy, insofar as doctoral origins are concerned, in selecting their staff."[37] Borrowing from Bernard Berelson, whose research is considered shortly, they reason: "In our profession, too, the evidence suggests "where a person gets the doctorate has a determining effect on where he winds up.'"[38]

As far as those attributes which political scientists are convinced are the principal contributors to their career success are concerned, school at which the doctorate was taken and "having the right connections" were listed right behind number of publications. Quality of publication was fifth, luck or chance was seventh, and teaching ability was again tenth or last.[39] Since over half of the doctorates in political science are granted by less well regarded institutions, Somit and Tanenhaus astutely note that the discipline as a whole is in the anomalous position of discriminating against the majority.[40]

In his inquiry into the education of sociologists, Elbridge Sibley reported that holders of doctoral degrees from the eleven most prestigious departments "are, as would be expected, relatively likely to be appointed to the staffs of leading universities; scarcely any of them are found teaching in junior colleges or lower schools Conversely, the universities belonging to the American Association of Universities seldom appoint Ph.D.'s from universities outside that group.[41]

Berelson also found that the most prestigious institutions have a higher rate of inbreeding than the less prestigious: in the top twelve universities (Chicago, Columbia, Cornell, Harvard, Yale, and so on) 47 percent of the faculty earned their highest degrees from the institution where they were teaching. The comparable figures for the ten universities ranked next (Minnesota, Pennsylvania, Stanford, U.C.L.A., and so on), other universities which were members of the association of graduate schools (Brown, Duke, Iowa, Kansas, North Carolina, Texas, and so on), and other universities with established graduate programs (Boston, Buffalo, Connecticut, Maryland, Oregon, Pittsburgh, Rutgers, and so on) were 27 percent, 20 percent, and 15 percent, respectively. Further, 85 percent of the faculty in the top twelve universities received their highest degrees from one of these institutions. Those who teach in prestigious institutions are trained in prestigious institutions.

The Effects of Social Class

Diana Crane's secondary analysis of Berelson's data—for both graduate faculty and recent Ph.D. recipients—suggests that the prestige of the institution from which a person receives his Ph.D. and his social-class origin are as important as publication for placement in leading universities. Her examination of this national sample representing a number of disciplines reveals that social-class background affects the quality of both the undergraduate and graduate degree of academics and consequently the likelihood of finding a position in a major university. Needless to say, those whose family of orientation (the family into which the individual was born and in which he was socialized) was lower class were more likely to have received their degree from lower-ranking institutions. In addition, when the quality of the institution where the graduate degree was obtained was statistically controlled by Crane, she was able to demonstrate that the higher the social class, the better the chances for younger academics—those who have yet to prove themselves—of finding their first position in a major university. Lower-class individuals from high-ranking universities are simply less likely than their middle-class counterparts to obtain positions in prestigious universities. Since not all institutions of higher learning offer the same resources and opportunities for research, and since resources and opportunities help determine research output, social-class origin affects productivity and the eventual course of the academic career.

Young academics with a disadvantaged social-class background apparently do not receive encouragement and help and are not sponsored by men from the departments in which they complete their graduate studies. It may well be that because of different experiences and values, lower-class students are unable to form close relationships with their middle-class instructors and advisers. The attitudes and behavior of lower-class students may appear inappropriate in a middle-class milieu, and this, in turn, would limit the amount of encouragement and help they receive from those who would be expected to sponsor them.

Various researchers, among them Stewart West and Jessie Bernard, have addressed themselves to the issue of how the careers of some individuals are given an extra boost, and there is general agreement that some sort of sponsorship can be decisive:

> The attitudes of professor toward student determine not only his granting or denial of financial help in the form of fellowships or assistantships, but also whether he brings opportunities to the attention of the student or otherwise encourages him.
>
> The association of the graduate student with his mentor may make all the difference between success or the lack of it in his subsequent career. If a top man takes him under his wing, doors will open for him and he will be in the club. If no one takes him on, or if a lesser faculty takes him on, he may never arrive professionally. He will not be recommended for the best job; he will not be in.

The picture sketched by Blau from an array of statistical correlations bearing on the social origins of faculty suggests "that academic institutions with superior reputations exhibit some class bias in faculty recruitment." A larger percentage of person with modest social-class origins from the 115 four-year institutions with liberal arts curriculums in Blau's sample were located at schools where heavy teaching loads and large class enrollments leave one little time for research. Consequently the possibility of moving into a spot where productivity can be maximized becomes even more remote. Blau explains this more fully:

> The scholarly research of individual faculty members depends to a considerable extent on the colleague climate in their institutions. To be sure, by the time a person joins a faculty, his ability to make contributions to knowledge has been largely formed. But

whether his or her scholarly potentials are stimulated and realized or stultified and dissipated hinges in large part on the colleague climate at the institution.

The salaries of those in Blau's study who started only a few steps from the bottom of the class structure were inferior to those not so handicapped, who were located in institutions where compensation is never niggardly—always reaching at least a middle-class standard. This is true in part because they are better prepared academically but also, as Blau puts it, "probably . . . owing to discrimination."

The Cumulative Effects of Ascriptive Qualities

Ascriptive qualities such as the social class into which one is born and where one takes his doctorate are not only as potent as those which are achievable in setting, in Caplow and McGee's words, "an indelible mark" on an academic career, but their additive, cumulative, and lasting effects—in the sense of bearing on the quality as well as on the quantity of one's scholarship—make it nearly impossible ever to escape their influence. This point becomes particularly evident from a review of the work of Lowell Hargens and Warren Hagstrom, Diana Crane, and Jonathan Cole.

Focusing on the 576 natural scientists from the Berelson study, Hargens and Hagstrom assessed the relative influence of both the school from which one took his doctorate and "scholarly merit" on the distribution of rewards in the academic community. Their most basic finding is that the institution where on received his doctorate was related to the prestige of the institution where he was teaching, even when productivity was controlled. This relationship was particularly strong among younger scientists. The prestige of a scientist's doctoral institution was almost as important as his productivity in recruitment into the top graduate institutions but had less effect in preventing placement in less well regarded institutions. Impressive credentials apparently can help one to find a good job, but by themselves they are not protection against downward mobility.

As has been suggested, a large university provides a very different environment for scholarly and scientific research from that of a small college where undergraduate teaching is supposed to be the foremost and almost singular concern of the faculty. Light teaching loads, access to research funds, opportunities for counsel and collaboration, and other supportive elements that are common in a university setting help the individual placed there to increase his productivity. Quite simply, where one is employed is a matter of great importance, which makes one's social class of origin, where one went to graduate school, and the like of great importance.

Logan Wilson has observed that papers submitted from major universities look better to the editors because of the institutional prestige and authority behind them. This assertion was probably as true in 1972 as it was in 1942, when it was made. Although not a great deal of evidence pertaining to this matter has been gathered, Crane has found that the academic characteristics of authors of articles selected for publication by scientific journals are similar to the academic characteristics of the journal's editors. The diversity in the academic affiliation of editors is related to the diversity in the academic affiliation of contributor, and the diversity in the doctoral origins of editors is related to the diversity in the doctoral origins of contributors. On the basis of this, she concluded, as we stated in chapter 3, that "the evaluation of scientific articles [by scholarly journals] is affected to some degree by non-scientific factors."

Moving on to what happens to work after it is published, Cole, who studied the citing practices of physicists, found that persons from the most prestigious departments made reference more to the research of others from the same types of departments than to the work of those from departments of lesser rank. The more eminent the physicist, the greater the probability that in his scientific papers he found the work of physicists at the most prestigious departments useful and ignored the work of physicists removed from centers of research.

When the quality of the work was controlled, the rank of the department where a physicist was located made a substantial difference in citation patterns. Research produced at undistinguished universities "is universally invisible," but when someone from these institutions is cited, it is at about the same rate by persons at both high- and low-ranked departments:

> If an obscure person has done something and then publishes it in an obscure journal, fewer people will look at it than if an outstanding person had done the same thing, because when people pick up a journal they scan the titles and look at the names of the authors . . . the work of certain authors will always be looked at. . . . It is also true that well-established people will have their work accepted quite readily, without too much refereeing.

In addition to having a not insignificant influence on whether someone will become professionally productive and have his papers accepted for publication by leading journals, ascribed attributes also have some influence on whether someone will receive scientific recognition and honors. Where one teaches is closely related, not only to productivity but also to recognition. In fact, Crane reports that "productivity did not make the scientist as visible to his colleagues in this discipline as did a position at a major university." Academic affiliation with a major university is of such importance in obtaining recognition because "contacts with scientists outside his own university [which this provides] have the most effect on a scientist's chances to recognition."

Such support might be necessary even to initiate a research program. The editor of *Science*, the official journal of the American Association for the Advancement of Science, writes:

> The system [of choosing men for review panels from eminent institutions] leads. . . almost inevitably to concentration of research support in a few institutions. A man of proved research productivity in a small school in the Middle West may submit an excellent proposal, but almost invariably his proposal will receive a rating below that of a comparable application originating at Harvard. . . . One group rated grants on the basis of a scale from one to five. The quality of applications originating from Harvard varied considerably, yet few if any were turned down, and most received a rating between one and two. Proposals from less well-known schools received severe scrutiny, were often rejected, and seldom were given a rating better than two.

Needless to say, the successful completion of one's research, particularly in the sciences, depends on adequate funding. All of this suggests an inescapable maze: who one is determines where one is, which determines how one's work is received, which determines where one is. It also suggests countless opportunities for some and dead-end careers for others.

Not unlike the case in chapters 3 and 4, the thrust of this chapter so far has been to suggest that the more closely one approximates what is held to be the model academic, the greater the probability of receiving more than one's fair share of amenities. Thus, those to whom the middle-class aptitude for articulateness and ready conviviality come easily, those with the most estimable pedigree, those whose attitudes and behavior are moderate rather than in the extreme—in other words, those who are no disreputably distinguishable from others—can expect to be more readily accepted in academic circles than are others.

Perhaps the largest category of academics who stand out—whose ascribed status makes them different—are females.

Academic Women

Females are not an insignificant minority in the academic world: though their proportion is only two-thirds of what it was at its peak in the 1930s, they are about one-fifth of those in university and college teaching, being primarily situated in the latter. Although in the late 1960s and early 1907s considerable attention has been given to increasing this proportion, one study conducted by the American Council on Education revealed that between 1968 and 1972 their representation rose from 19.1 percent to only 20.0 percent.

A great deal of evidence indicates that females are not evaluated in terms of merit, that something more than their competence is taken into account when they are candidates for a vacancy in a university. In Caplow and McGee's words:

Women scholars are not taken seriously and cannot look forward to a normal professional career.[71]

Women tend to be discriminated against in the academic profession, not because they have low prestige but because they are outside the prestige system entirely and for this reason are of no use to a department in future recruitment.[72]

This matter of the place of women in the academic world is now to be considered.

Females played essentially no part in the early history of higher learning in America. It was not until Georgia Female College was chartered in 1836, exactly two hundred years after the founding of Harvard, and Oberlin College became coeducational four years after its 1833 founding that it was possible for young women in the United States even to go beyond their somewhat spotty secondary education. After the Civil War, the number of institutions of higher learning admitting women began to grow at a slow but appreciable rate.

Impediments to Becoming "Academic Men"

By World War I, the number of females enrolled in graduate school had begun to grow substantially, though their total enrollment was still half of that for males. For some years after World War II, the ratio of females to males earning master's and doctor's degrees began to decline; by the end of the decade of the 1950s it was two-thirds of what it had been in its peak years, and by the end of the 1960s it was still lower than it had been between 1920 and 1940.[74] By 1967, although only 30 percent of graduate and professional students were female, they received 36 percent of all master's and first professional degrees awarded in 1968.[75] This is no mean achievement if the following comments made by female graduate students about a range of problems they encountered at the University of California at Berkeley are at all typical.[76]

A reported interview from a social science department:

"I suppose you went to another college?"
"I attended U.C., Berkeley."
"But you didn't finish?"
"I was graduated with a B.A."
"Your grades weren't very good?"
"I was named to Phi Beta Kappa in my junior
year and was graduated *Summa cum laude.*"
"You have to have 16 to 18 units of X. You don't have that, do you?"
"As my transcript shows, I had 18 units of
X, mostly A's, one or two B's."
"I'm going to disallow all 18, because they were so long ago. You understand that, don't you? There's no point in your trying to replace the undergraduate courses in order to qualify. You could not do it part-time; you would have to take 18 units in one year. Then you would probably not get into graduate school. If you did you would meet so much hostility that I doubt if you could stay in. Most women do not finish their work, and we couldn't take a chance on you. We don't want women in the department anyway, and certainly not older women. This may be unfair to you in the light of your record, but we just are not going to chance it."

On being discouraged from entering:

My faculty adviser was, and said he was, very much prejudiced against women, and often advised me against graduate work. Besides the discouraging advice ... my parents were told not to *allow* me to follow a science major! They were contacted privately and told they were very foolish to allow me to continue a major in physics or nuclear engineering because a woman would "never" be hired in these fields.

I was told "I'd never accept a woman graduate student unless she was unmarriageable," etc.

On being told scholarship is unfeminine:

I entered UC as a freshman and upon my first interview with an adviser, was advised that it was silly for woman to be serious about a career, that the most satisfying job for a woman is that of wife and mother, etc. . . . The advice was repeated upon several later occasions. . . . Now that I'm in graduate school, I am reminded that I am a risk, that I shall probably get married and forget my training, this coming from faculty and advisers. . . . "

I was asked . . . in a formal interview, with two other professors present, whether I felt that my husband and I were competing intellectually. I'm sure he would not have asked such a personal question of a male student.

A professor in the life sciences informed a student that women don't belong in graduate school because they didn't use their education; another in the same department suggested that women are intellectually inferior to men. "Women have trouble with science" said another. An adviser in the physical sciences steered women away from a course that only men take, and another spent part of the first class period explaining why women shouldn't get Ph.D.'s.

A woman in the biological sciences was told that for the fieldwork for her dissertation she should do something in the LSB courtyard "because women can't go out in the field and do a study." He also suggested that women aren't capable of mental work on a par with men.

On being excluded from informal training:

I received no help from faculty, other than that associated with courses, in securing a career. One faculty member even refused to review two manuscripts in his field when I asked where they should be sent for publication. I know that this was to the contrary regarding several males. Another told me that "women do not contribute," another that "women seeking Ph.D.'s must be personally disturbed."

On being denied support:

In our department at least one professor cut off funds to a married student when she became pregnant, thus forcing her to TA and increasing the time it took her to finish. He said the reason for cutting off funds was that "you should be home caring for your family."

The quotations below, gathered "from various institutions" by Ann Sutherland Harris for her inquiry into the status of women in the academic world, would lead one to believe that the University of California at Berkeley is not at all atypical.[77]

The admissions committee didn't do their job. There is not one good-looking girl in the entering class.

No pretty girls ever come to talk to me.

A pretty girl like you will certainly get married; why don't you stop with an M.A.?

You're so cute. I can't see you as a professor of anything.

Any woman who has got this far has got to be a kook. There are already too many women in this Department.

How old are you anyway? Do you think that a girl like you could handle a job like this? You don't look like the academic type.

Why don't you find a rich husband and give all this up?

Our general admissions policy has been, if the body is warm and male, take it; if it's female, make sure it's an A from Bryn Mawr.

Somehow I can never take women in the field seriously.

Jo Freeman collected other inimical remarks from the University of Chicago.[78]

They've been sending me too many women advisees. I've got to do something about that.

You have no business looking for work with a child that age.

I'm sorry you lost your fellowship. You're getting married aren't you?

I see the number of women entering this year has increased. I hop the quality has increased as well.

All of these statements may not only help explain why a higher percentage of women than men leave graduate school before completing their studies,[79] but they are also testimony that a large number of the mostly male faculty have different expectations—based on status and not ability—about the performance of male and female graduate students. Ann Heiss, who interviewed top administrators and faculty from ten prominent graduate universities, concluded:

> Not excluding academic qualifications, sex is probably the most discriminatory factor applied in the decision whether to admit an applicant to graduate school. It is almost a foregone conclusion that among American institutions women have greater difficulty being admitted to doctoral study and, if admitted, will have greater difficulty being accepted than will men. Department chairmen and faculty members frankly state that their main reason for ruling against women is "the probability that they will marry." Some continue to use this possibility as the rationale for withholding fellowships, awards, placement, and other recognition from women who are allowed to register for graduate work. . . .
>
> In the interviews for this study several department chairmen volunteered the information that women are purposely screened out as Ph.D. prospects and as faculty members. For example, the chairman of a department of biochemistry mentioned that the men on his faculty had a pact in which they agreed "not even to look at applications from women. . . ." In another interview the chairman of a psychology department worried about "what would happen to the department next year" as a result of admitting seven female students in a class of twenty-five. The imponderable effect of the military draft on male students had impelled the department to cover the available slots.[80]

The Durable: A Pool of Talent

Gaining admission to graduate school is actually not the first point where females encounter prejudice in institutions of higher learning. It would seem that they are dissuaded from becoming students even earlier, although as the figures below indicate, to the degree that there is prejudice against women, it is probably greater at the graduate level than at the undergraduate level.[81]

There is also an obvious implication here that from the beginning the hurdles females face on the way to the doctorate are more arduous than those for males, and as a consequence, they may well be better qualified after completing their graduate training. There is, in fact, some evidence that this is the case.[82]

Student category	Percentage of males	Percentage of females
High-school graduates who enter college	65–70	50–55
Entering freshmen with high-school grades of B+ or better	29	44
Bachelor degree recipients who go on to graduate school	44	29
College seniors with a grade average of B or better	35–40	43–48

When Lindsey Harmon compared the high-school records of a sample of men and women who were awarded their Ph.D.'s between 1959 and 1962, he found that the women had had higher intelligence test scores as youngsters and had achieved better academic records in high school.[83] The differences between test scores of males and those of females were largest in physical science, which suggests that women with the motivation and persistence to become scientists would be exceptionally able. It is such facts that have led Bernard to observe that: "As a whole, the women who receive the doctor's degree are, no doubt because of the greater selectivity involved, superior insofar as test-intelligence is concerned to men who receive the doctor's degree."[84]

Discrimination in the Recruitment of Women

A great deal of evidence indicates that females, regardless of their capacity, have a more difficult time than males in finding an academic position: they are less likely than males to be hired by universities and are instead placed in the less desirable four- or two-year colleges, where teaching as opposed to research is emphasized. Even when all of their qualifications, such as degrees, experience, publications, and other accomplishments, are on a par with those of males, in the end they are less likely than males to be offered a position.[85]

According to Brown, in recruiting, the better universities ("the top decile schools") "draw 29.1 percent big publishers, 40.1 percent small publishers, and 30.8 percent non-publishers."[86] On the basis of these figures, given the publication rate of women, 12.7 percent of the faculty at these institutions would be expected to be female. Actually, however, Brown found that only 8.8 percent were female.[87] Not only do these select universities discriminate against women, but so also did the top 60 percent of the institutions in Brown's study; they hire "too few of them [women], even after accounting for their differential research productivity."[88]

At the University of California at Berkeley, where between 1966 and 1969 women made up 42.1 percent of undergraduates, 26.2 percent of the graduate students, and 12.4 percent of those who received doctoral degrees, they accounted for only 3.8 percent of the faculty.[89] This is a marked decrease from 6.0 percent in 1948–49, 9.3 percent in 1938–39, and 8.3 percent in 1928–29.[90]

Arie Lewin and Linda Duchan did a survey of the potential for discrimination that could affect hiring decisions of all 179 graduate departments of a physical science discipline.[91] They developed four versions of a standardized resume in which the applicant was married with two children and had been an assistant professor for four years. The vitae were varied according to sex and professional accomplishments. The chairmen were asked to evaluate and to provide their overall impressions of and inclination to hire each applicant.

The results from the 111 departments which cooperated "showed a definite tendency for the chairmen to prefer the average male over the average female, but to recognize a superior woman."[92] Males were rated higher on educational background and were more often considered prospective candidates than females with identical resumes.[93] "The bias seems to hold especially for higher-quality schools, in departments with younger and newer chairmen, and for chairmen from schools located in the eastern and western parts of the country."[94]

On the basis of these results and of an analysis of the unsolicited comments that led to the hypothesis that different criteria "based on personal values and attitudes reflecting widely held socially accepted beliefs regarding the role of a woman in the family and the perceived difficulties regarding her compatibility with male colleagues" are utilized in evaluating women competing for academic posts, Lewin and Duchan concluded that "when two equally qualified applicants are being considered for an academic position, a male would be chosen over a female."[96]

Career Advancement: Blocked Passage

When a female is employed in a university, it is generally in the lower ranks. She is seldom part of the tenured, senior faculty. In the academic year 1959-60, women totaled 9.9 percent of the professors, 17.5 percent of the associate professors, 21.7 percent of the assistant professors, and 29.3 percent of the instructors in four-year colleges and universities. And the efforts to fill out the vertex of this pyramid that began in the last years of the decade had not taken hold by the 1971–72 academic year, when the figures were 8.6, 14.6, 20.7, and 39.4 respectively.[97] In 1972, of the 4,470 tenured professors in seven Ivy League institutions plus the Massachusetts Institute of Technology only 151 were women.[98] The ratio of women to men is even more unfavorable at the level of full professor. For example, for the 1969-70 academic year no full professor at Harvard was a woman (except the holder of one chair endowed for a female).[99] It was reported in *Science* in 1972 that in major universities one in fifty full professors was a woman.[100] Over a period of close to seventy years, no woman junior appointee in six social science departments at the University of Chicago was advanced to the rank of full professor.[102] In the spring of 1969, 11 out of 475 full professors at the University of Chicago were women (and only 16 out of 217 associate professors were women).[102]

All of this is consistent with Helen Astin and Alan Bayer's conclusion, arrived at through complex and thorough statistical procedures that controlled "for a large number of variables that account for rank differences among academic personnel," that much of the differential between men and women with respect to academic rank

> could still be attributed solely to sex. Indeed . . . sex is a better predictor of rank than such factors as number of years since completion of education, number of years employed at present institution, or number of books published.[103]
>
> When a woman attains the doctorate from a prestigious institution and demonstrates great scholarly productivity, she still cannot expect promotion to a high rank as quickly as her male counterpart.[104]

When they are employed alongside males, female academics are discriminated against in assignments to key university committees, in appointments to administrative positions, in the speed at which they are promoted, and in the rate of remuneration. Considering the question of their compensation in some detail, every study in which the salaries of males and females are compared has substantiated that females with the same rank and experience in the same or a comparable institution are paid less than males.

Unequal Pay for Equal Work

In the late 1960s, Bayer and Astin showed that female scientists earned less than male scientists, independent of field of specialization, employment setting, and academic rank.[106] At that time their median salary as a percentage of men's had decreased over the pervious thirteen years by almost six percent, from 63.9 percent to 58.2 percent.[107] In 1971, Michael La Sorte summarized the overall situation:

> the salary studies of the past two decades have shown discernible aggregate median and mean salary differentials between women and men academics. That this difference has persisted over a number of years is no longer debatable. What remains an issue, however, is whether the differential is a result of blatant sex discrimination against women academics or can be explained, in part or wholly, in terms of other factors.

To shed light on this questions, La Sorte undertook a comprehensive comparison of salary differentials of academic men and women from 1959 to 1968. He, of course, verified that very few females, regardless of professional status, make as much as their male counterparts.[109] Table 5.2 gives the figures by year and rank. Amplifying on these general disparities, La Sorte adduced two fine points. First, "men are rewarded above women regardless of whether they do research in addition to teaching or teaching only."[110] Second,

> women teachers upon entering academia initially encounter a small salary inequity which then increases in size with the acquisition of high rank, tenure, and professional experience. Accordingly, the most academically qualified women, those of greatest value to the institution, over time fall progressively behind in salary.[111]

All of this admits to "no other interpretation than that women are being treated unfairly."[112] Or as another highly statistical analysis concluded:

Table 5.2. Median Salary Differentials (in dollars)

	Year				
Rank	**1967–68**	**1965–66**	**1963–64**	**1962–63**	**1959–60**
Professor	1,400	1,125	1,450	1,900	1,275
Associate professor	500	750	775	1,050	700
Assistant professor	500	575	550	350	450
Instructor	500	400	400	525	300
Aggregate	1,200	1,550	1,400	1,275	1,050

SOURCE: Michael A. La Sorte, "Academic Women's Salaries: Equal Pay for Equal Work?" *Journal of Higher Education* 42 (April 1971): 269.

> To award women the same salary as men of similar rank, background, achievements, and work settings would require a compensatory *average raise* of more than $1,000 (1968–1969 standards). This is the amount of salary discrimination which is *not* attributable to discrimination in rank. The amount of actual salary discrimination, attributable to discrimination in the types of institutions that employ women, the opportunities they are given for administration or research, and advancement patterns, would substantially increases this figure of $1,000.[113]

An analysis conducted for the Carnegie Commission on Higher Education which controlled for a number of variables (such as highest degree, number of years employed, professional activities, prestige of institutions with which one had been associated, number of publications)[114] shows that "residual salary differences were largest" in the most prestigious institutions (See Table 5.3). It appears that the Women's Movement in the late 1960s to eliminate sex discrimination in institutions of higher learning had little impact in reducing the extent of his disparity. According to the Office of Education of the Department of Health, Education, and Welfare, females employed full-time in universities in 1972–73 earned on the average $3,500 less than their male counterparts, averaging $12,325, as compared with $15,829 a year. At the smaller two-year colleges the differential was smaller: $11,862, as compared with $12,889.[115]

Setting Aside Some Common Fictions and Half-Truths

The usual explanation for the relatively small proportion of females employed by universities is one or any combination of the following: females are less ambitious; females are less productive;

Table 5.3. Differences between Actual Salaries of Male and Female Faculty Members and Predicted Average Salaries, 1969

	Number of men (25% random sample)	Average differences for men (in dollars)	Number of women	Average differences for women (in dollars)
Research universities I	3,760	+ 2,729	2,649	−2,009
Research universities II and other doctoral-granting universities I and II	3,151	+ 2,303	2,551	−1,105
Comprehensive universities and colleges	985	+ 1,066	1,066	−385

SOURCE: Carnegie Commission on Higher Education, *Opportunities for Women in Higher Education* (New York: McGraw-Hill, 1973), p. 116. Used with permission of McGraw-Hill Book Company.

females earn their advanced degrees later in life than males and can expect a more modest career; females are trained at less prestigious institutions than males; females are more casual about their careers, which is evident by the way they frequently interrupt them to have and raise families or move with their husbands. Yet, regardless of which way they are permuted, there is as much evidence to refute many of these propositions as there is to support them.

For example, Helen Astin's study of two thousand female doctorates almost ten years after completing their graduate training showed that 91 percent were employed; of these 81 percent were working full-time, and 79 percent had worked continuously since beginning their careers. Those who took time out to raise children did so for a relatively short period—about fourteen months.[116] A second survey of almost the same number of females (1,764) three to nine years after receiving their doctorates found that 96 percent of the unmarried women were working full-time; 59 percent of the married women with children were working full-time, and almost 25 percent were working part-time. These figures are no as impressive as the 99 percent of the almost five hundred men also surveyed who were employed full-time,[117] but they should temper the exaggeration that "graduate training is wasted on women, most of them never find jobs, anyhow." Statistics gathered by the American Council of Education indicate that a higher percentage of men than women interrupt their careers.[118] To be sure, these data would not substantiate the contention that females are less professionally committed than males. We can better predict the turnover rate of a job by knowing its status than by knowing the gender of its holder: a part-time instructor will move from one position to another more frequently than will a full professor, regardless of sex.

On the matter of productivity the picture is somewhat mixed. Bernard believes that academic women

> tend to be less productive, as measured by published work, than academic men. When the major variables associated with productivity are held constant, however, the differential is reduced and academic position (college, university, or, in the case of scientists, laboratory) turns out to be a better predictor of productivity than sex.[119]

One national study of academics did show that 63 percent of the females in the sample had no publication, as compared with only 39 percent of the males, and that 11 percent of the males and only 2 percent of the females had twenty-one or more articles.[120]

In their examination of the research productivity of about fourteen hundred female Ph.D.'s employed full-time, Simon, Clark, and Galway found that "married women publish as much or more than men, and unmarried women publish slightly less than men. The differences on the whole are not great."[121] This, in spite of the fact that the research of women is not supported to the same extent as that of men:

> Men are more likely to receive research grants than women (married and unmarried) in the social sciences and the humanities. In education there is no difference among any of the categories and in the natural sciences the proportions are about the same for unmarried women and men. Married women are less likely to receive grants.[122]

That the productivity of females, particularly those who are unmarried, is not what it might be could be a function, as is suggested by some of the remarks collected from the University of California at Berkeley and elsewhere, of the milieu in which female academics must work and their placement outside of normal networks of communication. As was pointed out in one report at which the publication rate of females was found to be somewhat less than expected:

> The relatively low productivity of Radcliffe Ph.D.'s can hardly be ascribed to their training as such. It is more likely to result from the environment in which they find themselves, the tradition of scholarship, the amount of time and facilities available for research and writing, the attitude of their colleagues and the college administration, and the material inducements to publish. . . . In many smaller colleges atmosphere and opportunity are much less conducive to research and publication. Relatively few Radcliffe women hold professorial status in large institutions where scholarly pursuits are inspired by faculty and demanded by competition.[123]

Obviously, it is the institution where on teaches and not one's sex that is most directly related to productivity. Since females primarily teach in colleges, their overall productivity would not be expected to be high. That it is as high as it is, is remarkable. As Bernard has noted, females in universities are more productive than males in colleges.[124]

It is almost a truism to state that those who do not have a number of students, colleagues, or mentors to call new ideas to their attention, those who are not consulted by others for advice and information, those who are not in correspondence with those on the frontiers of research, those who do not have friends in high and important places who might help them advance their careers, are not in the best position to know what is going on in their field. And as far as such factors are concerned, women are in a more disadvantaged position than men. Bernard reports that women are less likely to be invited to participate in situations—visiting appointments, editorial boards, professional panels, committees, and research teams—leading to opportunities for informal communication than were men.[125] To be sure, most academics can recall one or more examples of a scholar or scientist who thrived in his isolation. But for most, productivity is a function of one's position in the communication system in a discipline.[126] In any case, it would appear that if enough variables were controlled, differential productivity between males and females would be reduced to insignificance.

The Benign and Tractable Invisible Hand

Brown's explanation of why females are underrepresented on the faculties of universities and why they generally make out so poorly in all types of institutions of higher learning reflects much of the conventional wisdom that has only hindered the cause of academic women. In discussing his finding that "women's colleges, on the average, pay men $1,200 more than women . . . paying men 16.8 percent more than women," Brown contends:

> Evidently, women prefer to work in women's colleges, even at some sacrifice in salary.
> . . . Only part of the discrimination is employer-initiated. Just as the woman's preference for women's colleges means that she will receive less remuneration, so also does her preference for emphasis upon teaching. Much of the apparent discrimination against women appears to be self-imposed.[127]

Brown is in effect arguing that females are discriminated against partly out of choice. They wish to be concentrated in women's colleges and other low-prestige institutions where they have heavier teaching loads but are paid less than men.[128] This is also the consequence of what he calls "differentiation"—

> treating two persons who are equal "in the eyes of God" as unequals—because they are not equally productive. It is allowing the best player, regardless of religion or race, to represent the U.S. in Davis Cup competition. . . . It is paying more to the better qualified and more productive professor. It is justifiably inequality.[129]

Thus, it is understandable why

> women *are* treated unequally. They are paid lower salaries (at least to start) and given lower academic rank but are assigned heavier teaching loads. They fill disproportionately high percentages of the positions at the least prestigious schools and are underrepresented in the most prestigious ones. As a rule they have fewer alternative job options from which to choose.[130]

It is simply a case of people getting what they deserve. His data, after all, do show that the percentage of women in academic positions who have earned their Ph.D.'s is only half of the percentage for men. Moreover, they appear to have considerably less interest in research, and the proportion of those with extensive bibliographies is one-third of that of men. Women also have less experience and are less often educated at the most prestigious schools.[131] Thus:

> To some degree the lower salaries paid to women professors, the lesser academic appointments in terms of both academic rank and institutional prestige, and the higher

teaching loads reflect the fact that, on the average, women are not as qualified and as committed to an academic career as are men.[133]

As Brown sees it, because

> 88 percent of the women spend more time teaching than researching, women want to teach. Women are not subject to the same prestige motivations as men. . . . Women actually prefer to accept jobs in institutions that emphasize teaching and do not expect research.[134]

Not only are women paid less because their employers know that they are less professionally committed to their work, but "even when women are equally qualified the nature of the products they produce are not as prestige-giving to their employer."

> Women, with their emphasis upon teaching, are of more economic value to the poorer schools. The types of products that they would be asked to produce at the top-rated schools are not ones they desire, whereas the lower echelon schools which emphasize teaching are willing to pay more for their services.
>
> All of these arguments simply show that women should earn less because they are less productive. They do not indicate how much less.[135]

This reasoning might not be as pernicious as alleging that the poor are poor because they are lazy and shiftless; but it is as fatuous as holding that they are poor because they want to be poor—that after weighing alternatives such as the heavy tax burdens of the rich, this is the choice that each has made.

Finally, citing a study which showed that female teachers had more success with less able students than with brighter ones and that male teachers did better with superior students, Brown concludes that "since the poorer students tend to be located at the poorer schools, it may be desirable that women are there also."[136] The world is indeed very rationally ordered.

These interpretations of Brown have for the most part remained unchallenged,[137] and it would seem that too few academics are as perceptive as Nobel laureate James D. Watson, who in the final paragraph of his "personal account of the discovery of the structure of DNA" has this to say about the most difficult individual with whom he had to deal during his tenure at Cambridge University:

> We both came to appreciate greatly her personal honesty and generosity, realizing years too late the struggles that the intelligent woman faces to be accepted by a scientific world which often regards women as mere diversions from serious thinking.[138]

However, the attribution of the unequal distribution of women between universities and colleges to preference is not a strictly masculine thesis. It is one of the four factors on which Jessie Bernard focuses in her consideration of the matter. Bernard believes that because universities "demand the man-of-knowledge" and women are not likely to fill this role (after all, how can a woman be a man?), they gravitate to college teaching.[139] "They may actually have preferred college positions, as some people apparently do . . . many may even have a vocation for college teaching";[140] "they prefer teaching to research."[141] It would appear that such decisions are well-taken: "There is some evidence that both men and women who teach in the less productive institutions do, in fact, like their positions."[142]

It is difficult to determine whether it is bad will or bad science that compels someone to hold women themselves accountable for what are, compared with those of men, generally modest academic attainments. To be sure, blaming the victim is not an unusual phenomenon, nor is it uncommon for those who must endure suffering to agree with those who inflict it about its indispensability and utility. It is as pointless to impute motivation to those whose questionable conjectures are more harmful than beneficial to academic women as it was for them to conjecture. The cause of understanding why female academics do not reach the same eminence that male academics do is perhaps best served, not by invention, but by a more positivistic thrust. Thus, we will turn our attention once again to letters of recommendation to consider the type of endorsements female academics seeking their first appointment receive from the graduate faculty who have trained them. The sources of this material are a document published in the official newsletter of the Modern Language Association and the completed dossiers containing sixty-one letters for nine females completing their graduate studies at five universities (three of which are Ivy League).

Mistresses, Wives, Mothers

The Modern Language Association's Commission on the Status of Women examined an unspecified number of recommendations looking for depreciative remarks touching on the (1) physical attributes and personality, (2) marital status, and (3) activities in women's studies and the contemporary feminist movement of young female literary scholars. Here is the body of their report:[143]

One young woman, for example, after completing numerous interviews and being offered no jobs was finally told by a frank department chairman that phrases in her dossier like feminine timidity and sweet, retiring nature suggested that she would be unable to survive in the competitive world of the university. Another young woman finally learned that being labeled intellectually assertive, aggressive—qualities appropriate to a male job applicant had kept her from being granted interviews; male dominated hiring committees are prejudiced against hard-headed women. And still another discovered that a benevolent, protective adviser had simply indicated that this mother's place was in the home, or perhaps a high school, a conclusion that prospective employers readily accepted. . . .

Physical appearance. Personality. Male dossiers do sometimes include phrases such as dresses well, poised, charming, but such language does not represent a tacit comment that what the male professor lacks in brains, he makes up in beauty. Our experience of women's dossiers confirms that a letter writer, often unselfconsciously, diminishes a female candidate's intellectual power by stereotyping her as too feminine, too pretty. These comments, a composite from a typical candidate's dossier, make a damning package: sweet, but not saccharine, quiet, unagressive, shy, but very pretty, a decoration to the classroom. Another letter of recommendation from a prestige graduate school confirms the formula that males see social grace as a substitute for intellectual brilliance: "While _____ probably doesn't have the stamina for independent scholarly work she loves big parties and mixes well."

Women candidates, to win entire approval, have to be both chic and brilliant, and so the woman who is plain-looking, a spinster-scholar type, evokes a negative response for she is not a complete woman; she lacks sociability, and will not flatter the egos of male department members. Dossier after dossier divulges irrelevant, negative commentary: "_____ is a large broad-boned somewhat awkward young woman who must be close to six feet in height"; her mousiness belies a sharp mind; "_____ is . . . tall and proportioned like an Olympic swimmer"; she is a steady woman who will never marry. And within a single paragraph from a male at an elite graduate school, she has a "comfortably upholstered" person and personality, she performed "athletically" in a particular course, she would be the "wheel-horse" of any committee on which she served. And of an older woman, "if she has any faults, they are those that usually accompany the ambitious woman of her age." In other words, the rare comment on a male's appearance is simply a footnote, the frequent comment on a female's, a thesis statement.

Dossiers betray a range of responses to the character of women candidates from the outright misogyny exemplified above to subtle doubt of intellectual equality. The subtle doubts would appear to any good critic of texts. For example, figurative language praising men shows that the writer conceptualizes the candidate's course as active, linear, progressing through time—from lowly instructor to full professor, from fledgling writer to serious scholar, from small reputation to appropriate renown. The young male candidate has "talent," "drive," is "at the start of a long career," "will be on the move," will continue "to surpass himself," to advance; he is "a live wire," "dedicated, industrious, dynamic"; in the classroom his posture is "commanding"; his prose style is "energetic, vigorous." The young woman candidate is praised for being "cooperative, sensitive"; she has "warmth," "good manners," humor, and particularly "rapport with students." She may even be endowed with a "lively intellectual curiosity," and her writing style, if mentioned, is "lucid," "witty," "elegant," or "graceful"—"truly readable," one writer said. (Does that mean "light?") If *her* future career is under consideration, it is most often to be a "good" one. Letter writers rarely create the expectation of remarkable success so common in recommendations of men. While one would not judge the vocabulary used to praise men as connoting higher moral or ethical value than that praising women, given the values of the university world, the concern for professionalism, the emphasis on publication, the shape of a scholarly career, the qualities ascribed to the woman candidate have a seriously limiting psychological impact. Universities as well as many colleges desire candidates with the traditional commitment to career and profession. Until these values change, the stereotype of the woman candidate that emerges here has the effect of damning her with faint and delicate praise. Though the letter writer himself may clearly admire the personal, private virtues, the gentleness and the modesty he considers appropriately womanly, he himself would never designate these qualities as befitting the public, dignified role of college professor. Men writing recommendations see women as objects of regard, pleasing or otherwise, I mean objects to be regarded, looked at, as mistresses, as wives, as mothers; women are already tracked in their minds, and they simply track them for employers, reinforcing the vision of woman as helpmeet or playmate, not as intellectual equal and full human being.

Marital Status. Dossiers on women show two distinct patterns—overt discrimination against older women—married divorced, or single—especially those just entering the job market; second, an almost humorous, but revealing tendency of male letter writers to praise, contrast, describe the work of a female candidate's husband rather than her own, while in men's dossiers wives are rarely mentioned, except as social adornments. . . .

Thesis directors and graduate advisers often speak sensitively of their older female students—"Mrs. _____ though a woman and older should be as well received as a younger man," "Mrs. _____ has an adolescent son, knows how to treat teenagers"—virulent prejudice is revealed in the notes hiring and review committees append to dossiers under their scrutiny. Said one reviewer's note on an older woman "Woman named _____. . . . Should direct mixed choral groups in Pinole." Let her run her household, not our department, said another. By contrast, the dossier of a forty-year-old man asserted that one should hire this man; his distinguished career record (army, public relations) "has been a better preparation for the university than uninterrupted schooling could have been. . . ."

The invisibility of the female job candidate emerges nowhere more unselfconsciously than in the dossiers of young, married graduate students. The dossiers of undeniably brilliant, serious, promising women, filled with letters of eminent advisers, very frequently compare the woman with her husband, stereotype her has the teacher not the scholar-thinker, and so the less valuable member of the couple. Indeed, one often wonders for whom the letter was written. One woman's letter contains this sentence: "Mrs. _____'s husband . . . is an excellent scholar, rather more disciplined and professional in his scholarship. Mrs. _____ compliments him with her more imaginative and enthusiastic. . . literary rather than historical perspective. . . . As in the case of her husband, I can recommend _____ without reservation. . . ." Or another begins: "_____ and her very able husband _____" and continues, "like her husband, she. . . . " Such letters affect the reader by reinforcing his notion that a woman is an appendage, her career second to her husband's; her talents shine in the light of his. . . .

Antifeminism. Some dossiers provide a commentary on the extent to which the women's liberation movement and its academic component, women's studies, present a threat to the university. One recommender praises his candidate by saying: "If you want a woman who can compete with men on absolutely equal terms—but does not take kindly to letters from the Women's Liberation Front addressed 'Dear Woman'—then I recommend _____." Another, enjoying his wit, says she is "feminine indeed, but no feminist. . . . " Another, apologizing for his candidate's decision to write a thesis on nineteenth-century women novelists, claims she is "no fem lib type," but " a real gentlewomen"; that is, her feminism is safely confined to the scholarly. But even with these disclaimers, two prospective employers who read dossiers of women writing dissertations on women were disposed to ask, "Do we need all this feminism that she so militantly carries with her?" and to jeer, "Let's interview her and Ms. _____ [already in the department] can protect the working males." The message, confirmed by this year's reports from the job market, is "we must hire women, but no feminist *activists* need apply."

Very, Very Bright . . . But Quite Feminine

A reading of the supplementary and heretofore unanalyzed sixty-one letters of recommendation also written for and by scholars of English language and literature bears out the theme that sexism is pervasive among faculty but that much of it is surely unconscious. Otherwise, why would so many of these letters ostensibly written in support of candidates be studded with remarks that many of the same would find empty and perhaps insulting ("In person [she] is very attractive, managing to appear both mod and chic")? For a female nearly fifty years old: "I should add that she is a very good-looking and very charming woman." This for an honors graduate, Woodrow Wilson Fellow, and Fulbright Scholar who passed her oral examination with distinctions:

> [She] is the kind of person for whom one writes letters of recommendation with pleasure, satisfaction and extreme confidence. She is outstanding in almost every way. She is charming, pretty, considerate, modest, thoughtful, versatile, and intellectually acute.

> [A]nd in the less formal atmosphere of the coffee lounge she mixes easily and gracefully, making friends without effort and earning the respect of all.

These are not meant to be unfriendly observations. In fact, it might be that the zealously sexist male would probably not be inclined to sponsor a female and/or be less apt to make his true sentiments part of the not strictly confidential record.

What seemed to the Commission on the Status of Women to be more or less irrational animosity on the part of those who would be expected to be the benefactors of individuals beginning their careers makes a great deal of sense if it is considered in the larger context of the thesis advanced at the beginning of this chapter—and throughout the book: there are relatively clear standards among academics regarding what is acceptable or socially normal behavior, and those who in one way or another are not prototypal are less welcome as colleagues than are those who conform. Females who by virtue of their sex-related physical and behavioral characteristics are initially stigmatized as different are, regardless of competence, attractiveness, or commitment to the Women's Movement, not expected to trade aggressively on their strength. This would serve only to make them anomalous, but not in a way that would bring credit to them or a department.

> She is a thoroughly professional grown-up young lady who knows what she can do and what she wants to do. She is self-confident and assured without the slightest touch of arrogance. . . .

> [W]ithout being aggressive she is inquiring and searching in the sort of questions she asks.

> Very, very bright . . . but quite feminine. . . .

> The most immediately striking thing about _____ is her physical beauty; she looks more like a Swedish starlet than a graduate student or what she is soon to be, a professor. It therefore took me some time to realize that behind [her] fair face is a keen, tough mind genuinely committed to the serious study of literature.

> She is active without being an activist; she is concerned over the profession without being a blithering blatherskate boiling over with bile and boreal blight. . . . As one talks with her, however, her mind and personality are the things that loom large in one's consciousness not her physical generosity of construction. . . .

> No petulant or peevish peregrinator, she.

(It is worth mentioning that this alliteration is from a professor and the dean of the college at one of the leading universities on the West Coast.)

By contrast, females are not supposed to be so passive that they would not be professorial.

> [She] is a very attractive young lady, charming in a rather quiet and reserved way, and yet outgoing.

> With the possible exception of her very soft speaking voice, I believe she has all the qualifications of being a good teacher.

> As a teacher she will, I dare say, give an early impression of meekness, but her authority shows through very soon after first acquaintance.

The ideal female is somewhere between the hag and the narcissist, between a Gorgon and the Graces—always engaging, never mousy. The message here is not really outrageous: in academia, the focus of the conquest is nature and the unknown, not other people. What is remarkable and reprehensible is that this message is almost always conveyed when the individual under consideration is a female, less often when it is a male.

Conforming to the Ideal

However, for the most part, the prejudice is against, not females per se, but the fact that they are unusual as academics; and, unless they greatly increase their representation on university faculties, by definition they will remain so. At present, they simply do not conform to very many people's conception of the typical university professor.

We have seen that any individual or category of individuals who deviates from the norm receives special attention, sometimes with a show of tolerance, sometimes with rigidity. As the final examples below from a matching set of twenty dossiers for young male literary scholars make clear, academics are expected to conform to an idealized image that the professoriate apparently hold of themselves or hope or believe is widespread throughout society—of someone who acts and looks as if he has what it takes to be on the side of truth, someone committed to tested and true ideas, not ideology.

> In person and character [he] is tall, broad shouldered and somewhat rugged, though slender. He gives the impression of dignity and confidence. His voice is quiet but clear. He seemed to me steady and dependable in every way.

> I was quickly attracted by his personality—a gentle and very perceptive spirit within a big bulk of a man, relaxed and alert like a handsome shepherd dog.

> Personally he is an attractive man, tall athletic-looking and in fact (so I hear) a good basketball player.

> [He is] a very short man . . . immature [and] precocious. . . . He is an energetic and ambitious personality, who expects to do well, and is ready to work at it.

> If he has any handicap as a teacher, it is his small stature. He is slight in build and only five feet in height. Remembering the late John Livingston Lowes, who was I think even shorter . . . but, who was an enormously effective teacher, I think [he] can overcome this handicap. He has not Lowes' great force, but his own quick mind, confidence [etc.]. . . .

> He has a rather high, unique voice range, which can be distracting until one gets used to it.

> Personally, despite his beard, he is a thorough gentleman, without any signs of eccentricity or the rebellious spirit presently fashionable in certain academic quarters.

> He is a very conventional man—and I *don't* mean stodgy. It's just that he really is profoundly interested in the rather old fashioned academic issues of renaissance scholarship and criticism, cuts his hair and wears neckies [sic], and worked systematically through his graduate requirements and exams on schedule and with very high marks.

Perhaps at this time when qualified Ph.D.'s are somewhat plentiful and calm campuses are not, personal qualities become more important than they have been in the past. His performance . . . is very much a part of his personal strength, and my description so far must convey some impression of his surprisingly well-balanced attitudes. . . . I believe that he is a whole and healthy person. . . .

During the T.A. [teaching assistant] strike he met and attended all his classes with the sense of loyalty and commitment which I expect of those who have a true sense of the meaning and importance of the intellectual life. As a mature member of a class containing younger students, he gave them an exemplary view of what it is like to be civilized though under thirty. I should emphasize, however, that he is not a reactionary; just decent middle-of-the-road. He has obviously been brought up to value and to use good manners and general civility.

He is a serious and competent young man, and I am confident he will never be seen leading any student demonstrations.

At present he leans towards a liberalism that sometime seems extreme, but he is a thoroughly responsible person. . . .

These letters were written at the culmination of a half-dozen years of frenzied political activity on campuses across the nation. At that time, and perhaps at all times, there was something more plausible, professorial, and professional about a Gargantuan and almost noble specimen (presumptive evidence of a large brain?) than about a dwarf, barely able to reach the blackboard, spewing forth quasi-Marxian rhetoric in a falsetto voice. If nothing else, the former could work to reverse the influence of the countless freaks trading in mischief on soap boxes, swarming the halls of the student union so that it looks like a scene from a Fellini movie, pilfering the dean's office, operating the vegetarian co-op in collegetown, or teaching in the free university (without even a Master's degree!).

Beyond Calumny: Get Thee to a College

By now it is fairly evident that those within the academic mainstream are ambivalent about the individual with one or more qualities that cast him outside of it. The question seems to be one of determining how serious the latter are. Even when there are assurances that the puritan ethic has been well internalized, some uneasiness is evident. Still, since the letter writer has an investment of emotion and time in and responsibility for the candidate, he must help him or her to secure an appointment. One way out of this paradox is to assist the applicant in finding a second-rate position. Apparently, the solution suggests itself to many writers. In slightly over half of the letters written for females, the candidate is commended to a teaching position, that is, to a college as opposed to a university.

[For a female with all A's in her 22 regular graduate courses (almost 90 hours) who had graduated Phi Beta Kappa from Radcliffe College] Altogether I recommend her quite strongly as a teacher.

[For a *magna cum laude*, Woodrow Wilson Fellow] Her work here has fulfilled and excelled every promise they made. . . . She will make an admirable and exciting teacher.[For an honors graduate who was awarded a Danforth Fellowship] It is, especially, her qualities as teacher I am most sure of: she is lively, adventurous intellectually, warm. . . . [She] will certainly prove competent in the field and well-informed on the level of undergraduate teaching.

She should be an especially attractive candidate to any department emphasizing vital and effective teaching. . . . I expect the dissertation to be . . . the basis of a solid book.

She was clearly to be ranked with the best two or three students in the seminar. . . .

I have not had an opportunity to observe her in the classroom. Some of my colleagues . . . will be able to speak to that topic. My guess is that . . . she would make a good teacher for lower-division students. . . .

Some comparative observations for males:

> He has the temperament and qualifications for becoming a first-rate scholar-teacher.

> I think that he will be an effective teacher, especially at the advanced undergraduate and graduate level, where his sophisticated knowledge and penchant for discussion will be most useful.

The implication of all of this is that, indeed, "women scholars are not taken seriously" and therefore are not matched with positions in the top universities. It is not so much a case of actual discrimination, although some persons contend that this occurs with some regularity:

> In one interview I had, about 8 women and one man were interviewed for the job. The man got it. And I know positively that nearly all the women, including myself, were better qualified for the job, better teachers, more conscientious, more interested in teaching, etc.[144]

Instead, what appears to be happening is that even before their professional debut females are tracked into colleges whence, as it should now be abundantly clear, it is very difficult to commence a research program that would make it possible to ascend to a university. Since one's first position essentially sets the course for one's career, frequently the point is not reached where males in universities even have an opportunity to discriminate against their female colleagues in promotions, the distribution of salary, and the granting of tenure.

Achievement and Ascription: Concluding Remarks

If the principle of merit were as potent as it is alleged to be, then there would have been considerably less evidence in the studies reviewed in this chapter signifying the influence of ascription on academic careers. For example, the fact cannot be overlooked that social class affects the appointment process in prestigious universities both indirectly and directly: the more modest one's class background, the less the likelihood that one will attend one of the better institutions from which similar institutions recruit. Leaving aside where someone takes his degree, the more modest one's class background, the less the likelihood that one will be recruited by one of the better institutions. Since most senior positions are filled by promotions from within, initial placement takes on added significance. And since the elite institutions are also more likely to hire their own graduates and to exclude females from their faculties, it would appear that in those institutions where we would expect the most marked emphasis on achievement we find—with the rejection of those outside the middle class, those with the wrong credentials, and females—the least.

The system is less open than is generally acknowledged, and as a consequence the access of some individuals "to the means of scientific [and scholarly] production" is severely limited. In the most simple terms, what is operating here can be called the Matthew effect: "for unto every one that hath shall be given, and he shall have abundance; but from him that hath not shall be taken away even that which he hath."[145] With differential opportunities, cumulative advantages, and "a basic inequity in the reward system that affects the careers of individual scientists [and scholars],"[146] the principle of merit cannot help but recede into the background.

Perspectives on the Professional Socialization of Women Faculty

A Case of Accumulative Disadvantage?

SHIRLEY M. CLARK AND MARY CORCORAN

Disproportionately fewer faculty women than men achieve high levels of success in academe. Although falling well short of parity, women have made small gains in hiring in the past several years, but securing an entry-level position and sustaining a successful academic career are two quite different things [11, 12, 24]. According to Cole [7], women who have persevered are survivors who have gone against the grain of occupational stereotyping to enter a primarily male profession. For those who have defied the tough odds of the gatekeeping processes, their occupation has always had a position of primary importance relative to marriage, family, and other pursuits. In spite of the salience of the career to faculty women and the lengths to which they go to sustain it, there is the well-documented issue of differential progress [1, 7, 11, 12, 24, 33, 36]. The problem is especially acute in elite, research-oriented institutions and in the ranks of tenured faculty [2, 32]. Possible explanations include overt and subtle sex discrimination, differential interests and preferences for teaching rather than research, lack of sponsorship and collegial networks, and others suggesting accumulative disadvantage in the structure of the occupational career.

Studies of social stratification in academe have paid most attention to men. Occasionally, quantitative data were gathered on the status of women as well. However, as Cole has noted in discussing limitations of his own substantial work, "there is a conspicuous absence of qualitative interviews with female scientists" [7, p. 15]. He further argues that it is time to describe in detail and to analyze the informal structure of activities and experiences of young scientists (academics) "that set in motion and sustain an accumulation of advantages and disadvantages" [7, p. 130].

Our objectives are both theoretical and policy-oriented. From study of faculty career vitality at a large, research-oriented public multiversity, illustrations will be drawn to demonstrate the applicability of a literature-based model of professional socialization to the career experiences of academic women. Selected hypothetical "explanations" for the different progress of women will be explored within the context of the connected, three-stage model, using content from focused, open-ended interviews with women respondents. Guiding our inquiry into academe's social stratification are the following questions: What experiences have women had in the anticipatory socialization and the entry stages of a career that have gender salience? Specifically, how were sponsorship processes (advising, mentoring, collegial) experienced by these women? What processes of accumulating advantages or disadvantages affected career progress and satisfaction for these women? Did these women perceive sex-based discrimination relative to educational preparation and employment processes, review procedures, assignments, rewards and recognition?

We then seek to illustrate processes of differential socialization that result in an accumulation of advantages and disadvantages affecting academic careers. Subjective perceptions of women respondents who were part of sample groups in the institutional study will be presented as illustrative excerpts shedding light on the forms of particularistic treatment and experience that are not easily quantified. The socialization framework will be extended by considering the "Matthew" and "Salieri" effects and the sponsorship process. Finally, we present concluding statements about the value of this approach for understanding the status problems of women and suggest some policy implications arising from the case data.

Professional Socialization

Socialization models have been postulated as being particularly useful for understanding sex differences in academic careers [7]. Conceptualizations of work socialization are variously termed organizational, occupational, or professional, but all direct attention to the setting in which the socialization of adults to work occurs. It is important to note that "at any age, socialization is a two-fold process; from the perspective of the group, socialization is a mechanism through which new members learn the values, norms, knowledge, beliefs, and the interpersonal and other skills that facilitate role performance and further group goals. From the perspective of the individual, socialization is a process of learning to participation in social life" [29, p. 422].

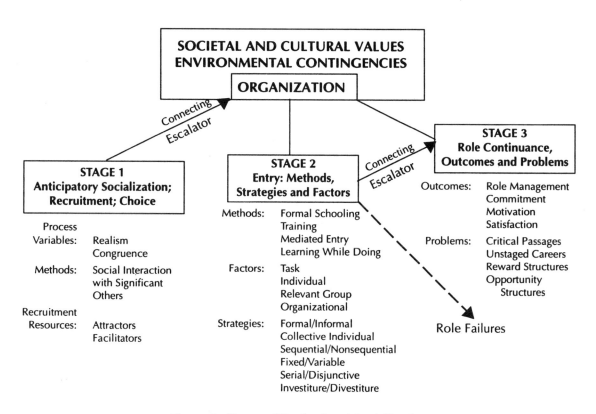

Figure 1. Stages of Professional Socialization

SOURCE: Partially based on a scheme in Feldman [10] and a revised version of Figure 1 from Mary Corcoran and Shirley M. Clark's "Professional Socialization and Contemporary Career Attitudes of Three Faculty Generations," *Research in Higher Education*, 20 (No. 2, 1984), p. 134; used by permission from Agathon Press, Inc.

Although extensive research and theoretical work dealing with socialization in professional schools (especially health sciences fields) has accumulated, few studies of faculty role socialization have been done. One relevant comparative occupational study is Lortie's *School-teacher* [23], an ethnography of a feminized occupation that probes how career decisions are made, what the strengths and weaknesses of the preparation programs are for long-term role performance, how share relations with peers are for long-term role performance, how shared relations with peers relate to professional success, how expectations of performance affect its quality, how reward and opportunity systems are structured, and more. Sociologists have identified several dimensions or strategies of organizational socialization and their consequences for the individual and the organization [40, 41]. A framework (see Figure 1) derived from the professional literature that envisions the individual as moving through three stages of experience is central to this study [6, 9]. Becker and Strauss [3] have used the metaphors "flow," "stream," and "escalators" to convey the relatedness of the stages.

Anticipatory socialization, recruitment, and choice is the first of the three stages. It includes the process by which persons choose occupations and are recruited to them, gradually assuming the values of the group to which they aspire and measuring the ideal for congruence with reality [10, 23, 26, and 43]. The second stage is occupational entry and induction; it includes or is preceded by formal schooling, preparation, or training for the occupation, and/or mediated entry, and/or learning while doing. For faculty members, the focus is on extensive formal training in graduate school, which also provides anticipatory socialization and a site for recruitment as well as facilitation of professional role commitment [42]. During this process, which includes passage into the status of neophyte faculty member, a variety of socialization strategies come into play [40, 41]. Particular emphasis is given here to the so-called "Matthew" effect and the sponsorship process.

The early stages of professional socialization are especially important, according to a social-psychological theory that attitudes, values, and beliefs tend to stabilize in young adulthood and to become less likely to change as personas grow older [15]. The aging-stability thesis emphasizes the importance of the early period of the career for developing commitment to work, for stimulating motivation, and for internalizing occupationally relevant attitudes and behaviors that sustain productivity and continued achievement throughout the career.

If all proceeds well, the third stage of role continuance is achieved. The new member has a set of internalized role specifications, a sense of satisfaction with work, and a high degree of job involvement and commitment. She or he is carried along within the structure of the career to later stages, which may involve the maturing, more independent professional in sponsoring, socialization, or other organizational leadership roles and generative activities.

The "escalator" metaphor is useful because it suggests that the career route may not be safe, smooth, or clear, particularly when careers are unstaged beyond an early point; when problematic elements of the organization's environment and broader social context intrude; or when "functionally irrelevant statuses" (gender or race, for example) are believed to affect evaluation [28].

The "Matthew" Effect: Accumulated Advantage or Disadvantage

The brunt of the sociological literature on scientific elites holds that scientists who are placed in structurally advantageous positions as a result of outstanding role performance accrue certain advantages due to attaining these positions. For example, there are accumulating advantages and visibility for being in an outstanding academic department as a graduate student. Merton [27] and Zuckerman [44] have described this process with Nobel laureates; in these cases, honored standing was converted into other occupational assets. The term "Matthew" effect is an allusion to Christ's description of accumulating faith: "For whosoever hath, to him shall be given, and he shall have more abundance; but whosoever hath not, from him shall be taken away even that he hath" (King James Version, Matt. 25:29). Merton, Zuckerman, Cole [7], Lorber [22], and others who have used the quotations are referring to social status advantages: a case of the rich getting richer and the poor getting poorer as time (or career in this case) goes on.

The "Matthew" effect tends to be considered fair. The "advantaged" scientist, after all, faces a series of challenges along the way. Success seems to be the result of a funnelling process: many begin the race, some drop out along the way, some finish in record time, others finish very slowly. Cole and Cole [8] explain that, because they apprentice in top departments and interact with productive, influential scientists, and because they have superior resources to carry out research, some male scientists have social advantages and rewards attributable to a strategic location and to interactions with high-status people. These advantages affect their achievement in positive ways.

The other side of this process that potentially influences the careers of women academics may be termed accumulative disadvantage. If women do not enroll in the best graduate programs, do not receive parity in financial aids, do not become protégés of productive, established academicians, do not have resources to carry out their research and scholarly work, do not penetrate the collegial networks where useful advice, advocacy, and patronage are dispensed, and so forth, they may begin with initial disadvantage and find that it grows with time. When they are reviewed for tenure and promotion, their publication records may be inferior to those of men; in turn, they have not accomplished much research, the funding gatekeepers may decide that there is little justification for granting financial support since the record of accomplishments is marginal. However plausible this reasoning may be, we do not have a full picture from the literature of the hypothesis of accumulative disadvantage as it applies to the career histories of women faculty. Cole suggests that "the processes of accumulative disadvantage may well begin at a far earlier age for women, and there may be processes that impede the progress of women which are not easily quantifiable" [7, p. 81].

An interesting modification of the "Matthew" effect is the "Salieri" phenomenon. In a recent paper, Lorber [22] discusses the interactive processes that keep women in academic medicine from positions of power and describes the "Salieri" phenomenon. She alludes to Peter Shaffer's play, *Amadeus* [35], in which Mozart's lack of social graces gives Salieri, the court composer and gatekeeper of musical patronage for the Emperor Joseph, the occasion to prevent Mozart's extraordinary accomplishments from receiving recognition. Salieri does recommend Mozart to the Emperor for a post, but he makes sure that the salary is set quite low. In the process, Salieri makes a pretense of being a benefactor to Mozart. Mozart, unhappy with the poor salary, is unaware that his career is actually blocked rather than advanced. Instead, he is grateful for the efforts which Salieri has made on his behalf. Not until after his death could Mozart's works be judged on their own merit, apart from the "functionally irrelevant" characteristic—lack of social graces—which so disturbed the prominent Salieri. Applying the "Salieri" phenomenon to the performance and behavior of academic women, we might consider that they are judged by a dominant, inner circle of men and may not measure up because of their social status. Women may not be blocked out entirely, but their progress is limited to a relatively low level of advancement in male-dominated occupations and societies.

Sponsorship

In *Fair Science*, Cole [7] calls for a detailed examination of the process of sponsorship in science to uncover significant differences in the training of women that are not easily captured in quantitative analysis. He doubts that the search for gross patterns of bias is likely to produce fruitful results. Rather, what is proposed is an analysis that would examine the nature of the relationship between women and their faculty advisors, the extent to which opportunities to learn to do scientific work are made available to women, the degree to which opportunities to participate in conferences, to enter the professional network, to collaborate on scholarly work, are offered to them. To be considered are both the claim that "intergenerational ties maintain a discipline's universe of discourse" [31, p. 143], thereby contributing to the development of scientific knowledge, and the practical career matters of obtaining good jobs, promotions, and salaries.

"Sponsorship," "role modeling," and "mentorship" are concepts whose time has come, as demonstrated by the attention devoted to them in the popular literature and the many recommendations devised to intervene in career development. "Professionals must have had one, been one, or be seeking one if they are to advance their careers" [37, p. 692]. The attention to mentoring, particularly, has reached (in one writer's term) "mania" proportions [4] in that readers are told that success depends "not only on what you know but whom you know" [21, p. 23]. This faith in the mentoring relationship, as a specific, two-person, mentor-protégé relationship, is not entirely supported by available research, according to Merriam's [25] critical review of the subject. Likewise, in an earlier, more encompassing review, Speizer [37] concluded that "role models," "mentors," and "sponsors" are concepts that still need to be defined and studied; until more methodologically sound studies are done, the concepts are suggestive rather than proven.

Although "sponsorship," "mentorship," and "role modeling" have not been defined with precision, for our purposes, sponsorship will include advancement of a favored protégé, mentoring and/or coaching a novice through the informal norms of the workplace and/or discipline. This process is thought to be important for upward mobility and career success in adult development generally, in business, in the professions, and specifically, in academic settings. Kanter [18] and others have recognized its importance even in "rationalistic" bureaucratic structures. Lorber argues that medicine, dependent as it is upon peer regulation, provides a good example of the processes of sponsorship and boycott—the "heart of the sorting process which results in colleague networks homogeneous in competence and ethicality" [22, p.6]. As a further consequence, this profession becomes homogeneous in social characteristics such as race (white) and religion (Protestant). Oswald Hall's classic study of physicians in a Canadian community [16] established that novice physicians (these included the few women in his sample) who were not sponsored by influentials had "friendly careers," but they never achieved the higher status, income, or leadership of the protégé group.

As we relate ideas of sponsorship to academic women, definitional problems notwithstanding, a series of questions come to mind: Are women less likely to pursue their graduate programs in the top departments in their fields? Are women's efforts to do scholarly work discouraged? Are women channeled into teaching-oriented institutions as they move into entry-level positions? Do they receive less post-degree help from advisors? Data collected from women in an exploratory study of faculty career vitality may sharpen images in an unclear picture of how sponsorship affects the sexes in academe.

An Exploratory Institutional Case Study

As part of an institutional case study of faculty career vitality at the University of Minnesota, Twin Cities campus, lengthy interviews with 147 faculty members were conducted during 1980-81 and 1981–82. Faculty respondents were drawn from four fields: The College of Biological Sciences, the physical sciences and mathematics departments of the Institute of Technology, and the social sciences and humanities departments of the College of Liberal Arts. Both reputational and stratified random sampling procedures were used to assure representation of the full range of faculty productivity in teaching, research, and service. All the faculty respondents were tenured associate or full professors whose median age was in the forties. Eleven percent, or twelve respondents, were women. Although this number is quite small, it is representative of the actual proportions of tenured women in the sample fields on the Minneapolis campus.[1]

The interview guide consisted of more than fifty, mostly open-ended questions on subjects such as (1) the decision to pursue an academic career; (2) graduate school dimensions of career socialization; (3) career stages and socialization as a faculty member; (4) work interests and preference orientations; (5) dimensions of productivity and success; (6) morale, satisfaction, and perceptions of change; and (7) appraisals and future considerations.

The applicability of the study is limited because of its attention to one case of a specific institutional type (research-oriented multiversity) and to only four fields, biological sciences, physical sciences and mathematics, social sciences, and humanities. It is arguable that there are different patterns of treatment for women in fields where they are token representatives of their sex and in fields where they are better represented, but there is little actual data regarding these differences and conflicting hypotheses abound. For example, Cole [7] asserts that one could argue that few women in a field do not represent a threat to the men in power, and so women are treated equitably. Conversely, one could argue that, in fields with few women, levels of sex discrimination are significant, for discrimination is not as visible or as frequently punished and men may be more apt to define women as incapable of doing the requisite work.

We turn now to the subjective perceptions of women respondents about their experiences in the anticipatory and entry stages of their careers.

Anticipatory Socialization: Women and the Career Choice

Among the significant others who influenced the career decision of respondents were parents, high-school teachers, and faculty members. We draw from the interviews three disparate selections to illustrate, first, the self-imposed limitations in choosing a graduate school, and second and third, the impact of parental support or lack thereof for career planning. In Berg and Ferber's [4] review of studies of men and women graduate students, it is alleged that women are less confident than men, are more conservative in choosing a graduate school, complain of lack of ability as a barrier to success, often lack maternal support for their choices, set lower goals for themselves, and receive less encouragement from male faculty. A woman scientist explains how she made her decision about which graduate school to attend:

> There were at the time maybe twenty good graduate departments in the country in my field. I probably applied to about half a dozen, and I got accepted at all of them. I didn't apply to what I called the top echelon because I was good academically, but I was a woman and I had some reservations. And I didn't want to go to Harvard or Princeton; I was from the Midwest, and socially I did not think I would be happy in those places. I received financial aid, I think, at all but one. And one of those places was ____. Actually, it turned out they made the best offer; that's why I went there.

Her mother's example and advice and a particular undergraduate teacher provided support for another faculty woman's decision to move ahead:

> She had married while she was in graduate school and dropped out to have three children. She felt that it probably would have been better if she had finished and had a career, but then she went back to having a career after I went to college. So she always told me that I should go right through! And that if I wanted a family, that I should combine it somehow, and I shouldn't give up my career for my family. So I think that she was a very big influence. I also had a teacher at my undergraduate school who was a woman—I was very impressed with her, and I think I identified with her, too.

Another distinguished woman talks of the mixed messages she received about graduate study and an academic career, even though she came from an academic family, and how this confusion kept her in graduate school but prevented her from clearly deciding to pursue an academic career:

> I wanted to be a scientist, but I didn't decide that I wanted to be a faculty member because I thought that would impossible because I was a female. I went to college at ____and to graduate school at ____, where there were no women faculty members. I come from an academic family and the way in which I was brought up was with the belief that this was not a career open to women. Period.
>
> In fact, my father felt very strongly that women should not go to graduate school because they were taking up a place that a man should occupy and he had potential and used his education—whereas women did not, so they should not go. So I'd say I made the decision to be a faculty member when I was thirty-five and was actually offered a job as a faculty member.

In response to further probes, she explained:

> My father was a professor and a scientist, so there was a lot of talk about science and a lot of approval for people who were academics and who were intelligent and well educated. So I was getting a lot of positive reinforcement for the idea that it would be desirable to be an academic, or to be a scholar, while at the same time getting the negative message that I shouldn't do this. It was rather confusing.

Later on, some little encouragement was forthcoming:

> I would say in college, I remember talking to one of the deans, and she quite surprised me by saying that she thought that women who had combined marriage and a career were probably the happiest. That was the first positive statement I'd heard from anyone that this was an option. At this time, I was trying to make up my mind to go to graduate school, but you see I wasn't really making up my mind to have a career. I would say outside my family I didn't get much positive reinforcement about this, either. I think I met a few people later on, after I had my PhD., who gave me positive reinforcement. Needless to say I'm very angry about this, thinking back on it.

These selections suggest, on the one hand, the early disadvantages that spring from negative or conflicting messages from significant others about career choice and planning, as well as the potential disadvantage of a conservative choice of graduate department. On the other hand, strong support for combining career and family aspirations was perceived as important, positive reinforcement from persons who mattered. In each of these excerpts and, indeed, throughout the interviews with women, the consciousness of gender and career is explicit, contrasting to the lack of expressed concerns about "being a man" or "combining marriage and career" among men faculty respondents.

We turn now to dimensions of graduate school preparation: the role relationship of the advisor and the advisee, its impact, the departmental environment, and the role of peers during formal training, induction, and after.

Work Entry: The Sponsorship of Women

Formal preparation of the faculty member takes place through graduate education in the departments of research-oriented universities. The department inducts students into the discipline, transmitting skills, knowledge, and a structure of values, attitudes, and ways of thinking and feeling. Trow asserts that the effects of this socialization "are often very strong, providing an individual with the perspectives and orientations that guide a lifetime of academic teaching and research" [39, p. 15].

The basic forms and functions of graduate education are similar across disciplines, but the actual processes vary among disciplines and departments, and even within departments among pairs of students and advisors. This situation is certainly true for men as well as for women, as our interview data attest. The result is that different environments and contexts for learning are experienced and that little is known of this variety even by academics themselves. Field differences in student environment (e.g., in history as compared to psychology), as well as sex differences in student expediences, have been reported by Hartnett [17]. The disadvantages faced by women students in finding sponsors and mentors, given the ratios of female faculty to female students in most graduate programs and fields, have been examined recently by Berg and Ferber's institutional case study of the University of Illinois at Urbana-Champaign [4]. They suggest that this disadvantage is an inevitable result of rising proportions of women students without related change in the sex composition of faculties. Particularly in male-dominated fields, women graduate students at Illinois reported knowing far fewer men faculty members well and experiencing junior collegial relations with men faculty far less often than did their male peers. It seemed clear to the researchers that "students and faculty of the same sex interact most comfortably" [4, p.639]. In earlier study by Katz and Hartnett [20], graduate students regarded their relations with faculty members as the single most important aspect of the quality of their graduate experience; sad to say, many also reported it as the single most disappointing aspect of their graduate experience.

One talented woman reflects on the absence of women role models in her environment, a typical experience of many of the respondents:

> I had a man advisor. Something that was very significant to me during this time was that there was only one woman who taught in the graduate school there, and she offered courses that were outside the field that I was working in. So the whole time I never did

work with any women professors. And this did have a clear impact on me, and I began to think, "Where do I fit in the system if there are no women in it, or very few?" And at that time, there were no women full professors in my department. So that was a very negative kind of message that I was getting. This subject was never talked about, the fact that some of were women and some of us were men. We were treated as though we had no gender whatsoever. And yet I could see that there was a big difference in the institution in terms of what happened to women and what happened to men. My advisor was and is a very kind man, and someone I respect a great deal. His expectations, as far as I could determine, were that I do well, that I work hard and write well and be conscientious, and that's about it. And he pretty much left me on my own to do that.

When this respondent was asked whether her advisor or other faculty members provided any specific encouragement to her to pursue an academic career, she expressed the bind she felt between marriage and career success:

I think when I look back on it that I got a set of double messages about my career. In fact, some people said very explicitly to me that I should not get married. Or that, if I did get married, I would ruin my career, or that I would not have a career. I found this sort of painful at the time, and I did get married in the course of graduate school. But three different professors suggested to me more or less openly that I would lose it all if I got married. On the other hand, the other side of that message was, "You're so good that you deserve to go on and do well." I couldn't see how I was supposed to live the life that they imagined me leading, or at least it was not the life I planned to live. But I didn't know how to reconcile my notion of what a career for me might be and their notion of what a career for me should be.

Not being taken seriously is a problem some women encountered:

I think the expectation was that the women, since no woman had ever graduated from there, were just taking some courses because our husbands were doing something else. Well I did a couple of things that made an impression on them, and they began to treat me more seriously. One is that I was the only one that finished the first semester without incompletes. And at the end of the first year, they gave me a summer fellowship which I didn't apply for and I had never heard of; they just decided that I had done the best job so they gave me the scholarship. The other thing I did toward the end of my first year was that I done an honors thesis in my undergraduate school which used some very elementary statistics, and in my statistics class we were talking about something and I raised my hand, and said "Well is that why I got such and such kind of results when I did this paper before?", and so the class started talking about it and my professor encouraged me to recalculate these things. And then he sort of said after that, "Oh you're serious about this, I thought you were just kind of hanging around here." And this professor was on my dissertation committee and became sort of my major mentor figure. So I worked on this article and submitted it; since it was in history, submitted it to a history journal and revised it, and it was accepted. Then people really started to notice me. What I'm trying to say is that they didn't have particularly high expectations at first, but they began to raise them very rapidly, especially this one person. And then they started to make comments about how, "Boy, they've sure taken a sow's ear and made a silk purse." They had a lot of fun telling the history department that I'd published an article in their leading journal, and they hadn't taken me as a graduate student, and so then it was this mutual patting themselves on the back and patting me on the back, that kind of thing.

Another woman, who admitted to being very ambivalent in the past about her own, now very successful career, began her relationship with her advisor in the following way:

When I came up here, it was not to be a graduate student. He was looking for a research assistant. I always loved research. And I applied for that job. And we had quite a go-around when we first met. It was a very hostile kind of interview between us. He wanted to know if I had any authoritative medical evidence that I couldn't have children. And I said I certainly didn't. Then he said, well what would you do if you got pregnant? I said,

I'd quit you. And I was very offended. And he, of course, did not like my attitude either. And so it ended on this rather sorry note, and I thought I would never hear from him again. Well, a month later I got this letter from him and he said I have examined the qualifications of all the people who have applied for the job, and you are the most qualified and if you want it, it is yours. Which was pretty white of him considering in those days they thought women would never finish graduate school, and men were stable and sturdy.

Doubting that she would be committed to her field because women's lives were likely to include marriage, the advisor of this woman provided help begrudgingly:

I was in graduate school between '65 and '69, and I was one of two other women in the graduate department at the time I was there. I definitely felt that my advisor's attitude towards me, his expectations of me, were highly dependent on my sex. He was never mean to me in any way, but I always felt that he had one or two other students, men, and it wasn't until they were out of the way (I was third in line) that he would spend some time with me. It was very near the end of my thesis, and I think he really wasn't expecting much to come out; he was very surprised at the end.

When she was attempting to obtain a postdoctoral position, she solicited his help:

When I was looking for a job, I actually asked my thesis advisor, "Won't you do anything for me? Aren't you going to help me get a job?" And he said, "Well now you do the work, you go out and you write the letters and write to all the places you're interested in and if any of them respond, then tell me and I'll follow them up." But this was quite different from what he did for the two men. He said to me in effect, "Okay, so I go out and I do this for you. And I get you a good job. And after a year or so you run off and get married, and you never do any work again. How am I to feel? I have stuck my neck out for you." And I said, "I personally didn't think that was any more reason against me than it should be against someone else. What guarantee did he have that two years from now those guys were going to be great guns?" My thesis had probably been better than theirs in some ways. But he was afraid that basically he was sticking his neck out because I was a woman. He made that specific.

As her reputation in her field grew, however, her advisor changed his mind about her:

My advisor and I are excellent terms now. It might have sounded like I'm bitter at him. At that time, I was very bitter. But since then, he's just been absolutely gushing. He's very proud of me, and he's very quick to tell me that and to tell all the people that I was his student.

Not all the women reported discriminatory treatment from their men advisors, although several did. For a more positive experience, this woman describes her advisor as a "real dynamo" who held "very high expectations and standards for the students":

Of course, in fact, I was a little intimidated by him because he was just so outstanding in every way. He knew so much, and he was so productive, and it was hard to think of being like him, or even working with him, but by the time I came to have to make the decision about who would be my advisor, he seemed the logical person, because he was interested in what I was interested in. We had a very formal relationship, I think. I never worked with him on his project, though he invited me to, because I felt very strongly that I should do my own thing. But it was a very good choice, I think, and he was excellent in helping me through, and reading everything very quickly, and getting me lots of good advice, and then he helped me get a job when I got out by writing recommendations. Then when it came time to make the transition here, he wrote letters and called people and so that was very helpful. But in terms of my career development, I've moved away from some of my original interests, and he's moved further in another direction.

Generally, the women respondents reported receiving some assistance, at least at a minimal level, from their advisors in obtaining positions after the doctorate was achieved. Frequently, however, this involved channeling or tracking women into certain positions and men into others, as perceived by these two respondents:

> This process was basically what is known as the Old Boy system. And I think what happened is that the director of placement would recommend to various people at other institutions which candidates they might seriously consider. So I had no insight into where they thought I should go, except that I figured out, I think pretty accurately after the fact, that they thought I should go to a small liberal arts college. They tended to channel most of the men into larger and sometimes more prestigious research-oriented institutions, and the women tended to be placed in small liberal arts colleges. Often these were colleges with wonderful reputations but known as teaching colleges rather than research colleges.
>
> The chairman of the department at the time pretty much told people where they would go to teach and this is one of the things that I resent now, that I was discriminated against as a woman. The plum jobs went to two men, and my advisor told me that there was a job at St. Cloud State, and I said I would never go there. Then he said, "Well there's a job at Iowa State," and that did seem like a reasonable place for me to go. There was also one in Utah. Now my colleagues, my peers, were going to Princeton, and I'm sure that it was because I was a woman, because I certainly had done as well in the program as my male peers. So there wasn't much encouragement and in fact, looking back, there was a sense of my being pushed into second-rate jobs. I was lucky that my husband was given incredible direction by his advisors, and he went to _____, and then I was able to get a job on my own, without any help from my department.

The channeling of women academics into colleges emphasizing teaching rather than research puts women at a disadvantage in beginning their research and scholarly work, in building their reputations as scientists and scholars. As Zuckerman [44] and Cole [7] put it, this is the "triple penalty" principle in operation, which states that certain groups (here, women) "suffer not only from direct discrimination and cultural definitions that define certain careers as inappropriate, but also from being placed initially into second-rate structural positions, which makes it difficult or impossible for them to produce the outstanding work that is necessary for moving out of such positions" [7, p. 79].

Peer relationships are an important part of socialization, for it is with peers that informal discussions, exchanges of aid and support, and friendships facilitate the learning that, in the present, tempers the "ordeal" aspects of professional preparation and, in the future, prepares the student for collegial structures. Women faculty have peers who, for the most part are men. Their consciousness of that fact stands out in the following comments:

> The first year, one of those ways in which I was pretty miserable was that I didn't have any friends among those students. It seemed that there were mostly single males, and I was a married woman, and you know that they didn't quite know how to relate to me, and so they just didn't. And then, over the first summer, these men all got girlfriends, or they got married; they became more able to interact as couples. And so then I started to see a lot of them socially, and their main way of relating to me was kind of like my brother used to relate to me. So they were important after the first year...that was really a way to get socialized.
>
> Well, when I was a student, we had a study group for the prelim, and I worked with two other men. There were hardly any women at all in the program, and so if you wanted to have relationships like that, they had to be cross-sex, because there was no one else by the time you reached the Master's. Beyond the Master's program, most of the women wound up dropping out. And the prelim study group kind of stands out in my mind, because it went on for a whole year; the prelim was the big milestone at _____. The third year would just be studying for this prelim, and we sued to meet every week, and go through all these reading lists, and talk about the ideas, and that was very good. Both of them wound up being good friends of mine, and that's continued even now.

Working in relative isolation characterized some graduate study environments:

> Graduate students as I remember them in my department, worked very hard, and they tended to work in isolation. They didn't do what I have heard has happened in other institutions, try to undermine each other's work. There wasn't that kind of nasty competition. On the other hand, they didn't share their work very much with their friends. We really didn't talk much about the papers we were writing or the subjects we were interested in, and there was a kind of reticence in that area. I'm now making contact again with some of the people I was with in graduate school, a lot of them women, and discovering that we have similar interests and sometimes it's very specific, in this field for instance. Those friendships are sort of latent and are now blossoming. We're also now able to share our work.

Many of the situations in which gender was conspicuous for women as graduate students (primarily male peers, primarily male faculty advisors, a predominantly male department milieu, problems of allocating time to both family and work, and so forth) continued to be experienced by many as they moved from the graduate school into postdoctoral or entry-level academic positions. There were certain pitfalls, for example, with colleagues and sponsors. One of the women who moved into a postdoctoral position found she needed to manage problems of dependency with a sponsor-colleague. As she explained it:

> A faculty member at another university provided me with encouragement and positive career advice. And he also gave me some financial support. Finally, I ended up being a postdoctoral fellow in his lab. Only I wasn't resident, I was living in another city where my husband was, and he was quite tolerant of that situation. So that was positive support from that one person who was more of a colleague than a mentor. I was very suspicious of accepting too much of this kind of help because, although I was very naive, I'd somehow caught on very early to the dangers of attaching myself to any such sugar-daddy type person who might absorb me into his research reputation. And with this man that did happen with some of the work that I did with him as a postdoc. There were certain hostilities between us for a while because I knew he was giving seminars and talking about the work I'd done, and so I extricated myself from that situation. I was very careful about not putting myself in a position of dependency. How I knew this I haven't figured out because I didn't see any role models for the situation, but I somehow knew that it was a danger for a young woman scientist.

Another woman, when asked about her perceptions of colleagues' expectations of her when she moved into her first faculty position, described her role as an outsider to a male culture.

> It wasn't clear to me what was expected of me, particularly at the small college where I held my first position. My experience there was not good. In part, because I was one of the very few full-time faculty members, the first full-time woman faculty member in my department. There really was difficulty among my male colleagues in associating with a woman as a colleague. I think they literally did not know how to talk to me, and as a consequence often just did not talk to me. They would ignore me. They would not invite me to have lunch with them, which was a very ordinary experience there. They all go up to the campus cafeteria and eat together. And it took me a long time to realize that they would walk past my office and ask the next person and never ask me. Late in my years there, when this finally dawned on me that I was being treated differently, I asked one of my colleagues why this was so. And he said, "You know what would happen if I asked you to lunch." I said, "No," and he said, "People would talk." And it wasn't until then that I began to understand how deeply conventional that society was and how much I was a strange element in it. That many people saw me as a subject of gossip if they associated with me. So that made me very uncomfortable. Also I had a baby my first year on the faculty, I was the only full-time woman faculty with a young child, in a society where all mothers of young children stayed at home. I also felt a kind of disapproval of my working and taking my daughter to a baby sitter for six hours a day. They never did articulate what they expected of me.

Societal expectations of wives and mothers bore heavily upon a woman who began her career thirty years ago. She commented:

> I did feel a very important role, like I was a pioneer when I started thirty years ago. And that was to show women that you could work and have successful kids, and it was this whole syndrome which is not much about being a woman and stuff. This whole thing of the working woman was neglecting her kids was looked down on. And I had to prove, I thought, that I could have good kids and work. And I worked very much; I mean I did all the outside things too. Scout leading, which I really enjoyed, it's one of the things that makes me a good teacher, I think. But I did all of those and I had the orange juice unfrozen every morning; that's a joke in our family!

Even, however, for the more recent women doctorates, the early stages of career often combined with childbearing, childcare, and required coordination with the husband's similarly emerging career, as demonstrated in the following response:

> You know, it was the dual-career, family business again, coordinating moves, and it just happened that my husband finished his degree one year before I did, and he wanted to take a post-doc position, so we planned to move to the area where his institution was located, and at that point, I had finished all of my dissertation research, but I hadn't written it yet. I had written parts of it, and I was also pregnant. So it seemed a reasonable idea at the time, and jobs were plentiful in those days, and there were a number of schools in the area, so I didn't consider it a very great risk to just move there, and then see what happened, and my plan was that I wouldn't be employed for a while, and I would finish my dissertation, I would have my baby, and then at some time maybe during the next year, I would try to get some employment....I had the baby in February, and at that time I was working very hard at trying to do the writing, and that was going well. But I was feeling very distressed at being alone in this unfamiliar place without friends or relatives, and having this new baby, and being cut off from professional colleagues. I was feeling very isolated, so I decided that I really had to get a job, even though I had thought I might not work so soon. So I applied around the area, and very soon I got a job on a part-time basis. I finished my dissertation during that first year, and then I was on a tenure track. It was rather strenuous, because I had this new baby, and I was trying to finish my dissertation and also preparing new classes that I hadn't taught before. I remember feeling like I was exhausted a lot of the time, getting low-grade colds and sore throats, and infections and things, and not being able to shake them. My husband was very helpful, and that wasn't the problem, but it was just too much for both of us.

She goes on to indicate that early crises brought on by "role overload" abated:

> After that first year, things really settled down, and then by the second year, I was feeling like I was able to handle it, and things weren't so stressful. I started sending things off to be published, got a grant proposal in, and then the people in my department were very supportive and really accommodating to my needs for special hours, arrangements, and things like that. I thought that was very nice to help. With women, these family concerns always enter in.

Being husbands and fathers rarely affects men's occupational involvement and commitment to the extent that women's marital and family roles affect their professional work engagement. Wifehood and maternity compete for resources that must be allocated among occupational and domestic spheres [30]. This allocation may create career discontinuity if it results in withdrawal from the workplace for childbearing and child care. Withdrawal may result in obsolescence of skills, loss of competitive position, attenuation of professional networks, and social isolation [13]. As if this were not problematic enough, the evidence suggests that women, regardless of marital and family status, tend to be marginals or outsiders to the male world of academe (in most field areas) to some greater or lesser extent. Outsiders are excluded from, or have limited access to, informal networks of communication that carry significant professional information. They, in turn, may feel awkward and self-conscious in the male milieu and further remove themselves from informal interactions. In devising strategies for change, it is important to consider the structure and processes within academe that are male-biased and to propose changes that will do more than simply increase the ratio of women on college and university faculties.

Conclusions

In many respects, American women faculty have succeeded in improving their status in this century. The earlier hostile climate of opinion about women's place, about married women working, about women's intellectual and creative capacities to become scholars and scientists has been neutralized. Women have many opportunities to pursue careers. It is also true that at least some types of institutions, including research universities, have hired more women as regular faculty than in the pre-World War II era. And these structural changes in academe seem to have been accompanied by social changes that have helped reduce sex discrimination—at least in its most blatant forms. A decade of concerted activity by women's interest groups, with the help of the federal government and the courts, has strongly influenced practices if not attitudes at many institutions. If one takes a long-term perspective, that is good news indeed.

The bad news seems to be that women have not completely overcome the effects of the "triple penalty." Among women like those we studied, who are in their thirties, forties, and fifties, there are reports of difficulties in first overcoming cultural barriers to entering academic careers. Second, during the training for and entry phase of their careers, there were particularistic experiences with advisors and others who doubted the women students' potential for, or likelihood of, having an academic career that would include research productivity. Third, structural impediments to success (in the form of opportunities for "best" positions and full participation in the collegial culture and networks) were easily recalled and described by many of the women respondents in the faculty career vitality study.

Qualitative data richly illustrate the utility of theoretical conceptualizations of professional socialization for understanding the quantitatively based sex differences in academic careers that have been established in numerous empirical studies. The idea of accumulated advantage or disadvantage, as suggested by the "Matthew" effect or the "Salieri" phenomenon, seems useful for understanding processes in academe that lead similarly talented graduate students into highly productive careers or less productive ones. Models of causal chains might be drawn up and tested once we better establish the nature of the relationships, choices, and interactive processes of advantage or disadvantage. We tend to think that the "Salieri" phenomenon (when gatekeepers to career advancement permit access but control achievement) is an interesting extension of sponsorship conceptualizations warranting further study. The diminished status of women's "triple penalty" and women's opportunity for so-called "friendly careers" in academe today suggests that, although women are no longer excluded, their place may be limited to some middle-range of career success.

Sponsorship—which is so important to vital faculty careers, as we learned from the larger study from which data about the women respondents are drawn [6]—needs a great deal of research and policy attention in the case of women. Descriptions of advisor behavior ranged from the very instrumentally helpful to the relatively unhelpful and even sex-biased. The cross-sex nature of most of the advisor, peer, and eventually, collegial relationships problematically affects the quality of the relationships in many instances.

As Finkelstein [11, 12] has noted, institutions of higher education are not, in and of themselves, able to attack sex-linked differential patterns of childhood socialization and family expectations directly. However, they are in a position to address practices and processes within academe that result in inequities and marginality in women's careers as graduate students, as neophyte scholars, and as full-fledged faculty members. We believe that sponsorship would be a more deliberate process, in which advisors and colleagues would relate to women and men according to universalistic principles appropriate to a meritocratic community—but this is more easily said than done while women represent a proportional minority of the professoriate.

Finally, at outset we accepted Cole's [7] descriptions of faculty women as "survivors" of a series of tests, challenges, and obstacles leading to and through their occupational lives. This assertion is in no way an exaggeration when applied to the women respondents in the faculty career vitality study. They have had to be successful academics, or they would not have persisted to tenured status and senior rank at the University of Minnesota, where several enjoy distinguished reputations in their fields. Yet in their descriptions of earlier experiences with advisors and colleagues, there was evidence of early preparation or career disadvantage. By their middle- and late-middle age, they overcame those early disadvantages of lack of sponsorship or little sponsorship, exclusion from the collegial culture, and significant "role-overloading" with marital and child-care demands. Many questions then arise as to how initial disadvantages were overcome, what kinds of careers these women might have had under more favorable circumstances, and what impact such earlier experiences have had on the mature, role-maintenance stage of their careers, relative to morale, commitment, work engagement, and satisfaction. We hope these questions will stimulate further inquiry into women's careers in the social system of academe.

References

1. Astin, H. S., and A. E. Bayer. "Sex Discrimination in Academe." In *Academic Women on the Move*, edited by A. Rossi and A. Calderwood, pp. 1399–79. New York: Russell Sage, 1973.

2. Baldridge, J. V., D. V. Curtis, G. Ecker and G. L. Riley. *Policy Making and Effective Leadership*. San Francisco: Jossey-Bass, 1978.

3. Becker, H. S., and A. L. Strauss. "Careers, Personality and Adult Socialization." *American Journal of Sociology*, 62 (November 1956), 253–63.

4. Berg, H. M., and M. A. Ferber. "Men and Women Graduate Students: Who Succeeds and Why?" *Journal of Higher Education*, 54 (November/December 1983), 629–48.

5. Bernard, J. "Women's Educational Needs." In *The Modern College*, edited by A. W. Chickering and Associates, pp. 256–78. San Francisco: Jossey-Bass.

6. Clark, S. M., and M. Corcoran. "Professional Socialization and Faculty Career Vitality." Paper read at the American Educational Research Association, Montreal, Canada, April 1983.

7. Cole, J. R. *Fair Science: Women in the Scientific Community*. New York: The Free Press, 1979.

8. Cole, J. R., and S. Cole. *Social Stratification in Science*. Chicago: University of Chicago Press, 1973.

9. Corcoran, M., and S. M. Clark. "Professional Socialization and Contemporary Career Attitudes of Three Faculty Generations." *Research in Higher Education*, 20 (1984), 131–53.

10. Feldman, D. "A Contingency Theory of Socialization." *Administrative Science Quarterly*, 21 (September 1976), 433–52.

11. Finkelstein, M. "The Status of Academic Women: An Assessment of Five Competing Explanations." *The Review of Higher Education*, 7 (Spring 19884), 223–46.

12. _____. *The American Academic Profession: A Synthesis of Social Scientific Inquiry Since World War II*. Columbus: Ohio State University Press, 1984.

13. Fox, M. F., and S. Hesse-Biber. *Women at Work*. Palo Alto: Mayfield Publishing, 1984.

14. Fury, K. "Mentor Mania." *Savvy* (December 1979), 42–47.

15. Glenn, N. D. "Values, Attitudes, and Beliefs." In *Constancy and Chance in Human Development*, edited by O. G. Brim, Jr. and J. Kagan, pp. 596–640. Cambridge: Harvard University Press, 1980.

16. Hall, O. "Types of Medical Careers." *American Journal of Sociology*, 55 (1949), 243–53.

17. Hartnett, R. T. "Sex Differences in the Environments of Graduate Students and Faculty." *Research in Higher Education*, 14 (1981), 211–27.

18. Kanter, R. M. *Men and Women of the Corporation*. New York: Basic Books, 1977.

19. _____. "Changing the Shape of Work: Reform in Academe." In *Current Issues in Higher Education: (1) Perspectives on Leadership*, pp. 225–27. Washington, D.C.: American Association for Higher Education, 1979.

20. Katz, J., and R. T. Hartnett. "Recommendations for Training Better Scholars." In *Scholars in the Making*, edited by J. Katz and R. T. Hartnett, pp. 261–80. Cambridge: Ballinger, 1976.

21. Kraft, B. S. "Substantial Need for Professional 'Mentoring' Seen by Project on Women." *Chronicle of Higher Education*, 11 January 1984, p. 23.

22. Lorber, J. "Women as Colleagues: The Matthew Effect and the Salieri Phenomenon." Paper presented at American Sociological Association Meetings, Detroit, 1983.

23. Lortie, D. C. *Schoolteacher: A Sociological Study*. Chicago: University of Chicago Press, 1975.

24. Menges, R. J. and W. H. Exum. "Barriers to the Progress of Women and Minority Faculty." *Journal of Higher Education*, 54 (March/April 1983), 123–44.

25. Merriam, S. "Mentors and Proteges: A Critical Review of the Literature." *Adult Education Quarterly*, 33 (Spring 1983), 161–73.

26. Merton, R. K. *Social Theory and Social Structure*. Revised ed. Glencoe: The Free Press, 1957.

27. _____. "The Matthew Effect in Science." *Science*, 199 (January 5, 1968), 55–63.

28. _____. In conversation with Jonathan Cole, as reported in pp. 81–83, Cole, J., *Fair Science: Women in the Scientific Community*. New York: The Free Press, 1979.

29. Mortimer, J. T., and R. Simmons. "Adult Socialization." *Annual Review of Sociology*, 4 (1978), 421–54.

30. Mortimer, J. T. and G. Sorensen. "Men, Women, Work and Family." In *Women in the Workplace: Effects on Families*, edited by D. Quarm, K. Borman, and S. Gideonse. Norwood, N.J.: Ablex Publishers, forthcoming.

31. Reskin, B. F. "Academic Scholarship and Scientists' Careers." *Sociology of Education*, 52 (July 1979), 129–46.

32. Rossi, A. "Status of Women in Graduate Departments of Sociology." *The American Sociologist*, 5 (1970), 1–12.

33. Sandler, B. R. "You've Come a Long Way, Maybe—Or Why It Still Hurts to Be a Woman in Labor." *Current Issues in Higher Education*, 11–14, Washington, D.C.: American Association for Higher Education, 1979.

34. Sarason, S. B. *Work, Aging and Social Change: Professionals and the One Life-One Career Imperative*. New York: The Free Press, 1977.

35. Shaffer, P. *Amadeus*. New York: Harper and Row, 1980.

36. Simon, R. J., S. M. Clark, and K. Galway. "The Woman Ph.D.: A Recent Profile." *Social Problems*, 15 (Fall 1967), 221–36.

37. Speizer, J. J. "Role Models, Mentors and Sponsors: The Elusive Concepts." *Signs*, 6 (Summer 1981), 692–712.

38. Trow, M. (ed.). *Teachers and Students: Aspects of American Higher Education*. A volume of essays sponsored by the Carnegie Commission on Higher Education. New York: McGraw-Hill, 1975.

39. _____. "Departments as Contexts for Teaching and Learning." In *Academic Departments*, edited by D. E. McHenry and Associates, pp. 12–33. San Francisco: Jossey-Bass, 1977.

40. Van Maanen, J. "People Processing: Strategies of Organizational Socialization." *Organizational Dynamics*, 7 (Summer 1978), 1936.

41. Van Maanen, J., and E. H. Schein. "Toward a Theory of Organizational Change." In *Research in Organizational Behavior*, edited by B. M. Staw, pp. 209–64. Greenwich: JAI Press, 1979.

42. Weiss, C. S. "The Development of Professional Role Commitment Among Graduate Students." *Human Relations*, 34 (1981), 13–31.

43. Wheeler, S. "The Structure of Formally Organized Socialization Settings." In *Socialization After Childhood*, edited by O. G. Brim, Jr. and S. Wheeler, pp. 53–116. New York: Wiley and Sons, 1966.

44. Zuckerman, H. A. *Scientific Elite*. New York: The Free Press, 1977.

Note

1. Percentages of tenured women (of total faculty cohort) in each field group at Minnesota according to the February personnel listings are: 5.06 percent in biological sciences; 4.38 percent in the Institute of Technology; 11.46 percent in the social sciences, and 22.56 percent in the humanities in the College of Liberal Arts.

This research was supported by funds from the University of Minnesota Graduate School Grant-in-Aid of Research Program and the College of Education.

Shirley M. Clark is professor of education and sociology and Mary Corcoran is professor of higher education and educational psychology at the University of Minnesota.

Making the Short List: Black Candidates and the Faculty Recruitment Process

ROSLYN ARLIN MICKELSON AND MELVIN L. OLIVER

The reappearance of overt racism on the campuses of the nation's predominantly white universities is merely a symptom of structural racism in higher education.[1] This situation is reflected by the declining number of minority enrollees and graduates, cutbacks in financial assistance, battles over multicultural curricula and over the broadening of canons to include the scholarship and artistry of women and members of minorities, and the precarious status of minority faculty.[2] Minority faculty members are declining in number; many who are hired fail to be tenured and promoted, and those who remain are frequently ghettoized in the lower ranks of the academic hierarchy.[3]

The number of minority Ph.D.'s who serve on university faculties depends on a three-phase process: (1) the production of Ph.D.'s (the so-called academic pipeline); (2) the search and hiring process in academic departments; and (3) the tenure and promotion process at individual institutions. In this essay we focus on the second issue as it pertains to black Ph.D.'s, specifically the process of recruiting prospective candidates for academic positions. Although a great deal has been written about this multistep process,[4] we argue that one additional factor is the fallacious assumption that "qualified" new Ph.D. candidates can be found only in the graduate departments of elite research universities.

According to this assumption, if black candidates are not trained in the graduate departments of universities considered to be the best in the field, it is concluded, often incorrectly, that no qualified black candidates are available. Search committees, often faced with a large volume of applications, frequently use the national reputation of a prospective candidate's Ph.D. department as a proxy for initially screening the individual's qualifications. "We know which are the top twenty economics departments in the country, and if an applicant was not trained at one of these schools, we are not interested in him [sic]," a department chair told one of the researchers. In this way many black Ph.D.'s from nonelite graduate programs are summarily disqualified from making the "short lists" of many university searches.

Although the assumption that the best potential academics are trained primarily at flagship research universities may be true for white, middle-class Protestant males, who until approximately 1950 filled most positions in the United States professoriate,[5] we argue that it is not true for blacks, members of other minorities and most women. We present evidence based on our analysis of data from the National Study of Black College Students (NSBCS),[6] which suggests that high-quality black Ph.D. students are found not only in premier institutions but also in a wide variety of graduate departments. We argue further that one way in which universities can increase their minority faculty is to abandon the fallacious notion that a graduate department's reputation is a suitable proxy for a candidate's potential, and to include on recruitment short lists qualified black Ph.D.'s from lesser-known universities. The results of our data analyses suggest that such a practice will enhance the likelihood of increasing the number of black academics in the coming decade without sacrificing the quality of the black professoriate.

The Crisis: Demographics of Black Academics

As this society enters the last decade of the twentieth century, a decade after the *Adams* case was first argued in federal courts, the proportion of minority faculty members at predominantly white institutions remains minuscule.[7] The proportion of black faculty members in these institutions has fluctuated from a mere handful before the 1960s to very low levels during the last three decades.[8] In the early 1960s blacks accounted for 3 percent of professors. This proportion dropped to 2.2 percent in the early 1970s, rose again in the early 1980s to the 4 percent shown in Table 1, and has fallen in 1989 to an estimated 3.3 percent.[9]

The representation of black faculty members at predominantly white universities is actually poorer than these figures suggest. Faculty members are stratified both by rank and by type of institution. The higher the rank, the less likely it is that a black person will be found in it. The same is true at more prestigious schools. These unpublished estimates, however, include faculty at both four-year and two-year schools, and thus suggest that the actual proportion of black faculty at four-year universities is overestimated in the 3.3 percent figure cited above. Unfortunately, available data from the Equal Employment Opportunity Commission (EEOC) do not control for type of college. Data from a nonrandom but comprehensively researched survey of 158 four-year colleges in *The Black Student's Guide to Colleges* show that black faculty at predominantly white universities average about 2 percent of the total, while nonblack faculty at historically black colleges averages about 30 percent.[10] This finding suggests that if the data analysis reported in Table 1 controlled for employment in historically black colleges, where large numbers of blacks teach, the representation of black faculty at predominantly white institutions would be even more disproportional than it already appears to be.

We are not suggesting that the significant numbers of black faculty members at historically black colleges are unwisely or poorly using their academic talent. On the contrary, the presence of large numbers of black faculty members at these institutions is often an advantage to the students at those schools.[11] Instead we note this fact to illustrate the dearth of black faculty at predominantly white institutions of higher education, where the majority of all college students, both black and white, attend school and where most university faculty members must find employment.

Table 1. U.S. Full-time Faculty in Four-Year Institutions, 1983

Rank	White	Blacks	All Races
Professor	119,219	2,857	128,142
Assoc. professor	102,246	3,969	111,887
Asst. professor	100,176	5,847	113,330
Instructor	73,206	5,117	82,211
Lecturer	8,274	618	9,480
Other	22,570	1,043	25,623
Totals			
N	425,691	19,451	470,673
%	90	4	100

SOURCE: NCES, *Digest of Educational Statistics* (Washington, DC: Government Printing Office, 1988), p. 177.

The Narrowing Pipeline

Although this chapter will not explore in detail the issue of the production of black Ph.D.'s, we will address briefly the importance of the educational pipeline for understanding the racial crisis in higher education. The absolute number of black Ph.D.'s produced each year in this country, as well as the proportion of the total degrees granted to blacks, declined between 1975 and 1985.[12] According to the U.S. Department of Education, 1,253 blacks received Ph.D.'s in 1975 (3.8 percent of the total doctorates awarded), as compared to 1,154 in 1985 (3.5 percent). Moreover, the rates at which blacks received bachelor's and master's degrees also declined during this period. This decrease is most dramatic at the master's level, where proportions of total master's degrees dropped from 6.6 percent in 1975 to 4.9 percent in 1985.[13] When we consider that more than 50 percent of all blacks' doctorates are in education, the actual pool of potential faculty members for academic positions in the physical and natural sciences, the humanities and the social sciences is actually smaller than the data initially suggest. Taken together, these statistics reflect a deepening crisis in the black academic pipeline.

Graduate Department's Reputation as a Proxy for Individual Merit

As we stated earlier, the available pool of black Ph.D.'s is not the only factor that inhibits schools from identifying and making offers to qualified blacks. The process by which candidates are identified, screened and selected is guided by a set of meritocratic norms and untested assumptions that work against the selection of qualified minority Ph.D.'s who are not graduates of the leading institutions.

It is well-established that merit is the overriding consideration guiding the selection process of university faculty members. Even so, one can question the ability of search committees to select new faculty on the basis of judgments of meritocratic criteria that do not inherently bias the decision-making process against minorities. Seen in its sociological context, the process of selection turns out to be less an expression of positive choices than the result of negative choices,[14] whereby inappropriate and supposedly less-qualified candidates are cast aside while the most appropriate and best-qualified candidates rise to the top of the list. At almost every turn, members of minorities seem to be excluded disproportionately by criteria that appear on the surface to be universalistic, but actually serve to decrease the probability of a minority candidate's rising to the top of the short list.

Proponents of the present system, which allows an autonomous faculty to choose its peers in the context of meritocratic values, argue that this system is minorities' best protection against biases in the selection process.[15] When selection is based on neutral, objective and universalistic criteria, the argument goes, blacks and other disadvantaged minorities are protected against the intrusion of particularistic and biased criteria that previously excluded them from participation in the academy. This view, however, disregards an established literature that finds the search process to be plagued by precisely the opposite situation:[16] "Objective standards are often vague, inconsistent, and weighted toward subjective judgments."[17] The implementation of meritocratic principles is thwarted somewhere between rhetoric and reality.

To understand where this disjuncture occurs, we look more closely at the search process itself. Several good studies offer considerable insight into this process.[18] Previous research indicates that affirmative action is one factor which has affected faculty recruitment. Affirmative action has made a marked difference in the initial stage of the search process, but unfortunately not in the results. Because of affirmative action, academic positions are now advertised more widely than ever. Advertisements are written to encourage women and minority candidates to apply. Studies and demographic data, however, show that the outcome of these searches continues to be largely the same as in the past. Those who rise to the top of the lists of qualified candidates are graduate students who studied at the most elite universities, who are recommended by the most eminent people in their field, and who were encouraged to apply, in many cases, by members of the hiring faculty. From the outset, then, the search process does not focus on candidates' individual qualifications, as the ideology of meritocracy would have us believe. Instead it focuses on institutional prestige. A graduate department's reputation becomes the proxy for a candidate's potential.

To aggravate the problem of reliance on institutional sources of merit in preliminary evaluations of candidates, faculties tend to rely heavily on the source of the recommendations that accompany an applicant's file. Because recruiting faculties cannot evaluate autonomously a candidate's record in light of conflicting or unclear standards, the nature and the source of an applicant's supporting letters become important. While they testify to candidates' abilities and potentials, they also locate the candidates in important disciplinary networks or exclude them from those networks. Thus Caplow and McGee argue that "personal influence among networks of colleagues" is the most important carrier of the prestige that really counts.[19] This suggests that the academic market is not an objective, competitive system based on merit but a system of "sponsored mobility" in which patronage from established scholars at elite institutions is a key factor in determining who makes the short list.[20]

In this context blacks seem to suffer more acutely because they lack the momentum generated by initial privilege. Blacks have severe difficulties in conquering the personal and institutional barriers they face in their quest for academic success. In the demography of higher education, they are more likely to attend the least prestigious and least elite institutions of advanced training. A 1977 report of the National Academy of Sciences states that blacks are least likely to earn their Ph.D.'s from the top-rated institutions and that the proportion of degrees earned by blacks from the top tier is less than the proportion of total degrees granted to blacks.[21] Recent evidence shows that this is still the case; blacks continue to be found in less prestigious graduate departments.[22] If graduation from top institutions is a prerequisite even for consideration by search committees in major colleges and universities, it is clear that blacks will be excluded systematically from short lists and ultimately from employment.

In view of these past findings, we address the following questions here: Are there any differences in quality among black graduate students in variously ranked graduate institutions? Do the backgrounds of these students differ, so as to confirm the notion that students from better institutions also come from more advantaged backgrounds? Do students from variously ranked graduate schools differ in aspirations regarding successful careers?

These questions test directly the assumptions that undergird present-day academic searchers. To the degree that we find differences in the present study, the current search process may well be the best way to identify minority talent. To the degree that we do not find such differences, we argue that the search process may affect blacks unfairly by overlooking an important source of black scholarly resources in nonelite institutions of graduate training.

Methods

Data Sources

Data used in this essay come from surveys administered to participants in the National Study of Black College Students. From 1981 through 1985 the NSBCS collected data on black undergraduates, graduates and professional students who attended eight predominantly white state-supported universities. Separate questionnaires were administered to graduate and professional students and to undergraduates. The instrument gathered comprehensive information on the respondents' background, achievements, experiences, attitudes and aspirations.[23] For more details about the methods, sample and data see Allen et al.'s *College in Black and White*.[24]

Sample

Our sample consists of all graduate and professional school students enrolled in the universities that contributed to the NSBCS in 1981 and 1982. Institutions that participated in this study were chosen on the basis of regional representations, diversity in the proportion of black enrollment, and accessibility of data and school records. Participants were the University of Michigan at Ann Arbor; Eastern Michigan University; the University of Wisconsin at Madison; the University of

North Carolina at Chapel Hill; Memphis State University; Arizona State University; the University of California at Los Angeles; and the State University of New York (SUNY) at Stony Brook. We drew a simple random sample of black students from computerized lists of graduate and professional students provided by each school's registrar. The overall response rate was 43 percent. The sample consists disproportionately of first-year graduate students and professional students.[25] We combined the 1981 and 1982 data sets primarily because of the small number of respondents in each year who attended schools in the lowest-ranked category. Without combining the two data sets we risked having too few cases in the lowest rank of colleges to make meaningful comparisons. (We discuss the basis for institutional ranking below). Our sample consists of 387 students from the top rank of universities, 224 students from the middle rank and 122 students from the lower group, a total of 733 students.

A potential problem arises from combining data sets from two separate years. There is a possibility that respondents from each year have different histories. The subjects from both years, however, are distributed throughout the three ranks. This situation compensates for any bias that may occur because our analyses are conducted across rather than between years.[26]

Variables

We used a performance-based model to examine the issues of quality differences among black graduate students. What skills are necessary for success in academia? What factors are academic search committees likely to examine? Four factors come to mind. First, we considered the student's academic performance as measured by grade point average. Outstanding grades indicate that a student has mastered the necessary coursework and subsequently has obtained the skills, theoretical background and knowledge to do good work in an academic discipline.[27] Second, we looked at the receipt of fellowships, research assistantships and grants; this step is a precursor to the competitive process of securing the grants and the prized fellowships that are part of a successful academic career. Third, we noted the presentation of scholarly papers at conferences and professional meetings. Finally, we considered the publication of scholarly articles and books. A combination of these four factors constitute our indicator of quality.

Because the students in the NSBCS sample range from first-year graduate students to those in the process of writing a dissertation, it would be inappropriate to demand that first-year students meet the same standards in our measure of quality as fourth- or fifth-year students. Therefore we used a sliding scale that takes into account the natural history, the development and the maturation of students in graduate school. Because first-year students do little more than take courses, we weight the criteria they are most likely to meet—a high grade point average and the receipt of the fellowship or grant—more heavily for them than for more advanced graduate students. For third- and fourth-year students all the criteria are applicable; in these cases excellence is based on wider range of factors. Ideally we would like to factor into this formula the number of papers presented and articles published, but the data do not permit this elaboration.

Respondents' quality index scores (QUALITY), our dependent variable, range from a low of 0.5 to a high of 8.0. The formula for ascertaining each student's score on our quality index works as follows: a first-year student with a high grade point average and a research grant would receive a score of 4.5 (GPA > 3.0 [2.0] + grant [2.5] = 4.5), whereas a third-year student would receive a score of 3.5 for the same accomplishments (GPA > 3.0 [1.5] + grant [2.0] = 3.5). In this way we weight the scale to the length of our respondents' graduate careers. We also adapt this formula to the extremes of our scale, however. Extraordinary first-year graduate students with high grades, grants, publications and a paper presentation or two can surpass the 8.0 scale. In these circumstances we truncate their scores to 8. Certain respondents, primarily a few first-year graduate students, show no papers, grants of publications and have a grade point average below 3.0. To prevent their quality index score from receiving a value of zero, which would cause their cases to be dropped from the data analysis, we assign them a score of 0.5 in order to retain their cases. Table 2 presents our formula for creating the students' quality index scores.

Table 2. Construction of Values of Quality Index

Year in Program	GPA*		Grant**		Paper***		Publication***	
	>3.0	<3.0	Yes	No	Yes	No	Yes	No
First or second	2.0	.5	2.5	0	2.5	0	2.5	0
Third	1.5	.5	2.0	0	2.5	0	2.5	0
Fourth or fifth	1.0	.5	1.5	0	2.0	0	2.5	0

* Missing values were assigned the value for first year.
** Missing values were assigned the value for undergraduate grade point averages.
*** Missing values were assigned the value for no.

We created our university rank variable (RANK) by dividing the eight graduate training institutions from the NSBCS into three groups based on the national reputations of their graduate departments. The top group represents institutions which in our sample of schools, across every discipline, have highly ranked departments whose size and influence have made them traditional suppliers of faculty for other elite institutions. This group includes the universities of Michigan at Ann Arbor, Wisconsin at Madison, and North Carolina at Chapel Hill. The middle group contains institutions that are ranked nationally in particular departments but are not consistently as strong as those in the first group. This group includes the University of California at Los Angeles, Arizona State, and SUNY at Stony Brook.[28] The lowest-ranked group, which includes Memphis State and Eastern Michigan University, represents schools without national reputations and with relatively new graduate programs. These institutions, located for the most part in urban areas, developed most rapidly during the 1960s, when expansion in higher education was common. Although they have recruited high-quality faculty, they have yet to gain more than regional (and in some cases local) recognition as important institutions of graduate training.

In addition to these key variables we introduced into our analyses a series of individual and structural variables, traditionally related to academic achievement, in order to elaborate our model. These variables are student's gender (GENDER), marital status (MARITAL), presence of young children in the home (KIDS), father's educational (DADED) and occupational attainment (DADOCC), mother's educational (MOMED) and occupational attainment (MOMOCC), respondent's age at first full-time job (AGE), the type of first job (FIRST JOB), and the respondent's motivation to succeed in a chosen career (HUNGER).

Findings

Differences in Quality

We began our data analysis with a series of analyses of variance (ANOVA), which examined mean differences in quality index scores for students who attended differently ranked graduate institutions. The first ANOVA revealed that the average score on the quality measure for students from the lower-ranked schools (3.35) was only slightly lower than for those from middle- and top-ranked schools (3.51 and 3.59). Table 3 shows that the differences were not statistically significant.

The analyses of variance also showed that institutional differences are less important than certain individual attributes in predicting how well students will perform in graduate school. Two such important attributes are gender and marital status. As table 3 shows, men and married graduate students have higher mean scores on our index of quality than do women and single graduate students. Both gender and marital status differences in graduate students' performance are statistically significant (gender, $p < .0001$; marital status, $p < .05$). Overall, the analyses of variance show that high-caliber black graduate students are found not only in the highest-ranking institutions but also in the lower-ranked schools. Indeed, gender and marital status are better predictors of quality.

Differences in Background

Implicit in the academic search process is the assumption that the best and brightest black students attend the best universities and become the best Ph.D.'s. This assumption implies that the educational attainment process for blacks in academia is similar to that for whites. The evidence regarding white students reveals a strong relationship among family background, academic achievement and the prestige of the university.[29] Thus the better white students are likely to come from more privileged backgrounds and to attend better graduate schools. Can we find evidence of this educational attainment process in our sample of black graduate students? If the same social forces are at work, we should find that the very best black graduate scholars come from more affluent families and are trained at the most elite research institutions. This is not the case, however.

Among black students at the variously ranked schools, the parents' educational and occupational backgrounds can be quite diverse (see Table 3). For example, the mean educational level of the mothers and fathers of students from the highest- and lowest-ranked graduate schools in our study are virtually the same (2.93 versus 2.95 for father's education and 3.10 compared to 3.00 for mother's education). Black students attending the middle-ranked schools appear to come from social backgrounds in which the parents are less well-educated and hold lower-status jobs than parents of blacks from both lower- and higher-ranked schools.

Black graduate students from all social backgrounds appear to attend a variety of graduate schools, possibly because the paths to graduate education taken by blacks differ markedly from those traditionally taken by middle-class white males. Blacks do not necessarily take the usual four years of baccalaureate work and then enter graduate school directly, as demonstrated by the work experiences of the graduate students in our sample. Students from the lowest-ranked universities worked full time at a much earlier age (18.91) than did students from either the middle or high category (20.72 and 20.40). Furthermore, they were likely to have less prestigious first jobs than their counterparts at more elite universities (p = <.05). Yet the marked differences in students' family backgrounds do not seem to affect their quality index scores. It becomes increasingly clear that black students differ minimally in terms of our measure of faculty potential across graduate training institutions.

Motivational Differences

Inherent in the notion that the best students train at the most prestigious universities is the assumption that students at elite universities are the most highly motivated, and therefore aspire to higher accomplishments in their chosen fields. To learn whether this difference exists among graduate students in our sample we examined an item related to this theme that appeared in the NSBCS. Students were asked the following question: "After you are in the profession which will be your life's work, when do you think you will be able to consider yourself successful enough so that you can relax and stop trying so hard to get ahead?" Students could choose one of five answers, which ranged from "when you are doing well enough to stay in the profession" (scored 1) to "when you are recognized as one of the top persons in the profession" (scored 5). We are labeled this the "hunger for success" questions: How hungry are these students to achieve at the highest levels possible? According to assumptions inherent in the evaluation of graduate students for jobs in the market today, the hungriest students are assumed to be found at the most elite institutions.

The data, however, demonstrate that for our sample the students from the most elite or most prestigious graduate programs are no more likely to be hungry for success than those from less prestigious universities. Although not statistically significant, mean hunger scores for students from the less highly ranked schools are higher (3.88) than for students at the most highly ranked schools (3.60). Once again, there is no evidence to support the notion that black academic resources, in the form of highly motivated black graduate students, are found exclusively in a narrow group of elite universities.

Table 3. Summary of Means and Standard Deviations of Selected Variables

Dependent Variable	N	Mean	Standard Deviation	F
Student Quality Index				.492
High rank	387	3.51	2.16	
Medium rank	224	3.59	2.11	
Low rank	122	3.35	2.23	
Student Quality Index				10.48***
Male	320	3.80	2.28	
Female	413	3.28	4.14	
Student Quality Index				4.28*
Single	427	3.37	4.53	
Married	219	3.74	5.01	
Father's Education (1 to 6 scale)				4.13**
High rank	375	2.93	1.48	
Medium rank	219	2.59	2.12	
Low rank	118	2.95	2.20	
Mother's Education (1 to 6 scale)				9.79***
High rank	386	3.10	1.31	
Medium rank	221	2.67	1.32	
Low rank	126	3.00	1.34	
Father's Occupation (Duncan SEI)				.82
High rank	345	40.40	28.75	
Medium rank	194	36.18	26.17	
Low rank	106	42.30	28.75	
Mother's Occupation (Duncan SEI)				1.47
High rank	338	40.51	24.94	
Medium rank	179	36.64	24.04	
Low rank	110	39.74	24.44	
Age at First Job				10.42***
High rank	285	20.40	9.78	
Medium rank	197	20.72	9.40	
Low rank	92	18.91	14.02	
Occupation Prestige of First Job (Duncan SEI)				5.57*
High rank	243	51.95	21.18	
Medium rank	151	56.11	17.31	
Low rank	106	42.34	28.75	
Motivation to Succeed ("Hunger")				1.159
High rank	222	3.60	2.25	
Medium rank	127	3.61	1.91	
Low rank	76	3.88	1.51	

*p = < .05

** p = < .01

*** p = < .001

Conclusions and Policy Implications

The racial crisis in higher education demands renewed efforts to eliminate institutional racism wherever it is located. This goal cannot be reached, however, without attention to faculty. Reasons to increase the number of minority faculty members include issues of employment equity for minority Ph.D.'s, the role of minority faculty in the enrollment, retention, achievement, persistence and graduation of minority students, and the necessity for the full and unfettered participation in American society by all of its members if this nation is to survive economically, socially and spiritually. This situation can come about only if every college student learns from a professoriate that reflects the racial, ethnic, gender and class diversity of the entire society.[30]

One policy used widely to increase the number of minority faculty members is affirmative action. Yet even the most rigorously enforced affirmative action programs have limitations because greater numbers of minority faculty per se are not their direct goal. Rather their primary objective is to open up the recruitment process by advertising widely and stating explicitly the employers' nondiscriminatory intentions. Affirmative action programs have been relatively unsuccessful in increasing the proportion of minority faculty in this country precisely because of the way in which qualified candidates are identified, screened and selected for the short list, the points at which affirmative action policies are relevant and operate most directly. An affirmative action policy is of little value if no minority candidates are selected for the short list.

In this essay we have attempted to examine critically an assumption that undergirds the traditional academic search process; we believe that this assumption reduces the likelihood that minority candidates will appear on the short list from which new faculty members are hired. Faculty members charged with securing a new colleague often rely on so-called proven categories of evaluation to assess potential candidates, namely the ranking of a candidate's graduate department and the recommendations of prestigious, influential, well-known scholars. In this initial screening the candidate himself or herself is not an issue; the school and the referee's reputation are used as proxies for the applicant's merit. To the degree that members of minorities are found less often at top institutions and are left out of prestigious patronage networks, the "institution as proxy" process tends to exclude qualified black candidates from reaching many short lists.

As our research demonstrates, the assumption that the best black graduate students are found only at the most elite, most prestigious colleges is unfounded. The assumption that quality rises to the top may reflect some truth in the case of blacks and other minority students, but such an assumption is flawed in the case of blacks and other members of minorities who continue to meet barriers to obtaining the prerequisites for higher education, and to higher education itself. Because of family obligations, community ties, hostile social and racial climates on elite campuses, inadequate social and psychological support systems at leading schools or limited financial support, well-qualified minority groups members may enroll in a wide variety of schools rather than following the path that leads to elite universities. The data we present in this essay suggest that one direct strategy to increase the number of minority faculty members is for recruitment committees to cast their nets more widely. This process will entail a critical assessment, and ultimately the rejection, of traditional reliance on institutional proxies (such as departments' reputation and referees' prestige) as indicators of minority candidates' potential.

A second strategy to make better use of the minority academic resources found in nonelite universities is the greater use of postdoctoral training programs at elite universities. These programs can be designed to provide black scholars with some of the resources to which they allegedly had limited access during their training in lesser schools. Minority Ph.D.'s can then become stronger candidates for positions at the university where they take their postdoctoral training or in the job market in general. In this way universities can assess for themselves whether a candidate from a lower-ranked school has the abilities, aptitude and skills necessary to contribute to the discipline at the highest levels.

We offer our research as a preliminary examination of this aspect of the minority faculty crisis in higher education. This study suffers from several problems, however. First, the sample of respondents relies too heavily on professional and first-year graduate students, and the sample of schools from which the subjects are drawn is not completely representative of all universities. Perhaps if we had included in our sample the most prestigious and most elite institutions, such as Harvard and Yale, the University of Chicago and Stanford, we would have found significant differences in our measure of students' quality. Moreover, problems always arise when researchers attempt to quantify or operationalize concepts such as student quality. Our dependent variable assumes that grades across institutions are equivalent. The results might have been different if we had controlled for the discipline or for the number and quality of the respondents' articles and presentations. Yet even with these flaws we submit this research as evidence that fresh, new, black academic talent is not isolated in prestigious graduate programs but is dispersed broadly throughout higher education. Future research into this topic must address these problems.

The issue at stake here is the subtle institutional racism inherent in the faculty recruitment and search process. Access to top research institutions and to eminent professors, whose reputations in turn attract the interest of search committees, is not yet free of discrimination. Thus to rely primarily on these criteria as the test of merit for new black scholars is essentially a racist practice. As long as "sponsored mobility" and attendance at premier institutions of higher education remains proxies for individual quality, the underutilization of minority talent will continue, as will the minority faculty crisis in higher education.

Notes

1. Walter C. Farrell, Jr. and Cloyzell K. Jones, "Racial Incidents in Higher Education: A Preliminary Perspective," *Urban Review* 20 (1988): 211–30.

2. Scott Heller, "Scholars Defend Their Efforts to Promote Literature by Women and Blacks, Decry Attack by Bennett," *Chronicle of Higher Education* 34 (February 17,1988): A1; Scott Heller, "Stanford Professors to Vote on Altering Freshman Reading List," *Chronicle of Higher Education* 34 (February 17, 1988): A13. And Stanley Aronawitz and Henry A. Giroux, "Schooling, Culture, and Literacy in the Age of Broken Dreams: A Review of Bloom and Hirsch." *Harvard Educational Review* 58 (may 1988): 172–94.

3. National Center for Educational Statistics (NCES), *Digest of Educational Statistics* (Washington, DC: Government Printing Office, 1988); "Shortage of Black Professors Is Forecast," *Chronicles of Higher Education* 35 (April 27, 1988): A23; Debra E. Blum, "Tenure for Black Professors Found to Lag at White Institutions in Nine Southern States," *Chronicle of Higher Education* 35 (September 21, 1988) A1; Howard R. Bowen and Jack H. Schuster, *American Professors: A National Resource Imperiled* (New York: Oxford University Press, 1986); Martin J. Finkelstein, *The American Academic Profession* (Columbus: Ohio University Press, 1984); Robert J. Menges and William H. Exum, "Barriers to the Progress of Women and Minority Faculty," *Journal of Higher Education* 54 (1983): pp. 123–44.

4. Bowen and Schuster, *American Professors;* Finkelstein, American *Academic Profession;* Neil Smelser and Robin Content, *The Changing Academic Market Place* (Berkeley: University of California Press, 1980).

5. Philip G. Altbach, "Stark Realities: The Academic Profession in the 1980's and Beyond," in *Higher Education in American Society*, rev. ed., eds. P. G. Altbach and R. O. Berdahl (Buffalo: Prometheus Books, 1980).

6. Walter R. Allen, Edgar G. Epps and Nesha Z. Haniff, eds., *College in Black and White: Black Students on Black and White Campuses* (Albany: SUNY Press, in press).

7. The *Adams case, Adams v. Califano,* Civil Action No. 3095-70, U.S. District Court, Washington, DC, was first heard in 1971 and continues in the federal courts today. The case is directed at the integration of public university student bodies in several states, primarily but not exclusively in the South. Over the last eighteen years, however, the many rulings in this case have alluded to faculty integration as a necessary component of institutional changes that will facilitate and solidify the integration of student bodies. (Telephone conversation between Roslyn Mickelson and Richard Robinson, Special Assistant to the President for Legal Affairs, The University of North Carolina, July 13, 1989.) The degree to which university faculties remain segregated is discussed in Denise K. Magner, "Nineteen Private Colleges Offer Fellowships to Minority Scholars," *Chronicle of Higher Education* 35 (December 14, 1988): A13.

8. The fact that data on minority faculty are difficult to obtain reflects the magnitude of the crisis. The situation of minority faculty in higher education has yet to become the object of widespread scholarly inquiry either by university, governmental or institutional researchers. For example, data on faculty members' race by rank in the most recent volume of the *Digest of Educational Statistics* consist of one table. Moreover, the data for this table come from an unpublished 1983 Equal Employment Opportunity Commission data set. As this essay goes to press, the U.S. Department of Education has begun to analyze data from the first-of-its-kind study of faculty members' race in higher education, the National Survey of Postsecondary Faculty. Academic researchers are no more likely than the government to pursue this issue, however. As Melvin L. Oliver and James H. Johnson, Jr. note in their article, "The Challenge of Diversity in Higher Education," *Urban Review* 20 (1988): 139–46, and as Ursula Elisabeth Wagener argues in her review essay, "Quality and Equity: The Necessity for Imagination," *Harvard Educational Review* 59

(May 1989): 241, most recent books on higher education still fail to address adequately the responsibilities of institutions of higher education to recruit and educate disadvantaged students. And greater numbers of minority faculty are crucially important if universities are to achieve these goals.

9. Joanell Porter (American Department of Education) reported these estimates from the unreleased National Survey of Postsecondary Faculty to Mickelson in a telephone conversation, July 3, 1989.

    Although books such as Alexander Astin's *Minorities in American Education* (San Francisco: Jossey-Bass, 1982), Michael Olivias's *Latino College Students* (New York: Teacher's College Press, 1986), and Jacqueline Fleming's *Blacks in College* (San Francisco: Jossey-Bass, 1984) address the issue of minority students, the corpus of research in higher education—with few exceptions—almost ignores the issue of minority faculty. Institutional researchers also generally fail to address the racial crisis in higher education faculty. For example, according to Maryse Eymoneri, consultant to the American Association of University Professor (AAUP) (phone conversation with Roslyn Mickelson, June 5, 1989), the AAUP collects data on faculty members' gender by rank but not by race. The Higher Education Research Institute (HERI) will launch its first survey ascertaining faculty members' race and ethnicity in fall 1989 (phone conversation between Mickelson and Guadalupe Anaya of HERI, June 15, 1989). We present these details to illustrate the depth of the problem, which we hope this volume will address.

10. Barry Beckham, ed., *The Black Student's Guide to College*, 2nd ed. (Providence: Beckham House Publishers, 1984).

11. Fleming, *Blacks in College*; Patricia Gurin and Edgar Epps, *Black Consciousness, Identity, and Achievement* (New York: John Wiley, 1975).

12. Michael W. Hirschorn, "Doctorates Earned by Blacks Decline 26.5 Percent in Decade," *Chronicle of Higher Education* 35 (February 3, 1988): A1; William Trombley, "Faculties Still Largely White," *Los Angeles Times* (July 6, 1986), p. A34. Actually, both the absolute number and the proportion of total doctorates awarded have declined more drastically for whites than for minorities during this period. According to the *Digest of Educational Statistics* (1988) the proportion of doctorates awarded to foreign students has increased steadily during the last decade.

13. NCES, *Digest of Educational Statistics*.

14. Smelser and Content, *Changing Academic Market Place*.

15. Nathan Glazer, *Affirmative Discrimination* (New York: Basic Books, 1978); Thomes Sowell, *Affirmative Action Reconsidered: Was it Necessary in Academia?* (Washington, DC: American Enterprise Institute, 1975).

16. Dorothy M. Gilford and Joan Snyder, *Women and Minority Ph.D.s in the 1970's: A Data Book* (Washington, DC: National Research Council, 1977); Troy Duster, "The Structure of Privilege and Its Universe of Discourse," *American Sociologist* 11 (May) 73–78; Lionel S. Lewis, *Scaling the Ivory Tower* (Baltimore: Johns Hopkins University Press, 1975); Bowen and Schuster, *American Professors*; Finkelstein, *American Academic Profession*.

17. William H. Exum, "Climbing the Crystal Stair: Values, Affirmative Action and Minority Faculty," *Social Problems* 30 (1983) 383.

18. Theodore Caplow and Reece McGee, *The Academic Marketplace* (New York: Basic Books, 1958); Finkelstein, *The American Academic Profession*; Smelser and Content, *Changing Academic Market Place*.

19. Caplow and McGee, *Academic Marketplace*, p. 120.

20. Ralph H. Turner, "Sponsored and Contest Mobility and the School System" *American Sociological Review* 25 (1960) 855–67.

21. Gilford and Snyder, *Women and Minority Ph.D.s*, p. 18.

22. Exum, "Climbing the Crystal Stair," p. 385.

23. Walter R. Allen, Angela Haddad and Mary Kirkland, *Preliminary Report: Graduate and Professional Survey* (Ann Arbor, MI: NSBCS, University of Michigan, 1982).

24. Allen, Epps and Haniff, *College in Black and White*.

25. Allen, Haddad and Kirkland, *Preliminary Report*.

26. We conducted parallel analyses with the graduate, professional and combined (graduate and professional) students with virtually identical results. We report the findings from the analysis that use the combined data set because of the greater statistical power in the larger sample.

27. Comparing grades across institutions is always difficult for researchers who seek a reliable indicator of performance. The question of whether an A from a top-tier institution means the same thing as an A from

a lesser school is beyond the scope of this essay. Used as the sole indicator of graduate students' quality across institutions, GPA might be problematic. Yet because grades are only one of the elements that constitute the quality index, we believe that the measure is sufficiently reliable to test our hypothesis.

28. Although some readers may question the placement of UCLA in the second tier of universities in this sample, many observers may be unaware of the commuter character of the Westwood campus. The effects of this character on the academic climate of graduate education militates against the intense form of graduate training that takes place in university communities such as Ann Arbor, Madison or Chapel Hill. It is unfortunate that the NSBCS sample contains no other comparable commuter campuses. Yet in view of the range of schools available in that sample, it is clear that from this perspective, UCLA does not belong in the top tier.

29. Denise Gottfredson, "Black and White Differences in the Educational Attainment Process," *American Sociological Review* 46 (1981) 448–572.

30. Michele N. K. Collison, "Neglect of Minorities Seen Jeopardizing Future Prosperity," *Chronicle of Higher Education* 34 (May 25, 1988) A1, A20; Astin, *Minorities in American Higher Education*, p. 205; Fleming, *Blacks in College.* And Melvin L. Oliver, Consuelo J. Rodriquez and Roslyn A. Mickelson, "Black and Brown in White: The Social Adjustment and Academic Performance of Chicano and Black Students in a Predominantly White University," *Urban Review* 17 (November 1985) 3–24.

A different version of this essay appears in College in Black and White: Black Students on Black and White Campuses, *Walter R. Allen, Edgar Epps and Nesha Haniff, eds. (in press, SUNY Press). The authors wish to thank Rodney D. Coates for his helpful comments on an earlier draft and Angela Detlev and Ginny G. Smith for their technical assistance in the preparation of this essay.*

PART IV
THE INSTITUTIONAL
LIFE OF FACULTY

INDIVIDUAL ISSUES

The Professor

To My Friend and Benefactor, Lorenzo the Insignificant

NICCOLITO MACHIAVELLI

How happy I am to hear, my friend, that you have set off on the long journey to become a professor. Don't be surprised if I am the only one to pass along felicitations. When I took a job on campus after graduation, I was greeted with nothing but expressions of disappointment and horror ("Oh, my God, not one of those witless hangers-on who winds up working in the alumni office"—my father). But you intend to become a true wanderer in the grove of academe—a professor—and I am so pleased for you.

It was many generations ago that one of my ancestors, Niccoló, wrote to one of yours, Lorenzo the Magnificent, about the intricacies of statecraft. Now I write to you regarding the stratagems of facultycraft. How fitting! In these past centuries, Niccoló's handbook of princely feint and parry has become as obsolete as its title. History ended not long ago—did you hear? Political power has oozed outward from the intense center of a single sovereign upon a throne to the flaccid fluctuations of millions of voters watching television from the BarcaLoungers. And, yet, there remains a place where a pinched intellect, a fisted heart, and the dread of elimination can still propel an ambitious soul toward a position of prestige: I speak, of course, of the faculty meeting. Its atmosphere is so petty because the stakes are so small—or so goes the maxim attributed to former professor Henry Kissinger (himself proof that the professor's stratagems and the prince's stage should never meet).

But are the stakes really that small? For the world, perhaps; for you, Lorenzo, they couldn't be greater. As one professor, who is a few monographs from tenure, told me: "Are you kidding? It's the last truly great deal. Tenure's the only feudal estate to survive the Renaissance—the modern equivalent of medieval knighthood. Look, pa, I've sat at the Big Table and supped from the cornucopia. I know what occult fruits lie deep in the horn: permanent employment, complete job security, total absence of responsibility, eternal income, abundant holidays, outdoor classes, and citizenship in a magical realm where adults act like kids and kids like adults. And I want more than anything in the whole wide world the chance to sit at that table from now until the end of my days, forever and ever. Amen."

And tenure is only where your new life begins. Matters great and small (mainly small) await you, Lorenzo. You are to become a professor, and when you don the elephant sleeves of your doctoral gown to parade in your first commencement, the epithet that has dragged behind you since childhood will suddenly lose its irony and become declaratively so. Thus, as a favor to you I have privately interviewed many of the best and most celebrated of your future peers to assemble for you, my patron, this humble, modest little (teeny-weeny, itsy-bitsy) booklet, The Professor.

I. How the Title of Professor is Acquired

Principally, the noble title is awarded after a six-year hazing ritual known as assistant professorship. Among the more progressive, trans-Mississippian campuses, the assistant professor is acknowledged in the halls with a suspicious grunt. In the traditional, cis-Mississippian colleges, the only difference between an assistant professor and a graduate student is orthographic.

II. On the Behavior of an Assistant Professor at a Meeting

At small colleges, the locus of power is called the faculty meeting; at large institutions, the maneuvers described below are best carried out in the departmental meeting. Power flourishes, according to one professor, wherever "there is a roomful of people, each of whom owns a piece of paper that says he or she is smart. This is the essential and lethal component."

Participation by junior faculty in such gatherings—even of the most unthreatening order—is considered impudence. On some campuses, junior faculty are encouraged to talk, but many assistant professors quite correctly suspect this generosity is a ruse to humiliate them. One full professor—normally a left-leaning, NPR-listening, celebrate-the-beautiful-mosaic gender-bender—found it "unthinkable" to listen to an assistant professor. "What do they have to say?"

An assistant professor at an Ivy League university, whispering unbulldoggishly from the shadows of gargoyles, offered these helpful hints:

> Remain silent unless your job is in danger or the room is on fire.
>
> Wear a somewhat glazed expression of otherworldly indifference on your face, as if you have just come from a conference with Edward Said and your mind is on far holier matters.
>
> Make significant, strategic eye contact with other nontenured faculty. Ferret out signs of dissidence (and diffidence), boredom, and tedium. These will serve as the foundation for future alliances.
>
> Don't sit too close to the front of the room or intervene in local concerns. Too many of my colleagues arrive late, looking like total wrecks. And they pipe up! I cast them withering glances and I think, *You fools! We are not fully limned individuals.* Junior faculty are invited to attend, but we're supposed to be like the glass flowers in the window boxes of the rare books library—things of beauty to behold, ornaments—nothing more.

III. How a Professor Can Raise or Lower the Chances for Tenure

Tenure is said to be connected to scholarship and achievement. True, and a presidential campaign is derived from constitutional principles. To procure tenure, said one professor of English at a state university (founded on Jeffersonian principles), one must comprehend the General Distribution of the Right to be Right. To wit: this professor arrived at a meeting bearing three irrefutably good ideas. One was approved immediately, but the other two were shelved amid mumbles. "I asked around about this peculiarity," the professor said, "and soon learned that no matter who you are, you can only be right a certain number of times." This number is arrived at by means of a complex formula that multiplies and divides one's rank, standing, publications, and personality. The formula itself is not reproducible, but over time a clever professor can instinctively produce its results as effortlessly as his own name. "Even if you are Socrates, you cannot be right all the time in a faculty meeting. And if you're an assistant professor with no books and no standing, you can barely afford to be right at all."

To acquire tenure, a professor must create the best conditions for this reward. In the words of this same professor:

> If you take to wearing two or three earrings and $1,500 worth of clothes, get your picture in the local paper, and drive an expensive car, then you'd better publish a lot of books and articles.

Whereas, if you wear really stupid shoes and an ugly plaid tie and adopt bad posture and kowtow to others, then three or four articles will do.

It's not that you can't get tenure being a confident, omnipresent media star teaching advanced sadomasochistic theory, but you've just upped the ante on what you have to do.

Coleridge said that poets create the standards by which they'll be appreciated. Well, assistant professors create the standards by which they'll be evaluated.

In doing so, the professor should heed the Principle of Sound Learning, first articulated a century ago by F. M. Cornford in his neglected masterpiece *Microcosmographia Academica*. This maxim assumes that "the noise of vulgar fame should never trouble the cloistered clam of academic existence. Hence, learning is called sound when no one has ever heard of it; and 'sound scholar' is a term of praise applied to one another by learned men who have no reputation outside the University, and a rather queer one inside it. If you should write a book (you had better not), be sure it is unreadable; otherwise you will be called 'brilliant' and forfeit all respect."

IV. How a Professor Can Obtain a Roomy, Well-Lighted, Book-Lined, Impressive Office

The very word "office" is enough to ignite in almost any professor eruptions of blubbering, harrumphing, and keening. Suffice it to say, Lorenzo, that none of the professors with whom I spoke neglected to mention it. The emblems of status are so scarce on a campus that almost any professor will lower his threshold of self-respect to the Joey Buttafuoco level when this subject comes up. Thus, ignominiously and irretrievably impelled, the most dignified professor will recast the most puerile plea—"I want to look important!"—into the absurdest euphemism—"I have an enormous computer for sorting out my vast collection of potsherds."

The surest path to a big office is a fat federal grant with plenty of indirect recovery costs (i.e., free money for the school). A professor at a university in a windy city won a gargantuan federal contract and was awarded a suite of mahogany-lined offices that glowed softly with the amber light reflected from the nearby lake. When the grant ran out, his suite was seized, his books boxed up and dispatched to library storage. In short order, this once proud man was shown a fourth-floor walk-up closet in an empty building six snowbound blocks from campus.

Since the scramble for office space is such a patently undignified matter to begin with, one can sometimes resort to shameless histrionics. A professor at a Palo Alto university remembered his arrival on campus. He'd already plied his chairman with every sort of entreaty to recognize his worth in hectarage: "I've got lots of books." "I entertain important visitors." "I've got *so many* potsherds. . . . " Nothing worked until, one night after his first year this professor (in his own words) "showed up quite drunk at the chairman's house and cried, 'My wife is going to leave me. She is moving back East with the children because I have all my books at home and she can't take it any longer.' This was a complete lie, by the way. But tears were streaming down my cheeks in front of *his* wife. She—she was southern—said, "You git thayat mayan a big awwfice bah tahmarruh, hunny, unnahstayand?' This is the level at which one must deal for an office, in the academy."

V. How a Professor Gets a Controversial Course into the Curriculum

The physical force of nature that drives change in a university is called inertia. Cornford associates this rare source of dynamism with the Principle of the Dangerous Precedent, which holds that "nothing should ever be done for the first time."

"On my campus," said one professor of science at cis-Mississippian university, "inertia is the administrators' most potent weapon against the faculty. They rarely schedule meetings—and they call it 'efficiency'. This is the way administrators lock us out of decisions. But stasis and impotence and languor can be turned to your advantage. If you want to teach a controversial course, just sign up for a gut and shape it into the course you want. They will *not bother* to intervene. Use their inert gaseousness against them."

Tradition-bound campuses require more delicate strategies. "The best tactic," said a professor of history, "is to propose the offending course as a one-time-only, just-this-semester special offering. This has a greater chance of passing through a recalcitrant committee. Once a course is in the curriculum, it is easier to renew and harder to kill. But there is work yet to do. At the end of the semester, explain that a certain number of students (make this up) have asked to take the course the following year. Also, present a sheaf of student evaluations lauding the course's breadth, rigor, and value. One can fill an accordion folder with this precious cargo by handing out the questionnaires the day after the wanton class banquet or on the morning of the final exam, which you cancel, because as you tell them, you know they are under a lot of pressure. Remember, the 'students' are to the faculty what the 'people' are to the politician—a wobbly fiction, yet utterly feared."

VI. How Rhetorical and Certain Oratorical Devices May Advantage the Professor

A faculty meeting is, according to legend, an assembly where reason prevails and principle is defended. But as in any human gathering, persuasion and perception matter more than syllogism and dialect. "A principle is a rule of inaction," Cornford warns, "which states a valid general reason for not doing in any particular case what, to unprincipled instinct, would appear to be right."

Remember these three handy absolutes: First, never be one of those who speaks at every gathering. No matter how clever you may be, you will be perceived as a crank and a fool. Second, don't bandy about beautiful rejoinders or clever turns of phrase. Others will resent your genius, and besides, to the average professor the rankest cliché falling from *his* lips rings as sonorously as the most freshly minted bon mot. Whereas, from yours . . . well, better not to put his innate generosity to the test. Third, if you have come with a compelling argument, allow the blabbermouths to sound off grandiloquently and early. Then present your position late in the game, close to the vote, when others will remember what you said.

The rhetoric of faculty meetings often devolves entropically into the declarative mood; at other times into *to quoque* arguments. But simple assertions of truth sound rude to the frail ears of professors and invite petty distinctions and fine-line arguments. Repair to the interrogative mode. As one professor of history, well known among his peers as a master of facultycraft, said:

> Never say to the president, 'Listen, you SOB, you promised us raises. . . . ' Many young professors mistake defiance for persuasion. No good. Instead, say: 'My memory may not be exactly correct on this, but I recall a statement about six-percent raises. I was wondering, will the other two-and-a-half percent be phased in, or has there been some unfortunate budgetary catastrophe?

A professor of English at a southern university (where students matriculate and Lentricchiate) also advocated the interrogatory approach: "It makes the answer to the question arise in the minds of others. They think *they* thought of it and will fight for that idea to the death." However, this professor added enigmatically, "The best strategy is to lose at basketball with Stanley."

VII. Showing a Professor/Chair/President to the Door: Three Variations

Indirection: The recent offing of an absentee president of an Ivy League school as widely portrayed as a simple resignation. Actually, it was a prime example of assassination by indirection, a stratagem commonly employed to rid a campus of an offending higher-up. This tactic compels the strategist to avoid a direct assault and to move, instead, against the offending superior's associates. Clausewitz and Sun-tzù would recognize this approach as the Attack to the Flank.

In this case, the young president had called for "restructuring," a *glasnostian* euphemism for dumping professors. Some professors went directly after the president in the news media. But this only won him sympathy from journalists (who instinctively toady to power and call it objectivity).

Other professors waited for an opening in the defense, and one fall it appeared.

The president's hatchet man was an abrasive dean. He was the kind of guy who publicly insulted his opponents and then whimpered that his enemies didn't appreciate his open and candid style. So long had his arrogance gone unchecked that he felt free to publish his Machiavellian scheme for undoing the humanities faculty in a magazine article. Adopting language that inevitably gave him away, the dean wrote of deploying this or that "weapon" against professors in the humanities. He suggested that administrators show preference to science because it is "the healthiest of the disciplines," thanks to its espousal of the "efficacy of reason" and the "possibility of truth." On the other hand, he said, "the woods are full of humanists," a "very funny bunch of guys" who don't teach but engage students in intellectual "mutual massage."

For some reason, the entire faculty did not cotton to the open and candid way in which the dean had depicted half the professors as intellectually sterile yahoos.

Several professors recognized an opening and put the article—not restructuring—on the next faculty meeting agenda. Attendance was the highest in memory, and the gathering had to be relocated to a larger room. For two hours, in what professors now refer to varyingly as the "roasting," the "massacre," and the "mayhem," the dean was sautéed in his own words. The humanities professors even objected to his pronouns, condemning the patronizing phrase "my faculty" in his writings.

Scientists attacked him for ignorance of their field's long acquaintance with Heisengergian uncertainty. The dean knew nothing of "the irrational aspect of science," a biophysicist declared—he made us sound like we slice off an inch of the salami of truth every day."

By the end of the evening, the faculty had issued a searing two-hour critique of the dean's reign—essentially a vote of no confidence—while the president watched in horror. By the end of the school year, the dean had resigned in a show of whining and pettiness. A month later, the president himself resigned—an entirely satisfactory outcome as far as many faculty were concerned. Except that he then embarrassed them, as one professor put it, by leaping to "the bosom of a third-rate media charlatan in search of some cheap prestige for his latest offering of educational snake oil."

Sabotage: "A popular tactic on my campus," said the professor from a windy city, "is to drive off a fellow professor by ruining his numbers. See, class enrollment—numbers like that—are important. Administrators make their intuitive decisions on whatever number they can grasp or grasp *at*, a subtle but critical distinction.

"So you counsel students not to take that professor's courses. It'll be a waste of time for *their* particular major, you say. You do this subtly, almost harmlessly.

"Then you edge the offending colleague out of staffing meetings. Assign him to poorly attended courses. Schedule other meetings when he is out of town. This will not only demoralize him: If it's done properly, he won't even know the source of his melancholy. Eventually, this handiwork will result in a merely mediocre pay raise—remember, those administrators are still measuring by the numbers. Soon he will feel isolated and hurt. He will send out feelers for a job offer from elsewhere to boost his stock. Meanwhile the dean knows the numbers (student enrollment is down, possibly he has attracted no good grants). When the professor presents his job offer to the dean for the usual counterproposal, he receives, instead, a "Hawaiian handshake.' This term refers to the fate of an unpopular professor who was offered a job by the University of Hawaii. When he went to the administration to use this offer as leverage for more money, the dean just shook his hand and said, 'Have a good time in Hawaii.' I have seen nontenured professors made to leave this way. Assiduously applied, this strategy can drive off a tenured professor as well."

Chaos: When affairs are moving against you, it is better to invite anarchy and churn the turbulence until an advantage arrives than to allow the mess to settle and set against you. The exploitation of chaos works only when you've got several confederates in your department and a few shills among the administrators. But, if you've been on campus longer than a single grading period, you will find that these people are already in place and awaiting your instructions.

A professor at a Far West university provided an exemplary tale of this popular technique:

> Our school was founded thirty years ago as a teaching college, so professors were hired merely to teach. After a burst of student enrollment not long ago, younger, more research oriented faculty were hired, and a ready-made split between teachers and scholars developed. The older folks outnumbered us and kept control, giving themselves raises and appointments. This was the source of the anarchy. In six semesters, I've seen five chairmen of my department. We learned how to eat them. But they are getting better, and *that's* the point.
>
> For example, one of the chairs had a habit of drinking just before meetings. And during one of them, he punched another professor. His defenders say he was putting his arm around him. But from where I stood, it looked like a slug. Anyway, he's gone.
>
> The next chair came in, and a memo war instantly broke out. People wrote vicious slurs and distributed them widely: 'How dare so-and-so talk about my work; he couldn't write his way out of a paper bag.'
>
> Then there were fistfights in the hall. Some professors were bailing out. Students were afraid to come up to the floor where our offices were. The dean intervened, forced the chair to quit, and brought in a professor from *another* department to serve as our chair. (Did I mention that I am not making this up?) He immediately ended the written war by announcing that the author of the next memo would be assigned 8 A.M. and 8 P.M. classes five days a week plus an 8 A.M. on Saturday. (Scheduling is a chair's only real power around here.)
>
> But one of the professors is also a state senator, and this is a state college, so for a while everyone thought she would use legislative power to settle matters for her side. But she had burned a lot of bridges. For example, when her graduate class asked to reschedule a final exam because it conflicted with another professor's exam, she said for all to hear, 'I wouldn't change a thing for that short, fat Persian.'
>
> The entire department is in receivership now, run by the dean. But things are looking up. We've found a chair who hasn't heard of us—but maybe that's because he's from Tasmania.
>
> Do you know that scene in *The Caine Mutiny* when the officers finally decide Queeg is completely insane? They all get together and visit the admiral's ship. When they get on board, they see this other ship is perfect. Everyone is stunning in dress whites. The deck is scrubbed, the sky blue. Everything is pristine, and the sailors are content. And Queeg's men realize they can't explain their situation because *no one will believe them*. They themselves will look crazy just by describing their situation. Do you know that scene? Have you watched the movie? Do you know that scene?

VIII. How One Professor Rose to College President and Pursued a Scorched-Earth Policy Against the Faculty: A Final Cautionary Tale

Most colleges endow their faculty with a little power to offset the administrative weight of the president. The most adept professor maneuvers between these two forces to gain resources for her department and honor for herself. ("Your best ally against the administration is the other faculty, and your best ally against the other faculty is the administration," reports one battle-scarred professor.) In Boston, however, on the less prestigious side of the Charles, is a university whose president has achieved a monstrous reputation for humiliating his faculty. Lorenzo, many were *afraid* to talk to me. At last, one survivor of the twenty-year Reign of Terror nervously agreed to speak. Although it has been years since he left, he was as shaken as a refugee newly escaped from some tyrannical land. As he told his story, he wheezed and honked in peristaltic breathlessness:

Oh, my. I remember when he first came. He isolated or destroyed all the faculty who were there. I was among the isolated. He had a business model for the university. Do you know it? There's a CEO. The junior officers have no power. NONE. And he was the CEO.

He drove the trustees to such distraction that many of them 'resigned in protest.' Soon the board was nothing but lickspittles.

He threw a monkey wrench into the system so that each professor had to sue the university for a pay raise. He drove out scores of professors by humiliation, degradation, and isolation. He told you your books were not worth the paper they were written on.

When he arrived, I was a prima donna, an exceedingly popular lecturer. He took away all the courses in which I starred. I was demoted from chairman of my department. I was removed from powerful committees. Some of us accepted this isolation and spent our new quiet time thinking beautiful thoughts, looking out at the lovely trees. But many couldn't deal with it and quit. One professor had a fatal heart attack, and his family blames the president outright.

It was like the Communist takeover of the Czech government in 1968. He wanted to get rid of *all* his predecessors. It didn't matter if you were good or bad. If you were *there* when he arrived, you were targeted—you could *remember* wielding power. He wanted to efface all our names from the triumphal arches.

And it worked: Suddenly you would see new dour faces, and *they* had power. The president had spies in the faculty meetings. Everything said in private was reported back to him. We wasted our days trying to figure out who the snitches were.

He made 'special appointments.' Then he would publicly announce how impressively they stood out among the drab fourth-rate minds of his tenured faculty. He would say that!

He was an incredibly intelligent, brilliant man. But he was also vicious, cruel, and loutish. I had always wondered what it was like to be a clerk at Woolworth's. How must if feel to be under the heel of a jerk, crushed by a petty boss? Well, he gave me a better understanding of the tragic sense of life.

You know, the committee that brought him in wanted to break with the past parade of presidents—each a piddly, Methodist, fuddy-duddy, goody-woody Milquetoast who forbade drinking at receptions. They wanted a university with balls! So they hired this tough guy, not anticipating the quality of mind of the Midwestern Protestant. Norman Mailer credits our walking on the moon to the same tight-lipped, invincible, inexorable, obsessive, Protestant zeal.

Well, that was this guy, and he targeted the very people who brought him in.

Now that the worst part of his reign is over, though, I wonder: By the middle of the twenty-first century, when we are all gone and he is dead, what will people say? They might say this man took an institution that was negligible in prestige and drawing power—a truly *tenth-rate* university—and made it second-rate. I often think of those ancient Egyptian peons pushing and dragging those huge stone blocks up the incline, every day, under the lash of Cheops. They were probably dreadfully unhappy and groused about the pharaoh. But now that all the slaves are dust and Cheops is dead, there, in the desert of Giza, is this pyramid, and, well, it's quite a pyramid, wouldn't you say?

Lorenzo, think of yourself as a pyramid builder. And know that if you follow all the advice contained here as diligently as you can, you will advance only from a peon who pushes to one who pulls. Maybe you figure that's not so great an achievement. Maybe you will ignore the secrets I have betrayed here. But when the giant stone block slips its tethers, where do you want to be?

With warmest personal regards,

Niccolito

Niccolito Machiavelli is a pseudonym for Jack Hitt, who is writing a book about the medieval road to Santiago, Spain. He is a contributing editor of Lingua Franca *and of* Harper's *magazine.*

Academic Careers

Tony Becher

Personality and Environment

In the preceding chapters, we have explored academic activity mainly in aggregative terms, tracing the common cultures, internal structures and modes of interaction of disciplinary tribes and their constituent networks. But just as there are new insights to be gained by moving from a broad to a narrow epistemological framework, so too there are benefits to be won in the social dimension from supplementing a conspectus of the large picture with a scrutiny of the small detail—the individual academics who might be labelled as the elementary particles of the intellectual world.

As one begins to speculate on the match between academic fields and the people in them, the familiar rivalry of nature against nurture manifests itself. Is it that particular kinds of people choose particular disciplines, or is it rather that disciplines shape and condition their adherents into becoming particular kinds of people? The classical escape route from most dilemmas is to repudiate them, arguing that the choices they pose are as false as they are stark. The claim in the present context must be that academic careers are subject to a range of causal factors, none of which can be shown as predominant in every case. The activities involved in the transmission and creation of knowledge, Ruscio (1987) writes, 'reflect individual preferences, disciplinary backgrounds and institutional imperatives' in a varied mix of ingredients. It is in the nature of the present study that the second of these should enjoy pride of place, since it is around the notion of disciplines that most of the evidence has been collected; something none the less needs briefly to be said about the first and third.

The relationship between personality and learning style is a longstanding topic of psychological enquiry. Some of the more recent research, including that reported by Wolfe and Kolb (1979), has a number of pertinent things to say. For one thing, it acknowledges more clearly than earlier work in the field that apparently homogeneous disciplinary categories may themselves embrace a fair amount of diversity. The Kolb-Wolfe review (drawing on a number of investigations of student learning styles, including Kolb's study of '800 practising managers and graduate students in management') remains cautious about the tendency discerned by Bereiter and Freedman (1962), 'of fields to attract people similar to those already in them':

> What these studies show is that undergraduate education is a major factor in the development of learning style. Whether this is because individuals are shaped by the fields they enter or because of selection/evaluation processes that put people into and out of disciplines is an open question at this point. Most probably both factors are operating—people choose fields that are consistent with their learning styles and are further shaped to fit the learning norms of their field once they are in it. When there is a mismatch between the field's learning norms and the individual's learning style, people will either change or leave the field.

In a more recent work, Kolb (1984) presses the argument further:

> For students, education in an academic field is a continuing process of selection and socialization to the pivotal norms of the field governing criteria for truth and how it is to be achieved, communicated, and used, and secondarily, to peripheral norms governing personal styles, attitudes and social relationships. Over time, these selection and socialization pressures combine to produce an increasingly impermeable and homogeneous disciplinary culture and correspondingly specialized student orientations to learning. . . . Students' developmental pathways are a product of the interaction between their choices and socialization experiences in academic fields such that choice dispositions lead them to choose educational experiences that match these dispositions, and the resulting experiences further reinforce the same choice disposition for later experiences.

Such claims are not inconsistent with, though they go a fair theoretical distance beyond, the observations about matches between personality types and subjects of study which I gleaned in my interviews. Although it was not part of my purpose to enquire into the private, as against the professional, lives of those I met, it was for example apparent from the incidental remarks they made that the physicists were inclined towards an interest in the theatre, art and music, whereas the engineers' typical leisure activities included aviation, deep-sea diving and 'messing about in boats'. The biologists , along with the historians, tended to the view that theirs was 'a discipline for loners'. Much as Evans-Pritchard (1951) had referred to anthropological fieldwork as requiring 'in addition to theoretical knowledge and technical training a certain kind of character and temperament, one of the physicists in my sample spoke of choosing a research area to match one's temperament, and another of picking a problem to suit one's personality; and a geographer observed that graduate students will usually have a good look at the mode of working as well as the content of subdisciplines, and make a selection on the basis of what they see as their own talents.

For undergraduates, the influence of the institution may be as strong as, if not stronger than, that of the discipline. As Parlett (1977), writing in the context of social psychology, reminds us:

> Everyday academic talk is full of statements such as 'he was a typical Balliol man'', or 'he absorbed the MIT philosophy', or 'the college made me what I am'. An individual's intellectual style, working habits, personal values, and even ways of speaking and mannerisms, may all be attributed to the lasting influence of his or her former place of education. Both in reminiscence and biography one finds a preoccupation with drawing out such connections.

Beyond the point of graduation, institutional influences remain, as has already been remarked in Chapter 4, a significant force in determining academic career chances. On the basis of nearly 150 interviews in a wide range of institutions with academics in physics, biology, political science, English, business studies and medicine, Ruscio (1987) concludes that 'the nature of research is determined in part by the organizational setting . . . other major influences . . . are its rationale or purpose and in the institutional attitudes towards it'. He shows convincingly how the interpretations of what research is, and the emphasis which is accorded to it, differ from one type of institution to another:

> Each sector seems to worship the god of research, but organized religion reflects the local culture. . . . At a leading research university, the demands for excellence in scholarship are apt to be precise and well understood. On the other hand, scholarship at a liberal arts college may be more broadly defined.

My study, concentrating as it did on élitist institutions, fully supported his contention about the strength of their research norms: virtually none of the people I interviewed—even the most junior postgraduate students—seemed in any doubt about the expectations placed on them. My findings also reinforced and elaborated his recognition (Ruscio 1987) that across the different disciplines there are different patterns, even within the same sector. It is the nature of those systematic differences which we shall now explore, as we follow though the main stages of the academic life-cycle.

Recruitment and the Choice of Specialisms

Disciplinary differences are evident at the very beginning of an academic career. In most subject areas it is now more or less obligatory to begin by acquiring a doctorate, but this is by no means the case in those applied, vocationally oriented disciplines in which the professional component is significant within academia as well as outside it. In pharmacy, as in the law, a professional qualification can only be acquired after at least a minimal period of practical experience in the field, and a majority of aspiring academics will choose the safety-net of becoming employable as working professionals before beginning to apply for posts within higher education. In engineering, the main motivation is different, though the outcome is the same: starting salaries in industry are so much more attractive than the financial prospects for a doctoral student that very few graduates are tempted to stay on at university. Recruitment to posts in engineering departments is therefore largely confined to those practising engineers who subsequently come to recognize the attractions of an academic life. It is understandable that in all such fields admittance to the relevant profession serves as at least an initial substitute for a doctoral degree—though the more ambitious academics, once appointed, make it their business to acquire a doctorate as well. The consequence is that in applied subjects, those entering the academic community tend to do so later in life than those in other disciplines (sometimes, in the case of mechanical engineering, at quite a senior level, in mid- to late career); that they may, atypically of academics at large, acquire tenured posts in élite institutions without a higher degree (in one leading law faculty in the early 1980s, there were only 5 members out of 32 with doctorates); and that, with some practical experience and professional contacts behind them, they may stand a good chance of augmenting their academic salaries with a reasonable amount of consultancy work.

For the rest, however, as the academic world has itself become more professionalized (Clark 1987a, 1987b), a doctorate has become a standard requirement, at least in the more élite institutions (only a negligible proportion of those I interviewed in hard pure and soft pure disciplines lacked such a handle to their names). It is therefore upon this rite of passage to the scholarly life that we shall for the moment concentrate attention.

In pure, as against applied, disciplines, a further series of broad distinctions emerges between the hard and the soft. In both alike, as has already been indicated in Chapter 4, it is prudent for the novitiate to seek out the most prestigious available department in his or her field (since this will serve to enhance initial research visibility), and to attach himself or herself to the most prestigious available research supervisor (since the benefits of patronage, at least in acquiring one's first paid job, are generally agreed to be more than negligible). There are certain trade-offs even here, since departmental prestige will no more guarantee a good match for a given individual's needs than will an eminent mentor necessarily have time to spare for providing the ideal amount of guidance and support. However, when the initial engagement is being negotiated between a successful applicant (the quality of whose first degree is, at this stage, though not so much later, an important consideration) and a potential supervisor, the extent of available choice of research topic is significantly different from one knowledge area to another.

Generally speaking, the stronger the contextual imperative, the less scope there is for negotiation over the subject matter of the doctoral thesis; the weaker the contextual association, the greater the latitude of decision allowed to the candidate. There are two related reasons for the constraints in hard pure settings. First, it is quite common for a graduate student to be taken on as a junior member of the supervisor's research team, and to be expected to carry out the task or tasks allocated to the team leader; secondly, the student, being relatively unfamiliar with the field, will not usually be in a good position to judge which problems or parts of problems are both relevant to current developments and at least in principle amenable to solution within the time-span of a doctoral programme. One of the requirements of a good supervisor, in subject areas of this kind, is to be able readily to supply newcomers with topics which are neither too easy nor too hard to meet the requirements, while at the same time ensuring a useful contribution to the work of the group as a whole.[1] Few such restrictions obtain in knowledge domains where the choice of theme is virtually unlimited, where a theme, once chosen may be addressed in a diversity of ways and at a variety of levels of sophistication, and where the norm (at least at the doctoral stage) is for individual rather than group research.

Research groups in laboratory-based and field-based sciences are for the most part closely knit, so that group leaders will tend to have regular weekly (and occasionally even daily) contact with their doctoral students, and will thus be quite strongly involved in guiding and overseeing their work. At the other extreme, a lone doctoral candidate working on, say, a relatively narrow topic in eighteenth-century history or the interpretation of a hitherto-neglected text in Renaissance Italian literature can expect nothing like the same degree of collective, corporate activity or close supervisory attention. Levels of contact between student and supervisor may vary over time, being generally more intense early and late in the evolution of the thesis; but monthly or less frequent sessions, interspersed with lengthy bouts of solitary reading and writing, are the common pattern.

This contrast throws up another, more complex and subtle distinction. There are some fields in which it is not unusual for a doctoral student to produce a paper of publishable standard. When it appears in print, there are certain disciplines or specialisms within disciplines in which it will be routinely expected to bear the name of the research supervisor as joint author. Various grounds for this practice were put forward by respondents, both in those disciplines where the practice is widespread (chemistry notable among them) and in those in which it is more patchy. One justification is that since the supervisor chose the topic and had a close hand in its resolution, he or she is rightly entitled to a share of the credit. ('The top man doesn't own the workers body and soul, but he does own the products of their labour.') One respondent compared it with the levying of a tithe by a landlord from his tenants; others saw it as a kindly way of giving the student the leg up by association with a more prestigious author, or as a way of underwriting the quality of a piece of work whose value it would otherwise be difficult to assess; whereas those who chose not to adopt the practice—or who were at its receiving end—confessed themselves embarrassed by its exploitative overtones and its implication that research students were 'slave labour' or 'cannon fodder'.

Much as standard lengths of articles differ between one knowledge domain and another, what is required in the way of a PhD thesis will vary from an occasionally highly concise proof of a significant theorem in mathematics to a treatise running to 300 or more typewritten pages on a topic in the humanities. Somewhere in the middle, even the more prestigious departments of economics will now allow a doctoral award for three scholarly papers published in a refereed journal or judged to be of comparable standard, one of which may be jointly authored with the research supervisor. This, it is argued, is more in keeping with the current professional research norms in the discipline than is the conventional lengthy and monolithic doctoral dissertation.

These considerations make it plain that even in their initial stages, the lines of academic development may vary substantially from one knowledge area to another; that there is no such thing as a standard career pattern which spans the range of intellectual activity. The claim, as we shall see, is borne out unequivocally in all the subsequent phases of the life-cycle.

The Achievement of Independence

Because the job market and the disciplinary traditions bear differently upon different subject areas, it will take longer in some than in others to become launched on an autonomous career as a scholar or researcher in an élite institution. In those disciplines in which there is a strong pattern of team activity, along with the availability of substantial grant funding—team activity, along with the availability of substantial grant funding—largely, that is, the pure sciences, together with some hard applied areas (notably medical and paramedical research)—the intending academic may be expected to occupy 3 years or more in the limbo of a postdoctoral research post before being offered a job leading to tenure. While this is regarded in some fields as useful further experience, it is essentially a period of marking time in career terms. Except in periods of expansion, it does not in any way guarantee a tenure-track post in a prestigious department. Even among those aspirants who survive the postdoctoral stage, many will end up in teaching jobs with few if any research opportunities, or in posts outside academia. Postdocs enjoy more independence and more responsibility than doctoral students, but they are still essentially what one non-scientist, critical of the system, regarded as an army of 'hired hands and dogsbodies.'[2] dependent largely on the goodwill of their seniors. Lacking the necessary institutional standing, they cannot in many universities supervise research students or apply for grants in their own names: they are not fully-fledged freemen in the scholarly community.

The academic career proper begins—in disciplines having a postdoctoral tradition, as in those that lack one—with a salaried but usually untenured and probationary appointment on the lower rungs of the promotion ladder (an already mentioned exception being through recruitment to more senior ranks on the basis of outside professional experience). The provenance of the first regular post is important, since it is less usual to move up the scale from a lower-ranking institution than it is to move down from a higher-ranking one. Let us, however, at this point, focus on the early research career of a successful survivor of the various initial hurdles, typically someone with a good first degree and a doctorate—both preferably acquired from well-regarded departments in leading institutions—together with, where appropriate, a spell of postdoctoral work in a group run by a well-known researcher.

Since my central concern is with the creation and development of knowledge rather than with its transmission, I will do no more than mention here the paradox that the standard route to a research career is through what is formally a teaching appointment, while a research post as such, except at the highest level, carries little status and no long-term prospects of advancement. It is none the less important to recognize that the common pattern in UK and US higher education—though it is not so pronounced in other national systems—is for elite researchers to have teaching obligations as well. These will often be quite substantial in the period before tenure is granted, so rendering it harder than it might otherwise be to make a major research contribution in early academic life.

The requirement to teach places a high premium on the choice of both an initial research specialism and a particular topic within it. To gain the early visibility commonly associated with a strong professional reputation, a budding researcher needs to concentrate the available research time, i.e. the time which remains after the necessary teaching commitments have been met, on an area of activity that is capable of yielding significant results in a reasonably short period. The selection of this activity is arguably the most strategic decision which faces academics in the initial stages of their careers.[3]

We shall need to distinguish more sharply at this point between a specialism and a specific research topic. Although the beginnings of a specialized interest may sometimes be traced back to the late undergraduate phase, intellectual identities necessarily become more pronounced in the course of choosing and pursuing a doctoral topic. Some individuals may stay with, or close to, their initial choice of specialism for the rest of their lives, selecting a series of research problems which continue to fall within it. On the whole, however, as we shall see in the next section, a strong academic reputation may depend on a reasonable degree of mobility between different specialist areas.

One of the most prized assets of an appointment to a tenure track academic post—identified as such by respondents in each of the 12 disciplines covered by my inquiry—is the perceived freedom to choose the subject matter of one's research. In reality, that freedom is hedged about by constraints—including the lack of necessary resources, the scarcity of time, and in some contexts the absence of incentives. None the less, the degree of autonomy, and in particular the liberty to determine the intellectual issues with which one wishes to engage, is held to be significantly greater than it would be in other walks of life.

The scope for matching activities to temperaments has already been noted. That scope is enhanced by the considerable variety of types of research on offer within virtually every discipline. The individual specialisms an apparently homogenous subject area embraces will often span the continuum from hard to soft modes of investigation. To give only a few examples, the quantitatively inclined historian may be free to register a commitment to economic or demographic history; the modern linguist may choose between the well-hedged confines of philology and the open pastureland of interpretive criticism; the economist may espouse the mathematical rigour of pure theory or the less easily tamed complexity of the labour market; the mechanical engineer may select from a menu which includes the creative uncertainties of design as well as the numerical precision of studies in fluid mechanics; the biologist may opt between the narrow and relatively certain worlds of taxonomy or microbiology and the broad and unpredictable studies of particular species or habitats; the physicist may escape the urban demands of research into particles or solid state by choosing to investigate such comparatively rural areas as meteorology, relativity or gravitation. The option may not of course be an entirely open one. Echoing a point made earlier in this chapter, one of my informants remarked that 'literature and linguistics demand different mind sets—once could view the choice between them as being temperamentally determined'.

Although a commitment to a given discipline does not dedicate one irrevocably to a specific pattern of thought or mode of enquiry, this is not to contradict the claim (argued in Chapters 1 and 2) that particular disciplines and groups of disciplines display certain aggregated characteristics which distinguish them clearly from others. It is merely to emphasize the variety within the uniformity: the fact that even the apparently softest subject may have hard edges, and that at its margins a seemingly hard one may allow for a fair measure of softness. The resulting catholicity within disciplines may be seen as a fortunate epistemological characteristic, in that it allows in the social dimension for a wide range of intellectual opportunity.

Even when the important choice of an initial research specialism has been settled—usually deriving, as we have seen, from the decisions entered into at the doctoral stage—there are still two well-marked escape routes from what may have transpired as a less than entirely successful match between them and temperament. The first, to which we shall return shortly, lies in the sometimes far-reaching decision to change from one specialism to another; the second, which we shall now consider, rests on the choice of a particular research topic within a specialism to which a firm commitment has already been made.

Inside their necessarily narrower limits, specialisms themselves may offer something akin to the options which most disciplines can be seen to provide. That is to say, certain topics will be seen as central, and others as more peripheral; some as demanding, and others as comparatively tame. The decision that this calls for, whether to gamble with large stakes for high dividends or to play safe for lesser rewards, is a quite serious one in career terms. As one of my respondents, a chemist put it:

> In underpopulated areas within the discipline, there are fewer grants and fewer fringe benefits—less communication, less meetings, less opportunities to share interests, less of the things that motivate people. Because such areas aren't competitive, they promise better results—but the credit is not so great. People drift into such an area if they are loners and isolated individuals who don't like the limelight. Highly competitive people wouldn't be attracted to fields of this kind.

Perhaps in part because the choice of topic is even more crucial in the brightly lit, jostling urban context than it is in the shadowy and less populous byways of rural research, many of those who have written about it have confined themselves to the domain of the hard pure sciences. Schatzman and Strauss (1966) offer an exception, in that their concern is with a soft applied field, the psychiatric profession:

> Psychiatrists-to-be . . . are very soon confronted with critical choices, since the psychiatric limb is itself many-branched. . . . By following one branch line rather than another, a psychiatric professional determines the kinds of interprofessional situations he will later select as appropriate to himself. He determines what situations he will be able to work in comfortably, if at all.

The strategic issues were elaborated in one of my interviews with chemists:

> Problems take different lengths of time to solve. It isn't necessarily a good strategy to go for the quick solutions. Although these result in a greater number of publications, they don't necessarily count for much. The result may just be 'shotgun science', with very little coherence or quality. In fact, you need to find a good balance between short and long problems as a matter of expediency. You have to do things with rapid results as well as tackling long-term issues. A large problem can be a large gamble too. It can bring a lot of credit—but you may not be able to complete its solution.

The successful selection of research themes in pure mathematics, incidentally, is celebrated by the epithet 'good taste'. Much like the same phrase used by a connoisseur of the arts, it denotes the independent identification of what is consequently recognized as valuable. It is 'a matter of finding significant and soluble problems not amenable to traditional approaches', problems that are 'difficult, deep as opposed to shallow, and worthwhile in terms of the new possibilities they give rise to'.

If the choice is less firmly underscored in soft pure, hard applied and soft applied domains, it is nevertheless there to be made. There are topics which, on most people's reckoning, are minor and perhaps rather trivial, but may none the less lead to a publication of sorts; and there are those on grander themes which promise to become the subject of widespread critical attention. Not everyone is prepared to make the large commitment which may, or may not, even after years of endeavour, be judged to result in a significant intellectual coup; as in the hard sciences, there is the countervailing temptation to stick to a series of minor, more manageable contributions.

Whatever the area of knowledge, however, the dividends are not necessarily confined to hot (mainstream or currently fashionable) topics. Indeed, the potentially greatest pay-offs may come from apparently marginal areas. It is there that many of the successful revolutions are bred: consider, for example, the lonely wilderness years of a Ladurie in history or an Einstein in physics. But to follow in their path is a high-risk strategy indeed, since the chances are that at the end of the day one's efforts will prove inglorious and one's endeavours remain unsung.

The Mid-Life Crisis

We shall need here to make a leap in imagination from the aspiring to the established. That is, we shall need to assume that the individuals with whose fates we have been concerned have duly achieved both the goal of a professional reputation and the status of a tenured appointment. The mid-career stage, though it does not mark an end to the demands and dilemmas of an academic life, will often signal the onset of a new set of challenges.

The main question which is posed at this point concerns whether or not to continue working within the same specialism, whether to switch to another one, or whether to begin the process of moving away altogether from active research. Consideration of the last of these options is conveniently deferred until later in the chapter, when we shall review the general phenomenon of ageing and burn-out; so we shall confine ourselves now to the issue of intellectual mobility.

The most important consideration must be what relative career gains and losses are likely to result from deciding to make a move: but there is of course the prior issue of why, if at all, a change of direction needs to be contemplated. We have already noted, from a collective standpoint, the inertia (though some would prefer the term conservatism) built into the academic enterprise as a result of the often substantial investment needed to attain a special expertise in a particular field (see Chapter 4). Anyone who has spent long, arduous years in the achievement of a close understanding of one particular knowledge area or in the acquisition of a particular type of expertise,[4] is unlikely without hesitation to abandon it and repeat the process in favour of a new one. The sense of reluctance, while apparent among my respondents in a variety of subject areas, seemed particularly acute where the linguistic and conceptual barriers between specialisms were high, or where one complex but well-established technical skill had to be replaced by another.[5]

Corroboration of this claim, at least in respect of the natural sciences, is provided by Reif and Strauss (1965):

> Once the scientist has acquired a certain amount of recognition and a reasonable position, there are many factors which reinforce further pursuits along similar lines. . . . The scientist has a large investment in his extensive training. He has also spent quite a few years viewing himself as a research scientist pursuing certain lines of work, and it is not easy to change his self-concept, role-models, and values.

Gilbert (1977a) makes a series of related points:

> As a result of his previous research experience, a scientist gains particular skills and knowledge and usually acquires specialised equipment suitable chiefly for his current

topic. To abandon work on that topic in favour of a new one involves learning new skills, perhaps demands the modification, construction or purchase of different apparatus and requires familiarity with additional sections of the scientific literature. In addition, moving to a new topic implies breaking some of his informal contacts with colleagues and neglecting the reputation which the scientist may have been careful to build up while working on his current topic.

It should be added that he may continue to receive invitations to write and speak on the theme for which he is best known, thus reinforcing his existing reputation at the expense of a new one.

In the face of such disincentives, the motive to change has to be a powerful one. The reasons for making a move tend to be more numerous in cumulative than in reiterative subject areas, being partly dependent on the way in which knowledge has progressed. It was a common theme of the testimony given to me by physicists that, in the words of one respondent, 'Ten years is about the maximum life-span of a fashionable topic' and that, in the words of another 'If you're lucky enough to hit on a new technique, your may be able to exploit it for up to a decade.' In the less rapidly moving areas in biology, 'your techniques can carry you through for about fifteen years after graduation, but you tend to run out of steam when your are around 40'.[6] Knowledge of instrumentation also becomes dated: 'my students do things with apparatus which I don't know how to do'.

Those who work in non-cumulative areas may be spared such problems, but they share others which arise from personal considerations. Even when the field itself is not subject to rapid development, it may be affected by the swings of fashion, leaving the researcher to feel that he or she has been left mouldering in an intellectual backwater. Or, more commonly, individuals may conclude that they have done all the work they want to do within a particular specialist area, or that they have become bored with it, or simply that they are stale and in need of a change.

The difficulties do not, however, end with the decision to migrate to another arena. The barriers to entry are sometimes even more daunting than the disincentives to departure. Hagstrom (1965) quotes a chemist he interviewed as saying, of the adoption of a new specialism, 'It takes at least one or two, sometimes up to five, years to get to the publication stage.' The time needed to become *au fait* with an unfamiliar field depends on several factors: conceptual compatibility between the old and the new, the amount of necessary background knowledge and know-how, the nature of the particular tops selected, and so on. Mention was made earlier of the practice in physics and biochemistry in particular, of applying a specialized technique in a diversity of different areas, 'skimming the cream' of significant but readily solvable problems. But many subject fields are not amenable to such an approach. At the other extreme, Crane (1965) quotes a psychologist as saying of his own specialism: 'There are no substantial contributions of the hit-and-run type. Substantial contributions come from ten to twenty years of working on basically one problem area.' Hagstrom (1965) contends that:

> Mobility seems to be easiest for experimental scientists in disciplines having powerful and general theories. It is hindered when the specialist must command much relatively unsystematic factual material, and it is also low among theorists working with elaborate and ramified theories.

There are social as well as cognitive constraints on intellectual mobility. Reif and Strauss (1965), in acknowledging that 'the scientist must acquire much unfamiliar knowledge before he can be creative in a new field', add that 'He will also have to compete against the young people trained *ab initio* in that discipline.' As several of my respondents in various subject areas pointed out—supporting the contention of Gilbert (1977a)—there is also the crucial difficulty that one is not necessarily able to transfer one's existing reputation to a new specialism; membership of new networks may need to be negotiated, and credibility with funding agencies re-established. Confronted with these challenges, it is perhaps predictable that most people who make a move do not compound their problems by choosing a more intellectually impenetrable area than the one with which they are already familiar. The tendency, discerned by Mulkay (1974), for migration to take place from areas of high precision to those of lower precision is borne out by the available evidence from my sample. To take a couple of cases in point: 'it's fairly common for theoretical economists to move into the history of economic ideas or to become economic historians'; 'it's only very rarely that people move from ecology to cell biology, but there are more examples of moves in the other direction'.

The strategy of hedging one's bets by keeping one foot in the old specialism while dipping the toes of the other in the new, is singled out by Gieryn (1978): 'complete substitution of one problem set for a completely different one is . . . a less common occurrence than simultaneous problem change and problem retention'. My own enquiries suggested that this practice was not confined to the sciences: respondents in other knowledge areas also argued that, to avoid a complete hiatus in one's publications, it was important to continue some writing in the field one was leaving while gearing up to contribute to the literature of the new affiliation.

So far, the discussion has been concerned with the reasons behind migration and the problems which beset it, rather than with its frequency and scope. But something also needs to be said on the latter two issues. Estimates of the incidence of mobility differ to a considerable extent; some commentators write it down as a relatively rare phenomenon, while others claim it to be comparatively common. The divergence may stem from the nature of the population under review. If the whole body of academics is in question, rather than the much smaller group of active researchers, then it could well be the case that 'few scientists change research area during their career' (Thagaard 1987); and that 'the vast majority of researchers stay in a single specialty or work in a related set of specialties' (Chubin 1976). But the evidence from my sample of academics from élite departments and institutions was supportive of Mulkay's (1972) claim that 'intellectual migration seems to occur very frequently . . . in most if not all scientific disciplines'; of Hagstrom's (1974) observation that 'scientists typically work in more than one specialty and change specialties often' (more than one-quarter of his sample, he claimed, had changed primary specialties in the preceding 5 years); and of Whitley's (1984) reference to the findings of the US National Academy of Sciences 1972 survey, that physicists do indeed "migrate" to a considerable degree between sub-fields with one-third of PhDs changing their major interests in 1968-70'.[7] The number of my respondents who reported some significant change in career direction was much higher in actuality than in expectation, and the extent of the changes was in some cases quite striking.

There were, among the apparently substantial shifts from one discipline to another, a number of physicists who had turned to chemistry and engineering; a chemist who had migrated to biology (as well as a number who had, more predictably, become pharmacists); a biologist about to take up a post in experimental psychology; an anthropologist in a history department (and again, more predictably, an archaeologist in another); a historian who had become a sociologist; and an economist who had changed allegiance to political science. Outside my sample, there are many other well-known cases of intellectual pluralism, including three singled out by those I interviewed: Herbert Simon, whose contributions to political science and economics were complemented by those he made to mathematics and psychology; Michael Polanyi, who abandoned a distinguished career in chemistry to become a philosopher of science; and Thomas Kuhn, who started his career as a physicist before establishing himself as a historian.

Movements across specialisms within the same discipline may also at times be quite radical. Examples among my respondents included a physicist who had switched from elementary particles to astrophysics to radioisotope dating to applied energy research; a plant pathologist who had made a new career in studying fish vision; an engineer who had moved on from research on missile structures to a study of machine tool vibration; and a French literature specialist whose interests had evolved from sixteenth-century poetry to modern drama. More limited changes were commonplace in almost every field, and perhaps especially in academic law, where 'there is a traditional notion that everyone should be able to teach every subject'', and in those disciplines, such as engineering and history, whose members are similarly encouraged to take the view that they are 'jacks of all trades'.

Career mobility of this kind is among the most potent sources of innovation and development within a discipline. Immigrants bring fresh ways of looking at familiar issues, and perhaps relevant but hitherto unfamiliar techniques as well. Documenting a celebrated case in point, Mullins (1972) was able to show that 17 of the 41 scientists in the community working on phage research in molecular biology were physicists and chemists by training: the physicists in particular had come to the conclusion that their original specialisms 'would provide no interesting research for some time', and that 'biology had the greatest number of unsolved problems which appeared open to fruitful investigation by physical methods'.[8] Ben-David (1960), looking at the more general pictures of 'roles and innovations in medicine' coined the term 'role-hybrids' (subsequently elaborated by Ben-David and Collins 1966) to encapsulate this process:

> the individual moving from one role to another, such as from one profession or academic field to another . . . may attempt to [fit] the methods and techniques of the old role to the materials of the new one, with the deliberate purpose of creating a new role.

The End-Point of Active Research

For the many academics who manage to survive the challenges and traumas of a mid-career change of life, there are many who do not; and yet others, as we have already seen, who have never faced the necessity or felt the urge to move out of their initial specialisms. They may for our present purposes be grouped together under the category of those whose research careers are at, or nearing, their end; though there are, as often before, significant differences to be discerned among them.

Let us begin by looking at the case of the researchers who, for one reason or another, conclude that they have no more to contribute within their existing fields of expertise, but who lack the incentive to start as virtual novices over again. The biologists I interviewed were particularly informative about the problems which arose and the career possibilities which remained open at this point, so I will take their observations as illustrative of a wider generality.

There was common agreement that the moment of crisis, at least among botanists and zoologists, occurred somewhere around the late 30s or early 40s. A number of respondents ascribed its incidence to an increasing administrative load which drained energies away from empirical research, and a mature professionalism which encouraged an emphasis on the theoretical and synoptic aspects of one's field, where necessary using research associates for data collection. An alternative response was to 'escape into administration' or, for people who were good at teaching, to concentrate on that. There were those again who simply opted to 'rest on their laurels and plod along'. As against this developmental-cum-structural view, however, other respondents offered an account of the matter more directly linked with the cognitive dimension of the research enterprise. According to the second school of thought, the intellectual menopause had less to do with the obligations of seniority and the growth over time of a reflective approach than it had with the average life expectancy of a research topic or an experimental technique that is, with the problems discussed in the preceding section. The appropriate response, on this interpretation, must be to 'retool your lab and rethink your problems'; to 'pick up the pieces, and update your techniques or change the emphasis of your research'.

Some who favoured the latter view were strongly critical of their older colleagues who had taken up the role of synthesizing elder statesmen: 'It is simply a way of maintaining their self-justification—a cheap and easy way out' said one. 'Such people do damned little work for their syntheses'. Another saw those senior scientists who were content to move out of the laboratory and adopt a supervisory function as 'people who want to "be scientists" rather than to do science in any genuine sense'.

The role of a senior academic as a supervisor of others' work, a synthesizer or philosopher about his or her discipline, is perhaps more common in hard pure subjects than in other fields—because, as we shall go on to argue, they show a more marked career hiatus. But it is fairly typical for those relinquishing an active research career in any subject to take on a sizeable administrative commitment, either in their own departments or at the institutional level. An added option is to seek office in a learned society or relevant professional association. A few people at this stage decide to leave academic life altogether. But the most common choice of all is to concentrate on undergraduate teaching at the expense of generating new knowledge or supervising the research of doctoral students.

It has already been suggested that the life-expectation of a specialist in a competitive urban field is relatively short. Reif and Strauss (1965) proffer two pertinent quotations: 'Young scientists . . . eat up old scientists . . . Well, they beat them down . . . you don't remain a scientist in the active progressive sense of the word for a great many years any more'; and '[I have the] feeling that I'm worn out or burned out, and this is the end of my career'. The phenomenon of 'burn out' is most widely recognized in pure mathematics, where the peak of performance is often said to occur in the 20s or early 30s.[9] The older mathematicians in my sample were skeptical about this claim, though some acknowledged that the subject called for lengthy periods of close concentration when working through an argument, and so tended to favour those with high intellectual energy and a capacity for prolonged introspection: 'You have to be able to concentrate intensely enough to see the whole solution to a problem in your head.' Some areas of physics too, particularly the more theoretical aspects closely akin to mathematics, were designated by my respondents as 'a young man's field'; though in many experimental specialisms experience was said to compensate for age, so that people tended to get better with increasing maturity. The testimony of engineers on this point was ambivalent—again, it may have been related to the level of theoretical content, though my sample was too small to lend confirmation to this suggestion. The majority view, however, was that 'the career profile is a straight gradient—experience counts for a lot'; 'some people remain productive well into their fifties'; 'no-one peters out completely—there are some very active oldsters'.

In soft pure and soft applied disciplines, burning out is not recognized at all as part of a typical career pattern. There is no discernible early peak in research productivity; an increase in age betokens a parallel increase in expertise. A respondent in the field of modern languages maintained that 'modern linguists probably do their best work after the age of 45'; another pointed out that 'late-blooming is partly a matter of the amount of material you have to assimilate and the amount of detail you have to master—but it's also partly a result of the need for emotional maturity, insightfulness and empathy'.

One source of the perceived difference between hard and soft may be traced to the contrast, noted by Hagstrom (1965) and mentioned in the previous section, between 'powerful and general theories' which can be rapidly assimilated and deployed by energetic newcomers, and 'relatively unsystematic factual material' or 'elaborate and ramified theories' which only long years of study can command. Another, as we have seen, lies in the differential importance of specialized apparatus and techniques, and the tendency for both to become outdated within a comparatively short period in cumulative knowledge areas. Research in the softer domains commonly demands no instrumentation, and such techniques as it calls upon are on the whole stable and relatively unchanging.

All that has been remarked so far about the relationship between career stage and research productivity has been based on the subjective impressions of the practitioners themselves. In principle, it should be possible to provide a more systematic, detached and impartial analysis, based on a correlation of published writings with chronological maturity. A number of researchers have in fact attempted such a task, though—with irritating perversity—the objective evidence is as confused and contradictory as the subjective is clear and unequivocal.

The pioneering work is that of Lehman (1953), who set himself the herculean challenge of relating age to achievement—subsequently translated as 'outstanding performances'—not only in academic subjects such as medicine, psychology, philosophy, mathematics and most of the natural sciences, but in music, art, creative literature, politics and 'public leadership positions' as well (though not, interestingly enough, in such fields as history, sociology, anthropology or literary studies). Most of those comprising his sample were deceased, some (e.g. Mozart and Beethoven) long so. He was thus able to compare individuals born in the 1700s with those born since 1850. In his analysis, peaking of productivity appears to occur mostly in the late 30s—the range for chemistry is given as 26-30,[10] for physics and mathematics as 30-34 and for geology and medical sciences as around 35-39. Philosophers, too, are quoted as peaking between 35 and 39, except for metaphysicians, who enjoy a relatively late maturity of 40-44.[11] Lehman stresses, however, that intellectual productivity continues, albeit at a reduced rate, after the peak is passed. Taken as a whole, people beyond the age of 40 make over half the total contributions in any field, but the greatest rate of achievement occurs between 30 and 39.

Critics of Lehman's methods and dissenters from his findings include Dennis (1956, 1958, 1966) and a number of others enumerated in the brief, workmanlike review of the research literature on the subject by Fox (1983). Dennis relies on ageing data in two senses of the phrase, since his sample covers 738 people, born between 1600 and 1820, living to the age of 79 and beyond. He maintains that:

> in many groups [but not among creative artists] the decade of the 20s was the least productive period. . . . The highest rate of output, in the case of nearly all groups, was reached in the 40s or soon after. From age 40 onwards the output of scholars suffered little decrement. After age 60 the productivity of scientists decreased appreciably.

His main contention, that 'productivity persists in the later years of life', is echoed in a number of subsequent writings; others discern a twin-peaked pattern, with a second efflorescence of creativity among those in their 50s.

A small group of studies have concentrated on the *crème de la crème* of academic researchers, in the form of Nobel prize winners. Manniche and Falk (1957) found the peaks to be in the late 30s and early 40s. Moulin (1955) gives somewhat higher mean ages for the Nobel prize winners 1901 to 1950.[12] Reif and Strauss (1965) state that 'during the past half dozen years . . . mean ages at the time of the award have been between 45 and 50 years in physics, chemistry and medicine' but that 'some men were in their late twenties when they did outstanding work leading subsequent awards of the prizes; indeed, their work was done at an average age of less than 35 years'. Zuckerman (1977), in her comprehensive exploration of the subject, would appear to dissent from this view, concluding that: 'Among Nobel laureates at least, science is not exclusively a young person's game; evidently it is a game the middle-aged can play as well.'[13]

Future generations of numerologists will doubtless continue to crunch out statistics, culled from diverse databases and generated from mutually incompatible assumptions, in the hope of producing a final, definitive statement on the relationship between age and productivity. Those lacking such inclinations, however, may conclude that there are too many complexities in all this to allow for more than a brace of unequivocal claims: first, that whatever the realities of the situation, the legend will die hard that subject areas making strong demands on abstractly symbolic or heavily quantitative reasoning are the main province of younger intellects; and, secondly, that for the rest, if custom has the scope to stale, yet age must lack the power to wither the propensity for intellectual excellence.

Personal Matters

One of the self-imposed limitations of my research was that it did not enquire into the lives of respondents as private individuals (and in particular that it eschewed the possibilities opened up by those egregious psychological studies whose design is to correlate academic with sexual characteristics). None the less, I did invite comment on issues relating to professional commitment and job satisfaction. The responses on these points, though they have no direct bearing on the shape and development of academic careers, deserve a brief resumé.

It was typical of the active researchers my sample comprised that they admitted to a strong sense of personal involvement in their work. However, the form that involvement took varied somewhat from one knowledge area to another. The academics who were subjected to the strong competitive pressures of urban research seemed to find it hardest to 'switch off'. In some areas of physics, to survive, you have to be 'dedicated and determined', 'monomaniac' and obsessed'. Several interviewees found it difficult to leave their work behind: 'I live my physics.' There are departments where the labs are seldom empty.

The patterns among engineers and biologists seem less consistent. A number of the former, especially in the hotter areas of the subject, spoke of their 'total absorption' in their research interests: 'It amazes me how much time people spend working—at least that's true if you're active; and if it's not true it means you've opted out.' One respondent went on to describe how his wife had instituted a customs-type search of the car to impound all contraband work from the holiday baggage. Others, however, had schooled themselves against 'getting overwound and overdoing things'. Again, while some biologists admitted that their professional concerns took up a large part of their lives ('you can't help carting your work round with you'),[14] others considered it essential to 'know when you have to stop working', and to avoid too much emotional intensity by the deliberate cultivation of other interests. By comparison, one respondent observed, 'physicists are more motivated and involved'.

There were fewer comments along these lines from those in the softer knowledge fields, though there remained a clear tendency to view the world from one's own disciplinary perspective. Much as a physicist might 'see everything from a physics point of view, 24 hours a day', or a biologist could discern 'a biological analogy in almost every situation', a number of historians claimed that their subject gave them a special understanding of life, 'a better feel for what is going on'; and a human geographer remarked that 'geography gives you a way of looking at the world: I can't imagine how I could stop being a geographer, especially when I'm in the countryside— seeing is an important part of geography to me'. But those who worked in disciplines concerned with human affairs were not perhaps as conscious of the dividing line between their occupational and their everyday lives, and seemed to adopt a more relaxed attitude towards their intellectual commitments.

The sense of personal pleasure to be derived from research activities was widely acknowledged, and there was not a single interviewee who confessed to being 'turned off' by, or uninvolved in, even its more routine aspects (it may be that, as one respondent suggested, most academics seem to end up in a field in which they find even the 'busy work' enjoyable, where others might find it tedious). This is not to say that there are no boring or unsatisfactory facets of an academic life. The most common candidates under this heading were administration, committee work and marking undergraduate essays and exam scripts (the actual process of teaching was generally held to be enjoyable and worth while, and could sometimes be found to have a broadening effect on one's research).[15] Many of the younger academics felt frustrated by the lack of career prospects, especially when compared with the expansionist opportunities enjoyed by their predecessors a generation before; and some of the more senior ones expressed concern that increasing professionalization, along with other forces pressing for uniformity, would rule out the making of imaginative or risky appointments, and so reward safe mediocrity at the expense of wayward brilliance.

Few of those with some years of professional experience would have wanted to live their lives differently. Among the special virtues of their own disciplines—the ability, say, to immerse oneself in and come to appreciate another culture in modern language studies, history or anthropology; the engineer's pride in 'knowing how to do things'; the physicist's sense of command in knowing how things work—most of the academics I interviewed would affirm the enjoyment that one expressed of 'a vivid intellectual life, full of satisfaction and exhilaration', and share with another the claim that 'I can't imagine doing anything else, or any other job where I would be paid to talk to lots of bright people and do what I want to do.'

This last point—the special opportunity which academia affords 'to exercise your own creative instincts—to be your own boss'—was a leitmotif of the testimony from virtually every discipline. There is no contesting the importance given by respondents to freedom of choice and freedom of action in their research. How far that freedom is a real one, or how far it persists only as a romantic illusion, must be a topic for the next chapter to consider.

Addendum: A Note on Gender

More than one reader of this chapter in its draft form pointed out that it had nothing specific to say about the careers of women in academics. The reason is straightforward enough: I made no conscious effort to control the sample for gender representation. Accordingly, out of the 221 academics I interviewed, only 22 were women.[16] This very small subsample failed to bring to light any systematic differences between male and female career patterns, particularly as there were no women in my groups of about a dozen respondents from mathematics, chemistry, geography and economics, and only two each from modern languages and pharmacy; there were a mere three in each larger group of some two dozen from biology, law, physics and sociology; none in engineering; and a significant proportion (6 out of 22) only in history.[17]

There is, however, a fairly substantial research literature, based mainly on US higher education. Apart from Bernard's (1964) influential study, much of this was published in the 1970s, when the topic would seem to have been in fashion. Both British and American findings suggest that women in academia have been marginalized in a number of respects. Not only are there far fewer of them: women PhDs tend to get posts in less prestigious institutions than do men PhDs from the same doctoral university level (Bernard 1964, Williams *et al.* 1974, Rendel 1984); they 'are more likely to receive initial appointments at lower ranks or in non-rank positions; they are promoted more slowly and receive tenure at a later age, if at all; they are less involved in administration' (Morlock 1973). Their salaries are lower (Morlock 1973, Carnegie Commission 1973, Williams *et al.* 1974), and more of them have part-time jobs (Carnegie Commission 1973); and they are less productive of research publications (Bernard 1964, Williams *et al.* 1974, Blackstone and Fulton 1975, Cole 1979). American findings suggest that women academics are more oriented to teaching and are given heavier teaching loads (Bernard 1964), though the British evidence suggests that the differences here are not significant (Williams *et al.* 1974).

It is widely remarked that there are different patterns between different subject fields.[18] As Bernard notes, 'it has been in languages and literature . . . that women have traditionally made their major contribution'. They are significantly under-represented in physical and social science, but they appear in sizeable numbers in female-oriented subject areas such as women's studies and home economics, and in relatively low-status fields such as library science and education (Bernard 1964, Carnegie Commission 1973, Blackstone and Fulton 1975). But, perhaps surprisingly, women's proportional share of professorial appointments is much higher in physics than it is in, for example, sociology; women physicists publish 'at rates equivalent with their male colleagues'; 'fare better in terms of rank'; and seem to be treated more closely on a par with men (Morlock 1973). The effects of differences in marital status are similarly unexpected. Married women with children are 'as likely to have a senior post as those without children', though both compare unfavourably in this respect with their unmarried women colleagues (Williams *et al.* 1974). However, married women in general appear to publish more than single women (Morlock 1973, Williams *et al.* 1974), as do married women scientists in particular, or at least those with small families (Cole 1979). Williams *et al.* offer a possible explanation: such women 'have to break existing social norms . . . they have to be women of exceptional drive and confidence . . . the pressures on them to achieve are greater than for other women'.

None of these studies is able to show much evidence of overt gender discrimination in the academic context. Bernard (1964) suggests that though some differentials are 'doubtless due to discrimination . . . it cannot be argued that all [academic women] were being seriously discriminated against'. Williams *et al.* (1974) state more categorically that 'it is impossible to demonstrate discrimination against women by the universities', while Cole (1979) remarks that 'the belief . . . that there is patterned and systematic bias and discrimination in hiring female PhDs is simply unsupported by data' and speculates that there could well be some measure of 'reverse discrimination in hiring'. The reasons postulated for the evident inequalities between men and women are various. They are generally agreed to reflect more subtle and pervasive considerations than a deliberate bias against women: 'a reflection of larger social differentiation'; the outcome of intermittent, mild, largely unconscious prejudice' (Blackstone and Fulton 1975); a consequence of 'accumulative disadvantage' (Cole 1979); or perhaps a matter of 'self-imposed' discrimination (Brown 1967, quoted in Williams *et al.* 1974), 'low self-evaluation' (Blackstone and Fulton 1975), or non-competitiveness among the female sex (Bernard 1964).

More specifically, it is suggested that there are psychological reasons (a lack of drive, low administrative ability) and socially induced expectations (role identities, a pressure to marry, and subsequent domestic commitments) to account for these differences between men's and women's career opportunities (Williams *et al.* 1974). Familiar considerations include careers interrupted for childbirth or hampered by other family obligations, together with the relative immobility of married women tied to their husbands' workplaces (Bernard 1964). In relation to scientific fields in particular, Zuckerman and Cole (1975) identify a 'triple penalty' for women: the definition of science as an inappropriate female career (reducing recruitment); the belief that women are less competent at quantitative reasoning than men (reducing motivation); and 'some evidence for actual discrimination against women in the scientific community'.

There are signs that the discrepancies are gradually diminishing over time (Rendel 1984, University Grants Committee 1987). But even allowing for changing social attitudes and values, for equal opportunities legislation and (less probably) for a requirement of positive discrimination, it will clearly be many years before anything approaching parity of career chances between the sexes is likely to be established.

Notes

1. In this connection, Mulkay (1977) observes that 'graduate students, who naturally find it difficult to compete with mature scientists, are often given research topics which are somewhat peripheral and which are, therefore unlikely to attract the attention of older and more experienced researchers.'

2. Knorr-Cetina (1982) argues that the exploitation here, as in the case of research students, is mutual. She cites the case of a postdoctoral researcher who complained that he was 'being used' by the head of his laboratory:

    The post-doc conducted all the research in a project [acted as overseer to] students and technicians, and came up with ideas. . . . His name appeared on papers but not on patents which resulted from the research, and it was the head of the laboratory who decided when and where to publish, and who presented the work at conferences. However, while the head of the laboratory was using the post-doc to 'run' the project, the post-doc was using the head of the laboratory to promote his own career. He came to the laboratory to get access to journals, research money and 'hot' research topics; and he thought that his affiliation with a prestigious institute would enable him to get a high-paying, high-prestige position.

3. "A scientist rarely makes a career decision more consequential than the selection of a problem for research' (Gieryn 1978).

4. Thagaard (1987), by way of illustration, writes: 'According to my interviews with physicists and chemists it was emphasized that 10 years (including the graduate study) was necessary in order to qualify for work at the research frontier.'

5. As one biologist in my sample observed, 'it can be traumatic to go back to being a student when you've earned a reputation in your field'. Another remarked, 'if you invest a lot of effort in learning a difficult technique, you naturally want to use it to the maximum advantage—you have to think twice about picking up a different one'.

6. It is interesting to note how closely these (epistemologically based) comments echo the (sociologically based) assertion by Griffith and Mullins (1972), quoted on p. 68, that the typical lifespan of a successful 'coherent social group' in science is 10–15 years.

7. In his study of 'specialization and change in academic careers', Ziman (1987) argues that 'most scientists do in fact change their research specialties substantially in the course of their lives', but adds that they 'actually change . . . quite gradually. . . . Again and again, scientists described the evolution of their research interests as an unplanned process of *gradual* drift.' His sample was, however, wider than that of most writers on the topic, in that it included career scientists in freestanding research establishments, government laboratories and private industry, along with a small minority holding academic posts.

8. A history of the key role played by physicists in the phage group, and more generally in 'the biological revolution' which led up to the Watson-Crick model of DNA, is narrated in Fleming (1969). Among its other virtues it throws an interesting light on the epistemological contrasts between the two disciplines in question.

9. A view which received authoritative endorsement from G. H. Hardy in his well-known and widely-read *Mathematician's Apology* (1941). The claim is directly contradicted, on the basis of citation analysis, by Stern (1978): 'no clear-cut relationship exists between age and productivity, or between age and quality of work. The claim that younger mathematicians (whether for physiological or sociological reasons) are more apt to create important work is, then, unsubstantiated.' Stern attributes an apparent dip in productivity in the 45–49 age group to increased administrative responsibilities at that career point.

10. This is surprising, in so far as the chemists among my respondents tended to the view that chemical physicists reached the end of their useful lives earlier than natural product chemists, but that in the case of the latter (to mix a metaphor) 'people usually blossom by their mid-thirties and then reach a plateau'. Comments were that 'there is no very obvious mid-career crisis—some people do allow themselves to become a bit out of date and old fashioned but there is always new stuff to assimilate and nothing to keep you from doing research', and that 'some people are productive to incredible ages'.

11. Lehman claims that these 'early maxima' are steadily decreasing. The peaks in most fields tend to occur at younger ages in the twentieth century than they did in the eighteenth or nineteenth centuries.

12. More specifically, he quotes the average age for physicists at 45–46 and for chemists as about 50. The youngest prize winner in physics was 25, and the youngest in chemistry 35. A total of 31 per cent of the physicists were under 40; the corresponding figure for chemists was only 13 per cent.

13. This is not altogether consistent with her earlier acquiescence with Lehman that the highest productivity is to be found in the 30s (see the chapter on 'Age, ageing and age structure in science' in Merton 1973).

14. Terman (1954) notes that the physical scientists who formed part of his study frequently cited their work as their greatest source of life satisfaction. Mitroff (1974) concurs with Roe (1953) that all eminent scientists seem to have a strong devotion to their work, and that this spills into their weekends, holidays and all the time available.

15. A typical comment was that of a physicist I interviewed: 'Teaching is one of the best ways to familiarise yourself with a new area of science which you aren't currently researching.'

16. The proportion is roughly comparable with recent statistics for the UK universities as a whole, which show the percentage of women full-time staff on academic and related grades as some 17 per cent of the total, and the percentage 'wholly university financed' as about 10 per cent (University Grant Committee 1987). Historically, the comparable US figures have been much higher, fluctuating between 20 and 28 per cent for the higher education system as a whole between 1889 and 1959 (Bernard 1964).

17. The UK statistics (University Grants Committee 1987) are not for individual subjects but for groupings of roughly cognate disciplines. The absence of a single female engineer in my sample of 22 is not out of keeping with the low UK representation (6.4 per cent) of women in 'Engineering and Technology' in 1984–5; physics is somewhat over-represented by 3 out of 223 as against a national total of 12.4 per cent for 'Biology, Mathematics and Physics', as is history by 6 out of 22 as against 14.5 per cent for 'Other Arts'; and sociology is under-represented by 3 out of 22 as against some 19 per cent for 'Administrative, Business and Social Studies'. But taken in all, I am satisfied that there are no gross discrepancies between my sample and the national figures for the UK.

18. McDowell (1984) advances an ingenious argument suggesting that women may be attracted to disciplines in which the obsolescence of knowledge is relatively low, and which therefore exact fewer penalties on interrupted careers.

Faculty Professionalism Reconsidered

James C. Palmer

Community college faculty still lack a shared sense of professional identity. Four frames of reference are examined within which a collective professional identity might be formed.

During the community college's greatest period of growth, 1965–1975, the questions of who should teach at the community college and how prospective teachers should be prepared for their jobs arose as key issues. With the demand for new faculty high (the number of faculty teaching at two-year colleges increased by 539 percent from 1953 through 1973), many pondered not only how faculty vacancies should be filled but whether junior college teaching was a distinct profession and, if so, how candidates for this profession should be trained. Articles appeared on the desired competencies of junior college faculty in individual disciplines. For example, biologists debated the question of whether those teaching biology at junior colleges require different and less specialized forms of graduate training in biology than colleagues teaching at four-year institutions (Hertig, 1971; Hurlburt, 1971). Many universities, responding to concerns that traditional master's degree programs produced subject-area experts who lacked pedagogical skills, initiated graduate tracks in junior college teaching, combining work in the discipline with courses and internships designed to hone teaching skills and introduce students to the junior college environment (Ross, 1972).

These graduate programs never became the primary source of new faculty members, and as growth in the number of institutions (and in the number of new faculty hired) tapered off in the mid 1970s, debates about the nature of a new community college teaching profession gave way to the administrative concerns of collective bargaining, faculty burnout, and the continuing education of faculty already hired. Writing on the heels of this growth period, Cohen (1973) observed that the professional status of community college faculty never fully developed. Many of the attributes of a profession, he wrote, could be at least partially conceded to community college faculty as an occupational group. For example, the master's degree had become the standard for entrance into the field; hence, practitioners needed to undergo a relatively long period of training and acquire a specialized body of knowledge not readily available to the layperson. In addition, faculty involvement in tenure and hiring decisions gave them a voice, albeit shared with administrators, in policing their own ranks. But a shared sense of professionalism, one toward which all members of the faculty could aspire, never emerged: "collectively, the image of the faculty may be quite different from any of its members' individual reflections. It is this collective image that must be clarified if community college teaching is to become more of a profession" (Cohen, 1973, p. 102).

Nonetheless, the issue of how community college teaching should be defined professionally may arise once again as college leaders prepare for a new era of faculty hiring brought on by the retirement of those employed in the 1960s and early 1970s. Almost one-fourth (23 percent) of all full-time faculty now teaching at public community colleges are fifty-five or older, and 62 percent are forty-five or older (Russell and others, 1990). Replacing these faculty over the next twenty years will not prove as dramatic an event as the expansion of the faculty ranks two decades ago. Those hired will fill existing positions in long-established institutions and not (as was the case earlier) newly created positions at newly established institutions. Yet the prospect of substantial turnover among faculty leads to questions not only about how replacements will be found but also about who those replacements should be professionally.

How is the latter question to be approached? At least four frames of reference have been proposed within which faculty professionalism can be conceptualized: (1) the institutional frame of reference, stressing responsibilities to the mission of the community college and the students that mission serves; (2) the scholastic frame of reference, stressing responsibilities to scholarship within the discipline; (3) the classroom research frame of reference, stressing responsibility to assess systematically the teaching and learning process; and (4) the pedagogical frame of reference, stressing responsibility to define and lead students to specific educational outcomes. This chapter examines each of these, drawing implications for how community college teaching might continue its evolution from a job to a profession.

Institutional Frame of Reference

Within the institutional frame of reference, which received its greatest support during the growth years of the 1960s and early 1970s, the faculty member ties his or her sense of responsibility to the comprehensive mission of the community college. Rejecting the university's emphasis on specialization within the discipline, instructors embrace the task of teaching a broad spectrum of related subjects at the lower-division level to students who may or may not intend to earn a baccalaureate. Gleazer (1967) was a strong proponent of this perspective, arguing that "at the heart of successful junior college teaching lies faculty understanding and acceptance of the diverse purposes of an 'open-door' type of educational institution" (p. 148). Because faculty "perceptions and attitudes will inevitably exert a major influence on the course of these institutions and their educational effectiveness" (p. 148), Gleazer continued, faculty who do not embrace the community college mission would at best become discouraged and at worst thwart the institution in its attempts to meet the educational needs of its broad constituency. He called for the development of master's degree programs in community college instruction, combining interdisciplinary study in related fields (such as biology, zoology, and botany) with supervised teaching experiences at a community college.

Focusing professionalism on the institution appeals to the ideas of those who identify the community college with the movement to open higher education to students previously unserved by the university. The resulting sense of mission has been a cohesive force among many community college educators. But those espousing the institutional frame of reference never structured it on a fully developed rationale that would link the perceived uniqueness of the community college to the practice of teaching. How exactly does teaching at the community college differ from teaching lower-division courses at four-year institutions? Without a clear answer, those outside the community college movement often looked askance at claims to a new teaching profession. As one biologist (Hertig, 1971) put it, "there has arisen a confusion about the difference between the overall mission of two-year colleges and the contribution that a given discipline makes toward the achievement of that mission" (p. 185). It may be granted, he continued, that two-year college biology classes prepare students for careers in medical technology as well as for baccalaureate degrees in biology. "But we are left with biologists teaching the discipline of biology" (p. 185).

One can therefore question the extent to which the institutional frame of reference actually took hold. Still, its legacy remains, notably in the limited extent to which community college faculty (in sharp contrast to university colleagues) identify with and remain active in their disciplines. Some deplore this lack of activity as a debilitating situation. Schmeltekopf (1983), for example, notes the relatively low participation of community college liberal arts faculty in discipline-based associations and views this limited participation as a symptom of intellectual stagnation. Others, however, are not so concerned. They see limited faculty ties to the discipline as an institutional strength, one that helps to focus faculty attention on teaching and student needs and away from outside commitments. Baker, Roueche, and Gillett-Karam (1990), for example, allude to this idea in their assertion that "a major challenge for the leadership of community colleges is to cause the faculty members to see themselves first as members of the college community and secondly as members of their specific professional community" (p. 291). Both points of view reflect the different tugs that all faculty members encounter when balancing professional responsibilities to the college with those that are owed the disciplines they teach.

Scholastic Frame of Reference

The scholastic frame of reference rejects the notion that intellectual work in one's discipline and commitment to the teaching-oriented, comprehensive community college are mutually exclusive goals. It embraces a broad definition of scholarship, one that includes traditional research, or the production of knowledge, as only one of many scholarly activities that may be undertaken by faculty. In embracing this broad definition, the scholastic frame of reference lays bare the false notion that research universities are the sole theater for scholarship in higher education. It recognizes the responsibility of community college faculty to imbue their teaching with the insights gained from active scholarship, rather than simply covering the course material.

Vaughan (1988) has been the leading advocate for attention to scholarship at the community college. He sees a clear tie between teaching effectiveness, which is at the heart of the community college mission, and scholarly endeavors, maintaining that "outstanding teaching requires constant learning and intellectual renewal" (p. 28). Noting that scholarship is the systematic pursuit of a topic through "rational inquiry and critical analysis," he points out that scholarly products may take many forms: "a book review, an annotated bibliography, a lecture, a review of existing research on a topic, [or] a speech that is a synthesis of thinking on a topic" (p. 27). These are clearly projects that do not require traditional, original research. But whatever the product, Vaughan continues, it is the obligation of the scholar to share it with others and open it to the criticism of those qualified to judge its merits.

In making his case, Vaughan concedes that the community college culture is often hostile to faculty involvement in scholarly activities outside of teaching. The failure of many college leaders to connect scholarship with teaching effectiveness and thus reward the scholarly activities of faculty has taken its toll. In addition, heavy teaching loads have sometimes fostered a work-by-the-hour mentality, one in which "obligations to the job overshadow a [professional] commitment to scholarship" (Vaughan, 1988, p. 29). As a result, faculty attitudes toward scholarship are mixed. In a recent national survey of community college faculty, Palmer (1922) found that most (86 percent) had completed at least one scholarly product, as broadly defined by Vaughan, within the past two years; 73 percent felt that work on these scholarly products improves teaching effectiveness. However, only 48 percent felt that community colleges should make scholarly work outside of the classroom a required condition of employment. Though the faculty recognize the value of remaining active in scholarship, most are reluctant to view it as a collective, professional responsibility.

Classroom Research Frame of Reference

Vaughan's call for the recognition of a broader definition of scholarship, one that makes room for those who do not spend their professional lives at research universities, has gained currency. Boyer (1990), for example, has warned that the intellectual vitality of the American professoriat demands that colleges recognize the many ways in which scholarly contributions can be made. Unlike Vaughan, Boyer focuses on the processes of scholarship rather than on its products. Some faculty, he notes, will continue work on basic research (the scholarship of discovery), while others will analyze and interpret research findings (the scholarship of integration), apply knowledge to the solution of technical or social problems (the scholarship of application), and convey knowledge and a love of learning to students (the scholarship of teaching).

The teaching emphasis of the community college leads naturally to a focus on the fourth scholarly process, the scholarship of teaching, and to a consideration of the faculty role in systematically analyzing the classroom as a learning environment. The Commission on the Future of Community Colleges (1988), for example, places the community college teaching profession squarely within this framework. "Community colleges," the commission argues, "should define the role of the faculty member as classroom researcher" (p. 27). Faculty should be analysts of the classroom environment who are "trained to be . . . careful observer[s] of the teaching process, to collect feedback on what and how well students learn, and to evaluate the effectiveness of instruction. This approach . . . asks faculty to make a clear connection between how they teach and what students learn. It establishes the classroom as both a teaching and research environment" (p. 27).

The use of the word *research* does not imply controlled experimentation; hence, faculty responsibilities as classroom researchers do not extend into the realm of social science. Cross (1989), the most outspoken advocate of today's classroom research movement and whose work was cited by the commission, stresses that classroom research does not require training or expertise in social science research methods. Procedures aimed at helping teachers assess student learning as classes proceed are key, rather than the production of research findings that are shared with the larger profession. As Cross explains, "our goal in Classroom Research [sic] is not to add research projects to already heavy teaching loads but to integrate research into everyday teaching. . . . A study of critical thinking in the classroom, for example, might begin with the assignment of a task that students approach the task and how well they perform. The Classroom Researcher [sic] would experiment with modifications in the design of the task and its presentation, followed by a reevaluation of the effectiveness of the changes" (p. 15).

Under the classroom research frame of reference, then, faculty professionalism is anchored in a process of teaching that has its roots, albeit unacknowledged by Cross, in the traditions of action research, which "is designed to yield practical results that are immediately applicable to a specific situation or problem" (Houston, 1990).

Unlike the scholastic frame of reference, fostering a sense of professionalism on the basis of classroom action research requires relatively little change on the part of colleges themselves. It does not take the teacher out of the classroom. By defining the faculty member's role as classroom researcher along the lines Cross suggests, the Commission on the Future of Community Colleges describes a faculty profession that, while not precluding work on out-of-class scholarly activities, does not threaten the suppositions of those who believe that such activities diminish the faculty member's teaching effectiveness. In this regard, today's emphasis on classroom research reflects the institutional frame of reference prevalent two decades ago; both tie the professional identity of faculty to the college and its teaching emphasis, although today's classroom research movement presupposes no need for specialized graduate training.

Pedagogical Frame of Reference

If faculty are to take responsibility for determining the extent to which their teaching results in desired student learning, they must have a clear idea of what it is that students should know or be able to do as a consequence of instruction. The need to specify desired student outcomes, acknowledged by Cross (1989) as a prerequisite of classroom research, places the faculty member not only in the role of classroom teacher but in the larger role of arbiter of the curriculum. In this role, faculty define the competencies that indicate successful completion of courses and degree programs; in turn, faculty are judged on the basis of the extent to which students demonstrate mastery of those competencies.

During the 1960s, Cohen, Brawer, and Prihoda (1967) argued forcefully for a community college teaching profession built around the discipline of instruction. They stressed faculty attention to the specification, in advance, of cognitive and affective behavioral objectives, to the use of varied instructional media in helping students master course material, and to the development of a sense of professional responsibility built around documented student learning. Faculty were to be judged solely on the basis of the proportion of students who meet specified goals;

hence, traditional modes of instruction would have to be changed. "This approach," they wrote, "differs from the usual one in which the teacher lectures, gives reading assignments, hopes all pupils do well on the examinations, and then cuts a curve of grades across his [or her] classes" (Cohen, Brawer, and Prihoda, 1967, n.p.).

While this vision of the profession never fully emerged, more recent calls for the documentation of student outcomes, emerging in the requirements of regional accrediting agencies, have once again underscored faculty responsibility to effect predetermined changes in students, not simply to cover the subjects outlined in course syllabi. Banta (1991) cites several examples of college efforts to involve faculty in specifying general education outcomes and developing assessment programs that monitor institutional success in leading students to those outcomes. Only through these efforts, she maintains, can institutional outcomes assessment programs succeed. While some colleges begin planning these programs by selecting or developing assessment instruments, they in effect place the cart before the horse. "They cannot proceed very far along this path," Banta maintains, ". . . without direction from a statement of expected student outcomes. That is, what do faculty hope students will know and be able to do as a result of their experience in the general education program?" (Banta, 1991, p. 1).

Will faculty be able to fulfill this professional role? Much will depend on their ability to define outcomes in ways that allows a measurement of the degree to which students have mastered course material. It will not be enough to agree that students passing a specific course should have "a good grasp" of the material covered in the class or that graduates should have certain attributes, such as critical thinking skills. Broad educational goals are useful, but faculty will need more specific measures that take the form of behavioral objectives, outlining both what students should know or be able to do and what criteria will be used to measure student success.

Conclusion

How should community college faculty define their profession? When asked, most faculty members would undoubtedly respond that teaching is their primary function and hence defines their role within the community college. A national survey conducted by the United States Department of Education in 1987 found that full-time community college faculty spent approximately 72 percent of their professional time in teaching or teaching-related tasks, compared to only 52 percent for full-time faculty at four-year institutions (Russell and others, 1990). In a subsequent national survey conducted in 1989 by the Carnegie Foundation for the Advancement of Teaching (1990), 92 percent of the responding faculty from community colleges indicated that teaching effectiveness should be the primary criterion for promotion.

Agreeing that teaching is what community college faculty do, however, says little about what community college faculty take responsibility for and hence who the faculty are as professionals. Without a defined scope of responsibility, teachers are hired hands who, because they hold specified credentials (usually the master's degree), are qualified to teach certain subjects for a specified number of hours per week. Dedication, hard work in the face of large teaching loads, and commitment to the student may all be conceded as qualities of most community college instructors. But within the community college professoriat, the gap between employment and membership in an identified profession has yet to be bridged. As Cohen and Brawer (1989) suggest, "community college instruction has become a career in its own right. Its flowering awaits a more fully developed professional consciousness on the part of its practitioners" (p. 90).

What can be done to foster this professional consciousness? Preservice education will be of little help; the master's degree within the discipline has long been established as the credential of entry into the profession, and specialized programs designed specifically for community college teachers are rare. Thus, the answer must come from within the institution and from the development of a college culture that has high expectations of its faculty. Before this culture can be developed, at least two barriers must be overcome.

The first is the recognition that the frames of reference discussed in this chapter are not mutually exclusive. For example, a commitment to the comprehensive mission need not preclude active involvement in scholarship; similarly, classroom research techniques are an ideal complement to course and curriculum development based on behavioral objectives. All may help to build a sense of profession. But when one is set against the other, discussions of faculty professionalism revolve around false dichotomies between activities (such as teaching versus research) rather than focusing on the ends toward which faculty work.

The second, noted by Cohen and Brawer (1989), is the tendency of the community college to be regarded as a passive agency that, like libraries and parks, prides itself on the number of clients served rather than on specified ways in which those clients are helped or changed. This aspect of the institutional culture is a legacy of the historical focus on access, which has often overshadowed concern for student outcomes. Without a delineation of the institution's responsibility toward students (other than to leave the doors of education open), faculty responsibilities will remain unclear. If the institute aims for high enrollments only, then the view of faculty as hired hands teaching a set number of hours will suffice. But if the institution hopes to lead students to the completion of curricula within defined fields of study, then faculty have responsibilities as practitioners within those fields of study. They must, as Ratcliff (1991) points out, help students understand the ways of knowing within their disciplines and thus ensure that students become able practitioners themselves. This demands that faculty understand the requisites of successful practice within the discipline, that they are able to define these requisites in the form of desired student outcomes, and that their teaching incorporates mechanisms to determine whether those outcomes have been achieved. Thus, faculty understanding of the discipline through active scholarship, a requisite of the scholastic framework, operates hand in hand with the pedagogical imperatives of classroom research and outcomes assessment.

The institution, discipline-based scholarship, classroom practice and research, and the specification of student outcomes all define the parameters of faculty work. Each poses a framework around which a collective professional identity might be formed. Yet each is insufficient as a basis for professional responsibility toward the student. Making a commitment to the institution and to its mission of serving all who can benefit leaves open the question of what those benefits are and how the college will know that those benefits have been gained. Stressing teaching and classroom research without reference to scholarship in the discipline trivializes the educational process, stripping if of the disciplinary context that shapes the ways of knowing that students will need as they pursue careers or further education. Emphasizing scholarship without reference to the constraints of the community college and its obligation to serve large, diverse student populations may unduly impose a definition of scholarship that, while appropriate at the university, leaves little room for scholarly participation on the part of community college faculty. The professional identity of faculty must, in the final analysis, incorporate all four frames of reference within an institution that bases its merits on predefined student outcomes.

References

Baker, G. A., III, Roueche, J. E., and Gillett-Karam, R. *Teaching as Leading: Profiles of Excellence in the Open-Door College.* Washington, D. C.: American Association of Community and Junior Colleges, 1990.

Banta, T. W. "Faculty-Developed Approaches to Assessing General Education Outcomes." *Assessment Update*, 1991, 3 (2), 1–2, 4.

Boyer, E. L. *Scholarship Reconsidered: Priorities of the Professoriat.* Princeton, N. J.: Carnegie Foundation for the Advancement of Teaching, 1990. 151 pp. (ED 326 149).

Carnegie Foundation for the Advancement of Teaching. *The Condition of the Professoriat: Attitudes and Trends*, 1989. Princeton, N. J.: Carnegie Foundation for the Advancement of Teaching, 1990. 162 pp. (ED 312 963).

Cohen, A. M. "Toward a Professional Faculty." In A. M. Cohen (ed.), *Toward a Professional Faculty.* New Directions for Community Colleges, no. 1. San Francisco: Jossey-Bass, 1973.

Cohen, A. M., and Brawer, F. B. *The American Community College.* (2ND ED.) San Francisco: Jossey-Bass, 1989.

Cohen, A. M., Brawer, F. B., and Prihoda, J. J. *Developing Specialists in Learning.* Los Angeles: Junior College Leadership Program, University of California, 1967. 19 pp. (ED 017 269).

Commission on the Future of Community Colleges. *Building Communities: A Vision for a New Century.* Washington, D. C.: American Association of Community and Junior Colleges, 1988. 58 pp. (ED 293 578).

Cross, K. P. "Improving Learning in Community Colleges." Paper presented at a conference of the Association of Canadian Community Colleges, Regina, Saskatchewan, May 29, 1989. 24 pp. (ED 308 888)

Gleazer, E. J., Jr. "Preparation of Junior College Teachers." *Educational Record*, 1967, 48 (2), 147–152.

Hertig, W. H., Jr. "Special Preparation for Two-Year College Biologists?" *BioScience*, 1971, 21 (4), 184–186.

Houston, J. E. (ed). *Thesaurus of ERIC Descriptors.* (12th ed.) Phoenix, Ariz.: ORYX Press, 1990.

Hurlburt, E. M. "Goals of the Tasks Force of Two-Year College Biologists." *American Biology Teacher*, 1971, 33 (3), 161–162.

Palmer, J. C. "The Scholarly Activities of Community College Faculty: Results of a National Survey." In J. C. Palmer and G. B. Vaughan (eds.), *Fostering a Climate for Faculty Scholarship at Community Colleges.* Washington, D. C.: American Association of Community and Junior Colleges, 1992.

Ratcliff, J. L. "Scholarship, the Transformation of Knowledge, and Community College Teaching." In J. C. Palmer and G. B. Vaughan (eds.), *Fostering a Climate or Faculty Scholarship at Community Colleges,* Washington, D. C.: American Association of Community and Junior Colleges, 1992.

Ross, N. V. *Community College Teacher Preparation Programs in the United States: A Bibliography with Introductory Notes.* University Park: Center for the Study of Higher Education, Pennsylvania State University, 1972. 30 pp. (ED 100 409).

Russell, S., Cox, R. S., Williamson, C., Boismier, J., Javitz, H., and Fairweather, J. *Faculty in Higher Education Institutions, 1988.* Washington, D. C.: National Center for Education Statistics, 1990. 209 pp. (ED 321 628).

Schmeltekopf, D. D. "Professional Status and Community College Faculty: The Role of the Associations." In S. F. Turesky (ed.), *Advancing the Liberal Arts.* New Directions for Community Colleges, no. 42. San Francisco: Jossey-Bass, 1983.

Vaughan, G. B. "Scholarship in Community Colleges: The Path to Respect." *Educational Record*, 1988, 69 (2), 26–31.

Jim Palmer is assistant professor of educational administration and foundations, Illinois State University.

Charting the Changes in Junior Faculty

Relationships Among Socialization, Acculturation, and Gender

ANNE REYNOLDS

I think just the sheer amount of pressure that is indigenous to being an assistant professor at a good school, you are going to change. You're going to have to change, or you're gonna leave, before you get fired or promoted. (Jeff)

As Jeff indicates, the beginning years in the academic environment are a time of change. But not all junior faculty go through the same kinds of changes. In this article I use case studies to illustrate some of the changes junior faculty experience as they interact with their departments and institution in the years prior to the tenure decision. The cases of Greta and Jeff illustrate how professors learn to adjust to a new department when their views of social interdependence closely resemble those of the existing department culture. The cases of Nancy, Steve, and Cathy demonstrate how beginning professors cope in an environment where their views of social interdependence differ from that of the existing culture. The article concludes with a discussion of the relationships among socialization, acculturation, and gender.

Theoretical Underpinnings

Although socialization and acculturation are often used interchangeably, they are theoretically distinct constructs. Socialization, or enculturation as it is commonly referred to in anthropology [22], refers to the process by which an individual acquires the norms, values, and behaviors of the group [10, 23, 24, 32]. In other words, socialization is the development of an initial world view. World view comprises seven logically and structurally integrated cognitive categories—self, other, relationship of self to other, time, space, causality, and classification [27]—as well as the ethos of a people, the "tone, character, and quality of their life, its moral and aesthetic style and mood . . . the underlying attitude toward themselves and their world that life reflects" [16, pp. 126–27]. Once initial socialization takes place, as in the rearing of a child, succeeding socialization experiences assume a *congruence* between the individual's world view and that of the new group. Acculturation, in contrast, is a process that assumes initial *differences* in world view between the individual and the group. Originally, acculturation was seen as a process of forced assimilation of a cultural world view [36]. Now it encompasses the strategies used by individuals who must cope with minority status in a new culture [37].

To understand the socialization and acculturation processes, we have to analyze the newcomer's experiences with others in the culture [24]. This means making sense of the individual's views in three of the world view categories: self, other, and relationship to other. The combination of these three categories is what I call "social interdependence" in this article. Unfortunately, there is a paucity of empirical research on the socialization and/or acculturation experiences of beginning professors from their own vantage points. We must turn to findings from studies in four major areas to gather pieces of the puzzle. The four areas of literature are: problems beginning professors face [29, 30, 33]; faculty career development [1, 2, 7, 14]; women in academia [6, 9, 25, 35]; and socialization outside of academia [3, 5, 13, 21].

From these studies we see that: (1) Junior faculty may find the new culture difficult to understand due to different norms, expectations, and practices; (2) They often feel unprepared for the various roles they must play (teacher, colleague, lone academic); (3) They are passing through a critical period for learning the job and forming attitudes about it, most notably, commitment to the academic way of life; (4) They may move from liberal, idealistic perspectives to more conventional, bureaucratic ones; (5) They are strongly influenced by significant others (peers, superiors) and highly regard their feedback and expectations; and (6) Women and men may experience different things during the early years, such as others' expectations concerning how they should allocate time to work and family life.

In light of current theories regarding socialization and acculturation, this last finding about gendered experiences is intriguing. If women and men have different experiences during their early years, is it due to gendered differences in world view, especially in views of social interdependence? If so, can we assume that all junior faculty go through a process of socialization [9, 11]? Or do some beginning professors, especially women [25], experience acculturation? Such questions lead to an examination of the literature on the development of gendered views of social interdependence.

Males and females go through early "genderization" that encourages their views of social interdependence to be more cooperative, competitive, or individualistic, or some combination of the three [8, 15, 17, 34]. Competitive social interdependence means that individuals are linked to others in a way that as one succeeds, the other fails [26]. Individualism signifies no interdependence; one works alone to attain predesignated criteria of success [26]. In such an environment, the "Separate Self" experiences relationships in terms of fairness and reciprocity between separate individuals and grounds itself in roles that are based on obligations and duties [17, 28]. Cooperation is characterized by positive interdependence, where individuals are connected with others in a way that one cannot succeed without the other [26]. The "Connected Self" experiences relationships as a response to others in their terms and maintains caring and connection with others [17, 28]. This cooperative, connected way of interacting with others is frequently posited as the hallmark of women's ways of knowing [4, 17, 28].

The incompatibility between women's ostensible cooperative view of social interdependence and the more competitive and individualistic views found in research-oriented faculty cultures [7, 14] prompted me to design a study in which I could examine more closely the changes junior faculty experienced. I turned a special eye toward possible gender differences in views of social interdependence that might result in acculturation rather than socialization. Specifically, I wanted to know:

1. Do women and men interpret differently their experiences as beginning faculty in a research university? If so, in what ways?
2. Do these interpretations reflect gender differences in views of social interdependence?
3. What happens to these views over time?

In the remainder of the article I describe this qualitative study of junior faculty, and then, in five case studies, I illustrate the differences I uncovered between and among the socialization and acculturation experiences. The case studies are not means to represent *all* possible experiences junior faculty may have; rather, they are offered as frames through which to view possible differences between socialization and acculturation.

Methodology

Despite a seemingly shared culture, humans give different meanings to actions that, on the surface, look identical. Therefore, to understand causal links among actions, we must uncover the meanings individuals give to their actions. This uncovering is the aim of interpretive study of the meanings junior faculty give to their experiences; thus, it utilizes qualitative data collection and analysis methods.

Nineteen faculty members formed the nucleus of the study. These key informants were criterion-base selected according to willingness to participate and representativeness of three areas of possible comparison/contrast in world view: gender (9 women, 10 men), status (11 pre-tenure, 8 tenured), and discipline (7 natural sciences, 8 social sciences, 4 humanities). Eight of the informants (3 men, 5 women) were married, and seven (5 men, 2 women) had children. Age-wise, three men were in their early 50s to mid-60s; the other informants split evenly above and below the mid-30s (3 men/5 women and 4 men/4 women, respectively). All but one informant grew up in the United States: six (2 men, 4 women) were raised in the Midwest; six (4 men, 2 women) were raised in the East; one woman was raised in the South; and five (3 men, 2 women) were raised in the West. One male informant was raised outside of the United States. All had attended well-respected schools, such as Harvard and Berkeley, for their undergraduate work and top research universities, such as Stanford and MIT, for their graduate work. All but seven informants began their academic careers at the West Coast research-oriented university where my research took place. Of those who started elsewhere, only one came to the present university after more than five years at other schools.

Over the course of a year, I collected data through four semi-structured, tape-recorded interviews with each informant. The interviews were designed to elicit information about the informants' experiences as beginning professors, thier feelings about life in the academy, their underlying values, and their professional duties as academics. I transcribed all of the interviews verbatim and returned them to the informants for any deletions, additions, or "off-the-record" comments. Informal conversations and observations of other faculty at faculty gatherings, such as an American Association of University Professors session on tenure, supplemented the interviews. Participant observation at talks given by faculty members and written documents and records from individuals and university archives, such as curricula vitae, job offer letters, and letters from professional associates rounded out the data collection efforts.

The conceptual framework I developed to structure both data collection and analysis was based on work by Kearney [27] and Geertz [16]. I coupled Kearney's world view universals, which define world view in cognitive terms, with Geertz's definition of world view, which focuses more on the individual's emotional interpretation of the world. The resulting framework comprised seven categories: *Self* refers to the perceptions and expectations junior faculty had of and for themselves prior to becoming professors and into their first year in the university. *Other* consists of the perceptions and expectations informants thought others had of and for them during their early years as professors. *Time* refers to informants' ideas about where their "year" began and ended, and what they considered "free" time and what was "work" time, how they spent their time in their professional lives (and personal lives where there was overlap or conflict with their professional lives), and so forth. *Causality* refers to the professors' sense of agency, that is, when did they see themselves as acting and when as being acted upon? *Classification* refers to the meanings professors gave to terms that describe and divide the academic world (for example, "good" versus "poor" scholarship, teacher/researcher). Conceptions of *Space* were reflected in the ways professors talked about and divided up their material world (for example, offices, labs) and their social world (for example, who were colleagues, who were not). Four other conceptual categories emerged during the data analysis: problems during the early years of a professorship, career influences, stories, and passages significant for a methodological appendix [38]. I used this conceptual framework to analyze the data inductively through qualitative methods, such as memoing and narrative text displays [31], the constant comparative method [18], and simple descriptive statistics.

For purposes of this discussion of junior faculty socialization and acculturation, I concentrate on three of the world view categories: "self," "other," and "relationship of self to other." These categories illuminate junior faculty perceptions about themselves in their interactions with others within the new social setting. I use the words "social interdependence" as a shorthand for these three categories in the remainder of the article.

Changes During the Early Years of the Professorship

Though all informants in the study spoke of changes in themselves during their years in the institution, the five case studies that follow demonstrate the contrast between socialization and acculturation. Jeff's and Greta's cases are interwoven to show the similarities between the sexes when both undergo a socialization experience. Nancy, Steve, and Cathy experienced accultura-tion; their cases represent three different acculturative strategies described by Spindler [37]. Nancy's case illustrates a cultural synthesis of conflicting cultural elements. Steve's case protrays a managed identity. And Cathy's case depicts a reaffirmation of traditional values and behavior patterns. Throughout each of the case studies, I focus on the individual's view of social interde-pendence and how it changed during the experiences of the early years.

Jeff and Greta: Learning the Ropes Through Socialization

The first years in the university were difficult for Jeff and Greta. The scientific side of work went well, but Jeff and Greta had problems interacting with students and other faculty members. As Jeff related, "It's no longer you against the scientific problem anymore. It's no longer that. It's *you* and graduate students, *you* and fellow assistant professors, fellow associate professors, senior faculty, post docs, *you* and granting agencies, *you* and reviewers—I mean, it's just wild—It's hard—not because of the science—if it was just that, I'd just skate right through it. It's hard because it's demanding in a number of other areas that are close to my Achilles heel." To Jeff, the department was a "fiefdom system" where there was "no collegiality" and "no shared interest." He found it hard to talk science with his colleagues because of the constant need to speak in a politically acceptable way. He summed up his feelings in this way: "I do not have a single senior colleague in this department that I trust at the level of being able to talk to. Not one."

Interactions with junior colleagues were much better, but still there was a self-imposed barrier between them. Jeff commented:

> Everybody's kinda living with that thing that some of us are going to make it, some of us aren't; none of us really know . . . who is and who isn't. So you try to be cooperative and help out one another as best you can, but there's a desire to maintain some distance on my part. I don't want to emotionally have to deal with that person's failure or that person's success. . . . You see, if they change when they're promoted, you don't know what they're going to do relative to what you've been open with them about. Essentially, I don't trust anybody in this department, and that is a statement not so much of paranoia as it is a practical way of operating.

While Jeff wanted to sequester himself in his laboratory to do science "at the bench," Greta sought interaction with other people and took on "more administrative duties than anybody had a right to expect," such as being the chairwoman of the graduate committee during her second year. She was vocal about getting students graduated and about professors pulling their weight in terms of advising students. She sent vitriolic memos to colleagues about these two issues, which angered students and a few faculty members. As Greta said, "I alienated a few faculty members when I called a spade a spade about a lot of their students, and just the way they were supervising their students." Greta also took on more graduate students than she could effectively handle, and her style of advising, modeled after her graduate advisor's directive style, antagonized them. Greta spoke of her experience this way: "What I didn't realize, and this was my big mistake, was that there are certain things you can pull off as a 6'5" sixty-year-old male that you can't pull off as a female that's only a few years older than most of the graduate students. That was really what I didn't understand, and that really was the source of all the problem. It was because there was a lot of resentment."

Over time, Greta learned that memos with negative comments about students and faculty only ostracized her from the very people with whom she had to interact. She also learned that diplomacy and tact, as they were defined by the departmental culture, were less alienating than her forthright style. She said, "These are all things that I think that I would back off from now, and I would have never done the way I did. I just would have been a little more diplomatic, a little more tactful. I think that if somebody had advised me, they might have suggested ways that I could have accomplished most of the same things but not with so much alienation of people." Unfortunately, Greta felt her colleagues left her to "sink or swim," though she remembered that one male colleague was instrumental in helping her through her early years.

The changes Greta and Jeff saw themselves going through centered mainly around becoming more politically wise. As Jeff said:

> When I came here, I had no political adroitness. Now I have pretty good savvy, I'm not nearly as good as I should be. I don't kiss as much ass as I ought to, and I don't pay homage to people's neuroses and paranoias as well as I should. But I'm significantly better than I was. I don't get as upset anymore. I don't know if I'm successful or not. There are some people that think I'm successful, and they welcome my opinions and I'd like to give them my opinions, but I have to stay in the position where I'll be able to give them my opinions, so—you either bend or you break, and if there's anything to this game, the amount you bend boggles the mind, and you cannot afford to be particularly bothered by it.

And Greta recalled, "I did change my behavior in the last year before tenure, in the sense that I kept my mouth shut a few times because I didn't want to antagonize people who I knew I'd already antagonized, and I thought I'd better back off." At the end of our talks, Greta had become the second woman in the department to be tenured and promoted to associate professor; Jeff was nearing tenure review.

The bending and breaking Jeff and Greta experienced are characteristic of both socialization and acculturation. However, in these cases, it is the socialization process that is at work. Jeff's and Greta's competitive and individualistic views of social interdependence were quite similar to what they believed their respective departmental cultures to be like, but the greatest difference between their views and that of their colleagues was brutal honesty with their students. Even though Greta interpreted her students' and colleagues' discontent to mean that her style was not appropriate for a young recently appointed woman professor, this style of interaction was also frowned upon by Jeff's colleagues. To reflect the expectations of their colleagues and students, both Greta and Jeff changed their behavior. However, as Greta's next comment suggests, in her case this behavioral change was largely a political move. She mused, "I think I'm probably more relaxed in terms of my interactions with my colleagues because of the tenure business being over. I'm much more willing to say what I think. Not that I've been all that shy about it, but it just makes things—it used to be that I could never stop myself from saying things, in fact, that was one of my big regrets. Then I did it, and I know it was wrong. Now I do it, and I don't care! That's the big difference." Given Jeff's pre-tenure position, he continued to bow to what he perceived to be departmental expectations, but it is likely that with tenure his comments would mirror Greta's.

Steve, Nancy, and Cathy: Coping through Acculturation

Before their dissertations were finished, Nancy, Steve, and Cathy took academic positions. Cathy moved directly into the university where she now works, and Nancy and Steve moved to teaching-oriented institutions. Nancy welcomed the opportunity to return to an environment similar to her undergraduate institution. She thoroughly enjoyed the work and, until she received an offer to apply for her current position, considered remaining there for the rest of her life. Steve took a job in another state due to financial straits at the university, which precluded fourth-year graduate support. The lack of time for research and writing, the heavy course load, and the unambitious students dissatisfied Steve. Within two years, both Steve and Nancy had received offers to work at their current university.

While Steve eagerly anticipated time to do research in this new position, both Cathy and Nancy felt ambivalent about working in a prestigious university. Cathy wanted to see if she would enjoy the rigorous academic environment where she could do research without a large teaching load. Yet, at the same time, she wondered if she were really committed to such a lifestyle: "I had a very `look and see' attitude about academic work at this place. And maybe that's significant in terms of the ambivalence I've had of sort of committing myself to the long work hours one has to do. The free time commitment of an academic is sort of assumed." Nancy also had mixed emotions about leaving her teaching-oriented college: "I think I was and continue to be very ambivalent about whether what I want is a small college and community and interactions with undergraduates—that whole thing, or whether what I really want is the research and the prestige and to be part of the action."

Like Jeff and Greta, Cathy, Steve, and Nancy experienced an intensive workload during their first years. Instead of spending most of their time just doing research, they were swamped with teaching and advising responsibilities for both undergraduate and graduate students and from people outside the university for talks and interviews about their work. Other faculty members expected Nancy, Steve, and Cathy to participate on departmental committees, as well as to continue to be top-notch researchers. The intense workload was especially difficult on Steve and Cathy, who had small children at home. Steve shared primary childcare responsibilities with his wife and felt pulls from two directions. He remarked, "And it's torture for me to go home and have dinner and say I'm gonna put in a couple more hours. I can't do that now because when I go home, I'm a family person." Shadowing all of Steve, Cathy, and Nancy's activities was the question of how everything either led to or away from a favorable tenure decision.

All three beginning professors found the intellectual stimulation at the university satisfying, but they bemoaned the lack of substantive interaction with their colleagues. As Nancy lamented, "People don't seem to talk very much about their research to each other, which I find sort of odd. Everything's very formalized. One doesn't know what people in the department are doing most of the time. . . . I found that very difficult last year. It made me extremely unhappy, because this is a place where you could sit in your office for weeks, literally, and no one would ever come by for any reason. . . . " Steve, too, had little substantive interaction with his colleagues beyond department meetings. In his first three years, no one shared papers they'd written, and no one asked to read papers Steve had written. A few colleagues talked to him about what he would need for tenure, though the advice wasn't always wise, for example, "write a textbook," which Steve knew to be lethal. In Steve's third year, two new assistant professors joined the department, and Steve felt happier. He finally had "someone to be an assistant professor with." Also Steve moved his office closer to his assistant professor colleagues. Cathy thought of her co-workers as colleagues, but she complained that "collegiality is not high, and it's not high because people don't have or don't take time to practice their colleagueship. Even the collaborative research model here tends to be a collection more than a collaboration—a collection of researchers where one meets together to share research, but not to be collaborative."

Over time, Steve, Cathy, and Nancy felt themselves changing as a result of interactions with the institution. Steve's change was slight. As he said, "I'm still me." Yet he did see some changes, such as going from feeling like an imposter (that is, someone whose word was given legitimacy because he was at the elite university and not at the local community college) to someone who was truly part of the university faculty. A second change was Steve's perception of the "big names" at the university—people who had written texts Steve had used—which changed from awe to distanced respect as Steve grew to see himself as an intellectual equal. A third change was in learning to say no to requests from others, in order to do the things that were important for tenure, such as publishing.

The changes Nancy saw herself going through were more dramatic. She lowered her expectations for interactions with her colleagues: "And what I find is that my norms have changed so that I no longer, if I walk by somebody's office and their door's open, it no longer occurs to me to stop and say hello. We have a new faculty member across the hall, and I used to think, how could somebody possibly be just a few steps away and not be constantly going [over there]—and now it never occurs to me to go over there and say hello. . . . So, clearly my behavior and my sense of what you do has changed a lot in the last year." To counterbalance this tendency towards isolation, Nancy tried to initiate contact with her colleagues by asking them to read her work and by participating in a lunchtime discussion group. She even vented her frustrations at faculty meetings, but found that "people who had been here for awhile didn't really understand your complaints. It was total noncomprehension. You'd say, `People never talk to each other.' And they'd say, `What do you mean, we have these seminars once a month.' They didn't understand that what I was talking about was informal interaction, or they believed that informal interaction was impossible because people were so busy. It was very hard for us who were new to talk to the people who were old about this thing because we were clearly thinking in different ways about it." Despite her attempts to change the cultural norms, Nancy felt herself becoming more and more like the typical colleague in the department. She remembered, "I kept thinking, I don't want to become like them, but it's become more clear to me that I've become much more like them. It's a lot easier for me, because it doesn't make me so unhappy because I'm used to it now." Nancy thought optimistically about the changes in herself and explained, "I think it's mostly a matter of sort of realizing that there are trade-offs and finding ways to deal with them. I mean, I guess finding ways to deal with them, coming to terms with them—those changes are for the good even if the world isn't always the way I'd like it to be."

Cathy also saw changes in herself. As tenure drew near, Cathy realized that she did not belong in this type of university. She stated, "It was more the second and third years that I began to really worry about productivity and certainly the conflict I felt right away between what I enjoyed in my job, which was working with students and also participating in intellectually stimulating things, and doing my own private work." Though she *could* meet the publication standards, Cathy was unwilling to put in the time and effort needed. Her expectations for herself as far as publications went were different from those of the institution and her colleagues: "I decided that I would do my job the way it was comfortable for me. . . . For me, if I do one good paper a year I'm perfectly satisfied with that. I don't see why that isn't sufficient. I mean, it is sufficient for me. It's just not for [this university]. [I] recognized that it was a misfit for me to be in a high pressure research-oriented university." Other factors were involved in Cathy's decision to leave, such as the desire to spend more time with her new husband and child and the desire not to ask her colleagues to vote on her tenure when she thought her work was not up to their standards. But Cathy's decision was largely based on the disparity between her own expectations for herself and those the university culture had for her.

After a sabbatical year away from the campus, Cathy announced her resignation. She continued to perform her duties as an assistant professor, but she investigated other job possibilities for a full-time research position outside of academia. When her resignation became effective, she took on a new administrative position in the university.

In each of these cases, a different acculturative strategy was used to cope with the new culture. While Nancy's view of social interdependence accentuated cooperation and interaction among people, she believed her department prized individualism. Nancy was forced to find a way to minimize her discomfort in the environment: she began to view the departmental interaction patterns as normal and to interact with others in an individualistic manner. She did not like interacting this way, but she wanted to fit into the culture, so she changed her behavior. Yet she didn't totally give up the behavior she was comfortable with. She found ways to remain in contact with other colleagues, for instance, during lunchtime meetings. In sum, Nancy coped with the discordant elements of her immediate culture by adopting some new behaviors while retaining the old. In acculturative strategy terms, Nancy's case depicts a cultural synthesis of conflicting cultural elements [37].

Steve's case offers a view of a managed identity [37]. He wanted the opportunity to research, write and teach in a cooperative environment. To some extent, he found this opportunity in his department. The departmental culture valued individualism with some collegial interaction. Yet, Steve also wanted to provide primary childcare to his two small children. This was not part of the work culture. In fact, Steve thought that the departmental expectations for a junior faculty member made outside activities almost impossible. Thus, Steve was forced to cope by being two people: the industrious beginning professor at work and the committed family member at home. The strain of such a double-identity was hard on him, and Steve thought seriously about leaving the culture for one in which he would be less stressed.

Though Cathy's view was in some ways similar to what she believed the departmental culture to be like, a very important aspect was quite different. As in Steve's case, this was the expectation that junior colleagues would be devoted to the academic values, norms, and behaviors as they existed. Cathy couldn't accept the standards, so she chose to leave the culture for one that was more compatible with her own view. In this choice, Cathy demonstrated the acculturative strategy of a reaffirmation of traditional values and behavior patterns.

Relationships among Gender, Socialization, and Acculturation

As the case studies in this article suggest, the changes junior faculty go through are not all the same. What appears to govern the changes that the individual experiences is the view of social interdependence with which the newcomer enters and the interaction of that view with the newcomer's perception of the view held by members of his or her department. If a beginning professor enters the department with a view of social interdependence that is different from what he or she perceives to be the department's view, for example, a view that is more cooperative than competitive or individualistic, then it's likely that the professor will undergo acculturation rather than socialization. We saw this in the case of Nancy. Or the professor may contemplate or actually leave the university in order not to change, as the cases of Steve and Cathy illustrate. On the other hand, if a professor enters the department with a view of social interdependence that is similar to what he or she believes is the existing departmental view, then it's likely that the professor will go through socialization. Jeff and Greta are cases in point.

The cases also suggest that it is not the sex of the assistant professor that is the major influence on the charges she or he will go through during the early years in the professorship. Nevertheless, the sex of the beginning professor may play a role in shaping the newcomer's experiences. In light of current descriptions of research faculty culture, it is not surprising to find women's experiences in the research university (or any competitive, individualistic culture, for that matter) reflective of acculturation more often than socialization. The reverse may hold for men's experiences. However, it is important to stress that even though genderization influences how one views social interdependence, both males and females can undergo either socialization or acculturation.

By itself, a discussion of whether junior faculty members undergo socialization or acculturation is pedantic. More important is the effect such changes have on the individual's research and teaching and, by extension, on society. Faculty members in universities construct knowledge through their research efforts. This knowledge is legitimized by members of similar thought collectives. The knowledge is then disseminated to the public via teaching, writing, and oral presentations. Given this situation, it seems critical to ask whether or not the acculturation process is encouraging a homogenized way of knowing and of sharing knowledge with others. Research by Gumport [19, 20] suggests that some individuals are able to resist the acculturative forces and find ways to maintain views of social interdependence that do not coincide with the dominant one while remaining in the institution. Such findings are encouraging, yet they do not diminish the importance of asking questions that challenge the status quo: should we not be concerned about the prevalence in research universities of individualistic and competitive views of social interdependence? About the exodus of people with divergent views from these universities? About the changes we see junior faculty undergoing—changes from cooperative views of social interdependence to those of individualism and competition? What kind of an effect do individualistic and competitive views of social interdependence have on the knowledge that is produced? On the methods used to diseminate that knowledge? On student learning?

As Jeff commented at the beginning of the paper, the junior faculty years are fraught with great change. It is important for us to examine critically the nature of these changes and their impact on the academy, for as Nancy explains, "I think coming here . . . wasn't just a change of jobs. It was a real choice of values, and I think it is likely to affect what I am as a human being, and part of my ambivalence about coming here is because I think the environment you put yourself in does affect the kind of person you become. I think I will become—I probably already am—a different person than I would have been had I stayed at [my former college]."

References

1. Baldwin, R. "Adult and Career Development: What Are the Implications for Faculty?" *Current Issues in Higher Education*, 2 (1979), 13–20.

2. Baldwin, R. G., and R. T. Blackburn. "The Academic Career as a Developmental Process: Implications for Higher Education." *Journal of Higher Education*, 52 (November/December 1981), 598–614.

3. Becker, H. S., et al. *Boys in White. Student Culture in Medical School.* Chicago: The University of Chicago Press, 1961.

4. Belenky, M. F., et al. *Women's Ways of Knowing. The Development of Self, Voice, and Mind.* New York: Basic Books, Inc., 1987.

5. Berlew, D. E., and D. T. Hall. "The Socialization of Managers: Effects of Expectations on Performance." *Administrative Science Quarterly*, 11 (September 1966), 207–23.

6. Bernard, J. *Academic Women.* University Park: Pennsylvania State University Press, 1964.

7. Brown, J. W., and R. C. Shukraft. "Personal Development and Professional Practice in College and University Professors." Ph. D. dissertation, University of California—Berkeley Graduate Theological Union, 1974.

8. Chodorow, N. "Feminism and Difference: Gender Relation and Difference in Psychoanalytic Perspective." *Socialist Review*, 46 (1979), 42–64.

9. Clark, S. M., and M. Corcoran. "Perspectives on the Professional Socialization of Women Faculty: A Case of Accumulative Disadvantage?" *Journal of Higher Education*, 57 (January/February 1986), 20–43.

10. Clausen, J. A. "Introduction," In *Socialization and Society*, edited by J. A. Clausen, pp. 1–17. Boston: Little, Brown, 1968.

11. Connolly, J. J. "Viewing Faculty Orientation as a Socialization Process." ERIC031 226, 1969.

12. Erickson, F. "Qualitative Methods in Research on Teaching." In *Handbook of Research on Teaching, Third Edition*, edited by M. C. Wittrock, pp. 119–61. New York: Macmillan Publishing Company, 1986.

13. Erlanger, H. S., and D. A. Klegon. *Socialization Effects of Professional School: The Law School Experience and Student Orientation to Public Interest Concerns.* Discussion Paper No. 434–77. Madison: University of Wisconsin, Institute for Research on Poverty, 1977.

14. Freedman, M. B., and J. W. Brown. *Academic Culture and Faculty Development.* Berkeley, Calif.: Montaigne, Inc., 1979.

15. Gardiner, J. K. "Self Psychology as Feminist Theory." *Signs: Journal of Women in Culture and Society*, 12 (Summer 1987), 761–80.

16. Geertz, C. *The Interpretation of Cultures.* New York: Basic Books, Inc., 1973.

17. Gilligan, C. *In a Different Voice.* Cambridge, Mass.: Harvard University Press, 1982.

18. Glaser, B. G. "The Constant Comparative Method of Qualitative Analysis." In *Issues in Participant Observation: A Text and Reader*, edited by G. J. McCall and J. L. Simmons, pp. 216–27. Reading, Mass.: Addison-Wesley Publishing Company, 1969.

19. Gumport, P. "The Social Construction of Knowledge: Individual and Institutional Commitments to Feminist Scholarship." Ph. D. dissertation, Stanford University, 1987.

20. _____. "Curricula as Signposts of Cultural Change." *Review of Higher Education*, 12 (Fall 1988), 49–62.

21. Hall, D. T., and B. Schneider. *Organizational Climates and Careers. The Work Lives of Priests*. New York: Seminar Press, 1973.

22. Herskovits, M. J. *Man and His Works*. New York: Alfred A. Knopf, 1948.

23. Homans, G. C. *The Human Group*. New York: Harcourt, Brace & World, 1950.

24. Hurrelmann, K. *Social Structure and Personality Development*. New York: Cambridge University Press, 1988.

25. Jensen, K. "Women's Work and Academic Culture: Adaptations and Confrontations." *Higher Education*, 11 (January 1982), 67–83.

26. Johnson, D. W., and R. T. Johnson. *Cooperation and Competition. Theory and Research*. Edina, Minn.: Interaction Book Company, 1989.

27. Kearney, M. *World View*. Novato, Calif.: Chandler & Sharp, Publisher, 1984.

28. Lyons, N. P. "Two Perspectives: On Self, Relationships, and Morality." *Harvard Educational Review*, 53 (May 1983), 125–45.

29. Mager, G. M., and B. Myers. "If First Impressions Count: New Professors' Insights and Problems." *Peabody Journal of Education*, 59 (January 1982), 100–106.

30. _____. "Developing a Career in the Academy: New Professors in Education." ERIC236 127. Portland, Oreg.: Portland State University, 1983.

31. Miles, M. B., and A. M. Huberman. *Qualitative Data Analysis. A Sourcebook of New Methods*. Beverly Hills, Calif.: Sage Publications, 1984.

32. Mortimer, J. T., and R. G. Simmons. "Adult Socialization." In *Annual Review of Sociology*, edited by R. H. Turner, J. Coleman, and R. C. Fox, pp. 421–54. Palo Alto, Calif.: Annual Reviews, 1978.

33. Reynolds, A. "Making and Giving the Grade: Experiences of Beginning Professors at a Research University." Paper presented to the American Educational Research Association, New Orleans, La., 1988.

34. Rossi, A. S. "The Biosocial Side of Parenting." *Human Nature*, 1 (June 1978), 72–79.

35. Simeone, A. *Academic Women. Working Towards Equality*. South Hadley, Mass.: Bergin & Garvey Publishers, 1987.

36. Spicer, E. H. "Acculturation." In *International Encyclopedia of the Social Sciences. Volume 1*, edited by D. L. Sills, pp. 21–27. U.S.: Crowell, Collier, and Macmillan, 1968.

37. Spindler, L. *Culture Change and Modernization: Mini-Models and Case Studies*. Prospect Heights, Ill.: Waveland Press, 1977.

38. Whyte, W. F. *Street Corner Society: The Social Structure of an Italian Slum*. Chicago: University of Chicago Press, 1943.

Anne Reynolds is a research scientist at Educational Testing Service in Princeton, N. J.

Practices of the Academy: Barriers to Access for Chicano Academics

MARÍA DE LA LUZ REYES AND JOHN J. HALCÓN

No set of data can properly set out the full range of problems that minorities face in America. Our malaise runs deep and is not easily described statistically. Since the Declaration of Independence was first written, we have lived a life unworthy of our stated ideals, and we are now paying a heavy price for our ambiguity—perhaps even our hypocrisy. We pass laws to protect minority rights and to increase minority opportunities, but too often we are satisfied with appearances.[1]

After a decade in which many of the bard-earned gains made by minorities in the 1960s and the early 1970s have been lost to ambivalence and retrenchment, the present crisis in the education of minorities has suddenly sparked a renewed sense of concern among leading educators. The call to increase opportunities for minorities in higher education is a recurring theme of the present reform movement and is now being heard on university and college campuses across the nation. The sense of urgency in that call can be best understood against the backdrop of two current education themes. On the one hand are current demographic projections which indicate that minorities are dramatically changing the face of student bodies in schools—warranting renewed efforts to improve their academic achievement.[2] On the other is the increase in racial conflict between white and minority students on university campuses, which prompts an unspoken fear of racial conflict spreading into the public elementary and secondary schools.[3]

These impending crises in higher education have led to a call for diversification among faculty and students in campuses across the nation. Most of these initiatives have not been successful and it is not surprising. We attribute this limited success to the discrepancy between the public "courting" of minorities and their actual incorporation (i.e., recruitment, retention and promotion) into institutions of higher education (IHEs). The barriers which limit minority access to IHEs under the guise of reform have proven to be among the most formidable of obstacles. With few exceptions, the renewed interest in minorities in higher education is proving to be nothing more than superficial flirtation and empty rhetoric about the value of cultural diversity. The call is intended to give the "appearance" of interest, a position powerfully captured in the opening quote by O. Meredith Wilson. Although the call for increasing the number of minorities in IHEs has gained momentum, it has been ineffective because it is rarely accompanied by a meaningful commitment to the realization of that goal. Diversification of college communities, including an increase in minority hiring, may indeed be incompatible with the current institutional power structures, which create the barriers to the attainment of those goals and perpetuate a status quo that favors majority groups.

Racism in Academia

Although most reports on racial conflicts focus on students, minority faculty are also victims of racism and are greatly affected by it. Accounts of racism experienced by minority academics receive less attention because racial incidents involving students are usually overt, often include racial slurs and occur in public settings. In many respects, these incidents are written off as harmless juvenile behavior, worthy only of fleeting concern. In contrast, racism involving minority faculty in institutions of higher education is generally covert and often masked by adherence to a mythical academic meritocracy regarding professional qualifications that subtly favors whites. To admit publicly that racism exists in academia is to question the very foundation of the academic enterprise.

Chicanos' experiences with racism in institutions of higher education have been well-documented and characterized as "academic colonialism."[4] Many Chicanos attribute the inability to penetrate a traditionally white male system to the existence of a pervasive racism.[5] The dismal number of Hispanics in faculty positions in institutions of higher education is ample evidence of this. Like other minorities, Hispanics have been surprised to learn that their earned doctorates have not translated into equal access or equal benefits even at the highest levels of the educational ladder, where the most educated and enlightened individuals are expected to behave fairly and treat others equitably. Instead, they have discovered that educational stratification[6] and discriminatory practices generally encountered at the lower levels of the educational pipeline are also present in academia, albeit under various disguises.[7]

A common explanation for the lack of Hispanics in academia is that the pool of Hispanics with Ph.D.'s is very small. Proportionately, this is true. Recent figures for Hispanics indicate that Hispanics represent only 2 percent of all Ph.D.'s in the country.[8] Although the overall percentage gain is small, there is a growing number of unemployed or underemployed Hispanic Ph.D.'s unable to gain access to faculty positions in institutions of higher education. Wilson and Justiz report that there are more candidates available than are finding appointments.[9] This situation makes us question whether it is realistic to talk about diversification or the elimination of racism in institutions of higher education without having provided minorities full incorporation and participation in the educational system.

The lack of public awareness of racism in academia, however, does not minimize its existence. Minorities know from personal experience that racism in higher education is vigorous and real. Nothing short of institutional racism could account for the magnitude of existing inequality and the minuscule number of minorities in academia.[10] In 1977, for example, Hispanic faculty in four-year institutions made up only 1.5 percent of the total full-time faculty, and in 1983 they represented only 1.8 percent.[11] The dearth of minorities in IHEs was underscored by the 1982 Commission on the Higher Education of Minorities which stated that "no amount of rhetorical commitment to the principles of equal opportunity, affirmative action, and pluralism can compensate for or justify the current degree of minority underrepresentation among faculty, administrators, staff members, and students in higher education."[12] Recent reports on the status of Hispanics in higher education have reached similar conclusions.[13] Institutional racism is a fundamental barrier to access and opportunity for minority faculty members.

Framework for Analysis

In this essay, we propose to examine institutional practices which promote racism and act as barriers to access and parity for Chicanos in academia. The framework for analysis consists of three interdependent sets of social relations: (1) the relative social status of Chicanos in American society; (2) the interactions between minority and majority faculty; and (3) the relationship between majority faculty and administrators in institutions of higher education. The term "Hispanic" as used here refers to the two major underrepresented Spanish-language background groups, primarily Chicano and Puerto Rican. To illustrate our points, we will use examples chiefly from the experiences of Chicano academics who represent the largest of the Hispanic groups in this country, but the application to other Hispanic, and non-Hispanic, minority groups will be self-evident. The purpose of this discussion is to examine the types of interactions, attitudes and practices that must be significantly altered to permit diversification and full participation of Chicanos and other minorities in the academy. Racism will be examined in light of these social relations which individually and collectively prevent Chicanos from achieving that access.

Chicanos in American Society

Although American society is rooted in the collective experiences of various immigrant groups who settled in this country, it has evolved into a monolithic system dominated by a strong ethnocentric perspective that generally views racial, cultural and linguistic differences as deficiencies and disadvantages. The dominant group in this monolithic system is composed of individuals from white, English-speaking, Anglo-Saxon backgrounds. Ramirez explains that in this system the "dominant cultural group has the power, resources, and authority to define itself in positive, normative ways and to define the out-group in negative, dysfunctional ways—thus rationalizing the continuation of vesting power in itself and away from other groups."[14] Individuals who do not belong to the dominant group, blacks, Hispanics, Native Americans and others, constitute the minority groups who occupy lower status positions, and comprise the poor and working class who have little voice in matters of government and policy-making. Not coincidentally, these same groups are also those most highly segregated in public schools and those least likely to graduate from high school, least likely to go on to college and least likely to occupy positions in academia.

The status of Hispanics relative to the dominant group in this country has been described as "second class citizenship."[15] Since the initial interactions between Mexican-Americans and Anglos in the Southwest, an attitude of "Anglo superiority" has predominated.[16] It is that attitude that has sustained prejudice and discrimination toward Mexican-origin individuals and continues to perpetuate negative stereotypes. These stereotypes suggest that Mexican-Americans are generally passive, are present-oriented, want immediate gratification, have low levels of aspirations, and are nonsuccess oriented.[17]

The notion that cultural differences imply inferiority are vestiges of those stereotypes and are reflected in educational institutions where differences arc treated as deficits. In elementary and secondary schools, these stereotypes serve to rationalize such educational practices as tracking of minorities, disproportionate representation in special education classes, poor career counseling and low expectations from teachers. These practices contribute to the small pool of college graduates available to fill academic positions in higher education.

Although the general public may cling to a naive perception that academicians who constitute the nucleus of intelligentsia are above racism,[18] "there is no reason to believe that there is less racism among academics than there is among other groups in society."[19] The academy mirrors the same attitudes and generalities about cultural/racial differences that plague the larger society. The low status that Hispanics occupy relative to the dominant group in society is reflected in what Garza refers to as Hispanics in "the role of second-class academic citizens."[20]

A culturally diverse professoriate is not valued in institutions of higher education. This is evidenced by the existence of pervasive "institutional ethnocentrism that ignores the perspectives and values of other cultures"[21] and the fact that stereotyping of minority academics is a common practice. The majority of Hispanics in academe, for example, are often relegated to ethnically oriented programs; Spanish department, Chicano studies, bilingual education and student support services (e.g., EOP, Upward Bound). In a 1987 National Latino Faculty Survey conducted by Garza, one respondent, a Puerto Rican faculty member from a midwestern university, summarized the barriorization of Hispanics in these words:

> There seems to be the assumption that all Latinos teach or should teach ethnic studies. I work on economic development of the Caribbean and Latin America. The problem is not that Anglos consider ethnic studies inferior [although they do], but Latinos in general inferior whether they do ethnic studies or not. I teach in a program that is the academic ghetto for Latinos at this university; the Spanish department is the other Latin ghetto.[22]

The concentration of Hispanics and other minorities in ethnically oriented departments is well-documented.[23] Rochin and de la Torre also reported in a 1986 affirmative action study that a disproportionate percentage of Chicano faculty at the University of California at Davis occupied positions in Chicano studies (41 percent), and Spanish and bilingual education programs.[24] The practice of specialized minority hiring for minority slots "is a more formal cooptation of Hispanic concern which relieves the institution of the need to integrate throughout their ranks"[25] and appears to be "the unofficial way of implementing affirmative action mandates and guidelines."[26]

The diverse representation of racial and ethnic groups in the larger society is not reflected in academia. On the contrary, there is little cultural or racial diversity among those who occupy the upper echelons of the educational pipeline and those in charge of developing and implementing educational policies. Wilson and Justiz report that minorities make up only 9.6 percent of all full-time faculty in higher education. Obviously then, white academics, who make up about 90 percent of total faculty, occupy a dominant status in the academy.[27]

The absence of a large diverse professoriate causes an unfair perception and evaluation of minority faculty. In an environment where there are few minority faculty or minority students, white students have an especially difficult time relating to minority faculty. Hispanic colleagues teaching at predominantly white colleges, for example, report that their student evaluations are replete with complaints that too much attention is given to "minority" issues, that "too many of the assigned readings focus on minorities" or are "too political," and that Hispanic professors "have a chip on their shoulders." We have also personally experienced the same type of criticism and know that it can leave a sharp sting, especially when students admit that they learned a great deal in spite of alleged biases in our teaching! This negative reaction from mainstream students occurs because a focus on race, discrimination, ethnicity, etc. makes people uncomfortable.[28] In a classic example of the old "double standard," minority faculty are perceived by Anglo students as "racial," "arrogant," or "on a personal bandwagon." Yet Anglo professors who espouse a non-mainstream perspective are regarded as sensitive and liberal. They emerge as forward thinkers and are generally accorded much respect. The tragedy of this double standard for minorities, however, is that when student evaluations are part of the evaluation, retention, promotion and merit pay decision-making processes, minority faculty pay a heavy price for being racially, culturally or linguistically different.

If more professors presented diverse perspectives on issues, the views of minorities would not seem at odds with the norm and the burden would not be so heavy for minority faculty. Additionally, white students would not be deprived of a healthy exposure to ethnically diverse points of view, which are desperately needed in an increasingly pluralistic society. Without the exposure to cultural diversity, it will continue to be difficult for students to develop mutual respect and learn how to coexist peacefully with other cultural or racial groups. The current increase in racial conflict between white and minority students on college campuses reflects that deprivation.[29]

Cultural diversity is not valued by educational systems. If it were, the success rate of minority academics would be higher and faculties in institutions of higher education would be more diversified.[30] Not appreciating cultural diversity as an asset is a major barrier to the full incorporation of Hispanics in the academy because it perpetuates the kinds of stereotyping about Hispanics faculty discussed above. Furthermore, it limits Hispanic opportunities to become full members of the academy.

In contrast, when cultural diversity is valued, ethnic, racial and linguistic diversity is not only respected, but nourished, and promoted. It means that differences are celebrated and viewed as means of enriching and benefiting the lives of both faculty and students. The Commission on the Higher Education of Minorities suggests that if IHEs were measured by the degree of "value added—that is, the difference made in quality of mind and self-respect of students, if value added were to become one of the measures used in assigning status to institutions, it is likely that . . . with this change in our national value premise, we might get commitment instead of lip service to minority opportunities in higher education."[31] If cultural diversity were valued, more opportunities would open up in all departments, and these would begin to pave the way to greater access for Chicano academics.

Majority-Minority Faculty Interactions

The interaction between majority and minority faculty in the academy mirrors the dominant/ subordinate paradigm of the larger society. Manifestations of covert racism emerge when educated "subordinates" interact within this paradigm. Although covert racism is difficult to prove, Chicanos and other minorities in academe frequently report the same type of recurring incidents against them that limit their access and opportunities for hiring, retention and promotion. In another paper, we discussed a number of typical examples of covert racism in academia.[32] Those examples can be grouped under the following categories: the "type-casting syndrome" (similar to stereotyping already discussed), tokenism, the "one-minority-per-pot syndrome", and "brown-on-brown" research taboo and the "hairsplitting concept". Each of these typify a patronizing, condescending attitude that mainstream faculty often demonstrate in interacting with minority faculty. These practices serve as barriers to parity for Chicano academics.

Although the implementation of affirmative action programs provided more access to minorities in certain job markets, it left all minority professionals and academics with a legacy of tokenism—a stigma that has been difficult to dispel. The myth that all minorities entered, and continue to enter, the system only under special admission is a result of that legacy. The fact is that the "availability pool" clause in the affirmative action regulations greatly limited the number of minority faculty who had to be hired under the guidelines. The clause was interpreted to mean that regulations applied only in cases where it could be proven that there were a significant number of available minorities who could be hired for the targeted positions. In the case of Hispanics, Holmes[33] reported this clause made it impossible for IHEs to comply with regulations because the number of Hispanics with Ph.D.'s constituted less than one percent of available persons in many academic fields at that time.[34] The former Department of Health, Education and Welfare responsible for overseeing the regulations, together with the University of California at Berkeley, for example, found that there were only three departments out of the entire campus where projected goals for minority hiring were required under affirmative action regulations.[35]

What this means is that the majority of Hispanic faculty who are now teaching in colleges and universities got there mainly by the strength of their own qualifications. There is little substance to the general assumption that they lack the appropriate qualifications to occupy their respective positions in academia. The myth that minorities are mere "tokens" and have been hired without the adequate experience or qualifications, however, still persists. In contrast, academics from the dominant group behave as if their positions were secured solely on the basis of high qualifications and merit. Our experience has taught us that this is simply not true. What is true is that doubts about a candidate's qualifications are more likely to emerge implicitly or explicitly when prospective candidates are minorities than when they are whites.[36]

Another negative result of tokenism is that it places undue pressure on minority academics to prove that they are as good as white academics. Moore contends that "Blacks are expected to be better in order to be equal."[37] The same is true for Hispanics. This sentiment begins in graduate school, where minority students report feeling "stigmatized" by their race and culture and frustrated by the continual need to prove themselves.[38] Tokenism has the added effect of reducing minority-occupied positions to second-class status providing an easy excuse for institutions to minimize and ignore Hispanic presence.

The minimizing of Hispanic presence is also manifested in the syndrome we call "one-minority-per-pot." This syndrome refers to a continued reluctance on the part of IHEs to hire more than one minority faculty per department. This common practice places an unwritten limit on minority hiring and prevents diversification of departments. The unwritten rule is that if a department has one ethnic minority, or if the department interviews without ultimately hiring a minority, the department has met its obligation. The result is that the members of the mainstream faculty are usually satisfied "good-faith efforts" have been exerted in hiring and integrating minorities. But, with the exception of minority-related programs, few mainstream departments can boast of more than one minority professor. When Chicanos apply for mainstream positions, they are often met with doubts about their qualifications outside of ethnically related areas or are automatically recommended for available "minority slots."[39]

This situation has happened to both authors and to many of our colleagues. In a job interview for a teacher education position where teaching reading was a requirement, one of these authors was met with the remark, "We know you teach bilingual reading, but can you teach real reading?" The assumption was that the teaching of reading as it applies to bilinguals is not based on the same core of processes and pedagogical principles of teaching reading to mainstream populations. That assumption is not only condescending, but absurd to those who understand that the teaching of reading to bilinguals requires additional specialization beyond the basic requirements for reading majors. In other cases where the authors have applied to separate institutions, both applications were automatically transferred or added to positions in ethnically related program areas. While it may be well-intentioned, this practice deprives Hispanics of serious consideration to qualifications in core disciplines, i.e., educational psychology, public policy, sociology, English, etc., and it classifies them according to their ethnic affiliation. The result of this practice is that Chicanos, like other minorities, are rarely recognized as full-fledged experts in their own right.[40]

The root of the one-minority-per-pot syndrome is a deep-seated belief that minorities are not as qualified as white academics. The unspoken truth is that there is an underlying fear that the presence of more than one minority faculty member in a traditionally mainstream program will lower the academic standards of the department.[41]

This syndrome is not limited to faculty positions. It also applies to administrative ranks. An example that comes to mind involved a Chicano department chair who applied for an associate deanship at his institution. In spite of his qualifications for the position, however, he was forewarned by the academic vice president, who was Anglo, that his candidacy would not likely receive serious consideration "because there were already three other Chicano administrators at the college." Convinced that submitting his application for the position was a futile exercise, he withdrew his name from consideration. It is important to note that when a non-Chicano applied for the same position, no one counted the number of Anglos already on the faculty or in administrative positions. The one-minority-per-pot syndrome prevents full integration and diversification of departments and serves to disempower and restrict the career goals and aspirations of Chicano academics.

The greatest obstacle to tenure for minority faculty is the taboo on "brown-on-brown" research.[42] This taboo refers to the practice of devaluing research on minorities when it is undertaken by minority researchers. Efforts on the part of Chicanos and other minorities to conduct research on minority-related topics, e.g., dropouts, bilingual education, second language literacy and the education of minorities, often meet with disapproval by white colleagues who sit as judges on the quality of their research and publications.[43] The research interest in these areas stems from Chicanos' need to define, label, describe and interpret their own condition from the inside out and to lend a sense of balance to existing theories about themselves. From the point of view of mainstream academics, however, brown-on-brown research is perceived to be narrow in scope and to lack objectivity. This paternal attitude is no more than a double standard which lends credibility to the research of whites on mainstream populations, but discredits minority academics who research minority issues. In fact, whites who undertake research on minorities are infinitely more likely to be admired and rewarded for the focus of their scholarship than are minorities who study the same populations. "White-on-white" research is accorded legitimacy, while brown-on-brown research is questioned and challenged.

The devaluing of research conducted by Chicanos affects promotion and tenure decisions. Although this practice has been difficult to prove, many Hispanics and blacks cite numerous examples of unfair evaluation of their research during promotion and tenure reviews.[44] The delegitimization of minority research by majority faculty is rooted in the values that undergird academe and that are characteristic of culturally monolithic systems. Those systems judge the quality of scholarship from the normative perspective of their own cultural group and thus deem deviations from the norm as inferior.[45] Under the guise of meritocracy and quality, they often sort out political, social and intellectual factors[46] that differ from traditional Eurocentric perspectives.[47]

Decisions about hiring, promoting and tenuring minority faculty are often based on what we call "hairsplitting" practices. This refers to the practice of making highly subjective and arbitrary judgment calls that frequently result in favor of whites over minorities. Many minority academics have now had opportunities to serve on faculty search committees. They have learned that final decisions are not as objective as minorities are led to believe. Far too often the best qualified candidate is not the person hired. It is not unusual for the second or third choice candidate to be hired because they are a better fit with the faculty. The minority candidate is rarely the "best fit" for a department. Because its application is so effective against minority faculty, we are convinced that the invocation of the "best fit" rule is one of the most significant barriers to access for minority candidates. The process of selecting a particular candidate is due much more to the personal preferences of the faculty committee than to the myth of objectivity or of equal opportunity hiring. Minorities, for example, are often not hired, promoted or tenured—not for lack of required qualifications, but on the basis of paternalistic attitudes of the decision-makers.[48] Or, they might be eliminated from academic positions on a presumption that they might not be happy in a predominantly white university.[49] Hairsplitting practices are dangerous because they exclude or limit Chicanos from full incorporation into the academy simply on the basis of minor, subjective, and often inconsequential factors.

One of the major conflicts in the academy is that majority faculty view merit, albeit mythical, as the overriding value in academia, while minority faculty emphasize worth. The "worth" of an individual is defined by the value he or she can add to the academic community, for example, the diverse perspective that a minority professor can add to a department.[50] While neither merit nor worth alone is sufficient, a balance of both can provide greater opportunity for minority access and parity. As a larger number of Chicano academics move into the ranks of the tenured professoriate, the current condescending and patronizing treatment of minorities will begin to wane. It will do so because full membership in the academy brings greater participatory power in the decision-making process. Minority voices in that process will ensure greater access and opportunities for other minorities. This will occur as minority academics begin to be treated more as equals and as full-fledged experts in their fields, and as their research interests are legitimized and put on a par with interests in mainstream issues.

Majority Faculty and Administration

Access and parity for minorities in IHEs lie in the hands of both majority faculty and university administrators. The call for the diversification of the faculty and greater opportunities for minorities begins at the highest levels. The typical approach is for the university president or chancellor to make a general, but public, declaration of concern for the recruitment, hiring and retention of more minorities. Sometimes this is echoed by school deans and other mid-level administrators and tacitly accepted by the general faculty. Neither administrators nor majority faculty, however, take a proactive stance in making the goal a reality. There are several reasons for this.

One reason is that the goals are set at the institutional level rather than at the individual department level. At the campus level, the entire campus community is charged with the responsibility, but no single individual or unit is held accountable. As a consequence, no minority gains are made because each department can always "pass the buck" and let another one do it, or satisfy their goal by hiring a white woman instead of an ethnic minority. "Playing off " white women against ethnic minorities in the hiring competition is a common practice that often leaves ethnic minorities on the short end.[51] Lack of performance monitoring in meeting the goals of the institution is another major reason why few institutions of higher education are successful in increasing their number of ethnic minorities.

Since departments are not individually charged with the hiring of minorities, majority faculty fall back on traditional ways of filling available positions. Without awareness of the unique educational experiences of minorities, they write the job descriptions and simply wait for ethnic minorities to apply. What they fail to recognize is that lack of flexibility and often the wording in their job descriptions (e.g., "Educational administrators with experience as public school superintendents preferred") discourage ethnic minorities from applying for positions for which they might otherwise be qualified. Then, when the national search yields no ethnic minorities, majority faculty blame the outcome on three possible reasons: (1) the pool of minority Ph.D.'s is too small; (2) minority candidates lack the appropriate qualifications for the job; or (3) the demands of minority candidates vis-a-vis their qualifications (defined in terms of publication record) are unreasonable. All these are symptoms of an internal resistance to the mission goals of the institution, and a strong indicator of a lack of a true commitment to increasing minority access to their ranks.

The excuse that the minority pool is too small to go around is a very common response. Olivas refers to this as the "high-demand/low-supply mythology" about minorities.[52] Although no one denies that the pool may indeed be small, the data indicate that the supply of minorities is greater than the number that is actually hired.[53] There is no justification for assuming or pretending that the minority pool is empty. When concerted efforts are made to recruit and hire minorities and when this goal is made a top priority, institutions always seem to be able to find enough eligible candidates to fulfill their objectives.

The experiences of Miami University of Ohio and the University of Massachusetts are potent examples of what can be done when both the faculty and university administrators are fully committed to the hiring of ethnic minorities. Under the helm of a new president, Miami University increased the number of black faculty from only seven in 1981 to twenty-seven in 1987.[54] At the University of Massachusetts blacks make up 8 percent of the faculty with 5.5 percent of them tenured. Recently, the faculty at Duke University has taken a similarly aggressive stand. It has approved a plan to require that each academic department hire at least one black faculty member by 1993.[55] These examples mitigate against the "empty pool" concept.

Majority faculty can find myriad reasons why minorities are not qualified for positions. As we discussed earlier, the qualifications of minorities alone are almost irrelevant; for sure, they are not sufficient to ensure admission into the ranks of the professoriate. Personal and political preferences, prejudices and fears of majority faculty and inaction of administrators play a larger role in the final decisions reached. The truth is that majority faculty are the "gatekeepers."[56] They have the power to confer membership on anyone they choose, but they lack a true commitment to achieving equity for ethnic minorities. When majority faculty want an individual badly enough they can find strong justification; they can bend or interpret rules as they wish. They alone determine the composition of their departments. Under the guise of objectivity, they select those who are deemed qualified, reject those who are not, and nominate their personal choices, based on highly subjective criteria reached in negotiation with other colleagues. The following excerpt by Moore clearly delineates their role:

> . . . they establish and chair search committees; they determine the criteria for selection, screen the applicants, conduct the interviews, influence the decision makers, and check their networks for nominations and references; they negotiate among themselves to determine which candidate to support if there is not a clear agreement on a specific candidate; and they submit their final subjective judgments with regard to who will be recommended to serve as faculty members in their institutions. The gatekeepers determine who is qualified and who is not; what rules to apply, break, or modify as it suits their objectives.[57]

Faculty recognize the power they have. The problem is that they do not always choose to exert that power, especially when minorities are concerned, so they deceive others into believing that opportunities for minorities are beyond their control.

A related barrier to minority hiring is the economic issue of supply and demand. Majority faculty understand the principles of supply and demand perfectly. They recognize, for example, that prominent scholars and underrepresented minority academics represent limited resources. Both bring an "added value" and, as a result, they are "worth" more than the average candidate. When majority faculty choose to hire a white prominent scholar, they readily respond to supply and demand principles. Like businesses, they understand that when the supply is low in any field, the demand for those few is high. As a consequence, they do not hesitate to engage in a "price war" to hire an individual whose presence meets the needs of the university, or enhances its prestige.

The relatively small pool of potential minority faculty and the current demands for diversification of IHEs puts minority candidates in a similar high demand category. But, when minorities demand higher compensation for the added perspective and presence that they bring to an institution, the principle of supply and demand begins to break down. Suddenly nonminority faculty who would ordinarily support the principles of supply and demand in any other context or forum, become the most vocal opponents of this fundamental law of economics. They grumble that the demands of minorities "are unreasonable," "too expensive," or that they "don't want to get into a bidding war with another university." The truth is that when the hiring of ethnic minorities is not really a priority, a double standard is applied. The end result is that minority candidates are not hired because the faculty is unwilling to pay them more than the established norm and to accord them equal consideration in the hiring process.

On the surface, the appearance of concern with increasing the number, of minorities on the faculty is sufficient for satisfying the public. Satisfying occurs, for example, when minority candidates are invited for interviews but, for various reasons which we discussed earlier, they do not get hired. Majority faculty pat themselves on the back for having tried and administrators justify the outcome by rationalizing that selection of colleagues is, after all, the prerogative of faculty—an academic freedom with which they refuse to interfere. So both majority faculty and administrators get off the hook, and the status quo remains undisturbed. The justification is unanimous: (1) there are few minority candidates in the available pool; (2) those who are available are either not fully qualified or they are already taken; and (3) those who are not taken are too expensive. In the end, all concerned can stand proud and united. They tried. Every effort was made. And, in the end, no minority candidate is hired. The self-fulfilling prophecy is once again fulfilled, and no one is held accountable.

There is no question that majority faculty and university administrators have the power to increase or restrict membership into the academy. Each plays an interdependent function. While the power to hire, promote and tenure may be vested in majority faculty, the power to ratify and fund those faculty decisions is the prerogative of administrators who control the budget. Administrators can make a difference in creating opportunities for minorities, as in the case of the president of Miami University in Ohio who had the courage to make a genuine commitment to increasing the number of black faculty. On the other hand, unwillingness of administrators to hold individual departments and their faculty accountable for the failure to hire minorities reinforces existing barriers to access and parity for all minority academics.

Conclusions

In this essay we have presented a framework for examining institutional strictures that function as barriers to access and parity for Chicanos in academia. Ensuring equity and increasing opportunities for Hispanics in institutions of higher learning will not be easy. We have seen that the major roadblocks to full membership in the academy center around three different but interdependent sets of social relations. The first of these describes the relatively low status that Hispanics occupy in the larger society and the negative attitudes toward those who are culturally, racially or linguistically different. The deficit perspective that colors all interactions between the dominant group and the minority groups in the larger society are mirrored in the academy.

Those manifestations of racism can be examined more closely in light of minority-majority interactions because it is in those interactions that they emerge. The practice of hiring underrepresented minorities only for certain specialized ethnic departments, of limiting their number in mainstream departments, of fueling and perpetuating the myth that they are not fully qualified for academic positions, the continual devaluing of minority research, and numerous other hairsplitting practices are all manifestations of covert racism that constitute roadblocks to full incorporation into the academy.

The interplay between majority faculty and university administrators constitutes the third set of social relations that affects minority access to the ranks of the professoriate. It is clear that majority faculty can play a major role in helping Hispanics to achieve parity. In their role as gatekeepers they can offer or deny membership to whomever they wish. University administrators share in this power. With the budget under their control they can persuade majority faculty to hire more minorities. They can hold individual departments accountable for achieving parity or setting specific goals and deadlines for increasing the number of underrepresented ethnic minorities on the faculty.

To be effective in providing greater opportunities to minorities, institutions (administrators, majority and minority faculty) must take a more aggressive and proactive stand in opening and creating opportunities for groups whose members are severely underrepresented in the system. Diversification of colleges and universities will not happen by chance or merely in time. The status quo contains too many loopholes that serve as internal resistance to equity, and work against the empowerment of minorities.

Universities must recognize that Chicano faculty are the key to recruitment, retention and promotion of other Chicanos, both students and other Hispanic faculty. Without full incorporation and integration into the various branches of the institution, not just in minority slots, they will be unable to empower other minorities to move successfully through the series of rituals necessary to achieve professional and academic success. The educational history of Chicanos in this country strongly suggests that without minority role models at all levels of the educational system, but especially in the centers of power—the ranks of the tenured professoriate—it will be difficult to extend membership in the academy to other minorities. So IHEs must learn how to market minority faculty so that they can serve as "educational brokers" who will attract large numbers of other capable minorities.

In order to reduce the existing racism in academia, leaders in higher education must recognize that the consequence of excluding a major segment of the population from taking an active participatory role in the educational design of the future will be a major catastrophe for a nation moving into the twenty-first century. Without full access to the ranks of the tenured professors where decisions are made, the numbers of minority faculty in tenure-line positions will be reduced even further, because minorities will not have the required votes to hire, promote and tenure others like them.

It is not sufficient to recognize that the sheer numbers of minorities in the larger society require greater diversification of educational institutions. Anyone can have a vision of what is needed for the future, anyone can pay lip service to the call for increased opportunities and access for minorities. Words are cheap. But it will take bold courage on the part of majority faculty, administrators and minority faculty to push for unpopular measures that have proven effective in other institutions, like setting quotas and deadlines for hiring and promoting minorities. A strong and genuine commitment to helping minorities achieve equity in higher education is needed, not only on grounds of justice, but because a minority presence will truly enrich the perspectives of all those engaged in attaining, sharing or imparting knowledge. That commitment, however, carries both a financial and moral price tag that few institutions may be ready to make.

Notes

1. Meredith Wilson, *The Commission on Higher Education of Minorities* (San Francisco, CA: Jossey-Bass, 1982), p. 5.

2. *From Minority to Majority: Education and the Future of the Southwest* (Boulder, CO: Western Interstate Commission of Higher Education, WICHE, 1987).

3. C. S. Farrell, "Black Students Seen Facing 'New Racism' On Many Campuses," *Chronicle of Higher Education* (January 27, 1988), pp. Al, A37–A38; C. S. Fanell, "Stung by Racial Incidents and Charges of Indifference, Berkeley to Become Model Integrated University," *Chronicle of Higher Education* (January 27, 1988), pp. A37–A38; C. S. Farrell, "Rising Concerns Over Campus Racial Bias Marked at Northern Illinois University," *Chronicle of Higher Education* (February 17, 1988), pp. A37–A38; C. S. Farrell, "Students Protesting Racial Bias at U. of Massachusetts End Occupation of Campus Building After Five Days," *Chronicle of Higher Education* (February 24, 1988), p. A41; J. McCurdy, "Nullification of Latino Students' Election Sparks Melee at UCLA," *Chronicle of Higher Education* (June 8, 1988), p. A23; Anita A. Williams, "Advice/Dissent," *Colorado Daily*, Oct. 12, 1987.

4. Carlos Ornelas, C. B. Ramirez and F. V. Padilla, *Decolonizing the Interpretation of the Chicano Political Experience* (Los Angeles: UCLA Chicano Studies Center Publications, 1975); Leonard Valverde, "Prohibitive Trends in Chicano Faculty Employment," *Chicanos in Higher Education*, H. J. Casso and G. D.

Roman, eds. (Albuquerque, NM: University of New Mexico Press, 1975), pp. 106–114; Carlos Arce, "Chicano Participation in Academe: A Case of Academic Colonialism," *Grito del Sol: A Chicano Quarterly 3* (1978): 75–104.

5. Casso and Roman, eds. *Chicanos in Higher Education*; Ornelas, Ramirez and Padilla, *Decolonizing the Interpretation*; Leonard Valverde, "Prohibitive Trends in Chicano Faculty Employment," pp.106–114; Cordelia Candelaria, "Women in the Academy," *Rendezvous: Journal of Arts and Letters 12 no. 1* (1978): 9–18; Steven F. Arvizu, "Critical Reflections and Consciousness," *Grito del Sol: A Chicano Quarterly 3* (1978): 119–123; Albert Ramirez, "Racism Toward Hispanics: The Culturally Monolithic Society," in *Eliminating Racism: Profiles in Controversy*. P. A. Katz and D. A. Taylor, eds. (New York: Plenum Press,1988), pp. 137–157.

6. Richard R. Verdugo, "Educational Stratification and Hispanics," in *Latino College Students*, M. A. Olivas, ed. (New York: Teachers College Press,1986), pp. 325–347.

7. Maria de la Luz Reyes & John J. Halcón, "Racism in Academia: The Old Wolf Revisited," *Harvard Educational Review 58* (August, 1988): 3.

8. *Minorities in Higher Education*, Sixth Annual Status Report (Washington, DC: American Council on Education,1987).

9. Reginald Wilson and Manuel Justiz, "Minorities in Higher Education: Confronting a Time Bomb," *Educational Record* (Fall 1987-Winter 1988), pp. 9–14.

10. de la Luz Reyes and Halcón, "Racism in Academia," p. 3.

11. *Minorities in Higher Education*.

12. *The Commission on the Higher Education of Minorities* (San Francisco, CA: Jossey-Bass,1982), pp. 5, 37.

13. R. J. Menges and W. H. Exum, "Barriers to the Progress of Women and Minority Faculty," *Journal of Higher Education 54*, no. 2 (1983): 123–144; Tomas Arciniega and Ann I. Morey, *Hispanics and Higher Education: A CSU Imperative* (Long Beach, CA: Office of the Chancellor, California State University, 1985); *Minorities in Higher Education; Minorities and Strategic Planning at the University of Colorado*, (Boulder: Office of the Associate Vice President for Human Resources, University of Colorado, 1987); Tomas Arciniega, *Hispanic Underrepresentation: A Call for Reinvestment and Innovation*, Hispanic Commission Follow-up Report (Long Beach, CA: Office of the Chancellor, California State University,1988); L. Gordon, "Second Report Criticizes UC on Its Policy Towards Hiring Latinos," *Los Angeles Times*, June 14, 1988, p. 3; C. M. Fields, "Hispanics, State's Fastest-Growing Minority, Shut Out of Top Positions at U. of California, Leaders Say," *Chronicle of Higher Education* (May 11, 1988), pp. A9–A10.

14. Albert Ramirez, "Racism Toward Hispanics," p. 138.

15. U.S. Commission on Civil Rights, "Stranger in One's Land" (Washington, DC: U.S. Commission on Civil Rights Clearinghouse, May 1970).

16. Julian Samora and P. V. Simon, *A History of the Mexican-American People* (Notre Dame, Indiana: Notre Dame Press,1977).

17. Albert Ramirez, "Racism Toward Hispanics," pp. 137–157.

18. de la Luz Reyes and Halcón, "Racism in Academia," p. 3.

19. William Moore, Jr., "Black Faculty in White Colleges: A Dream Deferred," *Educational Record* (Fall 1987-Winter 1988), pp. 117–121.

20. Hisauro Garza, "The 'Barriorization' of Hispanic Faculty," *Educational Record* (Fall 1987–Winter 1988): 123.

21. *Commission on the Higher Education of Minorities*, p. 22.

22. Garza, "The 'Barriorization' of Hispanic Faculty," p. 124.

23. Arciniega, *Hispanic Underrepresentation*; Gordon, "Second Report Criticizes UC," p. 3; Fields, "Hispanics, State's Fastest-Growing Minority," pp. A9–A10; de la Luz Reyes and Halcón, "Racism in Academia," p. 3; Garza, "The 'Barriorization' of Hispanic Faculty"; Wilson and Justiz, "Minorities in Higher Education"; Arciniega and Morey, *Hispanics and Higher Education*; Michael A. Olivas, "Research on Latino College Students: A Theoretical Framework and Inquiry," in *Latino College Students*, pp. 1–25; Arce, "Chicano Participation in Academe," pp. 75–104.

24. Rufio I: Rochin and Adela de la Torre in Garza, "The 'Barriorization' of Hispanic Faculty," pp.122–124.

25. Olivas, "Research on Latino College Students," p. 14.

26. Garza, "The 'Barriorization' of Hispanic Faculty," pp.122–124.

27. Wilson and Justiz, "Minorities in Higher Education," pp. 9–14.

28. Moore, "Black Faculty in White Colleges."

29. Farrell, "Black Students Seen Facing 'New Racism'," pp. Al, A37–A38; Farrell, "Berkeley to Become Model Integrated University"; Farrell, "Rising Concerns Over Campus Racial Bias"; Farrell, "Racial Bias at U. of Massachusetts"; McCurdy, "Nullification of Latino Students' Election"; Williams, "Advice/ Dissent."

30. Moore, "Black Faculty in White Colleges"; D. Carter, C. Pearson and D. Shavlik, "Double Jeopardy: Women of Color in Higher Education," *Educational Record* (Fall 1987-Winter 1988), 98–102.

31. *The Commission on the Higher Education of Minorities*, p. 5.

32. de la Luz Reyes and Halcón, "Racism in Academia."

33. Peter Holmes, "The Ineffective Mechanism of Affirmative Action Plans in an Academic Setting," in *Chicanos in Higher Education*, pp. 76–83.

34. *Minorities in Higher Education.*

35. Holmes, "The Ineffective Mechanism of Affirmative Action Plans."

36. D. E. Blum, "Black Woman Scholar at Emory U. Loses Three-year Battle to Overturn Tenure Denial, But Vows to Fight On," *Chronicle of Higher Education* (June 22, 1988), pp. A 15–A 17; S. Heller, "Some Colleges Find Aggressive Affirmative Action Efforts Are Starting to Pay Off, Despite Scarcity of Candidates," *Chronicle of Higher Education* (February 10, 1988) p. A12.

37. Moore, "Black Faculty in White Colleges:" p. 120.

38. *Commission on the Higher Education of Minorities.*

39. Garza, "The 'Barriorization' of Hispanic Faculty"; de la Luz Reyes and Halcón, "Racism in Academia."

40. Garza, "The 'Barriorization' of Hispanic Faculty"; Blum, "Black Woman Scholar at Emory. "

41. Blum, "Black Woman Scholar at Emory"; Heller, "Aggressive Affirmative Action Efforts"; Garza, "The 'Barriorization' of Hispanic Faculty"; Moore, "Black Faculty in White Colleges."

42. de la Luz Reyes and Halcón, "Racism in Academia."

43. Blum, "Black Woman Scholar at Emory"; D. E. Blum, "To Get Ahead in Research, Some Minority Scholars Choose to 'Play the Game'," *Chronicle of Higher Education* (June 22, 1988) p. A17; A. Ramirez, "Racism Toward Hispanics."

44. Blum, "To Get Ahead in Research"; Fields, "Hispanics, State's Fastest-Growing Minority"; Angela Simone, *Academic Women Working Towards Equality* (South Hadley, MA: Bergin and Garvey Publishers, Inc., 1987); M. D. Tryman, "Reversing Affirmative Action: A Theoretical Construct," *Journal of Negro Education* 55, no. 2 (1986): 185–199; Menges and Exum, "Barriers to the Progress of Women and Minority Faculty."

45. Ramirez, "Racism Toward Hispanics."

Yer Own Motha Wouldna Reckanized Ya: Surviving an Apprenticeship in the "Knowledge Factory"

SUZANNE SOWINSKA

And I? I will do everything and anything until the end of my days to stop anyone ever talking to me like that woman talked to my mother. It is in this place, this bare, curtainless bedroom that lies my secret and shameful defiance. I read a woman's book, meet such a woman at a party (a woman now, like me) and think quite deliberately as we talk: we are divided: a hundred years ago I'd have been cleaning your shoes. I know this and you don't.

Carolyn Kay Steedman, *Landscape for a Good Woman*

Everyone knows that a "woman of letters," which is what it seems as a graduate student in an English department, I am in training to become, is not someone who grew up in "the projects," a trailer court, a split-level exactly like all the rest on the block, in subsidized housing, or otherwise on the "wrong side of the tracks." Rather, the image of the female scholar, whose "job" is to pass her cultural knowledge of literary texts from one generation of students to the next, is one of refinement: she exudes an elegance of manners and intellect particular to that class of well-educated women to which she belongs. She is Virginia Woolf, arguing passionately for a "room of one's own"; she is Gertrude Stein, reinventing language—she is not Emma Goldman who, among her more newsworthy activities, lectured and wrote extensively about literature, nor is she Anzia Yezierska, who imagined a way to "authentically" represent the Russian and Jewish immigrant culture which was part of her verbal landscape as a child.

Although many English departments have become relatively comfortable with a critical agenda that asserts that the writers we study come from a multitude of race, class, and gender positions, the backgrounds of those of us who study those writers is not generally given much thought at all. The actual life experience of a female scholar is rarely discussed and generally her ascension through the ranks of academia is assumed to be an unproblematic acquisition of the written, verbal, and cultural skills needed to perform well in a university setting. The participation of most poor and working-class women in academia, however, is frequently not easy or comfortable and is often attended by chronic interruptions while we seek outside avenues of cultural validation, financial support, or whatever else is necessary in order for us to continue. Yet there are many of us who are successful in obtaining jobs inside academic institutions. We often stick out because we do not choose to adopt the largely middle-class (and, of course, white) discourse in which most academic institutions conduct their business. We rankle the various ranks of academia to which we belong. We demand texts that describe our concerns when we study, speak to a different audience when we teach, prescribe to different critical agendas when we argue, and write about different subjects when we write. We also write theory and find ourselves resisting theoretical models that refuse to include descriptions of the reality of working-class life. We participate in the activity of theory making even though theory can represent the very sort of abstract thought that has traditionally marked unfamiliar ground in our socially constructed experiences of working-class culture. If we are to accept, for example, current theoretical trends, which posit a notion of the "subject" secured by its "position" within "discourse" (and not by reference to some sort of transcendent essentialism), we accept both a limiting paradigm and a way of saying what we mean that linguistically alienates most of those "subjects" we intend to describe. In short, discourse theory with its formulation of passive subjects tends to overlook the ways that any symbolic system is subject to notions of "experience," the realm where class relations are understood, felt, and actually lived. The experiences of working-class women with the specific forms of knowledge gained from those experiences are never simply coded in one discourse but woven in between, through, and around a multitude of discourses. Forms of knowledge are ultimately discovered in what the fabric created by these often disparate discourses says or shows. To begin to describe ways in which working-class "subjects" might be construed as active agents rather than as passive subjects necessitates a discussion of the role of experience in social relationships which is often missing from theories that focus on a concept of subjectivity as merely a function of the structure of discourse. To describe experience allows an opportunity to see how social relations can be appropriated, resisted, and undermined; it can also provide the basis for action.[1] I will accordingly try to focus my comments here on experiences, beginning with my own and later discussing some of those related to me by other poor and working-class women who have struggled with their apprenticeships as academics. What is the role of women working-class intellectuals (if that's what our training in academia makes us) in reproducing class society? How do our experiences of being working class shape our relationships to academia?

When I was about twelve, a girl from one of my classes invited me to her house. Her mother wished to encourage a friendship between the two of us because we had the highest scores on that year's academic achievement tests. Her father was a neurosurgeon and her mother a part-time nurse. My father worked in a factory and my mother worked part time in a department store. The Murphys had a house in the country, about two miles outside of the town where our school was. My family's house was about one mile on the other side of town in what were referred to as "the developments." My friendship with the daughter didn't last too long. I was allowed to visit at her house but there was always an excuse as to why she couldn't come to mine. But her mother and I became mutually fascinated with one another. Mrs. Murphy (Audrey, she insisted but I never felt quite entitled to say) seemed to want to know everything about me and about my family. How long had my father been in this country? What about my mother? How was it that I had such a large vocabulary and could use such sophisticated phrases? Why did I think it was that the rest of my family wasn't as smart as me? No adult had ever had time to take such an interest in me before, and I wanted very much to be listened to.

In my best twelve-year-old reasoning I explained to my friend's mother that my sophistication had come from reading, that my mother read between four and six books a week, and that I had picked up "reading" from her. She told me that it was an admirable thing that my mother kept herself up through reading, especially with all my brothers and sisters, and became embarrassed when I attempted a defense by asking her how many books a week she read. With her response and a trip to the room that housed their family library, I acquired my first definition of what literature was: what Audrey read were called novels, my mother read paperbacks. From that day on my reading practices changed. I became determined to know whatever it was that Audrey got from reading novels that my mother didn't get from reading what she read. Along with coveting the books she owned, I coveted Audrey's confidence, graciousness, and apparent wisdom and I tried desperately to find it at our town's tiny branch of the public library. And, although I occasionally slipped back into reading a gothic novel or two, after that most of my time was spent reading what my sister and I (and most university English departments) referred to as "classics."

What I was unable to understand until many years later was exactly how much the barely discernible note of disdain in Audrey's voice, as she differentiated my mother's reading habits from her own, was able to change totally the arrangement of one small part of my world and cause me to negotiate an adjustment to what I privately began to think of as more accepted or normal. I was, of course, making similar negotiations in other parts of my life. The older I grew the more familiar it became to keep making adjustments on many different levels. Without understanding what I was doing or why I was doing it, I began to feel ashamed of who I was, who my family was, what they thought about, where they came from, and I began to alter myself and my appearance in an attempt to escape association with what they seemed to represent to others.

By providing me with a range of choices and an advanced vocabulary, the novels I read began to help me satisfy my desire to get free from what I then perceived as the constraints of the social class in which I was being raised. The seemingly better worlds and richer landscapes each individual narrative offered provided me with a fantasy of escape and helped me to see how it was possible to make up for whatever social sophistication I lacked through language. More and more I began to live in two very separate worlds, the one that I was born into and the one I was constructing out of various fictions of what I thought normal, intelligent, educated people were really like. Today, I've learned to label these self-limiting activities as attempting to "pass" for middle class, but for a long time, including all of my undergraduate years, I lived in a confused state of preconsciousness where I often, although not always, felt an urgent need to mask my working-class origins. Nowhere did I feel a greater need for disguise than inside academic institutions where the heightened level of discourse both fascinated and intimidated me and put me in situations where I most feared that someone would discover that I was only pretending to be "educated" and force me to leave. Although I felt a great deal of tension, confusion, and discomfort, I was not able to articulate these feelings as linked to class oppression. The mechanisms of a dominant discourse were fully in operation: I internalized my feelings as somehow related to something out of place or missing in me rather than as indicative of a system of oppression carefully masked by myths of equal access and opportunity.

A deep passion for reading, which is intricately connected to notions of escape, survival, and passing, is part of the reality of almost all the poor and working-class women in academia that I know. To pass means to attempt to disguise working class origins by outwardly adopting codes of behavior that come from outside working-class experience. Academic institutions present ideal situations for successful passing as they ostensibly operate under the premise that intelligence rather than background determines ability. Yet passing should also be seen positively as a skill that women from working-class backgrounds have developed in order to survive in academic environments. When used consciously, the ability to pass can become a valuable tool, capable of causing internal disruptions and potential manipulations of the institutions it operates within. But I'm jumping ahead of my argument here. Before I talk about how such experiences can be used for political ends, I must first describe their origins in class oppression.

For me, to be at college and to be able to read and interpret texts meant a freedom to experience words and worlds way beyond the grasp of what I had once considered to be available to me, but it also meant leaving behind the familiar validations of experience and community offered by my family and friends. My own passing included, among its other manifestations, altering my speech, changing the way I dressed, remaining silent during conversations about family, pretending to have enough money when I didn't, claiming I wasn't hungry when I was. I also developed a tendency toward automatic lying, filling in what I perceived as gaps in my background, telling people what I thought they wanted to hear, inventing, creating, making up stories. At that time in my life, these parts of me that I was giving up seemed unimportant, and I felt them as necessary sacrifices in order for me to be seen as legitimate. Nor did I think too much about the extra energy I was expending in my attempts to fit in: the trade-off was to become "educated," which would bring liberation.

Before I had developed any sense of class consciousness or a way to articulate class-based experience, I had learned to successfully negotiate my behavior away from the working-class culture I had been raised in to match that of the middle-class culture I had become immersed in. From this notion that there was a different set of cultural codes to adjust to eventually would come the recognition that the frames of reference for both sets of codes were illusory. At that time I was not concerned in any conscious or intentional way with identifying the nature of class relations as they operate within academic institutions. Nevertheless, through my experiences of difference eventually came the knowledge that exposed the central fallacy under which all educational systems operate: that success is determined by effort or ability rather than by class background. This was not an outside knowledge brought to me through a theory of class relations but something that arose out of my experience of class-based oppression.

Just as passing presents an aspect of experience that is unique to poor and working-class women in training to become academics, there are other social and intellectual survival strategies we use in attempts to continue to gain access to the cultural expertise offered by a university education. Where there are no family resources to provide us with the necessary financial or cultural prerequisites for our educations, we learn to do just about anything to be able to keep reading books. Economic survival is often the most basic of our concerns, and I will accordingly recount here some of the strategies other working-class women in academia have used in order to remain in school. I have one friend, for example, who described a period of about six weeks where she would take three or four books per night to sell at a used-book store on her way to the supermarket so she could have money to buy food. She was a Victorianist and, after being unable to part with Jane Austen, was alphabetically up to Dickens before her student-loan check finally arrived. This was after having sold off her classics, seventeenth-, eighteenth-, and twentieth-century texts and her copy of the abridged OED (which she was overjoyed to get thirty dollars for, describing the money as almost enough to feed her for two weeks).

Another friend had developed techniques for reading books without breaking their spines so she could return them a few days later claiming she was no longer enrolled in the course. Another shoplifted books but kept a record of every time she did, hoping to pay the money back in some future time when she had more cash. She knew that if she were caught she would have to agree never to "shop" at the university bookstore again, but she was hoping to make it through all her course work before that happened. She later acquired a stamp marked "used book" and began to change prices.

Another friend found a way to successfully hide her enrollment at a local university from the state so she could receive food stamps, which she then traded with others for money so she could buy books. Another worked every Monday night, the "single women and children" shift, at a local food bank. She told others that it was her way to help homeless women but privately confessed to me that it not only guaranteed her a meal but usually provided her with extra food she could take home. Another woman forged her father's name on a new income tax return when he refused to stop declaring her as his dependent.

One particularly desperate friend described how she frequently signed herself up as a paid participant for psychological and medical experiments conducted at the medical school of the university she was attending. She particularly liked the ones that involved only a few hours of her active participation but included two or three weeks of isolation and felt that she got some of her best studying done in hospital rooms. She stopped participating, however, after having agreed (for $460) to be part of an experiment comparing the spinal fluid of anorexics with that of "normal volunteers." Something went wrong with the spinal tap that her doctor-in-training performed on her; she spent two weeks in bed recovering from the botched procedure.

Another strategy common to women students from working-class backgrounds when faced with a lack of funding to continue their education is to seek employment within universities as clerical workers. There are a large number of working-class women in academia who have worked as secretaries, receptionists, filing clerks, word processors, or administrative assistants in universities, often in the very departments that will eventually grant them their degrees. In the English department where I am currently enrolled as an advanced graduate student, there has been a steady stream of fellow graduate students who also work as secretaries in our department. Many of them are relieved to find employment in such a familiar environment even though their jobs frequently put them in uncomfortable situations with both their professors and other students.

Of course, all students at one time or another find themselves in financially difficult situations. What makes the situation of poor and working-class women so unique is the way in which economic survival strategies are intimately connected to our self-esteem and collective notions of fear, shame, and defiance that make up our individual family or neighborhood landscapes. For the women I described above to have to "go on welfare" in order to stay in school meant she had to carry around a great deal of shame and a sense of having betrayed her familial and cultural values. In addition, her eventual employment as a secretary in a university left her feeling as though that was where she belonged: her proper place in the overall scheme of things was as a worker rather than as a thinker.

Much of what students from middle- or upper-class backgrounds take for granted and expect to be a part of college life is quite out-side the experience of those of us who were the first in our families to attend college. I can imagine that most students from middle-class backgrounds have not had the experience of enjoying dining hall food (because it is like "eating out" every night) nor do they delight in the privacy offered by a dormitory room shared with only one other person. Furthermore, they probably don't feel as though their delight and excitement at their new surroundings needs to be hidden. These feelings were all part of my first few days at college.

If I had remained only within university environments, I may never have discovered that I was raised working class. Although three generations on my mother's side and two generations on my father's side of my family had been laborers, they all thought of themselves as equal players in a mainly middle-class America, the land of opportunity for all. The members of the Polish side of my family, my grandmother, aunts, uncles, and cousins, had a concept of themselves as culturally distinct, but there were no class distinctions made even though a general mood of inferiority and lack of a sense of entitlement pervaded almost all their interactions outside their immediate neighborhood. Their struggle was so entirely defined as an attempt to rid themselves of the markers of their status as immigrants that the fact that some of those markers were class based did not occur to them as that important. It must have seemed to them that to stop sounding, acting, and looking Polish would unquestionably mean one had obtained the status of sounding, acting, and looking like middle-class Americans.

Having been "born and raised in America," both my parents had achieved their parents' goals of cultural proficiency, but the class-based markers remained. In terms of their dealings with the world, these translated into very little confidence, pride, or conviction in their own right to exist, and what I learned from them was that in most cases it was best to submit to those in positions of greater authority, power, and knowledge. Clichéd messages like "Don't rock the boat"; "It's best to just let a sleeping dog lie"; and "It doesn't do any good to try and buck the system," which had been passed to them from their parents, informed their personal vocabularies of self-debasement and shame, which they then passed on to me. This discourse of subjugation and deference to others had become so naturalized in them that they were unable to imagine any other, let alone begin to touch on the causes or reasons for the differences they must have felt.

Education was devalued in the white working-class culture in which I was raised.[2] My parents actively tried to discourage me from attending college. Prophesies of failure from my mother abounded; she was sure that I wouldn't finish my first year, let alone graduate. Although they could afford to, they provided no financial support; they did not want to participate in my separation from them. They did not want me to go outside their world, to become unfamiliar, to become a part of any of the institutions that they vaguely sensed were responsible for their manipulation and oppression. They were, it seems, at least somewhat correct in their fears: my college education made me no longer completely one of them. Not only did my vocabulary change by the time I had finished college, but I also had begun to dress differently, was eating different foods, and, among countless other small changes, insisted on fresh ground rather than instant coffee. I also began to notice a change in my family's responses to me. My mother occasionally now used the tone of humility and deference with me that she usually reserved for authority figures like police, bank officials, and bureaucrats while privately asserting her dismay to my brothers and sisters at how much better than the rest of the family I thought I had become.

My understanding of feminism, which had become much more grounded in the four years of relatively uninterrupted "reading" that college had provided, also helped to alienate me from my family and cultural roots. I had become an activist, organizing demonstrations, participating in acts of civil disobedience, attending conferences, and helping to publish a feminist newspaper. The feminist agenda to which I had committed myself, however, failed to include a class analysis. Nevertheless, my participation in feminist and radical communities did provide me with the tools of self-discovery that I needed to begin to analyze the sense of difference of which I had always been acutely aware.

Coming out as a lesbian was the main event that prepared me for the much more difficult ordeal of coming out as working class. As part of the powerful discourse of positive self-esteem and discovery present in most lesbian and gay communities, the experience of coming out taught me to turn shame and fear into anger and action. For me, a critique of power relations first came from the oppression I felt as a member of a sexual minority. The process of growing to understand myself as working class was very similar to the process of growing to understand myself as lesbian. Because of my early proclivities for "reading," I went to the library. When I began to think of myself as a lesbian, I took out every lesbian novel I could find. A whole new world and language was opened to me. When I began to think of myself as working class, I searched the library again. I wanted retellings of experience, not theory, yet this time I had a harder time knowing quite what headings in the card catalog to look under to find novels told from the perspective of working-class women.

My discoveries in the library gave me the beginnings of a class analysis, a reason to begin graduate school, and a subject to study once I got there. Talking with other women graduate students who also identified as being from poor or working-class backgrounds became the only way to ensure my sanity in graduate school and to validate my own class-based experience. Once I began to share the strategies I had used for survival with these women and began to listen to their experiences, my own no longer seemed so strange or even so extreme. Together we began to unravel the layers of shame, fear, and insecurity that represented our legacies as working-class scholars. We also began to imagine the beginnings of an analysis of class and gender relations that would not only describe our experience but also help us develop pedagogical approaches to use with other women students.

The lived experience of class-based oppression is what forces many working-class women academics from a cultural understanding of the operation of difference to a political recognition of the way in which social relations are ordered. We eventually learn to create rearticulations of our experience in order to discover a sense of identity. Leaving behind what is familiar to us in exchange for unfamiliar intellectual and economic survival strategies often provides a catalyst for critique and a desire to understand new terms in the subject/subjugated argument, allowing for the possibility of agency and real movement. The way that we exist as working class forms an identity not automatically written into the internal power relations of any particular context or discourse. What began as survival strategies have changed, for many of us, into powerful instruments we use to manipulate our environment. We have learned to reclaim the weapons of fear and shame once used against us, appropriating them for acts of defiance and creative undermining.[3]

There are, after all, advantages to our position. One fellow scholar argues that women from working-class backgrounds have nothing at stake in the middle-class ideologies that often pass for knowledge in academic institutions. She feels that her lack of complicity with the cultural values advanced by universities has put her in a better position than others to ask questions, "for bourgeois scholars, deconstruction is the latest critical theory, for working-class scholars it has always been a way of life."[4] The ability to see from at least two viewpoints at once, which the experience of passing provides, often makes it easier for working-class women to form alliances with members of other oppressed groups who experience similar disjunctions. We are also usually very adept at translating between individuals and institutions, exposing and demystifying self-perpetuating systems of authority. We tend to place the emphasis on individuals rather than on a set of invisible rules of conduct, trying to recognize and validate those students who seem to have a hard time adjusting to academic life.

The experience of feeling like an outsider in academic environments allows many of us access to a better understanding of the ideological function of the institutions we work within. One friend described to me how her position as working class gave her a clear understanding that the role of the state college she attended was to churn out teachers and low-level managers. She subsequently felt more knowledgeable and less pressured than those around her to adopt the façade of success that was being proffered by the institution. Another woman described how she used her ability to pass to gain access to classrooms. She knew what cultural knowledge she was supposed to be passing on to her students but instead chose to use her role as teacher differently. Common assignments for her included initiating discussions that, among other goals, would help students begin to deconstruct their experiences of difference and their complicity with the power relations at work within their immediate surroundings.

In general, we women graduate students from working-class backgrounds have an understanding of the nature of "work" that differs from those around us. On the one hand, our experience of work as physically difficult and labor intensive makes academic work seem easy, hardly like work at all. On the other hand, it is easy for us to see how institutions often disguise work as something other than work: where being nominated to serve on an undergraduate curriculum committee, for example, is presented as a helpful addition to a curriculum vitae instead of as the additional two hours per week work time that it is. Many working-class women academics also have more of a notion of work as separate from life: being an academic is what you do for a living as opposed to who you are the rest of the time.[5]

Working-class women academics who have also worked as secretaries in educational settings are quick to understand exactly where decision-making power lies within their departments. One friend describes using her sense of camaraderie with other secretaries to cut through much of the bureaucratic red tape experienced by her fellow graduate students. She was able to secure office and classroom assignments, keys to rooms, parking permits, and other everyday survival needs through her ability to interact with secretaries as peers. There is also no better way that I can think of for deconstructing the intellectual and cultural mystique of the ivory tower than being "on staff," where it becomes very clear that undergraduate acceptances, graduate appointments, faculty appointments, and tenure decisions are based on politics rather than merit.

Through the experience of living within the particular social relation of being both female and a working-class scholar comes the knowledge of how both articulations of dominant forms of discourse and resources against them are carried in permanent conflict. This recognition punctures and deflates the persistent myth of both working-class and female passivity just as our position as "educated" destroys the fiction of working-class ignorance and subordination. Although these comments should not be seen as an attempt to valorize the survival strategies used by working-class women in academia, they do recognize those strategies as forms of resistance being cultivated within the very system that has produced our subordination. It is equally important to note that the danger of our potential incorporation into the middle class is great and that we must learn new ways to resist the temptation to abandon our cultures and families of origin for the promised land of middle-class respectability. "The master's tools will never dismantle the master's house," but perhaps we apprentices will begin to see ways that the internal form of a particular discourse can be used to control the master.[6]

Even today I am sometimes haunted by echoes of the shame I once felt but had no words for. I feel a great deal of sadness for the young scholar who carried that shame around and at the same time I am embarrassed by the "simple beliefs" I once had. My newly gained sense of entitlement often seems too fragile to sustain me, and if I'm not careful I can still become too paralyzed to use the privilege of my education to speak. But at last, after a long struggle, I have not needed to discard my family or cultural values. I live instead in a strangely ambiguous middle ground, insisting on the validity of my working-class roots and experiences yet also feeling outside of them, transported by means of education and political awareness to another place I can't quite call home. My mother occasionally sends me what she calls "survival packages" to help me get by at school. They contain food, never money. In fact it always amazes me that she spends more money mailing the package to me than it would cost to send me a check and let me buy the food myself. But I'm glad she doesn't. Along with the canned beef stew that I no longer eat and always end up giving to a food bank, she inevitably includes a package or two of "International Coffees." These instant coffee drinks have pretentious packaging and names: Orange Cappuccino, Irish Creme,

Suisse Mocha, Double Dutch Chocolate, and Cafe Vienna. She never drinks what the box proclaims are "elegant drinks" herself; she only buys them because they match her perception of what I like now that I live and work in such a "classy" environment. Her gifts never fail to bring a smile. Her attempts to understand me almost seem an ironic recognition of the in-between space in which I am always finding myself. I guess these are the coffee spoons with which I get to measure out my life.

Notes

1. See Paul Willis and Philip Corrigan, "Orders of Experience: The Differences of Working Class Cultural Forms" in *Social Text 7* (Spring-Summer 1983) for an extensive discussion of the positioning of working-class "subjects" within discourse theory and the importance of "experience" in formations of meaning and knowledge.

2. My experience may be more typical of white working-class culture. In many experiences of working class culture, education is valued as a tool for upward mobility. For example, in a workshop on classism I attended at the 1989 NWSA Conference, many of the black and Jewish working-class women reported having had a great deal of pressure from their families to attend college. In cases where family resources were limited, however, preference was given to support the education of male members of the family.

3. I am especially indebted to my conversations with Helen Boscoe, Pamela Fox, Beth Hutchison, Barbara Schulman, and Rachel Stevens for their thoughts on both the subjugation and the resistances of working-class women in academia.

4. From a conversation with Rachel Stevens, November 1989.

5. For an in-depth study of the ideological role of the academic institution as workplace, see Evan Watkins, *Work Time: English Departments and the Circulation of Cultural Values* (Stanford UP, 1989).

6. Audre Lorde, "The Master's Tools Will Never Dismantle the Master's House," in *This Bridge Called My Back*, ed. Cherrie Moraga and Gloria Anzaldúa (Watertown, Mass.: Persephone, 1981).

The Politics of the Professors: Self-Identifications, 1969–1984

RICHARD F. HAMILTON AND LOWELL L. HARGENS

This study uses data from the 1969, 1975, and 1984 Carnegie surveys of faculty at U.S. colleges and universities to show that the distribution of political orientations among the professoriate changed minimally between the late 1960s and mid-1980s. The largest net shift, about 7% of the respondents, was from liberal to conservative self-identifications. The 1975 and 1984 surveys show the same patterns of disciplinary differences present in 1969, but the patterns by age and type of institution changed. Analyses by disciplinary political context and type of institution show that the incidence of leftism had been considerably exaggerated in much of the current literature. The institutional types with the largest numbers of students, moreover, have the most conservative or moderate faculties.

This article examines evidence on the political orientations of professors. The politics of the professors has been a persistent source of concern to observers throughout the modern era, at least from the time of the Reformation. In the United States, concern over the political orientations of college and university faculty dates from the beginning of this century. Then, as now, some were anxious that professors with leftist political orientations would use their positions to infect unsuspecting students with "alien concepts and ideals." It was reputed, for example, that the purpose of John D. Rockefeller's 1907 gift of $32 million to the General Education Board for higher education was "to head off, if possible, the teaching of socialism, which is on the increase . . . in a number of universities" (Brown 1979:50). Similarly, after World War I, some commentators denounced what they considered to be left-wing tendencies among college faculty (Lipset 1972: chaps. 4 & 5). In addition to the centuries-old fears about corruption of youth, more recent interest in the political persuasions of the professoriate stems from the great increase in the scale of U.S. higher education following World War II and from its central role in certifying scientific and cultural expertise (Ladd & Lipset 1975:2–3).

Comprehensive surveys of the political persuasions of faculty at U.S. colleges and universities date from the 1950s. They show that the professoriate was more likely to have leftist and liberal identifications than the population as a whole. But these studies also found considerable diversity among faculty in different fields and across levels of professional eminence (Ladd & Lipset 1975; Lazarsfeld & Thielens 1958). Following the late-1960s uprisings in the universities, most observers sensed a general moderation of professorial outlooks. Some commentators saw a growth of conservatism which paralleled the mood of the larger society. Some pointed to a tendency they labeled "neoconservatism, " a planned effort, with business support, for creation of "think tanks" and publication of books and magazines to further the new direction. Others indicated that the leading figures in this "movement" were basically liberals who subscribed to a different reading of appropriate liberal policies. One writer sounded the alarm on "the rise of a conservative elite"

(Blumenthal 1986:xiii) while another expressed skepticism about the importance of the threat (Muravchik 1986).

In the 1980s, the concern over a rightward drift in academia gave way to an opposite perception, that is, to claims of a resurgent Left in American universities. In 1986, Joseph Epstein, editor of the *American Scholar*, wrote of leftist views cropping up "nowadays . . . with a fair frequency" (Epstein 1986). In the same year, Stephen H. Balch and Herbert I. London, leaders of the Campus Coalition for Democracy (described as "an organization of college faculty concerned about ideological extremism within the academy") wrote that "the academy is a bastion of liberalism, a fact which most would take to be indisputable." But, "the liberalism of the academy . . . is now hard pressed to recognize its own principles, and even less capable of defending them when they come under attack from the Left" (Balch & London 1986). They cite data from a 1984 survey by the Carnegie Foundation for the Advancement of Teaching indicating that 5.8% of the professors described themselves as "left." Given a total population of some 600,000 professors, that would mean roughly 35,000 persons. The percentages of those identifying themselves as left were somewhat higher at institutions of "greater prestige and influence" and were considerably higher in some fields, notably in the social sciences and humanities. In four-year institutions, sociology was conspicuous: 37% identified their politics as left.

Several years later, Roger Kimball, managing editor of the *New Criterion*, published a book on the subject, *Tenured Radicals: How Politics Has Corrupted Our Higher Education* (1990). Another recent account arguing this tendency is by Dinesh D'Souza, *Illiberal Education: The Politics of Race and Sex on Campus* (1991a). Prior to its publication, excerpts had appeared in *The Atlantic*, the *American Scholar*, and *Forbes* magazines. The major news magazines picked up the themes and elaborated on them. One review described D'Souza's book as "the most complete study we have had of the capture and degradation of higher education by the Left" (Adelson 1991:55). Subsequent to the book's publication, a flurry of articles on "politically correct" tendencies within academia appeared, in the *New York Times*, *Newsweek*, *New York*, the *New Republic*, and eventually, in *Time* (for a review of these events, see D'Souza 1991b).

Some commentators, not too surprisingly, have disagreed with this portrayal of academia. Peter Mandler, writing in *Dissent* in 1989, challenged most of these basic claims. One conclusion reads: "Only the neoconservatives could transmute a mild resistance to prevailing ideological winds into a latter day Gunpowder Plot. "He points to examples of professors of the Left who were denied tenure by institutions that, supposedly, were bastions of leftist sentiment. Also citing Carnegie data, he points to a disregard of "the sharper shift to the right in the places where most Americans are educated" (Mandler 1989). Many others have challenged the claims of their critics (Gless & Smith 1992; Stimpson 1991). In September 1991, some of them launched a counteroffensive with the formation of an organization called Teachers for a Democratic Culture (DePalma 1991).

Much of the discussion has been based on anecdotes, incidents, and isolated examples. Depictions of incidents, not too surprisingly, have been hotly disputed. Authors taking both pro and con positions, as just indicated, have cited data from Carnegie surveys. There is, clearly, a need for more adequate information on the subject. To gain a better understanding of recent trends, we present results from three Carnegie surveys of the professoriate covering a fifteen year span, from 1969 to 1984.

The beginning point for this analysis is the major study by Ladd and Lipset, *The Divided Academy* (1975). That work, based on the 1969 Carnegie survey, contained many important findings, three of which are of special concern here. The first lesson, signaled in the title, is that of differentiation. It makes no sense to speak of "the universities" or "the professors." Within American higher education there are disciplines whose members are predominantly leftist and liberal in orientation, some whose members are generally middle-of the-road politically, and some where conservative tendencies dominate. This finding, of course, is no revelation; it is something known to all persons in and around academia. Ladd and Lipset's contribution was to provide specific magnitudes; their findings serve as a base of comparison with later studies. A second lesson was that in the late 1960s liberalism and leftism varied inversely with age. This pattern, taken in conjunction with low projected growth rates in the 1970s and the retirement of the older cohorts, suggested that liberal and leftist orientations might persist or become even stronger in American universities and colleges. A third and rather unexpected finding was that liberal and leftist orientations among professors were positively related to the prestige of the institution.

The basic questions we address here are, first, have the universities "moved left" since the 1969 study? And, second, what changes, if any, have occurred in the patterns by field, by age, and by institutional quality?

Methods

Our analyses are based on surveys conducted in 1969 and 1975 under the auspices of the Carnegie Commission on Higher Education, and in 1984 under the auspices of the Carnegie Foundation for the Advancement of Teaching. The surveys drew probability samples of U.S. college and university faculty, and mailed the sampled individuals questionnaires containing a broad range of questions about scholarly activities and beliefs about diverse social and educational issues. The response rates for the surveys ranged from 60% to 51%, and the respondents appear to be reasonably representative of the target populations. Reports by Trow and associates (1975) and Opinion Research Corporation (1984) indicate that data for survey respondents differed little from data yielded by special surveys of nonrespondents. The only consistent finding from both studies of respondent representativeness was that scholars whose interests lie exclusively in teaching were slightly less likely to respond than those primarily interested in research or in a mixture of those two activities.

A single self-identification question is used here to indicate political orientations. It reads: "How would you characterize yourself politically at the present time? Left, Liberal, Middle-of-the-Road, Moderately conservative, Strongly conservative." The identical question appeared in the 1975 and 1984 studies. In the 1969 survey, 112 respondents (0.296) checked both "left" and "liberal" in response to the political self identification question. In our analysis, we have assigned these cases to the "liberal" category.

Ladd and Lipset (1975:37–47) examined this question's correlations with other measures of political attitudes and found that it is the central item in a cluster of questions that tap a general "liberalism-conservatism" dimension. In addition, Ladd and Lipset (1975:66–67) report that disciplinary variation in a measure of political action—signing published statements against the Vietnam war—is almost identical to disciplinary variation in average responses to the political self-identification item. These results support the validity of the political self-identification item, and we therefore use it to gauge shifts in the political orientations of college and university faculty from the late 1960s to the mid-1980s. The Carnegie Foundation sponsored a fourth survey in 1989, but unfortunately changed both the wording of the political self-identification question and its answer alternatives. Thus, we are unable to use that survey to extend this review of the trends.

A word of caution. Two separate concerns are present in much of the current discussion, the question of the trend in political orientations and the question of behavior, of practices associated with the political directions. The most important of these, in recent discussion, have been subsumed under the heading of "the politically correct." This study, for the most part, addresses the first of those concerns. It provides some evidence about the frequency or incidence of political preferences. There is little information in these surveys allowing conclusions about the presumed correlated behaviors. Since political preferences and questionable behavior are separate and distinct subject matters, we should remember that the incidence of the former by itself says nothing about the frequency of the latter. Consider one formulation: "In American universities, faculty extremists are nearly all on the left: conservatives are never fascists and are rarely even devout Reagan Republicans. They are usually moderates . . . " (Bryden 1991:44). The statements, while possibly according with one's impressions, should be viewed as untested hypotheses. The first claim, if accurate, does not say all leftists are extremists.

Findings

Aggregate Results

Given the recent sounds of alarm, one would expect to find clear evidence of liberal and leftist growth. Evidence for the period 1969–84, however, does not confirm that expectation. The self-identified Left was fairly constant over this period, amounting to roughly one in twenty at all three points (Table 1). Liberal self-identifications declined by roughly seven points. This was the largest of the observed changes. Middle-of-the-road positioning, in the aggregate, was unchanged. Conservative identifications, both moderate and strong, showed increases, these together being approximately equal to the liberal losses. The overall or net tendency, clearly, was toward greater conservatism.[1] The direction of change within the academic world, in short, was the same as that found within the general population.[2] Most of the change, one should also note, occurred in the period from 1969 to 1975. The *only* support these data provide for those arguing that American university and college professors have shifted leftward is the small growth—amounting to roughly one percentage point—in the proportion who identified themselves with the left.

Differences by Field

Respondents were asked to indicate their department of teaching appointment and also their present primary field of interest. About one quarter of those interviewed in 1984 reported joint appointments. To reduce complication, we have classified people by their primary field of interest. Ladd and Lipset (1975: chap. 3) documented the divisions within the universities using a wide variety of measures. The basic pattern may be summarized as follows: The social sciences were the most liberal, followed by the humanities, law, and the fine arts. Several areas occupied a middle ground: physical sciences, biological sciences, education, and medicine. Business, engineering, and "other applied fields" were generally conservative. The most conservative of all was agriculture. Some sense of the differences may be gained by consideration of the extreme cases. The percentages of respondents identifying themselves as leftist and liberal in sociology as of 1969 were, respectively, 17 and 60, with most of the remainder indicating "middle-of the-road." The equivalent figures for agriculture were 0.1 and 17; nearly half of this group described themselves as moderately conservative (Ladd-Lipset:369).

Such internal differentiation, as indicated, comes as no great surprise. It is, simultaneously, one of those things that "everyone knows" but also one that "many people forget." The terms used in many critiques and analyses, as noted, are "the university" and "the professors." Commentaries that emphasize the "leftist tendencies" in American higher education typically overlook the center and right disciplines. This amounts to a part-for-whole substitution, what the literary specialists refer to as synecdoche. While in some contexts acceptable, here the procedure amounts to a sampling error and hence to a misrepresentation.

Table 1. Political Identifications

	Year			Change
	1969	1975 %	1984 %	1969–84 %
Political identification				
Left	4.8	5.4	5.7	+0.9
Liberal	40.6	35.6	33.8	−6.8
Middle of the road	27.1	28.4	26.6	−0.5
Moderate conservative	24.9	27.6	29.6	+4.7
Strong conservative	2.6	3.1	4.2	+1.6
Total percent	100.0	100.1	99.9	
N	58,313	24,534	4,944	

Table 2. Political Identifications by Disciplinary Context, 1969 and 1984

	Liberal-Left		Center		Conservative	
Disciplinary Context						
	1969	1984	1969	1984	1969	1984
Political Identification	%	%	%	%	%	%
Left	9.0	10.5	3.5	3.4	1.1	0.8
Liberal	53.6	43.2	39.2	32.4	24.1	18.4
Middle-of-road	21.2	24.8	29.5	28.1	32.7	26.8
Moderate conservative	14.6	19.1	25.6	32.7	37.7	44.5
Strong conservative	1.5	2.4	2.2	3.3	4.4	9.5
Total percent	99.9	100.0	100.0	99.9	100.0	100.0
N	20,295	1,860	17,971	1,901	7,704	745

We have simplified our exploration of trends by field by focusing on two points, 1969 and 1984 and by grouping the disciplines into three broad categories (disciplinary political contexts), these based on the combined liberal and leftist identifications in 1969 (see Appendix A for details). The political identifications for the two years and the three disciplinary contexts are shown in Table 2.

Liberal identifications declined in all three contexts, the greatest loss (of percentage points) coming in the liberal-left fields. Conservative identifications increased in all three. This shift, again measured in percentage points, was greatest in the conservative context. The proportion who identified themselves as middle-of-the-road changed little. It is likely that in the liberal-left context liberals shifted to the center. In the conservative context, centrists probably shifted to conservative positions. These, to be sure, are only guesses since individual changes cannot be demonstrated with two cross-sectional samples. There are, moreover, the possibilities of entrances and exits, that is, of new hires from among younger cohorts and retirements of the elderly. These possibilities will be explored below.

The most intriguing finding in Table 2 involves those identifying themselves as left. The minuscule increase seen in the overall result (Table 1) appears to hide two opposite trends. The increase was located principally within the liberal-left disciplines where in some fields sizable increases are indicated (see Appendix B for details). Within the center fields, no overall change in leftist strength is shown. The detailed breakdown (again in Appendix B) shows some gains and some losses, but all the differences were modest. In the conservative context, the small proportion identifying with the left became even smaller, disappearing entirely in some fields.

The basic trends, in short, were towards moderation and conservatism within the center and right disciplines. Within the liberal-left disciplines, a bifurcation occurred. Many professors moved with the dominant tendency, toward greater moderation, that being the larger of the two flows. But some moved against the "spirit of the times." It is, conceivably, this minor countertendency that has been picked up by many commentators and given such prominent attention. While small in the aggregate, in some fields clearly the changes are of much larger magnitude.

The Age Relationship

Ladd and Lipset reviewed the relationships between age (or, in two tables, the years when one was an undergraduate) and a wide range of political questions. They found conservative orientations strongest in the older cohorts and liberalism (or leftism) strongest in the younger ones. The extent of the differences between cohorts varied considerably, however, with some of them being rather small. Findings were presented from two surveys, these for five cohorts. The differences between the oldest and youngest age groups (60 and older, younger than 30) on four civil liberties questions contained in the 1955 Lazarsfeld and Thielens survey ranged from 24 to 33 points. The differences between these two age groups on six items from the Carnegie 1969 survey range from 16 to 28 points. One of the smaller differences involved political identification, the combined percentages of the liberal and the left for oldest and youngest cohorts, respectively, being 36 and 53, a matter of 17 points. Working with nine age categories based on the years respondents attended college, they found considerable differences in two items, support for campus activism and candidate preferences in the 1968 Democratic Convention, but differences in the percentages favoring an immediate withdrawal from Vietnam were modest. There were small differences in the percentages who reported that as undergraduates they viewed themselves as left. All age groups had between 2% and 6% who claimed this political position, with the highest proportions shown by those who were undergraduates between 1932 and 1948. Ladd and Lipset also showed that among older cohorts, fewer currently identified themselves as left, indicating some defection from the youthful preferences. An opposite pattern, some increase in leftist preferences, was found among the younger cohorts. The result was a consistent linear relationship for current political orientations, self-reported leftism ranging from 1 % in the oldest cohort to 9% in the youngest (Ladd & Lipset 1975:184–99).

Several explanations of the age patterns in political outlooks are available. It is easy to read them in terms of simple succession, with liberal and leftist cohorts replacing older conservative ones. There might also be period effects (e.g., those felt by the Depression generation, as suggested in the previous paragraph). Another familiar argument is that of conversion, conservatism supposedly increasing with age. These are not either/or options since all three processes may be operating in varying degree. While best approached with a long-term panel survey, some insight may be gained with these three cross-sectional surveys by following a given cohort across the surveys. Through this procedure, we may gain some sense of the patterns of stability and change in political orientations. For this analysis we examined the results for degree cohorts (with respondents classified by the year of the highest earned degree). The overall results allow assessment of the impacts of retirements, conversions, and new additions (Table 3).

Table 3. Political Identifications by Degree Cohort

	1969			1975			1984		
	Left %	Liberal %	Total %	Left %	Liberal %	Total %	Left %	Liberal %	Total %
Degree cohort									
To 1928	2.4	38.0	40.4						
1929–33	1.4	33.3	34.7	2.4	25.8	28.2[a]			
1934–38	1.7	34.8	36.5	3.4	32.3	35.7			
1939–43	1.5	37.6	39.1	1.8	34.6	36.4			
1944–48	2.4	39.2	41.6	2.7	34.2	36.9			
1949–53	2.7	39.3	42.0	2.8	34.4	37.2	3.6	34.0	37.6
1954–58	3.9	40.2	44.1	3.8	33.1	36.9	3.1	33.8	36.9
1959–63	5.1	41.5	46.6	4.5	33.9	38.4	4.9	30.5	35.4
1964–68	6.9	42.2	49.1	5.3	35.6	40.9	3.9	31.1	35.0
1969–73				7.2	37.7	44.9	4.8	35.5	40.3
1974–78				8.1	37.7	45.8	7.9	35.8	43.7
1979–84							9.1	34.6	43.7

[a]This is the smallest N in the table, N=101.

A first point to be noted is that the differences by degree cohort are not large. It would be a mistake, in other words, to claim that age is a major correlate of political identifications. The 1969 survey shows steady increases of leftist and liberal identifications for the younger cohorts. Leaving aside the aberrant earliest cohort (which had a relatively small number of cases), the combined total increases by 14 percentage points. A similar increase in leftist identifications appears in the 1975 results (again with some aberration in the early and smaller cohorts), but the link between age and liberalism at this point has all but disappeared. In the 1984 study, the inverse relationship between age and leftism again appears. That relationship, in short, is present at all three points. But again, as in 1975, the link between age and liberalism is irregular. If dichotomized, the difference would be no more than a few percentage points.

Comparisons for a cohort across two time points are possible in 14 instances. The examination of leftist identifications shows two distinct patterns. All six comparisons of the older cohorts (1949–53 and earlier) show increases in leftist identifications, a reversal of the conservatism-with-age expectation. Seven of the eight comparisons of younger cohorts, those from 1954–58 and later, show decreases in leftist identifications. Declines in liberal identifications exist in 13 of the 14 comparisons.

Given the prominence of claims about "tenured radicals," one might think that the highly visible campus protests of the late 1960s and early 1970s would have meant a peak of leftism for faculty receiving degrees in those years. But the subsequent surveys show further increases in leftist identifications among the later cohorts, the youngest in the 1984 survey having the highest figure, 9.1%. The generalizations based on the protests of the late 1960s overlook two important subsequent processes. There was, first, a subsequent increase in leftist identifications among new faculty cohorts, which continued the tendency present in the 1960s. And, second, there was a countering process of attenuation associated with time in the academic ranks. The 1964–68 cohort which began in 1969 with a 6.9% level of leftism was down to 3.9% in 1984, the same as the beginning level of the mid-1950s cohort.

The modest increase in leftist identifications noted in Table l, in short, hides three diverse processes: some conversions to the left in the older cohorts (a reversal of the pattern noted by Ladd and Lipset prior to 1969), the addition of young cohorts with relatively strong leftist sentiments, and a countering tendency toward moderation among those same cohorts associated with age (or years of employment).

Ladd and Lipset, writing in 1975, speculated briefly about future trends in political orientation among the professoriate and came to different conclusions at different points in their analysis. Based on evidence that older faculty were more conservative in 1969 than they remembered themselves to be during their undergraduate years (but ignoring the opposite pattern among younger faculty), they claimed that professors, like others, tend to become more conservative with age. Given projections that the expansion of American higher education would fall off during the 1970s and 1980s, they argued that the relatively left-oriented cohorts who earned their bachelor's degrees during the late 1950s and 1960 would become more conservative as they aged, and that the numerical preponderance of these cohorts over younger ones would, over the years, reduce the aggregate level of leftist sentiments (Ladd & Lipset 1975:197–98). In their chapter on "Concluding Observations," however, they argued that less favorable economic conditions, and expansion of the most "proletarianized" sectors of higher education, would lead to greater faculty unionism and increased leftist tendencies. "The initially more liberal views of the younger faculty," they argued, "reflecting the dominant orientations of the period when they entered the profession, the 1960s, may be reinforced rather than moderated as these faculty suffer frustrations imposed by a declining labor market and scarce financial resources" (303).

Our results are inconsistent with both of these arguments. Ladd and Lipset's projection that colleges and universities would grow at a much slower rate in the late 1970s and 1980s than in the 1960s was correct, but this did not mean small numbers of young Ph.D.s added to university faculties. Because the slower rate of growth was applied to a very large base, significant numbers of new faculty were added, a net of almost 300,000 between 1970 and 1982 (U.S. Bureau of the Census 1990:153). Data from the 1984 survey show that about one-sixth of the faculty at that date had received their highest degrees during 1979–84, and another fifth between 1974 and 1978. And as we have indicated, these new additions showed historically high levels of leftist identifications. Second, the proportions of those with leftist identifications increased in older cohorts, rather than decreasing. Thus, the slight increase in the proportions of leftist identifications shown in the overall result apparently stems from these two processes that outweigh the shifts away from the left found among those cohorts joining the faculties in the 1960s and after.

Quality of Institution

Ladd and Lipset (1975:142–44) found a positive relationship between institutional quality and various measures of liberalism. With institutions divided into elite, middle tier, and lowest tier, they found the following percentages classified as "very liberal" or "liberal" on their liberalism-conservatism scale: 55, 40, and 31. We have made use of the institutional classifications contained in the Carnegie surveys in our analysis. Unfortunately, different classification systems were used in 1969 and 1984. The change was introduced in the 1975 survey which classified institutions according to both systems.[3] Since precise 1969–84 comparisons are not possible, we have had to examine the changes in two steps, 1969 to 1975 and 1975 to 1984.

In the 1969–75 period, there are two distinct patterns (Table 4). In the high and medium-quality universities, leftist sentiment declined slightly and liberalism declined markedly. The extent of defection, from both leftist and liberal positions, it will be noted, varied with the quality of the university. The high-quality universities, those that were at the center of the student uprising of the late 1960s, were again in the vanguard, this time "leading the way"' to the moderation of the mid-1970s.

Table 4. Political Identifications by Quality of Institution

	1969				1975I			
	Left %	Liberal %	Total %	N	Left %	Liberal %	Total %	N
Universities								
High-quality	7.8	51.6	59.4	7,326	6.8	43.4	50.2	2,467
Medium-quality	6.3	44.9	50.9	10,595	5.4	40.3	45.7	3,346
Low-quality	4.3	39.4	43.7	9,197	4.4	36.7	41.1	3,879
Colleges								
High-quality	7.7	45.1	52.8	3,304	9.8	45.4	55.2	1,410
Medium-quality	4.3	37l7	42.0	6,386	7.4	36.3	43.7	2,597
Low-quality	3.4	39.2	42.6	13,013	5.2	32.3	37.5	6,510
Two-year colleges	2.3	29.5	31.8	8,510	3.0	27.6	30.6	4,325

It was the colleges, at all three quality Ievels, that showed an increase in leftist identification. The high quality colleges went against the aggregate trends in a second respect: they maintained their high levels of liberal sentiment. The regularly neglected two-year colleges also showed increased leftism, this accompanied by a modest fall-off in liberalism. The two-year colleges are distinguished by two characteristics: markedly lower levels of leftism and liberalism than was found in other institutions, and greater stability of orientations.[4]

We offer the following conclusions: (1) the high-quality universities showed the greatest aggregate change with relatively large declines in liberal identifications in all settings and declines of leftist identifications in two settings, (2) the high-and middle-quality colleges show minimal change, maintaining a high level of liberalism; the high quality colleges also showed an increase in leftism, and (3) the two-year colleges showed minimal change, having low levels of liberalism and leftism at both points. These changes altered the ordering of the institutions in terms of political orientations. In 1969, the high-quality universities were the clear leaders in liberal and leftist sentiment. In 1975, those institutions had yielded the lead to the high-quality colleges. At minimum then, there are three distinct patterns of change. The emphasis placed here on change, it should be noted, might be misleading since the largest change (difference between two percentages) is -8.2 points. The dominant fact in all settings is a relative stability in political orientations.

The 1975 and 1984 Carnegie surveys used a new institutional classification system, this having nine categories (Carnegie 1976). Rather than discussing results for all nine categories (described in Appendix C), the following summary conclusions will suffice. With only one exception, the levels of leftist identification were either maintained or increased although the changes, on the whole, were relatively small (Table 5). In the low-quality liberal arts colleges, the exception, a sharp drop in the percentage of the left was registered. The liberal percentages fell off in six of the nine categories. In two instances opposite tendencies appeared; increases in liberalism occurred in the better liberal arts colleges and in the category "comprehensive universities and colleges II." The latter appears to consist of less prestigious private institutions and state colleges. A cross-tabulation of the two institutional classification schemes indicates that most of them were previously classified as middle and low prestige liberal arts colleges. The two-year colleges, finally, again showed minimal change.

We offer the following conclusions as rough parallels to those drawn with respect to the 1969–75 changes:

(1) The high quality universities again showed, by a small margin, the greatest change. In the 1975–84 period the decline of liberal identifiers continued. In contrast to the earlier period, however, leftist identifications increased in all university settings although, to be sure, by very small amounts

(2) The high-quality liberal arts colleges showed a continuation of the previous trends, with both leftist and liberal identifications increasing slightly. The combined liberal and leftist sentiment, 59%, was well ahead of the equivalent figures in all other settings. The "comprehensive universities and colleges II" category showed similar tendencies and, as of 1984, had the second highest liberal-left total. The rank orderings, in short, were strikingly different from those found in 1969.

(3) The two-year colleges again showed minimal change and thus again showed the lowest levels of liberal and leftist identifications.

To guard against possible misinterpretation, some cautionary remarks may be useful. Discussions of the universities frequently focus on the most prestigious universities and colleges. If that meant the first and seventh categories listed in Table 5, one would be dealing, respectively, with 51 and 123 institutions having 1,144,000 and 154,000 students, the latter a trivial part of the grand total. Numerically, the most important segment was the two-year colleges, 1,147 institutions and nearly four million students. The second most important category was the comprehensive universities and colleges I segment with 381 institutions and 2,627,000 students. Overall, a majority of university-level students were found in those two categories.

Table 5. Political Identifications by Quality of Institution

	1975II				1984			
	Left %	Liberal %	Total %	N	Left %	Liberal %	Total %	N
Quality of institution[a]								
Research univ. I	6.1	43.0	49.1	3,866	6.4	39.0	45.4	707
Research univ. II	4.8	38.3	43.1	2,586	6.1	34.8	40.9	476
Doctoral univ. I	6.1	36.6	42.3	960	6.3	32.1	38.4	431
Doctoral univ. II	4.3	36.1	40.4	1,475	4.5	35.2	39.7	165
Comprehensive univ. & colleges I	5.8	36.8	42.6	4,409	5.9	34.9	40.8	1,283
Comprehensive univ. & colleges II	6.5	35.3	41.8	2,520	8.9	38.0	46.9	302
Liberal arts I	13.0	42.5	55.5	830	13.6	45.6	59.2	141
Liberal arts II	5.8	31.6	37.4	1,958	2.9	30.3	33.2	253
Two-year colleges	3.2	27.5	30.7	4,410	3.9	27.8	31.7	1,185

[a]See Appendix C for explanation.

Table 6. Political Identifications by Quality of Institution and Disciplinary Context: 1984

Institution and Political Identifications	Disciplinary Context			Differences between Liberal-Left & Conserv.
	Liberal-Left %	Center %	Conservative %	
Research univ. I				
Left	12.1	4.5	1.2	
Liberal	52.1	40.9	16.0	+47.0
N	188	356	119	
Percents across	28.4	53.7	17.9	100.0
High-quality colleges				
Left	17.7	4.0	—	
Liberal	47.1	46.1	—	
N	93	36	6	
Percents across	68.9	26.7	4.4	100.0
Comprehensive univ. & colleges I				
Left	11.8	2.8	0.7	
Liberal	45.9	32.0	16.1	+40.9
N	501	502	185	
Percents across	42.2	42.3	15.6	
Two-year colleges				
Left	5.4	3.0	1.2	
Liberal	36.6	24.6	23.6	+17.2
N	411	445	163	
Percents across	40.3	43.7	16.0	100.0

ªToo few cases for reliable estimates.

Quality of Institution and Field

One might expect that the combined effects of institutional quality and disciplinary political context would yield much higher levels of liberalism and leftism in certain cases. Some commentators, in fact, have drawn that conclusion and projected extremely high levels for some institutions. Because of the complication involved, only a partial presentation of results is possible. We will focus on the most visible institutions, the high-quality universities and colleges, and on those with the most students, the comprehensive universities and colleges I category and the two-year colleges.

We begin with the research universities I category. In the liberal-left disciplines of those 51 universities, professorial identifications with liberalism and the left are relatively strong (Table 6). One should note, however, that the combined result is not dramatically different from that seen in Table 2. Overall, we saw that liberal and leftist identifications in the liberal-left fields coming to 53.7%; in these high quality universities, the figure for those same fields is 64.2 (with four of five within the category, it should be noted, being liberals). Similarly, liberal and leftist identifications within the center disciplines was somewhat greater although the difference (compared to Table 2) is small. Since the political identifications of the professors in the right disciplines match the overall result, it follows that the differences between the liberal-left and right disciplines in this setting are relatively large, 47 percentage points.

The high-quality liberal arts colleges, as noted, are a minuscule factor, quantitatively, in American higher education. In the liberal-left disciplines, one finds the highest current level of leftist identification discovered thus far, approximately one in six making that choice. In addition, almost half identified themselves as liberal. Although based on very small numbers, the levels of liberal and leftist identifications in the center contexts in those colleges are also high. This is the only institutional setting in which the differences by disciplinary context, although present, are not statistically significant (a result stemming partly from the small numbers involved). The conservative fields (agriculture, business, engineering) have only a modest presence in these colleges (as may be seen in the N's of Table 6). In part at least, the relative homogeneity of political outlooks in the high-quality liberal arts colleges is due to this unusual compositional factor.[5]

The institutions in the comprehensive universities and colleges I category, as already signaled, provide a close match to the high-quality research universities. The levels of liberalism and leftism are lower but in most comparisons the differences are minor. This result, essentially, is a restatement of a previous conclusion, namely that the political differences associated with institutional quality are strikingly reduced since 1969.

The two-year colleges also show a distinctive pattern. Within the liberal-left disciplines, the levels of liberal and leftist identifications are remarkably low, the lowest in fact of all categories of institution. The differences between the center and right disciplines, moreover, are remarkably small. Like the high-quality liberal arts colleges, the discipline factor seems to be of less importance. In this setting, moreover, in both the center and right disciplines, conservatism is the modal tendency.

The highest level of leftist identifications found thus far in the 1984 Carnegie data was the 17.7% in the high quality liberal arts colleges. That falls far short of the figures given (or projected) in some of the literature cited above. Balch and London, citing the figures for leftist orientations from the same Carnegie survey, give the following percentages for specific fields within "4-year institutions"—sociology, 37.0; philosophy, 21.7; political science, 19.8; history,12.8. If percentages are for both liberal arts segments (liberal arts I and II in Table 5), it will be noted that the base figures must be very small. Taking segments I and II together, moreover, would "average" very diverse experience, the respective percentages of the left being 13.6 and 2.9. If those are combined results, our examination of the four fields listed shows history with the largest number of cases— a total of 13. There is little reason to doubt the principal conclusion, that leftist sentiment is high in those particular institutions and in that collection of fields. But one should be wary of the "precise" percentage figure for any given field within the liberal arts. One other point: exceptionally high figures in those fields would mean correspondingly low figures for other closely related fields in those institutions.[6]

The unusual distribution of preferences found in the high-quality liberal arts colleges is, from one perspective, not too surprising. The institutions are small in size and, on balance, attractive as places of employment. Given normal turnover, and given the overall political tendencies among the youngest cohorts (as shown in Table 3), it would be relatively easy for "large changes" to occur there as a result of, say, fifteen retirements and an equivalent number of new hires. Undoubtedly some nonrandom selection could be operating, with the current faculty choosing liberal and/or leftist candidates, and such candidates choosing such institutions. With no serious countering pressure from moderate or conservative fields, the political transformation of such an institution would be relatively easy. The impacts of committed liberal and leftist professors on the students in one such setting are reported in what is probably the most famous study of a liberal arts college, Theodore Newcomb's Bennington Study (1943, 1967). That institution was rather exceptional in the 1930s; the liberal-left tendency now appears to be much more pervasive.

Publication

The findings presented here leave something of a paradox. Some have sensed and reported a significant growth of the Left in U.S. colleges and universities. The evidence, as of 1984, shows a rather modest overall incidence of leftist identifications. Figures for fields and institutional contexts, moreover, fall far short of the more dramatic estimates. The measure used here, political identification, is in one respect like a blank check. A professor of a given political persuasion could use the classroom in an extremely tendentious way, taking every opportunity for advocacy of political values. Or, the opposite case, a professor could avoid any indication of personal preferences, instead reviewing all likely or frequently discussed options. The problem, of course, was a central concern of Max Weber who objected to Treitschke's fusion of politics and scholarship and·

his use of the lectern for political purposes (see Mommsen 1984:7–10). The opportunities for political advocacy, it will be noted, are not equally available to all professors. The civil engineer, the electrical engineer, the biologist, the music teacher (and many others) have fewer occasions for political advocacy than, for example, the political scientist or the sociologist.[7] Hence, as it stands, the data presented here provides little more than a body count—one third of the professors in 1984 indicated they were liberal—but we know nothing about the substance of that liberalism and we have shown nothing about their behavior in the classroom or in any other settings.

One measure of possible influence involves publication. A professor has some direct influence on students in class. In large lectures one may reach, possibly, up to several hundred. Publications too provide an opportunity for outreach. Depending on the medium, this kind of communication might reach thousands or tens of thousands. Publication, of course, varies systematically with the quality of institution. In the 1975 study, some 60% of the professors in high-quality universities reported publication of two or more articles in the last two years. At the opposite extreme, in the two-year colleges, 3.3% reported that level of productivity. In the high quality research universities where presumably all are obliged to publish, one would anticipate little difference either by field or by political identification. In other institutions, however, some variation would be possible. In those less demanding contexts, with remarkable consistency, frequency of publication shows a consistent pattern with political identifications: professors of the left have the highest rates and conservative professors the lowest (Table 7). Other things equal, the thoughts of leftist and liberal professors are more likely to be "seen." The straightforward "body count," therefore, as in a survey, is likely to understate their influence. There are again some unknowns here. Our procedure counts all articles as equal. But if professors in conservative disciplines produced highly technical articles for small audiences of specialists and the liberal and leftist professors produced pieces for general consumption, that too would alter the pattern of influence.

The university presses are of special interest in this connection. There are some 80 such organizations, most of them linked to prestigious institutions, those in the category research universities I. They account for just over 1% of publishers' annual sales, a trivial part of the total. About 10% of the 40,000 new titles published each year issue from the university presses. Although not ordinarily best sellers, "more than 20% of the awards and prizes made since 1950 have gone to books published by university presses" (Parsons 1989:8). Most of those books come from the fields we have referred to here as the liberal-left disciplinary context. Parsons provides an easy summary: "University presses publish primarily in the humanities and social sciences." A 1968 study of books published by these presses showed "52 percent in the humanities, 37 percent in the social sciences, and 11 percent in the natural sciences." Few university presses have publishing programs, that is, lists, in "such disciplines as computer science, social work, veterinary science, engineering, mathematics, and library science" (28, 31).

Substantive Issues

The three studies described in this article contained few questions that would allow research on the much-discussed issue of "politically correct" attitudes. Only one of the possibly relevant questions was posed in all three surveys, this dealing with affirmative action policy. Respondents were asked if they agreed or disagreed with this statement: "The normal academic requirements should be relaxed in appointing members of minority groups to the faculty here." This issue is frequently identified in discussions of "political correctness" with critics of U.S. higher education arguing that left-wing faculty, who allegedly favor vigorous affirmative action policies, have brought about a lowering of scholarly standards. This question allows some exploration of the issue orientations of faculty generally, and specifically of leftist and liberal identifiers, over the fifteen year period.

In 1969, half of the faculty members announced strong disagreement with the suggestion of relaxing standards in hiring and another quarter disagreed with some reservations. In 1975, strong disagreement had increased by about ten percentage points (Table 8). Unqualified support for the suggested relaxation of standards has never been strong and declined to a minuscule level by 1984. Support for that option is distinctively high among the leftist identifiers. In 1969, six of ten

Table 7. Publication by Political Identification in Selected Institutions, 1975

Institution and Publications	Left %	Liberal %	Middle of-Road %	Moderate Conservative %	Strong Conservative %
Low-quality college					
None	54.2	58.6	67.2	67.7	70.6
1–2	31.8	29.6	23.4	25.4	22.7
3 or more	14.0	11.8	9.4	6.8	6.8
N	336	2,084	1,903	1,860	257
Two-year college					
None	70.0	77.8	85.0	85.7	85.2
1–2	22.2	17.0	12.5	11.9	13.4
3 or more	7.8	5.1	2.5	2.4	1.4
N	132	1,168	1,261	1,553	145

identifiers of the left indicated some degree of support for such a policy, but that support fell to only three in ten by 1975. At that point, the Left was divided into three roughly equal segments, those favoring the relaxation of standards, those opposing with reservations, and those strongly opposed. An equally dramatic shift, a halving of support, occurred among the liberal identifiers. Support for this affirmative action option was stronger in the liberal-left disciplines but even there, in 1984, it gained only about one supporter in eight (and most of them agreed only with reservations). At that point more than three fifths of the professors in those disciplines strongly opposed such relaxation. Even in the social sciences, strong opposition was the modal choice (47.0%) with reserved opposition the second most frequent (35.3%). At one point, Balch and London offered a hypothetical equivalence: "If 'Left' is taken as a synonym for 'radical'. . ." (1986:43). On this issue, the equation is not justified. Three tenths of the "Left" has signaled agreement with the majority faculty position on standards and another two fifths lean in that direction.[8]

Conclusions

Many writers, already in the mid-1980s, sensed a growth of leftism in American universities. Our aggregate results for the period 1969–84 provides only modest support for that conclusion, the identifiers of the left increasing from 4.8% to 5.7%. The overall growth, in short, amounted to roughly one percentage point. Much larger changes appeared elsewhere on the political spectrum. Liberalism declined by roughly seven points; conservatism gained just over six points.

There are substantial differences by field. This is the case in all three studies. The aggregate result hides two diverse tendencies. Identifications with the left increased (by 1.5 percentage points) in the liberal-left disciplines. They remained constant in the center disciplines and declined in the right disciplines. Liberal identifications declined in all three contexts; conservatism increased in all three. The commentators are correct in detecting an increase in leftism but are mistaken about the magnitude of the change and in sensing it as occurring throughout the universities.

The original study (Ladd & Lipset 1975) showed both liberalism and leftism varying inversely with age, results that suggested a persistent long term development for the universities. The subsequent surveys show a more complex set of changes. The percentage of leftist identifiers was greater in more recent cohorts, those employed first in the 1970s and early 1980s. But the rate of defection in those segments also appears to be high. Although the younger cohorts moved away from identification with the left, within older cohorts there was some movement toward the left. Finally, the inverse relationship between age and leftist identifications was still present in 1984, but the relationship between age and liberal identifications all but disappeared.

Table 8. Relax Standards in Appointing Minorities by Political Identification

Should standards be relaxed?	1969 %	1975 %	1984 %
All faculty			
Strongly agree	4.2	2.3	1.6
Agree with reservations	17.6	9.7	10.3
Disagree with reservations	27.9	27.0	27.6
Strongly disagree	50.4	61.1	60.4
N	59,231	24,981	4,950
Left identifiers			
Strongly agree	21.2	6.2	7.1
Agree with reservations	39.3	24.9	21.2
Disagree with reservations	23.2	34.9	41.8
Strongly disagree	16.2	34.0	29.9
N	2,757	1,310	271
Liberal identifiers			
Strongly agree	5.5	2.3	1.9
Agree with reservations	26.3	13.4	14.0
Disagree with reservations	32.0	33.4	35.5
Strongly disagree	36.1	50.9	48.6
N	23,445	8,664	1,645

The original study found a clear, but modest, relationship between quality of institution and the frequency of both liberal and leftist identifications. By 1984 that pattern was substantially changed. The most prestigious universities, those leading the late-1960s insurgency, showed substantial rates of defection from both positions between 1969 and 1975. There was a slight increase in leftist identification by 1984 but the loss of liberal sentiment continued. The high-quality liberal arts colleges showed a striking opposite pattern with both liberal and leftist sentiments increasing over the fifteen years. This put them at "the top of the list" of combined liberal-left sentiment, well ahead of the prestigious research universities.

There is some reason to believe that the count of identifications understates the impacts of liberal and leftist professors. In several contexts, the leftist identifiers report the highest rates of publication, followed by the liberals. The strong conservatives, typically, had the lowest rates.

The identifications themselves reveal nothing of the teaching or research style or usage, whether serious and scholarly or agitational and tendentious. One question in the Carnegie studies allowed some exploration in this area, that asking about relaxing standards for the sake of affirmative action, a position said to be favored by "politically correct" faculty members. The trend, as was seen, is in opposition to any suggested relaxation of standards. The shift toward greater support for merit alone was particularly large among the leftist identifiers, a category which, as of 1984, was seriously divided on this issue.

Discussion

The public discussions of a growing and influential left in the universities and colleges appear to be seriously misleading. They do not accurately portray the tendencies nor do they satisfactorily indicate the differentiation within American higher education. As indicated above, the "body count" cannot do justice to the complexities involved. A determined minority may have an impact far out of proportion to its numbers. A department is basically a small work group, and its members will often yield to the sentiments of a minority to avoid internal division. Thus, although the dominant sentiment in 1984 strongly favored unbending standards, serious inequities have appeared in practice (Lynch 1989, 1990).

One curiosity deserves some attention. It is often argued, especially by those on the left, that the best universities are training grounds for children of the upper and upper-middle classes.

They are being prepared for succession, for continuation of class rule. Those institutions, it is said, with some supporting evidence, are controlled by members of the ruling class and they are thought to be ardent defenders of the status quo. This might be the case with respect to governing boards, but the students in those institutions, especially those in the liberal-left fields, are likely to be receiving an education that would challenge inherited privilege (as shown in Table 6). Where meritocratic practice prevents the entry of upper-class children into the best universities, they would probably fall back on the best of the liberal arts colleges where currently the liberal and leftist political orientations are more strongly represented. Working-class and lower-middle class children, in contrast, are most likely to be educated by conservative and moderate professors in two-year institutions and comprehensive universities.

One major study of mass political orientations provides some evidence that is at least consistent with this description of influences. Using the National Election Studies from the 1950s and the 1970s, Nie, Verba, and Petrocik (1979) constructed a liberal-conservative attitude profile to show the distributions and trends for various segments of the population. They provided graphic representations showing the percents in each decile of the left-right continuum. Overall, in the 1950s, the pattern was an inverted-U shape with strong clustering in center deciles. In the 1970s, the U appeared upright, shifts having occurred to both left and right. Those authors show a fair-sized shift to conservatism among "middle and lower status" northern white Protestants. Among higher-status northern white Protestants, they show liberal attitudes going from an initial minuscule presence, 4%, to a significant minority, 13% (Nie, Verba & Petrocik 1979: 245, 261, 263). While not specifically linked to higher-education influence, this line of research does seem an appropriate direction for subsequent study.

Another important line of research undertaken in this period has focused on the growth of postmaterialist value orientations (Inglehart 1977, 1990). Those values are said to result from some major system-level changes, economic, and technological development, distinctive cohort experiences, rising levels of education, and expansion of mass communications. The two latter factors are said to increase the proportions of the population "having skills to cope with politics" on a national scale (Inglehart 1977:5; for further discussion see Hamilton & Wright 1986: 42–44, 95–100). As opposed to that focus on "skills," we suggest two alternative hypotheses: liberal and leftist professors would ordinarily be advocates of postmaterialist values. Those values, we hypothesize, would be communicated (with varying degrees of intensity, to be sure) in lectures, discussion, and texts. Increasingly, also, with the relaxation of formal and informal controls over mass media content, there too one would find advocacy (favorable portrayals of) postmaterialist values. The combination of influences would be most strongly felt by those present in the leading institutions of higher education, specifically, by those in the liberal-left disciplines.

Students in the liberal-left disciplines, it will be noted, are disproportionately female and students in the right disciplines are disproportionately male. Among students from conservative upper- and upper-middle-class backgrounds, one should expect to find conversion among the females and continuity among the males. The disparate experience might, perhaps, have had some impact in the reversal of a long-standing pattern in order to create the new pattern, the so-called gender gap. These too seem appropriate subjects for further research.

Notes

1. Small differences between percentages in our study are statistically significant because the three surveys obtained data from so many respondents. For example, the .9% increase in those who identified themselves as having leftist political orientations across the three surveys is highly significant statistically (x^2=18.2, d.f.=2; $p<.001$), meaning that we can be quite confident in rejecting the null hypothesis of no change in political orientations among the population of college and university faculty during the period. Whether the change in leftist identifications shown in Table 1 is substantively important is, of course, a different issue. Because our large sample sizes almost guarantee statistically significant results, we will not routinely report levels of statistical significance below and will instead briefly note only those results that are not statistically significant.

2. The National Opinion Research Center's General Social Surveys first asked a political self-identification question in 1974 and have repeated it regularly since. Seven options are provided, three degrees of

liberalism and of conservatism plus a "moderate, middle of the road" option. The latter has regularly been the modal choice of the general population. The distributions, generally, closely approximate a normal bell-shaped curve. In 1974, the combined liberal and conservative percentages were, respectively, 30 and 30. In 1984, the date of the last Carnegie study analyzed here, the equivalent figures were 24 and 36. The much-discussed wave of conservatism amounted to an increase of six points. These figures were calculated from the General Social Survey codebooks.

3. The earlier institutional classification system was based upon published "quality" ratings of US. colleges and universities, such as The Gourman Report (see Trow and Associates 1975:367–71). The latter system employs explicit concrete criteria for assigning institutions to categories (see Appendix C), thereby making possible analysis of the changing composition of institutions of higher education (Carnegie Foundation for the Advancement of Teaching 1976).

4. Professors at leading universities sometimes have an opposite impression about the community colleges, sensing them to be centers of radicalism. This appears to be based on a very selective awareness of the recruitment processes. Some of them know radical graduate students who dropped out of the program and later ended up teaching in a junior college. That flow doubtlessly exists and might account for the increase of leftism there (to 396 in 1975). It shows the problems involved in generalizing from small and atypical samples.

5. The 1975 study, which had many more cases (N=830), showed much the same pattern. The conservative fields in the high quality liberal arts colleges had an even smaller presence in that study. Most other university settings closely matched the results shown for the research University I category. The percentages of identifiers of the left in the liberal-left disciplines for the six university categories shown in Table 5 are, respectively: 12.1, 11.3, 12.5, 10.4, 11.8, and 14.6. The latter figure is for the comprehensive universities and colleges II category, the transformed liberal arts colleges. They are, therefore, closer to the high quality liberal arts colleges. Those institutions, reflecting their origins perhaps, like the colleges, had relatively small representation in the right disciplines.

6. Cantor (1985) says that "in leading academic departments, at least 50% of the best minds are now committed to other ideologies [i.e., the Marxists, feminists, deconstructionists, and their allies] and among scholars below the age of forty, 75% are so committed" (38).

    Some figures contained in Appendix B suggest a sizable increase in leftist sentiment within the law faculties -10.3% in 1969 and 23.7% in 1984. But the latter result is based on 38 cases which would mean the difference vis-a-vis 1969 is due to five respondents. The 1975 result, based on 285 cases, showed the level of identification with the left in law faculties at 6.2%.

7. Most discussions of "the university" portray faculty as the movers in the recent innovations. For an interesting case study, one in which the Kenyon College administration is portrayed as attempting to "make women's studies an integral part of the liberal arts"—over the opposition of a reluctant faculty—see Lilla 1986. (Many letters, pro and con, reacting to her position appeared in *Commentary* 81[5]:13–19.)

8. There are other possibilities, of course. One might favor an affirmative action program that, rather than relaxing standards, instead required a more extended search. The option specified in the question clearly would go beyond that procedure.

    Space limits do not allow detailed reporting of other findings. One of these, however, deserves at least passing mention. Most of the discussions about trends within the universities appear without consideration of regional differentiation. The 1975 study, the only one asking about region, showed fair-sized differences. The highest levels of liberalism and leftism were found in the New England and Pacific states; the lowest in the areas from the Great Lakes to the mountain states together with the South and Southwest.

Appendix A: Classification of Disciplines

We grouped the academic disciplines in terms of the combined liberal and left percentages in the 1969 study. The three categories are: liberal-left, 50% or more; center, 35–49%; conservative, 34% or less. The 1969 survey provided results for 70 disciplinary categories. These were grouped into 14 broadly comparable fields (e.g. social science, humanities, engineering, etc.). The disciplines within the general categories showed remarkable similarity in political identification patterns in that only rarely does one diverge from the tendency of the category. Collectively the five disciplines grouped as fine arts fell in the liberal-left category. Music, one of the five, with 39.6%, was an exception, a center group. Ten of eleven humanities disciplines were liberal-left; only Spanish, 43.8%, was center in orientation. Since precise comparison of the detailed categories with the 1984 results was not possible (and also since the number of cases was very small in some instances), we chose to work with the fourteen categories. A miscellany of nine categories (including "none") remained after we constructed the 14 broad disciplinary groups. Eight of these were relatively homogeneous and we classified them as "center" according to the above scheme. The ninth category, "none; is difficult to interpret. There was a sizeable increase in the proportions choosing this option (1969, N=434 or 0.7% of the total; 1984, N=438, 8.8% of the total). They do not show the same tendencies as the other "right" fields (both left and liberal choices increased sharply between 1969 and 1984). Our guess is that many of them are in the rapidly growing interdisciplinary programs. Some of them, we suspect, would have been in liberal-left disciplines in the previous surveys. Because of these uncertainties, we have not included them in the analysis by discipline. Because of the importance of some fields in the recent discussions, where the number of cases in the 1984 study was sufficient, we have presented the detailed figures. This was possible for economics, political science, sociology, English and history. Sociology at that point led all fields in left identifications: three of ten made that choice.

Appendix B: Political Identification by Discipline

Discipline	1969				1984			
	Left	Liberal	Total	N	Left	Liberal	Total	N
Liberal-left								
Social work	12.8	69.7	82.5	322	19.3	48.1	67.4	25
Social sciences	12.4	57.6	70.0	3,976	17.4	41.2	58.6	444
Economics	7.7	57.1	64.8	1,250	5.5	22.2	27.7	112
Sociology	18.7	60.3	79.0	961	29.8	48.6	78.4	140
Political science	12.2	57.7	69.9	1,096	17.8	48.3	66.1	99
Psychology	7.2	59.4	66.6	2,133	8.1	56.9	65.0	155
Architecture	7.1	55.4	62.5	368	10.2	27.1	37.3	48
Humanities	9.6	52.6	62.2	9,354	10.3	43.9	54.2	755
Engish	9.2	53.6	62.8	3,404	9.1	45.4	54.5	387
History	11.8	53.7	65.5	2,095	10.0	46.0	56.0	127
Law	10.3	47.7	58.0	455	23.7	29.5	53.2	38
Fine Arts	4.6	47.7	52.3	3,686	2.5	41.6	44.1	396
Center								
Journalism	1.8	44.3	46.1	222	2.1	44.6	46.7	32
Physical science	3.9	41.4	45.3	4,172	4.0	32.6	36.6	369
Biology	3.3	41.4	44.7	3,860	4.1	35.3	39.4	300
Geography	3.6	40.3	43.9	357	2.1	24.9	27.0	27
Mathematics	6.4	35.9	42.3	2,519	4.0	32.0	36.0	269
Education	2.7	38.8	41.5	3,600	4.3	34.2	38.5	375
Other[a]	2.8	37.5	40.3	416	0.0	28.4	28.4	60
Library science	2.8	37.1	39.9	295	0.0	45.1	45.1	21
Medicine/health	1.6	36.5	38.1	2,532	1.9	28.8	30.7	449
Right								
Engineering	2.2	26.1	28.3	2,900	1.7	21.7	23.4	250
Business	0.6	27.3	27.9	2,235	.7	15.9	16.6	221
Physical education	0.3	21.2	21.5	1,063	0.0	17.6	17.6	87
Home economics	0.4	21.0	21.4	355	0.0	21.8	21.8	61
Industrial arts	0.6	16.9	17.5	225	0.0	26.7	26.7	15
Agriculture	0.1	16.1	16.2	926	0.0	13.4	13.4	111
Unclassified								
None	2.6	20.6	23.2	434	4.2	26.1	30.3	438

[a]Other in 1969; a residual, vocational technical in 1984.

Appendix C: Classification of Institutions

Abbreviated descriptions of the nine categories indicated in Table 5 follow Carnegie Foundation for the Advancement of Teaching, 1976.

Research Universities I

"The fifty leading universities in terms of federal financial support of academic science in at least two of the three academic years,1972–72,1973–74, and 1974–75, provided they awarded at least 50 Ph.D's (plus M.D.'s if a medical school was on the same campus) in 1973–74." Rockefeller University also included.

Research Universities II

The next 50 of the top 100 in terms of federal financial support. Awarded at least 50 Ph.D.'s (plus M.D.'s) in 1973–74.

Doctorate Granting Universities I

Awarded 40 or more Ph.D.'s in at least five fields in 1973–74 (plus M.D.'s) or received at least $3 million in total federal support in either 1973–74 or 1974–75.

Doctorate Granting Universities II

Awarded at least 20 PhD.'s in 1973–74 without regard to field or 10 Ph.D.s in at least three fields.

Comprehensive Universities and Colleges I

Offered a liberal arts program as well as several other programs; many offered master's degrees but lacked a doctoral program or had very limited one.

Comprehensive Universities and Colleges II

State colleges and private colleges with liberal arts program and at least one professional or occupational program. Many former teachers colleges that broadened programs.

Liberal Arts Colleges I

High scoring institutions on a "selectivity index" or, by another measure, had large numbers or graduates subsequently achieving Ph.D.s at leading institutions.

Liberal Arts Colleges II

All those liberal arts colleges that did not meet criteria for inclusion in first group. The distinction between liberal arts colleges and the comprehensive universities and colleges II category is "necessarily partly a matter of judgment."

Two-Year Colleges and Institutes

In addition, several kinds of professional schools and specialized institutions were listed but these have been excluded from our analysis.

References

Adelson, Joseph. 1991. Review of D'Souza, Illiberal Education. *Commentary* 91(6): 55–58.

Balch, Stephen H., and Herbert I. London.1986. "The Tenured Left." *Commentary* 86(4): 41–51.

Blumenthal, Sidney. 1986. *The Rise of the Counter-Establishment.* Times Books.

Brown, E. Richard. 1979. *Rockefeller Medicine Men: Medicine and Capitalism in America.* Berkeley: University of California Press.

Bryden, David P.1991. "It Ain't What They Teach, It's the Way That They Teach It." *Public Interest* 103(Spring): 38–53.

Cantor, Norman.1985. "The Real Crisis in the Humanities Today," *New Criterion* 3(10): 28.38.

Carnegie Foundation for the Advancement of Teaching.1976. *A Classification of Institutions of Higher Education.* Rev. ed.

DePalma, Anthony. 1991. "In Battle on Political Correctness, Scholars Begin a Counter-offensive." *New York Times,* 25 Sept.

D'Souza, Dinesh. 1991a. *Illiberal Education: The Politics of Race and Sex on Campus.* Free Press.

_____. 1991b. "'PC' So Far" *Commentary* 92(4): 44–46.

Epstein, Joseph.1986. "A Case of Academic Freedom." *Commentary* 82(3): 37–47.

Gless, Darryl J., and Barbara Herrnstein Smith (eds.).1992. *The Politics of Liberal Education.* Duke University Press.

Hamilton, Richard F., and James D. Wright. 1986. *The State of the Masses.* Aldine.

Inglehart, Ronald. 1977. *The Silent Revolution: Changing Values and Political Styles among Western Publics.* Princeton University Press.

_____. 1990. *Culture Shift in Advanced Industrial Society.* Princeton University Press.

Kimball, Roger. 1990. *Tenured Radicals: How Politics Has Corrupted Our Higher Education.* Harper Collins.

Ladd, Everett Carll, Jr., and Seymour Martin Lipset. 1975. *The Divided Academy: Professors and Politics.* McGraw-Hill.

Lazarsfeld, Paul R, and Wagner Thielens, Jr. 1958. *The Academic Mind.* Free Press.

Lilla, Elizabeth. 1986. "Who's Afraid of Women's Studies?" *Commentary* 81(2): 53–57.

Lipset, Seymour Martin. 1972. *Rebellion in the University.* Little, Brown.

Lynch, Frederick R. 1989. *Invisible Victims: White Males and the Crisis of Affirmative Action.* Greenwood Press.

_____. 1990. "Surviving Affirmative Action Research—More or Less. " *Commentary* 90(2): 44–4,7

Mandler, Peter.1989. "The 'Double Life' in Academia: Political Commitment and/or Objective Scholarship." *Dissent* (Winter): 94–99.

Mommsen, Wolfgang J. 1984. *Max Weber and German Politics:1890–1920.* University of Chicago Press.

Muravchik, Joshua. 1986. "Review of Blumenthal, Rise of the Counter-Establishment" *Commentary* 82(4): 84–88.

Newcomb, Theodore M. 1943. *Personality and Social Change.* Dryden.

Newcomb, Theodore M., K.E. Koenig, R. Flacks, D.P. Warwick. 1967. *Persistence and Change: Bennington College and Its Students After 25 Years.* John Wiley.

Nie, Norman H., Sidney Verba, and John R. Petrocik. 1979. *The Changing American Voter,* enlarged ed., Harvard University Press.

Opinion Research Corporation. 1984. "Technical Report:1984 Carnegie Foundation National Surveys of Higher Education." Princeton, N.J.: Opinion Research Corporation.

Parsons, Paul.1989. *Getting Published: The Acquisition Process at University Presses*. University of Tennessee Press.

Stimpson, Catherine. 1991. "New 'Politically Correct' Metaphors Insult History and Our Campuses." *The Chronicle of Higher Education*, 29 May.

Trow, Martin, and Associates.1975. "A Technical Report on the 1969 Carnegie Commission Survey of Faculty and Student Opinion." Pp. 297–371 in *Teachers and Students: Aspects of American Higher Education*, edited by Martin Trow. McGraw-Hill.

U.S. Bureau of the Census. *Statistical Abstract of the United States: 1990*. Government Printing Office.

INSTRUCTIONAL ISSUES

Teaching Performance Norms
in Academia

JOHN M. BRAXTON, ALAN E. BAYER, AND MARTIN J. FINKELSTEIN

As most faculty have autonomy in their teaching, social control mechanisms to guide teaching in the interests of clients are needed. Thus, this study posed the question: What is the normative system for undergraduate college teaching? To answer this question the College Teaching Behaviors Inventory was administered to a sample of 800 faculty holding appointments in biology, history, mathematics, and psychology at Research I Universities and Comprehensive Colleges and Universities II. Principal components analysis was used to identify four patterns of teaching norms: interpersonal disregard, inadequate planning, moral turpitude, and particularistic grading. Analysis of variance was used to test for differences in the degree of impropriety accorded to these normative patterns by academics in the two types of institutions and in the four academic disciplines included in our inquiry. Although institutional differences were observed for interpersonal disregard and inadequate planning, disciplinary differences were not found for any of the four normative patterns. Conclusions and implications of these findings are presented.

The functionalist perspective on professions holds that the mastery and control of a basic body of abstract knowledge and the ideal of service—the client's welfare above that of the professional— are the core generating traits of professionalism (Goode, 1969).[1] Claims made to professional status by occupational groups are derived from these core traits. Larger society grants autonomy to those occupational groups that control the work of members in the interest of their clients (Goode, 1969).

Such control of individual professional behavior is exercised through the community of the profession (Goode, 1957). Formal and informal codes of conduct serve to exercise such control as they provide guides for professional behavior. Such social control mechanisms define appropriate and inappropriate behavior with respect to the larger community, colleagues, and clients (Goode, 1957).

Although there is no formally proclaimed code of conduct in the academic profession, a normative structure of science has been identified and described by Merton (1942, 1973). These norms constitute an ethos of science or an affectively toned complex of attitude, values, and norms. Norms are prescribed and proscribed patterns of behavior (Merton, 1942, 1973) that function as mechanisms of social control.

The four norms of science are communality, disinterestedness, organized skepticism, and universalism. As these four norms are derived from the goals and methods of science (Merton, 1942, 1973), compliance with them enhances the advancement of knowledge. Thus, the norms of science act as mechanisms of social control for the scholarly and research activities of academic professionals. Although teaching and research form an integrated core of activities for the academic profession (Braxton and Toombs, 1982; Parsons and Platt, 1973), and teaching is the primary activity of most college and university faculty (Baldridge, Curtis, Ecker, and Riley, 1978), little is known about the mechanisms of informal social control that guide teaching role performance in the academic profession (Braxton, 1986). The question that emerges, then is: What is the normative system for college teaching?

Herein, we put forth a theoretical framework to pursue this fundamental question, raise a set of questions that need to be addressed in an empirical treatment of this topic, and provide the results of pilot study designed to address the conceptually prior questions of this theoretically derived set of questions.

Theoretical Framework

Goals and Norms

The goals of social groups are coupled with regulations that specify permissible procedures for realizing these goals (Merton, 1968). Although these regulations may be prescriptions for procedures and methods, they may also be value-laden sentiments that are prescriptions, preferences, permissions, or proscriptions for conduct in pursuit of group goals (Merton, 1968). Such value-laden sentiments are regulatory norms or informal mechanisms of social control.

As the implicit goal of the professions is attending to the welfare of clients, norms serve to guide the behavior of the individual professional in pursuit of this implicit goal by prescribing appropriate and inappropriate behavior with respect to clients and colleagues (Goode, 1957). In the case of college teaching, the clients served are the academic discipline (Schein, 1972), students in groups (Schein, 1972), and students as individuals (Blau, 1973). Thus, we anticipate that teaching role performance is guided by norms that attend to the welfare of these clients. However, consensus on these norms may vary. Violations of teaching norms may evoke various levels of moral indignation and outrage (Durkheim, 1934). As such reactions signal the social significance of these norms, it is posited that the degree of impropriety ascribed to a given norm will vary as a function of the degree of emphasis placed on teaching across different types of colleges and universities. As faculty in research-oriented universities may place a lower value on teaching, the social significance of various teaching norms may be less for such individuals than for academics in colleges and universities where teaching is emphasized to a greater extent. Consequently, the degree of impropriety ascribed to teaching norms may be greater in educational institutions where faculty stress teaching more than they do research.

Likewise, the degree of impropriety accorded to teaching norms may vary across different academic subject matter areas or academic disciplines. Academic subject matter areas have been found to differ in the level of commitment to teaching espoused by faculty (Biglan, 1973; Creswell and Roskens, 1981). As the level of commitment to teaching may be indexed in the social gravity bestowed to various teaching norms, we might expect that faculty in academic subject matter areas that place a higher degree of importance on teaching accord a higher degree of impropriety to teaching norms than do academics in subject matter areas that declare less commitment to teaching. Although endorsement of teaching norms is necessary for effective social control, faculty conformity to these norms is critical.

Compliance with Teaching Norms

For teaching role performance to best serve the interests of clients, faculty compliance with identified norms is necessary. Put differently, conformity with teaching norms is necessary for effective informal social control.

Sources of control that induce conformity to norms have been described by Reiss (1951). These sources are personal controls, and social controls emanating from the community, institutions, and primary groups. Deviancy occurs when personal and social controls are not of sufficient magnitude to influence compliance with norms.

Personal controls that induce individual conformity to teaching norms are internalized to varying degrees through the graduate school socialization process. Graduate school attendance in general and doctoral study in particular are regarded as a powerful socialization experience (Hagstrom, 1965). The potency of this process lies not only in the development of knowledge, skills, and competencies, but also in the inculcation of norms, attitudes, and values (Merton, Reader, and Kendall, 1957). This socialization process entails the total learning situation (Toombs, 1977) and is composed of formal gateways (courses, qualifying examinations, dissertation), interpersonal relationships between faculty and students, and exchanges with the ambient environment. Interpersonal relationships involve both formal and informal relationships with faculty. Through these interpersonal relationships with faculty, values, knowledge, and skills are inculcated (Cole and Cole, 1973). Thus, the norms of teaching are internalized to varying degrees by individuals through the graduate school socialization process.

Given that the thrust of the graduate school socialization process is toward the inculcation of skills, attitudes, and values on research and scholarship (Cole and Cole, 1973; Hagstrom, 1971), this process tends to instill a deprecating attitude toward teaching role performance (Heiss, 1970; Katz, 1976; Taylor,1976). However, graduate departments vary in the degree of emphasis placed on socialization for scholarly role performance given that faculty scholarly role performance differs across departments of varying degrees of prestige (Hagstrom, 1971). Hence, the extent to which individuals develop a disparaging stance toward teaching may be influenced by the emphasis placed on research in the graduate school socialization process. The degree to which the norms of teaching are internalized by individuals may, in turn, be affected by the emphasis placed on research and scholarship in the graduate school socialization process.

In addition to personal controls that induce conformity to teaching norms, social controls that emanate from the community of the academic subject matter area, the college or university of employment, and the academic department also induce conformity to teaching norms. However, the effectiveness of these sources of social control depend on the intensity of commitment to teaching held by these social groups (Reiss, 1951). Where commitment to teaching is strong, the ability of these sources of social control to induce compliance with teaching norms will also be great. Obversely, deviancy from these norms will occur when commitment to teaching is weak or absent. As a consequence, individual faculty will be free to perform the role of teaching according to their own preferences.

The Reward System and Social Control

These personal and social controls are buttressed by a system of positive and negative sanctions (Zuckerman, 1977). Such a reward system is also necessary for norms to be effective as mechanisms of informal social control of teaching role performance. Positive sanctions are allocated for conformity with teaching norms and negative sanctions are meted out for deviancy from these norms. The allocation of negative sanctions is necessary to deter deviancy (Zuckerman, 1977). Moreover, the sanctioning of offenders is necessary to preserve the prestige and reputation of the profession as well as its autonomy (Goode, 1957, 1969).

These theoretical formulations raise several questions that guide this research on the norms of teaching. The obvious and most basic question is: To what degree do norms for college teaching exist? Once these teaching norms are identified, then the following questions are pertinent: Do faculty in different types of colleges and universities vary in their endorsement of these norms? Do faculty in the various academic disciplines differ in their endorsement of these norms? Are faculty rewarded for compliance with teaching norms and sanctioned for deviancy from them? Although these basic questions are pertinent to both undergraduate- and graduate-level teaching, this inquiry will focus on undergraduate college teaching.

As norms are prescribed, preferential, permissive, or proscribed patterns of behavior (Merton, 1942, 1968, 1973), the degree of impropriety faculty members ascribe to various teaching behaviors provides a suitable operational definition of norms for this inquiry. Moreover, the measurement of the degree of impropriety is assessed herein through the type of sanctions individuals believe should be meted out for each behavior stated in the form of a violation of a possible norm. Thus, the Durkheimian principle of ascertaining norms by assessing the opinions of individuals concerning the type of sanction that might be allocated for deviance was followed in this study. Only those behaviors for which relatively strong sanctions were believed to be fitting were defined as being a norm.

Research Methods

Sampling Design

The population of inference for this study is the faculty in the academic subject matter areas of biology, history, mathematics, and psychology holding full-time academic appointments at Research Universities I and Comprehensive Colleges and Universities II categories of the Carnegie Classification of Institutions of Higher Education (1987). Although Research I Universities (RUI) and Comprehensive Universities and Colleges II (CUCII) are not polar opposite types of collegiate institutions, these two types do differ on the degree of emphasis placed on teaching and research. Teaching is more heavily emphasized in Comprehensive Universities and Colleges II, whereas research receives greater emphasis at Research Universities I. Thus, these two types of colleges and universities provide suitable settings for taking the initial steps toward addressing the exploratory question raised above.

Research on the Biglan model for the classification of academic subject matter areas indicates that individual academic disciplines differ on the amount of time spent on teaching and on the preference or amount of importance attached to teaching (Creswell and Roskens, 1981). Thus, faculty in different subject matter areas may differ on the degree of importance accorded to the various teaching norms discerned. Consequently, the four academic subject matter areas were selected to test for differences in the degree of impropriety accorded to the teaching norms identified.

The model generated by Biglan (1973) assorts academic subject matter areas into eight categories using three dimensions: pure-applied, hard-soft, and life-nonlife. The following four categories of Biglan's model are represented herein: hard-life (biology), hard-nonlife (mathematics), soft-life (psychology),and soft-nonlife (history). In this study, only pure subject matter areas are represented.

A cluster sampling design was used to select a random sample of the population of inference of this research. The two types of institutions and the four academic subject matter areas represented are the elements in this sampling design. This design entailed the random selection of specific institutions from the two categories of the Carnegie Classification of Institutions of Higher Education (1987): Research Universities I and Comprehensive Universities and Colleges II. Each specific institution represents a cluster from which the faculty sample was drawn.

From the population of 70 institutions classified as Research I Universities, 11 universities were randomly selected, and 25 institutions were randomly drawn from the population of 171 Comprehensive Universities and Colleges II. To construct the faculty sample, the specific names of faculty were derived from the most recent university and college catalogues or bulletins of the randomly chosen colleges and universities. All faculty holding the rank of assistant professor or higher and listed under one of the four academic departments represented in this research were eligible for selection.

Eight lists of faculty were formed, one list for each academic subject matter and institutional type combination. From these eight lists, a random sample of 800 faculty was drawn. This sample was comprised of 200 faculty from each of the four subject matter areas, or 400 faculty from each of the two types of colleges and universities included in this study.

During April 1989, the data collection instrument designed and constructed for this study was mailed to this sample of 799 faculty.[2] After an initial mailing, a postcard reminder, and a second mailing of the survey form to nonrespondents, a total of 356 individuals responded with completed survey forms. Thus, a response rate of 44.5 percent was realized. Although 356 completed survey instruments were gathered, this sample size was reduced to 302 by the application of three criteria for inclusion in the data analysis. These three criteria were the individual holds a full-time academic appointment, the individual is tenured or holds a tenure-track appointment, and the individual holds the academic rank of assistant professor or higher. Responses to survey items pertaining to these criteria were used to select this group of 302 individuals.

Analyses of variance by groups of mailings to nonrespondents indicated no bias on either the specific behaviors meeting the criterion for designation as a norm, or the four patterns of norms (which are described later).[3] This method for determining a sample's representativeness is consistent with procedures outlined by Goode and Hatt (1952) and Leslie (1972).

Data Collection Instrument

A data collection instrument "College Teaching Behaviors Inventory" was designed and constructed for this research. This instrument was mailed to the sample of 799 individual academics described above. This instrument was comprised of 126 specific items classified a priori into eight categories of teaching behaviors. These categories were: Preplanning for the Course (14 behaviors), First Day of Class (14 behaviors), In-Class Behaviors (21 behaviors), Treating Course Content (9 behaviors), Examination and Grading Practices (25 behaviors), Faculty-Student In-Class Interactions (9 behaviors). Relationships with Colleagues (16 behaviors), and Out-of-Class Practices (18 behaviors). The specific teaching behaviors subsumed under each category were negatively worded so as to cast each behavior in the form of a violation of possibly preferred conduct. This approach is consistent with the general principle advanced by Durkheim (1934) that norms are best known or recognized by individuals when violated.

Individuals were asked to indicate their opinion on each specific behavior as it might ideally apply to a faculty member teaching a lower-division college course in his or her field of about 40 enrolled students regardless of whether the individual teaches such a course himself. To indicate their reactions to each behavior, the following response categories were provided: (1) appropriate behavior, should be encouraged, (2) discretionary behavior, neither particularly appropriate nor inappropriate, (3) mildly inappropriate behavior, generally to be ignored, (4) inappropriate behavior, to be handled informally by colleagues or administrators suggesting change or improvement, and (5) very inappropriate behavior, requiring formal administrative intervention. Through these reactions, the types of sanctions individuals believe should be appropriated for deviance are assessed. Only those behaviors for which the mean value on this scale was 4.00 or higher were delineated as being norms.

The specific behaviors included in the College Teaching Behaviors Inventory were derived from literature on ethics in college teaching (Baumgarten, 1982; Robertson and Grant, 1982; Schurr, 1982; Scriven, 1982; Wilson, 1982), from analogies to the four norms of science identified by Merton (1942, 1973), and from the suggestions of a panel of 23 experts on college teaching.[4]

An inventory of specific behaviors derived from the literature on ethics in college teaching and analogies to the norms of science were submitted to the panel of experts on college teaching. These individuals were asked to indicate whether each of the specific behaviors provided was a strong norm, a discretionary norm, or not a norm at all. The panel of experts was also asked to suggest additional norms. The reactions and suggestions of this panel were used to develop an instrument for field testing. This draft of the instrument was field tested and refinements to the items and response categories were made to produce the trial version of the College Teaching Behaviors Inventory.

Data Analysis Design

Simple descriptive means were used to delineate those behaviors that meet the criterion for delineation as a norm. As previously indicated, only those behaviors that have a mean value of 4.00 or higher on the scale of possible sanctions were subsequently employed in the analysis. The means and standard deviations for the 126 behaviors included in this inventory are displayed in Table 1.

Analysis of variance was used to address the question of whether faculty in different types of colleges and universities and in different academic subject matter areas vary in the level of impropriety they ascribe to the norms delineated. The two factors of the analyses of variance were academic departments and institutional type.[5] The academic department factor was composed of four levels—biology, history, mathematics, and psychology—and the institutional type factor was comprised of two levels—RUI and CUCII. All the statistical tests employing analyses of variance were conducted at the .025 level of statistical significance. This relatively conservative level of statistical significance was chosen to reduce the probability of committing type I errors. As cluster sampling was utilized in this study, an increase in the probability of committing type I errors above the level of statistical significance selected is possible. Kish (1957) states that the mean of a sample derived from cluster sampling is an unbiased estimator of the population mean, but that the variance of the population may be underestimated because of the homogeneity of the elements of the clusters selected. Consequently, the .025 level of statistical significance was selected.

Findings

The Delineation of Teaching Norms

From Table 1, it can be observed that 25 behaviors meet the criterion of 4.00 or higher on the sanctioning actions scale. With the exception of Treating Course Content, all of the a priori categories of teaching behaviors contain at least one behavior that can be delineated as a norm. Examination and Grading Practices (6 items) and Out-of-Class Practices (7 items) have the most behaviors and Relationships with Colleagues has the fewest (1 item).

The norm perceived to be of the highest level of impropriety was an instructor who frequently attends class while obviously intoxicated (mean = 4.87). Following this norm are two norms that proscribe making suggestive sexual comments (mean = 4.82) and having sexual relationships with students enrolled in class (mean = 4.82). Two additional norms perceived to be highly inappropriate are allowing personal friendships with students to intrude on the objective grading of their work and changing the meeting time of a class without first consulting students.

In order to discern the underlying pattern of meaning of the proscriptions of these norms, a factor analysis was conducted. As no theory undergirded the development of the 126 teaching behaviors, principal components analysis was selected to derive a set of factors that could account for the covariation among these 25 specific behaviors (Kim and Mueller, 1978). Following the principal components analysis the scree test was used to arrive at the number of factors to be extracted and rotated. The scree test suggested that a four-factor solution was appropriate. With the restriction of a four-factor solution applied, the initial principal components analysis was rotated using the varimax method. The rotated factor structure accounted for 48.14 percent of the variance. The proportion of variance explained by each factor is exhibited in Table 2. Additionally, Table 2 shows the factor loadings of the specify norms for each of the four factors discerned as well as the Cronbach alpha estimates of internal consistency reliability computed for each of these factors.

The first factor or normative pattern was named *Interpersonal Disregard*. The behaviors included in this pattern of norms suggest a disregard for the feelings and opinions of both students and colleagues. *Particularistic Grading* is the label given to the second normative pattern discerned. This configuration of norms prescribes that the assessment of student academic performance and the awarding of grades should be both fair and according to merit. The third configuration of norms was designated *Moral Turpitude*, where behaviors such as an instructor attending class while intoxicated, making suggestive sexual comments, and having sexual relationships with students enrolled in one's course had high factor loadings. *Inadequate Planning* was the name given to the fourth normative pattern. The prohibited behaviors associated with this pattern of norms deal with inattention to detail in such matters as changing classroom locations and class meeting times without consulting students, not ordering required texts in time to be available for the first class, and not preparing a course outline or syllabus for a course.

Table 1. Means and Standards Deviation for Behaviors Included in the College Teaching Behaviors Inventory

Behaviors	Mean	S.D.
A. PREPLANING FOR THE COURSE		
A1. Required texts and other reading materials are not routinely ordered by the instructor in time to be available for the first class session.	4.24*	0.84
A2. A course outline or syllabus is not prepared for a course.	4.00*	1.01
A3. Prior to the first meeting of a class, the instructor does not visit the assigned classroom and assess its facilities.	2.68	0.85
A4. A course outline or syllabus does not contain dates for assignments and/or examinations.	3.12	1.10
A5. Objectives for the course are not specified by the instructor.	3.60	0.94
A6. Changes in a course are made without seeking information from students who have previously taken the course.	2.30	0.78
A7. The instructor does not read reviews of appropriate textbooks.	2.66	0.88
A8. The course is designed without taking into account the needs or abilities of students enrolling in the course.	3.79	0.89
A9. Colleagues teaching the same or similar courses are not consulted on ways to teach the particular course.	2.76	0.94
A10. Required course materials are not kept within reasonable cost limits as perceived by students.	3.23	0.95
A11. New lectures or revised lectures that reflect advancements in the field are not prepared.	3.83	0.85
A12. In-class activities are not prepared and anticipated in advance, but are developed while the class is in session.	3.10	1.04
A13. The instructor does not request necessary audiovisual materials in time to be available for class.	3.68	0.86
A14. Assigned books and articles are not put on library reserve by the instructor on a timely basis for student use.	3.83	0.85
B. FIRST DAY OF CLASS		
B1. Class roll is not taken.	2.56	1.05
B2. The instructor does not introduce her/himself to the class.	3.37	0.86
B3. Office hours are not communicated to the students.	3.92	0.77
B4. The instructor changes classroom location to another building without informing students in advance.	4.22*	0.87
B5. The instructor changes class meeting time without consulting students.	4.60*	0.66
B6. Students are not informed of the instructor's policy on missed or make-up examinations.	3.97	0.87
B7. Students are not informed of extra credit opportunities available in the course during the term.	3.52	0.98
B8. Students are not asked to record their background, experiences, and interests for reference by the instructor.	2.15	0.61
B9. An overview of the course is not presented to students on the first day.	2.72	0.86
B10. An introduction to the first course topic is not begun on the first day.	2.49	0.84
B11. The first class meeting is dismissed early.	2.53	0.92
B12. The first reading assignment is not communicated to the class.	3.42	0.93
B13. A course outline or syllabus is not prepared and passed out to students.	3.75	1.04
B14. The instructor does not ask students if they have questions regarding the course.	3.32	0.91

TABLE 1. (Continued)

Behaviors	Mean	S.D.
C. IN-CLASS BEHAVIORS		
C1. Class sessions are begun without an opportunity for students to ask questions.	2.64	0.92
C2. The topics or objectives to be covered for the day are not announced at the beginning of the class.	2.66	0.85
C3. Joke-telling and humor unrelated to course content occurs routinely in class.	3.02	1.02
C4. The instructor frequently uses profanity in class.	4.14*	0.87
C5. Class is usually dismissed early.	3.99	0.87
C6. The instructor meets the class without having reviewed pertinent materials for the day.	3.95	0.86
C7. The instructor routinely allows one or a few students to dominate class discussion.	3.52	0.77
C8. Instructions and requirements for course assignments are not clearly described to students.	3.97	0.71
C9. Class does not begin with a review of the last class session.	2.31	0.72
C10. Joke-telling and humor related to course content occurs frequently in class.	1.96	0.85
C11. The instructor does not end the class session by summarizing material covered during the class.	2.31	0.63
C12. The instructor is routinely late for class meetings.	4.25*	0.69
C13. The instructor routinely holds the class beyond its scheduled ending time.	3.94	0.72
C14. The instructor does not take class attendance every class meeting.	2.03	0.72
C15. The instructor does not introduce new teaching methods or procedures.	2.60	0.87
C16. The instructor does not provide in-class opportunities for students to voice their opinion about the course.	2.91	1.00
C17. The instructor calls on students to answer questions in class on a non-voluntary basis.	2.00	0.62
C18. The instructor does not follow the course outline or syllabus for most of the course.	3.81	0.86
C19. The instructor practices poor personal hygiene and regularly has offensive body odor.	4.06*	0.84
C20. The instructor routinely wears a sloppy sweatshirt and rumpled blue jeans to class.	3.19	1.14
C21. While able to conduct class, the instructor frequently attends class while obviously intoxicated.	4.87*	0.44
D. TREATING COURSE CONTENT		
D1. The instructor does not have students evaluate the course at the end of the term.	3.30	1.13
D2. The instructor insists that students take one particular perspective on course content.	3.74	0.94
D3. The instructor's professional biases or assumptions are not explicitly made known to students.	2.91	0.94
D4. The instructor frequently introduces opinion on religious, political, or social issues clearly outside the realm of the course topics.	3.78	0.98
D5. The instructor does not include pertinent scholarly contributions of women and minorities in the content of the course.	3.43	1.00
D6. Memorization of course content is stressed at the expense of analysis and critical thinking.	3.52	0.93
D7. Connections between the course and other courses are not made clear by the instructor.	2.95	0.89
D8. The relationship of the course content to the overall departmental curriculum is not indicated.	2.91	0.89
D9. A cynical attitude toward the subject matter is expressed by the instructor.	3.72	0.99

TABLE 1.

Behaviors	Mean	S.D.
E. EXAMINATION AND GRADING PRACTICES		
E1. The instructor does not give assignments or examinations requiring student writing skills.	3.15	1.11
E2. When examinations or papers are returned, student questions are not answered during class time.	2.86	0.99
E3. Graded tests and papers are not promptly returned, to students by the instructor.	3.61	0.75
E4. Individual student course evaluations, where students can be identified, are read prior to the determination of final course grades.	4.48*	0.76
E5. Examination questions do not represent a range of difficulty.	3.27	0.95
E6. Grades are distributed on a "curve."	2.50	1.07
E7. An instructor lowers course standards in order to be popular with students.	4.28*	0.76
E8. The standards for a course are set so high that most of the class receives failing grades for the course.	4.37*	0.81
E9. Individual students are offered extra-credit work in order to improve their final course grade *after* the term is completed.	4.35*	0.90
E10. Explanation of the basis for grades given for essay questions or papers is not provided to students.	3.83	0.84
E11. Written comments on tests and papers are consistently not made by the instructor.	3.52	0.94
E12. The instructor allows personal friendships with a student to intrude on the objective grading of his or her work.	4.54*	0.64
E13. Student papers or essay examination questions are not read at least twice before a grade is given.	2.63	0.95
E14. Social, personal, or other nonacademic characteristics of students are taken into account in the awarding of student grades.	4.43*	0.84
E15. Final examinations are administered during a regular class period rather than at the official examination period.	3.84	1.16
E16. Student class participation is considered in awarding the final course grade.	1.85	0.77
E17. Student attendance in class is weighed in determining the final course grade.	2.21	0.85
E18. Student opinions about the method of grading are not sought.	2.29	0.86
E19. Students' work is not graded anonymously.	2.73	1.07
E20. The final course grade is based on a single course assignment or a single examination.	3.59	1.07
E21. Examination questions do not tap a variety of educational objectives ranging from the retention of facts to critical thinking.	3.33	0.95
E22. Sexist or racist comments in students' written work are not discouraged.	3.84	1.01
E23. An instructor does not hold review sessions before examinations.	2.34	0.79
E24. All student grades are publicly posted with social security numbers and without names.	2.38	1.32
E25. Graded papers and examinations are left in an accessible location where students can search through to get back their own.	3.36	1.18
F. FACULTY STUDENT IN-CLASS INTERACTIONS		
F1. Stated policies about late work and incompletes are not universally applied to all students.	4.07*	0.87
F2. Students are not permitted to express viewpoints different from those of the instructor.	4.16*	0.81
F3. The instructor expresses impatience with a slow learner in class.	3.91	0.75
F4. The instructor does not encourage student questions during class time.	3.31	1.00
F5. An instructor makes condescending remarks to a student in class.	4.09*	0.76

TABLE 1. (Continued)

Behaviors	Mean	S.D.
F6. The instructor does not learn the names of all students in the class.	2.68	0.82
F7. A clear lack of class members' understanding about course content is ignored by the instructor.	3.82	0.81
F8. Shy students are not encouraged to speak in class.	2.75	0.89
F9. The instructor does not allow students to direct their comments to other members of the class.	2.74	0.91
G. RELATIONSHIPS WITH COLLEAGUES		
G1. A faculty member refuses to share academic information about mutual students with colleagues.	2.75	1.03
G2. A faculty member does not tell an administrator or appropriate faculty committee that there are very low grading standards in a colleague's course.	2.71	0.95
G3. A faculty member does not tell an administrator or appropriate faculty committee that a colleague's course content largely includes obsolete material.	2.96	0.99
G4. A faculty member refuses to share course syllabi with colleagues.	3.32	1.04
G5. A faculty member avoids sharing ideas about teaching methods with colleagues.	3.19	0.96
G6. A faculty member refuses to allow colleagues to observe his or her classroom teaching.	3.30	1.08
G7. A faculty member assumes new teaching responsibilities in the specialty of a colleague without discussing appropriate course content with that colleague.	3.31	0.93
G8. A faculty member makes negative comments in a faculty meeting about the courses offered by a colleague.	3.54	1.04
G9. A faculty member makes negative comments about a colleague in public before students.	4.33*	0.70
G10. A faculty member aggressively promotes enrollment in his or her courses at the expense of the courses of departmental colleagues.	3.78	0.92
G11. The requirements in a course are so great that they prevent enrolled students from giving adequate attention to their other courses.	3.74	0.87
G12. A faculty member refuses to team teach a course.	2.68	1.04
G13. A faculty member avoids talking about his or her academic specialty with departmental colleagues.	3.02	0.92
G14. A faculty member gives unsolicited advice on the content of a colleague's course.	2.79	0.96
G15. A faculty member gives unsolicited advice to a colleague about teaching methods.	2.70	0.93
G16. A faculty member refuses to participate in departmental curricular planning.	3.86	0.91
H. OUT-OF-CLASS PRACTICES		
H1. Office hours scheduled for student appointments are frequently not kept.	4.24*	0.66
H2. Individual counseling on matters unrelated to course content is not provided to students enrolled in one's course.	2.44	1.02
H3. A faculty member criticizes the academic performance of a student in front of other students.	4.15*	0.80
H4. A faculty member avoids spending time with students outside of class time and/or regular office hours.	2.80	1.05
H5. A faculty member insists on never being phoned at home by students regardless of circumstances.	2.61	0.99
H6. A faculty member makes suggestive sexual comments to a student enrolled in the course.	4.82*	0.46

TABLE 1.

Behaviors	Mean	S.D.
H7. A faculty member has a sexual relationship with a student enrolled in the course.	4.82*	0.53
H8. A faculty member does not refer a student with a special problem to the appropriate campus service.	3.70	0.84
H9. An advisee is treated in a condescending manner.	3.99	0.73
H10. A faculty member avoids giving career or job advice when asked by students.	3.38	0.95
H11. A faculty member refuses to write letters of reference for any student.	3.71	1.13
H12. A faculty member neglects to send a letter of recommendation that he or she had agreed to write.	4.26*	0.68
H13. A faculty member refuses to advise departmental majors.	4.21*	0.88
H14. A cynical attitude toward the role of teaching is expressed by an instructor.	3.96	0.92
H15. A faculty member's involvement in scholarship is so great that he or she fails to adequately prepare for class.	4.19*	0.72
H16. Scholarly literature is not read for the purpose of integrating new information into one's courses.	3.70	0.87
H17. A faculty member avoids reading literature on teaching techniques or methods.	2.97	0.95
H18. A faculty member avoids professional development opportunities that would enhance his or her teaching.	3.36	0.97

Table 2. The Four Patterns of Teaching Norms with Items Loading .38 or Higher on Each Pattern

Normative Pattern/Item		Loading
I.	INTERPERSONAL DISREGARD (10 items)	
F5.	An instructor makes condescending remarks to a student in class.	.73
H3.	A faculty member criticizes the academic performance of a student in front of other students.	.65
C4.	The instructor frequently uses profanity in class.	.62
C19.	The instructor practices poor personal hygiene and regularly has offensive body odor.	.59
G9.	A faculty member makes negative comments about a colleague in public before students.	.57
F2.	Students are not permitted to express viewpoints different from those of the instructor.	.57
E7.	An instructor lowers course standards in order to be popular with students.	.47
H12.	A faculty member neglects to send a letter of recommendation that he or she had agreed to write.	.45
C12.	The instructor is routinely late for class meetings.	.44
H1.	Office hours scheduled for student appointments are frequently not kept.	.39

Percent Explained Variance = .32
Cronbach Alpha = .85

	II. PARTICULARISTIC GRADING (5 items)	
E14.	Social, personal, or other nonacademic characteristics of students are taken into account in the awarding of student grades.	.70
E12.	The instructor allows personal friendships with a student to intrude on the objective grading of his or her work.	.65
E9.	Individual students are offered extra-credit work in order to improve their final course grade after the term is completed.	.57
E4.	Individual student course evaluations where students can be identified are read prior to the determination of final course grades.	.57
F1.	Stated policies about late work and incompletes are not universally applied to all students.	.50

Percent Explained Variance = .06
Cronbach Alpha = .73

	III. MORAL TURPITUDE (4 Items)	
C21.	While able to conduct class, the instructor frequently attends class while obviously intoxicated.	.81
H7.	A faculty member has a sexual relationship with a student enrolled in the course.	.69
H6.	A faculty member makes suggestive sexual comments to a student enrolled in the course.	.67
E8.	The standards for a course are set so high that most of the class receives failing grades for the course.	.41

Percent Explained Variance = .05
Cronbach Alpha = .66

	IV. INADEQUATE PLANNING (6 Items)	
B4.	The instructor changes classroom location to another building without informing students in advance.	.70
B5.	The instructor changes class meeting time without consulting students.	.67
A2.	A course outline or syllabus is not prepared for a course.	.55
H13.	A faculty member refuses to advise departmental majors.	.53
H15.	A faculty member's involvement in scholarship is so great that he or she fails to adequately prepare for class.	.44
A1.	Required texts and other reading materials are not routinely ordered by the instructor in time to be available for the first class session.	.39

Percent Explained Variance = .05
Cronbach Alpha = .66

With the delineation of these four patterns of norms, the second research question pursued in this inquiry is to address whether academics in disparate types of colleges and universities and in various academic subject matter areas vary in their level of endorsement of these four configurations of norms. In this case, level of endorsement is expressed in terms of the degree of impropriety accorded to the specific behaviors of each of these four patterns of norms.

In order to address this question composite measures were developed to appraise the degree of impropriety ascribed by academics to each of the four normative patterns. These composite measures are factor-based scores (Kim and Mueller, 1978) as only those specific norms that had a loading of .38 or higher on the target factor (pattern) were included in the construction of each composite variable.[6] Each of the four composite measures were computed by summing the values of the specific behaviors having a loading of .38 or higher on the target factor and then by taking the mean value of these summations. The four composite measures appear to be reliable as the Cronbach alpha estimates for these four normative patterns range from .66 to .85 (see Table 2 for the specific estimates computed for each normative pattern).

Institutional and Academic Subject Matter Area Differences

With the computation of the four composite measures in place, it is now possible to determine whether faculty in different types of colleges and universities and in different academic subject matter areas differ on the degree of impropriety they accord to each of the four patterns of teaching norms. As previously indicated, 4 x 2 analyses of variance were used to test for such differences. Four such tests were conducted, one for each of the four normative patterns.

Table 3 contains the means and standard deviations for each of the four patterns of teaching norms by institutional types and by academic subject matter area. Table 4 displays summary statistics from each of the four 4 x 2 analyses of variance performed. Prior to conducting each of the analyses of variance, tests for the homogeneity of the variances of the four patterns of teaching norms were made. Although heterogeneous variances were conducted for each normative pattern, the probability of committing type I errors is assessed as minimal for all of the patterns of norms except Inadequate Planning. For Inadequate Planning, the analysis of variance was conducted at a .01 level of statistical significance.[7]

Interpersonal Disregard

Although faculty in the four academic subject matter areas have similar assessments of the level of impropriety accorded to the normative pattern of Interpersonal Disregard, academics in Comprehensive Universities and Colleges II (x = 4.27) bestow a somewhat higher level of indiscretion to this normative pattern than do their counterparts in Research I Universities (x = 4.07).

Particularistic Grading

Academics in Research I Universities differ little from their counterparts in Comprehensive Universities and Colleges II on the degree of impropriety they ascribe to grading that is unfair and based on personal and social characteristics of students. Moreover, faculty in biology, mathematics, history, and psychology also hold comparable views on the extent of imprudence they accord to particularistic grading practices.

Moral Turpitude

Although statistically significant variation for both institutional type and academic subject matter areas was not detected, the interaction between these two factors was statistically significant (F = 3.18, p < .024). To interpret this interaction, two analyses of variance were conducted. One of these analyses was based only on Research I University faculty, whereas the other analysis of variance included only Comprehensive University and College II faculty.

Table 3. Means and Standard Deviations for Four Patterns of Teaching Norms

	Pattern of Norms											
	Interpersonal Disregard			Particularistic Grading			Moral Turpitude			Inadequate Planning		
	$\bar{x}$	S.D.	N*	$\bar{x}$	S.D.	N*	$\bar{x}$	S.D.	N*	$\bar{x}$	S.D.	N*
Institutional Type												
CUC II	4.27	0.49	165	4.42	0.57	171	4.75	0.41	169	4.36	0.47	170
RU I	4.07	0.47	120	4.31	0.51	122	4.68	0.39	122	4.07	0.53	117
Academic Subject Matter Areas												
Biology	4.28	0.49	73	4.45	0.49	73	4.79	0.32	73	4.33	0.48	71
History	4.08	0.54	78	4.33	0.63	79	4.69	0.54	81	4.28	0.57	79
Mathematics	4.29	0.47	62	4.41	0.55	67	4.73	0.33	64	4.20	0.52	64
Psychology	4.14	0.45	74	4.35	0.50	76	4.69	0.35	75	4.18	0.46	75

*N's vary due to missing values on specific norms.

Both analyses of variance failed to detect any statistically significant variation among the four academic subject matter areas. Thus, this interaction appears to be specious. Consequently, we can infer that academics in Research I Universities and in Comprehensive Universities and Colleges II accord equivalent levels of impropriety to the normative pattern of Moral Turpitude, as do faculty holding appointments in biology, mathematics, history, and psychology.

Inadequate Planning

Statistically significant variation between the two types of institutions was observed. However, the interaction between academic subject matter areas and institutional type was also found to be statistically significant. Consequently, it was necessary to interpret the interaction by using the same set of procedures as used above.

Table 4. F-Ratios for the Sources of Variance in the 4 X 2 Analyses of Variance of the Four Patterns of Teaching Norms

Normative Pattern	Institutional Type F-Ratio	Academic Department F-Ratio	Institutional Type X Academic Department F-Ratio
Interpersonal Disregard	13.94***	2.78	2.07
Particularistic Grading	3.64**	0.69	1.64
Moral Turpitude	3.56	1.33	3.18*
Inadequate Planning	29.91***	2.55	4.48**

* $p < .025$
** $p < .01$
*** $p < .001$

Statistically nonsignificant variation across the four academic subject matter areas was found for both analyses of variance conducted. Therefore, the statistically significant variation found for institutional type rather than the interaction between institutional type and academic subject matter area is of interest herein. Hence, we observe that Comprehensive University and College II faculty ($x = 4.27$) tend to attribute a higher level of impropriety to the normative pattern of Inadequate Planning than do faculty holding appointments at Research I Universities ($x = 4.07$).[9]

Discussion

One marker of professionalism is the presence of formal or informal codes of conduct and associated normative prescriptions and proscriptions, generally first conveyed to new inductees to the profession through the training and schooling provided prior to certification. Yet codification or delineation of codes and norms for the profession of college teaching is markedly absent. Indeed, Liebert and Bayer (1975) note:

> The standards and values of the academic professions have historically had little direct bearing on most aspects of undergraduate teaching. . . . It is a common observation that the discipline-based professions in academe do not develop pedagogic skills in any systematic way. (pp. 195-196)

This is not to say, however, that there is not a substantial body of literature on improving teaching and on conceptualization of the goals of teaching. Additionally, as noted earlier, there is likewise a growing literature on ethics in college teaching (e.g., Baumgarten, 1982; Robertson and Grant, 1982; Schurr, 1982; Scriven, 1982; Wilson, 1982). However, there are no extensive attempts to delineate an *explicit list* of norms of teaching behavior. For example, Neff and Weimer's (1990) compilation, entitled *Teaching College: Collected Readings for the New Instructor*, avoids any compilation of prescriptive and proscriptive behaviors for the beginning college teacher. Similarly, McKeachie's (1986) *Teaching Tips: A Guide for the Beginning College Teacher*, a recognized standard handbook for college teaching now in its eighth edition, provides few normative statements of behavior for professionals in college teaching.

Consequently, this present research is very much an exploratory study. Our College Teaching Behaviors Inventory was necessarily *not* derived from a robust literature base. Rather, it was largely compiled from an extensive process of suggestions and opinions from individual academics. Consequently, the 126 items may not represent an exhaustive listing of behaviors subject to normative standards. Nor does the format of alternative levels of sanctioning action derive from a strong literature base. The analytic results above indicate that this instrument has substantial utility, but its exploratory nature invites subsequent revision and extension.

This study is restricted to faculty in only four disciplines, selected to be representative of several dimensions in the Biglan classification system. Disciplinary differences are generally profound and extensive (Becher, 1989; Biglan, 1973; Creswell and Roskens, 1981), yet the results of this study show nonsubstantial variations of teaching performance norms across the four fields, suggesting that the norms for the college teaching profession may be relatively monolithic.

Additionally, this exploratory study is restricted to faculty in only two types of higher education institutions. Furthermore, the response context is circumscribed to a classroom setting involving lower-division undergraduate students in a moderate-size course. It is likely that other types of institutional settings and other levels of teaching context might engender different normative proscriptions. For example, different norms and patterns of norms may apply to large, lower-division courses. Different norms and normative patterns might also be identified for liberal arts colleges and for two-year colleges.

Finally, we followed the Durkheimian principle of ascertaining norms by assessing sanctioning opinion that might be prescribed for deviance. However, it is a well-established observation that what individuals believe should be sanctioning actions for various normative violations may not correspond closely with *actual* sanctions that may be imposed by institutional authorities or by colleagues. Indeed, there are few documented cases each year of extreme administrative sanction (i.e., dismissal) in academe for violation of teaching norms. The following discussion of findings is offered within the context of these limitations.

As norms are functional to adherence to the ideal of service, it is useful to assort the four normative patterns delineated in this study according to the client(s) of teaching role performance served. In the case of college teaching, the clients served are students as individuals and as a group and the academic discipline or field of study. Moreover, norms may also be classified as being either social or cognitive (Zuckerman, 1977, 1988). Social norms pertain to social relationships between clients and colleagues, whereas cognitive norms ordain technical or methodological procedures.

The four patterns of teaching norms identified may be regarded as being social norms, as social relationships among colleagues, clients, and the individual professional are proscribed by these four normative patterns. Although Interpersonal Disregard and Moral Turpitude may affect the social context of learning for students, it is the individual qua individual who is directly harmed by these teaching transgressions. Thus, these two norms seem to address the interpersonal relationships between the client and the teaching professor rather than social relationships, which directly affect learning. To elaborate, Interpersonal Disregard can disrupt the pattern of social relationships within an institution and within an academic department by creating a climate of strain and disharmony due to an individual who hurts the feelings of colleagues and students alike and has little respect for their opinions. Likewise, Moral Turpitude has a similar effect, as the sensibilities and rights to privacy of individuals are adversely affected by individuals with drinking problems and by individuals who sexually exploit students in their classes. Such a pattern of social relationships can have a detrimental effect on the social context for student learning within an academic department.

Certainly, the enhancement of student learning of course content is the intent of service to students as clients of teaching role performance. The prohibited normative patterns of Particularistic Grading and Inadequate Planning are injurious to this intent. Grading students on any criteria other than merit can be detrimental to individual student learning. If particularistic criteria rather than universalistic standards are employed in the grading of student course assignments, then a biased assessment of student learning obtains. Such biased assessments communicate erroneous information about the achievement of a student(s) in a given course. Such inaccurate information, in turn, can be harmful to not only the students' estimates of their learning, but also to their performance in future courses and future career. The normative pattern of *Particularistic Grading* is equivalent to the norm of universalism for research role performance identified by Merton.

Student learning of course content can also be adversely affected by teaching role performance in accord with the proscriptions of Inadequate Planning. Inadequate Planning for a course can hinder the progress of students in a course by creating situations that put students behind in their reading and completion of assignments. Thus, this particular normative pattern affects students as a group rather than the student as an individual.

Whereas social norms that pertain to students as clients were identified as being normative in this inquiry, cognitive norms that prescribe techniques or procedures that enhance student learning were absent from this delineation. Such behaviors as beginning class sessions without an opportunity for students to ask questions (C1), not announcing the topics or objectives to be covered during class time (C2), not beginning class with a review of the last class session (C9), not ending class by summarizing material covered during that class (C11), not making clear the connections between the course and other courses (D7), and not indicating the relationship of course content to the overall departmental curriculum (D8) do not enhance student learning of course content. For teaching role performance to serve the learning needs of students as clients, cognitive norms such as the above, expressed in prescriptive terms, are needed to guide the teaching role performance of faculty. Given the neglect of training in the methods and skills of teaching during the graduate school socialization process (Jencks and Reisman, 1968; Liebert and Bayer, 1975), it is not surprising that such cognitive norms are not in place in the institutions and academic subject matter areas represented in this inquiry.

Also missing from the set of specific behaviors that met the criterion for delineation as a norm are specific behaviors that are pertinent to the academic subject matter area as a client of teaching role performance. Such behaviors as not preparing or revising lectures that reflect advancements in knowledge (A11) and not reading scholarly literature for the purpose of integrating new information into one's courses (H16) are harmful to the transmission of disciplinary knowledge. Such behaviors lead to the communication of obsolete material to students which, in turn, adversely affects the knowledge base of an academic field of study. If the less stringent criterion of a mean value of 3.50 or higher had been used, then these two behaviors would have been identified as teaching norms. Moreover, it is possible that faculty in some types of colleges and universities and in some academic subject matter areas may accord a level of impropriety to these behaviors that meets the 4.00 criterion.

Additional behaviors that can affect the content of an academic subject matter area transmitted to students are as follows: insisting that students take one particular perspective on course content (D2), not making explicit to students professional biases or assumptions (D3), frequently introducing opinion on religious, political, or social issues clearly outside the realm of the course topics (D4), and not including the pertinent scholarly contributions of women and minorities in the content of courses (D5). Such behaviors lead to a biased transmission of academic subject matter area content to students. Again, the application of a 3.50 criterion would have resulted in the inclusion of insistence that students take one particular perspective on course content (D2) and frequently introducing opinion on religious, political, or social issues clearly outside the realm of course content. Nevertheless, these behaviors may be ascribed to a level of imprudence by academics in some institutional and disciplinary settings that would meet the 4.00 criterion.

The findings of this study suggest that a normative structure for lower-division courses of moderate enrollment exists in Research I Universities and in Comprehensive Universities and Colleges II. Although faculty in Comprehensive Universities and Colleges II accord a higher degree of impropriety to Interpersonal Disregard and Inadequate Planning than do their counterparts in Research I Universities, this difference is one of degree rather than kind. However, these two normative patterns meet the criterion for delineation of a norm by the endorsements given by faculty in both types of institutions. For Particularistic Grading and Moral Turpitude, equivalent levels of indiscretion were assigned by faculty in both types of institutions. Moreover, the level of impropriety accorded to each of the four normative patterns is invariant across the academic subject matter areas of biology, history, mathematics, and psychology.

These findings are heuristic. The specific norms and the four normative patterns identified herein may not emerge in other institutional settings such as liberal art colleges and two-year colleges. For example, cognitive norms that are functional to the student as a client might be operative in such types of institutions where teaching is the preeminent mission. Consequently, research should be conducted that seeks to identify specific norms and normative patterns in such institutions. The theoretical framework and the methodology of this study could serve as a basis for such research.

Moreover, we need answers to some additional fundamental questions before it might be concluded that teaching norms identified by this research and by the research suggested above are informal mechanisms of social control. These fundamental questions, which are derived from the theoretical framework advanced above, include: Are teaching norms inculcated through the graduate school socialization process? Do such sources of social control as the college or university of appointment, the academic discipline, and the academic department induce conformity to teaching norms? Do individual faculty conform to these norms? Does faculty compliance with these norms vary across various types of colleges and universities and different academic subject matter areas beyond those used in this exploratory study? Are sanctions apportioned for deviancy from these norms? If faculty do conform to these norms and if sanctions are meted out for deviancy from these norms, then we might conclude that the identified norms of teaching do function as informal mechanisms of social control for teaching role performance. Research should be conducted to provide answers to these necessary and sufficient conditions for such a conclusion.

Given the high degree of autonomy most academics have in teaching role performance, an understanding of the processes of social control of this role performance in the interests of such clients of teaching as individual students, groups of students, and the knowledge base of an academic subject matter area is of fundamental significance. The findings of this study as well as those of future inquiries will increase our knowledge and understanding of this process. One such additional needed study is the administration of an instrument parallel to that used herein to a cross-section of college students. Such an understanding is of some substantial importance given the attention of the lay public and the clients (students) of the professorate to the improvement of the quality of the undergraduate college experience.

Moreover, a different perspective on the current condition of undergraduate college and university teaching may also be provided. To elaborate, considerable national attention has focused on the improvement of the quality of undergraduate education. This concern has been expressed in reports issued by the Study Group on the Conditions of Excellence in American

Higher Education (1984), the American Association of Colleges' *Integrity in the College Curriculum* (Association of American Colleges, 1985), and Bennet's *To Reclaim a Legacy* (1984). Without an understanding of the informal social control mechanisms and normative structures that guide undergraduate college teaching, it is difficult to develop policy, programs, and procedures that address the issues raised in such reports. Such improvement efforts may be fostered or impeded by prevailing faculty (and student) views on teaching behaviors deemed to be of varying degrees of impropriety. Moreover, if there are no norms governing desired behaviors prescribed for improvement, then these needed behaviors will not be enacted by academics (Wilson, 1982). In other words, informal (and formal) control mechanisms, together with explication of the normative system, are necessary to assure the preferred performance of the role of the undergraduate teacher. Thus, a knowledge and understanding of the normative structure of undergraduate college teaching is needed if colleges and universities are to develop policies, programs, and procedures designed to improve undergraduate instruction.

Appendix: College Teaching Behaviors Inventory©

Teaching is a complex activity composed of many behaviors and expectations. Listed below are some behaviors related to college teaching. These may appear to be inappropriate to some faculty members but not to others. Using the response codes listed below, please indicate your opinion on each of the listed behaviors as you think they might best ideally apply to a faculty member teaching a *lower-division college course in your field of about 40 enrolled students, whether or not you teach such a course yourself.* The response categories are as follows:

1 = Appropriate behavior, should be encouraged

2 = Discretionary behavior, neither particularly appropriate nor inappropriate

3 = Mildly inappropriate behavior, generally to be ignored

4 = Inappropriate behavior, to be handled informally by colleagues or administrators suggesting change or improvement

5 = Very inappropriate behavior, requiring formal administrative intervention

A. PREPLANNING FOR THE COURSE

		Appropriate/encourage	Discretionary	Mildly inappropriate/ignore	Inappropriate/handle informally	Very inappropriate/requires intervention
A1.	Required texts and other reading materials are not routinely ordered by the instructor in time to be available for the first class session.	1	2	3	4	5
A2.	A course outline or syllabus is not prepared for a course.	1	2	3	4	5
A3.	Prior to the first meeting of a class, the instructor does not visit the assigned classroom and assess its facilities.	1	2	3	4	5
A4.	A course outline or syllabus does not contain dates for assignments and/or examinations.	1	2	3	4	5
A5.	Objectives for the course are not specified by the instructor.	1	2	3	4	5
A6.	Changes in a course are made without seeking information from students who have previously taken the course.	1	2	3	4	5
A7.	The instructor does not read reviews of appropriate textbooks.	1	2	3	4	5
A8.	The course is designed without taking into account the needs or abilities of students enrolling in the course.	1	2	3	4	5
A9.	Colleagues teaching the same or similar courses are not consulted on ways to teach the particular course.	1	2	3	4	5
A10.	Required course materials are not kept within reasonable cost limits as perceived by students.	1	2	3	4	5
A11.	New lectures or revised lectures that reflect advancements in the field are not prepared.	1	2	3	4	5

A12.	In-class activities are not prepared and anticipated in advance, but are developed while the class is in session.	1	2	3	4	5
A13.	The instructor does not request necessary audio-visual materials in time to be available for class.	1	2	3	4	5
A14.	Assigned books and articles are not put on library reserve by the instructor on a timely basis for student use.	1	2	3	4	5

B.   FIRST DAY OF CLASS

B1.	Class roll is not taken.	1	2	3	4	5
B2.	The instructor does not introduce her/himself to the class.	1	2	3	4	5
B3.	Office hours are not communicated to the students.	1	2	3	4	5
B4.	The instructor changes classroom location to another building without informing students in advance.	1	2	3	4	5
B5.	The instructor changes class meeting time without consulting students.	1	2	3	4	5
B6.	Students are not informed of the instructor's policy on missed or make-up examinations.	1	2	3	4	5
B7.	Students are not informed of extra credit opportunities available in the course during the term.	1	2	3	4	5
B8.	Students are not asked to record their background, experiences, and interests for reference by the instructor.	1	2	3	4	5
B9.	An overview of the course is not presented to students on the first day.	1	2	3	4	5
B10.	An introduction to the first course topic is not begun on the first day.	1	2	3	4	5
B11.	The first class meeting is dismissed early.	1	2	3	4	5
B12.	The first reading assignment is not communicated to the class.	1	2	3	4	5
B13.	A course outline or syllabus is not prepared and passed out to students.	1	2	3	4	5
B14.	The instructor does not ask students if they have questions regarding the course.	1	2	3	4	5

C.   IN-CLASS BEHAVIORS

C1.	Class sessions are begun without an opportunity for students to ask questions.	1	2	3	4	5
C2.	The topics or objectives to be covered for the day are not announced at the beginning of the class.	1	2	3	4	5
C3.	Joke-telling and humor unrelated to course content occurs routinely in class.	1	2	3	4	5
C4.	The instructor frequently uses profanity in class.	1	2	3	4	5
C5.	Class is usually dismissed early.	1	2	3	4	5
C6.	The instructor meets the class without having reviewed pertinent materials for the day.	1	2	3	4	5
C7.	The instructor routinely allows one or a few students to dominate class discussion.	1	2	3	4	5
C8.	Instructions and requirements for course assignments are not clearly described to students.	1	2	3	4	5
C9.	Class does not begin with a review of the last class session.	1	2	3	4	5
C10.	Joke-telling and humor related to course content occurs frequently in class.	1	2	3	4	5

C11.	The instructor does not end the class session by summarizing material covered during the class.	1	2	3	4	5
C12.	The instructor is routinely late for class meetings.	1	2	3	4	5
C13.	The instructor routinely holds the class beyond its scheduled ending time.	1	2	3	4	5
C14.	The instructor does not take class attendance every class meeting.	1	2	3	4	5
C15.	The instructor does not introduce new teaching methods or procedures.	1	2	3	4	5
C16.	The instructor does not provide in-class opportunities for students to voice their opinion about the course.	1	2	3	4	5
C17.	The instructor calls on students to answer questions in class on a nonvoluntary basis.	1	2	3	4	5
C18.	The instructor does not follow the course outline or syllabus for most of the course.	1	2	3	4	5
C19.	The instructor practices poor personal hygiene and regularly has offensive body odor.	1	2	3	4	5
C20.	The instructor routinely wears a sloppy sweatshirt and rumpled blue jeans to class.	1	2	3	4	5
C21.	While able to conduct class, the instructor frequently attends class while obviously intoxicated.	1	2	3	4	5

D. TREATING COURSE CONTENT

D1.	The instructor does not have students evaluate the course at the end of the term.	1	2	3	4	5
D2.	The instructor insists that students take one particular perspective on course content.	1	2	3	4	5
D3.	The instructor's professional biases or assumptions are not explicitly made known to students.	1	2	3	4	5
D4.	The instructor frequently introduces opinion on religious, political, or social issues clearly outside the realm of the course topics.	1	2	3	4	5
D5.	The instructor does not include pertinent scholarly contributions of women and minorities in the content of the course.	1	2	3	4	5
D6.	Memorization of course content is stressed at the expense of analysis and critical thinking.	1	2	3	4	5
D7.	Connections between the course and other courses are not made clear by the instructor.	1	2	3	4	5
D8.	The relationship of the course content to the overall departmental curriculum is not indicated.	1	2	3	4	5
D9.	A cynical attitude toward the subject matter is expressed by the instructor.	1	2	3	4	5

E. EXAMINATION AND GRADING PRACTICES

E1.	The instructor does not give assignments or examinations requiring student writing skills.	1	2	3	4	5
E2.	When examinations or papers are returned, student questions are not answered during class time.	1	2	3	4	5
E3.	Graded tests and papers are not promptly returned to students by the instructor.	1	2	3	4	5
E4.	Individual student course evaluations, where students can be identified, are read prior to the determination of final course grades.	1	2	3	4	5
E5.	Examination questions do not represent a range of difficulty.	1	2	3	4	5
E6.	Grades are distributed on a "curve."	1	2	3	4	5

E7.	An instructor lowers course standards in order to be popular with students.	1	2	3	4	5	
E8.	The standards for a course are set so high that most of the class receives failing grades for the course.	1	2	3	4	5	
E9.	Individual students are offered extra-credit work in order to improve their final course grade *after* the term is completed.	1	2	3	4	5	
E10.	Explanation of the basis for grades given for essay questions or papers is not provided to students.	1	2	3	4	5	
E11.	Written comments on tests and papers are consistently not made by the instructor.	1	2	3	4	5	
E12.	The instructor allows personal friendships with a student to intrude on the objective grading of his or her work.	1	2	3	4	5	
E13.	Student papers or essay examination questions are not read at least twice before a grade is given.	1	2	3	4	5	
E14.	Social, personal, or other nonacademic characteristics of students are taken into account in the awarding of student grades.	1	2	3	4	5	
E15.	Final examinations are administered during a regular class period rather than at the official examination period.	1	2	3	4	5	
E16.	Student class participation is considered in awarding the final course grade.	1	2	3	4	5	
E17.	Student attendance in class is weighed in determining the final course grade.	1	2	3	4	5	
E18.	Student opinions about the method of grading are not sought.	1	2	3	4	5	
E19.	Students' work is not graded anonymously.	1	2	3	4	5	
E20.	The final course grade is based on a single course assignment or a single examination.	1	2	3	4	5	
E21.	Examination questions do not tap a variety of educational objectives ranging from the retention of facts to critical thinking.	1	2	3	4	5	
E22.	Sexist or racist comments in students' written work are not discouraged.	1	2	3	4	5	
E23.	An instructor does not hold review sessions before examinations.	1	2	3	4	5	
E24.	All student grades are publicly posted with social security numbers and without names.	1	2	3	4	5	
E25.	Graded papers and examinations are left in an accessible location where students can search though to get back their own.	1	2	3	4	5	

F. FACULTY-STUDENT IN-CLASS INTERACTIONS

F1.	Stated policies about late work and incompletes are not universally applied to all students.	1	2	3	4	5	
F2.	Students are not permitted to express viewpoints different from those of the instructor.	1	2	3	4	5	
F3.	The instructor expresses impatience with a slow learner in class.	1	2	3	4	5	
F4.	The instructor does not encourage student questions during class time.	1	2	3	4	5	
F5.	An instructor makes condescending remarks to a student in class.	1	2	3	4	5	
F6.	The instructor does not learn the names of all students in the class.	1	2	3	4	5	
F7.	A clear lack of class members' understanding about course content is ignored by the instructor.	1	2	3	4	5	

F8.	Shy students are not encouraged to speak in class.	1	2	3	4	5
F9.	The instructor does not allow students to direct their comments to other members of the class.	1	2	3	4	5

G. RELATIONSHIPS WITH COLLEAGUES

G1.	A faculty member refuses to share academic information about mutual students with colleagues.	1	2	3	4	5
G2.	A faculty member does not tell an administrator or appropriate faculty committee that there are very low grading standards in a colleague's course.	1	2	3	4	5
G3.	A faculty member does not tell an administrator or appropriate faculty committee that a colleague's course content largely includes obsolete material.	1	2	3	4	5
G4.	A faculty member refuses to share course syllabi with colleagues.	1	2	3	4	5
G5.	A faculty member avoids sharing ideas about teaching methods with colleagues.	1	2	3	4	5
G6.	A faculty member refuses to allow colleagues to observe his or her classroom teaching.	1	2	3	4	5
G7.	A faculty member assumes new teaching responsibilities in the specialty of a colleague without discussing appropriate course content with that colleague.	1	2	3	4	5
G8.	A faculty member makes negative comments in a faculty meeting about the courses offered by a colleague.	1	2	3	4	5
G9.	A faculty member makes negative comments about a colleague in public before students.	1	2	3	4	5
G10.	A faculty member aggressively promotes enrollment in his or her courses at the expense of the courses of departmental colleagues.	1	2	3	4	5
G11.	The requirements in a course are so great that they prevent enrolled students from giving adequate attention to their other courses.	1	2	3	4	5
G12.	A faculty member refuses to team teach a course.	1	2	3	4	5
G13.	A faculty member avoids talking about his or her academic specialty with departmental colleagues.	1	2	3	4	5
G14.	A faculty member gives unsolicited advice on the content of a colleague's course.	1	2	3	4	5
G15.	A faculty member gives unsolicited advice to a colleague about teaching methods.	1	2	3	4	5
G16.	A faculty member refuses to participate in departmental curricular planning.	1	2	3	4	5

H. OUT-OF-CLASS PRACTICES

H1.	Office hours scheduled for student appointments are frequently not kept.	1	2	3	4	5
H2.	Individual counseling on matters unrelated to course content is not provided to students enrolled in one's courses.	1	2	3	4	5
H3.	A faculty member criticizes the academic performance of a student in front of other students.	1	2	3	4	5
H4.	A faculty member avoids spending time with students outside of class time and/or regular office hours.	1	2	3	4	5
H5.	A faculty member insists on never being phoned at home by students regardless of circumstances.	1	2	3	4	5
H6.	A faculty member makes suggestive sexual comments to a student enrolled in the course.	1	2	3	4	5

H7.	A faculty member has a sexual relationship with a student enrolled in the course.	1	2	3	4	5
H8.	A faculty member does not refer a student with a special problem to the appropriate campus service.	1	2	3	4	5
H9.	An advisee is treated in a condescending manner.	1	2	3	4	5
H10.	A faculty member avoids giving career or job advice when asked by students.	1	2	3	4	5
H11.	A faculty member refuses to write letters of reference for any student.	1	2	3	4	5
H12.	A faculty member neglects to send a letter of recommendation that he or she had agreed to write.	1	2	3	4	5
H13.	A faculty member refuses to advise departmental majors.	1	2	3	4	5
H14.	A cynical attitude toward the role of teaching is expressed by an instructor.	1	2	3	4	5
H15.	A faculty member's involvement in scholarship is so great that he or she fails to adequately prepare for class.	1	2	3	4	5
H16.	Scholarly literature is not read for the purpose of integrating new information into one's courses.	1	2	3	4	5
H17.	A faculty member avoids reading literature on teaching techniques or methods.	1	2	3	4	5
H18.	A faculty member avoids professional development opportunities that would enhance his or her teaching.	1	2	3	4	5

A Few Questions About You and Your Institution

1. Are you considered a full-time faculty member by your institution for the current academic year? (check one)

   _____ Yes, full-time

   _____ No, part-time but more than half-time

   _____ No, half-time

   _____ No, less than half-time

2. Your academic rank: (check one)

   _____ Professor

   _____ Associate Professor

   _____ Assistant Professor

   _____ Instructor

   _____ Lecturer

   _____ Other (specify:_____)

3. Your tenure status: (check one)

   _____ Tenured

   _____ Untenured, but on tenure track

   _____ Untenured, and not on a tenure track

4. Are you, or have you ever been, a Department Head/Chair or a Dean? (check one)

   _____ No

   _____ Yes, but not now

   _____ Yes, and am currently

5. Your gender:

   _____ Female

   _____ Male

6. Name of your present employing institution: _____

7. What kind of academic year calendar is there at your institution? (check one):

   _____ Semester calendar

   _____ Quarter system

   _____ Other (specify: _____)

8. Year you were first employed at present institution: _____

9. Discipline of your present academic department: _____

10. Which one statement do you think best reflects the attitude of the principal administrator for your department or program? (check one):

    _____ Consistently strong advocate of quality undergraduate teaching

    _____ Intermittently advocates maintaining or improving teaching quality

    _____ Laissez-faire on teaching: generally neither emphasizes nor deprecates teaching

    _____ Stresses other professional roles (e.g. research and writing) over teaching

11.   Information concerning your highest earned degree:

Highest earned degree: _____

Year highest degree received: _____

Name of degree-granting institution: _____

Discipline/field of highest degree: _____

12.   During the past three years how many of each of the following have you published:

Journal articles (circle one):   None   1–2   3–4   5–10   11 or more

Books and monographs (circle one):   None   1   2   3 or more

13.   How many classes did you teach during the past full academic year? _____

14.   How many *different course preparations* did you have during the past full academic year? _____

15.   During the past full academic year have you taught any lower-division (freshman or sophomore) courses? (check one)

_____ yes

_____ no

16.   During the past full academic year what is the approximate total number of *undergraduate* students enrolled in all the classes you taught: (check one)

_____ none

_____ 100 or less

_____ 101 to 200

_____ 201 to 500

_____ over 500

17.   In the space below, please note any comments or clarifications of your answers which you would like to provide:

Notes

1. Functionalist and power theories are two broad categories of theories on professions discerned by Abbott (1988). Abbott states that power theories of Johnson (1972) Freidson (1970a, 1970b) Berlant (1975), and Larson (1977) seriously question the functionalist view that professions are self-regulating and worthy of trust by clients and larger society. Taken together these power theories suggest that professions are concerned with dominance, autonomy, and monopoly rather than the ideal of service.

2. Because of a clerical error, one individual was deleted from the sample of 800 individuals. Thus, the final sample was comprised of 799 individuals.

3. Three groups of respondents comprised the three levels of the factor comprising these one-way analyses of variance. These three groups were respondents to the initial survey mailing, respondents after a postcard reminder sent to nonrespondents, and individuals who responded to the second mailing of the survey instrument.

4. We are indebted to Carla Howry of the American Sociological Association and to members of the ASA Project on Teaching for this assistance.

5. The least-squares or regression approach to ANOVA was used because of unequal cell sizes in each of the analyses of variance conducted.

6. Although factor loadings of .40 or higher are recommended for the development of factor-based scores (Kim and Mueller 1978), loadings of .38 or higher were used in this study. A slightly lower criterion was used so that all 25 norms were subsumed under one of the four factors.

7. When sample sizes and variances are negatively correlated, the probability of committing type I errors increases above the level of statistical significance set due to the violation of the assumption of homogeneous variances (Boneau, 1960). Conversely, a positive correlation between sample sizes and variances deflates the probability of committing type I errors. The correlations between sample sizes and variances for the four patterns of norms were as follows: Interpersonal Disregard ($r = .38$), Particularistic Grading ($r = .36$), Moral Turpitude ($r = .30$), and Inadequate Planning ($r = .19$). Thus the probability of committing type I errors above the level of statistical significance set is minimal for Interpersonal Disregard, Particularistic Grading, and Moral Turpitude but may be above the level of statistical significance set for Inadequate Planning. Consequently the more conservative .01 level of statistical significance was chosen for the analyses of variance pertaining to this particular normative pattern.

8. Following the statistical significant F-test for Institutional Type, post-hoc mean comparison using the Scheffe method was used. This comparison indicated that the differences between the means for the two types of institutions were statistically significant.

9. The post-hoc mean comparison conducted using the Scheffe method detected this statistically significant difference between the means of these two groups of faculty.

References

Abbott, A. (1988). *The System of Professions.* Chicago: University of Chicago Press.

Association of American Colleges (1985). *Integrity in the College Curriculum: A Report to the Academic Community.* Washington, DC: Association of American Colleges.

Baldridge, J. V., Curtis, D. V., Ecker, G., and Riley, G. L. (1978). *Policy Making and Effective Leadership.* San Francisco: Jossey-Bass.

Baumgarten, E. (1982). Ethics in the academic profession: A Socratic view. In *Ethics and the Academic Profession,* David D. Dill (ed.). *Journal of Higher Education* 53: 282–295.

Becher, T. (1989). *Academic Tribes and Territories: Intellectual Enquiry and the Cultures of Disciplines.* Milton Keynes, UK: Open University Press.

Bennet, W. J. (1984). *To Reclaim a Legacy: A Report on the Humanities in Higher Education.* Washington, DC: National Endowment for the Humanities.

Berlant, J. G. (1975). *Profession and Monopoly.* Berkeley, CA: University of California Press.

Biglan, A. (1973). Relationships between subject matter area characteristics and output of university departments. *Journal of Applied Psychology* 57: 204–213.

Blau, P. (1973). *Organization of Academic Work*. New York: Wiley.

Boneau, C. A. (1960). The effects of violations of assumptions underlying the *t* test. *Psychological Bulletin* 57: 49–64.

Braxton, J. (1986). The normative structure of science: Social control in the academic profession. In *Higher Education: Handbook of Theory and Research, Vol. II.*, John C. Smart (ed.), pp. 309–357. New York: Agathon Press.

Braxton, J., and Toombs, W. (1982). Faculty uses of doctoral training: Consideration of a technique for the differentiation of scholarly effort from research activity. *Research in Higher Education* 16: 265–282.

Carnegie Foundation for the Advancement of Teaching (1987). *A Classification of Institutions of Higher Education*. Princeton: The Carnegie Foundation for the Advancement of Teaching.

Cole, J. R., and Cole, S. (1973). *Social Stratification in Science*. Chicago: University of Chicago Press.

Creswell, J., and Roskens, R. (1981). The Biglan studies of differences among academic areas. *Review of Higher Education* 4: 1–16.

Durkheim, E. (1934). *The Elementary Forms of Religious Life*. London: Allen and Unwin (original work published in 1912).

Freidson, E. (1970a). *Profession of Medicine*. New York: Dodd Mead.

Freidson, E. (1970b). *Professional Dominance*. Chicago: Aldine.

Goode, W. J. (1957). Community within a community. *American Sociological Review* 22: 194–200.

Goode, W. J. (1969). The theoretical limits of professionalization. In *The Semi-Professions and Their Organization*, A. Etzioni (ed.), pp. 263–313. New York: The Free Press.

Goode, W. J., and Hatt, P. K. (1952). *Methods of Social Research*. New York: McGraw-Hill.

Hagstrom, W. (1965). *The Scientific Community*. New York: Basic Books.

Hagstrom, W. (1971). Inputs, outputs, and the prestige of university science departments. *Sociology of Education* 44: 375–397.

Heiss, A. M. (1970). *Challenges to Graduate Schools*. San Francisco: Jossey-Bass.

Jencks, C., and Reisman, D. (1968). *The Academic Revolution*. Garden City, NY: Doubleday.

Johnson, T. J. (1972). *Professions and Power*. London: Macmillan.

Katz, J. (1976). Development of the mind. In *Scholars in the Making: The Development of Graduate and Professional Students*, J. Katz and R.T. Hartnett (eds.). Cambridge, MA: Ballinger Publishing.

Kim, J. O., and Mueller, C. W. (1978). *Factor Analysis: Statistical Methods and Practical Issues*. Beverly Hills: Sage Publications.

Kish, L. (1957). Confidence intervals for clustered samples. *American Sociological Review* 22: 154–165.

Larson, M. S. (1977). *The Rise of Professionalism*. Berkeley: University of California Press.

Liebert, R. J., and Bayer, A. E. (1975). Goals in teaching undergraduates: Professional reproduction and client-centeredness. *American Sociologist* 10: 195–205.

Leslie, L. L. (1972). Are response rates essential to valid surveys? *Social Science Research* I: 323–334.

McKeachie, W. J. (1986). *Teaching Tips: A Guide for the Beginning College Teacher*, 8th ed. Lexington, MA: D.C. Heath.

Merton, R. K. (1942). Science and technology in a Democratic order. *Journal of Legal and Political Sociology* 1: 115–126.

Merton, R. K. (1968). *Social Theory and Social Structure*. New York: The Free Press.

Merton, R. K. (1973). *The Sociology of Science: Theoretical and Empirical Investigations*. Chicago: University of Chicago Press.

Merton, R. K., Reader, G. G., and Kendall, P. L. (1957). *The Student-Physician*. Cambridge, MA: Harvard University Press.

Neff, R. A., and Weimer, M. (eds.) (1990). *Teaching College: Collected Readings for the New Instructor*. Madison, WI: Magna Publications.

Parsons, T., and Platt, G. M. (1973). *The American University*. Cambridge, MA: Harvard University Press.

Reiss, A. (1951). Delinquency as a failure of personal and social controls. *American Sociological Review* 16: 196–207.

Robertson, E., and Grant, G. (1982). Teaching and ethics: An epilogue. In *Ethics and the Academic Profession*, David D. Dill (ed.). *Journal of Higher Education* 53: 345–357.

Schein, E. H. (1972). *Professional Education: Some New Directions*. New York: McGraw Hill.

Schurr, G. M. (1982). Toward a code of ethics for academics. In *Ethics and the Academic Profession*, David D. Dill (ed.). *Journal of Higher Education* 53: 318–334.

Scriven, M. (1982). Professional ethics. In *Ethics and the Academic Profession*, David D. Dill (ed.). *Journal of Higher Education* 53: 307–317.

Study Group on the Conditions of Excellence in American Higher Education (1984). *Involvement in Learning: Realizing the Potential of American Higher Education*. Washington, DC: National Institute of Education.

Taylor, A. R. (1976). Becoming observers and specialists. In *Scholars in the Making: The Development of Graduate and Professional Students*, J. Katz and R.T. Hartnett (eds.). Cambridge, MA: Ballinger Publishing.

Toombs, W. (1977). Awareness and use of academic research. *Research in Higher Education* 7: 743–765.

Wilson, E. K. (1982). Power, pretense, and piggybacking: Some ethical issues in teaching. In *Ethics and the Academic Profession*, David D. Dill (ed.). *Journal of Higher Education* 53: 268–281.

Zuckerman, H. E. (1977). Deviant behavior and social control in science. In *Deviance and Social Change*, E. Sagarin (ed.), pp. 87–138. Beverly Hills: Sage.

Zuckerman, H. E. (1988). The sociology of science. In *Handbook of Sociology*, N.J. Smelser (ed.), pp. 511–574. Newbury Park, CA: Sage.

The Influence of Gender on University Faculty Members' Perceptions of "Good" Teaching

LAURA D. GOODWIN AND ELLEN A. STEVENS

What is "good" teaching? The question has been asked numerous times and has been addressed from many different perspectives. Although there is no clearly definitive answer to the question, there are some generally accepted characteristics of "good" teachers and teaching situations: enthusiasm, knowledge of the subject area, stimulation of interest in the subject area, organization, clarity, concern and caring for students, use of higher cognitive levels in discussions and examinations, use of visual aids, encouragement of active learning and student discussion, provision of feedback, and avoidance of harsh criticism [12, 16, 22, 24, 32, 35, 40, 41, 47, 59]. This list has largely been generated from studies that explored college and university students' opinions about effective teaching, as well as from some that explored the opinions of elementary and secondary teachers. In addition to teacher characteristics, McKeachie [40] noted almost thirty years ago how difficult it was to define and measure the appropriate *outcomes* of "good" teaching, and this is still a major concern and unsolved problem today.

In this study we were interested in obtaining university faculty members' views on what they perceived to be the teacher or teaching characteristics that resulted in "good" teaching and on what they perceived to be the appropriate outcomes of "good" teaching. We were especially interested in investigating the nature and extent of any relationships between the gender of the faculty respondents and perceptions about good teaching and the appropriate outcomes of good teaching.

What differences, if any, exist between male and female faculty members in their opinions about effective teaching is a timely question, and one that few researchers have investigated—although there has been a fairly large number of publications in the last decade or so that have dealt with the status of women in academic settings and with gender differences as perceived by students. Many authors [for example, 1, 3, 26, 33, 45, 51, 58] have noted the increase in the number of women faculty members. Lomperis [37] provided statistics showing that women represented about one-fifth of all university faculty twenty-five years ago, and about one-third by 1990. As these and other authors have also pointed out, however, real differences continue to exist in terms of such factors as proportionate representation by discipline or field, salary, rank, part-time versus full-time employment, and type of appointment (tenure-track versus non-tenure track). Finkelstein [27], in summarizing an extensive review of studies on female faculty, found that women tended to be segregated by discipline and by institutional type; to be disproportionately represented at lower ranks; to get promoted at a slower rate than their male colleagues; to participate less in governance and administration; and to be compensated at a rate that averaged only 85 percent of that of their male colleagues. Newell and Kuh [45], who had conducted a fairly large national survey of professors of higher education, reported that women had generally lower academic-year salaries and heavier teaching loads than men and that they perceived more pressure to publish and were less happy with the structure of their departments. Differences such as these have led some authors to use the term "chilly" to describe the academic climate experienced by women faculty members [49, 60].

The research on gender differences as perceived by students has produced some conflicting results. One possible reason for some of the discrepancies in this body of literature was discussed by Bennett: "Evidence for gender stereotyping and performance evaluation bias [often] comes from studies that use quasiprojective procedures and hypothetical descriptions designed intentionally to elicit stereotypic response patterns. The evidence of such studies is mixed and occasionally conflicts with that based on direct rating techniques" [8, p. 170]. Although type of design used in these studies is an important factor, the "mix" of results is not completely explained by the difference between hypothetical situations and naturally occurring classroom situations. Feldman [23], who summarized much literature on gender differences in student ratings, also pointed out other factors that could account for the conflicting results across these studies. For example, some researchers have analyzed student rating data at the item level, whereas others have looked at differences in a more global way. Further, relationships between gender of instructors and their seniority could confound examinations of the relationships between gender and student ratings.

Recognizing the many factors that make it difficult to summarize this literature, we attempt the following brief description of some of it. Although a number of researchers have reported no significant differences between male and female professors' evaluations due to gender differences alone [for example, 2, 5, 6, 8, 11, 14, 28], others have found female professors receiving somewhat higher ratings than males on a variety of specific or global dimensions [for example, 10, 19, 20, 21]. By contrast, Wilson and Doyle [61] found that male professors tended to receive significantly higher ratings on clarity of presentation than did female professors. Other researchers have found differences in student ratings according to discipline—for example, Ferber and Huber [25], who reported that female professors received higher ratings in traditionally female disciplines (such as home economics) compared to female professors in traditionally male disciplines (such as engineering).

These same researchers, and others, also have found interactions between the gender of the professors and the gender of the students. For example, Ferber's and Huber's [25] work showed that, whereas male faculty members were rated similarly by male and female students, the female students rated the female professors higher than did the male students and also higher than they rated the male professors. In contrast, Kaschak [34] found that male students consistently favored male professors, but female students rated male and female faculty members equally. Similar results were reported by Lombardo and Tocci [36]. Basow and Silberg [7] conducted a study involving one thousand students in classes taught by sixteen male and female professors; the professors were matched for type of course, years of teaching experience, and tenure status. Findings included significantly lower ratings of female professors by male students—compared to ratings of male professors by male students—on six evaluative dimensions. The female students also rated female professors less positively than male professors on three of the dimensions. These authors pointed out that male students' lower ratings of female professors might be attributed, at least in part, to the fact that college teaching is generally considered a male occupation. "Less favorable ratings of women are most likely to occur when women are seen as not fitting gender stereotypes" [7, p. 312]. Berry echoed this notion when she commented, "Extensive research supports the contention that women faculty members are evaluated differently than males and women are evaluated less favorably, especially when they step outside of traditionally `feminine' areas of knowledge" [9, p. 3].

Compared to the amount of published research findings pertaining to gender differences in student ratings, there is a dearth of information about actual differences between male and female professors in their teaching practices or methods. A few studies have investigated differences in communication styles between male and female instructors. Markham [39] studied the effects of gender and the perceived "expertness" of a speaker on recall of orally presented material; the subjects listened more attentively to male rather than female speakers, although the "expertness" factor neutralized this gender difference somewhat. Berry [9] reported that female professors tended to generate more class discussion, more interaction, and more give-and-take than male professors. Similarly, in a review article, Treichler and Kramarae wrote that, "At the college level, investigators . . . consistently report more interaction in classes taught by women, with more student input, more teacher and student questions, and more feedback" [60, p. 121]. After analyzing data from a fairly large-scale study of sixty classrooms, Macke, Richardson, and Cook [38] discovered that there were greater levels of student participation in classes taught by women—regardless of department, course level, class size, and ratio of female to male students. However, the more student participation that was generated, the less competent the instructors were rated by the students. (See also, Statham, Richardson, and Cook [54].)

Finally, what do we know about professors' own perceptions of what constitutes "good" teaching and about differences and similarities between male and female professors in such perceptions? We found very few works that attempted to answer this specific question. Miron [44] surveyed fifty-one Israeli instructors regarding their conception of the characteristics of the "good professor." The answers given most frequently included the ability to stimulate intellectual curiosity and develop thought processes and the preparation and organization of lessons. Chism [13] questioned two hundred faculty members at one university on a variety of topics, especially ones pertaining to the type and extent of changes they had initiated in their teaching practices. She found a few gender differences—for example, the female professors placed greater value on talking with peers about teaching, observing their colleagues, attending workshops, and experimenting personally as being potentially useful activities in the pursuit of more effective teaching strategies.

In a previous study [56], we compared the attitudes toward teaching of faculty members at three quite different types of higher education institutions. Although gender comparisons were not central to that study, we did discern some interesting differences—ones that led to the design of the present study and, especially, the construction of the questionnaire (described below). Again, then, the major purpose of this study was to investigate similarities and differences between female and male professors in their attitudes toward teaching, especially toward "good" teaching. The general areas about which we wanted to obtain opinions included: the behaviors and characteristics that constitute "good" teaching, the appropriate outcomes of good teaching, attitudes toward various teaching and grading practices, and favored teaching and grading methods. In addition to studying gender differences, we were secondarily interested in investigating the extent of differences according to campus, rank, and discipline.

Method

Subjects and Sampling

The accessible population for this study consisted of 2,555 faculty members holding the ranks of assistant, associate, and full professor at the four campuses of the University of Colorado (CU). Each campus's 1990-91 directory was used to identify the members of this population: 1,365, CU-Boulder; 284, CU-Denver; 179, CU-Colorado Springs; and 727, CU-Health Sciences Center (which included some faculty in the School of Pharmacy who were still located on the Boulder campus but were being moved to the Health Sciences Center campus). Virtually all academic disciplines were represented. From an original list of over fifty separate disciplines or fields of study, we derived twelve disciplinary groups for stratification of the faculty prior to sampling. Those twelve groups, and the percentages of faculty members in each (for the entire CU system) were as follows: arts and humanities (15.5 percent); social sciences (16.4 percent); sciences and mathematics (18.3 percent); engineering (10.8 percent); business (4.5 percent); education (3.5 percent); public affairs (.8 percent); law (1.7 percent); dentistry (1.3 percent); medicine (23.9 percent); nursing (2.0 percent); and pharmacy (1.2 percent).

After stratifying the faculty by campus and by discipline, a systematic sampling procedure was used. Within each category (campus-by-discipline), every third faculty member was selected. Due to the fact that there were some faculty with joint appointments and some who had retired, the ultimate size of the sample was slightly less than one-third the size of the original accessible population. The total sample size was 762: 417, CU-Boulder; 88, CU-Denver; 57, CU-Colorado Springs; and 200, CU-Health Sciences Center.

Instrumentation

A questionnaire was designed specifically for this study, although we retained some items from a questionnaire that had been used in an earlier study [56], especially those items for which we had found statistically significant differences in the mean responses given by male and female respondents. We also consulted a number of other sources, including some that provided already developed measures [13, 15, 17, 18, 29, 30, 31, 43, 46, 48, 50, 52, 53, 55]. Approximately seventy questions were initially generated. They included a variety of types of format—Likert-type, open-ended, ranking, and so on—and were intended to solicit responses in the following areas: teaching behaviors that are indicative of "good" teaching; whether or not those behaviors are perceived to be more common among "good" female professors as compared to "good" male professors; the appropriate outcomes that reflect "good" teaching; teaching styles, teaching methods, and grading practices used most often; aspects of one's teaching that had been the focus of an attempt at change or improvement and the ensuing results; perceptions of the usefulness of a variety of activities and information in terms of improving teaching; and demographic information.

The first draft of the questionnaire was reviewed by twelve faculty members and administrators. They critiqued it in terms of such factors as clarity, length, relevance, interest level, and sufficiency. We then revised it by eliminating or rewriting some items that had been viewed as unclear or redundant. The final questionnaire was organized into four major sections: "Good Teaching," which solicited ratings of behaviors that might be indicative of "good" teaching, perceptions of any gender differences in terms of the use of these behaviors, and opinions about what outcomes best reflect "good" teaching; "Teaching Roles, Methods, and Evaluation Practices," which solicited favorite methods and attitudes toward the use of various practices; "Change," which solicited opinions about what areas of improvement were most important and what attempts had been made to improve teaching; and "Demographic Information."

Data Collection Procedures

The questionnaire and a cover letter were sent by campus mail to the 762 faculty members who were selected by the stratified, systematic sampling procedure. Addressed campus mail envelopes were included to facilitate the return of the questionnaire. Anonymity of respondents, assured by not asking for names, hopefully encouraged honest answers. Unfortunately, the anonymity precluded the possibility of conducting a follow-up mailing to nonrespondents to increase the response rate.

Completed and usable questionnaires were received from 250 professors; another twelve questionnaires were returned uncompleted (due to professors being on sabbatical leave, or having recently left the university). This return rate of 34.4 percent, including the returned incomplete questionnaires, was close to what can typically be expected in survey research using mailed questionnaires [4, 42]. In table 1, demographic information about the respondents is given. In general, the breakdown on these variables compared favorably with the institutional profiles available to us at the time the study was conducted.

Table 1. Demographic Information about the Respondents (*n* = 250)

Variables	Percentages of Respondents
Campus	
CU-Boulder	50.6
CU-Denver	15.2
CU-Colorado Springs	10.3
CU-Health Sciences Center	23.9
Discipline	
Arts and Humanities	16.7
Social Sciences	20.6
Sciences and Mathematics	14.0
Engineering	8.3
Business	4.8
Education	5.3
Public Affairs	2.2
Law	3.9
Dentistry	1.3
Medicine	16.7
Nursing	3.1
Pharmacy	3.1
Tenure Status	
Tenured	57.7
Untenured	42.3
Gender	
Male	66.9
Female	33.2
Rank	
Assistant Professor	30.9
Associate Professor	30.8
Professor	38.3
Type of Appointment	
Full-time	95.1
Part-time	4.9
Type of Teaching Assignment	
Undergraduate Courses Only	9.1
Graduate Courses Only	28.1
Undergraduate and Graduate Courses	62.8

NOTE: The percentages in this table are based on non-missing data. A few respondents did not answer every question.

Data Analysis Procedures

Preliminary analyses were conducted to estimate the reliability of the items. There were three sets of items that used a Likert or Likert-type response format. The first set consisted of thirteen characteristics or behaviors; the respondents were asked to indicate the extent to which they agreed that each was indicative of "good" teaching, using a five-point Likert scale (strongly agree to strongly disagree). The second set of this type of item, which also used a five-point Likert response scale, consisted of eleven statements dealing with a variety of teaching and grading practices. A third set of nine items used a three-point Likert-type scale (not helpful, somewhat helpful, very helpful). These items solicited perceptions of the usefulness of various factors (for example, observing other faculty) in the improvement of their teaching. To estimate internal consistency reliability, Cronbach's alpha was calculated for each set of items. The reliability estimates were 0.82, 0.56, and 0.75, respectively. (The items in the second set covered a more diverse range of topics than did the items in either of the other two sets, which is probably the reason for the lower reliability coefficient.)

Another preliminary activity consisted of deriving categories for the coding of the responses to the open-ended question. For each open-ended question, all of the respondents' answers were listed. We then determined the number and nature of coding categories, and a research assistant coded all of the responses. To estimate the interrater reliability of the coding, 10 percent of the completed questionnaires were randomly selected, and a second person independently coded the responses. The overall percentage of agreement between the two raters (or coders) was 92 percent.

The intended analyses for the Likert and Likert-type items were multivariate analyses of variance (MANOVAs) on each of the three sets of items. We chose this approach because we were interested in examining responses, and mean differences, to each item rather than to summated indexes. Realizing that the probability of a Type I error (alpha) for a fairly large number of separate analyses would become too high, we chose MANOVA to control somewhat for that too-large alpha, at least for each set of items. Nevertheless, an acknowledged limitation of the study is the heightened probability of a Type I error for all of the analyses combined. For that reason, we interpret the findings somewhat tentatively. The statistical tests were useful, primarily, to provide helpful gauges of the relative importance of the differences that emerged.

Although gender was the major variable of interest, we also examined differences according to campus, rank, and discipline. Due to a high relationship among the four independent variables—especially between gender and rank, and between gender and discipline—we were not able to include them in a factorial ANOVA.

Finally, we also conducted some contingency table analyses to investigate the relationship between gender and those dependent variables that were ordinal- or nominal-level. With these analyses, the statistic of interest was chi-square. For all analyses, alpha was set at 0.05.

Results

"Good" Teaching

The MANOVA for the first set of Likert items—those that pertained to characteristics of "good" teaching—yielded a statistically significant F-ratio ($F = 2.16$; $df = 13, 202$; $p = 0.01$). Each item in that set, along with the means and standard deviations for female and male respondents, are in Table 2. The results of the univariate ANOVAs are also given. As can be seen, statistically significant differences were found for five of the items. In each case, the mean for the female respondents was higher than the male respondents' mean. These items described "good" teaching in terms of concern about improving students' higher-order thinking, concern about students' self-esteem, encouraging student interaction via small-group activities, seeking a variety of learning levels via exams and discussions, and using a variety of visual aids. Although the mean differences were not statistically significant for the other eight items, it can be seen that the females' mean was higher than the males' mean for all items except the first one, "is enthusiastic about teaching."

Following the ratings on the Likert scale for these items, the respondents were given the following question and instruction: "Do you think that the above behaviors/characteristics are more common among `good' female professors as compared to `good' male professors? If you think that the characteristic is more common among `good' female professors, generally, put an "F" on the line to the far *right* of the characteristic. If you think that the characteristic is more common among "good" male professors, generally, put an `M' on the line to the far *right* of the characteristic." The respondents were further instructed to leave the right-hand line blank if they felt that there was no difference or they had no opinion. The majority of the respondents did leave all of the lines blank; because of this, we were unable to conduct contingency table analyses to examine the relationship between the gender of the respondent and the gender of the response. The total number of responses to nine of the items—items 1 through 4, 7 through 9, 11, and 13— was less than 20. For item 5, 69 respondents (34 female and 35 male) said that the characteristic— being concerned about students' self-esteem—was more characteristic of "good" female professors than "good" male professors; no one said that it was more common among "good" male

Table 2. Means and Standard Deviations for "Good" Teaching Items, by Gender

Items	Females (n=72)		Males (n=144)		
	$\bar{X}$	s	$\bar{X}$	s	p
Is enthusiastic about teaching	4.54	0.73	4.69	0.57	0.11
Is enthusiastic about the subject matter	4.63	0.70	4.59	0.54	0.47
Is knowledgeable about the subject matter	4.76	0.62	4.73	0.51	0.66
Is concerned about improving students' higher-order thinking	4.51	0.77	4.24	0.77	0.01
Is concerned about students' self-esteem	4.17	0.79	3.88	0.88	0.02
Encourages student interaction via small-group activities	3.74	0.95	3.46	0.91	0.04
Seeks a variety of learning levels via exams and discussions	4.17	0.82	3.82	0.82	0.01
Uses a variety of visual aids	3.68	0.98	3.44	0.94	0.05
Given feedback often	4.26	0.75	4.15	0.69	0.25
Avoids criticism or sarcasm	4.13	1.06	3.97	1.10	0.33
States clearly course/class objectives	4.51	0.73	4.35	0.73	0.12
Is friendly and approachable	4.22	0.86	4.21	0.80	0.95
Gives fair tests	4.40	0.76	4.29	0.84	0.32

NOTES: Only the data from those respondents who answered every item in this set were included in this multivariate analysis of variance.

The p-values are the significance levels from the univariate analysis of variance on each item.

The stem for this set of items was, "To what extent do you agree that each of the following characteristics or behaviors listed below is generally indicative of 'good' teaching?" The response format was a five-point Likert scale, where 1 = strongly disagree; 2 = disagree; 3 = unsure; 4 = agree; 5 = strongly agree.

professors. The next item—encouraging student interaction via small-group activities—showed a similar response pattern, although again there were few respondents. Twenty-eight respondents (6 male and 22 females) said it was more common among "good" female professors. To item no. 10, dealing with the avoidance of sarcasm, 42 professors (20 male and 21 female) responded; 41 of them said that the behavior was more common among "good" female professors. To item no. 13, 42 respondents (evenly divided by gender) also said that the behavior (giving fair tests) was more frequent for "good" female professors.

The most frequently occurring answers to the question, "In your view, what are the appropriate *outcomes* that reflect 'good' teaching?", are in table 3. There was no statistically significant relationship between gender and type of response given to this question. As can be seen, the most common outcomes cited by both male and female professors involved student cognitive variables. For the males, relatively specific types of cognitive outcomes, for example, learning the subject matter of the course, were the most common. The female professors had a *very slight* preference for more general types of cognitive outcomes, for example, becoming better problem solvers or critical thinkers.

Teaching Methods, Evaluation Practices, and Improvement

When asked what percentages of their "work" time was devoted to teaching, to research and creative activities, and to service, the female and male respondents gave similar (and not statistically different) average percentages. The female means for teaching, research, and service were 39.6 percent, 36.8 percent, and 23.0 percent, respectively. The mean percentages for the males were 36.4 percent (teaching), 37.5 per cent (research), and 23.6 percent (service).

Table 3. Percentages of Responses to the "Outcomes" Question, by Gender

Types of Outcomes	Females	Males
Cognitive: students learn new information, become proficient in the subject matter, learn the course material	27.3	31.2
Cognitive: students become better problem-solvers, critical thinkers; are better able to apply and transfer information	28.3	29.3
Cognitive/affective: students "learn to be better learners," show a desire to pursue subject matter further; go on to graduate school	15.2	15.6
Affective: students become more enthusiastic, self-motivated; have an improved self-image or more positive self-esteem	21.2	14.1
Other indicators: e.g., high student course ratings; high grades	8.1	9.8

NOTES: Up to two responses per respondent were coded and analyzed. The total number of responses given by female respondents was 99; the total number given by male respondents was 205. The percentages are based on these numbers.

This open-ended question was stated as follows: "In your view, what are the appropriate *outcomes* that reflect 'good' teaching?"

There also were no statistically significant differences between males and females in their preferred teaching methods and end-of-semester grading practices. In response to a question about what teaching methods they used most often, 64.0 percent of the males and 53.2 percent of the females said "lecture"; 20.0 percent of the males and 29.9 percent of the females said "discussion." Fewer than 10 percent of either male or female respondents chose "case study," "small-group activities," or "other," which usually was explained to be a combination of the various methods. In terms of preferred end-of-semester grading practices, criterion-referenced approaches were said to be used most often by both females (68.5 percent) and males (51.4 percent). Norm-referenced approaches were preferred by 13.7 percent of the females and by 23.6 percent of the males. Other approaches—contract-based, pass-fail, and combination approaches—were chosen by fewer than 10 percent of the respondents.

In Table 4, the means and standard deviations, by gender, for the second set of Likert items are given. The MANOVA on these data yielded a statistically significant multivariate F-ratio ($F = 2.72$; $df = 11, 200$; $p = 0.003$). Three of the items had statistically significant univariate F-ratios. The female respondents were significantly more likely to agree (or agreed more strongly) with the statements, "I consult with colleagues in order to help improve my teaching" and "Competition for grades in a class should be avoided." The male professors had a significantly higher mean than the females for the statement, "Student course evaluations provide useful information for course improvement purposes."

The final set of results we present is in Table 5. These items solicited opinions, on a three-point scale, about the usefulness of a variety of factors in improving the respondents' teaching. The MANOVA F-ratio was statistically significant ($F = 2.36$; $df = 9, 191$; $p = 0.02$). The univariate ANOVAs yielded significant mean differences for three factors (and a fourth item had a p-value of 0.07). The females had higher average usefulness ratings for observing other faculty as they teach, having other faculty observe and comment on their own teaching, attending work shops on teaching, and working with a consultant on their teaching.

Differences by Campus, Rank, and Discipline

As expected, there were statistically significant relationships between gender and both rank and discipline. For the gender-by-rank comparison ($X^2 = 13.72$; $df = 2$; $p = 0.001$), 46.2 percent of the males were full professors, 29.1 percent were associate professors, and 24.7 percent were assistant professors. Among the females, 22.8 percent were full professors, 34.2 percent were associate professors, and 43.0 percent were assistant professors. To examine the relationship between

Table 4. Means and Standard Deviations of Teaching Practices and Attitudes Items, by Gender

Items	Females (n=70)		Males (n=142)		
	$\bar{X}$	s	$\bar{X}$	s	p
I am primarily responsible if most of my students do not perform up to my course expectations	2.99	1.22	3.19	1.15	0.24
I consult with colleagues in order to help improve my teaching	4.10	.80	3.69	1.03	0.01
Marked improvement in student learning can occur if I make course modifications	3.42	1.00	3.45	0.94	0.79
The teacher's predominant role should be content expert	2.83	0.98	3.06	1.02	0.12
Competition for grades in a class should be avoided	3.40	1.03	3.07	1.22	0.05
If students appear disinterested and unmotivated, an effective teacher should be able to change the situation and "turn it around"	3.61	0.77	3.78	0.84	0.18
My predominant role should be a guide who collaborates with students	3.56	1.06	3.38	1.11	0.27
In assigning end-of-semester grades, a student's effort is as important as the quality of her/his work	2.59	1.06	2.53	1.06	0.71
Teachers should make changes in courses and assignments to enhance student involvement in the course	4.11	0.73	4.00	0.79	0.31
Giving grades undermines students' natural curiosity and intrinsic desire to learn	2.37	0.78	2.26	1.09	0.45
Student course evaluations provide useful information for course improvement purposes	3.11	1.11	3.61	1.01	0.01

NOTES: Only those respondents who answered every item in this set were in the multivariate analysis of variance for the items.

The p-values are the significance levels from the univariate analysis variance on each item.

The stem for this set of items was, "Below are some statements concerning teaching practices and attitudes. Please indicate how strongly you agree or disagree with each item, using the following scale: 1 = strongly agree; 2 = agree; 3 = unsure; 4 = disagree; 5 = strongly disagree."

gender and discipline we collapsed the twelve discipline groups into five (so that each cell would have, at least, a sample size of five). The five groups were arts and humanities; social sciences and education; sciences, mathematics, and engineering; professional schools (business, public affairs, and law); and health sciences (nursing, medicine, dentistry, and pharmacy). The chi-square was significant ($X^2 = 17.54; df = 4, p = 0.002$). Proportionately, the largest difference between numbers of female and male respondents was in the sciences, mathematics, and engineering group (90 percent male and 10 percent female). In the arts and humanities group, by contrast, 54.1 percent were male professors and 45.9 percent were female professors. As stated earlier, these significant relationships precluded the inclusion of rank and discipline in factorial ANOVAs along with gender.

When we analyzed the responses to the questionnaire items separately by campus, rank, and discipline, we found virtually no significant differences by campus. By rank, there also were few statistically significant differences in the mean responses to the items. The significant differences that emerged all showed the same pattern: significantly lower means for the full professors as compared to the associate or assistant professors. Those items included the eighth item in table 2—that "good" teaching is reflected in the use of a variety of visual aids—as well as the second

Table 5. Means and Standard Deviations for Items Relating to Supportive or Helpful Factors, by Gender

Items	Females (n=67)		Males (n=134)		
	$\bar{X}$	s	$\bar{X}$	s	p
Feedback from students	2.46	0.56	2.59	0.56	0.13
Feedback from other faculty	2.40	0.61	2.28	0.67	0.22
Talking with other faculty about teaching generally	2.22	0.69	2.26	0.65	0.71
Experimenting on my own	2.60	0.49	2.56	0.53	0.63
Observing other faculty as they teach	2.40	0.65	2.18	0.61	0.02
Having other faculty observe and comment on my teaching	2.40	0.63	2.08	0.67	0.01
Reading about college teaching	1.63	0.67	1.53	0.60	0.30
Attending workshops on teaching	1.94	0.81	1.76	0.71	0.07
Working with a consultant on my teaching	2.13	0.82	1.78	0.79	0.01

NOTES: Only those respondents who answered every item in this set were included in the multivariate analysis of variance for the items.

The p-values are the significance levels from the univariate analysis of variance on each item.

The stem for this set of items was, "Below are some factors that might be supportive or helpful in improving your teaching. Rate the extent to which you think that each would be helpful." The response format was a three point Likert-type scale, where: 1 = not helpful; 2 = somewhat helpful; 3 = very helpful.

item in table 4, and the last three items in table 5. The items in tables 4 and 5 dealt with consulting with colleagues about teaching, and with reading about teaching, attending workshops, and working with a consultant to improve their teaching. When responses were examined by the five discipline groups, the significant differences that emerged pertained to percentages of time devoted to teaching and to research. For teaching ($F = 6.44$; $df = 4,223$; $p = 0.001$), the health sciences professors' mean percentage (25.53 percent) was significantly lower than the other groups' means, especially arts and humanities (42.45 percent). The results for research ($F = 4.02$; $df = 4,223$; $p = 0.0004$) showed the arts and humanities faculties' mean (26.13 percent) to be significantly lower than the other groups' means; the health sciences mean was highest (41.13 percent).

Discussion

Before discussing the findings, some limitations of the study should be noted. The response rate was only about 35 percent. Although this is not unexpected in a study of this sort, and the profiles of the respondents appeared to compare well with the available institutional profiles, the unknown type and extent of response bias is still a limitation. A second limitation is inherent in the type of measure that we used, a self-report questionnaire with Likert and Likert-type items. The extent to which the answers were faked or to which social desirability occurred is unknown.

This study produced many interesting findings and has suggested questions and methods for future investigations. We were somewhat surprised that relatively few significant gender differences were found. The significant differences that emerged for the "good" teaching items (table 2) showed that the female respondents tended to agree more strongly than the male respondents about the extent to which "good" teachers are concerned about students higher-order thinking skills, are concerned about their self-esteem, encourage student interaction via small-group activities, seek a variety of learning levels via exams and discussions, and use a variety of visual aids. The mean for the males was higher, although not significantly, for one characteristic: being enthusiastic about teaching. Another aspect of the results in table 2 worth noting is the high level of the means for most of the items for both male and female respondents. The highest possible value of those means was 5 ("strongly agree"), and many of them are above 4, and a few are above 4.5. Overall, then, this sample of faculty agreed that the behaviors and characteristics we listed were indeed characteristics of "good" teaching. The two items with the lowest means (although still quite high) were the ones that dealt with encouraging student interaction via small-group activities and using a variety of visual aids.

We also were intrigued with the data that we obtained when we asked the respondents to indicate whether they thought that any of the behaviors and characteristics in table 2 were more common among "good" female professors or among "good" male professors. As we stated earlier, most respondents did not indicate either "M" or "F" in the spaces provided. From many unsolicited written comments on the questionnaires, we concluded that most of the "blanks" were because the respondents did not think that there were any gender differences. The few items that received some attention (around 40 respondents) dealt with students' self-esteem, the encouragement of interaction via small-group activities, and fair tests; those faculty who responded to these items almost unanimously agreed that these behaviors were more common among "good" female professors as compared to "good" male professors. The interaction item (no. 6 in table 2) was one for which the female respondents' mean was significantly higher than the male respondents' mean *and* was viewed by some respondents as being a characteristic more common among "good" female professors. These results are consistent with reports of greater interaction and student participation in classes taught by female faculty members [9, 38, 60]. However, given Macke and her colleagues' [38] finding of a relationship between lower student ratings and higher levels of student participation, these findings are somewhat troubling and definitely suggest an area for further study.

The opinions of our respondents about the appropriate outcomes of "good" teaching were similar across gender and showed heavy emphasis on cognitive outcomes. Over 50 percent of the outcomes given pertained either to relatively specific types of cognitive outcomes (for example, students learn the specific course material) or relatively general cognitive outcomes (for example, students' critical thinking skills are improved). Outcomes that included or focused on affective variables were mentioned less often by both male and female respondents. These findings, in conjunction with the lesser value placed on student interaction and participation, suggest another area for further study: the nature and extent of the relationship between various classroom techniques and types of outcomes deemed most relevant to "good" teaching.

Examining the results shown in tables 4 and 5, a few interesting points emerge. The items in table 4 (which covered a "mixed bag" of teaching practices and attitudes) yielded relatively few gender differences. The significantly higher mean for females on the second item—"I consult with colleagues in order to help improve my teaching"—is consistent with findings reported by Chism [13], Thoreson and his colleagues [57], and with our findings from an earlier study [56]. When we analyzed our data from that earlier study to explore the types and extent of gender differences, we also found significant differences such as several of those found here. For example, the females' mean was significantly higher than the males' mean for the item, "Competition for grades in a class should be avoided." The males agreed more strongly than the females with the statement, "Student course evaluations provide useful information for course improvement purposes." The similarity in findings between the two studies (in terms of non-significant differences, too) showed some support for the external validity of our findings.

The higher usefulness ratings for the female professors in table 5 for some activities—having other faculty observe their teaching, observing other faculty themselves, working with a consultant on their teaching, and attending workshops on teaching—were also consistent with findings reported by Chism [13]. Female professors seem to place greater value than male professors on seeking "outside" help from peers and others. In general, too, the means in table 5 illustrate that the respondents thought that feedback from students and from faculty, experimenting on their own, and observation were potentially useful activities for improving teaching. However, the other factors—reading about teaching, attending workshops, and working with a consultant—received lower usefulness ratings. This result may be explained, in part, by the absence on three of the campuses of a faculty development office; such an office typically provides resources such as books about teaching, workshops, and consultants. It is interesting to note, nonetheless, that faculty preferences—for discussions and reciprocal visits with colleagues, as opposed to read-ings—reflect an emphasis on active learning; in their own classes, however, the most commonly used teaching method was the lecture method.

Interestingly, we found no significant differences between male and female professors in the self-reported percentages of time spent on teaching and on research. Finkelstein [27] cited many references in which differences have been found, usually showing that female professors spent relatively more time on teaching and males spent relatively more time on research and related activities. We also were surprised that very few differences were found when we analyzed the data by discipline. Our sampling approach, which was intended to yield a broad representation across a large university system, precluded an in-depth investigation of discipline differences, and gender-by-discipline interactions. Perhaps a methodological approach like that taken by Thoreson and his colleagues recently [57], in which matched pairs (one male, one female) of professors were selected within a number of departments, might be a useful approach to finding the type and extent of gender-by-discipline differences on some of these dimensions. Interesting, too, is that Thoreson found few gender differences, although female professors reported signifi-cantly greater levels of stress and lower satisfaction levels than did males. Their overall conclusion was that their findings showed "no consistent gender differences in either attitudes or behaviors related to enactment of the academic role" [57, p. 207].

Although we found relatively few gender differences, the ones that emerged were consistent with others' works and are interesting. In general, the findings suggest that female professors might place greater value or importance on, or be more interested in, enhancing students' self-esteem and in encouraging student interaction and participation in class. Female professors also appear to be more interested in seeking "outside" assistance in attempting to improve their teaching; male professors appear to place greater value on students' evaluations than females. However, all professors seem to share similar views about what constitutes "good" teaching, and about the appropriate outcomes of "good" teaching.

References

1. Abel, E. K. *Terminal Degrees*. New York: Praeger, 1984.

2. Aleamoni, L. M., and M. Yimer. "An Investigation of the Relationship between Colleague Rating, Student Rating, Research Productivity, and Academic Rank in Rating Instructional Effectiveness." *Journal of Educational Psychology*, 64 (1973), 274–77.

3. American Association of University Professors, Committee 2 on the Status of Women in the Academic Profession. "Academic Women and Salary Differentials." *Academe*, 74 (1988), 33–34.

4. Babbie, R. R. *Survey Research Methods*. Belmont, Calif.: Wadsworth, 1973.

5. Barnett, L. T., and G. Littlepage. "Course Preferences and Evaluations of Male and Female Professors by Male and Female Students." *Psychonomic Society Bulletin*, 13 (1979), 44–46.

6. Basow, S. A., and M. S. Distenfeld. "Teacher Expressiveness: More Important for Males than Females?" *Journal of Educational Psychology*, 77 (1985), 45–52.

7. Basow, S. A., and N. T. Silberg. "Student Evaluations of College Professors: Are Female and Male Professors Rated Differently?" *Journal of Educational Psychology*, 79 (1987), 308–14.

8. Bennett, S. K. "Student Perceptions of and Expectations for Male and Female Instructors: Evidence Relating to the Question of Gender Bias in Teaching Evaluations." *Journal of Educational Psychology*, 74 (1982), 170–79.

9. Berry, E. *Taking Women Professors Seriously*. Paper presented at the annual meeting of the American Association for Higher Education, San Francisco, April 1989.

10. Brandenburg, D. C., J. A. Slinde, and E. E. Batista. "Student Ratings of Instruction: Validity and Normative Interpretations." *Research in Higher Education*, 7 (1977), 67–78.

11. Brown, D. L. "Faculty Ratings and Student Grades: A University-wide Multiple Regression Analysis." *Journal of Educational Psychology*, 68 (1976), 573–78.

12. Cahn, S. M. "The Art of Teaching." *American Educator*, 6 (1982), 36–39.

13. Chism, N. *The Process of Development in College Teachers: Toward a Model.* Paper presented at the annual meeting of the American Educational Research Association, New Orleans, April 1988.

14. Choy, C. "The Relationship of College Teacher Effectiveness to Conceptual Systems Orientation and Perceptual Orientation." Ed.D. dissertation, Colorado State College, 1969.

15. Cohen, P. A., and W. J. McKeachie. "The Role of Colleges in the Evaluation of Teaching." *Improving College and University Teaching*, 28 (1980), 147–54.

16. Ebel, K. E. *The Craft of Teaching.* San Francisco: Jossey-Bass, 1977.

17. Eison, J. *Gender: The Issue that Won't Go Away.* Cape Giradeau, Mo.: Southeast Missouri State University, Center for Teaching and Learning, 1987.

18. Eison, J., H. Pollio, and O. Milton. *Manual to Use with LOGO II.* Knoxville, TN: University of Tennessee, Learning Resource Center, 1982.

19. Elmore, P. B., and K. A. LaPointe. "Effects of Teacher Sex and Student Sex on the Evaluation of College Instructors." *Journal of Educational Psychology*, 66 (1974), 386–89.

20. _____. "Effects of Teacher Sex, Student Sex, and Teacher Warmth on the Evaluation of College Instructors." *Journal of Educational Psychology*, 67 (1975), 368–74.

21. Elmore, P. B., and J. T. Pohlman. "Effect of Teacher, Student, and Class Characteristics on the Evaluation of College Instructors." *Journal of Educational Psychology*, 70 (1978), 187–92.

22. Feldman, K. A. "The Superior College Teacher from the Students' View." *Research in Higher Education*, 5 (1976), 243–88.

23. _____. "Seniority and Experience of College Teachers as Related to Evaluations They Receive from Students." *Research in Higher Education*, 18 (1983), 3–124.

24. _____. "Effective College Teaching from the Students' and Faculty's View: Matched or Mismatched Priorities?" *Research in Higher Education*, 28 (1988), 291–344.

25. Ferber, M. A., and J. A. Huber. "Sex of Student and Instructor: A Study of Student Bias." *American Journal of Sociology*, 80 (1975), 949-63.

26. Finkelstein, M. J. "The Status of Academic Women: An Assessment of Five Competing Explanations." *Review of Higher Education*, 7 (1984), 233–46.

27. _____. *The American Academic Profession: A Synthesis of Social Scientific Inquiry since World War II.* Columbus: Ohio State University Press, 1984.

28. Freedman, R. D., S. A. Stumpf, and J. C. Aguanno. "Validity of the Course-Faculty Instrument (CFI): Intrinsic and Extrinsic Variables." *Educational and Psychological Measurement*, 39 (1979), 153-59.

29. Geisinger, K. F. "Who's Giving All Those A's?" *Journal of Teacher Education*, 31 (1980), 11-15.

30. Geisinger, K. F., and A. J. Abedor. "Organizational Change and the Development of Faculty Evaluation Systems." *Journal of Instructional Development*, 8 (1985), 22-25.

31. Goldman, R. D., and B. N. Hewitt. "Adaptation Level as an Explanation for Differential Standards in College Grading." *Journal of Educational Measurement*, 12 (1975), 149–61.

32. Goldsmid, C. A., J. E. Gruber, and E. K. Wilson. "Perceived Attributes of Superior Teachers (Past): An Inquiry into the Giving of Teacher Awards." *American Educational Research Journal*, 14 (1977), 423-41.

33. Hyer, P. B. "Women Faculty at Doctorate-granting Universities: A Ten-Year Progress Report." *Journal of Educational Equity and Leadership*, 5 (1985), 234–49.

34. Kaschak, E. "Sex Bias in Student Evaluations of College Professors." *Psychology of Women Quarterly*, 2 (1978), 235–43.

35. Lewis, K. G., and P. J. Woodward. *What Really Happens in Larger University Classes.* Paper presented at the annual meeting of the American Educational Research Association, New Orleans, March 1984.

36. Lombardo, J., and M. E. Tocci. "Attributions of Positive and Negative Characteristics of Instructors as a Function of Attractiveness and Sex of Instructor and Sex of Subject. *Perceptual and Motor Skills,* 48 (1979), 491–94.

37. Lomperis, A. M. T. "Are Women Changing the Nature of the Academic Profession?" *Journal of Higher Education,* 61 (November/December 1990), 643–77.

38. Macke, A. S., L. W. Richardson, and J. Cook. *Sex-typed Teaching Styles of University Professors and Student Reactions.* Columbus: The Ohio State University Research Foundation, 1980.

39. Markham, P. L. "Gender and the Perceived Expertness of the Speaker as Factors in ESL Listening Recall." *TESOL Quarterly,* 22 (1988), 397–405.

40. McKeachie, W. J. "Research on Teaching at the College and University Level." In *Handbook of Research on Teaching,* edited by N. L. Gage, pp. 1118-72. Chicago: Rand McNally, 1963.

41. _____. "Student Ratings of Faculty: A Reprise." *Academe,* 65 (1979), 384–97.

42. McMillan, J. H., and S. Schumacher. *Research in Education: A Conceptual Introduction.* 2nd ed. Glenview, Ill.: Scott, Foresman, and Company, 1989.

43. Milton, O., H. R. Pollio, and J. Eison. *Making Sense of College Grades.* San Francisco: Jossey-Bass, 1986.

44. Miron, M. "The 'Good Professor' as Perceived by University Instructors." *Higher Education,* 14 (1985), 211–15.

45. Newell, L. J., and G. D. Kuh. "Taking Stock: The Higher Education Professoriate." *Review of Higher Education,* 13 (1989), 63–90.

46. Orban, D. A., and A. J. Abedor. "Organizational Change and the Development of Faculty Evaluation." *Journal of Instructional Development,* 8 (1985), 22–25.

47. Rosenshine, B. "Teaching Behaviors Related to Student Achievement." In *Research into Classroom Processes: Recent Developments and Next Steps,* edited by I. Vestbury and H. Bellack, pp. 51–98. New York: Teachers College Press, 1971.

48. Sadler, D. R. "Evaluation and the Improvement of Academic Learning." *Journal of Higher Education,* 54 (January/February 1983), 60–79.

49. Sandler, B. R. *The Campus Climate Revisited: Chilly for Women Faculty, Administrators, and Graduate Students.* Washington, D.C.: Association of American Colleges, Project on the Status and Education of Women, 1986.

50. Seldin, P. *Changing Practices in Faculty Evaluation.* San Francisco: Jossey-Bass, 1984.

51. Simeone, A. *Academic Women: Working toward Equality.* Hadley, Mass.: Bergin and Garvey, 1987.

52. Sorcinelli, M. D. "An Approach to Colleague Evaluation of Classroom Instruction." *Journal of Instructional Development,* 7 (1984), 11–17.

53. Stancato, F. A., and C. F. Eiszler. "When a C is Not a C: Meaning of Grades in Educational Psychology." *Journal of Instructional Psychology,* 10 (1983), 158–62.

54. Statham, K. A., L. Richardson, and J. Cook. *Gender and University Teaching: A Negotiated Difference.* Albany, N.Y.: State University of New York Press, 1991.

55. Stevens, E. "Tinkering with Teaching." *The Review of Higher Education,* 12 (1988), 63–78.

56. Stevens, E., L. Goodwin, and W. Goodwin. "How Are We Different? Attitudes and Perceptions of Teaching across Three Institutions." *Journal of Staff, Program, and Organizational Development,* 9 (1991), 1–12.

57. Thoreson, R. W., C. M. Kardash, D. A. Leuthold, and K. A. Morrow. "Gender Differences in the Academic Career." *Research in Higher Education*, 31 (1990), 193–209.

58. Touchton, J. G., and L. Davis. *Fact Book on Women in Higher Education.* New York: American Council on Education/Macmillan Series on Higher Education, 1991.

59. Travers, R. M. W. "Criteria of Good Teaching." In *Handbook of Teacher Evaluation*, edited by J. Millman, pp. 14–22. Beverly Hills, Calif.: Sage, 1981.

60. Treichler, P. A., and C. Kramarae. "Women's Talk in the Ivory Tower." *Communication Quarterly*, 31 (1983), 118–32.

61. Wilson, D., and K. G. Doyle, Jr. "Student Ratings of Instruction." *Journal of Higher Education*, 47 (July/August 1976), 465–70.

Laura D. Goodwin is associate dean and professor of education and Ellen A. Stevens is assistant professor of education at the School of Education, University of Colorado at Denver.

Institutions Matter: Campus Teaching Environments' Impact on Senior Faculty

MARK W. LaCELLE-PETERSON AND MARTIN J. FINKELSTEIN

Institutional support is a key to sustaining the vitality of higher education's most experienced teachers. Research on eleven campuses shows that institutions need to create collaborative teaching structures and to broker significant opportunities for individual growth.

Senior faculty members' individual and collective engagement in teaching is vital to both the immediate and the long-term future of higher education in the United States. Today, tenured associate and full professors, directly or through their oversight of adjunct faculty and graduate students, bear the lion's share of responsibility for college teaching. In addition, because they select and socialize the new faculty who will eventually replace them, they are building the foundation for college teaching in the next century. Clearly, higher education's present and future success as a teaching enterprise depends on the senior faculty. What is all too frequently overlooked, however, is the crucial corollary: *senior faculty members' success as teachers depends on the support of their institutions.* Too often observers assume that senior faculty, securely tenured and with years of teaching experience under their belts, are impervious to circumstance. Their styles and levels of success as teachers were presumably set in graduate school or during their first academic appointment, and any variations in enthusiasm or skill they display as teachers are simply evidence of inherent individual differences, neither the result of, nor amenable to, institutional policies.

Contrary to this common wisdom, the findings of a study of 111 senior faculty members on eleven New Jersey campuses show that teaching vitality is, at least in part, a product of a positive teaching climate: one that affords professors opportunities to work together on teaching and to experience professional growth as teacher-scholars within their disciplines. The study ought to answer three questions: First, how do senior faculty members as individuals experience teaching? Do they remain engaged in teaching after years in the classroom? Why or why not? Second, how do institutions enhance or diminish the teaching experience for senior faculty? Do institutional policies or characteristics matter in relation to faculty members' individual or collective "teaching engagement?" Third, given the answers to the first two questions, can institutions and their senior faculty, working together, do more to create institutional climates that support vital, engaged teaching for all faculty members?

A two-year action research project shaped by these questions is described in five sections below. The first section presents the origins of the project, the questions that drove it, and the process set up to answer them. The second section presents what we learned from senior faculty about the role of institutions in supporting them as teachers. The final two sections outline the wider policy implications of these findings.

Eleven-Campus Study

The desire to explore these questions grew out of the realization that the faculty side of the demographic equation sketched in Chapter One of this volume held true for the state of New Jersey. A study of faculty demographics revealed that, in the short run, senior faculty were, and would remain, the dominant cohort in all sectors of higher education (Finkelstein, 1988). In the long run, however, once the faculty cohort hired between 1965 and 1973 begin to retire, a tremendous turnover can be expected. In both the short and the long term, senior faculty are clearly the key to the quality and effectiveness of college and university teaching.

In light of these demographic realities, and inspired by the great success of its Partners in Learning Program in engaging faculty on very different kinds of campuses—senior faculty in particular—in reflection-based teaching innovation (see Smith and Smith, this volume), the New Jersey Institute for Collegiate Teaching and Learning conceptualized an action research project to explore the role of institutional support in sustaining the development of senior faculty as teachers, and to encourage greater institutional efforts to create and/or maintain positive teaching climates. Eventually, eleven campuses—public and private, two-year, four-year, and university— agreed to participate (see Table 2.1).

Two groups—"a campus advisory board" composed of the chief academic officers from the eleven campuses and a "research advisory board" made up of recognized scholars on faculty in higher education—guided the project. Separate discussions with each advisory group began with two questions: how should we define "senior faculty"? and whom within the defined group ought we to interview? In answer to the first question, a general demographic definition emerged in both groups: senior faculty were those tenured individuals who had taught full time in colleges or universities for at least fifteen years; these faculty members were typically forty-five years of age or older, and could look forward to as many as twenty more years of teaching. In considering the second question—how to sample this large and diverse group—discussion centered on two characteristics of faculty: their degree of engagement in teaching, and their degree of influence among colleagues. These characteristics defined, on the basis of administrators' perceptions (not empirical evidence), three potentially overlapping subgroups of senior faculty who could provide important perspectives on the research questions. Those recognized by faculty colleagues and administrators as exceptionally engaged in teaching could provide "best case" exemplars to guide and inspire. Those faculty seen as exceptionally disengaged teachers, on the other hand, were of particular interest to administrators alarmed at the student complaints they provoked. Given the action orientation of the project, the insights of a third group, faculty "opinion leaders" who helped shape the campus environment, would contribute to a clearer understanding of how teaching was valued and could be enhanced.

In the end, twelve senior faculty members were nominated from each campus; each list included professors from a wide range of disciplines as well as some who were perceived to exhibit different degrees of influence and engagement. Though these categories played no role in the subsequent research or analysis, their use ensured that a wide variety of views would be expressed. From eight to twelve professors on each campus agreed to participate in one- to two-hour structured interviews. Table 2.2 presents gender and disciplinary distributions of those interviewed.

The interviews themselves consisted of fifty open-ended questions focused on two areas: teaching experience and teaching environment. The former included questions about respon-

Table 2.1. Participating Campuses by Type

	Public	Private	Total
Two-year	3	—	3
Four-year	1	4	5
University	2	1	3
Total	6	5	11

Table 2.2. Faculty Participants by Gender and Discipline

Discipline	Men	Women	Total
Anthropology	1	—	1
Architecture	—	1	1
Art	2	—	2
Art History	1	—	1
Biology	7	1	8
Business education	—	2	2
Chemistry	5	1	6
Community health	1	—	1
Comparative literature	—	1	1
Computer science	1	—	1
Ecology	1	—	1
Economics	7	2	9
Education	—	2	2
Engineering	7	—	7
English	10	8	18
History	5	—	5
Humanities	1	—	1
Languages	1	4	5
Management	5	—	5
Mathematics	4	3	7
Nursing	—	5	5
Philosophy	2	1	3
Physics	4	—	4
Political science	—	1	1
Psychology	5	3	8
Religion	2	—	2
Sociology	1	—	1
Theater	1	—	1
Total	76	35	111

dents' early teaching experiences, how the teaching of a particular course had changed over the years, the kinds of assignments they gave students, and how they maintained interest in frequently taught courses. The latter included questions about changes in students over the years, how colleagues in and outside the department influenced their teaching, the role of formal faculty development programs, and institutional promotion and tenure policies. The sample was not drawn randomly, nor did each interview cover all possible questions; as in Clark's (1987) study of academic life, the conversations followed the individual respondents' interests and circumstances.

What We Found

Analysis of the interviews yielded three major findings, elaborated in the following sections. First, senior faculty members care a great deal about teaching and experience it as fulfilling. Second, however, in the normal course of "business as usual," they typically find little opportunity—formally or informally—to focus on teaching. Teaching is isolated, and poorer for that isolation. Without periodic opportunities to revitalize their professional lives generally and their teaching lives in particular, faculty members report that their "teaching vitality" tends to slip. Third, two ways emerged in which institutions support and enhance faculty development as teachers: *creating structural alterations* in the teaching situation to eliminate the isolation of teaching, and *brokering individual opportunities* to revitalize individual professors.

Senior Faculty Enjoy Teaching. The first question considered was "How do senior faculty members as individuals experience teaching?" Since many had taught hundreds of courses and thousands of students, did these campus veterans still find joy in teaching? The data were clear: *the overwhelming majority enjoy teaching and care a great deal about student learning.* Though a number expressed greater and lesser degrees of dissatisfaction about students' level of academic preparation in recent years, and though those whose teaching assignments were repetitive noted the difficulty this posed, senior faculty members cared a great deal about teaching. Not only did most express a strong commitment to their roles as teachers, many answered the question "What keeps you fresh as a teacher?" with the emphatic reply, "The students!"

While faculty members generally reported a positive attitude toward teaching, some reported relatively more frequent innovation and revision in their teaching than did others. Some, in fact, reported that the repetition that characterized their teaching assignments was wearying—though the occasional spark of interest by a student made it worthwhile. A few individual faculty members reported great variations in teaching vitality across their own careers. These faculty, whom we have called "turn arounds," reported periods in their careers during which they "burned out" on teaching or on their institution as a whole. They did not, however, remain in this state, but instead eventually found renewed vitality. In analyzing what all of the senior faculty told us about their teaching experiences and the "milestones" in their teaching careers, we found that, to greater and lesser degrees, such swings in teaching vitality were common to many faculty careers—and that the swings "up" were often mediated by an institutional variable, a point to be elaborated below.

In the big picture, the data suggest that while professors are highly motivated as individuals by the intrinsic rewards of teaching—interaction with students and material or "performances" (as clearly illustrated by faculty members who reported "getting energy" from performing well in front of a roomful of students)—their teaching vitality cannot be sustained indefinitely without extrinsic or institutional support.

How can institutions support teaching vitality among their senior professors? In the interviews, we inquired into three vehicles that might, logically, provide such support. First, given the high level of autonomy among professors and the value placed on collegiality, we explored the role of informal collegial interactions in sustaining teaching. Second, given that the department or division is often the faculty member's most meaningful unit of membership, we asked how departmental policies and routine departmental interactions influenced faculty members' teaching. Third, as each of the participating campuses had faculty development policies or programs in place, we asked how these supported faculty in their roles as teachers. After reporting briefly on these vehicles, we will elaborate on the two types of institutional interventions that mattered most for senior faculty.

Collegial Interaction Regarding Teaching Is Limited. Despite their individual interest in and commitment to teaching, professors report little collegial interaction around it. Half of the interviewees do not discuss teaching with their colleagues. One in five discusses teaching with his or her colleagues around the department, another one in ten talks about things related to teaching, like books, lab materials, or complaints about students, with his or her colleagues. One in ten reports discussions about teaching with colleagues across disciplines. The patterns of informal interaction around teaching reflect the fact that teaching is the very part of faculty work that is most individual and that is almost always conducted in isolation.

One additional finding: informal interaction is, in the experience of some, shaped by institutional factors. Several professors at one private campus mentioned that the disappearance of a popular faculty gathering place reduced the amount of collegial interaction—including interaction around teaching—since the informal venue for those conversations was no longer available. Respondents at two community colleges and two private institutions commented that increased use of adjuncts for teaching, and the resultant burden on the remaining fulltimers to take care of department business, left them feeling more harried with less time for conversation. Faculty at two universities noted that, even for those interested in talking about teaching, it was hard to find time and interested partners.

Departmental Discussion of Teaching Is Scarce. We also asked faculty whether they discuss teaching formally at the department level. Here, even more pronouncedly than with regard to informal conversation, they report little if any interaction around teaching. One in fourteen faculty members said that teaching was a topic of discussion in department meetings. Three-quarters of those interviewed reported no interaction around classroom teaching in department meetings; one-quarter said that occasional discussions of curriculum revision were the only teaching-related agenda items. In all cases, informational and business matters dominated departmental agendas. As one reflective faculty member characterized it, "We talk a lot about the prerequisites to teaching, but not about teaching itself." To many, the status quo was quite acceptable. Several went so far as to express satisfaction that the department was not "intrusive" in regard to teaching—being left alone to do one's own thing was the best some faculty members could wish from their departments. In some cases, faculty members opined that keeping teaching off the agenda was just as well because their departmental colleagues had been together for too long to learn from each other about teaching: each had a position to reiterate, and the arguments were worn and predictable.

Though departments generally turned out to be the missing player in interaction around teaching, there were important exceptions. Nursing departments in particular structured their teaching work collaboratively and provided for significant interaction around teaching, both formally and informally. Natural science departments likewise, in a more limited way, found a common focus for teaching interaction in their laboratory experiences. In addition, faculty members in one English department reported frequent interaction around classroom teaching issues: this was carried on outside official departmental channels, however. Most faculty members who wanted to focus on teaching together with their colleagues, however, did so through institution-wide faculty development programs—not through departmental structures.

Faculty Development Programs Attracted Many. Some faculty members reported significant interaction around teaching in other institution-wide programs. Each of the eleven participating campuses was home to at least one, in most cases two or three, ongoing faculty development programs (such as the Partners in Learning program, a Writing Across the Curriculum program, or a Race, Class, and Gender (Multicultural) faculty seminar) in which faculty from across the institution participated voluntarily. In addition, each campus sponsored occasional series of teaching workshops. One in four faculty members participate (or have participated) in one or more of the ongoing programs. These programs provide a structure for reflection on teaching, and often require faculty member participants to revise a course, in terms of both content and teaching methods. Participants in these programs are self-selected; those who participate in them found them to be beneficial, and others who did not personally participate often knew them to have positive reputations. Valuable though they were to participants, many were hesitant to participate in non-discipline-based programs. Two of five faculty members interviewed had not participated in any faculty development effort; one in five had only attended occasional seminars.

What Made a Difference?

While collegial interaction and structured faculty development programs provide important sustenance for faculty interest in teaching, analysis of the mass of interview data suggests that, from the organizational perspective, two classes of opportunities provide the most meaningful structure and support for vital engagement in teaching. Near the end of the interview with each faculty member, after having discussed the issues already noted, we asked two questions that promoted reflection on what mattered over the course of their careers. The first asked what milestones or stages they had passed through as teachers; the second asked what sustained them, that is, what gave them the energy to keep going semester after semester. As already noted, to the latter question, a number of faculty responded "the students"; many also noted their love of the discipline. But in addition to these factors faculty members talked about opportunities for collaboratively structured teaching and for significant personal growth.

Collaboration on Teaching. Teaching experiences that were reported with greatest enthusiasm and appreciation by those who were still involved, and with a great sense of loss by those whose involvement has ceased, involve collaboration on teaching marked by substantive discussion of content in connection with a common group of students. Frequently, faculty report these interactions in the context of team teaching—an arrangement that on some campuses has become less common these days due to resource constraints, but that was becoming more common on others in the form of "core course clusters" through which students fulfilled general education requirements, or as part of special honors programs or retention programs. Faculty who had taught in such course clusters at the freshman or sophomore level in which two or more faculty members collaborate in teaching a common group of students with some degree of coordination report that the experience was the occasion for their most meaningful teaching interactions.

Departments much less frequently provide a forum for teaching-embedded interaction; only nursing and, to a lesser degree, science departments commonly do. Faculty in nursing, for example, report frequent cooperative interaction both in team teaching individual courses and in constantly monitoring the real-world success of their students in clinicals and of their graduates on state nursing board examinations. The addition of these very real and externally monitored standards led to intense and focused interaction on teaching. Two nursing faculty members in separate institutions noted that, in their perception, faculty colleagues in other departments who were looking for ways to improve teaching to help their students were struggling with issues nursing departments had dealt with for years.

Limited dimensions of collaboration arose in departments that structured interaction around particular aspects of teaching. In laboratory sciences, for example, faculty report their most significant interactions with colleagues and students took place in laboratory settings. Teaching one on one or with small groups in the laboratory setting seems to many scientists to be the essence of science teaching. Faculty members' collegial teaching interactions likewise are often centered around shared laboratory space and equipment; they interacted less around the teaching of classroom sections of courses. Finally, faculty in English departments on two campuses report intensive interaction focused around departmental grading of final writing assignments from all sections of composition courses. The economics department on a third campus, and an engineering department on a fourth, framed teaching-embedded interactions by using common examinations (or at least common portions) in multiple-section courses.

Significant Brokered Opportunities. In addition to valuing structured interaction around teaching, faculty report significant benefits from opportunities to venture outside of the classroom for a time for renewal. The traditional faculty development practices of periodic sabbaticals and support for travel to scholarly or professional meetings are highly valued by faculty members. For some faculty members, spending a sabbatical semester or year in scholarship or research is literally revitalizing. For others, participation in a fellowship program that takes them off campus to interact around teaching issues with other scholars in their discipline is remembered as a significant turning point in their career. Such opportunities were particularly significant for those few faculty who were isolated as lone specialists or lone members of a discipline on their campuses (though these were not the only faculty who benefited from them). Still others noted that time spent at their own institution outside the classroom—for example, a stint as department chair or as an acting administrator—provides a break that leaves them eager to return to teaching and energized for the task.

Two points about such brokered opportunities stand out. First, their significance comes from the break in the routine, regardless of whether the professor leaves the campus. Second, faculty members typically avail themselves of these opportunities via the encouragement of their colleagues or administrators. That means that these opportunities can be "missed" in the absence of such second-party intervention. It also means that when the opportunity comes, it is experienced as an outside recognition of ability—an extrinsic reward.

What Can Campuses Do?

In light of the findings above, what can campuses do to support the continuing development of their senior professors as teachers? While no one answer fits all campuses, the patterns that emerged on the diverse group of campuses participating in the study suggest concrete strategies.

Provide a Stimulus-Rich Environment. If there is one general principle to be drawn from the data, it is that even a small faculty will benefit from having a wide variety of options available. Indeed, the two smallest institutions in terms of number of faculty had the widest array of opportunities available, the highest degree of participation in them, and the highest degree of satisfaction with the teaching situation, even among the few who knowingly chose not to participate. Judging from the evidence gathered on the eleven campuses, it appears that variety is important both because it provides a wider range of options for faculty members as individuals (who may find different options valuable at different points in their personal and professional development) and because the options seem to have a multiplier effect. The impact of the whole range of options on a given campus appears to let greater than the sum of the parts.

Provide Opportunities for Collective/Collaborative Teaching. Changes in the structure of teaching that foster collaboration allow individuals to rethink their own teaching practice. Faculty who had experienced team teaching found it to be a revitalizing experience. Austin and Baldwin (1992) report on a range of models that support faculty collaboration around teaching, including inter- and multidisciplinary models. Their discussion underscores the point that opportunities for fostering collective interaction around teaching need not come only in the form of providing for expensive double-staffing of existing courses. Several models in which faculty teams teach multiple courses might be considered. Other institutional efforts might also present opportunities. For example, campuses that are considering changes in freshman core requirements or general education revisions might find in them a valuable opportunity for faculty growth.

The benefits that accrue include development of teaching ability, intellectual stimulation, and closer connection to the campus community (Austin and Baldwin, 1992, p. 41). In addition to benefiting students, creating community around teaching is important for faculty members themselves.

Broker Opportunities for Individuals. As important as collective engagement in teaching is for many faculty members, the individual dimension is also of vital importance. Systematic (not serendipitous) brokering of opportunities to individuals is experienced as an act of valuing the individuals' past contributions and future potential. Encouraging faculty members to apply for fellowships or awards can be a form of validation, a vote of confidence. Whether opportunities are created within the institution or are identified outside it, providing information, encouragement, and whatever support is appropriate can enhance individual vitality.

One illustrative example comes from a community college where the teaching load is heavy. This institution developed a program of "mini-sabbaticals" through which faculty received a one-course reduction in teaching load to carry out a proposed project of research or scholarship, the results of which they presented to their faculty colleagues. Though the award is relatively modest, the payoff to the individuals participating *and to their colleagues who look forward to each semester's presentations* is significant.

Such small-scale awards alone are, of course, not enough, but each additional increment probably adds significantly to the overall perception of an environment that values teaching and teachers. In order for such strategies to succeed, those in the position to broker the opportunities must know their faculty members' individual strengths and interests.

Bring the Departments into the Picture. While departments are the administrative center of teaching on most campuses, they are often not the center of faculty interaction around teaching. The data from this study provide only a few examples of departments that focus faculty energies on teaching. Those faculty members who decline to participate in campus wide, teaching-related, faculty development programs, however, often note that such generic faculty development programs are limited, and that programs related to teaching their chosen discipline would be of greater interest. At least one faculty member, a department chair at a private university, was determined to institute departmental seminars on teaching. Campuses might also look for in-house examples of departments where beneficial collaboration around teaching is already taking place for close-to-home models.

Maintain Institution-wide Faculty Development Programs. These programs are of great benefit to many faculty; they are not the answer for all. Faculty and administrators alike spoke of the limits of generic faculty development. Still, the value of these programs is in providing a forum for faculty from a range of disciplines to share a common focus and to learn from each other. While they do not meet all needs, they can have a significant impact and contribute to some sense of campus wide community.

Epilogue

Thus far, we have focused on the question of how campuses are now, or could better be, supporting their senior faculty's continuing development as teachers. But would faculty on any given campus respond to such support? One result of our conversations with these faculty suggests they would. In addition to asking about their histories as teachers and about the current state of their institutional teaching environments, we asked them to tell us what they would like to see in the "best of all worlds" in regard to teaching. While some of the answers given to the question might strike administrators as predictable and impossible to create—such as reduced course loads, particularly in community colleges, and better-prepared students—many of the answers matched the recommendations above.

Faculty said they want more of what their experiences suggest make for growth and development as teachers. For example, faculty want more intellectually oriented collegial interaction in general, and feel that it will contribute to their development as teachers. Faculty want opportunities to expand their horizons through fellowships, even in small doses such as the minisabbaticals described above, or through interinstitutional exchange, in order to bring new perspectives into the classroom. Faculty, especially those who have experienced team teaching, also want to work collectively again in teaching. Finally, many faculty members would like to see good teaching recognized and rewarded. By focusing attention on brokering opportunities for senior faculty and on creating multiple supports on campus for excellent teaching, institutions can indeed matter for the vitality of their faculty and, ultimately, for the experience of their students.

References

Austin, A., and Baldwin, R. *Faculty Collaboration.* ASHE-ERIC Higher Education Research Report, no. 7. Washington, D.C.: ASHE-ERIC Higher Education Reports, George Washington University, 1992.

Clark, B. R. *Academic Life: Small Worlds, Different Worlds.* Princeton, N.J.: Carnegie Foundation for the Advancement of Teaching, 1987.

Finkelstein, M. J. *Staffing New Jersey's Colleges and Universities of the 21st Century: Faculty Supply and Demand, 1987-2014.* Trenton: New Jersey Department of Higher Education, 1988.

MARK W. LaCELLE-PETERSON is assistant professor of education, State University of New York, Geneseo.

MARTIN J. FINKELSTEIN is director of the New Jersey Institute for Collegiate Teaching and Learning at Seton Hall University, South Orange, New Jersey.

The research reported here was supported by a giant from the Pew Charitable Trusts to the New Jersey Institute for Collegiate Teaching and Learning at Seton Hall University.

INSTITUTIONAL ISSUES

Faculty and Administrator Perceptions of Their Environments:

Different Views or Different Models of Organization?

Marvin W. Peterson and Theodore H. White

Individuals' perceptions of the culture and climate of the organizations in which they work influence their motivation and individual performance. Using a theoretical model of institutional culture, organizational climate, and faculty motivation, this study examines how faculty and academic administrators differ in their perceptions; whether these differences in perceptions are affected by institutional type; and to what extent faculty and administrators have different implicit models of their institutions (i.e., see different organizational variables as predictors of faculty motivation and involvement). The goals of this investigation are to shed additional light on the relationship between institutional variables and faculty performance, to examine the existence of differing implicit models, and to provide new insights for administrators in managing their post secondary institutions.

> Managers who work with each other often use "implicit models" composed of their own somewhat subjective and biased views of the managerial problem. Such implicit models create a great deal of difficulty in resolving differences. . . . Organizational models filter and focus perceptions. They underlie and guide our perceptions about organizations. (Tichy, 1983, pp. 39–40).

Numerous studies of colleges and universities have consistently identified differences between administrator and faculty perceptions of their institutions (White, 1990). Except for the commonly held assumption that colleges and universities should have common purposes (Carson, 1960) and that the faculty and administrator constituencies must work together effectively to achieve those purposes, the implications of these differences are seldom examined and may be substantial. A critical implication is the observation raised by Tichy that different managers (or constituent groups) in an organization may not only have different views, but may have different "implicit (organizational) models" of how their institutions function. In summarizing extensive literature and research on leadership in higher education, Bensimon (1987) emphasized the importance for administrators of recognizing multiple "cognitive frames" or different implicit models of how their institutions functioned:

> Leaders who incorporated elements of several frames are likely to be more flexible in responding to different administrative tasks because they are able to enact different images of the organization and provide different interpretations of events. (p. 4)

This belief suggests that perceptions of different constituent groups may reflect more than just consistent differences and may reflect different "implicit models" of how their institution functions. Thus, if two groups hold very different "cognitive" or implicit models of how their institution functions, they may assume different variables influence key dependent variables. For example, if administrators have a hierarchical, rational model, they may assume that obtaining board approval (authoritative power) and rationally distributing salary increments (financial rewards) may enhance faculty commitment to the enterprise. Faculty, on the other hand, may have a professional collegial model assuming that peer agreement (consensual power) and recognition (professional status) may enhance their commitment. Thus, their disagreements are not just in the relative perceptions of organizational variables but in what variables are most influential in effecting a key variable.

A recent study of the Organizational Context for Teaching and Learning identified consistent differences between faculty and administrator perceptions of organizational variables both within institutions and across three types of institutions. The purposes of this research paper are twofold: to examine the pattern of differences between faculty and administrator perceptions of their institutions as organizations and to investigate the relationships among organizational variables that faculty and administrators perceive in order to determine whether they have, not just differing views, but different "implicit models" of how their institutions function. The focus is on organizational dimensions that examine differences in administrator and faculty perceptions of their institution's academic purpose and institutional culture, its organizational and administrative climate, and the faculty motivational climate for undergraduate education and teaching. The paper addresses the following questions:

1. Do faculty and academic administrators' differing perceptions of their institution's academic purpose and culture, organizational and administrative climate, and faculty motivational climate for undergraduate education reflect a consistent descriptive pattern that suggests a different implicit organizational model?

2. Are these differences in academic administrator and faculty perceptions affected by the type of institution in which they work?

3. To the extent that there are consistent differences, do faculty and administrators have different implicit models of how their institutions function (i.e., do they see different organizational variables as predictors of faculty motivational climate)?

Conflicting Views of the Organizational Context

Numerous studies of organizational phenomena in colleges and universities present differences in faculty and administrative beliefs about and perceptions of their institutions, both within and across institutional types. They are based largely on faculty perspectives (Austin and Gamson, 1983; Bowen and Schuster, 1986; Rice and Austin, 1988); research on what administrators believe about faculty is much less extensive (Blackburn, Pitney, Lawrence, and Trautvetter, 1989).

A few recent studies underscore the differences in faculty and administrator beliefs and perceptions of their organizations. In a study of individual perceptions of organizational goals in higher education, Birnbaum (1987) did a content analysis of the responses of senior administrators and faculty leaders to open-ended interviews on 32 campuses. He concludes that there is great inconsistency toward goals among institutional participants, with respondents in universities and community colleges expressing the least consistency in articulation of the goals of their institutions. In a national sample of college and university presidents and faculty officers, Neumann (1987) found that presidents and faculty officers disagreed on the attributes of good faculty leadership. Blackburn, Lawrence, and Associates (1990), in a representative national survey of faculty and administrators, found consistent differences between faculty and adminis-

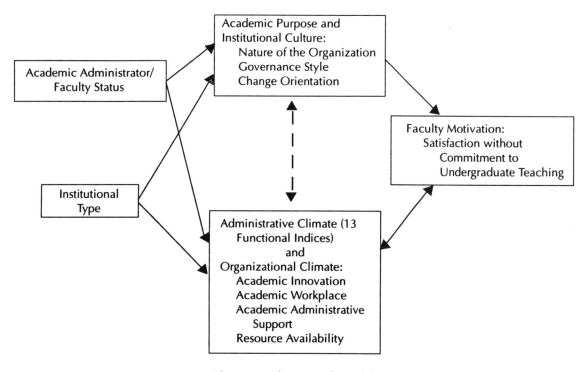

Figure 1. Theoretical model

trator views of the organization on several dimensions, including views of the organizational climate, academic workplace, and administrative supportiveness.

These studies reflect the results of a comprehensive literature review that concludes: (1) that there are faculty and administrator differences on many separate organizational variables, (2) that these differing perspectives occur in all institutional types, (3) that there are differences by institutional type, and (4) that those differences may be counterproductive. The literature is less clear on whether there is a consistent pattern of differing faculty and administrative views across several variables. No study was identified that examined the degree to which faculty and administrators see different patterns of variable interactions that reflect different "implicit models" of organizational functioning.

Conceptual Framework

The conceptual framework for this research focuses on faculty and administrative perceptions of the organizational and administrative environment for undergraduate teaching and learning on their campus. Figure 1 depicts the framework for this study. The model focuses on three broad categories of organizational variables. Faculty Motivation toward undergraduate teaching is seen as the primary dependent variable category. The institution's Academic Purpose and Institutional Culture and its Organizational and Administrative Climate are conceived as the primary intervening variable categories. Since the study is based on individual survey responses and seeks to examine differing patterns, the respondents' Faculty or Administrator Status and the Institutional Type in which they reside are the primary independent or conditioning variables. The implicit assumptions of this model are that the institution's academic purpose and culture and its perceived organizational and administrative climate influence how faculty feel about their work and that this motivational or psychological climate is an effective predictor of faculty performance. (This study did not provide actual measures of faculty teaching performance. Student learning outcomes are, of course, the desirable dependent variable but common measures were not available for inter institutional comparison.)

Culture and Climate: A Distinction

Before discussing the variable categories in the model, a critical distinction in this conceptual framework is between organizational culture and climate. Although culture and climate are often used interchangeably, these concepts have varying definitions. For the purpose of this study, culture is defined as:

> The deeply embedded patterns of organizational behavior and the shared values, assumptions, beliefs, or ideologies that members have about their organization or its work.

Climate is:

> The current, common patterns of important dimensions of organizational life or its members' perceptions of and attitudes toward them.

Several dimensions help highlight the definitional distinction (for a thorough discussion of the distinction see Peterson and Spencer, 1990). Culture represents a *holistic* perspective while climate is focused on more specific phenomena. Culture is more *embedded* and less *malleable*.

Organizational culture focuses on those primary patterns of behavior that reflect deeply embedded values, beliefs, and assumptions that members share about their institutions and that make it *distinctive*. Climate, on the other hand, can focus on common perceptions of many different organizational phenomena (Allaire and Firsirotu, 1984). Further, because measures of climate focus on organizational phenomena, which are more specific and objective than those of culture, the participants' views of the organizational climate are based on more *explicit content* and are more easily discerned. The embedded assumptions shared by members of the organization are based more on the *implicit content* of culture, which is more difficult to identify. Finally, culture may be distinguished from climate by its *continuity* and resistance to change. As ephemeral and transient changes occur in the organization, participants' perceptions of the climate often change. Organizational culture, on the other hand, represents values closely held, less easily forsaken, and thus, it has more continuity over time. Culture has often been compared to the seasons and climate to the daily weather.

In essence, culture represents those aspects of organizational and higher educational life that provide important *meaning* to our life and work in and for the institution whereas climate is more akin to changing conditions around us. For example, an institution's faculty could believe strongly in their institution's and their own commitment to a highly individualized pattern of undergraduate education or close student-faculty community (culture). Yet, they could also have very differing views of the institution's support for this pattern of undergraduate education depending on leadership, resources, and curricular requirements (climate) that changed more often while the cultural belief (meaning) continued.

Individual Variables

Faculty versus administrative status is the key independent or conditioning variable in which this study is interested. The critical nature of this distinction and its relationship to measures of organizational culture, climate, and motivational variables were discussed earlier.

A substantial amount of research exists regarding the relationships between individual variables including age, gender, education, and position on both perceived and psychological climate (Moussavi, Jones, and Cronan, 1990; James and Jones, 1974; Jones and James, 1979). Specific differences in perceptions of psychological climate were found for faculty by gender (Thoreson et al., 1990). Austin and Gamson (1983) found that individual characteristics such as age, stage in career, and gender may predict faculty members' perceptions of the academic workplace and their commitment to undergraduate education. Since age, gender, and degree levels were not found to influence other variables in preliminary analyses for this study, only faculty and administrative status were included as the key status variable.

Institutional Type

Other studies have shown substantial variation on academic purpose, institutional culture, organizational climate, and even teaching-learning performance by institutional type (e.g., Martines, 1985; Cardozier, 1984; Howell and Edison, 1985). Thus, its effects as an independent or conditioning variable must be examined and controlled to understand the influence of faculty and administrator status.

Academic Purpose and Institutional Culture

While higher education studies have shown some differences in institutional purpose and culture by institutional type, most studies of institutional culture study culture for its own sake (Peterson and Spencer, 1990). They attempt to understand its nature, its development, or to gain holistic insight into the institution rather than to treat it as a variable affecting or affected by other variables (e.g., Clark, 1970; Chaffee and Tierney, 1988; Tierney, 1989). Yet it is widely assumed that an institution with a strong culture attracts members and enhances their motivation, which makes it central as a key variable in this study.

While there is a preference in the literature for ethnographic, qualitative studies when examining culture in the work environment, Schein (1985) presents an opposite perspective and differentiates the views of the "ethnographer" from those of the "clinician." He dismisses qualitative results because of the unavoidable bias of the researcher. While the large study that is the source of this paper incorporates qualitative and quantitative methods, this paper considers only the quantitative data on culture.

The higher education literature suggests four major content dimensions of culture that are often used to study participants' beliefs about their institution and that seem to provide a central sense of meaning in a college or university: the institution's Academic Purpose, the nature of its Organization Culture, its Academic Governance Style, and its Organizational Change Orientation.

The Nature of Organizational Culture topology in this study is based on a framework developed by Cameron and Ettington (1988) that uses four elements (dominant characteristics, leadership style, criteria of success, and management style) to examine culture on two primary dimensions: internal-external orientation and emphasis on flexibility-stability. The resulting culture types are "clan or teamwork" (internal/flexible), "hierarchy or formal/rational" (internal/stable), "market" (external/stable), and "adhocracy or innovative" (external/flexible). (See Figure 2.)

The Academic Purpose topology addresses the primary purpose of undergraduate education and is drawn from literature reviews and instruments developed at NCRIPTAL (Peterson et al., 1991). They are: improving society: educating students who contribute productively, emphasizing general or liberal education, clarifying student values, and enhancing student intellectual skills.

The Governance Styles topology is also drawn from a NCRIPTAL literature review and instrument development (Peterson et al., 1986). They are: collegial, rational, political, autonomous, and anarchic.

The Change Orientation topology (Peterson et al., 1978) assesses the dimensions of future versus current orientation of change strategy and internal organization versus external environment locus of control. The resulting topology indicates that institutions respond (current/organization), resist (current/environment), adapt (future/environment), or lead (future/organization). (See Figure 3.)

Organizational and Administrative Climate and Faculty Motivation

These two categories of variables highlight a second critical distinction in this conceptual framework between three constructs of climate (Peterson et al.,1986): the "perceived climate" of the social psychologist, the "psychological or felt climate" of the cognitive psychologist, and the "objective" climate of the organizational behaviorist. (Observed behavior is not a focus of this study.)

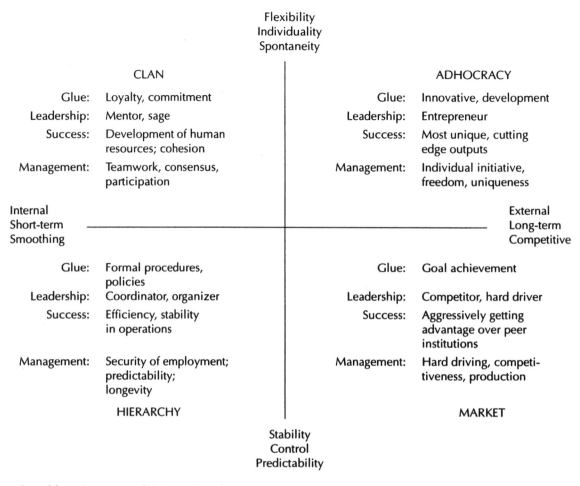

Adapted from Cameron and Ettington (1988).

Figure 2. Cultural models of organizations

The perceived climate reflects members' shared common perception of the "patterns of organizational behavior." It usually focuses on explicit organizational behavior or phenomena. The psychological, or felt, climate is the "shared sense of how members feel about their organizations or their roles in it." This differentiation of the climate concept allows us to measure and to interpret behavior in organizations more accurately.

"Organizational and Administrative Climate" in this framework includes members' perceptions of five types of organizational and administrative behavior related to undergraduate education in their institutions: the institutional emphasis on the Academic Management Policies or Practices in thirteen functional areas, on patterns of Academic Innovativeness, on the challenge of work and professional treatment in the Academic Workplace, on Academic Resource Availability, and on the degree of Academic Administrative Support. All of these factors have been identified in the literature, as related to faculty motivation or performance (Blackburn, Pitney, Lawrence, and Trautvetter, 1989).

"Faculty Motivational Climate," the dependent variable in this framework, is defined as the faculty member's psychological or felt climate. It focuses on measures of Faculty Satisfaction with and Commitment to Undergraduate Education. Respondents were asked to indicate both personal and peer perceptions of these dimensions. The importance of this set of dependent variables is highlighted by Blackburn, Pitney, Lawrence, and Trautvetter's (1989) finding that faculty satisfaction and commitment to teaching are related to improved teaching performance.

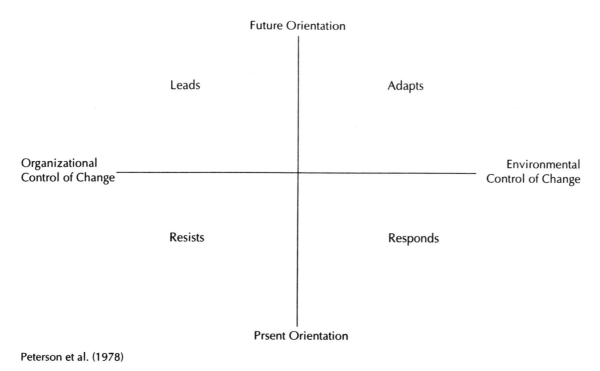

Peterson et al. (1978)

Figure 3. Institutional change orientation

Methodology

Three community colleges, three private liberal arts colleges, and four comprehensive universities participated in a study of the Organizational and Administrative Context for Teaching and Learning conducted at the National Center for Research to Improve Postsecondary Teaching and Learning (NCRIPTAL), the setting for this research. These institutions were selected from a population of 1053 institutions that responded to an earlier national survey of "Academic Management Practices" that was sent to 2300 institutions of postsecondary education with undergraduate programs. The 10 institutions reported a broad array of academic management practices existing on their campuses and an institution-wide effort to improve undergraduate education. The Community Colleges varied in urban-rural location while the Liberal Arts and Comprehensive institutions represented both urban-rural location differences and differing selectivity.

The data used for this paper are from a survey instrument, the *Organizational Climate for Teaching and Learning* (OCTL), developed at NCRIPTAL. The survey included sections measuring the institutional culture, organizational and administrative climate for undergraduate teaching and learning, and faculty motivation. It was used as a means of providing corroborating data for case studies of the ten institutions. The survey was given to all academic administrators and tenure-track faculty with appointments greater than 50 percent at all ten institutions. The overall response rate was 50 percent. A total of 1123 faculty responses and 381 administrator responses were received.

The Organizational Climate Survey instrument consists of 164 items in 9 sections. Institutional culture was measured by four indices of Organizational Culture and 14 discrete items measuring Academic Purpose, Academic Governance Style, and Educational Change. These are based on the conceptual framework from which they were created and not on factor analysis. Factor analysis with varimax rotation was used to identify 20 Organizational and Administrative Climate and 4 Faculty Motivation factors for this analysis. All statistical analyses were conducted using SPSSx. Each item was included in the factor cluster in which it had the highest loading, providing its factor loading was greater than .40 and the item made conceptual sense in the new index. Culture and climate indices were created based on the average value of all items included in the index. The alpha coefficients of reliability for the 24 indices ranged from .65 to .85. These 14 items and 28 indices serve as variables and fall into three broad categories that are the conceptual framework for this study. (See Table 1 for a list of all indices and reliabilities.)

To measure the Academic Purpose and Institutional Culture quantitatively, ipsative measures were used. Respondents distributed 100 points over four or five response items on dimensions measuring Academic Purpose (5 items), Organizational Culture (4 indices) Academic Governance Style (5 items), and Educational Change Orientation (4 items) to indicate the "degree to which the item characterized their institution." We believe they provide a better understanding of the degree to which personal values and beliefs are strongly held than would have been possible with simple Likert-scaled items. The trade-off for better intraindividual discrimination is the set of well-documented problems associated with the statistical analysis of nonindependent measures (e.g., Clemans, 1966; Davis and Chissom, 1981; Johnson, Wood, and Blinkhom, 1988). However, Tamir and Lunetta (1977) found that "When ipsative procedures are preferred on the ground of construct validity . . ., the danger of distorted relationships is not as severe as might have been expected" (p. 92). As noted above, the ipsative data items were assigned to indices for conceptual reasons, not through factor analysis.

To measure Organizational and Administrative Climate, respondents reported their perceptions of the "institution's emphasis on policies, practices or processes supporting undergraduate education" on a 5-point Likert scale of "None" (1) to "Very Strong" (5). Organizational and Administrative Climate indices include measures of Academic Management Climate (13 indices), Academic Innovation (1 index), Academic Workplace (2 indices), Administrative Support (2 indices), and Resource Availability (2 indices).

Finally, to measure the Faculty Motivational Climate, respondents used a 5-point Likert scale to indicate their own and their perception of their peers' "Satisfaction with and Commitment to Undergraduate Education at their institution." Four indices measuring Personal and Faculty Colleague Satisfaction with Undergraduate Education (2 indices) and Personal and Faculty Colleague Commitment to Undergraduate Education (2 indices) emerged. The two measures dealing with "Personal Satisfaction" and "Personal Commitment" are inappropriate for administrators and were not included in this analysis.

Patterns of Differences

Analysis

Analyses of variance was used to determine differences between administrator and faculty status and among institutional types for all respondents on the measures of Academic Purpose and Institutional Culture, Organizational and Administrative Climate, and Faculty Motivational Climate (see Table 2). Additional analyses compared faculty versus administrator status within institutional type: community college, liberal arts, and comprehensive university (see Table 3.)

Results and Discussions

The analysis of variance by faculty and administrator respondent and by institutional type showed no significant differences on Faculty Commitment to Undergraduate Education (See Tables 2 and 3). On the other hand, the variance on Faculty Satisfaction with Undergraduate Teaching was significantly different for faculty and administrators overall and between the community college and comprehensive university respondent group and those in private liberal arts colleges. This suggested that institutional type was an important control variable in predicting the satisfaction variable.

Table 1. Reliabilities of the Purpose, Culture, Climate, and Motivational Indices

Indices	Alphas	(Number of Items)
I. Academic Purpose and institutional Culture		
A. Nature of the Organizational Culture		
1. Teamwork	.67	(4)
2. Innovation	.72	(4)
3. Rational	.75	(4)
4. Market	.72	(4)
B. Academic Purpose		(5)
1. General Improvement of Society*		
2. Contribute Productivity to Society*		
3. General/Liberal Educations*		
4. Individual Values Clarifications*		
5. Enhance Individual Thinking Skills*		
C. Academic Governance Style		(5)
1. Collegial*		
2. Formal/Rational*		
3. Autonomous/Loosely Coordinated*		
4. Anarchist*		
5. Political		
D. Educational Change Orientation		(4)
My institution		
1. Leads*		
2. Adapts*		
3. Responds*		
4. Resists*		
II. Organizational and Administrative Climate		
E. Academic Management Climate		
1. Educational Mission and Goals	.79	(8)
2. Academic Planning	.79	(5)
3. Governance	.83	(5)
4. Resource Allocation	.83	(5)
5. Communication/Information	.79	(6)
6. Student Recruitment and Enrollment Mgt	.68	(4)
7. Academic, Curricular, and Program Mgt	.79	(5)
8. Educational Technology	.76	(3)
9. Faculty and Instructional Development	.80	(3)
10. Faculty Selection, Evaluation, and Reward	.83	(5)
11. Student Academic Support Services	.75	(4)
12. Student Entry Assessment	.82	(2)
13. Student Outcomes Assessment	.81	(4)
F. Academic Innovation		
1. Academic Innovation	.82	(5)
G. Academic Workplace		
1. Challenge of Academic Work	.83	(3)
2. Professionalism in the Academic Setting	.80	(6)
H. Administrative Support		
1. Academic Administration	.71	(5)
2. Student Affairs	.82	(4)
I. Resource Availability		
1. Educational Resources	.78	(8)
2. Institutional Facilities	.67	(3)

III. Faculty Motivational Climate

J.	Satisfaction with Undergraduate Education and Teaching		
	1. Peer Satisfaction with Teaching	.78	(3)
	2. Personal Satisfaction with Teaching	.85	(4)
K.	Commitment to Undergraduate Education		
	1. Peer Commitment and Motivation	.65	(3)
	2. Personal Commitment and Motivation	.72	(4)

*Single-item variables.

For a complete definition of all indices and a copy of the OCTL survey instrument, see: M. Peterson et al., *Assessing the Organizational and Administrative Context for Teaching and Learning.* Ann Arbor, MI: NCRIPTAL, 1991.

The Effects of Institutional Type

The analysis of variance by institutional type for all respondents revealed great diversity in the perceptions of community college, liberal arts college, and comprehensive university respondents on the Academic Purpose and Institutional Culture, Organizational and Administrative Climate, and Faculty Motivation indices (see Table 2). Significant differences at the .05 level occurred on 34 of the 40 indices. Such differences indicate that institutional type may confound the results of other analyses. However, the results of a two-way analysis of variance of institutional type and faculty or administrator status on all indices showed that only four variables displayed significant interaction effects: Teamwork as the Nature of the Organization, Collegial Governance, Student Entry Assessment, and Institutional Facilities. Thus, any confounding effects of institutional type should be minimal. While these differences can lead to interesting insights about differences in implicit organizational models by institutional type, the small sample of institutions makes any analysis speculative.

Faculty and Administrator Differences

The analysis of the variance between all faculty and administrator respondents showed significant differences at the .05 level on 28 of the 40 indices in this study (see Table 2). More agreement occurred on the Institutional Culture indices than on the Organizational and Administrative Climate indices. Faculty and administrators differed on only 7 of 18 indices of Academic Purpose and Institutional Culture but on all 20 of the Organizational and Administrative Climate indices. A statistically significant difference occurred on one Motivational Climate Index, but the actual differences were small.

In the Academic Purpose and Institutional Culture indices, administrators, as opposed to faculty, see greater emphasis on values clarification as an educational purpose, governance as more collegial (and less anarchic), and their institutions as leading (not responding), more innovative, and less rational. Among the Organizational and Administrative Climate indices, administrators see their institutions placing greater emphasis on all areas: academic management practices, support for academic innovation, having a challenging and professional work setting, having supportive administrators, and having more available educational resources and facilities. Interestingly, while administrators in these ten institutions see levels of Faculty Commitment to and Satisfaction with Undergraduate Education as high (as do faculty), they seem to have a much more positive or idealized view of their institutions as being more value oriented and collegial as well as more innovative than do faculty.

A clearer pattern emerges when we analyze faculty and administrator differences by institutional type (see Table 3). Community college faculty and administrators disagreed on 28 of the 40 indices used in the study and comprehensive university faculty and administrators disagreed on 26 of the 40 indices. Liberal arts participants, on the other hand, perceived differences on only 7 of those same measures. Community college faculty and administrators disagreed on 9 of 18 measures of Academic Purpose and Organizational Culture and on 18 of 20 measures of the

Table 2. One-Way ANOVA of Purpose, Culture, Climate, and Motivational Indices (Faculty vs. Administrator and by Institutional Type for all Respondents)

	Overall	Faculty	Admin	ComCol	LibArts	CompreUniv
I. Academic Purpose and Institutional Culture						
Nature of the Organization						
Index 1 Culture: Teamwork	28.53	28.47	28.95	25.70	29.93	29.51**
Index 2 Culture: Innovation	21.71	20.40	25.50**	25.97	14.76	21.9**
Index 3 Culture: Rational	30.38	31.49	27.15**	33.26	33.33	27.84**
Index 4 Culture: Market	18.78	18.94	18.32	14.27	20.95	20.45**
Academic Purpose						
Item 1 Purpose: General improvement of society	13.50	13.48	13.56	11.08	16.88	13.57**
Item 2 Purpose: Contribute productivity to society	38.02	38.81	35.72	54.88	23.12	34.42**
Item 3 Purpose: General/Liberal education	13.21	13.06	13.65	6.91	16.95	15.20**
Item 4 Purpose: Individual values clarification	16.02	15.34	17.99**	10.60	22.10	16.72**
Item 5 Purpose: Enhance indiv. critical thinking	18.80	18.71	19.06	15.79	20.01	19.96**
Academic Governance						
Item 1 Collegial	28.03	26.86	31.42**	26.67	31.50	27.52*
Item 2 Formal/Rational	22.07	21.87	22.67	20.55	23.74	22.27
Item 3 Autonomous/Loosely coupled	15.33	15.39	15.15	17.88	12.33	16.18**
Item 4 Anarchic	8.55	9.15	6.83*	19.64	6.88	8.11**
Item 5 Political	25.62	26.28	23.71	26.25	24.55	25.69
Academic Change Orientation						
Item 1 Leads	31.87	30.20	36.76**	38.64	26.19	30.33**
Item 2 Adapts	33.98	34.38	32.80	31.86	32.96	35.43*
Item 4 Resists	7.63	7.87	6.93	8.41	10.59	6.17**
II. Organizational and Administrative Climate						
Academic Innovation						
Index 1 Academic Innovation	33.33	3.30	3.42*	3.52	3.05	3.33*
Academic Workplace						
Index 1 Challenge of Academic Work	3.34	3.29	3.50**	3.27	3.33	3.34
Index 2 Professionalism in the Academic	3.41	3.34	3.60**	3.43	3.38	3.40
Workplace						
Academic Management Climate						
Index 1 Educational Mission and Goals	3.73	3.69	3.84**	3.64	3.69	3.79**
Index 2 Academic Planning	3.41	3.38	3.51**	3.43	3.20	3.48**
Index 3 Governance	3.01	2.94	3.20**	2.98	3.01	3.02
Index 4 Resource Allocation	3.06	2.99	3.24**	3.03	3.13	3.04

Table 2 (Continued)

	Overall	Faculty	Admin	ComCol	LibArts	CompreUniv
Index 5 Communication/Information	2.98	2.93	3.12**	2.91	2.96	3.02**
Index 6 Student Recruitment and Enrollment Mgt	3.74	3.69	3.88**	3.59	3.80	3.79**
Index 7 Academic and Curricular Mgt	3.08	3.04	3.22**	3.06	2.88	3.17**
Index 8 Educational Technology	3.30	3.24	3.49**	3.53	3.18	3.23**
Index 9 Faculty and Instructional Development	3.20	3.12	3.44**	3.03	3.43	3.20**
Index 10 Faculty Selection, Evaluation, and Reward	3.21	3.13	3.46**	2.80	3.45	3.33**
Index 11 Student Academic Support Services	3.33	3.29	3.43**	3.22	3.16	3.45**
Index 12 Student Entry Assessment	3.55	3.50	3.69**	3.94	2.92	3.53**
Index 13 Student Outcomes Assessment	3.20	3.13	3.37**	3.13	2.96	3.33**
Academic Administrative Support						
Index 1 Institutional Academic Administrative Support	3.85	3.77	4.06**	3.73	3.93	3.88**
Index 2 Student Academic Administrative Support	3.13	3.03	3.38**	2.97	3.29	3.17**
Resource Availability						
Index 1 Educational Resources	3.22	3.14	3.45**	3.23	3.28	3.19
Index 2 Institutional Facilities	3.17	3.13	3.28**	3.81	3.67	2.92**
III. Faculty Motivational Climate						
Index 1 Peer Commitment	3.75	3.73	3.81	3.73	3.90	3.71*
Index 2 Personal Commitment	N/A	3.92	N/A	N/A	N/A	N/A
Number of Respondents						
Total	1522	1123	381	438	291	793
Male/Female	N/A	723/382	264/116	N/A	N/A	N/A
Tenured/Nontenured	N/A	761/303	N/A	N/A	N/A	N/A

Significant Levels:
* < .05
** < .01

Table 3. One Way ANOVA of Purpose, Culture, Climate, and Motivational Indices (Faculty vs. Administrator for Each Institutional Type)

	Community Colleges				Liberal Arts Colleges				Compre. Universities			
	Means				Means				Means			
	FAC	ADM	F Ratio	Prob.	FAC	ADM	F Ratio	Prob.	FAC	ADM	F Ratio	Prob.
I. Academic Purpose and Institutional Culture												
Nature of the Organization												
Index 1 Culture: Teamwork	25.04	28.00	5.37	.02*	31.91	24.91	7.44	.01**	29.10	30.98	4.32	.04*
Index 1 Culture: Teamwork	25.04	28.00	5.37	.02*	31.94	24.91	7.44	.01**	29.10	30.98	4.32	.04*
Index 2 Culture: Innovation	24.30	31.25	14.36	.00**	14.24	16.01	.28	.59	20.48	26.08	15.92	.00**
Index 3 Culture: Rational	35.55	25.99	11.26	.00**	33.43	33.98	.01	.94	28.66	25.27	1.27	.26
Index 4 Culture: Market	14.04	14.81	1.17	.28	19.15	24.72	8.56	.00**	21.47	17.66	6.20	.01*
Academic Purpose												
Item 1 Purpose: General improvement of society	11.05	13.29	.01	.92	16.98	16.60	.04	.85	13.55	13.64	.01	.93
Item 2 Purpose: Contribute productivity to society	55.89	51.81	2.16	.14	22.79	24.03	.19	.66	35.32	31.79	3.78	.05
Item 3 Purpose: General/Liberal education	6.76	7.37	.33	.57	16.73	17.57	.24	.63	15.12	15.41	.09	.77
Item 4 Purpose: Enhance indiv. critical thinking	15.60	16.37	.30	.58	19.84	20.49	.12	.73	19.98	19.91	.00	.95
Academic Governance												
Item 1 Collegial	24.04	34.45	14.78	.00**	31.79	30.69	.12	.73	26.60	30.18	3.55	.06
Item 2 Formal/Rational	20.28	21.36	.21	.65	21.86	29.10	8.02	.01**	22.71	20.98	1.11	.29
Item 3 Autonomous/Loosely coupled	15.60	16.23	.10	.76	13.73	8.33	6.26	.02*	15.87	17.09	.69	.41
Item 4 Anarchic	11.83	6.65	5.41	.02*	7.27	5.76	.55	.46	8.40	7.29	.83	.36
Item 5 Political	27.82	21.42	4.62	.03*	24.15	25.69	.26	.61	26.22	24.15	.97	.33
Academic Change Orientation												
Item 1 Leads	35.65	44.61	6.02	.01*	25.12	29.33	1.77	.18	28.58	35.45	8.80	.00**
Item 2 Adapts	21.19	30.88	.26	.61	34.24	29.17	2.90	.09	23.74	20.73	.11	.74
Item 3 Responds	21.88	16.64	5.02	.03*	30.50	28.81	.24	.62	29.11	24.16	6.29	.01*
Item 4 Resists	8.88	6.99	.70	.40	9.78	12.97	1.75	.19	6.66	4.72	2.99	.08
II. Organizational and Administrative Climate												
Academic Innovation												
Index 1 Academic Innovation	3.47	3.68	5.03	.03*	3.05	3.08	.17	.68	3.31	3.42	3.26	.07
Academic Workplace												
Index 1 Challenge of Academic Work	3.19	3.53	10.43	.00**	3.35	3.30	.12	.72	3.32	3.55	9.48	.00**
Index 2 Professionalism in the Academic Workplace	3.35	3.66	10.33	.00**	3.33	3.52	.13	.71	3.34	3.60	10.01	.00**
Academic Management Climate												
Index 1 Educational Mission and Goals	3.59	3.78	5.67	.02*	3.68	3.72	.29	.59	3.75	3.92	11.03	.00**
Index 2 Academic Planning	3.37	3.61	6.49	.01*	3.20	3.18	.00	.95	3.44	3.58	4.69	.03*
Index 3 Governance	2.87	3.30	23.25	.00**	2.96	3.16	3.65	.06	2.98	3.16	8.29	.00**
Index 4 Resource Allocation	2.93	3.35	18.33	.00**	3.10	3.24	1.67	.20	2.99	3.18	7.94	.01**
Index 5 Communication/Information	2.87	3.04	3.75	.05	2.94	3.03	.69	.41	2.96	3.21	14.82	.00**
Index 6 Student Recruitment and Enrollment Mgt	3.51	3.82	14.67	.00**	3.80	3.78	.00	.98	3.74	3.95	15.22	.00**

Table 3 (Continued)

	Community Colleges Means				Liberal Arts Colleges Means				Compre. Universities Means			
	FAC	ADM	F Ratio	Prob.	FAC	ADM	F Ratio	Prob.	FAC	ADM	F Ratio	Prob.
Index 7 Academic and Curricular Mgt	3.00	3.22	6.24	.01*	2.83	3.06	5.37	.02*	3.13	3.29	6.60	.01**
Index 8 Educational Technology	3.46	3.73	7.27	.01**	3.15	3.28	1.17	.28	3.15	3.44	13.56	.00**
Index 9 Faculty and Instructional Development	3.92	3.36	17.19	.00**	3.37	3.61	3.98	.05*	3.13	3.42	15.78	.00**
Index 10 Faculty Selection, Evaluation, and Reward	2.71	3.09	12.82	.00**	3.43	3.49	.23	.63	3.24	3.63	32.56	.00**
Index 11 Student Academic Support Services	3.21	3.27	.38	.54	3.11	3.27	2.08	.15	3.41	3.58	7.91	.01**
Index 12 Student Entry Assessment	3.84	4.26	14.09	.00**	2.93	2.97	1.07	.30	3.48	3.67	5.22	.02*
Index 13 Student Outcomes Assessment	3.04	3.37	10.74	.00**	2.93	3.04	1.01	.32	3.26	3.49	11.49	.0088
Academic Administrative Support												
Index 1 Institutional Academic Administrative Support	3.64	3.99	13.86	.00**	3.92	3.99	.40	.53	3.79	4.12	27.23	.00**
Index 2 Student Academic Administrative Support	2.89	3.20	7.85	.01**	3.18	3.56	9.93	.00**	3.06	3.42	18.29	.00**
Resource Availability												
Index 1 Educational Resources	3.12	3.57	35.33	.00**	3.25	3.39	3.58	.06	3.12	3.41	29.18	.00**
Index 2 Institutional Facilities	3.42	3.77	12.41	.00**	3.38	3.32	.37	.54	2.89	3.02	4.23	.04*
III. Faculty Motivational Climate												
Index 1 Peer Commitment	3.72	3.74	.09	.76	3.90	3.91	.03	.87	3.68	3.81	2.45	.12
Index 2 Personal Commitment												
Index 3 Peer Satisfaction	3.68	3.90	6.73	.01**	3.74	3.76	.06	.08	3.60	3.80	12.13	.00**
Index 4 Personal Satisfaction												
Number of Respondents	323	115			214	77			589	204		

Significance Levels:
    * < .05
    ** < .01

Table 4. Academic Purpose, Institutional Culture, and Organizational Climate 3 as Predictors of Faculty Commitment to Improve Undergraduate Education (Regressions by Respondent Group)*

Faculty		Administrators
$R_\wedge 2$	Institutional Culture	$R_\wedge 2$
.007	Purpose: Contribute productivity to society	
	Purpose: Enhance individual critical thinking skills	.010
.044	Governance: Collegial	
	Governance: Political	.013
.101	Change Orientation: Leads	.129
.013	Culture: Teamwork	
	Culture: Rational	.020
.166	Total	.178
	Organizational Climate	
	Challenge of Academic Work	.031
.297	Institutional Academic Administrative Support	.299
.057	Educational Resources	
.013	Educational Mission and Goals	
.007	Faculty and Instructional Development	
	Faculty Selection, Evaluation, and Reward	0.67
.373	Total	.397
	Culture & Climate	
	Challenge of Academic Work	.031
.297	Institutional Academic Administrative Support	.299
.057	Educational Resources	
.013	Educational Mission and Goals	
.007	Faculty and Instructional Development	
	Faculty Selection, Evaluation, and Reward	.067
.373	Total	.397

*Based on step wise regressions. Variable's contribution to $R_\wedge 2$ shown only for those at the .05 level.

Organizational and Administrative Climate. Comprehensive university faculty and administrators' perceptions disagreed less frequently on Academic Purpose and Organizational Culture indices (6/18) than on the Organizational and Administrative Climate indices (19/20).

In other words, community college faculty and administrators disagreed more than those in the other two institutional types both on Academic Purpose and Institutional Culture, and on Organizational and Administrative Climate dimensions. At the liberal arts colleges, faculty and administrators in the study are largely in agreement on both. Faculty and administrators at comprehensive universities differ to some degree on Academic Purpose and Institutional Culture but disagree on all Organizational and Administrative Climate measures.

The direction of faculty and administrator responses reflects that for all respondents, perceptions vary by institutional types. In the liberal arts colleges, there is strong agreement on the purposes, culture, and climate patterns. Community college administrators saw their institutions as more concerned about values (still low) and perceive governance as collegial in an entrepreneurial and innovative setting, while their faculties were more likely to view governance as a political process in a more formal-rational organization. Comprehensive university administrators viewed their institutions as having a concern for values education and as leaders in undergraduate education in a more innovative teamwork-oriented institution faculty see their institution as a responsive market-driven place. Community college and comprehensive university faculty both exhibit lower means than their administrative colleagues on all the Organizational and Administrative Climate indices.

The highest agreement on Academic Purpose and Institutional Culture occurs in the liberal arts institutions, less occurs in the comprehensive, and the least agreement occurs in the community colleges. This supports the argument that commonality of purpose and strength of institutional culture is most likely in the liberal arts colleges, and least clear in the community college or larger public institutions. The degree of faculty and administrator consensus on the varied dimensions of climate in the Liberal Arts and the sizable differences in both the Community Colleges and Comprehensive Universities may suggest either the importance of culture in supporting cohesive climate or the effect of institutional differences.

Predicting Motivational Climate: Implicit Models

Analysis

To go beyond the descriptive differences in the way they viewed their institutions and to investigate whether faculty and administrators held different implicit organizational models (i.e., saw different variables associated with the dependent variables), a series of regressions was run. Because of the strong influence of institutional type (Table 2), dummy-coded institutional-type variables were used to partial out the influence of institutional type.

Using only faculty response data, each of the two dependent variables (Faculty Commitment to and Faculty Satisfaction with Undergraduate Teaching) were regressed separately against each of the two categories of independent variables (Academic Purpose and Institutional Culture, and Administrative and Organizational Climate). Separate regressions were run because of limitations in the sample size. Then the dependent variables were regressed once more, in a step wise regression, against all the indices (Institutional Type, Academic Purpose and Institutional Culture, and Organizational and Administrative Climate) that were statistically significant predictors in the previous regressions. The whole sequence was repeated using the administrator data. Table 4 displays the results of the separate regressions for faculty and for administrative respondents predicting Faculty Commitment. Table 5 displays the same information for Faculty Satisfaction. Only the indices that made statistically significant contributions (.05 level) to explaining the variance (R^2) are shown.

Results and Discussion

The previous analysis of patterns of differences in faculty and administrator perceptions of the academic purposes, organizational culture, and organizational and motivational climate of their institutions suggests that faculty and administrators may see different "implicit descriptive models." However, it does not make clear whether they have different "implicit causal models" of how the institution actually functions. If faculty and administrators have different mental models of how their institutions function, then one would expect different organizational variables to predict the Motivational Climate (dependent) variables in this study. The regression analysis examined these dynamics.

Commitment

The regression of the Academic Purpose and Institutional Culture indices against the Faculty Commitment to Undergraduate Education (Table 4) accounted for only 17 percent of the variance for faculty and 18 percent of the variance for administrators. The primary contributing variables for both respondent groups was Academic Change Orientation (Institution is a "leader"), which explained 10 percent of the variance in the faculty model and 13 percent in the administrator model.

The regression of Faculty Commitment against the Organizational and Administrative Climate indices accounted for 37 percent of the variance for faculty and 40 percent for administrators. In both sets of results, emphasis on Institutional Academic Administrative Support (i.e., "support for improving undergraduate education" by board members, the president, the execu-

Table 5. Academic Purpose, Institutional Culture, and Organizational Climate as Predictors of Faculty Satisfaction with Undergraduate Education (Regressions by Respondent Group)*

(Regressions by Respondent Group)*

Faculty		Administrators
$R_\wedge 2$	Institutional Culture	$R_\wedge 2$
.005	Purpose: Contribute productivity to society	
.014	Governance: Collegial	
	Governance: Political	.052
.101	Change Orientation: Leads	.149
.033 (–)	Change Orientation: Resists	
.145	Culture: Teamwork	
	Culture: Rational	.030
.298	Total	.231
	Organizational Climate	
	Professionalism in the Academic Workplace	.241
.030	Institutional Academic Administrative Support	.030
.013	Educational Resources	
.285	Educational Mission and Goals	.011
	Academic Decision Making	.059
.068	Faculty and Instructional Development	
.397	Total	.340
	Culture & Climate	
.003	Governance: Collegial	
.006	Change Orientation: Leads	
.004	Change Orientation: Resists	
.022	Culture: Teamwork	
	Culture: Rational	.019
	Professionalism in the Academic Workplace	.241
.030	Institutional Academic Administrative Support	.030
.015	Institutional Resources	
.285	Educational Mission and Goals	
	Academic Decision Making	.059
.068	Faculty and Instructional Development	
.433	Total	.348

*Based on step wise regressions. Variable's contribution to $R_\wedge 2$ shown only for those at the .05 level.

tive officers, deans, and department chairs) was the major contributing variable, predicting 30 percent of the variance in both respondent models. The second variable of consequence is emphasis on the availability of Educational Resources (for Teaching) in the faculty model (6% of variance in R^2) and on Faculty Selection, Evaluation, and Reward (7% of variance in R^2) in the administrative model. Each makes a very small contribution, however.

In the combined regression, the influence of the larger climate predictors superseded the influence of the culture indices. These results are the same for both respondent groups, which suggests that faculty and administrators have a similar "implicit" organizational model of how the institution functions. The notion is a "top down" model in which emphasis on "institutional academic administrative support" seems to reinforce "faculty commitment to undergraduate education." This is consistent with an institution whose members see it as a "leader" in undergraduate education. In a very minor way, faculty see the "availability of educational resources" as reinforcing their commitment while administrators see manipulation of "faculty selection, evaluation, and rewards for teaching" as reinforcing faculty commitment.

Satisfaction

The regression of Faculty Satisfaction with Undergraduate Education on the Academic Purpose and Institutional Culture indices yielded somewhat different predictors for faculty than for administrators (Table 5). The faculty model accounts for 30 percent of the variance and sees an organizational culture emphasizing "teamwork" (15% of the variance) and an institutional change orientation emphasizing "leadership" in undergraduate education (10% of the variance) as the key dynamics influencing faculty satisfaction. The administrative model accounts for only 23 percent of the variance with an institutional "leadership" orientation as the major contributor (15% of the variance) and with "political" governance style in a "rational" organization as minor influences.

The results of the regression of Faculty Satisfaction with Undergraduate Education on the Organizational and Administrative Climate indices suggest further distinctions between faculty and administrators (Table 5). The faculty model accounts for 40 percent of the variance and sees an emphasis on "educational mission and goals" stressing undergraduate education as the primary variable (29% of the variance) influencing Faculty Satisfaction with some contribution from an emphasis on "faculty and instructional development" (7% of the variance). The administrative model accounts for 34 percent of the variance but sees an emphasis on "professionalism in the academic workplace" (24% of the variance) as the key contributing variable followed by an emphasis on "academic decision making" (6% of the variance).

As with the prediction of Faculty Commitment, in the combined model predicting Faculty Satisfaction, the influence of the climate predictors supersedes that of the purpose and culture indices (Table 5). The faculty model now accounts for 43 percent of the variance, with emphases on "educational mission and goals" stressing undergraduate education (35% of the variance) and "faculty and instructional development" (7% of the variance) as the primary predictors. The administrative model remains essentially unchanged stressing "professionalism in the workplace" (24% of the variance) with an emphasis on "academic decision making" (6% of the variance).

The patterns in these regressions do suggest slightly different "implicit causal models" of the organizational dynamics affecting Faculty Satisfaction with Undergraduate Education. For faculty, an institution with a cultural belief that it employs "teamwork" in a climate that emphasizes "educational mission and goals" stressing undergraduate education (that is, one that appears to be consistent with a cohesive collegial model), appears to be one model that is related to Faculty Satisfaction. Administrators also have a model stressing a "leadership" role or culture but one in which a climate of "professionalism in the academic workplace" is the primary predictor of Faculty Satisfaction. There is seemingly less emphasis on teamwork and "educational mission and goals" for undergraduate education, and more reliance on a professional model of organization.

Conclusions

This paper began with three questions regarding differences in faculty and administrator perceptions of their academic organizational context. The results lead us to conclude that faculty and administrators do seem to differ consistently in their perceptions of Academic Purposes and Institutional Culture, of the Organizational and Administrative Climate, and of the Faculty Motivational Climate for undergraduate education. Administrators appear to reflect a more idealized view. They place more stress on values as the primary educational purpose, view the nature of the organization as slightly more entrepreneurial, see a more supportive organizational and administrative climate, and have a more favorable view of faculty motivation.

Regarding institutional type, faculty and administrator differences were more pronounced in the community colleges and the comprehensive universities than in the liberal arts colleges. Culture and climate were more distinctive, easier to identify, and more cohesive in the liberal arts colleges. In this small sample, institutional type was a slightly larger predictor of differences than faculty versus administrator status but did not eliminate the effects of role.

Finally, the regression analysis of faculty and administrative respondents on "faculty commitment to undergraduate education" suggested similar "implicit models." A similar analysis of "faculty satisfaction with undergraduate education" suggests slightly divergent "implicit models."

Implications for Future Research

Clearly the institutional sample size is too small for extensive generalizations about faculty and administrative differences, the implications of institutional type, and the existence of different models of organization. However, the significant contrasts in faculty and administrative perceptions in a consistent direction points to the need to examine the impact of such differences on other institutional variables. In addition, the variation in those patterns of difference by institutional type suggests the need for further study of these differences in perceptions of organizational culture and climate in a larger sample of institutions. Finally, the descriptive and relational evidence of possible different "implicit models" of organization among faculty and administrative constituents suggests a fruitful line of conceptual as well as practical research. Further, exploration of different "implicit models" by incumbents of more specific roles (e.g., student affairs and academic administrators, faculty in different fields, etc.) and by participants in different institutional types is needed.

References

Allaire, Yuan, and Firsiruto, Mihaela E. (1984). Is "organizational culture" culture bound? *Human Resource Management* 25: 72–90.

Austin, Ann E., and Gamson, Zelda F. (1983). *Academic Workplace: New Demands, Heightened Tensions.* ASHE-ERIC Higher Education Research Report No. 10. Washington, DC: Association for the Study of Higher Education.

Bensimon, Estella M. (1987, November). The meaning of "good presidential leadership": A Frame analysis. Paper presented at the annual meeting of the Association for the Study of Higher Education, Baltimore.

Birnbaum, Robert (1987, November). Individual preferences and organizational goals. Consistency and diversity in the futures desired by campus leaders. Paper presented at the annual meeting of the Association for the Study of Higher Education, Baltimore.

Blackburn, Robert T., Lawrence, Janet, and Associates (1990). *Same Institution, Different Perceptions: Faculty and Administrators Report on the Work Environment.* Publication of the National Center for Research to Improve Postsecondary Teaching and Learning. Ann Arbor, MI: The University of Michigan.

Blackburn, Robert T., Pitney, Judith A., Lawrence, Janet H., and Trautvetter, Lois. (1989, March) Administrators' career backgrounds and their congruence with faculty beliefs and behaviors. Paper presented at the annual meeting of the American Educational Research Association, San Francisco.

Bowen, Howard R., and Schuster, Jack H. (1986). *American Processors: A National Resource Imperiled.* New York: Oxford University Press.

Cameron, Kim S., and Ettington, Deborah R. (1988). The conceptual framework of organizational culture. In John C. Smart (ed.), *Higher Education: Handbook of Theory and Research,* vol. 6, pp. 356–396. New York: Agathon Press.

Cardozier, V. R. (1984). Upper-level colleges yesterday, today, and tomorrow. *Educational Record* 65(3): 30–35.

Chaffee, Ellen E., and Tierney, William G. (1988). *Collegiate Culture and Leadership Strategies.* New York: American Council on Education and Macmillan Publishing Co.

Clark, Burton, R. (1970). *The Distinctive College: Antioch, Reed, and Swarthmore.* Chicago: Aldine Publishing Co.

Clemans, William V. (1966). *An Analytical and Empirical Examination of Some Properties of Ipsative Measure.* Psychometric Monograph, Number 14. Richmond, VA: The William Byrd Press, Inc.

Carson, John J. (1960). *Governance of Colleges and Universities.* New York: McGraw-Hill .

Davis, Todd M., and Chissom, Brad. (1981, October). Factor analysis (*R*-technique) of ipsatized data may be misleading. *Psychological Reports* 49(2): 643–647.

Howell, Joe A., and Edison, Donald R. (1985). *The Idea of an Ideal Liberal Arts College.* Lanham, MD: University Press of America.

James, L. R., and Jones, A. P. (1974) Organizational climate: A review of theory and research. *Psychological Bulletin* 81: 1096–1112.

Johnson, Charles E., Wood, Robert, and Blinkhorn, S. F. (1988, June). Spuriouser and spuriouser: The use of ipsative personality tests. *Journal of Occupational Psychology* 62(2): 153–162.

Jones, A. P., and James, L. R. (1979). Psychological climate: Dimensions and relationships of individual and aggregated work environment perceptions. *Organizational Behavior and Performance* 23:201–250.

Marines, Lauro (1985, Spring). Large and little school teaching: Reed College and UCLA. *American Scholar* 54:194–203.

Moussavi, Farzad, Jones, Thomas W., and Cronan, Timothy P. (1990, April). Explaining psychological climate: Is perceptual agreement necessary? *Journal of Social Psychology* 130: 239–248.

Neumann, Anna (1987, November). Defying "good faculty leadership": Interpretations of professors and presidents. Paper presented at the annual meeting of the Association for the Study of Higher Education, Baltimore.

Peterson, Marvin W., and Spencer, Melinda G. (1990). Assessing academic culture and climate. In William G. Tierney (ed.), *Assessing Organizational Climate and Culture* (New Directions in Institutional Research, No. 68), pp. 3–18. San Francisco: Jossey-Bass.

Peterson, Marvin, W., Blackburn, Robert, Gamson, Zelda F., et al. (1978). *Black Students on White Campuses: The Impacts of Increased Black Enrollments.* Ann Arbor, MI: Institute for Social Research.

Peterson, Marvin W., Cameron, Kim S., Mets, Lisa A., Jones, Phillip, and Ettington, Deborah R. (1986). *The Organizational Context for Teaching and Learning: A Review of the Research Literature.* Publication of the National Center for Research to Improve Postsecondary Teaching and Learning. Ann Arbor, Ml: The University of Michigan.

Peterson, M. W., Cameron, K. S., Knapp, A., Spencer, M. G., and White, T. H. (1991). *Assessing the Organizational Context for Teaching and Learning: An Institutional Self-Study Manual.* The University of Michigan, Ann Arbor, MI: NCRIPTAL.

Rice, Eugene, and Austin, Ann E. (1988, March-April). High faculty morale: What exemplary colleges do right. *Change 20*: 50–58.

Schein, Edgar H. (1985). *Organizational Culture and Leadership: A Dynamic View.* San Francisco: Jossey-Bass.

Tamir, Pinchas, and Lunetta, Vincent N. (1977, November-December). A comparison of ipsative and normative procedures in the study of cognitive preferences. *Journal of Educational Research* 71(2): 86–93.

Thoreson, Richard W., Kardash, Carol Anne M., Leuthold, David A., and Morrow, Kelly A. (1990). Gender differences in the academic career. *Research in Higher Education 31*(2): 193–209.

Tichy, Noel (1983). *Managing Strategic Change: Technical, Political, and Cultural Dynamics.* New York: Wiley.

Tierney, William G. (1989). *Curricular Landscapes, Democratic Vistas: Transformative Leadership in Higher Education.* New York: Praeger.

White, Theodore H. (1990). Differences in faculty and administrator perceptions of their institutions: Implications for institutional performance. Unpublished doctoral preliminary examination. Ann Arbor, MI: University of Michigan.

Marvin W. Peterson and Theodore H. White, University of Michigan, 2117 School of Education, 610 East University, Ann Arbor, MI 48109.

The research reported in this paper is part of the Research Program on The Organizational Context for Teaching and Learning in the National Center for Research to Improve Postsecondary Teaching and Learning (NCRIPTAL). The research is supported by a grant from the Office of Educational Research and Improvement (OERI), U.S. Department of Education (ED), to the University of Michigan (grant number G008690010). The opinions expressed herein are those of the authors and do not necessarily reflect the position or policy of the OERI/ED or the Regents of The University of Michigan, and no official endorsement should be inferred.

The Role of the Chairperson in Support of Junior Faculty

Daniel W. Wheeler

Department chairpersons can facilitate the success of junior faculty members through the use of a variety of strategies.

Department chairs at some seventy institutions across the United States identified one of their top priorities as helping new and junior faculty achieve success (Creswell and others, 1990). One of the chairs, from a research university, emphasized the importance of investing time, energy, and resources in new and junior faculty: "It's the responsibility of the department chair to help new faculty succeed. When we recruit an individual, we are convinced that this person has the skills that will really benefit our program. Our responsibility, once we hire, is to provide him or her with the resources and support to be successful."

This chapter draws on my consultations with many chairs about issues confronting junior faculty and strategies for success. The premise of the chapter is that chairs can help junior faculty acclimate to the institution and can provide guidance to enhance their likelihood of success. The enormous investment of time and resources involved in hiring new faculty members makes the provision of support for these junior colleagues an important aspect of the department chair's role. This chapter posits that a chairperson can facilitate the success of junior faculty members by identifying their needs, examining the potential roles in which he or she can be helpful, and taking specific actions and using a number of concrete activities to support junior faculty.

If a chairperson addresses these three facets of working with junior faculty members, the levels of their achievement and advancement can be greatly enhanced. Without systematic attention, the "sink-or-swim" model will prevail, a result that can be costly both to individual faculty members and to the institution.

Junior Faculty Needs

Research on junior faculty (Boice, 1991; Fink, 1984; Sorcinelli, 1989) and the role of chairpersons in faculty development (Creswell and others, 1990) suggests that all faculty members need to develop the following expertise and abilities:

Understanding Institutional Roles and Expectations. The institutional context greatly affects the roles and expectations of faculty. Considerable clarification may occur during the hiring process, but many junior faculty members contend that often the expectations of their departments and the institution are unclear, or worse, in conflict. Whatever the expectations for junior faculty, they should be clear and mutually accepted.

Learning How the Institution Operates in Getting Things Done. New faculty members must find out how to get things done on campus. The best of their ideas may not come to fruition because they lack an understanding of policies and procedures, written and unwritten, and are unaware of the most appropriate channels for achieving results.

Finding Resources. Many kinds of resources are necessary for faculty members to progress professionally. Library, laboratory, and various support services are just a few. Departmental, disciplinary, and institutional expectations determine the press for additional financial resources. For example, to begin a research program in the sciences, junior faculty may be faced with the need for $100,000 to $300,000 to develop a laboratory and obtain the necessary equipment. This can be a daunting task.

Developing Collegiality. New junior faculty consistency indicate that positive working relationships with fellow faculty members are an important aspect of their careers. Yet, work by Boice (1991) and Sorcinelli (1989) suggests that the desire often goes unfulfilled and these connections are not achieved. Boice adds that lack of collegiality may be an even greater problem for minorities and women. This lack of explicit support from established colleagues may be due either to a philosophy that new faculty need to stand on their own or to the fear of established faculty that suggestions for collaboration will be treated as intrusions unless they are requested by the new faculty members.

Obtaining Feedback on Professional Progress. Academics are fiercely independent and often skeptical about evaluation, but they do want feedback about their progress. New faculty are especially concerned about early evaluation of their teaching and progress in research. Heightened anxiety results from lack of feedback or the expectation that "no news is good news." Insufficient feedback can create difficulty down the road when colleagues and administrators need to make personnel decisions.

Improving Skills and Performance in Professional Roles. Ongoing professional development is critical to junior faculty. Strategies for growth in teaching and instructional skills are addressed at some professional society meetings. However, researchers (Creswell and others, 1990; Fink, 1984) have found that many junior faculty need additional interventions to become effective teachers.

Finding a Balance in Work-Life Expectations. Junior faculty express frustration that their lives are consumed by their careers (Sorcinelli and Near, 1989). Particularly with the tight timelines for tenure decisions, faculty may experience alienation from "significant others" and burn out. The necessity of carving out time for family, relationships, leisure, and community activities needs to be recognized and addressed during these initial years.

Potential Chairperson Roles

Given the range of junior faculty needs, chairs can take on several important roles to help facilitate progress in the early years of colleagues' careers. Each of these roles should be considered, although no single chair is likely to be able or willing to attend to all of them. The following are major roles that chairpersons can assume.

Chair as Resource Link. Tucker (1984) characterized the importance of this role in his work on department chairs. Whether referred to as *broker* or *matchmaker*, the role of making a connection between junior faculty resources and resource people is crucial both within the university and in the community at large. Chairs can address some faculty needs for information and understanding of the context of the institution and community through orientation sessions. But because orientation is an ongoing process that requires constant facilitation rather than a one-time activity, chairs should think through some of the following questions.

What orientation resources and information beyond the department are available to faculty? Is there a campuswide new faculty orientation in which faculty are given information about available programs and policies as well as an opportunity to meet other new faculty with similar concerns? Does the chair encourage attendance at these activities for new faculty? Timelines for these activities is critical; many opportunities will not have the same value several years into the career.

What will be the chair's role in a departmental orientation? Some chairs design a whole sequence of departmental sessions to address issues that they know junior faculty will have to face. Such formal orientations often include information about academic performance standards, policies and practices for working with graduate students, possible funds for research and issues related to the pursuit of grants, effective teaching techniques, important record keeping, faculty service responsibilities, duties of department heads, tenure and promotion, and library resources. Chairs may include information on issues not addressed by other orientations such as student services, benefits and personnel, purchasing, and the physical plant.

Some chairs develop and present an orientation on their own, while others draw on campus resource people. One advantage of introducing junior faculty to resource people is that the newcomers have an opportunity to meet individuals face to face before actually calling them to request services.

Other chairs, especially those from smaller departments or institutions, believe that they can provide an orientation by "meeting around the coffee pot" or dropping in to visit new junior faculty members in their offices. Informal get-togethers can be powerful tools in building relationships but are often overlooked because of the press of time or the lack of initiative by either the chair or the junior faculty members.

A combination of both formal and informal activities, including mentoring, seems to be the best orientation strategy. Effective chairs ensure that departmental orientation efforts have high priority and are maintained throughout the early years of faculty members' careers.

Chair as Mentor. Many chairpersons see themselves as mentors for junior faculty. Certainly, many have accepted the role of department chair because of their interest in working with others. In some ways, chairs make for good mentors because of their knowledge of the ways in which the institution operates and of what it takes to be successful. Also their commitment to new faculty members often develops early in the hiring process.

On the other hand, there are complications in mentoring relationships between the chair and junior faculty. New faculty may feel intimidated by and insecure with the chair, who not only hired them but also is probably responsible for their evaluation. For chairs to be successful as mentors, they must be clear with mentees about their responsibilities to provide both support and evaluation. Straightforward discussion is necessary to head off potential conflicts between the roles of mentor and chair.

Chair as Facilitator of Mentor Relationships. A number of chairpersons have initiated procedures or structures to encourage senior colleagues within their departments to take on mentoring roles. Some departments assign faculty members to serve as mentors, and others provide various opportunities for new faculty to select a mentor or sometimes multiple mentors. In research on the socialization of new junior faculty, Egly (1991) found that junior faculty often have more than one mentor, each of whom is associated with a particular function: teaching, research, service, or career development.

Chair as Institutional Authority or Representative. The department chair is often the first institutional representative who defines and negotiates what the institution expects of faculty. The chair thus plays a crucial role in the development of verbal and written correspondence that pertain to, but are not limited to, job descriptions, written contracts, and job offers.

Clarification of expectations is always important, but it becomes critical in institutions that are in the midst of change. An instructive example is the comprehensive university, which historically has had a primarily undergraduate teaching focus but more recently has emphasized the development of its graduate programs. For both new and senior faculty, stress abounds. Both groups face heavy teaching loads, new demands for research activity, and shortages in institutionally available research resources. Senior faculty often feel conflict because they were hired primarily as teachers but now face new expectations. Some of these long-term faculty complain that "the rules of the game have changed." They feel alienated from the administration, the new institutional emphasis on research, and, often, the institution as a whole.

At the same time, new faculty members in this situation need counsel on "navigating the muddy waters," especially when they hear conflicting views from their peers and the administration. Chairs can help to set priorities, provide reinforcement to the junior faculty member who says no to a request that does not fit priorities, and serve as an advocate for junior faculty members with senior colleagues and higher administrators who will eventually make decisions on tenure and promotion. In short, for junior faculty, protection from distractions and minutia is helpful, and reminders and clarifications of what is expected in order to be successful and remain at the institution are necessary. As one chair exclaimed, "Without some protection, new faculty can become cannon fodder." Even in the most straightforward situations with congruent expectations, guidance of junior faculty by the department chair can prevent missteps and distractions from priorities.

Chair as Evaluator. Chairpersons play a major role in helping junior faculty assess their own progress. New faculty members typically understand what progress means in their respective disciplines or content areas, but the tasks of identifying the institutional benchmarks for progress in teaching, establishing research programs, and meeting other departmental and institutional expectations may be difficult.

Chairs need proficiency in giving specific feedback, coaching on a short-term basis, and conducting annual evaluation conferences. For instance, new faculty often initially spend an inordinate amount of time preparing for their classes. Chairs can demonstrate ways to shorten preparation time and ensure that effective teaching is achieved in an efficient manner.

In the research conducted by Creswell and others (1990), a priority constantly stated by chairs was to be honest and direct in evaluation and other interactions with junior faculty. Their view was that inflated assessments and avoidance of difficult issues caused complications later when hard decisions (such as tenure and promotion) must be made. Without honest feedback, junior faculty members become confused and unclear about their status and progress. As a result, unfavorable decisions may be blamed on politics or personality conflicts rather than on substantiated records of unmet performance expectations.

Certainly, some faculty will not succeed or may be mismatched in terms of personal and institutional goals. For example, an individual who is a successful teacher but a less than enthusiastic researcher may be better placed at an institution that focuses primarily on teaching. The chair can help the junior faculty member make a realistic assessment of his or her strengths and weaknesses and, if necessary, facilitate redirection to a more appropriate institution.

Chair as Faculty Developer. Chairpersons can help directly, provide referral to other professors in the department, or link new faculty to instructional or faculty development centers. To give appropriate referrals, a department chair must be aware of the abilities of all faculty in the department as well as familiar with campus resource people who can provide help. The chair's attitude about a faculty member seeking help is critical. If the chair conveys the attitude that a referral is remedial, rather than a stage through which most new faculty progress, newcomers will be hesitant to reach out for help. What is to be avoided at all costs is a new faculty member who waits until the situation is so desperate and demoralizing that radical interventions are necessary.

If the chairperson chooses to be a direct developer, then refined consulting skills are required. Lucas (1989, 1990) and Creswell and others (1990) provide many strategies and suggestions to chairs for developing effective teaching among junior faculty. One strategy is to visit the classroom, and perhaps videotape the activities, with subsequent feedback to the faculty member regarding particular aspects of teaching and learning. Detailed teaching consultation strategies are provided in Lewis and Povlacs (1988), and numerous suggestions about course structure and classroom operations are offered by McKeachie (1986).

In a more generic vein, Creswell and others (1990) suggest a series of steps through which chairs can stay in tune with faculty on any situation or problem and help them address any needed changes. The steps are to (1) detect the signs of faculty needs, (2) explore the options individually with the person, (3) collaboratively develop a plan for action, and (4) enact the plan and monitor its results.

Beyond these four steps, the practice of staying in touch with new faculty requires a developmental perspective and an awareness that while faculty have many common concerns, they also have unique needs that can be determined through careful observations and in-depth conversations. Baldwin (1990), Schuster, Wheeler, and Associates (1990), Bowen and Schuster (1986),

Menges (1985), Baldwin and Blackburn (1981), and Mathis (1979) provide a solid grounding in the assessment of concerns and stages associated with the development of faculty.

Skill in listening to faculty also was found by Creswell and others (1990) to be crucial for the chairperson as developer. Chairs in their study suggested questions such as "What do you want to do?" and "How can I help you do it?" to increase the exchange of information and to identify ways to be of assistance. Whatever the questions or strategies employed, direct interactions in a supportive atmosphere help to prevent misconceptions or improper assumptions. They also help build trust and good faith, which can provide a basis to overcome what at times seem insurmountable difficulties to newcomers. These are high expectations for chairs, but the times demand new levels of skill and commitment to attract and retain quality junior faculty.

Chair as Model of Balance. Academic careers have the potential to consume new faculty members in the absence of guidance from institutional authorities or admired colleagues. Efforts are needed to prevent faculty burnout and alienation of family members. Chairs can encourage junior faculty to make time for family and themselves, to build it into their schedules. To be sure, many chairs also have difficulty in achieving balance between their academic and personal lives, but those who are able to model this strategy not only benefit personally but are able as well to make the expectation believable to their junior colleagues.

Support Mechanisms and Actions

As outlined above, the chair should try on various roles to facilitate junior faculty growth. Equally important, the chair should help the junior faculty member to set out a specific plan for development. Exhibits 8.1 and 8.2 list support mechanisms that the department chair can put into place so that the new faculty member can develop a realistic and comprehensive plan for development. The suggestions in Exhibit 8.1 pertain to tangible, material resources that are helpful in years one through five. The suggestions in Exhibit 8.2 pertain to collegial support needed at different points during the first five years.

With a grasp of junior faculty needs, a thoughtful choice of roles to facilitate faculty growth, and the development of support mechanisms to assist junior faculty in career planning, chairs can greatly facilitate the success of the newest members of their departments. If junior faculty perform well, chairs who have assisted them certainly will share in the credit and be applauded for their efforts.

Exhibit 8.1. Tangible Resources for Professional Support, Years One Through Five

Year One

1. Provide symbols of institutional identification or belonging. Items could be writing materials, briefcases, clothing, or pins with institutional logos and other identification.

2. Provide a list of community services and resources available. This list could include recreational, housing, and medical entries. Sometimes these lists are already available elsewhere (for example, the local Chamber of Commerce), but they can be tailored to the institution.

3. Provide start-up funds for laboratory and equipment, secretarial support, graduate research or teaching assistants, and computers, as needed.

4. Pay dues for the appropriate professional society for the first year. Some chairs take this action as a symbolic gesture of commitment to faculty development as well as in recognition that the process of becoming established the first year requires financial resources that some new faculty do not have.

5. Provide travel funds for professional society meetings. Once again, while the new faculty member is becoming established and finding out how to obtain resources, chairs often make support available, with the expectation that new faculty will progressively find more of their own resources.

6. Reduce teaching load or provide other load reduction to encourage good teaching as well as to establish a research program. Particularly for new faculty without previous teaching experience, chairs have found that overpreparation for classes can result in poor teaching as well as inadequate time devoted to research and writing.

Years Two Through Five

7. Encourage junior faculty to use internal and external resources to meet professional obligations. Chairs can nominate junior faculty for fellowships, society positions, and review panels to help them become known and better connected to resources.

8. Provide resources with an expectation that junior faculty members can find and parlay other resources over time to meet their goals. Often, a faculty member can consolidate diverse sources of modest funding into one complete, well-funded package.

Exhibit 8 2. Collegial Resources for Professional Support, Years One Through Five

Year One

1. Introduce the faculty member to campus leaders and resource people. Some faculty become isolated and unaware of resources available to improve their professional lives.

2. Provide an orientation to the institution and the department. This orientation is most effective when conducted as an ongoing process and not as a one-time activity.

3. Arrange or facilitate mentor relationships. Although all faculty may not desire mentors, these relationships have proved helpful to junior faculty success.

4. Periodically schedule sessions (over coffee or lunch breaks) to discuss concerns and answer "how to" questions. In addition to being useful to the junior faculty members, these sessions enable the chair to monitor progress and make appropriate interventions as needed.

5. Facilitate professional development plans for a period of two to five years. This planning helps to ensure that both short-term needs and long-term goals are addressed.

6. Ensure that professional progress is discussed beyond the annual evaluation conference. Feedback from the chair, the promotion and tenure committee, and senior faculty needs to be interpreted for the junior faculty member.

Years Two Through Five

7. Periodically schedule sessions to discuss concerns and to facilitate growth and development. Listen and ask "What do you want to do?" and "How can I help you do it?"

8. Invite junior faculty to participate in projects and proposals, whether the chair's own projects or those of the department.

9. Continue to encourage junior faculty to make appropriate time allotments for priority activities and to eliminate unnecessary commitments. They often need help in learning to say no and in preventing overcommittment.

10. Encourage participation in development activities both on and off campus to meet needs and to strengthen professional expertise and skills. Faculty often need guidance to address areas of professional performance that need to be strengthened. Chairs should have open and honest communications about strengthening areas of weakness or underdevelopment.

11. Provide evaluation and feedback on professional progress. Evaluative feedback helps to ensure that individuals are realistic about their roles and expectations and that they make the necessary adjustments for success.

References

Baldwin, R. G. "Faculty Career Stages and Implications for Professional Development." In J. H. Schuster, D. W. Wheeler, and Associates (eds.), *Enhancing Faculty Careers: Strategies for Development and Renewal.* San Francisco: Jossey-Bass, 1990.

Baldwin, R. G., and Blackburn, R. T. "The Academic Career as a Developmental Process: Implications for Higher Education." *Journal of Higher Education,* 1981, *52,* (6), 598–614.

Boice, R. "New Faculty as Teachers." *Journal of Higher Education,* 1991, *62,* (2), 150–173.

Bowen, H. R., and Schuster, J. H. *American Professors: A National Resource Imperiled.* New York: Oxford University, 1986.

Creswell, J. W., Wheeler, D. W., Seagren, A. T., Egly, N. J., and Beyer, K. D. *The Academic Chairperson's Handbook.* Lincoln: University of Nebraska Press, 1990.

Egly, N. J. "Academic Socialization and Faculty Development Assistance: A Study of New Tenure-Track Faculty Members in the Institute of Agriculture and Natural Resources." Unpublished doctoral dissertation, Department of Vocational and Adult Education, University of Nebraska, 1991.

Fink, L. D. (ed.) *The First Year of College Teaching.* New Directions for Teaching and Learning, no. 17, San Francisco: Jossey-Bass, 1984.

Lewis, K. G., and Povlacs, J. T. *Face to Face: A Sourcebook for Individual Consultation Techniques for Faculty/Instructional Developers.* Stillwater, Okla.: New Forums, 1988.

Lucas, A. F. (ed.) *The Department Chairperson's Role in Enhancing College Teaching.* New Directions for Teaching and Learning, no. 37. San Francisco: Jossey-Bass, 1989.

Lucas, A. F. "The Department Chair as Change Agent." In P. Seldin and Associates (eds.), *How Administrators Can Improve Teaching: Moving from Talk to Action in Higher Education.* San Francisco: Jossey-Bass, 1990.

McKeachie, W. J. *Teaching Tips: A Guidebook for the Beginning College Teacher.* Lexington, Mass: Heath, 1986.

Mathis, B. C. "Academic Careers and Adult Development: A Nexus for Research." *Current Issues in Higher Education,* 1979, *2,* 21–24.

Menges, R. J. "Career-Span Faculty Development." *College Teaching,* 1985, *33,* 181–184.

Schuster, J. H., Wheeler, D. W., and Associates (eds.) *Enhancing Faculty Careers: Strategies for Development and Renewal.* San Francisco: Jossey-Bass, 1990.

Sorcinelli, M. D. "Chairs and the Development of New Faculty." *Department Advisor,* 1989, *5,* (2), 1–4.

Sorcinelli, M. D., and Near, J. "Relationships Between Work and Life Away from Work Among University Faculty." *Journal of Higher Education*, 1989, *60*, (1), 59–81.

Tucker, A. *Chairing the Academic Department*. New York: Macmillan, 1984.

This chapter is based on the National Chairperson Study, conducted from 1986 to 1988 and supported by the Lilly Foundation and the Teachers Insurance and Annuity Association-College Retirement Equities Fund.

Daniel W. Wheeler is coordinator of the Office of Professional and Organizational Development at the Institute of Agriculture and Natural Resources, University of Nebraska, Lincoln.

Full-time Non-tenure-track Faculty: Current Status, Condition, and Attitudes

JAY L. CHRONISTER, ROGER G. BALDWIN, AND THERESA BAILEY

Introduction

Over the past decade, many U.S. colleges and universities have undertaken a number of strategies designed to meet institutional needs for flexibility in faculty staffing. One popular strategy at colleges and universities with tenure systems is employing faculty in full-time non-tenure-track appointments (El-Khawas 1990; AAUP 1986, 1978). Eighty-six percent of the institutions responding to the 1990 Campus Trends survey reported that they had made term or contract appointments (non-tenure-track) of full-time faculty as compared with 77 percent of the institutions reporting such types of appointments two years earlier (El-Khawas 1990, 19; 1988, 23). Robert Blackburn and Neil Wiley (1990) found that about 30 percent of the total faculty at a select group of private liberal arts colleges were not tenure eligible. Figures derived from the U.S. Department of Education's National Survey of Postsecondary Faculty showed an estimated 10 percent of all full-time faculty not on the tenure track (National Center 1990).

The American Association of University Professors (AAUP) has described three types of non-tenure-track faculty appointments. The first are indefinitely renewable appointments which place no limit on the number of times a one- or two-year appointment may be renewed for a faculty member. The second category, restricted renewable appointments, can be renewed only a specified number of times—for example, a maximum of three one-year contracts. The third type is called a "folding chair." This appointment is explicitly terminal at the end of the original appointment period, which is usually for two or three years (AAUP 1978). A key feature of all three categories is the lack of an explicit expectation of continued employment that a tenure appointment conveys and the potential for security that an untenured, but tenure-track, appointment offers for those who successfully complete the probationary period.

The AAUP has emphasized in several of its reports the potential negative impact of non-tenure-track appointments on the careers of faculty (AAUP 1978, 1986). Martin Finkelstein observed that non-tenure-track appointments are "developed less for the express academic purpose of providing new roles to convey a very specialized skill" than as an institutional convenience with little consideration given to the impact of their use on academic program quality or on faculty careers (1986, 33).

As higher education plans to meet staffing needs for the next several decades, it must almost certainly deal with a short-fall of qualified faculty (Bowen and Schuster 1986; Bowen and Sosa 1989). In addition to a dwindling supply of students enrolled in graduate school who are the logical replacements for the professorate, attractive alternative careers are available for many recent graduates as well as for those currently enrolled in graduate school. A 1989 report shows that the proportion of doctoral recipients employed in academe declined from 66.6 percent of the

1968 graduates to 49.8 percent of the 1988 recipients, a loss in actual numbers as well as a proportionate decline (National Research Council 1989, 42).

These conditions—actual and projected shortages of replacement faculty and increased competition for those in the shrinking pool—urge the reexamination of current faculty personnel policies and practices. Colleges and universities need to determine whether any current policies are, or have the potential of, exacerbating the demand/supply problem. In particular, higher education institutions should determine how non-tenure-track appointments are related to professors' work orientation and professional morale. Do professors in non-tenure-track appointments have more negative images of academic life than their tenure-track colleagues? Are non-tenure-track faculty more likely to consider alternative employment outside of higher education? The answers to these questions, addressed in this study, will clarify the implications of a personnel practice that has increased on campuses across the nation.

Faculty Careers

The higher education literature devotes very little attention to the issue of non-tenure-track faculty. Other than statistics on the magnitude of this faculty subgroup, we know little about this distinct component of the academic profession. There are some parallels between the experiences of beginning academics and non-tenure-track professors. Members of both groups typically have worked at their institutions for only short periods of time and have probationary or peripheral status. Because of these parallels, the literature on novice college professors offers some insight concerning the experiences of non-tenure-track faculty. For example, Dee Fink (1984) found that first-year geography professors experienced a host of stresses (e.g., isolation from colleagues, exhaustion from excessive demands on their time, and insecurity about their future) closely associated with their transitional circumstances. Similar experiences and concerns may characterize non-tenure-track faculty who never achieve the security of a permanent appointment. However, in spite of parallels with other faculty groups, non-tenure-track professors occupy a unique position in higher education that deserves closer examination.

To anticipate the effects of non-tenure-track appointments on faculty careers, it is necessary to provide a model of careers that is amenable to analysis. Our discussion relies on the model of faculty careers presented by Light, Marsden, and Corl in 1972, and on Baldwin's research on faculty career stages (Baldwin 1990; Baldwin and Blackburn 1981).

The Light, Marsden, and Corl conceptualization of the academic career consists of three analytically distinct but interrelated strands which at different times and to differing degrees contribute to the potential for a successful career. The three strands are the disciplinary career, the institutional career, and the external career. Although analyzed separately, the activities and events in one strand have meaning and effects in the others.

The disciplinary career generally begins in graduate school and is at least partially reflected in the choice of a major (the discipline), undertaking specialized preparation or training (graduate school), and becoming involved with organizations that represent the discipline. This strand includes those events specifically connected with the discipline and its goals, rather than with a specific job.

The institutional career consists of events associated with an individual's employment at a specific college or university and is based on some type of contractual relationship between the faculty member and the institution. The institutional career strand is important for development and success because the institution provides the environment, resources, and recognition necessary for advancement.

The external career strand usually begins later in the life of faculty members and involves recognition and work outside of the institution but directly related to the discipline. This strand may be an "alternative" career strand that develops because of disciplinary commitment and expertise and disaffection with the institutional career.

Although the three career strands are interrelated, the institutional career and the disciplinary career are especially central to the lives of new and probationary faculty like non-tenure-track professors. These two strands comprise the principal environment in which these faculty work.

Negative conditions in either domain can adversely affect the performance and morale of professors ineligible for tenure.

Baldwin's conceptualization of faculty career stages draws extensively on adult development and career development literature and research (Baldwin 1990; Baldwin and Blackburn 1981). The four-stage career model he describes as a basis for understanding the professional development needs of faculty is directly relevant to the circumstances of non-tenure-track faculty. We focus primarily on the first two stages: career entry and the early academic career (Baldwin 1990, 31–34). These two stages relate directly to the expectations of career support inherent in the institutional strand described by Light, Marsden and Corl (1972).

Baldwin's career entry process (the novice professor) is complex and challenging, the introduction to the professorate. He cites the competing demands that the novice faces in terms of designing courses, developing a repertoire of teaching skills, developing an understanding of available institutional resources and support services, initiating the scholarly dimensions of the academic role, and attempting to maintain some semblance of family life. Baldwin indicates that the novice needs sensitive guidance and support from senior colleagues and the department chair.

The early academic career falls between career entry and full membership status as signified by receiving tenure or its equivalent. At this period in the academic career, the new faculty member settles in, makes a name for himself or herself, and "wishes to master the principal roles"; as a "prominent goal," the faculty member also desires to make some kind of a meaningful achievement (deserving of recognition within one's institution or broader discipline)" (Baldwin 1990, 33). The institution expects him or her to become involved through committee work and cooperative activities with colleagues. In fact, interacting with colleagues in intellectual and governance activities is part of the acculturation process for novices and helps them adjust to career demands. During this "probationary" period, adequate resources to support growth in both institutional and disciplinary roles are of paramount importance, particularly the expectation of some defined multi-year probationary period and the mentorship or guidance of an established senior colleague.

It appears from these two models that non-tenure-track faculty may be at a distinct disadvantage in trying to build a solid foundation for a productive, multi-dimensional academic career. Their temporary and peripheral status both in their institution and discipline often excludes them from many of the opportunities, resources, and forms of support associated with success in the academic profession. The uncertain and sometimes unstable employment experiences of non-tenure-track professors may be inconsistent with the conditions needed to initiate successful academic careers.

The remainder of this paper focuses on factors which influence the early stages of faculty career development. In particular, we scrutinize employment conditions associated with non-tenure-track appointments and the influence of these conditions on professors' career orientation and outlook.

The Study

Our goal in this study was assessing the condition/status of non-tenure-track faculty in American higher education in comparison to their non-tenured but tenure-track faculty. The models of career development that guided this study (Light, Marsden, and Corl, 1972; Baldwin, 1990; Baldwin and Blackburn, 1981) suggest that non-tenure-track faculty may have distinctly different career orientations and experiences due, at least in part, to their differentiated academic status. We organized our research around three questions:

1. What is the primary career orientation of non-tenure-track faculty (i.e., teaching vs. research, discipline vs. institution, local vs. cosmopolitan) and how does this orientation compare with non-tenured, tenure track faculty?

2. How do non-tenure-track faculty perceive their work environment in terms of participation in institutional governance, intellectual environment, etc.?

3. Given the conditions under which they are employed and their career experiences, how do non-tenure-track faculty perceive (assess) their career future?

Data Source

The data used in this study were generated by the 1989 survey of the professoriate conducted by the Carnegie Foundation for the Advancement of Teaching. The Carnegie study involved a two-stage, stratified, random-sample design to select college and university faculty for the study. The first stage involved selecting 306 four-year and two-year institutions from the Carnegie Foundation data bank. The second stage involved the random selection of 9,996 faculty, distributing them equally among the nine classifications of institutions. A total of 5,450 of the 9,996 faculty surveyed responded to the instrument for a response rate of 54.5 percent (Carnegie 1988, 55).

Among the 5,450 respondents were two cohorts of faculty whom we chose for this study. These sub-samples consisted of 832 full-time untenured but tenure-track faculty and 183 full-time non-tenure-track faculty who had no guarantee of continuing contracts. Faculty members in both of these cohorts were employed on at least nine-month appointments at four-year institutions during the 1988–89 academic year.

This project was designed as an exploratory study which would rely heavily on descriptive statistics. When appropriate, we analyzed responses through cross-tabulations and chi-square tests.

Characteristics of the Sample Populations

The non-tenured professors in the Carnegie study reflect the changing composition of the academic profession. (See Table 1.) The tenure-track faculty averaged forty-one years of age; the non-tenure-track cohort averaged forty-three. These ages are slightly higher than might be expected for a group of faculty whose careers are not yet established. More noteworthy, perhaps, is their gender mix. More than one-third (35.7 percent) of the tenure-track faculty and more than half (50.8 percent) of the non-tenure-track professors are women. The larger number of women in the non-tenure-track classification comes as no surprise because women traditionally have had to accept less favorable employment opportunities to balance marriage and family obligations while pursuing a professional life. However, this discrepancy between men and women faculty should be viewed with concern. If the tenure system and the possibilities of achieving tenure are integral components of a successful academic career, then many women academics work at a distinct disadvantage. The large numbers of women professors working off the tenure track may be permanently handicapped in trying to establish a permanent academic career.

A quick examination of the employment histories of tenure-track and non-tenure-track professors helps to illuminate their differing career paths. On average, the non-tenure-track faculty have worked more years in higher education than their tenure-eligible colleagues (8.4 vs. 6.7). Similarly, they have been employed at their current institutions for longer periods. However, the non-tenure-track faculty have been employed at fewer higher education institutions (1.53, non-tenure-track 1.78, tenure-track) as their tenure-eligible counterparts. This combined evidence indicates that non-tenure-track faculty are not as professionally mobile as their colleagues on the tenure-track, do not move between institutions (and perhaps do not move up the career ladder) as rapidly as those who have the tenure option. This condition is clearly evident from the average number of years the non-tenure-eligible faculty have served higher education and their institutions without the benefit of employment security.

Table 1. Characteristics of the Sample Populations

	Tenure-Track	Non-Tenure-Track
Number of faculty	832	183
Mean age	41.1	43.2
Gender*		
Male	64.3%	49.2%
Female	35.7%	50.8%
Type of Employing Institution**		
Research university	22.8%	16.4%
Doctorate-granting university	26.1%	19.6%
Comprehensive college/university	25.2%	30.6%
Liberal arts college	25.8%	33.3%

Chi-square tests:
* significant at the .001 level.
** significant at the .01 level

The employment options of tenure-track faculty seem more diverse than those of college teachers not on the tenure-track. Table 1 shows that tenure-track faculty in the sample are quite evenly distributed among four types of higher education institutions. In contrast, larger proportions of non-tenure-eligible faculty work in comprehensive universities and liberal arts colleges, institutions which impose heavier teaching assignments and offer fewer opportunities for research and publication, the "coin of the realm" in academe today. Being employed in institutions with limited resources and a more restricted definition of the faculty role may inhibit the career development of some academics who could blossom professionally in a more supportive environment.

The primary professional orientation of tenure-eligible and non-tenure-eligible faculty differs significantly ($p < .001$), as well. Table 2 shows that non-tenure-track faculty, as a rule, are more teaching-oriented than their tenure-track colleagues. A much larger percentage of the non-tenure-track participants (81.4 percent) in the study indicated that their professional interest was tilted toward teaching rather than research. The actual work assignments and scholarly activities of the two faculty groups appear to parallel these differing interests. A substantially larger portion of the non-tenure-track faculty work at the undergraduate level while nearly 40 percent of the tenure-track faculty had some experience working with graduate students as part of their assigned teaching load.

The scholarly activity of the two groups is consistent with their professional interests and teaching level. Fewer non-tenure-track faculty indicate that they are currently involved in research and scholarship. This finding is not surprising given the uncertain nature of the non-tenure-track professor's careers, the limited resources that typically are available to them, and the large proportion of them who are employed at schools which have teaching as their primary institutional mission. Perhaps more remarkable is the fact that more than two thirds of the non-tenure-track faculty indicated that they were engaged in scholarship activities.

In some important respects, the two groups of faculty are quite similar, however. Table 3 shows that both tenure-track and non-tenure-track faculty view their disciplines and their departments as very important aspects of their professional lives. The great majority of both types of faculty also agree that their institutions and relationships with undergraduates are important to them.

On the other hand, the familiar local-cosmopolitan dichotomy (Gouldner 1957) helps to clarify differences between tenure-track and non-tenure-track faculty. Slightly larger percentages of the non-tenure-eligible faculty indicated that their institutions and undergraduates were important to them professionally. In contest, more tenure-track faculty highlighted the importance in their careers of national disciplinary societies. These differences, though not large, suggest that professors' orientation to their work life may vary with the employment situation/ circumstances they encounter.

Table 2. Academic Areas of Interests and Responsibilities

	Tenure-Track	Non-Tenure-Track
*Primary professional interests**		
Primary interest in research	8.5%	4.9%
In both, lean toward research	37.7%	13.7%
In both, lean toward teaching	34.3%	31.7%
Primary interest in teaching	19.6%	49.7%
*Currently involved in scholarly works**		
Yes	87.5%	67.2%
No	12.5%	32.8%

*Chi-square test significant at the <.001 level.

Table 3. Importance of Career Elements/Variables

Variables	Tenure-Track	Non-Tenure-Track
Discipline		
Very important	78.4%	73.2%
Fairly important	19.6%	24.6%
Fairly unimportant	1.6%	2.2%
Not at all important	.5%	.0%
Department		
Very important	47.2%	45.9%
Fairly important	43.8%	39.9%
Fairly unimportant	7.5%	12.6%
Not at all important	1.4%	1.6%
Institution		
Very important	30.5%	33.3%
Fairly important	49.3%	49.7%
Fairly unimportant	17.4%	13.1%
Not at all important	2.8%	3.8%
Relationship with Undergraduates		
Very important	53.7%	70.0%
Fairly important	38.6%	26.7%
Fairly unimportant	6.7%	2.2%
Not at all important	1.1%	1.1%
National Discipline Societies		
Very important	20.3%	17.5%
Fairly important	47.9%	33.9%
Fairly unimportant	25.5%	36.0%
Not at all important	6.3%	12.9%

Non-Tenure-Track Faculty's Perceptions of Their Work Environment

As we indicated in our introduction, the institutional career of faculty members is critical to their academic career because it is through such affiliations that the individual acquires the environment, support services, and resources necessary for advancement. During the early academic career stage, faculty members attempt to master the roles associated with academic life and establish the groundwork for a productive multi-dimensional professional life. For non-tenured tenure-track faculty members, this early career period is generally a probationary period prior to the award of tenure. For non-tenure-track faculty, the only reward may be achieving some type of long-term contract. Does the absence of a defined probationary period adversely affect non-

Table 4. Summary of Chi-Square Tests of Difference
Between Groups on Work Environment Variables

Variable	Chi-square	df	Group@
Feelings about the institution	2.22	2	
Feelings that junior faculty have little say in running department	8.17	4	
Feelings about ability to influence departmental policies	15.79***	3	TT
Feelings about ability to influence institutional policies	11.28**	3	TT
Participation in department faculty meetings	13.69***	2	TT
Involvement in faculty senate	.92	3	
Involvement in administrative advisory committees	4.28	3	
Involvement in academic budget committees	3.23	3	
Involvement in campus faculty committees	10.88**	3	TT
Rating of teaching load	3.00	3	
Rating of current teaching load with load of five years ago	9.60*	4	TT
Rating of salary	10.76**	3	TT
Rating of institution's intellectual environment	1.16	3	
Rating of quality of life at the institution	1.43	3	
Rating of sense of community at the institution	5.13	3	

* significant at the .05 level
** significant at the .01 level
*** significant at the .001 level
@ group expressing most positive feelings about item
TT = Tenure-track NTT = Non-tenure-track

tenure-track faculty? How do they perceive their work environment and do their perceptions differ from those of non-tenured but tenure-track faculty?

The vast majority of the non-tenured but tenure-track (85.2 percent) and non-tenure-track (81.9 percent) faculty in the sample studied felt that their employing institution was either a very good or fairly good place for them. Table 4 describes the variables about the institutional work environment which we assessed.

When asked to assess whether junior faculty have too little say in running their department, the majority of both groups responded in the negative with no statistically significant differences. The two groups differed significantly ($p < .001$) in their perceptions of their opportunity to influence departmental policies. Approximately 67 percent of the tenure-track faculty felt they had "a great deal" or "quite a bit" of opportunity to influence policy; only 52.5 percent of the non-tenure-track faculty agreed. Neither group felt it had "a great deal" or "quite a bit" of influence over institutional policy; but the non-tenure-track faculty were more likely to feel they had no influence (52.5 percent) or only "some influence" (37.0 percent), while tenure-track faculty responses to the same items were 39.0 percent and 46.7 percent respectively.

Involvement in institutional governance is an important aspect of a faculty member's career role. Tenure-track faculty reported significantly greater involvement than non-tenure-track faculty in department faculty meetings ($p < .001$) and in campus-wide faculty committees ($p < .01$). Neither group reported much involvement at all in faculty senate, administrative advisory committees, or academic budget committee activities. Such lack of involvement in institution-wide committee work by junior faculty, whether tenure-track or non-tenure-track, was not unexpected. In assessing their teaching loads, 58.2 percent of non-track faculty rated that aspect of employment as fair or poor with an additional 34.6 percent rating it as good. They did not differ significantly from their tenure-track colleagues on this variable. In comparing current teaching loads with their teaching loads of five years ago, however, the two cohorts of faculty who provided a five-year comparison were significantly different ($p < .05$). Approximately 24 percent of the tenure-track faculty, in contrast with 13 percent of the non-track faculty, reported their load was lighter than it had been five years earlier. In contrast non-track faculty reported loads that were about the same (52.6 percent vs. 45.4 percent) or heavier (34.1 percent vs. 30.9 percent).

The vast majority of non-tenure-track (80.7 percent) and tenure-track (70.3 percent) faculty rated their salaries as poor or fair. It is evident from these ratings that neither cohort felt the salary received was adequate, but the groups differed ($p < .01$) on this variable with a larger proportion of tenure-track faculty (29.7 percent vs. 19.3 percent) rating their salary as good or excellent.

When assessing the intellectual environment, the quality of life, and the sense of common unit at their institution, non-tenure-track faculty had generally negative (fair or poor) evaluations of those factors (60.2 percent, 56.4 percent, and 61.3 percent, respectively). These assessments did not differ significantly from those of the tenure-track respondents.

Non-Tenure-Track Faculty's Feelings about Their Careers

In view of the findings cited above and with the problems projected in replacing the retiring professorate with competent new faculty, institutional leaders should be interested in the plans of today's untenured faculty members. How do these faculty feel about their careers and what is their reaction to their careers to date?

Nearly 42 percent of the non-tenure-track faculty in this study have given "serious consideration" to leaving academic life permanently during the two years prior to the survey. Another 27.3 percent had considered leaving, but not "seriously." They differed significantly ($p < .05$) from their tenure-track colleagues on this variable; 31.8 percent of the tenure-eligible faculty had given serious consideration to departing, while 34.2 percent reported less serious thought. The figures for both sets of untenured faculty should be a point of concern in view of higher education's needs, but the degree of seriousness expressed by non-tenure-track personnel indicates a degree of disenchantment that may have negative consequences for faculty staffing in the near future.

It has become evident that many recent Ph.D. graduates, who are potential faculty members, obtain positions in a wide variety of professional fields outside of academe (National Research Council 1989). Seventeen percent of the non-tenure-track faculty in this study indicated that it was "very" (6.0 percent) or "somewhat" likely (11.0 percent) that they will seek a research position outside of academia in the next five years. On this variable, their responses differed significantly ($p < .05$) from those of their tenure-track colleagues; 24 percent saw such action as "very" (7.0 percent) or "somewhat" likely (17.0 percent). This difference is probably related to the difference in career orientation reflected earlier in this paper—that more of the tenure-track than non-tenure-track faculty indicated a stronger professional interest in research.

When queried whether they would seek an administrative position outside of academy in the next five years, approximately 29 percent of the non-tenure-track respondents reported that it was "very" (6.6 percent) or "somewhat" likely (22.5 percent). Among non-tenured respondents, 19.2 percent reported respective percentages of 5.2 percent and 14.0 percent for such action. This was again a significant difference ($p < .05$) between the groups, with the non-tenure-track group more likely to seek administrative positions.

The insecurity of non-tenure-track faculty members is further highlighted by their response to whether their "academic position would be in jeopardy if there were faculty cutbacks in the next five years?" A sizeable minority (42.6 percent) said it was "very likely" and 14.8 percent it was "somewhat likely." In contrast, only 15.9 percent of tenure track faculty indicated it was "very likely" and 21.7 percent felt it was "somewhat likely." The groups differed significantly ($p < .001$) on this item and although both cohorts perceived their positions as being in possible jeopardy, the non-tenure-track faculty were the most sensitive to the issue.

We also asked them to indicate the degree to which their job was a source of "considerable personal strain." The two groups did not differ significantly, although it is important to note that 48.6 percent of non-track and 57.5 percent of tenure-track faculty agreed that it was a strain. Possibly the strain for the tenure-track faculty is directly related to the "probationary period" in which they find themselves, while non-track faculty feel strain because of the general uncertainty of the future. Nearly 50 percent of non-track faculty strongly agree, or agree with reservations, that they "hardly ever get time to give a piece of work the attention it deserves" but their concern differed significantly ($p < .05$) from that of their tenure-track colleagues who felt even more time constrained.

Table 5. Summary of Chi-Square Tests of Differences Between Groups on Career Attitude Variables

Variable	Chi-square	df	Group[@]
I have considered permanent departure from academia in past two years.	6.75*	2	NTT
I may seek a research position outside academy in next five years.	10.35*	4	TT
I may seek an administrative position outside academy in next 5 years.	10.21*	4	NTT
My position is in jeopardy if faculty cutbacks are made in the next 5 years.	65.94***	4	NTT
My job is a source of considerable personal strain.	7.22	4	
I hardly ever get time to give a piece of work the attention it deserves.	11.06*	*/4	TT
This is a poor time for a young person to begin an academic career.	5.96	4	
I may consider entering another career due to limited prospects for advancement.	30.73***	4	NTT
I may leave the profession in the next five years.	23.31***	4	NTT
I often wish I had entered another profession.	9.12	4	
I feel trapped in a profession with limited advancement opportunities.	22.08***	4	NTT
I am more enthusiastic about work than when I began my career.	11.92*	4	NTT
If had to do it again, I would not become a college teacher.	4.14	4	

* significant at the .05 level
** significant at the .01 level
*** significant at the .001 level
@ Group most in agreement with statement
TT = Tenure-track NTT = Non-tenure-track

Slightly in excess of 25 percent of the non-track faculty strongly agreed (9.9 percent), or agreed with reservations (15.4 percent) that this is a poor time for any young person to begin an academic career, and 17.5 percent either strongly agreed (7.1 percent) or agreed with reservations (10.4 percent) that, if they were recommencing their careers, they would not become college teachers. On these two variables they did not differ significantly from their tenure-track colleagues. In addition, nearly 38 percent strongly agreed (14.8 percent) or agreed with reservations (23.0 percent) with the statement, "I am considering entering another line of work because prospects for academic advancement seem limited now." On this variable they differed significantly ($p <$ .001) from tenure-track faculty for whom the "strongly agree" and "agree with reservations" percentages were only 6.3 and 13.9, respectively.

Additional conformation of this apparent disaffection with academic careers among a large segment of non-track faculty was confirmed by another set of responses: Nearly 20 percent strongly agreed and an additional 35.7 percent agreed with reservations that they may leave the profession within the next five years. On this possible decision, they differed significantly ($p <$ .001) from tenure-track faculty, 11 percent of whom strongly agreed and 26 percent of whom agreed with reservations. In reviewing their decision to enter the professorate, 23 percent of non-track faculty agreed (strongly or with reservations) with the statement "I often wish I had entered another profession." Sixteen percent of their tenure-track colleagues had similar responses to the item. Although the differences in response were not significant, non-track faculty were less apt to strongly disagree with the statement.

Non-tenure-track faculty also differed significantly from tenure-track faculty on two other factors related to career satisfaction. Non-track faculty were more apt ($p <$ .001) than tenure-track faculty to express feelings of being "trapped" in a profession with "limited opportunities for advancement" (32.8 percent vs. 18.8 percent), and were more likely ($p <$ .05) to disagree strongly or disagree with reservations to the statement, "I am more enthusiastic about my work now than I was when I began my academic career" (37.7 percent vs. 29.2 percent).

Discussion and Summary

The results of this study indicate that untenured faculty in general experience considerable stress and uncertainty in the early stages of their careers. In many ways, the faculty in this study expressed many similar perceptions and concerns, regardless of whether they were non-tenure-track appointees or untenured but on the tenure track. Both groups mentioned dissatisfaction with their teaching loads, their role in academic governance, and their salaries. Similarly, the tenure-track and non-tenure-track faculty both expressed reservations about their prospects for future employment in higher education.

These data reinforce the hypotheses of career development theory that the early career phase of academic life is challenging for virtually all professors. Colleges and universities should be sensitive to these challenges, support new professors' current performance, and encourage their long-term professional development regardless of whether they are on the tenure track.

The results of this study also support the commonly held assumption that faculty appointed to non-tenure-track positions have distinctive attributes and operate in a different institutional environment than that experienced by their tenure-track colleagues. The non-tenure-track faculty who served as the basis for this analysis were more likely to be oriented to teaching as their primary career orientation, to be more committed to their interaction with undergraduates, and to be less committed to national disciplinary associations than their tenure-track colleagues. It is true that a significantly larger proportion of non-tenure-track faculty work at institutions that define teaching as their primary mission than their tenure-track colleagues. Therefore, it is difficult to ascertain whether these "preferences" are actual initial career orientations or have developed from employment circumstances.

Also significant to young faculty's progress and success are the institutional context and environment. Our findings indicate that non-tenure-track faculty are generally more negative about selected aspects of the institutional context than their tenure-track colleagues. Specifically, non-track faculty in this study felt that they had less influence on departmental and institutional policies, felt less involved in departmental faculty meetings and in campus faculty committees, felt more negative about their teaching loads, and also felt that their salaries were inadequate.

If these non-tenure-track faculty are an important human resource for higher education in meeting expected future faculty staffing needs, institutions must review the policies and/or practices that create these negative perceptions and feelings among full-time non-track faculty. The alternative is to lose them as faculty for the future.

Furthermore, at a time when institutions are recognizing the need for equity in recruiting and retaining women, it was disconcerting to find that women comprise about 50 percent of non-tenure-track faculty but only about one-third of the tenure-track personnel. The different proportion of women in the two categories is troublesome. First, women are the largest proportion of personnel filling full-time positions that are considered least secure in terms of long-term career development. Second, the fact that women hold only one-third of the tenure-track positions is disturbing on its face.

Perhaps the most noteworthy difference between the two groups of non-tenured professors concerns their perceptions about their career prospects. Both groups expressed some uncertainty about their futures in the academic profession. However, non-tenure-track faculty are more pessimistic about the future than tenure-track faculty. Their assessment of their situation is regrettable but seems realistic, given the peripheral status and expendable nature of non-tenure-track appointments in most higher education institutions.

Overall, this study demonstrates that the early phase of an academic career is an unsettled time that places great demands on new professors. Colleges and universities must recognize and respond to these stresses if they wish to maintain vigorous, high-quality faculty. Sensitivity to the distinctive concerns of different types of non-tenured faculty is essential if higher education is to attract and retain the high quality personnel needed to meet the educational challenges of the twenty-first century. Consistent with Light, Marsden, and Corl's (1972) career model, this study's findings reveal differences in both the institutional and disciplinary dimensions of the groups under investigation. Although the early career years are challenging for faculty in general, as developmental theory asserts, non-tenure-track-professors appear to confront more obstacles to long-term career advancement than professors on the tenure-track.

Bibliography

American Association of University Professors. "On Full-Time Non-Tenure-Track Appointments." *AAUP Bulletin 64* (September 1978): 267–73.

_____. "1986 Report on Full-Time Non-Tenure-Track Appointments." *Academe* 74 (July-August 1986): 14a–19a.

Baldwin, Roger G. "Faculty Career Stages and Implications for Professional Development." In *Enhancing Faculty Careers: Strategies for Development and Renewal*, by Jack H. Schuster, Daniel W. Wheeler, and Associates, 20–40. San Francisco: Jossey-Bass, 1990.

Baldwin, Roger G., and Robert T. Blackburn. "The Academic Career as a Developmental Process: Implications for Higher Education." *Journal of Higher Education* 52, no. 6 (1981): 598–614.

Blackburn, Robert T., and Neil R. Wiley. "Current Appointments and Tenure Practices: Their Impact on New Faculty Careers." *CUPA Journal* (Fall 1990): 9–20.

Bowen, Howard R., and Jack H. Schuster. *American Professors: A National Resource Imperiled*. New York: Oxford University Press, 1986.

Bowen, William G., and Julie Ann Sosa. *Prospects for Faculty in the Arts and Sciences*. Princeton, N.J.: Princeton University Press, 1989.

Carnegie Foundation for the Advancement of Teaching. *1989 National Survey of Faculty: Technical Report and Detailed Tabulations*. Princeton, N.J.: Carnegie Foundation, 1989.

El-Khawas, Elaine. *Campus Trends, 1988*. Higher Education Panel Report Number 77, Washington D.C.: American Council on Education, 1988.

_____. *Campus Trends, 1990*. Higher Education Panel Report Number 80, Washington D.C.: American Council on Education, 1990.

Fink, L. Dee. *The First Year of College Teaching*. New Directions for Teaching and Learning, No. 17. San Francisco: Jossey-Bass, March 1984.

Finkelstein, Martin. "Life of the 'Effectively Terminal' Tenure Track," *Academe*, 72 (January-February 1986): 32–36.

Gouldner, Alvin. "Cosmopolitans and Locals: Toward an Analysis of Latent Social Roles." *Administrative Science Quarterly* 2 (December 1957): 281–306.

Light, D. W., Jr., L. R. Marsden, and T. C. Corl. *The Impact of the Academic Revolution on Faculty Careers*. AAHE-ERIC Higher Education Report, No. 10. Washington, D.C.: American Association for Higher Education, 1972.

National Center for Education Statistics. *Faculty in Higher Education Institutions, 1988 (NSOPF 88)*. Washington, D.C.: U.S. Department of Education, March 1990.

National Research Council. *Summary Report 1988: Doctorate Recipients from United States Universities*. Washington, D.C.: National Academy Press, 1989.

Jay L. Chronister is a Professor at the Center for the Study of Higher Education, University of Virginia, in Charlottesville. Roger G. Baldwin is an Associate professor in the School of Education at The College of William and Mary, in Williamsburg. Theresa G. Bailey is an Associate Professor in the School of Education, Liberty University, in Lynchburg, Virginia. The source of data in this study is the 1989 Natioal Survey of Faculty by the Carnegie Foundation for the Advancement of Teaching.

Employment Profiles of Part-Timers

Judith Gappa and David Leslie

Part-time faculty come from extraordinarily varied and interesting work lives. We interviewed corporate executives and "starving poets," medical doctors and massage therapists, chemists and coaches, musicians and politicians, entrepreneurs and entertainers. Typically, part-time faculty have other work and sources of income. The large majority spend less than half their time teaching and derive an average of 18 percent of their total income from this source (NSOPF '88).

To explore how teaching fits in with their other work and activities, we asked about professional experiences, other jobs, and other teaching assignments. We also asked whether part-time faculty experienced conflicts among their roles and what their career aspirations were. Our goal was to understand the whole person so that we could better understand why people chose to teach part-time and what this decision meant to their lives and careers.

We were able to recognize four major clusters of academic background, employment history, and motivations. These clusters are only partly consistent with the popular and widely referenced topology generated a number of years ago by Howard Tuckman's (1978) research, which we summarize for the purpose of comparison.

We can see clearly that part-timers are not a monolithic group of marginal employees. We have identified four distinct subpopulations that we describe in this chapter. We show how individuals within each of these groups need varying career options and patterns of work and compensation in order to better meet their needs and those of the institutions they serve.

Categorizing Part-Timers' Employment Experiences

The diversity of employment experience we encountered in our site visits was first recognized and documented in a path-breaking study by Howard Tuckman in 1978. From the results of a survey of 3,763 part-time faculty members, Tuckman and his associates developed a taxonomy of part-timers based on their reasons for choosing part-time employment. This taxonomy contains seven categories:

1. *Semiretireds* (2.8 percent of Tuckman's total sample) were former full-time academics or professionals who were teaching fewer hours and were less concerned about future job prospects than the part-timers in other categories.

2. *Graduate students* (21.2 percent of the total sample) were usually employed as part-timers in institutions other than the one in which they were pursuing a graduate degree. They were teaching to gain experience and to augment income.

3. *Hopeful full-timers* (16.6 percent of the sample) were those who could not find full-time academic positions but wanted them. Tuckman also included those who were working enough part-time hours at one or more institutions to constitute full-time

employment but under several contracts, each of which only provided part-time status.

4. *Full-mooners* (27.6 percent of the sample) were individuals who held another primary job of at least thirty-five hours a week. Tuckman characterized these individuals as spending relatively little time preparing lectures and other teaching activities and limiting the number of hours they taught. He also included here tenured faculty teaching overload courses.

5. *Homeworkers* (6.4 percent of the sample) worked part-time because they cared for children or other relatives. Part-time employment might be the sole source of support for the homeworker's household or it might supplement the income of a spouse.

6. *Part-mooners* (13.6 percent) consisted of people working part-time in one academic institution while holding a second job of fewer than thirty-five hours a week elsewhere. Reasons given for holding two jobs simultaneously were economic necessity, psychic rewards not obtainable from one job only, concern about future employment prospects, and highly specialized skills that could be used by one employer only to a limited extent.

7. *Part-unknowners* (11.8 percent) were part-time faculty whose reasons for working part-time were either unknown, transitory, or highly subjective. (See Tuckman, 1978.)

Tuckman's topology continues to provide a foundation for viewing part-time faculty employment experiences and motivations. While Tuckman and Pickerill (1988) note that no recent data permit a new test of this topology, we encountered part-timers who fit neatly into the topology among the 240 part-timers we interviewed. Our interviews indicate, however, that there are some important changes to be taken into account. For example, we found that the "full-mooners" were very dedicated to their teaching and spent a great deal of time in preparation, and we found that the label "homeworkers" now encompasses a much broader array of people with a wide variety of care-giving roles and life-style concerns. Because the interview data gave us much more information about other components of people's lives, we found the patterns of work experience and motivation too complex to fit into the narrow categories Tuckman's topology suggests.

On the basis of our interviews, we have broadened Tuckman's topology into four loose categories: career enders; specialists, experts, and professionals; aspiring academics; and freelancers. We will briefly define these four categories from the perspective of Tuckman's topology and then look at each one in turn, using our site visit interviews to draw a more comprehensive picture.

We have retained Tuckman's category of semiretired but renamed it *career enders*. We have broadened it to include those who are already fully retired and those who are in transition from well-established careers (mostly outside of higher education) to a preretired or retired status in which part-time teaching plays a significant role. From our interviews, we would estimate that the percentage of part-timers who are retired or semiretired is now much higher than Tuckman's figure of 3 percent would suggest.

We have changed Tuckman's category of full-mooner to a designation of *specialist, expert,* or *professional* with a primary, usually full-time, career elsewhere. This group of people comes to higher education from a wide range of fields and careers and teaches for the love of it rather than because of a need for income. Some are hired as specialists to teach in their discipline; others are specialists in their primary occupation but teach as generalists. These specialists, experts, or professionals formed a significant portion of our total sample.

We have relabeled Tuckman's hopeful full-timers *aspiring academics* because the focus of their career aspiration is not necessarily to teach full-time but to be fully participating, recognized, and rewarded members of the faculty with a status at least similar to that currently associated with the tenure-track or tenured faculty. We include as aspiring academics only those part-timers who possess the terminal degree and want full-time academic careers and ABD doctoral students. Among the aspiring academics, we distinguish between only part-time faculty and those who have managed to become "full-time" part-timers because they have a combination of part-time appointments at the same institution or at several institutions. (This latter group is frequently referred to as "freeway fliers.") In some cases, these full-time part-timers carry teaching loads that are greater than full-time. We also include in this group those who are fully qualified but who are "stuck," the geographically immobile who have chosen a part-time teaching career because of family or other obligations.

We have been unable to estimate how common the freeway flier phenomenon may be. We found individual part-timers at virtually every institution in our sample who held more than one part-time teaching job. Yet nowhere did it appear to be the principal mode of employment for part-timers, contrary to the standard myth we have heard repeated many times. A study conducted by the Office of the Chancellor of the California Community Colleges (1987, p. 8) estimated the number of aspiring academics in this subgroup at about one-quarter of all part-timers, a proportion that was found to be increasing. An earlier study conducted by Dykstra (1983), on the other hand, found little evidence of "crosstown teaching" in the Columbus, Ohio, metropolitan area. Anecdotal evidence from our study suggests that this form of employment, undertaken out of economic necessity, is probably more common in large metropolitan areas, and it may be more consequential for individuals and institutions in those areas. Further direct study of this phenomenon is needed, with particular attention to geography.

Our final category is a composite of Tuckman's part-unknowners, part-mooners, and homeworkers that we have broadened and relabeled *freelancers*. It is a composite of all part-timers whose current career is the *sum* of all the part-time jobs or roles they have, only one of which is part-time teaching in higher education. Freelancers are part-time faculty in higher education by choice; they are not aspiring academics.

We found a good example of the mixture of part-timers among the different groups in our interviews at one large community college. Of the forty-four part-time faculty members we interviewed, eight were otherwise unemployed (four of these by choice), six were self-employed in their own businesses, six had other full-time jobs at the same institution, five were teaching elsewhere, five were retired, three were artists, three had corporate jobs, three were graduate students, two were musicians, two were state government administrators, and one reported that he was a starving poet and massage therapist. Seventeen of the forty-four part-timers considered their part-time employment at the community college to be their primary employment.

Career Enders

Among the career enders we interviewed, one had just begun teaching international economics at a university. He had done his graduate work in the 1950s and had been a full-time faculty member for four years. He then went into the foreign service as an economic adviser in Vietnam and other Asian locations. Subsequently, he was employed by the Department of Commerce, U.S. Agency for International Development (USAID), and several major corporations. Upon his retirement from the government, he established a real estate partnership to buy inner-city property in Washington, D.C. Continuously seeking a challenge, he had just taken up part-time teaching.

Another career ender we interviewed had been retired for a longer period of time but continued to work part-time where he had spent his career, in education:

> I taught in the public schools for twenty years and then was a principal. I spent thirty-three years in public education. I've been teaching at the local community college and at _____ for three years. I'm retired, but I currently serve on a part-time basis as the truant officer for the schools and sell as much fish as I can catch in my spare time.

Others we interviewed had more prosaic reasons for teaching in retirement, such as those offered by a woman recently retired from teaching:

I'm glad to be out of the junior high school setting. Now that I'm retired, I need a routine and a structure. This provides me with that.

Another, a man retired from a career in public administration, said,

I've always taught, and now that I'm retired the routine is useful to keep me on track. I enjoy this because it keeps me in touch with young people and intellectually alive. I do four courses a term and love teaching.

As current faculty members reach retirement age in progressively larger numbers in the coming years, we expect that many will choose to teach part-time while phasing into full retirement. If this trend develops, it will mean that substantial numbers of experienced faculty may become available, altering the present marketplace for faculty in ways we do not yet foresee.

Specialists, Experts, and Professionals

According to NSOPF '88 data, over half of the part-time faculty in all institutions (52.5 percent) have other full-time employment. This ranges from a low of 37 percent at liberal arts colleges and public doctorate-granting institutions to a high of 67 percent at private doctorate-granting universities. There is also variation among disciplines. Only 19 percent of those in the humanities have full-time positions elsewhere, while 59 percent of those in education, 67 percent in business, and 73 percent in engineering work full-time at other jobs.

Those who do have full-time positions elsewhere tend to have been employed at their colleges or universities as part-time faculty members for a longer period of time. About 60 percent of the part-timers who have full-time positions elsewhere have been employed more than four years as compared with an average of 48.6 percent for all part-time faculty. Similarly, the higher the terminal degree, the more likely the part-time faculty member is to have full-time employment elsewhere. Across all types of institutions, 61 percent of the part-time faculty who have doctoral or professional degrees also have full-time employment elsewhere, but only 47 percent of those with master's degrees and 52 percent of those with bachelor's degrees work full-time elsewhere (NSOPF '88).

At virtually every institution in our study, we interviewed part-timers who have full-time jobs as professionals or managers. They have advanced training in fields such as medicine, allied health, biochemistry, mathematics and statistics, public administration, business, education, social work, law, and criminal justice. Some of them teach courses closely related to their primary occupation; some of them were hired as generalists for courses such as basic mathematics. For almost all, their teaching represents a professional commitment, a community service, and a source of personal satisfaction.

Since most of the part-time faculty we interviewed who also have full-time positions elsewhere already enjoy comparatively high salaries and relative employment security, they have little economic need or motive to teach part time. They are teaching because they want to. Usually, they do not experience conflict with their full-time jobs:

My superiors and subordinates on my full-time job are supportive. They don't see my teaching as competitive. This job keeps me fresh and enthused. I recruit volunteers from classes to help out at the facilities. I can use real life examples in class.

At San Jose State University, we interviewed the dean of the School of Engineering who talked about his proximity to Silicon Valley and the need to graduate quality engineers:

To make sure we graduate quality engineers, we must have part-timers. Industry understands this. People from the companies come in at all times of day. [We have] a partnership concept. . . . Teaching at San Jose State is part of the part-timers' outside work assignment with their companies.

Some fast-track professionals enjoy the intrinsic rewards of teaching but do not always appreciate or understand the folkways of academic life. One Ph.D. in economics had worked for a

Big Eight accounting firm and subsequently formed his own company. He currently teaches macroeconomics and would be well qualified for a tenure-track position, but he has reservations:

> I just enjoy teaching. The rest of what [the faculty] are involved in is a pain in the butt. Committee work is redundant and a waste of time. Also, academic work is not as financially rewarding as work in the private sector. I decided to leave academe because of finances. But I like being in the classroom. Teaching is much more fulfilling than work in the private sector. Right now I have the best of both possible worlds.

One individual with a Ph.D. in mathematics and statistics had originally considered an academic career. Instead he had become a statistical systems analyst for a research institute. Then he worked at the Department of Health, Education and Welfare setting up medical data bases and data analysis systems. He is currently employed in a management position as a senior statistician with another major federal agency. Despite his decision to forego an academic career, he has been teaching evening courses since receiving his Ph.D.

> It is *fun*. I enjoy teaching, but I don't want to do it full-time. I had that option after I got the Ph.D. I looked at it as a career. I could have gotten an academic job in 1973, but [the job market] was discouraging. I've learned a lot about myself. I'm not much of a publisher. I have published ten to twelve articles in sixteen or seventeen years, and these are policy interpretation stuff. I've lost the cutting edge. I enjoy the teaching, but I don't want the rest of the full-time responsibility.

Another part-time faculty member also currently works as a biochemist for a major corporation. His research, while satisfying, does not fulfill his interests in teaching:

> I love teaching! I work full-time in the private sector for the money and because I have a chance to do research. But I wanted to grow personally and am looking to options for a postretirement career—teaching is high on the list. I love the challenge of dealing with students who aren't intrinsically interested and who are required to be in my class. I feel I can bring real world examples to help motivate and interest them in the study of biology.

Over and over again, we interviewed executives, health care specialists, engineers, artists, public school teachers, and others who teach in addition to their full-time careers. They teach because they love to and are rejuvenated by their students. But they often teach at considerable personal sacrifice.

> When you work full-time, it is hard to find the time to teach. It is hard to juggle the schedule. I teach at most twice a year here. Employers are supportive of the concept [of teaching] but the work doesn't go away. Employers are expecting nothing; in return they are neutral. It is your choice to teach.

Part-timers in the School of Extended Education at Saint Mary's College whom we interviewed were commuting to off-campus teaching sites from homes and jobs all over the greater San Francisco Bay area, frequently at peak commuting hours.

> My personal life is very scheduled, and my children recognize this. My wife is also in health care. I schedule time with the children. I keep a calendar, and the kids know this. I am working in Pleasanton, living in Richmond, and teaching in San Francisco. But the students are also driving and preparing and they have full-time jobs.

Still, the personal price tends to be worth the costs to those with primary jobs elsewhere. As one part-timer put it:

> Teaching at _____ is the only stable part of my life. CEOs in health care have rapid turnover.

Some careerists mentioned their desire eventually to switch from full-time executive jobs to teaching positions:

Teaching is very rewarding personally. In five or six years I would like to make a career change to full-time teaching and part-time consulting. Now I have two children.

Aspiring Academics

Aspiring academics include relatively new Ph.D.'s seeking tenure-track appointments and some Ph.D. recipients who have been teaching on a part-time basis for years in the hope of attaining a full-time, tenure-track position. Under better circumstances, they would be part of the tenured faculty. Aspiring academics also include ABD doctoral students who are simultaneously employed as part-timers.

Many of these long-term part-timers, while still retaining a wish that they could be part of the "regular" faculty, have found ways to build academic careers within their part-time status. In the most satisfactory arrangements, they have successfully put together several part-time assignments within their institutions and/or have taken leadership positions in faculty governance.

One part-timer exemplifies this group of individuals. With a Ph.D. from a leading university in 1972, he held a tenure-track position for four years before deciding to return to California. Employed in higher education for several years, he was laid off in the wake of California's Proposition 13. He then took courses in computer science at his local community college. In 1978 he returned to the university in a half-time faculty position in medieval studies and in a staff position created for him because of his knowledge of the use of computers in the humanities. Now he teaches courses in his discipline in three different departments and is also employed as a data base manager. All of his part-time assignments, when put together, are more than full-time. This ability to put together a full-time "position" out of pieces of part-time assignments is characteristic of more than a few of the part-timers we interviewed. While the pieced-together temporary assignments may constitute a full-time work load, they remain without the status, salary, benefits, and security normally associated with full-time or regular employment. At any time one of the part-time assignments can easily "disappear."

For other aspiring academics we interviewed, waiting and hoping had extended for substantial periods of time without bearing fruit. Some of these people realized that they were now falling behind the newer doctoral graduates and had become less attractive as potential full-time faculty. One assessed his situation this way:

> I am ambivalent as to whether part-time faculty should be thankful they've had an opportunity to teach or whether they should be regretful that they've pursued teaching too intensely at the expense of other things. You teach part-time here at the expense of research, and this forecloses opportunities. . . . There are also psychological issues: part-time faculty sometimes wonder if they are living in an artificial world; my kids think I'm a professor, but I know nothing is guaranteed beyond the current semester. I feel I am under scrutiny all the time. I worry about how I am doing and am oversensitive to student reactions. Every year, you are judged. You have to perform all the time and can't rely on the colleagueship or goodwill of full-time faculty. I also can't take time to do research. I teach ten to fifteen hours each semester with hundreds of papers, and I don't have time for research or even to prepare properly for class. I know I've devoted too much energy to teaching and should have done more research. I deeply regret this choice, but [I] had no alternative at my age and with my family commitments. I needed to provide a stable income.

This person was acutely conscious that he had essentially foregone the opportunity for a full-time position and was now "stuck" in a marginal role in academic life. A major reason for being stuck is lack of geographical mobility. Another part-timer we interviewed is teaching at a large comprehensive regional university in an urban area. She has all her degrees, including her doctorate from the institution where she is currently employed as a part-timer. She started teaching part-time as a graduate student in 1978. By the mid 1980s she had achieved a full-time teaching load while retaining part-time status.

> I wanted an academic career, and this is the only way I could do it. . . . Part-time work was the only route to go. . . . I am not terribly satisfied. I am paying a mortgage and am overworked to meet this obligation. I need to work hard to survive. . . . [There is] not enough time to do a lot of research. Also, I am committed to one institution. As a part-timer, I basically have to take the work that is available to me. I want to teach a philosophy course. I am teaching humanities, social sciences, English, extended education. [I am] teaching all over the university. . . . Our experience is a mile wide but an inch deep. . . . I can use my seniority to get part-time positions all over the university, but I can't use it to get a tenure-stream appointment.

These two individuals exemplify a small but important and vocal part of our total sample: those dedicated, well-prepared individuals who still hope to move to tenure-track status but who have pursued, for whatever reasons, the wrong strategies for achieving that goal. They feel stuck, and their future prospects are uncertain at best.

Other aspiring academics are more recent Ph.D.'s. Some begin teaching part-time immediately after completing the Ph.D.while they seek tenure-track positions. Others are teaching part-time because of family responsibilities. While we interviewed several men who are the trailing spouses in dual-career couples (see Chapter Two), by far the majority are women. These women are caught in their prime childbearing years in an unresolvable conflict between their desire to have a family and the lack of alternatives and flexibility in an academic career. Through its rigidity, this career system fails to use considerable available talent and also demonstrates a systemic, if not intentional, gender bias. Such bias wreaks havoc with the lives and plans of superbly well-qualified individuals:

> I came from England where I did my B.A. I came to _____ on a four-year fellowship to do my Ph.D. I did not originally plan to stay here. I met someone who became my husband, and now I'm on my second child. The first child was born in 1987. The consequence of this decision is that my husband is in his own business here and I am not mobile. My career plans changed. I have been working here as a lecturer since 1987, sometimes full-time, sometimes part-time. I'm almost forty; my husband is fifty. We did not plan to have children. I planned to have regional mobility and come home weekends or whatever. I looked for a tenure-track position. Then I got pregnant. Having a child changed my plans. I wasn't willing to commute long distances. Decisions have come after life changes. It has been *difficult*. I was always at the top in fellowships, scholarships. For example, I published my honors thesis as an undergraduate student. The institution loses out because I have lots more to offer than they are taking advantage of. The institution could gain from accommodating my needs. Until very recently I was not eligible for research grants.

In our interviews we encountered evidence of unused potential over and over again. Many women (and increasingly men, too) feel exploited by an academic career system that does not adequately address the interrelationship between the personal and professional lives of faculty and that takes advantage of their training and talent without providing rewards and incentives.

A small subset of those we interviewed were doctoral students close to completion of their Ph.D.'s and employed as part-timers. Aspiring academics who are also aspiring Ph.D. recipients can lead very hard lives. The Ph.D. candidates we interviewed had been struggling for years to earn a living by teaching part-time while finishing degrees. Said one,

> I came to the University of Minnesota to get a Ph.D. I am in my fourth year at _____. I am also teaching at three other institutions. I am primarily here as a Ph.D. student. The relationship between jobs is rough. I don't like what I am doing. It is hard on me and has slowed down my progress on the dissertation. I have to work hard to make a minimum income to support me and my family. It would be nice to have a job in one place so I wouldn't have to run around. My wife is not allowed to work because of immigration, and we have two children. It is not easy. Our last child had major medical problems. I hope to finish the Ph.D. in a year and a half.

Another interviewee had been working on her Ph.D. for seven years. She had received her undergraduate degree in 1968, worked as a librarian, had three children, and now is divorced.

> I am going to have to skip doing academic jobs in order to get ahead in my academic career. I need the money. I am a single mother with three teenagers. ABDs teaching part-time are having a real struggle. It's a full-time job just to be employed enough to support myself in getting the Ph.D. Colleges and universities are using us as a cheap source of labor.

A final subgroup of aspiring academics are "freeway fliers," those part-timers who have teaching assignments at several institutions at the same time. They represented a small portion of our total sample of part-timers. Their "packages" of teaching assignments in multiple locations contribute to the marginal nature of their affiliation with each of their institutions and to the little that is known about them by their departments. One young man's situation illustrates the rigors of multiple teaching assignments in different locations:

> I have a lot of roots in [the area]. I don't want to relocate. I wanted to keep a foot in each door as an inroad to a full-time job. . . . I have taught part-time a lot. One year I taught at five colleges simultaneously. Thursdays I started at the university for an 8 A.M. class. Then I went [across town] for a 9:45 A.M. class, which went to 11 A.M., then to [a nearby institution] for early afternoon and to [a fourth institution] for mid afternoon. Finally, I returned] to the university for an evening extension class. I finished teaching at 9 P.M. I think I taught well. I never sacrificed the classroom. The colleges lost the out-of-class interaction. It really compromised my personal life. But it would be too embarrassing to be unprepared for class.

Another part-timer in a large city had been teaching at three different institutions for the past eleven years, having begun her career as a part-timer more than twenty years ago. During our interview, she said,

> I used to teach seven or eight classes a semester. I'd come home and read *The Faerie Queen, Paradise Lost*, and *The Sun Also Rises* at the same time. I started retrenching. I try to coordinate. Here I have one class and work with the learning-disabled students. I also do tutoring ten hours a week. I have cut down on the work. Now I teach four courses a semester and a bit in the summer. I make $20,000. I don't think about the money. My primary job is at all three places. I am the oldest living adjunct (here). Nasty rule they have here—three-courses-a-year limit. That hurts. I used to teach two each semester and one in the summer. Doing the preparation for one class doesn't pay. But I like the variety. . . . I don't want to spend time on bureaucracy. I don't want committees. I don't like office politics. A number of things that go along with full-time work don't interest me. I would prefer the variety of three schools to the convenience of three composition courses here. I like the sense of freedom I have.

This part-timer is both a freeway flier and a freelancer. While she commented that there are aspects of the academic career she values, she also values her freedom and the variety that a series of part-time positions can offer. Thus, she provides a good introduction to our final employment group, the freelancers.

Freelancers

In our interviews, we encountered as many career profiles as we encountered freelancers. Their reasons for working part-time make sense in the context of their lives. The composite group of freelancers includes homemakers or primary care people artists and others seeking affiliation with an institution for a variety of reasons; individuals who choose to build their careers around a series of part-time jobs that are generally interrelated but occasionally capitalize on varied skills and talents; and individuals who at the time of our interviews occupied part-time positions for reasons beyond their control. A substantial number of the part-time faculty we interviewed were freelancing to support themselves. They held a variety of "jobs," including writing, consulting, and teaching and preferred not to have ties to any particular institution or position.

One woman we interviewed exemplifies the freelancers. She had moved to a rural area as a "life-style émigré" after her husband left corporate life. She now writes education books and manuals for teachers, offers in-service teacher training as an independent contractor, holds a one-quarter-time position as director of a state energy education program, and teaches part-time at a public institution in her area. Her various jobs and roles reinforce each other; what she learns in one arena she puts to use elsewhere. Her teaching job, for example, serves as a laboratory for new ideas that she can later pass along in her writing and consulting. Although she reported being isolated from the full-time faculty and her department chair, she prefers not to have any greater involvement in the institution because she values the free time she can devote to her other roles and activities.

There are many variations on this theme. Generally speaking, freelancing part-time faculty have much to offer the colleges and universities where they teach. They have varied experiences that they put to good use in the classroom. They tend to be resourceful and are able to use their contacts and connections to benefit the college or university. All in all, they constitute a resource not easily found in other ways. The part-timers who are freelancers are also usually uninterested in tenure-track appointments. They vary in whether or not they are dependent upon their part-time positions for salary or benefits.

Some of the freelancers we interviewed were experimenting at the time. They had not yet found a career that ideally suited their needs. One of the women we interviewed has bachelor's and master's degrees and a teaching credential. She had tried full-time teaching but had not found it a viable career alternative. So she had gone to Maine to write the great American novel and run out of money!

> It took me ten years to pay off the two degrees. I worked in a press office for a U.S. senator. He lost. My thirtieth birthday was spent in unemployment offices. I became the communications director of a company. Then I went to Lexington, Kentucky, as a spouse. There I taught business writing at the university and really liked it. But I hated Kentucky so we moved back. I worked for a trade association. I hate office politics, working twelve-hour days, feeling out of control of my life. So I went to part-time work. The head of my department was in a class in Gaelic [with me]. She hired me. Now I am putting together a Ph.D. program, teaching three courses, and making money as a freelance editor. I take the summers off and work on my fiction.

This ability and desire to handle multiple jobs and interests simultaneously was common in our interviews.

Some part-timers have already experimented and, at the time of our interviews, were quite satisfied with their career choice to be a freelancer. One of our interviewees had started out with a Ph.D. in English (Shakespeare). She had gone into publishing and opened her own consulting firm in textbook development. From there she had moved into business communication and teaching business writing. Recently married to a tenured faculty member, she has continued her consulting business and teaching, in combination with enjoying a new marriage and stepson. Experiencing a variety of roles or jobs simultaneously meets her personal needs at this point in her life.

At most of our site institutions we found a substantial number of freelance studio artists. One member of the art department at a comprehensive regional university in a large city was teaching at two other institutions and was also a professional painter when we spoke with her. Because of her financial needs and the benefits package the university offered, she commuted to the regional campus three days a week, leaving home at 5:30 A.M. and returning at 7:30 P.M. The other two days she taught at the other institutions. Another artist whom we interviewed talked about her commitment to staying in a major city in order to be part of its art world, to retain her affiliations with a gallery and an art institute. She talked about how she was balancing her life between the loneliness of painting in her studio and her teaching:

I want contact with people. I want to offer people things. It is a thrill to teach people how to draw or to help the advanced people into careers.

A music teacher at an urban community college maintained an intimidatingly energetic schedule, dividing her work among a number of activities. She told us:

I wanted to teach at the college level and wanted time for composing, arranging, and concertizing. In addition to teaching here, I also teach at [a local] music school, serve as church choir director, give concerts around the country, and provide private music lessons. I like the flexibility part-time teaching allows me.

Conclusion

The profiles of academic and employment experience show that the bifurcated employment system that lumps all tenure-track faculty in one class and all part-time faculty in another does not nearly fit the current realities. Part-time faculty come from enormously varied backgrounds and life situations. They need a far more flexible set of options, rewards, incentives, and recognitions for their work. Some depend almost completely on their part-time teaching to survive, but others are primarily committed to other professional careers in which they are well compensated. Some part-time faculty aspire to academic careers, but others have no interest in them at all. Yet most institutions treat all part-time faculty alike. They see part-timers as marginal, temporary employees with no past and no future beyond the immediate term and give them no incentive to stay and make a commitment.

Institutions should make a greater effort to understand who is teaching for them, what each person has to offer, and what kind of incentives and support would help part-timers make a greater contribution. For example, are aspiring academics being developed as a legitimate future pool for tenure-bearing appointments? Are career enders seeking part-time employment as an attractive transition to retirement? Are specialists, experts, and professionals recognized as an untapped resource with great potential for enriching academic programs? Could freelancers make more enduring contributions if they enjoyed a more stable employment relationship with their institutions? We found these questions rarely raised and even more rarely addressed because part-timers are treated as an invisible, indistinguishable mass and dealt with arbitrarily.

The Peer Review Process
Confidentiality and Disclosure

KENT M. WEEKS

During the 1980s courts have been required to address and to attempt to resolve the conflict between peer review confidentiality and the disclosure of such peer review materials. The initial results of this litigation produced confusion and a lack of uniformity. Despite the frequent recurrence of this academic dilemma, many colleges have failed to develop a consistent and workable policy to resolve this conflict. As a result, faculty members turned to the courts for relief even though the courts would prefer that these disputes be resolved by the institutions [4, 5, 6, 7, 21]. However, after eight years of litigation a framework for college administrators to respond to these issues is beginning to develop.

This article focuses on techniques and methods some courts have utilized to balance the tensions between the aggrieved faculty members who allege discrimination—sex, race, national origin, handicap, age—in the tenure or promotion process or who allege some other civil wrong and who seek disclosure of some aspect of the peer review process and the colleges at which the charges are levied and their assertions of confidentiality. In addition, the article analyzes four recent federal appellate court decisions and the application of these decisions by federal, district, and state courts and identifies the general guidelines that are clearly emerging from the litigation. Finally, the conclusion contains some suggestions on how to avoid litigation and offers some alternative approaches that would serve the best interests of all concerned parties.

Current Status of the Litigation

To date, four federal United States Circuit Courts of Appeals whose decisions apply to federal litigation in Connecticut, New York, Vermont [17], Delaware, New Jersey, Pennsylvania [11], Alabama, Georgia, Florida, Louisiana, Mississippi, Texas [9], Illinois, Indiana, and Wisconsin [13] have ruled on claims for an academic or evidentiary privilege when challenging disclosure of various inputs into the personnel decision-making process. With the exception of the Seventh Circuit, in a case involving Notre Dame University [13], the circuits have not been overly sympathetic to claims to a qualified privilege. In the Notre Dame litigation, the court sustained a privilege and ruled that a "particularized need" had to be demonstrated prior to disclosure of certain materials deemed to be confidential. Two other federal circuits in cases involving Professor Dinnan and the University of Georgia [9], and Franklin & Marshall College [11], have rejected the notion that there is any privilege available to protect peer review materials or votes. In the Second Circuit *Gray* decision [17], the court did balance the competing claims but held that the balance was on the side of the faculty member and therefore ordered disclosure of the votes of several members of the tenure committee.

Sooner or later, other federal appellate courts will be asked to review lower court decisions. Even though the United States Supreme Court has been provided two opportunities to review the issues and to clarify the judicial terrain, it has refused to do so.[1] When the Supreme Court denied the request for review filed by Franklin & Marshall College, Justices White and Blackmun noted that in light of the different approaches between the circuits in the decisions involving Franklin & Marshall College and Notre Dame University they would grant review in "order to resolve this conflict" [12].

Litigation, however, continues in both the federal district courts and in state court systems. Federal district courts have issued opinions involving Harvard University [19], Stanford University [24], the University of California, Berkeley [27], the University of Central Arkansas [26], and Macalester College [23]. Rutgers University [10], Skidmore College [8], Stanford University [2] and Middlebury College [3] have each defended requests for confidential material in state courts.

Competing Claims and Peer Review Materials

The issue of the confidentiality of the peer review system typically arises when a faculty member claims that a tenure denial or some other employment decision was based on various forms of discrimination. In order to substantiate this claim, the faculty member or the Equal Employment Opportunity Commission (EEOC) to which the faculty member has filed a discrimination claim attempts to acquire all relevant information, including access to peer review materials, in order to prove that the adverse personnel decision had a discriminatory basis.

Specifically, a faculty member alleges that a personnel decision violates Title VII of the Civil Rights Act of 1964 that prohibits employment decisions from being made on the basis of race, sex, national origin, or religion. Other statutes protect age or handicapping conditions. However, in order to meet the burden generally required by the courts to prove a discrimination claim, the faculty member must introduce evidence of intentional discrimination, bias, or animus. The best evidence of such discrimination may be to demonstrate that an evaluator discriminated against the faculty member or that other faculty with qualifications similar to those of the litigant were promoted when the aggrieved faculty member was not. If the faculty member is unable to obtain the requested data during the discovery process, litigation ensues over disclosure of the information. Thus, the battle lines are drawn between the aggrieved faculty member who desires access to all the materials necessary to show discrimination exists and faculty members and the college that want to protect the confidentiality of the peer review process and its materials.

The advocates of a qualified academic privilege maintain that "the peer review process is essential to the very life blood and heartbeat of academic excellence and plays a most vital role in the proper and efficient functioning of our nations colleges and universities" [13, p. 336].

These supporters of confidentiality claim a loss of confidentiality would result in overcautious and noncommittal evaluations. They portray the failure to allow a privilege from compulsory disclosure as seriously undermining the "effective self-government of a university organized on a collegial basis" [17, p. 907]. Consequently, these advocates claim that an educational institution, unlike a business organization, must have a privilege from compulsory disclosure to enable the college to maintain the special character of the peer review process.

On the other hand, the faculty member who alleges substantial violation of his or her constitutional or statutory rights argues that the evaluative personnel files must be disclosed in order to pursue a discrimination claim in court. These advocates claim that any denial of access to peer review materials creates an obstacle to the truth seeking function of the American judicial system [13, p. 337]. They further point out that a privilege from compulsory disclosure could still be used to cover up discrimination in the peer review process and argue that from a public policy vantage point the stamping out of discrimination has a higher priority than preserving the confidentiality of the personnel process [13, p. 337].

Discovery

A faculty member alleging employment discrimination, like all litigants in the legal system, is entitled to a very liberal discovery process [18, pp. 170–75]. The discovery process may be defined as a pretrial procedure in which both parties seek information and documents that enable them to prepare for a full and fair hearing. A specific request for information on a personnel decision occurs when the faculty files a formal request for personnel material or during a deposition when a colleague is requested to produce documents, to disclose a vote, or to discuss certain aspects of the peer review process.

According to the Federal Rules of Civil Procedure, the parties "may obtain discovery regarding any matter, *not privileged*, which is *relevant* to the subject matter involved in the pending action" [16]. Despite this broad statement of law, the same rules of procedure allow federal judges to limit the scope of discovery if a judge believes that a party should be protected from annoyance, embarrassment, oppression, undue burden, or expense. One may wonder why a privilege is necessary if the courts possess the discretionary power to refuse to order discovery. The fact remains that this protection is discretionary and, subsequently, fails to provide guidance to participants who need to know in advance what protections apply to the confidential information. Problems arise when aggrieved faculty members request the courts to compel colleges to disclose information because they believe the information in the personnel file is relevant[2] and would help them win their lawsuit. This request, in turn, is rejected by the institution on the grounds that the materials obtained in a peer review process are privileged.

Privileged information

Privileged information is an *exception* to the rule that a party may obtain information that is relevant during the discovery process [22]. Some privileges, such as that protecting a person from self-incrimination, are constitutional while others are based upon statute.

The constitutional basis for a qualified privilege protecting peer review material emanates from the notion of academic freedom. The argument is that the First Amendment, even though not explicitly stating so, contains an academic freedom protection within its free speech provisions. To support the argument, various judicial pronouncements are offered regarding the importance of academic freedom and its protections. For example, in 1967 the United States Supreme Court in *Keyishian* [20] stated that the nation is committed to "academic freedom which is of transcendent value to all of us and not merely to the teachers concerned. That freedom is therefore a special concern of the First Amendment. . . . The Nation's future depends upon leaders trained through wide exposure to that robust exchange of ideas which discovers truth" [20, p. 603]. And in the more recent *Bakke* decision [25] Justice Powell stated that academic freedom even "though not a specifically enumerated constitutional right, long has been viewed as a special concern of the First Amendment"[25, p. 312]. However,the use of the academic freedom privilege generally has been employed by colleges or individual professors to divert inquiries or attacks from outside the university. In the litigation over confidentiality and disclosure of peer review materials, the challenger is generally a member of the faculty or a party seeking disclosure on behalf of the faculty member.

Most privileges are based on common law or judicial sanction; that is, they have been established over the years by courts. In order to determine whether certain information is privileged and not subject to disclosure, a two-step procedure is undertaken by the court [5].

The first step is to determine whether a specific case presents the kind of information or relationship that ought to be protected [30]. In establishing a privilege against a disclosure of information, the court must determine if certain conditions are present regarding the value of confidentiality and the harm from disclosure. Under these conditions, a number of privileges have been recognized by the courts, such as the attorney-client privilege, the privilege protecting the confidential communications between priest and penitent, and the privileged communications between spouses.

Privileges, however, need not be absolute; some privileges are qualified. Thus, the second step requires the court to determine if a privilege must yield to the claim of a person seeking disclosure. In making this determination, courts generally consider a host of factors relating to the significance of the requested information to the litigant's claim and whether alternative sources for the information are available [28, p. 436]. In the end, the court would have to balance the party's right to discover against protecting the confidentiality of the peer review system.

Despite the federal court's ability to create privileges, the trend in the law is against finding the existence of a privilege except in the most unique situations [9, p. 429]. As noted in the Notre Dame litigation: "If an academic freedom privilege could be used to totally prohibit disclosure of tenure review records, the privilege could be used as a shield to hide evidence of discrimination" [13, p. 337]. Thus, even if a court creates a new privilege the trend is to narrowly limit its use.

Dinnan

The first major and most dramatic decision addressing this issue was delivered by the United States Court of Appeals, Fifth Circuit's decision in *In re Dinnan* [9]. At that time, the Fifth Circuit's jurisdiction included the states of Texas, Louisiana, Georgia, Mississippi, Alabama, and Florida. Professor James Dinnan served on the University of Georgia's Promotion Review Committee that denied promotion to a female faculty member allegedly on the basis of sexual discrimination. During the course of discovery, Professor Dinnan was requested in his deposition to reveal how he had voted in the aggrieved faculty member's bid for tenure. Professor Dinnan refused to answer the question under court order and subsequently was found in contempt of court and served a ninety-day sentence in the federal penitentiary. Professor Dinnan claimed he had a privilege not to testify grounded in the concept of academic freedom, which he argued protects an institution and its members from compulsory disclosure of materials that are a part of the evaluation process.

In addressing Professor Dinnan's argument that an evidentiary privilege must be established to protect academic freedom, the court noted that the nature of academic freedom usually has been used to protect a college or university from various forms of government intrusion to suppress the free exchange of ideas [9, p. 430]. In Dinnan's situation, government intrusion was not an issue, but to the contrary, an injured faculty member was trying to assert certain constitutional and statutory rights via the discovery process. Viewed in this light, the court determined that if Professor Dinnan's expansive definition of academic freedom were to be adopted, its implications would be "staggering" [9, p. 430] and various other important societal goals, such as the end of employment discrimination, would be "frustrated" [9, p. 431].

In bolstering its conclusion, the court devised a hypothetical fact scenario in which it stated that if a "tenure committee attempted to stop the promotion of all faculty members who were not pro-abortionists, a right-to-life music professor's attempt at discovery would be barred by the concept of academic freedom" [9, p. 436]. The court feared that the claim of academic freedom would shield the tenure committee from having to reveal its votes, even though the decision had nothing to do with any academic grounds. This probable result, grounded on the academic freedom privilege, "would serve to obstruct the vindication" [9, p. 431] of the rights of the injured faculty member. As the court concluded, "[T]his possibility is a much greater threat to our liberty in academic freedom than the compulsion of discovery in the instant case" [9, p. 431].

Accordingly, the court resoundingly rejected Professor Dinnan's attempt to claim that a privilege existed. The court based its decision on "fundamental principles of law and sound public policy" [9, p. 427]. Furthermore, the court recognized the inhibiting effect on litigation that imposition of a new privilege creates. In concluding its discussion of the feasibility and desirability of creating a privilege, the court stated: "[W]here there is no compelling justification for a new privilege, the vital truth-seeking function of our justice system must carry the day" [9, p. 430].

The court then proceeded to characterize Professor Dinnan's failure to testify as an attempt to avoid responsibility for his action [9, p. 432]. The claim of academic freedom cannot be used to avoid making tough tenure decisions. People in positions that inevitably would be called upon to make tough decisions "must have the courage to stand up and publicly account for [their] decision" [9, p. 432]. The court determined that if faculty members could not handle such responsibility, they should not accept positions in the personnel decision-making process. As the court concluded, "If it means that a few weak-willed individuals will be deterred from serving in positions of public trust, so be it; society is better off without their services" [9, p. 432].

AAUP Responds

In light of the Dinnan episode and the rejection of a claim to an academic freedom privilege, the AAUP prepared a "Preliminary Statement on Judicially Compelled Disclosure in the Nonrenewal of Faculty Appointments" [1]. Although deploring Dinnan's imprisonment and characterizing it as a "harsh action," the statement attempts to balance the competing claims of a faculty member's need for disclosure of personnel material with the interests of the institution and of the faculty members who participate in the peer review process.

First, the statement reaffirms the traditional AAUP position that a faculty person ought to have the right to an internal review of a nonrenewal decision when the faculty member alleges a violation of academic freedom or prejudice with respect to race, sex, religion, or national origin. Second, the statement recognizes that institutions "ought to be free from impermissible external intrusions or constraints in making nonrenewal decisions" [1, p.27]. Accordingly, the statement attempts to balance the value of maintaining institutional integrity and the need for faculty persons to have access to data from the evaluative process [1, p. 27].

Third, the AAUP position supports a qualified privilege for the motivations and actions of faculty participants in the appointment process. A number of factors are identified that a court should consider in determining whether the privileged nature of the communication must yield because a court believes that the "facts and circumstances raise a sufficient inference that some impermissible consideration was likely to have played a role to overcome the presumption in favor of the integrity of the academic process." The factors include:

> the adequacy of the procedures employed in the nonrenewal decision, the adequacy of the reasons offered in defense of the decision, the adequacy of the review procedures internal to the institution, statistical evidence that might give rise to an inference of discrimination, factual assertions of statements or incidents that indicate personal bias or prejudices on the part of the participants, the availability of the information sought from other sources, and the importance of the information sought to the issues presented [1, p. 28]

The AAUP statement was not without its critics. Both from within and outside the organization, faculty persons argued that it did not go far enough in protecting the integrity of the peer review process and conversely that it went too far and did not adequately protect the rights of faculty complainants.

AAUP Applied in *Gray*

The United States Court of Appeals, Second Circuit, did adopt a "balancing approach" in addressing the issue of confidentiality in the peer review process [17]. Simpson Gray, a black professor at the City University System of New York, LaGuardia Community College, challenged his denial of reappointment with tenure alleging racial discrimination.

Through his discovery attempts Professor Gray sought to uncover how two of the faculty members on the tenure committee voted on his application claiming such evidence was "material" and "indispensable" to the resolution of his case. The lower court created a "qualified privilege for tenure committee votes because confidentiality is integrally related to safeguarding academic freedom" [17, p. 902]. Thus, Gray was prohibited from discovering the votes.

On appeal, the United States Court of Appeals, the Second Circuit, however, adopted a balancing approach utilized in part by the lower court, but unlike the lower court it concluded that Professor Gray's need to obtain the votes outweighed the college's confidentiality interest. The Second Circuit s decision stemmed from its conclusions that the faculty members votes "were an indispensable element . . . without which proof of an intent to discriminate would be impossible" [17, p. 906]. The AAUP submitted a brief which served as the basis of the court's rationale in establishing the balancing approach enunciated.

After considering the various factors offered by the AAUP, the court stated: "Our decision . . . holds that absent a statement of reasons, the balance tips toward discovery and away from recognition of privilege" [17, p. 908]. In the future, if a detailed statement of reasons given by the peer review committee existed, then confidential materials in personnel files would not be routinely discoverable. However, in Professor Gray's case, no written statement of reasons was produced, and thus the court felt that the slight infringement on the confidentiality of the peer review system was outweighed by the various concerns of fair employment, academic excellence, and freedom.

Notre Dame

In 1983 the United States Court of Appeals, Seventh Circuit, expressly recognized the existence of a "limited academic freedom privilege in the context of challenges to college or university tenure decisions" [13, p. 337]. This decision represents the federal law that will be applied in Illinois, Indiana, and Wisconsin. In this case, Oscar T. Brookins, a black assistant professor of economics, filed a charge of unlawful discrimination with the Equal Employment Opportunity Commission (EEOC) against the university, claiming he was denied tenure on the basis of race. He alleged that the university had not provided him with a written statement of reason on why he was denied tenure; the economics department had never extended tenure to a black professor; and the economics department chairman had made statements to Brookins' Caucasian wife in which the chairman made known that he did not believe the races should be mixed.

Upon receiving this complaint, the EEOC initiated an investigation which culminated in the issuing of a subpoena demanding that the university turn over the personnel files of Brookins and others considered for tenure during the time period in question. The university refused to comply and argued that the personnel files contained confidential peer review evaluations protected by a qualified academic privilege. Moreover, the university proposed to delete the names and identifying information of those individuals who participated in the peer review process and argued that the EEOC should execute a nondisclosure agreement prior to any release of faculty personnel files.

Because the university refused to comply with the EEOC request, the EEOC sought enforcement of the subpoena in federal district court. The university wanted the court to recognize a qualified academic privilege and to prohibit the disclosure of the persons involved in the peer review process. It did not ultimately refuse to produce the documents requested by the EEOC. The district court did not recognize Notre Dame's claims. On appeal, the Seventh Circuit, acknowledging the university's precarious position, maintained that confidentiality is critical to the decision-making process but yet must not be absolute because substantial interests on both sides are at stake.

The court set forth elaborate procedures for the lower courts to follow to ensure that the confidentiality of the peer review system was maintained. The university would be permitted to redact all of the identifying information of the reporting scholars in the personnel files. Upon doing so, the university should produce redacted files plus the original unredacted files to the lower court. The lower court then, outside the presence of both parties, would determine if the redactions were "reasonably necessary' to prevent disclosure of the reporting scholar or scholars. If found to be reasonably necessary, the court would give the redacted file to the EEOC and the original file back to the university.

The process does not end when the EEOC receives the "altered" personnel file. The EEOC may decide it needs identifying information from the files in order to substantiate the charge of discrimination. To receive more information, the court set a high standard to be achieved before such additional information will be revealed. The EEOC must "make a substantial showing of 'particularized need' for relevant information" [13, p. 338]. The aggrieved faculty member must "show a 'compelling necessity' for the specific information requested" [13, p. 338] before a court will order disclosure of privileged information. In stating what is necessary to meet this high standard, the court maintained that a party must engage in extensive and exhaustive discovery "to exploit each and every possible source of information" [13, p. 338] before it seeks privileged material.

What then is the consequence of requesting a party to show a "particularized need" for relevant information? The answer is simple. As the court states, "We foresee the identities of the scholars would be released only under the most limited circumstances" [13, p. 339]. The Seventh Circuit decision does not categorically bar any complainant from acquiring any privileged information, but rather due to the qualified nature of the privilege, the decision sets up procedures whereby certain privileged information will be revealed only after all other possible avenues of discovery have been exhausted.

Franklin & Marshall

In 1985 the United States Court of Appeals, Third Circuit, followed *Dinnan* and refused to recognize a qualified academic freedom privilege or to adopt a balancing approach similar to the ones utilized by other federal courts. The decision involving Franklin & Marshall College represents the law in the states of Delaware, New Jersey, Pennsylvania, and the Virgin Islands [11]. Gerald Montbertrand, an assistant professor of French, claimed that Franklin & Marshall College refused his tenure application because of his French origin in violation of Title VII of the 1964 Civil Rights Act. After unsuccessfully following the college's appellate and grievance procedures in attempting to reverse the decision, Montbertrand filed his charge of discrimination with the EEOC which then requested certain materials from the college in order to pursue its investigations of Montbertrand's claims.

The college complied with some of the requests for materials such as grade surveys, enrollment data, student evaluations, but refused to provide other materials including "tenure recommendation forms prepared by faculty members, annual evaluations (except those prepared by the Dean), letters of reference, evaluations of publications, evaluations by outside experts, and all notes, letters, memoranda, or other documents considered during each tenure decision" [11, pp. 112–13]. As a result of the college's resistance, the EEOC went to court to force the college to comply. The lower federal court ruled that Franklin & Marshall had to comply but would allow the college to delete the names and identifying data in the confidential personnel files. As a result, the college appealed the decision, but the Third Circuit affirmed the lower court decision.

Several liberal arts colleges requested the court to sustain a qualified privilege and to acknowledge the particular nature of the peer review process within a small college and more specifically, the need for confidentiality and honest assessments because "in such close educational settings of the size of the appellant, . . . tenure applicants and tenure decision makers continue to work side-by-side" [11, p. 114]. The court acknowledged that Franklin & Marshall, in addition to other liberal arts colleges, had "forcefully argued the increased importance of confidentiality based upon the relatively small size of the teaching staffs and administrative personnel. They cite[d] embarrassment, confrontational situations, and the fear of less than honest evaluations as likely results of a lack of confidentiality [11, p. 114].

The college's position was clear: "The court should adopt a qualified academic peer review privilege which would prevent disclosure of confidential peer review material absent a showing of an inference of discrimination" [11, p. 113]. However, the court rejected this suggestion and concluded that "[a] privilege or Second Circuit balancing approach which permits colleges and universities to avoid a thorough investigation would allow the institutions to hide evidence of discrimination behind a wall of secrecy" [11, p. 115]. The court acknowledged the probable burden on the tenure process by the EEOC's ability to review the confidential materials but concluded, "[W]e have no choice but to trust that the honesty and integrity of the tenured reviewers in evaluation decisions will overcome the feelings of discomfort and embarrassment and will outlast the demise of absolute confidentiality" [11, p. 115].

Upon losing the qualified academic privilege argument, the college argued that the EEOC must show that the alleged discrimination charge by the aggrieved faculty member has some merit before the college has to turn over the confidential materials. The college feared that unless the EEOC was required to show some evidence to substantiate the charge, the subpoena could be used as a "fishing expedition" to see what was in the personnel file. Furthermore, the college believed other avenues of discovery could be used to determine if there had been discrimination. However, the court did not accept this argument, claiming that the standard which limits the EEOC's subpoena power is relevancy. Based upon this standard, the court found the materials relevant to the investigation and affirmed the lower court's order.

During and following the decisions from these four federal appellate courts, activity at both federal district courts and state courts increased. Faculty members continued to seek disclosure of their own and other faculty personnel files, materials from committee deliberations, and the names of evaluators. These decisions point to further refinements in the judicial saga on confidentiality of the peer review process.

Disclosure of Third Party Files

The New Jersey Supreme Court recently held that the academic freedom privilege did not protect confidentiality of material contained in promotional packets of faculty members at Rutgers, the State University of New Jersey [10].

In accordance with university procedures, Dr. Ruth Dixon, a black female and assistant professor at Rutgers Camden College, was evaluated for promotion and tenure by an ad hoc faculty committee, the Appointments and Promotions Committee, and the Dean of the College. After receiving a unanimous recommendation for tenure and promotion, her promotion packet was sent to the Promotion Review Committee (PRC). This committee is appointed by the university president to review all evidence previously considered in the proposed promotion and granting of tenure, including confidential letters of recommendation from sources outside of the university. The PRC decided that there was "insufficient evidence of distinction in teaching, creativity and research," which precluded its recommendation of Dixon for promotion and tenure. The previous day the PRC had recommended Henry Eng for tenure and William Jones for tenure and promotion. These two recommendations were adopted by the Rutgers Board of Governors.

Utilizing the internal grievance procedures, Dixon appealed the decision. After a further review which supported Dixon, the Promotion Review Committee recommended against tenure and promotion. For some unstated reasons, the Board of Governors granted Dixon tenure but sustained the recommendation to deny her promotion to associate professor.

Dixon filed a complaint with the state Division of Civil Rights (DCR) alleging discrimination based on race and sex. The DCR examined the promotion packets including confidential letters of the outside reviewers of Dixon, Eng, and Jones under a protective stipulation and found probable cause to credit the sex discrimination claim in the denial of tenure and promotion to Dixon. No support was found for the racial discrimination claim after noting that Eng was oriental and Jones was black.

The case was transferred to the Office of Administrative Law to be prosecuted by the attorney general. The Administrative Judge denied Rutgers' preheating motion to preclude the admission of the promotion packets of Dixon, Eng, and Jones. The administrative law judge did permit Rutgers to excise the names of the outsider reviewers; however, Rutgers was prohibited from placing greater weight on one outside specialist over another because of reputation in the academic community.

Rutgers appealed. A New Jersey appellate court rejected Rutgers' claim citing *Dinnan* for the presumption against recognizing additional privileges in the absence of compelling reasons. The court ruled that the potential damage to the peer review process was heavily outweighed by the strong public interests of disclosing relevant evidence and opposing discrimination. Because comparative materials were imperative in demonstrating discrimination, full disclosure of the relative qualifications of Eng, Jones, and Dixon along with the information contained in their promotional packets was necessary, particularly when no alternative sources were available.

On appeal to the New Jersey Supreme Court by Rutgers, the court first rejected Rutgers' argument that the promotional packets of Eng and Jones were not relevant to a determination of whether sex bias entered into the denial of tenure and promotion. Even though the other two professors might have had different responsibilities or been evaluated by different persons, or comparisons were not made during the review process, the court stated:

> Only through comparison can she show that male faculty members received promotion and tenure though less qualified; and only by comparing her record with others can she show that the rationale for her denied tenure and promotion was not equally applied to exclude others [10, p. 1053].

Second, both Rutgers and Princeton through an *amicus* brief also argued that a qualified privilege protected the packets from disclosure. They argued that before such confidential material should be disclosed, Dixon had to demonstrate a "particularized need" or a compelling necessity for the specific information requested.

Even though the court rejects the academic freedom privilege, it does assess how disclosure and confidentiality claims can be reconciled. Dixon, according to the court, had to show that her claim had some real substance and that the documents requested were truly relevant to her claim. Moreover, the court orders trial courts to be creative in designing protective procedures to assure confidentiality.

According to the New Jersey Supreme Court, trial courts should "examine the strength of the complaint" and consider the various factors offered by the AAUP in determining whether a claim "is valid" [10, p. 1058]. Following a determination of the *validity* of the claim, the courts must determine the *relevancy* of the material requested. The court encourages trial courts to utilize appropriate protective measures such as: (1) limiting access to persons directly involved in the case; (2) limiting access to those persons who prepared them or who had access to them; (3) sealing certain portions of depositions until required for trial; (4) confining use of materials to particular litigation and requiring return once the litigation is completed; (5) limiting scope of discovery; and (6) redacting names and other identifying features contained in the promotion packets with the court to review the original and redacted copies and settle any disputes about further disclosure.

In summary, the New Jersey Supreme Court ruled:

> Our State's strong public interest in eradicating discrimination in employment outweighs the public interest in preserving the confidentiality of peer review material through the creation of a qualified academic privilege. Academic freedom cannot be used as a shield to conceal discrimination. Hence, we do not create a qualified privilege to protect the confidentiality of peer review materials used by a university in its tenure and promotion decisions. Instead we find that the use of protective orders that substantially limit access to the materials and provide for redaction procedures will best accommodate the competing interests [10, p. 1061].

Tenure Deliberations

Michael J. Desimone, an assistant professor of business at Skidmore College sued the college and attempted to take the deposition of a member of the Promotions and Tenure Committee of the Business Department [8]. The college objected to the effort to obtain evidence about the deliberations of the Promotions and Tenure Committee.

On two occasions, the Committee had evaluated Desimone and on both occasions had recommended his reappointment. However, he was denied reappointment by the dean. During deposition, a member of the committee was directed by the college's attorney not to answer any questions relating to the deliberations of the committee, discussions of the committee members or statements made by committee members.

Accordingly, Desimone brought a lawsuit to compel the faculty member, Betty Belevic, to testify. The court reasoned that the deliberations of the committee had nothing to do with Desimone's denial of reappointment because the committee had recommended his reappointment.

The court noted that "without extraordinary cause" the court was not inclined to allow discovery. If Desimone had a dispute it was with the dean and not with the committee. Because the discovery request related to "deliberations which appear to be unconnected with the ultimate decision to deny the plaintiff reappointment" [8, p. 881], the court denied the discovery request.

Nanette Rollins was employed as assistant professor by the University of Central Arkansas in 1978. She was denied tenure in 1984. She subsequently filed a lawsuit in which she alleged that the denial of tenure was based on discrimination for reasons of age and sex [26]. She also alleged denial of due process. Furthermore, she argued that some of the reasons for her denial of tenure were based on false rumors. She was not given any reasons for the denial of her tenure.

During discovery, Rollins took the deposition of Sarah McAuley, a member of the Tenure Committee. When asked certain questions about Rollins' application for tenure and negative comments evoked by it by members of the committee, McAuley refused to answer asserting an academic freedom privilege from disclosure. McAuley did state that the minutes of the Tenure Committee contained some of the reasons for the adverse decision of the committee. McAuley also testified that two persons who were considered for tenure immediately prior to Rollins were routinely approved after it had been determined that their applications met the specific criteria listed in the college handbook.

Rollins sought to obtain the tenure files of various faculty members and the minutes of the faculty committee that considered her application. The college argued that there was a qualified academic peer review privilege "which would prevent disclosure of confidential peer review material absent a showing of an inference of discrimination, in order to 'balance' the needs of the employee and the university's 'academic freedom' and interest" [26, p. 716].

The district court after analyzing each of the four United States Court of Appeals decisions concluded that Rollins could obtain the votes, minutes, and deliberations of the tenure reviewing body because, the allegations concerned employment discrimination in which proof of intent to discriminate was necessary.

The court, however, did place some limitations on access to these documents. In order to obtain disclosure, a faculty member must allege that the documents sought through compelled discovery will produce evidence needed for the litigation. For example, if a faculty member seeks confidential information that has no utility to the litigation, the court should not compel discovery. As the court reasoned, if a faculty member "is falsely accused of tardiness, missed classes, or drunkenness on the job, these allegations could possibly be shown to be pretextual in nature without reference to the confidential deliberations" [26, p. 719].

Rollins's claims of discrimination, however, related to the fact that the Tenure Committee applied criteria to Rollins that were not listed in the handbook. Accordingly, the minutes of those deliberations were critical to an assessment of Rollins's claim. Finally, the court acknowledged in this case that in balancing the competing claims the infringement on the peer review process was outweighed by the demands of fair employment as well as those of academic excellence and freedom.

Cynthia Orbovich was a political science professor at Macalester College. In June of 1987 she was denied tenure and given a terminal contract for the academic year 1987–88. She filed a complaint of sex discrimination with the EEOC and eventually filed a lawsuit in federal district court [23].

The political science department and the Faculty Personnel Committee both had recommended Orbovich for tenure. However, it was the provost and the president who denied the tenure. Upon an appeal to a faculty committee, the committee recommended that the president reverse the negative decision. But that was not done.

A skirmish arose over the information that the college would make available to Orbovich. Orbovich requested that she be given access to all of the peer review materials reviewed by the Tenure Committee and access to files of other tenured faculty at Macalester College. The college resisted these claims by asserting an academic freedom privilege. The college also asserted that it had promised confidentiality to all outside reviewers who participated in the review process and that comparative treatment of other employees did nothing to determine Orbovich's eligibility for tenure. Orbovich filed a motion to compel answers to interrogatories and to produce certain documents.

After reviewing the various court approaches, the court decided that the approach taken in the University of Central Arkansas litigation was appropriate [26]. In order to pursue her discrimination claim, access to personnel files, disclosure of evaluators, and access to other tenure files were necessary. Furthermore, the court ruled that comparative assessment of files of other faculty members was relevant to Orbovich's claim. The court concluded that full disclosure must be made, but a protective order was issued prohibiting the disclosure of the personnel file material to any person other than the parties in the litigation.

Disclosure of Evaluators

Several female faculty members brought suit against the University of California at Berkeley, alleging sex discrimination in employment [27]. Specifically they alleged that the "old boy network" was operating at the same time they applied for employment. Jacqueline Desbarats applied for a job in the geography department. The position was awarded to a male candidate who was a close friend of one of the professors in the geography department. Furthermore, Desbarats alleged that certain information in the confidential personnel file of the male applicant was changed and that the job description also was changed to accommodate the male protégé.

Desbarats as one of the litigants requested access to the confidential letters of recommendation. The university was willing to provide the litigants with the substance of the letters but argued that it had a privilege that protected it from identifying the letter writer. However, Desbarats insisted that she needed to know who wrote each letter.

Again, after reviewing various court's approaches to the confidentiality and disclosure issue, the federal district court concluded that a balancing approach should be applied. The court reasoned that even if the university did have an interest in confidentiality, Desbarats's need for disclosure outweighed that interest and accordingly ordered the university to provide that information:

> Alleged irregularities in the process resulted in the hiring of a male (who allegedly did not have the original expertise required) over a female (who allegedly did have the original expertise required). Those alleged irregularities could only be demonstrated through the identity of the evaluator, not by the substance of the evaluation. Thus, plaintiffs have shown a particularized need in this case for the identity of the evaluator [27, p. 4].

Summary

The best preventive strategy is to make sure that discriminatory factors do not influence a personnel decision. It has been the litigation involving allegation of discrimination that has prompted most of the disclosure litigation. However, the issue of the confidentiality of the peer review system remains. Several techniques or alternatives can be gleaned from the various court decisions which enable colleges to respond to discovery proceedings without violating confidentiality. These include:

1. A college could provide a summary of data so that a faculty member would have adequate information in order to pursue litigation without having to seek the original documents or notes. The problem with this alternative may be the reluctance of an aggrieved faculty member to accept this data summary as being truthful. The faculty member may be inclined to believe the college fabricated the summary and thus would press for the disclosure of the original documents or votes.

2. The college could follow the procedures enunciated in the *Notre Dame* case. In essence, the college would edit all the information identifying the reporting scholars in the personnel files and then submit these files plus the original file to the court. Upon receipt of these files, the court would determine, outside the presence of both parties, whether the editing was "reasonably necessary" to prevent the scholar's disclosure.

3. If the college fails to convince the court to adopt one of the above alternatives and orders full disclosure, the college should ask the court for a protective order which would limit the use, access, and dissemination of the confidential data.

Even though the litigation over confidentiality and disclosure will continue, several common themes emerge in both federal and state courts. Those themes can be summarized as follows:

1. The courts will recognize the competing interests and the underlying policy issues in this litigation. There is the need of college and faculty reviewers for confidentiality in some aspect of the peer review process. Also, a faculty complainant has a legitimate right to obtain relevant material to pursue the claim. More importantly, the courts have clearly acknowledged the stated national policy on eliminating discrimination in employment. Since both congress and state legislatures clearly have affirmed this social policy, courts do not want to frustrate it by preventing disclosure of information required to expose alleged discrimination.

2. The courts generally want the faculty member seeking peer review materials to demonstrate some legitimate basis for the claim of discrimination. The courts have characterized this approach in different ways.

3. The courts generally will apply the relevancy standard to discovery requests to limit unreasonable or unnecessary requests. For example, courts have ruled that there are situations when access to certain peer review materials is not appropriate because the validity of the alleged claim could not be demonstrated by the requested material.

4. Courts generally agree that protective orders should be used to protect the confidential nature of peer review materials. Generally, such protective orders have limited access to the compelled material and allow the college to eliminate identifying references on recommendations obtained under assurances of confidentiality.

5. Courts use various labels in their approach to resolving faculty and college disputes on access to information. Some have embraced the concept of a qualified academic privilege, some have invoked a balancing test, and some have used the rules of the discovery process to resolve the claims of confidentiality and disclosure.

6. The more specific the objection to disclosure, the more able the courts are to deal with the objection to disclosure.

In summary, courts will implement the national public policy on nondiscrimination in employment. Therefore, colleges still need to tailor objections to disclosure of confidential material to claims that clearly do not have a reasonable basis or to those requests for materials that are not relevant.

The best preventive approach, of course, is to eliminate any form of discrimination and to develop fair review procedures that apply reasonable criteria uniformly. If the procedures are fair and access is provided to certain material, a college should have a stronger claim for preserving the confidentiality of certain peer review materials.

References

1. AAUP. "A Preliminary Statement on Judicially Compelled Disclosure in the Nonrenewal of Faculty Appointments." *Academe*, 67 (February-March, 1981),

2. *Board of Trustees of Leland Stanford University v. Superior Court*, 119 Cal. App.3d 516 (1981).

3. *Cockrell v. Middlebury College*, 536 A.2d 547 (Vt. 1987).

4. Comment, "A Qualified Academic Freedom Privilege in Employment Litigation: Protecting Higher Education or Shielding Discrimination?" *Vanderbilt Law Review*, 40 (1987), 1397–1432.

5. Comment, "Preventing Unnecessary Intrusions on University Autonomy: A Proposed Academic Freedom Privilege." *California Law Review*, 69 (1981), 1538–68.

6. Comment, "Title VII and Academic Freedom: The Authority of the EEOC to Investigate College Faculty Tenure Decisions." *Boston College Law Review*, 28 (1987), 559–94.

7. Delano, M. "Discovery in University Employment Discrimination Suits: Should Peer Review Materials Be Privileged?" *Journal of College and University Law*, 14 (1987), 559–94.

8. *Desimone v. Skidmore College*, 517 N.Y.S.2d 880 (Sup.Ct. 1987).

9. *In re Dinnan*, 661 F.2d 426 (5th Cir. 1981), *cert. denied*, 457 U.S. 1106 (1982).

10. *Dixon v. Rutgers*, 521 A.2d 1315 (N.J. App. 1987), 541 A.2d 1046 (N.J. 1988).

11. *EEOC v. Franklin & Marshall College*, 775 F.2d 110 (3rd. Cir. 1985), *cert. denied*, 476 U.S. 1163 (1986).

12. *EEOC v. Franklin & Marshall College*, 476 U.S. 1163 (1986).

13. *EEOC v. University of Notre Dame*, 715 F.2d 331 (7th Cir. 1983).

14. *EEOC v. University of Pennsylvania*, 850 F.2d 969 (3rd Cir. 1988).

15. *Federal Rules of Evidence*, Rule 401. In *Federal Civil Judicial Procedure and Rules*. St. Paul: West Publishing, 1989.

16. *Federal Rules of Civil Procedure*, Rule 26. In *Federal Civil Judicial Procedure and Rules*. St. Paul: West Publishing, 1989.

17. *Gray v. Board of Higher Education*, 692 F.2d 901 (2nd cir. 1982).

18. *Herbert v. Lando*, 441 U.S. 153 (1979).

19. *Jackson v. Harvard University*, 111 F.R.D. 472 (D. Mass. 1986).

20. *Keyishian v. Board of Regents of New York*, 385 U.S. 589 (1967).

21. Lee, B. A., "Balancing Confidentiality and Disclosure in Faculty Peer Review: Impact of Title VII Litigation." *Journal of College and University Law*, 9 (1982–83), 279–314.

22. *McCormick on Evidence*, edited by E. Cleary, Section 72. St. Paul: West Publishing, 3rd ed. 1984.

23. *Orbovich v. Macalester College*, 119 F.R.D. 411 (D. Minn. 1988).

24. *Paul v. Sanford University*, 39 EPD 35, 918 (N.D. Cal. 1986).

25. *Regents of the University of California v. Bakke*, 438 U.S. 265 (1978).

26. *Rollins v. Ferris*, 108 F.R.D. 714 (E.D. Ark. 1985).

27. *Rubin v. Regents of University of California*, 114 F.R.D. 1 (N.D. Cal. 1986).

28. *Silkwood v. Kerr-McGee Corp.*, 563 F.2d 433 (10th Cir. 1977).

29. *University of Pennsylvania v. EEOC*, F.Supp.2d (D.C.D.C.)

30. Wigmore, J. *Evidence in Trials at Common Law*. Vol. 8, Section 2285, edited by J. McNaughton. Boston: Little, Brown and Co., 1961.

Notes

1. In *EEOC v. University of Pennsylvania*, 850 F.2d 969 (3rd Cir. 1988) the University of Pennsylvania challenged a federal district count decision which refused to stay a subpoena issued by the EEOC for certain peer review materials. Rosalie Tung, a member of the Wharton School who was denied tenure, filed a lawsuit in which she alleged race (Asian) and sex discrimination in the tenure decision. The University provided some material to Tung from the peer review process but refused to provide Tung confidential peer review materials relating to Tung and five other male candidates. The EEOC filed a court action seeking the files. The University challenged this action because it had previously filed a suit in the United States Federal District Court in the District of Columbia challenging the EEOC's position on peer review materials on administrative and constitutional grounds, arguing that the EEOC action was unenforceable or unconstitutional. The United States Court of Appeals, Third Circuit, refused to stay the subpoena, and the University has now appealed to the United States Supreme Court which granted review of the issue. A decision of the United States Supreme Court could add further clarity on the scope of the EEOC subpoena powers. In the University of Pennsylvania challenge the Third Circuit reaffirmed its position in *Franklin & Marshall* permitting extensive access by the EEOC to peer review materials. The court did permit the University to redact identifying names from the personnel files.

2. Federal Rules of Evidence, Rule 401 defines relevant evidence as "evidence having any tendency to make the existence of any fact that is of consequence to the determination of the action more probable or less probable than it would be without the evidence."

Kent M. Weeks is a professor of the practice of education at Peabody College, Vanderbilt University, and a practicing attorney.

Academic Values and Faculty Rewards

The social and economic contributions which faculty make to society through teaching, research, and service have historically had both demonstrable value and cultural acceptance. Viewed as a "social good, "investment in higher education has been fundamental to maintaining the American social fabric (Bowen 1977; Leslie and Brinkman 1988, 80–82). This support is now eroding. Some critics view the role of faculty as educators—training citizens to participate in the workforce—as insufficient, particularly in a global economy where more direct involvement in technology transfer may be needed (Chmura, Henton, and Melville 1988; Tomatzky and Fleisher 1990, 236–57). The recent overhead expenditure fiascoes at leading research universities also have tarnished the image of higher education, raising questions about the ethical use of funds received from public and private sources. In the name of accountability, some state officials have asked (or in some cases required) colleges and universities to demonstrate the productivity of their faculty (Jacobsen 1992).

Reacting to these external criticisms, the American Association of Higher Education set "Reclaiming the Public Trust" as its theme for the 1992 annual conference. Ernest Boyer (1987) and Derek Bok (1992), echoing the recommendations of the Study Group on the Conditions of Excellence in American Higher Education (Study Group 1984), argued that renewing investment in undergraduate education is paramount to restoring this trust. In particular, Boyer and Bok emphasized that achieving a balance between teaching and research is essential to restore higher education to favorable social status.

Recommendations for changes in faculty time allocation require an examination of faculty reward structures and the values embedded in them about the relative importance of teaching, research and scholarship, and service. Also needed is examination of the contribution of administrative action to faculty rewards (Alpert 1985). Most of the research on faculty reward structures has been attitudinal, focusing on promotion and tenure (e.g., Bowen and Schuster 1986; Carnegie Foundation 1989; Cook, Kinnee, and Owens-Misner 1990; Peters and Mayfield 1982). Less often studied are faculty and administrative behavior and how faculty are rewarded through compensation for the way they spend their time.

Compensation is an annual "reward," reflecting at least in part the value placed by the institution or department on the work of individual faculty. Although studies of compensation abound, the focus has been descriptive—for example, research to see whether faculty salaries have kept pace with inflation (AAUP 1989; CUPA 1986a, 1986b; Dillon and Marsh 1981; Hansen 1985; Keister and Keister 1989). A few articles have focused on the relationships between compensation and faculty activities. Katherine Kasten's (1984) literature review found that faculty research activity was consistently and positively related to promotion and salary (see also Fulton and Trow 1974; Katz 1973; Rossman 1976; Siegfried and White 1973; Tuckman, Gapinski, and Hagemann 1977; Tuckman and Hagemann 1976; Tuckman and Leahy 1975). The relationships between teaching, promotion, and salary were ambiguous. Some researchers have found teaching positively related to salary and promotion (Hoyt 1974; Katz 1973; Rossman 1976; Salthouse, McKeachie, and Lin 1978; Siegfried and White 1973), unrelated to salary and promotion (Tuckman, Gapinksi, and Hagemann 1977; Tuckman and Hagemann 1976), and negatively related to salary and promotion (Marsh and Dillon 1980). In her own work at a single research university, Kasten found research and teaching positively related to compensation, although research activity was more highly predictive of salary than time spent on teaching (1984, 505–8).

Previous research on the relationships between faculty pay, behavior, and productivity has been limited, typically relying on information about a single school and using a small set of explanatory variables because of their availability. The few studies based on national data used correlational analyses rather than examining combined relationships between faculty behavior and pay (e.g., Marsh and Dillon 1980). The different findings about the importance of teaching in faculty compensation may be a function of these data and analytical limitations but we simply have had no national portrait of the relationship between pay and how faculty spend their time.

We have also needed a portrait of what administrators believe about the importance of teaching and research in their own institutions and the relationships between these beliefs and their behavior. Daniel Alpert (1985) suggests that understanding administrator beliefs and behaviors is crucial both in changing faculty rewards and in responding wisely to external demands for increasing the emphasis on undergraduate education. He views academic institutions as matrix organizations where administrators represent external demands and institutional obligations, acting as a counterweight to disciplinary interests reflected in departmental emphases on publishing and research. The reward which administrators most obviously influence is compensation.

Purpose

In this article, I examine the beliefs of a national sample of department chairs about the relative importance of teaching and research in faculty rewards. Next, I study the relationships between faculty activity and productivity with pay using a national sample of faculty from all types of four-year institutions. Despite the claims that we "already know" that research is highly valued and that teaching is not, the data used to support these claims are often attitudinal and/or based on only one or two institutions. Moreover, the relationship between teaching and pay is not as clear as previously assumed. Finally, I examine the correspondence between stated beliefs by administrators (department chairs) and pay.

If Alpert is correct, administrator behavior inherently conflicts with departmental values because it represents institutional rather than disciplinary norms. Accordingly, the results should show departmental values in favor of research and against teaching and instruction, at least in research universities. In addition, the results should show a positive relationship between pay and activities for which the institution is responsible, namely teaching and service. As Alpert notes: "The administrative leaders play only a limited role in developing research initiatives on the home campus; they are, however, necessarily involved in the instructional programs and public service activities" (1985, 275–76). In sum, in this paper I examine whether administrative behavior is actually a countermeasure to the research-and-scholarship model espoused by the disciplines or whether administrative action reinforces disciplinary norms.

The Study

I gathered data for this research from the 1987-88 National Survey of Postsecondary Faculty (NSOPF), sponsored by the National Center for Education Statistics. One component of NSOPF surveyed department chairs nationwide. Departments were stratified into ten program areas, including agriculture, business, education, engineering, fine arts, health sciences, humanities, natural sciences, social sciences, and other fields. I used data pooled across program area from 2,423 department chairs in 424 institutions (response rates of 88 and 80 percent, respectively) as reported by Russell, Cox, and Boismier (1990) to examine the perceived role of teaching in faculty rewards.

NSOPF also examined a nationally representative sample of 11,071 faculty (i.e., individuals who had some instructional duties during fall term, 1987) from 480 colleges and universities. In all, 8,383 full- and part-time faculty from 424 institutions responded, a response rate of 76 percent (Russell, Fairweather, Cox, Williamson, Boismier, and Javitz 1990, 98). The institutional sample was stratified by institutional type (Carnegie Foundation 1987), source of control, and size (estimated number of faculty).

For the analysis of faculty compensation, I used data on *full-time, tenure-track* faculty from four-year institutions (n = 4,481; weighted n= 343,343). The range of institutional types includes research universities, whose faculty train the majority of doctorates in the United States and which house the majority of funded research; doctoral-granting universities, whose faculty also train doctoral students and conduct research but generate fewer doctorates and research funds than their counterparts in research universities; comprehensive colleges and universities, which focus on liberal arts and professional programs at the undergraduate and masters-degree levels; liberal arts colleges; and other four-year institutions, which in this study were predominantly professional schools of engineering and medicine.

The study is limited by the lack of data about the quality of faculty teaching (as distinct from workload and productivity). Another limitation is the lack of data on institutional wealth, which can affect the distribution of faculty salaries. Finally, the sample size of the faculty survey is insufficient to simultaneously address analyses by institutional type, rank, and field of study.

Department Chair Beliefs

The NSOPF survey asked department chairs to rate the relative importance of thirteen factors in granting promotion and tenure: quality of teaching, quality of research, number of publications, quality of publications, community or professional service, reputation in professional field, reputation of the individual's graduate program, highest degree awarded, affirmative action considerations, ability to obtain outside funding, "fit" with the department, and "fit" with students (Russell, Cox, and Boismier 1990, 11). Table 1 shows the ranking of criteria based on the percentage of department chairs claiming a criterion was "very important" in granting tenure or promotion, by type of institution.

Table 1. Department Chair Rankings of Criteria for Promotion and Tenure, by Type of Institution

Criteria	Type of Institution	
	Doctoral	Other 4-Year
Teaching quality	3	1
Highest degree	4	2
Fit with department	7	3
Institutional service	10.5	4
Research quality	1	6
Quality of publications	2	7
Fit with students	10.5	5
Professional reputation	5.5	9.5
Number of publications	5.5	11
Affirmative action	9	8
Community/public service	12	9.5
Ability to obtain outside $	8	13
Reputation of individual's graduate school	13	12

SOURCE: Russell, Cox, and Boismier (1990)

The results indicate that department chairs in doctoral-granting institutions, which include the Carnegie classifications of research and doctoral-granting institutions, had higher expectations than their colleagues in other four-year institutions (comprehensive and liberal arts colleges) for research productivity. The rank-order correlation between the two types of institutions was only .38 for this reason. Despite clear differences in the ranking of research and publishing, department chairs in distinct types of institutions rated the quality of teaching high on their list of criteria (first in comprehensive and liberal arts, third in doctoral-granting institutions).

If compensation follows the stated beliefs of department chairs, we should see distinct patterns in the correlates of pay by type of institution. Research and publishing should be more prominent factors in faculty pay at doctoral-granting universities than in comprehensive and liberal arts colleges. Regardless of type of institution, teaching productivity should be positively related to pay.

Faculty Compensation

Howard Bowen and Jack Schuster (1986, 15), describe the faculty role as encompassing instruction, research, public service, and institutional governance and operation (i.e., administration). Each generic activity category contains distinct concepts of workload, time allocation, and productivity. Measures of "instructional activity," for example, might include the number of hours per week spent on teaching; the relative percentage of time spent on teaching activities to other tasks and the number of student contact hours generated, a measure of productivity.

I used the Bowen and Schuster framework to guide the selection of variables from the NSOPF for analysis. Variable categories included compensation, demographic characteristics, length of service, teaching/instruction, research/scholarship, administration, and public service.

Study Variables

The measure of compensation used in this research was basic salary from the institution for the calendar year 1987 (i.e., gross earnings before taxes).

Faculty demographic characteristics included age during fall term 1987, gender, ethnic/racial minority status, highest degree awarded (doctorate or not), and program area. A respondent was classified as a member of a racial or ethnic minority if she or he was of Hispanic descent, American Indian, Asian/Pacific Islander, or black. Program area was the primary field of study in which a faculty member worked: agriculture/home economics, business, education, engineering, fine arts, health sciences, humanities, natural sciences, social sciences, and other fields. For multivariate analyses, I categorized primary field of study into a three-part variable called high-paying field based on average basic salary (1 = program areas with average salaries above the mean—engineering and health sciences, 0 = at the mean—agriculture/home economics, business, natural sciences, -1 = below the mean—education, fine arts, humanities, social sciences, other fields).

Length of service included time in current rank (i.e., the number of years since achieving the rank held at the institution in question during fall term 1987) and the number of years in the current position at the institution in question (irrespective of changes in rank).

Faculty instruction-related activities consisted of measures of how faculty spent their time, workload, and productivity. The measures of instruction-related activities and workloads included percent of time spent on teaching and instruction, hours spent in the classroom per week, and the type of student taught (undergraduate, graduate, or both). Percent of time spent on teaching and instruction encompassed time spent on working with student organizations; teaching, advising, and supervising students; and grading papers, preparing courses, and developing new curricula.

In addition, total student contact hours generated during fall term 1987 measured instructional productivity. I calculated student contact hours as the sum across all courses taught of the number of hours a class met per week times the number of students enrolled in the class.

I measured faculty emphasis on research according to the percent of time spent on research and scholarship—which included time spent on research, scholarship, preparing or reviewing articles or books, and attending or preparing to attend professional meetings or conferences giving performances in the fine or applied arts and seeking outside funding for research. Research productivity included total refereed publications during the career (refereed articles, chapters in edited volumes, textbooks, other books, monographs, and reviews of books, articles, or creative works), and whether or not the respondent was a principal/co-principal investigator on an externally funded research project during fall term 1987. Being designated as a principal/co-principal investigator meant having at least one research project during fall term 1987 funded by the federal government, state or local governments, foundations or other nonprofit organizations, or industry.

To fill out the picture of the faculty workload, I included estimates of the percent of time spent on administrative activities and time spent on public or community service.

Scales

High positive correlations between age, time in rank, and years at current institution (.65 to .69), and a high negative correlation between percent of time spent on teaching and research (-.62), suggested the need to create composite variables prior to proceeding with multivariate analyses. A principal components analysis with an oblique rotation successfully combined highly correlated indicators into two composites. The first was seniority, which combined age, time in rank, and years at the current institution into a single scale. The second composite—more research/less teaching—reflected the "exchange" relationship between teaching and research; i.e., the more faculty spent on one activity, the less they spent on the other.

Analyses and Results

Using weighted estimates of population parameters,[1] I first compared the bivariate relationships between various measures of faculty activity and compensation. I used quartiles to form groupings of variables for cross-tabulation analyses to examine results by type of institution. All differences between means or proportions described as "significant" are statistically significant at $p < .05$ (two-tailed test).

To study the combined relationships between faculty demographic characteristics, activities and workload, and productivity with compensation, I carried out multiple regression analyses by type of institution and by academic rank within type of institution, the latter to control better for seniority and length of service.

Bivariate Analyses

This section examines the relationships between basic salary and various indicators of teaching, research and scholarship, administration, and public service.

Teaching/Instruction

For tenure-track, full-time faculty, the more time spent on teaching and instruction, the lower the basic salary. (See Table 2.)[2] Average basic salary varies in a linear pattern from a high of $56,181 for faculty spending less than 35 percent of their time on teaching, to a low of $34,307 for faculty spending more than 72 percent of their time on teaching. By type of institution, the same pattern holds for faculty in research universities, doctoral-granting institutions, and comprehensive colleges. Time spent on teaching is not related to basic salary for faculty in liberal arts colleges.[3]

For full-time, tenure-track faculty, the fewer hours spent in class, the higher the pay.[4] Average basic salary ranges from a high of $50,927 for faculty spending the fewest hours in class (less than six per week),to a low of $36,793 for faculty spending the most time in class per week (twelve or

Table 2. Mean Basic Salary by Teaching-related Variables: Fall 1987

	All 4-year	Research	Doctoral	Compre-hensive	Liberal Arts	Other 4-year
Percent of Time Spent on Teaching/Instruction						
< 35%	56,181	57,893	46,349	50,189	*	67,202
SE	914	1,131	1,839	2,067	*	4,639
35–52%	42,935	47,445	39,180	37,814	30,908	54,345
SE	465	709	875	659	1,283	4,833
53–71%	37,244	43,142	36,008	34,551	30,672	40,876
SE	357	817	716	423	976	2,184
72% +	34,307	38,113	34,138	34,366	30,023	38,869
SE	320	1,149	903	379	708	2,254
Number of Hours per Week Teaching in Class						
< 6	50,927	53,239	43,558	45,162	33,897	60,928
SE	732	936	1,512	1,758	2,176	3,924
6–8	43,191	48,100	38,679	38,817	33,142	46,531
SE	488	770	823	830	1,295	3,232
9–11	38,060	40,845	36,706	36,181	29,708	*
SE	503	927	769	481	1,023	*
12 +	36,793	47,542	35,263	34,251	29,139	49,180
SE	433	1,612	1,092	385	673	4,121
Number of Student Contact Hours per Semester						
< 110	49,267	53,026	40,042	42,758	30,742	61,512
SE	712	954	1,326	1,615	1,472	3,628
110–217	38,442	43,887	38,233	36,225	30,649	*
SE	378	729	871	513	852	*
218–359	37,632	45,523	36,852	35,076	29,524	*
SE	444	1,144	894	416	775	*
360 +	43,159	51,433	38,726	36,417	32,945	54,649
SE	602	1,205	1,097	583	1,662	3,833
Type of Students Taught						
Taught only under-graduate students	44,176	48,223	42,002	42,129	31,296	*
SE	883	1,402	1,627	1,351	2,793	*
Taught both types of students	41,478	48,785	37,795	36,238	30,565	57,598
SE	287	545	533	316	533	3,351
Taught only graduate students	56,661	57,118	52,914	61,210	NA	54,457
SE	1,365	1,742	3,072	5,824	NA	2,495

* = Too few cases for reliable estimate
NA = Not applicable

more hours), although the difference between salary for those spending nine to eleven hours in class per week versus those spending twelve or more is not significant.

The same negative relationship between time spent in class and compensation holds for faculty in doctoral-granting universities, comprehensive institutions, liberal arts colleges, and other four-year institutions.[5] The relationship between hours spent in class and compensation for faculty in research universities is curvilinear—faculty spending the least time in class earn the highest salaries, faculty spending the most time in class earn the second highest salaries, and faculty spending between six and 11 hours in class are paid the least.

For student contact hours, the distribution of basic salary is also curvilinear. The highest income is earned by those with the least number of student contact hours, dropping to a low point through the mid-range of contact hours, and rising again to the second highest salary for those with the most contact hours.[6]

The same general pattern holds for faculty in all institutions except liberal arts colleges. Statistical comparisons show, however, that for faculty in comprehensive colleges and universities only those with the fewest contact hours are paid more than their colleagues with heavier teaching loads. Similarly, student contact hours are not significantly related to basic salary for faculty in doctoral-granting institutions, liberal arts colleges, or other four-year institutions.[7]

Faculty who teach only graduate students are paid more than their counterparts who teach both undergraduates and graduate students, or who teach only undergraduate students.[8] The same pattern holds true for faculty in research, doctoral-granting, and comprehensive institutions.[9]

Research/Scholarship

In contrast to time spent on teaching, faculty who spend the greatest time on research and scholarship receive the highest compensation. (See Table 3.)[10] Salaries range from a low of $36,963 for faculty spending less than 5 percent of their time on research, to a high of $48,711 for those spending the most time on research—34 percent or more.

The same pattern holds for faculty in doctoral-granting universities. For faculty in research universities, comprehensive colleges, and other four-year institutions, only the faculty most committed to research—34 percent or more of their time—have a significantly higher salary. Time spent on research is not related to basic salary at liberal arts colleges.[11]

The ratio of total refereed publications to number of years since achieving the highest degree—i.e., the average annual number of refereed publications—shows that the greater the publication record, the higher the compensation.[12] Faculty averaging less than .20 publications per year during their careers averaged $35,500, while their counterparts averaging two or more publications per year averaged $51,901. The relationship between publications and basic salary does not vary by institutional type. Publishing is as strongly related to compensation for faculty in liberal arts colleges and comprehensive institutions as it is for their peers in research and doctoral-granting universities.[13]

Having research grants experience, as a variable, is associated more strongly with a higher salary than not having research grants experience. The same pattern holds true for faculty in research universities, doctoral-granting universities, comprehensive colleges and universities, and other four-year institutions. The relationship is nonexistent among faculty in liberal arts colleges.[15]

Administration and Service

Faculty spending the greatest time on administration earn higher salaries than their peers who spend less time on administration, both overall[16] and in research universities, doctoral-granting institutions, and comprehensive colleges. (See Table 4.)[17] Percent of time spent on administration is only weakly related to compensation for faculty in liberal arts colleges; it is not related to compensation for faculty in other four-year institutions.

Faculty who spend the most time on public service tend to make lower basic salaries.[18] There is no significant difference, however, when the relationship between public service and compensation is examined by type of institution.

Summary

Bivariate analyses and cross-tabulations show negative relationships between several measures of teaching activity and productivity with basic salary, while the relationships between compensation and indicators of research activity and productivity are positive. These patterns hold true for faculty overall and, in most cases, for faculty in each type of institution.

Multivariate Analysis

Although strongly suggestive, bivariate analyses can be misleading. The relationship between percent of time spent on research and compensation, for example, may be influenced by seniority. For this reason, the next set of analyses explores the combined relationships between faculty demographics, behavior, and compensation to determine their relative importance in faculty salaries. I examine multiple regression models using basic salary as the criterion, focusing on results by type of institution and by academic rank within type of institution. Only relationships which are significant at $p < .05$ are reported in the tables. The regression models generally accounted for between .30 and .60 of the variance in basic salary across the various analyses.[19]

Type of Institution

Faculty in research universities who are paid the most focus their efforts on working with graduate students, conducting research (while spending less time on teaching activities), and publishing. Being a senior male in a high-paying field also is positively related to compensation. (See Table 5.)

Highly paid faculty in doctoral-granting institutions have the same profile as their counterparts in research universities: emphasizing research and scholarship with a focus on graduate programs and publication, spending more time on research and less on teaching, spending time on administration, and being a senior male in a high-paying field. Having an externally funded grant is more strongly related to compensation in doctoral-granting universities than in research universities, where it is nonsignificant.

The predictors of compensation for faculty in comprehensive institutions are similar to the model for research university faculty, including the positive relationships between pay and emphasizing research, scholarship, and graduate programs.

Faculty in liberal arts colleges who receive the most pay focus more on research and less on teaching, publish, and spend fewer hours in class per week. Being a senior male in a high-paying field is also positively related to compensation.

Faculty in other four-year institutions, which in this study are principally medical and engineering schools, are rewarded for publishing, bringing in grant money, and spending time on administration.

Summary

Faculty who follow a research- and scholarship-oriented model are paid the most at each type of institution regardless of mission, including comprehensive and liberal arts colleges which historically have emphasized undergraduate education. The most important demographic factors in predicting pay are seniority, gender (i.e., male), and field of study.

Academic Rank by Type of Institution

Table 6 presents the significant predictors ($p < .05$) for faculty compensation by rank and by type of institution, discussed below.

The highest paid full professors in research universities have substantial publication records and teach graduate students. They also spend more time on administration and work in higher paying disciplines. Associate professors are rewarded for publishing, teaching graduate students, and spending a high proportion of time on research, but also for spending time in the classroom and on service. In addition, being a principal investigator on a funded research project is negatively related to basic salary. The compensation of assistant professors, however, suggests early socialization in the research university model: publishing and teaching graduate students are the only significant behavioral predictors of compensation.

Table 3. Mean Basic Salary by Research-related Variables

	All 4-year	Research	Doctoral	Compre- hensive	Liberal Arts	Other 4-year
Percent of Time Spent on Research/Scholarship						
< 5%	36,963	45,581	34,453	35,805	30,389	46,424
SE	549	2,129	1,070	515	943	4,946
5.0–15.9%	36,638	48,384	37,249	36,974	30,281	52,394
SE	475	1,220	737	571	789	5,356
16.0–33.9%	44,062	50,990	37,799	36,711	29,615	58,935
SE	588	1,043	929	670	1,191	4,089
34.0% +	48,711	50,060	42,825	40,044	*	60,713
SE	620	736	1,326	1,220	*	4,480
Average Publications per Year						
< .20	35,550	44,421	33,450	34,731	28,417	42,731
SE	422	1,519	938	512	676	3,214
.20–.78	39,549	44,521	38,095	37,183	31,701	*
SE	414	955	828	515	1,106	
.79–1.99	45,451	49,383	40,613	40,239	36,496	54,064
SE	508	817	807	852	1,455	2,811
2.00 +	51,901	54,074	42,879	40,639	*	70,609
SE	833	1,001	1,551	1,281	*	6,771
Status as Principal Investigator on Research Project						
Not principal investigator	39,567	46,779	36,585	36,273	30,536	49,456
SE	284	625	478	349	566	2,448
Principal investigator	51,517	53,980	44,973	41,364	31,572	68,240
SE	761	957	1,667	1,107	1,494	5,240

* = Too few cases for reliable estimate

Table 4. Mean Basic Salary by Administrative- and Service-related Variables

	All 4-year	Research	Doctoral	Compre- hensive	Liberal Arts	Other 4-year
Percent of Time Spent on Administration						
< 5%	38,491	45,214	35,608	35,137	32,517	*
SE	489	1,118	1,002	557	1,291	*
5.0–9.9%	40,410	49,569	38,257	34,154	27,012	*
SE	588	1,189	1,278	546	906	*
10.0–19.9%	41,720	46,200	38,830	35,522	30,782	58,716
SE	466	785	832	538	797	3,516
20.0% +	48,546	56,694	41,026	42,315	32,430	62,272
SE	688	1,128	1,150	910	1,288	5,733
Percent of Time Committed to Public Service						
< 5.0%	42,738	49,409	38,416	36,952	30,655	57,019
SE	307	560	565	363	569	2,552
5.0% +	40,174	50,120	38,998	35,768	30,388	*
SE	z731	1,669	1,464	808	1,536	*

* = Too few cases for reliable estimate

Table 5. Significant Predictors of Basic Salary, by Type of Institution

Predictor	Research Universities R-square = .38 N (unweighted) = 1269	
	Beta	Standardized Beta
Publications (career)	4593	.29****
High-paying field	5795	.24****
% time, administration	4501	.22****
Seniority	3830	.20****
Taught only graduate students	1816	.12****
Male	2243	.11****
More research/less teaching	1802	.09***
Hours in class/week	1405	.08**
	Doctoral Universities R-square = .41 N (unweighted) = 711	
Seniority	4839	.35****
Taught only graduate students	3890	.22****
Publications (career)	2636	.16****
Male	2107	.16****
Highest degree, doctorate	2184	.14****
High-paying field	2581	.14****
More research/less teaching	1944	.12***
Principal investigator, funded	1455	.10**
Hours in class/week	1537	.08*
% time, administration	941	.07*
	Comprehensive Universities R-square = .47 N (unweighted) = 1491	
Seniority	4658	.35****
Taught only graduate students	5121	.23****
High-paying field	3687	.20****
% time, administration	2416	.19****
Highest degree-doctorate	1885	.17****
Male	1691	.14****
Publications (career)	2859	.13****
More research/less teaching	1582	.09****
Minority faculty member	776	.06***
	Liberal Arts College R-square = .47 N (unweighted) = 367	
Seniority	5194	.49****
Male	2133	.20****
More research/less teaching	3201	.18****
Publications (career)	4947	.17****
Highest degree, doctorate	1535	.17***
Hours in class/week	−2049	−.14**
	Other 4-Year Institutions R-square = .40 N (unweighted) = 115	
% time, administration	10670	.30***
Taught only graduate students	−4764	−.26**
Publications (career)	5389	.26**
Principal investigator, funded	6320	.25*

**** $p < .0001$
*** $p < .001$
** $p < .01$
* $p < .05$

Table 6. Significant Predictors of Basic Salary, by Academic Rank and Type of Institution

	Research Universities Professor *R*-square = .24 *N* (unweighted) = 611	
Predictor	**Beta**	**Standardized Beta**
Publications (career)	3257	.17****
High-paying field	6231	.26****
% time, administration	3822	.22****
Taught only graduate students	1804	.13**
Highest degree, doctorate	−2887	−.09**

	Associate Professor *R*-square = .45 *N* (unweighted) = 367	
High-paying field	7023	.34****
Hours in class/week	3226	.30****
Publications (career)	9693	.27****
Principal investigator	−2067	−.14**
Taught only graduate students	1991	.13**
More research/less teaching	2333	.13**
% time, service	1781	.09*
Highest degree, doctorate	2105	.09*

	Assistant Professor *R*-square = .33 *N* (unweighted) = 276	
High-paying field	5408	.35****
Publications (career)	8269	.20***
% time, Administration	2703	.16**
Male	1762	.15**
Seniority	−3271	−.13*
Highest degree, doctorate	1951	.12*
Taught only graduate students	1190	.12*

	Doctoral-Granting Universities Professor *R*-square = .21 *N* (unweighted) = 278	
Taught only graduate students	4354	.29****
Seniority	3297	.21***
Principal investigator	2308	.17*
Publications (career)	1483	.12*

	Associate Professor *R*-square = .45 *N* (unweighted) = 244	
High-paying field	5146	.35****
Taught only graduate students	4523	.29****
Male	2523	.23****
Hours in class/week	4443	.23***
More research/less teaching	2564	.22***
% Time, Administration	2277	.21***
Highest degree, doctorate	2272	.18***
Seniority	2374	.17**

	Assistant Professor *R*-square = .20 *N* (unweighted) = 174	
High-paying field	2268	.18*
Seniority	2246	.17*

Table 6 (Continued)

	Comprehensive Colleges and Universities Professor R-square = .34 N (unweighted) = 638	
High-paying field	3896	.25****
More research/less teaching	3602	.23****
Taught only graduate students	3248	.17****
Seniority	2237	.17****
Publications (career)	1870	.15****
% Time, administration	1278	.14***
% time, service	−1223	−.12***
Hours in class/week	934	.09*
Highest degree, doctorate	1099	.08*
	Associate Professor R-square = .25 N (unweighted) = 452	
Seniority	2172	.26****
High-paying field	2368	.22****
% Time, administration	1449	.21****
Male	1078	.16***
Hours in class/week	−1590	−.15**
Taught only graduate students	−1692	−.13**
Minority	760	.11**
% time, service	710	.11**
Student contact hours	1380	.09*
Taught only undergraduates	781	.09*
	Assistant Professor R-square = .35 N (unweighted) = 358	
Taught only graduate students	6631	.38****
High-paying field	3115	.28****
Seniority	2604	.25****
% time, administration	−2097	−.14**
Male	942	.13**
Highest degree, doctorate	777	.12*
More research/less teaching	1295	.12*
	Liberal Arts Colleges Professor R-square = .50 N (unweighted) = 146	
Seniority	5229	.35****
Male	5526	.34****
Taught only undergraduates	−3580	−.31***
More research/less teaching	5358	.28***
Publications (career)	7232	.26***
% time, service	−3338	−.20**
Highest degree, doctorate	2093	.19**
	Associate Professor R-square = .51 N (unweighted) = 109	
Hours in class/week	−2595	−.31**
Male	1489	.28***
Highest degree, doctorate	1203	.25**
High-paying field	2194	.23**
More research/less teaching	1716	.19*

Table 6 (Continued)

	Assistant Professor R-square = .36 N (unweighted) = 103	
Hours in class/week	−3096	−.40***
Student contact hours	10902	.39**
Minority	−2731	−.35***
Publications (career)	16253	.34**
Seniority	3458	.23*

**** $p < .0001$
*** $p < .001$
** $p < .01$
* $p < .05$

The three behavioral predictors of compensation for professors in doctoral-granting universities are teaching graduate students, publishing, and securing research funding. Highly paid associate professors teach graduate students and spend more time on research than teaching; they also, however, spend significant hours in the classroom and spend time on administration. Two demographic characteristics are significant predictors of compensation for assistant professors: working in a high-paying discipline and seniority.

Seniority, working in a high-paying field, and having a doctorate are important predictors of compensation for professors in comprehensive institutions. The strongest behavioral predictors of basic salary are spending more time on research and less on teaching, publishing, and spending time on administration. Time spent on public service is negatively related to compensation. Hours spent per week in the classroom is positively though weakly related to basic salary.

Demographic characteristics are strongly related to pay for associate professors—seniority, being in a high-paying program area, and gender (male). Time spent on administration is positively related to compensation, as is time spent in providing service to the community. The number of hours spent in class is negatively related to compensation, while student contact hours are positively related (suggesting the benefits of teaching fewer but larger classes). No indicators of research or scholarly productivity are related to compensation.

The assistant professor rank tells a different story. Assistant professors at comprehensive colleges and universities who are paid the most teach only graduate students, spend more time on research and less on teaching, and participate in administrative activities. Seniority, gender (i.e., male), having a doctorate, and working in a high-paying discipline also are positively related to compensation.

Gender (i.e., male), seniority, and holding a doctorate are positively related to compensation for full professors in liberal arts colleges. Behavioral indicators which are positively associated with compensation include publishing and spending more time on research and less on teaching. For associate professors, spending fewer hours in class per week and spending more time on research are positively related to compensation. Demographic predictors of pay include holding a doctorate, gender (i.e., male) and working in a high-paying field. Assistant professors who publish, spend fewer hours in class teaching larger numbers of students, and who are not members of a racial or ethnic minority are paid more than their peers.[20]

To summarize, the analyses of compensation by academic rank within type of institution show a more varied picture of the reward structure than the bivariate analyses. Full professors in each type of institution, including comprehensive colleges and liberal arts colleges, are rewarded for publishing and for spending more time on research (and less on teaching). In research universities, doctoral-granting institutions, and comprehensive colleges and universities, associate professors are rewarded for research, administration, teaching, and, in one case, service. Teaching remains a negative factor in compensation for associate professors in liberal arts colleges.

The earliest point of socialization in the academic career—the assistant professor rank—shows the extent of the research model orientation in American postsecondary education. Producing a substantial publication record and spending more time on research and less on teaching are the dominant factors in compensation for assistant professors.

Discussion and Conclusions

Department chair beliefs about the importance of teaching and research in faculty rewards vary by type of institution along the lines suggested by the Carnegie typology (Carnegie Foundation 1987). Department chairs in comprehensive and liberal arts colleges say they most value a professor's teaching ability and accord research and scholarly productivity a more modest value than their colleagues in doctoral-granting universities. Despite their emphasis on scholarly productivity, department chairs in doctoral-granting institutions also say that faculty reward systems place high value on teaching. The results of this study suggest that the homogeneity of the beliefs of department chairs about the relative importance of teaching and research in faculty rewards, implied by studies of faculty attitudes by the Carnegie Foundation (1989) and by Bowen and Schuster (1986), is inaccurate.

Patterns of faculty pay, however, *do* follow the emphasis suggested by studies of faculty attitudes. Teaching is at best a neutral factor in pay. Research and scholarship are the most valued activities. These results suggest that pay, which reflects, at least in part, administrative values placed on faculty behavior, does not follow the stated values placed on teaching by department chairs. Pay is instead consistent with disciplinary emphases on research and scholarship, thus conflicting with Alpert's (1985) view that administrative behavior is a countermeasure to the emphasis on research in the disciplines.

The findings demonstrate the dominance of the research- and scholarship-oriented reward structure for faculty in four-year colleges and universities. Regardless of institutional type or mission, faculty who spend more time on research and who publish the most are paid more than their teaching-oriented colleagues. Analyses either show teaching as a negative factor in compensation, especially the percent of time spent on teaching and instruction, or show teaching as unrelated to compensation. Research-related indicators, especially teaching graduate students, publishing, and spending time on research, are positively related to compensation.

Even when teaching productivity is positively related to compensation, the implications for instructional *quality* are not promising. Student contact hours generated are almost always positively related with compensation when faculty spend fewer hours in class per week. This finding reflects the institutional reliance on larger classes. Although there maybe substantial financial benefits in teaching larger numbers of students, the associated consequences of spending less time with them hardly suggests an approach likely to result in higher quality instruction (McKeachie 1986).

The findings also suggest that assistant professors in all types of institutions are socialized early to follow a research and scholarship model. Most likely this result is simply a continuation of expectations created during training in graduate school. Assistant professors in each type of institution except doctoral-granting universities are socialized to publish, teach graduate students, and generally spend as little time teaching as possible.

These results suggest that Kasten (1984) was incorrect in her belief that the impact of research on the faculty reward structure would be constrained because the funding formulae for most colleges and universities were based on the number of students served rather than on research productivity. The nature of institutional funding apparently has not constrained the role of research in faculty compensation at all. Kasten's speculation about the consequences of a faculty reward structure which did not maintain a balance between faculty roles, however, may be correct: "Professional orientation becomes harmful when it entails loss of support from clients, governing bodies, and funding groups, many of whom are more likely to be familiar with the more locally visible aspects of faculty work" (1984, 512).

In addition, the results of my study strongly suggest that the focus of graduate training, early socialization in the profession, and peer values which emphasize publishing only partly explain the emphasis on research and publishing at colleges and universities. Administrative behavior as reflected in compensation reinforces the values dear to the disciplines: publishing and spending less time with undergraduate students. Far from acting as a counterweight to the drift toward a single acceptable norm for faculty behavior, administrative practice reinforces this view. The talk about the increased importance placed by administrators on teaching is unconvincing when we see the relationship between teaching and faculty pay.

As academic institutions attempt to deal with severe financial constraints being placed on them by state legislatures, federal agencies, and parents who pay tuition for their children, the emphasis of faculty rewards on research, not teaching or public service, must be recognized as a widespread, actively encouraged phenomenon, not a pattern limited to a handful of faculty in elite universities. If teaching, particularly the teaching of undergraduates, is to be allocated any value in academy, which the public is surely demanding, academic administrators must face their role in perpetuating the unbalanced emphasis on research and publishing. Administrators should reassert their role by requiring as much devotion by faculty to institutional needs as they have to the disciplines, paying their faculty in line with the institutional obligations rather than simply reinforcing the dominant research-and-scholarship model.

Bibliography

Alpert, Daniel. "Performance and Paralysis: The Organizational Context of the American Research University." *Journal of Higher Education* 56 (May/June 1985): 241–81.

American Association of University Professors (AAUP). "The Annual Report on the Economic Status of the Profession, 1988–89." *Academe* 75 (March/April 1989): entire issue.

Bok, Derek. "Reclaiming the Public Trust." *Change* 24 (July/August 1992): 12–19.

Bowen, Howard R. *Investment in Learning: The Individual and Social Value of American Higher Education.* San Francisco: Jossey-Bass, 1977.

Bowen, Howard R., and Jack H. Schuster. *American Professors: A National Resource Imperiled.* New York: Oxford University Press, 1986.

Boyer, Ernest L. *College: The Undergraduate Experience in America.* New York: Harper and Row, 1987.

Carnegie Foundation for the Advancement of Teaching. *A Classification of Institutions of Higher Education.* Princeton, NJ.: Carnegie Foundation for the Advancement of Teaching, 1987.

_____. *The Condition of the Professoriate: Attitudes and Trends,* 1989. Princeton, NJ.: Carnegie Foundation for the Advancement of Teaching, 1989.

Chmura, Thomas, Douglas Henton, and John Melville. *California's Higher Education System: Adding Economic Competitiveness to the Higher Education Agenda.* Menlo Park, Calif.: SRI International, 1988.

College and University Personnel Association (CUPA). *National Faculty Salary Survey by Discipline and Rank in Private Colleges and Universities, 1985–86.* Washington, D.C.: College and University Personnel Association, 1986a.

_____. *National Faculty Salary Survey by Discipline and Rank in State Colleges and Universities, 1985–86.* Washington, D.C.: College and University Personnel Association, 1986b.

Cook, Ellen P., Peggy Kinnetz, and Neva Owens-Misner. "Faculty Perception on Job Rewards and Instructional Development Activities." *Innovative Higher Education* 14 (Spring/Summer 1990): 123–30.

Dillon, Kristine E., and Herbert W. Marsh. "Faculty Earnings Compared with Those of Nonacademic Professionals." *Journal of Higher Education* 52 (November/December 1981): 615–23.

Fulton, Oliver, and Martin Trow. "Research Activity in Higher Education." *Sociology of Education* 47 (Winter 1974): 29–73.

Hansen, W. Lee. "Starting the Upward Climb?" *Academe* 71 (March-April 1985): 3–7.

Hoyt, D. P. "Interrelationships among Instructional Effectiveness, Publication Record, and Monetary Reward." *Research in Higher Education* 2, no. 1 (1974): 81–89.

Jacobsen, Robert L. "Colleges Face New Pressure to Increase Faculty Productivity." *Chronicle of Higher Education* 38 (15 April 1992): 1.

Kasten, Katherine L. "Tenure and Merit Pay as Rewards for Research, Teaching, and Service at a Research University." *Journal of Higher Education* 55 (July/August 1984): 500–514.

Katz, David A. "Faculty Salaries, Promotion, and Productivity at a Large University." *American Economic Review* 63 (June 1973): 469–77.

Keister, Stephen D., and Lekha G. Keister. "Faculty Compensation and the Cost of Living in American Higher Education." *Journal of Higher Education* 60 (July/August 1989): 458–74.

Leslie, Larry L., and Paul T. Brinkman. *The Economic Value of Higher Education.* New York: ACE/Macmillan, 1988.

Marsh, Herbert W., and Kristine E. Dillon. "Academic Productivity and Faculty Supplemental Income." *Journal of Higher Education* 51 (September/October 1980): 546–55.

McKeachie, Wilbert J. *Teaching Tips: A Guidebook for the Beginning College Teacher,* 8th ed. Lexington, Mass.: D.C. Heath, 1986.

Peters, Dianne S., and J. Robert Hayfield. "Are There Any Rewards for Teaching? *Improving College and University Teaching* 30 (Summer 1982): 105–10.

Rossman, Jack E. "Teaching, Publication, and Rewards at a Liberal Arts Colleges." *Improving College and University Teaching* 24 (Autumn 1976): 238–40.

Russell, Susan H., Robert C. Cox, and James M. Boismier. *A Descriptive Report of Academic Departments in Higher Education Institutions.* Washington, D.C.: U.S. Department of Education, 1990.

Russell, Susan H., James S. Fairweather, Robert C. Cox, Cynthia Williamson, James M. Boismier, and Harold Javitz. *Faculty in Higher Education Institutions.* Washington, D.C.: U.S. Department of Education, 1990.

Salthouse, Timothy A., Wilbert J. McKeachie, and Yi-Guang Lin. "An Experimental Investigation of Factors Affecting University Promotion Decisions." *Journal of Higher Education* 49 (March/April 1978): 177–83.

Siegfried, John J., and Kenneth J. White. "Teaching and Publishing as Determinants of Academic Salaries." *Journal of Economic Education* 4 (Spring 1973): 90–98.

Study Group on the Conditions of Excellence in American Higher Education. *Involvement in Learning: Realizing the Potential of American Higher Education.* Washington, D.C.: U.S. Department of Education, 1984.

Tornatzky, Louis G., and Mitchell Fleisher. *The Process of Technological Innovation.* Lexington, Mass.: Lexington Books, 1990.

Tuckman, Howard P., James H. Gapinski, and Robert P. Hagemann. "Faculty Skills and the Salary Structure in Academe: A Market Perspective." *American Economic Review* 67, no. 4 (1977): 692–702.

Tuckman, Howard P., and Robert P. Hagemann. "An Analysis of the Reward Structure in Two Disciplines." *Journal of Higher Education* 47 (July/August 1976): 447–64.

Tuckman, Howard P., and Jack Leahy. "What Is an Article Worth?" *Journal of Political Economy* 83 (October 1975): 951–67.

Notes

1. I based population estimates from survey data on weights derived from the inverse of the probability of a faculty member in a particular type of institution being selected. The probability of selecting a faculty member for the sample was a function of the odds of an institution being selected from the universe of accredited postsecondary institutions, the probability of a faculty member being selected from the population of faculty within his or her institution, and the sampling rate for employment status (full- or part-time) and program area (Russell, Fairweather, Cox, Williamson, Boismier, and Javitz 1990, 99).

2. All four-year: $t(35/35-52) = 12.92, p < .001$; $t(35-52/53-71) = 9.71, p < .001$; $t(53-71/72) = 6.13, p < .001$.

3. Research: $t(35/35-52) = 7.83, p < .001$ $t(35-52/53-71) = 3.98, p < .001$; $t(53-71/72) = 3.57, p < .001$.
   Doctoral: $t(35/35-52) = 3.52, p < .001$: $t(35-52/53-71) = 2.81, p < .01$.
   Comprehensive: $t(35/35-52) = 5.70, p < .001$: $t(35-52/53-71) = 4.17, p < .001$.
   Other: $t(35-52/53-71) = .2.54, p < .05$.

4. All four-year: $t(6/6-8) = 8.79, p < .001$ $t(6-8/9-11) = 7.32, p < .001$.

5. Research: $t(6/6-8) = 4.24, p < .001$: $t(6-8/9-11) = 6.02, p < .001$; $t(9-11/12) = -4.09, p < .001$.
   Doctoral: $t(6/6-8) = 2.25, p < .05$.
   Comprehensive: $t(6/6-8) = 3.26, p < .01$; $t(6-8/9-11) = 2.75, p < .01$; $t(9-11/12) = 3.13, p < .01$.
   Liberal arts: $t(6-8/9-11) = 2.08, p < .05$.
   Other: $t(6/6-8) = 2.83, p < .01$.

6. All four-year: $t(110/110-217) = 13.43, p < .001$; $t(218-359/360) = -7.39, p < .001$.

7. Research: $t(110/110-217) = 7.61, p < .001$ $t(218-359/360) = -3.56, p < .001$.
   Comprehensive: $T(110/110-217) = 3.48, p < .001$.

8. All four-year: $t(both/grad) = -10.89, p < .001$; $t(und/grad) = -7.68, p < .001$.

9. Research: $t(both/grad) = -4.57, p < .001$; $t(und/grad) = -3.98, p < .001$.
   Doctoral: $t(both/grad) = -4.85, p < .001$; $t(und/grad) = -3.14, p < .01$.
   Comprehensive: $t(both/grad) = -4.28, p < .001$; $t(und/grad) = -3.19, p < .01$.

10. All four-year: $t(5/5-15) = 3.61, p < .001$: $t(5-15/16-33) = 5.85, p < .001$; $t(16-33/34) = 5.44, p < .001$.

11. Research: $t(5/34) = 1.99, p < .05$.
    Doctoral: $t(5/5-15) = 2.15, p < .05$; $t(16-33/34) = 3.10, p < .01$.
    Comprehensive: $t(16-33/34) = 2.39, p < .05$.
    Other: $t(5/34) = 2.14, p < .05$.

12. All four-year: $t(.20/.20-.78) = 685, p < .001$; $t(.20-.78/.79-1.99) = 9.01, p < .001$; $t(.79-1.99/2) = 6.61, p < .001$.

13. Research: $t(.20-.78/.79-1.99) = 3.87, p < .001$; $t(.79-1.99/2) = 3.63, p < .001$.
    Doctoral: $t(.20/.20-.78) = 3.71, p < .001$; $t(.20-.78/.79-1.99) = 2.18, p < .05$.
    Comprehensive: $t(.20/.20-.78) = 3.38, p < .001$; $t(.20-.78/.79-1.99) = 3.07, p < .01$.
    Liberal arts: $t(.20/.20-.78) = 2.53, p < .05$; $t(.20-.78/.79-1.99) = 2.62, p < .01$.
    Other: $t(.20/.79-1.99) = 2.65, p < .01$; $t(.79-1.99/2) = 2.26, p < .05$.

14. $t(all four-year) = 14.71, p < .001$.

15. $t(res) 6.30, p < .001$; $t(doc) = 4.84, p < .001$; $t(comp) = 4.39, p < .001$; $t(other) = 3.25, p < .01$.

16. All four-year: $t(5/5-9) = -2.51, p < .05$; $t(10-19/20) = -8.21, p < .001$.

17. Research: $t(5/5-9) = -2.67, p < .01$; $t(5-9/10-19) = 2.36, p < .05$; $t(10-19/20) = -7.63, p < .001$.
    Doctoral: $t(5/10-19) = -2.47, p < .05$; $t(5/20) = -3.55, p < .001$.
    Comprehensive: $t(10-19/20) = -6.42, p < .001$.

18. All four-year: $t = -3.23, p < .01$.

19. Estimates of regression coefficients were unbiased. A study of residuals showed no evidence of heteroskedasticity or need to transform variables. The analysis of residuals showed no evidence of interaction effects or need to explore quadratic or other polynomial equations. Multicollinearity was successfully controlled for by creating composite variables from highly correlated measures. Statistical procedures showed no indication of multicollinearity in regression analyses.

20. The number of respondents in other four-year institutions was insufficient to carry out analyses by rank within type of institution.

James S. Fairweather is Associate Professor and Senior Research Associate, Center for the Study of Higher Education, Penn State University. A version of this paper was originally prepared for the 1992 Conference of the Association for the Study of Higher Education in Minneapolis. Data were collected under a contract supported by the National Center for Education Statistics. Analyses were supported by grants from TIAA-CREF and from OERI, U.S. Department of Education, as part of the National Center on Postsecondary Teaching, Learning and Assessment. The views expressed in this paper are solely those of the author.

Campus Leaders and Campus Senates

BARBARA A. LEE

Case studies of the dynamics of campus governance indicate that the effectiveness of academic senates depends on structure, culture, and administrative posture toward faculty involvement in institutional decision making.

Surveys of faculty attitudes toward campus governance conducted over the past three decades have revealed a consistent theme: Faculty are dissatisfied with the quality, quantity, and outcome of their involvement beyond the department level in academic governance (American Association for Higher Education, 1967; Ladd and Lipset, 1975; Mortimer, Gunne, and Leslie, 1976; Carnegie Foundation for the Advancement of Teaching, 1982). Although little systematic information is available about the attitudes of academic administrators toward governance, it is safe to say that they, too, are unhappy with campus governance, although often for different reasons. Despite variations in the issues facing higher education over the years—from increases to declines in enrollment, from student activism to apathy, from glutted faculty job markets to faculty shortages—governance problems have been seemingly impervious to resolution.

The interplay between leadership and governance is of special importance at times when institutions are under stress, whether they are facing financial difficulty, the need to adapt to a changing student population, or pressure to perform more efficiently or effectively. A governance system on a campus is usually in place when a leader (president, provost, or dean) arrives, and the leader must decide whether to work within the existing governance system (both formal and informal), attempt to modify it, or completely restructure it. Irrespective of the alternative selected, the governance system may pose a formidable constraint on the leader's ability to effect change.

The research discussed in this chapter reports the results of visits to eight institutions of higher education where data were collected on the interplay between leadership and governance and, more specifically, on how leadership both affected governance and was affected by it. The eight institutions were a subset of a larger sample of thirty-two institutions participating in the Institutional Leadership Project, a five-year longitudinal study sponsored by the National Center for Postsecondary Governance and Finance. The eight institutions included two universities (one public, one private), two state colleges recently renamed "university," two private comprehensive colleges, and two public community colleges. Respondents included presidents, provosts, other vice-presidents, deans, department chairs, faculty senate leaders, union leaders, and faculty not formally involved in the senate. Because the focus was campus-level governance and, more particularly, the interaction between faculty and administration through the operation of the governance system, the term leadership was broadly defined. It included both academic administrators (the president and the provost or similar position) and faculty governance representatives.

What Is Governance?

For purposes of this study, governance was defined as the way that issues affecting the entire institution, or one or more components thereof, are decided. It included the structure, both formal and informal, of decision-making groups and the relationships between and among those groups and individuals. It included the process used to reach decisions and the outcome of recommendations from governance groups to higher-level individuals or groups. The governance "system" (and, more particularly, the institution's senate) and how it affected and was affected by leadership was the focus of attention.

The number, role, and interaction of governance groups vary by institution or campus, but most governance systems have a campuswide body such as a senate or faculty council. It is this group and its relationship with academic administrators and other significant faculty organizations (such as a faculty union) that this chapter examines. Although senates have a number of roles and purposes, this chapter does not attempt to evaluate whether the senate's role was appropriate or whether it was fulfilling that role (Millet, 1978). The senate's role and function on each campus were taken as a given; this research assessed the characteristics of senates and the apparent effects of those characteristics on each senate's perceived effectiveness, as well as the reciprocal relationship between senates and leaders.

Both faculty and administrators value senates, although for different reasons (Birnbaum, this volume). While some argue that the value of a senate is primarily symbolic (Millet, 1978; Birnbaum, this volume), others assert that a senate can play a significant role in managing a college or university (American Association for Higher Education, 1967). Yet others commend a faculty role in governance so that administrators will have "someone with whom to share the blame for mistakes" (Keller, 1983, p.61). Given the substantial amount of time, energy, attention, and nurturing that is needed to create and maintain an academic governance system, senates are obviously perceived either as useful or as a necessary evil. Because senates are unlikely to "go away" (Birnbaum, this volume), assessing the characteristics of useful senates as well as senates that are necessary evils should enhance our understanding of how senates and academic leaders function within a governance system.

Characteristics of Senates

Senates on the eight campuses differed in their perceived effectiveness and credibility with faculty and administrators. There is much literature on organizational effectiveness (for example, Cameron, 1978); it is beyond the scope of this chapter to define effective governance or to attempt to explain why faculty and administrators believe that a certain governance system is effective or ineffective. In this chapter, perceived effectiveness is an expression of a positive view of the governance system by both faculty and administrators and a belief that little or no change in the system is needed. Analysis of both the functional and dysfunctional governance systems revealed three dimensions that appeared to contribute to a system's perceived effectiveness. These are the system's broadly defined structure, the cultural context in which the system operated, and the interaction between the faculty governance structure and the administration. Each of these contributed to the system's perceived effectiveness. Several of the elements emerging from the eight campus visits were also included in a national study of faculty governance systems (Gilmour, this volume). Although the survey data were not available until the research described in this chapter was completed, the Gilmour data confirm or supplement several findings of the field research.

Structural Issues. The single most important structural issue in the governance system's perceived effectiveness was its composition, including the identity of its chair. Senates that included large numbers of nonfaculty (this category includes academic administrators) were viewed by both faculty and administrators as less effective than faculty-dominated or all-faculty bodies. Gilmour (this volume) found that nearly two-thirds (59 percent) of all senates included administrators as members and that students and professional staff were members of approximately one-fourth of the senates. In the present study, one institution was attempting to add nonfaculty professionals to the senate, and the faculty were furious at the usurpation of their primacy in the senate. At another institution in this study, the senate was chaired by the president, while the senates of five institutions were chaired by faculty. At the institution where the president chaired the senate, the faculty did not believe that the senate represented their views or was a legitimate faculty governance vehicle.

Another important issue encompassed the size and complexity of the senate. At one institution, the senate had thirty-one committees, leading to numerous disagreements about which committee should deal with certain issues, while at another institution where governance was perceived to be effective, there were only three standing senate committees. Respondents reported that it was difficult to staff a large number of committees with faculty who would devote the necessary time and attention to committee work. It seemed that greater senate size and complexity resulted in the perception of inefficiency, leading in turn to a perception of the senate's ineffectiveness.

A third structural element that affected a senate's perceived effectiveness was the composition and role of its executive committee. Because of the size of most senates, the executive committee did the most important work of the senate—setting the agenda, often determining committee assignments (both members and issues), framing issues for presentation to the body, and cutting deals with the administration. Gilmour's (this volume) study found that 73 percent of the senates had an executive committee, and of these, 84 percent set the senate agenda, 76 percent met with the president or provost, and 60 percent established and appointed committee members. At the institution where the president chaired the senate, there was no executive committee and thus no ability for faculty and administrative leaders to discuss important issues informally or shape issues collaboratively. The senate was viewed as illegitimate by faculty on that campus. How the executive committee saw its role and how it was perceived by the senate itself clearly contributed to the senate's perceived effectiveness.

Closely related to the composition of the executive committee was the agenda-setting process. As noted previously, at institutions where a president or provost set the agenda nearly unilaterally, the faculty viewed the senate as illegitimate. On the other hand, if the faculty controlled the agenda completely, the probability was high that issues important to the administration would either not be addressed or would be deferred indefinitely.

The way that issues were framed for the senate, and by whom, was also important, particularly at institutions preparing for substantial change in mission, size, or quality standards. Unilateral framing of issues, either by administrators or faculty, was often counterproductive; interaction between the two groups, either through the executive committee or a more informal mechanism, was perceived to produce better-quality decisions with less lengthy deliberation.

The boundaries of the senate role, particularly on campuses where faculty were unionized, were less important than expected. Although early writing about faculty bargaining predicted that unions would either destroy senates or usurp their functions, research on dual-track governance has found, instead, that unions play a protective role vis-a-vis the senate, often because the leadership overlaps (Baldridge and Kemerer, 1976; Lee, 1979). Gilmour's study (this volume) found no difference, in either the presence of a senate or its characteristics, between unionized and nonunionized campuses. In the research conducted for this study, little evidence of role conflict with the union was found, although occasionally, administrators and senates disagreed on the proper boundaries for the senate (and it was not necessarily the faculty seeking to expand the senate's role).

In sum, structural elements were important primarily because they influenced the way that the senate functioned and its ability to deal with complex issues. While poorly functioning senates were not solely a result of structural problems, it would be difficult for a senate to function well if the structure militated against it.

Cultural Issues. The impact of an institution's culture on its values, structure, and priorities has been well documented (Masland, 1985; Chaffee and Tierney, 1988). For senates, as well, the cultural context in which they operated had important effects on their functioning. One of the most dramatic and obvious cultural elements was the governance history of the institution. On several campuses, old disputes between long-gone provosts or presidents and the faculty had shaped the governance system in ways that even two or more decades could not change. At one campus, widespread faculty distrust of an unpopular president focused the faculty on the process, almost to the exclusion of the outcome, of any governance issue. The cultural context shaped the posture of the senate leadership; on that campus it was guardian of the process and the status quo, while on others it was a positive agent for change.

Another contextual factor that influences governance is the faculty's attitude toward the senate. A senate viewed as illegitimate, for structural or other reasons, is not viewed as an attractive leadership opportunity for faculty. Often the faculty's attitude toward the senate is shaped not by the characteristics of its leaders but by the way the administration responds to it.

A third cultural element that is viewed as critical to governance effectiveness is the quality of faculty who choose to participate. Although administrators on some campuses complained that only faculty with axes to grind or who were poor researchers or teachers participated in governance, this was not true across the eight institutions. Some respondents noted that the quality of senate leadership varied with the intensity of faculty emotions about certain issues in certain years, with the better leaders being energized by anger over an issue. Birnbaum (this volume) has noted that views of administrators toward the senate are often influenced by their attitudes toward its leaders. In Gilmour's data (this volume), administrators were less likely than the senate chairs to believe that the senate's leaders were "capable people," although only 69 percent of the chairs believed that the senate attracted capable people. It is difficult to separate this element from the others in this section and even more difficult to trace cause-and-effect relationships between the quality of faculty leadership and the way that faculty leaders are treated by academic administrators.

A critical factor to a governance system's success, and one that was not addressed satisfactorily on any of the eight campuses, was the development of leadership continuity. At best, a president-elect served for a year as the president's assistant. At worst, offices turned over annually with little communication between new and old officers, no attempts by leaders (either faculty or administrative) to help new officers learn their roles, and inadequate exploitation of the knowledge of former officers. At institutions where the senate was perceived to be functioning appropriately, more attention was given to continuity, but surprisingly, only minimal efforts were made to provide information, training, or advice to prospective or new officers, even on the good governance campuses.

Administrative Posture. The third dimension of governance systems found to be critical to perceived effectiveness was the posture of the president and/or provost toward the system. The degree to which the administration permitted the system to operate, the amount of interaction between faculty governance leaders and top administrators, and the responsiveness of top administration to recommendations from the governance group shaped faculty and administrative attitudes toward the legitimacy and effectiveness of the system.

Although it might be expected that an important component of an effective senate would be the commitment of institutional resources to senate use, the data did not support this conjecture. Gilmour (this volume) found that 44 percent of senate chairs received release time, 72 percent of senates were given secretarial support and telephone service, and 43 percent were given office space. In Lee's study, all but one institution gave the senate an office, at least a part-time secretary, a telephone, and release time for its officers, but there were substantial differences in perceived effectiveness of senates among these institutions. It may be that senates need institutional resources in order to function at a minimal level of effectiveness but that such resources do not predict that a senate will be perceived as effective.

On campuses where governance was viewed as relatively effective, there was a routinized formal relationship between faculty governance leaders and the administration. On several campuses, this involved inviting the senate chair (and on one campus, the chair-elect also) to all presidential cabinet meetings. Depending on the campus, the senate chair gained access to confidential and often sensitive information and provided a faculty voice at the cabinet level. Inclusion of the senate chair, on occasion and depending on the chair, was also used as a co-optation device. On one campus, it became the custom for senate officers to sit with an administrative committee that advised the provost on promotion and tenure recommendations. The faculty were not permitted to participate in the discussion or to vote, but their presence at these meetings increased the faculty's confidence in the fairness of personnel decisions and promoted trust between the governance leaders and top administrators.

An important supplement to the formal relationship was an informal relationship between the senate chair and either the president or the provost. If the president had a limited internal role in governance, then the senate chair's relationship with the provost was the important element. Regular interaction appeared to result in greater trust and more inclination on the part of both sides to resolve problems informally.

Most important in this dimension was top administration's deference to the governance system for most issues that affected the academic core of the institution or the faculty's welfare. This does not mean that the administration always accepted faculty recommendations, but that it allowed the senate to deal with any issue within the senate's purview, whether it was a matter of institutional survival or a trivial matter. Although several presidents reserved to themselves and their administrative team the responsibility for long-range planning, on those campuses where governance was perceived to be effective, administrators shared the outline of plans with governance leaders, and the implementation of the plans was delegated to the faculty governance structure.

Another important feature of governance relationships perceived to be effective was the administration's accountability to the senate. The "batting average" for faculty recommendations was less important here than the administration's practice of explaining why, on occasion, it could not accept the senate's recommendation, or why it felt that some modification was necessary. On some campuses, the administration worked with the senate to achieve the modifications the administration believed necessary. On those campuses where senate leaders were included in the administrative cabinet, the need to reject or modify senate recommendations was infrequent.

The administration's deference to the governance system and inclusion of its leaders in institutional management was either facilitated or constrained by the other two dimensions: the governance structure and the institutional governance culture. Administrative attempts to defer to the governance system were hampered by negative cultures or overly complex structures, and of course, negative cultures were created in the first place by faculty perceptions that administrators were unwilling to defer to the governance structure. This intertwining of the three dimensions made it difficult for either faculty leaders or administrators to improve governance relationships that had been historically poor, but on those campuses where all three dimensions were favorable it resulted in a governance system that was viewed as relatively effective (to the degree that any such system can be so viewed).

An Assessment of Three Senates

Of the eight institutions visited, two institutions had no campuswide governance system, which caused serious communication problems among academic units. Another had a governance structure so atypical that its analysis would not be useful to other institutions. A fourth had a governance structure created completely by collective bargaining agreement, a structure that addressed only curricular matters and left all other governance issues to the union contract. A fifth was in the process of changing its structure to reduce the number of committees and to add nonfaculty representatives.

Of the remaining three institutions, one had a governance system that both faculty and administrators viewed as reasonably effective. The governance system of the second could be safely characterized as paralyzed. A third had a governance system that could be characterized as "troubled" because its cultural context was the stumbling block. We will now describe the senates on these three campuses using the framework developed in the previous section.

Respecting the System

Structure. Urban College (UC) is a large comprehensive public institution with a wide range of programs. The basic governance structure is the faculty senate which is the executive body of the faculty assembly (all full-time faculty) and consists of four officers and twelve additional senators elected from the academic divisions. No administrators serve on the senate or meet with it regularly. One counselor attends meetings but may not vote. The senate has three committees: one for personnel decisions, one for minor resource allocation decisions, and a third for academic matters (including curriculum issues).

There are other bodies with responsibilities that overlap some of the senate's: for example, an instructional council (which includes senators, deans, and chairs) that handles curriculum matters and an academic council that deals with instructional concerns and consists of a large number of administrators and chairs. The provost meets with the senate executive committee regularly to set the agenda and help shape the issues to be addressed. There is no faculty union; in fact, it was clear that the president's decision to defer all academic and faculty status matters to the senate was a union-avoidance technique. No instances of administrative failure to respect the senate's purview were reported.

Culture. UC, although founded over a century ago, was fortunate from a governance standpoint that it attained its present size and complexity, as well as most of its faculty, within the past decade. The current president arrived at that time and created the governance system; he has supported and encouraged the faculty's governance role ever since.

Although the faculty supported the senate and viewed it as legitimate, many believed that the administration did not pay enough attention to faculty views. There was no dispute, however, over the credibility of the senate.

With regard to the quality of faculty leaders, one senior administrator believed that faculty complacency with the governance system resulted in the selection of mediocre leaders. According to this administrator, "The weakest thing [about governance at UC] is that faculty put a low priority on the senate and governance, and they are willing to elect less than the best faculty for leadership roles. This makes working with the senate more difficult for the administration. The faculty feel that they're treated fairly already, so it doesn't matter who the senate president is." No system was in place for the continuity of senate leadership. The senate chair met regularly with the provost and somewhat less regularly with the president, and despite the fact that the chair-elect was designated a year in advance, only the current chair dealt with top administrators. This lack of attention to leadership continuity may have contributed to the perceived poor quality of senate leadership.

Administrative Posture. Although administrative support for the faculty governance system at UC was strong and consistent, it was motivated by pragmatism rather than ideals. A senior administrator disparaged faculty governance, saying, "With the rapid change facing higher education today, I have some real doubts about the ability of academic governance to succeed. Governance focuses on keeping the status quo." But this distaste for faculty governance was exceeded by a distaste for faculty unions, and the administrator viewed deference to faculty governance as a quid pro quo for union avoidance.

Although another senior administrator's support for governance was consistent with institutional policy, the expressed attitude was completely different: "The ability to effect change is difficult in a mature organization with very powerful faculty. It takes patience if you want the faculty to come along with you. I would rather take longer and have the faculty on board than push something through." The senate chair is a member of the president's cabinet (a forty-member body that includes various administrators, support staff, and students). The chair does not meet with the president's council (the vice-presidents and the president). The cabinet is an information-sharing group; the senate chair had asked to attend president's council meetings but had been rebuffed.

Informal meetings between the senate chair and top administrators are frequent; the chair meets weekly with the provost and at least monthly with the president. The chair reported that both administrators were always available and that the president encouraged even more frequent meetings.

The administration's commitment to the senate is evident in its allocation of resources for senate use. The chair receives a 40 percent teaching reduction, the chair-elect receives approximately a 15 percent reduction, and the senate secretary receives approximately a 6 percent reduction. The senate has a budget, an office, a telephone, and the unlimited use of the provost's clerical staff. Although assigning the provost's secretary to the senate appears to be a conflict of interest, the provost stated that the secretary maintained the confidentiality of senate material.

Administrative deference to the senate's role was reported to be high and consistent. A faculty leader asserted that neither the president nor the provost would permit "end runs" but would insist that the matter be taken up by the senate. Although the faculty leader remarked that "the administration does look at the senate as a necessary entity that needs to be" and viewed its motives as political rather than normative, both sides reported that the system worked well.

The studied deference of administrators to the governance system was reflected in their accountability to the system. Only one faculty recommendation—on salary levels—had been rejected by the administration in recent years. The low level of conflict between the senate and the administration appeared to be a result of the substantial informal interaction between the senate chair and other senate leaders and top administrators. A senior administrator remarked, "It's important that they [the senate] be perceived as legitimate and effective," and the administration's policy was calculated to that end.

Although perceived as reasonably effective, respondents at UC were not without criticism of the governance system. Some faculty criticized the structure as too complex and lengthy (a curriculum matter, for example, would be addressed by five layers of groups or individuals). Senior administrators criticized its slowness, and one viewed his role as "developing a sense of urgency for issues" because the system took so long to resolve a problem. Nevertheless, top administrators viewed their acceptance of and deference to the senate as critical to responding to their constituency, improving quality, and avoiding a faculty union.

A System Paralyzed

Structure. System College (SC) is part of a major state university system with a systemwide governance code. The code requires that the senate include only faculty and that it develop recommendations on matters of academic concern and faculty welfare.

SC's president is an ex officio member of the senate and attends meetings and makes reports but does not chair the meetings (as the former president did). Although the code gives the president the power to appoint all committee members, he has delegated that power to the executive committee. Twenty-nine standing committees (at a college employing 500 faculty) report to five councils that report to the senate. There are also numerous ad hoc committees. Both faculty and administrators were critical of the senate's structure as overly bureaucratic—a system that "gets in the way of communication."

The president meets regularly with the senate executive committee to set the senate agenda, to shape issues for senate action, and to encourage the officers to take a stronger leadership role. There is no faculty union (although one may be developing), so the senate's purview is broad.

Culture. SC's culture is the governance albatross. Former presidents ran the college as a patriarchy, and the faculty, until now, has been given no real governance role. The senate under previous presidents was the president's captive—chaired by the president and dominated by administrators. Faculty are now expected to participate fully in institutional governance; however, they say they do not know how. Senior administrators are impatient with the faculty's know-nothing attitude and criticize the senate and its leadership for being ineffective.

The faculty's attitude toward the senate is equally critical. A long-time faculty member remarked:

> My largest criticism of the faculty senate is that it continues to operate under [the prior] constraints even though there has been an open invitation from the president to take part in the governance of the institution. It may be the goldfish bowl syndrome—when goldfish who have spent their lives in a goldfish bowl are put in a stream, they still swim in a circle. Mostly senate committee members do what they're supposed to do, but others don't get around to it with the alacrity that they should. Another problem with the faculty senate is that too many people are elected who aren't wholly committed to the

work of the senate and the institution—who will be present and prompt. Sometimes there is no quorum, so the senate cannot do its work.

Another faculty member criticized the senate for not communicating with the faculty. He said, "The faculty senate here works better than it used to, but there is little communication between the senate and the faculty. At my former institution, the senate minutes were typed and distributed to all faculty. I said in a faculty meeting that we should get a report from senators, but it is not yet being done." This faculty member put the blame squarely on the senate. He believed that the faculty finally had an opportunity to participate in governance but were squandering it.

The criticism of the senate extends to its leadership as well, although the criticism is less severe. Respondents seemed to recognize that the leaders were fighting a difficult and unsuccessful battle to stir the demoralized senators into effective action. An administrator said "I have more faith in the faculty governance system than those inside it do. The senate leaders really need help." A senate leader admitted that personal efforts had not been successful: "Senate committees won't study these problems. I can't seem to generate the kind of movement that the senate needs. Committee chairs need to be more active. For example, take the faculty evaluation form [that is used to determine pay increases]. The faculty have been dissatisfied with it for five years, and the senate still hasn't revised it. At a time when change has to occur quickly, resistance slows it down."

There is little attention to leadership continuity at SC. Although the senate chair is involved in many committees (discussed in the next section) the chair-elect is not. In fact the chair-elect is selected in April and takes office in May, so there is no time for sensitizing or training the chair-elect.

The faculty's inexperience in governance and the former patriarchal culture of the institution were cited by every respondent as the reason for the system's paralysis. Although everyone agreed on the reason for the dysfunction, no one suggested interventions, such as training, retreats, or other mechanisms to boost faculty expertise and confidence in their governance role. Everyone blamed people who were gone (former presidents) and bemoaned the result, while failing to move ahead with the critical matter of building a system that could work.

Administrative Posture. A senior administrator simultaneously expressed hope and frustration with the governance system. In an effort to avoid dominating the senate, the administration has insisted that the senate solve its own problems, revise its own structure, and begin addressing important issues in a timely way. The situation is especially grave because the SC is under considerable external pressure to raise its admission standards, improve its curriculum, and enhance the performance of its students. This external pressure exacerbates the senate's paralysis because many faculty are resisting these changes.

The president has established several formal settings for interaction with the senate chair. The chair is invited to the president's meetings with the vice-presidents, and the college's planning committee includes the senate chair. Furthermore, the president meets regularly with the senate chair and the executive committee.

Informal meetings are also frequent and usually initiated by the administration. One administrator said "My relationship with the senate is probably more trusting than they may be comfortable with. I have regular heart-to-heart talks with the senate chair." The chair confirmed that administrators were always available and were very supportive.

The administration has provided resources for the senate—an office, a telephone, a part-time secretary, and three hours of release time, a 25 percent reduction. No release time is provided for the chair-elect, since that person is only in that role for one month.

The administration has made it clear that it expects the senate to perform its role and has refused to make the faculty's decisions for them. But simultaneously, the administration is pressured to make major changes in the curriculum, student quality, and student outcomes to comply with state requirements. This pressure has led administrators, frustrated with the senate's paralysis, to create other governance structures to deal with some issues or to make the decisions without the senate. This behavior, of course, reinforces the paralysis of the senate and permits the doubting faculty to point fingers at autocratic administrators. A faculty leader concluded that the college needs "marriage counseling" to help all groups deal with conflict and resolve it. This leader said, "We need more tolerance by both administrators and faculty. They [administration] have to realize that [change] is not going to happen overnight. There is so much impatience and frustration. Some decisions are painful. The faculty are turned off by being told that they are the problem. The administration is in too much of a hurry." A relatively new administrator agreed with this assessment, replying, "There are several faculty who have their Mary Kay or real estate businesses and spend minimal time on campus. But there are others, especially a group of older faculty, who really want to try, but they don't understand that the rules have changed. There are some new faculty who are pretty good or very good, but they're reacting badly to the president's strategies because his management tactics are aimed at the lowest group of faculty. The good faculty are insulted, and they'll either retreat into their shells or will leave if they get a better offer."

At SC, all three dimensions of the governance system contribute to its paralyses. Its structure is overly complex and bureaucratic, its culture is not conducive to faculty confidence in the governance system, and the administration, while evidencing considerable support for the system, has undermined it through its impatience with the system's paralysis. All parties are so busy pointing fingers at each other that little constructive progress is being made to resolve the situation. Particularly when the system is stressed by external pressures for change, the energy devoted to blaming drains the institution's ability to focus on how that change will occur.

A Fixation on Process

Structure. The senate at Rural College (RC) is dominated by faculty, but it also includes all deans, the president and provost, the library director, other nonfaculty members, and six students. Membership totals 62 (the college employs 500 faculty). The senate chair, in recent years always a faculty member, is elected by the senate. The senate addresses all academic matters and has the final say on curriculum matters.

The president attends all senate meetings and makes some initial remarks, but then does not participate in senate discussion. The senate executive committee includes the president, provost, senate officers, and two at-large members. The executive committee sets the agenda, screening issues to determine whether to take them to the senate or drop them. It appoints members to standing committees and creates ad hoc committees as well. It also develops resolutions for senate consideration.

RC faculty have been unionized for two decades, and the boundaries between senate and union turf appear well established. The same people held senate and union office, although usually not concurrently. Although the senate works closely with the president and provost, the union has no relationship with either leader. The union president deals with a member of the business vice-president's staff and has no communication, either formal or informal, with academic administrators. Both union leaders and academic administrators are satisfied with this arrangement.

Culture. The culture of this institution had an important effect on governance. A senior administrator explained, "We recruited a bright, young faculty fifteen years ago, and they got caught in the academic crunch [the stagnant job market]. They had not planned to stay, but they are still here. . . . There is an activist core, made up of faculty from the arts and sciences. They want the college to be different than it is . . . more graduate education and more research and all the trappings that go with research." The college's history was troubled by a series of presidents that the arts and sciences faculty believed to be autocratic. The union was formed in response to faculty dissatisfaction with a president. A faculty leader said, "Atrocity precedes a union. There was an autocratic president who denied raises to people he disliked. The AAUP [American Association of University Professors] censured [the college.] Faculty were fired. The academic senate was reorganized." The senate was reorganized following the censure to remove all administrators except the deans, provost, and president. Although the union has survived one decertification attempt, the union leadership acknowledged that it would not call a strike, because the faculty would not support it.

Subsequent presidents were also reported to be insufficiently deferential to faculty concerns or recommendations (one administrator described former presidents as "strong-arm, benevolent dictators"). In recent years, the board of trustees' rejection of a faculty search committee recommendation for a new president outraged faculty and nearly destroyed the governance system. The college's history of troubled governance has resulted in a faculty that is focused on guarding the governance process, while substantive issues are of secondary importance. An administrator described the governance culture as one of intense faculty interest in the minutiae of decision making. For example, he said, "Faculty spend hours allocating peanuts [small amounts of dollars] for faculty travel."

The faculty view the senate as critical to maintaining a strong voice in institutional matters. Faculty support for the senate is so strong that administrators know better than to attempt to circumvent it. One said, "The faculty is very interested in governance. The academic senate is very important. I wouldn't dream of doing anything about curriculum—that's their territory." Conversations with both faculty and administrators suggested that it was the system the faculty valued, not the outcomes or the way the system dealt with issues.

Because the system was the faculty's focus, there was less pressure on faculty leaders to be effective. An administrator criticized senate leaders, saying, "The faculty leadership that emerges, I have found, is not the best and the brightest of the faculty. It is made up of those who love the intrigue of faculty governance, who are politically active. The faculty abdicated the senate leadership to a small arts and sciences group a long time ago. They [faculty] would all have more clout if the others [beyond arts and sciences] were more involved in leadership functions. . . . I don't think the faculty have good leadership." No other respondents mentioned senate leadership.

Leadership continuity in formal terms is restricted to the election of a chair-elect and the inclusion of the immediate past chair on the senate executive committee. Formal attempts to train or sensitize new leaders may be less important at RC because of the small number of faculty who seek leadership roles and their tendency to hold the same office several times.

Administrative Posture. The formal relationship between the president, provost, and senate chair appears to be confined to meetings of the senate executive committee. The senate chair does not attend meetings of the president's administrative team. Informal meetings, however, are frequent, especially between the provost and the senate chair.

RC provides resources for the senate in the form of an office, a budget, and a secretary. The senate chair gets a 50 percent teaching reduction, but the chair-elect gets no release time.

Administrative deference to the governance system has been noted previously. Because of the college's history and the intensity of faculty interest in protecting the governance process, administrators feel constrained to defer to the process on some issues (for example, personnel decisions or major curricular matters) in which some of them would like to have a stronger voice.

Part of the current president's credibility with the faculty is that the president was selected on the advice of a faculty search committee. In reflecting on the faculty's view of the president, a faculty leader said, "I'm not sure the president himself has made the difference [in governance], or just that he was selected using the proper channels—it's the process that the faculty have primarily reacted to. . . . The processes were developed in the mid 1960s under an unpopular president [and the faculty guard them very jealously]." Because the president was new, it was too early to tell whether the president would continue to defer to the governance system and what the reaction would be if he did not. Furthermore, the college was under no real external pressure to make the kinds of changes that SC was facing, so neither the governance system nor the faculty's relationship with the president were stressed.

Impact of Governance on Leadership

At each of the three colleges included in this chapter, the presidents were respected by the faculty and viewed as strong leaders. UC's president was respected both within and outside the college as a strong advocate for the institution, an effective fund raiser (from both private and state sources), and a creative leader. SC's president was respected for administrative experience at other institutions and a strong vision for the college. At RC, the president was very new and the faculty's respect was due primarily to the fact that the president was their candidate for the job.

Despite the evident ability of these leaders and the faculty's generally favorable reaction to them, each was constrained, albeit in very different ways, by the governance system. While one used those constraints to build faculty support for administrative ideas and plans, another was unable to shock the system into functioning as a partner rather than an impediment. The third was struggling to shift the faculty's concern from guarding the process to dealing with substance.

Although the president at UC lamented the additional time that it took to process issues through the faculty senate, it did not appear that the institution suffered greatly as a result. The college was thriving, had adequate resources, and was viewed as very responsive to community and business needs. While the faculty were not at all fooled by the administration's pragmatic approach to governance, they were supportive of administrative policies and generally viewed the president as an effective leader.

The president at SC was frustrated by the paralysis of the governance system but chose to work around it rather than taking strong measures to heal it. This approach alienated the faculty because of the conflicting messages that the faculty governance system is critical to a high-quality institution but that the low-quality faculty are the reason for the institution's problems. The president did not seem to see that these strategies further weakened the senate. The institution appeared to be on a collision course, and a faculty group had been formed that was discussing unionization, no-confidence votes, and other measures to express the faculty's dismay.

The impact of RC's governance system on its new president was not clear, but it did result in the president's deciding to use the first year at RC as a learning experience rather than attempting to make change right away. The strong faculty concern over process cannot help but slow the pace of change at RC, if, in fact, change occurs at all. Hailing from an institution with a relatively weak faculty role in governance, this president will have to move cautiously, respect the process in all its details, and develop strong informal channels to faculty who are not involved in the formal process if the president expects to effect change.

Impact of Leadership on Senates

This chapter described governance at three colleges, one with a governance system judged by both its members and the researcher to be relatively effective and two with troubled governance systems. To what degree did the president and provost contribute to the relative effectiveness of these governance systems?

Although academic administrators on all three campuses stated their firm commitment to the process, only on one campus did they make good on that commitment. Despite their personal reservations about delegating important college issues to the senate, UC's administrators consistently deferred to the system. They did not create alternatives to the system. They did not openly criticize the system or the effectiveness of its leaders, although they had doubts on both scores. They made it clear that a strong faculty governance system was a sine qua non of a well-managed college.

On the second campus, administrators, while espousing deference to the faculty governance system, took actions that further weakened it and neglected to take steps to strengthen it. Their simultaneous exhortations that the senate assume more responsibility conflicted with the message they were sending that the institution's problems were the faculty's fault. They disparaged the senate members' ability to function without creating ways for them to learn how to function. They created governance mechanisms to deal with matters that the senate had not been able to deal with. While their impatience is understandable in light of the considerable external pressure for institutional change, these administrators' actions simply failed to improve the governance situation and, in fact, added to its problems.

It was really too soon to ascertain what effect the new top administrators at RC would have on the governance system. They were watching and listening, rather than working closely with the system, and faculty leaders were frustrated with administrators' refusal to communicate their plans for the institution. Because of the faculty's emphasis on process, the administrators understood that they first had to win the faculty's trust in their intention to defer to the system before they could try to have an impact on either that system or institutional problems.

How Can Senates Be More Effective?

While a sample of eight institutions is too small to produce valid generalizations about campus governance, observing how these systems operate and the factors that either enhance or impede their work suggest several strategies for campus leaders, both administrative and faculty, to consider. The data also suggest that some factors may be beyond the control of campus leaders and that leaders must find ways to work around these factors if they cannot be changed.

While structure, culture, and administrative posture toward the senate were all found to be important, structure was the least important. Certainly, a senate dominated by administrators, or including a large proportion of nonfaculty, was not supported by faculty, but the mere absence of nonfaculty did not guarantee that a senate would function effectively. A few elements—faculty domination, resources for the senate, and clarity on the boundaries of the senate's role—seemed to play an important role, and their absence could have seriously impeded a senate's work. But much more was needed for a senate to be viewed as reasonably effective by campus actors.

Negative Culture. A negative culture can impede the best-intentioned leaders. On two campuses, well-intentioned leaders were hampered by faculty distrust or fixation on the past. Any attempts to change the system or to pressure the faculty to address serious institutional needs were viewed with suspicion. Faculty at one college simultaneously complained that the administration never listened to them while grousing that they did not know how to participate in governance and the president was pushing them too hard. Faculty at another institution insisted that they participate in all decisions while criticizing the president for not "leading" the institution. Part of the problem at both these institutions may have been an aging faculty made up of locals who had never taught anywhere else. One might speculate that the anticipated increase in faculty retirements (Bowen and Schuster, 1986) and the orientation of younger faculty to research and their disciplines may ease the pressure for substantial faculty involvement. Nevertheless, at many institutions, leaders faced with negative cultures and an aging faculty cadre with little turnover will find it most difficult to build faculty trust and expertise in shared governance.

Respect and Reward Needed. Governance leaders are rarely respected or rewarded. Even on campuses where the system appeared to function reasonably well, both faculty and administrators criticized the quality of faculty governance leaders. They complained that few faculty were active and that the same ones held office almost all of the time. While Birnbaum (this volume) has noted that giving a faculty "troublemaker" a governance role is one way to diffuse some negative energy, some respondents seemed to believe that nearly all governance leaders fit this description. One reason for the difficulty in attracting good governance leaders is that there are few or no rewards for such service. Release time from teaching is very likely inadequate to compensate an individual for the time spent on governance matters. Furthermore, many institutions are shifting their reward systems to emphasize research and publication, and many others have never rewarded service to the institution, through governance or other activities, even to the degree that teaching is rewarded. So there is little incentive for faculty to participate if they are unrewarded and especially if they are criticized for inadequate research because they spent the time on governance instead.

But how can an institution reward governance activity? If the institution's priority is increasing its prestige to external groups by mimicking higher-status research institutions, can it afford to reward faculty whose research productivity is low or nonexistent? And what of those governance leaders who struggle to maintain the status quo, resisting change and stirring up the faculty to protest leaders' efforts to improve quality? Should individuals who work against what the leaders perceive to be the interests of the institution be rewarded for that? And if not, is it politically feasible, or even desirable, for an institution to reward only those leaders who support the administration's efforts?

Tailoring the reward system to encourage higher-quality faculty participation in governance, while superficially appealing, may be more difficult than it sounds. Nevertheless, campus leaders cannot expect to entice productive, respected faculty to assume governance roles if they are either disadvantaged or not rewarded for their participation.

Leadership Development. Governance leaders need training and seasoning. Although the data are not reported here, faculty and administrators were asked to comment on the characteristics of a good faculty leader. Their answers fell into two categories: personal attributes and an understanding of how the system works. If understanding the system is necessary for effective governance participation, how can we expect an individual to chair a senate if that person has not been actively involved in some other leadership role in the senate? While it is likely that many senate chairs had held committee offices or other leadership positions, there was no mechanism on some campuses to sensitize incoming chairs to recent developments, informal agreements, pending concerns, or the dynamics of the chair's relationship with administrative leaders. And because senate leaders generally held office for only one year, the knowledge of the immediate past chair was often tapped only informally and at the initiative of the incoming chair.

While statewide senates or associations of campus senates at the state level helped sensitize leaders to state-level concerns and how they were implemented on other campuses, there appeared to be no formal opportunity to develop future senate leadership. Given the importance to the faculty of their governance role and given administrative recognition of faculty interest in governance, the lack of leadership development is striking.

It would seem that at a minimum, the past senate chair and the incoming chair should work with the current chair for the year that he or she is in office. The past chair can provide important insights to both the current chair and the chair-elect. The chair-elect will have a year of on-the-job training before he or she assumes the chair's position. This system may cost the institution somewhat more in release time, but if the institution's leadership believes that an effective senate is important, it will find the necessary resources.

Consistent Deference. Deference is inconvenient but necessary. Even on the campus where governance appeared relatively effective, administrators bemoaned the need to defer to the faculty governance system. They believed, however, that consistent deference was the key to effective shared governance.

Deference does not mean abdication of the administrative role. On several campuses where the senate made recommendations on all important institutional matters, faculty conceded that the administration had a right to reject faculty recommendations at least occasionally, as long as an explanation was forthcoming. Faculty did not appear to expect the president or provost to agree with them 100 percent of the time; they did expect that their views would be listened to and considered thoughtfully and that administrators would explain their reasons for rejecting a senate recommendation.

Communication for Consensus. Frequent formal and informal communication builds consensus. While simply communicating does not mean that people will agree, the practice of inviting senate chairs to administrative staff meetings and frequent informal meetings seemed to enhance the effectiveness of campus governance. It is likely that these meetings sensitized both parties to each other's concerns and helped shape the way that the senate discussed issues referred by the administration. At UC, the senate chair and provost both noted that they spent many hours discussing issues until both were clear on each other's position, the president's position, and the faculty and administration's view of the college's needs. They believed that a high level of institutional consensus resulted from these discussions.

What Is the Role of Research?

Although several surveys have been conducted on the characteristics of governance structures and the perceptions of senate leaders and administrators on their effectiveness (Kemerer and Baldridge, 1975; Adler, 1977; Gilmour, this volume), it is only through case studies that a researcher can assess the dynamics of the governance system, the factors that enhance or impede its ability to function, and the degree to which faculty and administrators support it. One of the weaknesses of the case-study methodology is its limited generalizability, but case studies of governance are useful because they can identify practices or structures on one campus that may be either adopted or avoided by other institutions with similar cultures, missions, and problems.

Because a campus senate must deal with a multitude of agendas and because of its substantial symbolic role, it may be insufficient to try to study these bodies with tools of rational analysis. Whatever insights are gained from this study of three senates are of limited predictive value, although they may identify weaknesses or good practice that will inform the efforts of other institutions as they struggle to improve shared governance. This is not to say that one should not try to understand academic governance, but that whatever success one has in identifying factors that enhance or impede governance, there is more happening than can be understood or appreciated.

References

Adler, D. L. *Governance and Collective Bargaining in Four-Year Institutions 1970–1977*. Academic Collective Bargaining Information Service Monograph No. 3. Washington, D.C.: Academic Collective Bargaining Information Service, 1977.

American Association for Higher Education. *Faculty Participation in Academic Governance*. Washington, D.C.: American Association for Higher Education, 1967.

Baldridge, J. V., and Kemerer, F. R. "Academic Senates and Faculty Collective Bargaining." *Journal of Higher Education*, 1976, 47, 391–411.

Bowen, H. R., and Schuster, J. H. *American Professors: A National Resource Imperiled*. New York: Oxford University Press, 1986.

Cameron, K. D. "Measuring Organizational Effectiveness in Institutions of Higher Education." *Administrative Science Quarterly*, 1978, 23, 604–632.

Carnegie Foundation for the Advancement of Teaching. *The Control of the Campus: A Report on Governance of Higher Education*. Princeton, N.J.: Princeton University Press, 1982.

Chaffee, E. E., and Tierney, W. G. *Collegiate Culture and Leadership Strategies*. New York: American Council on Education/Macmillan, 1988.

Keller, G. *Academic Strategy: The Management Revolution in American Higher Education*. Baltimore, Md.: Johns Hopkins University Press, 1983.

Kemerer, F. R., and Baldridge, J. V. *Unions on Campus*. San Francisco: Jossey-Bass, 1975.

Ladd, E. C., Jr., and Lipset, S. M. *The Divided Academy*. New York: McGraw-Hill, 1975.

Lee, B. A. "Governance at Unionized Four-Year Colleges: Effect on Decision-Making Structure." *Journal of Higher Education*, 1979, 50, 565–585.

Masland, A. T. "Organizational Culture in the Study of Higher Education." *Review of Higher Education*, 1985, 8, 157–168.

Millett, J. D. *New Structures of Campus Power: Successes and Failures of Emerging Forms of Institutional Governance*. San Francisco: Jossey-Bass, 1978.

Mortimer, K. P., Gunne, M. G., and Leslie, D. W. "Perceived Legitimacy of Decision Making and Academic Governance Patterns in Higher Education: A Comparative Analysis." *Research in Higher Education*, 1976, 4, 273–290.

Barbara A. Lee is associate professor of industrial relations and human resources, Rutgers University.

PART V

THE PROFESSIONAL LIFE OF FACULTY

SCHOLARSHIP ISSUES AND DEFINITIONS

Linking Teaching and Research

A Critical Inquiry

Ronald Barnett

Introduction

What is the relationship between research and higher education? Is there one? By speaking of a relationship, I want to raise the question as to whether or not there is a conceptual connection between the two. Clearly, much research goes on in institutions of higher education. Indeed, we can probably find some kind of research in progress in each of the two hundred or more institutions which offer some kind of higher education in the UK. The question, though, is whether or not, qua institutions of higher education, they have an obligation to sponsor research. Is it part of the meaning of "institution of higher education" such that we would not be prepared to grant the name to an institution in which there was no research taking place?

This issue has formed a key element in the historical debate over the idea of higher education.[1] Or, rather, over the idea of the university. Views are to be found on both sides. Amongst those who have argued that the university need not or, indeed, should not engage in research, we find Newman, Ortega y Gasset and Sir Walter Moberly. On the other side, in arguing that research is indeed part of the meaning of "university," we see Jaspers, Phillips Griffiths and Wegener.[2] So there is no unanimity of view on this issue.

Today, this is not just a philosophical issue: it has political importance. The UK government has suggested that universities should be separated and funded on the basis of their research capability, so that we might have "research" universities and "teaching" universities.[3] However, our concern is higher education. It might make sense to argue that no bona fide university could exist which did not also conduct research. But even if that were the case, we could still maintain that research is not part of what we understand higher education to be. That is the argument I shall make here.

Before we get into the argument, there will be two objections to what I have just said. Firstly, that making a conceptual distinction in this way between "university" and "higher education" is to engage in philosophical pedantry. Secondly, that it is politically naive, since such an argument could be said to justify the kind of political move I have just mentioned, in which some institutions of higher education might be denied research funding: for research might then be seen to be a mere luxury add-on, not an essential part of what it is to be an institution of higher education.

Against the first objection, I hope to show that the conceptual distinction is far from mere pedantry. It forces us to consider what we mean by higher education and, indeed, I shall argue that research is not an essential part of the process of higher education as such.

So far as the second objection is concerned, any such political argument would be missing the point. Precisely because my focus is the relationship between higher education and research, I am not concerned with research per se. But, in distinguishing higher education and research, nothing said here will imply that research is not worth conducting or supporting. Indeed, I shall argue that while research is not part of the idea of higher education, it is presupposed by higher education. Any attempt to withdraw research funding on the basis of the argument I am offering would, therefore, be quite illegitimate.

The Ideology of Research

Over the last thirty years, research has become big business, and has been a key element in the formation of new academic disciplines. The aspiration to conduct research on the part of the academic community has been a vital ingredient in the process of "academic drift," of new institutions of higher education measuring their performance against the more established and elite institutions.[4] Being a costly enterprise and having many uses to the modern state, research has at the same time come under increased scrutiny from the paymaster. The debate over research has become the battleground for the competing ideologies of the academic community and of the state.

Quite apart from the rhetoric, what is the character of research in reality? Clearly, there are differences across subject areas, and so general observations are fraught with difficulty. Nonetheless, certain aspects stand out. Firstly, a significant element of research is not only funded by the government, or quasi-governmental agencies, but also organized on a customer-contract basis.[5] The initiative for a project very often comes from the funding agency, which adopts a "proactive" stance (in the jargon), setting the agenda, administering a steering committee, and ensuring that the project is running towards the desired end. Under this set of structural conditions, research has taken on an instrumental character, extrinsically oriented to external goals. Accordingly, in many fields, the conventional idea of a disinterested researcher having his or her own idiosyncratic interest and pursuing it wherever it might lead is a matter of history.

Secondly, this form of research endeavour can all too easily produce a state of alienation in those conducting the research. I use the term "alienation" in its marxian sense of the workers being separated from their work; for literally their work is not their own.[6] This is especially the case where large budgets generate research "teams" with different grades of research workers, the individual members having little control over their work.

Thirdly, research is largely uncontrolled by democratic means even though it is directed by state agencies.[7] The fiction is that those state agencies are able to and do exert democratic influences; or at least, they impose a measure of accountability to the public. But the argument should be recognized for the fiction it is.

Finally, research is increasingly conducted outside institutions of higher education. It is pursued not just in specially funded research institutes, but on a large scale in industry, and by private foundations and policy institutes.

How do these broad-brush sociological observations help us to understand the conceptual connections between higher education and research? On the picture just conveyed, research appears to have something of the character of a commodity, largely unconnected with "improvement," whether improvement of society or of the individual. The metaphor of commodity suggests itself (with its marxian overtones) precisely because research has become part of academic currency, bestowing credibility on those who possess a curriculum vitae listing their research publications. That kind of curriculum vitae brings a reward in terms of career advancement, with the inevitable monetary gains. And those rewards bear more of a relationship to the length of the publications list than its quality. There should be nothing surprising about this: in a competitive market, where the number of would-be senior academics considerably exceeds the posts available, an "objective" means is required to allocate the scarce goods. The publications list meets the bill: it is a form of intellectual capital, bartered in exchange for the sought-for advancement.[8]

The general point of all this is very simple: knowledge in the context of discovery and knowledge in the context of transmission are entirely different enterprises. Sometimes they are to be found in close proximity; and there are certainly empirical connections between them. Curricula which are project-based can be linked to staffs' research programmes. Alternatively, curricula which are weak in certain areas may prompt the need for particular kinds of research. The key point remains, however: research is seldom driven by curricular considerations but is normally given direction by an interest structure based on academic careers and the public use of knowledge.

The significance of career advancement in driving research is evident enough; but the use of knowledge in determining the shape of research should not be overlooked. In an age of the commercial exploitation of discoveries, and the marketing of research work, the division between pure and applied research has almost vanished.[9] Certainly, there remain some domains of research which are disinterested, but the incentive to have an eye to the main chance grows. Not only in biotechnology and in computer science; even in archaeology and fine art, we see that academics (advising new museums and making television films) are finding with no little alacrity that their intellectual capital is highly marketable.

Research, then, is born by a coincidence of social interests: of the academic community, of industry, and of the state. Whether it is the academics' interests in the livings that come in the wake of a research career; or industry's wish to produce new drugs or insecticides; or the state's desire to develop new military armaments or better traffic flows or even to reduce truancy in schools; these are motivations quite unconnected with the education of students in higher education.

All this leads to a distortion in academic life. Academic excellence comes to be defined in terms of research excellence, irrespective of an academic's qualities as a teacher. Correspondingly, high level achievements in research all too easily serve as a sufficient criterion for academic excellence. We have to see through this framework of thought for what it is: nothing short of academic ideology.

The Logic of Research and Higher Education

By the logic of research and higher education, I mean the general conceptual relationships that exist between these two sets of activity; and I should like to explore those relationships in the following six theses.

First thesis: Research is public; higher education is private. Research and higher education share much in common. Both activities are built around structured inquiries, which are persistent, deliberative, more or less organized, and set within a context of present knowledge, and which contain elements of interaction, dialogue, problem-solving, creativity and criticism. This is such a formidable list that we might be tempted to assume that research and higher education must at least be species of the same genus of activity even if not actually identical. But such a conception is to overlook a fundamental distinction about the two activities.

Research is an attempt to produce objective knowledge, independent of personal viewpoint. It is the knowledge which inhabits World III of Popper's schema. The point of research is that it is a systematic human endeavour intended to produce a level of impersonal knowledge, standing outside individuals. And, as Popper reminds us, this is so in a literal sense: we can find the outcomes of research on the library shelves, or on the computer disc. Its public character has a solidity and a substance to it.

Higher education, on the other hand, is oriented differently. It is directly concerned with individuals, with their minds and with their own way of looking at things. In that sense, it is deliberately idiosyncratic. This is a genuine kind of knowledge but it is shot through with subjectivity. To return to Popper, his schema allows for this form of knowledge, but as forming the inhabitants of World II, the personal knowledge contained in the human consciousness. Qua researcher, the academic may inhabit World III; but qua teacher, he or she works in the realm of World II. Admittedly, from time to time, the development of the student's mind is assessed, and the student is required to give a semi-public demonstration of the extent to which his or her consciousness has advanced. But in the end, higher education is a matter of what goes on in the mind of the individual; it is essentially a personal affair.

Second thesis: Research is a matter of outcome; higher education is a matter of process. Research is a painstaking business. Much time is spent getting anywhere. Progress is often slow, and can be counted in years. Sometimes, the model or theory being examined leads into a blind alley or the methodology turns out to be faulty, and the researcher feels as if the effort involved was worthless. Outcome is everything. And not just any outcome. The outcome, whether a journal article or a book or a commercial patent, has to be significant and recognized as such. First, it has to get past the gatekeepers, the publishers and the journal editors, the referees and reviewers. Secondly, it has to beat the clock. Particularly in the sciences, time presses heavily as research teams around the world struggle to be first to the finish, and then engage in priority disputes to determine just who was successful. But other areas are not without their temporal aspects: even philosophy has its intellectual fashions.[10] Then, if a new thought does see the light of day, it still requires the approval of the researcher's peer group within the academic or professional world. The outcome can be conventional or revolutionary; to develop another of Popper's metaphors, it can amount to mere filling in of the mortar, an additional brick or two, or even a completely new building.[11] Either way, in research, the outcome is all. Except for the historians and the sociologists of knowledge, the process of getting there is signally uninteresting.[12]

In higher education, it is entirely the other way around. There, there is no outcome as such. This may seem odd. After all, the government, employers and other agencies are talking precisely about student outcomes.[13] That is understandable, given the desire of those agencies to ascertain that the three years or more spent in higher education lead to some definite outcome. Higher education, though, is a matter of getting students launched on a process of self-development, in which they take responsibility for enlarging and deepening their own consciousness. Admittedly, after graduation, many students go no further in their reading and thinking. But at least, they have sufficient grounding to do so, if they wish.

Seen in this way, the moment of graduation is just an arbitrary point in the formation of the individual's consciousness. Graduation day symbolizes no end-point; merely perhaps a getting-off point, or an interlude, or a marker in the continuing process. The degree cannot be an outcome; for the development of the human consciousness has no outcome. It is a process which can be continuous, or halted, or intermittent. In one sense, though, there is an outcome. And that is— perhaps when receiving the undergraduate degree—that the student has reached the point when he or she intellectually can take off on his or her own, if so desired. The BA or BSc is a symbol to the world that the student has attained a level of intellectual independence. But the key point remains: higher education is a continuing developmental process.

Third thesis: In higher education, learning is intended; in research, it is a by-product. In higher education, the focus is the mind of the student, and its development. For the moment, let us call this developmental process "learning." It is the private world of the student's mind that is at issue, a world that should expand and take on a rich array of colours, within the course of studies.

In research, however, with its emphasis on demonstrable outcomes and the public world of knowledge, we are completely uninterested in the mind of the researcher. Still less do we want to know if the production of the book or research paper represented a learning experience for the academic concerned. Even if we were, there would be no necessary relationship between research as public outcome and research as personal learning. A modest journal article might have produced for the author a significant learning experience. In reverse, we can imagine a researcher producing a paper which had a profound impact on the research community and even the wider society, but for some strange reason had little personal impact. In reality, of course, such events are rare; researchers do undergo a process of intellectual development in the course of their work. But this is incidental, for it is not a condition of research taking place.

Research and learning, then, are conceptually unrelated, while higher education and learning are conceptually interwoven.

Fourth thesis: Higher education is open; research is closed. Research is highly specific. The researcher has to have some idea of what he or she is looking for, even though the outcome may be unpredictable. Sometimes, the sought-for object may be entirely predicted in advance, as with the "discovery" of the planet Neptune in 1846 (which in reality was just the astronomers' confirmation of the mathematicians' predictions). On other occasions, a model or theory may emerge in an act of discovery; but that is the result of deliberate endeavour, perhaps over several years, devoted to some particular inquiry.

Higher education, as the opening of a person's consciousness, is in contrast unpredictable. Certainly, that movement of mind normally takes place in a bounded framework of study, the student's "course." The very term "course" implies a definite path of study; the student is not going to go wandering all over the intellectual map. But higher education produces a dynamic interaction between the mind of the student, the teachers, the other students in the course and even on other courses in other subjects, and the array of resources the institution has to offer. And students are expected to make their own responses to what is put in their way. There is, accordingly, an element of uncertainty about the educational processes in higher education. Indeed, the better the course, the more the students will feel welcome to offer their own insights, reactions, and ideas to which the staff will want to respond in turn. Higher education, as we have seen, has the character of a conversation: the participants may have their own roles, but improvisation breaks out continually as they interact with each other.

One way of putting this difference between the bounded nature of research and the comparatively unbounded nature of higher education is to say that, in research, the researcher starts off with a fairly hazy idea of what might emerge and ends with a precise formulation or conclusion; in higher education, this is reversed. The student starts off with a fairly definite hold on the world, built on reasonably stable concepts and ideas, but at the end of the course has grasped that very little of the intellectual world has enduring substance and that there are always more cognitive spectacles to put on. In theory, students should always be welcome to go beyond the immediate limits of their studies, and "read round their subject." The pity is that we do not sufficiently encourage them to conduct those explorations.

Fifth thesis: Research is a necessary but not a sufficient ingredient for higher education. Precisely because others have conducted research in the past, and knowledge has "exploded," the opportunities for the development of the student's mind have grown and widened. Not all research is important in this way: it is not the accumulation of detailed findings, but the occasional additions to our conceptual frameworks which make possible the expansion of the student's understanding. The position that Newman held, in seeing higher education as unconnected with the search for new knowledge, is no longer tenable. Over the last one hundred and fifty years, the world of knowledge and understanding created through research has opened up infinite possibilities for higher education, and so research has become undeniably linked to our modern understanding of higher education. For a genuine higher education to take place, research has to have been undertaken somewhere, upon which programmes of study will in part be based. It does not follow, though, that an institution offering a course of study should be conducting research in that topic. It does not even follow that the research base should have been developed in any institution of higher education. (It could be established in research institutes and, in some branches of science, it largely is.)

While, then, higher education and research are separate and separable activities, higher education inescapably draws on research. But if institutionalized research is a necessary condition of higher education taking place, it cannot be a sufficient condition. Introducing research into the curriculum is justifiable provided it is used to expand the student's intellectual horizons, and not because it propels students towards becoming embryonic researchers. The relationship between research and higher education is such that someone, somewhere, should have engaged in research; but that does not mean that research is part of the meaning of higher education.

Sixth thesis: The academic community is directly related to research, but indirectly related to higher education. There is no single group which forms the academic community. Academics are intertwined in networks which operate at different administrative levels, from the department to the institution itself. More importantly, they are locked into their own epistemic community, composed of others who are working in the same subject areas. That community not only traverses frontiers, to form an invisible college; it also extends, for some subjects, beyond institutions of higher education to include research institutes, industrial laboratories, professionals working in the field, and the individual scholar who (no longer based in an institution) still goes on contributing to the literature.

Kogan and Becher have argued that, beyond the individual academic, the department is the basic unit of academic life.[14] Certainly academics will tend to identify with their department more than their institution; but there is a sense in which the world-wide subject-based invisible college could be said to be basic. For academics qua researchers can operate without a department in an institution of higher education; many academics are located in quite different settings, as I have just mentioned. As researchers, though, they cannot operate without reference to that wider community of others who are active in research, wherever those others are based. It follows that the academic community and research are directly interrelated.

The academic community figures much less prominently in higher education. Clearly, students are not (or only exceptionally) full members of the academic community. Occasionally, a student—perhaps in mathematics, or logic — can be seen actually to make a contribution to the research literature, but that is so rare as to appear precocious. Many of their teachers will certainly be making a contribution to research, but in their role as researchers, not as teachers. And the process of higher education is not, or should not be, intended to produce new cohorts of researchers. We have seen, however, that it is entirely proper that the results of research will be drawn on, within that educational process.

It follows that we can describe the human transactions between students and staff that constitute the processes of higher education without mentioning "the academic community." The academic community is not directly part of that process. It is on the fringes of higher education, through its contribution to research which provides an educational resource for students. Accordingly, we can say that the academic community stands in a direct relationship to research but in an indirect relationship to higher education.

Teaching Staff and Students

What are the implications of these rather abstract remarks for the key people in higher education?

Teaching staff. We have seen that for effective teaching in higher education to take place, someone, somewhere should have engaged in research. This does not imply that all teachers should engage in research. It does suggest that teachers corporately have a responsibility to assist in keeping alive the research tradition, but that there is also only a minimal obligation on individuals to participate in the research enterprise. On the other hand, every teacher has a professional obligation to understand the key conversations going on in the research community. This is sometimes called "scholarship," but that term carries unfortunate overtones of separateness and aloneness. A better term might be "informed eavesdropping."

Some might be willing to grant the general thrust of what has been said, that teaching and research are different kinds of activity, but still be reluctant to accept that teachers in higher education do not have a major responsibility to conduct research. Is that not one of the distinguishing characteristics of an institution of higher education, that its staff do, by and large, conduct research and feel themselves under an obligation so to do? As an empirical observation, that is normally the case; that set of shared norms *is* part of the culture of institutions of higher education. But my argument is that that culture should not be accepted uncritically. Indeed, the balance between teaching and research obligations as they are felt is too much weighted towards research for, in some respects, the research culture can have deleterious effects on the teaching process.

I have in mind, for example, that research can often consist of narrow problem-solving routines, with little theoretical content and even with little empirical content.[15] Researchers, too, can sometimes be carried away in delving deeply into some issue in the minutest detail. This may be entirely proper for the evolution of knowledge in a particular field; or it may be simply that the researcher has developed a tunnel vision, and is unable to see beyond a very narrow focus. Whatever the reason, that kind of perspective is anathema to higher education, where we are trying to widen students' horizons.

Another counter to this argument might be to point out that one of the defining characteristics of higher education is that students are brought to the "frontiers of knowledge" in a particular field. Students, the argument continues, can hardly be brought to this level of understanding unless their teachers are active in research. But the argument does not work. The notion of bringing students to "frontiers of knowledge" is tendentious. A corpus of knowledge does not have a single well-defined boundary; it has many fuzzy debates going on. Secondly, as a matter of fact, it is accepted in many areas of the higher education curriculum that the basic conceptual understanding cannot be fully accomplished at the undergraduate stage, in which case the "frontiers of knowledge" can be shown only to students who follow on to a postgraduate programme.

But apart from these largely empirical objections, the argument is flawed theoretically. One can reach a frontier without crossing it. Teachers in higher education are bound to have a close understanding of much of the current thinking and work in their intellectual field. They have professional obligations to engage in that kind of scholarly work; and, in that sense, be right up against the "frontiers." It does not follow that the teacher has to be engaged in actually moving the frontier.

The relationship of the teacher to research is analogous to the relationship of the musical soloist to the score. There is no demand on the soloist that he or she be a composer, be able to produce new scores. But it is paramount that the soloist be so directly acquainted with the score that he or she is able to offer us a personal interpretation of it; in a sense, a critical commentary on it. Indeed, being a composer may even be a drawback; for it might lessen the critical distance that the soloist needs to maintain in order to bring a fresh interpretation to bear.

Put this analogy into the teaching situation, where the argument often runs that the teacher in higher education should not just be doing research, but that that research should be brought into the curriculum. The musical analogy suggests that there is no general obligation of that kind; the responsibility of the teacher lies much more in having an intimate understanding of other academics' research and in being able to give an interpretation of it. But the musical analogy also suggests that the picture of the teacher giving an interpretation of his or her own research is likely to reduce the chances of an independent viewpoint being brought to bear. This is vital; for ultimately we want students to branch out on their own, to develop their own viewpoints, and not simply to imitate the views of the teacher bound to a particular research methodology or paradigm. Higher education is notorious for producing disciples, as students take on the mantle of a teacher who has created a great impression. The teacher in higher education should be trying to promote genuine independence of mind, rather than act in the guise of a pied piper.[16]

The point I have just made, about the dangers of the teacher being so bound up in her or his research that a genuinely critical perspective is made more unlikely, links to another argument that is often heard. This is that the research effort in a department should underpin the courses it offers. There are two assumptions at work here. Firstly, that there should be a direct transfer of that knowledge base into the curriculum. Secondly, that there is a more general "spin-off" in terms of the intellectual energy and commitment which staff will put into their teaching responsibilities.

I have partly dealt with the first argument. It is simply undesirable for there to be a direct transfer of research findings into the curriculum, particularly the undergraduate curriculum. Course design should be led by educational objectives, and not by research perspectives.

The second argument is more diffuse and therefore more difficult to counter. If it were true that research effort in the area of the curriculum promoted teaching commitment, few would quarrel with the proposed obligation on the department. But is there any evidence for it?[17] It admittedly makes intuitive sense, and fits in with the general observation about staff's professional identities being a function of their research identities. If that is the prime source of their professional motivation, then the more their research is oriented towards their students' courses, the more likely is their commitment to those students. So, yes, if staff are conducting research, the more they can be persuaded to work in areas which directly "underpin" the curriculum, the less is the intellectual distance between their teaching and research activities. But this is an argument about departmental and institutional management, as much as it is a matter of professional ethics. It does not amount to an argument that staff should be conducting research as such; merely that if they are engaged in it, there is advantage to it being undertaken with an eye to their teaching commitments.

Some may think that these are just nice debating points, and that they bear little relationship to what actually happens. For, in reality, the research and teaching activities are so closely interwoven that they are in inseparable. There is good reason for this; at its best, the teaching situation takes on much of the character of the research process, with an open dialogue between the students and teacher, the teacher being the first amongst equals. The teacher may lead the discussion or the activity, but he or she is also learning from the students. That is a very common situation.[18] Indeed, not infrequently, a teacher in higher education will use a set of lecture notes—polished over the years through interactions with students—as the basis of a book. This kind of close integration between research and higher education is obviously highly desirable: discussion with students so advancing the teacher's understanding and insight that a stronger publication emerges. That being so, suppose we have another member of staff who is equally as effective as a teacher but who does not work up the lecture notes in the same way: could we not say that his or her teaching is integrated with research to the same degree? Critical reflection is there; so too is the dynamic dialogue with the students and with it the continuing development in the teacher's own thinking. The only difference is that the work simply does not get published.

That difference, while immaterial from the point of view of teaching, is vital from the research point of view. It is the difference between Worlds II and III, between the private and the public worlds of knowledge (thesis one). Getting one's work published and counted by one's peers as a contribution to the intellectual debate is a significant step in its own right. The individual teacher may well have made a significant development in his or her own understanding, but that is not a sufficient condition of securing publication (thesis three). That is why the academic community has erected its appraisal systems, with anonymous referees and appraisers.

But to go down this path of analysis is to put things in an unreasonably negative light. It suggests that the difference between the successful teacher and the successful researcher is that the teacher is a failed researcher. It misses the point that being an effective teacher, leading students to a measure of intellectual and professional independence such that they are able to articulate with others their own viewpoint, is a major achievement. There are many gifted teachers who are extraordinarily successful in this way, who are not just animated interpreters of complex concepts and theories but who are able to galvanize their students into grappling with the issues for themselves. From the student point of view, and from the point of view of their higher education, whether the teacher is also involved in research is quite irrelevant.

From all this, we can say quite simply that the roles of teacher and researcher are distinct. Individuals may perform either role by itself; or they might be active in both roles, and successfully at that; or they may be strong in one but not in the other. There is nothing odd in that, for the two activities call for separate sets of accomplishments.

If we sense that academics could improve the quality of their teaching—if, for example, we find that there is a high rate of students failing to complete their courses—the attention of the academics concerned should be directed to their teaching rather than their research activity. It is a truism, but worth stating for all that: as teachers, academics' first responsibility is to their teaching (that is, to their students); it is not to their research.

The student. I have tried to indicate that the role of the student should not be construed as that of embryonic researcher. The intellectual, emotional and practical development that goes on—or should go on—is much wider than that. For that reason, it is a second order matter whether the student is actually brought to the "frontiers of knowledge," even putting aside the tendentiousness of that notion. It is much more important that the student is given an understanding of a conceptual structure, is able to take up stances within it, to understand something of the fundamental debates taking place within it, to see the difference between sense and nonsense, and to be able to stand back and form critical evaluations of the wider social role of the form of thought.

Certainly, in writing essays, conducting experiments, citing sources, marshalling one's findings, reading part of the relevant literature, and finding one's way around information sources, students are undertaking tasks which are found in the research enterprise. But these tasks are not expected of students *because* they are quasi-research activities. Rather, being quasi-research activities, they are a means of promoting in students the higher order thinking and reflection that are characteristic of a higher education. Those higher order levels include being critical, forming independent judgements, authenticity of thought and action, and problem-setting and problem-solving by the student. It is in these higher order achievements that we can talk of a logical correspondence, although not identity, between the roles of student and of researcher.

So the idea of the student as an embryonic researcher turns out to be a metaphor referring, at its best, to just some of the activities employed by the student. At its worst, the metaphor is misleading and dangerous. It can reflect an academic ideology, seeing the student programme of study as a narrow training which initiates the student into the world of research. On the contrary, the higher education experience should be a challenging and unsettling experience, opening the student's mind to a sense of ever-widening possibilities, in concept, supposition and approach to the world.

The research student. Even if all this is granted, even if it is accepted that higher education and with it the roles of teacher and student are in principle separate from the world of research, the skeptic still has one final card to play. It could be suggested that my argument has merit in relation to undergraduate education, but that it makes no sense at all at the level of postgraduate education. There, research and education are surely intimately connected. We would have to say, for example, that staff responsible for research students have a definite obligation to engage in research. The point appears to come through even more strongly in the role of the postgraduate student, particularly the research student. For that looks like a situation in which research and higher education are one and the same process. There we have a student who is in receipt of a higher education (almost by definition); and at the same time, an individual who is engaged in research.

This counter has point to it, but it is one-sided reading of the situation. In preparing a thesis at the Master's or the Doctorate level, the student is clearly engaged in research. Indeed, particularly in the humanities, and perhaps in the social sciences and in professionally related fields, it will be a substantial work of research when considered against any criterion. But it is still wrong to think that here research and higher education are one and the same thing. To see research students in that way is educationally shortsighted.

Given the way that research is structured, where for instance research students in the sciences and social sciences are often engaged to assist staff in large-scale research projects, research students as a matter of fact are part of the total research enterprise of the academic community. That much has to be admitted. But precisely on that account, it is all too easy for the work of the research student to be governed by the interests of the director(s) of the research project. As a result, the student is directed into exceedingly narrow channels, and the work is a matter of going through some methodological routines and writing up the results. Pressures of this kind have led the PhD work to become a narrow research training, rather than a proper educational process of making ever-wider connections and expanding one's intellectual compass.

In other words, the pretence that research and higher education are inseparable results in driving out higher education. Is it possible now, given the huge weight of academic ideology and the interests of the research councils bearing down on it, to inject an educational dimension into the work of the research student? Or is the situation beyond retrieval? This is not to press for a reversal of the present position, but to understand that if the work of research students is to be understood in educational terms, then the first step is to accept that the role is a hybrid of research and of higher education. The point also holds for those postgraduate courses which are hardly more than programmes of professional training. If they are to be more than mere training, then a process of informed reflection has to go on at the same time. Research theses and postgraduate courses can fulfil ends other than purely educational ones; but they cannot become, as part of higher education, simply instrumental whether in the direction of academic careers or professional careers. They also have to fulfil the higher order objectives implied by the title "higher education."

Conclusion

Institutions of higher education do not need to conduct research in order to justify the title "institution of *higher* education." We have so distorted our conception of higher education that it is difficult to realize the point. Research and higher education seem so inseparable that they are almost synonymous. Admittedly, there is some substance in this way of thinking. A genuine higher education today cannot be offered entirely separately from some kind of research base. But that does not mean that either institutions of higher education or their staff are obliged to conduct research. Staff, though, do need to have the time and resources to so keep up with their field of study that they are immersed in its conversations. So the argument here is not just theoretical: it has policy implications.[19]

There are, however, major forces at work sustaining the present occlusion of research and higher education. Research is the fulcrum of the academic community. It is the point on which the academic community turns, and it is by their research performance that academics take on their professional identity and are judged by their peers. Teaching accomplishments take a back seat. One justification for this has been given: research is public while higher education is private. Exposing teaching performance is tantamount, in Lawton's phrase, to invading "the secret garden" of the curriculum.[20] But if we are seriously interested in promoting the quality of higher education, of improving the effectiveness by which teachers teach and students learn, it is to the teaching process that we must look. In short, if we are concerned about higher education, it is to higher education that we must turn, rather than research.

Notes

1. Gilman, the first President of Johns Hopkins University, observed that "The term research . . . was presented to the English-speaking world in 1875, in a volume called *The Endowment of Research*, . . ." quoted in Wegener, C. *Liberal Education and the Modern University*. Chicago and London: University of Chicago Press, 1978, p. 10. One of the contributors to the volume was Mark Pattison, and some inkling of the way in which the meaning of the term has changed can be glimpsed in Pattison's view that "the university . . . is a national institute for the preservation and tradition of useful knowledge. It is the common interest . . . that such knowledge should exist, should be guarded, treasured, cultivated, disseminated, expounded." Sparrow, J. *Mark Pattison and the Idea of a University*. London: Cambridge University Press, 1967, p. 123. In other words, the nineteenth century view was much more one of research, rather than today's conception of the systematic advancement and public demonstration of fresh knowledge.

2. Newman's idea of higher education centered on the enlargement of the individual mind. This had nothing to do with the acquisition of knowledge: indeed, "knowledge, in proportion as it tends more and more to be particular, ceases to be knowledge." Newman, J. H. *The Idea of a University* (ed. I. T. Ker.) Oxford: Oxford University Press, 1976, p. 104. (Originally published 1853.) Ortega y Gasset. *Mission of the University*. London: Routledge and Kegan Paul, 1946, p. 58: "scientific investigation has no place in any direct, constituent capacity among the primary functions of the university." Moberly, W. *The Crisis in the University*. London: SCM Press, 1949, p. 184: "For God's sake, stop researching for a while and begin to think." Jaspers, K. *The Idea of the University*. London: Peter Owen, 1965 (originally published 1946), p. 55: "the university is simultaneously a professional school, a cultural centre, and a research institute." Phillip Griffiths. "A Deduction of Universities." In *Philosophical Analysis and Education*, edited by R. E. Archambault, pp. 187-208. London: Routledge and Kegan Paul, 1965. In his chapter Phillips Griffiths argues that the university is essentially a centre for the pursuit of truth (pp. 192-93). Wegener, *Liberal Education and the Modern University*, p. 75, where he picks out research as one of the diverse "necessities inherent in the enterprise [of the liberal university]."

3. Advisory Board for the Research Councils. *A Strategy for the Science Base*. London: HMSO, 1987. Also, Cm 114, *Higher Education: Meeting the Challenge* (White Paper). London: HMSO, 1987, par. 3.18.

4. This is a worldwide phenomenon. See Burgess, T. *Education after School*. London: Victor Gollancz, 1977, pp. 31 et seq.

5. The "customer-contract" principle was adumbrated by Lord Rothschild, 1971, and developed in subsequent Green and White Papers. See references in papers by S. Blume, R. J. H. Beverton and G. W. D. Findlay, and C. Smith, in *The Future of Research*, vol. 4, edited by G. Goldham. Leverhulme Programme of Study into the Future of Higher Education, Guildford: SRHE, 1982.

6. For Marx, "the work is external to the worker . . . it is not his work but for someone else . . . the activity is not his spontaneous activity . . . his labour becomes an object, takes on its own existence, it exists outside

him. . . ." Quoted in Bottomore, T. B., and M. Rubel. Karl Marx: *Selected Writings in Sociology and Social Philosophy*. London: Penguin, 1971, pp. 177-78. Herbst, P., in his essay "Work, Labour and University Education," argues that the alienating character of universities is spreading, from research to teaching itself. In *Philosophy of Education*, edited by R. S. Peters. Oxford: Oxford University Press, 1973.

7. Habermas, J. *Toward a Rational Society*. London: Heineman, 1972, chap. 5: "The Scientization of Politics and Public Opinion." Rose, H., and S. Rose (eds.). *The Political Economy of Science: Ideology of/in the Natural Sciences*. London: Macmillan, 1976, esp. chaps. 2, 3, 6, 7. Maxwell, N. *From Knowledge to Wisdom*. Oxford: Blackwell, 1987.

8. Shaw, M. *Marxism and Social Science: The Roots of Social Knowledge*. London: Pluto, 1975, pp. 50–51.

9. Sklair, L. *Organized Knowledge*. St. Albans, England: Paladin, 1973, p. 168. Sklair's book is a useful conventional analysis of science, from a sociological point of view. For example, it examines the value and rewards systems inherent in science.

10. Gellner, "The Crisis in the Humanities and the Mainstream of Philosophy." In *The Crisis in the Humanities*, edited by J. H. Plumb. Harmondsworth, England: Penguin, 1964.

11. Popper, K. R. *Objective Knowledge: An Evolutionary Approach*. Oxford: Oxford University Press, 1975, pp. 121, 185.

12. Popper makes a philosophical point out of this, in declaring that our sources of knowledge are irrelevant to our assessments of our theories; his essay, "On the Sources of Knowledge and Ignorance." In *Studies in Philosophy*, edited by J. N. Findlay. London: Oxford University Press, 1966.

13. For example, par. 3.15, Cm 114, *Meeting the Challenge* (White Paper), London: HMSO, which talks of judging standards in higher education "mainly by reference to students' achievements . . ."; it also talks of drawing on data on graduates' employment patterns and degree results.

14. Kogan, M., and T. Becher. *Process and Structure in Higher Education*. London: Heineman, 1980, p. 12. (A new edition of this book is in press.)

15. This is the logic of Kuhn's analysis of the growth of science.

16. Peters, R. S. *Ethics and Education*. London: George Allen and Unwin, 1966, p. 62.

17. Elton says that there is little evidence of mutual linkages between teaching and research, but that that is due to the limited way in which the investigations have been conducted. He goes on to argue for a link through scholarship, or the reinterpretation of existing knowledge. My argument is that it is possible to distinguish research and scholarship: the latter is a necessary obligation for the academic as teacher; the former is not. Elton, L. "Research and Teaching: Symbiosis or Conflict?" *Higher Education*, 15 (1986), 299–304.

18. Cf. Minogue, K. *The Concept of a University*. London: Weidenfeld and Nicolson, 1973, p. 71: "there is a certain crudeness about distinguishing the work of universities into teaching and research . . . teaching undergraduates is, in part, rethinking the fundamentals of a subject: it constitutes a kind of research." In other words, the dialogue between the teacher and the students is parallel to the dialogue between the teacher and other fellow academics. Also, Freire, P., and I. Shor. *A Pedagogy for Liberation*. London: Macmillan, 1987, p. 179, where the story is recounted of a liberating educator working with immigrant Spaniards in Germany. To do his work effectively, the educator had to conduct a kind of "research" by working with the immigrants in order to understand them and to perceive the educational possibilities that could be realized by them: "the teacher learnt how to read reality, changing his practice . . . the educator did not separate research from teaching."

19. For example, at the levels of the system (its planning and resourcing); at the levels of the institution (which should develop appropriate staff development and staff appraisal policies, alongside internal "research" policies which recognize the need for scholarship as a professional duty); and the level of the individual teacher, in recognizing the professional ethic implied by the analysis.

20. Lawton, D. *The End of the Secret Garden? A Study in the Politics of the Curriculum*. London: University of London Institute of Education, 1982.

Ronald Barnett is Senior Lecturer at the Centre for Higher Education Studies, Institute of Education, University of London.

This article is a reprint of "Research," chapter 9 of *The Idea of Higher Education*, by Ronald Barnett. Buckingham, England: Open University Press, 1990. In the United States this book can be obtained through Taylor & Francis, Inc., at 1900 Frost Road, Suite 101, Bristol, Pa. 19007.

Publication, Performance, and Reward in Science and Scholarship

Mary Frank Fox

The reward structure of any social system centers upon the relationship between the performance of roles and the return on that performance. In science and scholarship the central activity, performance, and social processes involve the communication of findings of research (Allison, 1980; Merton, 1973b; Price, 1963). The social structure of scholarship (disciplines, specialties, and networks) is organized around communication, and publication is the principal means of that communication (Mullins, 1973).[1] Through publication, scholars are kept abreast of a field, verify information, obtain critical response to work, and redirect research interests.

Publication, is, in turn, the primary basis of scholarly recognition and esteem (Cole and Cole, 1973; Gaston, 1978; Price, 1963; Storer, 1966). And recognition—symbolized in awards, citations, editorial appointments, and board and panel memberships—is the prime reward for scholarly performance (J. Cole, 1979; Merton, 1973a; Storer, 1973; Zuckerman, 1977). In economic analogy, scholarly recognition has been called the equivalent of property (Cole and Cole, 1973)—in the "coin of the realm" of scholarship (Storer, 1973).

Scholars and scientists sometimes maintain that the research process is its own reward and that they require no further compensation (Hagstrom, 1965). One problem with this claim is that the "significance" and "importance" of research depend upon the response and evaluation of the relevant social—collegial—group (Mulkay, 1977). The link between research, recognition, and reward is highlighted further in the priority disputes that have raged throughout the history of science (Merton, 1961, 1973a). Being the first, or the second, or the simultaneous party to a discovery does not diminish the quality of the work process or the satisfaction of research. But it does determine recognition derived.

Beyond recognition, other, more extrinsic, rewards such as salary and promotion also result from publication.[2] Across fields and institutions, Tuckerman (1976) shows an increasing probability of promotion to associate professor with increasing publication of articles. In salary also, Tuckman (1976) and Tuckman and Hagemann (1976) report that those who publish are rewarded more highly than those who do not, with higher returns accruing over the lifetime from articles than from books; with greatest incremental returns from the first compared to subsequent articles; and with diminishing returns with increased output. In analysis of data from a large university, Katz (1973) found that number of publications was paramount in determining salary, while public service and committee work gave some returns, and teaching inconsequential returns. Using data from a national sample of academics across fields and institutions however, Gregorio, Lewis, and Wanner (1982) caution that the publication of books and articles is related to salary but that the effects are not as great as those of high rank or experience (seniority).

Beyond seniority, the relation of publication to salary is also determined by functionally irrelevant characteristics—especially sex. In an analysis of data from a national survey of faculty, Bayer and Astin (1975) show much higher correlations between publication and salary levels for men than for women. David (1971) reports that while 70% of the male scientists who had published were in the highest salary group, only 29% of the women who had published were in this group. However, data from the faculty in twenty-two disciplines (Tuckman, 1976, Table 6-1) suggest that sex-specific salary returns may vary by *level* of publication. Specifically, for a single article, salary returns are twice as great for men compared to women; for five articles, returns are also higher for men. But at the highest levels of productivity—15, 20, or 25 articles—salary returns are more equitable for the sexes. One must note, on the other hand, that few academics are in the highest producing groups, and thus for the vast majority, male returns to productivity are much higher.

Salary returns relative to publication also vary by discipline and institutional location (Johnson and Kasten, 1983; Smart and McLaughlin, 1978; Tuckman and Hagemann, 1976). Further, within a given university, Marshall and Perrucci (1982) show that publication is more critical in determining salaries within high-consensus compared to low-consensus fields.[3] In addition, at major research universities compared to more minor universities, the association between publication and salary is especially strong (see Katz, 1973; Koch and Chizmar, 1973).

These variations suggest institutional diversity in academic reward structures. Yet diversity in salary and promotional criteria at an institutional level coexists with a national (and international) reward structure that is monolithic rather than plural.[4]

> The aspiring academic may draw his paycheck locally, but the most valued kudos of recognition and reward are often conferred elsewhere as a consequence of the judgments made by members of the larger community of scholars and scientists who are "referees" and "gatekeepers" of merit symbols. The most widely publicized estimates of scholarly and scientific worth—special fellowships, distinguished lectureships, major awards, listings in citation indexes, honorary degrees, editorial appointments, board and panel memberships, memberships in the National Academy of Sciences, and so on—are all symbols of visibility and esteem. [Wilson, 1979, p. 141]

In this larger scholarly community, research productivity and recognition are the central aspect of the reward structure.

Teaching is a significant activity for many academics, but it does not bring national recognition and esteem. Those academics who define themselves primarily as researchers rather than teachers get more outside funding, have more opportunities for paid consulting, and report higher job satisfaction (Astin, 1984). This lower recognition accorded to teaching is due to several factors. First, teaching has limited visibility. A reputation for outstanding teaching rarely extends beyond a given institution. As Lewis (1975, p. 27) says: "Who in the chemistry department at the University of Minnesota can name the superior teachers in the state university in neighboring Wisconsin? Who in the multiuniversity in Bloomington, Indiana, knows the master teachers at her sister school, Purdue?" Second, compared to publication output, the products of teaching are difficult to measure and success is difficult to quantify (Tuckman, 1976). Third, standards of judgment about effective teaching differ from one campus to another, while standards of excellence in research are much the same nationally (and at the upper reaches as in Nobel science awards, internationally) (Wilson, 1979). Finally, since World War II the needs for productive technology in industry and commerce have become increasingly dependent upon research and the institutions that do research (see Shils, 1975). As this occurred, the teaching role has lost esteem (Altbach, 1980).[5] For these reasons, accomplishment in teaching "lacks universal currency" (Wilson, 1979, p. 140) in the scholarly community.

Along with research and teaching, professional service is a third—and catchall—component of academic performance. Professional service includes activities ranging from local committee work and guest lectures to the refereeing of papers for national journals, reviewing of grant proposals, and holding of offices in professional associations. In the latter case, the service is a recognition in itself, and in fact it correlates with publication productivity (see Jauch and Glueck, 1975).

Functions of Rewards of Publication

The central rewards of publication act as both a "stimulus" and a "control" in academia (Wilson, 1979). Recognition and esteem validate past performance by bringing attention to accomplishments judged to be of high quality. The rewards also provide motivation for future performance by encouraging successful scholars to continue to be productive (Cole and Cole, 1973; Zuckerman, 1970). These mechanisms in turn reinforce standards of performance by focusing attention upon work that helps set the pace of scholarly achievement. If, in fact, honor follows excellence, then the most visible rewards can evoke performance in others by conveying research standards of a high order (see Merton, 1973b). In this way, recognition and reputation both reflect and generate productivity (Gaston, 1978). Fame may be a reward that few will attain, but its elusive promise serves as an incentive for many others (Blau, 1973).

On the flip side of these purposes are more subtle functions of the scholarly reward system. By reinforcing standards of success, the reward structure can serve to perpetuate intellectual hegemony and obstruct innovative paradigms that threaten established intellectual traditions. It can function to control junior members of the academy, disguise power struggles, and justify decisions that are, in fact, particularistic (see Lewis, 1975; Martindale, 1976). Beyond this, by focusing upon publication and recognition, the academic reward structure helps support faculty control of the university. Because research originates with and is governed by faculty, it provides for peer review and evaluation, and thus increased faculty authority in the university (Skiff, 1980).

Performance Levels in Publication

Despite the centrality of publication to science and scholarship, average levels of performance are low. In a sample of academics of both natural and social sciences, J. Cole (1979) found that one or two years after the doctorate, 53% had failed to publish a single paper and 34% had published just one. In most years, 70% of these academics published nothing. With a national sample of faculty across fields, Ladd and Lipset (1975) also document astonishingly low levels of publication: over half of the full-time academics had never written or edited any sort of book; more than one-third had never published an article; and more than one-quarter had never published a scholarly work of any kind over the course of their careers.

Within-discipline analyses show variations by field, but at the same time confirm the global pattern of low productivity. In a study of academics in three discipline areas, Wanner, Lewis and Gregorio (1981) show that natural scientists publish almost two and a half times as many articles as humanists, and 40% more than social scientists. In publication of books, the social scientists lead, followed by the humanists, and then the scientists (the mean rates are 1.80, 1.44, and .89, respectively). The differences can be partly accounted for by different styles of reporting research. In the natural sciences, articles are shorter—frequently just research notes—and in the social sciences, and especially the humanities, articles are longer essays. In addition, large-scale laboratory projects, requiring diverse specialists and expensive equipment, have led increasingly to team work in the sciences. In many cases, the name of the principal investigator appears—together with the names of the others working on the project—on publications coming out of the lab. This also influences rates of publications between disciplines.

Yet even in the more prolific scientific disciplines, publication rates are low. For example, in a random sample of chemists Reskin (1977) reported that in any given year 60% of the chemists had not published a single article. Likewise, among physical scientists in colleges and universities, Ladd and Lipset (1977) reported that 29% had published nothing while another 24% had published one or two articles.

While average levels of publication are low, the variation between academics is very high. Whether one considers publication over the past two years, past five years, or professional lifetime, publication varies enormously. Since Lotka's (1926) analysis of articles published in physics journals, it has been known that productivity is strongly skewed, with a small group producing the bulk of publications and the vast majority publishing little or nothing.

In any analysis of long-term patterns, Price (1963) estimated that 10% of scientists contributed over one-third of the papers in print, and that only 3% of all scientists were "highly prolific, major contributors." Other studies between and within fields confirm Price's general conclusion about the concentration of publication. In a sample of academics in the social and natural sciences, J. Cole (1979) reports that 15% of the group accounted for half of all papers published. Reskin (1977), likewise, found that 15% of chemists contributed half of the papers published in a sixteen-year period. Allison and Stewart (1974) similarly show high concentration of publication among physicists and mathematicians, as well as chemists.

Thus the data on publication show conclusively that (1) the average level of performance is low, and (2) it is highly variable. But beyond these two facts, agreement splinters and explanation of the determinants of these patterns is a central problem in the study of science and scholarship.

Explaining Differential Publication

Explanations of productivity in publication fall broadly into three categories.[6] The first emphasizes the role of personal or individual characteristics, such as psychological traits, work habits, and demographic factors. The second perspective emphasizes aspects of the work environment, especially prestige of department. A third perspective of "cumulative advantage" and "reinforcement" focuses upon feedback processes of the environment and its presumed resources and rewards.

Personal Characteristics

Among the studies of personal characteristics, the largest number have focused on psychological factors. One version of this perspective has been termed the "sacred spark" theory because it attributes productivity to "inner compulsion" which persists even in the absence of external rewards (Cole and Cole, 1973). A second variant of this perspective focuses not so much on motivation and attitude as on "stamina" or the capacity to work hard, tolerate frustration, and persist in the pursuit of long-range goals (Merton, 1973b; Zuckerman, 1970). A third variety of the psychological perspective is represented by clinical investigations of (1) the emotional styles (Cattell and Drevdahl, 1955; Knapp, 1963; Roe, 1953, 1964); (2) the biographical backgrounds—early childhood experiences, sources of satisfactions and dissatisfactions, attitudes, values, and interests (Chambers, 1964; Roe, 1952; Stein, 1962; Taylor and Barron, 1963; Taylor and Ellison, 1967); and (3) the cognitive structure of productive scientists (Cropley and Field, 1969; Eiduson, 1962; Gordon and Morse, 1970; Selye, 1964, Wilkes, 1980).

From the above studies, we find that certain psychological and attitudinal factors do correlate with publication. The biographical studies, especially, show that autonomy or self-direction is characteristic of the most productive. This is apparent in their early preferences for teachers who let them alone, in attitudes toward religion, and in personal relations. Productive scientists and scholars tend to be detached from their immediate families and wider social relations and attached, instead, to the inanimate objects and abstract ideas of their work (Chambers, 1964; Stein, 1962; Taylor and Ellison, 1967).

Further, data suggest the superior stamina of the high producers, revealing them as absorbed, involved, and indefatigable workers (Bernard, 1964; Eiduson, 1962; Pelz and Andrews, 1976; Zuckerman, 1970). Driven by curiosity, ambition, or need for achievement, high producers tend to organize their lives around work.

In cognitive and perceptual styles, productive scholars and scientists also show certain modes of perceiving and thinking, including a capacity to play with ideas, stave off intellectual closure, and tolerate ambiguity and abstraction (Eiduson, 1962; Gordon and Morse, 1970; Selye, 1964). The emphasis here is upon *style* rather than level of ability. Measured ability level, in fact, correlates very weakly with productivity and achievement in science (Cole and Cole, 1973). Although high IQ may be a prerequisite for doctoral training, once the degree is obtained, differences in measured ability do not predict subsequent levels of performance (Cole and Cole, 1973). Rather, persons with equal ability differ markedly in the ways in which they deploy intellectual resources (see Cropley and Field, 1969).

The fundamental problem of the psychological perspective is that personality traits and attributes do not exist in a vacuum (Andrews, 1976). These individual traits and dispositions are strongly affected by the social and organizational context in which they exist. Andrews shows that measured creativity, for example, does not result in productivity unless scientists have strong motivation, diverse activities, and the capacity to exercise power and influence over decisions. Likewise, other studies fail to show a direct relationship between measured creativity and measured performance (Connor, 1974; Gordon and Morse, 1970), and suggest the "interface of psychological capability and organizational requisite" (Gordon and Morse, 1970) as the nexus of research performance. However, unlike Andrews' investigation, these others do not actually test the extent to which organizational context mediates psychological characteristics and productivity. Thus the link between individual attributes and environment remains a critical area for investigation.

Compared to the large number of psychological studies, those on work habits are few, and the commentary on the subject tends to be speculative (see, for example, Stinchcombe, 1966). Exceptions include Hargens' (1978) study, which focuses upon disciplinary context, and Simons' (1974) study of the work practices of eminent scholars. Hargens' work reports that habits relate to productivity according to the level of "routine" or "predictability" in the work. Thus in chemistry, a more routinized discipline, time spent in research and engagement in multiple projects are associated with productivity, while in less routinized fields such as mathematics these work practices have weak to nonexistent impact upon output. Simon's study reports that, as a group, eminent scholars have certain work patterns: they devote enormous times to research (some work 365 days of the year); they work on several projects at once; they tend to devote mornings to writing.

While studies of work habits are few, they are suggestive, and strongly appealing for further research—because work routines (unlike factors such as "insight" or "imagination") are more adaptive strategies available to aspiring scholars.

Finally, among investigations of individual characteristics and productivity are studies of demographic characteristics: age and, more recently, gender. Almost fifty years ago, Lehman (1936, 1944, 1953) began presenting evidence that major contributions occur in scientists' late thirties and early forties and decline thereafter. In subsequent work (1958, 1960), he elaborated that the age peaks occur earlier in more abstract fields (such as mathematics) and later in more empirically based fields (such as biology). He also observed that the age peak is sharper for major contributions and flatter for more minor contributions.

Although Lehman's conclusions have gained wide acceptance in scientific lore, his work is methodologically flawed (see S. Cole, 1979; Reskin, 1979b). Instead of determining the proportion of scientists in each age group who had made important discoveries, Lehman simply compared the proportion of all important discoveries made by scientists of different ages. In failing to take into consideration the number of scientists in each age group, he assumed equal proportions in each group. However, because science has been growing exponentially over the past two centuries, scientists are disproportionately young and thus discoveries—both important and unimportant—will have been made disproportionately by younger persons.

Other investigations have modified Lehman's findings, and shown that the association between age and productivity is neither linear nor monotonic. Pelz and Andrews (1976) report a productivity peak in scientists' late thirties and early forties—but also a second peak ten to fifteen years later at age fifty. In analyses of data from academics in seven fields, Bayer and Dutton (1977) obtain results similar to Pelz and Andrews'. In five of the fields, Bayer and Dalton observe a "spurt-obsolescence" function between age and articles published in the past two years, with the first productivity peak reached about the tenth year of career age followed by a second peak near retirement age. However, the reported relationships are weak in all fields, and age accounts for little variation in publication levels.

For a cross section of academics in six fields, S. Cole (1979), on the other hand, reports a slightly curvilinear relationship between age and quantity of publication. Publication rates rise gradually with age, peak in the late thirties and early forties, and then drop off. Additional longitudinal data from mathematics, and cohort effects, show the same curvilinear pattern. Yet despite these variations, productivity does not differ significantly with age.

Most studies of age and productivity, however, have been cross-sectional. As such, they are unable to distinguish between the effects of generational differences in socialization, training, and access to resources which might be responsible for the lower productivity of older scholars (Reskin, 1979b). A recent and intriguing exception to this cross-sectional work is Hammel's (1980) longitudinal study of chemists in the University of California system.

Challenging the notion of productivity declines with age, Hammel reports that "productivity increases strongly with age and decreases strongly with the square of age, so that the pattern is one of gradually decelerating increase" (p.5).[7] In other words, he finds that productivity increases with age—with some flattening but not necessarily decline. Further, he reports that these increases are more dramatic for recent cohorts, and that declines apparent in a mean rate across persons are "attributable to 'shooting stars'—the high producers who climb to a peak and then decline" (pp. 4–5).

Other studies may have failed to capture a pattern of decelerating increase with age because they do not separate behavior by birth cohort. Hammel's analyses, which do separate by cohort, show that only the very oldest cohort (over age 61) manifests a decline in mean productivity over age 40, and that the two cohorts prior to it (age 51–55 and age 56–60) exhibit only a leveling off of productivity with increasing age.

Along with the problems of cross-sectional analyses, studies of age and productivity are flawed in other ways (see Reskin, 1979b). First, the predominant bivariate analyses (analyses limited simply to measures of age and productivity) fail to control for factors such as early experience, institutional location, primary work activity, and availability of resources. Further, failure to report the *magnitude* of the association between age and productivity can be misleading. Studies that have reported the strength of the association (Bayer and Dutton, 1977) have shown a weak impact of age upon productivity. This strongly cautions against any educational policy on the basis of age and productivity relationship *per se*.

The most recent studies of individual characteristics have focused on gender. These studies converge on one point: as a group, academic women publish less than men. Although the data vary somewhat, they indicate that, within a given period, women publish about half as many articles as men. Thus, among academics in the fields of chemistry, biology, psychology, and sociology, J. Cole (1979) found that over a twelve-year period the median publication was 8 papers for men and 3 for women. Likewise, among a sample of male and female scientists in six fields, who were "matched" for year of Ph.D. and doctoral department, Cole and Zuckerman (1984) report that men had published 11.2 papers compared to 6.4 for women.

Analyses within fields also show sex differentials in publication. Over a three-year period male psychologists were significantly more productive than women, publishing an average 1.7 papers compared to women's .7 (Helmreich et at., 1980). Among educational researchers—two-thirds of whom were in education and one-third in other social science fields—Persell (1983) found that throughout their careers the average number of articles published by men was 12.6 and the average for women 7.6. For chemists, however, Reskin (1978a) reports slighter differences, which suggest "a true but small sex difference between the populations" in this field (p. 1236).

The data above show the central tendencies—means and medians—in the publication of women compared to men. In variability, on the other hand, there are smaller proportions of women than men among the prolific (Astir, 1978; Bayer, 1973; Cole and Zuckerman, 1984; Ladd and Lipset, 1976), but women's publication is as skewed, or more so, than that of men. This indicates that among both gender groups most of the work is published by a few persons, while the majority publish little or nothing. Specifically, in J. Cole's (1979) sample of academics in both social and physical sciences, 15% account for about 50% of the total papers published by each gender group. Further, in their sample of male and female scientists, Cole and Zuckerman (1984) found that the most prolific women account for an even larger proportion of all papers published by women than do their counterparts among men.

Documenting sex-differential productivity is one thing, and accounting for it quite another. While the sex differential is certain, the explanations are not. In accounting for sex-differential productivity, studies have controlled for variables such as institutional location, family status, years of experience, and age at Ph.D.

Some studies (Astir, 1978; Persell, 1983) show that controls for institutional location and marital status do reduce the differential—although not always in the expected direction. Astin's work shows that married women publish more than single women, rather than the other way around. This she attributes in part to the marriage of academic women to other academics, which, she argues, puts these women into contact with male colleagues and collegial networks (Astin and Davis, 1985). Other studies, however, have found that significant sex differences in publication remain even after controlling for family status or institutional affiliation (see J. Cole 1979; Helmreich et al., 1980). On the other hand, within a particular occupational location—the most distinguished research universities—Helmreich et al. report minimal sex differences in the productivity of psychologists.

In assessment of sex-differential productivity, a major shortcoming of the studies is their failure to assess organizational variables as they affect the productivity of men and women. These variables include level and type of teaching (undergraduate versus graduate, lecture versus seminar), collegial interaction, mentoring and support, research assistance, and funding information and networks—factors that are discussed in the following sections.

Environmental Location

The second major category of productivity studies focuses on the structural context often overlooked in investigations of individual characteristics. These studies emphasize the importance of early academic environment (i.e., graduate school background) and characteristics of subsequent environment, particularly prestige of location.

Graduate school background is important not only because it develops knowledge, skills, and competencies, but also because it cultivates norms, values, and opportunities. Graduate education shapes conceptions of the scholarly role, styles of work, and standards of performance (Zuckerman, 1977). In fact, most academics do not significantly alter their ideas and approaches following graduate school (Kuhn, 1970; Mullins, 1973). Given the salience of this socialization, investigators have looked to graduate school background to explain publication levels. Despite variation in the findings, prestige of doctoral program, along with predoctoral productivity, emerge as predictors of productivity.

In an early study of academics in three fields—biology, political science, and psychology—at universities of varying prestige levels, Crane (1965) reported that the setting in which an academic receives training is more decisive for productivity than the setting in which one works after obtaining the degree. More specifically, Crane reports that academics with degrees from a major university are more likely to be productive independent of present location, while academics trained at minor universities are unlikely to be productive unless currently located at a major university. Crane attributes the stronger effect of current environment for graduates of minor universities to two factors—motivation and judgment in selecting research topics.

Subsequent studies of graduate school background and productivity have extended the investigation by differentiating training processes, refining the measures, and further specifying the effect of graduate school upon publication productivity. With data from chemists, Reskin (1979a) analyzes the effect upon both pre- and postdoctoral publication and citation of three different aspects of graduate school background: caliber of doctoral program, training with a productive sponsor, and collaborative publication with a sponsor. Reskin's findings indicate that sponsorship may be important in launching early—predoctoral—publication, but once the degree is obtained, the quality of the doctoral program as a whole is more critical in facilitating sustained—postdoctoral—publication.

Long, Allison, and McGinnis (1979) challenge these findings. Analyzing data from biochemists, they report that while prestige of doctoral department and sponsor's eminence are positive in their effects on productivity, the associations are weak. Instead, they find that the strong and direct determinant of productivity is predoctoral publication, and that the effects of doctoral program are indirect, influencing productivity by way of prestige of first appointment.

Another group of researchers, Chubin, Porter, and Boeckman (1981), question the generalizability of these findings to fields beyond chemistry. Replicating aspects of Long et al.'s work on doctorates in engineering, physics, psychology, sociology, and zoology, as well as biochemistry, they support Long's contention that early publication influences later publication. But they also maintain that prestige of doctoral program is critical.

Beyond studies of graduate school background, the strongest and most consistent of all correlates of publication is the prestige of institutional affiliation (see Blackburn, Behymer, and Hall, 1978; Blau, 1973; Long, 1978; Long and McGinnis, 1981; Wiley, Crittenden, and Birg, 1981), suggesting that more prestigious locations foster, and less prestigious hinder, the research orientation and activity of their members. Of course, the causal relationship between productivity and location might operate in the effect of productivity upon location as well as the other way around—so that more prestigious departments are selecting more productive scholars. However, recent longitudinal studies, which have actually monitored the publication histories of scientists between locations and over time, indicate a stronger causal effect of location upon publication rather than vice versa.

Among these studies, Long (1978) reports that while the effect of publication upon prestige of location is weak, the effect of location upon publication is strong. For academics moving into first position, publication is not immediately affected by location rather, it is affected by early, predoctoral publication levels. However, after the third year in the job, productivity is more strongly related to prestige of department than to previous predoctoral publication. Specifically, those in prestigious departments increase their publication, and those in less prestigious settings begin to publish less. Among those who switch institutions, the change in publication level after the move is more clearly related to the prestige of the new department than to that of the old department. Long's findings suggest a process of cumulative advantage: even if later job mobility is based upon more objective criteria, the prestige of first appointment, which is independent of earlier productivity, has an impact upon subsequent productivity and, in turn, prestige of second appointment.

In a subsequent study, Long and McGinnis (1981) extend these analyses beyond the prestige of academic department to the effects of larger organizational contexts—the research university, non-research university or four-year college, and nonacademic or industrial sectors. They report that the chance of obtaining employment in a given context is unrelated initially to publication level. However, once in the job, publication comes to conform to the context. Location in four-year colleges and in industrial settings depresses publication, while location in research universities fosters publication. Moreover, when changes occur in context, the new location takes hold as the determinant of publication—but only after three years in the new job. The fact that it takes some time for new location to take effect suggests that productivity levels are not simply a result of changes in individuals' goals or of global barriers to publication in some settings.

A major gap in these investigations, however, lies in their failure to explain how environment fosters or impedes publication. Specifically, the research has failed to determine the extent to which institutional location promotes productivity through the cultivation of individual habits or dispositions, or through the influence of institutional factors such as research facilities, graduate assistance, or a favorable reward structure. Among the environmental factors which might mediate productivity levels, however, one variable—collegial exchange and communication—does emerge with some consistency.

Data indicate that collegial exchange stimulates research involvement by testing ideas, activating interests, and reinforcing work (Blau, 1973; Reskin,1978b; Pelz and Andrews, 1976). Explaining the collegial process, Blau (1973, p. 113), argues:

> Whether a faculty member's interests are stimulated or stifled in an academic institution depends on his colleagues. The discussions of such colleagues about their research experiences—the problems encountered and the exciting discoveries made with those who share research interests, and primarily with them, are incentives likely to activate any latent interest in research a person may have. To become a genuine member of a

colleague group of this kind, one must be involved in research and thus be able to participate fully in discussions about research. These processes of social exchange are a continual source of rewards for scholarly endeavor and create group pressure to engage in scholarly research by depriving those failing to do so of social rewards.

The prestigious academic departments which are said to provide a context favoring productivity are also reported to have stronger patterns of scholarly exchange (see Parsons and Platt, 1968). Further, certain accounts (Blau, 1973; Mandell, 1977; Martindale, 1980) suggest that the collegial atmosphere in minor institutions may actually discourage research and publication by belittling or beleaguering its significance. Martindale's (1980, p. 238) account is chilling:

> When one does write and publish extensively in the teaching universities, a new ambivalent situation develops between an individual and his colleagues. One's achievement then becomes a source of envy and fear—lest the administration demand this in addition to its teaching and service requirements. The individual also becomes a source of mixed pride and anxiety to the administration—lest it lead productive writers and scholars to demand salary increases and free time to pursue their research.

Because the scholarly community—and its central reward structure—is national rather than local, collegian networks clearly transcend immediate environment. Attachments, loyalties, and reference groups outside the institution constitute a "cosmopolitan" compared to "local" professional orientation (Gouldner, 1957; 1958 Merton, 1942). "Locals" identify with their employing institution, its organization and rewards. "Cosmopolitans" are committed to achievement and recognition within the discipline as a whole. The cosmopolitan orientation is associated with research productivity among scientists and scholars further, while it is possible to score high on both local and cosmopolitan dimensions, the interaction of both dimensions is not more strongly associated with productivity than is the cosmopolitan orientation alone (Jauch, Glueck, and Osborn, 1978; Stahl, McNichols, and Manley, 1979).

However, collegial exchange (as opposed to local identification or loyalty) within the unit or department does appear to facilitate productivity. Ongoing, face-to-face contact helps provide ideas, catch errors, and stimulate development (see Pelz and Andrews, 1976). In a particular study of theoretical high-energy physicists, J. Blau (1976) concludes that for this group the best departmental environment is one in which the physicists have *few* colleagues working in the same specialized environment but *many* who share the general theoretical orientation. Such departmental heterogeneity promotes both collective emphasis upon research and stimulating cosmopolitan contacts outside the department.

Beyond collegial exchange, certain organizational and management studies have reported that higher levels of organizational freedom support publication productivity. But these investigations focus on levels of freedom as they operate in industrial and nonacademic labs rather than in academic settings (see Box and Cotgrove, 1968; Stahl and Stevens, 1977 Vollmer, 1970). Related studies focus on factors such as group coordination or style of leadership as they influence productivity of the research aggregate (e.g., lab unit or team) rather than the individual, or they focus on productivity through patents, reports, and other products in primarily nonacademic settings (Jitendra, 1974; Kowalewska, 1979; Smith, 1971; Visart, 1979). Although these studies suggest the general importance of organizational climate, they tell us little about particular processes of environment as they affect publication in academic settings, specifically.

Feedback Processes: Cumulative Advantage and Reinforcement

While the psychological theories assume a simple additive relationship between publication and individual characteristics, the environmental perspective begins to suggest feedback processes— whereby initial appointment affects productivity and, in turn, subsequent employment and productivity patterns. These reciprocal processes of environment, resources, and reward are the very focus of the cumulative advantage perspective.

From this perspective, scholars who experience early success are able to command increased time, facilities, and support for continued research. Once these rewards are obtained, they have an independent effect upon the acquisition of further resources and rewards. Thus the accumulation of advantage involves "getting ahead initially and moving further and further out front" (Zuckerman, 1977, p. 61).

One variation of cumulative advantage has been called the "Matthew effect" (after the Gospel of St. Matthew).[8] This effect consists of the accrual of greater recognition to contributions of those with considerable repute and lesser recognition to those with limited repute (Merton, 1973b). Heightened recognition can then be converted to resources for further performance. This effect applies especially in cases of collaboration and independent multiple discoveries by those of unequal rank (Merton, 1973b). In both instances, the already eminent get disproportionate credit.

Although the perspective of cumulative advantage is well developed, tests of the hypotheses are difficult, since they require data on the research resources of scholars. Lacking these data, findings have supported the perspective only indirectly. Showing almost perfect linearity between career age and productivity differences, Gaston's (1978) longitudinal data, for example, indirectly suggest a pattern whereby productivity differences become ever larger between those initially advantaged and those not so advantaged. Allison and Stewart's (1974) data, which are merely cross-sectional, also show strong linear increases in publication differences with increasing career age.

The cumulative advantage and reinforcement perspectives are frequently lumped together. However, the reinforcement perspective focuses not on how productivity is advanced, but rather on why it is sustained. The perspective derives from the fundamental behaviorist principle that behavior which is reinforced continues to be emitted, and that which is not rewarded tends to be extinguished. Applied to productivity, early publication and citation should result in continued performance, while failure to produce early on should result in continued nonproductivity.

The problem with the reinforcement perspective is that the social context of scholarly productivity is much more complex than the laboratory settings and animal experiments (Skinner, 1938, 1953, 1969) from which the reinforcement principle derives. Further, while reinforcement and cumulative advantage are conceptually distinct, the processes are related in ways that make it difficult to untangle the effects analytically. Positive reinforcement alone will not account for much productivity unless it is accompanied by the cumulation of resources for research. Cumulative advantage, on the other hand, does not exist without some prior reinforcement; thus reinforcement almost always accompanies the enabling resources of advantage.

Despite the difficulties in assessing reinforcement, certain studies have attempted to do so, and the data lend support to the perspective. For example, with data on the publication records of 83 sociologists, Lightfield (1971) found that among those who published and received citations to their work in the first five years following the doctorate, the majority (73%) continued to publish and to be cited in the second five-year period. In contrast, only 6% of those who published and were cited dropped out in the second period. Most critically, of the 21 sociologists who published but did not receive citation to their work during the first period, only one received citation during the second period. With these data, Lightfield concludes that "unless a person achieves a qualitative piece of research during the first five years, it seems unlikely that he will do so during the next five years—if at any time during his career" (p. 133).

Data from other fields also support the reinforcement principle of publication. Among physicists, Cole and Cole (1973) report those whose work is uncited are much less likely to continue publishing than those whose work is cited. With a sample of men and women in six scientific fields—astronomy, biochemistry, chemistry, earth sciences, mathematics, and physics—Cole and Zuckerman (1984) also found that later productivity relates strongly to early publication and its citation. Specifically, 29% of those who had published four or fewer papers in an earlier period, but who receive citation, were prolific publishers in a later period. However, only 9% of those who published fewer than five papers, but went uncited, were prolific later on. Correspondingly, two-thirds of those who both published five or more papers and were comparably cited in an earlier period continued to be as productive later, while less than one-half of those who were equally productive but uncited continued to be productive.

Among chemists, likewise, Reskin (1977) found that early publication and citation support productivity in the following decade. However, she adds an important qualification: the strength of the effects varies by type of first employment. For those employed in research universities, early publication in itself is important for continued productivity. But for those in settings with less emphasis on research, citation is particularly important. These patterns suggest that for those in research universities the informal and immediate response of colleagues may be more important than the formal but delayed reinforcement of citation. However, in settings with less emphasis on research, the formal acknowledgment of citation may be especially important, because it can symbolize ties to the research community and its norms and activity.

These findings highlight the role of organizational context in the operation of reinforcement. They also point to the limitations of the studies in their reliance on citation as the sole measure of reinforcement. We do not know the extent to which scholars are aware that they are being cited, nor do we know whether a few citations from prominent researchers are more sustaining than numerous citations from the rank and file (Cole and Zuckerman, 1984). Further, it may be the awards, honors, and grants—associated with citation—that actually support and sustain publication.

Agenda for Future Research

In studies of productivity, the major problem of the psychological perspective is that personal traits and dispositions do not exist in a vacuum. By themselves, psychological factors do not necessarily translate to productivity. Studies show no direct relationship between measured creativity or intelligence, for example, and research performance, and suggest that social and organizational variables interact with, and affect, the manifestation of these characteristics. Yet only one study (Andrew, 1976) actually tests and demonstrates a social process that creativity results in research productivity only with motivation, diverse activities, and the capacity to influence the organizational environment. Although ability, creativity, and other characteristics are undoubtedly important in research activity, studies need to specify the way in which these factors translate to productivity and the organizational and environmental processes involved.

Another underdeveloped area of inquiry is that of work habits and productivity. The relationship between work habits and productivity is intriguing because work routines and practices (unlike insight and imagination) are more adaptive strategies available to individual scholars. Practices such as when one works, with whom, for how long, and on how many projects may be pertinent to productivity. Another pertinent factor is the proportion of time spent in research compared to nonresearch activities. In an unpublished paper (reported in Pelz and Andrews, 1976), Meltzer found that full-time researchers published less than those spending three-quarters of their time on research. Likewise, Pelz and Andrews and Knorr et al. (1979) found that some mixture of research and teaching or administration is associated with higher productivity. But a confounding factor—and one worthy of future research—is the causal relationship between habits and productivity. Thus practices such as simultaneous work on several projects or diverse activities of research and administration can either be the cause or the result of productivity. We need to untangle the ordering of the variables.

Studies of the age and productivity relationship also need fine tuning—with controls for mediating and moderating factors. The study of age and productivity has a long research tradition stemming back some 50 years to Lehman's investigations of productivity declines with increasing age. While subsequent studies have modified Lehman's work and showed curvilinear and bimodal relationships between age and productivity, most of the studies have been cross-sectional. Thus they have failed to distinguish the effects of generational differences in socialization, training, and access to resources that might be responsible for lower productivity of older scientists. Since the growth of science and scholarship is leveling off and the age of the participants is increasing as fewer positions are available for the young, the age and productivity relationship becomes more important. Studies need to get beyond simple, cross-sectional bivariate analyses and begin to assess how factors such as generational differences, environmental location, primary work activity, and availability of resources figure into the age and productivity relationship. At present, the methodological shortcomings of current studies plus the weak association between age and productivity, reported in one of the few studies showing magnitude of relationship, provide little basis for any standard policy such as "early retirement" (Bayer and Dutton, 1977).

Likewise, the study of sex and productivity suffers from failure to consider organizational factors. First, we need to determine how factors such as type of teaching, inclusion or exclusion from collegial networks, research assistance, and funding opportunities affect the productivity—and productivity differences—of men and women. Secondhand this is more subtle—we must consider whether the same type of institutional setting (major research university, minor university, or liberal arts college) may, in fact, offer different organizational opportunities and constraints for one sex compared to the other. Thus, although research opportunities are frequently more limited in liberal arts colleges than in universities, such an environment does not necessarily operate uniformly. The women may have patterns of heavier teaching loads, less access to released time, fewer claims on in-house grants, limited opportunities for collaboration, and fewer administrative favors for travel funds and the like.

Moving yet more broadly to the relationship between environment and productivity, fundamental questions are left unanswered. First, we lack adequate data about the ways in which "group climate" vary in academic institutions and the way it relates to productivity. From studies of nonacademic (industrial, government, and agency) research settings, we know that higher levels of freedom support publication productivity. When scientists are free to select, initiate, and terminate their own research projects or influence the process, publication productivity is higher (Box and Cotgrove, 1968; Pelz and Andrews,1976; Vollmer, 1970). Further, in scientists' own subjective impressions about group climate and productivity, they stress the importance of organizational freedom and autonomy (see Parmerter and Garber, 1971). In nonacademic settings, the more creative researchers value a "loose rein" and "minimal structure" in their work (Gantz, Stephenson, and Erickson, 1969).

Academic settings generally do permit more academic freedom and autonomy for researchers than do nonacademic organizations in which goals of profit and direct application frequently conflict with individual research initiative. Yet within the academic setting work climates differ, and we need to specify (1) how factors such as organizational freedom, as well as style of administrative leadership, degree of group coordination, and lines of communication, vary in academia, and (2) how they affect the productivity of its faculty.

Freedom and independence are certainly strong precepts in science and scholarship, and as a correlate to these structural norms, scholarship tends to attract the "solitary mind." Yet the solitary dispositions and independent norms of science and scholarship are contravened by the communalism of the work (see Fox and Faver, 1984). The communalism and exchange of research engender cooperation and interdependence. Correspondingly, collegial exchange emerges with some consistency in the literature as an environmental correlate of productivity. However, we need to know much more about the way in which collegiality operates. For example, what constitutes collegial exchange—group colloquia and the interchange of papers and written work, as well as interpersonal communication? How do such types of exchange vary in their relationship with productivity? What is the optimal frequency of collegian communication? For productive outcomes, is collegiality best as a "monogamous" or "polygamous" arrangement—that is, to support productivity, is it better to have one significant colleague or a more diverse but less intensive circle? In collegial exchange, are parallel or divergent intellectual approaches, skills, and perspectives more effective for research productivity? How do factors of colleagues' academic rank and gender affect collegiality and productivity—what are the relative costs and benefits of peer compared to junior-senior alliances and cross-sex relationships compared to same-sex ones? Further, how do each of these issues of collegiality and productivity vary (1) by discipline, (2) by inter- versus intradepartmental (and university) exchange, and (3) for formal collaboration and team work compared to informal exchange?

Better data on organizational processes and productivity would also increase understanding of feedback processes of cumulative advantage. So far, studies showing that productivity differences become greater with career age have offered only indirect support for the cumulative advantage perspective. To make an adequate test of the perspective that the initially advantaged move further and further ahead and those not so advantaged further behind, we need data on scholars' productivity and organizational resources—time, assistance, funding, networks—as they vary over time.

We also need better tests of the reinforcement perspective. While data do indicate that early publication and citation support continued performance, Reskin's (1977) work suggests that the effects vary by type of first employment. For those in settings with less emphasis on research, the formal citation is important; for those in research universities, the informal and immediate acknowledgment of colleagues may be more important than formal but delayed citation. This points again to the importance of organizational context and collegial exchange. In doing so, it also indicates once more the need for future work that further specifies how collegiality varies between contexts and does, or does not, reinforce productivity in research. Future work also needs to assess the extent to which scholars are aware that they are being cited, and the extent to which it is other awards, honors, and grants—associated with citation—that actually reinforce performance.

Implications and Recommendations for Equity and Performance

Achievement—along with objectivity and rationality—are the manifest values that guide and control the behavior of scientists and scholars (Cole and Cole, 1973; Merton, 1949). In academia, achievement is not merely a criterion for reward. Rather, it has intrinsic value for the very activity and goals of the institution:

> In the university, the achievement ideology explains and justifies reward and supports and maintains inequality, as does ideology everywhere But, as part of the scientific work ethos, the university's achievement and performance standards justify the presence, the purpose, and the activity, itself. [Fox, 1981, p. 81]

Manifest values notwithstanding, academia is hardly immune from particularistic processes. As Max Weber said years ago: "Academic life is a mad hazard. If the young scholar asks for my advice with regard to habilitation, the responsibility of encouraging him can hardly be borne" (Weber, [1919] 1946, p.133). Politicking, committeeing, and power-wooing continue to beset academic life—to the particular disadvantage of women and other marginal members (Fox, 1984; Reskin, 1978b). Still, as a standard of activity and reward, the academic achievement value persists. Scholarship (along with organized sports) is said to offer an approximation to structured situations in which individual rewards stem from performance (Goode, 1967).

But while a meritocratic standard helps to provide normative pressure for rewards to follow performance, it does not guarantee equal opportunity to acquire the credentials and produce performance. We have seen that achievement through publication is not a simple function of motivation and ability. It is the result also of organizational background, environment, and access to the means of performance—training, resources, and support.

Structural barriers, however, restrict the access to performance and reward in academia. At the onset, a small and select group of students derives advantages from contact with eminent scholars. These scholars selectively provide students the opportunity to pose important questions, solve problems, and set goals. Moreover, for these favored groups of students, elite scholars provide access to informal communication networks and fashionable, emergent areas of research (Crane, 1972; Hagstrom, 1965; Mulkay, 1976). These opportunities to enter a growing field—when the chances for making a significant contribution are greater—may be a major determinant of early and continued success in scholarship (Mulkay, 1976). Accordingly, 50% of American Nobel laureates were themselves students of laureates (Zuckerman, 1970). While this may be due to "an extremely efficient albeit uncoordinated process of selective recruitment," it is also attributable, in large part, to selective patronage, support, and opportunity (Mulkay, 1976).[9]

Such patterns of selection help create and maintain a class structure in science and scholarship by providing stratified chances for performance and reward. To point to a high correlation between citation and other types of awards as evidence of meritocracy begs the question. The correlations merely show that both kinds of rewards go to the same group of persons (Mulkay, 1980) without explaining how a select group gains access to the ways and means of performance and reward, and without explaining how opportunity is affected by structural access.

For some academics, research and publication may be a questionable aspiration. Bayer (1973) found that only about a third of American faculty would want lighter teaching loads to pursue research. It would be a mistake, then, to impute to the vast group of academics the motivations of the most productive. But at the same time, we must recognize that aspirations tend to reflect levels of available opportunity (Kanter, 1977). Academics, like other groups, limit and modify their choices in favor of socially realistic and attainable options. Although there may be little that can be done to raise the performance of the least productive, and least motivated, academics (Hammel, 1980), organizational resources and a facilitating environment are potentially important for a large group of academics who have not benefited from the cumulative advantage—elite scholarship, prestigious appointments, early performance, and recognition—that supports productivity. Resources and a favorable environment are also important to sustain the performance of the already productive. What, specifically, can universities do to activate and sustain the productivity of their faculty?

First, despite the shortcomings of the psychological studies, data do point to tendencies of the "research mind and personality," and administrators would be wise to take heed. Biographical and clinical studies show that productive scientists and scholars are independent, self-sufficient, and self-directed persons. As a group, they tend to be detached from personal relations, adverse to personally toned controversy, and attached to abstractions and ideas rather than people (see Chambers, 1964; Roe, 1952; Stein, 1962; Taylor and Ellison, 1967). If administrators want to encourage such researchers, they should minimize both the pressures and the rewards for social—"gadabout"—behavior. Productive, creative researchers are apt to be frustrated by an interpersonally centered climate and resentful about deflections from their work.

At the same time, the solitary disposition of scholars is to some extent contravened by communal norms of the work. Collegiality facilitates productivity. It is wise, then, to encourage colloquia and professional meetings on site, with an aim to create collegiality such that one can gain significant membership and rewards by active involvement in research. The aim is to foster not simply collegiality but *research-based* collegiality, with interaction and exchange centering on scholarly inquiry. In departmental groups without interests and rewards based on research performance, opposite normative pressures can stifle research, and berate it with criticisms of "careerism" and "publish or perish."

Furthermore, since productivity is associated with "cosmopolitan" rather than "local" orientations, academic institutions can help activate productivity by subsidizing travel to meetings where faculty may gain wider recognition and reinforcement for research by participation in panels and symposia. Moreover, these meetings impose external deadlines for completion of papers that can be subsequently prepared for publication.

Access to funding is also important to support research, which is increasingly technical, large-scale, and costly. Thus intramural seed money can be useful in developing the research productivity of faculty with potential, but without the external funding advantages of the academic superstars (Hammel, 1980).

Colleges and universities can affect work behavior through the manipulation of the reward structure for promotion, salary, honors, and awards.[10] To foster achievement and equity and minimize bias and particularism, institutions need to standardize the criteria for evaluation. Schools have resisted this, however, and defended shifting criteria as a "flexible" standard. "Flexibility" may be a favored organizational word, but the problem is that "it keeps other things from being equal" (Huber, 1973), especially for women and minorities. Studies indicate that the more loosely defined the criteria, the more likely that white males will be perceived as the superior candidates and the more likely that bias will operate (see Deux and Emsmiller, 1974; Nieva and Gutek, 1980; Pheterson, Kiesler, and Goldberg, 1981; Rosen and Jerdee, 1974).

To counter these tendencies and promote both equity and performance, schools should take steps to standardize criteria for evaluation—with research productivity as a principal component. In an effort to distribute merit increases fairly, Bowling Green University recently developed one criterion-based point system (see Partin, 1984). In the interests of publication productivity, I would argue with the weights assigned—since more peripheral activities such as presentation of a paper earns 14 points, preparation of an in-house report 8 points, reviewing a book for a publisher 5 points, and editing a newsletter 7 points, while publication of an article in a refereed journal returns, in comparison, only 20 points.[11]

Nonetheless, as a tool for objectivity and accountability—and as a potential device for relating rewards to productivity—a standardized instrument for evaluation would be a valuable step. Without objective standards, functionally irrelevant attributes can govern evaluation to an appalling degree. In a survey of deans of liberal arts colleges, Seldin (1984) found that "personal attributes"—one's dress, politics, and friends—were a "major factor" in overall evaluation of faculty among 38% of the deans in 1978 and 28% in 1983. Publication, by contrast, was a major consideration for only 19% in 1978 and 29% in 1983.

While standardized criteria can promote equity and performance, administrators must be careful to avoid applying a single standard of productivity across disciplines. As discussed earlier, short research reports and patterns of team collaboration account in part for a higher rate of publication in the natural sciences; in the social sciences, and especially in the humanities, longer essays and books are more frequent and account in part for fewer publications in these fields.

Efforts to activate and sustain faculty research performance can and should be a central institutional concern. The Ph.D. is, after all, a degree in research, and all doctorate holders have been trained to design, carry out, and report research projects. Further, academic research is critical, since 90% of all discoveries come out of institutions of higher learning (Kolstoe, 1975). Thus, when the dissertation is the single and last rather than the first of one's scholarly works—as it is for almost half of American academics (Mandell, 1977)—the loss is considerable to the nation, to the colleges and universities, and to the academics themselves.

Notes

1. In some fields, particularly those in rapidly changing, technical areas, research findings are communicated with preprints. The preprints tend to be circulated, however, to a limited group of researchers working on closely related problems. Wider communication comes with publication, and publication legitimizes authorship of the work.

2. As Smelser and Content (1980) argue, however, in academia monetary rewards simply act as a kind of "floor" for comfortable existence and moreover as a symbolic reflection of prestige and esteem for the productive. In this way, "monetary rewards should be regarded not as inducements proffered to secure specific performance, but rather as a symbolic recognition of past, present, or promised performance" (p. 6).

3. "Consensus" (also called "paradigm development" or "codification") refers to level of agreement within a field on prevailing theory, methods, and significant areas of research. In this sense, fields such as physics and mathematics have high consensus and fields such as sociology and psychology have low consensus.

4. The "nationalization" of the scholarly reward structure occurred especially after World War II—with increased speed of modern communication, concentration of research efforts, and mobility of students and faculty (see Altbach, 1980).

5. Of course, in certain cases, most notably in the supervision of doctoral work, the research and teaching roles are integrated.

6. This section draws upon the author's "Publication Productivity Among Scientists: A Critical Review," *Social Studies of Science*, 1983, 13, 285–305.

7. Hammel's productivity index includes measures of teaching and service performance as well as publication. However, publication measures correlate very strongly with the other two—suggesting that those who do a lot in one area do a lot in the other areas as well. When publication measures are separated, they show the same age and productivity patterns as the combined measures.

8. "For whomever hath, to him shall be given, and he shall have more abundance: but whomever hath not, from him shall be taken away even that he hath." Matthew 13:12.

9. Even when procedures are formally open and universalistic, they can produce the same consequences—in elite formation and cumulation of advantage—as do informal patterns of exclusion. In a sobering account of "open" hiring at Berkeley, Smelser and Content (1980, p. 175–176) conclude:

> Though we advertised widely and we encouraged the application of minorities and women, the final results of the search—in terms of persons invited for interviews and in terms of persons actually appointed—was much the same as it would have been if we had simply written letters to colleagues in the dozen leading departments and asked them to name their best students. We were aware of this at the time of the search. Toward the end, when we knew generally who the successful candidates were going to be, we developed a somewhat bitter joke that the whole thing could have been done for the cost of two 13-cent stamps to send letters to a colleague at Chicago and a colleague at Harvard.

10. When collective bargaining schedules fix salary increments, merit increases may not be possible. Faculty collective bargaining can, however, provide better assurances of objectivity and accountability.

11. Thus with these weights, one can accumulate more points, more readily, through peripheral activities than through the central activity of doing research and publishing the results.

References

Allison, P. D. *Processes of Stratification in Science.* New York: Arno Press, 1980.

Allison, P. D., and Stewart, J. A. "Productivity differences among scientists: Evidence for accumulative advantage." *American Sociological Review*, 1974, *39*, 596–606.

Altbach, P. "The crisis of the professoriate." *Annals of American Academy of Political and Social Science*, 1980, *448*, 1–14.

Andrews, F. "Creative process." In D. Pelz and F. Andrews (eds.), *Scientists in Organizations.* Rev. ed. Ann Arbor, Mich.: Institute for Social Research, 1976.

Astin, H. S. "Factors affecting women's scholarly productivity." In H. Astin and W. S. Hirsch (eds.), *The Higher Education of Women*, New York: Praeger, 1978.

Astin, H. S. "Academic scholarship and its rewards." In M. W. Steinkamp and P. Maehr (eds.), *Advances in Motivation and Achievement*, vol 2. Greenwich, Conn.: JAI Press, 1984.

Astin, H. S., and Davis, D. E. "Research productivity across the life and career cycles: Facilitations and barriers for women." In M. F. Fox (ed.), *Scholarly Writing and Publishing: Issues, Problems, and Solutions.* Boulder, Colorado: Westview Press, 1985.

Bayer, A. E. "Teaching faculty in academe: 1972–73." *ACE Research Report 8*, 1973.

Bayer, A. E. and Astin, H. S. "Sex differentials in the academic reward system." *Science*, 1975, *188*, 796–802.

Bayer, A. E., and Dutton, J. E. "Career age and research-professional activities of academic scientists." *Journal of Higher Education*, 1977, *48*, 259–282.

Bernard, J. *Academic Women.* University Park, Pa.: Pennsylvania State University Press, 1964.

Blackburn, R. T., Behymer, C. E., and Hall, D. E. "Research note: Correlates of faculty publications." *Sociology of Education*, 1978, *51*, 132–141.

Blau, J. R. "Scientific recognition: Academic context and professional role." *Social Studies of Science*, 1976, *6*, 533–545.

Blau, P. *The Organization of Academic Work.* New York: Wiley, 1973.

Box, S., and Cotgrove, S. "The productivity of scientists in modern industrial research laboratories." *Sociology*, 1968, *2*, 163–172.

Cattell, R. B., and Drevdahl, J. D. "A comparison of the personality profile of eminent researchers with that of eminent teachers and administrators, and that of the general population." *British Journal of Psychology*, 1955, *46*, 248–261.

Chambers, J. "Creative scientists of today." *Science*, 1964, *145*, 1203–1205.

Chubin, D. E., Porter, A. L., and Boeckman, M. "Career patterns of scientists." *American Sociological Review*, 1981, *46*, 488–496.

Cole, J. R. *Fair Science: Women in the Scientific Community*. New York: Free Press, 1979.

Cole, J. R., and Cole S. *Social Stratification in Science*. Chicago: University of Chicago Press, 1973.

Cole, J. R., and Zuckerman, H. "The productivity puzzle: Persistence and change in patterns of publication among men and women scientists." In M. W. Steinkamp and M. Maehr (eds.), *Advances in Motivation and Achievement*, vol. 2. Greenwich, Conn.: JAI Press, 1984.

Cose, S. "Age and scientific performance." *American Journal of Sociology*, 1978, *84*, 958–977.

Connor, P. E. "Scientific research competence as a function of creative ability." *IEEE Transactions on Engineering Management*, 1974, *EM-21*, 2–9.

Crane, D. "Scientists at major and minor universities: A study of productivity and recognition." *American Sociological Review*, 1965, *30*, 699–715.

Crane, D. *Invisible Colleges*. Chicago: University of Chicago Press, 1972.

Cropley, A. J., and Field, T. W. "Achievement in science and intellectual style." *Journal of Applied Psychology*, 1969, *53*, 132–135.

David, D. *Career Patterns and Values: A Study of Men and Women in Science and Engineering*. Columbia University, Bureau of Social Science Research, 1971.

Deux, K., and Emsmiller, T. "Explanations of successful performance in sex-linked traits." *Journal of Personality and Social Psychology*, 1974, *22*, 80–85.

Eiduson, B. T. *Scientists: Their Psychological World*, New York: Basic Books, 1962.

Fisch, R. "Psychology of science." In I. Spiegel-Rosing and D. Price (eds.), *Scientific Technology and Society*, London: Sage, 1977.

Fox, M. F. "Sex, salary, and achievement: Reward-dualism in academia." *Sociology of Education*, 1981, *54*, 71–84.

Fox, M. F. "Women and higher education: Sex differentials in the status of students and scholars." In J. Freeman (ed.), *Women: A Feminist Perspective*, Palo Alto, Calif.: Mayfield, 1984.

Fox, M. F., and Faver, C. A. "Independence and cooperation in research: The advantages and costs of collaboration." *Journal of Higher Education*, 1984, *55*, 347–359.

Gantz, B., Stephenson, R., and Erickson, C." Ideal research and development climate as seen by more creative and less creative research scientists." *American Psychological Association Proceedings*, 1969, 605–606.

Gaston, J. *The Reward System in British and American Science*. New York: Wiley, 1978.

Goode, W. "The protection of the inept." *American Sociological Review*, 1967, *32*, 5–19.

Gordon, G., and Morse, E. V. "Creative potential and organizational structure." In M.J. Cetron and J.D. Goldhar (eds.), *The Science of Managing Organized Technology*, Vol. II, New York: Gordon and Breach, 1970.

Gouldner, A. W. "Cosmopolitans and locals: Toward an analysis of latent social roles—I." *Administrative Science Quarterly*, 1957, *62*, 281–306.

Gouldner, A. W. Cosmopolitans and locals: Toward an analysis of latent social roles—II. *Administrative Science Quarterly*, 1957, *62*, 444–480.

Gregorio, D., Lewis, L., and Wanner, R. "Assessing merit and need: Distributive justice and salary attainment in academia." *Social Science Quarterly*, 1982, *63*, 492–505.

Hagstron, W. *The Scientific Community*. New York: Basic Books, 1965.

Hammel, E. "Report on the task force on faculty renewal." Berkeley, Calif.: University of California, Program in Population Research, January 1980.

Hargens, L. L. *Patterns of Scientific Research: A Comparative Analysis of Research in Three Scientific Fields.* Washington, D.C.: American Sociological Association, 1975.

Hargens, L. L. "Relations between work habits, research technologies, and eminence in science." *Sociology of Work and Occupations*, 1978, 5, 97–112.

Helmreich, R., Spence, J., Beane, W., Lucker, G. W., and Matthews, K. "Making it in academic psychology: Demographic and personality correlates of attainment." *Journal of Personality and Social Psychology*, 1980, 39, 896–908.

Huber, J. "Criteria for hiring, promotion, and tenure." *ASA Footnotes*, March 1973, p. 3.

Jauch, L., and Glueck, W. "Evaluation of university professors' research performance." *Management Science*, 1975, 22, 66–75.

Jauch, L., Glueck, W., and Osborn, R. "Organizational loyalty, professional commitment, and academic research productivity." *Academy of Management Journal*, 1978, 21, 84–92.

Jitendra, S. *Management of Scientific Research.* New York: International Publications, 1974.

Johnson, M., and Kasten, K. "Meritorious work and faculty rewards: An empirical test of the relationship." *Research in Higher Education*, 1983, 19, 49–71.

Kanter, R. M. *Men and Women of the Corporation.* New York: Basic Books, 1977.

Katz, D. A. "Faculty salaries, promotions, and productivity at a large university." *American Economic Review*, 1973, 63, 469–477.

Knapp, R. "Demographic, cultural, and personality attributes of scientists." In C. Taylor and F. Barron (eds.), *Scientific Creativity: Its Recognition and Development.* New York: Wiley, 1963.

Knorr, K., Mittermeir, G., Aichholzer, G., and Waller, G. "Individual publication productivity as a social position effect in academic and industrial research units." In F. Andrews (ed.), *Scientific Productivity: The Effectiveness of Research Groups in Six Countries.* Cambridge, England: Cambridge University Press, 1979.

Koch, J. V., and Chizmar, J. F. "The influence of teaching and other factors upon absolute salaries and salary increments at Illinois State University." *Journal of Economic Education*, 1973, 5, 27–34.

Kolstoe, O. P. *College Professoring.* Carbondale, Ill.: Southern Illinois University Press, 1975.

Kowaleska, S. "Patterns of influence and the performance of research units." In F. Andrews (ed.), *Scientific Productivity: The Effectiveness of Research Groups in Six Countries,* Cambridge, England: Cambridge University Press, 1979.

Kuhn, T. *The Structure of Scientific Revolutions.* Chicago: University of Chicago Press, 1970.

Ladd, E. C., and Lipset, S. M. "How professors spend their time." *Chronicle of Higher Education*, October 14, 1975, p. 2.

Ladd, E. C., and Lipset, S. M. "Sex differences in academe." *Chronicle of Higher Education*, May 10, 1976, p. 18.

Ladd, E. C., and Lipset, S. M. "Survey of 4,400 faculty members at 161 colleges and universities." *Chronicle of Higher Education*, November 21, 1977, p. 12, and November 28, 1977, p. 2.

Lightfield, E. T. "Output and recognition of sociologists." *American Sociologist*, 1971, 6, 128–133.

Lehman, H. C. "The creative years in science and literature." *Scientific Monthly*, 1935, 43, 162.

Lehman, H. C. "Man's most creative years: Quality v. quantity of output." *Scientific Monthly*, 144, 59, 384–398.

Lehman, H. C. *Age and Achievement.* Princeton, N.J.: Princeton University Press, 1953.

Lehman, H. C. "The chemist's most creative years." *Science*, 1958, 127, 1213–1222.

Lehman, H. C. "The age of decrement in scientific creativity." *American Psychologist*, 1960, 15, 128–134.

Lewis, L. *Scaling the Ivory Tower: Merit and Its Limits in Academic Careers*. Baltimore: Johns Hopkins University Press, 1975.

Long, J. S. "Productivity and academic position in the scientific career." *American Sociological Review*, 1978, *43*, 899–908.

Long, J. S., Allison, P. D., and McGinnis, R. "Organizational context and scientific productivity." *American Sociological Review*, 1981, *46*, 422–442.

Lotka, A. J. "The frequency distribution of scientific productivity." *Journal of the Washington Academy of Sciences*, 1926, *26*, 317.

Mandell, R. D. *The Professor Game*, New York: Doubleday, 1977.

Marshall, H., and Perrucci, R. "The structure of academic fields and rewards in academia." *Sociology and Social Research*, 1982, *66*, 127–147.

Martindale, D. *The Romance of a Profession: A Case History in the Sociology of Sociology*, St. Paul, Minn.: Wildflower, 1976.

Martindale, D. "King of the hoboes: Portrait of an international cultural workman." In D. Martindale and R. Mohan (eds.), *Ideas and Realities: Some Problem Areas of Professional Social Science*, Ghaziabad, India: Intercontinental Press, 1980.

Merton, R. "Science and technology in a democratic order." *Journal of Legal and Political Sociology*, 1942, *1*, 115–126.

Merton, R. "Science and democratic social structure." In *Social Theory and Social Structure*, Glencoe, Ill.: Free Press, 1949.

Merton, R. "Singletons and multiples in scientific discoveries." *Proceedings of the American Philosophic Society*, 1961, *105*, 470–486.

Merton, R. "Priorities in scientific discovery." In *The Sociology of Science*, Chicago: University of Chicago Press, 1973(a).

Merton, R. "The Matthew effect in science." In *The Sociology of Science*. Chicago: University of Chicago Press, 1973(b).

Mulkay, M. "The medicating role of the scientific elite." *Social Studies of Science*, 1976, *6*, 445–470.

Mulkay, M. "Sociology of the scientific research community." In I. Spiegel-Rosing and D. Price (eds.), *Scientific Technology and Society*, London: Sage, 1977.

Mulkay, M. "Sociology of science in the West." *Current Sociology*, 1980, *28*, 1–184.

Mullins, N. C. *Science: Some Sociological Perspectives*. Indianapolis: Bobbs-Merrill, 1973.

Nieva, V., and Gutek, B. "Sex effects on evaluation." *Academy of Management Review*, 1980, *5*, 267–276.

Parmerter, S. M., and Garber, J. D. "Creative scientists rate creativity factors." *Research Management*, 1971, *14*, 65–70.

Parsons, T., and Platt, G. M. "Considerations of the American academic system." *Minerva*, 1968, *5*, 497–523.

Partin, R. "A case study: Evaluating faculty at Bowling Green State University." *Change*, 1984, *16*, 31ff.

Pelz, D. C., and Andrews, F. M. *Scientists in Organizations: Productive Climates of Research and Development*. Ann Arbor, Mich.: Institute of Social Research, 1976.

Persell, C. H. "Gender, rewards, and research in education." *Psychology of Women Quarterly*, 1983, *8*, 33–47.

Pheterson, G. T., Kiesler, S. G., and Goldberg, P. A. "Evaluation of women as a function of their sex, achievement, and personal history." *Journal of Personality and Social Psychology*, 1971, *19*, 110–114.

Price, D. *Little Science, Big Science*. New York: Columbia University Press, 1963.

Reskin, B. F. "Scientific productivity and the reward structure of science." *American Journal of Sociology*, 1978(a), *83*, 1235–1243.

Reskin, B. F. "Social differentiation and the social organization of science." *Sociological Inquiry*, 1978(b), *48*, 6–37.

Reskin, B. F. "Academic sponsorship and scientists' careers." *Sociology of Education*, 1979(a), *52*, 129–146.

Reskin, B. "Age and scientific productivity." In M. McPherson (ed.) *The Demand for New Faculty in Science and Engineering*, Washington, D.C.: National Research Council, 1979(b).

Roe, A. "A psychologist examines 64 eminent scientists." *Scientific American*, December 1952, pp. 21–25.

Roe, A. *The Making of a Scientist*. New York: Dood, Mead, 1953.

Roe, A. "The psychology of scientists." In K. Hill (ed.), *The Management of Scientists*. Boston: Beacon Press, 1964.

Rosen, B., and Jerdee, T. H. "Influence of sex-role stereotypes on personal decisions." *Journal of Applied Psychology*. 1974, *59*, 9–14.

Seldin, P. "Faculty evaluation: Surveying policy and practices." *Change*, 1984, *16*, 29–33.

Selye, H. *From Dream to Discovery: On Being a Scientist*. New York: McGraw Hill, 1964.

Shils, E. "The academic ethos under strain." *Minerva*, 1975, *13*, 1–37.

Simon, R. J. "The work habits of eminent scientists." *Sociology of Work and Occupations*, 1974, *1*, 327–335.

Skiff, A. "Toward a theory of publishing or perishing." *American Sociologist*, 1980, *15*, 175–183.

Skinner, B. F. *The Behavior of Organisms*. New York: Appleton-Century, 1938.

Skinner, B. F. *Science and Human Behavior*. New York: Macmillan, 1953.

Skinner, B. F. *Contingencies of Reinforcement*. New York: Appleton-Century-Crofts, 1969.

Smart, J. C., and McLaughlin, G. W. "Reward structures of academic disciplines." *Research in Higher Education*, 1978, *8*, 39–55.

Smelser, N. J., and Content, R. *The Changing Academic Market: General Trends and a Berkeley Case Study*. Berkeley: University of California Press, 1980.

Smith, C. G. "Scientific performance and the composition of research teams." *Administrative Science Quarterly*, 1971, *16*, 486–495.

Stahl, M., McNichols, C., and Manley, R. "Cosmopolitan-local orientations as predictors of scientific productivity, organizational productivity, and job satisfaction of scientists and engineers." *IEEE Transactions on Engineering Management*, 1979, E-M26, 39–43.

Stahl, M. J., and Stevens, A. E. "Reward contingencies and productivity in a government research and development laboratory." Paper presented at the Joint National TIMS/ORSA Meeting, San Francisco, May 9, 1977.

Stein, M. I. "Creativity in the scientist." In B. Barber and W. Hirsch (eds.), *The Sociology of Science*, New York: Free Press, 1962.

Stinchcombe, A. L. "On getting "hung up" and other assorted illnesses." *Johns Hopkins Magazine*, 1966, 25–30.

Storer, N. W. *The Social System of Science*. New York: Holt, Rinehart and Winston, 1966.

Storer, N. W. *The Sociology of Science*, Chicago: University of Chicago Press, 1973.

Taylor, C. W., and Barron, F. *Scientific Creativity: Its Recognition and Development*. New York: Wiley, 1963.

Taylor, C. W., and Ellison, R. L. "Biographical predictors of scientific performance." *Science*, 1967, *155*, 1075–1080.

Tuckman, H. P. *Publication, Teaching, and Academic Reward Structure*. Lexington, Mass.: Lexington Books, 1976.

Tuckman, H. P., and Hagemann, R. P. "An analysis of the reward structure in two disciplines." *Journal of Higher Education*, 1976, 47, 447–464.

Visart, N. "Communication between and within units." In F. Andrews (ed.) *Scientific Productivity: The Effectiveness of Research in Six Countries*, Cambridge, England: Cambridge University Press, 1979.

Vollmer, H. M. "Evaluating two aspects of quality in research program effectiveness." In M.J. Cetron and J.K. Goldhar (eds.), *The Science of Managing Organized Technology*, Vol IV, New York: Gordon and Breach, 1970.

Wanner, R., Lewis, L., and Gregorio, D. "Research productivity in academia: A comparative study of the sciences, social sciences, and humanities." *Sociology of Education*, 1981, 54, 238–253.

Weber, M. "Science as a vocation." In H. H. Gerth and C. Wright Mills (eds.), *From Max Weber: Essays in Sociology*, New York: Oxford University Press, 1946.

Wiley, M. G. Crittenden, K. S., and Birg, L. D. "Becoming an academic: Early vs. later professional experience." *Sociological Focus*, 1981, 14, 139–145.

Wilkes, J. M. "Styles of thought, styles of research, and the development of science." Worcester, Mass.: Worcester Polytechnic Institute, 1980.

Wilson, L. *American Academics: Then and Now*. New York: Oxford University Press, 1979.

Zuckerman, H. "Stratification in American science." In E. O. Laumann (ed.), *Social Stratification: Research and Theory for the 1970s*, New York: Bobbs-Merrill, 1970.

Zuckerman, H. *Scientific Elite: Nobel Laureates in the United States*. New York: Free Press, 1977.

Research Productivity and Teaching Effectiveness at a Small Liberal Arts College

STANLEY J. MICHALAK, JR. AND ROBERT J. FRIEDRICH

"Publish or perish!" has long been an accepted imperative for faculty at major universities. The rationale most often advanced for this dictum is that scholarly research contributes, directly and indirectly, to two of the traditional missions of these institutions—directly to perhaps the primary mission of many of these institutions, the advancement of knowledge, and indirectly to another important mission, the education of new generations of students. In the latter case, the underlying assumption is that faculty members who engage in research will be better teachers than those who do not.

In recent years, however, the norm of "publish or perish" has gained currency in other quarters of the academic world, including the smaller liberal arts colleges. More than ten years ago, Jencks and Riesman [12] identified several developments contributing to this. Universities were graduating from their advanced degree programs college instructors who were socialized to be "less and less preoccupied with educating young people, more and more preoccupied with educating one another by doing scholarly research which advances their discipline" [12, p. 13]. At the same time, career-minded undergraduates more and more saw a graduate degree as a prerequisite to success in life. They therefore sought to compile an academic record that was good enough—and at a college that was good enough—to gain them admission to a respectable graduate program.

These two developments fostered a third—the rise of the "university college," a high-quality undergraduate school serving essentially as a prep school for graduate school. Some small colleges, that is, sought to meet the students' demand for a certifiably high-quality education by hiring faculty from the best graduate schools—faculty who were, as just noted, increasingly socialized to prefer research over teaching [12, p. 24].

The number of "university colleges" was not large—Jencks and Riesman estimate that no more than 100 out of the 2,000 undergraduate colleges in the United States really fit the description—but these schools' adoption of the norm favoring research proved to have a more pervasive effect. As Jencks and Riesman put it, "drawn by emulation on the one side and pushed by accrediting agencies on the other" [12, p. 25], faculty and administrators at many of the 1,900 other undergraduate colleges began to try to model their institutions on the "university college." In particular, they sought to build faculties of not just "instructors," but "scholars" [12, pp. 24–25]. Early in the period, "the shortage of Ph.D.'s, especially 'productive' ones" [12, p. 21], impeded this effort. But more recently, the oversupply of Ph.D.'s and the continuing desire of such institutions to increase their prestige in order to attract the dwindling number of students have probably helped it along. So it is that many small colleges have come to rely more and more on research productivity in coming to decisions about which faculty to hire and which to fire, about which to promote, and about how much faculty should be paid. Such has certainly been the case at the institution where the research described in this article was conducted.

These developments raise important questions because, unlike major universities, small colleges have traditionally devoted themselves primarily to the mission of educating students and only secondarily, if at all, to the mission of generating knowledge. At the university level, the relationship between research and teaching is not a particularly crucial issue for, if research does not enhance teaching or even if it interferes with teaching, it can always be justified in terms of the other institutional mission. But at small colleges the issue is more crucial: given the mission of these institutions, research must be justified primarily in terms of its contribution to teaching.

The spreading acceptance of the norm that faculty members should engage in substantial research activity thus raises two basic empirical questions. First, is it generally the case that research enhances the quality of teaching? Second, even if it is generally the case that it does, research enhance the quality of teaching in the particular context of the smaller liberal arts colleges, where such norms have more recently been invoked? These are the principal questions to be addressed in this study. They will be pursued through a unique study of the relationship between research and teaching conducted at a small liberal arts college. Because the study was conducted at only a single institution, the findings can, strictly speaking, be applied only to that institution. Nevertheless the findings should be of interest to those at other similar institutions and at larger ones as well.

Some Theoretical Considerations

Does research in general enhance teaching? Clearly there are good reasons to think that it might. Research may expose the scholar to new information and ideas that improve and enliven his or her teaching. It may stimulate the scholar's sense of intellectual adventure, which may be transmitted to, and thereby motivate, students. It may foster intellectual self-discipline, which may manifest itself in clearer and better-organized classroom presentations.

At the same time, though, there are reasons to think that research may have little effect on teaching or even have an adverse effect on it. Research with the demands it makes on self-discipline, isolation, and concentration, may do little to enhance the interpersonal skills that seem so important to good teaching—and may even detract from them. Much research may proceed at too advanced a level to have an impact on undergraduate teaching, where lower-level treatment is the order of the day. More simply, as every scholar who tries to do both knows, limits on time and energy may lead to a difficult trade-off: those who focus on teaching may do so at the expense of their research and those who focus on research may do so at the expense of their teaching.

But even those possibilities do not exhaust the factors that must be considered in an examination of this question. Thus far the assumption has been that research influences teaching, whether positively or negatively. An empirical examination of this question must also confront the problem that any relationship that emerges between the two may be attributable to some other causal mechanism. For one, whatever relationship emerges between research and teaching may result from the latter influencing the former rather than the other way around. To illustrate, what teacher has not seen a research possibility flash into his or her mind as a result of preparing to teach a course or of a student's insightful comment in class? For another, the two may relate not because one influences the other, but because they both are influenced by some third factor. A positive but spurious relationship could result if good teaching and good research both stemmed from intelligence, self-discipline, or organization. On the other hand, a negative spurious relationship might result if personality qualities that led to good research—introversion, for example—also led to poor teaching.

So, strictly on theoretical grounds, there is good reason to think that the relationship between teaching and research may be more complicated than many have supposed. What follows, we think, will provide ample empirical evidence to support this view.

Previous Research

Despite the importance of the "publish or perish" issue and the controversy that surrounds it [3, 4, 6, 7, 11, 13, 15, 17, 18, 19, 22], fewer than a dozen systematic studies have been done on the relationship between research and teaching. And it is startling to note, in the face of the widespread acceptance of the link by those charged with faculty evaluation, that hardly any of the studies have found any relationship worth noting between research and teaching [1, 5, 8, 9, 10, 14, 20, 21]. Only Bresler [2] found a statistically significant relationship between the two variables and even that was a small one. On face, then, it would appear that either research has nothing to do with teaching or, at most, that its positive effects are balanced out by negative effects.

However, a closer look at these studies engenders caution about coming to any firm conclusions. In every case, assumptions and procedures seem flawed enough that serious questions can be raised about the validity of the results. The problems can be grouped into four major categories: problems with research setting, measurement, time span, and over-simplification.

Research setting poses a problem because all but one of the studies have been carried out at large public institutions. This makes it difficult to generalize about the effects of research on teaching because large institutions constitute only one segment of the higher education community. The problem is particularly acute for those at the smaller liberal arts colleges because it is difficult to know whether the results obtained in studies at large, often research-oriented, institutions have any applicability to their situations.

The means of measuring research and teaching pose another major problem for most of the studies. Consider first some of the measures of research activity. Harry and Goldner [8] measure productivity by asking faculty to estimate the time they spend on research, a procedure that leaves the definition of research up to each individual respondent and is highly vulnerable to distorted reporting. Bresler [2] uses government awards and contracts obtained by faculty members, but this neglects all research carried out under nongovernmental aegis. Hicks [9] employs a simple dichotomy between those who have published anything in an academic year and those who have not. This obscures both quantity and quality. Bresler [2], as an alternative measure to the one previously noted, uses the number of published articles—again neglecting the qualitative dimension. Dent and Lewis [5], along with Linsky and Straus [14], use the number of citations in the *Social Sciences Citation Index*. While the number of citations reflects, to some extent, both quantity and quality, its utility as a measure is reduced because not all pertinent publications are indexed and not all worthwhile research is necessarily cited. (Further, what if a scholar's work is cited as an example of poor research or specious logic? Presumably, though, peer review processes minimize the extent of this.) Perhaps the most intuitively appealing measures are those used by Voeks [21], Aleamoni and Yimer [1], and Linsky and Straus [14], which combine quantity and quality by awarding points for different types of scholarly output. Minsky and Straus, for example, assign a 1 for each article, a 2 for an edited book, a 4 for a jointly authored book, and a 6 for a singly authored book, and then add up values. Though such a formulation does recognize the degree of scholarly effort, it is weakened by the essentially arbitrary assignment of values.

The measures of teaching proficiency used vary less widely than the measures of research proficiency. Most common are measures, in mean or percentage terms, taken from student course evaluations of faculty performance [2, 8, 9, 21]. The literature is rife with controversy about the validity of this approach (see, e.g., Wittrock and Lumsdaine [23] and McKeachie [16]), but, in spite of the weaknesses, these student perceptions of faculty performance seem to be about the best that any researcher has been able to do, at least until now.

Almost all the studies examine the relationship between research and teaching for a single semester or year. This seems an inordinately narrow time span, given the improbability of research activity producing instantaneous improvement in teaching. More likely its effects are subtle and cumulative over time. In addition, it seems plausible (and our own early results tended to support this) that the relationship between the two may vary substantially from year to year, for essentially idiosyncratic reasons.

Finally, none of the studies has, at least in our view, been sensitive enough to theoretical complexities of the sort raised at the end of the previous section. Previous researchers have come to conclusions on the basis of an examination of the uncontrolled relationship between research and teaching. They have not considered the possibility that those slight relationships that do emerge may be artifacts of the effects of other variables such as intelligence, self-discipline, organization, or even field of study. Nor have they considered the possibility that other variables may be acting to suppress the relationship so that the real relationship between teaching and research is actually stronger than the observed one. Perhaps most important, they have cast the question of the relationship between teaching and research in very broad terms without considering the possibility that the answer may be a conditional one. That is, it may be that only in certain kinds of circumstances does research have an effect on teaching. This is a possibility that makes considerable sense in view of the theoretical considerations raised earlier. For example, research in some disciplines may be progressing at such an advanced level that it can contribute little to undergraduate teaching. Alternatively, research in some areas may be so demanding and time-consuming that it simply cannot be done without detracting seriously from teaching. We believe that by failing to recognize these sorts of complications, those who have previously studied this question may have made the mistake of looking for a general answer where there is none. Finding none, they may have then compounded the mistake by dropping the question altogether without having first looked for more complicated sorts of effects.

Research Design

The study described in the following pages has been designed to advance our understanding of the effects of scholarship on teaching by avoiding, or at least minimizing, each of the problems with previous research just identified. We aim to broaden the context within which research on the topic has been done by employing data gathered at a small liberal arts college. Specifically, the data were gathered at Franklin and Marshall College, a small liberal arts college in Lancaster, Pennsylvania. The institution has a student body of about 2,000 and a faculty of about 125. Because the school attracts students of relatively high quality—*Barron's Profiles of American Colleges* for example, rates it as very competitive plus—pressures for good teaching are strong. At the same time, as was said to be typical of such institutions at the beginning of this article, pressures for research are strong too.[1] This research setting is no more typical of higher education than any of the previous research settings, but it does contribute to our ability to generalize about the effects of research on teaching by shedding some light on another important sector of higher education. And it does, as suggested at the beginning of this article, focus attention on the research-teaching question in a setting where it is particularly controversial.

We also seek to improve on previous research by using measures of research and teaching more valid than those employed in previous research. For scholarship, we employ two distinct measures. One, essentially duplicating Dent and Lewis's [5]; and Linsky and Straus's [14] procedures, is the number of citations of a scholar's work in the *Science Citation Index* and the *Social Science Citation Index*. (Because no comparable indexes exist for disciplines outside the natural and social sciences, scholars from other fields were excluded from this part of the analysis.) While this measure does have the problems mentioned earlier, it can be defended on the grounds that the ultimate test of a scholar's research is the degree to which it stimulates other scholars to think and write about it.

Our uncertainty about this measure, though, does lead us to propose another—one novel in the field. It is the scholarship merit rating assigned by the college administration to the faculty member in the course of its usual annual faculty evaluation. Before the reader dismisses this choice as reflecting the rankest expediency, let us hasten to describe the measure and state why we think it is not just an adequate measure, but even a good one.

At Franklin and Marshall College, faculty members scholarship is rated along an ordinal scale according to the following standards:

Rate a 0 on this criterion if the faculty member has, during the past year, (1) had no publications and (2) had no systematic program of research and study.

Rate a 1 on this criterion if the faculty member has, during the past year, (1) published a book review or its equivalent or (2) pursued a systematic program of research and study leading toward further publication or the presentation of a new course.

Rate a 2 on this criterion if the faculty member has, during the past year, displayed activity in scholarship by having (1) published an article or equivalent series of book reviews or subsidized studies and (2) pursued a systematic program of research and study leading toward further publication or the presentation of a new course.

Rate a 3 on this criterion if the faculty member has, during the past year, displayed good scholarship by having (1) published one or two high-quality articles or edited an anthology or book of readings and (2) pursued a systematic program of research and study leading toward further publication or the presentation of a new course.

Rate a 4 on this criterion if the faculty member has, during the past year, displayed excellence in scholarship by having (1) pursued a systematic research and study program leading toward further publication or the presentation of a new course and (2) published a book or equivalent of articles and/or monographs, or the equivalent in the fine arts or (instead of 2) (3) devised a set of procedures or syllabus that could be expected to affect the teaching of the discipline in first-rate colleges and universities.

Rate a 5 on this criterion if the faculty member has, during the past year, displayed outstanding excellence in scholarship by having (1) pursued a systematic research and study program leading toward further publication or the presentation of a new course and (2) authored a high-quality book or an equivalent set of articles and/or monographs, or the equivalent in the fine arts or (instead of 2) (3) devised a set of procedures or syllabus that can be expected to substantially change the teaching of the discipline in first-rate colleges and universities.

Ratings along this scale are first devised by two judges working independently—the chairperson of the faculty member's department and the dean of the college. They confer and reconcile any differences. The rating agreed upon is then reported to the faculty member, who can take issue with it and ask the dean to reconsider. The dean makes the final decision.

This measure offers both advantages and disadvantages. On the positive side, it goes beyond the strictly quantitative measures described earlier to include some qualitative elements. Further, the procedure involving independent judgments by the chairperson and the dean, followed by their reaching a consensus and the faculty member then being allowed to challenge that consensus parallels a consensus coding procedure and is thereby likely to enhance the reliability and validity of the results. On the negative side because the procedures reflect the particular administrative routines of this institution they might be difficult to replicate elsewhere.

Constituting neither a clear plus nor minus is the broader coverage of the measure compared to those used in other studies. It includes not just publications, but also research in progress, systematic programs of study, and involvement in professional associations and conferences, exhibits, and shows. In other words it differs from the usual measures that, by focusing on publication, favor "hard research"—original research that advances the state of knowledge in a discipline—over "soft research"—secondary research in which a scholar assimilated and integrates others' research so as to advance his or her own state of knowledge. This greater latitude has the disadvantages of differing from the tack taken in other studies and because it includes activities that maybe directly related to teaching of possibly biasing results in favor of the research-teaching hypothesis. But it does capture the sort of intellectual activity that is at the base of all scholarship and particularly important here it does reflect the implicit definition of worthy scholarly activity employed at small liberal arts colleges.

Our measure of teaching effectiveness is novel in the same way as our measure of research productivity. It is the teaching merit rating assigned by the institution to the faculty member in the course of its usual annual faculty evaluation. In this case faculty members are rated on the basis of five different elements: evaluations from the students in all of the courses the faculty member teaches, "exit interviews" with departing seniors, "grapevine" feedback from students, examination of course syllabi, and in some cases firsthand observation of the person's teaching. They are rated along the following scale:

Rate a 0 on this criterion if on the basis of the evidence it can be said that the faculty member was below average on all measures and counts.

Rate a 1 on this criterion if on the basis of the evidence it can be said that the faculty member was below average, taking all counts and measures as a whole even though on some measures or counts he or she may have been above average.

Rate a 2 on this criterion if on the basis of the evidence it can be said that the faculty member was average taking all counts and measures as a whole.

Rate a 3 on this criterion if on the basis of the evidence it can be said that the faculty member was above average, taking all counts and measures as a whole.

Rate a 4 on this criterion if, on the basis of the evidence, it can be said that the faculty member was above average on all counts and measures.

Rate a 5 on this criterion if, on the basis of the evidence, it can be said that the faculty member was clearly excellent on all counts and measures.

As with the scholarship measure, the chairperson of the department and the dean of the college work independently. Their task of determining whether a faculty member is above or below average is eased by the fact that they have available to them mean scores for the college on all the items on the student evaluation form. The process of reconciling differences, allowing faculty challenge, and final decision making by the dean is the same as for the scholarship measure.

While this procedure admits of some subjectivity and has the same problem of replicability as the scholarship measure, it has a number of advantages. Unlike the measures described in the extant literature, this measure does not rely on student evaluations in one course. It encompasses all the courses taught by a faculty member and taps the quality of teaching from a number of different angles—not just the immediate reaction of students, but also the longer-term assessment of graduating seniors, the more amorphous judgments of the grapevine, and the more professional perspective of syllabus examination and classroom observation. Presumably these multiple sources of information combine to average out errors and thereby enhance validity. And, like the scholarship measure, this measure's validity is enhanced by the "consensus coding" type of procedure.

One problem that does arise with the use of these two institutionally determined measures is a problem not with either of the measures themselves but with the use of the two of them in combination. Because the same people determine both the scholarship and the teaching rating, it is possible that judgments made on one may contaminate judgments made on the other. For example, a chairperson or dean who rates a particular faculty member as an outstanding teacher may tend also to rate the faculty member as a strong scholar. It would be preferable, therefore, to have different people making assessments about research and assessments about teaching in order to prevent "halo effects." Unfortunately, that is not possible within this institutional context. Here all that can be done is to recognize this as a factor that may inflate the correlation between research and teaching and to pay special attention to the relationship between the citation-based measure of scholarship—which, because it is determined separately from the other two measures, cannot be contaminated—and teaching effectiveness.

We aim to avoid the problems raised by the short time span of earlier studies by looking at the relationship between research and teaching not just in a single semester or year, but over a period of several years. This approach recognizes that research may improve teaching only on a more subtle and long-term basis and also probably enhances validity by averaging out short-term measurement errors. We have adopted a five-year time span for our study. That is, our final measures of research and teaching are the measures just described, but averaged over a five-year period (from academic year 1972–73 to academic year 1977–78). We chose the five-year span because it seemed a long enough period of time in which to pick up any subtle and cumulative effects. At the same time, because the presumably poorer researchers and teachers leave the college after six years as the result of an unfavorable tenure decision, the five-year period was not so long as to result in a selection out of the group of the relatively weak performers and thus in an unrepresentative group. This narrowing of the focus of the study to five-year continuing faculty results in a reduction of the number of faculty studied to eighty-six cases.

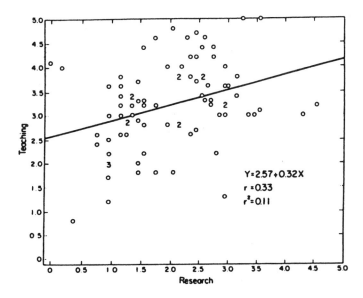

Figure 1. The Relationship Between Research Merit Rating and Teaching Merit Rating, Each Averaged Over Five Years

Finally, we have tried to improve on previous studies by recognizing some of the logical and theoretical complexities of the relationship between research and teaching. Our ability to do this has been hampered by the difficulty of measuring many of the factors that might play an important role, but we feel that by explicitly introducing some of them—in particular, the faculty member's rank and discipline—and at least considering the role that others of them may play, we have advanced our understanding of the relationship.

Data Analysis

Does research enhance teaching? We can begin to answer this question by examining the relationship between research performance and teaching performance, each averaged over the five-year period, for the eighty-six members of the Franklin and Marshall College faculty. As Figure 1 shows, there is a moderate tendency for those rated as better researchers also to be rated as better teachers. The slope of the regression line, or the straight line that best approximates the underlying trend in the relationship, is 0.32. This means that a faculty member rated one point higher than another on the research dimension is rated, on average, about one-third of a point higher on the teaching dimension.

However, while this provides some evidence that better researchers are also better teachers, an important point must be made. The relationship observed is not a particularly strong one. In the figure, many of the cases deviate substantially from the underlying trend. Note, for example, in the upper left-hand corner of the figure the two faculty members who rank at the absolute bottom of the scholarship scale, but among the best of the teachers. Note as well, at the right-hand side of the figure, that the two best scholars are not rated very highly on teaching. These impressions of substantial variation from the underlying trend are communicated most succinctly in the summitry statistics for the relationship. The r (Pearson product-moment correlation coefficient) of +0.33, relative to a scale ranging from −1 to +1, indicates, at best, only a moderate positive relationship, while the r^2 of 0.11 indicates that only about one-tenth of all the variation in teaching quality and research performance is shared. So the overall impression conveyed by the data is that research and teaching have something to do with each other, but not very much.[2]

While these simple results may seem unexceptional, they do add measurably to our understanding of the relationship between research and teaching. First, they run directly counter to the view that, either due to conflicting skill requirements or limitations on time, research and teaching are antithetical and that one cannot do both well at the same time. In general, the better researchers tend to be the better teachers, and the poorer researchers tend to be the poorer teachers. Second, the results diverge from the bulk of the previous research, finding little or no relationship between the two factors. Whereas most previous studies have found little merit in the proposition that research improves teaching, we have obtained results that are moderately consistent with it.

But for one study to obtain results that are consistent with a hypothesis that other studies have disconfirmed does not prove the hypothesis true nor the other studies wrong. We will deal with these two issues in turn.

Our results show that better research performance is related to better teaching performance. But is this because research improves teaching? One possible threat to this as a valid conclusion is the potential for contamination raised by the fact that the same people determine both the research and teaching ratings. Apart from noting that the raters are instructed to make separate judgments on the basis of separate criteria, our primary defense against this threat is to examine the relationship between the independently determined measure of scholarship, the citation measure, and teaching effectiveness. Data on citations are available only for faculty in the social sciences and natural sciences, so that the comparison cannot be a direct one. Nevertheless, the correlation between number of citations and teaching merit rating is +0.20. This smaller correlation—compared to the +0.33 observed between teaching and the other measure of research—suggests that judgments made along those two dimensions may influence each other to some degree, but the persistence of a positive correlation between the two measures derived independently of each other indicates that the observed relationship between research and teaching is not wholly or even primarily due to this sort of contamination. (An alternative interpretation of these results will be presented shortly.)

So the relationship survives the first test of its validity. The next step is to see whether the relationship survives the imposition of controls. Controls, as we said, are justified in these circumstances on two grounds. First, they are essential to ensure that the relationship observed is not the spurious product of some other factor that influences both research and teaching and makes it appear that they are causally related when they really are not. Second, we have argued that the effect of research on teaching may vary from one circumstance to another—in particular, because different types of research could be expected to have varying effects on teaching. This latter possibility is what we, following the statisticians, will call interaction.

Ideally, one would prefer to control for all the potentially complicating factors discussed earlier—intelligence, self-discipline, organization, introversion-extroversion, and so on. Unfortunately, our database, derived from institutional sources, is limited to only two—the faculty member's rank and discipline (broadly defined). It will be most convenient to discuss these two factors in succession, considering the possibilities of both spurious and interactive relationships stemming from each.

Faculty members of higher rank might, by reason of their greater experience, be expected to be better at both research and teaching. Thus differences in rank might make research and teaching appear to be causally related when they really are not. Alternatively, we might conjecture that the relationship between research and teaching would diminish with increasing rank, as more senior professors become less and less willing to tamper with what they see as a long-perfected series of lectures. The data in Table 1 show that the latter possibility, rather than the former, is the better supported of the two. For neither measure of scholarship does the relationship completely disappear in every category of the control variable, as would be the case if the relationship between research and teaching were simply a spurious one. Instead, the relationship diminishes as rank increases, suggesting that research does tend to enhance teaching, but more so for the junior than the senior members of the faculty, perhaps for the reason suggested above.

Table 1. Correlations Between Measures of Research and Teaching, Each Averaged Over Five Years, by Rank of Faculty Member

	Rank of Faculty Member		
	Assistant Professor	Associate Professor	Full Professor
Research merit rating by teaching merit rating	0.45	0.34	0.29
(n)	(13)	(33)	(40)
Number of citations by teaching merit rating	0.55	0.28	−0.01
(n)	(7)	(22)	(24)

The other factor for which it is possible to control is the discipline, broadly defined, of the faculty member. The possibility of a spurious relationship between research and teaching arises in these data because, at Franklin and Marshall College in recent years, faculty members in the natural and social sciences have tended to rate relatively high on teaching and research, while those in the humanities have rated relatively low. Alternatively, it may be, as noted earlier, that research in some areas may be of the sort that has little payoff in the classroom. In particular, it might be expected that the sort of advanced research more common in the natural sciences may contribute little to instruction at the undergraduate level.

Table 2 allows an assessment of these possibilities by displaying the correlations between the two measures of research and the measure of teaching within each of the three major disciplinary divisions of the college. The relationship between research and teaching clearly persists under most circumstances with this control, which rules out discipline as a possible source of a spurious relationship between the two variables. At the same time, though, it is immediately apparent that research and teaching do relate more strongly in some disciplines than in others. Whereas research and teaching are quite strongly correlated for humanities and social science teachers, they are much more weakly related for natural science teachers. This is consistent with our hypothesis that research in the natural sciences, in contrast to research in the social sciences and humanities, may be at a level of abstraction and complexity that renders it of little utility in the classroom.

So our confidence in the research-teaching hypothesis has been increased by results showing that neither is the observed relationship due, in any important measure, to contaminated ratings nor is it the spurious product of the effects of experience or discipline. Other threats to its validity remain, of course. Other factors ought to be controlled for—though, to the extent that they correlate with rank or discipline (as it is plausible to think they might), they may have already been dealt with to some degree. The nettlesome question of what causes what persists—does research influence teaching, as most (including us) are inclined to assume, or does teaching

Table 2. Correlations Between Measures of Research and Teaching, Each Averaged Over Five Years, by Discipline of Faculty Member

	Discipline of Faculty Member		
	Humanities	Natural Sciences	Social Sciences
Research Merit rating by teaching merit rating	0.48	0.07	0.57
(n)	(24)	(38)	(24)
Number of citations by teaching merit rating		0.20	0.54
(n)		(33)	(20)

influence research? But these threats are ones that cannot be resolved given the research design and data that we have employed here. All that we can say is that we have obtained results that are mildly consistent with the hypothesis that research improves teaching and that suggest that the nature of the effects varies substantially, depending on the rank and the discipline of the professor.

Whereas previous research has pretty much rejected the research-teaching hypothesis out of hand, our research has found some support for it. It may be instructive to consider briefly why the results diverge. The most benign approach would be to say that this has happened because the hypothesis is really true and that it has been supported for the first time because of the sophistication of our procedures—specifically, measurement techniques that, because they rely on explicit criteria employed by two independent, expert raters and because they are applied over a period of years, produce scales of superior reliability and validity. We believe there is some truth in this.

At the same time, though, we must admit that there may be other reasons as well. One may have to do with the research setting. It might in fact be the case that involvement in research at small liberal arts colleges—or at least at this particular small liberal arts college—influences teaching more than it does at large universities. Such a view is certainly consistent with our findings of substantial variation in the relationship between teaching and research. That is, there may be no general answer to the question of whether or not research enhances teaching. Rather, the answer may be that it depends—depends on the position of the faculty member and his or her discipline, as we have shown, but also perhaps on the facilities for research and teaching, the atmosphere of research and teaching (e.g., are good research and good teaching fostered by the creation of a conducive atmosphere or by compulsion?), the kind of teaching that is done, and the kind of research.

The last point regarding the kind of research that is done is particularly important because it constitutes another possible explanation for why our results diverge from previous results. Earlier we noted that our operational definition of research productivity differed from others in that it subsumed activities beyond just publication—what we called "soft" as opposed to "hard" research. It may be that we have found more of a relationship between research and teaching than other studies because our measure of research includes this soft research and it is this soft research—particularly "systematic program[s] of research and study leading toward . . . the presentation of a new course" and "[devising] a set of procedures or syllabus which could be expected to affect the teaching of the discipline in first-rate colleges and universities"— which may have an especially beneficial effect on teaching. This may also be another reason why we found, overall, a stronger relationship between teaching merit and the relatively soft measure of research merit than between teaching merit and the relatively hard measure of the number of citations. (This pattern is not as clearly manifested in Tables 1 and 2, but we are inclined to put more faith in the correlations calculated for the population than in those calculated for its subdivisions, given the numbers of cases involved.) Finally, it may also be that this distinction helps to explain why research correlates with teaching so much more strongly in the social sciences and humanities than in the natural sciences. Because of the nature of their disciplines, social scientists and humanists may tend to engage in the softer sort of research that does pay off in teaching while natural scientists engage in harder research that does not.

Summary and Conclusions

In a study conducted at a small liberal arts college, we have found that faculty members who are active researchers tend to be somewhat better teachers than those who are not, though the relationship is by no means a strong one. The relationship is strongest in the lowest rank of the faculty and weakest in the highest rank. It varies as well across disciplines, with moderately strong relationships observed for the social sciences and the humanities, and hardly any relationship at all for the natural sciences. These differences probably reflect changing patterns of motivation among faculty as the years pass and differences in the relevance of scholarly activity to undergraduate teaching across the disciplines. The generally stronger relationships between research and teaching found in this study, compared to others, may be due to improved measurement procedures, the novel research setting, or perhaps to the greater weight that our operational definition of research quality puts on "soft" research as opposed to "hard" research, since soft research encompasses activities that seem especially likely to bolster teaching performance.

In light of the weakness of previous research results, the net effect of these results is to increase slightly empirical support for the premise that better research leads to better teaching. The correlation of +0.33, while not strong, is certainly a noteworthy one, especially in comparison to previous results. At the same time, though, these results make it difficult for us to endorse the policy of pressing faculty to do more and better research on the theory that it will help to improve their teaching. For one thing, the relationship is not, overall, that strong. For another, it is not that consistent—better research may lead to better teaching among junior faculty and in the social sciences and the humanities, but there is little evidence that it does so among senior faculty and in the natural sciences. For a third, the inability to control for many important factors and the necessity of relying on a nonexperimental design leave us very much in the dark about what, in general, the mechanism relating the two variables is and what, in particular, causes what. To put it differently, to show that better researchers tend to be better teachers does not mean that pressing a faculty member to do more and better research is going to improve his or her teaching.

Clearly there is a need for more research of high quality on this question. Better measures, ones that separate out the hard and the soft aspects of research, as well as explore the different facets of teaching, are needed. Research designs that operationalize other important variables in the complex of factors that may link research and teaching should be devised so that the precise set of mechanisms connecting the two can be identified. And, continuing on the path followed by this study, research should be undertaken in a variety of different institutional settings so that the appropriate sphere of generalization for assertions about the relationship between teaching and research can be established.

In the interim, while our empirical knowledge about the relationship is limited, it is difficult to make policy recommendations with any great sense of confidence. What we can say with considerable confidence, though, is this. There are many reasons why a small college might want to encourage its faculty to pursue scholarly research and publication. Such activities may, in some cases, make significant contributions to mankind's store of knowledge and insight. They may publicize the name of the college among academic and intellectual elites. They may help to keep faculty members intellectually alive. They may serve to enhance morale by giving faculty members the sense that they work at an institution of high academic quality. But it is unclear whether scholarly research and publication contribute at all to teaching and quite clear that they do not contribute much. In the end, institutions of higher education—large and small—and those who populate them—faculty and administrators—might do better to regard scholarship as an end in its own right rather than as a means to the end of improving teaching. Then they could rationally choose to pursue these two ends separately, in proportion to the degree that they value them.

References

1. Aleamoni, L. M., and M. Yimer. "An Investigation of the Relationship Between Colleague Rating, Student Rating, Research Productivity, and Academic Rank in Rating Instructional Effectiveness." *Journal of Educational Psychology*, 64 (June 1973), 274–77.

2. Bresler, J. B. "Teaching Effectiveness and Government Awards." *Science*, 160 (April 1968), 164–67.

3. Buswell, J. O. "Publish or Perish?" *Improving College and University Teaching*, 23 (August 1975), 219.

4. Carroll, J. D. "The Process Values of University Research." *Science*, 158 (November 1967), 1019–24.

5. Dent, P. L., and D. J. Lewis. "The Relationship Between Teaching Effectiveness and Measures of Research Quality." *Educational Research Quarterly*, 1 (Fall 1976), 3–16.

6. Fischer, J. "Is There a Teacher on the Faculty?" *Harper's*, 230 (February 1965), 18–28.

7. Hammond, P. E., J.W. Meyer, and D. Miller. "Teaching Versus Research: Sources of Misperceptions." *Journal of Higher Education*, 40, (December 1969), 682–92.

8. Harry, J., and N. S. Goldner. "The 'Null' Relationship Between Teaching and Research." *Sociology of Education*, 45, (Winter 1972), 47–60.

9. Hicks, R. A. "The Relationship Between Publishing and Teaching Effectiveness." *California Journal of Educational Research*, 25 (May 1974), 140–46.

10. Hoyt, D. P., and R. K. Spangler. "Faculty Research Involvement and Instructional Outcomes." *Research in Higher Education*, 4 (1976), 113–22.

11. Hutchinson, W. R. "Yes, John, There Are Teachers on the Faculty." *American Scholar*, 35 (Summer 1966), 430–42.

12. Jencks, C., and D. Riesman. *The Academic Revolution.* Garden City, N.Y.: Anchor-Doubleday, 1969.

13. Killian, J. R., Jr. "Teaching Is Better than Ever." *Atlantic Monthly*, 216 (December 1965), 53–56.

14. Linsky, A. S., and M. A. Straus. "Student Evaluations, Research Productivity, and Eminence of College Faculty." *Journal of Higher Education*, 46 (January/February 1975), 89–102.

15. McGrath, E. J. "Characteristics of Outstanding College Teachers." *Journal of Higher Education*, 33 (March 1962), 148–52.

16. McKeachie, W. J. "Student Ratings of Faculty: A Reprise." *Academe*, 65 (October 1979), 384–97.

17. Sample, S. B. "Inherent Conflict Between Research and Education." *Educational Record*, 53 (Winter 1972), 17–22.

18. Schmitt, H. A. "Teaching and Research: Companions or Adversaries?" *Journal of Higher Education*, 36 (November 1965), 419–27.

19. Showalter, D. E. "Publication and Stagnation in the Liberal Arts College." *Educational Record*, 59 (Spring 1978), 166–72.

20. Stallings, W. M., and S. Singhal. "Some Observations on the Relationship Between Research Productivity and Student Evaluation of Courses and Teaching." *American Sociologist*, 5 (May 1970), 141–43.

21. Voeks, V. W. "Publications and Teaching Effectiveness." *Journal of Higher Education*, 33 (April 1962), 212–18.

22. Wilson, J. H., and R. S. Wilson. "The Teaching-Research Controversy." *Educational Record* 53 (Fall 1972), 321–26.

23. Wittrock, M. C., and A. A. Lumsdaine. "Student Ratings of Teachers." *Annual Review of Psychology*, 28 (1977), 446–49.

Notes

1. To illustrate, criteria for initial appointment at the institution (which were developed during the 1960s and made explicit in the early 1970s) include the following: "The candidate must be able to demonstrate the potential to develop and pursue programs of research and study. We believe that effective teaching is enhanced by scholarly activity, customarily manifested by scholarly publication or equivalent public artistic presentation."

   For tenure, one of the major criteria reads: "It is expected that effective teaching must be informed through research and scholarship. Publication is the most obvious demonstration of significant research." In addition, annual salary increases can depend as much on research prowess as on teaching ability.

2. Unlike many other researchers in this field, we do not employ tests of statistical significance in our analysis. The reason is simple: a test of statistical significance indicates whether the results of an analysis of a sample are clear-cut enough to warrant a generalization about the population from which the sample was drawn. In this case the results describe the entire population about which we wish to make

generalizations—all the faculty members at Franklin and Marshall College who worked through the five-year period. Thus there is no need to make an inference from a sample to a population. To those who would justify the use of significance tests by seeing the Franklin and Marshall faculty as a sort of sample from a broader population, we would respond that, even if it is viewed as such a sample, it is clearly not a probability sample so that none of the usual tests of significance could properly be applied. To those who recognize this but still see significance tests as a useful standard against which to judge results, we can report that the +0.33 value for r reported here exceeds the 0.21 value necessary for significance at the 0.05 level with eighty-six cases. So our acceptance of a relationship that others have rejected cannot be attributed to the fact that others rely on significance tests and we do not.

Stanley J. Michalak, Jr., is professor, and Robert J. Friedrich is assistant professor, Department of Government, Franklin and Marshall College.

The Distinctive Scholarship of the Selective Liberal Arts College

KENNETH P. RUSCIO

Introduction

The main issue addressed in this article is the effect of America's diverse higher-education system on its academic profession. As higher education in the United States evolved from a privilege enjoyed by a small minority to an option for nearly every member of society, colleges divided their labor and coalesced into sectors, each sector offering a form of education designed for a segment of the market. Institutions differ greatly in size, quality, and clientele, and each blends teaching, research, and public service in a manner compatible with its chosen mission. Whether the academic profession followed a similar path is a more complex proposition. Institutional expectations for balancing teaching and research certainly differ, but almost all colleges, even community colleges to some extent, require or at least encourage faculty to be active professionally. This usually means faculty should be engaged in their disciplines—making a contribution to the discipline—which results in faculty being evaluated, in part, by criteria that cut across institutional sectors. As models of institutional success become more complex, the criteria for success in the academic profession seem to remain intact. A successful member of the academic profession is someone who not only educates students, but who also advances his or her field of study. Jencks and Riesman [6, p.13] phrased it this way: "College instructors have become less and less preoccupied with educating young people, more and more preoccupied with educating one another by doing scholarly research which advances their discipline." Edward Shils [11, p. 104] had a similar view.

> The fundamental obligations of university teachers for teaching, research and academic citizenship are all the same. . . . Not all academics are equally endowed or equally inclined, for whatever reason, to the activities needed to meet these obligations. . . . Nevertheless, to abstain from any of these totally and to show no respect for them is contrary to the obligations of an academic career.

To investigate this broader proposition, and to amend it, this article looks at faculty scholarship in the selective liberal arts college. Their strong reputation for quality teaching notwithstanding, these colleges have historically expected their faculty to perform research, and the level and quality of research suggest a professional affinity between faculty in the research universities and in the selective liberal arts colleges. For example, in one extensive survey of faculty, 65 percent of the professors in "high-quality four-year colleges" expressed at least some interest in research, a figure almost as high as that for research universities of low quality (67 percent), medium quality (77 percent), and even high quality (85 percent). Rates of publication showed a similar trend, leading to the conclusion that professors in selective liberal arts colleges "by virtue of their continuing research activity, are raising the same kinds of questions, reading the same research and scholarly literature, as are men of the leading graduate departments" [4, p. 67]. Jencks and Riesman [6, p. 24] echoed this finding. A "university college" (which they defined as an undergraduate college whose primary purpose is to prepare students for graduate education) "is almost certain to draw its faculty from the same manpower pool as the graduate schools of arts and sciences, seeking the same virtues and looking askance at the same presumed vices." This apparently has become the conventional wisdom. "Even small liberal arts colleges primarily oriented to undergraduate education," writes Daniel Alpert, "exhibit strong loyalties to the values of the research universities, particularly in their dependence on the disciplinary communities for measuring professorial performance, for providing faculty mobility, and for strengthening professional identity" [1, p. 259].

If others are struck by the similarities, I am struck by the differences. In interviews conducted for a study of the academic profession, faculty at selective liberal arts colleges expressed subtle but important differences between their attitudes toward scholarly work and those of faculty in research universities. Data from the 1985 Carnegie Faculty survey support the interview responses. (See Appendix A for a description of the methodology.) The differences reflect the faculty members' commitment to the goals of the selective liberal arts college and their contentment with their professional home. The differences are also significant enough to suggest the development of a distinctive model of scholarship. The components of this model will be discussed in detail, but the fundamental contention is that although liberal arts and research university faculty both revere scholarship, the form of worship is not the same. Faculty at selective liberal arts colleges accept the norm of research, but reject the way it is practiced at the leading research universities. The academic profession, in other words, has indeed complicated its model for success.

Research and the Liberal Arts Setting

Before sifting through the data, a few background points deserve mention. They are intertwined, although the connections are not apparent. The undergraduate years are the forgotten years in American higher education. Incorporating research into the higher education system resulted in a concentration of resources and talent at the upper levels. Rewards for educating the masses of undergraduates are slight compared to the prestige, wealth, and power of the elite graduate programs. Graduate education pulls the system. Research confers professional prestige on the academic and institutional prestige on the institution.

The selective liberal arts colleges are somewhat of an exception. These colleges devote almost all their resources to a small number of highly qualified students who, upon graduation, typically enter the best graduate programs. Faculty also boast of impeccable credentials. Degrees from elite universities are virtually a prerequisite for employment. Thus, although the organizational settings are quite different, ties between the sectors remain.

To understand the relationship between the research universities and the selective liberal arts colleges better, imagine each sector enclosed in its own circle. The two circles partially overlap, and contained in the area of intersection is a set of shared activities and beliefs. New faculty flow from the universities to the colleges; highly qualified students flow from the colleges to the universities; members of a discipline communicate with each other at conferences and through journals; and a spirit of inquiry feeds upon itself, with each new discovery providing a foundation for the next. But the size of the area of intersection is not fixed. Conditions change, and currently there are some trends that increase the interaction and some that lessen it.

One trend which fortifies the links is the funneling of highly qualified students from the selective liberal arts colleges to the research universities. It occurs at a highly impressive rate. Consider the following: Of the three hundred leading colleges which awarded bachelor's degrees to students who went on to obtain doctorates in science and engineering between 1960 and 1981, fifty-three were liberal arts I colleges.[1] One does not have to read far down the list to find them. Oberlin is 47th; Swarthmore is 77th; Reed is 101st; and Pomona is 103rd [8]. These colleges and others like them have historically attracted students interested in science. As Table 1 shows,

Table 1. Freshmen Educational and Career Plans, 1985 (In Percentages)

| | National Norms | Private Nonsectarian Four Year Colleges | | Highly Selective Universities |
		High Selectivity	Very High Selectivity	
1. *Intended Field of Study:*				
a. Biology	1.8	3.5	6.0	4.0
b. Biochemistry	0.6	1.4	2.5	1.8
c. Chemistry	0.8	1.5	2.5	1.8
d. Physics	1.4	0.7	2.0	1.4
e. Electrical Engineering	4.1	7.4	3.5	6.3
f. Pre-Medicine	3.2	5.4	5.8	6.4
2. *Probable Career*				
a. College Teacher	0.3	0.4	1.2	0.5
b. Engineer	10.4	14.9	8.5	15.1
c. Scientific Researcher	1.5	2.8	4.3	3.4
d. Physician	4.0	7.7	13.2	11.1
e. Lawyer	4.1	6.9	11.0	7.7
3. *Highest Degree*				
a. Ph.D. or Ed.D	1.7	17.2	24.4	16.7
b. M.D. or Other Medical	1.4	10.8	16.6	14.0
c. J.D.	0.9	7.1	12.8	8.3

SOURCE: Alexander W. Astin and Associates, "The American Freshman: National Norms for Fall 1984." Cooperative Institutional Research Program: ACE, UCLA, December 1984.

interest in scientific careers and postgraduate plans is extremely strong among freshmen in highly selective four-year colleges, at least as strong as that of freshmen in highly selective research universities, and far higher than the national norm.

Although the interest in scientific careers among students in selective liberal arts colleges ensures continued links between the sectors, developments in the conduct of science run in the opposite direction. Research is concentrated in a small number of organizations, primarily because of the elaborate and expensive support structure (equipment, support staff, and so forth) required to perform modern science. Eighty-five percent of federal money for academic science goes to one hundred institutions (out of a post secondary population of over three thousand). None of these institutions is a liberal arts college. In fact, the first liberal arts college to appear on the list is Pomona, which ranks 280th, followed by Occidental (284th), Amherst (289th), and Harvey Mudd (298th) [9]. Given the primary criterion for research support, which has been to produce science and not necessarily scientists, as well as the enormous differences in enrollment between the two sectors, this distribution is predictable and no cause for undue controversy. Still, it casts doubt on the ability of scientists at selective liberal arts colleges to keep pace in some areas of research.

Thus, while flows of personnel persist, the nature of the research enterprise grows increasingly different because of the organizational differences. The model of contemporary academic science does not fit well in the contemporary liberal arts college.

A final trend also relates to the contemporary model of academic science, but this one favors the liberal arts college. Pathbreaking research no longer conforms, if it ever did, to the constraints of disciplinary purity. Solving a significant problem requires crossing the boundaries of specializations. The National Science Foundation [9, p. 29] offered these examples.

> Solid state physics has merged with materials science and with chemical engineering and computer science to produce new catalysts and microelectronic fabrication methods . . . optics, solid state physics, and cellular biology have merged in the creation of flow

cytometry for analyzing cell components; . . . robotics and neurobiology merge in their analysis of vision. Fundamental studies of how a smoothly flowing liquid becomes a turbulent one devolve into work in mathematics, in physiology, in the dynamics of the atmosphere, and in galactic structure. The search to uncover the structure of cell receptors needs the recombinant DNA techniques of molecular biology. And fundamental work in receptor biology has in turn sparked the discovery of peptide receptors governing neurological events.

In the social sciences, Clifford Geertz has written of "blurred genres," the mingling of different perspectives to interpret society's problems [5]. Such disregard for disciplinary boundaries should reassure researchers at the selective liberal arts colleges, where the fixation on disciplines is attenuated by the belief in a broad, liberal approach to the world of knowledge. Despite the practical limitations on their research, faculty find that their approach is legitimate espistemologically as well as pedagogically. This is not to suggest that specialized research driven by disciplinary concerns is ineffective, or that large universities resist interdisciplinary efforts, or even that liberal arts colleges have the characteristics most conducive to overcoming disciplinary boundaries. The issue cannot withstand such flat assertions. The only contention at this stage of the discussion is that the temperament which promotes integrative scholarship is at home in a liberal arts college, and as the value of that kind of research receives recognition, the legitimacy of the liberal arts college as a setting for research will not suffer any harm, even though other circumstances put them at a disadvantage.

With this background, it is possible to analyze the ways in which faculty in selective liberal arts colleges differ from faculty in the research universities.[2]

The Distinctive Scholarship

1. *Research in the selective liberal arts college is more individualistic than bureaucratic.* In a liberal arts setting research is individualistic. It is unlike the highly organized and entrepreneurial research that often requires an intricate administrative structure. This might vary by discipline, but research in universities is typically very "organized"—bureaucratic—whereas at liberal arts colleges it remains in the hands of the individual.

Table 2 clarifies this assertion. The Carnegie survey asked those who do research to describe the characteristics of their activities. Liberal Arts I professors do not depend on financial support from other organizations, nor do they enlist the support staff found in research universities.

As a result, investigators in selective liberal arts colleges might modify their plans, choose different topics, or approach a problem differently than they would in a setting with more extensive resources. A physicist changed his research agenda after leaving graduate school because of "practicalities." "We don't have the facilities here to do the kind of work I used to do," he explained, "and I do not think the previous work is all that well suited for undergraduate participation. It is a little too esoteric and substantially too expensive." Moreover, the less pressure there is to obtain funds for research, the less pressure to establish a well-defined research program or to "carve out a niche in the profession. "A political scientist compared his "ability to move around as the mood strikes" with a friend at a research university whose office resembles a "war room because he has everything mapped out." Another political scientist put the matter clearly: "I think it is indubitably the case that the kind of institution this is limits the kind of professional career the faculty can have."

As already noted, trends in science place the liberal arts professor at somewhat of a disadvantage. The sheer cost of research impedes some sophisticated research plans. An electron microscope costs nearly a million dollars; Haverford's R & D expenditures in 1980 were $438,000. A basic spectrometer costs $500,000; it would have taken all of Denison's federal R & D funding for 1979 and 1980 to purchase one of them [9]. As Donald Kennedy has pointed out, universities may be reaching the point where the equipment and special facilities needed to support a faculty member's research will exceed "the capital values of the endowment necessary to yield the faculty member's salary" [7, p. 481]. That was Kennedy's definition of "Big Science"; and liberal arts

Table 2. Research Contexts in Universities and Liberal Arts I Colleges

	Sectors		
Research Characteristics	**Research I Universities**	**Research II Universities**	**Liberal Arts I Colleges**
1. *Received Funds from the Following Sources:*			
a. Federal Agencies	51.2%	35.0%	9.2%
b. State & Local Agencies	15.9	19.5	0.8
c. Private Foundations	21.1	13.6	20.7
d. Private Industry	21.8	18.4	2.5
e. Other Sources Outside the Institution	10.2	7.0	1.6
2. *Support Staffs*			
a. Postdoctoral Researchers	26.1	8.7	0.0
b. Research Assistants	59.8	51.9	5.6
c. Permanent Staff	36.9	28.1	11.3
3. *Working Association with Research Institute or Research Center*	43.9	34.4	13.9

SOURCE: 1985 Carnegie Faculty Survey, Carnegie Foundation for Advancement of Teaching. Used with permission.

NOTE: Question asked of those who do research. N = 641 faculty for Research I Universities; 410 for Research II Universities; 109 for Liberal Arts I Colleges.

colleges, despite their high per capita endowments, must face the reality of partaking in equipment-intensive research through special arrangements: sabbaticals for professors, consortia, or summer grants. Even the social sciences, which occasionally require the purchase and manipulation of large data bases, are not immune.

Although cost is a conspicuous barrier, a less visible one is the organization structure. Over the last two decades universities have rearranged the principal units for housing research. New units have arisen for a variety of reasons, including, for example, the desire to buffer the autonomous core of the university from threats posed by organizations supplying money for research. These structures fall under a variety of headings, such as research institutes or cooperative research centers. There are many examples.

California's MICRO program, funded by the state and the micro-electronics industry, supports research and graduate programs at the University of California campuses. A coalition that includes the University of Maryland, the National Bureau of Standards, and Montgomery County in Maryland plans to establish a Center for Advanced Research in Biotechnology. A majority of the seventy-five hundred nonprofit research centers listed in the 1984-85 Research Centers Directory are university related. At MIT only $81 million of their $218 million in research expenditures was accounted for by the departments; the rest was spent in interdisciplinary centers [12, pp. 150–52]. In short, the scale of complexity in universities far surpasses the simple departmental structure of the selective liberal arts colleges. And that surely is one measure of bureaucratization.

As research becomes tied to sophisticated technology and equipment, more expensive, dependent on external funding, and housed in hybrid organizational units, the research contexts of universities and selective liberal arts colleges will diverge. The Carnegie Institute stated,"[The] time may be passing when an individual can produce significant discoveries without support and present them as pure gifts to society. Universities once provided most of our scientists with an independence that allowed them to pursue their research at least part-time. As research activities have become an explicit commitment on the part of both the individual and the institution . . .

conflicting pressures and constraints appear" [2, p. 672]. To maintain a high level of research, the selective liberal arts college will have to adjust.

2. *Faculty in selective liberal arts colleges are less "taxonomically upstanding."*[3] Faculty in Liberal Arts I colleges are critical of the work in their disciplines. They perceive their fields to be preoccupied with narrow, specialized topics and marginal, incremental contributions to an arcane literature. They blame this on the counterproductive pressure to publish which compels those in research universities to conduct professionally safe, risk-free research. For one liberal arts professor, an "outstanding academic" was someone who "is willing to go out on a limb with some pretty wild ideas." But that is likely to occur only rarely in a field where, according to another respondent, "half to three-quarters of what I read, if I ask myself why was this written, the answer normally is promotion." A political scientist found that academics in universities "generate a lot of studies that confirm or slightly extend (the work) of someone else. And those seem to me to be useful exercises, but they are not ground-breaking, they don't organize the way people think about a subject or the way they see it. They don't fundamentally change anything. . . . There's a lot of self-promotion in academia which is problematic." In the field of English literature, the pressure of mandatory publication has led to work that "seems increasingly trivial or increasingly making use of a very technical and sophisticated apparatus that somehow does not end up enhancing the work or some aspect of the work or anything else." Another literature professor expressed puzzlement about why someone would "want to succeed in knowing more about the Elizabethan use of the comma than anybody needs to know."

Criticism is less severe in the sciences, perhaps because of the consensus on major problems and agreement on the methods of investigation. But the natural or physical scientist must still make some adjustment to his or her organization. For example, the small size of the departments and the broad range of courses to be taught means that there will never be a core of individuals in a particular specialization. The young professor fresh from graduate school where the departments are large and several scientists are working on related questions will find the liberal arts college radically different. In some cases, according to a molecular biologist, a scientist might have to perform "horizontal" research—research that crosses over into neighboring subfields or even neighboring disciplines—instead of the "vertical" research found in a university setting. A biochemist found this had some advantages. He explained, "I am better prepared to ask interesting questions about membrane biochemistry because I am forced to keep up with a pretty wide area." This same professor had branched out from his biology department to establish ties with his chemistry colleagues. "I think if we were all at a big university," he said, "we would not be making much of an effort to understand one another because we would not need that community. There would be another dozen membrane biochemists to talk to and I wouldn't have to keep up with what the molecular geneticist is doing. One of the virtues of a small college is that you are forced to be aware of other people's fields, but I think out there in the big world people are not very aware of the whole subject matter of biochemistry."

The relationship of the liberal arts professors to the mainstream of the discipline is not easy to delineate. Scholarly work has a high priority, but the boundaries of specializations and the taxonomies of the disciplines are considered artificial and constraining. Transcending these boundaries is not only tolerated but encouraged. A political scientist, who conceded his work was not fashionable in the discipline, found his liberal arts home ideal because "if I had set my sights on a position in a major graduate school, it would have been hard with my current interests. Here I could follow precisely where my curiosities led without having to answer to anybody or to feel that I was professionally imperiling myself." Similarly, a literature professor who was turning her dissertation into a book contrasted her situation with being in a major research university: "If I had to establish myself as the Americanist at Big X University I might feel I had to direct my book more toward the American subject. Now I feel quite free to do what I really want to do, which is comparative."

But neither are these professors out of touch with their disciplines. They attend national professional meetings almost as frequently as their university counterparts (Table 3). And they have a credible record of publication (Table 4). Over 80 percent said they devoted at least some time each week to research, and only 30 percent said their interests were totally in teaching. Most

Table 3. Attendance at National Professional Meetings by Sector

Sector	Number of Meetings Attended in the Last Year			
	None	One	Two/Three	Four or More
1. Research I Universities	15.4%	27.5	44.3	12.7
2. Research II Universities	21.7	28.7	41.3	8.2
3. Liberal Arts I Colleges	21.3	34.1	37.1	7.5

SOURCE: 1985 Carnegie Faculty Survey. Used with permission.

Table 4. Publication Rate by Sector (Total Number of Articles and Articles Published Last Two Years)

Number of Articles Published	Research I Universities		Research II Universities		Liberal Arts I Colleges	
	Total	Last 2 Yrs	Total	Last 2 Yrs	Total	Last 2 Yrs
None	6.1	13.4	17.0	22.1	26.9	38.4
1 – 4	21.5	47.4	18.0	51.5	35.7	52.4
5 – 10	14.4	25.2	18.3	18.7	14.3	7.7
More than 10	58.0	14.0	46.8	7.7	23.1	1.4

SOURCE: 1985 Carnegie Faculty Survey. Used with permission.

faculty in selective liberal arts colleges are deeply engaged in scholarship, but they feel less compelled to contribute to the discipline in the conventional manner, to be "taxonomically upstanding." There is a tolerance for a broader range of activities under the heading of scholarship.

3. *Research is justified as an investment in students.* Professors at Liberal Arts I colleges have their own reasons for conducting research. It is justified for its educational benefits. The distinction between liberal arts and university professors in this regard is a subtle one. In diplomacy, when two parties are on opposite sides of a dispute, it is usually "body languages rather than the formal statement that conveys the true feelings of the negotiators. And so it is with the educational attitudes of professors in the research and liberal arts sectors. Their commitments to broadly phrased values and beliefs are nearly indistinguishable. Contrary to usual perceptions, university professors do not always ignore students nor do they find teaching unfulfilling. By the same token, liberal arts professors poorly conform to their stereotype of an academic whose sole purpose in life is the moral and intellectual development of his or her students: 36 percent of the Liberal Arts I professors believe students demand too much of their attention. But as we review survey and interview responses, comparing the two sets of academics, different postures are evident. Liberal arts professors lean sharply toward exposing students to a variety of ideas and subjects, whereas university professors lean less in that direction, sometimes tilting the other way toward concentration and specialization. Attitudes towards research are part of that package. The assertion can be argued only by combining bits and pieces of evidence.

From the responses to the survey questions (Table 5), a profile of the Liberal Arts I professor begins to emerge. First, values have a place in education. Compared to university professors, a higher percentage of Liberal Arts I professors believe that from moral values, self-knowledge, and a tolerance for diversity are "very important" undergraduate goals. A much greater percentage believe their institutions perform an "excellent" job in teaching values.

Second, practical education, if that is defined as imparting knowledge directly useful for a career, is not a central concern. Compared again to university professors, liberal arts professors do

Table 5. Profile of Faculty Attitudes

Sector	Research I Universities	Research II Universities	Liberal Arts I Colleges
1. *Percent Who Strongly Agreed or Agreed with Reservations:*			
a. Undergraduate education would be improved if less emphasis on specialized training, more on broad liberal arts.	50.6	53.2	70.7
b. Prefer teaching undergraduates with a clear idea of career plan.	41.3	43.5	20.1
2. *Percent Who Consider the Following to be "Very Important" Goals of Undergraduate Education:*			
a. Appreciation for literature and arts	40.8	44.6	70.7
b. Development of firm moral values	35.5	37.5	47.7
c. Preparation for career	26.3	30.5	14.2
d. Tolerance for diversity	58.4	64.0	77.0
e. Acquiring self-knowledge	53.4	57.0	65.4
3. *Percent Who Judge Their Institutions to be Doing an "Excellent" Job in the Following Areas:*			
a. General education	20.9	13.2	64.0
b. Vocational training	28.0	16.7	16.6
c. Allows students to express personal interests through electives	19.7	12.7	46.3
d. Allows students to express personal interests/arts	16.1	12.7	46.3
e. Teaches values	6.3	4.8	27.8

SOURCE: 1985 Carnegie Faculty Survey. Used with permission.

not prefer teaching undergraduates with a clear idea of their career plans and only a few think their institution performs an excellent job in vocational training.

Finally, although knowledge in a particular area is important for students, knowledge of other subjects is also highly valued. Higher percentages of liberal arts professors think an appreciation for literature and the arts is a very important undergraduate goal and that undergraduate education would be improved if there were less emphasis on specialized training and more on a broad liberal education. Perhaps most striking, liberal arts professors have more confidence in their institutions' ability to impart a general education and to provide opportunities for students to express personal interests. These attitudes, some starkly different from the universities, some not so different, form the first part of the argument.

Next we look at qualitative evidence. In a liberal arts college, the members of an economics department felt that teaching and advising responsibilities prevented them from conducting research and reading the current literature. In response the department instituted a policy setting aside one day a week for "future students." By conducting research—which would mean time away from their current students—the faculty could acquire the skills necessary to teach later generations. Another "student-capital" reason for research was frequently mentioned. Undergraduates in Liberal Arts I colleges, especially those students in the sciences, are often called upon to do research, whether for an honors program or as a basic graduation requirement. Professors consider it imperative to serve as models for these students, because it would be somewhat hypocritical to encourage research while not engaging in it. Research, to put it another way, fulfilled educational goals.

Whether it was a concern for future generations or current apprentices, the liberal arts professors justified their research as a benefit to students as well as a contribution to their peers outside the college. Undoubtedly, they conduct research because they choose to do so. But the choice derives from a complex set of reasons, one of the most salient being that students learn by actually searching for knowledge and that professors teach these skills by demonstrating them. Scholarship promotes the students' intellectual development if properly conducted and carefully crafted it would also, conveniently, advance the professor's field of study.

Blending the interview and survey responses provides an additional observation. If research is justified as an investment in students and if the view of student education is slightly different in liberal arts colleges than in research universities, then the nature of the research, to the extent that it is linked to the student's education, will differ from that in research universities. There is little empirical information about the influence of organization setting on the choice of research topics, but the responses from the professors suggest that the topics will reflect the values of the institution. For a liberal arts professor, the standard for credible research is not only peer acceptability but also use of the research in the undergraduate classroom. As mentioned already, the relationship of the liberal arts professors to the discipline, compared to their university counterparts, is not as tight; their students are also influential. Thus, the marginal contribution to the literature is not pursued; the emphasis is on major, reflective publications; the insightful synthesis ranks alongside the purely original formulation; and student involvement is encouraged.

Faculty in Liberal Arts I colleges must achieve a balance between the specialization required to perform credible research and the breadth required to translate the material for students. In weighing the two demands the latter is usually treated more carefully. A literature professor decried the excessive specialization that made it impossible to talk to students or even colleagues. Another respondent defined an outstanding academic as someone having an "ability to see outside the framework of one's discipline . . . and to empathize directly and quickly with students who do not understand what you are saying or talking about." A political scientist acknowledged that "writing for one's peers constitutes a kind of intellectual discipline," but teaching was a "real activity: The opening and exposing of minds is something that is necessary and constantly beneficial."

Conclusions

Sociologists debate whether the academic profession is a single profession or an awkward conglomerate of many separate professions, whether the different types of colleges and universities will give rise to disparate professional outlooks, and whether the centrifugal forces of the specialized disciplines will dissolve any common core. Is the profession "one or many?" Comparing faculty in research universities and selective liberal arts colleges is an especially appropriate way to answer the question. Previous studies found strong links between the faculties despite widely different organizational environments. This strengthened the position of the "one" advocates: in the midst of competing organizational missions, academics preserved a common bond.

Although some links remain, there are also important differences in professional outlooks and behaviors of the faculty. And because of developments in science beyond the control of higher education, those differences are likely to increase, suggesting that the profession will slowly but inevitably tolerate distinctive models for performance across the sectors. Scholarship will not lose its sacredness, but each sector might develop variations on the research university model of scholarship, accepting broader definitions of "a contribution to the discipline," and rejecting the characteristics of university scholarship inappropriate in other sectors.

The consequences of such an evolution go beyond the ivory towers, influencing relationships between the colleges and their constituencies. For example, a recent study of science in the selective liberal arts colleges (called "research colleges" in the report) described the high level of research among the faculty. The report seemed partly designed to develop a rationale for greater public support. It emphasized, though perhaps not strongly enough, the distinctive forms of scholarship in these colleges, especially the level of undergraduate student involvement and the ease with which faculty crossed disciplinary boundaries [3]. Laying a claim on public resources will necessitate an articulation of distinctiveness. At the same time, however, funding, because of the peer review system, subtly steers scientists towards disciplinary conformity. Liberal arts researchers face a strategic choice between emphasizing their distinctiveness or their conformity. The observations here suggest following the path of distinctiveness: a continuing effort to involve undergraduates in research and a continuing respect but not subservience to the dictates of the disciplines.

The involvement of undergraduates in research entices students into scientific and academic careers. Most academics choose their careers because of an interest in the subject; they first wish to be biologists, chemists, or political scientists, and only then do they realize that college teaching is a means to achieve that end. The undergraduate years mold the unformed interest; and the bachelors degree is the conduit guiding students into fields of study. By including undergraduates in research, the selective liberal arts colleges provide a service that graduate-oriented universities and the large teaching-oriented colleges provided only incidentally.

Moreover, a broad liberal arts curriculum, in theory, fosters a sensitivity for the social implications of research. In a world where science and scientists are moving closer to centers of power, that function should not be slighted. That the selective liberal arts colleges are distinctive in this regard is a hard claim to verify. Research universities and teaching colleges would possibly object. But the liberal arts colleges, more than others, make this goal explicit and deliberately design curricula to meet this objective.

Conditions which foster cross-disciplinary research also distinguish the selective liberal arts faculty from their counterparts. Disciplines will not wither away. They provide standards for conveniently evaluating scholarly work, and perhaps more significant, the means to introduce academics to their career. But as the credibility increases for interpretive, interdisciplinary research, professors in liberal arts colleges will emphasize the advantages of their setting. One of the strongest messages to emerge from the interviews was that these faculty valued the ability "to move around as the mood strikes" and to pursue interesting but possibly unproductive research projects without fear of jeopardizing their position. They were not dilettantes. But the college seemed to allow individuals the discretion to attach themselves to the scholarly world as they saw fit and to choose research out of the mainstream of the discipline. The grip of the discipline was looser than in research universities.

Finally, we return to the larger issue: the impact of a diverse higher education system on the academic profession, for it does appear that distinctive models of scholarship can arise in different sectors. This is not a "deprofessionalization" nor is it a dissolving of the common core which Shils described as the fundamental obligation of all academics. But if the selective liberal arts college develops its own breed of scholarship, that is yet another sign of the complexity of our higher educational system. The academic profession mirrors the diversity of the institutions in which it resides.

References

1. Alpert, D. "Performance and Paralysis: The Organizational Context of American Research Universities," *Journal of Higher Education*, 52 (May/June 1985). 241–81.

2. Carnegie Institute, "Annual Report of the Staff, The Program in Science Policy 1980–81," Washington, D.C., 1982.

3. Davis-Van Atta, D., S.C. Carrier, and F. Frankfort, "Educating American Scientists: The Role of the Research Colleges," A report prepared for the Conference on "The Future of Science at Liberal Arts Colleges," Oberlin College, 9-10 June 1985.

4. Fulton, O. and Trow, M. "Research Activity in American Higher Education," *Sociology of Education*, 47 (Winter 1974), 29–73.

5. Geertz, C. "Blurred Genres: The Refiguration of Social Thought," *The American Scholar*, 40 (1980), 165–79.

6. Jencks, C., and D. Riesman. *The Academic Revolution*, New York: Doubleday Anchor, 1969.

7. Kennedy, D. "Government Policies and the Cost of Doing Research," *Science*, 227 (1 February 1985), 481.

8. National Science Foundation. *Science and Engineering Doctorates: 1960-1981*, Washington, D.C. 1983.

9. _____. *Academic Science: R & D Funds, FY1980*, Washington, D.C. 1983.

10. _____. *Annual Science and Technology Report to the Congress*, 1982.

11. Shils, E., *The Academic Ethic*, Chicago: University of Chicago Press, 1984.

12. Walsh, J., "New R & D Centers Will Test University Ties," *Science* 227 (11 January 1985), 150-52.

Notes

1. In 1973 and again in 1976, The Carnegie Commission on Higher Education developed a typology for the institutions of postsecondary education in the United States. In 1976, 52 were classified as "Research Universities I," 40 were classified as "Research Universities II", on the basis of graduate degree production and federal funding for research, and 146 were classified as "Liberal Arts Colleges I." These colleges had a selective admissions program and granted undergraduate degrees in the liberal arts. Other categories included communities colleges; doctoral granting universities (I and II); comprehensive colleges (I and II); and liberal arts colleges II. See The Carnegie Commission on Higher Education, *A Classification of Institutions of Higher Education*, Berkeley, Calif.: The Carnegie Foundation for the Advancement of Teaching, 1976.

2. The following propositions could vary by disciplines, but it is enough of an initial task to describe the general contours, leaving more precise distinctions for later efforts.

3. Clifford Geertz [5] uses the term in a slightly different context.

Appendix

Methodology

This comparison between the attitudes of liberal arts faculty and research university faculty is part of an extensive study of the academic profession. The study was designed to explore the disciplinary and institutional foundations of the profession. The core of the research consisted of in-depth interviews with faculty members who represented a range of disciplines and institutional types. Also, The Carnegie Foundation for the Advancement of Teaching granted us access to their recent survey of over five thousand faculty members. The responses to the questionnaire complemented the qualitative responses from the interviews.

During 1983–1985, we visited sixteen institutions. The Carnegie classification of postsecondary institutions (1973 and 1976) was the guide for selecting the colleges and universities. On each campus, we selected at least two faculty members (usually a junior and senior member) from each of the following departments: physics, biology, political science, English, business, and medicine. Adjustments were sometimes necessary. For example, not all campuses had medical schools and for those that did, it was necessary to interview several additional faculty in order to understand the complexity of those professional schools. We also conducted several background interviews with administrators, campus faculty representatives, and part-time faculty. The composition of this background sample varied considerably from campus to campus; the purpose was simply to inform the core faculty interviews.

We contacted the interviewees by phone a week or two before our visit. They were promised anonymity and were told that the quote would be identified only by type of institution and discipline (e.g., 'a political scientist at a research university'). Refusals to be interviewed were rare. They occurred most often because of an inability to arrange a mutually convenient time. Only three individuals refused because they simply did not want to participate. Two others did not permit us to tape the conversation. The rest of the interviews were taped, and half of those were fully transcribed. The average time for each interview was approximately an hour and fifteen minutes.

The total interview sample was 236 (169 faculty; 67 background). The sub-samples pertinent to the comparison of liberal arts and research university faculty were as follows:

	Research University I Faculty (3 Institutions)	Research University II Faculty (2 Institutions)	Liberal Arts I Faculty (2 Institutions)	Total
Physics	6	4	4	14
Biology	7	3	4	14
Political Science	6	3	4	13
English	6	4	5	15
Business	6	3	2	11
Medical Care	10	4	—	14
Totals	41	20	19	

The interview format is best described as "structured flexibility." The topics were complex and necessitated more than simple responses. Answers frequently shaded into other topics. The interviewer often departed from the sequence of the interview schedule and still covered the specific topics. The ability to temporarily digress from the sequence but not from the main purpose was critical to the success of the fieldwork.

Kenneth P. Ruscio is assistant professor of social science and policy studies at the Worcester Polytechnic Institute.

PROFESSIONAL CULTURE
AND AFFILIATIONS

Academic Freedom at the End of the Century: Professional Labor, Gender, and Professionalization

SHEILA SLAUGHTER

In this chapter I review the academic freedom cases investigated by the Association of American University Professors (AAUP) between 1980 and 1990, and compare them to those in my 1983 article on academic freedom cases for the decade 1970–1980.[1] Given that challenges to academic freedom shift as historical conditions change, I thought that a comparison between the two decades would be useful, allowing us to see how closely we need to guard established danger zones, and to see if there are new terrains in need of protection.[2] I use a broad construction of academic freedom, similar to that used by the American Association of University Professors.[3] I see academic freedom as encompassing faculty rights to free inquiry under all circumstances and to free communication in the classroom; faculty rights to hire, fire and promote colleagues; and collective faculty rights to self-governance. Generally, I assume that faculty are the heart of the university, and understand that all faculty rights have corresponding responsibilities related to sustaining the common good of the professoriate's teaching, research and service endeavors.

Very generally, there were a number of changes in academic freedom cases during the past two decades. Financial exigency or retrenchment cases accounted for the largest numbers of dismissals of tenured faculty in both decades.[4] In the 1970s, retrenchment was usually preceded by declarations of financial exigency, and was an unexpected, cataclysmic event. In the 1980s, retrenchment initiated a general restructuring of postsecondary education. In the 1970s, gender did not figure in the academic freedom cases; in the 1980s, sex discrimination emerged as a category. In the 1970s, cases related to the student movement and faculty opposition to the war in Vietnam were numerous; in the 1980s, there were fewer cases that turned on the faculty's ideological deviance. Administrative abuse cases, in which administrators arbitrarily and capriciously abrogated faculty rights, occurred in both decades, increasing somewhat in the 1980s.

My analysis of the academic freedom cases concentrates on the cases of the 1980s. I use the cases of the 1970s primarily to illuminate the changes that have occurred. In addition to analysis of specific cases of the 1980s, I try to contextualize these cases in broad social and political economic perspectives that have implications for academic freedom. The perspectives to which I give most mention are: (1) challenges to academic freedom that result from concentration of decision-making powers in university management; (2) threats to academic freedom that arise from a broad restructuring of professional labor; (3) problems that stem from contested gender ideologies; (4) difficulties created by the failure of faculty professionalization to curb or counter administrative exercise of power, especially at small, non-elite institutions.

Data and Method

The data for this article are all of the cases reported in the Committee A "Academic Freedom and Tenure" section of *Academe* between January 1980 and December 1990. The AAUP is probably the best central, national data source for academic freedom cases. However, the AAUP has several weaknesses as a data source: it is not comprehensive, and it is not the only source. Many violations of academic freedom are probably not reported at all. Although the AAUP investigates complaints regardless of whether or not faculty members who bring them are members of the association, the timorous, deviant or cynical may never contact the Association. Faculty who choose to pursue violations of academic freedom have a number of alternatives to the AAUP. They can resort to institutional grievance procedures. They can litigate. They can turn to unions or other academic organizations, such as associations of learned or professional societies. They can approach the press. Faculty who take these routes usually do not involve the AAUP, and their cases are not captured in this sample.

The cases reported in *Academe* present another problem as a data source; they are not necessarily representative of the complaints received by the AAUP.[5] *Academe* publishes only a fraction of the complaints the AAUP receives. The cases finally reported in *Academe* are the most serious, the ones that the AAUP staff thought were worth pursuing, the ones that could not be settled by informal mediation, the ones that call for a formal investigation by a committee of AAUP members, or the ones that result in censure. However, the process by which the AAUP staff chooses cases for *Academe* probably compensates for their unrepresentativeness and serves well my concern with understanding threats to academic freedom. The AAUP staff selects cases for *Academe* because they illuminate pressing problems facing the academic community.

As I read each of the forty-seven cases from the 1980s, I developed categories based on substantive topics. The development of categories was informed but not dictated by the categories that emerged from my previous study of the 1970s, which, in turn, was guided but not definitely shaped by the historical and sociological literature treating academic freedom cases.[6] The categories for the 1980s cases were retrenchment and program restructuring, administrative abuse, civil liberties, and sex discrimination. The cases were analyzed in terms of years they occurred, the issues involved, the characteristics of the faculty—race, gender, area of specialization—and what they said about power relations within the academy, and then treated in terms of the broader perspectives outlined above.

In the interests of brevity, at the beginning of each section and subsection of this article, I outline what I take to be the important trends in the several cases that constitute a category or subcategory. I select cases to illustrate the points I am making, but do not speak to each case nor to any case in great depth. Those interested in fuller presentation of data can look at the cases themselves, or, for retrenchment or program restructuring cases, at my article, "Retrenchment Cases in the 1980s: The Politics of Prestige and Gender."[7]

The document that constitutes a case—the reporting appearing in *Academe*—was prepared by an investigating committee with the aid of the AAUP staff. An investigating committee usually consists of two or three persons selected by AAUP staff and Committee A members. Their reports are based on examination of available documents and on-campus interviews with the faculty and administrators who are willing to talk to them. In interpreting these reports, I may make judgments and reach conclusions with which the investigating committees, Committee A and the AAUP may disagree.

Retrenchment and Program Restructuring Cases

In the 1970s, financial exigency cases accounted for approximately 10 percent of the AAUP cases, and 85 percent of the firings reported in *Academe*. In the 1980s, financial exigency cases represented 36 percent of such cases, and 81.5 percent of dismissals (see Table 1). In the 1970s, economic justification for dismissals usually involved a declaration of a financial exigency, or a statement that the institution as a whole was in serious financial straits. Substantial numbers of faculty were fired, as was the case with the City University of New York (CUNY), from which roughly one

**Table 1. Number of Cases and Number of Faculty Fired in AAUP
Academic Freedom Cases, 1980–1990**

Category	Retrench-ment/ Program Restructuring	Adminis-trative Abuse	Religious	Civil Liberties	Sex Dis-crimina-tion	Misc.	TOTAL
Number of Cases*	17(36%)	16(34%)	5(10%)	2(4.5%)	2(4.5%)	5(10%)	47
Year	**Number of Faculty**						
1980	04	3	0	1	0	1	9
1981	22	0	0	0	0	2	24
1982	21	2	0	0	0	0	23
1983	30	2	0	1	0	0	33
1984	41	0	0	0	0	0	41
1985	35	7	1	0	0	0	43
1986	10	5	1	0	0	2	18
1987	27	1	1	0	0	1	30
1988	0	2	0	1	1	0	4
1989	0	1	3	0	0	0	4
1990	0	3	0	1	0	0	4
TOTALS	191** (82%)	26(11%)	6(2.5%)	2(11%)	2(11%)	6(2.5%)	233

SOURCE: Academic Freedom cases reported in *Academe*, 1980–1990.

*Number of cases are different from number of faculty because each case may include faculty.

**The number of faculty retrenched in Table 1 differs somewhat from the number in Table 2 because Table 2 records all faculty who received dismissal notices, some of whom are later reinstated. Table 1 reports only those faculty who were clearly dismissed.

thousand faculty were fired.[8] Usually there was some concern with seniority and tenure, as in the CUNY case, in which nearly all the fired faculty were untenured. If more selective cuts were employed, administrators usually felt compelled to cut an entire unit or program rather than a single individual, and to dismiss the most senior faculty last.[9]

In the 1980s, retrenchment was not conceived of as an isolated event unlikely to occur again in the near future. "Retrenchment," as a concept, gave way to "restructuring." Academic managers—presidents, chancellors, provosts and other high level campus or system administrators—no longer declared states of financial exigency prior to terminating faculty. Instead, projected economic difficulties were used to justify firing faculty who were unproductive, a criterion that was variously defined. Academic administrators who engaged in restructuring never utilized across-the-board cuts and were rarely concerned with seniority and tenure. They no longer cut whole programs, but cut selectively within programs. Almost all faculty were vulnerable to consideration for dismissal during restructuring.

The 17 cases of financial exigency involved 190 faculty, 81.5 percent of all faculty fired between 1980–1990. Cases were almost evenly divided between public (9) and private (8) institutions. The number of faculty fired in the public higher education sector was much greater than the private, undoubtedly because of the larger size of public institutions. Four of the 17 institutions, all public, were organized to bargain collectively.[10]

Program Restructuring and Academic Freedom

The most obvious opportunity that program restructuring offered for violation of academic freedom was dismissal under cover of retrenchment of professors whose speech was for some reason offensive to the administration. Although the investigating committees had difficulty proving selective firing under the guise of financial exigency, administrators occasionally were so flagrant in their pursuit of their faculty critics that their intentions were fairly obvious. Sonoma State College provided an example of an administrator who used financial difficulties as a pretext for firing faculty who disagreed with him.

In early 1982, in response to declining enrollments, the president at Sonoma State announced that he was restructuring existing programs to deal with students' shift in interests. To inform the faculty of the dimension of the restructuring proposed, he issued a "jeopardy list" that named fifty-three faculty as candidates for termination.[11] The professors at risk were on the list because their Teaching Services Area (TSA) faced "lack of funds or lack of work."[12] Although the president claimed to honor seniority in dismissals, the flexibility of the unit of retrenchment made determination of seniority difficult. A professor's TSA was determined by the administration, either in individual negotiations with faculty or unilaterally. TSAs were not co-terminous with departments. For example, in biology, the administration could define a TSA in molecular biology and a TSA in conventional biology, keep the former and eliminate the latter. The TSA was essentially a mechanism that allowed the president to consider each faculty member individually.

Professor William Crowley, chair of geography, publicly disagreed with the president about issues pertinent to the football program. Crowley was fourth in seniority in his TSA, and the president decided to keep only three tenured faculty. Crowley was terminated, even though one of his junior colleagues escaped dismissal because the untenured professor was able to transfer his TSA from geography to the "safe area" of computer science. Using the TSA as the unit of retrenchment, the administration was able to rid itself of a senior member of the department who acted as a critic, and keep a junior professor deemed more valuable.

Strategic Planning and Academic Freedom

Eight (47 percent) of the seventeen financial exigency cases explicitly used the planning process to identify faculty for dismissal. Administrators faced with declining enrollments or a marked shift in enrollment patterns used strategic planning to reshape programs by identifying faculty they termed non-productive. Although faculty participated in the planning process, administrators usually had the last word.

Goucher College provided an example of how strategic planning was used. Goucher had wrestled with declining enrollments and a precarious financial situation in the 1970s and had survived by aggressively building endowment and recruiting students.[13] By the early 1980s, Goucher had turned itself around: it substantially increased its enrollment, created a budget surplus and built up a healthy endowment. However, institutional projections for the 1980s indicated that the future was perilous. The president interpreted this data to mean that Goucher could survive the 1980s only by getting rid of classes in low enrollment fields and by building new programs more attractive to students. The president shared her data with faculty, who interpreted them differently, objecting to making courses' popularity with students the basis of curricular decisions, and questioning the economic necessity for retrenchment. Despite faculty requests for reconsideration of the projection, the president fired five faculty, three of whom were tenured.

Temple University provided an example parallel to Goucher, but at a large, doctoral-granting public institution.[14] The president at Temple, like Goucher's president, saw himself as addressing the future with his plans for faculty terminations. He thought he would preempt future crises by firing faculty in fields with declining enrollments, better preparing the institution for the future. The faculty of the college most deeply affected by the president's strategic planning developed an alternative plan, but it did not satisfy the administration, and thirty-four faculty were dismissed.

Temple was unionized; the AAUP was the collective bargaining agent. The Chapter brought two grievances aimed at halting the dismissals. One alleged lack of faculty participation in the terminations, the other argued that the faculty could have been reassigned to areas related to their expertise. Both grievances went to outside arbitration and both lost, in part because the AAUP had negotiated a relatively weak retrenchment protection clause for the period during which the firings took place.[15]

Through strategic planning, college and university administrations asserted their right to make long-range decisions about the curriculum. The authority to make such decisions was often formally vested in the administration through state administrative codes, as was the case at Sonoma State. In private institutions, as was the case at Goucher College, Boards of Trustees often specifically delegated power to retrench to administrators, excluding faculty from financial deliberations. Although administrators had formal authority for institutional decision making, they were also often bound by faculty by-laws and personnel policies that called for faculty participation in shared governance. The faculty devoted a great deal of effort to these processes. At Yeshiva, Goucher, Metropolitan Community Colleges (Missouri), Temple, and Morgan State, the faculty, through either the Senate or a collective bargaining agency, opposed administrative efforts, offered alternative analyses of institutional fiscal health, and developed strategies for institutional savings that preserved tenured faculty positions.[16] This activity drew on a deep reservoir of creative energy and institutional commitment on the part of faculty. The alternative strategies for retrenchment devised by the faculty were politely received by the various administrations, and largely ignored.

Administrators saw their plans as embodying broad concern for institutional health and for the institution as a whole. In other words, they saw themselves as concerned with student enrollments, work load patterns, the development of new and marketable areas of study, and the preservation of a core of basics. Administrators portrayed faculty as primarily concerned with saving their jobs and promoting their specialties. In the words of the Temple university attorney:

> The AAUP [chapter] seems to be ideologically unable to grasp the notion that it might be eminently reasonable for a university to spend its limited money strengthening academic departments in which student enrollments are stable and rising rather than subsidizing the salaries of faculty members who have no students to teach.[17]

Administrators took the moral high ground and were successfully able to preempt claims to represent the public interest or common good of the institution, while faculty, resting their authority on academic freedom, tenure, and expertise, was represented as a special interest.

Strategic planning posed problems to academic freedom because the process often undercut faculty authority with regard to curricular decisions and faculty review. In effect, administrators took over long-range curricular decision making when they, not faculty, made decisions to expand some programs and cut others. Administrators also reviewed all faculty, tenured or not, when decisions to cut were made, effectively substituting their judgments about hiring and firing for peer review committees' judgments on promotion and tenure.

Part-Time Labor and Academic Freedom

In the 1970s, there were no cases involving the use of part time labor; in the 1980s, there were three. Faculty salaries were the largest fixed cost of an institution. The use of part-time labor allowed institutions to reduce faculty costs significantly. Part-time professionals were paid a fraction of full-time faculty costs, received few or no benefits, and could be laid on or off to meet fluctuating institutional requirements. Part-time professional workers usually performed what were regarded as the most onerous institutional tasks—teaching and grading of undergraduate students.

At Eastern Oregon State College, program restructuring raised the possibility of the institution's rehiring fired full-time faculty on a part-time basis. Professor Carol E. Rathe, Music Education, was one of four faculty who were terminated in program reduction. Initially, she was kept on as a part-time tenured faculty. In other words, she was paid for a fraction of her tenured appointment. She was then reduced to a "teach only" basis.[18] This new status meant that she was re-hired to teach part of her former load, but on a per course basis rather than at a fraction of her former salary. The rationale for the very low "teach only" salary was that she was not engaged in student advising, curriculum planning, supervising, and research. Finally, she was let go altogether.

The case caused a great deal of furor in the college and the system. Faculty passed a vote of no confidence on the president. A state system investigating committee was appointed. The state system committee eventually found that program reduction needed to be more clearly defined, but thought that the specific decision to fire Rathe was justified in order "to maintain strong programs and a sound budget." The faculty at Eastern Oregon State College took a position against tenuring faculty whose load was less than 1.0 FTE, on the grounds that the possibility of part-time tenure for faculty would be an invitation to reduce institutional costs by changing full-time faculty to part-time status. At Temple University the part time labor issue was quite different than at Eastern Oregon State. At Temple, the issue was not change in the status of tenured faculty from full- to part-time, but reassignment of tenured faculty from one area to another.[19] A number of faculty slated for retrenchment at Temple claimed that they were able to teach in general education or in remedial programs, areas in which the university was currently hiring. Indeed, several of the faculty were already regularly teaching courses in these areas. However, the administration did not want to assign (relatively) highly paid, full-time faculty to low cost slots. The administration had a policy that kept the ratio of part to full-time faculty high in order to reduce costs through the use of graduate students and full-time non-tenured staff. At the Metropolitan Community Colleges (Missouri) the administration tried to increase faculty productivity by "speed-ups"—eliminating faculty, increasing the teaching load of the remaining faculty, and increasing the number of part-time faculty. Faced with a projected budget shortfall, the administration used strategic planning in an attempt to change the Master Plan ratios of full- to part-time faculty. The trustees and administrators changed the institution staffing parameters so that full-time faculty, who taught 80 percent of the credit hours, would teach 65 percent, thereby creating an excess 21 full-time faculty, who were slated for retrenchment. During a protracted struggle with the administration, lay-off notices were issued to 21 full-time faculty. Several of those faculty, in an attempt to protect their jobs, began working part-time on a substantially lower salary scale. A number of new part-timers were hired, and "overloads were assigned in most of the disciplines from which tenured faculty members had either been placed on layoff or, while continuing to teach, had been removed from tenured status."[20] Ultimately, the board and the administration compromised on the ratio of full- to part-time faculty, and only eight faculty were fired. In the part-time labor cases faculty were able to contain administrators' attempts to convert numerous full-time faculty members into part-time faculty, but they were not able to halt administrators' increased use of part-timers. The increased use of part-timers often meant speed-ups for full-time faculty. Because part-time faculty were usually hired on a per-course basis, that meant full-time faculty had to give more time to advising students, committee work, planning and curriculum, and supervising part-timers. Every time ratios of part- to full-time faculty increased, full-time faculty workload increased. The increased use of part-time faculty probably heightened the antagonism between part- and full-time faculty, increasing the distance between the two groups, with full-time faculty attempting to codify their rights and privileges in relation to part-time faculty. Indeed, these cases suggested the development of a two tier labor force, one full-time, the other part-time. The full-time tier had benefits and a degree of job security, and was at one and the same time supported and threatened by part-timers, who made full-timers workload possible even as they increased that workload and constituted a reserve labor pool, implicitly challenging the continued security of full-time jobs.

A two-tier work force posed many problems for academic freedom. A two-tier work force often resulted in a divided academy, marked by internal inequities and unequal rights. Faculty in the second tier were generally not incorporated into the system of rights and responsibilities that had evolved for faculty. Increased reliance on second tier faculty for cheap labor meant that few faculty generally had access to tenure and to the academic freedom that accompanies tenure.

Patterns of Preference

When administrators provided rationales for retrenchment and reallocation, they usually talked about productive and non-productive faculty, programs or departments. Generally, they presented cut-backs as a rational response to student choice, which had shifted from the arts and sciences to professional schools and programs. However, none of the administrators advocated making cuts solely on the basis of numbers of students served. Administrators usually took the position that they were able to assess intangible factors, such as quality or centrality, that influenced patterns of reallocation and retrenchment.[21]

In practice, what patterns of preference emerged in the cuts made in the 1980s? Which programs and departments were privileged, which were cut, and why? At first glance, the AAUP sample (see Table 2) suggests that those programs *least* likely to be cut were those best able to position themselves close to the upper end of the market. For example, the physical sciences, medical schools, business schools and law schools were unlikely to be cut. Those programs *most* likely to be cut were those associated not with the market, but with the social welfare functions of the state, as was the case with education and home economics. Fields with an indeterminate and unclear relationship to the market, for example, the liberal arts and social sciences, were also quite vulnerable to cuts.

Although administrators invoked the market as if an invisible hand were making the choices as to which programs would be cut, the workings of the academic market were far from free. Department of Defense spending shaped the demand for scientists and engineers much more strongly than private sector labor force needs.[22] Similarly, the demand for physicians remained high because the supply of doctors was artificially contained by professional limits set on the number of medical students and schools.[23] Fields such as business and law were directly concerned with commerce, but demand for graduates was irregular and uneven. The sometimes considerable distance of these fields from the market was masked by the high salaries and broad privileges that some, but certainly not all, graduates from these fields were able to attain. Moreover, professors within these fields actively attempted to position themselves close to the market, often associating growth and discovery in science with productivity and general prosperity.[24]

The field that was more deeply cut than any other in the 1980s was education. Of the faculty fired in the AAUP sample, 36.7 percent were educators (see Table 2). Like faculty in the sciences and engineering, law, business and medicine, educators often tried to position themselves close to the market, arguing that their services were essential for human capital development and ultimately for increased productivity. However, education was strongly associated with the social welfare function of the state. Indeed, education was singled out by the Reagan and Bush administrations as a signifier of state agency incompetence. Although educators tried to position themselves close to the market, their claims were not taken seriously, even though there was continued strong demand for teachers. Perhaps not coincidentally, teachers were members of the largest and strongest labor unions in the country.

Liberal arts faculty in the AAUP sample, including social scientists, accounted for 36.2 percent of those fired. Faculty in the liberal arts and social sciences generally did not try to position themselves close to the market. Faculty in those fields easily could have made a case for their contribution to productivity, but they usually did not. Instead, new fields, such as communications and media arts, used a vocation rhetoric and the techniques and methods of the humanities, fine arts, and the social sciences, and grew rapidly in the early 1980s. In other words, faculty in some fields, for whatever reasons, chose not to try to position themselves close to the market. These fields were often cut.

The faculty in heavily restructured fields were predominantly male, as were the faculty fired. However, there tended to be more women faculty in the restructured fields than in the unrestructured ones.[25] Education, liberal arts, and home economics and social sciences, all fields that draw many women, both as faculty and students, accounted for approximately 82.9 percent of fired faculty.[26] In terms of students, the heavily restructured fields, with the exception of social sciences, currently at 43.8 percent women, had majority female student populations.[27]

Table 2. Fields Retrenched*

Field	Number of Faculty Cut	Percentage
Allied Health	1	0.5
Journalism, Communication	2	1
Pharmacy	2	1
Mathematics	4	2
Science	5	2.5
Life	4 (2%)	
Physical	1 (.5%)	
Social Science	21	10.7
Agriculture & Industrial Technology	39	19.9
Liberal Arts**	50	25.5
Education	72	36.7
	196+	99.8

*Data were compiled from the dismissals listed by Committee A, "Academic Freedom in Tenure," in *Academe* 1980–1990.

**Includes humanities and fine arts.

The data include all instances in which colleges or universities issued termination notices, regardless of whether or not faculty were finally terminated. The total number of faculty who received notice was 221. The discipline or filed of the faculty was unknown in 25 cases (11.3%) of the total. Table 1 reports only those faculty where field was known.

SOURCE: Sheila Slaughter, "Retrenchment in the 1980s: The Politics of Prestige and Gender," *Journal of Higher Education* 64 (May–June 1993): 250–82.

In sum, those fields best able to represent themselves as close to the market were generally least likely to be cut, even though the strength of these markets often called for a good deal of state maintenance. These were usually the same fields that were best able to provide external resources, resources above and beyond fixed formula allotments, whether through grants or gifts. The fields that were cut were often seen as part of the social welfare function of the state, did not hold out the promise of external resources for their institutions, and tended to have majority female student bodies. The patterns of preference expressed in the AUP sample suggests that full academic citizenship does not extend to fields with heavily female student populations, that faculty in these fields are somehow different, that they do not have the same rights and freedoms of faculty in other fields, given that their tenure is fairly easily abrogated.

Sex Discrimination, Ideologies, and Beliefs

As gender was an underlying element in financial exigency cases, so gender escaped the boundaries of sex discrimination and spilled over into cases concerned with ideologies and beliefs. Gender issues were not limited to equal representation in the academic labor force; they were also at the heart of the majority of cases in which faculty were fired for their ideologies, beliefs and practices. Male and female faculty were dismissed because they explored nontraditional gender issues and questions in public forums, in their classrooms and in their lifestyles. In the 1970s, Committee A did not investigate any sex discrimination cases. In the 1980s, it investigated two (see Table 1). In the 1970s, only eleven women, 5 percent of the faculty in the cases where gender was known, were involved in academic freedom cases. In the 1980s, twenty-one women (33 percent) of the cases where gender was known, were involved in academic freedom cases. In part, the increase in numbers of women in the 1980s is explained by the greater number of women who joined the academic labor force. However, the pervasiveness of gender issues in the 1980s academic freedom cases—whether these were financial exigency cases, as discussed in the previous section, or cases related to ideologies and beliefs—suggests that gender issues go far beyond questions of work force equity and raise questions about the nature of power and authority in the academy.

Sex Discrimination and Academic Freedom

Auburn University provided the only clear cut finding of sex discrimination by the AAUP.[28] The Auburn case brought together some of the issues faced by the first wave of women to enter the academy: problems associated with child rearing, paternalistic treatment, unclear career lines, spousal roles. The AAUP's interest in Lida Mayfield's complaint led to a broad investigation of the status of women at Auburn.

Lida Mayfield was hired by a long time family friend, the chair of the Music department, where her father had worked as an adjunct instructor. She alleged that when she was hired she was told she did not have to get a master's degree. The Dean and the department chair indicated that they had not wanted to pressure Mayfield about the MA degree because she had two small children. Although Mayfield always worked full-time, even while her children were young, the administrators initially classified her appointment as temporary, without informing Mayfield. Over time, the character of the department changed, and the majority came to hold advanced degrees. Mayfield was told she had to acquire one or face termination. She quickly attained an MA and was put up for tenure after having served as a full-time faculty member for 12 years. Her department was very hostile to her, perhaps in part because she had received special treatment from an earlier administration, perhaps in part because Mayfield's husband, an administrator in the School of Education, sat on a committee dealing with the relation between the Music Department and the School of Education and that committee made a decision regarded by the Music Department as detrimental. To Mayfield's surprise, she was not given tenure. The portion of the faculty review available to Mayfield characterized her as a "very difficult person to work with," "lacking in restraint and professional demeanor," "highly opinionated and quite self-serving," as "severe and even abusive" in her criticisms, and as having a "generally uncooperative and uncompromising attitudinal stance."[29]

Mayfield's case illustrated the difficulties faced by women in an institution which defined the normative employees as male. Although she did not opt-out for child rearing, the senior administrators in her department put her on a "mommy track" without consulting or informing her. This treatment, at once patriarchal and preferential, delayed her tenure clock and probably heightened her colleagues' antagonism toward her. Her spouse held a position in which he could and did exercise indirect and negative authority over his wife's colleagues, all without violating any nepotism rules.

Mayfield was probably not a feminist, nor even concerned with women's issues. She may well have filed a sex discrimination charge because such a complaint provided her only hope of redress. Mayfield initially benefited, perhaps even explored her statuses as daughter, wife and mother to gain the support of the administration, and in so doing turned the faculty against her. However, Mayfield's intentions are largely unimportant. What is important is that she had to deal constantly with her gender status, facing issues that men rarely had to deal with at all.

Mayfield was not the only woman to encounter problems at Auburn. The university had over 30 faculty who had served more than seven years who were working full time at the rank of instructor, 25 of whom were women. Shortly before the AAUP investigation of the Mayfield case, each of these instructors had received a letter from the administration, asking them to sign an acknowledgment that as instructors they were untenurable and would never seek tenure at Auburn. A number of the instructors said they thought that if they had not signed the letters, they would have been fired immediately. Although Auburn probably did not treat all women faculty as it did these instructors, a disproportionate number of persons in the instructor category—a category marked by lack of full-time benefits, full-range salary scales and the protection of tenure—were women.

The irregularities in women's faculty positions—indeterminate probationary periods, unclear status with regard to the tenure track, permeable boundaries between work and home—posed problems for academic freedom. As the threatening letter from the Auburn administration suggested, faculty were vulnerable to pressure because of job insecurity. Lack of tenure made those in the instructor category unwilling to speak out.

In the case of Marcia Falk at the University of Judaism, it was difficult to discern what occupied the foreground: sex discrimination or faculty hostility to Falk's religious beliefs, which were intertwined with her feminism. I was uncertain about whether I should put this case in the category of ideological deviance or sex discrimination. I finally opted for sex discrimination, largely because the AAUP investigating committee thought, but could not prove, that sex discrimination was a major factor.[30]

Marcia Falk was a poet, a translator from Hebrew to English, and a feminist. Her scholarship involved re-writing traditional Jewish prayers to include women. The University of Judaism was associated with the conservative wing of the Jewish religion. When Falk joined the faculty, only men, most of whom were rabbis, held tenure. Falk was on the only women ever evaluated for tenure at the University of Judaism.

The committee at the University of Judaism that reviewed Falk was completely anonymous; it never reported to the faculty as a whole, or to a faculty body to whom Falk could appeal. The committee's report on Falk was very negative. The Committee claimed its report was based on Falk's external letters of reference. On the basis of the faculty committee review, Falk was denied tenure.

Unbeknownst to the anonymous faculty review committee at the University of Judaism, four of Falk's referees sent her copies of their letters, as did the remaining two after they discovered she did not receive tenure. Falk read the letters as overwhelmingly positive, as did the AAUP investigating committee. The AAUP investigating committee compared the anonymous faculty review committee's treatment of the external letters with the letters themselves. As an Association staff letter to the President of the University of Judaism put it, one "did not overstate the case in asserting that 'one has difficulty recognizing the letter and the report were discussing the same publications and the same person.'"[31] In other words, the faculty review committee at the University of Judaism had so distorted the external referees' evaluation of Falk that very positive recommendations became negative.

The Falk case suggested the limits of academic freedom as defined by the AAUP. The AAUP rested its case against the University of Judaism on procedure. The AAUP took the position that the faculty review committee should not have been anonymous, that Falk had a right to know the committee membership and to appeal to them. However, Falk's knowledge of the names of the faculty review committee would not have helped her. Only her knowledge of the content of the external reviewers' letters allowed her to challenge the decisions. In the normal course of events, she would have known the names of the faculty review committee, but not the content of the external letters.

She would have appealed to the faculty review committee, and have been turned down. The substance of the case—the deep disparity in judgment between the faculty review committee and the external letters—would never have become public. The Falk case points to the problems in the AAUP's heavily procedural approach to academic freedom, an approach that assumes that the collective conscience of the senior faculty exercising judgment over their junior colleagues is fair, just and wise, especially when junior faculty members differ from senior with regard to gender, beliefs and ideology.

Religious Cases and Academic Freedom

Marcia Falk's case bore a disturbing resemblance to a number of other cases involving religion and gender. In all but one of the religious cases, conservative groups in church administrations precipitated the firing of faculty, or the cancellation of the speaking engagements of faculty who spoke out on gender issues or engaged in practices contrary to religious norms on gender. It was tempting to dismiss these cases as anachronistic, vestiges of a time when higher education was more strongly informed by religious than scientific beliefs. However, the hierarchies or officialdom of the churches in these cases had all at one point expressed a commitment to secular standards of academic freedom, and then pulled back. The faculty in the cases were caught in conflicts engendered by changing standards of belief. These cases seemed to reflect the resurgence of conservative and evangelical forces within conventional churches. The churches involved were those to which the large majority of believers in the U.S. belong—Jewish (Falk, discussed above), Catholic, Lutheran and Baptist.

A comparison between the cases of the 1970s and the 1980s pointed to a greater conservatism and a stronger focus on gender. In the 1970s, there were two religious freedom cases; in the 1980s there were five cases (see Table 1). In the 1970s, the central issue in the two religious cases turned on student and faculty concerns over issues related to social justice and the student movement. In one of the 1970s cases, forty faculty supported a dismissed colleague by declaring a moratorium on classes, eventually establishing a university in exile. In the 1980s, the main issue was gender, and faculty apparently did not collectively protest the dismissals of their colleagues. In the 1980s cases, church hierarchies or officialdom reasserted traditional positions on gender issues, resulting in the firing of six faculty.

The Maguire case turned on women's procreative rights. During the Reagan-Mondale campaign, Professor Daniel Maguire worked with Vice-Presidential candidate Geraldine Ferraro in an organization called Catholics for Free Choice to let voters know that there was more than one position on abortion in the church. Archbishop O'Conner publicly denied the legitimacy of Maguire's position, saying: "There is no variance and no flexibility—there is no leeway as far as the Catholic Church is concerned. . .Pope John Paul II has said that the task of the church is to reaffirm that abortion is death."[32] The head of the Vatican's Sacred Congregation for Religious and Secular Studies demanded a public retraction on the part of the priests and nuns involved with Catholics for Free Choice. The priests made a pro-forma retraction; the nuns refused. Maguire, a former priest, refused to retract. Following his refusal to retract, his scheduled appearances at four Catholic institutions were canceled. Although Maguire threatened legal action of breach of contract, all but one of the institutions, Boston College, were steadfast in their refusal to allow him to speak.

At the Catholic University of Puerto Rico, the issue was not belief but practice.[33] Professor Jeannette Quilichini Paz, a tenured professor in English and Foreign language, was divorced. The administration informally advised her that if she remarried in a civil ceremony, she would be fired. She did and was, even though the issue of the sacramental status of marriage was never broached in her classroom or writings. On investigation, the AAUP committee discovered that up to the point of the Quilichini Paz case, the administration at Catholic University had not consistently enforced the informal rule on civil marriages. The Quilichini Paz case represented a reassertion of the Church's traditional position on the sanctity of Catholic marriage, which, like many other religions, made an analogy between the church and the family, likening the head of the church to Christ, and the head of the family to the husband, affirming male leadership. Moreover, Catholic University of Puerto Rico expanded its arena of authority from the university to faculty's private life.

At Southeastern Baptist Seminary, conservatives made a clean sweep in Board of Trustee elections and made a number of changes at the institution, including the non-reappointment of adjunct professors M. Mahan Siler, Jr., and Janice Siler.[34] Both Mahans' connections with the school were severed because Mahan Siler, Jr., was not firmly against homosexuality. His wife, Janice, had taken no public position on homosexuality, but she was treated as her husband's adjunct and not reappointed as well. In its position against homosexuality, the Trustees at Southeastern Baptist were concerned with maintaining traditional gender roles, focusing in this instance on the male rather than the female role.

At Concordia Theological Seminary (Indiana), Dr. Alvin A. Schmidt, a tenured and widely published sociologist, was fired because he taught "false doctrine."[35] He "(a) consistently advocated the view that there are no valid theological or biblical grounds for excluding women from the Office of the Public Ministry of Word and Sacrament, and. . .(b) applied hermeneutical principles and procedures of Holy Scripture which, in the absence of further constraints, would have the effect of substituting cultural relativism for all moral absolutes."[36] At issue was not only gender, but cultural relativism. The seminary was against cultural relativism in general, and against cultural relativism that diminished scripturally sanctioned male dominance of clerical offices, in particular.

Taken together, the sex discrimination cases and religious cases that turned on gender issues revealed the tension feminism and gay liberation have caused in the academy by challenging established gender roles. In religious institutions, where it was still possible to invoke traditional hierarchies, changing gender roles were viewed as threatening established doctrine in which power relations were embedded. The gender of the speaker did not matter. The men who spoke for women's right to choose, for women's right to priestly office, for men's freedom with regard to sexual preference were all punished, with sanctions ranging from abrogation of speaking contracts to dismissal. The ability of men and women to address gender issues in religious schools was sharply constrained, in clear violation of their secular claims to academic freedom.[27]

The 1940 statement of academic freedom exempted religious institutions acknowledging the centrality of particular doctrines to church schools.[38] However, in the 1960s, many religious institutions, among them Catholic and Lutheran ones, voluntarily accepted the AAUP statement of principles in an effort to broaden their scope and approach.[39] In the 1980s, the hierarchies of some of these churches, and the boards of some institutions, moved away from their accommodation to secular codes central to faculty norms. The denominations in the AAUP samples that experienced power struggles between liberal and conservative factions were not isolated occurrences in the 1980s, but part of the broad struggles for dominance between contending groups in these churches. In other words, the question of the sanctity of academic freedom at church-sponsored colleges and universities has been re-opened, and the AAUP may once again have to caution prospective faculty that alternative norms prevail at these institutions.

Politics, Ideologies, and Beliefs

In the 1970s, fifty-five faculty (4 percent of faculty in AAUP reported academic freedom cases) were involved in twenty-two civil liberties or political ideology cases. In the 1980s, two faculty (1 percent of all cases) were involved in two cases (see Table 1). In the 1970s, the cases generally involved faculty participation in the civil rights movement, the student movement, protest against the war in Vietnam, and the black power movement. Faculty who were fired engaged in behavior that ranged from public criticism of political figures and university administrators to flag burning, draft card burning, illegal teach-ins and sit-ins. Among the more famous and notorious cases were the Angela Davis case at UCLA and the Morris Starsky case at Arizona State University. In the 1980s, faculty were apparently less active in social movements and outspoken protest, at least within the university. However, the cases in the 1980s, like many of the cases in the 1970s, reflected the major foreign policy issues of the decade. In the 1980s, these were Central America, South Africa and the Middle East.

Barbara Foley was an assistant professor of English at Northwestern University.[40] She was an ardent supporter of the Sandinista regime in Nicaragua. She thought that allowing Contra leader Adolpho Calero to speak at Northwestern would be countenancing a Fascist rally. She believed that campus events such as the Calero rally were no different from political events held off campus. She thought that heckling and other forms of disruptive audience behavior were acceptable. In other words, she took the position that Calero's right to be heard by the university community did not take precedence over her right to disruptive protest against him. Before Calero's arrival, Foley stood up on the stage and spoke in favor of preventing the rally. When Calero appeared, she participated in the chanting that made it impossible for him to speak. Someone other than Foley threw red liquid at Calero, and the rally was canceled.

Foley faced the Northwestern faculty disciplinary machinery as a result of her actions. The disciplinary committee was disturbed when Foley showed no remorse for her action, but were somewhat mollified when she agreed not to engage in similar behavior again. The punishment the faculty committee arrived at was an official reprimand, to be placed permanently in her file.

At the same time that Foley went before the disciplinary committee, she began the promotion and tenure process. As her case went up the elaborate system, the faculty tried to keep her disciplinary hearing and her promotion and tenure evaluation separate, apparently taking the position that her political behavior should not effect their judgment of her as a scholar. Although the votes on her promotion and tenure were sometimes split at the various levels of the process, there was always a clear majority in her favor. However, the provost turned her down, arguing that he could not separate her "citizenship" from her ability as a scholar.

The faculty was very upset with this decision, and 77 signed a letter expressing their anger. They were convinced that President Weber had made a mockery of the lengthy promotion and tenure deliberations because he had irrevocably made up his mind to fire Foley shortly after the precipitating incident occurred. They thought their deliberations had been spurned.

In fighting against the President's judgment, Foley claimed sex discrimination, arguing that if she had been a man, her behavior would have been evaluated differently. The EEOC gave her the right to sue, probably because Northwestern had a bad statistical record with regard to promoting women. The AAUP investigating committee did not take up the charge of sex discrimination, and did not censure Northwestern, even though the faculty will with regard to the Foley case had been overturned. The cases of the 1970s suggest that Foley was probably not on solid ground when she claimed that had she been a man her actions against Calero would have been evaluated differently, although comparisons were difficult because of the very different numbers of women in the academy in the two decades. Had she been an African-American woman, she might have had a stronger case. In the 1970s, four women faculty, all African-Americans, were involved in cases where they spoke out forcefully or protested against political events. The remaining 51 faculty fired for similar behavior were men.

Northwestern's President Weber probably considered Foley's case particularly egregious because she prevented a speaker from being heard, violating norms with regard to freedom of speech, which are closely related to norms regarding academic freedom.[41] The faculty too were very upset by Foley's behavior, particularly by her lack of remorse. Like President Weber, most faculty were committed to the concept of free speech, regardless of how reprehensible or offensive the words of the speaker. Although the faculty did not condone Foley's actions, they did not take such a harsh view of her citizenship as the president, and defended her right to tenure.

As with the Northwestern case, the SUNY-Stony Brook case involved the administration turning down the advice of faculty on a promotion and tenure decision.[42] Professor Ernest D. Dube was a native of South Africa and an African National Congress member. He was imprisoned on Robben Island for political activity, and released on the condition that he leave South Africa. He did graduate work in cognitive psychology at Cornell University, and then took a job at SUNY Stony Brook, a joint appointment in African Studies and Psychology. On the basis of a student complaint, a visiting Israeli professor accused Dube of linking Zionism with Nazism as a form of racism, of being an anti-Semite and engaging in "gross perversion and blasphemy."[43] The executive committee of the Faculty Senate investigated Dube and found that he had not exceeded the bounds of academic freedom. After deliberating on the executive committee's report, the faculty senate as a whole endorsed the committee's resolution and decision not to pursue the matter further. The New York Jewish community was unhappy with the faculty committee's decision and brought tremendous pressure to bear on Stony Brook's administration to repudiate Dube's position on Zionism. Jewish alumni threatened not to give; legislators threatened to cut SUNY-Stony Brook's budget; Governor Cuomo condemned Dube; the Jewish Defense League disrupted Dube's classes, vandalized his home, and made harassing phone calls.

During this campaign against him, Dube, who had a weak publication record, came up for tenure. By and large, the numerous faculty committees constituted to make and review this decision voted for tenure, on the basis of Dube's citizenship, but against promotion, on the basis of his scholarship. The President turned him down for promotion and tenure, as did the SUNY system Chancellor, Clifton Wharton.

The two political cases raise questions of citizenship and faculty authority. Citizenship is a code word for the intangible factors that go into promotion and tenure decisions. In the two cases, faculty and administration construed citizenship differently. In the Northwestern case, the faculty thought that Foley had not offended the norms of academic citizenship so much as to warrant dismissal; the provost thought she had. In the SUNY-Stony Brook case, the faculty thought Dube merited tenure on the basis of citizenship; the president and chancellor claimed he did not. These cases indicated the limits of faculty power. The faculty had decision-making authority with regard to promotion and tenure delegated to them until the administration disagreed with the decisions that faculty made. At that point, the administration overrode the faculty, and had the bureaucratic and legal authority to do so. Like retrenchment decisions, the administrations' decision in the Foley and Dube cases suggested that faculty were not part of the university management if circumstances departed from the normal. If this is the case, academic freedom is precarious indeed.

Anti-Administration Cases

In the 1970s, thirty-eight faculty (3 percent of those fired) were dismissed for challenging or criticizing the administration on matters relating to management of the institution. In the 1980s, twenty-six faculty (11 percent) were dismissed in sixteen anti-administration cases (see Table 1). Like the 1970s, the 1980s cases centered on faculty efforts to assert or obtain a voice in decision making: faculty wanted a meodicum of professional autonomy. As in the 1970s, the cases in the 1980s were at mid-sized state colleges, small private colleges, and optometry or osteopathic colleges. Again like the 1970s, in the 1980s, when gender was known, men (80 percent) tended to figure in these cases to a greater degree than women (19 percent).

The degree of conflict in a typical anti-administration case was intense and all-consuming, permeating the professional lives of the participants. Conflict was usually prolonged, sometimes continuing for years. In a number of cases, faculty throughout the institutions were drawn into the conflict. The issues were almost always the same. Faculty critical of the administration's management of the institution sought a degree of self-governance. They were fired for their criticism, and for their efforts to inaugurate or renovate forums such as faculty senates and councils.

Illinois College of Optometry was illustrative.[44] Professors Alexander and Shansky, who held Ph.D.s in psychology from University of Washington and Syracuse, respectively, had served the college well over seven years, but were still on term contracts, as were all faculty. They attempted to establish a faculty senate and adopt AAUP guidelines as institution personnel policy.

Alexander was chair of the Faculty Organizing Committee. Alexander and Shansky regularly confronted the administrator who simultaneously held the position of dean and chair of the division in which they worked. They dealt with him in his capacity as dean on issues of curriculum. Given that the administrator did not have a degree in an area related to the division specialization, he was somewhat uncertain of his authority. At a meeting with the dean/chair dealing with curriculum, Alexander and Shansky walked out in protest over the time-frame in which the issue was being handled. The dean's chair and the president warned the faculty members that their behavior was unacceptable, and immediately rescheduled the meeting for the afternoon of the same day of the walkout. Alexander and Shansky claimed prior commitments, did not attend, and were fired.

The charges brought against Alexander and Shansky were "irresponsibility, insubordination, and evidence of an unwillingness to cooperate in furthering the purposes of the College."[45] They were summarily dismissed: "The professors were escorted from the College by uniformed campus security police and were subsequently allowed to retrieve their effects only in the presence of the police and the College legal counsel."[46] The professors filed charges with the National Labor Relations Board, to no avail. They instituted a civil suit, but failed to win a preliminary injunction to forestall dismissal.

A number of the anti-administration cases (5, or 38 percent) were at historically African-American institutions. Like faculty at other institutions, faculty at these colleges were attempting to professionalize, and in the process confronted autocratic administrators. In the years after 1965, the demand for African-American faculty at predominantly white institutions grew, creating many more options than were previously available for them. Faculty with greater market options probably felt more able to challenge administrators.

Talladega College illustrated the problems encountered by faculty at traditionally African American institutions. Howard Rogers chaired the social science division, which sent a memo to the board of trustees, voicing:

their concern . . . the general academic environment at the college and a perceived absence of administrative commitment to open dialogue and communication with the faculty, an absence of administrative concern for the integrity of the academic program . . . , and an absence of any administrative vision for the future of this college beyond mere survival.[47]

The faculty doubted "the capacity of this administration to address these concerns."[48]

The president charged the faculty with attempting to "preempt [his] office" and "circumvent established lines of communication."[49] Faculty complaints about the administration were taken up by the Faculty Concerns Committee, which eventually charged the administration with trying to pack the committee with college personnel who did not have voting status in order to secure outcomes sought by the administration. The Faculty Concerns Committee brought these and other charges to the board of trustees, the members of whom heard out the faculty and then gave full academic support to the president, delegating to him virtually complete discretion for management of the institution. Shortly thereafter, the president terminated the services of Rogers and several other professors who had engaged in criticism of his administration. Two of the professors were locked out of their offices and escorted from the campus by security police. The faculty appealed unsuccessfully to the trustees, and then turned to the courts. The county court judge dismissed their suits, and the case went to appeal.

Whether at predominantly white or at historically African-American institutions, these sixteen cases polarized relations between faculty and administration over issues of faculty autonomy. In many of the cases, the administrations made few concessions to faculty claims to professional status. The administrators treated faculty like "mere employees" rather than like professionals. They charged faculty with "insubordination," "trouble-making," even "sedition." As the AAUP investigating committee remarked in one case, the reasons given by the administration for the dismissals were "more appropriate to a military organization or an industrial enterprise than to an institution of higher learning."[50] The treatment of faculty in these cases seemed designed to illustrate their powerlessness. Boards of trustees emphasized their legal authority over the institutions, the administrations demonstrated their power by using the campus police to supervise faculty as they physically left the institutions, the courts generally refused to recognize professional claims to some degree of participation in government. These administrations, then, defined themselves as management and treated faculty like workers.

In eight of the sixteen cases, the faculty as a whole engaged in some sort of collective action designed to support their fired colleagues. Support ranged from writing letters protesting treatment of the dismissed faculty to administrators or trustees to participating in the organization of an informal caucus or even AAUP chapters. In most cases, the administration was able to use its superior bureaucratic and legal powers to defeat the opposition. In a number of these cases, administrative victories may have been pyrrhic, given that the faculty seemed to divide into relative stable pro- and anti-administration factions, ensuring a high degree of continuing conflict.

Generally, professors have assumed that if faculty obtain the proper credentials and engage in scholarship and expert service, then administrators will give them a participatory institutional voice. In other words, faculty believe that administrators will eventually acknowledge that faculty expertise commands authority, especially in terms of the curriculum, hiring and firing, and academic governance. This benign view of the professionalization process is based largely on the study of elite institutions in periods not marred by social conflict, and does not do justice to the struggle for professional authority in which many professors were and are forced to engage.[51] This view of professionalization minimizes the history of complex negotiations and compromises which faculty at elite institutions have made with administrations in an effort to maintain autonomy.[52] Generally, the array of faculty power bases at elite institutions—positions in associations of learned disciplines, access to external sources of power and status, such as national and international prizes and honors, access to federal and foundation grants, to consulting opportunities—are not figured into conceptions of maintenance of faculty governance and academic freedom. Because of this general lack of attention to the high levels of conflict surrounding efforts at professionalization, central to which is self-governance, faculty, especially those with degrees from research universities who find positions at non-elite institutions, are often unprepared for the viciousness and intensity of struggles over self-governance. By diminishing the degree to which connections with powerful external organizations and agencies, organizational skills and ability to engage in conflict contribute to professional authority, current views of professionalization do faculty a disservice by leaving them unprepared for the conflicts that many will face. And unless faculty are able to achieve a degree of self-governance, they are unlikely to be able to protect their academic freedom.

Conclusion

The seventeen financial exigency cases point to changes that have occurred over the past several decades with regard to faculty rights and privileges, such as tenure and participation in faculty governance. In the mid 1960s, faculty tenure was widely recognized by colleges and universities and in the courts, usually on the basis of personnel policies and Fourteenth Amendment claims. Once granted, tenure was viewed as inviolable, other than for cause or moral turpitude, the first of which was difficult to prove, the second of which was increasingly difficult to define. In the 1970s, tenure as an institution was weakened when financial exigency became grounds for dismissal. However, tenure and seniority remained key criteria for making cuts in the 1970s. In the 1980s, financial exigency cases become reorganization and reallocation cases, seriously undermining tenure. Tenure and seniority did not guide the way in which decisions to fire faculty were made in reorganization and retrenchment cases.

The undermining of tenure that occurred in the 1980s was due in part to university administrators' increased sophistication with regard to tactics and strategies for managing professional labor. In the private sector, the Yeshiva decision, perhaps contrary to its intent, made collective action on the part of faculty almost impossible, clearing the way for university administrators to become primary decision makers. In the public sector, university managers were able to use bureaucratic rules, often embodied in state personnel policies, which vested institutional authority for making decisions about reorganization and reallocation in administrators rather than faculty. Tenure ceased to give faculty meaningful protection because administrators were able to substitute their judgment for collective faculty judgment about personnel and curricula. During reorganization and reallocation crises, administrators reviewed all faculty on criteria that were usually ill-defined and vague, and fired those who were found wanting on the basis of unclear guidelines.

In the 1980s, university managers were engaged in restructuring the professional labor force, using many of the same tactics and strategies that corporate CEOs had used against blue collar labor in the 1970s. In the 1970s, corporate CEOs pushed the blue collar labor force into job loss, speed-ups, give-backs and fragmented labor as a collectivity through increased use of part timers, all of which resulted in the creation of a two tier labor force.[53] In the 1980s, academic administrators pressured faculty into loss of academic lines, heavier teaching loads, reduction of benefits, and the fragmentation of faculty as a collectivity through the increased use of part-timers, all of which resulted in the creation of a two-tier labor force. The general political climate during the Reagan and Bush years favored encroachment on the rights of professional labor. Union-busting in the public sector, exemplified by the PATCO strike, was supported, and the Reagan and Bush appointees on the courts and on the NLRB generally favored management.

Reorganization and retrenchment cases revealed a pattern of preference in firing that reinforced commitment to a conservative status quo. Professors were most frequently cut in fields that had as students the greatest number of new entrants to higher education—women and minorities. Those fields were also often the same fields from which a critique of the status quo had been developed in the 1960s and 1970s—the social sciences and the liberal and fine arts.

Gender ran like a threat through all the academic freedom cases other than the anti-administration category, testifying to the difficulties that the academy has had in incorporating women. In the reorganization and reallocation cases, the fields in which women were mostly likely to concentrate as students were usually the fields that experienced the heaviest cuts. Sex discrimination cases emerged as an AAUP category of academic freedom cases for the first time in the 1980s.

These cases pointed to women's place in academe—in the bottom tier of a two tier labor force, usually in part time positions with few, if any benefits. In the ideological deviance cases, faculty who challenged conventional gender ideology were even more likely to be fired than faculty who challenged prevailing political ideologies.

Finally, many faculty at small, undistinguished state colleges and private liberal arts colleges were unable to secure a modicum of professional autonomy. Their lives continued to be dominated by administrators. Efforts that these faculty made to achieve a role in governance, in hiring, firing and promotion, were interpreted by university officials as insubordination and resulted in faculty dismissals. Although anti-administration cases were a factor in the 1970s, they increased in the 1980s, suggesting that the political climate of the 1980s provided less sustenance for professional labor then the climate of the 1970s.

Overall, the academic freedom cases of the 1980s point to the ways in which threats to academic freedom shift as historical conditions change. The financial exigency and retrenchment cases of the 1970s were replaced by reorganization and reallocation, and a deepening threat to tenure. Challenges to political orthodoxy that characterized the 1970s became challenges to gender ideology in the 1980s. Only the struggle on the part of faculty to gain professional autonomy remained fairly constant, although this struggle may have become more difficult.

Notes

1. Sheila Slaughter, "Academic Freedom in the Modern University," in *Higher Education in American Society*, rev. ed., ed. Philip G. Altbach and Robert O. Berdahl (Buffalo, N.Y.: Prometheus Books, 1987), pp. 77–105.

2. Sheila Slaughter, "The Danger Zone: Academic Freedom and Civil Liberties," *Annals of the American Academy of Political and Social Science* 448 (March 1980): 781–819.

3. American Association of University Professors, *American Association of University Professors: Policy Documents and Reports* (Washington, D.C.: AAUP, 1990).

4. The basis of comparison between the 1970s and the 1980s is between my 1983 article (rev. ed. 1987) cited in note 1, and the data presented in this article.

5. A complaint is the registration by a professor of a suspected violation of academic freedom. A complaint becomes a case when the AAUP staff finds it merits further investigation. Forty-three percent of the 2,135 complaints (1975–1979) received were handled by AAUP staff without ever achieving "case" status. Although 1,312 (57 percent) became cases calling for further probing, only 23 cases (2 percent) were subject to full-dress investigation and public report by Committee A. Even if the 366 cases (27 percent) said to be successfully closed are omitted on the grounds that positive resolution does not result in publication, approximately 70 percent of the cases are unaccounted for. "Report of Committee A, 1978–1979," *AAUP Bulletin* 65 (September 1979): 296. For an explanation of the processing of complaints received by the AAUP see "Report of the Special Committee on Procedures for the Disposition of Complaints under the Principles of Academic Freedom and Tenure," *AAUP Bulletin* (May 1965): 210–24.

6. See, for example, Richard Hofstadter and Walter P. Metzger, *The Development of Academic Freedom in the U.S.* (New York: Columbia University Press, 1957); Robert Melver, *Academic Freedom in Our Time* (New York: Columbia University Press, 1955); Walter P. Metzger, "Academic Tenure in America: A Historical Essay," in *Academic Tenure: A Report of the Commission* (San Francisco: Jossey-Bass, 1973), pp. 93–105; Sheila Slaughter, "The Danger Zone: Academic Freedom and Civil Liberties," *Annals of the American Academy of Political and Social Science* 448 (March 1980): 46–61; Ellen W. Schrecker, *No Ivory Towers: McCarthyism and the Universities* (New York: Oxford University Press, 1986); Lionel S. Lewis, *Cold War on the Campus: A Study of the Politics of Organizational Control* (New Brunswick, N.J.: Transaction Books, 1988); William W. Van Alstyne, "Freedom and Tenure in the Academy: The Fiftieth Anniversary of the 1940 Statement of Principles," *Law and Contemporary Problems Special Issue* 52 (Summer 1990).

7. Sheila Slaughter, in "Retrenchment in the 1980s: The Politics of Prestige and Gender," *Journal of Higher Education* 64 (May/June 1993): 250–82, also provides a theoretical explanation of the phenomenon of retrenchment.

8. Committee A, "Academic Freedom and Tenure: City University of New York: Mass Dismissals Under Financial Exigency," *AAUP Bulletin* 63 (1977): 60–81.

9. Committee A, "Academic Freedom and Tenure: The State University of New York," *AAUP Bulletin* 63 (August 1977): 237–60.

10. J. M. Douglas with B. G. Or, *Directory of Faculty Contracts and Bargaining Agents in Institutions of Higher Education* (New York: National Center for the Study of Collective Bargaining in Higher Education and the Professions, Baruch College, City University of New York, 1990), vol. 16.

11. Committee A, "Academic Freedom and Tenure: Sonoma State University (California)," *Academe* 69 (May-June 1983): 4.

12. Ibid.

13. Committee A, "Academic Freedom and Tenure: Goucher College," *Academe* 69 (May-June 1983): 13–23.

14. Committee A, "Academic Freedom and Tenure: Temple University," *Academe* 71 (May-June 1985): 16–27. Goucher had been involved in the termination of four tenured faculty during efforts to stave off budgetary difficulties in 1974–75.

15. Committee A did not condone the work of the AAUP chapter engaged in collective bargaining at Temple, and castigated the chapter for weakening tenure safeguards.

16. Committee A, "Academic Freedom and Tenure: Yeshiva University," *Academe* 67 (August 1981): 187–95; Committee A, "Academic Freedom and Tenure: Goucher College," *Academe* 69 (May-June 1983): 12–23; Committee A, "Academic Freedom and Tenure: The Metropolitan Community Colleges (Missouri)," *Academe* 70 (March-April 1984): 23a–32a; Committee A, "Academic Freedom and Tenure: Temple University," *Academe* 71 (May-June 1985): 16–27; Committee A, "Academic Freedom and Tenure: Morgan State University (Maryland)," *Academe* 73 (May-June 1987): 23–32.

17. Committee A, "Academic Freedom and Tenure: Temple University," *Academe* 71 (May-June 1985): 21.

18. Committee A, "Academic Freedom and Tenure: Eastern Oregon State College," *Academe* 68 (May-June 1982): 2a.

19. Committee A, "Academic Freedom and Tenure: Temple University."

20. Committee A, "Academic Freedom and Tenure: The Metropolitan Community Colleges (Missouri)," *Academe* 70 (March-April 1984): 28a.

21. For a detailed treatment of administrator's positions on retrenchment see Sheila Slaughter, "Retrenchment in the 1980s: The Politics of Prestige and Gender," *Journal of Higher Education* 64 (May-June 1983).

22. L. L. Leslie and R. L. Oaxaca, "Scientist and Engineer Supply and Demand," in *Higher Education: A Handbook of Theory and Research,* ed. John Smart (Bronx, N.Y.: Agathon, 1993).

23. Paul Starr, *The Social Transformation of American Medicine* (New York: Basic, 1983).

24. Gary Rhoades and Sheila Slaughter, "Professors, Administrators and Patents: The Negotiation of Technology Transfer," *Sociology of Education* 64 (April 1991): 65–77; Gary Rhoades and Sheila Slaughter, "The Public Interest and Professional Labor: Research Universities," in *Culture and Ideology in Higher Education: Advancing A Critical Agenda,* ed. W. G. Tierney. (New York: Praeger, 1991), pp. 187–211.

25. A. M. T. Lomperis, "Are Women Changing the Nature of the Academic Profession?" *Journal of Higher Education* 61 (November-December 1990): 643–77.

26. Agriculture and industrial technology accounted for thirty-nine firings, or 19.9 percent of all firings. Agriculture is usually where home economics is housed. I assumed that half of the firings in agriculture and industrial technology were in home economics to come up with the figure 82.9 percent.

27. National Center for Educational Statistics, *The Condition of Education 1990. Vol. 2: Postsecondary Education* (Washington, D.C.: USGPO, 1990); National Center for Educational Statistics, *Digest of Education Statistics 1990* (Washington, D.C.: USGPO, 1991).

28. Committee A, "Academic Freedom and Tenure: Auburn University," *Academe* 69 (May-June 1983): 24–32.

29. Ibid., 27.

30. Committee A, "Academic Freedom and Tenure: University of Judaism (California)," *Academe* 74 (May-June 1988): 29–40.

31. Ibid., 38.

32. "Academic Freedom and the Abortion Issue: Four Incidents at Catholic Institutions, Report of a Special Committee," *Academe* 72 (July-August 1986): 2a.

33. Committee A, "Academic Freedom and Tenure: The Catholic University of Puerto Rico," *Academe* 73 (May-June 1987): 33–38.

34. Committee A, "Academic Freedom and Tenure," *Academe* 75 (May-June 1989): 35–45.

35. Committee A, "Academic Freedom and Tenure: Concordia Theological Seminary (Indiana)," *Academe* 75 (May-June 1989): 62.

36. Ibid., 59.

37. One of the religious cases did not involve gender ideology. Professor Volenski, a Roman Catholic priest, left the priesthood, and in doing so, lost his job at Seton Hall. Committee A, "Academic Freedom and Tenure: Seton Hall University (New Jersey)," *Academe* 71 (May-June 1985): 28–36.

38. AAUP, *American Association of University Professors: Policy Documents and Reports* (Washington, D.C.: AAUP, 1990).

39. "Academic Freedom and the Abortion Issue: Four Incidents at Catholic Institutions, Report of a Special Committee," *Academe* 72 (July-August 1986): 1a–13a.

40. Committee A, "Academic Freedom and Tenure: Northwestern University: A Case of Denial of Tenure," *Academe* 74 (May-June 1988): 55–70.

41. E. T. Silva and Sheila Slaughter, *Serving Power: The Making of the American Social Science Expert, 1880–1920* (Westport, Conn.: Greenwood, 1984), chapter 2, "Defense of the Expert Role: Social Science Leaders in the AAUP," pp. 273–95.

42. Committee A, "Academic Freedom and Tenure: State University of New York at Stony Brook," *Academe* 76 (January-February 1990): 55–66.

43. Ibid., 55.

44. Committee A, "Academic Freedom and Tenure: Illinois College of Optometry," *Academe* 68 (November-December 1982): 17a–23a.

45. Ibid., 20a.

46. Ibid.

47. Committee A, "Academic Freedom and Tenure: Talladega College (Alabama)," *Academe* 72 (May-June 1986): 7a.

48. Ibid.

49. Ibid.

50. Committee A, "Academic Freedom and Tenure: Illinois College of Optometry," *Academe* 68 (November-December 1982): 22a.

51. See for example, Burton R. Clark, *The Academic Life: Small Worlds* (Princeton, N.J.: Carnegie Foundation for the Advancement of Teaching, 1987).

52. E. T. Silva and Sheila Slaughter, *Serving Power: The Making of the American Social Science Expert*, chapter 2, "Defense of the Expert Role: Social Science Leaders in the AAUP."

53. B. Bluestone and B. Harrison, *The Deindustrilization of America* (New York: Basic Books, 1982); Barry Bluestone and Bennett Harrison, *Plant Closings, Community Abandonment and the Dismantling of Basic Industry* (New York: Basic, 1982). For the way in which movement of capital in deindustrialization affected faculty, see Sheila Slaughter and E. T. Silva, "Toward a Political Economy of Retrenchment: American Public Research Universities," *Review of Higher Education* 8 (Summer 1985): 38–69.

Disciplinary Adaptations to Research Culture in Comprehensive Institutions

DOROTHY E. FINNEGAN, ZELDA F. GAMSON

Many commentators have noted how higher education in the United States became more homogeneous in the 1960s. (Clark 1984; Hodgkinson 1971; Jencks and Riesman 1968; Pace 1974). In a general trend away from localism and single purposes, denominational colleges became more secular, single-sex colleges went co-ed, and teachers' colleges and other specialized institutions broadened their curricula. The exhilaration of expansion during the 1950s and 1960s propelled these colleges to increase public support in the following decades by broadening their missions and curricula.

Absent was a cultural model by which the institutions, transformed by the expansionary period, could articulate their new identities. Older sources of legitimacy became less serviceable, and the transformed institutions sought new markets of legitimacy. The situation was ripe for what Paul DiMaggio and Walter Powell (1983) term "mimetic isomorphism," the imitation of apparently successful organizations. Imitation is likely when organizations have ambiguous goals or face uncertainty about their future or legitimacy. Many colleges and universities during the 1960s and 1970s allowed themselves to be pulled toward what appeared to be the only worthwhile model to emulate: the research culture, or, what we are here calling the culture of scholarship.

The culture of scholarship draws its essential character from graduate faculty in research universities. Through the socialization of new generations of scholars, through invisible colleges of researchers across the country working in similar subdisciplines, and through the peer review of grant applications and publications, these faculty define the content, methods, and research problems addressed in funded projects, journals, and professional associations (Becher 1989; Clark 1987). The preeminence of the culture of scholarship is underscored by almost a century's worth of institutional ranking schemes. These ranking systems ensure not only visibility to those at the top, but they also legitimate an institutional hierarchy based on measures that are closely related to the research culture (Webster 1986).

Through these means, a kind of invisible hand guides the competition for faculty reputation, power, and prestige and, by extension, institutional prestige. Darwin Sawyer noted in his study of career mobility of faculty in ranked research university: "The professional status of an individual is as much an organizational resource in the institutional career of the department(s) which employ him/her as the institutional status of the department is a personal resource in the organizational careers of its members" (1981, 86). Prestige is a resource that enables universities to garner more tangible resources (Sorensen 1989). An institution can offer its prestige by extension to its other constituents who, in return, place additional resources at its disposal. The greater the prestige generated by the institution, the more advantage it has in the competition for research funds, graduate students, and undergraduate enrollments.

No wonder many formerly specialized colleges and universities copied the overwhelmingly successful culture of scholarship. This mimicry became especially apparent during the contraction period of the 1970s when the scramble for resources became intense and the administrators sought new means of support to sustain the level of security and growth of the 1960s. The buyer's market of the 1970s allowed many institutions to hire faculty with more prestigious pedigrees than they had previously attracted (Finnegan 1993; Muffo and Robinson 1981). With them, this new breed of faculty brought a commitment to scholarly work that corresponded to their administrators' desire for institutional prestige. This match resulted relatively quickly in the inclusion of scholarship criteria for faculty recruitment, retention, and promotion (Finnegan 1993; Queval 1990). Through the late 1970s and the 1980s then, the shift toward prestige and scholarship eroded the institutional emphasis on teaching and service in many formerly teaching institutions (Austin and Gamson 1983; Rau and Baker 1989) just as resources became more scarce and public support for higher education began to wane (Massy 1990).

The Conceptual Framework

To this point, we have presented the spread of the culture of scholarship across higher education as relatively straightforward, albeit problematic in its effects. Diffusion, however, is a complex and messy process (Rogers and Shoemaker 1971; Zaltman, Duncan, and Holbek 1973). Ideas and practices developed under one set of circumstances change as they are adapted to other circumstances. The changes occur not only because human beings are endlessly inventive and subversive, but because they interpret the meaning, worth, and utility of the same ideas and practices in different ways. Not only must new ideas and practices be acceptable to the participants and to the unique circumstances of the host community, but the resources necessary to support the new customs must be dedicated as well. When an institution adopts something as new as the culture of scholarship with implications for almost every facet of life of the collegiate organization and its members, we can expect that adoption might be complex indeed.

In this paper, we trace how the culture of scholarship was adopted in four comprehensive universities.[1] Comprehensive institutions are especially germane to understanding the diffusion of scholarship culture because of their historical commitment to teaching and their local or regional orientation. Resources in this understudied sector are typically scarce; and they therefore present an especially difficult situation for the adoption of the culture of scholarship. Because the culture of scholarship is defined by the disciplines and must be implemented in academic departments within the larger organization of an academic institution, we examine how faculty members in two disciplines, English and mathematics, have interpreted and adapted the culture of scholarship. We look at the effects of these interpretations and adaptations—their benefits as well as their costs—on the departments and the four institutions.

We are guided in our analysis by William Sewell's recent analysis of the relationship between cultural schemas and resources (1992). *Cultural schemas* are rules of social life expressed as formal prescriptions, metaphors, or assumptions. These rules exist at both conscious, surface levels as well as at unconscious, deeper levels. *Resources* can be either human or nonhuman. Nonhuman resources are objects, animate or inanimate, naturally occurring or manufactured, that can be used to enhance or maintain power and the schema. Human resources are physical strength, dexterity, knowledge, and emotional commitments that can be used to enhance or maintain power and the schema. Knowledge, according to Sewell, also includes understanding "the means of gaining, retaining, controlling, and propagating either human or nonhuman resources" (1992, 9). In academe, resources therefore include such things as travel funds, released time, equipment, library acquisitions, faculty and staff personnel lines, and perhaps most important within the culture of scholarship, reputation and standing in the academic hierarchy.

Schemas are affected by resources. A schema cannot be judged to have been reproduced or enacted if it is not supported by adequate and apposite resources. Conversely, schemas affect resources by directing and providing meaning for their use. When cultural schemas and resources are mismatched, one or the other will be abandoned, will dissipate, or will be transformed. Efforts to make general education requirements more coherent, for example, provide a sad example of the effects of a mismatch. With the best intentions, colleges and universities periodically pour enormous energy into changing their general education programs (Gaff 1991). But the ambitious programs newly designed are rarely implemented as intended, if at all. General education, as the "spare room" of the undergraduate curriculum (Boyer and Levine 1981, 3), most often does not command the substantial human and nonhuman resources necessary to carry out the cultural schema of coherence. Curricular resources are located almost exclusively in the academic department, whose first priority is disciplinary coursework. General education courses other than those already offered as departmentally controlled requirements end up underfunded. The reward system seldom supports faculty initiative and achievement in this type of teaching. The match between the schema of coherence in general education and the resources needed to achieve coherence is difficult to achieve (Gamson 1992; Kanter, London, and Gamson 1992).

Cultural schemas are generalizable in the sense that they are not simply associated with a particular practice or location but can be applied and extended to a variety of situations that may differ greatly from their origins (Sewell 1992). Resources, on the other hand, are local. The interplay between generalizable schemas and local resources almost guarantees that the process whereby a cultural schema is applied or extended to a new situation is neither orderly nor predictable. What eventually develops may not necessarily be consistent with, or even a good reproduction of, the original cultural schema. As Sewell indicates, "the resource consequences of the enactment of cultural schemas is never entirely predictable"; indeed, "if the enactment of schemas creates unpredictable qualities and quantities of resources, and if the reproduction of schemas depends on their continuing validation by resources, this implies that schemas will . . . be differentially validated when they are put into action and therefore will potentially be subject to modification" (1992, 18). Particular contexts must be examined closely to determine how this process actually works.

We examine the processes of differential validation in our account of how faculty in the comprehensive sector have adopted the research culture. For the purpose of this argument, we define the cultural schema of scholarship as consisting of three main elements: (1) It is based on national, rather than local allegiances, with loyalty to the discipline or subdiscipline outweighing loyalty to the institution; (2) It values research over teaching and service; and (3) It prizes pure over applied research activities (Becher 1989; Bailey 1977; Gouldner 1957, 1958; Ruscio 1986). We demonstrate that this cultural schema has been interpreted and adapted in different ways within the comprehensive institutions we studied. Further, we demonstrate how the four mathematics and four English departments generated and deployed resources to support their versions of the culture of research.

We briefly trace the historical routes to the scholarship culture in the comprehensive sector and in the four institutions. We then discuss differences between mathematics and English as disciplines. Finally, we analyze how these disciplines operated within the four institutions through the departments, how the departments interpreted and adapted the research schema, and what implications the patterns hold for higher education policy.

Methods

We collected our data in a 1990–91 qualitative study of the academic labor market in four New England comprehensive universities and colleges. During the second half of the 1980s, scholars warned of impending shortages of qualified faculty when, beginning in the mid-1990s, unprecedented numbers of faculty would begin to retire (Bowen and Schuster 1986; Bowen and Sosa 1989). In an effort to discover if and how comprehensive institutions—considered by some to be the most vulnerable sector—were preparing for the forecasted retirements and replacements, we joined with two other scholars in 1990 to collect data on recruitment, retention, and retirement practice and planning from faculty members, department chairs, and chief academic offices (CAOs) at the four institutions.

After an extensive telephone survey concerning academic labor market issues with representatives in twelve comprehensive colleges and universities conducted in February and March 1990, the team purposively selected four metropolitan institutions that represented different historical origins within the current comprehensive sector, that were located in several New England states, and that, through the president's assent, were willing to participate in the study. We additionally selected the institutions according to the size of their enrollments and for their vision of the public they served. The two public universities, Technical State and Regional State,[2] enroll 13,000–14,000 students; the two private institutions, Merger and Parochial, enroll 6,000 and 8,000 respectively. One private university, Merger, and one public university, Technical State, have national and even international orientations, while the other private college, Parochial, and the other public university, Regional State, have more regional ones.

The Comprehensive Academic Labor Market Study (CALMS) team,[3] after developing interview schedules for each role, conducted lengthy interviews with 159 respondents: the chief academic officers, deans, and chairs of institution-wide institutional promotion and tenure committees. We also interviewed the chair, faculty from each rank, and search committee chairs in five departments—English, mathematics, management, education, and a fifth department that varied across the four institutions. Interviews averaged two hours.[4] We asked for information, attitudes, and beliefs about the experiences with recruitment, retention, affirmative action, and retirement. We also asked about departmental and institutional planning and responses to the possibility of faculty shortages.

Team members then coded our computerized field notes after extensive cross-checking and analyzed them according to various conceptual perspectives (Gamson, Finnegan, and Youn 1991; Finnegan 1992, 1993; Youn and Gamson forthcoming). For this study, we limited our analysis to the English and mathematics departments to ascertain if the nature of the department's discipline reflected differential patterns of schema adoption. We isolated both faculty and administrative interview responses that identified the actors and circumstances surrounding the shift from the former institutional cultural schema of teaching toward the adoption of the culture of scholarship. We also tagged the resources (or lack thereof) sponsored by the various institutional actors—presidents, academic officers, deans, and chairs—that indicated a range of actions from sustaining to deterring the adoption of the new schema within the departments in the four institutions.

Routes to the Culture of Scholarship

The advent in 1973 of the new Carnegie category of comprehensives followed the almost simultaneous shift by a large number of four-year colleges from single-purpose to multi-purpose missions. Between the mid-1960s and the mid-1970s, the largest changes occurred among institutions that evolved into comprehensives (Birnbaum 1983). These institutions, having traditionally responded to their constituents, also now reacted to fluctuations in the larger American social environment. When national and state recessions diminished available resources, comprehensive universities and colleges reacted at first by retrenching faculty, then by restructuring academic programs and personnel policies. When students demanded vocational preparation and eschewed the liberal arts, these colleges refocused on applied programs (Geiger 1980). When demographic analysts projected smaller traditional-age cohorts in the 1980s, they opened their doors to older, part-time students. To remain competitive in an ever-increasing environment where consumers questioned public expenditures (Singletary 1975), many institutions saw university status as the answer. State colleges, now boasting diversified professional and arts and science schools, became state universities and many four-year independents and denominationals merged with local specialized schools to become universities (Harcleroad and Ostar 1987).

As these shifts in structure and mission occurred, the professional background and nature of the faculty employed at these institutions also changed. When faculty shortages in the early to mid-1960s made it difficult to recruit faculty with doctorates, they hired faculty with master's degrees. By 1968, the academic labor market began to shift to a buyer's market and institutions could attract new faculty with doctorates. Although many of these new recruits brought an interest in scholarship, they were primarily attracted to the teaching role still required by these institutions (Finnegan 1992, 1993).

By the mid-1970s, however, administrators within the comprehensives took advantage of the oversupply of Ph.D.'s to advance the standing of their institutions by hiring new faculty with more prestigious degrees than their senior colleagues. These new hires were also committed to scholarly work and to the transformation of their institution toward greater scholarship (Muffo and Robinson 1981). It was senior administrators and, in some cases, governing boards, who initially demanded that publications be part of promotion and tenure decisions. But as time passed, the faculty hired in the late 1970s adopted the same value and began to change the norms for faculty recruitment, evaluation and promotion. These bearers of the culture of scholarship encountered opposition from faculty hired in earlier periods and from mid-level administrators who often had to find the resources to support the new orientation.

When a model such as the cultural schema of scholarship is imposed on an organization like comprehensives, the participants may possess a range of assumptions, values, and role definitions that may not be consonant with the new expectations. Further, when the participants within an organization differ in their interpretations and acceptance of a cultural model, they will undoubtedly disagree about the distribution of resources to support it. Such a model has implications for almost every aspect of these colleges and universities. When an institution adopts this schema, we expect that the process might be complex indeed. The adoption of the cultural schema of scholarship served distinct purposes directly related to the changes experienced during the 1970s and 1980s at each of the four comprehensives discussed in this paper. We turn now to accounts of how this happened.

The Four Comprehensive Institutions

The four institutions are examples of several historical streams out of which the current comprehensives flowed. Merger University is an independent university that was established in 1957 when three separate institutions merged. Technical State University, like Merger and many other comprehensives, is an amalgamation of two different institutions brought together in a state system in 1975. Established as a regional public normal school in 1893, Regional State University was authorized to grant baccalaureates as a state teachers' college in 1934, became a state college in 1959, and earned university status in 1983. Finally, Parochial College, a men's college chartered during World War I, which became coeducational in 1970, has been controlled throughout its history by a Catholic men's clerical order. A sketch of how each of the four comprehensives incorporated the research schema provides the backdrop for our analysis of the departments' adaptation to the research and scholarship culture.

Merger University

The story of Merger University, common to many institutions like it, is one of an ambitious president who was hired during the buyer's market of the late 1970s and who raised the aspirations of the university community. Merger University was established when four distinct institutions merged into one university. Each of the four—a baccalaureate college that offered liberal arts and engineering programs, an art school, music conservatory, and a proprietary electronics school—contributed faculty and curricula to create a new whole in 1957. Gradually through the 1960s and 1970s, Merger built a new campus on a tract of land on the outskirts of the city.

By adding new slots and converting part-time positions into full-time ones, the university increased the number of faculty from 170 in 1960 to 396 in 1982. By the end of the 1960s, the university recruited only Ph.D.'s. Hired primarily because of the value they placed on teaching, only a few wrote scholarly papers and textbooks (Finnegan 1992).

As the period of expansion ended, the university seemed directionless. A new president was hired in 1977 with the charge to invigorate the university. He implemented a strategic plan to enhance the reputation of the university through "upgrading" the faculty; less scholarly faculty were either pressed to retire or denied tenure ([Merger] Planning Committee 1980). Through these tactics, he was able to replace almost one-quarter of Merger's faculty with a new, more research-oriented cadre. New faculty with extensive publication records and degrees from prestigious graduate programs, hungry for a position in the bleak academic labor market, arrived with a research agenda in mind. Their aspirations reinforced the president's, and the atmosphere of the university became more energetic and lively. The criteria for tenure heightened annually from an exclusive focus on teaching to a few publications, and then to multiple publications.

The president succeeded in attracting grants to support curriculum and faculty development projects. For a few senior faculty, these opportunities provided a welcome renewal of dormant skills; for some junior faculty, the projects permitted a modicum of support for their research. But these opportunities were limited to a small group of faculty. More importantly, the teaching load of four courses a semester did not change for most faculty.

Technical University

Technical University followed a more targeted strategy to introduce the culture of scholarship. The institution's roots include both a technical institute and a former normal school, which for seventy-five years had little connection with each other, although they existed in the same industrial city. The promise of a large dowry from the state and the appeal of university status brought the two institutions together in a marriage of convenience in 1975. A series of short-lived presidencies in the years immediately after the merger ensured a continued distance between the two colleges. With the accession in the early 1980s of a strong president, a local man who had held faculty and senior administrative positions in the technical institute, Technical University adopted a unified mission: to build nationally recognized departments in a selected number of scientific and technical fields. This university rode the roller coaster of state funding for public higher education through the 1980s and aggressively pursued national recognition by adding doctoral programs in education, engineering, and computer science and by receiving accreditation for twenty-three professional programs.

From 1975 to 1983, the number of faculty doubled in size. The departments of focus were permitted to recruit nationally recognized scholars. To support this effort, the president shifted significant resources from the humanities and social sciences toward the targeted departments. Dozens of faculty were hired in some departments very quickly, creating a frontier quality that appealed to the academic stars who arrived from all parts of the country in response to promises of research support, lower teaching loads, and the freedom to develop new programs. With these faculty in place, the criteria and standard for promotion and tenure emphasized research and publication. Simultaneously, the commitment to teaching declined.

Regional State University

Regional State University, continually attempting to serve the needs of its regional constituents, has followed the classic pattern of development from normal school through university status. Like many of its counterpart state teacher colleges, it expanded its academic programs after World War II. Its faculty rose from 132 in the mid-1960s to 446 by 1972 (Finnegan 1992).

As a result of fluctuations in the academic labor market, departments hired two distinct groups of faculty. During the mid-1960s seller's market, a master's degree was not an unusual hiring credential. By the early 1970s, however, a terminal degree plus some teaching experience became the standard. Although these later hires were recruited primarily to teach and upgrade the curriculum, they carried on some scholarly activity. These new doctorate-holders paved the way for shifting an institutional culture from prizing teaching and devaluing research toward a greater appreciation of scholarship.

The original pressure to move toward the scholarship schema came from outside the institution—from regents of the centralized state college system. In 1975, the regents began to urge that scholarship be considered along with teaching and service in promotion and tenure decisions. Faculty union negotiators, all tenured faculty with doctorates, forestalled the requirements of scholarship as a separate criterion, knowing how unsettling the change would be to their colleagues. For fifteen years, the regents pressed for more weight to be attached to scholarly activity with small gains during every negotiated contract. In 1990, scholarship was finally separated from service as a distinct criterion for promotion and tenure. By this time, many of the faculty had developed scholarly agendas.

With a state recession in process, a reduction in the four-course teaching load was impossible when the regents initiated the move toward scholarship. The first faculty union negotiators succeeded in getting a course-release program, a set number of credit hours that released some faculty from one course assignment each semester for scholarly work. With few other internal resources to support research, released time has been a prized resource at Regional. Internal competition for released time has benefited faculty who were inclined to write and disadvantaged those who could not or would not do so, thus widening the gap between those who publish and those who do not. Many of the faculty with doctorates have consistently profited professionally from the released-time program, while the senior master's-prepared faculty have carried a full teaching load year after year.

Parochial College

The national trend toward secularization in church-related colleges overlapped with the buyer's market that brought more scholarship-oriented faculty to Parochial College. Parochial was chartered in 1917 to serve the Catholic youth of the diocese and state (McDade 1992). The college opened with a faculty of twelve priests, many of whom spent their entire careers at Parochial. By 1932, four years after the first lay faculty member was hired, one-third of the faculty were not clerics. The shift from religious to lay faculty accelerated during the 1970s at the same time that the college admitted women students. Like many Catholic colleges, Parochial over the years had turned to Catholic lay faculty when they could not fulfill their teaching needs from the shrinking supply of priests and nuns. In 1973, the proportion of clerics on the faculty had dropped to 22 percent.

While Parochial continued to reiterate its mission as a Catholic teaching institution, it discovered in the 1970s that it could hire faculty from well-known universities more easily than it could in the postwar period. The academic vice president during this period, the first layman to hold a vice presidency in the order's colleges, capitalized on the buyers' market to recruit more faculty with doctorates. In the early 1970s, 35 percent of the faculty had doctorates; in the early 1980s, 45 percent did; by the early 1990s, the proportion had risen to 63 percent. The heightened preparation among the faculty had an effect on promotion and tenure decisions, making publications more important than they had been in the past. The actual impact on retention and promotion decisions has not, however, been extensive. Teaching at Parochial is still highly prized and good teachers with a minimum of scholarly activity have not found rank and tenure difficult to achieve.

Disciplinary Adaptations to the Culture of Scholarship

Although the four institutions have traveled different routes, by the 1980s they were following the same trajectory toward a greater emphasis on research and scholarship. Once the institutional direction was established, the task of translating this new emphasis was left to the departments. They did so in different ways, depending on the discipline involved. As we will demonstrate, mathematics departments were able to adapt the culture of research in ways that were congruent with their institutions' mission and character and with their teaching obligations, while within the English departments, adaptations were more individual than collective. Clues to differences in adaptation are more apparent in the labor market conditions that candidates faced, the nature of the two disciplines, and the cultures of the particular departments we studied. First, we analyze differences between the disciplines of English and mathematics independent of faculty expression within the particular departments and institutions. This general disciplinary discussion forms the context for an examination of the cultures of the English and mathematics departments in our study. We then show how departmental differences, set against disciplinary differences, shape the adaptations to the culture of scholarship.

Disciplinary Differences

Disciplines are demarcated knowledge domains with distinctive epistemologies and methods. They are also cultures that are embodied in the social relations among members. These two aspects of the discipline—the cognitive and the social—can be understood separately, although they interact and influence each other (Becher 1989).

A number of writers have analyzed the distinctive cognitive aspects of the disciplines according to a variety of schemes (Becher 1989; Biglan 1973a, 1973b; Kolb 1981; Kuhn 1970). For our purposes, Tony Becher's (1989) contrast between convergent paradigm and divergent paradigm disciplines is apposite. In convergent paradigm disciplines—primarily the physical sciences and mathematics—members agree widely about the core subject matter to be encompassed by the discipline and about acceptable methods to employ in working with the subject matter. Criteria for evaluating new knowledge are fairly clear and growth is cumulative. In divergent paradigm disciplines, the humanities and several of the social sciences, members hotly debate what constitutes core subject matter and methods. Criteria for evaluating new contributions are complex and diverse. Growth tends to be recursive, returning to old questions and exemplars. In Becher's (1989) metaphor, convergent paradigm disciplines grow like branches on a tree, while divergent paradigm disciplines evolve like an organism.

Social relations among members of the disciplines mirror these cognitive differences. Members of convergent paradigm disciplines exhibit a shared intellectual style and high levels of mutual identity. In contrast, divergent paradigm disciplines encompass a variety of intellectual styles and members exhibit high levels of fragmentation (Becher 1989). The two types of disciplinary paradigms produce different political outcomes. Convergent paradigm "communities are favorably placed to advance their collective interests (since they know what their collective interests are, and enjoy a clear sense of unity in promoting them)." These disciplines command great prestige, while divergent paradigm disciplines are often politically vulnerable and seen as "lacking in good intellectual standing" (Becher 1989, 160).

The differences between convergent and divergent paradigm disciplines is perhaps no more sharply pointed than in the comparison between mathematics and English. Mathematicians feel they share "'common modes of discourse'; universal agreement on 'the notions of proof and definition, and on the criteria for acceptability'; and 'the need for a special talent'" (Becher 1989, 156). While mathematicians often work alone, they talk over their work and their professional disciplinary concerns with their colleagues.

Mathematics as a field has had a flooded internal labor market for the past few years, even though fewer than 1,000 new Ph.D.'s are awarded each year (Cipra 1991). The ratio of applications to job openings swung from 1:2 in the mid-1908s to almost 3:1 in 1991. The profession is also currently struggling with the fact that native English speakers earned only 441 new doctorates in 1989-90 while nonresident aliens earned 464 (National Center for Education Statistics 1992). Several faculty and chairs with whom we spoke voiced concern about the discipline's future labor pool. One chair predicted that within a few years the department's faculty searches would produce no native-born applicants. A middle-aged newly hired white male assistant professor who had spent several years in non-tenure track positions felt that the labor market had become more receptive to him with the increase in foreign nationals.

In an effort to increase a national and diverse faculty, the American Mathematics Society has been urging mathematics departments to encourage more undergraduates, especially women and minorities, to do graduate work in mathematics. Within the departments in our study, a greater acceptance of applied mathematics, pedagogical research, and the publication of teaching materials indicates a conscious attempt to recruit and retain faculty who are concerned with the needs of their students and the traditional niche of the comprehensives.

English faculty live in a very different world. They disagree about almost everything, and this seems to have been true since English departments were first established (Graff 1987). Rather than confronting their differences, English departments have followed the principle of "systematic non-relationship in which all parties tacitly agree not to ask how they might be connected or opposed" (Graff 1987, 8). Becher (1989) suggests that English is "a cluster of related disciplines, rather than a single unity," in which "each of its constituent communities is split, not only between literary critics and linguistic scholars, but also within the former between advocates of conflicting theories—the psychoanalytic approach, deconstruction, structuralism, and the like" (Becher 1989, 157).

The contemporary scene in English brings the additional voices of feminists and multiculturalists, critical theorists and postmodernists, proponents of film studies and popular culture, teachers of writing and rhetoric—all of whom stimulate questions about the genres and periods framework of the traditional literature curriculum. Graduate departments of English began changing in the early middle 1970s, leading to sharp differences between faculty who received their degrees before the 1970s and those who received their degrees during and after the 1970s.

In the 1970s and 1980s, an abundance of well-qualified job-seekers heightened the competition for the limited number of positions available around the country. Nineteen seventy-three was the peak year for English with 1,631 doctorates earned; by 1982, the output stabilized around 940 per year (National Center for Education Statistics 1992). The accumulation of a decade of overproduction of Ph.D.'s in English, however, devastated the market for most graduates.

Gender also divides English departments, for the rapid entry of women into graduate departments of English coincides almost exactly with changes in the curriculum. Four men received their doctorates in English for every woman in 1970; by 1988, the gender ratio reversed with women receiving more degrees than men (Finnegan 1992). As new epistemological perspectives emerged from women's studies and proponents of multi-culturalism, English departments incorporated faculty with diverse disciplinary perspectives and specialties. While the paradigmatic battles are being fought out most fiercely in the research universities, skirmishes have emerged in the departments in the four comprehensive universities as well.

Departmental Cultures: Cohesiveness and Collective Action

The contrasts between mathematics and English as disciplines are strikingly reflected in the departments we studied. Two structural elements of the departments have an impact on how they have adapted the culture of research and capture the resources to support it. Cohesiveness—the degree to which members feel connected to one another through shared emotional or ideological values (Etzioni 1968)—is an internal characteristic of the departments. Not surprisingly, given the disciplinary differences we have discussed, the mathematics departments display higher levels of cohesiveness than English departments. Collective action within the institution—the degree to which the department acts together to advance its goals within the framework of the institutional objectives or departmentally approved small group action—is a characteristic that relates the departments to their immediate environment (Etzioni 1968; Finnegan 1992). Our data suggest that collective action and cohesiveness are associated but independent aspects of life in departments. Two of the mathematics departments act in a highly collective manner within their institutions; two are slightly less collective. In contrast, the faculty in the four English departments characteristically do not act collectively. Instead, faculty act independently to advance their own interests or within short-lived and shifting coalitions.

The Four Mathematics Departments

The mathematics departments[5] are congenial worlds. Faculty members know what they are supposed to do and why they are doing it. Hiring and tenure decisions are made without much disagreement, and the criteria for making those decisions echo throughout each department. Faculty used words and phrases like "I belong, it's home"; "it's a family"; "most of us have grown up [professionally] together" to describe their departments. "We are a friendly department with no built-in hierarchy," a junior faculty member at Parochial said. "I like my colleagues," another commented. "They are decent people." And most junior members feel support from their elders. For example, when a prized untenured ABD faculty member reached the end of the period permitted for his doctoral studies, his degree was in jeopardy and so was his continued employment in the department. However, the senior faculty at Regional pleaded successfully with his dissertation chair for leniency.

Three of the four departments are approximately the same size with thirteen to sixteen faculty members; the department at Technical employs three times as many faculty as the others.[6] Women comprise approximately 20 percent of the faculty in each of the departments and three departments employ one or more minority and international faculty members.

The majority of the full-time tenured and tenure-track faculty in all four departments have earned doctorates; only a few hired in the mid-1960s have not pursued a terminal degree. Some senior faculty arrived at Technical, Regional, and Parochial with a master's degree or as "ABDs" and finished their degrees subsequently. Most of the senior faculty earned their doctorates at the Ivy Leagues (Brown, Yale, Columbia, Cornell) and other eastern research and doctoral universities (M.I.T., Boston College, Lehigh, Connecticut). The junior faculty, hired when the labor market was less congenial for applicants, hail from degree programs at major research universities across the country (Michigan State, Texas A&M, SUNY-Albany, Yale, Cornell, Rhode Island, Brown, Penn State), evidencing recent national recruiting strategies. Most faculty studied in graduate departments that specialized in applied mathematics or concentrated in applied areas within more eclectic programs.

The degree of collective action within the mathematics departments is fairly high; the mathematics departments at Merger and Technical are particularly strong cohesive units, even though their professional profiles differ. The mathematics faculty at Merger has maintained a cohesive culture for almost twenty-five years; the recently retired department chair, who headed the expansion effort in the late 1960s, hired selectively to create a cohesive unit. Subsequent chairs, emulating her model of management, involve the faculty in articulating departmental goals that fit those of the larger university. The faculty's scholarly interests, supported by departmental interest groups established by the current chair, are distributed almost exclusively according to when they were hired: most senior faculty work together on problems in applied mathematics; the mid-cohort, hired in the late 1970s to early 1980s, tend toward theoretical scholarship; and the junior faculty pursue both pedagogical and theoretical research projects (Finnegan 1992). Senior and junior faculty alike head subcommittees or task groups that advance the interests of the department and the university. One junior member, hired for a high-demand specialty and employed on a permanent nontenure line, supervises adjunct faculty, ensuring that departmental curricular objectives are met. An associate professor, given released time and summer support by the department and the university, learned computer applications to facilitate the department's role in a university project to consult with and train local secondary teachers.

Likewise at Technical, the math faculty, only half of whom until a few years ago held doctorates, have responded enthusiastically to one of the president's goals for the university[7] by recently hiring dedicated researchers. Despite the enormous professional gap in their ranks, the faculty act as a unit within the university. By aiming to become a major national department with their own doctoral program, they espouse institutional goals, and for that, a senior faculty member said, "we will let everything else go."

Of the four comprehensives, Technical has advocated the adoption of the cultural schema of scholarship to the greatest extent. Those new recruits who accept the department and university goals, which translates into research and publications, blend in and find support. A junior member explained: "Within the department, we are working together very well. This is a good climate. You ask questions, you need help professionally, they are there. . . . [Senior] members will give up one-tenth of their salaries to [avoid] possible department layoffs."

A former faculty member after being denied tenure secured a position at another New England public comprehensive. An Ivy League Ph.D., he describes himself as "on the leading edge of a hiring wave in the department [in 1985] and was typical of these people in quality of training. . . . I was less intensely research-oriented than [others in his hiring cohort]." The faculty members hired after him had "some personal connection with faculty already in the department or a close overlap of research with a department person. Neither condition held in my case, though my field did correspond to most of those being hired at the time." At the end, his four theoretical math articles and good teaching evaluations were not enough for tenure. "There were all kinds of opportunities to talk about my research. The deans were always offering support for research, travel money, and supplies. I did not pursue it as actively as I might have."

Until recently, the Regional and Parochial mathematics faculty had not defined many collective department goals. Due to Regional's historical roots, the department has maintained its institutional position as a support service to the education school and to a dwindling number of majors. But until recently the department was lethargic. As one senior member stated, "The department as a whole hasn't moved vertically, but everyone has been happy. They have been individuals rather than a department. It should be a team effort." Several textbook writing teams have existed at various times over the past twenty-five years, so that the collective action has been contained in subgroups that support the faculty and their professional needs. Recently, as teacher-education requirements have come under scrutiny and the number of mathematics majors has decreased, the department has begun to formulate collective goals and activities, such as recruiting math majors and solidifying the link to education through setting up a funded mathematics education computer lab.

Of the four institutions, Parochial is the most oriented towards teaching. A senior mathematician noted that the shift toward research began around the mid-1970s but has heated up recently. He explained, "We tenure people for good teaching. Research is primarily for the purpose of promotion. . . . But we will not put any more emphasis on research than we already have. We do not want to turn into a research department." A junior member maintained that "the administration is ambivalent about publishing versus teaching. . . . They want you to do research with no equipment." The most prominent collective activity beyond maintaining a good working environment is preliminary discussions on the merit of a master of arts in teaching for mathematics.

Like many cohesive communities, these mathematics departments have trouble assimilating people who do not "fit in." "Performance is what matters," a junior Parochial faculty member explained, "although there is also your image. There is a little bias around against abrasive, anti-establishment people. They are really conservative here." A personality that is defined as "abrasive" or "self-centered" is not welcome in these departments. Nonconformists either do not embrace the collective values held in the department or do not participate in group action. And the departments react to the nonconformists according to their employment status.

For newer faculty, denying tenure eliminates the issue of lack of fit. A self-reported theoretician at Merger not only failed to publish on his own but refused to join an existing departmental professional interest group that might have lent the support needed to further his scholarship. At Parochial, a specialist with degrees from elite institutions complained that his colleagues "never said that I was doing something wrong—no one! . . . These people have been smiling at me for four years!" He charged that the department never made it clear what he needed to do to gain tenure. Colleagues described him to us as abrasive. Neither man received a department recommendation for tenure and their contracts subsequently were not renewed.

For faculty who are tenured, desirable professional behavior that promotes departmental activity is rewarded, while inaction, rather than undesirable behavior, results in either mild forms of ostracism initiated by the unit or disengagement initiated by the individual. One Regional faculty member, originally a high school teacher with a master's degree, was hired in 1965 and tenured three years later. Currently, one of the few without a doctorate, he is also one of the few who has not been asked to join a textbook writing team, the normative scholarly activity in the department. His bids for promotion to associate rank were unsuccessful until the mid-1980s. Both he and another faculty member who does little research or writing, a 1968 Ph.D. hire, are rarely given responsible assignments within the department and receive little encouragement from their colleagues. On the other hand, at Merger, a senior faculty member, who led the department in scholarship fifteen years ago and has an extensive but now dated list of publications, is no longer interested in research. By choice, he has sought stimulation from moonlighting as an adjunct faculty member in the business school; he participates only in a few department social gatherings.

The definitions of "fit" does not appear to extend to issues of gender and ethnicity. None of the women or the few minorities and foreign nationals in the mathematics departments voiced any discomfort in this respect. All of the departments are actively looking for women and minorities. One senior member at Parochial explained that "the department is 60 percent women students in class and we want the role models. Minorities are very scarce." At the same time, many of the faculty are concerned with the number of foreign nationals who earn Ph.D.'s in mathematics but who usually do not speak English well. "Over the next five years, we will have to be willing to take non-U.S. Ph.D.'s because we do not have the clout of [a local Ivy League] University. . . . But we will insist on the ability to speak English well."

Both women and minorities appear to share with their white male colleagues a common understanding of the discipline, similar intellectual styles, and joint departmental goals. Their full membership is not doubted. Two senior scholars at Regional—the sole woman member until recently and a male naturalized citizen—have collaborated with other colleagues for almost two decades in textbook publishing. The man recently served as the department's elected acting chair, standing in for the woman chair who was on a sabbatical. At Merger, the department has been proactive in an effort to recruit and retain women. An informal recruitment goal to add more women faculty to serve as role models for undergraduate women majors recently has attracted a third woman, who is also an Asian. In several personnel disputes in which the university or college has not decided favorable for women in the department, senior male faculty have championed their causes successfully.

One of the by-products of the collective action and the linkage that these mathematics faculty and departments have to their institutions is institutional acceptance and legitimacy. The mathematics faculty across the four institutions are active on such important university-wide committees as search, promotion, and tenure committees; several have held administrative positions over the years. As we will demonstrate, these linkages and the resulting institutional visibility and approval seem to increase access to institutional resources and thus, become self-reinforcing.

The Four English Departments

English departments, in contrast, are comprised of shifting alliances or of individuals who pursue their own goals. The faculty hold conflicting epistemological perspectives about their discipline, specialties, and professional activities. Collective action, as a result, is almost impossible. At Parochial, sharp divisions among younger scholarly faculty who have been recruited in the last decade and older teaching-oriented faculty have created "a real mess in the department," as a senior faculty member described it. The department is split between the "fundamentalists," the adherents to the traditional canon, and the "pluralists," between the pre-modernists and the modernists (not post-modernists yet!), the humanists and the "anti-humanists." At Technical, faculty described their department as "filled with hatred and riddled with internecine conflict." At Regional, faculty conflicts are "vituperative"; "the harassment of nonliterature faculty is public and emotional with sickening rumors." Departmental relations appear to be slightly more civil at Merger, although mutual respect for professional ability, worth, and productivity is equally lacking and tends to be split according to the length of employment.

The departments range in size from a low of seventeen faculty at Merger to a high of twenty-eight at Technical. Within the Regional and Parochial departments, women represent just under half of the faculty with most at the junior rank. At Merger, the four women (23 percent) span the ranks with two in senior and two in junior positions. Seven of the nine women in the Technical English Department are in the senior ranks. Only Regional and Parochial have hired respectively one or two African American males in recent years, the only minority faculty across the four departments.

Both of the public institutions, Regional and Technical, hired some faculty members with master's degrees during the expansion years of the mid-1960s;[8] although senior in longevity, most of these faculty remain at the assistant rank or have only recently attained the associate level because of their length of service. The majority of the faculty across the departments have now earned Ph.D.'s. Like the mathematics departments, their degrees are from the Ivy League research programs at Yale, Harvard, Brown, Princeton, or from several eastern (Boston College, Boston University, Brandeis, New York University) and midwestern (Wisconsin, Chicago) research and doctoral universities.

The differences of opinion simultaneously that permit shifting alliances to coalesce and prohibit more collective action are entirely professional and result in radically different values and attitudes about appropriate faculty roles and pursuits. The few senior faculty who remain without doctorates or who have few publications tend to be dismissed professionally by most of the newcomers. Among the senior faculty, however, many of the males have managed to wield power mainly through verbal intimidation and positional power. They have resisted change, whether because of an inability to accept new perspectives in the field, a strong commitment to tradition and teaching, an unwillingness to give up their influence, or shrinking access to perquisites as the competition favors the researchers. At Technical, senior males have tried to hold the line against pressures from the larger university to upgrade the department. Unable to take jobs elsewhere or unwilling to leave their tenured, high-salary positions, these "dinosaurs" (as another senior male in the same department calls them) have blocked the hiring and promotion of people, especially women, with prestigious doctorates and scholarly interests. A senior woman brought a discrimination suit against the department in the mid-1970s because "the unstated policy was not to promote women. . . . The power struggles therefore were over promotion, and there was a definite desire to prevent women from being promoted—a real vendetta against achieving women by a small coterie of men who are still around."

The Regional English Department is the most balanced by gender across the ranks but is also perhaps the most battle-scarred of the four. "The senior faculty loathe each other," explained a junior woman. "Sometimes they show it in public. Literally, there have been fist fights in the hall." Some of the senior men are active scholars; others are primarily teachers, several of whom are feeling very disgruntled. Although the senior women in the main have had little power in the department, they joined with several of the active scholars to strengthen their position. A junior male explained: "The way that the women have been treated [in the department] was shameful. The older women [some of whom possess master's degrees only] did not do anything to gain the respect of the men and so [the men] have no respect for their views or positions. The older women did help to get new women in, though. The three new women [all feminists] are powerful and pretty much run the department." Many of the women and junior men pursue interests in both traditional genres and contemporary applied specialties but through the lenses of new epistemological perspectives. A male associate professor, who is "mostly interested in community, both with faculty and students," feels caught between one group of senior males who are "interested in nothing" or those hired after him who are mainly concerned with "the profession-at-large," rather than the university.

At Merger, the primary dispute occurs between teachers and scholars. The senior faculty were hired specifically because they valued teaching above other professional duties, although some actively have pursued scholarship in addition to their heavy teaching load. One senior member, the author of "a high-powered book on style . . . in its fourth edition" assumes that his junior colleagues value his teaching since "I have regular visitors to my lectures and seminars and they take notes." But he cannot figure out what some of his own cohort members do besides teaching: "[A] never did much in writing—what does he do in his personal life? [B] never published. [C] does his teaching and nothing else. Some get unhappy. For example, [D] stopped functioning about the early 1970s." One of these named colleagues says that he was very clear about his aversion to writing when he was hired. Now, he says, "I don't expect to be promoted; I don't like it but it is my choice not to publish."

When the new president decided to "upgrade" the institution in the late 1970s, an entirely different group of faculty were hired. Although the senior and middle cohorts of faculty share professional ties as genre and period specialists, the middle cohort values a life of research and publications and criticizes the quality of most of the senior faculty's scholarly work. A third group, hired since the mid-1980s, are not quite as research oriented; they arrived with fewer publications and more teaching experience. The junior members have brought specialties in newer applied areas of the humanities—film, composition, and western, journal, and travel literature to the department. These specialties have increased student appeal but are disdained by some senior faculty.

Needless to say, the English departments do not act collectively and the new generation has yet to reach the critical mass to develop a consensus about departmental objectives. Provisional faculty alliances form to realize short-term goals, but long-term departmental objectives seem to be impossible to establish, due to strong differences in epistemological opinions. Unfortunately, as Becher has noted, the faculty within these departments often let their "domestic quarrel to erupt into public view" (1989, 160), which only deepens the gulf between colleagues and estranges others in the university at large from the department. Without clear departmental goals, faculty members typically act independently to secure their own goals. Those department members whose activities parallel university interests succeed in attaining their individual professional agendas.

At Regional, the junior faculty have the advantage in the competition for released time to pursue scholarship. Many senior faculty—some of whom have continued to write, albeit not in refereed journals and others who have not pursued scholarship—cannot make a satisfactory case in their applications for released time. Many junior faculty have successfully reduced their teaching loads semester after semester, while senior faculty continue to teach a full load. One associate professor with an M.A., who "get[s] tortured without the Ph.D.," summed up the difference between many of the senior faculty and the junior faculty: "There has been a dramatic shift from service and teaching to 'how can I get ahead in my career?'"

The dedication to individual goals is further reinforced by extra-departmental involvement. Although many senior faculty have been active as union negotiators and faculty senate representatives, mid-level faculty are active on faculty welfare committees (which are not recognized by the Merger administration), bury themselves in nonacademic activities with students, or moonlight at other local universities. Junior faculty, attempting to simultaneously gain recognition across the campus and promote their disciplinary specialties, head campus-wide programmatic initiatives and teach in the university-wide general education program. None of these service activities contributes to the department.

Departmental "fit" is an ephemeral issue. As the departments have become more sophisticated in their hiring strategies, the definition of fit arises out of recruitment. One chair noted that faculty were beginning to recognize the power that department search committees possess. Interest in serving on searches has mounted as philosophical arguments escalate. Although candidates without outstanding credentials are not asked to interview, several junior faculty indicated that informal conversations about sports and mutual acquaintances with certain committee members seemed to make a difference in their hiring. The sustained definition of fit depends on the number of advocates a faculty member can secure both in the department and within the university. Needless to say, a sufficient number of these advocates has to serve on the department personnel committee in a year in which personnel issues are brought forth.

Adaptation to the Culture of Scholarship: Departments and Their Institutions

As we noted at the beginning, the interpretation of a new cultural model depends on the evolving social structure of the organization and the constant interplay between cultural schemas and resources (Sewell 1992). In the case of the incorporation of the culture of scholarship in comprehensive institutions, these forces operate through the relationship between departments and the larger institution. All four comprehensive institutions moved during the 1970s to a greater emphasis on scholarship. Departments and faculty did not usually initiate the shift; senior administrators did. This shift was most evident at Technical and Merger, whose presidents deliberately chose this course in search of greater prestige. The transformation was less obvious at Regional but equally important as its administration responded to pressures from the central state system to raise the scholarly productivity of its faculty. Only at Parochial was the shift toward scholarship initiated by the faculty, and even then, only by a small group of research-oriented people recruited when the college was downplaying its Catholic roots.

How departments interpreted the new institutional emphasis on research varied considerably, and their adaptations refract their interpretations of the research schema and teaching in different ways. The mathematics departments at Merger and Technical have made the integration of research a group effort, backed up by a considerable investment of resources. They have been able to garner these resources from the university because of the prestige and centrality of their discipline, as well as because of their willingness to adapt the scholarship model. These two strongly collective departments are among the most respected and influential departments in their institutions. They are successful in capturing such institutional resources as positions, travel money, space, equipment, and released time. Such departmental influence accumulates and attracts new recruits. "If I can get the [most desirable] candidates on campus," the chair at Merger boasted, "I have a shot at recruiting them." The resources also support retention. A junior mathematician at Technical benefited by departmental leverage. "The department has tried to make the teaching role lighter for nontenured faculty—two courses a semester instead of three."

At Technical, research is clearly dominant and the university will do whatever is necessary to shift its focus to research in certain fields. The "high-flyers" recruited into the Mathematics Department from major universities around the country have been offered larger salaries, a lower than average teaching load,[9] courses in their specialties, and the promise of a new doctoral program in one of the largest mathematics departments in the country. A Technical professor explained additional resources that have spun out of the departmental and university culture:

> I enjoy the work and there are great opportunities here. I have taught the applied math seminar for the last eight years, which is very enjoyable. I put on math festivals which have brought in fifty to a hundred students. I brought the math honor society to campus. I have traveled a lot. I have had a half dozen NSF grants for individualized teaching. . . . I got written up in the [major private research university] Bulletin, which gave me a chance to tie into individualized instruction. That is how I met [major private research university] people like [two prominent mathematicians]. . . . I have also gotten to work with the consortium for math and its application. I have enjoyed it here.

Even with severe cutbacks at the university, members of the Mathematics Department receive support to attend national meetings, buy software, and apply for grants.

While less national in its orientation, the department at Merger is also very ambitious. After receiving seed money from the president, Merger mathematics faculty are now producing a dozen or more grant proposals each year and the effort is beginning to pay off with funding. Some of the grant proposals seek support for departmental activities, while others are aimed at sustaining individual research. At the same time, the department has paid considerable attention to both the faculty's representative interests—to teaching and research. Small task groups ensure the integrity of teaching within the various mathematics specialties, engage in institution-sponsored professional activities serving local and international communities, or promote the research projects of its members primarily through mutual support. University support and an external grant enabled the department to establish a dedicated computerized classroom that not only assists their majors but also facilitates the work of junior faculty who write computer application teaching manuals.

Similarly, even in the very ambitious Mathematics Department at Technical, the faculty recognize that they have to do a good job at teaching. If they do not, the departments they serve—engineering, for example—could offer their own courses, with obvious resource implications for the mathematics department. Indeed, the chair who was brought to Technical to build up the department declared to us that he may have "overshot the mark" and that the department will need to "self-correct" to do a better job with teaching. These two departments engage in strong collective action based on the evolving institutional mission and are able to attract resources, which then support and reinforce the new schema. Collective action on behalf of this new synthesis breeds greater influence, which attracts resources, which reinforces the schema, and so on.

If the cultural schema of scholarship at Technical and Merger's mathematics departments is "Scholarship Is Necessary," the cultural schemas for Regional and Parochial are still very much based in teaching. At Regional, the schema is "Scholarship Serves Teaching," and for Parochial it is "Scholarship Is Nice But Not Necessary." When the majority of the Regional faculty were hired during the second half of the 1960s, pure research was viewed as detrimental to teaching because it took teachers away from the classroom. Through the 1970s, the mathematics faculty, many of whom specialize in mathematics education and several of whom were active in the first union negotiations in which the regents began to argue for scholarship, changed the departmental culture by working in small teams to produce high school and collegiate textbooks. Thus, the faculty were collectively moving in the same direction as the larger institution in its efforts to promote research.

At Parochial, teaching is preeminent and is the basis for gaining tenure. Research at Parochial has grown in importance, especially for promotion but is still not as valued as teaching. As a senior professor at Parochial who maintains an active research program put it, "We don't want to turn into a research department. We cannot and will not keep high-level research people in the future." New hires must demonstrate teaching skills, and most of the tenure-track faculty teach "in the trenches," in contrast to mathematics faculty in more research-oriented institutions, who do not teach lower-division courses or sometimes any undergraduate classes.

Parochial does, however, give individuals the freedom and some resources to carry out their research. A junior member explained, "I have been allowed to teach upper-level courses in the department . . . [and] have also been free to schedule my courses when I want. I teach early in the morning and have time for research and for seminars at [local public university]." Half of the faculty in the department do not have doctorates, and about 70 percent do not conduct any research. Consequently, those who do research, like the junior faculty member just quoted, look to colleagues outside of Parochial but are supported through scheduling flexibility and informal encouragement to sustain their research interest without pressure to publish a certain number of articles.

In contrast to the mathematics departments, the English departments operate as purely administrative units with little collective action. On a national level, faculty in the humanities have been engaged in profound debates about the nature of the canon and the boundaries of the field. Within the daily activities of department members, the process by which these debates appear to be played out fosters power coalitions that fuel mistrust. Individuals, regardless of length of service, pursue their own agendas and/or those of the small coalitions with whom they align on temporary bases.

The more scholarly faculty within these departments emulate the model they know—that of the graduate department in a research university, which emphasizes individual pursuit of professional reputation and achievement and deemphasizes organizational mission and values. "In this department, the kind of scholarship that is acceptable is what people do at Princeton, Brown, and Columbia," an associate professor at Merger explained. Few faculty who engage in scholarship have ways to integrate their research with teaching. This segregation of professional activities has led to even more conflict. When some faculty offer adaptations of the schema to fit their institution, their colleagues have spurned the ideas. In the English Department at Technical, for example, several faculty suggested that the curriculum and the scholarly activities of the faculty be geared to the university mission by offering technical writing, science fiction, and computer applications. Their colleagues vehemently rejected the suggestion.

On the other hand, implementing the scholarship schema within the context of such philosophical disputes has engendered a variety of problems for the English departments. They now have trouble recruiting new faculty who exemplify that schema. Several faculty reported that colleagues with a "graduate school complex" have talked about hiring "exceptional candidates" and "people with national reputations," but they have not succeeded in doing so more recently. The chair of one English Department described "one faculty member on the college promotion and tenure committee who asked whether a candidate was a scholar of national worth. The chances are slim that such people will come to this institution, especially with the growing shortages in fields like composition and rhetoric." Faced with the same issue, a Parochial faculty member said, "We aren't Harvard or Yale, after all."

The English departments also have trouble defining the standards for promotion and tenure that exemplify the scholarship schema. Beyond general agreement that a doctorate and scholarly promise have become more important than in the past for new faculty and that some publication is necessary for promotion, common understanding about the kinds of scholarship they should consider is minimal. "We promote a medievalist for writing a good mystery story or a metaphysical poetry specialist for an article in American literature," complained a senior member of the English Department at Parochial, "because we don't know how to evaluate people." None of the departments is employing external peer review in their promotion and tenure evaluations. Thus, without clear criteria for formal personnel decision, the disputes between faculty about the worth of their colleagues' scholarship tend to occur informally within the departments rather than affecting tenure or promotion decisions. At this point, the inclusion of scholarship as a separate criterion in personnel issues is either so new or so contentious that quantity is the primary standard used to determine professional worth.

Finally, the lack of consensus concerning the scholarship schema appears to reduce the departments' potential for resources. They fare poorly in the competition for university resources. At both Technical and Merger, the cost to the English Department has been enormous. While mathematics at Technical has received additional faculty lines for a national hiring blitz in the last five years, positions in English have been "borrowed" or confiscated by the administration to fill needs in other departments. Similarly, at Merger, mathematics faculty have received seed money from the administration to seek grants, permission to reconfigure their course credit system to reduce the number of courses faculty teach, and support for a dedicated math-computer classroom. The English Department, on the other hand, continues to have the enrollment limits for its composition classes increased by the administration, houses its junior faculty in makeshift hallway offices whose walls do not reach the ceiling, and, due to a lack of secretarial support, expects a junior faculty member to paste mailing labels on the twenty-year-old departmental journal that he edits. At Parochial, the administration has intervened in departmental business, overturning negative tenure decisions and pressing the department to stop its practice of hiring from nearby universities. This kind of administrative intervention is not unusual in English departments, but it is rare in mathematic departments.

Many of the English faculty believe that the lack of resources arises from their local administration. "[The president] says, 'Upgrade', but there is no support to the humanities. It is not [the state's public flagship university] after all. With respect to the humanities, I do not think that [the president] can do what he says he wants to do. There is just not much coming our way, people or library resources." The lack of university support for the departments means that faculty with scholarly agendas must fend for themselves. The most productive English faculty have found collaborators and funding outside of their departments, either at nearby universities or in women's studies or communications programs in their own institutions. At Regional, the feminists in the English Department have successfully developed strong ties with other feminists across the campus and have garnered university resources to organize seminars and workshops for the university and local communities. Yet few bridges span the tenuous coalitions within the department; the resources benefit individuals without effecting positive change in the department itself.

Unlike the mathematicians, whose discipline would seem to be less accessible, English faculty members experience an enormous gap between their teaching and research. Those faculty who engage in scholarship must do it on the side, taking time here and there for sabbaticals and leaves and getting reduced course loads and small grants from the administration. "My scholarship is internationally recognized," said a senior faculty member at Technical, "yet I do not teach in my field." "How can you have people who are scholars as well as teachers if you cannot teach graduate students and if all courses are surveys?" pleaded a junior faculty member. To manage this perceived role discrepancy, faculty divorce their scholarship from their teaching. An associate professor at Merger sighed, "The irrelevance of scholarship is what gets to you. The last time I taught my specialty, I was so depressed. The students couldn't understand what I was talking about." A department chair summed up the dilemma facing faculty at a comprehensive university: "The department is trying to recruit faculty that fit the university and its students, to hire faculty that can produce students who can read, to produce scholarship but not to go wild. However, we don't want to bring in people who cannot get tenured or promoted. . . . How many undergraduates actually come to study specifically with these people? None."

In summary, we have found that the mathematics departments, compared to the English departments in the same institutions, have adapted the culture of scholarship to their teaching and institutional setting. In doing so, they have enhanced their own professional development and served their institutions' ambitions for greater scholarly prestige at the same time. Their convergent disciplinary paradigm provides sufficient direction to develop consensus and enhance collective departmental goals. The profession's concern with its future supply of Ph.D.'s has encouraged the development of applied and pedagogical research, which more closely aligns with the values of the majority of the mathematics faculty and simultaneously satisfies institutional needs. The resulting benefits are both internal and external to the departments. Individually, faculty feel supported, departmental goals are realized, resources for individuals and departmental activities are accessible, and institutional needs are addressed.

On the other hand, faculty in the English departments hold diverse views about their discipline, which prevents consensus about collective goals. Faculty criticize the professional work of their colleagues without having a clear standard for what constitutes scholarship. They may develop ties temporarily with some in the department, but more often they act alone to secure their own goals and resources. As a result, English departments have adopted, but not adapted, the research schema of graduate departments in research universities. Scholarly faculty, then, find integrating research with teaching difficult at best. Without a strong departmental connection with the larger university, the English departments pay a penalty in lost faculty lines and other budgetary support.

Conclusions and Policy Implications

Clearly, the diffusion of the scholarship model to nonresearch institutions has been a complex process. Recent appeals to contextualize research by sector have recognized the mixed nature of the comprehensives (Clark 1987; Ruscio 1987). As we have demonstrated, administrators and institutional governing boards within the comprehensive sector adopted the cultural schema of scholarship to seek legitimacy. To these leaders, imitation or mimetic isomorphism (DiMaggio and Powell 1983) of the successful, prestige-generating scholarship model appeared to be a viable way to build a reputation and to attract resources as their former missions and resource base began to shift.

The opportunity to lay the foundation for this new cultural schema arose when the academic labor market changed in the late 1960s from a seller's to a buyer's market. With a plethora of new Ph.D.'s, comprehensive colleges and universities began to require a terminal degree for new hires, when only a few years before a master's degree was sufficient. These new faculty, unlike their predecessors, were trained to execute research. Although they did not aspire to research careers, many did take scholarship seriously. By the mid-1970s, administrators could take their pick from even more qualified faculty, and many hired faculty with higher research aspirations. These new hires increased the number of faculty who accepted the importance of scholarly productivity. Between the two cohorts of faculty, the model was no longer merely a product of imitation fostered by administrators but simultaneously became a product of diffusion through the faculty who embraced these professional values from their graduate training. Therefore, the new process of adopting the new cultural schema was twice blessed.

But the espousal of a new cultural schema is only one element in its adoption (Sewell 1993); resources are necessary to sustain it. Comprehensive institutions have failed to secure or allocate resources needed to carry out the cultural schema of scholarship. Without adequate resources, an adaptation may be open to multiple interpretations. This study of mathematics and English departments indicates that the adaptation of the scholarship culture differs by discipline. While we make no claims that mathematics and English departments in all comprehensive institutions have responded in a manner similar to those in our study, we do urge attention to certain variables that mediate adaptation of the research culture: (1) the nature and current discourse in the disciplines, (2) departmental cohesion, (3) departmental collective action, and (4) congruence of goals between the department and the institution.

Although faculty as a class of employees within a particular institution have shared similar institutional pressures, our analysis of the mathematics and English departments in four comprehensive universities indicates that different disciplines have expressed these adaptations distinctly. The adaptations appear to reflect the distinctive values and imperatives related to Beher's concept of convergent and divergent paradigms (1989) rather than to the distinct properties of the two disciplines per se. Mathematics, as a hard science, is a discipline that values convergence; the evidence demonstrates that these departments operate through intradepartmental and interinstitutional mission and activity congruence, supporting those faculty who cooperate and excluding those who do not. The departments have managed to bridge the professional concern for the diminished number of undergraduate mathematics majors detailed by their national associations with the changing role demands of their institutions.

They adapted the cultural schema of scholarship by deliberately recruiting and retaining faculty who first of all are equally interested in scholarship and teaching. But second, they have harmonized these two activities with an overarching goal of resolving the professional dilemma. Thus, the departments have pursued goals that have coincided with the ebb and flow of administrative goals for the institution. Many of the faculty have practiced applied and pedagogical scholarship through the encouragement of the department or have engaged in institutionally conceived consulting projects for external constituents. The departments have also backed faculty who pursue theoretical research by encouraging their quest for external funding that would in turn contribute resources to the department. The institutional administrators have rewarded the collective and organizationally supported behavior by conferring and conceding tangible and intangible resources that then reinforce the positive relationship.

In comparison, English is a composite of soft humanistic specializations with different epistemologies, methodologies, and scholarly values. English departments are loose associations of individuals who promote their own agendas and question the legitimacy of other colleagues. Individual faculty pursue goals in support of their specialty and consistently override departmental objectives. Even though many of the faculty consider themselves superlative and caring teachers, their professional allegiances inhibit even discourse on the art of teaching. Departmental recruitment, retention, and the distribution of incentives and rewards rely on individual productivity and temporary coalitions; the distribution of resources within the department and by the institution, therefore, further justifies and affirms the primacy of individual professional achievement. In the end, the contentiousness and resulting lack of common departmental goals preclude marshaling the forces necessary to attract additional resources from university administrators or even to withstand losing existing resources.

Policy Implications

Lessons from this analysis can be drawn for organizational and governance practice, professional socialization, and faculty personnel policies. As higher education moves toward another major hiring period, policy and practice should be reconsidered in light of our findings.

Most obviously, a cultural schema cannot be adopted wholesale without the resources to support it. The diffusion of a model is a more complex social phenomenon than merely deciding that the outcome is attractive. The diffusion of the cultural schema of scholarship occurred because administrators sought prestige and legitimacy and found, as a result of the vagaries of the labor market, an easy means to that end. Institutional upward mobility may have been possible during the 1960s, but we doubt that we shall see this situation again. A strength of the American higher education system is its diversity, yet aspirations for prestige have the potential to destroy that very diversity. It seems more advantageous to define a secure and effective mission that answers the needs of a particular constituency than to imitate poorly the external glamour of another organizational type.

Contextualizing not only according to institutional sector but by discipline focuses our attention squarely on the faculty and on the departments in which they carry out their work. Faculty are socialized to be members of their disciplines; in graduate school, they are steeped in the values, beliefs, and methods espoused by their fields' "invisible colleges." Then, as faculty members, they play out their careers with diverse "work styles, reference groups, objectives, organization of authority, and attitudes" as moderated by their separate institutions (Ruscio 1987, 331). Few gain an understanding of other disciplines at a level sophisticated enough to appreciate the differences among them in the execution of scholarly work. Because no "cross-training" occurs among the disciplines, faculty (and administrators, too, for that matter) may not understand that diverse but legitimate approaches to scholarship influence how faculty manage their organizational life. Further, educating graduate students about differences in mission among the institutional sectors and the different expectations for faculty in them would encourage better preemployment career choices.

We question whether some departments, as a result of their disciplinary proclivities, are ordained to act in certain ways. Do some paradigms lend themselves to more congenial relationships with the larger organization than others? In other words, are some departments doomed to negativity? We think not. Administrators, whether on the institutional or departmental level, can delineate an appropriate schema for their institutional type and, with the collaboration of the faculty, ensure that the schema is widely understood. Then they can assess the relationship between the cultural schema and the resources available to determine to what degree they support or hinder one another. Our analysis shows that the means do exist by which faculty and institutional needs may be met simultaneously. But these means do not surface without careful analysis and collective work. What might work in mathematics departments, for example, may not work in English departments.

Most institutions have established institution-wide retention, reward, and incentive policies and practices. This analysis questions the wisdom of such homogeneity. Few faculty handbooks have detailed specific criteria and standards, and certainly fewer undoubtedly relate to the particular mission of the institution. At least two issues result from this state of affairs. First, faculty personnel policies are intended to provide motivation and reinforcement for certain behaviors. They may promote the intended outcomes for some faculty and some departments. However, these same policies may suppress desirable behaviors in others. Further, they also may encourage competition when resources are scarce and inhibit progress toward collective goals. Personnel policies should advance both the goals of the institution and the professionals it employees. To accomplish this end, policy makers, department chairs, and faculty members should analyze the values implicit in their disciplines and evaluate the consequences that certain types of reward systems have on the development of individual faculty and on the realization of departmental and institutional goals.

Second, when the institutional mission is not used to define the criteria and standards within faculty personnel policies, faculty are actually encouraged to apply the professional standards by which they were socialized, that is, the cultural schema of scholarship. Given the lack of resource support, this application can only be inept. Administrators and faculty must determine the type, quality, and quantity of products (both students and publications) as well as the quality and effect of the process behind those products that express continued professional involvement based on the particular mission of their institution.

As the field of higher education grows, case studies of successful models abound. As we try to cope with an era of scarce resources, proven models become attractive alternatives to current practice. However, the adoption of a model that works in another organization is highly dependent upon the amount and type of resources available in the receiving system. This study suggests that the adoption of a cultural schema that has been successful in one sector is fraught with potential problems for other sectors. Perhaps the answers lie within more often than without.

Bibliography

Austin, Ann E., and Zelda F. Gamson. *Academic Workplace: New Demands, Heightened Tensions.* ASHE-ERIC Higher Education Research Report No. 10. Washington, D.C.: Association of Higher Education, 1983.

Bailey, F. G. *Morality and Expediency: The Folklore of Academic Politics.* Chicago: Aldine, 1977.

Becher, Tony. *Academic Tribes and Territories: Intellectual Enquiry and the Culture of Disciplines.* The Society for Research into Higher Education. Milton Keynes, England: Open University Press, 1989.

Biglan, A. "The Characteristics of Subject Matter in Different Scientific Areas." *Journal of Applied Psychology 57* (1973a): 195–203.

_____. "Relationships between Subject Matter Characteristics and the Structure and Outputs of University Departments." *Journal of Applied Psychology 57* (1973b): 204–13.

Birnbaum, Robert. *Maintaining Diversity in Higher Education.* San Francisco: Jossey-Bass, 1983.

Bowen, Howard R., and Jack H. Schuster. *American Professors: A National Resource Imperiled.* New York: Oxford Press, 1986.

Bowen, William G., and Julie A. Sosa. *Prospects for Faculty in the Arts and Sciences.* Princeton, N.J.: Princeton University Press, 1989.

Boyer, Ernest L., and Arthur Levine. *A Quest for Common Learning: The Aims of General Education.* Washington, D.C.: The Carnegie Foundation for the Advancement of Teaching, 1981.

Carnegie Commission on Higher Education. *A Classification of Institutions of Higher Education.* Berkeley: The Carnegie Foundation for the Advancement of Teaching, 1973.

Carnegie Foundation for the Advancement of Teaching. *A Classification of Institutions of Higher Education.* Princeton, N.J.: Author, 1987 edition.

_____. *A Classification of Institutions of Higher Education.* Princeton, N.J.: Author, 1994 edition.

Cipra, Barry. "Math Ph.D.'s: Bleak Picture." *Science 252* (26 April 1919): 502–3.

Clark, Burton R. *Perspectives on Higher Education.* Berkeley: University of California Press, 1984.

_____. *Academic Life: Small Worlds, Different Worlds.* Princeton, N.J.: The Carnegie Foundation for the Advancement of Teaching, 1987.

DiMaggio, Paul J., and Walter W. Powell. "The Iron Cage Revisited: Institutional Isomorphism and Collective Rationality in Organizational Fields." *American Sociological Review* 48 (1983): 147–60.

Etzioni, Amitai. *The Active Society: A Theory of Societal and Political Processes.* New York: Free Press, 1968.

Evangelauf, Jean. "A New 'Carnegie Classification.'" *Chronicle of Higher Education* 40, no. 31 (6 April 1994): A17–A26.

Finnegan, Dorothy, E. "Academic Career Lines: A Case Study of Faculty in Two Comprehensive Universities." Ph.D. diss., The Pennsylvania State University, University Park, 1992.

_____. "Segmentation in the Academic Labor Market: Hiring Cohorts in Comprehensive Universities." *Journal of Higher Education* 64 (1993): 621–56.

Gaff, Jerry. *General Education Today: A Critical Analysis of Controversies, Practices, and Reforms.* San Francisco: Jossey-Bass, 1991.

Gamson, Zelda F. "The Realpolitik of Reforming General Education." *Proceedings of the Asheville Institute on General Education.* Washington, D.C.: Association of American Colleges, 1992, 70–72.

Gamson, Zelda F., Dorothy E. Finnegan, and Ted I. K. Youn. "Assessing Faculty Shortages in Comprehensive Universities." *Metropolitan Universities: An International Forum* 1, no. 4 (1991): 87–97.

Geiger, Roger. "The College Curriculum and the Marketplace: What Place for Disciplines in the Trend Toward Vocationalism?" *Change* 12, no. 6 (1980): 17–23, 54–55.

Gouldner, Alvin W. "Cosmopolitans and Locals: Toward an Analysis of Latent Social Roles." *Administrative Science Quarterly* 2 (1957): 281–306; and 2 (1958): 444–80.

Graff, Gerald. *Professing Literature: An Institutional History.* Chicago: University of Chicago Press, 1987.

Harcleroad, Fred, and Alan W. Ostar. *Colleges and Universities for Change: America's Comprehensive Public State Colleges and Universities.* Washington, D.C.: American Association of State Colleges and Universities Press, 1987.

Hodgkinson, Harold L. *Institutions in Transition: A Profile of Change in Higher Education.* The Carnegie Commission on Higher Education. New York: McGraw-Hill, 1971.

Jencks, Christopher, and David Riesman. *The Academic Revolution.* New York: Doubleday, 1968.

Kanter, Sandra, Howard London and Zelda F. Gamson. "General Education Reform: Moving Beyond the Rational Model." *Perspectives* 22 (1992): 58–68.

Kolb, David A. "Learning Styles and Disciplinary Differences." In *The Modern American College,* edited by Arthur W. Chickering, 232–55. San Francisco: Jossey-Bass, 1981.

Kuhn, Thomas S. *The Structure of Scientific Revolutions.* 2d ed. Chicago: University of Chicago Press, 1970.

Massy, William F. "A New Look at the Academic Department." *Policy Perspectives.* Philadelphia: Pew Higher Education Research Program, 1990.

McDade, Sharon. "Profile of [Parochial College]." Unpublished manuscript. Boston: New England Resource Center for Higher Education, 1992.

[Merger University] Planning Committee. *Five-Year Planning for [Merger University], A Working Paper.* [River City, New England]: May 5, 1980.

Muffo, John A., and John R. Robinson. "Early Science Career Patterns of Recent Graduates from Leading Research Universities." *The Review of Higher Education* 5 (1981) 1–13.

National Center for Education Statistics, U.S. Department of Education. *Digest of Educational Statistics, 1987.* Washington D.C.: Office of Educational Research and Improvement, 1989, 1992.

Pace, C. Robert. *The Demise of Diversity? A Comparative Profile of Eight Types of Institutions.* Princeton, N.J.: Carnegie Foundation for the Advancement of Teaching, 1974.

Queval, Francoise A. "The Evolution Toward Research Orientation and Capability in Comprehensive Universities: The California State System." Ph.D. diss., University of California, Los Angeles, 1990.

Rau, William, and Paul J. Baker. "The Organized Contradictions of Academe: Barriers Facing the Next Academic Revolution." *Teaching Sociology* 17 (1989): 161–75.

Rogers, Everett M., with F. Floyd Shoemaker. *The Communication of Innovations A Cross-Cultural Approach.* New York: Free Press, 1971.

Ruscio, Kenneth P. "Bridging Specializations: Reflections from Biology and Political Science." *Review of Higher Education* 10 (1986): 29–45.

_____. "Many Sectors, Many Professions." In *The Academic Profession: National, Disciplinary, and Institutional Settings,* edited by Burton R. Clark, 331–68. Berkeley: University of California Press, 1987.

Sawyer, Darwin O. "Institutional Stratification and Career Mobility in Academic Markets." *Sociology of Education* 54 (April 1981): 85–97.

Sewell, William H., Jr. "A Theory of Structure: Duality, Agency, and Transformation." *American Journal of Sociology* 98, no. 1 (July 1992): 1–29.

Singletary, Otis. "Accountability and Higher Education." *Efficiency and Effectiveness in Higher Education: Proceedings of 24th Southern Regional Board Legislative Work Conference, August 1975, Biloxi, Mississippi.* 4–9. Biloxi: SREB, 1975.

Sorensen, Aage. "Academic Careers and Academic Labor Markets." Paper presented at the Ringberg Symposium, Max-Planck-Gesellschaft, May 1989, Schloss Ringberg, Tegernsee, Federal Republic of Germany.

Webster, David. *Quality Rankings.* Springfield, Ill.: Thomas Crown, 1986.

Youn, Ted I. K., and Zelda F. Gamson. "Organizational Responses to the Labor Market: A Study of Faculty Searches in Comprehensive Colleges and Universities." *Higher Education*, forthcoming.

Zaltman, Gerald, Robert Duncan, and Jerry Holbek. *Innovations and Organizations*. New York: Wiley, 1973.

Notes

1. By 1973, a recognizable institutional type emerged out of the multitude of formerly distinctive colleges and universities, leading the Carnegie Commission (1973) to acknowledge the existence of a "comprehensive" sector. According to its most recent edition, Carnegie classifies 532 colleges and universities as comprehensive (or "Master's Universities and Colleges"); slightly more than half are public (Carnegie Foundation for the Advancement of Teaching 1994). In the 1987 classification, the 595 institutions were defined as enrolling a minimum of 1,500 students, graduating more than half of their classes with degrees in professional subjects, and most offer some master's degrees. The 1994 classification (Evangelauf 1994) includes colleges and universities that offer the master's degree as their highest academic award.

2. All four institutions have been given pseudonyms to ensure the anonymity of the faculty and administrators who participated in the study.

3. The research team consisted of Dorothy E. Finnegan, Zelda F. Gamson, Ted I. K. Youn, and Robert Ross. All four team members conducted interviews using the team-generated interview schedules.

4. In addition to the CLAMS interviews, Finnegan interviewed forty additional faculty in three of the five departments at two of the institutions. Those interviews focused on the career lines of faculty in comprehensive universities (Finnegan 1992, 1993).

5. Unless otherwise noted, when we refer to the mathematics or English departments, we are referring to those of all four institutions collectively.

6. Faculty data are deliberately general to ensure their anonymity.

7. The president, in our interview with him, delineated his program for the university dating from 1981, which was to gain accreditation for all possible programs, to balance the graduate and undergraduate programs in a 1:4 ratio, and to develop quality programs in particular areas of the curriculum, especially engineering sciences and management, teacher preparation, and health sciences.

8. At Technical, the faculty who originally were employed by the teachers' college primarily had doctorates, while technical college faculty usually had a master's; however, these degrees came from Harvard, Brown, Boston College, and Ohio State.

9. The junior faculty recruited for their research talents recently had to assume a three-course load due to state budget cuts.

The Ties of Association

Burton R. Clark

In every case, at the head of any new undertaking, where in France you would find the government or in England some territorial magnate, in the United States you are sure to find an association.
—*Alexis De Tocqueville*, Democracy in America

For what to us is the praise of the ignorant? Let us join together in the bond of our scientific societies, and encourage each other, as we are now doing, in the pursuit of our favorite study; knowing that the world will sometime recognize our services, and knowing, also, that we constitute the most important element in human progress.
—*Henry A. Rowland, "A Plea for Pure Science" (1883)*

Individuals who are not bound together in associations, whether domestic, economic, religious, political, artistic, or educational are monstrosities.
—*John Dewey*, Individualism Old and New *(1930)*

American academic specialists do not long remain monstrosities—in John Dewey's vivid imagery—unbound by solid organization that promises to consolidate and further their intellectual effort. They settled a century ago upon the department as their main tool of controlled development inside universities and colleges, a unit primarily centered on individual subjects and devoted to furthering individual disciplines, while it also served as the building block of academic enterprises. But something more was needed to tighten the hold of specialization upon academic life, a device that would serve externally as a carrying mechanism for a discipline at large, a way of furthering specialties without regard to institutional boundaries. By the end of the nineteenth century, American academics en masse found that external arm in the learned society or disciplinary association, a form at once specialized in scope and national in membership and orientation.

Near the end of the twentieth century, we cannot imagine academic life without this type of professional linkage. It serves many interests of academics, idealistic and practical, right down to the "flesh market" realities of job seeking. No academic specialty amounts to anything unless it has a national association, or a section of one—or, as we later see, an "invisible" substitute—to help it develop, spread its influence, and enhance its sense of solidarity. Among the associations operating in 1985, two-thirds had originated since 1940, with 150 starting up after 1960 (Table 4 and Appendix B), clear evidence of the widespread and increasing importance of this form of linkage. Disciplinary associations multiply as fast as specialties develop; they have also begun to reflect the division of academics among institutional sectors.

The Patterns of Association

The first distinction we need to grasp is between associations of professors and associations of administrators. The duality of disciplines and institutions in American higher education is reflected in the division of national associations into those that center on faculty interests and those that are organized around the interests of college and university administrators. Institutionally tied associations are exemplified and semiofficially capped by the American Council on Education (ACE), a "presidents' club" established in 1918 at the same time as the National Research Council (NRC) and the Social Science Research Council (SSRC). All were voluntary associations established to help link higher education and the national government.[1] While the NRC and the SSRC served as multidiscipline associations organized by and for professors, the ACE became an association of universities and colleges, hence administrator-driven, that was to serve, in part, as an association of associations. Its present locale at One Dupont Circle, an edifice in Washington, D.C., houses the headquarters of many other associations in which institutional members are represented by their top administrators, as in the powerful National Association of State Universities and Land-Grant Colleges (NASULGC) that dates itself in an earlier form as far back as 1887, or in which individuals represent a segment of administration as well as their whole institutions, as in the Council of Graduate Schools (CGS), where graduate school deans, committed primarily to the welfare of graduate education, serve as members. The programs of the annual meetings of these associations do not take up academic subjects, other than, occasionally, the minor specialty known as the study of higher education. They explore not Wittgenstein and Weber, but student personnel services and strains of the college presidency. Representing the interests of administrators in the welfare of whole institutions or major parts thereof—and in personal advancement in administrative careers—an entire set of associations runs on a separate track from the discipline-by-discipline representation we find in the faculty associations.

When graduate deans, business officers, admissions officers, presidents, chancellors, and other clusters of administrators represent institutional concerns, their efforts may well serve faculty interests. They may help to increase financial resources and, generally, to enhance the good name of academia; they may specifically lobby to strengthen the humanities or the sciences. Leaders in these associations may go down two roads simultaneously, running with the faculty hare as well as with the administrator hound. But often they do not: The agendas quite naturally diverge. The administrators tune to governmental actions that would strengthen or adversely affect entire institutions. They are interested in overall institutional leadership and hence in effective administrative controls. They seek counsel on "management." Their agenda stretches from legislative actions on student aid, to relations with universities in other countries, to the never-ending battle to bring big-time collegiate sports under some semblance of control.

In contrast, faculty members operate within disciplines, either individual ones or in combinations of them—the natural sciences, the social sciences, the humanities, the arts—to influence governmental and private-sector actions that will strengthen the research and scholarly base of their own fields. The academicians are particularly strong in the science councils, penetrating by means of peer review the ordinary routines of such major agencies as the National Science Foundation and the National Institutes of Health. And, most of the time, their associations turn inward upon periodic meetings in which papers are read and criticized and specialized knowledge is otherwise pursued. Hence it is not surprising that faculty members and administrators from the same campus may go separate ways in representing interests in Washington, D.C., to the point where one does not know what the other is doing, and uncoordinated if not conflicting action is taken, to the surprise of all. Clark Kerr pointed out in the 1960s that the heads of campuses can readily feel things are out of control, and their own authority threatened, when professors strike their own deals in Washington.[2] One story used to illustrate the problem is about the research professor who strolled into the president's office in an Eastern private university to announce that he had just arranged, on a recent trip to Washington, for a research grant that included not only a new laboratory but an entire new building. The professor was sure the president would welcome this good news.

Natural conflict between administrator and faculty associations is exemplified in arguments over the size of "institutional overhead" in the budgeting of federal research grants. Researchers are inclined to see every dollar for overhead as one less dollar for research itself. They strongly prefer to have granting agencies limit the amount allotted to "indirect costs" that goes to the institution as a whole and hence into the hands of central administrators. On the other hand, campus administrators have constantly urged the government to raise the overhead rate. They maintain that big science has long had major hidden costs on university campuses, that "in the early days of indirect costs, everyone was under-recovering."[3] Further, science is steadily becoming more capital intensive, requiring more equipment and buildings that entail significant increased costs in depreciation, maintenance, and administration, which ought to be charged to research projects. At major private universities, the indirect cost rates had climbed by 1984 to between 65 and 70 percent, a very major addition to the allocations made directly for the research itself. Hence, income from this source becomes a major item in the overall budgets of research universities: At Stanford, "indirect cost recovery from government is characteristically the second most important income source, behind tuition but well ahead of all endowment income."[4] A million here and a million there soon add up to real money.

Sharp hostilities broke out over this issue in 1983, when the National Institutes of Health (NIH)—the principal supporter of research in the biological sciences—proposed to withhold 10 percent of indirect cost reimbursement in order to allocate more money to the research projects themselves. NIH was backed by the Federation of American Societies for Experimental Biology (FASEB), which accused university administrators, in true fighting language, of playing a "four-dimensional shell game" with indirect costs and described them as having made a "triumphant tour de force in evading the issue in the past three years." The serious conflict called out the skills of some of the best academic diplomats, who were soon at work forming another coalition, one of "university associations and scientific groups" that would help to obtain "full funding for both direct and indirect costs." FASEB reversed its position and passed a resolution calling for cooperation.[5] However, this issue is a sore point, a matter on which administrators and professors naturally divide, and on which their associational voices are prone to speak in divergent and often conflicting terms. Administrative associations and faculty associations see the world differently.

Of the disciplinary associations to which faculty members belong, some are almost completely restricted to academics, others center on the outside members, and still others blend the two. The American Historical Association and the American Sociological Association are known as academic associations: Academics heavily predominate, and the organization has a "learned-society" heritage that may have made a simple name change from "society" to "association" a wrenching decision. Such academic organizations are understood to be inside higher education, parts of the academic profession. In contrast, the American Medical Association and the American Bar Association are outside higher education, positioned in major domains of professional practice, with academics a small proportion of their members.

But the lines are rarely hard and fast, and some associations extensively mix academics and others. Academic chemists use the American Chemical Society as their primary association, but they constitute only one-third of its members; membership of the other two-thirds indicates that chemistry is a field in which the Ph.D. degree leads mainly to employment in industry. Founded in 1876, this association has evolved in a century into a complex organization that stretches quite naturally across the boundary between academia and industry. By the standards of wholly academic associations, it is huge, with a membership of 125,000, a budget of over one hundred million dollars, a dozen or more journals, and a fully professionalized administrative staff of 1,600 people (in a major building of its own in Washington, D.C.) that annually oversees 1,700 local, regional, divisional, and other meetings.[6] Academic and nonacademic concerns naturally cross-hatch, for whatever the differences between the academics and the industrial chemists, they have powerful mutual interests in such specialties as food chemistry, organic chemistry, and physical chemistry. This association epitomizes a longstanding and increasingly more prevalent subject-centered form of organization that bridges between higher education and other sectors of society, particularly industry. This form is now common in engineering and the sciences, including biology, as a rapidly expanding field in which Ph.D.'s increasingly spread out from the academy to posts in government and private firms.

What gradually emerged in our probing of the associational structure of the profession, particularly in the accounts that respondents provided in field interviews, is the way associations mirror the ongoing contest between centrifugal and centripetal academic forces. "Splinteritis" is everywhere. Each academic association finds itself subdividing into numerous major divisions along subject-matter lines, which then divide still further into subsections. As they grow substantively, incorporating more specialties, associations sow the seed of their own fragmentation. The large associations also tend to divide by institutional sector: One community college president pointed out that in the Modern Language Association and in the National Council of Teachers of English, "there is usually a community college component or at least a series of workshops dealing with community colleges at these annual meetings." If a major association does not strategically subdivide itself, it faces the constant threat of the loss of autonomy-seeking groups of specialists who move to set up their own organizations. In the older mainline associations that have managed to remain intact, unitary organization drifts toward a more federative form.

Interests in some fields—preeminently the biological sciences—have been so scattered and diversified from the beginning that no one organization ever established hegemony. Biologists of varying specialties turned to different associations, which then became integrated confederatively from the bottom up by coming together officially in one or more mammoth umbrella organizations. A well-informed observer of the associations in biology did his best to tell us how a confusing reality was composed:

> The discipline is divided in this country into perhaps a hundred subdisciplinary societies: the ecologists, the physiologists, the microbiologists, the biochemists, and so on. These societies are really independent, but there are two major groups that are umbrellas. One, [the Federation of American Societies for Experimental Biology] has seven societies, and the other group is under the American Institute of Biological Sciences. . . . There are about thirty or forty societies in that group. But, you see, there are many societies that don't belong to either one, and there are some societies that belong to both. The physiologists belong both to AIBS and to FASEB. . . . Now the American Chemical Society, although there are many subdivisions of chemistry, has stuck together as the American Chemical Society. The American Institution of Physics has all of the nine major physics societies in the country under the American Institute of Physics. The biologists are scattered.
>
> *(Is that because of what biology is, or is it some historical thing that happened?)* That is a very difficult question. It is historical certainly, to a degree. The chemists organized early and stuck together; and the biologists, it seems, as soon as a discipline of biology forms, there are subdisciplines which splinter off. Their jealousies and egos and territorialities become important. For one reason or another, biologists seem to have much more difficulty working together than do the physicists or the chemists or even the engineers, although the engineers are somewhat split too. There is an American Association of Engineering Societies [total membership, one million!], which has recently been structured to pull together the electrical engineers, and so forth, under one umbrella. The point is that in Washington . . . or [in] a national posture, you almost need a strong unified group. . . . The nation simply can't listen to hundreds of little subdisciplines, each one purporting to represent science in their field, because the fields get too small and get too specialized. It's just like medicine. Medicine is also splintered, but somehow the AMA has held together, and the American Association of Medical Colleges has held together. But the biologists probably have the worst case of splinteritis of anyone in the country. . . .
>
> You'll find that each individual society feels that it has the key to the future. The ecologists feel that the rest of biology is really not at all important. This is the pinnacle of science. The biochemists, at the other end of the spectrum, say you get anything above the molecule [and] it just becomes hokus-pokus and phenomenological. There is, perhaps, a great deal more sheer arrogance from discipline to discipline in biology than you

find anywhere else. I don't understand it completely, and I have been observing it my whole life.

In the set of disciplines known as "the biological sciences," there are numerous associational keys to the kingdom. But a good share of the groups feel they ought to associate loosely with each other in umbrella organizations, just as small individual political states often feel the need to confederate, federate, or band together as a united larger state to exert influence. In biology, however, the larger nation is inherently weak; the individual states have separate historical identities and interests. Still, superimposed upon a resource- and knowledge-rich academic base, umbrella organizations in biology offer impressive credentials. The Federation of American Societies for Experimental Biology, with a combined membership of over 20,000, can rightfully claim it is a powerful and wealthy organization. It publishes over thirty scientific journals, counts over 100 Nobel Prizes earned by its members, and is organized to do massive reports for the federal government and other authorities on food safety and food additives, toxic waste disposal, and other significant, practical issues.[7] Confederative or not, it is a major, busy corner of academia. And its identity and membership blur the lines between the pure and the applied, the private lives of academic disciplines and the public concerns of legislators and public executives.

In efforts to counter splinteritis, multidisciplinary associations interpenetrate one another. Umbrellas are raised over umbrellas. A professor of biology who had been active in the American Zoological Society pointed to the two umbrella organizations mentioned above as larger amalgams, and then noted that he belonged to and had been an officer in yet another wider umbrella organization, the American Association for the Advancement of Science (AAAS), whose interests were very diffuse and included the social sciences and beyond. He continued:

> Then, there are global organizations. For example, there is the International Union of Immunological Societies (IUIS), which is the umbrella for all national immunological societies. For example, the American Association of Immunologists holds a seat in IUIS; so does the French Society of Immunologists; so does the British Society of Immunologists. Then there is another one . . . the International Union of Biological Societies. . . .

Umbrella is one metaphor, spider web another, and pyramid yet another that points to the many ways in which proliferating associations constitute a larger maze of linkages. Many relatively small associations do not particularly acknowledge the overtones of shelter and possible subordination inherent in the umbrella concept, yet they weave themselves around a larger national association by holding their annual meeting in the same city, presenting their own programs right before, right after, or during the meeting of the major group. In the social sciences, the Society for the Study of Social Problems (SSSP) has long attached itself in this fashion to the American Sociological Association; most of its members also hold memberships in the ASA, while backing a vehicle for more practical concerns. The Policy Studies organization, newly sprung largely from political science and public administration, meets with the American Political Science Association, again with an extensive overlap of membership. In turn, the associational networks include pyramids within individual disciplines, as smaller regional associations feed loosely into national associations that, in turn, offer the institutional building blocks plus the members for international associations. In a confusing manner only partially caught in any one metaphor, associations structure the metainstitutional life of the academic profession.

That metastructure has begun to reflect significantly the allocation of academics to types of institutions other than research universities. In at least three major ways, the associational network is adapting to the interests of faculty located in the middle and lower rungs of the institutional hierarchy. For one, national associations themselves have been adjusting their own inner lives, since about 1970, to attract and retain faculty located in state, small private, and community colleges. More attention is paid to teaching the discipline: A teaching specialist is placed in the headquarters staff; a separate budget allocation is made for work on the problems of teaching; a subdivision is organized; and space for discussion of the problems of teaching is inserted in the annual program. Second, regional disciplinary associations take on the character of a home for those who cannot get on the programs of the national associations, and especially for those unable to obtain travel funds to attend distant meetings. Regional associations are also much smaller, and their meetings in most cases seem friendlier as well as more accessible. Coast to coast, lack of travel funds is a major irritant particularly noticeable in the state-college sector. On one coast we heard: "I don't have the money to go. . . . I can't, even if I am invited to present a paper. . . . I couldn't go last year." And on the other coast: "We don't have any money within this system to send people to those things . . . If they [the meetings] are in the neighborhood, I will go to them." The regional associations are also joined by more localized state and city counterparts, which serve as small worlds attractive to teachers and researchers of less than national renown. Those who serve as officers and members of the many committees of these associations may receive some local and regional notice in their disciplines in lieu of national accolades.

A third, and most recent, adaptive evolution is the most telling: Disciplinary associations are now forming along sector lines. The more a sector is organizationally set off, the more do associations break off. The community college sector is, therefore, the principal center of this type of proliferation. A community college biology instructor explained how and why a sectoral association was organized in her discipline, in her part of the country, just a few years earlier:

> [We] got a notice that a group of biology professors from various two-year schools were putting together an organization. The purpose of the organization is for communication, [for] exchange of ideas between people who have the same problems, community college biologists that saw a certain type of student, a student that for one reason or another didn't go to a four-year school, either because of money or . . . often because of academic reasons. You know, what textbooks we should use at this level, and how we can use the computer in our courses, and how we can get across this idea at this level. . . . If I go to real high-powered meetings occasionally, and they speak about technologies that I have no idea about anymore, being out of it, [then] I can bring back almost nothing to our students; but from these meetings I bring back a lot because they are geared for the teacher of the two-year institution.

Localization in this case took place on two dimensions simultaneously: The association is statewide instead of national, and it limits itself to the community-college part of the biology professoriate.

Such doubly local associations are both more within reach of the pocketbook, when colleges provide little or no travel funds, and more relevant to substantive interests. A social science instructor in a metropolitan community college told us he wanted to attend disciplinary meetings, but for the last four of five years he had only been able to attend one taking place in his own metropolitan area. He had gotten out of the main national association some time ago:

> I used to belong to the American Political Science Association but found in recent years there was such a disparity between what they were doing and what I was doing that I didn't find it to be terribly intellectually stimulating. . . . Given where my students are at and where they are likely to go, given their socio-economic backgrounds and their language limitations, and their heterogeneity, a lot of things that I see in the journals don't correspond very much to what I can do in class. . . . I mean, reality dictates.

Astute observers have argued cogently that community college faculty are not in a position to follow the cosmopolitan road to professionalism so heavily traveled by university professors: "The community college faculty disciplinary affiliation is too weak, the institutions' demands for scholarship are practically nonexistent, and the teaching loads are too heavy for that form of professionalism to occur." Community college faculty will either undergo more deprofessionalization, slipping further toward the weak professionalism of American school teaching, or they will have to bootstrap themselves into a different set of appropriate forms that "reconceptualize the academic disciplines themselves to fit the realities of the community colleges."[8] In this effort, associations and journals are crucial tools. Moves in this direction have included the formation of the Community College Social Science Association and the Community College Humanities Association, together with the establishment of journals directed toward two-year college instructors in such fields as mathematics, journalism, and English.

National surveys have shown clearly that faculty members vary greatly across sectors in attendance at national meetings. In the 1984 Carnegie survey, half of the community college faculty members reported they had not made their way to a meeting during last year, compared to about 20 percent not having done so in leading liberal arts colleges and 15 percent in leading research universities (Table 17). About one-half of leading liberal arts college faculty members and research university faculty members had attended two or more meetings, with proportions in the other sectors diminishing to one-fourth in the two-year colleges. But the other side of the coin is that, even in the community college sector, one-half of the faculty managed at least one meeting, and one out of four, by personal expense or otherwise, negotiated two more meetings. Clearly, the urge to meet with other academics outside of one's own institution does not die even in the most adverse settings. Unfortunately, the survey data do not reveal what type of national meeting was attended or how far respondents had to travel. As national associations move their annual meetings from one city to another, a common practice, many faculty members can readily catch a meeting in their region at least every third or fourth year. And, as sector associations develop, principally in the community college area, they can find gatherings appropriate to their own cause.

In short, as the cutting edges of academic specialization become sharply honed, reality dictates that national associations centered on university professors become inappropriate for a good share of the faculty who are so involved in undergraduate teaching that they are "out of it." National meetings replete with the papers reporting the latest research results are not relevant to the vast majority of community college teachers and to a large proportion of professors located in four-year institutions. We can predict further proliferation of associations localized by type of institution as well as by geographic area. Only the top third or so of the institutional hierarchy, consisting of the better colleges as well as the research universities, is thoroughly national in interest. Academics in the rest of the system find their way to types of associations their own realities dictate, including responsiveness to a local undergraduate student clientele in place of responsiveness to a national group of peers. The critical divide between students and peers as primary clientele is increasingly reflected in the associational maze of the professoriate.

Table 17. Faculty Attendance at National Meetings, by Type of Institution

Type of Institution	Number of Meetings		
	None	One	Two or More
	(Percent of Faculty)		
Research Universities I	15	28	57
Research Universities II	22	29	49
Doctoral-Granting Universities I	27	32	41
Doctoral-Granting Universities II	33	27	40
Comprehensive Universities and Colleges I	31	32	37
Comprehensive Universities and Colleges II	41	27	32
Liberal Arts Colleges I	21	34	45
Liberal Arts Colleges II	38	32	30
Two-Year Colleges	49	26	25
All Institutions	33	29	38

Total respondents, 4,863.

Question: "During the last year, how many national professional meetings did you attend?"

SOURCE: The Carnegie Foundation for the Advancement of Teaching, Faculty Survey 1984.

The Role of Invisible Associations

A major unanticipated finding that emerged from our interviews is the extent to which university researchers themselves are sometimes finding their major national associations to be empty shells, too general in scope to be relevant to special interests, too large to facilitate interaction among like-minded peers. National associations try to cope with this problem by elaborate sectioning, creating smaller worlds of subject-centered divisions, all with formal names, their own officers and members, perhaps a small budget, and definitely their own piece of the annual programming. The internal life of one association after another in the post-World War II decades has been characterized by a tension between the centrists, who wish to maintain a unitary organization and the section leaders who are busy developing separate parts whose strength and autonomy give the whole organization a confederative cast. History rides with the separatists; there are limits to how much their interests can be appeased by well-integrated generalist organizations.

At the interdisciplinary association level, the problem has struck particularly hard at the American Association for the Advancement of Science, where attendance at annual meetings slipped over 70 percent in a decade and a half, dropping between 1969 and 1985 from 8,000 to 2,300. Association officials have reported a sense of ebbing vitality; they bemoan the lack of announced major new scientific discoveries at their meetings; that "the young scientist who is doing the exciting experiment isn't at this meeting"; that only white-haired veterans, "long past the stage of active scientific work," still come. The cause of the AAAS problem is seen to be that "the increasing specialization of science is ending the popularity of big general meetings that consider scientific and public policy issues of interest to a great range of scientists, not just those from a narrow specialty." As a result, the AAAS, looking to its own vitality and value, has been shifting its center of gravity from the annual meeting, long the flagship activity, into such activities as publishing a science magazine for laymen and programs for improving the quality of precollege science and mathematics education.[9]

At the discipline level, the American Physical Society has seen attendance at its annual meeting slip drastically, from about 7,000 in 1967 to 800 in 1985. The society's executive secretary has concluded that "the general meetings are just disappearing. . . . The only way to have a successful meeting is to have specialized topics," that is, meetings that are themselves limited to such specific topics as basic properties of optical materials or radio-frequency plasma heating. The society has turned to sponsoring two dozen such smaller topical conferences a year, which might be attended by 150 to 300 physicists.[10] University faculty members we interviewed concurred: I do not go "to these gigantic Physical Society meetings, but very often to smaller workshop-things"; "nobody goes to the conferences any more very much. I mean, not the standard APS meetings. I never go; very few of my colleagues go. Instead, we tend to go to special topical meetings, which are set up just for one time only."

Similarly, in biology, where the field is already radically subdivided among national associations, processors speak of seeking smaller networks, some of which can be worked up regionally:

> I tend to go to small, local meetings. There is a guild of population biologists that meet in the Rocky Mountains. There is a prairie states ecology conclave of about five local universities. I find I get to know the people better, and I actually learn more by going to these local meetings, than the big, frustrating national ones.

Another biologist at a leading university viewed meetings of the national associations as "monster meetings." He, too, sought out informal and semiformal "meetings during the year which are smaller and, therefore, more focused. Those are the preferred ones to go to." Where specialization is most advanced, academics have learned to use disposable meetings. They deformalize their networks to better adjust to the shifting contours of research interests.

In the narrowly focused world of topical meetings, we enter a vast underbrush of semiformal and informal linkages characteristic of American academia, ties that also weave, weblike, around the mainline associations. Faculty members speak of going to meet others in their "network" when they go off to attend sessions of their "division" within the national association ("the Business Policy and Planning Division of the Academy of Management is where most of the people in my network are"). Of growing importance also are the ties not dependent on formal associations for their footing, connections that we can view as visible associations, in line with the fruitful concept of invisible colleges, which has been widely used in the sociology of science. The idea of an invisible college has meant a communication "network of productive scientists" that links "separate groups of collaborators within a research area."[11] We can broaden the idea so that it is not limited to "productive scientists," but instead refers more inclusively to the informal arrangements by which academics connect and communicate on campus and, especially, in the system at large.

Even at top universities, where cosmopolitan ties are strongest, informal associations, for some, may be largely local. A political scientist at a leading university reported that although he often discussed intellectual matters with one important colleague at another university 2,000 miles away, all the others with whom he sought close interaction—a goodly number—he found by roaming his own campus, branching out from his own department to a major campus institute that contained members of several departments and then on to numerous other departments:

> Right now I have just initiated some discussions with a colleague in the linguistics department, and I talked to a colleague in the anthropology department. I have been interested in the evolution of behavior, and I have gotten a lot out of a colleague in the biology department. I have occasional dealings with colleagues in the sociology department and the business school who are also interested in organization theory—and the school of public health—because we have had a group of organization theorists that has gotten together.

This professor felt that he did "a different kind of work," and therefore, did not "feel very strongly identified with any particular group." His own department was satisfactory as "a professional home," but to pursue his own research agenda he needed to fashion his own set of ties, a flexible set of local exchanges.

A major campus is a vast collection of such highly disposable individualized networks, interpersonal ties fashioned by professors with those outside as well as with those within their own departments, as they follow the thrust of their intellectual interests. The social inventions here are many. "Journal clubs," one of them, was described by a professor of biology in a leading university:

> I interact with people in the medical school because there are not other immunologists in this department. . . . Right now, we're not actually connecting on a given project, though we may be starting something like that soon, but we share journal clubs. You know what journal clubs are? That is where you get together with people working in your area and review current papers from the literature that are of interest. So we share a weekly journal club with three other labs in the medical school. . . . This is fairly common in biology, at least.

Two political scientists told us about larger invisible associations of which they are a part; mentor-student ties played an important role here. One, who indicated his closest professional ties were elsewhere, not in his own department, added, "I also have Ph.D.'s all over the place. When you have been at it as long as I have, you are pretty well connected nationally." The informal can stretch to become a whole "school of people" lasting over several academic generations. The second professor spoke of having close friends elsewhere—at Cornell and Harvard and in the government—and went on to describe his main network as an informal and "highly controversial school of people . . . who are identified with a man who taught at Chicago for many years, Leo Strauss, and I am a student of students of Strauss. People who know my work think of me as Straussian."

In all the disciplines, from the humanities to the sciences, the invisible associations have a primary role in self-identity, communication, and the bonding of members of the profession. A humanist declared, "I have better relations with colleagues at other universities simply because they share my interests in Joyce, O'Casey, and Yeats, my interest in Anglo-Irish literature, and it is healthy to meet colleagues." The informal then shades into small-scale associations: "I belong to organizations within my specific field: the Committee for Irish Studies, the James Joyce Society, the O'Casey Society." At the same time, this humanities professor continued his membership in "the major organization in our field. . . . The Modern Language Association."

In the sciences, too, there are extended families that form around a mentor and several generations of students and research associates. In physics: "There are several groups that basically have the same parentage, which sprang from John Wheeler at Princeton University, and he had some great students who spawned some great groups. . . . That family I identify with. I wasn't a student of his, but I was a colleague and a research associate, and that's whom I identify with."

Another physics professor spoke of his professional home as being the "collection of people I sort of professionally grew up with over the last twenty years. . . . My closest collaborators tend to be people immediately around me, but all over there are people who have been close to me and have worked with me in the past." For those struggling to do research in second- and third-level universities, the dominant informal associations were all the more likely to be elsewhere, even abroad, since relevant immediate colleagues are in short supply:

> The persons that I have most contact with in terms of my research goals are not in this department. . . . [They are] people at IBM research labs, or at the Max Planck Institute of Stuttgart, and some other universities.
>
> [My] closest professional colleagues in the sense of people who do what I do—certainly, they are somewhere else. There is nobody here that does what I do, which is, I guess, typical, at least at a small school.

So segmented is the academic labor market that many specialists in large and small places are hired as one-of-a-kind experts. Their intellectual sustenance then depends largely on associations, informal and formal, which bridge the boundaries of their own institutions.

Weakest in associational ties, of course, are the many reluctant part-time and temporary full-time faculty, whose marginal careers leave them hanging by their fingertips to the edges of academe. They are least likely to have personal or institutional travel funds to attend meetings. They are outside or peripheral to the regular faculty circles that spawn the more informal ties. Associationally, as well as organizationally they get left out. But even here, the drive to associate does not die: Indeed, those in a common weak position have good reason to band together to support one another, to find strength in numbers, to share tips on employment opportunities, and to have intellectual discussions. Thus, in sociology in the 1980s, "independent scholars" became a new network of the unemployed and underemployed, with officers, meetings, a newsletter, and formal affiliation with the mainline national association.

The Associational Webbing of Academic Groups

To solve their institutional problems, professors turn to such place-bound tools as departments and senates. To solve their disciplinary problems, they reach for subject-based associations that extend to wherever like-minded peers can be found. The larger the national system, the more academics seem to need to create such ties; they need to bring a cohort of over 500,000 "colleagues," as in the United States, down to the more manageable size of 50,000, or better 5,000 or even better 500 or 50, and sometimes 5. The more a national system is decentralized, the more academics are encouraged to turn a voluntary action, since there are no formal embracing schemes that even pretend to bring them together. Then, too, the individual and small-group autonomies of academia provide the freedom and moral authority to voluntarily associate. Even in the most managerial settings, academics do not have to ask permission from "the boss" before reaching outside their own departments, and then beyond their university or college, to fashion meaningful ties with others. There are virtually no product secrets. Academics communicate with colleagues readily and band together in formations of their own devising as soon as they face new problems or generate new bodies of knowledge. They would rather be association persons than "organization men."

Without any person or group planning it, or even setting the general direction, a division of labor has evolved in America in which postsecondary associations of institutions attend to institutional and student issues while disciplinary associations concentrate, field by field, on issues of research and scholarship. With this division, many issues affecting professors are beyond the bounds of their primary national associations: Organized institutional interests, then readily predominate over the professional ones. When government officials and legislators, state or national, want advice on "higher education," they turn to institutional heads and their associations. In turn, especially in the national capital, the presidents' clubs develop a lobbying capacity to represent higher education. But when the state turns directly to "science"—or "the humanities" or "the arts"—do its officials turn to disciplinary groupings. And it is mainly around the needs of scholarship that professor-run associations reciprocally develop a presence as a lobby and learn to penetrate governmental agencies. The many disciplinary associations thereby fashion connections with government that bypass the institutions.

As a class of organizations, American disciplinary associations are more pervasive and powerful than their counterparts in other countries, but their power is narrowly focused. As they concentrate on the research and scholarship of direct interest to their members, they leave other aspects of higher education to administrators. The division of influence parallels the bargain struck within the authority structures of universities and colleges, but the professional base is more dampened. The associational structure reflects the simple fact that the higher the level in the American system, the more pervasive is the sway of management. Senates may be powerful locally, but there are no powerful professor-dominated senates nationally to pull academics together as a professional class.

Since specialization is what counts in the professional network, right down to professors withdrawing from their own major associations because they view them as too general, all-inclusive associations have a difficult time. They are cast in a secondary role because they deemphasize disciplinary distinctions, swimming against the tide of the proliferating pursuit of such separations. Membership in the American Association of University Professors, for example, then seems relatively costly; one first pays membership dues to a set of regional, national, and possibly international, disciplinary associations and then squeezes the family budget still further to pay the AAUP its annual dues. For those in top places, disciplinary memberships are relatively essential; joining and serving in the AAUP is more in the nature of *noblesse oblige*, done with a sense that less fortunate colleagues in other places need a defense league to protect them against the batterings of politicians, trustees, and administrators.

When the National Education Association and the American Federation of Teachers seriously entered the picture in the late 1960s and the 1970s, in full union dress, they not only deemphasize disciplinary distinctions but also those of status. As we have seen (Chapter VI), they run up against the stubborn fact that successful people in every discipline want the rewards of status. Thus, in a system so much given to diversity, competition, and hierarchy, there are powerful reasons why inclusive bodies in the form of unions are strongest where discipline and status matter least, and weakest where discipline and status count the most. Issues left for unions are then largely economic and managerial in a domain where leadership and stature flow to those who most effectively attend to their focused scholarship and take up the roles of salaried entrepreneurs. For their members, the disciplinary associations, able to build on a substantial consciousness of kind, are often impressive symbols of professional community. The NEA, the AFT, and sometimes the AAUP, in contrast, have only a weak base of common consciousness upon which to operate as vehicles of shared identity. Their base lies in local strains between "workers" and "management."

American higher education is simultaneously underorganized in certain respects and overorganized in others.[12] It has no national ministry and no national formal system of control. Seen in comparative perspective, it is only loosely structured by normal bureaucratic and political tools of state authority. But voluntary association then substitutes for systemwide formal organization. The substitute system is bewildering and hard to capture, quantitatively or qualitatively. It is simultaneously formal, semiformal, and informal; it is visible and invisible. Overall hierarchy is minimal: loop through and around one another, with no regard for unifying principles of order, logic, and accountability. The gaps and redundancies are too numerous to count.

American academics associate voluntarily from the bottom up. Their national network forms from the intellectual and practical interests of thousands of clusters of practicing academics scattered in the vast array of disciplines and institutions that compose the system. What the bottom does not like, the bottom disposes of. More than in other countries, the voluntary lines make for a disposable structure of coordination, thereby promoting system flexibility. Voluntary associating is a good way to have structure follow knowledge, rather than the other way around. Professionals have known for a long time that, as a general form, association is more malleable than bureaucracy. It follows particularly well the many contours of academe. In the American setting, it is deeply a part of the logic of the academic profession.

Paralleling the cultural overlap identified in Chapter V, associational overlap provides some integration in an otherwise chaotic domain. Even in the most narrow specialties, professors face outward from their own campus, joining hands across organizational boundaries. They take up multiple memberships: They join specialty associations and larger disciplinary ones; they belong to a pyramid of regional, national, and international associations; they maneuver in the invisible groupings as well as the formal ones. Specialties in one discipline converge on those in another: Some molecular biologists run some of the time with physicists and chemists. As a biologist put it, "My area of research carries me into other professional societies of which I am also a member." It is hard to distinguish political sociologists from behavioral political scientists; they cross associational lines accordingly, even to occupy high office. The inclusive faculty associations, such as the American Association of University Professors, provide some additional linkage, however secondary its importance. As for liaison among the associations themselves, there are the interdisciplinary umbrella associations and the councils of the umbrella organizations.

In American academic life, where scholars are so scattered by type of institution as well as discipline, reasons for singularity and division abound. Following the division of labor, fragmentation is necessarily—as emphasized throughout this study—the dominant theme. But if there are reasons to isolate, there are reasons to associate. Academics who occupy a common corner in fields of knowledge coalesce so they will not be monstrosities of individualized isolation. As their limited associations, formal and informal, overlap one another, a larger network emerges. In a profession of professions, overlapping voluntary linkages are the nearest thing to a social structure that provides order and integration.

References

1. Bloland, Harland, G., *Higher Education Associations in a Decentralized Education System* (Berkeley: Center for Research and Development in Higher Education, University of California, 1969), pp. 77–99.

2. Kerr, Clark, *The Uses of the University* (Cambridge, Mass., Harvard University Press, 1963), pp. 56–60.

3. Kennedy, Donald, "Government Policies and the Cost of Doing Research," *Science*, February 1, 1985, pp. 480–484. Quotation, p. 482.

4. Ibid., p. 483.

5. Ibid., pp. 480, 483.

6. American Chemical Society, *Programs and Activities of the American Chemical Society* (Washington, D.C., 1983).

7. Federation of American Societies for Experimental Biology, *Annual Report*, 1982 (Washington, D.C., 1982).

8. Cohen, Arthur M., and Florence B. Brawer, *The American Community College* (San Francisco: Jossey-Bass, 1982), pp. 88–90.

9. Boffey, Philip M., "Prestigious Forum Slides into a Troubling Decline," *New York Times*, June 4, 1985, pp. C1–C2.

10. Ibid.

11. Crane, Diana, *Invisible Colleges: Diffusion of Knowledge in Scientific Communities* (Chicago: University of Chicago Press, 1972), pp. 54, 35.

12. Wilson, Logan, *American Academics: Then and Now* (New York: Oxford University Press, 1979), pp. 155–159.

The Matthew Effect in Science, II

Cumulative Advantage and the Symbolism of Intellectual Property

ROBERT K. MERTON*

The subject of this essay is a problem in the sociology of science that has long been of interest to me. That problem, a candid friend tells me, is somewhat obscured by the formidable title assigned to it. Yet, properly deciphered, the title is not nearly as opaque as it might at first seem.

Consider first the signal emitted by the Roman numeral II in the main title. It informs us that the paper follows on an earlier one, "The Matthew Effect in Science," which I finally put into print a good many years ago.[1] The ponderous, not to say lumpy, subtitle goes on to signal the direction of this follow-on. The first concept, cumulative advantage, applied to the domain of science, refers to the social processes through which various kinds of opportunities for scientific inquiry as well as the subsequent symbolic and material rewards for the results of that inquiry tend to accumulate for individual practitioners of science, as they do also for organizations engaged in scientific work. The concept of cumulative advantage directs our attention to the ways in which initial comparative advantages of trained capacity, structural location, and available resources make for successive increments of advantage such that the gaps between the haves and the have-nots in science (as in other domains of social life) widen until dampened by countervailing processes.

The second phrase in the subtitle directs us to the distinctive character of intellectual property in science. I propose the seeming paradox that in science, private property is established by having its substance freely given to others who might want to make use of it. I shall argue further that certain institutionalized aspects of this property system, chiefly in the form of public acknowledgment of the source of knowledge and information thus freely bestowed on fellow scientists, relate to the social and cognitive structures of science in interesting ways that affect the collective advancement of scientific knowledge.

That is a long agenda for a short disquisition. Since that agenda can only be discharged by dealing with these matters in the large, I shall not attempt to summarize the detailed findings that derive from a now widely dispersed program of research on cumulative advantage and disadvantage in the social stratification of science.

An obscure title can also have a latent function: to keep one from assuming that the title truly speaks for itself, and thus to make it necessary to elucidate one's intent. As for the main title: what, you may well ask, does "The Matthew Effect in Science" refer to? A mercifully short reprise of the work introducing this notion will get us into its further elucidation.

The Matthew Effect

We begin by noting a theme that runs through Harriet Zuckerman's hours-long interviews with Noble laureates in the early 1960s. It is repeatedly suggested in these interviews that eminent scientists get disproportionately great credit for their contributions to science while relatively unknown ones tend to get disproportionately little for their occasionally comparable contributions. As a laureate in physics put it: "The world is peculiar in this matter of how it gives credit. It tends to give the credit to already famous people."[2] Nor are the laureates alone in stating that the more prominent scientists tend to get the lion's share of recognition; less notable scientists in a cross-sectional sample studied by Warren O. Hagstrom have reported similar experiences.[3] But it is the eminent scientists, not least those who have received the ultimate contemporary accolade, the Nobel Prize, who provide presumptive evidence of this pattern. For they testify to its occurrence, not as aggrieved victims, which might make their testimony suspect, but as "beneficiaries," albeit sometimes embarrassed and unintentional ones.

The claim that prime recognition for scientific work, by informed peers and not merely by the inevitably uninformed lay public, is skewed in favor of established scientists requires, of course, that the nature and quality of these diversely appraised contributions be identical or at least much the same. That condition is approximated in cases of full collaboration and in cases of independent multiple discoveries. The distinctive contributions of collaborators are often difficult to disentangle; independent multiple discoveries, if not identical, are at least enough alike to be defined as functional equivalents by the principals involved or by their informed peers.

In papers jointly published by scientists of markedly unequal rank and reputation, another laureate in physics reports, "the man who's best known gets more credit, an inordinate amount of credit." Or as a laureate in chemistry put it, "If my name was on a paper, people would remember *it* and not remember who else was involved."[4] The biological scientists R. C. Lewontin and J. L. Hubby have lately reported a similar pattern of experience with a pair of their collaborative papers, which have been cited often enough to qualify as "citation classics" (as designated by the Institute for Scientific Information). One paper was cited some 310 times; the other, some 525 times. The first paper described a method; the second

> gave the detailed result of the application of the method to natural populations. The two papers were a genuinely collaborative effort in conception, execution, and writing and clearly form an indivisible pair, . . . published back-to-back in the same issue of the journal. The order of authors was alternated, with the biochemist, Hubby, being the senior author in the method paper and the population geneticist, Lewontin, as senior author in the application paper. Yet paper II has been cited over 50 percent more frequently that paper I. Citations to paper I virtually never stand alone but are nearly always paired with a citation to II, but the reverse is not true. Why? We seem to have a clearcut case of Merton's "Matthew Effect"—that the already better known investigator in a field gets the credit for joint work, irrespective of the order of authors on the paper, and so gets even better known by an autocatalytic process. In 1966 Lewontin had been a professional for a dozen years and was well known among population geneticists, to whom the paper was addressed, while Hubby's career had been much shorter and was known chiefly to biochemical geneticists. As a result, population geneticists have consistently regarded Lewontin as the senior member of the team and given him undue credit for what was a completely collaborative work that would have been impossible for either one of us alone.[5]

At the extreme, such misallocation of credit can occur even when a published paper bears only the name of a hitherto unknown and uncredentialed scientist. Consider this observation by the invincible geneticist and biochemist, J. B. S. Haldan (whose *not* having received a Nobel Prize can be cited as prime evidence of the fallibility of the judges sitting in Stockholm). Speaking with Ronald Clark of S. K. Roy, his talented Indian student who had conducted important experiments designed to improve strains of rice, Haldane observed that

Roy himself deserved about 95 percent of the credit. . . ."The other 5 percent may be divided between the Indian Statistical Institute and myself," he added. "I deserve credit for letting him try what I thought was a rather ill-planned experiment, on the general principle that I am not omniscient." But [Haldane] had little hope that credit would be given that way. "Every effort will be made here to crab his work," he wrote. "He has not got a Ph.D. or even a first-class M.Sc. So either the research is no good, or I did it."[6]

It is such patterns of the misallocation of recognition for scientific work that I described as "the Matthew effect." The not quite foreordained term derives, of course, from the first book of the New Testament, the Gospel according to Matthew (13:12 and 25:29). In the stately prose of the King James Version, created by what must be one of the most scrupulous and consequential teams of scholars in Western history, the well-remembered passage reads: "For unto everyone that hath shall be given, and he shall have abundance; but from him that hath not shall be taken away even that which he hath."[7]

Put in less stately language, the Matthew effect is the accruing of large increments of peer recognition to scientists of great repute for particular contributions in contrast to the minimizing or withholding of such recognition for scientists who have not yet made their mark. The biblical parable generates a corresponding sociological parable. For this is the form, it seems, that the distribution of psychic income and cognitive wealth in science also takes. How this comes to be and with what consequences for the fate of individual scientists and the advancement of scientific knowledge are the questions in hand.

The Accumulation of Advantage and Disadvantage for Scientists

Taken out its spiritual context and placed in a wholly secular context, the Matthew doctrine would seem to hold that the posited process must result in a boundlessly growing inequality of wealth, however wealth is construed in any sphere of human activity. Conceived of as a locally ongoing process and not as a single event, the practice of giving unto everyone that hath much while taking from everyone that hath little will lead to the rich getting forever richer while the poor become poorer. Increasingly absolute and not only relative deprivation would be the continuing order of the day. But as we know, things are not as simple as that. After all, the extrapolation of local exponentials is notoriously misleading. In noting this, I do not intend nor am I competent to assess the current economic theory of the distribution of wealth and income. Instead, I shall report what a focus upon the skewed distribution of peer recognition and research productivity in science has led some of us to identify as the processes and consequences of the accumulation of advantage and disadvantage in science.

(Unkind readers will no doubt describe this part of my report as rambling; critical ones, as convoluted; and kindly, understanding ones, as complex. Myself, I should describe it as the slow, laborious emergence of an intellectual tradition of work in the evolving sociology of science.)

I first stumbled upon the general question of social stratification in science in the early 1940s. One paper of that period alludes to "the accumulation of differential advantages for certain segments of the population, differentials that are not [necessarily] bound up with demonstrated differences in capacity."[8] It would not be correct or, indeed, just to say that that text is no clearer to me now than the notoriously obscure *Sordello* was clear to Robert Browning, when he confessed: "When I wrote that, God and I knew what it meant, but now God alone knows."[9] However, I can report that the notion of the accumulation of advantage just rested there as only a proto-concept— inert, unnoticed, and unexplicated—until it was taken up, almost a quarter century later, in my first paper on the Matthew effect. Until then, the notion of cumulative advantage in science had led only a ghostly existence in private musings, sporadically conjured up for oral publication rather than put in print.[10]

Further investigation of the process of cumulative advantage took hold in the latter 1960s with the formation of a research quartet at Columbia consisting of Harriet Zuckerman, Stephen Cole, Jonathan R. Cole, and myself. There has since emerged an "invisible college"—to adopt the brilliant terminological recoinage by Derek Price—which has grown apace in contributing to a program of research on cumulative advantage and disadvantage, in social stratification generally and in science specifically. Notably including Price himself until his recent lamented death, that college also numbers Paul D. Allison, Bernard Barber, Stephen J. Bensman, Judith Blau, Walter Broughton, Daryl E. Chubin, Dale Danefer, Simon Duncan, Mary Frank Fox, Eugene Garfield, Jerry Gaston, Jack A. Goldstone, Warren O. Hagstrom, Lowell L. Hargens, Karin D. Knorr, Tad Krauze, J. Scott Long, Robert McGinnis, Volker Meja, Roland Mettermeir, Edgar W. Mills, Jr., Nicholas C. Mullins, Barbara Reskin, Leonard Rubin, Dean K. Simonton, Nico Stehr, John A. Stewart, Norman W. Storer, Stephen P. Turner, and Herbert J. Walberg, among others.[11]

This, surely, is not the occasion for providing a synopsis of that now considerable body of research materials. Rather, I shall only remind you of a few of the marked inequalities and strongly skewed distributions of productivity and resources in science, and then focus on the consequences of the bias in favor of the precocity that is built into our institutions for detecting and rewarding talent, an institutionalized bias that may help bring about severe inequalities during the life course of scholars and scientists.

First, then, a quick sampling of the abundance of conspicuously skewed distributions and inequalities identifiable at a given time.

- The total number of scientific papers published by scientists differs enormously, ranging from the large proportion of Ph.D.s who publish one paper or none at all to the rare likes of William Thomson, Lord Kelvin, with his six hundred plus papers, or the mathematician Arthur Cayley, publishing a paper every few weeks throughout his work life for a total of almost a thousand.[12]

- The skewed distribution in the sheer number of published papers is best approximated by variants of Alfred J. Lotka's "inverse square law" of scientific productivity, which states that the number of scientists with n publications is proportional to n^2. In a variety of disciplines, this works out to some 5 or 6 percent of the scientists who *publish at all* producing about half of all papers in their discipline.[13]

- The distributions are even more skewed in the use of scientists' work by their peers, as that use is crudely indexed by the number of citations to it. Much the same distribution has been found in various data sets: typical is Garfield's finding that, for an aggregate of some nineteen million articles published in the physical and biological sciences between 1961 and 1980, 0.3 percent were cited more than one hundred times; another 2.7 percent between twenty-five and one hundred times; and, at the other extreme, some 58 percent of those that were cited at all were cited only once in that twenty-year period.[14] This inequality, you will recognize, is steeper than Pareto-like distributions of income.

When it comes to *changes* in the extent of inequalities of research productivity and recognition during the course of an individual's work life as a scientist, the needed longitudinal data are much more scarce. Again, a few suggestive findings must serve.

- In their simulation of longitudinal data (through desegregation of a cross section some two thousand American biologists, mathematicians, chemists, and physicists into several strata by career age), Paul D. Allison and John A. Stewart found "a clear and substantial rise in inequality for both [the number of research publications in the preceding five years and the number of citations to previously published work] from the younger to the older strata, strongly supporting the accumulative advantage hypothesis."[15]

- Allison and Stewart also confirmed the Zuckerman-Merton hypothesis that decreasing research productivity with increasing age results largely from differing rates of attrition in research roles and that this approximates an all-or-none phenomenon. The hypothesis held that "the more productive scientists, recognized as such by the reward-system of science, tend to persist in their research roles," while those with declining research productivity tend to shift to other indispensable roles in science, not excluding and conventionally maligned role of research administrator.[16]

- Derek Price pointedly reformulated and developed that hypothesis, "because there is a very large but decreasing chance that any given researcher will discontinue publication, the group of workers that reaches the [research] front during a particular year will decline steadily in total output as time goes on. Gradually, one after another, they will drop away from the research front. Thus the yearly output of the group as a whole will decline, [and now comes the essential point Zuckerman and I tried to emphasize] even though any given individual within it may produce at a steady rate throughout his [or her] entire professional lifetime. We need, therefore, to distinguish this effect [of mortality at the research front] from any differences in the actual rates of productivity at different ages among those that remain at the front."[17]

With regard to the Matthew effect and associated cumulation of advantage,

- Stephen Cole found, in an ingeniously designed study of a sample of American physicists, that the greater their authors' scientific reputation, the more likely that papers of roughly equal quality (as assessed by the later number of citations on them) will receive rapid peer recognition (by citation within a year after publication). Prior repute of authors somewhat advances the speed of diffusion of their contributions.[18]

- Cole also found that it is a distinct advantage for physicists of still small reputation to be located in the departments most highly rated by peers: their new work diffuses more rapidly through the science networks than comparable work by their counterparts in peripheral university departments.[19]

Accumulation of Advantage and Disadvantage Among the Young

I now focus on the special problems in the accumulation of advantage and disadvantage that derive from an institutionalized bias in favor of precocity. The advantages that come with early accomplishment taken as a sign of things to come stand in Matthew-like contrast to the situation confronted by young scientists whose work in judged as ordinary.[20] Such early prognostic judgments, I suggest, lead in some unknown fraction of cases to inadvertent suppression of talent through the process of the self-fulfilling prophecy. Moreover, this is more likely to be the case in a society, such as American society, where educational institutions are so organized as to put a premium on relatively *early* manifestations of ability—in a word, on precocity. Since it was that wise medical scientists Alan Gregg who led me to become aware of this bias institutionalized in our educational system, and since I cannot improve on this formulation, I transmit it here in the thought that you too may find it revealing.

> By being generous with time, yes, lavish with it, Nature allows man an extraordinary chance to learn. What gain can there be, then, in throwing away this natural advantage by rewarding precocity, as we certainly do when we gear the grades in school to chronological age by starting the first grade at the age of six and college entrance for the vast majority at seventeen and a half to nineteen? *For, once you have most of your students the same age, the academic rewards*—from scholarships to internships and residences—go to those who are uncommonly bright *for their age*. In other words, you have rewarded precocity, which may or may not be the precursor of later ability. So, in effect, you have unwittingly belittled man's cardinal educational capital—time to mature.[21]

The social fact noted by Gregg is of no small consequence for the collective advancement of knowledge as well as for distributive justice. As he goes on to argue, "precocity thus may succeed in the immediate competitive struggle, but, in the long run, at the expense of mutants having a slower rate of development but greater potentialities."[22] By suggesting that there are such slow-starting mutants who have *greater* potentialities than some of the precocious, Gregg is plainly assuming part of what he then concludes. But, as I noted almost thirty years ago, Gregg's

> argument cuts deeply, nevertheless. For we know only of the "late bloomers" who have eventually come to bloom at all; we don't know the potential late bloomers who, cut off from support and response in their youth, never manage to come into their own at all. Judged ordinary by comparison with their precocious "age-peers," they are treated as youth of small capacity. They slip through the net of our institutional sieves for the location of ability, since this is a net that makes chronological age the basis for assessing relative ability. Treated by the institutional system as mediocrities with little promise of improvement, many of these potential late bloomers presumably come to believe it of themselves and act accordingly. At least what little we know of the formation of self-images suggests that this is so. For most of us most of the time, and not only the so-called "other-directed men" among us, tend to form our self-image—our image of potentiality and of achievement—as a reflection of the images others make plain they have of us. *And it is the images that institutional authorities have of us that in particular tend to become self-fulfilling images: if the teachers, inspecting our Iowa scores and our aptitude-test figures and comparing our record with [those] of our "age-peers," conclude that we're run-of-the-mill and treat us accordingly, then they lead us to become what they think we are.*[23]

Of even more direct import and for our immediate subject is the further observation back then that the institutionalized bias toward precocity, noted by Gregg, may have notably different consequences for comparable youngsters in differing social classes and ethnic groups.

> The potential late bloomers in the less privileged social strata are more likely to lose out altogether than their counterparts in the middle and upper strata. If poor [youths] are not precocious, if they don't exhibit great ability early in their lives and so are not rewarded by scholarships and other sustaining grants, they drop out of school and in many instances never get to realize their potentialities. The potential late bloomers among the well-to-do have a better prospect of belated recognition. Even if they do poorly in their school work at first, they are apt to go on to college in any case. The values of their social class dictate this as the thing to do, and their families can see them through. By remaining in the system, they can eventually come to view. But many of the [presumably] more numerous counterparts in the lower strata are probably lost for good. The bias toward precocity in our institutions thus works profound [and ordinarily hidden] damage on the [potential] late bloomers with few economic or social advantages.[24]

Such differential outcomes need not to be intended by the people engaged in running our educational institutions and thereby affecting patterns of social selection. And it is such unanticipated and unintended consequences of purposive social action—in this case, rewarding primarily early signs of ability—that tend to persist. For they are *latent*, not manifest, social problems, that is, social conditions and processes that are at odds with certain interests and values of the society but are not generally recognized as being so.[25] In identifying the wastage that results from marked inequalities in the training and exercise of socially prized talent, social scientists bring into focus what has been experienced by many as only a personal problem rather than a social problem requiring new institutional arrangements for its reduction or elimination.

Mutatis mutandis, what holds for the accumulation of advantage and of disadvantage in the earliest years of education would hold also at a later stage for those youngsters who have made their way into fields of science and scholarship but who, not having yet exhibited prime performance, are shunted off into the less stimulating milieus for scientific work, with their limited resources. Absent or in short supply are the resources of access to needed equipment, an abundance of able assistance, time institutionally set aside for research, and, above all else perhaps, a cognitive microenvironment composed of colleagues at the research front who are themselves evokers of excellence, bringing out the best in the people around them. Not least is the special resource of being located at strategic nodes in the networks of scientific communication that provide ready access to information at the frontiers of research. By hypothesis, some unknown fraction of the unprecocious works in the vineyards of science are caught up in a process of cumulative disadvantage that removes them early on from the system of scientific work and scholarship.[26]

Other social and cognitive contexts may make for such patterned differentials of cumulative advantage and disadvantage. Harriet Zuckerman suggests, as an example, that just as class origins may differentially affect the rates at which potential late bloomers remain in the educational system long enough to bloom, so academic disciplines may differ in an unplanned tolerance for late blooming. Disciplines in which scholars often develop comparatively late—say, the humanities—presumably provide greater opportunities for late bloomers than those in which early maturation is more common—say, mathematics and the physical and biological sciences. Generalized, these conjectures hold that *contextual differences* such as social class or fields of intellectual activity as well as *individual differences* in the pattern of intellectual growth affect the likelihood of success and failure for potential late bloomers.[27]

Differences in individual capabilities aside, then, processes of accumulative advantage and disadvantage accentuate inequalities in science and learning: inequalities of peer recognition, inequalities of access to resources, and inequalities of scientific productivity. Individual self-selection and institutional social selection interact to affect successive probabilities of being variously located in the opportunity structure of science. When the scientific role performance of individuals measures up to or conspicuously exceeds the standards of a particular institution or discipline—whether this be a matter of ability or of chance—there begins a process of cumulative advantage in which those individuals tend to acquire successively enlarged opportunities for advancing their work (and the rewards that go with it) even further.[28] Since elite institutions have comparatively large resources for advancing research in certain domains, talent that finds its way into these institutions early has the enlarged potential of acquiring differentially accumulating advantages. The systems of reward, allocation of resources, and other elements of social selection thus operate to create and to maintain a class structure in science by providing a stratified distribution of chances among scientists for significant scientific work.[29]

Accumulation of Advantage and Disadvantage Among Scientific Institutions

Skewed distributions of resources and productivity that resemble those we have noted among individual scientists are found among scientific institutions. These inequalities also appear to result from self-augmenting processes. Clearly, the centers of historically demonstrated accomplishments in science attract far larger resources of every kind, human and material, than research organizations that have not yet made their mark. These skewed distributions are well known and need only bare mention here.

- In 1981, some 28 percent of the $4.4 billion of federal support for academic research and development went to just ten universities.[30]

- Universities with great resources and prestige in turn attract disproportionate shares of the presumably most promising students (subject to the precocity restriction we have noted): in 1983, two thirds of the five hundred National Science Foundation graduate fellows elected to study at just fifteen universities.[31]

- Those concentrations have been even more conspicuous in the case of outstanding scientists. Zuckerman found, for example, that at the time they did the research that ultimately brought them the Nobel Prize, 49 percent of the future American laureates working in universities were in just five of them: Harvard, Columbia, Rockefeller, Berkeley, and Chicago. By way of comparison, these five universities comprised less than 3 percent of all faculty members in American universities.[32]

- Zuckerman also found that these resource-full and prestige-full universities seem able to spot and to retain these prime movers in contemporary science. For example, they kept 70 percent of the future laureates they had trained, in comparison with 28 percent of the other Ph.D.s they had trained. Much the same pattern, though less markedly, held for a larger set of sixteen elite institutions.[33]

But enough about these details of great organizational inequalities in science. This only raises the question anew: If the processes of accumulating advantage and disadvantage are truly at work, why are there not even greater inequalities than have been found to obtain?

Countervailing Processes

Or to put the question more concretely and parochially, why have not Harvard, rich in years—350 of them—and in much else, and Columbia, with its 230 years, and, to remain parochial, the Rockefeller, with its 75 years of prime reputation both as research institute and graduate university, jointly garnered just about *all* the American Nobel laureates rather than a "mere" third of them within five years after the prize?[34] Put more generally, why do the posited processes of accumulating advantage and disadvantage not continue without assignable limit?

Even Thomas Macaulay's ubiquitous schoolboy would nowadays know that exponential processes do not continue endlessly. Yet some of us make sensible representations of growth processes within a local range and then mindlessly extrapolate them far outside that range. As Derek Price was fond of saying in this connection, if the exponential rate of growth in the number of scientists during the past half century were simply extrapolated, then every man, woman, and child—to say nothing of their cats and dogs—would have to end up as scientists. Yet we have an intuitive sense that somehow they will not.

In much the same way, every schoolgirl knows that when two systems grow at differing exponential rates, the gap between them swiftly and greatly widens. Yet we sometimes forget that as such a gap approaches a limit, other forces come into play to constrain still further concentrations and inequalities of whatever matters are in question. Such countervailing processes that close off the endless accumulation of advantage have not yet been systematically investigated for the case of science—more particularly, for the distribution of human and material resources in research universities and of scientific productivity within them. Still, I would like to speculate briefly about the forms countervailing processes might take.

Consider for example the notion of an excessive density of talent. It is not a frivolous question to ask: How much concentrated talent can a single academic department or research unit actually stand? How many prime movers in a particular research area can work effectively in a single place? Perhaps there really can be too much of an abstractly good thing.

Think a bit about the patterned motivations of oncoming talents as they confront a high density of talented masters in the same department or research unit. The more autonomous among them might not entirely enjoy the prospect of remaining in the vicinity and, with the Matthew effect at work, in the shadow of their masters, especially if they felt, as youth understandably often comes to feel—sometimes with ample grounds—that those masters have seen their best days. Correlatively, some of the firmly established masters, in a pattern of master-apprentice ambivalence, may not relish the thought of having exceedingly talented younger associates in their own or competing research terrains, who they perceive might subject them to premature replacement, at least in local esteem, when, as anyone can see, they, the masters, are still in their undoubted prime.[35] Not every one of us elders has the same powers of critical self-appraisal, and the same largeness of spirit, as Isaac Barrow, the first occupant of the Lucasian Chair of mathematics at Cambridge, who stepped down from that special chair at the advanced age of thirty-nine in favor of his twenty-seven-year-old student—a chap named Isaac Newton. In our time, of course, at least during the years of seemingly limitless academic affluence and expansion, Barrow would have stayed on and Newton would have been given a new chair. But again, as we have ample cause to know, continued expansion of that kind in any one institution also has its limits.

Apart from such forces generated *within* universities that make for dispersion of human capital in science and learning, there is also the system process of social and cognitive competition *among* universities. Again, a brief observation must stand for a detailed analysis. Entering into that external competition is the fact that the total resources available to a university or research institute must be allocated somehow against its constituent units. Some departments wax poor even in rich universities. This provides opportunities to institutions of considerably smaller resources and reputation. These may elect to concentrate their limited resources in particular fields and departments and so to provide competitively attractive microenvironments to talents of the first class in those fields.

As another countervailing process, populist and democratic values may be called into play in the wider society, external to academic institutions and to science, and lead governmental largesse to be more widely spread in a calculated effort to counteract cumulating advantage in the great centers of learning and research.

But enough of such speculations. I must not further defer examination of the symbolism of intellectual property in science by continuing with observations on countervailing forces that emerge to curb the accumulation of advantage that might otherwise lead to a permanent institutional monopoly or sustained oligopoly in fields of science and the sustained domination of a few individuals in those fields. Just as there is reason to know that the preeminence of individual scientists will inexorably come to an end, so there is reason to expect that various preeminent departments of science will decline while others rise in the fullness of time.[36]

The Symbolism of Intellectual Property in Science

To explore the forms of inequality in science registered by such concepts as the Matthew effect and the accumulation of advantage, we must have some way of thinking about the distinctive equivalents in the domain of science of income, wealth, and property found in the economic domain. How do scientists manage to perceive one another simultaneously as peers and as unequals, in the sense of some being first among equals—*primus inter pares,* as the ancients liked to say? What is the distinctive nature of the coin of the realm and of the intellectual property in science?

The tentative answer to the coinage question I proposed back in 1957 seems to have gained force in light of subsequent work in the sociology of science.[37] The system of coinage is taken to be based on the public recognition of one's scientific contributions by qualified peers. That coinage comes in various denominations: largest in scale and shortest in supply is the towering recognition symbolized by eponyms for an entire epoch in science, as when we speak of Newtonian, Darwinian, Freudian, Einsteinian, or Keynesian eras. A considerable plane below, though still close to the summit of recognition in our time, is the Nobel Prize. Other forms and echelons of eponymy, the practice of affixing the names of scientists to all or part of what they have contributed, comprise thousands of eponymous laws, theories, theorems, hypotheses, and constants, as when we speak of Gauss's theorems, Planck's constant, the Heisenberg uncertainty principle, a Pareto distribution, a Gini coefficient, or a Lazarsfeld latent structure. Other forms of peer recognition distribute to far larger numbers take further graded forms: election to honorific scientific societies, medals and awards of various kinds, named chairs in institutions of learning and research, and, moving to what is surely the most widespread and altogether basic form of scholarly recognition, that which comes with having one's work *used and explicitly acknowledged* by one's peers.

I shall argue that cognitive wealth in science is the changing stock of knowledge, while the socially based psychic income of scientists takes the form of pellets of peer recognition that aggregate into reputational wealth. This conception directs us to the question of the distinctive character of intellectual property in science.

As I suggested at the outset, it is only a seeming paradox that, in science, one's private property is established by giving its substance away. For in a long-standing social reality, only when scientists have published their work and made it generally accessible, preferably in the public print of articles, monographs, and books that enter the archives, does it become legitimately established as more or less securely theirs. That is, after all, what we mean by the expression "scientific contribution": an offering that is accepted, however provisionally, into the common fund of knowledge.

That crucial element of free and open communication is what I have described as the norm of "communism" in the social institution of science—with Bernard Barber going on to propose the less connotational term "communality."[38] Indeed, long before the nineteenth-century Karl Marx adopted the watchword of a fully realized communist society—"from each according to his abilities, to each according to his needs"—this was institutionalized practice in the communication system of science. This is not a matter of human nature, of nature-given altruism. Institutionalized arrangements have evolved to motivate scientists to contribute freely to the common wealth of knowledge according to their trained capacities, just as they can freely take from that common wealth what they need. Moreover, since a fund of knowledge is not diminished through exceedingly intensive use by members of the scientific collectivity—indeed, it is presumably augmented—that virtually free and common good is not subject to what Garrett Hardin has aptly analyzed as "the tragedy of the commons": first the erosion and then the destruction of a common resource by the individually rational and collectively irrational exploitation of it.[39] In the commons of science it is structurally the case that the give and the take both work to enlarge the common resource of accessible knowledge.

The structure and dynamics of this system are reasonably clear. Since positive recognition by peers is the basic form of *extrinsic* reward in science, all other extrinsic rewards, such as monetary income from science-connected activities, advanced in the hierarchy of scientists, and enlarged access to human and material scientific capital, derive from it. But, obviously, peer recognition can be widely accorded only when the correctly attributed work is widely known in the pertinent scientific community. Along with the motivating *intrinsic* reward of working on a scientific problem and solving it, this kind of extrinsic reward system provides great incentive for engaging in the often arduous and tedious labors required to produce results that enlist the attention of qualified peers and are put to use by some of them.

This system of open publication that makes for the advancement of scientific knowledge requires normatively guided reciprocities. It can operate effectively only if the practice of making one's work communally accessible is supported by the correlative practice in which scientists who make use of that work acknowledge having done so. In effect, they thus reaffirm the property rights of the scientist to whom they are then and there indebted. This amounts to a pattern of legitimate appropriation as opposed to the pattern of illegitimate *ex*propriation (plagiary).

We thus begin to see that the institutionalized practice of citations and references in the sphere of learning is not a trivial matter. While many a general reader—that is, the lay reader located outside the domain of science and scholarship—may regard the lowly footnote or the remote endnote or the bibliographic parenthesis as a dispensable nuisance, it can be argued that these are in truth central to the incentive system and an underlying sense of distributive justice that do much to energize the advancement of knowledge.

As part of the intellectual property system of science and scholarship, references and citations serve two types of functions: instrumental cognitive functions and symbolic institutional functions. The first of these involves directing readers to the sources of knowledge that have been drawn upon in one's work. This enables research-oriented readers, if they are so minded, to assess for themselves the knowledge claims (the ideas and findings) in the cited source; to draw upon other pertinent materials in that source that may not have been utilized by the citing intermediary publication; and to be directed in turn by the cited work to other, prior sources that may have been obliterated by their incorporation in the intermediary publication.

But citations and references are not only essential aids to scientists and scholars concerned to verify statements or data in the citing text or to retrieve further information. They also have not-so-latent symbolic functions. They maintain intellectual traditions and provide the peer recognition required for the effective working of science as a social activity. All this, one might say, is tucked away in the aphorism that Newton made his own in that famous letter to Hooke where he wrote: "If I have seen further, it is by standing on ye shoulders of Giants."[40] The very form of the scientific article as it has evolved over the last three centuries normatively requires authors to acknowledge on whose shoulders they stand, whether these be the shoulders of giants or, as is often the case, those of men and women of science of approximately average dimensions for the species *scientificus*. Thus, in our brief study of the evolution of the scientific journal as a sociocognitive invention, Harriet Zuckerman and I have taken note of how Henry Oldenburg, the editor of the newly invented *Transactions of the Royal Society* in the seventeenth-century England, induced the emerging new breed of scientist to abandon a frequent long-standing practice of sustained secrecy and to adhere instead to "the new form of free communication through a motivating exchange: open disclosure in exchange for institutionally guaranteed honorific property rights in the new knowledge given to others."[41]

That historically evolving set of complementary role obligations has taken deep institutional root. A composite cognitive and moral framework calls for the systematic use of references and citations. As with all normative constraints in society, the depth and consequential force of the moral obligation to acknowledge one's sources become most evident when the norm is violated (and the violation is publicly visible). The failure to cite the original text that one has quoted at length or drawn upon becomes socially defined as theft, as intellectual larceny or, as it is better known since at least the seventeenth century, as plagiary. Plagiary involves expropriating the one kind of private property that even the dedicated abolitionist of private productive property, Karl Marx, passionately regarded as inalienable (as witness his preface to the first edition of *Capital* and his further thunderings on the subject throughout that revolutionary work).

To recapitulate: the bibliographic note, the reference to a source, is not merely a grace note, affixed by way of erudite ornamentation. (That it can be so used, or abused, does not of course negate its core uses.) The reference serves both instrumental and symbolic functions in the transmission and enlargement of knowledge. Instrumentally, it tells us of work we may not have known before, some of which may hold further interest for us; symbolically, it registers in the enduring archives the intellectual property of the acknowledged source by providing a pellet of peer recognition of the knowledge claim, accepted or expressly rejected, that was made in that source.

Intellectual property in the scientific domain that takes the form of recognition by peers is sustained, then, by a code of common law. This provides socially patterned incentives, apart from the intrinsic interest in inquiry, for attempting to do good scientific work and for giving it over to the common wealth of science in the form of an open contribution available to all who would make use of it, just as the common law exacts the correlative obligation on the part of the users to provide the reward of peer recognition by reference to that contribution. Did space allow—which, happily for you, it does not—I would examine the special case of tacit citation and of "obliteration by incorporation" (or, even more briefly, OBI): the obliteration of the sources of ideas, methods, or findings by their being anonymously incorporated in current canonical knowledge.[42] Many of these cases of seemingly unacknowledged intellectual debt, it can be shown, are literally exceptions that prove the rule, that is to say, they are no exceptions at all since the references, however tacit, are evident to knowing peers.

Once we understand that the sole property right of scientists in their discoveries has long resided in peer recognition of it and in derivative collegial esteem, we begin to understand better the concern of scientists to get there first and to establish their priority.[43] That concern then becomes identifiable as a "normal" response to institutionalized values. The complex of validating the worth of one's work through appraisal by competent others and the seemingly anomaly, even in a capitalistic society, of publishing one's work without being directly recompensed for each publication have made for the growth of public knowledge and the eclipse of private tendencies toward hoarding private knowledge (secrecy), still much in evidence as late as the seventeenth century. Current renewed tendencies toward secrecy, and not alone in what Henry Etzkowitz has described as "entrepreneurial science,"[44] will, if extended and prolonged, introduce major change in the institutional and cognitive workings of science.

Since I have imported, not altogether metaphorically, such categories as intellectual property, psychic income, and human capital into this account of the institutional domain of science, it is perhaps fitting to draw once again upon a chief of the tribe of economists for a last word on our subject. Himself an inveterate observer of human behavior rather than only of economic numbers, and also himself a practitioner of science who keeps green the memory of those involved in the genealogy of an idea. Paul Samuelson cleanly distinguishes the gold of scientific fame from the brass of popular celebrity. This is how he concluded his presidential address, a quarter century ago, to an audience of fellow economists: "Not for us is the limelight and the applause [of the world outside ourselves]. But that doesn't mean the game is not worth the candle or that we do not in the end win the game. In the long run, the economic scholar works for the only coin worth having—our own applause."[45]

Notes

1. Robert K. Merton, "The Matthew Effect in Science," *Science*, 5 January 1968, *159*(3810:56–63; rpt. in Merton, *The Sociology of Science*, ed. Norman W. Storer (Chicago: Univ. Chicago Press, 1973), Ch. 20.

2. Harriet Zuckerman, "Nobel Laureates: Sociological Studies of Scientific Collaboration" (Ph.D. diss., Columbia Univ., 1965). The later fruits of Zuckerman's research appear in Zuckerman, *Scientific Elite: Nobel Laureates in the United States* (New York: Free Press, 1977); an account of the procedures adopted in these tape-recorded interviews appears in Zuckerman, "Interviewing an Ultra-Elite," *Public Opinion Quarterly*, 1972, 36:159–175. This is occasion for repeating what I have noted in reprinting the original "Matthew Effect in Science": "It is now [1973] belatedly evident to me that I drew upon the interview and other materials of the Zuckerman study to such an extent that, clearly, the paper should have appeared under joint authorship." A sufficient sense of distributive and commutative justice requires one to recognize, however belatedly, that to write a scientific or scholarly paper is not necessarily sufficient grounds for designating oneself as its sole author.

3. Warren O. Hagstrom, *The Scientific Community* (New York: Basic Books, 1965), pp. 24–25.

4. Zuckerman, *Scientific Elite* (cit. n. 2), pp. 140–228.

5. R. C. Lewontin and J. L. Hubby, "Citation Classic," *Current Contents/Life Sciences*, 28 Oct. 1985, No. 43, p. 16.

6. Ronald W. Clark, *J. B. S.: The Life and Work of J. B. S. Haldane* (New York: Coward-McCann, 1969), p. 247.

7. The term and concept "Matthew effect" has diffused widely since its coinage a quarter century ago. Geographically, it has become common usage in the West and, my colleague Andrew Walder informs me, has traveled to mainland China where it is known as "mati xiaoying." Substantively, it has diffused into diverse domains other than the sociology and history of science. As examples, it has been adopted in welfare economics and social policy (e.g., by Herman Deleeck, *Het Matteüseffect: De ongelijke verdeling van de sociale overheidsuitgaven in België* [Antwerp: Kluwer, 1983]); in education (Herbert J. Walberg and Shiow-Ling Tsai, "Matthew Effects in Education," *American Educational Research Journal*, 1983, 20:359–373); in administrative studies (James G. Hunt and John D. Blair, "Content, Profess, and the Matthew Effect among Management Academics," *Journal of Management*, 1987, 13:191–210); and, to go on further, in social gerontology (Dale Dannefer, "Aging as Intracohort Differentiation: Accentuation, the Matthew Effect and the Life Course," *Sociological Forum*, 1987, 2:212–236.)

   Despite that wide diffusions, it is also the case that the term "Matthew effect," though not concept, has been questioned from the start on several grounds. In 1968, soon after its first appearance in print, my colleague and later collaborator, David L. Sills, based his reservations about the term "(1) the issue of the priority of the words in Matthew 25:29 (Mark 4:25 said them first [to say nothing of Luke 8:18 and 19:26 probably being indebted to them both]); (2) the authorship issue (it is almost certain that Matthew did not write the Gospel According to Matthew); (3) the attribution issue (the words are Christ's, not those of the author-compiler of the gospel); and (4) the interpretation issue (it is quite unlikely that the point of the parable is 'the more, the more')": Sills to Merton, 29 Mar. 1968.

   These objections have been variously reiterated over the years. Thus the astronomer Charles D. Geilker (*Science*, 1968, 159:1185) maintains that since the three evangelists were all quoting Jesus, I might just as well have called it "the Jesus effect." But then, this would have precluded my having neutralized or educed the Matthew effect of the term by the very act of calling it "the Matthew effect." Most recently, I am indebted to M. de Jonge, professor of theology at the University of Leyden, who has made some of the same observations as Sills. He notes further that "it is highly likely that [Jesus] took over a general saying, current in Jewish (and/or Hellenistic) Wisdom circles—see, e.g., Proverbs 9:9, Daniel 2:21, or Martialis, Epigr. V. 81: 'Sempre pauper eris, si pauper es, Aemiliane. Dantur opes nullis [nunc] nisi divitibus.'" And de Jonge concludes: "The use made of this sentence [in Matthew] by modern authors neglects the eschatological thrust inherent in the saying in all versions, and (in all probability) in Jesus's own version of it. It links up, however, with one thing, you get more; if you have not a penny, they will take from you the little you have.'" M. de Jonge, summary of lecture, "The Matthew Effect," 24 July 1987.

   It is not for me to adjudicate these matters. The priority question of Matthew, Mark, Luke, Q, or still earlier proverbial wisdom had best be left to historians specialized in the matter. In coining the term, I was plainly transferring the pertinent sentence from its theological context into a secular one. Having studied the various interpretations of the five similar passages in the synoptic gospels—principally as summarized and advanced by Ronald Knox, *A Commentary on the Gospels* (New York: Sheed & Ward, 1952)—I decided to give public expression to my preference for Matthew. It was a comfort to learn recently that Wittgenstein had chosen Matthew as *his* favorite gospel: M. O'C. Drury, "Conversations with W," in *Ludwig Wittgenstein: Personal Recollection,* ed. Rush Rhees (Oxford: Blackwell, 1981), p. 177.

8. Robert K. Merton, "The Normative Structure of Science" (1942), rpt. in Merton, *Sociology of Science* (cit. n. 1), p. 273.

9. There are other versions of that confession. Edmund Gosse reports that he "saw him [Browning] take up a copy of the first edition, and say, with a grimace, 'Ah! the entire unintelligible "Sordello"': Gosse, "Robert Browning," *Dictionary of National Biography,* First Supplement (London: Smith, Elder, 1901), Vol. 1. pp. 306–319, on p. 308. The remark has also been attributed to the eighteenth-century poet Friedrich Klopstock and to Hegel. Once again, it is not for me to adjudicate priority claims.

10. The central idea was presented briefly in the National Institutes of Health Lecture in February 1964 and later that year in expanded form at the annual meeting of the American Association for the Advancement of Science. It then underwent several more editions in a succession of public lectures, notably one at the University of Leyden in 1965, before it found its way into print in *Science* (see n. 1).

11. Price had extended Robert Boyle's seventeenth-century term "invisible college" to designate the informal collectives of scientists interacting in their research on similar problems, these groups being generally limited to a size "that can be handled by interpersonal relationships": Derek J. de Solla Price, *Little Science, Big Science . . . and Beyond* (New York: Columbia Univ. Press, 1986; 1st ed., 1963), pp. 76–81, *passim.* For a key paper on cumulative advantage see Price, "A General Theory of Bibliometric and Other Cumulative Advantage Processes," *Journal of the American Society for Information Science,* 1976, 27:292–306. For detailed analysis and history of the idea and a substantial bibliography see Harriet Zuckerman, "Accumulation of Advantage and Disadvantage: The Theory and Its Intellectual Biography," paper presented to the Amalfi Conference of the Associazione Italiana di Sociologia, 1987; forthcoming in *L'opera di Robert K. Merton e la sociologia contemporanea,* ed. Carlo Mongardini (Rome).

12. Silvanus P. Thompson, *The Life of William Thomson, Baron Kelvin of Largs,* 2 vols. (London: Macmillan, 1910), Vol. II, pp. 1225–1274; J. D. North, "Arthur Cayley," *Dictionary of Scientific Biography,* ed. Charles C. Gillispie (New York: Scribners, 1970–1980), Vol. III, p. 163.

13. Alfred J. Lotka, "The Frequency Distribution of Scientific Productivity," *Journal of the Washington Academy of Sciences,* 1926, 16:317–232; and Price, *Little Science, Big Science. . .and Beyond* (cit. n. 11), pp. 38–42.

14. Eugene Garfield, *The Awards of Science and Other Essays* (Philadelphia: ISI Press, 1985), p. 176.

15. Paul D. Allison and John A. Stewart, "Productivity Differences among Scientists: Evidence for Accumulative Advantage," *American Sociological Review,* 1974, 39:596–606. But see Michael A. Faia, "Productivity among Scientists: A Replication and Elaboration," *Amer. Sociol. Rev.,* 1975, 40:825–829, and the following Allison-Stewart "Reply," pp. 829–831; also Roland Mettermeir and Karin D. Knorr, "Scientific Productivity and Accumulative Advantage: A Thesis Reassessed in the Light of International Data," *R & D Management,* 1979, 9:235–239. A later study by Paul D. Allison, J. Scott Long, and Tad Krauze, based on actual rather than simulated age-cohort data for chemists and biochemists, finds increasing inequalities in research publication as a cohort ages but, as yet inexplicably, finds no such increases in rates of citation: "Cumulative Advantage and Inequality in Science," *Amer. Sociol. Rev.,* 1982, 47:615–625.

16. Allison and Stewart, "Productivity Differences" (cit. n. 15); Harriet Zuckerman and Robert K. Merton, "Age, Aging and Age Structure in Science" (1972), rpt. in Merton, *Sociology of Science* (cit. n. 1), pp. 497–559, on pp. 519–537.

17. Derek de Solla Price, "The Productivity of Research Scientists," *1975 Yearbook of Science and the Future* (Chicago: Encyclopedia Britannica, 1975), pp. 409–421, on p. 414. Stephen Cole's studies of age cohorts in various sciences confirm this pattern of a steady rate of publication by a significant fraction of scientists; see Cole, "Age and Scientific Performance," *Amer. J. Sociol.,* 1979, 84:958–977.

18. Stephen Cole, "Professional Standing and the Reception of Scientific Discoveries," *Amer. J. Sociol.,* 1970, 76:286–306, on pp. 291–292.

19. *Ibid.,* p. 292.

20. Jonathan R. Cole and Stephen Cole, *Social Stratification in Science* (Chicago: Univ. Chicago Press, 1973), pp. 112–122, *passim.*

21. Alan Gregg, *Four Future Doctors* (Chicago: Univ. Chicago Press, 1957), pp. 125–126 (emphasis added).

22. *Ibid.*, p. 125.

23. This sociological extension of Gregg's biopsychosocial observation remains as formulated in 1960: R. K. Merton, "'Recognition' and 'Excellent': Instructive Ambiguities," in *Recognition of Excellence: Working Papers*, ed. Adam Yarmolinsky (New York: Free Press, 1962), rpt. in Merton *Sociology of Science* (cit. n. 1), pp. 419–438, on p. 428 (emphasis added). Much theoretical debate and hundreds of empirical studies of this kind of self-fulfilling prophecy in American schools have resulted from the pioneering work of Robert Rosenthal. See, to begin with, Robert Rosenthal and Lenore Jacobson, *Pygmation in the Classroom: Teacher Expectation and Pupils' Intellectual Development* (New York: Holt, Rinehart & Winston, 1968); the critical monography by Janet D. Elashoff and Richard E. Snow, *Pygmalion Reconsidered* (Worthington, Ohio: Jones Publishing, 1971); and a monograph on the "decade of research and debate" by Harris M. Cooper and Thomas L. Good: *Pygmalion Grows Up: Studies in the Expectation Communication Process* (New York/London: Longman, 1983).

24. Merton, "'Recognition' and 'Excellence,'" pp. 428–429.

25. On the first concept see R. K. Merton, "The Unanticipated Consequences of Purposive Social Action," *Amer. Sociol. Rev.*, 1936, 1:984–904; on the concept of manifest and latent social problems see R. K. Merton, *Social Research and the Practicing Professions*, ed. Aaron Rosenblatt and Thomas F. Gieryn (Cambridge: Abt Books, 1982), pp. 43–99, esp. pp. 55ff.

26. Late-bloomer patterns in science remain a largely unexplored area of research. Jonathan R. Cole and Stephen Cole found (in a sample of 120 university physicists that by design overrepresents productive and eminent physicists) that "three-quarters of these physicists began their professional careers by publishing at least three papers soon after their doctorates. There are few 'late bloomers'; only five of the thirty physicists who started off slowly ever became highly productive (averaging 1.5 or more papers a year)": Cole and Cole, *Social Stratification in Science* (cit. n. 20), p. 112. Whether one writes that "only" five of thirty (17 percent) or "as many as" 17 percent proved to be late bloomers is, of course, a matter of tacit judgment. See also Stephen Cole, "Age and Scientific Performance" (cit. n. 17); Nancy Stern, "Age and Achievement in Mathematics: A Case-Study in the Sociology of Science," *Social Studies of Science*, 1978 8:127–140; and Barbara Reskin, "Age and Scientific Productivity: A Critical Review," in *The Demand for New Faculty in Science and Engineering*, ed. Michael S. McPherson (Washington, D.C.: National Academy of Sciences, 1979).

27. Zuckerman, "Accumulation of Advantage and Disadvantage" (cit. n. 11).

28. In terms of a clinical rather than statistical sociology, I have tried to trace the process of accumulation of advantage in the academic life course of the historian of science and my longtime friend Thomas S. Kuhn, as I have done more recently in tracking my own experience as apprentice to the then world dean of history of science who has been honored by the establishment of the George Sarton Chair in the History of Science at the University of Ghent. For the case of Kuhn see R. K. Merton, *The Sociology of Science: An Episodic Memoir* (Carbondale: Southern Illinois Univ. Press, 1979), pp. 71–109; for my own case see Merton, "George Sarton: Episodic Recollections by an Unruly Apprentice," *Isis*, 1985, 76:47–486.

29. On processes of stratification in science see Harriet Zuckerman, "Stratification in American Science," *Sociological Inquiry*, 1979, 40:235–257; Zuckerman, *Scientific Elite* (cit. n. 2); Cole and Cole, *Social Stratification in Science* (cit. n. 20); Jonathan R. Cole, *Fair Science: Women in the Scientific Community* (New York: Free Press, 1979); Jerry Gaston, *The Reward System in British and American Science* (New York: Wiley, 1978); G. Nigel Gilbert, "Competition, Differentiation and Careers in Science," *Social Science Information*, 1977, 16:103–123; Hagstrom, *Scientific Community* (cit. n. 3); Lowell Hargens, Nichoals C. Mullins, and Pamela K. Hecht, "Research Areas and Stratification Processes in Science," *Soc. Stud. Sci.*, 1980, 1055;74; Hargens and Diane Felmlee, "Structural Determinants of Stratification in Science," *Amer. Sociol. Rev.*, 1984, 49:685–697; Norman W. Storer, *The Social System of Science* (New York: Holt, Rinehart & Winston, 1966); Jack A. Goldstone, "A Deductive Explanation of the Matthew Effect in Science," *Soc. Stud. Sci.*, 1979, 9:385–392; and Stephen P. Turner and Daryl E. Chubin, "Chance and Eminence in Science: Ecclesiastes II," *Soc. Sci. Info.*, 1979, 3:437–449.

30. National Science Foundation, *Federal Support to Universities, Colleges, and Selected Nonprofit Institutions, Fiscal Year 1981* (Washington, D.C.: U.S. Government Printing Office, 1983), pp. 79–80.

31. *National Science Foundation, Grants and Awards for Fiscal year 1983* (Washington, D.C.: U.S. Government Printing Office, 1984), pp. 215–217.

32. Zuckerman, *Scientific Elite* (cit. n. 2), p. 171.

33. *Ibid.*, Ch. 5.

34. *Ibid.*, p. 241.

35. R. K. Merton and Elinor Barber, "Sociological Ambivalence" (1963), rpt. in Merton, *Sociological Ambivalence* (New York: Free Press, 1976), pp. 3–31, esp. pp. 4–6; Vanessa Merton, R. K. Merton, and Elinor Barber, "Client Ambivalence in Professional Relationships," in *New Directions in Helping*, ed. B. M. DePaula *et al.* (New York: Academic Press, 1983), Vol. II, pp. 13–44, on pp. 26–27.

36. Surveys of the quality of graduate departments in American universities have been conducted from time to time, with the last three of them, in 1966, 1970, and 1982, having adopted more-or-less similar methods of inquiry. I am indebted to an unpublished study by Donald Hood that identifies patterns of substantial change in the assessed quality of academic departments in the course of quite short intervals.

37. R. K. Merton, "Priorities in Scientific Discoveries" (1957), rpt. in Merton, *Sociology of Science* (cit. n. 1), pp. 286–324.

38. R. K. Merton, "The Normative Structure of Science" (1942), rpt. *ibid.*, pp. 267–278, esp. pp. 273–275; and Bernard Barber, *Science and the Social Order* (New York: Free Press, 1952), pp. 130–132.

39. Garrett Hardin, "The Tragedy of the Commons," *Science*, 1968, *162*:1243–1247.

40. George Sarton was long interested in the history of the aphorism. Since it says much in little about one of the ways in which scientific knowledge grows, I indulged in a Shandean account of its historical adventures: R. K. Merton, *On the Shoulders of Giants* (1965; New York: Harcourt Brace Jovanovich, 1985).

41. Harriet Zuckerman and R. K. Merton, "Patterns of Evaluation in Science: Institutionalization, Structure and Functions of the Referee System," *Minerva*, 1971, *9*:66–100.

42. I easily resist the temptation to begin a discourse on this pattern in the transmissions of knowledge. Short proleptic discussions of "obliteration by incorporation" are found in Merton, *Social Theory and Social Structure* (New York: Free Press, 1968), pp. 25–38; Merton, foreword to Eugene Garfield, *Citation Indexing: Its Theory and Application in Science, Technology, and Humanities* (New York: Wiley, 1979); and Garfield, *Essays of an Information Scientist* (Philadelphia: ISI Press, 1977), pp. 396–399.

43. For the claim that the race for priority derives from the culture of science itself see Merton, "Priorities in Scientific Discoveries" (cit. n. 37), pp. 286–308. It is further proposed (pp. 309–324) that the extreme emphasis upon significant originality in the culture of science can become pathogenic, making for such occasional side effects as the cooking of fraudulent evidence, the hoarding of one's own data while making free use of others' data, and the breaching of the mores of science by failing to acknowledge the work of predecessors one has drawn upon.

44. Henry Etzkowitz, "Entrepreneurial Scientists and Entrepreneurial Universities in American Academic Science," *Minerva*, 1983, *21*:198–233.

45. Paul Samuelson, "Economics and the History of Ideas" (delivered in 1961), rpt. in *The Collected Scientific Papers of Paul A. Samuelson*, ed. Joseph E. Stiglitz (Cambridge, Mass.: MIT Press, 1966), Vol. II, pp. 1499–1516.

Fayerweather 415, Columbia University, New York, New York 10027.

E Pluribus Unum?
Academic Structure, Culture, and the
Case of Feminist Scholarship

PATRICIA J. GUMPORT

E pluribus unum—out of many, one. Higher education scholars have used this phrase both descriptively and prescriptively. Both as metaphor and motto, the phrase suggests that, despite a plurality of interests and specialties in academic life, there is cohesion within the organization of academic work and that this cohesion corresponds to lines of formal structure based on one's disciplinary and institutional affiliation. In this article, I call into question the utility of this idealized image as a conceptual frame for understanding complex variations in academic culture. Drawing on recent empirical data about the formation of intentional intellectual communities, I analyze feminist scholarship as a contemporary current in academic life.

Two significant findings are: (1) Faculty seek and find intellectual communities beyond lines of formal structure (e.g., department, institution); and (2) The departmental organization of academic work does not necessarily function as an integrating framework for resolving conflicting interests and advancing common ones. This analysis concludes with an invitation to rethink the premises about culture and structure that are implicit in prevailing conceptual frameworks for studying change in higher education organizations.

Frameworks for Understanding Academic Change

The current configuration of departments and disciplines across campuses evolved in an evolutionary process of intellectual and social differentiation, according to functionalist accounts of academic change in American higher education (e.g., Blau 1973; Clark 1983; Rudolph 1981; Trow 1984). From this perspective, disputes over curricula and new academic programs have been handled by additive solutions—that is, expanding to cover a plurality of interests rather than replacing what counts as worthwhile academic pursuits. Regardless of whether this explanation is the definitive historical explanation, it is apparent that differentiation has its limits. Fewer resources and more capital-intensive academic endeavors render infinite expansion an untenable solution for solving conflicting academic visions.

With varying degrees of urgency over the past decade, some scholars have challenged higher education to "pull itself together" against the current proliferation of new fields and the "blurring of genres" (Geertz 1983; Clark 1983, 1987). Other scholars have warned that "faculty are even more sharply divided than in previous years, . . . and the end of this . . . fragmentation is not in sight" (Bowen and Schuster 1986, 152). One assessment of this state of academic affairs is to assure us of *e pluribus unum*, that is an enduring, harmonious system where faculty are held together by a devotion to knowledge, dual commitments to one's discipline and institution, a unified system albeit constituted by a pluralistic landscape of interests, as Clark (1987, 145) has proposed. An alternative assessment is to view the contemporary scene as a site of oppositional discourses, imbued with fundamental conflicts of vision and resistance to new ideas, such that the revision of the current departmental organization may be imminent (Lincoln 1986).

Such divergent assessments of how things are and how they may be in the future compel us to reconsider some assumptions about academia. In the broadest sense, when we speak of the organization of academic work or of the academic profession, we usually presuppose some degree of integration, whether it be cohesion among people around a knowledge base by discipline or by department, or whether it be cohesion around a professional ideal of purpose or service.

Yet, both within and across disciplines as well as within and across departments on any given campus, such cohesion appears to be waning or, if present, is buried under an array of dramatically different visions of the nature and content of academic knowledge. Debates over the value of Euro-centric scholarship and Western culture undergraduate requirements in the curricula, to name two recent examples, illustrate not only different but conflicting interests. Although the metaphor of organizational culture has been implicitly used in higher education for over two decades (e.g., Clark 1970, 1972), the increased popularity and refinement of cultural perspectives among higher education researchers and managers attest to the pervasive interest in understanding the glue that holds academia together. The theoretical and empirical work on organizational culture in higher education is, at least in part, a response to this functionalist concern.

Whether positing structural dimensions of organizations as a foil or merely as an analytical complement, deliberate cultural analysis in higher education settings has provided an alternative set of concepts and methods for studying cultural artifacts (e.g., myths, symbols, and rituals) in higher education organizations. The purpose of such research is to uncover beliefs and values among organizational participants, with the promise of more accurately portraying organizational life (Clark 1983; Dill 1982; Gumport 1988; Harman 1988; Masland 1985; Tierney 1988).

Most of such higher education research has been constructed and disseminated within a functionalist paradigm that implicitly seeks to uncover layers of academic order and mechanisms of integration. For example, Andrew T. Masland proposes that culture be seen as "a force that provides stability and a sense of continuity" (1985, 165). Along similar lines, William G. Tierney suggests that the study of cultural dynamics can help us "to decrease conflict" and "to understand and, hopefully, to reduce adversarial relationships" (1988, 18, 5).

Grounded in an *e pluribus unum* premise of organic solidarity (Durkheim 1933), such frameworks for understanding academic organization may be appealing for their currency as a motto, if not as a metaphor, for the hoped-for, ensuing coordination. However, as a conceptual frame for analyzing academic culture, the approach limits inquiry by assuming equilibrium rather than investigating it as an open empirical question. Conflict among organizational participants is seen as either a transient condition that erupts in an otherwise smoothly running system or as a more substantial difference of interest that nonetheless can and should be remedied or resolved. The solution may be structural (by creating a new organizational unit) or cultural (by accepting a divergence of beliefs). Conflict in academic culture is conceptually rendered part of a trend toward differentiation and pluralism.

An alternative starting point for the analysis of academic culture is to ask a different question than what glue is holding everything together, for it may be that things will fall apart or fall out along different lines. Rather than beginning with integration as an *a priori* analytical strait-jacket, we can examine what faculty do—"not what others think they do or should be doing," as George Kuh and Elizabeth Whitt have proposed (1988, 109). What becomes centrally problematic is to examine the nature of individuals' interests and commitments. In other words, the researcher should try not only to find out whether faculty really have dual commitments to their disciplines and institutions, but also to describe faculty perceptions of how their comments are constructed in different academic settings. This approach leaves open the possibility for ambiguity, with an enduring interest in the sociology of knowledge and of science to determine the interplay between social structures and the development of ideas.

Accordingly, my analysis is framed by two questions: First, how do faculty seek and find intellectual community? And second, how do patterns of association differ in different campus organizational settings? I have found that the emergence of feminist scholarship and its associated academic networks call into question the accuracy of the *e pluribus unum* framework. The analysis is based on interview data from twenty-seven full-time faculty located on two campuses and case study data analyzing how different organizations frame the possibilities for forming intentional communities. These data are drawn from a larger two-year study in which I conducted seventy-five semi-structured, in-depth interviews with administrators and a stratified, random sample of women faculty across ten campuses and three disciplines (Gumport 1987). By supplementing the interviews with case study research and by conceptually anchoring faculty at the center of the analysis, I examined how faculty are constrained by, yet contribute to, their academic settings.

A major substantive line of inquiry in the interviews was examining whether and how these faculty became involved with feminist scholarship and its teaching arm, women's studies. Some of the faculty were located in conventional departments (sociology, history, and philosophy); others were in autonomous women's studies programs. Since they were all women who were in academia at a time of heightened gender consciousness, the contemporary emergence of academic feminism provided a set of intellectual, social, and political interests that they could ignore or embrace. Voluntary association was the major mechanism whereby faculty became participants in this newly emerging, not-yet-legitimate academic specialty. Feminist scholarship is interdisciplinary, potentially of interest to faculty in a wide range of disciplines, and controversial. Some scholars interpret it as having an explicitly political and oppositional agenda. These factors make it a suitable empirical opportunity to examine contemporary lines of academic culture on different campuses.

Analysis

Through an iterative, grounded theory analysis of the interview data (Glaser and Strauss 1967), I discerned patterns that reflected a complex process of finding intellectual affinity and forming intentional networks that cross-cut structural lines of departments. Faculty described individual and group processes as characterized by ambiguity of purpose and conflict of vision as well as by an absence of forethought, conscious planning, or likelihood of academic rewards. In fact, more often than not, the reference group and source of authority were identified as outside the department and sometimes outside academia entirely. Visible communities of feminist scholars emerged across departments as well as across campuses.

Faculty career histories and intellectual biographies enable us to examine what compelled them to associate and what subsequent senses of intellectual and organizational community emerged. First, I address the individual level of how faculty conceive of their intellectual community. Second, I analyze the campus levels for the distinctive informal networks that emerged.

Although individual variations may be interesting in and of themselves, different patterns among individuals provide greater insight for the analysis of social action. The faculty in this sample may be grouped into the following four patterns: (1) scholars whose interests matched their conventional departments and who had no interest or participation in feminist thinking; (2) feminist scholars working primarily in their department and discipline of training but who had some dual or mixed loyalties; (3) feminist scholars in departments yet whose primary loyalty was to women's studies as an autonomous unit separate from the conventional department; and (4) feminist scholar-activists located in women's studies programs who saw themselves as change agents to develop women's studies as an autonomous unit, and whose primary affinity was to the broader national feminist movement.

In this sample, those in the first group were fewer in number, especially among those who entered graduate school in the 1960s. The other three groups reflected some involvement with feminist scholarship and conveyed varying experiences of fragmentation and conflict in academia, both internally and interpersonally. They expressed a sense of conflicting membership within their departments and even internally within an emerging women's studies subculture. I examine each group in turn.

Faculty Identifying with Departments

The scholars who were oriented to their department and discipline agendas did not see their work as intersecting with feminist scholarship in a meaningful way. They did not become involved with feminist research or teach women's studies, deeming them either irrelevant or inappropriate due to the perceived political nature of feminist scholarship.

Four quotations illustrate this sense of detachment. A philosopher commented, "I was conscious of there being a feminist movement; but since there weren't any differences for me as a women at the time, I more or less ignored all of it."

"I could see it as an area of interest but not something that can stand alone," said a sociologist. "It could get into trouble if it becomes a matter of taking sides rather than material that can be analyzed and looked at critically. It's fine to see women as victims, but that should be separate from the academic milieu. I feel uncomfortable with that."

"I just don't understand it," admitted a second sociologist, and added, "I don't think I agree with it. It worries me a little . . . because I can see people saying we need a Catholic or Jewish sociology; we need a sociology of white supremacy or anti-white supremacy. It gets off into directions I feel real uncomfortable with. . . . I'm not very comfortable with a larger political role. I don't have any problem with people trying to shift the agenda of the discipline as an intellectual activity, but I have problems with combining the roles—using their academic credentials to legitimate a particular political position. . . . I prefer to keep them separate."

"The label is a disservice," a historian charged. "I've had enough ideologies and dogmas. I have not found [feminist scholars] a natural audience. . . . I'm mistrustful. . . . They want something more doctrinaire, much more ideological."

These four scholars conceived of themselves and their sense of community as clearly anchored in their departments and disciplines. Their networks and associations were not problematic, since they followed the formal structure; but they were only a few voices in my sample.

Faculty with Mixed Loyalties

The second group tried to balance the dual loyalties of their department/discipline and their emerging interests in feminist scholarship.

For some, the balancing act worked. These were usually historians who found a niche in the emerging subfield of women's history. For example, one historian explained she "fell into" feminist scholarship "by accident." Initially she was worried about possible consequences and

> . . .toyed briefly with not telling anyone here that I was working on it, because I was afraid of how it might be perceived, especially as I was coming up for tenure at the time. But I decided not to. There was the practical reason that people would wonder what I was working on. . . . Then it also just didn't seem right. Then I presented some of it in the form of a paper to colleagues in my department. It went very well. I was amazed. Some of the issues that I dealt with are at the intersection of sex and power. They are interested in that. . . . They were very supportive and made good suggestions, and I was much relieved.

Recalling her relations with departmental colleagues prior to her feminist research, she realized in retrospect that there was no need to worry: "I had established such a moderate or really a conservative facade in my department that . . . I felt it would not be detrimental." This scholar thus conceived of herself and her community as centered in history, yet able to accommodate a feminist research project.

Others found no convergence between interests in historical and feminist scholarship. They either felt pulled in two different directions or tried to enact a new kind of scholarly identity.

Another historian described herself as "balancing on women's history and French history. Each of them takes me in a direction away from the other. I do pursue women's history outside of France and French history outside of women's history. But in different periods of my life, I'm concentrating either on one or the other."

Her primary professional involvement was the American Historical Association, although she characterized that group as "not exciting." In contrast, she was "attached to" the Berkshire Conference of women's historians and feminist scholars with related interests: "It's special and it's a happening. To go to a place where you know you're going to be indulging your professional interests with other women . . . perks you up in a sense because it takes away a burden you don't even know is there when you're working in a male-dominated place like this." In spite of her identification with those who attend the Berkshire Conference, her sense of her work and community was still problematic. She felt pulled apart, unable to find a home entirely in either location.

In trying to reconcile this kind of tension, some scholars in history, sociology, and philosophy generated a research agenda and tried to establish a new intellectual and organizational identity created from the intersection of disciplinary and feminist interests. Historians were most likely to succeed in making this a viable option, although others made concerted efforts.

One historian, who described herself as a pioneer, characterized her efforts:

> I was putting together the politics and the scholarship and feeling like it had to be done. . . . I still do it that way. You can see all my articles start out with the contemporary political issue and end up with it, too. And I do the history in between. . . . Now I define myself as someone in women's history and a feminist. I have a network of women's historians around the country. It's an intellectual community: we read each others' work and comment on it . . . and go to conferences. We also socialize at those gatherings and other times. It's also active as a political network.

She had a clear sense of belonging in a feminist scholarly community. Rather than feeling pulled in two separate directions or working in two separate worlds, she had constructed a new primary identity as a "feminist historian." Simultaneously she retained a strong disciplinary orientation, which reflected a comfortable congruence with her being located in the history department at a leading research university: "I'm very wedded to history," she described herself. "I read in other fields, but I really believe in history and in having strong disciplinary training, that without it people can float too much. So my primary identity is as a feminist historian."

It is noteworthy that both this historian and the one who described herself as "balancing" between feminism and history were in the same department at the same institution. Yet their experiences differed, one ending up with dual loyalties while the second ended up constructing a new sense of self and community.

Two philosophers also spoke of finding a new scholarly path which united their divergent scholarly interests. However, they characterized this orientation as more problematic, both in the process and in the outcome, than for the historians. Both philosophers described the difficulty of, first, establishing an intellectual and organizational niche and, second, finding an audience for their research.

The first philosopher observed, "In college I was definitely not a feminist," but over the past two decades, she became a self-described "feminist and a philosopher." She described the process: "The challenge for me as my own person and independent thinker was to get the blend that is desirable. I felt that it was too difficult . . . to meet the narrow constraints of the discipline, so I shifted into a women's studies program for a while. That context was invaluable for me [in being] able to develop my thinking freely." Then she took a position in a philosophy department. Her sense of her work was that "it is not straight philosophy." Her most recent paper probably will not be accepted for the American Philosophical Association annual conference because "it's too bizarre in its multidisciplinary approach." In sum, this scholar did not see herself fitting comfortably into her discipline.

A second philosopher also sought to "have something to say to both feminist and philosophical audiences," a task she conceived of as doing something new for her field.

> I take the current [feminist] agenda and ask myself is there something useful a philosopher can do here. . . . When I'm speaking to a feminist audience . . . , I have to make my work relevant in ways that I don't have to when I'm speaking to a philosophical audience. . . . After the initial encounter between the disciplinary work and feminist concerns, then the work develops its own momentum and generates its own sort of questions, so that it no longer seems appropriate to talk about my work as bridging some gap between my subfield in philosophy and separate [feminist] concerns.

This philosopher still saw negative consequences for not "doing straight philosophy," so she spent time developing a feminist scholarly network and trying to publish in both feminist and philosophy journals.

In sum, the pattern characteristic of this group was mixed loyalties that they tried, with different degrees of success, to balance or blend through different strategies. Historians tended to find more resolution in carving out an intellectual and organizational niche for themselves and their community.

Faculty Identifying Primarily with Women's Studies

A third pattern in this sample was scholars who, although located in conventional departments, found their intellectual and social center outside the department. For the most part, they were extensively involved with a campus women's studies program and read, attended, and published primarily in women's studies forums. They consistently reported feeling "more and more distance" from their departments. (Not surprisingly, these scholars were employed at a comprehensive state university, not a research university, which is a point I will address later in the analysis.)

As an example of this pattern, a historian described how she has struggled with this dimension of academic life since graduate school in the late 1960s. She stayed in history, even though her identity and interests gradually moved into women's studies. As a graduate student, she recalled, the discipline was more a heavy hand than an intellectual home. "Where there was a question of my values being in direct conflict with the trajectory of the disciplinary career, I got slapped down and I was very well aware of that. I could see that happening. I cried. I wept. I said it was unfair. And I changed."

Years later, her intellectual affinities turned toward women's studies, even though she had a full-time position in a history department. She did not find it feasible to be in both worlds, so she, in effect, "dropped out of the history department." She remembered: "I wouldn't serve on any committees and I wouldn't socialize with anyone. I had nothing to do with the department. . . . All of my orientation was with the women's studies program. Because that was a confrontational program at the time, the separation was absolute. I could be here, or I could be there. But I couldn't be in both places."

In retrospect, she characterized herself as having been "professionally dumb" to make primary commitment to women's studies without thinking about the consequences. Still, her identification with women's studies was so strong that "if someone had said don't risk it, it would have to have been the leader of our feminist movement. If the chair of the [history] department had said to me, 'Look, I'm with you and I love what you're doing for the women's studies but I'm not going to be able to get you through the department,' I would have said 'screw you.'" She gained tenure in her department, probably because of her outstanding teaching record; her courses, which were cross-listed with women's studies, were popular and consistently well-enrolled.

Naturally faculty located in women's studies programs most frequently expressed the feeling of having an intellectual and organizational home in women's studies. Since they were not located in conventional departments, they would have a greater opportunity to find congruence between their interests, expertise, and organizational niche. However, such positions lacked the security of appointments in more traditional departments. Only some women's studies faculty had "retreat rights" to another department in the event of program dissolution. However, the perceived marginality of women's studies coupled with a lack of common intellectual interests made those future scenarios unsatisfactory. One women's studies program director, who was simultaneously a full professor in a sociology department, explained her own situation: "The loss of collegiality with my 'home' department is something I hadn't anticipated would happen. I no longer go to their meetings—on campus or nationally in the association. I can't do both." The center of her academic life was clearly in women's studies, locally, regionally, and nationally—an orientation shared by some other women's studies scholars who had departmental appointments.

Faculty Identifying with Feminism

Some faculty with positions in women's studies differed from their department colleagues in having a distinctive nonacademic orientation, where the faculty member conceived of her work and her community as lying outside the academy. In those cases, the primary loyalty and reference group became more the political movement than the academy.

For example, one faculty member reported having had a series of terminal appointments over the last seven years, part-time on and off, later full-time in a women's studies program. "Basically I've been a gypsy scholar and to me it [politics and academics] is not an internal conflict. If it's a choice between my political convictions and a job, the job can go to hell. . . . I will never make those kinds of compromises. It's not an internal conflict, but it's a conflict with the system." She identifies herself as a feminist scholar and black scholar who believes in women's studies programs as "an essential institutional power base . . . not . . . in it being a safe harbor, but in it being a real space for women . . . scholars and women students." She describes having a primary political agenda.

She is located in a women's studies program on a campus where the program functions much like a department; a handful of other full-time faculty in women's studies ostensibly share her feminist scholarly interests. However, this setting has not become a complete home. As a woman of color, she felt that she was hired to boost enrollments; and the other women's studies faculty felt threatened when she wanted to change things, "threatened enough to complain to the administration." She felt betrayed:

> Most of the tension has come in women's studies because they didn't realize what it'd mean to have a woman of color who is not a clone of traditional feminist theory. . . . They put on file with the administration a criticism saying that I was not collegial because I did not validate the work of the women who went before me, that I moved too fast. And they refused to talk with me about it. . . . So that's saying to me we don't want you here, and if we want you here we want you under our control.
>
> Although this particular case may seem extreme, it is a useful reminder that the basic organizing units of academic life do not necessarily convey cohesion of purpose and loyalty. Both on the individual level and the interpersonal level, fragmentation and conflict may be pervasive. Even in a case where women's studies functions like a department, there may be less cohesion than we presume. In fact, faculty involved with women's studies and feminist scholarship admit to internal lack of consensus on program content, visions for change, and even who qualifies as members in their enterprise (Gumport 1990). As one director of a women's studies program observed: "People differ in what they mean by feminist and feminist scholarship, and some programs have been torn apart over it."

Campus Networks

These four patterns of faculty orientations also coincide with different higher education organizational settings. Individuals oriented toward conventional departments without interest or involvement in feminist work as well as individuals who felt pulled in two directions from conflicting departmental and feminist scholarly associations were located at a leading research university. Those whose primary affinities were in autonomous women's studies programs or who were highly politicized and oriented outside academia entirely were located at a comprehensive state university.

At the common-sense level and in a functionalist framework, this pattern is no surprise. One obvious hypothesis is that either the individual women self-selected organizational settings that matched their interests or the research-oriented and teaching-oriented institutions each selected faculty with orientations that fit their particular campus culture. However, rather than assuming conscious choice on either part, and examining desegregated individual behaviors, it is more illuminating to examine the kinds of informal networks that developed in each campus setting.

The reward system within research universities for departmental and disciplinary research and the emphasis in comprehensive state universities on teaching suggest that the different organizational settings provide different possibilities for cross-departmental networks among feminist scholars. The case study data from the two campuses point to a distinctive pattern: the comprehensive university had a thriving cross-departmental feminist, scholarly network; the leading research university had a floundering one.

At the comprehensive university, the faculty in general were described as "progressive" and "having a radical bent." The core of the feminist scholarly community revolved around the women's studies program, which was established in the early 1970s and, at the time of this research, boasted fifty undergraduate majors, eighteen courses a semester, and a dozen faculty (including part-timers) with women's studies appointments. The faculty network also included over a dozen more active feminists located in departments.

The faculty network originated in and has been sustained by students' grass-roots efforts to establish a women's studies program. In the early years, there was a student alliance, where students either ran the courses or taught them informally. Since the courses were well-enrolled and highly politicized, the administration took notice. As an administrator remembered: "It scared the administration. The mere size of the thing, the numbers of people involved, the energy generated around it! I think all that was significant enough to carry us ultimately into the women's studies program itself." Years later, the alliance became an ad hoc committee which has been the intellectual, social, and political center for feminist faculty and students ever since. Many departmental faculty became connected formally by cross-listing courses or serving on committees, or informally by socializing. Their efforts are constrained by time; "we're all teaching heavy loads." Their focus shifted to formulating a master's program in women's studies and whether to make women's studies a general education requirement, thereby changing small, personal classes into large required ones.

As faculty described the campus milieu, they often referred to "the administration." "The administration," they said, "does not penalize us for being involved in women's studies." What seemed to count most was generating and sustaining high enrollment programs. Since departmental involvement and women's studies involvement were not differentially valued, participating in a feminist network on campus had a pay-off.

In contrast to the thriving feminist scholarly network at the comprehensive university, the research university has had a small though growing faculty group, whose members tended to keep an intellectual and organizational anchor in their departments. The women's studies program at the research university was small and had no permanent autonomous faculty lines; except for an occasional visitor, the program relied on cross-listed departmental courses. Established relatively late vis-a-vis the national scene, the program did not grant degrees; students petitioned individually to an interdisciplinary majors committee for a bachelor's degree in women's studies.

At the time of this research, the dozen or so most visible feminist faculty in the departments wanted the teaching program to flourish but recognized the constraints in faculty recruitment and hiring practices in the departments. A historian explained: "The reality of the university is so discipline-based that you do a disservice to create something outside the disciplines. . . . Strategically, people need to be based in the disciplines. . . .And it's not just strategically but intellectually as well." However, the women's studies program director acknowledges that the institution was willing to support women's studies, provided that it demonstrated "strong scholarship" and an "assurance of respectability." The willingness came from the competitive drive for excellence—the fact that "entrepreneurs get their way here. . . . it's survival of the fittest. . . . You survive if you get a high level of visibility, if you are judged by your peers as at the top."

Participating in an emerging informal feminist scholarly network on this campus would have little pay-off for faculty, given the strong disciplinary orientations and time constraints from pressure to publish. In addition, according to one observer in the humanities:

> It's a little risky that no matter how committed you are; you have to draw the line somewhere because there is so much to be done. There are considerations of practicality, of what you need to do and can do if you want to stay here. . . . Most people are much more cautious about getting involved in anything besides writing their books. . . . It's getting labeled—not as a feminist or a women's studies person per se. It's getting labeled as a person who will do non-scholarly, collaborative, student-oriented things. . . . It's the kiss of death.

In spite of the risk, participating in a feminist network on a small scale provides intellectual, social, or political support for faculty who are trying to balance or blend feminist with disciplinary interests. Although informal feminist networks connect people who would otherwise be dispersed and isolated in conventional departments, they may also do a disservice. A philosopher explained: "In general there isn't a location for feminist work in the field. . . . The status of feminist work is still fairly fragile. . . . It's mostly women doing it. And so, of course, [since] women are all engaged in this funny kind of work just really confirms people's initial prejudice that women can't do real philosophy . . . [but] are doing this other thing which isn't real philosophy." In any case, despite the scrutiny and stigma, a scholar with this orientation may still seek a feminist scholarly network as an intellectual and organizational home. Another philosopher explained her own decision to do so and remarked on the same inclination of her colleagues:

> If you are working on feminist stuff, you are likely to feel embattled. . . . The women in philosophy who see themselves as feminist scholars will generally be the only person doing feminist work in a department and may sometimes be the only woman period. [They] may feel cut off or deprived of collegial relationships among departmental colleagues and may develop closer relationships with colleagues in women's studies [located] in other departments. . . . Those are the only places where you get both philosophical colleagueship and feminist colleagueship. You get both of them at the same time, in the same place, in the same sentence. And for most women philosophers that is extremely rare.

Thus, both the advantages and disadvantages of associating with a feminist scholarly network are heightened in the constraints of the research university than in the comprehensive university.

The contrast between two campuses raises questions about the organizational factors that might account for these differences. The inability of the research university to generate—let alone sustain—a thriving feminist scholarly network reflects a distinctive structure and culture which stand in dramatic contrast to that of the comprehensive university.

At the research university, faculty were oriented primarily to their disciplinary colleagues; and departments did the essential work of research and graduate education. In a sense, this peer culture became coercive, guiding faculty behavior and time management as a means of social coordination. In effect, it kept people on their assigned academic tasks, not only junior faculty who faced the "publish or perish" criteria for tenure but senior faculty who earned merit increases in promotion. Since departmental senior faculty held the power, other faculty were not inclined to spend too much time and energy on voluntary associations. Those who chose to do so essentially ran against the grain at their own risk by leaping across the discrete departmental building blocks on which the university organization rests. When it comes to peer review, they ran an even greater risk of not fitting in (Gumport 1990). A feminist scholar who had been denied tenure at a leading research university explained it this way: "It's harder to work when it's not fitting into your discipline in a particular way. You can't expect to get clear judgments and rewards, although you'll get different opinions about it. . . . The problem is the people who could judge it are out there and not in here in my department and my discipline."

In contrast, the locus of power at the comprehensive university lay with administrators, not with a departmental/disciplinary peer culture. Administrators' power was linked to their discretion over academic programs and teaching loads. Enrollment-driven data carried clout. Consequently, there was a greater organizational distance between the faculty and the central administration. Faculty and administrators ended up antagonists, no matter what voluntary associations faculty formed. Since course enrollments were the currency for leverage, it was less important whether a feminist faculty member was participating in women's studies centrally, marginally, or in a conventional department. The issue simply lacked the salience it assumed in the disciplinary peer culture of the research university.

In light of these fundamental differences in organizational settings, it becomes clear that overarching academic beliefs like academic freedom and devotion to knowledge are mediated by local settings. Moreover, each setting coordinates academic work with a different emphasis so that faculty are encouraged to attend to different concerns. Thus, each setting is more likely to raise different possibilities for the formation of a cross-departmental feminist scholarly network. Although these patterns appear to warrant an *e pluribus unum* conclusion, such a conclusion would be overly simplistic and premature. As the first part of this analysis shows, participants interpret and reenact beliefs according to their subjective perceptions and have the potential to reconstitute the settings in which they work.

Conclusion

In an analysis of recent empirical data, I reexamine the functionalist premise of *e pluribus unum*— out of many, one. Rather than beginning with the assumption of the past, present, or future cohesion among organizational participants, as other higher education scholars have, I bring the analysis down to the level of individuals to examine how they enter, negotiate, and play out structural and cultural dimensions of their particular organizational settings. The interview data reveal that faculty conceive of their commitments and their sense of community in ways that do not always correspond with idealized conceptions of academic organization in which departmental and institutional affinities reign supreme.

Setting aside the sub-group in this small sample whose orientations did correspond to their departments, the three other groups of women scholars exemplify a kind of intellectual and social incongruence with their organizational locations. There are plenty of academics whose work does not fit neatly into their so-called home departments and disciplines. In fact, many of the quotations cited in the preceding analysis could have been spoken by faculty in such fields as area studies, urban studies, environmental studies, science policy studies, and ethnic studies—to name a few. These are contemporary fields whose scholarly content and practice do not match the current departmental organization. These are fields where, in an effort to reconstitute academic knowledge, people seek and find intentional communities that are cross-departmental and sometimes even nonacademic.

In a fundamental sense, the emergence of faculty with orientations that diverge significantly from their departments/disciplines of training remains a puzzle. Are they self-chosen outliers, deviants, or examples of inadequate disciplinary socialization? Do they reflect the particular dynamics of those with distinctive special interests? Or are their experiences characteristic of academics who are engaged in the formation of new specialties or interdisciplinary fields?

While I am not proposing generalizability from this small sample of women faculty, I am suggesting that the data may illuminate some persistent dynamics of conflict and ambiguity in academic life that are overlooked when one begins in the aggregate by attributing cohesion of purpose to departments and institutions. Whether it be for academics who engage in not-yet-legitimate academic pursuits or even for those who apparently have conventional disciplinary and departmental affiliations, the process of forming a scholarly identity, the nature of interpersonal communication, and positioning oneself within the academic reward system may be central features of academic organizational life that have been understudied and undertheorized.

The nature of academic organization needs to be reconceptualized because departmental units do not necessarily or inevitably determine behavior, interests, and, more profoundly, the pace and direction of knowledge change. That is, the formation of intentional communities may be integral to the process of negotiating the tension between constraints of the academic reward structure and personal ambitions, between the designation of what is cutting edge versus trivial, and between determining what is legitimately innovative versus what is off the map. The consequences for innovation in higher education are significant, as there is a perennial need to consider which administrative frameworks foster scholarly creativity. As Dean MacHenry has noted: "In scholarship, as in farming, the most fertile soil may be under the fences, rather than at the center of long-established fields" (1977, ix). Similarly, Angela Simeone has proposed that "there are some who would argue that these networks constitute the most vital development within the recent history of American higher education" (1987, 99).

Functionalist conceptions do not make problematic how, where, and why faculty seek and find intellectual community, since a premise of overlapping memberships assures that affinities will converge along two primary lines of disciplinary and campus affiliations. Such an orientation assumes that beliefs lead to commitments (Clark 1987, 106–7) and commitments lead to community. Beliefs and increasingly specialized orientations more or less correspond to, or at least complement, one's departmental affiliation; otherwise, a new unit will be differentiated. A further functionalist presupposition is one of coordination, where the organization of academic work and knowledge acts as a "framework for both resolving conflicting interests and advancing common ones" (Clark 1987, 109). In spite of "narrow groups that in turn generate their own separate subcultures," cultural overlap emerges from a common commitment to shared, overarching principles and beliefs (Clark 1987, 109, 140–42).

While my analysis challenges Clark's rationalistic premises, one functionalist proposition finds support in this analysis: beliefs get played out differently in organizational settings (Clark 1987, chap. 5). At research universities, disciplinarity and cutting edge scholarship are valued; whereas in the comprehensive college sector, both faculty and administration, the "they" to whom faculty often refer, turn their attention to teaching and undergraduate enrollments. Using this analytical distinction, I examine how these different organizational settings may inhibit or foster informal, cross-departmental faculty networks.

As the analysis revealed, location was linked with distinctive patterns of association among faculty. Feminist scholarly activity at the comprehensive university most closely approximates a subculture, although this particular subculture seems more likely to subvert the status quo enterprise than enhance it. The research university could not generate and sustain a viable cross-departmental network; instead faculty behavior tended to either correspond to, or complement, lines of differentiation in the formal structure. Both patterns illustrate that structural and cultural features of organizational life may be a coercive force. Yet faculty are active agents who may try to reshape their immediate academic settings; further, faculty's innovative interests may be tied to the wider external culture. Thus, when supposedly shared beliefs are viewed in their respective organizational embodiments, far more variation, fragmentation, conflict, and ambiguity exist than the *e pluribus unum* framework presumes.

For those who study higher education, a theoretical and methodological directive is clear. The kinds of questions we need to ask about academic life need to reflect complexity, not only of structures but of processes; not of distinct levels but of the mechanisms that cross-cut and potentially undermine the levels; not of daily life inside an organization but of how daily life is necessarily situated in wider socio-cultural circumstances. The questions locate both the realities of organizational life and the potentials for change in people's subjective experiences, not solely in *a priori* notions of formal structure, dominant norms, and beliefs as determinative.

Indeed, an even further diversity of perspectives is necessary to understand something as complex as the nature of academic change. As illustrative of one emerging approach, a critical cultural perspective signifies a marked departure from functionalist premises in order to take seriously the interplay between prevailing social structures and individuals' perceptions of agency (Tierney 1991). The intention is to yield a more accurate portrayal, not only of the variation in academic life in its myriad settings, but also of the ways in which research from a functionalist perspective advance a myth of unity in pluralism. The aim is to examine how interests may conflict and come to be differently valued, "not to celebrate organization as a value, but to question the ends it serves" (Smircich 1983, 355). Nor is the intention to remain silent on the unresolved and unacknowledged controversies underlying established departmental categories, but rather "to think about them and to recognize they [themselves are] the product of theoretical choices" (Graff 1987, 8).

Although some proponents of this line of inquiry approach their data with an etic standpoint from the top down, other proponents of a critical cultural analysis advocate inductive inquiry that begins at the local level from the inside out. From either perspective, a cultural analysis makes problematic conventional functionalist analyses of such essential academic processes as curricular change, faculty hiring and promotion, and academic program planning. It forces us to rethink concepts such as hierarchy—an all-important context of academic life. For instance, rather than seeing hierarchy as an ordered arrangement that promotes coordination and excellence, hierarchy may also be examined as a means of social control which is contested between the Weberian bureaucratic interests of central administrators and the faculty's professional interests for self-regulation and autonomy.

From this line of inquiry, empirical study on the problem of social integration generates a wider range of questions worth pursuing, ultimately for revising theoretical explanations of the nature of academic organization. For example, how and under what conditions do academic organizations reflect enduring systemic disequilibria, either in the contemporary era or historically? Are there new types of social and intellectual integration that have emerged beyond the administratively decentralized, rational organizational order; if so, how has the formation of intentional communities played a role in academic change? Are current faculty commitments pointing to a disintegration of the modern academic role, or possibly to a postmodern legitimacy for explicit expression of political and economic commitments, or perhaps to an institutionally mediated academic role in which certain commitments and behaviors—such as political protest or economic entrepreneurship—are deemed acceptable lines of partisanship in certain kinds of campus settings but not in others?

As researchers of higher education define directions for further organizational studies, they will determine whether the various structural and cultural analyses of higher education may be used in a complementary manner or may be judged incompatible on the basis of divergent directives for what to study, how to study it, and to what end. It remains to be seen whether this uncertainty should be interpreted as a sign of knowledge growth and differentiation in a maturing field of study or as a sign of impending fragmentation and cultural ambiguity in a field of study that is itself inescapably embedded in multiple nested contexts.

Bibliography

Blau, Peter. *The Organization of Academic Work.* New York: John Wiley & Sons, 1973.

Bowen, Howard, and Jack Schuster. *American Professors: A National Resource Imperiled.* New York: Oxford University Press, 1986.

Clark, Burton R. *The Distinctive College.* Chicago: Aldin, 1970.

_____. "The Organizational Saga in Higher Education." *Administrative Science Quarterly* 17 (June 1972): 178–84.

_____. *The Higher Education System: Academic Organization in Cross National Perspective.* Berkeley: University of California Press, 1983.

_____, ed. *The Academic Life: Small Worlds, Different Worlds.* Princeton: The Carnegie Foundation for the Advancement of Teaching, 1987.

Dill, David D. "The Management of Academic Culture: Notes on the Management of Meaning and Social Integration." *Higher Education* 11 (May 1982): 303–20.

Durkheim, Emile. *The Division of Labor in Society.* 1933; reprint ed., New York: The Free Press, 1984.

Geertz, Clifford. "The Way We Think Now: Toward an Ethnography of Modern Thought." In his *Local Knowledge: Further Essays in Interpretive Anthropology,* 147–66. New York: Basic Books, 1983.

Glaser, Barney, and Anselm Strauss. *The Discovery of Grounded Theory: Strategies for Qualitative Research.* New York: Aldine, 1967.

Graff, Gerald. *Professing Literature: An Institutional History.* Chicago: The University of Chicago Press, 1987.

Gumport, Patricia J. "The Social Construction of Knowledge: Individual and Institutional Commitments to Feminist Scholarship." Ph.D. diss., Stanford University, 1987.

_____. "Curricula as Signposts of Cultural Change." *Review of Higher Education* 12 (Autumn 1988): 49–61.

_____. "Feminist Scholarship as a Vocation." *Higher Education* 20 (October 1990): 231–43.

Harman, Kay. "The Symbolic Dimension of Academic Organization: Academic Culture at the University of Melbourne." Ph.D. diss., La Trobe University, 1988.

Kuh, George, and Elizabeth Whitt. *The Invisible Tapestry: Culture in American Colleges and Universities.* ASHE-ERIC Higher Education Reports, Washington, D.C.: Association for the Study of Higher Education, 1988.

Lincoln, Yvonna S. "Toward a Future-Oriented Comment on the State of the Profession." *Review of Higher Education* 10 (Winter 1986): 135–42.

MacHenry, Dean. "Preface." In *Academic Departments,* edited by Dean MacHenry and Associates, ix–xvi. San Francisco: Jossey-Bass, 1977.

Masland, Andrew T. "Organization Culture in the Study of Higher Education." *Review of Higher Education* 8 (Winter 1985): 157–68.

Rudolph, Frederick. *Curriculum: A History of the American Undergraduate Curriculum Since 1936.* San Francisco: Jossey-Bass, 1981.

Simeone, Angela. *Academic Women: Working Toward Equality.* South Hadley, Mass.: Bergin and Garvey, 1987.

Smircich, Linda. "Concepts of Culture and Organizational Analysis." *Administrative Science Quarterly* 28 (1983): 339–58.

Tierney, William G. "Organizational Culture in Higher Education: Defining the Essentials." *Journal of Higher Education* 59 (January/February 1988) 2–21.

_____, ed. *Culture and Ideology in Higher Education: Advancing a Critical Agenda.* New York: Praeger, 1991.

Trow, Martin. "The Analysis of Status." In *Perspectives on Higher Education,* edited by Burton Clark, Chap. 5. Berkeley: University of California Press, 1984.

PART VI

LOOKING TOWARD
THE FUTURE

Turning Points in Graduate Student Socialization: Implications for Recruiting Future Faculty

DEBORAH KIRK AND WILLIAM R. TODD-MANCILLAS

Higher education faces major recruiting problems in the years ahead. Howard Rothman Bowen and Jack H. Schuster (1986) report that fewer post-baccalaureates are pursuing careers in academe and that 40 percent of the current faculty will retire by 1995, with the balance retiring no later than 2010. Unless a deep pool of faculty applicants becomes available, universities may be forced to employ less than fully qualified individuals, and a few universities may even lose their accreditations (Erekson and Lundy 1986). At the very least, a shortage of doctoral-level faculty will certainly have a negative impact on research and development. For these reasons, the academy must consider how to encourage qualified and interested post-baccalaureates to pursue academic careers.

One logical solution is to encourage well-qualified, master-level students to continue with their graduate studies, obtain Ph.D.s, and pursue careers in academe. Information useful in considering how to strengthen graduate students' commitment to academe would be an understanding of how graduate students are socialized while pursuing masters' degrees. Because socialization experiences allow graduate students to develop the competencies necessary to cope with their roles (Corcoran and Clark 1984; Gottlieb 1961; Rouse 1984; Weiss 1981), we assume that these experiences either attract or repel graduate students who are considering a potential career in academe.

Recently, three researchers have studied graduate students socialization processes. Ann L. Darling (1987) focused on graduate assistants' interactions with their peers and faculty. She argued that these communication encounters provided the primary vehicle for socializing graduate students into their roles and departments. Interestingly, her study revealed that graduate students used passive strategies with faculty and experienced graduate students but interactive strategies with peers.

Connie Bullis and Betsy W. Bach (1987) developed a typology of fifteen "turning points"—experiences that positively or negatively affected beginning instructors' socialization and identification (sense of belonging) with their departments. Borrowing from Bullis's and Lesley Baxter's (1986) earlier work, Bullis and Bach (1987) defined a turning point as any occurrence perceived as signaling and accentuating relationship change. They found that informal recognition, (for example, a compliment from a peer or faculty member) was associated with significant and positive identification, while even slight rejection (for example, a comment that one's presentation was too long) was associated with reduced identification. They also found that mere frequency of socialization, was associated with positive identification with the student's department.

Bullis's and Bach's promising findings suggest how graduate students' socialization can become more positive — for themselves, their institutions, and the students they serve. Accordingly, our exploratory study furthers their research in two ways: (1) We identify and categorize turning points that graduate students perceive as most significantly affecting their socialization and identification with their departments, and (2) We identify turning-point types that increase graduate students' commitment to advanced graduate studies.

Method

Participants

We collected data from twenty-nine graduate-student teachers at California State University, Chico. Owing to the exploratory nature of this study and the limited number of graduate-student teachers available, we invited every eligible graduate-student teacher (thirty-eight) to participate. Those eligible had not completed more than four semesters of graduate work nor taught more than four semesters. These criteria assured that participants would be "organizational newcomers," who, according to Cynthia Stohl (1986), are better able to recall significant socialization experiences than persons who are already fully socialized.

Our interview pool of twenty-nine represented nine departments: biology, geology, English, communication, computer science, mechanical engineering, management information systems, finance and marketing, and accounting. Sixteen participants were male; thirteen female; twenty-four were Americans; five were foreign nationals. Ages ranged from twenty-two to forty-nine.

Instrumentation and Procedure

The first author, Deborah Kirk, greeted each participant courteously, explained the propose of the study, assured the interviewee of the confidentiality of the audio-taped interview, and demonstrated the Turning Point Graph (Figure 1). On the ordinate axis, participants indicated their degree of identification with their departments ("0" indicated minimal, "10" maximum).The abscissa represented the period, in monthly intervals, transpiring between the participant's acceptance as a graduate student and the time of interview.

Kirk asked participants to recall, plot, and describe all subsequent changes (turning points) in identification. She sometimes used neutral prompting to clarify explanations of the events and circumstances associated with these changes. The interviews ranged from twenty-five to ninety minutes.

Data Analysis

We analyzed and interpreted the data's contents, carefully designing categories on the basis of turning-point consequences for the participants. This approach seemed to be consistent with the study's objective of identifying different types of substantive turning points as perceived by the participants themselves (see Appendix). We trained two coders to use the category system. Interrater reliability (percentage of agreement) was achieved in excess of .90.

Results

The twenty-nine graduate-student teachers identified and discussed 171 turning-point experiences as influencing identification with their departments. We eliminated ten events from the analysis because their descriptions were too imprecise to allow for reliable categorization and assigned the remaining 161 turning points to three categories as shown in the appendix: (1) intellectual identity; (2) socio-emotional identity; and (3) occupational identity.

Figure 1. Identification with Department

Identification:
Sense of Similarity, Belonging and Membership with Department.

10
9
8
7
6
5
4
3
2
1
0

AUG SEP OCT NOV DEC JAN FEB MAR APR MAY JUN JUL AUG SEP OCT NOV DEC JAN FEB MAR

Scale
10 = Complete and Total Identification
5 = Moderate Identification
0 = No identification

Participation $_____   Subject Matter: _____
M or F
Age _____   American Student: Y   N

Category I: Intellectual Identity

Participants reported a total of seventy-three turning-point events (42 percent of the total) as either enhancing or threatening their intellectual identity. This major category is divided into two subcategories: (1) intellectual competence and (2) intellectual compatibility.

Intellectual competence. The subcategory of intellectual competence contained turning-point events which signaled to the graduate student his or her intellectual competence or incompetence. They reported a total of sixty-two events in this subcategory. These events predominantly fall into three areas of evaluation: the individual's evaluation of himself or herself as a teacher, the individual's evaluation of himself or herself as a student, and the individual's evaluation of himself or herself in relationships with superordinates—confirming or disconfirming communication interactions with superordinates that signal to the graduate student his or her intellectual competence.

In the sub-subcategory of self-evaluation as a teacher, interviewees reported a total of sixteen points—thirteen events as signaling teaching competence and three as signaling incompetence. When students demonstrated to the beginning teacher that "learning" had actually taken place (for example, by applying theoretical concepts to class discussion), the beginning teacher felt successful. However, when students did not participate in classroom discussion or performed poorly on assignments, three interviewees questioned their qualifications and abilities as instructors.

Another difficult obstacle is the graduate-student teacher's proximate age with their students. One graduate student reported that a student incredulously asked him on the first day of class, "Are you *really* our teacher?" Already uneasy about his teaching abilities and credibility, this beginning teacher felt decreased identification.

In the second sub-subcategory, self-evaluation as a student, interviewees reported twenty-six turning points, twenty-one indicating academic competence. As the graduate student successfully completed major assignments, passed qualifying exams, or received good grades, his or her level of confidence increased, reinforcing the "I-can-do-this!" feeling. Among other significant signals of intellectual competence were receiving fellowships and awards, admission to Ph.D. programs, being awarded financial assistance for a special department project, or having an opportunity to make presentations at conferences.

They reported five events as indicating intellectual incompetence. When projects or academic efforts did not meet the graduate student's expectations (for example, performing poorly on papers or exams, or receiving low grades), feelings of identification with the department decreased. Interviewees confessed to "feeling stupid" when they did not understand material covered in their courses.

In the third sub-subcategory, self-evaluation with superordinates, interviewees reported twenty-one turning points, nineteen of them with superordinates giving confirming feedback and two where feedback was negative. Most of the confirming communication events consisted of a superordinate giving advice to the graduate student about course-work, projects, or research possibilities, telling the student that he or she was "Ph.D. material," and/or saying that he or she would like the student to enroll in his or her course. Other examples were positive teaching evaluations, being asked to proctor an exam, and receiving letters of recommendation from superiors.

Only two events were classified as disconfirming. In one instance, the graduate student received a lower-than-expected grade for class work. In the other, a superordinate told the graduate student that she was too young to handle a beginning teaching position and strongly suggested that she wait another semester before applying again. In both instances, the graduate students felt inadequate and angry; and identification with their departments decreased.

Intellectual compatibility. Eight of the ten turning-point events in this category signaled to the graduate student that his or her research agenda and/or intellectual objectives were not compatible with those of the department. Two exceptions were that one graduate student indicated a strong desire to adopt the same teaching style as her professor, while another graduate student reported feeling inspired and intellectually stimulated by her professor.

The eight turning points that signaled incompatibility involved preferred subject matter or research methodologies. These events usually motivated an individual to consider taking classes in other departments or leaving the university to pursue studies at a different academic institution.

Category II: Socio-emotional Identity

Interviewees reported thirty-eight turning points, which signaled acceptance, belonging and emotional support between and among peers and superordinates, as enhancing or threatening their socio-emotional identity. These events grouped into (1) dyadic interactions with peers or superordinate and (2) small group interactions.

Dyadic interaction with peer or superordinates. The seventeen events in this category signal the presence or absence of support, camaraderie, or acceptance. The most frequently reported dyadic interaction between peers involved receiving needed information about one's graduate program. The students considered these events significant because prior to the interaction very little information was available about how to conduct the assignments and the day-to-day paper work expected of graduate students. Peers would also give advice about grading and coping with problem students. In the sole event that signaled an absence of support or acceptance, the graduate student said that her study partner stopped interacting with her personally and intellectually, leaving her feeling isolated and less identified with the department.

Only one turning point with a superordinate was classified as supportive or strengthening identification, while three were classified as signaling an absence of support or weakening identification. The supportive turning point occurred when a faculty member said to a graduate student, "You belong; you just don't know you belong." In contrast, one graduate student felt alienated when her professor "reluctantly" agreed to write a letter of recommendation. Another reported that the department chair (with whom she felt "bonded" prior to this interaction) acknowledged her decision to pursue academic interests at another university but "brushed it off" and changed the topic of conversation. And another graduate student reported feeling isolated when his major advisor took a job at another university.

In the second area, *small group interaction*, the graduate student was involved in an exchange with more than two peers or superordinates that signaled a presence or absence of acceptance or belonging. The twenty-one reported incidents that we further classified into academic socializing, nonacademic socializing, and disassociation.

In the seven cases of academic socializing, graduate students met with colleagues to coordinate efforts in deciding the department's common essay, common exams, or common lab assignments. They also met with thesis committee members or with members of an academic club. All of these events were reported as strengthening identification.

In the eight cases of non-academic socializing, the students became involved with a social club, partied with other graduate students and professors, and participated in departmental sports like a softball game or golf tournament. All of these cases enhanced interpersonal relationships and strengthened identification with the department.

Six of the turning-point events signaled disassociation. Graduate students either felt separated from or chose to sever connections with peers or professors because of differing academic interests or socially unacceptable behavior. One graduate student reported a "passive disassociation" by simply withdrawing from peers working on theses much different from his. Another graduate student "severed ties" with several other graduate students whom she discovered gossiping in a "vicious" manner about other graduate students.

Another participant described a troubling interaction with a professor hosting a faculty party. The professor attempted to persuade the graduate student to interact more with his protégés because she "certainly could" and "certainly should." The graduate student felt "cornered" and resentful.

Category III: Occupational Identity

Interviewees reported fifty turning points involving organizational structure and climate as enhancing or threatening their occupational identity. These events can be grouped on two subcategories: status classification and structural support/cooperation.

Status classification . Of the seven events reported, the graduate students discussed a positive awareness of "place" or position in the department in three, a negative awareness in four. As an affirmation of positive status, one graduate student recalled being invited as a "member" of the department to attend a Christmas party. Although the invitation was an announcement that everyone received and hence might not be considered a "big deal," the student felt as if "it was one time when it wasn't explicitly stated that there was a distinction in classification." Another graduate student recalled as a positive turning point the first time he saw his name on the department phone list. Similarly, another student identified as a positive turning point the appearance of his name in the class schedule.

Events signaling negative status classification or distinction were reported four times. One participant received a letter from the department chair announcing that she was hosting a beginning-of-the-semester party at her home for all returning faculty and requesting the student "serve" hors d'oeuvres and drinks. The letter added she should "show up promptly." The graduate student, far from feeling honored by the demand, resented the department chair's "throwing her weight around" and declined the "invitation."

Another student reported feeling discouraged after the college dean told him that his request for funding had not been approved. The discouraged feelings stemmed not from the funding but from "how he treated me." The graduate student described the dean's manner as a "professional wall"; he explained that, because there were comparatively so few graduate students in the department, the undergraduates were more important.

Other graduate students similarly reported having to overcome "bureaucratic answers" and "being a peon in a monarch department." In addition, several respondents described themselves as "part-time slime," "lowly T.A.s," or "a sling-shot" (the department chair's self-proclaimed title was "Big Gun"). This terminology signals self-deprecating position awareness within the hierarchy of the university.

Structural support and cooperation. The forty-three turning points classified in this area signaled administration policies and procedures that either supported (or failed to support) the graduate student. Thirty-two were positive and eleven were negative.

The event graduated students reported most frequently as strengthening their identification was being hired as a teaching assistant. In addition, many interviewees identified as supportive the process of meeting and establishing both an interpersonal and organizational relationship with the department secretaries—for example, receiving a mailbox, getting an office key, and obtaining access to the copy machine. The graduate students reported that these events were the first signs of acceptance and trust by "the department." Graduate students also reported that merely receiving information about necessary teacher/graduate student procedures strengthened identification with their departments. Their uncertainty decreased and they felt more secure and satisfied with how the system operated.

As another example, a department chair helped one graduate student disenroll a particularly obnoxious student. This was a devastating experience for the beginning teacher, but her chair's much appreciated assistance left her feeling satisfied with how the situation turned out.

Eleven turning points were reported as signaling distrust or dissatisfaction with administrative intervention. Receiving a teaching assistantship offered verbally (rather than in writing) and receiving the teaching contract three days after the semester had already begun were both interpreted as unprofessional. Other graduate students reported receiving unclear instructions (or none) about formal procedures to successfully complete student-teacher responsibilities. One graduate student reported that nobody in the department administration knew about his final exam: "It could have been a sports trivia quiz and not one person from the department would have known about it. They didn't know what I was doing, and it didn't seem like they cared. To them I wasn't really a teacher, I was just someone to plug [into] a section." This event, along with others, communicated to this graduate student that the administration neither valued nor understood his need to have access to important procedural information.

Summary and Implications

The results of this study reveal that graduate-student teachers can identify and describe specific events (turning points) that influence their identification with their departments. The large number of turning points (seventy-three) in the intellectual identity category indicate how vital it is for graduate students to feel intellectually appreciated and compatible with their departments. They rate their intellectual competence against departmental standards, as communicated with them formally and informally by subordinates (students), peers (other graduate students), and superordinates (faculty and administrators).

In addition to feeling competent, graduate students also need to feel that their intellectual interests are compatible with their departments'. Often graduate students become disenchanted with particular ("narrow") intellectual foci of their department. While no department can be all things for all graduate students, a nurturing department would acknowledge such discrepancies and respect divergent interests through counseling, frequent discussions with mentors, visiting lecturers, and studies in other departments.

Events in the socio-emotional identity category indicate the importance of supportive interpersonal relationships with peers and faculty. Peers primarily demonstrate their support by giving advice (for example, clarifying an attendance policy) and sharing teaching experiences (for example, dealing with students who complain about low grades). Through this guidance from peers, graduate-student teachers reduce some of the anxiety associated with their academic roles. Additionally, graduate students reported that working with full-time faculty members and other graduate students to establish common course-work and assignments strengthened their feelings of acceptance and belonging.

All of the turning points in the occupational identity category were related to organizational structure and climate. In describing these events, graduate students signaled an awareness of the system and their "place" in it. While positive affirmation of status strengthened graduate students' sense of membership, negative affirmation (sometimes self-assigned) weakened these feelings.

One of the most important turning-point types identified as strengthening occupational identity was receiving information from the department on how to successfully fulfill the department's required procedures (how and when to complete forms, construct exams, and submit grades, etc.). Because this information reduces uncertainty and strengthens identification, departments should frequently and clearly disseminate information about performance policies and standards.

Interestingly, only three events were identified as possibly affecting the student's decision to pursue further graduate study— all three negative and related to economic security. The message is clear. If graduate students are to be encouraged to pursue academe as a career, then they must also be assured that they will have a livelihood to which they can look forward. They cannot, as some interviewees in this study reported, be told at the last moment that they had received a teaching assistantship or that they were getting the assistantship because part-timers were fired. Further, when dire circumstances do occur, making it necessary to terminate part-timers or hire teaching assistants at the last moment, then graduate students should be clearly advised of the reasons for these last-minute adjustments. Otherwise, graduate students are left to infer the worst—namely, that academe cannot offer economic security.

We feel that our exploratory study successfully replicated Bullis's and Bach's (1987) findings about factors that aid or discourage graduate-student teachers socialization. Our findings underscore the fruitfulness of considering, from graduate students' perspective, events affecting their socialization and identification with departments. In addition, these results suggest a number of pragmatic actions that might increase both outcomes in a positive way.

It is, however, important to emphasize the exploratory nature of these findings. We interviewed only graduate student teachers and only those at one university. While the sample was comprehensive for that particular university, it is also limited to that institution. The results may not be generalizable without additional replication and extension. More research will also help assess whether certain turning points are significantly more important than others, a useful point that this descriptive study did not undertake.

As further caution, we note that these recommendations, though perhaps effective in positively socializing greater numbers of graduate students toward doctoral study and ultimate careers in academe, may not be effective for all masters' candidates. Moreover, masters' candidates who choose a different career path may do so for any number of reasons besides not enjoying their graduate work. Inappropriate socialization, in short, could be the least significant of all the factors weighed in such a decision.

Even so, if improved socialization and identification were to result in only modest—or even slight increases in the number of graduate students pursuing doctoral studies and academic careers, the effort will be well justified.

Bibliography

Bach, Betsy W., and Connie Bullis. "A Critique of State and Phase Models of Socialization Using Turning Point Analysis." Paper presented at the annual meeting of the Speech Communication Association, Boston, 1987. Photocopy in our possession.

Baxter, Lesley, and Connie Bullis. "Turning Points in Developing Romantic Relationships." *Human Communication Research* 12 (Summer 1986): 469–94.

Bowen, Howard Rothman, and Jack H. Schuster, *American Professors: A National Resource Imperiled.* New York: Oxford University Press, 1979.

Bullis, Connie, and Betsy W. Bach. "Organizational Identification in an Educational Setting: A Comparative Study." Paper presented at the annual meeting of Speech Communication Association, Boston, 1987. Photocopy in our possession.

Bullis, Connie, and Lesley Baxter. "A Functional Typology of Turning Point Events in the Development of Romantic Relationships." Paper presented at the annual meeting of the Speech Communications Association, Chicago Ill., 1986. Photocopy in our possession.

Corcoran, Mary, and Shirley M. Clark. "Professional Socialization and Contemporary Career Attitudes of Three Faculty Generations." *Research in Higher Education* 20, no, 2 (1984): 131–53.

Darling, Ann L. "Communication in Graduate Teaching Assistant Socialization: Encounters and Strategies." Paper presented at the Speech Communication Association Convention, Boston, 1987. Photocopy in our possession.

Erekson, Thomas L., and Lyndall L. Lundy. "Supply/Demand for Industrial Education University Faculty Based on Retirement Projections: Implications for Industrial Teacher Education, Research, and Development." Paper presented at the annual meeting of the American Educational Research Association, San Francisco, 1986. Photocopy in our possession.

Gottlieb, David. "Processes of Socialization in American Graduate Schools." *Social Forces* 40 (December 1961): 124–31.

Rouse, Linda P. "Breaking into Academe." *Academe* 70 (May/June 1984): 39.

Stohl, Cynthia. "The Role of Memorable Messages in the Process of Organizational Socialization." *Communication Quarterly* 34 (Fall 1986): 231–49.

Weiss, Carin S. "The Development of Professional Role Commitment among Graduate Students." *The Journal of Human Relations* 34 (January 1981): 13–31.

Appendix: Categories of Turning Point Experiences

I. Turning point events enhancing or threatening one's intellectual identity.

  A. Intellectual competence: situations, events, acts signaling to self one's intellectual competence.

    1. Individual's evaluation of self as teacher.

      a. Feeling competent about one's ability as a teacher by fulfilling responsibilities, realizing that students are performing and responding positively to instruction.

      b. Feeling incompetent about one's ability as a teacher, feeling concerned about being "too young," doubting whether one is really helping students become better educated.

    2. Individual's evaluation of self as a student.

      a. Feeling competent about one's scholarly ability as a student, (e.g., performing well on papers and exams, receiving good grades, making good progress on one's thesis).

      b. Feeling incompetent about one's scholarly ability as a student (e.g., performing poorly on papers and exams, receiving grades that are lower than expected, having difficulty with one's thesis project, finding theoretical concepts or course material too difficult or complex to understand).

    3. Superordinates' intellectual evaluation and acknowledgment.

      a. Superordinate gives confirming feedback about intellectual competence (e.g., giving advice about courses, project, or research possibilities; offering software or financial assistance for research; inquiring about interest in a teaching position; asking one to proctor an exam; making encouraging comments about teaching performance; or indicating to student that he/she is Ph.D. material, and/or would like the student to take the professor's course).

      b. Superordinate gives disconfirming feedback about intellectual competence (e.g., giving the student a lower-than-expected grade, communicating doubts about the student's ability to handle a teaching position because of age, refusing to write a letter of recommendation).

  B. Intellectual compatibility: situations, events, or acts signaling one's compatibility with the department's research agenda or intellectual objectives.

    1. Students realize that the department's intellectual objectives are compatible with their own (e.g., finding the course work stimulating and challenging, "linking" intellectually with a professor in the department).

    2. Students realize that the department's intellectual objectives are incompatible with his/her own (e.g., departmental philosophy too narrow-minded, course work not rigorous enough or too much so, not enjoying or interested in the course work, or failing to "link" with the department or from other departments or leaving the institution.

II. Turning-point events enhancing or threatening one's socio-emotional identity.

  A. Interpersonal interactions: situations, events, or acts with peer, superordinate, or both, signaling acceptance, belonging, and/or emotional support.

    1. Dyadic interaction with peer presence or absences of support, camaraderie, acceptance.

      a. Interaction with a peer signaling presence of support or acceptance (e.g., receiving an offer to share work space, receiving advice about grading or dealing with problem students, receiving help with new language, having a peer cover one's class, receiving directions as how to proceed in graduate program, empathetic listening).

b. Interaction with a peer signaling absence of support or acceptance (e.g., peer imposing conditional regard, study partner physically separates him/herself).

2. Dyadic interaction with superordinate signaling a presence or absence of support or acceptance.

a. Interaction with professor, advisor, or other superordinate signaling a presence of support or acceptance (e.g., casual chit-chat).

b. Interaction with professor, advisor, or other superordinate signaling an absence of support or acceptance (e.g., major professor temporarily leaves the university for own academic pursuits, department chair does not indicate support of student's decision to leave department for other interests).

3. Small group interaction with both superordinates and/or peers signaling a presence or absence of acceptance or belonging.

a. Socializing academically (e.g., meeting with thesis committee members, joining academic club, coordinating with part- and full-time faculty about common essays, exams, or lab assignments for the department).

b. Socializing non-academically (e.g., joining and interacting with a club, going to luncheons and outings, partying with other graduate students and professors, or participating in departmental sports activities).

c. Disassociation. The graduate student feels separated from or chooses to sever connections with peers or professors because of different academic interests, imposed conditional regard, gossip, etc.

III. Events related to organizational structure and climate affecting one's occupational identity.

A. Structural support and cooperation: situations, events, interventions, or acts signaling administrative support, supportive policy, supportive procedures, etc.

1. Events signaling trust and satisfaction with administrative intervention, decisions, or how the system operates (e.g., interviewing for and/or receiving assistantship in department, receiving formal permission to take a class outside department, receiving support in dealing with disruptive students, receiving information about how to proceed with graduate school, feeling validated for one's representation at professional seminar or contribution to interdepartmental coordination efforts, or receiving secretarial support).

2. Events signaling distrust or dissatisfaction with administrative intervention, decisions, or the manner in which the system operates (e.g., structural decisions adversely affecting a peer or one's own economic and/or occupational security, being offered a teaching assistantship verbally instead of in writing, or receiving unclear or no instructions about procedural requirements for successfully completing student teaching responsibilities).

B. Status classification: situations, events, or acts signaling an individual's awareness of "fit," "place," or status in the organization.

1. Events signaling positive status classification or distinction (e.g., being invited to a party as a "member" of the department or seeing one's name in the class schedule).

2. Events signaling negative status classification or distinction (e.g., administrator giving bureaucratic answer, establishing and/or maintaining a professional wall, or administrator "throwing weight around").

IV. Other: Events that do not belong in a specific category.

Faculty Career Stages and Implications for Professional Development

ROGER G. BALDWIN

A brief stroll down a corridor of "Old Main" reveals the seasons of academic life. In one office sits a new professor frantically preparing notes for her afternoon lecture. The chair of the faculty senate hurries from the next office as he races to catch a plane. Tomorrow morning he will deliver a paper on an exciting new research project. The door to the third office is closed for the day. By 2:00 PM its occupant, a midcareer professor, is up to the eighth green of the local golf course. The last office before the elevator belongs to one of the university's senior professors. He is having coffee with a younger colleague while helping him with a complex statistical procedure.

A casual observer of faculty lounges or committee meetings can divide the academic career into a series of loosely ordered stages. Research design specialists might take issue with this "soft" methodology, yet most academics would agree that—while exceptions abound—professors change as they progress through the faculty ranks and as their careers gradually place different demands on them. Typically, however, colleges and universities fail to acknowledge the developmental nature of faculty careers. They maintain basically the same expectations and apply the same policies to all professors, regardless of their age or career stage. By viewing all faculty members synonymously, higher education institutions overlook some basic facts of academic life, and in doing so they forgo important opportunities to fashion policies that could benefit faculty members and their institutions.

Colleges and universities that wish to maintain a vital professional workforce must be cognizant of the powerful development forces that influence faculty members. Faculty development policies and practices, such as those described in this book, should accommodate the varying needs of professors at successive points in the academic career. Effective strategies to renew faculty and enhance their performance must take into account the special character of each phase of the academic life cycle.

Growth and Change During Adulthood

People change through the course of their lives and careers in fairly predictable ways. The adult years may be viewed as a series of stages characterized by changing developmental tasks, concerns, activities, values, and needs (Hall, 1976). Focusing on academic life through a developmental lens can reveal subtle, but important, differences among professors at successive stages.

Development theorists portray adulthood as a variegated and dynamic phase of life. Erik Erikson defines the adult years in terms of three sequential objectives: intimacy, generativity, and ego integrity. The young adult seeks intimacy, meaning involvements and commitments beyond oneself. Establishment of meaningful interpersonal relationships and choice of a vocational role,

551

for example, help to satisfy the natural drive for connections with the larger world. Erikson views the core years of adulthood as a quest for generativity. The goal at this stage is to produce or create things (such as children, theories, buildings, new scholars) of enduring value. The task of late adulthood is a drive for ego integrity. The individual at this stage seeks a feeling of fulfillment, of satisfaction with life. This assessment phase permits the late adult to disengage from life's commitments with a sense of closure. Erikson's framework broadly illustrates the varying forces that exert themselves at different points of life and significantly shape the concerns and behavior of adults (Erikson, 1963).

Levinson (1984; and others, 1978) describes the adult years as a series of alternating stable and transitional periods. During a stable period the basic task is to produce clearly defined priorities and goals and enhance one's life within that framework. However, after seven to ten years of one life-style, "we are propelled by certain psychological forces to assess what . . . we are doing with our lives" (Bardwick, 1986, p. 110). Hence the adult moves into a transitional phase (lasting four to five years). The task during transition is to evaluate the existing life structure, explore alternatives, and make some initial commitments that will form the basis of a new, more satisfactory life plan. According to Bardwick, this assessment always reveals some disparity between reality and a person's expectations or dreams. Internal negotiation and compromise are often necessary before one can establish new or revised objectives for the next stable phase of life. For this reason, transitional periods sometimes become major life crises.

This sequence of stable and transitional periods repeats itself regularly. According to Levinson and others (1978), the cycle never becomes routine. Each season has its special character and presents distinctive tasks to be completed.

Most academic careers begin near the end of Levinson's early adult era and continue until the transition into late adulthood. Early adulthood is a time for choices and initial commitments. This is a period of heavy burdens as the young person struggles to form a vocation, marry, and start a family, often concurrently. The settling-down period, which in Levinson's scheme concludes early adulthood, is strongly achievement-oriented. During this period one often feels pressured to accomplish specific goals (for example, tenure, senior partnership) on a certain timetable (often by the age of forty). Essentially, the objective is to earn recognition, to become a full-fledged member of a valued segment of the adult world.

No matter how successful a person may be, however, the onset of mid-life triggers another transition phase. Levinson calls it the mid-life transition; the popular media label it the mid-life crisis. Bardwick says that this is the point at which the future no longer seems endless, and at which it seems to extend with a "frighteningly unvarying script" (1978, p.131). At this stage there is a sudden realization: "This is your work; this is your spouse; this is your place; this is your level; this is your life" (Bardwick, 1978, p 132). Long-neglected parts of the self seek expression during the mid-life transition. For example, artistic interests and nurturing drives overshadowed by career demands may suddenly reemerge (Levinson and others, 1978). The task of the adult in mid-life transition is to work through anxieties about aging, to set priorities, and to define new goals that will form a more satisfactory life structure.

The outcome of the mid-life transition influences the subsequent course of life. A flawed life structure (composed of unrealistic ambitions, unsatisfying relationships, and so on) can cause some people to decline in mid-life. For many, however, middle adulthood can be "the fullest and most creative season in the life cycle" (Levinson and others, 1978 p. 62). Mature men, for instance, are less driven by the illusions, passions, and ambitions of youth and are freer to become deeply attached to others (Levinson and others, 1978).

Evidence suggests that the sequence of stable and transitional stages continues to the end of the life cycle (Levinson, 1986). Reassessment and revision are repeatedly necessary as one adapts to the changing demands of relationships and careers. Satisfactory adjustments can lead to fulfillment at any stage of life. Failure to adapt to changing circumstances can promote disappointment, despair, even withdrawal from major life roles.

Stage models of adult development should be applied with caution. Critics object, for example, to the rigid sequence of age related stages that schemes such as Levinson's present. Models that conceptualize the adult years as a routine series of common tasks may oversimplify the complexities and diverse forms of post-adolescent life. Levinson's theory, based on a small sample of men only, no doubt fails to portray the distinctive development experiences of women and other groups not adequately represented in his research. (This omission should be partially remedied soon, however. Levinson has been studying the adult development of women and is scheduled to publish *The Seasons of a Woman's Life* in the near future.)

Yet in spite of these valid criticisms, theories of adult development offer an enlightening perspective from which to examine faculty. Contrary to the popular myth, college and university professors do not reside in an ivory tower. They are subject to the same psychosocial forces as are other adults. Alternating periods of goal seeking and reassessment are common as academics proceed through their careers. Higher education should acknowledge the changing character of these periods and help professors travel through them successfully.

The Evolving Career

The work career is a major anchor of adult life. Especially for highly job-involved professionals, work is an important component of identity and a vehicle for pursuing dreams (Levinson and others, 1978).

The career consists of "a sequence and combination of roles a person plays during the course of a lifetime" (Super, 1986, p. 96). Like other aspects of adulthood, a career follows a developmental path. Even when an individual continues in the same broadly defined occupation, qualitative changes usually occur over time in workplace, status, and meaning and mode of work (Levinson and others, 1978). Hence career stages can help to explain the different attitudes and behavior of people in complex organizations such as universities (Hall, 1976).

Career stages and their associated tasks have been conceptualized by many occupational theorists (Voydanoff, 1980). Each model views the career development process slightly differently, but a comparable evolutionary process emerges from the various schemes. Most careers progress from an initial entry and establishment period to a period of growth and advancement. Eventually careers cease to expand; they level off to a stable plateau in a maintenance stage. Finally they move into a disengagement phase, during which people's involvement with their occupation decreases in anticipation of retirement. Each career stage poses distinctive challenges that significantly influence the concerns and performances of workers.

Career Entry. The initial stage of any career is a time of learning and socialization. The novice learns the basic rules and expectations of the profession or organization and is judged in terms of long-term potential (Bailyn and Schein, 1976). Career entry can be a stressful experience. Research with young AT&T managers, for example, has shown considerable concern for "career safety." Typically the new professional wishes to achieve competence, establish him- or herself securely in the organization, and receive some preliminary recognition from superiors or higher-ranking colleagues (Hall and Nougaim, 1968).

Substantial changes in a person's self-image, attitudes, and aspirations can occur during the early years of a career. Often these changes are negative rather than positive. To prevent a negative outcome, efforts to make career entry a satisfying experience are desirable (Hall, 1976).

Early Career. Further learning occurs during the early-career phase as the individual tries to master the organization or profession. But this stage is qualitatively different from career entry. The experienced worker is more capable of functioning fully and of performing meaningful work (Bailyn and Schein, 1976). This is a good period for creativity and innovation; junior members of an organization tend to be work-engaged and unbridled by years of habit and tradition. Advancement and promotion are often dominant concerns of the early career (Glaser, 1964). Bardwick (1986) describes this phase of life as a time of "full-out striving, grabbing for long-range opportunity" (p. 10). This is an exciting period in a person's work life as he or she strives to carve out an area of specialization, move up professionally, and make a name.

Midcareer. The midpoint of a career represents a watershed for many, especially for highly career-involved professionals. It is the point at which an individual feels established and has achieved perceived mastery of his or her work (Hall, 1986a). This is the period of maximum productivity and greatest influence for persons in many occupations. Yet it may also be the time when the career begins to be, when the limits of one's achievements come into view. At this stage the need or opportunity to compete may decrease (Hall, 1976). For many, midcareer brings the onset of a career plateau of few new challenges or creative achievements.

Midcareer is a time for reexamination of personal values and needs as well as professional concerns (Rabinowitz and Hall, 1981). Questions about the future and what it has to offer naturally emerge. According to Hall (1986a), the issue of balance between one's work roles and personal roles becomes more salient. He suggests that careers often become less of a priority as one ages and assumes additional life roles. This may necessitate some reordering of priorities. The reassessment process can be uncomfortable, but it is necessary in order to redefine one's relationship with work and to identify new goals for a rewarding future.

Late Career. The final years of a career present their own challenges. Senior members of an organization or profession are usually beyond the point of maximum productivity, but their knowledge and experience enable them to continue making valuable contributions (Bailyn and Schein, cited in Voydanoff, 1980). Two primary tasks dominate the late-career period: Concluding the career in a personally satisfactory manner and preparing for retirement. Termination of a career requires considerable adjustment—especially for professionals, who must accept a significantly altered identity. The central emotional need is to achieve a sense of personal integrity—the feeling that one has achieved worthwhile goals, that one's work truly mattered (Hall, 1976). Often there is a strong desire to leave some kind of legacy that will have value in the future. The later years of a career can be very fulfilling, if one is given the opportunity for stimulating work and satisfying professional relationships. Alternatively, if one's professional life is stale and the future is uncertain, this can be a devastating period.

Career Plateau. The career plateau is a developmental phenomenon that deserves special attention here, because it is common in the academic profession. A plateau is "a stage in work or life where there is no growth or movement" (Bardwick, 1986, p. *vii*). Career plateauing is most common at mid-life, but it can occur whenever work becomes routine and is no longer engrossing. Once the sensation of progress ceases, motivation, commitment, and productivity may well decline (Bardwick, 1986). A person who feels stuck gradually withdraws psychologically from work in search of other sources of gratification (Kanter, 1977).

Faculty members are susceptible to two forms of plateauing: structural and content. Structural plateauing results when opportunities for advancement are constrained by the organization's hierarchical arrangement. The faculty career ladder from assistant to full professor provides only a short path for formal career development. Thus professors quickly plateau structurally, often by the age of forty (Bardwick, 1986).

Content plateauing is a more serious problem. It occurs when work is mastered, when there is nothing new to learn. In *The Plateauing Trap* Bardwick (1986) claims that it is difficult to maintain a sense of growth if work remains essentially the same for more than three years. She estimates that after five years of the same responsibilities, a sense of mastery turns into a feeling of boredom. Professors who continue teaching the same course or studying the same narrow research questions are easy victims of content plateauing.

Fortunately, plateauing is not an irreversible phenomenon. Hall (1986b) recommends that "flat" organizations, such as universities, identify alternatives to promotion that provide opportunities for genuine professional growth. Bardwick (1986) advocates that people alter their work responsibilities often enough to sustain a continuous sense of challenge and learning: "When people have the opportunity to engage in new work, be creative, and make things happen, enormous amounts of psychic energy can be released so that they work well and feel good" (p. 82).

Sources of Variation in Development

Developmental concepts and models enhance understanding of major forces that shape the concerns and behaviors of adults, including college and university professors. Theories of adult and career development describe common life patterns. However, much latitude exists within the models for individual and group differences. Development during the adult years does not follow a uniform, unvarying course. Levinson (1986; and others, 1978), for example, believes that certain developmental issues emerge in a set chronological sequence, yet his stages occur over flexible age ranges, not at fixed points for everyone. Other models are even more flexible than Levinson's, suggesting that adult and career development are contextual processes that are significantly influenced by individual attributes and intervening circumstances. Career timing, for one thing, may affect the development process. Hall (1986a) suggests that the pattern of work life influences when various career stages occur. A person with an uninterrupted career will experience a midcareer transition sooner and in a different way than a person whose career has followed an irregular course. Career stages may even recur, depending on how often work responsibilities change and then become routine again.

The length and dynamics of career stages may also vary by occupation (Voydanoff, 1980). Obviously the prime of professional life is different for football players and orchestra conductors. Similar variations may occur within the academic ranks. Blackburn (1985) reports that "career advancement differs across disciplines and even within subspecialties in the same field" (p. 69). Variation most likely occurs for faculty in different types of higher education institutions as well. Nuclear physicists at Berkeley and philosophers at Oberlin do not progress professionally in the same ways or at the same pace.

Gender is another major source of variation in the development process. Woman's development has received scant attention from researchers, but theorists presume significantly different life patterns. Woman's occupational development is often more complex than men's. Clark and Corcoran (1986) report that women find it more difficult than men do to locate sponsors and mentors to facilitate their career advancement. Similarly, Clark and Corcoran observe that women's marital and family roles affect their professional work engagement much more than men's work is affected by their marital and family roles. Women in American society are more likely than men to have interrupted careers due to family obligations. Also, transition stages for women may occur in a somewhat different manner than those for men. The biological clock can prompt women to confront life's basic issues at different times than men confront those issues. Theorists suggest that men and women start at opposite ends of a psychodynamic continuum but gradually move closer together. With age, men become more involved in their internal psychological needs and less driven by external career demands. Women, on the other hand, become more externally oriented as their relational commitments decrease (Bardwick, 1980). Frequently this trend includes a greater interest in careers.

Life confronts both genders with many of the same tasks, but the distinctive nature of each sex in this society surely influences the manner in which they respond to these challenges. The demands of academic life in theory are identical for women and men, yet the timing of major career events (for example, job entry, onset of a career plateau) may vary significantly for professors from the two genders. Hence the salient professional issues concerning male and female faculty members may sometimes differ in qualitative ways that affect career orientation and job performance.

Distinctive career patterns may be true for individuals from different ethnic groups as well. The developmental forces that shape adults' identity and behavior may vary in significant ways according to ethnic origins. For instance, the growing presence of Asian Americans and the diminishing presence of black males in college campuses suggest that their respective backgrounds do not position people of those backgrounds equally well for successful careers in the academic profession. The relative availability of role models, mentors, and peers from similar origins is among the factors that may account for developmental differences among faculty from distinctive sociological subgroups.

Developmental models provide a valuable lens that enhances understanding of academic life. Within the developmental framework, however, there is wide latitude for individual and group differences. Together, these sources of variation account for rich diversity that exists within the overall developmental pattern that characterizes members of the academic profession.

Developmental Research on Faculty

Developmental research on faculty has identified notable differences among professors at successive ages and career stages. For example, interest in various faculty roles seems to vary among professors with different levels of experience. Scholars have found among older faculty a decreased interest in research (Baldwin, 1979; Fulton and Trow, 1974; Ladd and Lipset, 1976a) and increased enthusiasm for teaching (Fulton and Trow, 1974; Ladd and Lipset, 1976a) and institutional service (Baldwin, 1979). Several studies report differing time allocations among the principal faculty roles. Apparently teaching responsibilities require less of experienced professors' time (Durham, Wright, and Chandler, 1966; Thompson, 1971; Baldwin, 1979), while institutional service activities require more (Mortimer, 1969). Professors' perceived strengths and weaknesses also seem to differ over the academic career. A study of liberal arts college faculty, for instance, revealed greater comfort with teaching and institutional service at successively higher academic ranks but less comfort with scholarly activity (Baldwin, 1979). Limited research also suggests that faculty problem solving and professional development behavior differ at successive career points. Senior professors appear more likely to solve problems independently than do their junior colleagues, for example, and they are less likely to participate in formal professional development activities (Baldwin, 1979).

Blackburn (1985) concluded from several studies that faculty research productivity seems cyclical. Research productivity appears to follow a complex developmental pattern, with alternating periods of increased and decreased achievement common among professors. This recurring phenomenon, in Blackburn's view, supports the contentions of adult development theorists.

The relationship between professional and personal life appears to vary over the career cycle as well. A study at a major research university found that assistant professors reported more negative "spillover" (that is, they reported that feelings associated with work directly influenced life outside of work, and vice versa) between work and family life and between work and leisure activities than did associate and full time professors. Junior faculty in the study reported "conflicts between time and energy for work and for spouses, children, dual careers, and commuter marriages" (Sorcinelli and Near, 1987, p. 18). They also noted the lack of time for pleasure reading, exercise, and social and civic activities. The study suggests that balance between professional and personal roles is most difficult to achieve during the early years as a faculty member.

Evidence on faculty satisfaction also reveals noteworthy differences across the academic career. Some researchers (Eckert and Williams, 1972: Ladd and Lipset, 1976b) have reported that career satisfaction increases steadily with age. Baldwin and Blackburn (1981) likewise found that satisfaction was greatest among senior faculty, but they also found some evidence of decreased satisfaction at transition points in academic life.

More comprehensive research is needed to clarify the developmental nature of the academic career. To date, few national studies of the professoriate have been completed that are representative of the range of academic disciplines and institutions (Blackburn, 1985), yet available evidence on faculty across the career is sufficiently compatible with developmental theory to justify a close look at stages of academic life.

Faculty Career Stages

It is possible to translate various developmental schemes into a sequential model of the academic career. This generic view of academic life covers at least four distinct phases from the time of career entry to retirement. In some (perhaps many) cases the career surely follows an even more differentiated course. As has been noted, the pattern may vary for professors from different fields, institutions, genders, and ethnic groups. The framework outlined here is thus not a definitive model of academic life; many successful academic careers do not fit this precise developmental pattern. Still, because the model addresses developmental issues common to many professors throughout higher education, it provides a basic foundation for understanding the evolving interests, activities, and development needs of college and university faculty members.

Novice Professor: Getting into the Academic World. Beginning an academic career is a complex and demanding process. The new professor's major concern is competence. How can he or she learn quickly to perform all the duties of a college teacher? With so many things to do at once, how does a person set priorities and balance these new roles successfully? This entry period (lasting from one term to several years) is a time of intense pressure and considerable growth. Numerous tasks must be completed as the new professor establishes a solid base for a successful career. The novice must design several courses in a brief period of time. Often these cover subjects in which the individual has limited expertise. More fundamentally, the beginner must develop a repertoire of teaching skills. It is one thing to lead a small discussion section as a graduate assistant; it is considerably more demanding to have full responsibility for lecturing, sequencing assignments, designing examinations, and motivating students with diverse needs. Not surprisingly, developing effective teaching skills is perhaps the most immediate concern of the new professor.

Early learning tasks extend beyond the classroom, however. The novice must gain knowledge of the institution's resources and support services. He or she must also become acquainted with the formal policies of the institution and, more importantly, with its mores and expectations. It would be regrettable, for example, if a new college teacher failed to hear of the instructional development center on a campus, and it would be fatal for a beginning professor to remain ignorant of the values and manners of his or her department or institution.

Successful career entry also requires attention to the scholarly dimensions of academic life. The new teacher must avoid becoming so consumed by instructional responsibilities that professional development and research are neglected.

Initiation to the academic ranks presents many competing demands. Young professors are often juggling new family responsibilities and related financial obligations in addition to a full menu of professional duties. Unfortunately, if the early years as a professor are unsatisfying, they can diminish enthusiasm and create a negative attitude that may persist throughout the career.

The distinctive demands of entering the academic profession call for special efforts on the part of the institution to smooth this important transition. Work assignments should acknowledge the extra time required of a new teacher—time to design new courses and take on other new roles. It is unrealistic to assume that a beginning professor can effectively carry the same range of duties as a veteran professor. Some reduction of normal teaching, advising, or committee work is appropriate at this stage. Information on policies and services relevant to a professor's diverse responsibilities should be shared systematically rather than in a haphazard fashion. A well-planned orientation strategy can facilitate adjustment to the institution and reduce initial career anxiety. Finally, sensitive guidance from established professionals may be the most effective way to ease the initial career transition. A supportive department chair or senior colleague willing to give advice and respond to questions can remove many hurdles confronting a new professor. Higher education institutions should foster mentoring relationships of this nature to promote the rapid adjustment of new faculty members. Well-planned strategies to meet the unique needs of new professors can promote the feeling of competence so important at the beginning of a career.

Early Academic Career: Settling Down and Making a Name. Achievement and confirmation are the dominant themes of the early-career years—that is, the period between career entry and full membership in the academic ranks. These objectives are especially manifest in the academic profession, where full membership status is awarded only after a lengthy probationary period. Although the early-career years are substantially different from the initial entry period, they also have a make-or-break quality to them. A professor at this stage wishes to master the principal faculty roles, and some kind of meaningful achievement (deserving of recognition within one's institution or broader discipline) is usually a prominent goal as well. The desire for publication of respected articles, chapters, or a book, or for acquisition of a major research grant, often focuses the efforts of an early-career professor. This is a task-oriented phase with concrete goals. Beneath the stability offered by a clear sense of propose, however, may linger a nagging concern about the future. The early-career professor recognizes that denial of tenure could provoke a major transition in his or her life.

The clear objectives of the early career demand much of the junior academic. On the basis of initial experience in the classroom, courses must be redesigned and teaching strategies refined. Participation in institutional service must be increased; more time must be allotted to meeting with committees and preparing reports. The quest for confirmation often demands involvement in external scholarly communication networks, professional associations, and editorial boards, in addition to research and writing. The press of fixed responsibilities leaves little time to stay broadly informed of developments in one's field or to plan for an uncertain future. Stress at this career stage is an everyday experience.

Higher education institutions should acknowledge the special burdens of the early academic career. It is in their best interest to help junior faculty members prosper. Support should be available to facilitate young professors teaching and research endeavors. (A small number of institutions even provide sabbatical leaves for non-tenured, junior faculty. This provides an opportunity to organize one's research agenda when it is most needed.) Perhaps most important, academic administrators should be willing to adjust faculty assignments during the early-career years to help professors accomplish their highest professional priorities. Keeping the demands of the early career manageable can prevent burnout and preserve fragile faculty morale.

Midcareer: Accepting a Career Plateau or Setting New Goals? Reaching midcareer (the long period after one feels established but before the career disengagement process begins) signals another major phase in the academic life cycle. This is often a very productive and rewarding phase, a time when professors enjoy maximum professional influence. Extrinsic goals, such as promotion to full professor, may direct faculty efforts during the early years of this period. Likewise, the desire for true senior status within one's institution and discipline is common among midcareer faculty members.

For many, it is also a transitional phase. Interests and concerns that were dormant during the intense early-career years may bubble to the surface. The midcareer professor may become aware that family obligations have been shortchanged and hobbies or recreation neglected. Mid-life increases one's awareness that time is finite. This realization may provoke some effort to achieve more balance among life's competing roles.

Frequently, midcareer parallels the onset of a career plateau. After many years in the classroom or laboratory, a professor may begin to note a monotonous sameness about his or her work. A fear that professional challenge and growth have ended may develop. Worries about falling behind in one's field and about potential obsolescence are also common at this stage. Additionally, the professor who has reached a plateau lacks the concrete goals and clear sense of direction that make the early career so exciting.

Even for professors who have not reached a plateau, one pervasive question of midcareer is, What should I do with the rest of my professional life? For many academics, midcareer stimulates a period of assessment; priorities and goals are reexamined. Do I want to continue teaching full time? Would I make a good administrator? Is it too late to learn to use the computer? Could team teaching with the new member of our department help me catch up with new developments in my field? Ideally, this process of assessment should identify new goals that can be energize subsequent phases of a professional career.

The costly toll of faculty "deadwood" is sufficient reason for higher education institutions to devote special attention to midcareer professors. Veteran faculty need opportunities to review and redefine career goals from time to time. Career-planning workshops may benefit some, while formal growth contracts outlining new goals and development strategies may help others. Sometimes an informal conversation with the dean or department chair can enable a midcareer professor to define new career challenges. Regardless of the method employed, professors need periodically to examine their careers and identify exciting new paths for the future.

Acceptance of this point of view has implications for faculty policies and work assignments also. Policies must be sufficiently flexible to foster professors' growth in new directions. For example, sabbatical plans that require faculty members to conduct research in their established area of specialization may be too rigid to meet the distinctive needs of midcareer professors. In addition, colleges and universities must be willing to revise work assignments to maintain a spark of variety and challenge in professor's careers. It must be acknowledged that a lifelong career in higher education is not the best course for everyone. Policies that make career change and early retirement feasible alternatives can help some midcareer academics leave campus for other types of work that they may find more invigorating.

Late Career: Leaving a Legacy. The last phase of an academic career (the years prior to retirement, when gradual disengagement from work ordinarily occurs) can be filled with paradox. Senior professors express considerable satisfaction with their careers (Eckert and Williams, 1972; Ladd and Lipset, 1976b; Baldwin and Blackburn, 1981). Many enjoy a respected position in their institutions and can look with pride at the achievements of a long life in higher education. Concurrently, however, a professor nearing retirement may feel increasingly out of touch with developments in a rapidly changing field. As one of the oldest members of a department, this individual may have little in common with younger colleagues and feel isolated and somewhat irrelevant. On many campuses, shifting values—a new emphasis on research productivity over teaching, for example—leave senior faculty members feeling neglected and underappreciated. These feelings are sometimes reinforced by the efforts of market-driven salaries that favor young faculty members in "hot" fields. Concerns about retirement security—both financial and psychological—may likewise trouble a person whose identity is closely tied to the work role. This combination of positive and negative factors can leave a senior professor feeling ambivalent about the end of his or her career and anxious about what lies ahead.

The final stage of academic life need not be a mixed bag, however. In fact, from the perspective of overall faculty morale, it ought to be a gratifying period, and an institution can do much to ensure that it is. Helping faculty prepare for a secure retirement is one way to reduce their stress at concluding a career. Retirement-planning assistance well in advance of the actual separation date is essential. Such assistance should address personal and psychological aspects of retirement as well as financial considerations. Individual counseling and group discussion sessions in addition to informative seminars can ease the adjustment process. Phased retirement, which enables a faculty member to reduce work commitments gradually, is another way to smooth the path to emeritus status.

Senior professors should be treated as full-fledged faculty members, not as old-timers waiting to be put out to pasture. They deserve challenging teaching assignments and support for their professional development. Professors approaching retirement have much to offer their institution and the academic profession. Roles that capitalize on seasoned professors' special skills and their natural desire to leave a legacy can be particularly satisfying to senior faculty. For example, academic veterans are uniquely qualified to orient new colleagues to academic life. Some are well prepared to lead workshops on teaching strategies, while others can help novice scholars with research methodology or committee duties. Such opportunities for junior and senior colleagues to work together can bridge generational barriers and provide both generations with avenues for exciting professional growth. Special service to the department or institution is another way senior professors can make a lasting contribution before retirement: work with important task forces, the admissions or alumni offices, or the president can offer stimulating challenges for the last years of an individual's professional life. Meaningful work that is recognized and respected by others is important at all stages of work life, of course, but it may be *essential* in bringing a long academic career to a satisfying conclusion.

Conclusion

The academic profession does not lend itself to neat classification schemes. Professors comprise an exceptionally diverse occupational group; they differ by field and by institution as well as by age and career stage, and they represent both genders and many ethnic groups. Above all, they are individuals who possess unique interests, talents, and expertise.

Yet a shared value system and a spirit of community pervade the academic ranks. As Bowen and Schuster (1986) conclude from a nationwide study, "Despite the variety that exists in academe, it is appropriate for many purposes to treat the professoriate as a closely knit social group and not merely as a collection of disparate individuals or unrelated small groups" (p.13). Widespread socialization practices and similar work roles help to unify the profession. So does the developmental process common to academic life.

The developmental framework outlined in this chapter clarifies major themes and events that dominate successive seasons in the careers of many faculty members. It suggests why a new college teacher with superb credentials can be scattered and ineffective. It indicates why a prolific young scholar may become the sedentary campus curmudgeon. It helps to explain why a professor on the verge of retirement spends his weekends working in the laboratory with a new colleague.

A developmental model of the faculty career sensitizes higher education to the changing demands of academic life. It helps colleges and universities to define policies and work assignments in light of differing professional circumstances rather than by a rigid standard. It enables a dean or department chair to offer faculty development support when it can be most beneficial.

No model can fully capture the rich variety that exists within the professoriate. No two academic careers are identical, and professors deserve to be treated as the talented *individuals* they are. A developmental frame of reference, however, illuminates powerful forces that influence many faculty members at different points of the career. This insight can empower higher education to serve more effectively the distinctive needs of individual professors. Ideally, it will help to extend the most creative phases of academic life and abbreviate unproductive career plateaus.

References

Bailyn, L., and Schein, E. "Life/Career Considerations as Indicators of Quality Employment." In A. D. Biderman and T. F. Drury (eds.), *Measuring Work Quality for Social Reporting.* Beverly Hills, Calif.: Sage, 1976.

Baldwin, R. G., "The Faculty Career Process—Continuity and Change: A Study of College Professors at Five Stages of the Academic Career." Unpublished doctoral dissertation, Center for the Study of Higher Education, University of Michigan, 1979.

Baldwin, R. G., and Blackburn, R. T. "The Academic Career as a Developmental Process: Implications for Higher Education." *Journal of Higher Education,* 1981, 52 (6), 598–614.

Bardwick, J. M. "Middle Age and a Sense of Future." *Merrill Palmer Quarterly,* 1978, 24 (2), 129–138.

Bardwick, J. M. "The Seasons of a Woman's Life." In D. G. McGuigan (ed.), *Women's Lives: New Theory, Research, and Policy.* Ann Arbor: University of Michigan Center for the Continuing Education of Women, 1980.

Bardwick, J. M. *The Plateauing Trap.* New York: AMACOM, 1986.

Blackburn, R. T. "Faculty Career Development: Theory and Practice." In S. M. Clark and D. R. Lewis (eds.), *Faculty Vitality and Institutional Productivity: Critical Perspectives for Higher Education.* New York: Teachers College Press, 1985.

Bowen, H. R., and Schuster, J. H. *American Professors: A National Resource Imperiled.* New York: Oxford University Press, 1986.

Clark, S. M., and Corcoran, M. "Perspectives on the Professionalization of Women Faculty: A Case of Accumulative Disadvantage?" *Journal of Higher Education,* 1986, 57 (1), 20–43.

Durham, R. E., Wright, P. S., and Chandler, M. O. *Teaching Faculty in Universities and Four-Year Colleges.* Washington, D. C.: U. S. Office of Education, 1966.

Eckert, E. H., and Williams, H. Y. *College Faculty View Themselves and Their Jobs.* Minneapolis: College of Education, University of Minnesota, 1972.

Erikson, E. H. *Childhood and Society.* (2nd ed.) New York: Norton, 1963.

Fulton, O., and Trow, M. "Research Activity in American Higher Education." *Sociology of Education,* 1974, 47 (1), 29–73.

Glaser, B. G. *Organizational Scientists: Their Professional Careers.* Indianapolis, Ind.: Bobbs-Merrill, 1964.

Hall, D. T. *Careers in Organizations.* Pacific Palisades, Calif.: Goodyear, 1976.

Hall, D. T. "Breaking Career Routines: Midcareer Choice and Identity." In D. T. Hall and Associates, *Career Development in Organizations*. San Francisco: Jossey-Bass, 1986a.

Hall, D. T. "Introduction: An Overview of Current Development Theory, Research, and Practice." In D. T. Hall and Associates, *Career Development in Organizations*. San Francisco: Jossey-Bass, 1986b.

Hall, D. T., and Nougaim, K. "An Examination of Maslow's Need Hierarchy in an Organizational Setting." *Organizational Behavior and Human Performance*, 1963, 3, 12–35.

Kanter, R. M. *Men and Women of the Corporation*. New York; Basic Books, 1977.

Ladd, E. C., and Lipset, S. M. "The Aging Professoriate." *The Chronicle of Higher Education*, 1976a, 12 (13), 16.

Ladd, E. C., and Lipset, S. M. "What Do Professors Like Best About Their Jobs?" *The Chronicle of Higher Education*, 1976b, 12 (5), 10.

Levinson, D. J. "The Career Is in the Life Structure, the Life Structure Is in the Career: An Adult Development Perspective." In M. B. Arthur, L. Bailyn, D. J., and H. A. Shepard, (eds.), *Working with Careers*. New York: Center for Research in Career Development, Columbia University, 1984.

Levinson, D. J. "A Concept of Adult Development" *American Psychologist*, 1986, 41 (1), 3–13.

Levinson, D. J., and others. *The Seasons of a Man's Life*. New York: Knopf, 1978.

Mortimer, K. P. "Academic Government at Berkeley: The Academic Senate." Unpublished doctoral dissertation, School of Education, University of California, Berkeley, 1969.

Rabinowitz, S., and Hall, D. T. "Changing Correlates of Job Involvement in Three Career Stages." *Journal of Vocational Behavior*, 1981, 18, 138–144.

Sorcinelli, M. D., and Near, J. P. "Relations Between Academic Work and Personal Life: Conflicts and Strategies for Change." Paper presented at annual meeting of American Educational Research Association, Washington, D. C., Apr. 1987.

Super, D. E. "Self-Realization in Work and Leisure." In D. T. Hall and Associates, *Career Development in Organizations*. San Francisco: Jossey-Bass, 1986.

Thompson, R. K. *How Does the Faculty Spend Its Time?* Seattle: University of Washington, 1971. (Mimeographed.)

Voydanoff, P. "Work-Family Life Cycles Among Women." In D. G. McGuigan (ed.) *Women's Lives: New Theory, Research, and Policy*, Ann Arbor: University of Michigan Center for the Continuing Education of Women, 1980.

The Academic Profession In Transition: Toward a New Social Fiction

R. Eugene Rice

In 1837, Ralph Waldo Emerson delivered "The American Scholar," an address that Oliver Wendell Holmes described as "our intellectual Declaration of Independence" (quoted in Jones, Leisy, and Ludwig 1952, p. 424). Using the images and issues of that time and place, Emerson articulated a vision of the scholar in a new democracy, a vision that resonated across nineteenth-century America. He called for the rejection of a past that was alien and debilitating and for the adoption of a new approach to scholarship and a new role for the scholar in society—a role that would be vital and self-confident, or in his words, "blood warm" (Jones, Leisy, and Ludwig 1952, p. 437).

Emerson's address was not so much an assertion of intellectual nationalism as a statement of his own struggle with the problem of vocation, with the nature and meaning of scholarly work in a changing society (Smith 1939). It is this same issue—what it means to be a scholar in a evolving democracy—that confronts us today. Just as Emerson's American scholar was struggling to break away from the cultural tyranny of "the learning of other lands," from patterns of deference that engendered self-doubt and the depreciation of new, adaptive roles, so the academic professional of today is wrestling with the legacy of a social fiction that came to dominate the lives of faculty from the mid-1950s to the mid-1970s, what is all too frequently referred to as the golden age of higher education.

During the past 15 years, most of our academic institutions have experienced monumental changes. The structural contexts in which we work have been transformed, but the normative conceptions by which the majority of faculty measure success in the profession remain unaltered and largely unexamined. The purpose of this paper is to initiate the search for a new conception of the academic professional, one more adaptive for both institutions and ourselves.

The Professionalization of Scholarship

It is significant that Emerson did not use the title "The American Professional," for in the middle of the nineteenth century, the professionalization of scholarship had just begun. Emerson's scholar was "man thinking," whether he was a physician, lawyer, minister, lecturer, writer, or teacher. During the second half of the nineteenth century, the process of professionalization began with a vengeance. The historian Burton J. Bledstein (1976) provides a critical review of the beginning of that process in his important book *The Culture of Professionalism: The Middle Class and the Development of Higher Education in America*. He argues that the self-doubt and status anxieties engendered by a democratic society with little reverence for tradition and no formal class boundaries created a culture of professionalism, which provided middle-class Americans with a basis for authority, an opportunity for mobility, and the standards for judging merit and success.

The institution that provided the organizational context and structure for this important cultural development was the American university. Bledstein shows that the American university and the culture of professionalism are intrinsically linked, and he traces their development back to the period between 1870 and 1900.

As a part of this critical cultural and structural development, scholarship in America was segmented into professions and disciplines and was institutionalized in newly organized professional associations and a burgeoning system of higher education. The process of professionalization and the institutionalization of scholarship continued during the opening decades of this century. Veysey (1973) contends that the academic revolution Jencks and Riesman (1968) describe actually took place between 1890 and 1910. During those years, the discipline-based departments became the foundation of scholarly allegiance and political power in academic life (Riesman 1980). It was not until after World War II, during the expansionist years in higher education, that this two-edged process, the professionalization of scholarship and its institutionalization in higher education, came to full power in society.

The financial resources and employment opportunities available to the professional scholar in the academic sector were unprecedented. Prestige, status, and influence also accrued to the academic professional. This was consistently demonstrated in the periodic rankings of occupations. For example, between 1953 and 1962, in Gallup poles assessing the suitability or attractiveness of nine leading professions, academic scholars rose from seventh place to third place, a rank they held until 1973 (Metzger 1975). In addition to relatively high status in the eyes of the general public, the faculty member enjoyed considerable influence inside academic institutions. [1]

During the years of incredible growth and expansion in higher education, scholarly activity that had previously been conducted in nonacademic settings was drawn under the extended umbrella of colleges and universities. Prior to this period of educational affluence, scholars— particularly those in such fields as economics and psychology—carried out their work independently of academic institutions. The new sources of funding, the expansion of programs, and the rising prestige in influence of the academic scholar made a college or university appointment not only convenient but almost irresistible. Within a relatively short period of time, being a scholar became virtually synonymous with being an academic professional, and a powerful image of what it meant to be an academic professional took hold.

The Dominant Image of the Academic Professional

Much about life is defined and shaped by socially constructed fictions, by patterns of meaning that cohere in a particular time and place. The great American poet Wallace Stevens said it best:

> The final belief is to believe in a fiction, which you know to be a fiction, there being nothing else. The exquisite truth is to know that it is a fiction and that you believe in it willingly (Stevens 1957, p. 163).

Nowhere in the contemporary world do socially constructed fictions have more power than in the professions. And no profession—with the possible exception of medicine—takes its own professional imagery more seriously than the academic profession. Reference needs only to be made to the years of graduate school socialization and to the power that academic mentors have in the lives of their protégés to make the argument.

The image that dominated the academic profession prior to World War II , particularly in the liberal arts colleges that then played a larger role in higher education, was that of the teacher-scholar. After a two-year study of faculty development programs in twenty of the nations better liberal arts colleges, Nelson (1981) published a book calling for the "renewal of the teacher-scholar." The call for renewal is, itself, testimony to the demise of that occupational ideal. During the earlier decades of this century, however, the teacher-scholar was an image widely shared. Nelson finds the teacher-scholar ideal articulated best in the *Davidson College Faculty Handbook*:

> Ideally the college professor would be a widely respected scholar excited about learning and capable of communicating this excitement to others, a teacher deeply concerned

with the welfare of students and eager to have them learn and grow, one who teaches imaginatively both by books and by personal example, a demanding yet compassionate person who respects the moral worth of students and their potential for growth (Nelson 1981, p. 7.)

Sometime after the mid-1950s, after the impact of the G. I. Bill of Rights and the launching of Sputnik, a major shift took place in the image of what it meant to be an academic professional. The older image of the teacher-scholar was celebrated in the Harbison Awards, sponsored by the Danforth Foundation. These widely publicized awards were given to ten outstanding teacher-scholars each year between 1962 and 1972. The Harbison Award was, however, little more than a nostalgic gesture; the image was dying or already dead, and the award series was established posthumously—in memoriam.

Scholarship became research, and teaching and research became activities that competed for the faculty member's time (Light 1974). The term *scholarship*, if it was used at all, referred to research, not teaching. In the consciousness of the faculty, as they thought about their working lives, the teacher-scholar as a model to be emulated had migrated from the core of the profession to the margins.

The magnitude of the growth and change in higher education that began in the late 1950s is still difficult to comprehend. A few statistics are instructive. Between 1956 and 1966, the proportion of high school graduates that went directly to college went from 32 percent to 53 percent. Between 1960 and 1970, the number of Ph.D.'s granted per year tripled, rising from about 10,000 to about 30,000 (Dressel and Mayhew 1974), and the increase in expenditures in the academic sector outstripped both the increase in enrollments and the rise in cost of living. Much of this early expansion was a direct response to demographic shifts and societal demand. Toward the end of the 1960s, however, growth in higher education had developed a momentum of its own and became what Carter referred to as "a binge of reckless expansion" that lasted well into the 1970s (quoted in Riesman 1980, p. 7).

This period of rapid growth in highest education brought with it a new conception of the academic professional. The constituent parts of this new professional image existed in nascent form throughout the early history of American higher education, but it was only the heady days of what seemed to be limitless growth, affluence, and societal influence that the component elements fused to form a powerful and dominant conception.

Parsons (1968), in a major essay on the professions, described the "educational revolution" that he saw coming to full fruition in American society after World War II. Fundamental to this revolution was the process of professionalization, a process that he regarded as "the most important single component in the structure of modern societies" (p. 545). According to Parson's influential theory, the keystone in the arch of the professionally oriented society is the modern university, and "the profession *par excellence* is the academic" (p. 545). He also described the impact of professionalization on the role of the typical faculty member:

> The typical professor now resembles the scientist more than the gentleman-scholar of an earlier time. As a result of the process of professionalization, achievement criteria are now given the highest priority, reputations are established in national and international forums rather than locally defined, and the center of gravity has shifted to the graduate faculties and their newly professionalized large-scale research function (Parsons 1968, p. 545).

What is most striking about this statement is that what he describes is not the typical professor. What he articulates is the dominant fiction by which the typical professor measures himself and his colleagues as professionals. The image of the academic professional that emerged during the expansionist days of higher education not only shaped the self-conceptions of faculty but informed institutional policies and determined, in large part, who received promotion, tenure and such amenities as leaves of absence and funding for travel and research.

The Assumptive World of the Academic Professional

In his work on psychosocial transitions, Parkes (1971) demonstrates the significance of what he calls the assumptive world in efforts to cope with change. In periods of stability, a complex of basic assumptions is established. Then in times of transition, this assumptive world is challenged and fundamentally restructured. In the mid-1960s, at the height of affluence and expansion in higher education, a consensus emerged regarding what it meant to be fully professional academically. Clustering around this image were the following basic assumptions:

1. Research is the central professional endeavor and the focus of academic life.

2. Quality in the profession is maintained by peer review and professional autonomy.

3. Knowledge is pursued for its own sake.

4. The pursuit of knowledge is best organized according to discipline (i.e., according to discipline-based departments).

5. Reputations are established through national and international professional associations.

6. The distinctive task of the academic professional is the pursuit of cognitive truth (or cognitive rationality).

7. Professional rewards and mobility accrue to those who persistently accentuate their specializations.

This professional vision and the interrelated complex of assumptions on which it was built contributed to an extraordinary advancement of knowledge. The increased specialization, the new levels of funding for research, and the rigorous exchange and critique of ideas produced undeniable benefits. The several interrelated elements listed above were woven into a fabric of consensus that became the assumptive world into which the large number of new Ph.D.'s from the rapidly expanding graduate schools were initiated. The men and women who were in graduate school during those expansionist days now form the majority of mid-career faculty who are struggling with the problems of steady-state staffing, or worse, retrenchment.

This conception of the academic professional is questioned here not because it is inappropriate but because it has created a one-dimensional view of the academic career, a view that continues to be normative for the majority of faculty regardless of the type of institution in which they work. This conception has had an especially debilitating effect on higher education; it has been a major stumbling block in efforts to adapt to the profound social, economic, and political changes confronting colleges and universities in these difficult times.

As faculty members look toward what is at best an ambiguous future, they cling tenaciously to that established professional image internalized during graduate school days. Rather than looking for new ways of dealing with the difficult problems confronting higher education or responding to opportunities for renewal or new career options, they accentuate and narrow further the older, established career path. In times of stress, they choose familiar.

New Context, Old Image

John Kenneth Galbraith takes pleasure in reminding us that everyone is a genius in a bull market. The older image of the academic professional could be accommodated without serious dissidence in the area of expansion. New programs and activities could be added on the margins of higher education without challenging the assumptive world at the core. Individuals committed to ideas and practices that moved them toward the margins of the profession (e.g., to the innovations initiated in the experimental colleges during the 1960s) could pursue their dreams with impunity. The context and conditions have changed dramatically in the 1980's but the older professional image continues to exert a debilitating influence on higher education's capacity to proactively shape and adapt to those changes.

The changing context in higher education has been reviewed so frequently that we now have a kind of demographic litany that is recited at the beginnings of most academic conferences. Rather than rehearse what is already too familiar, I focus on a basic organizational shift that is occurring in higher education and relate that shift to the professional self-understanding of faculty.

Shifting Organizational Cultures

American higher education has its deepest roots in the *collegial culture* of the British and Protestant colonial colleges. The collegial culture was also shaped by the German research university, which was based on research specialization and peer review—a pattern first introduced in this country at Johns Hopkins University. The assumptive world of the academic professional identified above was most directly informed by the collegial culture found in the contemporary liberal arts colleges and in research universities, where most faculty in the established disciplines received their graduate education and socialization into the profession.

Much of American higher education is now being profoundly influenced by a competing culture—the *managerial culture*. This culture in higher education can be traced back to the urban colleges and universities that grew out of the Catholic school system. These institutions, which were founded to provide educational opportunities and upward mobility for recent immigrants and the urban poor, were administered by priests and nuns who had strong administrative authority and often previous experience as educational managers. The origin of leadership in the managerial culture was dramatically different from that of the collegial culture, where leaders emerged from the ranks of faculty in the liberal arts colleges or from the successful research scientists in universities. The managerial culture is now being fostered by the increased complexity of the managerial task, by collective bargaining, and by the new professional specialization—educational administration—which has its own training programs, degrees, and associational life. This culture has been adopted by the community colleges and technical schools, and is being rapidly incorporated as the dominant organizational culture in regional state colleges and universities.[2]

The strains between the collegial and managerial cultures are having a major impact on faculty. The self-perceptions of faculty are rooted in the collegial tradition, but the currents of institutional change, including areas of expansion and power, are strengthening the managerial culture. Faculty committed to the peer review process are being evaluated by clients (students), and established liberal arts disciplines have lost ground to burgeoning interdisciplinary programs (business and computer science). Furthermore, knowledge is valued not as an end in itself but because it is economically useful and can be directly applied. Schuster and Bowen (1985) have shown that these changes are having their most profound effects on liberal arts faculty in mid-career, those individuals who were socialized into the profession during the expansionist days, when the collegial culture was stronger. Professional school faculty and those recently recruited into the new applied, technology programs (i.e., those more attuned to the managerial culture) are not faced with the same decline in real income and deteriorating work environments. Particularly galling to liberal arts faculty is the differential salary structure. The split that is developing between professional school faculty (who are often more recently appointed) and liberal arts faculty (who are generally older and in mid-career) is exacerbated by the tension between the managerial and collegial cultures, a tension that is making the collegial orientation less viable. The professional commitments of liberal arts faculty are anchored in the collegial culture, but the currents of change are strengthening the managerial culture.

The impact of these changing conditions on the lives of faculty can be conceptualized in a variety of ways. Austin and Gamson (1983) have captured the plight of faculty in their discussion of extrinsic and intrinsic rewards in academic careers (see Figure 1).

Austin and Gamson's conclusions coincide with Herzberg, Mausner, and Synderman's (1959) two-factor theory that intrinsic characteristics relate more to satisfaction and commitment and extrinsic factors have more to do with dissatisfaction. Austin and Gamson argue that in the current educational climate, the balance between the extrinsic and intrinsic is delicate indeed.

Figure 1. The Impact of Current Conditions on Extrinsic and Intrinsic Rewards

Extrinsic Rewards	Impact of Conditions
Salary	Decreasing
Opportunities	Limited
Workload	Increasing
Supervision	Centralized
Intrinsic Rewards	Impact of Condition
Intellectual challenge	Problematic for midcareer faculty
Interaction with students	Students perceived as unprepared
Autonomy	Limited
Trust	Eroding
Variety/wholeness	Depending upon discipline
Contribution (feedback)	Not as evident

Intrinsic characteristics may help keep satisfaction and commitment fairly high. The conclusion that is especially important for our work here, however, is that intrinsic characteristics may not be able to compensate for serious erosion of the extrinsic rewards. Schuster and Bowen (1985) have reached a similar conclusion.

A key factor in understanding the plight of faculty in the present situation is the professional self-perception of faculty cultivated during the expansionist period of higher education. The present conditions under which faculty labor do not seem particularly bleak when compared to income levels and working conditions prior to 1955. To use 1970 as the baseline in a comparative assessment of working conditions (as a number of recent studies do) is to make standard for the profession conditions that were, in fact, quite unique.

The problem is made worse by the age distribution of the present faculty. The majority of faculty are in mid-career and were inducted into the profession during that same period of growth. The structural conditions have changed, but the social fiction that defines success in the profession remains intact. I want to take several of the basic assumptions undergirding that dominant conception of what it means to be a professional and examine briefly the ways in which they distort our perception of the new context and conditions.

Research as the Focus of Academic Life

Even in the period of affluence in higher education the model of the academic professional was based upon a distorted view of the working lives of most faculty. Research was never the central professional endeavor or the focus of academic life, as is assumed in the prevailing model. As Ladd (1979) shows, most college and university professors do not think of themselves as researchers; in fact, a clear majority have published little or nothing. Their interests lie primarily in teaching, and they spend most of their time in teaching-related activities. Ladd (1979, p, 5) summarizes the situation forthrightly: "An ascendant model in academe, positing what faculty should be doing, is seriously out of touch with what they actually do and want to do. . . . [it] is also profoundly at odds with the primary goal of promoting the best possible teaching—that is, the best educational experience—in the nation's colleges and universities." The assumptions surrounding the relationship between teaching, research and the reward structure in most institutions were easy to tolerate in the period of affluence, but the conditions in higher education have changed, and those misleading assumptions must now be challenged.

Wilson (1977) argues that research can no longer be "piggybacked" on teaching, and objects on ethical grounds. Consumer-oriented students have raised the issue in terms of instructional quality, and legislatures and boards of trustees are concerned about cost. The academic professional model assumes an easy, complementary relationship between teaching and research— good teaching will follow from good research. But as Light (1974) has pointed out, the two activities compete for the faculty member's time and for most create a source of severe strain.

Good teaching of undergraduates requires the kind of scholarship that does not feed easily into research publication. Thus, the high priority placed on research fosters resentment of the demanding undergraduate and, particularly, of the underprepared student. The academic professional model establishes a normative climate—a professional culture—that fosters a sense of failure and encourages faculty members to withdraw from more difficult (and often more time-consuming) teaching challenges that are a part of the profession today.

The academic professional model is especially pernicious in its effect on tenure and promotion decisions. In the expansionist period, when Ph.D.'s were in demand and faculty were highly mobile, tenure could be taken for granted. But under current conditions, a negative tenure decision can terminate one's academic career. Mauksch (1980) found that the normative pressures to support research are so great that members of faculty promotion committees often vote against their own preferences. He argues that this discrepancy is very similar to the discrepancy between public behavior and private attitudes described by Gunnar Myrdal in *The American Dilemma*. In confidential interviews with members of tenure and promotion committees, Mauksch found that although 75 percent of the committee members wanted to give more weight to teaching in their voting, they did not, because they were certain that their colleagues and the administration had "stacked the cards against such judgments." Ladd (1979, p. 5) supports this conclusion: "When a particular norm is ascendant within a group and is institutionalized in various ways, it is very hard for a member of a group to deny its claim, even if intellectually he is fully convinced of its serious deficiency." In the current period of retrenchment, when tenure quotas are being imposed and promotions are being limited for fiscal reasons, the publication productivity standard is even more stringent. The older academic professional mode is being used to rationalize very difficult and often arbitrary judgments. In institutions in distress, it is being used as an anesthesia in the management of pain.

Peer Review

Peer review (colleague rather than client evaluation) has long been considered one of the primary characteristics of a profession (Carr-Saunders and Wilson 1928). The medical and legal professions have gone to great lengths to maintain that aspect of professionalism. In the academic world, peer review remains a hallmark of the profession, but it is under severe assault. Student evaluation is becoming an established procedure in most institutions, despite occasional protests, particularly among faculty who do not take peer review seriously. A professional prerogative has been challenged, in part, because it was not responsibly maintained. Students also serve on tenure and promotion committees in a number of institutions and have become deeply involved in the appointment process. In years ahead, client evaluation of professionals promises to become even more important in higher education.

Peer review as a professional prerogative is being eroded not only by the encroachments of the clients (students) but by the increased authority of administrators. This is reflected in the changes taking place in the organizational culture in higher education—i.e., in the shift from a collegial culture to a managerial culture. Supervision, evaluation, and the maintenance of standards are increasingly in the hands of academic managers. Peer review is giving way not only to new demand from below but to more authoritative directives from above.

Even in the arena of scholarly research, where peer review is most appropriate, the process has been redefined. Papers submitted to many journals are subjected to blind review. Thus, no longer is the reputation of the author and his or her mentor, the prestige of the author's institution of affiliation, or the general perception of the author's quality of mind allowed to influence directly the decisions regarding publication. Empirical studies demonstrating the unreliability of nonblind peer review are persuasive (Ceci and Peters 1982). The legitimacy of those older patterns of deference, which at one time passed for standards of excellence, has been eroded.

According to the older academic model, peer review keeps the academic hierarchy open and rational, so that "superiority of competence is the general legitimizing base of superiority of status in the academic system" (Parsons 1978, p. 105). But few would claim that the academic system in America has ever been fully open and rational, that the best always rise to the top. Discrimination based upon ascribed characteristics (e.g., race, religion, and sex) and the incessant press for homogeneity have continued to plague the profession. The changing conditions in higher education, however, are making the system even less open and the legitimizing basis for the superiority of status is losing ground (see Schuster and Bowen 1985, pp. 18–19). In departments that are fully tenured or in departments that have established a tenure quota, temporary faculty with non-tenure-track appointments are frequently as qualified as or better qualified than older, established faculty, and senior faculty often impose standards that even they could not meet. Strains between junior and senior faculty make colleagueship across age cohorts especially difficult. Even the gains that have been made by women and minorities through affirmative action are being threatened as the system contracts (Menges and Exum 1983).

The new conditions in higher education are even making it difficult to identify one's professional peers. Are the temporary non-tenure-track faculty to be regarded as fully enfranchised peers? What about the increasing number of part-time faculty? In community colleges, over half of the teaching faculty are already part-time. The preservation of older notions of peer review could lead to what Wilke (1979, p. xii) refers to as "a dramatic but relatively unnoticed structural transformation of higher education: the emergence of a quasi-closed elite at the top and a permanent underprivileged strata of untouchables at the bottom." To invoke the specter of the caste system is perhaps extreme, but if the one-dimensional academic professional model continues to be accepted as normative, higher education might well develop its own dual labor market.

Peer review is valued because it promotes informed critique, minimizes the abuses of the dilettante, and maintains the autonomy of the disciplines. In so doing, however, peer review keeps the critique inside, limiting contracts with not only other academic disciplines but other sectors in the society. What is needed now is a renewed capacity to reach out to that broader world, not reinforcement of the distance.

Centrality of the Discipline

A key element in the academic professional model is the centrality of the discipline. The commitment to a body of specialized knowledge has become the center point around which the other components turn. In American culture, where professionals already function with narrowly circumscribed work-encapsulated egos, professional identity among academicians is disciplinary: "I am a psychologist," or "I am a physicist." There is a kind of bonding to a disciplinary perspective, a way of thinking (theory) and doing (method). There is a body of literature, a mode of inquiry, and a history. Many faculty can trace their intellectual genealogies back to the founders of their disciplines. Introductory textbooks are often organized in that way and faculty offices are filled with the totems of discipline: books, pictures, and even charts of the lineage.

According to the older academic professional model, there is a distinct ordering of the disciplines, ranging from those that stand at the intellectual core of academic life to those that are obviously on the periphery. Parsons put it bluntly: "It seems quite clear that the faculties of arts and sciences constitute the structural core of the university complex" (1978, p. 103). Within this context, the major task of faculty members in relationships to students is to prepare them for academic careers. The most successful professors are expected to reproduce themselves, a process that is disparagingly referred to as academic cloning. The inappropriateness of this process for most of higher education is obvious.

The strength of the discipline at the center of the profession is institutionally buttressed locally by the discipline-based departmental structure and in more cosmopolitan settings by professional associations (national and international) that honor and reinforce the commitments of the discipline. The intellectual bonding to the discipline, which is nurtured in graduate school, is reinforced at every turn. In this assumptive world, to be a scholar is to be an academic professional within a discipline.

Given the wedding of academic professionalism and the discipline, interdisciplinary studies are by definition marginal. During the expansionist era, interdisciplinary programs were added on at the periphery of institutions without threatening the disciplinary core. During the 1960s, American studies, urban affairs, and various area studies programs flourished. Experimental "cluster" colleges focusing on interdisciplinary themes received much attention. But when budgets tightened in the 1970s, these interdisciplinary programs were the first to be eliminated. The more controversial programs focusing on the study of blacks, Chicanos, and women faced a discipline-based discrimination that was every bit as entrenched as the racism and sexism they were established to confront.

The disciplinary fortress that withstood these earlier assaults is now beginning to crumble in the face of a new interdisciplinary thrust driven by the demands of the market. Enrollment shifts from the arts and sciences to applied interdisciplinary programs in business, communications, and computer sciences are altering the basic character of colleges and universities. Confronted with this major structural tiff, liberal arts faculty argue for the integrity of the discipline and inveigh against the erosion of curricular turf. The legitimate case for the discipline has been tarnished by a contentiousness that is transparently self-serving.

The disciplines—particularly in the humanities and the social sciences, where there is limited consensus in the first place—have been heavily politicized, and the struggle to defend departmental hegemonies has profoundly distorted the educational mission of colleges and universities. Constructive debate over the distinctive intellectual substance separating the disciplines and the contribution each specialization makes to the whole educational enterprise has given way to the development of strategies to maintain FTEs (full-time equivalents) and faculty positions.

This zealous commitment to the discipline—exacerbated by the older academic professional model—has exacted heavy institutional and personal costs. The ideological defense of the discipline and the attendant political posturing have become major stumbling blocks in efforts to reallocate faculty responsibilities to meet changing needs. The adaptive capacity of institutions is being attenuated. For individual faculty, particularly those in mid-career, an inordinately close identification with the discipline limits opportunities for growth and development within the institution and renders the exploration of career options outside higher education virtually unthinkable.

The Pursuit of Knowledge for its Own Sake

No tenet in the established conception of the academic professional has been more enduring than the commitment to knowledge for the sake of knowledge, to dispassionate reason, to the objective (value-free) study of nature, society, and the individual. Nisbet (1971) lamented the assault upon this ancient belief in his book *The Degradation of the Academic Dogma*. His argument was weakened somewhat when he began to write a regular column for the *Wall Street Journal*. No tenet has been the subject of more rancorous debate or betrayed greater evidence of a "false consciousness" within the profession—a discrepancy between what is said and what is done, between the ideal and the real.

In the early 1960s, scholars, particularly those in the social sciences, claimed to be engaged in the "scholarship of civility," a scholarship that was, if not value-free, certainly "beyond ideology."

During that period, many of these same scholars joined the march to Washington, D. C., and moved into positions of incredible power and influence. In a series of articles published in *Life* magazine in June 1967, Theodore White celebrated the new American action-intellectuals:

> In the past decade this brotherhood of scholars has become the most provocative and propelling influence on all American government and politics. Their ideas are the drivewheels of the Great Society: shaping our defenses, guiding our foreign policy, redesigning our cities, reorganizing our schools, deciding what our dollar is worth. . . . For such intellectuals now is a Golden Age, and America is the place. Never have ideas been sought more hungrily or tested against reality more quickly. From White House to city hall, scholars stalk the corridors of American Power (quoted in Steinfels 1979, p. 280).

By the late 1960s, it became evident that much of this scholarship, far from transcending biases, was deeply rooted in narrow ideological distortions of class, culture, sex, and race. Knowledge and power were being mixed in ways that became publicly evident. Those who argued for a scholarship of civility, for a scholarship that could rise above ideology, initiated a process that was self-discrediting. The radical caucuses in the professional associations—particularly in the social science associations—forced members to recognize that much of American scholarship had been shaped by and served the interests of rather select groups. The new scholarship produced by women, blacks, and representatives of various Third World groups strengthened the argument. By the end of the decade, the professional commitment to scholarship for its own sake had been severely undermined both within and outside the academy.

The professional arrogance of the early 1960s and the turmoil of the late 1960s produced a demand for a new approach to scholarship. The graduate students and young faculty who formed the new caucuses in the professional associations argued that all knowledge is rooted in a value context, and the radicals among them called for the international politicization of scholarship. Activities within the American History Association are representative. In 1969, the *AHA Newsletter* urged educators to "[broaden] historical abilities and knowledge among the general public ... [to] demystify the holders of power and serve democracy" (cited in Lightman and Negrin 1981, p. 9). There was a call to reassess the relationship between the roles of scholar and citizen.

By the mid-1970s, scholars were being pressured by more established groups to address immediate public concerns. With the shrinking of available funding for scholarship, public agencies and private foundations became increasingly interested in projects that addressed public-policy issues. In 1976, the congressional reauthorization of the National Endowment for the Humanities mandated support for state councils established to provide public-issue programming for the adult out-of-school population. Participants in a major conference on the "New Scholarship on Women" in 1981 argued that education, itself, is a profoundly political act, that what is taught and learned "controls destinies, gives some persons hope for a particular kind of future, and deprives others even of ordinary expectation for work and achievement" (Howe 1982, p. 28). The commitment to knowledge for its own sake must be fundamentally reconceptualized if it is to make sense to faculty in colleges and universities that are now dominated by applied programs, where the slogan itself has been ideologically tainted by its most vociferous defenders.

Professional Rewards and Mobility Accrue to Those Who Persistently Accentuate Their Specializations

The assumptive world of the academic professional that took full form during the heyday of higher education has implied in it a career development pattern that was assumed to be normative for all. Like other professionals in America, academicians take as a guide for their working lives what Seymour Sarason (1977, p. 123) has called "the one life, one career imperative." Buttressed by the additional commitment to the discipline and to their specialization, academic professionals take this imperative one step further and view their career trajectory as one that continues to narrow and become more firmly focused in the specialization. The reward structure, in both professional associations and local institutions, reinforces this conception of career development. Leaves of absence and research grants are awarded to those who continue to build on and narrow the thrust of their specializatons. Efforts to move in new directions or to develop competencies in other areas are systematically discouraged within the context of that older assumptive world.

My own work with faculty has focused primarily on arts and science faculty in mid-career. It is that large group of mid-career faculty—the majority in most colleges and universities—who are struggling to maintain vitality in their careers and who are having the greatest difficulty accepting the normative conception of what they should be doing with their careers (Rice 1980, 1985).

The literature on adult development and the new research that is being done on careers in other occupational settings indicate that what is needed for continual growth and development in mid-life is not pressure to extend and narrow further our specializations but the opportunity to attend to the development of the other parts of ourselves that has been neglected because of the specialized choices made at an earlier time. Kolb's (1981, 1984) work on adult learning is especially helpful here. He begins with Carl Jung's notion that the age of forty is the noon of life, and believes that "fulfillment in adult development is accomplished through efforts at integration and the cultivation of nondominant modes of dealing with the world" (1981, p. 250).

Kolb argues that what is needed in early career is the opportunity to develop and extend one's specialization; then, in mid-life, the change to move in new directions, to develop other modes of learning, becomes more important. The movement in mid-life is from specialization to integration. For example, a theoretical physicist should move from an assimilative learning style (combining abstraction and reflection) into a policy-making position combining concrete experience and active experimentation. For Kolb, this is a movement toward wholeness, toward integration, toward the more complete development of the self. He is fond of quoting Yeats: "Nothing can be sole or whole that has not been rent."

The conception of career development that currently dominates the academic professional's self-perception and that informs our staff development policies promotes the perpetual pursuit and narrowing of one's specialization. Professors in their forties, looking ahead to twenty or thirty more years in the same department with the same colleagues teaching the same courses, feel stuck (Kanter 1977). To revitalize our institutions and the individuals within them, we must utilize the talents of this large group of faculty in new and imaginative ways. Again, the assumptive world of the academic professional stands in the way.

Toward a New Fiction

The primary difficulty with the dominant conception of what it means to be professional in the academic world is that it is one-dimensional, that it is applied to an increasingly varied occupational context, and that it is made normative for all. It is a complex of assumptions that developed in a unique period of affluence and expansion. It is probably too soon and would certainly be presumptuous to attempt to construct an alternative conception. Whatever the new professional image, it will emerge in response to the challenges of the new context and will be an elaboration on much of the old. Certainly, the new conception should lend dignity and give support and challenge to faculty where they are—in their everyday working lives—and where they need to be for the good of their students, the society, and the advancement of learning. There are some themes that stand out, however, and might well be included in a more multidimensional approach. I will list those themes and comment briefly.

A key issue is the place of scholarship in the profession. The older professional model takes for granted the bifurcation of the profession into teaching and research and identifies scholarship almost exclusively with the latter. There needs to be a primary focus on scholarship more broadly defined. It may very well lead to publication in highly specialized disciplinary journals, or it may be disseminated in some other, more applied form.

In the older conception, teaching became a secondary activity that, it was assumed, would benefit from scholarly research. The particular kinds of scholarship required for quality teaching were largely neglected; if one was not engaged in substantive research—which is true of the majority of faculty—scholarship could also be deferred. The new conception should make scholarship the central focus of the profession. The demonstration of scholarship should be required, but the form it takes should be allowed to vary broadly, and its ties to teaching and learning should be assessed and honored.

The new image of the profession should also be multifaceted; it should recognize the full legitimacy of a variety of career paths and allow people to build on individual strengths. Heterogeneity should be valued. Despite the pitfalls, there is much to be learned from the corporate sector. Research on managerial careers has demonstrated that organizations benefit from recognizing and rewarding individual differences. The work of Schein (1978) and Driver (1979, 1982), which matches individual career orientations with organizational structure, is helpful here.

This new approach will require deans and department chairpersons to know more about the changing commitments and interests of faculty in their units. They will also need to know about the opportunities available (both within their institutions and without) for enabling faculty to grow and change in ways that benefit both the individual and the organization. Individualized approaches that take into consideration both age and career stage will be necessary.

In the older model, the disciplinary career (research, publication, and associational life) became disassociated from the institutional career (teaching, governance, and program development). A new and more appropriate conception should bridge the two. Autonomy is highly valued by most faculty, and the older academic professional model built upon and extended this concern to the point at which many faculty felt cut-off and isolated from their institutions and even their colleagues. Faculty want their professional lives to be institutionally useful. They want to participate meaningfully in program development and institutional innovation, but they feel de-classed professionally if they become involved in program perceived to be marginal, programs such as general education or adult learning.

The academic career has three strands: the disciplinary career, the institutional career, and the external career. During the expansionist era, faculty lost connection with the larger society's purposes and tasks. This disconnectedness was caused by the rapid growth and the estrangement of the 1960s and was exacerbated by the high levels of specialization. Faculty are now being called upon to make new connections with what is regrettably called the world of work or, worse, the real world. The descriptions depict the problem. Younger students (aged 18 to 22) are seeking advice on nonacademic careers, and the increasing number of older students are bringing to the classroom a wealth of work experience that needs to be integrated into the process of teaching and learning. Co-op programs and internships abound (Rice 1983). Consulting is now regarded as an asset rather than a liability (Patton 1978, 1980). A number of faculty are having to consider, for the first time, the possibility of nonacademic employment. The disciplinary currency that has been so highly valued in academic settings suffers rapid devaluation in that external market.

The new conception of the academic professional must encompass that external world. The walls between the university and that other world will have to become more permeable to allow for greater movement both ways. At the same time, what is distinctive about the academic profession must be clearly articulated and carefully preserved.

Many of the challenges confronting academic professionals in the years ahead are integrative. They must tie the specialties together and transcend the polarities implied in the older model—i.e., teaching and research, theory and practice, content and process, peer and client. This is not to say that we should return to a simpler, less complex past. The new professional should not be a generalist, the gentleman scholar of an earlier time. Rather, the emerging challenge is to provide new forms of reintegration and build upon the advancements made possible through specialization. During the golden age of higher education, the advances in disciplinary specializations were many and the achievements significant. That effort must be sustained and enhanced. But there is also a need for critical integrative work, which is every bit as legitimate professionally. Relating the parts to the whole and preventing the fragmentation that is always a threat is also of value and must be given priority. Only then will we begin to overcome the culture of separation that pervades society and, especially, higher education (Bellah et al. 1985).

Finally, like Emerson in the 1830s, we must reexamine the place of scholarship in a changing democracy. Much of what we have identified as the dominant conception of the academic professional is rooted in a cultural hegemony that is no longer viable in an open, pluralistic society. Scholars in a democracy have a responsibility not only for what is referred to as scholarly productivity but for what is learned, for how students "make meaning" out of what is written in journals, presented in the classroom, and performed in the laboratory. A developmental approach to the student as learner is required (see Perry 1981). Diversity in background and preparation should be seen as a central vocational challenge rather than a distraction from the real world. Scholarship must be defined in these broader terms to sustain a democracy that is committed to both honoring a plurality of communities and breaking through debilitating ascriptive barriers.

The new conception of the academic profession should take responsibility for learning in the general society, for what has been referred to as the ecology of learning. In the 1960s and 1970s, while the disciplinary specializations were growing and higher education was expanding, the quality of teaching and learning in the schools was seriously eroding (Rice 1984). Whether or not there was a causal connection, the culture of separation evident here can no longer be tolerated.

In his book *The Emergence of Professional Social Science*, Thomas Haskell (1977, p. 67) argues that during the early years of the social science disciplines, the new man of science had to "exchange general citizenship in society for membership in the community of the competent." The professional conception discussed above accepted that exchange. The new view needs to reject the choice and affirm the academic professional's responsibility to both the specialized community and the larger society. Bellah et al. (1985) persuasively argue that higher education in our society has become primarily an instrument of individual careerism and that this orientation can provide neither the personal meaning nor the public commitment required to sustain a free society. The American professorate must restructure its own professional commitments if it is to provide constructive leadership in a changing democracy.

References

Austin, A. E. and Z. F. Gamson, 1983. *Academic Workplace: New Demands, Heightened Tensions.* ASHE-ERIC/Higher Education Research Report No. 10. Washington, D. C.: Association for the Study of Higher Education.

Bellah, R. N., R. Madsen, W. Sullivan, A. Swindler, and S. Tipton. 1985. *Habits of the Heart: Individualism and Commitment in American Life.* Berkeley: University of California Press.

Bergquist, W. H. 1982. "The Future of Professional Development." Keynote address delivered to the Professional and Organizational Development Network in Higher Education, Montebello, Quebec.

Bledstein, B. J. 1976. *The Culture of Professionalism.* New York: Norton.

Carr-Saunders, A. M., and P. A. Wilson. 1928. *Professions: Their Organization and Place in Society.* Oxford: Clarendon.

Ceci, S. J., and D. P. Peters. 1982. "A Naturalistic Study of Peer Review in Psychology: The Fate of Published Articles, Resubmitted." *Behavior and Brain Sciences* 5:187–252.

Dressel, P. L., and L. B. Mayhew. 1974. *Higher Education as a Field of Study.* San Francisco: Jossey-Bass.

Driver, M. J. 1979. "Career Concepts and Career Management in Organizations." Pp. 79–139 in *Behavioral Problems in Organizations,* edited by C. L. Cooper. Engelwood Cliffs, NJ: Prentice-Hall.

_____. 1982. "Career Concepts: A New Approach to Career Research." Pp. 38–52 in *Career Issues in Human Resource Management,* edited by R. Katz. Engelwood Cliffs, NJ: Prentice-Hall.

Haskell, T. L. 1977. *The Emergence of Professional Social Sciences: The American Social Science Association and the Nineteenth-Century Crisis of Authority.* Urbana: University of Illinois Press.

Herzberg, F., B. Mausner, and B. Snyderman. 1959. *The Motivation to Work.* New York: Wiley.

Howe, F. 1982. "The New Scholarship on Women: The Extent of the Revolution." *Women's Studies Quarterly* 10:26–29.

Jencks, C., and D. Riesman. 1968. *The Academic Revolution.* Garden City, NY: Doubleday.

Jones, H., E. Leist, and R. Ludwig. 1952. *Major American Writers.* Vol. 1 3rd. ed. New York: Harcourt Brace.

Kanter, R. M. 1977. *Men and Women of the Corporation.* New York: Basic.

Kolb, D. A. 1981. "Learning Styles and Disciplinary Differences." Pp. 232–55 in *The Modern American College: Responding to the New Realities of Diverse Students and a Changing Society,* edited by A. L. Chickering and Associates. San Francisco: Jossey-Bass.

_____. 1984. *Experimental Learning: Experience as the Source of Learning and Development.* Engelwood Cliffs, NJ: Prentice-Hall.

Ladd, E. C. 1979. "The Work Experience of American College Professors: Some Data and an Argument." *Current Issues in Higher Education* 22:135–54.

Light, D. 1974. "Introduction: The Structure of the Academic Professions." *Sociology of Education* 47:2–28.

Lightman, M., and H. Negrin. 1981. *Outside Academe: New Ways of Working in the Humanities*. New York: Simon and Schuster.

Mauksch, H. O. 1980. "What Are the Obstacles to Improving Quality Teaching?" *Current Issues in Higher Education* 2:49–56.

Menges, R. J., and W. H. Exum. 1983. "Barriers to the Progress of Women and Minority Faculty." *Journal of Higher Education* 54:123–44.

Metzger. W. P. 1975. "The American Academic Profession in 'Hard Times'." *Daedalus* 104:25–44.

Nelson. W. C. 1981. *Renewal of the Teacher Scholar*. Washington, D. C: Association of American Colleges.

Nisbet, R. 1971. *The Degradation of the Academic Dogma*. New York: Basic.

Parkes, M. C. 1971. "Psycho-social Transitions. A Field of Study." *Social Science and Medicine* 5: 101–15.

Parsons. T. 1968. "Professions." *International Encyclopedia of the Social Sciences* 12:536–46.

_____.1978. *Action Theory and the Human Condition*. New York: Free Press.

Patton, C.V. 1978. "Mid-Career Change and Early Retirement." Pp. 69–82 in *New Directions for Institutional Research*, edited by P. Heistaud and J. Warren. Cambridge, MA: ABT Books.

_____. 1980. "Consulting by Faculty Members." *Academe* 66:181–85.

Perry, W. C. 1981. "Cognitive and Ethical Growth: The Making of Meaning." Pp. 79–116 in *The Modern American College: Responding to the New Realities of Diverse Students and a Changing Society*, edited by A. L. Chickering and Associates. San Francisco: Jossey-Bass.

Rice, R. E. 1980. "Dreams and Actualities: Danforth Fellows in Mid-Career." *AAHE Bulletin* 32:3–16.

_____. 1983 *Strategies for Relating Career Preparation and Liberal Learning*. St. Paul, MN: Northwest Area Foundation.

_____. 1984. *Toward Reform in Teacher Education: Strategies for Change*. Washington, DC: The Fund for the Improvement of Postsecondary Education.

_____. 1985. *Faculty Lives: Vitality and Change*. St. Paul, MN: Northwest Area Foundation.

Riesman, D. 1980. *On Higher Education*. San Francisco: Jossey-Bass.

Sarason, S. B. 1977. *Work, Aging, and Social Change: Professionals and the One Life-One Career Imperative*. New York: Free Press.

Schein, E. H. 1978. *Career Dynamics: Matching Individual and Organization Needs*. Reading, MA: Addison-Wesley.

_____. 1985. *Organizational Culture and Leadership*. San Francisco: Jossey-Bass.

Schuster, J. H., and H. P. Bowen. 1985. "The Faculty at Risk." *Change* 17:12–21.

Smith, H. N. 1939. "Emerson's Problem of Vocation: A Note on the American Scholar," *New England Quarterly* 12:52–67.

Steinfels, P. 1979. *The New Conservatives: The Men Who Are Changing America's Politics*. New York: Simon and Schuster.

Stevens, W. 1957. *Opus Posthumous*. New York: Knopf.

Veysey. L. 1973. "Stability and Experiment in the American Undergraduate Curriculum." Pp. 1–64 in *Content and Context: Essays on College Education*, edited by C. Kaysen. New York: McGraw-Hill.

Wilke, A. S. 1979. *The Hidden Professorate: Credentialism, Professionalism, and the Tenure Crisis*. Westport, CT: Greenwood Press.

Wilson, E. K. 1977. "Sociology: Scholarly Discipline or Profession?" Paper presented at the annual meeting of the American Sociological Association, Chicago.

Notes

1. Jencks and Riesman's (1968) book describing the increase in faculty domination in colleges and universities was published in the year that faculty domination peaked.
2. This analysis of organizational cultures was first brought to my attention by Bergquist (1982). The most useful book on organizational cultures is Schein (1985).

The Aging of Faculty in American Colleges and Universities: Demographic Trends and Implications

Ira E. Robinson and Everett S. Lee

Introduction

In the United States, as in other industrialized countries, the aged are already a large segment of the population and the rate is increasing. In 1990 only one in twenty-five Americans was sixty-five or older and one in ten was fifty-five or over. Currently, one in eight is sixty-five or over and one in five is fifty-five or over. By 2030, a year for which we must now begin to plan, one in five will be sixty-five or over and one in three will be fifty-five or older. We are moving toward a time when for every two years a person spends in the labor force there will be a full year of retirement.

Already our resources are strained by the related burdens of retirement and health costs. According to Richard Darman, former director of the U. S.. Office of Management and Budget, health costs alone could rise from the current 12 percent to one-third of the gross national product. Other than reforming our medical system, we can continue to meet these costs in only two ways. The first is to increase the number of working years per person by earlier entry to and later exit from the work force. The second is to increase overall productivity, a task in which colleges and universities must play a leading role. We can no longer expect non-high school graduates like Edison and Ford to spring forward with inventions or renovate industrial systems. Even a high school education equips one for little more than a minor role in the work force. It is primarily in colleges and universities that the basic research and innovative ideas that can be developed by business and industry or applied by government to improve the environment and living conditions flourish.

This role, however, will not be easy. College and university faculties, upon whom much of this burden will fall, are aging at a faster rate than the general population. President Sovern of Columbia University noted in an article for the *New York Times Magazine* that at his university "nearly half of the tenured professors in the arts and sciences will retire in the 1990s. Colleges and universities all over the country are facing a massive wave of retirements."[1] Indeed, the pace of faculty retirement will resemble a torrent in the next few years. For example, Brigham Young University currently has thirty to forty vacancies a year and expects to see a rise to fifty or sixty because of an increase in the retirement rate. By the year 2000 over one-third of its faculty will have retired.

Already vacancies are difficult to fill, and it may be impossible in the near future to replace retirees with equally qualified people. Many campuses report trouble in recruiting for "hard to hire" disciplines like business and engineering.[2] An article in the Journal of the American Associa-

577

tion for the Advancement of Science entitled "The Graying of Physics" features a chart which shows an almost linear increase in the average age of physics faculty members from 40.7 in 1973 to 51.6 in 1989.[3]

This, of course, sets up a movement throughout the college and university hierarchy in which the better faculty from lesser institutions move up to those with higher salaries, fewer class hours, and better facilities. Still, a number of institutions are tempting professors to leave early by offering extra retirement benefits, a program not unlike that undertaken by the federal government some years ago. Occasionally the reason is to remove dead wood, but mostly it is because financially troubled institutions seek to lower total salaries by replacing full professors with those of lower rank. However, when colleges and universities have state retirement plans, this can result in greater public expense since the state winds up paying two persons rather than one.

One might claim that the retirement of the aging faculty is not a completely bad thing. There are many tenured but poorly qualified professors who entered academe as colleges and universities experienced unprecedented growth in the 1960s. Even the best colleges and universities were forced to appoint and promote persons who would not meet today's standards. This was particularly true of institutions that entered late into the category of research universities and of many four-year and two-year colleges. Often these schools had to accept those who would not be employed by more prestigious institutions or those who drifted down as they were denied tenure in the weeding-out process in the 1970s. Given the pace of change in knowledge and technology, it could be desirable to hire persons who have been better trained or are more comfortable with new techniques.

But who is there to take the vacant places? Have we trained enough Ph.D.'s in specific disciplines to replace the professors who will soon be gone? More important in the long run is whether the best and the brightest of undergraduate and graduate students are willing to be trained for a notoriously underpaid profession that in recent years has fallen in public and legislative esteem. Have we trained enough American students to replace the professors leaving the fields of mathematics, science, and engineering? If not, can we attract to our shores the likes of Einstein, Fermi, Bohr, Stern, Rabi, Pauli, Bloch, Kusch, Wigner, Lee, Yang, Goeppert-Mayer, and Bethe, who with limited native help established the American lead in physics? Or the Kuznets, Leontiefs, and Koopmans who won Nobel prizes in economics?

As will be detailed later, the answer to all of these inquiries is *no*. Faculty salaries have not risen with the cost of living from the 1970s to the present, and yearly increases have fallen well behind those of workers outside academe, including most federal and state employees. Fewer persons with high test scores and fewer honors graduates see college or university teaching as a desirable career. Of those receiving Ph.D.'s an ever-increasing proportion choose other vocations. Enrollment in sciences, engineering, and mathematics is well below future needs, and fewer graduates in these disciplines are interested in college or university teaching. In many universities those departments maintain present levels of faculty employment only because of the influx of foreign students and the increasing enrollment of the Asian-American children of immigrants.

That we have so bluntly answered the questions posed above with an unqualified "no" should trouble everyone and cause many to challenge our conclusions. To understand why faculties are aging at such a rate and why the resulting problems are suddenly so acute, we have to consider the past as we project future trends. In dealing with the future we almost always use previous conceptions and expect to solve problems with methods that formerly worked. That can be dangerous in times of accelerating changes.

Magnitude of the Problem

As detailed in the *Digest of Educational Statistics, 1990,* American institutions of higher education are numerous. In the fall of 1987, the latest date for which information is available, the 3,587 institutions of higher learning had 2,337,534 employees, about 2 percent of the national labor force. And the direct economic effect of these universities is great. It would surprise almost no one to learn that the University of North Carolina at Chapel Hill and the University of Georgia at

Athens are the largest employers in their cities, but it is astonishing to learn that the University of Pennsylvania is the largest private employer in Philadelphia.

Most of this growth has taken place since World War II. Just before that war began (academic year 1939–40), there were 1,708 higher educational institutions enrolling 1,494,203 students. Soon after the end of the war (1949–50), there were 1,851 institutions with 2, 659,021 students—a near doubling in enrollment. That was the beginning of an extraordinary expansion of higher education in the United States. Ten years later an additional one million students were counted, and in the decade of the 1970s the number more than doubled—from 3.6 to eight million. Another three million were added by the academic year 1979–80, after which growth was moderate. Currently, over thirteen million students are enrolled in colleges or universities.

The increase in faculty, however, has not kept pace with enrollment. Faculty expanded from academic year 1939–40 to 1987–88 5.4 times. while enrollment went up 8.5 times. Of course, faculty are the smaller part of college and university employment. Almost 40 percent of the employees of institutions of higher learning are nonprofessionals, and about half of these are clerical or secretarial. Of the 60 percent who are professionals, only 34 percent are faculty. However, faculty members are aided by the 7 percent of employees who are instruction or research assistants.

The rest are administrators; for every six faculty members there is a manager or administrator. But to dispel the common charge of a bloated bureaucracy, remember that administrators supervise not only the 793,000 faculty members, but also the other 1.5 million employees in addition to caring for thirteen million students. Fully 15 percent of employees of institutions of higher education are non-faculty professionals. Administrators, too, are aging, but it is only for faculty that we have good data. A needed review of the non-faculty staff must await data that are classified both by age and by type of activity.

The Ideal Age Distribution of Faculties

Educational institutions are no different from other industries in having ideal age distributions for different segments of their work forces. In general, it is best to have an age balance that permits vacancies to be filled from within by those in lower positions and hire others as trainees who eventually may move up. Of course, not all positions can be filled in this way, and persons must be brought in from outside to fill some jobs. This is especially true of faculty, for whom transfers from campus to campus are generally necessary for quick promotion, higher salary, or improved working conditions. Perpetrating such transfers is the fact that colleges and universities are held to tight standards advertising faculty openings and making appointments which either satisfy fair employment requirements or bring in the best qualified applicants.

Faculty employment is further complicated by tenure requirements. Instructors and assistant professors go through an agonizing period in which they struggle to acquire tenure, while most associate and full professors, the great majority of whom have tenure, cannot be removed or demoted except for the most serious offenses. Whereas deans, presidents, and other officials can be instantly removed, tenured faculty can hang on to their jobs even if they only partly fulfill the teaching, research, and community service expected from them.

Thus, more than in most occupations, upper faculty levels tend to be filled by the oldest professors. For financial, if for no other reasons, the number of full, associates, or assistant professors is limited, and promotion from lower ranks depends upon vacancies in higher ranks. Retirement is the major way in which full professorships become open, and for the older to linger too long slows promotions all down the line. Especially in nonresearch institutions or in rapidly changing disciplines, older faculty may be out of touch with new developments. However, it should be kept in mind that older faculty members with good records have contacts others do not have and can play an important role in suggesting avenues of research to younger faculty and in helping them secure funding. In addition, as pointed out by Zuckerman in her study of Nobel Prize winners, there is the personal contact that means so much in steering people toward the cutting edges of a field.[4] "Smoked-out volcanoes" are sometimes better at this than younger, more active professors.

In sum, the ideal age distribution for faculty is one that expands downward, but not in extreme fashion. Its overall size should be such that there is relatively little reliance on part-time lecturers or instructors. Within the associate and full professor ranks there should be a graduation of age so that retirements are regularly spaced and the prospect of promotion is always there for productive persons of low rank. The increase in numbers as rank decreases allows for a trial period before tenure is granted and for more rigorous selection as rank increases.

Deviations from the Ideal Age Distribution

There are different ways to approach the subject of faculty aging and these depend largely upon the definition of faculty. Contrary results may be obtained if only full-time faculty are considered, if full- and part-time faculty are lumped together, or if all who teach are included. Insofar as aging is concerned, however, all definitions point in the same direction. Faculties are aging rapidly and the present distribution by age is far from ideal. This is clear from the age distributions given in Table 1 for the full- and part-time regular instructional faculty in the fall of 1987. Full-time regular faculty are at the heart of college and university endeavors and largely determine their programs. Included below are 489,000 full-time faculty which make up 62 percent of the total faculty.

There is, in fact, a great deal of variance in the rate and effect of aging for different institutions and for different departments in the same college or university. Useful data for such comparisons are limited. Fortunately, Bowen and Sosa have used special tabulations from the Survey of Doctoral Recipients, conducted biennially by the National Research Council, to take such estimates for several types of colleges and universities.

Using a fivefold classification of institutions that award bachelor's or higher degrees, they computed the proportions of faculty under forty, forty to forty-nine, and fifty or over in 1987. These are shown in Table 2.

At first glance, deviations from the average age may not seem great, but a closer examination indicates quite large differences between different types of institutions. In the "Other Four-Year" category, 43 percent of the faculty in 1987 was fifty and over, as compared with only 33 percent in the more prestigious Liberal Arts colleges. At the other end of the scale, 29 percent of the faculty of Liberal Arts 1 colleges were under the age of forty as compared with 17 percent at the lesser-ranked colleges.

Differences among the research and doctorate universities are not great, and for no age group do they differ very much from the average for all institutions. The Comprehensive 1 colleges, which generally offer master's degrees but not doctorates, have about average proportions of older faculty and a low proportion under the age of forty. It would appear that the lease prestigious institutions have smaller proportions of young faculty who would move upward to fill the slots vacated by older faculty.

Table 1. Full and Part-time Regular Faculty in Institutions of Higher Learning by Age, 1987

| Age | Full-time | | Part-time | | Percent |
	Number (thousands)	Percent	Number (thousands)	Percent	Part-time
Less than 30	8	1.6	9	5.3	0.53
30–34	41	8.3	17	9.9	0.29
35–39	72	14.7	39	22.4	0.35
40–44	82	16.7	34	19.4	0.29
45–49	92	18.9	25	14.2	0.21
50–54	74	15.1	19	11.0	0.20
55–59	59	12.0	19	10.9	0.23
60 and over	62	12.7	19	10.9	0.23
Total	489	100.0	174	100.0	0.26

Table 2. Faculty Age Distribution by Sector, 1987

Sector	Under 40 (%)	40–49 (%)	50 & Over (%)
Research	24.2	36.6	39.3
Other Research/Doctorate	22.4	38.8	38.7
Comphensive 1	17.9	43.2	38.5
Liberal Arts 1	29.3	37.2	33.4
Other Four-Year	17.3	40.0	42.5
Total	21.7	39.4	38.9

SOURCE: William G. Bowen and Julie Ann Sosa, Prospects for Faculty in the Arts and Sciences: A Study of Factors Affecting Demand and Supply, 1987 to 2012 (Princeton, Princeton University Press, 1989).

Table 3. Faculty Age Distribution by Sector, 1987

Field of Study	Under 40 (%)	40–49 (%)	50 & Over (%)
Humanities	16.4	39.8	43.8
Social Sciences	25.2	40.3	34.5
Humanities/Social Sciences	20.3	40.0	39.7
Mathematics	28.5	40.2	31.3
Physics/Astronomy	17.6	34.1	48.3
Chemistry	19.3	38.9	41.8
Earth Sciences	26.2	35.5	38.3
Mathematics/Physical Sciences	22.9	37.7	39.4
Biological Sciences	22.6	41.1	36.3
Psychology	25.0	38.0	37.0
Biological Sciences/Psychology	23.6	39.8	36.6
All Arts/Sciences	21.7	39.4	38.9

SOURCE: William G. Bowen and Julie Ann Sosa, Prospects for Faculty in the Arts and Sciences: A Study of Factors Affecting Demand and Supply, 1987 to 2012 (Princeton, Princeton University Press, 1989).

Differences by field of study are much greater than those by type of institution. As shown in Table 3, mathematics stands out as the field with the youngest faculty. In 1987, only 31 percent of its faculty were fifty and over and 28 percent were under forty. That contrasts with humanities where 44 percent were fifty and over and only 16 percent were under forty.

Since mathematics is a field in which maximum productivity comes at young ages, something which is not true for most fields, these findings are somewhat reassuring. Physicists are also known for having made their major inputs while they were relatively young. Nevertheless, faculty members in physics/astronomy are the oldest; 48 percent were over fifty in 1987, while only 18 percent were under forty. As indicated earlier, the aging of physicists has continued, apparently adding another percentage point to the count of the oldest each year since 1987. Since physics is basic to the other physical and biological sciences and to technology, this is of major concern.

Demography of Faculty Aging

Though the aging of college and university faculties has only recently become a major concern, the process has been going on for a long time. When enrollments jumped in the 1950s and 1960s, it was necessary to employ large numbers of young people. When enrollments leveled off or fell, aging of the faculty occurred, a process which is now accelerating. The simplest expression of the aging of a group is obtained from the median age, that at which 50 percent are younger and 50 percent are older. This, however, can be a misleading figure. For example, for the academic year 1947–48 the median age of the American professorate was forty-two and by 1980–81 it had advanced to forty-eight. Currently, it is estimated at forty-nine for total and fifty-two for tenured faculty. In just ten years the figures will be forty-nine for total and fifty-five for tenured faculty. As all averages do, these figures mask the changes which occur on either side of the median.

In 1947–48, only 22 percent of the faculty members were over fifty; by 1980–81, 43 percent were of that age. Currently, the estimate is about 52 percent for the faculty as a whole and 60 percent for tenured faculty. At the turn of the century, those figures will probably have jumped to fifty-five and sixty-seven.[5]

Changes of this sort mean there have been major reductions in the proportion at the lower end of the age spectrum. In 1947–48, almost one-third of faculty members were under thirty-five. Currently, it is 13 percent and only 2 percent are tenured. Since new hires will be mostly young scholars, the proportion under thirty-five must rise. Indeed, the estimate is that this youngest group will make up 20 percent of total faculties at the turn of the century. The median age, however, will not move downward because at that time 41 percent of the total faculty will be fifty-six and over, as compared with the current 31 percent. The middle segment of the professorate, that aged thirty-five to fifty-five, will undergo an equally striking change. In 1980–81, 66 percent were in that age group. Already, the proportion is down to 46 percent and in 2000 it will be 36 percent. For tenured faculty, the progression was from 75 percent in 1980–81 to 63 percent in 1990–91 and is estimated to be 43 percent in 2000–01. This is of special importance because it is within these ages that most books and articles are written and discoveries made. As discussed more fully below, a decreasing proportion in these middle ages would seem to indicate a less-productive faculty and one which would have less effect upon creative students.

Aging faculties are not unique to the United States. This trend is partly a reflection of changes in the age distribution of population over time, but it is also related to world events and to economic and social conditions. To understand the future of college faculties we should therefore consider social and economic as well as population changes since World War II.

World War II was a watershed for demographic, social, and economic change in the United States. Throughout the nineteenth century and into the 1930s, there was a continuous fall in the birth rate, a fall in the proportion of persons in their late teens, and a drifting upward in the median age of the total population. In the early 1800s the U. S. birth rate was estimated at fifty-five per 1,000 population, the highest the world had ever known for a population so large. A quite steady decline reduced the birth rate to 17.6 per 1,000 population in 1933, the bottom of the Depression. Thereafter, the rate moved up slowly, but as the boys came home from World War II marriages skyrocketed and the birth rate rose to a peak of 26.6 in 1947, a higher level than at any time since 1921. It remained above twenty until 1965 and is now lower than in the Depression.

From 1954 through 1964 there were more than four million births per year. The years 1946–65 are usually referred to as the "baby boom" years. As the baby boomers grew up, enrollments soared—in the 1950s in elementary schools and in the 1960s in colleges and universities. Most of the baby boomers are now through college, and the decrease in persons of college age will continue until 1995. It will then rise again as the children of the baby boomers finish high school.

Non-Demographic Factors in Faculty Aging

The number of persons of college age was but one factor in the increasing enrollment in colleges and universities after World War II. A major factor was that returning soldiers sought higher education; it was then that the national government, with the G.I Bill, made its best investment ever in human resources. With increasing prosperity, more parents moved into the middle class and prepared their children for higher education. Greater proportions finished high school, more went on to college, and more followed up with graduate or professional training. Demographic groups that had seldom gone beyond high school further swelled enrollments in colleges and universities. The largest such group was white women, who now outnumber men as college students and form an increasing share of graduate and professional students and college faculties. With the Civil Rights Movement, blacks and Hispanics increased their share at all levels of higher learning.

Clearly the world's center for scientific achievement and the development of technology, the United States was also the major supplier of manufactured goods and high technology to the world into the 1970s Nobel Prizes and other distinctions in science shifted from Europe to the United States, and electronics, the cutting edge of modern technology, was initially developed in American universities and made widely available by innovative manufacturers.

World War II and the astonishing scientific and technological development that followed transformed the traditional anti-intellectual view Americans took of professors. Professors did not replace the "Marlboro man" as the virile ideal and astronauts, rather than the scientists who made their trip possible, were the heroes of the trip to the moon. Nevertheless, professors became recognized as holding the keys to progress and were respected, if not revered. Consequently, many white men sought college and university positions. Increasingly, their ranks were swelled by white women and Asians and to a lesser extent, blacks and Hispanics. For a time, faculty pay increased faster than inflation. It was a heyday for American colleges and universities and their professors. It was also a time when research institutes proliferated.

The redevelopment of Europe and Japan, the Vietnam War, and the many civil disturbances of the 1960s and 1970s radically changed the U. S. position in the world and the status of academe within the United States. As the United States lost its preeminence in manufacturing and became a debtor nation, there was a pronounced shift toward conservatism and anti-intellectualism. With the possible exception of economists, social sciences were generally derided, and sociologists, considered the most liberal of all, were favorite whipping boys. As the earnings of lawyers, stockbrokers, and money manipulators soared, the brighter college students turned away from arts and sciences and into schools of business and law.

Even while the federal government and the American people went on a binge with borrowed money, there arose a swelling cry, "You can't improve education by throwing money at it." The president tried to abolish the Department of Education. Support for education was shifted to states and within some states, to cities or counties. Major support for research was allocated to Star Wars or similar efforts, and, as state and federal budgets were increasingly crunched, money for higher education became a smaller part of national and state expenditures.

This can best be shown by contrasting faculty salaries with the cost of living. An excellent report on this topic was made by W. Lee Hansen.[6] He showed that from 1970–71 to 1984–85 the average faculty salary increased by 124 percent. However, during that time the consumer price index rose by 166 percent. In real dollars, that is in dollars adjusted for inflation, there was a net loss of 15 percent over the fourteen year period. Since then, there has been further decline in real dollar earnings. From 1970–71 to the present there was not a year when increases in faculty salaries exceeded the cost of living, and sometimes the difference was great. From 1973–74 to 1974–75, the loss in real earnings was 4.7 percent; from 1978–79 to 1979–80 it was 5.5 percent.

Figures computed in a slightly different way show a loss of real earnings of 19 percent for faculty members from 1970–71 to 1983–84. This compares with a loss of 1.3 percent for government employees in general and a gain of 3.3 percent for employees in manufacturing. Looking at a somewhat longer period, we find that the gain in real income for the period 1960–61 to 1983–84 for faculty members was 0.0 percent as compared to 27 percent for government workers and 21 percent for workers in manufacturing.

Another useful comparison is with full-time state and local employees. For the instructional staff of public colleges and universities the increase in real earnings was 13 percent between 1960–61 and 1983–84. For the noninstructional staff of such institutions the increase was more than twice as high, 29 percent. For the remainder of state employees the increase was 32 percent. If the salary of faculty members had risen annually by the same percentage as did the salaries of other state employees, a full professor would have made $60,000 more than actually received. Hansen concluded that "state governments were biased in favor of state employees other than instructional staff." His explanation for the lower increases for faculty is that faculty funding is for persons, that for other state employees is for positions. Thus, when a nonfaculty position is vacated, it is filled by someone who receives the same salary as the person who left the job. However, when a full professor leaves his or her position, it is frequently filled by an assistant professor at a much lower salary.

Hansen also compared the actual average salary of full professors in 1983–84 ($37,400 for all types of institutions) with what would have been received if pay increases had matched tuition price increases. The amount lost by not having such increases is astonishing—$64,000 dollars per professor.

Again we note that averages can be misleading. Within universities there is considerable variation in salaries from department to department, largely in response to demand for persons with similar training in outside organizations. Thus, the highest-paid professors, when we deal only with entire schools and not with specific disciplines, are generally in law or medical schools. At the bottom of the heap are professors of fine arts or home economics.

These differences tend to widen over time. For example, the average salary of a full professor of law in 1976–77 was $30,951, while that for a full professor of fine arts was $22,045, a difference of $8,906 or 40 percent. By 1983–84, the salary for a full professor of law was $52,994 and that for the full professor of fine arts was $34,202. The percentage increase for the former was 71 percent while that for the latter was 55 percent. Consequently, the absolute difference between the two had widened to $18,792 and the percentage difference, to 55 percent.

Over the years the low opinion that Americans have for teachers has been expressed in the near-poverty salaries for elementary and secondary school teachers and in such statements as, "If you can't do something, teach it." How the public views college teaching is also a matter of great importance since that view is communicated to high school and college students as they consider lifetime careers. It also affects the way legislators and governmental executives set salaries and perquisites and provide the necessary buildings and equipment for colleges and universities.

There are indications, however, that attitudes may again become more favorable. An excess of imports over exports and growing international competition have caused business leaders to focus on education as the key to progress. The cover story of *Fortune* magazine of June 3, 1991, was "Brain Power: How Intellectual Capital Is Becoming America's Most Valuable Asset" by Thomas A. Stewart. In it, Polaroid is cited as a company "far ahead of the pack," in part because it has its employees taking courses at Harvard, M. I. T., and Northeastern and has hooked into a satellite relay from the National Technological University, a consortium of graduate institutions. In the same issue, a full page ad aims to attract industry to Georgia by touting the state university and its other educational institutions.

An increasing number of businesses are sponsoring or buying university research, and more and more want their employees to take language courses. Japanese as well as American entrepreneurs are making such arrangements with U. S. universities, and the prospects are for increasing international connections. Some business schools now require or advise prospective MBAs to take language courses, and businessmen are becoming aware of the need to have knowledge of other cultures. This will affect enrollment in courses outside the business school.

Faculty Demand and Supply

The future demand for faculty depends largely, but not entirely, upon growth in population. Projections of the number of college students, made by applying slightly modified past rates of enrollment to the total populations estimated for coming years, can be deceptive. Even if present enrollment rates remain static, there will be a modern upswing in enrollment after 1995 as the late teenage and early adult populations begin to rise. That rise, however, will be moderate and will soon level off. The most reassuring aspect of this demographic swing is that there will be no sharp fall in the prospective number of teenagers and young adults in the near future.

But, even if the number of persons in the usual ages of college and university attendance remains nearly constant, there are major factors that point in the direction of higher enrollment. Of considerable importance is the increasing proportion of children with parents who have college and high school degrees. Fully aware that their achievements have resulted from or have been limited by their own education, such parents will push their children toward college and advanced degrees. Eighty-five percent of the children born in 1987 were to mothers who had finished high school, 42 percent were born to those who had some college education, 19 percent of mothers were college graduates, and 6 percent had five or more years of college training. The older women who had children in 1987 were even more likely to be college graduates and 9 percent had further training. [7]

One can also foresee major increases in adult education and in programs which permit college and university degrees to be earned through part-time attendance. The pace of change is such that an increasing and eventually high percentage of workers must reconcile themselves to remaining students for most of their working lives. A number of corporations have already made arrangements for further college and university training for their employees, and we may expect this practice to be widespread—so much so, in fact, that college and university location will become an increasingly important factor in industrial location as well as for federal, state, and local governments.

Another factor influencing enrollment, and perhaps the major one in the long run, is the increasing belief by the American people that American students do so poorly in international comparisons that our economy and security are threatened. Sooner or later the need for major overhaul of the educational system will become generally apparent, and the idea that "you can't improve education by throwing money at it" will be somewhat challenged by the realization that "you can't improve education by taking money away from it." When indeed we do have improvement in elementary and secondary education, requests for college admission will increase.

Related to such concerns is the fact that real improvement in the economic and social position of the so-called "underclass," in which blacks, Hispanics, and rural and central city whites are heavily represented, can only come with longer school terms and more years of increasingly rigorous schooling. As that improvement is made and teenage childbearing is reduced further, increases in enrollment in higher education within these groups will occur.

Projections by Bowen and Sosa, the most comprehensive now available, indicate relatively little change in enrollment between now and 2012, that is thirteen or fourteen million students each year until 2012. However, they also give a "high estimate" which indicates a fairly steady increase to eighteen million by the end of that period. Our inclination is to accept the higher estimate, based in part upon arguments advanced previously but also upon a faith that our leaders and citizens will stop hiding their heads in the sand and look seriously at the potential future if we continue our apathetic approach to educational reform. It is possible that we may be shocked from our present state by dramatic changes in technology in Japan or Europe or by any of a wide series of world events.

It should now be clear that a shortage of prospective faculty already exists and that it will threaten higher education as it increases sharply in the following decades. This raises several questions. Will there be a sufficient number of trained persons to fill vacated positions as they become open? Will the quality of replacements match that of those leaving? Will the faculty mix move closer to that of the general population with regard to gender, sex, and ethnic composition? What are the disciplines for which shortages are most threatening? Upon which institutions will the shortages bear most heavily?

Recall that the distribution of faculty by rank is far from ideal and that the number of full professors is greater than that of associate professors, which, in turn, is greater than that of assistant professors. Thus, filling positions by movement upward from the lower ranks is only a partial answer to the problems to be faced as faculty vacancies increase.

Further exacerbation of this situation will be evident if we examine the reasons why vacancies occur. Bowen and Sosa have divided these into three groups: deaths, retirements (voluntary or involuntary) and "quits" (voluntary or involuntary).

Of these three, death is by all odds the least important factor. College and university teaching is one of the "safest" occupations. For faculty members under fifty-five, the probability of survival for five years was estimated by Bowen and Sosa as 0.969 to 0.966. Even for those age sixty-five it was 0.927. Given present and prospective age distributions, we could expect only two or three per thousand to die in any five-year period. These, of course, will be predominantly older faculty.

Retirement also involves older faculty. The average age at retirement for faculty is sixty-five, three years greater that for workers in general, and is of little consequence before the age of sixty. Of those still on faculty at ages sixty to sixty-four, only 45 percent continue past sixty-five and close to none after seventy. The removal of the seventy-year retirement requirement will have very little effect. Rees and Smith endorse this conclusion and note that faculty are most likely to defer retirement in institutions where SAT scores of students are high and where research is emphasized.[8]

Especially disturbing are the "quits" because they are greater for younger faculty. Less than 5 percent of faculty members fifty and over are likely to quit within a five-year period, but for ages thirty to thirty-four, a 17 percent loss is estimated by Bowen and Sosa. By ages forty to forty-four it is only 7 percent. As indicated by the authors, different calculations based on the available data could have given much higher "quit rates," a possibility that should be considered given the likelihood that faculty salaries will fall further behind inflation and the salaries accorded persons with equal education or abilities outside academe. However, computed quit rates are tentative because it is uncertain how many people leaving an educational institution simply move to another and how many leave the fold permanently.

Putting the three kinds of attrition together produces overall estimates of survival on college and university faculties for the five-year period 1992–97 that are low at the youngest ages, 83 percent at ages thirty to thirty-four, but rising to a peak of 92 percent at ages forty-five to forty-nine. Thereafter, five-year survival rates fall at an increasing rate to 76 percent at ages fifty-five to fifty-nine, 41 percent at ages sixty to sixty-four, and 7 percent at ages sixty-five to sixty-nine. At the early ages the overall rates are dominated by quit rates and at the older ages, by rates of retirement. Not until ages sixty to sixty-four would mortality reduce faculty numbers by as much as 1 percent per year. Using "standard quit assumptions," those that seem most likely, Bowen and Sosa estimate that 67 percent of the faculty of 1987 will be gone by 2007. The proportion leaving will be highest for physics/astronomy at 76 percent and lowest for the social sciences at 67 percent. For 1997–2002, they foresee only eighty-three new doctorates for each 100 leaving the faculty, a situation which improves to only 94 per 100 in 2007–12. While their study deals with only a fraction of the total faculty in all kinds of institutions (139,000 out of the 793,000 considered in earlier sections of this chapter), there is good reason to believe that similar shortages will penetrate to the lowest levels of higher education if present standards or preparation and individual ability are maintained. In sum, forthcoming faculty exits from colleges and universities are such that adequate replacement throughout the system will require major shifts in attitudes toward institutions of higher education and their faculty.

Adequacy of Replacements

There are several ways of dealing with a shortage of workers. One is to increase the productivity of the faculty by increasing the number of students per faculty member. As suggested previously, this has been in progress for some time. One aspect of this could be the combining of small institutions. There are many small colleges; some are located near each other, and others were created as a way of maintaining racial segregation. While combinations might have the effect of reducing faculty-student interrelations, they could also increase the number of available courses and the number with optimal enrollment.

It is also likely that a number of private colleges, as well as some of the more isolated state colleges, will be eliminated simply because the shortage of prospective faculty members will push salaries beyond the ability of faltering institutions to meet them. This will result in increasing pressures for admission to larger institutions, and more state universities will reach the 40,000 to 60,000 mark.

The more usual result, however, will be a lowering of standards for faculty. In general, vacancies will be filled with the best candidates available to a particular institution. The institutions of top rank will, of course, get the best candidates and they will increasingly drain off the better faculty of lesser institutions. Black and women's colleges will be especially at risk because of the rising demand that faculties be balanced in terms of gender and ethnic identification.

While the difficulty of maintaining standards will be greatest for the lesser-known and worst-financed institutions, almost all will have such difficulty. There are at least two reasons for this. One is that in recent years so many students have rejected arts and sciences for the more immediate rewards available to graduates of law and business schools. Perhaps more important, however, is the competition increasingly offered by business and industry for graduates in almost the whole range of sciences.

For these and other reasons, excellent students have chosen to enter industry or business rather than pursue the doctorate. And even if they continue to obtain higher degrees, greater proportions elect professions other than college or university teaching. One of the best examples is the professions chosen over time by Phi Beta Kappa's. Of the 1950–54 electees, 22.3 percent took up careers in colleges or universities; for those elected in 1975–79, the proportion was only 7.2 percent, and it has since fallen further. Of those elected in 1945–49, only, 9.1 percent entered legal or medical professions; for the cohort of 1975–79 that percentage was 40.1 percent. For the 1965–69 cohort of Phi Beta Kappa's the leading choice for a career was college or university educator. As early as 1970–74, however, business, law, and medicine each attracted larger proportions.[9]

The seeming adequacy of doctoral supply, as measured by the number of persons receiving doctorates can be misleading, not only because such persons are increasingly attracted to nonacademic fields, but also because of the high proportion of foreign students, especially those receiving doctorates in mathematics and sciences. No less than 23 percent of all doctorates awarded in 1978–88 were to persons with foreign citizenship. In engineering the proportion was 49.8 percent; in mathematics, 46.3 percent; in physical sciences, 32.5 percent; and in business and management, 32.4 percent. Only in those fields where the proportion of women receiving doctorates was high was the proportion of foreign citizens low.

Operating against the intent to balance faculties by sex and ethnic group are the low percentages of doctorates obtained by women, blacks, and Hispanics in several fields. Asians accounted for 5 percent of the doctorates received in all fields in 1987, while blacks and Hispanics each received less than 4 percent. Whereas Asians received 15.5 percent of the doctorates in engineering, 8.6 percent of those in mathematics, and 9.4 percent of those in business, blacks received only 1.5 percent of those in engineering, 0.7 percent of those in mathematics, and 2.8 percent of those in business and management. For women, the spread was better. They received 35 percent of all doctorates, and, while they took only 6.8 percent of the doctorates in engineering, they accounted for 16.2 percent of those in mathematics, and 23.8 percent of those in business and management.[10]

To determine the adequacy of supply, we must consider much more than the ratio of faculty to students. In addition to teaching, professors in universities and major colleges are expected to engage in community service and research. Both are invaluable to the progress of the nation. We have already discussed the key role played by universities in basic research, and we could elaborate at length on the benefits, for example, of applied research in agriculture and biology that led to the exceptional productivity of American farmers.

The United States has lagged behind Japan and will fall further behind other nations if it does not find better ways to implement basic discoveries by integrating colleges and universities with business and industry. In the future, we will be even more reliant upon university researchers, especially those at institutions that can provide the increasingly elaborate and expansive materials needed for much of today's research. Only in universities can research spread over wide areas, bring together people from diverse fields, and inspire thousands of young people to enter fields which often seem exotic and financially unrewarding as was true of physics in the 1930s, when it was just on the edge of the atomic and electronic breakthroughs.

Much of the research and the most rewarding teaching is now done by professors with long-term attachments to academia. We cannot foresee their replacement by similarly oriented and capable persons unless there is a major change in the way the nation and its people are willing to support higher education, both in funding and in respect for its accomplishments. Doubting there will be a sudden change in national attitudes, we may expect the following to happen:

1. Because well-qualified replacements will be hard to find, there will be a flow of the better faculty from smaller or lesser colleges and universities to better-paying or better-known institutions.

2. The number of institutions that now offer good teaching and research faculties will decrease as faculty members retire or accept positions at higher-rated institutions.

3. The best of the private institutions will fare quite well, but their tuition and other fees will be so high that only the wealthy and the highly subsidized can afford to attend.

4. State colleges will receive a higher proportion of total applications for admission because their tuition fees are relatively low. These, however, will rise since tuition fees are only a fraction of total costs per student, and legislators will be reluctant to provide needed amounts.

5. Middle-class students will find it increasingly difficult to afford the best colleges and universities. This will especially be true if the bulk of federal and state aid is reserved for minorities or the poor.

6. A number of black colleges will close their doors either because they will be combined with other institutions or are unable to pay higher salaries. Only a few will be able to keep their most qualified faculty because of higher salaries and opportunities offered by other institutions and by government, business, and industry, all of which will be searching for minority employees.

Steps to Remedy the Situation

The situation in higher education is bound to get worse before it gets better. The nation and the states are caught in a financial crunch which demands economies of all sorts, and the electorate seems more concerned about taxes than about our standing in elementary and secondary education and the worsening plight of colleges and universities. There are, however, steps that could be taken to remedy the situation.

There must be an awakening of the public to the real situation of colleges and universities and to the crucial role they play in the nation's economy, security, and general well-being. Leading industrialists are already taking the stump to address this matter, and it is of greatest importance that presidents and legislators recognize this as one of their highest priorities.

One of the lessons they must teach the general public and then apply themselves is that the amount of money spent on higher education is inadequate to maintain good teaching or good research. College and university salaries are so low and have lagged so far behind inflation that the needed brains and energy cannot be obtained. The money needed to rectify this situation would be returned many times over through research and the training of better qualified entrants into business, industry, and government.

Notes

1. W. G. Bowen and J. A. Sosa, *Prospects for Faculty in the Arts and Science: A Study of Factors Affecting Supply and Demand, 1987–2012* (Princeton, N.J.: Princeton University Press, 1989), 15.

2. *Chronicle of Higher Education* (April 18, 1990), 14.

3. "The Graying of Physics," *Science* (may 31, 1991), 1249.

4. Harriet Anne Zuckerman, Nibel Laureates in the United States: A Sociological Study of Scientific Collaboration (Ann Arbor: University Films, Inc., 1965), 392ff.

5. H. R. Bowen and J. H. Schuster, *American Professors: A National Resource Imperiled* (New York: Oxford University Press, 1986).

6. Ibid.

7. Bureau of the Census, *Statistical Abstracts of the United States: 1989* (Washington, D.C.: Government Printing Office, 1989).

8. A. Rees and S. P. Smith, The End of Mandatory Retirement for Tenured Faculty," *Science* (August 23, 1991).

9. Bowen and Schuster, *American Professors,* 227.

10. National Center for Education Statistics, *Digest of Education Statistics: 1990* (Washington, D.C.: NCES, February 1991) table 263.

Select Bibliography

General

Altbach, Philip G. "Stark Realities: The Academic Profession in the 1980s—and Beyond." In *Higher Education in American Society*, revised edition, edited by Philip G. Altbach and Robert O. Berdahl. Buffalo: Prometheus Books, pp. 247–265.

Altbach, Philip G. and Robert O. Berdahl (Eds.). *Higher Education in American Society*, revised edition. Buffalo: Prometheus Books, 1987.

Anderson, Martin. *Impostors in the Temple*. New York: Simon and Schuster, 1992.

Bailey, F. G. *Morality and Expediency: The Folklore of Academic Politics*. Chicago: Aldine, 1977.

Becher, Tony. *Academic Tribes and Territories: Intellectual Inquiry and the Culture of Disciplines*. Milton Keynes, England: Society for Research into Higher Education and Open University Press, 1989.

Benda, Julien. *The Treason of the Intellectuals*, translated by Richard Aldington. New York: W. W. Norton and Company, 1969.

Bess, James L. *University Organization: A Matrix Analysis of the Academic Professions*. New York: Human Sciences Press, 1982.

Bourdieu, Pierre. *Homo Academicus*. Stanford, CA: Stanford University Press, 1988.

Bowen, Howard R. and Jack H. Schuster. *American Professors: A National Resource Imperiled*. New York: Oxford University Press, 1986.

Chamberlain, Miriam K. *Women in Academe: Progress and Prospects*. New York: Russell Sage Foundation, 1988.

Clark, Burton R. *The Academic Life: Small Worlds, Different Worlds*. Princeton, N.J.: Carnegie Foundation for the Advancement of Teaching, 1987.

Clark, Burton R. (Ed.). *The Academic Profession: National, Disciplinary, and Institutional Settings*. Berkeley: University of California Press, 1987.

Cohen, Arthur M. and Florence B. Brawer. *The American Community College*. 2nd edition. San Francisco: Jossey-Bass. 1989.

Coser, Lewis A. "Academic Intellectuals." in *Men of Ideas: A Sociologist's View*. New York: Free Press, 1965, pp. 275–293.

Finkelstein, Martin J. *The American Academic Profession: A Synthesis of Social Scientific Inquiry Since World War II*. Columbus: Ohio State University Press, 1984.

Hagstrom, Warren O. *The Scientific Community*. New York: Basic Books, 1965.

Jencks, Christopher and David Riesman. *The Academic Revolution*. New York: Doubleday, 1968.

Lazarsfeld, Paul F. and Wagner Thielens, Jr. *The Academic Mind*. Glencoe, Ill.: Free Press, 1958.

Light, Donald, Jr. "Introduction: The Structure of the Academic Professions." *Sociology of Education* 47 (1974), pp. 2–28.

McGee, Reece. *Academic Janus*. San Francisco: Jossey-Bass, 1971.

Metzger, Walter P. (Ed.). *Reader on the Sociology of the Academic Profession.* New York: Arno Press, 1977.

_____. "The American Academic Profession in 'Hard Times.'" *Daedalus* 104 (1975), pp. 25–44.

Riesman, David. "Some Personal Thoughts on the Academic Ethic." *Minerva* 21 (1983), pp. 265–283.

Simeone, Angela. *Academic Women: Working Towards Equality.* South Hadley, Mass.: Bergin and Garvey, 1987.

Sykes, Charles J. *ProfScam: Professors and the Demise of Higher Education.* Washington, D.C.: Regnery Gateway, 1988.

Trillin, Calvin. *Remembering Denny.* New York: Farrar, Straus, Giroux, 1993.

Washington, Valora and William Harvey. *Affirmative Rhetoric, Negative Action: African-American and Hispanic Faculty at Predominantly White Institutions.* ASHE-ERIC Report #2. Washington, D.C.: George Washington University, School of Education and Human Development, 1989.

I. Data Tables

The Condition of the Professoriate: Attitudes and Trends. 1989. Princeton, N. J.: Carnegie Foundation for the Advancement of Teaching, 1989.

II. History of the Profession

Adams, Hazzard. *The Academic Tribes.* New York: Liveright, 1976.

Ben-David, Joseph. "Universities and the Growth of Knowledge in Germany and the United States." *Minerva* 7 (1968), pp. 1–35.

Berelson, Bernard. *Graduate Education in the United States.* New York: McGraw-Hill, 1960.

Bernard, Jessie. *Academic Women.* University Park, PA: The Pennsylvania State University Press, 1964.

Brown, David G. *The Mobile Professors.* Washington, D.C.: American Council on Education, 1967.

Caplow, Theodore, and Reece J. McGee. *The Academic Marketplace.* New York: Basic Books, 1958.

Carrell, William D. "American College Professors: 1750–1800." *Higher Education Quarterly* 8 (#3, 1968), pp. 289–305.

Cartter, Alan. *Ph.D.'s and the Academic Labor Market.* New York: McGraw-Hill, 1976.

Chamberlain, Miriam K. *Women in Academe: Progress and Prospects.* New York: Russell Sage Foundation, 1988.

Crane, Diane. "Scientists at Major and Minor Universities: A Study of Productivity and Recognition." *American Sociological Review* 30 (1965), pp. 699–714.

_____. "The Academic Marketplace Revisited: A Study of Faculty Mobility Using the Cartter Ratings." *American Journal of Sociology* 7 (1970), pp. 953–956.

Daniels, George H. "The Process of Professionalization in American Science: The Emergent Period, 1820–1860." *ISIS* LVIII (1967), pp. 151–166.

Davis, John W. *Land-Grant Colleges for Negroes.* West Virginia State College Bulletin, April, 1934.

Diehl, Carl. *Americans and German Scholarship, 1770–1870.* New Haven. 1972.

Finkelstein, Martin J. "The Emergences of the Modern Academic Role." In *The American Academic Profession: A Synthesis of Social Scientific Inquiry Since World War II.* Columbus: Ohio State University Press, 1984.

Gouldner, Alvin W. "Cosmopolitans and Locals: Toward an Analysis of Latent Social Roles." *Administrative Science Quarterly* 2 (1957), pp. 281–306; 2 (1958), pp. 444–480.

Hansen, W. Lee. "Changing Demography of Faculty in Higher Education." In *Faculty Vitality and Institutional Productivity: Critical Perspectives for Higher Education*, edited by Shirley M. Clark and Darrell R. Lewis. New York: Teachers College Press, 1985, pp. 25–54.

Hawkins, Hugh. "University Identity: The Teaching and Research Functions," in *The Organization of Knowledge in Modern America*, edited by Alexandria Oleson and John Voss. Baltimore: Johns Hopkins University Press, 1976, pp. 285–312.

Hofstadter, Richard and Walter P. Metzger. *The Development of Academic Freedom in the United States.* New York: Columbia University Press, 1955.

Jencks, Christopher and David Riesman. *The Academic Revolution.* New York: Doubleday, 1968.

Kuhn, Thomas S. *The Structure of Scientific Revolutions.* 2nd ed. Chicago: University of Chicago Press, 1970.

Lipset, Seymour Martin. "Faculty and Students: Allied and in Conflict," in *Rebellion in the University*. New Brunswick, N.J.: Transaction Publishers, 1993, pp. 197–235.

McCaughey, Robert. "The Transition of American Academic Life: Harvard University, 1821–1892." *Perspectives in American History* 8 (1974), pp. 239–334.

Metzger, Walter P. "Academic Tenure in America: A Historical Essay," in *The Commission on Academic Tenure in Higher Education, Faculty Tenure*. San Francisco: Jossey-Bass, 1973, pp. 93–159.

Metzger, Walter P. (Ed.). *The American Concept of Academic Freedom in Formation: A Collection of Essays and Reports.* New York: Arno Press, 1977.

Moore, Kathryn McDaniel. "The War with the Tutors: Student Faculty Conflict at Harvard and Yale, 1745–1771." *History of Education Quarterly* (1978), pp. 115–127.

Palmieri, P. "Here was Fellowship: A Social Portrait of Academic Women at Wellesley College, 1895–1920." *History of Education Quarterly* 23 (1983), pp. 195–214.

Rossiter, Margaret W. "Doctorates for American Women, 1868–1907." *History of Education Quarterly* 22 (1982), pp. 159–183.

Rossiter, Margaret W. *Women Scientists in America; Struggles and Strategies to 1940.* Baltimore: Johns Hopkins University Press, 1982.

Sawyer, Darwin O. "Institutional Stratification and Career Mobility in Academic Markets." *Sociology of Education* 54 (1981), pp. 85–97.

Smelser, Neil and Robin Content. *The Changing Academic Labor Market.* University of California Press, 1980.

Stevenson, Louise L. "Between the Old-Time College and the Modern University: Noah Porter and the New Haven Scholars." *History Of Higher Education Annual* 3 (1983), pp. 39–57.

_____. *Scholarly Means to Evangelical Ends: The New Haven Scholars and the Transformation of Higher Learning in America, 1830–1890.* Baltimore: Johns Hopkins University Press, 1986.

Storr, Richard J. *The Beginnings of Graduate Education in America.* Chicago: University of Chicago Press, 1953.

Willie, Reynold, and John E. Stecklein. "A Three-Decade Comparison of College Faculty Characteristics, Satisfactions, Activities, and Attitudes," *Research in Higher Education* 16 (1982), pp. 81–93.

Wilson, Logan. *American Academics: Then and Now.* New York: Oxford University Press, 1979.

_____. *The Academic Man: A Study in the Sociology of a Profession.* New York: Oxford University Press, 1942.

III. The Academic Labor Market: Recruitment and Recruits

Allison, Paul D. and J. Scott Long. "Interuniversity Mobility of Academic Scientists." *American Sociological Review* 52 (1987), pp. 643–652.

Allison, Paul D. and John A. Stewart. "Productivity Differences Among Scientists: Evidence for Accumulative Advantage." *American Sociological Review* 39 (1974), pp. 596–606.

Astin, Helen S. *The Woman Doctorate in America; Origins, Career and Family.* New York: Russell Sage Foundation, 1969.

Austin, Ann E. and Zelda F. Gamson. *Academic Workplace: New Demands, Heightened Tensions.* ASHE-ERIC Higher Education Research Report No. 10. Washington, D.C.: Association of Higher Education, 1983.

Bailey, F. G., *Morality and Expediency: The Folklore of Academic Politics.* Chicago: Aldine, 1977.

Baldwin, Roger G. and Robert T. Blackburn. "The Academic Career as a Developmental Process: Implications for Higher Education." *Journal of Higher Education* 52 (1981), pp. 598–614.

Banks, W. M. "Afro-American Scholars in the University: Roles and Conflicts." *Behavioral Scientist* 27 (1984), pp. 325–338.

Bayer, Alan E. and Helen S. Astin. "Sex Differences in Academic Rank and Salary Among Science Doctorates in Teaching." *Journal of Human Resources* 3 (1968), pp. 191–199.

Berg, H. M. and M. A. Ferber. "Men and Women Graduate Students: Who Succeeds and Why?" *Journal of Higher Education* 54 (1983), pp. 629–48.

Bernard, Jessie. *Academic Women.* University Park, PA: Pennsylvania State University Press, 1964.

Bowen, Howard R. and Jack H. Schuster. *American Professors: A National Resource Imperiled.* New York: Oxford Press, 1986

Bowen, William and Julie Ann Sosa. *Prospects for Faculty in the Arts and Sciences.* Princeton, N.J.: Princeton University Press, 1989.

Breneman, David W. and Ted I. K. Youn (Eds.). *Academic Labor Markets and Careers.* Philadelphia: Falmer Press, 1988.

Brown, David G. *The Mobile Professors.* Washington, D.C.: American Council on Education, 1967.

Burke, Dolores L. *The New Academic Marketplace.* Westport, CT: Greenwood Press, 1988.

Caplow, Theodore and Reece McGee. *The Academic Marketplace.* New York: Basic Books, 1958.

Centra, John. *Women, Men and the Doctorate.* Princeton: Educational Testing Service, 1974.

Cole, Jonathan R. and Stephen Cole. *Social Stratification in Science.* Chicago: University of Chicago Press, 1973.

Cole, Jonathan R. and Harriet Zuckerman. "The Productivity Puzzle: Persistence and Change in Patterns of Publication of Men and Women Scientists." In *Advances in Motivation and Achievement*, edited by M. W. Steinkamps and M. L. Maehr. Greenwich, CT: Jai Press, 1984.

Crane, Diana. "The Academic Marketplace Revisited." *American Journal of Sociology* 75 (1970), pp. 953–964.

_____. "Social Class Origin and Academic Success: The Influence of Two Stratification Systems on Academic Careers." *Sociology of Education* 42 (1969), pp. 1–17.

De la Luz Reyes, Maria and John H. Halcon. "Practices of the Academy: Barriers to Access for Chicano Academics." In *The Racial Crisis in American Higher Education*, edited by Philip G. Altbach and Kofi Lomotey. Albany: State University of New York Press, 1991, pp. 167–186.

Dunham, E. Alden. *Colleges of the Forgotten Americans: A Profile of State Colleges and Regional Universities.* Carnegie Commission on Higher Education. New York: McGraw-Hill, 1969.

Exum, W. H., Robert J. Menges, B. Watkins, and P. Berglund. "Making it at the Top: Women and Minority Faculty in the Academic Labor Market." *American Behavioral Scientist* 27 (1984), pp. 301–324.

Finnegan, Dorothy E. *Academic Career Lines: A Case Study of Faculty in Two Comprehensive Universities.* Ph.D. diss., The Pennsylvania State University, University Park, 1992.

Gamson, Zelda P., Dorothy E. Finnegan, and Ted I. K. Youn. "Assessing Faculty Shortages in Comprehensive Colleges and Universities." *Metropolitan Universities* 1 (1991), pp. 87–97.

Gappa, Judith M. and Barbara S. Uehling. *Women in Academe: Steps to Greater Equality.* AAHE-ERIC/ Higher Education Research Report No. 1. Washington, D.C.: George Washington University, 1979.

Gouldner, Alvin W. "Cosmopolitans and Locals: Toward an Analysis of Latent Social Roles." *Administrative Science Quarterly* 2 (1957), pp. 281–306; 2 (1958), pp. 444–480.

Harcleroad, Fred and Alan W. Ostar. *Colleges and Universities for Change: America's Comprehensive Public State Colleges and Universities.* Washington, D.C.: American Association of State Colleges and Universities Press, 1987.

Hargens, L. L., J. C. McCann, and Barbara F. Reskin. "Productivity and Reproductivity: Fertility and Professional Achievement Among Research Scientists." *Social Forces* 57 (1978), pp. 154–163.

Hargens, Lowell L. and Warren O. Hagstrom. "Sponsored and Contest Mobility of American Academic Scientists." *Sociology of Education* 40 (1967), pp. 24–38.

Heath, Julia A. and Howard P. Tuckman. "The Impact on Labor Markets of the Relative Growth of Female Doctorates." *Journal of Higher Education* 60 (1989), pp. 704–715.

Hite, L. M. "Female Doctoral Students: Their Perceptions and Concerns." *Journal of College Student Personnel* 26 (1985), pp. 18–22.

[Hitt, Jack.] "The Professor." *Lingua Franca* 3 (July/August, 1993), pp. 1; 24–29.

Holland, Jearold W. *Relationships Between African American Doctoral Students and Their Major Advisors.* Paper presented at American Educational Research Association, Atlanta, 1993.

Holstrom, Engininel and Robert Holmstrom. "The Plight of the Woman Doctoral Student." *American Educational Research Journal* 11 (1974), pp. 1–17.

Kaplowtiz, Richard A. *Selecting College and University Personnel: The Quest and the Questions.* ASHE-ERIC Higher Education Report No. 8. Washington, D.C.: Association for the Study of Higher Education, 1986.

Kim, S. *A Study of the Advantage of Organizational Context on Academic Research Productivity: The Case of Chemistry Faculty.* Ph.D. diss., University of Pittsburgh, Pittsburgh, PA, 1990.

Lewin, Arie Y. and Linda Duchan. "Women in Academia." *Science* 173 (3 September, 1971), pp. 892–895.

Lipset, Seymour M. and Everett C. Ladd, Jr. "The Changing Social Origins of American Academics." In *Qualitative and Quantitative Social Research: Papers in Honor of Paul F. Lazarsfeld,* edited by Robert K. Merton, James S. Coleman, and Peter H. Rossi. New York: Free Press, 1979, pp. 319–338.

Long, J. Scott, Paul D. Allison, and Robert McGinnis. "Entrance in the Academic Career." *American Sociological Review* 44 (1979), pp. 816–830.

Long, J. Scott and Robert McGinnis. "Organizational Context and Scientific Productivity." *American Sociological Review* 46 (1981), pp. 422–442.

Marshall, Howard D. *The Mobility of College Faculties.* New York: Pageant Press, 1964.

McGee, Reece. *Academic Janus: The Private College and Its Faculty.* San Francisco: Jossey-Bass, 1971.

McGinnis, Robert and J. Scott Long. "Entry into Academia: Effects of Stratification, Geography and Ecology." In *Academic Labor Markets and Careers,* edited by David W. Breneman and Ted I. K. Youn. New York: The Falmer Press, 1988.

Merton, Robert K. "The Matthew Effect in Science." *Science* 159 (1968), pp. 55–63.

Mickelson, Roslyn Arlin and Melvin L. Oliver. "Making the Short List: Black Candidates and the Faculty Recruitment Process" In *The Racial Crisis in American Higher Education,* edited by Philip G. Altbach and Kofi Lomotey. Albany: State University of New York Press, 1991, pp. 149–166.

Mommsen, Kent G. "Black Ph.D.s in the Academic Marketplace: Supply, Demand, and Price." *The Journal of Higher Education* 45 (1974), pp. 253–267.

Monroe, Charles R. "Faculty." In *Profile of the Community College*. San Francisco: Jossey-Bass, 1977, pp. 245–271.

Moore, Jr., William. "Black Faculty in White Colleges: A Dream Deferred." *Educational Record* 68 (1987–88), pp. 116–121.

Muffo, John A. and John R. Robinson. "Early Science Career Patterns of Recent Graduates from Leading Research Universities." *The Review of Higher Education* 5 (1981), pp. 1–13.

Queval, Francoise A. *The Evolution Toward Research Orientation and Capability in Comprehensive Universities: The California State System*. Ph.D. diss., University of California, Los Angeles, 1990.

Rafky, David M. "The Black Scholar in the Academic Marketplace." *Teachers College Record* 74 (1972), pp. 225–260.

Reskin, Barbara F. "Scientific Productivity and the Reward Structure of Science." *American Sociological Review* 42 (1977), pp. 491–504.

_____. "Academic Sponsorship and Scientists' Careers." *Sociology of Education* 52 (1979), pp. 129–146.

Reynolds, Anne. "Charting the Changes in Junior Faculty: Relationships among Socialization, Acculturation, and Gender." *Journal of Higher Education* 63 (1992), pp. 637–652.

Roby, Pamela. "Structural and Internalized Barriers to Women in Higher Education." In *Toward a Sociology of Women*, edited by C. Safilios-Rothschild. Lexington, MA: Xerox College Publishing, 1972.

Ruscio, Kenneth P. "Many Sectors, Many Professions." In *The Academic Profession: National, Disciplinary, and Institutional Settings*, edited by Burton R. Clark. Berkeley: University of California Press, 1987.

Ryan, Jake and Charles Sackrey. *Strangers in Paradise: Academics from the Working Class*. Boston: South End Press, 1984.

Sands, Roberta G., L. Alayne Parson, and Josann Duane. "Faculty Mentoring Faculty in a Public University." *Journal of Higher Education* 62 (1991), pp. 174–193.

Sawyer, Darwin O. "Institutional Stratification and Career Mobility in Academic Markets." *Sociology of Education* 54 (1981), pp. 85–97.

Smelser, Nell and Robin Content. *The Changing Academic Market: General Trends and a Berkeley Case Study*. Berkeley: University of California Press, 1980.

Sorensen, Aage. "Academic Careers and Academic Labor Markets." Paper presented at the Ringberg Symposium, Max-Planck-Geeselschaft, Schloss Ringberg, Tegernsee, FRG, 1989.

Thompson, Fred and William Zumenta. "Hiring Decisions in Organized Anarchies: More Evidence on Entrance into the Academic Career." *The Review of Higher Education* 8 (1985), pp. 123–138.

Tokarczyk, Michelle M. and Elizabeth A. Fay. *Working-Class Women in the Academy: Laborers in the Knowledge Factory*. Amherst: The University of Massachusetts Press, 1993.

Tuma, Nancy Brandon and Andrew J. Grimes. "A Comparison of Models of Role Orientations of Professionals in a Research-Oriented University." *Administrative Science Quarterly* 26 (1981), pp. 187–206.

Turner, Ralph H. "Sponsored and Contest Mobility and the School System." *American Sociological Review* 25 (1960), pp. 855–867.

Youn, Ted I. K. "Patterns of Institutional Self-Recruitment of Young Ph.D.s: Effects of Academic Markets on Career Mobility." *Research in Higher Education* 29 (1988b), pp. 195–218.

Youn, Ted I. K. and Zelda F. Gamson. "Organizational Responses to the Labor Market: A Study of Faculty Searches in Comprehensive Colleges and Universities." *Higher Education*, forthcoming.

Zey-Farrell, M. and P. J. Baker. "Faculty Work in a Regional Public University: An Empirical Assessment of Goal Consensus and Congruency of Actions and Intentions." *Research in Higher Education* 20 (1984), pp. 399–426.

IV. The Collegiate Life of Faculty

Individual Issues

Becher, Tony. *Academic Tribes and Territories: Intellectual Enquiry and the Culture of Disciplines.* The Society for Research into Higher Education. Milton Keynes, England: Open University Press, 1989.

Berger, Bennett M. *Authors of their Own Lives: Intellectual Autobiographies by Twenty American Sociologists.* Berkeley: University of California Press, 1990.

Boyer, Ernest. *Scholarship Reconsidered: Priorities for the Professoriate.* Princeton: Carnegie Foundation for the Advancement of Teaching, 1990.

Carnegie Foundation for the Advancement of Teaching. *Conditions of the Professoriate, Attitudes and Trends, 1989.* A Technical Report. Princeton: Carnegie Foundation for the Advancement of Teaching, 1989.

Diener, Thomas. "Job Satisfaction and College Faculty in Two Predominantly Black Institutions." *Journal of Negro Education* 54 (1985), pp. 558–565.

Exum, William H. "Climbing the Crystal Stair: Values, Affirmative Action, and Minority Faculty." *Social Problems* 30 (1983), pp. 383–399.

Finkelstein, Martin J. *The American Academic Profession: A Synthesis of Social Scientific Inquiry Since World War II.* Columbus: Ohio State University, 1984, p. 96.

Flynn, Elizabeth A., John F. Flynn, Nancy Grimm, and Ted Lockhart. "The Part-Time Problem: Four Voices." *Academe* 72 (1986), pp. 12–18.

Garza, Hisauto. "The 'Barriorization' of Hispanic Faculty." *Educational Record* 68 (1987–1988), pp. 122–124.

Goodman, Paul. *The Community of Scholars.* New York: Random House, 1962.

Gouldner, Alvin W. "Cosmopolitans and Locals: Toward an Analysis of Latent Social Roles—I." *Administrative Science Quarterly* 2 (1957), pp. 281–306.

Gouldner, Alvin W. "Cosmopolitans and Locals: Toward an Analysis of Latent Social Roles—II." *Administrative Science Quarterly* 3 (1958), pp. 444–480.

Jackson, Kenneth W. "Black Faculty in Academia," In *The Racial Crisis in American Higher Education,* edited by Philip G. Altbach and Kofi Lomotey. Albany: State University of New York Press, 1991, pp. 135–148.

Johnsrud, Linda K. and Christine D. Des Jarlais. "Barriers to Tenure for Women and Minorities." *The Review of Higher Education* 17 (1994), pp. 335–353.

Katz, Joseph. "White Faculty Struggling with the Effects of Racism," In *The Racial Crisis in American Higher Education,* edited by Philip G. Altbach and Kofi Lomotey. Albany: State University of New York Press, 1991, pp. 187–196.

Kolodny, Annette. "I Dreamed Again That I Was Drowning." In *Women's Writing in Exile,* edited by Mary Lynn Broe and Angela Ingram. Chapel Hill: University of North Carolina Press, 1989, pp. 170–178.

Ladd, Jr., Everett C. "The Work Experience of American College Professors: Some Data and an Argument." *Current Issues in Higher Education.* Washington, D.C.: American Association for Higher Education, 1979, pp. 3–12.

Menges, Robert J. and William H. Exum. "Barriers to the Progress of Women and Minority Faculty." *Journal of Higher Education* 54 (1983), pp. 123–144.

Olivas, Michael. "Latino Faculty at the Border." *Change* 20 (1988), pp. 6–9.

Rau, William and Paul J. Baker. "The Organized Contradictions of Academe: Barriers Facing The Next Academic Revolution." *Teaching Sociology* 17 (1989), pp. 161–175.

Schuster, Jack M. Daniel W. Wheeler, and Associates. *Enhancing Faculty Careers: Strategies for Development and Renewal.* San Francisco: Jossey-Bass, 1990.

Tack, Martha W. and Carol L. Patitu. *Faculty Job Satisfaction: Women and Minorities in Peril.* ASHE-ERIC Higher Education Report No. 4. Washington, D.C.: George Washington University School of Education and Human Development, 1992.

Tuckman, Howard P. "Who Is Part-Time in Academe?" *AAUP Bulletin* (December, 1978), pp. 305–315.

Washington, Valora and Harvey William. *Affirmative Rhetoric, Negative Action: African-American and Hispanic Faculty at Predominantly White Institutions.* Report No. 2. Washington. D.C.: George Washington University, School of Education and Human Development, 1989.

Willie, Reynold and John E. Stecklein. "A Three-Decade Comparison of College Faculty Characteristics, Satisfactions, Activities, and Attitudes." *Research in Higher Education* 16 (1982), pp. 81–93.

Instructional Issues

Austin, Ann E. and Roger G. Baldwin. *Faculty Collaboration: Enhancing the Quality of Scholarship and Teaching.* ASHE-ERIC Higher Education Report No. 7. Washington, D.C.: George Washington University School of Education and Human Development, 1991.

Barnett, Ronald. "Linking Teaching and Research: A Critical Inquiry." *Journal of Higher Education* 63 (1992), pp. 621–636.

Berger, Bennett M. "Motivations to Teach." *Journal of Higher Education* 68 (1977), pp. 243–258.

Blackburn, Robert T., Glenn R. Pellino, Alice Boberg, and Colman O'Connell. "Are Instructional Improvement Programs Off-Target?" *Current Issues in Higher Education* 2 (September, 1980), pp. 32–48.

Boice, Robert. "New Faculty as Teachers." *Higher Education* 62 (1991), pp. 150–173.

Eble, Kenneth E. and Wilbert J. McKeachie. *Improving Undergraduate Education through Faculty Development.* San Francisco: Jossey-Bass, 1985.

Feldman, Kenneth A. "The Superior College Teacher from the Students' View." *Research in Higher Education* 5 (1976), pp. 243–288.

Goodwin, Laura D. and Ellen A. Stevens. "The Influence of Gender on Faculty Members' Perceptions of 'Good' Teaching." *Journal of Higher Education* 64 (1993), pp. 167–185.

Hagstrom, Warren O. *The Scientific Community.* New York: Basic Books, 1965.

Maitland, Christine. "Tales of a Freeway Flyer: Or Why I Left College Teaching After Ten Years." *Change* 19 (1987), pp. 8–9, 54.

Michalak, Jr., Stanley J. and Robert J. Friedrich. "Research Productivity and Teaching Effectiveness at a Small Liberal Arts College." *Journal of Higher Education* 52 (1981), pp. 578–597.

Smith, Page. "Teaching." In *Killing the Spirit: Higher Education in America.* New York: Viking, 1990, pp. 199–222.

Wilson, Robert C., Lynn Woods, and Jerry G. Gaff. "Social-Psychological Accessibility and Faculty-Student Interaction Beyond the Classroom." *Sociology of Education* 47 (1974), pp. 74–92.

Institutional Issues

AAUP Policy Documents & Reports. Washington, DC: American Association of University Professors, 1990.

Astin, Helen S. and Mary Beth Snyder. "Affirmative Action, 1972–1982—A Decade of Response." *Change* 14 (1982), pp. 26–31; 59.

Auerbach, A. J. "Professors in Retirement: The Emeritus College Model." *College Board Review* 141 (1986), pp. 22–36.

Austin, Ann E. and Zelda F. Gamson. *Academic Workplace: New Demands, Heightened Tensions.* ASHE-ERIC Higher Education Research Report No. 10. Washington, D.C.: Association for the Study of Higher Education, 1983.

Baldwin, Roger G. and Robert T. Blackburn. "The Academic Career as a Developmental Process." *Journal of Higher Education* 52 (1981), pp. 598–614.

Banks, W. M. "Afro-American Scholars in the University: Roles and Conflicts." *Behavioral Scientist* 27 (1984), pp. 325–338.

Bayer, Alan E. and Jeffrey E. Dutton. "Career Age and Research-Professional Activities of Academic Scientists." *Journal of Higher Education* 68 (1977), pp. 259–82.

Becher, Tony. *Academic Tribes and Territories: Intellectual Enquiry and the Culture of Disciplines.* The Society for Research into Higher Education. Milton Keynes, England: Open University Press, 1989.

Bess, James L. "Patterns of Satisfaction of Organizational Prerequisites and Personal Needs in University Academic Departments." *Sociology of Education* 46 (1973), pp. 99–114.

Blackburn, Robert T., Jeffrey P. Bieber, Janet H. Lawrence, and Lois Trautvetter. "Faculty at Work: Focus on Research, Scholarship, and Service." *Research in Higher Education* 32 (1991), pp. 385–413.

Blau, Peter M. *The Organization of Academic Work.* New York: Wiley, 1973.

Boice, Robert. *The New Faculty Member.* San Francisco: Jossey-Bass, 1992.

Bowen, William G. and Julie Ann Sosa. *Prospects for Faculty in the Arts and Sciences: A Study of Factors Affecting Demand and Supply, 1987–2012.* Princeton, N.J.: Princeton University Press, 1989.

Boyer, Carol M. and Darrell R. Lewis. *And on the Seventh Day: Faculty Consulting and Supplemental Income.* ASHE-ERIC Higher Education Report No. 3. Washington, D.C.: Association for the Study of Higher Education, 1985.

Brown, Ralph and Jordan Kurland. "Academic Tenure and Academic Freedom." In *Freedom and Tenure in the Academy.* Durham, NC: Duke University Press, 1993, pp. 325–355.

Cameron, Susan W. and Robert T. Blackburn. "Sponsorship and Academic Career Success." *Journal of Higher Education* 52 (July/August, 1981), pp. 369–377.

Chait, Richard. "Make Us an Offer: Creating Incentives for Faculty to Forsake Tenure." *AGB Trusteeship* 2 (January/February 1994), pp. 28+

Chait, Richard P. and Andrew T. Ford. *Beyond Traditional Tenure.* San Francisco: Jossey-Bass, 1982.

Chronister, Jay L., Roger G. Baldwin, and Theresa Bailey. "Full-time Non-tenure-track Faculty: Current Status, Condition, and Attitudes." *Review of Higher Education* 15 (1992), pp. 383–400.

Chronister, Jay L. and T. R. Kepple, Jr. *Incentive Early Retirement Programs for Faculty: Innovative Responses to a Changing Environment.* ASHE-ERIC Higher Education Report No. 1. Washington, D.C.: Association for the Study of Higher Education, 1987.

Clark, Shirley M., Mary Corcoran, and Darrell R. Lewis. "The Case for an Institutional Perspective on Faculty Development." *Journal of Higher Education* 57 (1986), pp. 176–195.

Dresch, Stephen P. "Tenure and Faculty Quality in Post-Growth Academe." *PS: Political Science and Politics* 21 (Winter, 1988), pp. 68–71.

Fairweather, James S. (coordinator). *Teaching, Research, and Faculty Records: A Summary of the Research Findings of the Faculty Profile Project.* University Park, PA: National Center on Postsecondary Teaching, Learning, and Assessment, 1993.

Finkelstein, Martin. "Life on the 'Effectively Terminal' Tenure Track." *Academe* 72 (1986), pp. 32–36.

Floyd, Carol E. *Faculty Participation in Decision Making: Necessity or Luxury?* ASHE-ERIC Higher Education Report No. 8. Washington, D.C.: Association for the Study of Higher Education, 1985.

Gappa, Judith M. and David W. Leslie. *The Invisible Faculty*. San Francisco: Jossey-Bass, 1993.

Garbarino, Joseph W. *Faculty Bargaining: Change and Conflict*. New York: McGraw-Hill, 1975.

Gmelch, Walter H., Nicholas P. Lovrich, and Phyllis Kay Wilke. "Sources of Stress in Academe: A National Perspective." *Research in Higher Education* 20 (1984), pp. 477–490.

Green, Madeleine (Ed.). *Minorities on Campus: A Handbook for Enhancing Diversity*. Washington, D.C.: American Council on Education, 1989.

Honan, William. "Wary of Entrenchment in the Ranks, Colleges Offer Alternatives to Tenure." *New York Times* 20 April, 1994, B13.

Hammond, P. Brett and Harriet Morgan, (Eds.). *Ending Mandatory Retirement for Tenured Faculty: The Consequences for Higher Education*. Washington, DC: National Academy Press, 1991, pp. 103–111.

Johnson, Gail E. R. "Post-Tenure Review: Practical Considerations." *Journal for Higher Education Management* 8 (1993), pp. 19–29.

Keeton, Morris . *Shared Authority On Campus*. Washington, D.C.: American Association for Higher Education, 1971.

Kerlin, Scott P. and Diane M. Dunlap. "For Richer, for Poorer: Faculty Morale in Periods of Austerity and Retrenchment." *Journal of Higher Education* 64 (1993), pp. 348–377.

LaCelle-Peterson, Mark W., and Martin J. Finkelstein. "Institutions Matter: Campus Teaching Environments' Impact on Senior Faculty." In *Developing Senior Faculty as Teachers*. New Directions for Teaching and Learning, no. 55. San Francisco: Jossey-Bass, 1993.

LaNoue, George R. and Barbara A. Lee. *Academics in Court: The Consequences of Faculty Discrimination Litigation*. Ann Arbor: University of Michigan Press, 1987.

Lewis, Darrell R. and William E. Becker, Jr. *Academic Rewards in Higher Education*. Cambridge, Mass.: Ballinger, 1979.

Lewis, Lionel S. *Scaling the Ivory Tower: Merit and its Limits in Academic Careers*. Baltimore: Johns Hopkins University Press, 1975.

Licata, Christine M. *Post-tenure Faculty Evaluation: Threat or Opportunity?* ASHE-ERIC Higher Education Report No. 1. Washington, D.C.: Association for the Study of Higher Education, 1986.

Licata, Christine M. and Hans A. Andrews. "Faculty Leaders' Responses to Post-Tenure Evaluation Practices." *Community Junior College Quarterly of Research and Practice* 16 (1992), pp. 47–56.

Lipset, Seymour M. and Everett C. Ladd. "The Changing Social Origins of American Academics." In *Qualitative and Quantitative Social Research*, edited by Robert K. Merton, et al. New York: The Free Press, 1979.

London, Howard B. "In Between: The Community College Teacher." *Annals of the American Academy of Political and Social Science* (March, 1980), pp. 62–73.

_____. "Tension Management and Perspectives in the Community College: The Teachers." In *The Culture of a Community College*. New York: Praeger, 1978, pp. 115–150.

McClelland, Katherine E., and Carol J. Auster. "Public Platitudes and Hidden Tensions: Racial Climates at Predominantly White Liberal Arts Colleges." *Journal of Higher Education* 61 (1990), pp. 607–642.

Metzger, Walter P. "Academic Tenure in America: A Historical Essay." In *The Commission on Academic Tenure in Higher Education, Faculty Tenure*. San Francisco: Jossey-Bass, 1973, pp. 93–159.

Moore, Kathryn M. and Marilyn J. Amey. "The Uses of Compensation." in *Making Sense of the Dollars: The Costs and Uses of Faculty Compensation*. ASHE-ERIC Report #5. Washington, D.C.: The George Washington University School of Human Development, 1993, pp. 31–57.

Morris, Arval. *Dismissal of Tenured Higher Education Faculty: Legal Implications of the Elimination of Mandatory Retirement.* Topeka, KS: National Organization on the Legal Problems of Education, 1992, pp. 7–16; 78–87.

Mortimer, Kenneth P., Marque Bagshaw, and Andrew T. Masland. *Flexibility in Academic Staffing: Effective Policies and Practices.* ASHE-ERIC Higher Education Report No. 1. Washington, D.C.: Association for the Study of Higher Education, 1985.

Mortimer, Kenneth P. and T. R. McConnell. *Sharing Authority Effectively.* San Francisco: Jossey-Bass, 1978.

Neumann, Anna. "Double Vision: The Experience of Institutional Stability." *Review of Higher Education* 15 (1992), pp. 417–447.

O'Toole, James. "A Conscientious Objection." *Change* 26 (May, 1994), pp. 78–87.

Richlin, Laurie. *Preparing Faculty for the New Conceptions of Scholarship.* New Directions for Teaching and Learning No. 54. San Francisco: Jossey-Bass, 1993.

Seidman, Earl. *In the Words of the Faculty: Perspectives in Improving Teaching and Educational Quality in Community Colleges.* San Francisco: Jossey-Bass, 1985.

Selden, Peter (Ed.). *Coping with Faculty Stress.* New Directions for Teaching and Learning No. 29. San Francisco: Jossey-Bass, 1987.

Sorcinelli, Mary Deane and Austin, Ann E. (Eds.). *Developing New and Junior Faculty.* New Directions for Teaching and Learning, no. 50. San Francisco: Jossey-Bass, 1992.

Tierney, William G. and Robert A. Rhoads. *Faculty Socialization as Cultural Process: A Mirror of Institutional Commitment.* ASHE-ERIC Higher Education Report No. 93–6. Washington, D.C.: George Washington University, School of Education and Human Development, 1994.

Tucker, Allan. *Chairing the Academic Department: Leadership among Peers.* Washington, D.C.: American Council on Education, 1981.

Van Alstyne, William W. "Tenure, A Conscientious Objective." *Change* 26 (May, 1994), pp. 88–89.

_____. William. "Tenure: A Summary, Explanation, and 'Defense'." *AAUP Bulletin* 57 (September, 1971), pp. 328–333.

Waggaman, John S. *Faculty Recruitment, Retention, and Fair Employment: Obligations and Opportunities.* ASHE-ERIC Higher Education Research Report No. 2. Washington, D.C.: Association for the Study of Higher Education, 1983.

Webster, David S. "600 Days of Angst . . . and Counting." *Thought and Action* 2 (1986), pp. 73–78.

V. The Professional Life of Faculty

Scholarship Issues and Definitions

Allison, Paul D. and J. Scott Long. "Departmental Effects on Scientific Productivity." *American Sociological Review* 55 (1990), pp. 469–478.

Allison, Paul D. and John A. Stewart. "Productivity Differences among Scientists: Evidence for Accumulative Advantage." *American Sociological Review* 39 (1974), pp. 596–606.

Blackburn, Robert T., Charles E. Behymer, and David E. Hall. "Research Note: Correlates of Faculty Publications." *Sociology of Education* 51 (1978), pp. 132–141.

Cole, Jonathan R. and Harriet Zuckerman. "The Productivity Puzzle: Persistence and Change in Patterns of Publication of Men and Women Scientists." In *Advances in Motivation and Achievement,* edited by M. W. Steinkamps and M. L. Maehr. Greenwich, CT: Jai Press, 1984.

Cole, Jonathan R. and Stephen Cole. *Social Stratification in Science.* Chicago: University of Chicago Press, 1973.

Dill, David D. "Research as a Scholarly Activity: Context and Culture." In *Measuring Faculty Research Performance*. New Directions for Institutional Research, no. 50. San Francisco: Jossey-Bass, 1986, pp. 7–23.

Feldman, Kenneth A. "Research Productivity and Scholarly Accomplishment of College Teachers as Related to Their Instructional Effectiveness: A Review and Exploration." *Research in Higher Education* 26 (1987), pp. 227–298.

Fox, Mary Frank. "Publication, Performance, and Reward in Science and Scholarship." In *Higher Education: Handbook of Theory and Research*, vol. 1, edited by John C. Smart. New York: Agathon Press, 1985, pp. 255–282.

_____. "Publication Productivity Among Scientists: A Critical Review." *Social Studies of Science* 13 (1983), pp. 285–305.

Fox, Mary Frank and Catherine A. Faver. "Independence and Cooperation in Research." *Journal of Higher Education* 55 (1984), pp. 347–359.

Fulton, Oliver and Martin Trow. "Research Activity in American Higher Education." *Sociology of Education* 47 (1974), pp. 29–73.

Gabelnick, Faith, Jean MacGregor, Roberta S. Matthews, and Barbara Leigh Smith. *Learning Communities: Creating Connections Among Students, Faculty, and Disciplines.* New Directions for Teaching and Learning No. 41. San Francisco: Jossey-Bass, 1990. See especially "Teaching in Learning Communities," pp. 53–60 and "Faculty Responses to Learning Communities," pp. 77–87.

Gamson, Zelda F. and Patrick J. Hill. "Creating a Lively Academic Community." In *Liberating Education*, edited by Zelda F. Gamson and Associates. San Francisco: Jossey-Bass, 1984, pp. 83–94.

Keller, George. "Trees without Fruit: The Problem with Research about Higher Education." *Change* 17 (1985), pp. 7–10.

Long, John. "Productivity and Academic Position in the Scientific Career." *American Sociological Review* 43 (1978), pp. 899–908.

Long, J. Scott and Robert McGinnis. "Organizational Context and Scientific Productivity." *American Sociological Review* 46 (1981), pp. 422–442.

Reskin, Barbara. "Scientific Productivity and the Reward Structure of Science." *American Sociological Review* 42 (1977), pp. 491–504.

_____. "Academic Sponsorship and Scientists' Careers." *Sociology of Education* 52 (1979), pp. 129–146.

Soldofsky, Robert M. "Age and Productivity of University Faculties: A Case Study." *Economics of Education Review* 3 (1984), pp. 289–298.

Webster, David S. "Does Research Productivity Enhance Teaching?" *Educational Record* 66 (1985), pp. 60–62.

"Women as Faculty Members and Scholars." In *Women in Academe: Progress and Prospects*, edited by Miriam K. Chamberlain. New York: Russell Sage Foundation, 1988, pp. 163–313.

Professional Culture and Affiliations

Bloland, Harland G. *Associations in Action: The Washington. D.C. Higher Education Community.* ASHE-ERIC Report No. 2. Washington, D.C.: Association for the Study of Higher Education, 1985.

Bloland, Harland G. and Sue M. Bloland. *American Learned Societies in Transition.* New York: McGraw-Hill, 1974.

Bok, Derek. "Academic Freedom." In *Beyond the Ivory Tower: Social Responsibilities of the Modern University*. Cambridge, Mass: Harvard University Press, 1982, pp. 17–36.

Brown, E. Richard. *Rockefeller Medicine Men: Medicine and Capitalism in America.* Berkeley: University of California Press, 1979.

Clark, Burton R. *The Academic Life: Small Worlds, Different Worlds.* Princeton: Carnegie Foundation for the Advancement of Teaching, 1987.

Cohen, Arthur M. and Florence B. Brawer. *The Two-year College Instructor Today.* New York: Praeger, 1977.

Cosand, Joseph P., Gerald Gurin, Martin W. Peterson, and Frank R. Brister. *Presidential Views of Higher Education's National Institutional Membership Associations: Summary Report.* Ann Arbor: University of Michigan, Center for the Study of Higher Education, 1980.

Crane, Diana. *Invisible Colleges: Diffusion of Knowledge in Scientific Communities.* Chicago: University of Chicago Press, 1972.

Crimmel, Henry H. "The Myth of the Teacher-Scholar." *Liberal Education* 60 (1984), pp. 183–198.

Hofstadter, Richard and Walter P. Metzger. *The Development of Academic Freedom in the United States.* New York: Columbia University Press, 1955.

Jencks, Christopher and David Reisman. *The Academic Revolution.* New York: Doubleday, 1968.

Jensen, Katherine. "Women's Work and Academic Culture." *Higher Education* 11 (1982), pp. 67–83.

Ladd, Everett Carll, Jr. and Seymour Martin Lipset. *The Divided Academy: Professors and Politics.* New York: McGraw-Hill, 1975.

Light, Donald Jr. "Thinking about Faculty." *Daedalus* 103 (1974a), pp. 258–264.

_____. "Introduction: The Structure of the Academic Professions." *Sociology of Education* 47 (1974b), pp. 2–28.

Lazarsfeld, Paul F. and Wagner Thielens, Jr. *The Academic Mind: Social Scientists in Times of Crisis.* Glencoe, Ill: Free Press, 1958.

McCarthy, Mary. *The Groves of Academe.* New York: Harcourt Brace, 1952.

Metzger, Walter P. "The American Academic Profession in 'Hard Times'." *Daedalus* 104 (1975), pp. 25–44.

_____. (Ed.). *The American Concept of Academic Freedom in Formation: A Collection of Essays and Reports.* New York: Arno Press, 1977.

_____. "The Academic Profession in the United States." In *The Academic Profession: National, Disciplinary and Institutional Settings,* edited by Burton Clark. Berkeley, CA: University of California Press, 1987.

Metzger, Walter P. (Ed.). *Professors on Guard: The First AAUP Investigations.* New York: Arno Press, 1977.

Metzger, Walter P., Sanford H. Kadish, Arthur DeBardeleben, and Edward J. Bloustein. *Dimensions of Academic Freedom.* Urbana: University of Illinois Press, 1969.

Murray, Michael A. "Defining the Higher Education Lobby." *Journal of Higher Education* 57 (1976), pp. 79–92.

Olswang, Steven G. and Barbara Lee. *Faculty Freedoms and Institutional Accountability: Interactions and Conflicts.* ASHE-ERIC Research Report No. 5. Washington, D.C.: Association for the Study of Higher Education, 1984.

Snow, C. P. *The Masters.* New York: Macmillan, 1951.

VI. Looking Toward the Future

Moore, Kathryn M. "Women's Access and Opportunity in Higher Education: Toward the Twenty-First Century." *Comparative Education* 23 (1987), pp. 23–34.